EMPLOYMENT DISCRIMINATION STATUTES

APPLICABLE TO EMPLOYMENT	APPLICABLE TO NON-EMPLOYMENT ACTIVITIES	AVAILABLE REMEDIES	SOURCE OF ATTORNEYS' FEES
Yes	Yes	—Against individual government official defendants sued in their individual capacities, including state officials (*Hafer v. Melo*). Prospective relief and full, uncapped compensatory damages for actual injuries (*Carey v. Piphus*), as well as punitive damages when defendant acts with evil motive or reckless indifference (*Smith v. Wade*) —Against government entity defendants: same, except no punitives (*City of Newport v. Fact Concerts, Inc.*) —Against state officials sued in their official capacities: prospective relief only (*Will v. Michigan Dep't of Police*)	42 U.S.C. § 1988(b). Experts' fees includable. § 1988(c)
Yes	Yes, but contract rights only	Same as § 1983 above	Same as above
Yes	Yes, but contract rights only	Same § 1983 as above	Same as above
Not if Title VII available (*Great Am. Fedl S & L Ass'n v. Novotny*)	Yes	Same § 1983 as above	Same as above
Only to employment and including claims of unequal pay for equal work covered by equal pay act and certain other intentionally discriminatory gender-based compensation practices, unless differentiation authorized by an equal pay act affirmative defense. (*County of Washington v. Gunther*)	No	—For any violation, injunctive relief, including reinstatement or hire orders; back pay running from no earlier than two years before EEOC charge filed; and front pay, to the extent equitable—§ 706(g), 42 U.S.C. § 2000e–5. —For intentional violations, compensatory and if appropriate punitive damages also available, capped at a combined total, per plaintiff, of $50,000 to $300,000 depending on employer size. 42 U.S.C. §§ 1981(a)(1), (b) —Where employer carries "same-decision" burden, plaintiff limited to injunctive relief and attorneys' fees. § 706(g)(2)(B), 42 U.S.C. § 2000e–5(g)(2)(B). —Where "after-acquired evidence" shows employer would have terminated plaintiff under uniformly applied work rules, liability limited to back pay ending at date evidence discovered, attorneys' fees, and possibly compensatory and punitive damages. (*McKennon v. Nashville Banner*) (case under ADEA)	Title VII, § 706(k), 42 U.S.C. § 2000e–5(k). Experts' fees includable. 42 U.S.C. § 1988(c)
Yes	No	Hire, back pay, variable civil penalties. 8 U.S.C. § 1324b(g)	8 U.S.C. § 1324b(h), (j)(4)
Only to employment	No	—Prospective relief including reinstatement or hire orders, back wages and front pay; for "willful" violations, an equal additional amount of "liquidated" damages. 29 U.S.C. §§ 216 & 217 —No express textual counterpart to Title VII § 706(g)(2)(B) (the "same-decision" limitation on liability) —*McKennon v. Nashville Banner*, discussed under Title VII above, was decided under ADEA	29 U.S.C. § 216(b)
Only to employment	No	Same as ADEA	29 U.S.C. § 216(b)
Yes, except perhaps if Title VII available (circuits split) see § 9.10	Yes	Prospective relief and, at least for intentional violations, full uncapped compensatory and, if appropriate, punitive damages. (*Franklin v. Gwinnett County Pub. Schs.*)	42 U.S.C. § 1988(b)
No, unless providing employment is a primary objective of the federal funding. 42 U.S.C. § 2000–d	Yes	Prospective relief and, at least for intentional violations, full uncapped compensatory and, if appropriate, punitive damages. *See Guardians Ass'n v. Civil Serv. Comm.* and *cf. Franklin v. Gwinnett County Pub. Schs.*	42 U.S.C. § 1988(b)

CIVIL RIGHTS LAW AND PRACTICE

Second Edition

By

Harold S. Lewis, Jr.
Walter F. George Professor of Law
Mercer University

and

Elizabeth J. Norman
Member of Georgia Bar

HORNBOOK SERIES®

THOMSON
WEST ™

Mat #40180764

610 Opperman Drive
P.O. Box 64526
St. Paul, MN 55164–0526
1–800–328–9352

ISBN 0–314–15011-0

TEXT IS PRINTED ON 10% POST CONSUMER RECYCLED PAPER

Dedication

To Leslie for love and support, and to Isabel, Bailiff and Puzzle for zestful refreshment for the soul. The authors also dedicate this work to the memory of the late Justice Harlan, whose concurring opinion in *Monroe v. Pape* cut to the heart of the matter.

*

Preface

To serve the needs of law students, this book tracks the materials surveyed in a number of widely used civil rights casebooks, including: Abernathy's *Civil Rights and Constitutional Litigation* (3d ed. West 2000); Brown and Kinport's *Constitutional Litigation under Section 1983* (Lexis Nexis, 2003); Eisenberg's *Civil Rights Legislation* (Lexis Nexis 5th ed. 2004); Jeffries, Karlan, Low and Rutherglen's *Civil Rights Actions: Enforcing the Constitution* (Foundation 3d ed. 2000); and Nahmad Wells and Eaton's *Constitutional Torts* (Lexis Nexis 2d ed. 2004). Hence the reader will find coverage not only of the Principal Reconstruction Acts—42 U.S.C. Sections 1981, 1983 and 1985(3)—but also of Title VI of the 1964 Civil Rights Act; the Civil Rights Attorney's Fees Act of 1976; 42 U.S.C. Section 1982 and Title IX of the Education Amendments of 1972. Lawyers and law students alike will note that the authors have proceeded from one bedrock understanding: procedural, remedial, and evidentiary rulings shape the outcome of litigation in these areas at least as much as substantive decisional doctrine.

In fact, many of the most significant Section 1983 decisions of the past decade have worked refinements to defenses, procedures and remedies. This is not surprising, since by 1989 the Supreme Court had completed the principal foundation work for Section 1983 actions against individual government officials and the government entities they serve. After *Monroe v. Pape* widened the scope of the damages claim against individual defendants, *Carey v. Piphus* and *Memphis v. Stachura* insisted on specific proof of compensatory loss, *Smith v. Wade* circumscribed punitive damages, and *Harlow v. Fitzgerald* and *Anderson v. Creighton*—more recently elaborated by *Hope v. Pelzer* and *Saucier v. Katz*—dramatically reformulated and expanded the qualified immunity defense. As for damages from government entities, *Monell v. Dep't of Social Services* recognized the claim; *Pembaur v. Cincinnati, St. Louis v. Praprotnik*, and *City of Canton v. Harris* substantially limited its scope; *Owen v. City of Independence* rejected a formal affirmative defense; *City of Newport v. Fact Concerts* precluded punitive damages; and *Will v. Mich. Dep't of State Police* precluded any application to the states. And *Maine v. Thiboutot* opened up a vast potential array of claims under Section 1983 for violations of federal statutes.

The Supreme Court decisions since 1990, while occasionally breaking new ground, have for the most part filled in crucial details. *Hafer v. Melo* reminds us that state officials remain subject to damages liability when sued in their individual capacities even though their employing entities are not. *United States v. Lanier* helps a bit on when law may be considered "clearly established" for purposes of qualified immunity; *Crawford-El v. Britton* ends the debate over whether unlawful intent or motive defeats that defense; and *Behrens v. Pelletier* lays out a blueprint enabling individual defendants to stretch out litigation of the defenses over two motions and successive appeals. *Wilson v. Layne* reflects the Supreme Court's insistence that trial courts assess whether a particular claim is currently cognizable before deciding whether a cognizable claim was clearly established when an individual defendant acted—a sequence that ensures Section 1983 can perform its function as the principal procedural vehicle for testing constitutional boundaries in cases against government officials as well as their employing entities. *Leatherman v. Tarrant County* facilitates notice pleading, even as *Bryan County v. Brown* erects overwhelming proof obstacles to proving an entity's unlawful failure to train. *Texas v. Lesage* applies the *Mt. Healthy* "same-decision" defense to all claims under Section 1983, observing, however, that a reverse discrimination plaintiff is eligible for injunctive relief against a formal, race-conscious program despite a successful same-decision showing. *Kolstad v. American Dental Ass'n*, a Title VII decision, clarifies indirectly the *Smith v. Wade* predicates for punitive damages against individual Reconstruction Act defendants. And in *Suter v. Artist* and *Blessing v. Freestone* and more recently *Gonzaga University v. Doe*, the Court has tried to close the doors somewhat to Section 1983 actions based on federal statutory claims.

Given the ever-growing number of liability restrictions, procedural impediments, and remedy limitations hamstringing Section 1983 actions, Section 1981 claims against individual defendants have assumed increasing importance. But recent circuit decisions are in agreement that the Civil Rights Act of 1991 failed effectively to overrule *Jett v. Dallas Ind. Sch. Dist.*, and accordingly have held that Section 1981 is unavailable as a distinct, stand-alone remedy for race discrimination by government entities. And the Supreme Court's decision in *Bray v. Alexandria Women's Health Center* has rendered Section 1985(3) a virtual nullity as a practical remedy against racially or otherwise invidiously motivated conspiracies by private parties.

Since the arrival of the millennium, the Supreme Court's highly publicized, federalist-driven expansion of Eleventh Amendment immunity has begun to intrude on civil rights enforcement. Its decisions in *Kimel v. State Bd. of Regents* and *Univ. of Alabama v. Garrett* have rejected use of the Age Discrimination in Employment Act and the employment title of the Americans With Disabilities Act against state employers. A key unanswered question is the degree if any to which this resurgent federalism will limit the use against state employers of Title VII of the 1964 Civil Rights Act, but the Court's recent, more forgiving applications of the Amendment in *Nevada Dep't of Human Resources v. Hibbs* and *Tennessee v. Lane* suggest that Title VII will remain viable in those cases.

Two areas that have burgeoned in the 1990's warrant special mention. One is Title VI, which, however, has recently been impaired in its scope by Alexander v. Sandoval. The other is Title IX, under which the Supreme Court has recognized certain claims against school districts, by teachers and students alike, for sex discrimination, including sexual harassment, in federally funded education programs. Here we survey four key cases, *Franklin v. Gwinnett County Public Schools, Gebser v. Lago Vista Ind. Sch. Dist., Davis v. Monroe County Bd. of Education* and *Barnes v. Gorman.*

Finally, on attorney's fees recoverable by prevailing parties, the text surveys the Supreme Court's restrictive *Farrar v. Hobby and Buckhannon Bd. and Care Home* decisions, as well as the recent circuit court decisions applying the offer of judgment rule, FRCP 68.

H.S.L, Jr.
E.N.

*

Acknowledgements

The authors gratefully acknowledge the support of the Walter F. George Foundation, Mercer Law School, and Deans Michael Subbath and Daisy Floyd.

*

WESTLAW® Overview

Civil Rights Law and Practice offers a detailed and comprehensive treatment of basic rules, principles and issues relating to civil rights law and practice. To supplement the information contained in this book, you can access Westlaw, a computer-assisted legal research service of West Group. Westlaw contains a broad array of legal resources, including case law, statutes, expert commentary, current developments and various other types of information.

Learning how to use these materials effectively will enhance your legal research abilities. To help you coordinate the information in the book with your Westlaw research, this volume contains an appendix listing Westlaw databases, search techniques and sample problems.

THE PUBLISHER

*

Summary of Contents

*

Table of Contents

Page

C. RECENT PROCEDURAL LIMITATIONS ON THE RECONSTRUCTION CIVIL RIGHTS ACTS

CHAPTER TWO. SECTION 1983

A. INTRODUCTION

B. Section 1983 CONDUCT "UNDER COLOR OF STATE LAW" VERSUS CONSTITUTIONAL "STATE ACTION"

Page

D. PREVAILING DEFENDANTS

E. RULE 68 OFFERS OF JUDGMENT

CHAPTER FIVE. PROCEDURAL ASPECTS OF LITIGATING UNDER THE RECONSTRUCTION STATUTES AND CONTEMPORARY CIVIL RIGHTS AND EMPLOYMENT DISCRIMINATION LEGISLATION

A. OVERVIEW—THE NEW FEDERALISM IN CIVIL RIGHTS FORUM SELECTION: STATE PRIMACY REASSERTED

B. FEDERAL SUBJECT MATTER JURISDICTION

C. *YOUNGER* NONINTERVENTION

L. MOOTNESS

M. GAP–FILLING FROM STATE LAW UNDER SECTION 1988: SURVIVORSHIP AND LIMITATIONS

N. PLEADING

O. FEDERAL RULE OF CIVIL PROCEDURE 11, AS AMENDED—RELATIONSHIP TO PLEADING

Page

P. DISCOVERY, EVIDENCE, PRE–TRIAL ORDERS, WAIVER OF OBJECTIONS, AND RELATED ISSUES

Q. SUMMARY JUDGMENT (F.R.C.P. 56), SETTLEMENT, AND JUDGMENT AS A MATTER OF LAW UNDER F.R.C.P. 50(a) ("DIRECTED VERDICT") AND 50(b) ("J.N.O.V.")

R. SECTION 1983 ACTIONS AGAINST INDIVIDUAL AND ENTITY DEFENDANTS—BIFURCATION OF CLAIMS FOR TRIAL

S. CLASS ACTIONS

T. CLAIM AND ISSUE PRECLUSION IN ACTIONS UNDER TITLE VII AND THE RECONSTRUCTION CIVIL RIGHTS ACTS

CIVIL RIGHTS LAW AND PRACTICE

Second Edition

*

Chapter One

OVERVIEW OF RECONSTRUCTION–ERA CIVIL RIGHTS LEGISLATION

Analysis

A. THE CIVIL RIGHTS ACTS OF 1866, 1870, AND 1871

§ 1.1 In General

The Civil Rights Acts of 1866, 1870, and 1871 are generally referred to as the Reconstruction Civil Rights Acts, and they were originally intended to enforce the 13th and 14th Amendments in the post-Civil War era. The most frequently invoked provisions are codified at 42 U.S.C.A. §§ 1981, 1983, and 1985(3). These acts remained dormant for many years but were resurrected in the 1960's.[1]

What is now § 1981 was first enacted in 1866 under authority of the 13th Amendment, and re-enacted in 1870, two years after ratification of the 14th Amendment. This history has spawned doctrinal schisms and jurisprudential inconsistencies. On one hand, the Supreme Court has relied on the 13th Amendment origins of § 1981 (and § 1982, its legislative companion that bars discrimination in the acquiring, holding and disposing of property) to apply these statutes to purely private defendants, at least with respect to transactions held open to the public.[2] On the other, the court has relied on the 14th Amendment origins of § 1981 to limit its reach to violations that reflect race discrimination that is intentional in character.[3] And while the Court has insisted that it is the intent of the enacting Congress that controls the breadth of the §§ 1981 and 1982 definitions of "race,"[4] its reliance on the 13th Amendment origins of these statutes seemingly caused it to depart from the norms of that Congress by holding the statutes to bar purely private discrimination, subject only to possible First Amendment limitations related to freedom of association.[5]

Section 1985(3), like § 1983 and in contrast to §§ 1981 and 1982, creates no rights of its own but simply provides damages and perhaps injunctive relief for the conspiratorial deprivation of certain rights independently secured by the federal Constitution and, perhaps, other federal statutes. But when the conspiracy is among purely private actors, very few rights are protected against such deprivation, and § 1985(3) offers no protection unless the conspirators, public or private, act with a specific class-based animus or motive that goes beyond the intent requirement of §§ 1981 or 1982.[6]

§ 1.2 Section 1981

Section 1981 secures equal contracting rights without regard to race. It affords "all persons" in the United States "the same right ... to make and enforce contracts ... and to the full and equal benefit of all laws ...

§ 1.1

1. *See Jones v. Alfred H. Mayer Co.*, 392 U.S. 409, 88 S.Ct. 2186, 20 L.Ed.2d 1189 (1968).

2. *Jones v. Alfred H. Mayer Co.*, 392 U.S. 409, 88 S.Ct. 2186, 20 L.Ed.2d 1189 (§ 1982); *Runyon v. McCrary*, 427 U.S. 160, 96 S.Ct. 2586, 49 L.Ed.2d 415 (1976); *Patterson v. McLean Credit Union*, 491 U.S. 164, 109 S.Ct. 2363, 105 L.Ed.2d 132 (1989) (§ 1981).

3. *General Building Contractors Ass'n v. Pennsylvania*, 458 U.S. 375, 102 S.Ct. 3141, 73 L.Ed.2d 835 (1982).

4. *McDonald v. Santa Fe Trail Transp. Co.*, 427 U.S. 273, 96 S.Ct. 2574, 49 L.Ed.2d 493 (1976); *St. Francis College v. Al–Khazraji*, 481 U.S. 604, 107 S.Ct. 2022, 95 L.Ed.2d 582 (1987) (§ 1981); *Shaare Tefila Congregation v. Cobb*, 481 U.S. 615, 107 S.Ct. 2019, 95 L.Ed.2d 594 (1987) (§ 1982).

5. *See, e.g., Runyon*, 427 U.S. at 186, 96 S.Ct. at 2602 (Powell, J., concurring).

6. *See Bray v. Alexandria Women's Health Clinic*, 506 U.S. 263, 113 S.Ct. 753, 122 L.Ed.2d 34 (1993).

as is enjoyed by white citizens."[1] By its terms § 1981 reaches not just employment but a host of contracting relationships—with private schools, to name just one—not reached by Title VII of the Civil Rights Act of 1964, as amended.[2] And § 1981, unlike Title VII, has no minimum-employee numerical threshold for employer liability; § 1981 also provides for individual liability in several circuits.[3] Section 1981 has been interpreted to provide a civil damages remedy for racial discrimination arising from contracts of employment, even though Congress has comprehensively addressed employment discrimination much more recently in Title VII.[4] Moreover, the Supreme Court has held, *Runyon v. McCrary*,[5] and reaffirmed, *Patterson v. McLean Credit Union*,[6] that § 1981, long assumed to reach only state action, also reaches purely private conduct.

A contract for § 1981 purposes is not necessarily the legalistic agreement that the word conjures up in one's mind. In *Patterson*, the Supreme Court impliedly acknowledged that an at-will employee may bring an action under § 1981. The Court stated that Patterson, an at-

§ 1.2

1. Thus, where African–American plaintiffs conceded that various tobacco companies sold the same menthol cigarettes to African–Americans and whites, plaintiffs could not state a claim under § 1981 for race-based disparity in the making and enforcement of contracts. *Brown v. Philip Morris Inc.*, 250 F.3d 789 (3d Cir. 2001). Plaintiffs argued that the companies targeted African–Americans in marketing mentholated tobacco products, which were alleged to be more dangerous than non-mentholated products.

2. The First Circuit has written that a § 1981 defendant can be liable to an independent contractor for a racially hostile work environment. In *Danco, Inc. v. Wal–Mart Stores, Inc.*, 178 F.3d 8 (1st Cir.1999), *cert. denied*, 528 U.S. 1105, 120 S.Ct. 843, 145 L.Ed.2d 712 (2000), Wal–Mart contracted with Danco, solely owned by Benjamin Guiliani, to maintain a Wal–Mart store's parking lot. Racist graffiti was spray painted in the area near Guiliani's truck and a Wal–Mart employee made racist remarks to Guiliani. These incidents were reported to Wal–Mart management, who subsequently fired Danco. Guiliani could have pursued a § 1981 hostile work environment claim, despite his status as an independent contractor, the court wrote, if he (rather than his company) had been a party to the contract with Wal–Mart.

In *Webster v. Fulton County*, 283 F.3d 1254 (11th Cir.2002), an independent contractor stated a claim for violation of § 1981 when that contractor alleged that a governmental entity refused to award a contract to the contractor in retaliation for the contractor's filing of a lawsuit charging the governmental entity with a custom or policy of disparate-treatment racial discrimination that was applied against the contractor in violation of § 1981.

3. *Whidbee v. Garzarelli Food Specialties, Inc.*, 223 F.3d 62, 75 (2d Cir.2000) (in order to make out a claim for individual liability under § 1981, a plaintiff must demonstrate some affirmative link to causally connect the actor with the discriminatory action); *Allen v. Denver Pub. Sch. Bd.*, 928 F.2d 978, 983 (10th Cir.1991) (apparently assuming § 1981 allows individual liability but finding no evidence of personal involvement); *Jones v. Continental Corp.*, 789 F.2d 1225, 1231 (6th Cir.1986) ("[T]he law is clear that individuals may be held liable for violations of § 1981"); *Faraca v. Clements*, 506 F.2d 956, 959 (5th Cir.1975). Likewise, district courts have allowed individual liability under § 1981. *See, e.g., Hicks v. IBM*, 44 F.Supp.2d 593, 596–97 (S.D.N.Y.1999); *Amin v. Quad/Graphics, Inc.*, 929 F.Supp. 73, 78 (N.D.N.Y.1996); *O'Connor v. 11 W. 30th St. Rest. Corp.*, 1995 WL 354904, at *7 (S.D.N.Y.1995); *Sheppard v. Dickstein, Shapiro, Morin & Oshinsky*, 59 F.Supp.2d 27, 33 (D.D.C.1999).

4. *See Johnson v. Railway Express Agency*, 421 U.S. 454, 95 S.Ct. 1716, 44 L.Ed.2d 295 (1975); *McDonald v. Santa Fe Trail Transp. Co.*, 427 U.S. 273, 96 S.Ct. 2574, 49 L.Ed.2d 493 (1976).

5. 427 U.S. 160, 96 S.Ct. 2586, 49 L.Ed.2d 415 (1976).

6. 491 U.S. 164, 109 S.Ct. 2363, 105 L.Ed.2d 132 (1989).

will employee, might have a cause of action against her employer for failure to promote: "the question whether a promotion claim is actionable under § 1981 depends upon whether the nature of the change in position was such that it involved the opportunity to enter into a new contract with the employer. If so, then the employer's refusal to enter the new contract is actionable under § 1981."[7] Justice Stevens, writing separately in *Patterson*, explained that an "at-will employee . . . is not merely performing an existing contract; she is constantly remaking that contract."[8] As noted by the Fifth Circuit, early federal decisions on the issue were few, and were not unanimous.[9] The 1998 Supreme Court decision in *Haddle v. Garrison*[10], wherein the Court held that an at-will employee can state a claim under § 1985(2), apparently has put this issue to rest. Every circuit to consider the issue since *Haddle* has held that at-will employees can state a claim under § 1981.[11]

The Supreme Court has construed the language that secures to all the same contracting rights as "white citizens" to refer only to the racial (as opposed to, say, gender-based or religious) character of the prohibited discrimination, rather than to limit the class of appropriate plaintiffs to non-whites. Accordingly, while the lower courts are in agreement that the statute does not prohibit discrimination because of gender, it is also settled that whites as well as blacks may assert contract denial claims under § 1981 on the basis of race.[12]

The Supreme Court has construed § 1981's ban on "race" discrimination to include also discrimination on the basis of ancestry. The Court has understood ancestry, in turn, to mean membership in an "ethnically

7. *Id.* at 185, 109 S.Ct. at 2377.

8. *Id.* at 221, 109 S.Ct. at 2396 (Stevens, J., concurring in part).

9. *Compare, e.g., Fadeyi v. Planned Parenthood Ass'n of Lubbock, Inc.*, 160 F.3d 1048, 1049 n. 11 (5th Cir.1998) (allowing at-will to proceed under § 1981) and cases cited therein *with Gonzalez v. Ingersoll Milling Mach. Co.*, 133 F.3d 1025 (7th Cir. 1998) (suggesting that no contract exists in an at-will employment relationship to support a cause of action under § 1981).

10. 525 U.S. 121, 119 S.Ct. 489, 142 L.Ed.2d 502 (1998).

11. *See Skinner v. Maritz, Inc.*, 253 F.3d 337 (8th Cir.2001); *Whidbee v. Garzarelli Food Specialties, Inc.*, 223 F.3d 62 (2d Cir.2000); *Lauture v. International Business Machines Corp.*, 216 F.3d 258 (2d Cir.2000); *Fadeyi v. Planned Parenthood*, 160 F.3d 1048; *Spriggs v. Diamond Auto Glass*, 165 F.3d 1015 (4th Cir.1999) (at will employment relationship is contractual); *Perry v. Woodward*, 199 F.3d 1126, 1133–34 (10th Cir.1999), *cert. denied*, 529 U.S. 1110, 120 S.Ct. 1964, 146 L.Ed.2d 796 (2000). *See also Faulk v. Home Oil Co., Inc.*, 184 F.R.D. 645 (M.D.Ala.1999). *But cf. Bishop v. Avera*, 177 F.3d 1233 (11th Cir.1999) (granting § 1981 defendant qualified immunity in light of the unsettled law governing availability of § 1981 claim to at will employee). The Eleventh Circuit did not mention *Haddle* in its decision. The Fifth Circuit also appears to assume that qualified immunity is available to § 1981 individual defendants sued for damages in their individual capacity. *Felton v. Polles,* 315 F.3d 470 (5th Cir.2002).

12. *McDonald v. Santa Fe Trail Transp. Co.*, 427 U.S. 273, 96 S.Ct. 2574, 49 L.Ed.2d 493. But race, rather than mere discipline, must be the subject matter of the complaint. *Hughes v. Ortho Pharm. Corp.*, 177 F.3d 701 (8th Cir.1999). The Fifth Circuit has held that discrimination on the basis of the plaintiff's interracial relationship constituted actionable race discrimination under § 1981. *See Deffenbaugh–Williams v. Wal–Mart Stores, Inc.*, 156 F.3d 581, 588–89 (5th Cir.1998), *vacated on grant of reh'g en banc*, 169 F.3d 215 (5th Cir.1999), *reinstated in relevant part*, 182 F.3d 333 (5th Cir.1999).

and physiognomically distinctive sub-grouping.''[13] This somewhat vague formulation has generated predictable confusion among the lower federal courts. We do know that § 1981 ''ancestry'' does not mean national origin, religion, or alienage status as such.[14] On the other hand, these latter characteristics are often statistically correlated with an individual's descent from a particular ancestry. For example, in one recent case, a hiring supervisor disparaged the plaintiff's Israeli background, and in particular his prior sales experience in Israel, saying ''Israel doesn't count.'' The appellate court ruled that the jury was entitled to treat these comments not just as discrimination on the basis of national origin . . . actionable under Title VII . . . but also as discrimination based on the plaintiff's Israeli ancestry, and thus ''race'' within the meaning of § 1981.[15] It reasoned that the Israeli population was composed primarily of members of a particular ancestry and therefore the jury might have concluded that by disparaging Israel the defendant was really, or also, discriminating against plaintiff because of his ''race'' . . . in the nineteenth century sense defined by the Supreme Court.

Although § 1981, like Title VII, does not prohibit discrimination on the basis of alienage *per se*, a limited protection from employment discrimination on the basis of non-citizenship status is now provided by the Immigration Reform and Control Act of 1986. But aliens, like other ''persons within the jurisdiction of the United States,'' may complain of race or ancestry and alienage, i.e. non-citizenship[16] discrimination under § 1981, or of race, gender, religious, or national origin, but not ancestry or citizenship discrimination under Title VII.[17] None of the Reconstruction Civil Rights Acts reaches gender or religious discrimination as such, although discrimination on those grounds might violate Equal Protection and accordingly would be redressable under § 1983.

13. *St. Francis College v. Al–Khazraji*, 481 U.S. 604, 107 S.Ct. 2022, 95 L.Ed.2d 582 (1987) and *Shaare Tefila Congregation v. Cobb*, 481 U.S. 615, 107 S.Ct. 2019, 95 L.Ed.2d 594 (1987) (protection against ancestry, as opposed to religious, discrimination available to, respectively, Arabs and Jews).

14. *See id.*

15. *Sinai v. New England Tel. & Tel. Co.*, 3 F.3d 471 (1st Cir.1993).

16. *Contrast Anderson v. Conboy*, 156 F.3d 167 (2d Cir.1998) (allowing § 1981 alienage discrimination claim against a private defendant and noting that all circuits recognize a § 1981 claim for alienage discrimination by government defendants); *Duane v. GEICO*, 37 F.3d 1036 (4th Cir. 1994) (§ 1981 prohibits private defendant alienage discrimination against a lawfully admitted, permanent resident alien) *and Bhandari v. First Nat'l Bank of Commerce*, 829 F.2d 1343 (5th Cir.1987) (*en banc*) (§ 1981 does not prohibit private alienage discrimination). The Fifth Circuit's position was based largely on its unwillingness to ''extend'' to discrimination based on alienage the application of § 1981's race discrimination ban to private defendants, which the Supreme Court had upheld in *Runyon v. McCrary*, 427 U.S. 160, 96 S.Ct. 2586, 49 L.Ed.2d 415 (1976). The Court's reaffirmation of *Runyon* in *Patterson v. McLean Credit Union*, 491 U.S. 164, 109 S.Ct. 2363, 105 L.Ed.2d 132 (1989) may have eroded the continuing vitality of *Bhandari*, although on remand the Fifth Circuit held that *Patterson* did not affect its holding in *Bhandari v. First Nat'l Bank of Commerce*, 887 F.2d 609 (5th Cir.1989). The Fourth Circuit in *Duane* stressed that even undocumented aliens are among the ''persons'' granted rights by § 1981.

17. *Espinoza v. Farah Mfg. Co.*, 414 U.S. 86, 94 S.Ct. 334, 38 L.Ed.2d 287 (1973) (Title VII); *Bhandari v. First Nat'l Bank of Commerce*, 829 F.2d 1343 (5th Cir.1987) (§ 1981).

The federal judiciary began to place significant limitations on the utility of § 1981 in *General Building Contractors Association v. Pennsylvania.*[18] There the Supreme Court held that a showing of disparate impact does not suffice to prove a § 1981 employment violation, which requires instead a direct or inferential demonstration of discriminatory intent.[19] Consistent with this ruling, the Court in *Patterson* approved for use in § 1981 actions the Title VII intentional yet inferential disparate *treatment* mode of proof first outlined in *McDonnell Douglas Corporation v. Green.*[20] Those requirements continue to be routinely applied to actions under § 1981.[21]

Yet at times one encounters some suggestion in the cases that the showing of intent required in § 1981 cases by *General Building Contractors* in practice demands somewhat more "direct" evidence of discrimination than would usually be required under Title VII.[22] And it remains uncertain whether, in § 1981 "mixed motive" situations, the courts will hew to the complete-defense approach mandated for at least some constitutional violations in actions under § 1983[23]; to the more limited

18. 458 U.S. 375, 102 S.Ct. 3141, 73 L.Ed.2d 835 (1982).

19. The court has since explicitly confirmed in the majority opinions in the last text paragraph of *Grutter v. Bollinger*, 539 U.S. 306, 123 S.Ct. 2325, 156 L.Ed.2d 304 (2003), and the last footnote of *Gratz v. Bollinger*, 539 U.S. 244, 123 S.Ct. 2411, 2430 n. 23, 156 L.Ed.2d 257 (2003), that the type of intentional race discrimination that violates the Equal Protection clause of the Fourteenth Amendment is coextensive with that which violates Section 1981.

20. 411 U.S. 792, 93 S.Ct. 1817, 36 L.Ed.2d 668 (1973). *Patterson*, 491 U.S. at 186, 109 S.Ct. at 2377; *St. Mary's Honor Ctr. v. Hicks*, 509 U.S. 502, 506 n. 1, 113 S.Ct. 2742, 125 L.Ed.2d 407.

21. *See, e.g., Arguello v. Conoco, Inc.*, 330 F.3d 355 (5th Cir.2003) (requirement of proving damages in § 1981 claim demands evidence that plaintiff was unable to enter into contractual relationship, an element not satisfied when gas station customers in fact successfully completed their transaction despite racially discriminatory conduct of defendant's employees); *Saulsberry v. St. Mary's Univ. of Minnesota*, 318 F.3d 862 (8th Cir.2003) (African–American plaintiff failed to show that preferably treated Caucasian student was similarly situated with respect to their job responsibilities); *Lockridge v. Bd. of Trustees of Univ. of Arkansas*, 315 F.3d 1005 (8th Cir.2003) (§ 1981 promotion claim fails for want of evidence that plaintiff applied, despite his contention that employer typically promoted from within, absent evidence that application would have been futile).

22. *See Durham v. Xerox Corp.*, 18 F.3d 836 (10th Cir.1994). Compare the standards the Tenth Circuit applied in *Durham* in upholding district court's grant of summary judgment to the employer on the § 1981 claim with the lower court decisions after *St. Mary's Honor Ctr. v. Hicks,* 509 U.S. 502, 113 S.Ct. 2742, 125 L.Ed.2d 407 (1993) that deem it inappropriate to grant the defendant summary judgment when the plaintiff produces sufficient prima facie evidence of race discrimination under Title VII.

23. *See Mt. Healthy City Sch. Dist. Bd. of Educ. v. Doyle*, 429 U.S. 274, 97 S.Ct. 568, 50 L.Ed.2d 471 (1977). *Mt. Healthy* itself involved a First Amendment violation. So it is not controversial to apply the complete-defense approach to successful same-decision showings in Reconstruction Act actions based on First Amendment violations. *See Ballard v. Muskogee Reg'l Med. Ctr.*, 238 F.3d 1250 (10th Cir.2001). But another circuit decision applies the *Mt. Healthy* approach—which altogether relieves the defendant of liability upon its showing that it would have reached the same challenged decision even had it not considered an unconstitutional factor—to a § 1983 claim alleging a violation of equal protection based on race discrimination. *See Harris v. Shelby County Bd. of Educ.*, 99 F.3d 1078 (11th Cir.1996). This extension of *Mt. Healthy* is in tension with a line of Supreme Court and circuit decisions beginning with *Regents of Univ. of Cal. v. Bakke*, 438 U.S. 265, 98 S.Ct. 2733, 57 L.Ed.2d 750 (1978), that permit plaintiffs who challenge racial preferences as equal protection violations to

defense mandated by the 1991 Civil Rights Act for post-November 21, 1991 employment practices that violate Title VII; or to the complete defense stipulated by the Supreme Court in *Price Waterhouse v. Hopkins*, which governed Title VII violations before they were modified by the 1991 Act.[24] The uncertainty is fueled by the fact that the 1991 Act, which in other respects expressly and materially modifies § 1981, refers only to Title VII, not to § 1981, in the provisions that modify *Price Waterhouse*.

Section 1981 has also been read more narrowly than Title VII with respect to the ability of plaintiffs to assert the rights of third parties. The problem has recently arisen in connection with suits by "testers" to challenge discriminatory referrals by employment agencies. Testers have been defined as persons of the opposite race "equipped with fake credentials intended to be comparable" who apply for employment to an agency or employer without an intention to accept an offer if one is forthcoming.[25] The typical ensuing claim is that the employment agency, on grounds of race, failed to refer the African–American (or female) tester but did refer the other (white or male) tester. Title VII provides that any "person claiming to be aggrieved" by an unlawful employment practice may, after exhausting administrative remedies, sue such an agency in court.[26] Consequently, testers may be able to state a Title VII claim despite their own lack of a bona fide interest in employment.[27]

By contrast, the text of § 1981 suggests that only a person deprived of what is otherwise a legal right to make or enforce a contract has standing. Reasoning that testers could not have enforced an employment

obtain limited remedies despite a defendant's "same decision" showing. This tension was noted neither in *Harris* nor in a subsequent decision of the same circuit that extends the *Mt. Healthy* complete defense approach to race discrimination claims under § 1981. *Mabra v. United Food & Commercial Workers Local Union No. 1996*, 176 F.3d 1357 (11th Cir.1999). The two Eleventh Circuit decisions correctly contrast §§ 1983 and 1981 with the 1991 Civil Rights Act amendments to Title VII, which, unlike those Reconstruction-era statutes, limit the force of the mixed-motive defense by expressly providing that the Title VII plaintiff may establish liability and recover prospective relief and attorneys' fees notwithstanding a "same decision" showing. But the decisions then assume that a same-decision showing constitutes a complete defense to *all* actions under the Reconstruction Acts, without considering whether § 1983 actions based on Equal Protection violations represent an exception, at least as respects prospective relief, because of the contrary implications of the *Bakke* line of cases. The issue is also acute in actions under § 1981. To prevail under that statute, the plaintiff must show intentional race discrimination, see *General Bldg. Contractors, supra*, similar to the kind that generated the *Bakke* exception which permits the plaintiff to establish liability and obtain limited relief despite the defendant's "same decision" showing. It remains unresolved, in other words, whether the consequence that *Mt. Healthy* attaches to a mixed-motive showing (a judgment of nonliability) serves as an across-the-board defense to all actions under §§ 1983 and 1981, or only to those constitutional and statutory claims under § 1983 (like the First Amendment claim in *Mt. Healthy* itself) whose policies may not be offended by a complete judgment for defendant. See § 2.26, *infra*.

24. *Id.*

25. *See Fair Employment Council of Greater Wash., Inc. v. BMC Mktg. Corp.*, 28 F.3d 1268 (D.C.Cir.1994).

26. 42 U.S.C.A. §§ 2000e–5(b), (c), (f)(1).

27. *Fair Employment Council of Greater Wash. v. BMC Marketing*, 28 F.3d 1268; *but see* n.1 of that decision, which reserves decision on the question whether the lack of a bona fide interest in employment defeats standing.

contract offer because of the material misrepresentations of fact they made to the defendant employment agency about their intentions to secure employment, several appellate courts have held that tester plaintiffs cannot state a claim for damages under § 1981: "the loss of the opportunity to enter into a *void* contract ... i.e., a contract that *neither* party can enforce ... is not an injury cognizable under § 1981, for a void contract is a legal nullity."[28] In *Kyles*, the Seventh Circuit explained that Congress created "a substantive right, the denial of which alone gives rise to a cognizable injury and the right to sue."[29] By its terms, § 1981 protects only the contractual relationship, and the class of persons who can sue is therefore generally limited to those wishing to enter in, or remain in, that relationship.[30] Thus a shareholder may not maintain such an action for harm caused to her corporation, unless the defendant's conduct that injures the corporation causes distinct injury to the shareholder.[31] The corporation itself probably does have standing if it is an indirect target of racial discrimination in contracting, for example when it suffers loss profits resulting from unlawful discrimination aimed at a member of a class protected under § 1981.[32]

This standing problem, however, should be distinguished from the question of how broadly a violation of the plaintiff's own rights under § 1981 may be defined in relation to discriminatory actions immediately directed against another. Here the courts have shown considerable flexibility, permitting the assertion of § 1981 claims where intimate or associational rights of the plaintiff are allegedly invaded by a defendant whose conduct was aimed at third parties.[33] A related, but distinct

28. *Fair Employment Council of Greater Wash. v. BMC Marketing,* 28 F.3d 1268. *See also Kyles v. J.K. Guardian Sec. Servs., Inc.*, 222 F.3d 289 (7th Cir.2000) (finding that testers lack standing to sue under § 1981 for employment discrimination, but can pursue a Title VII claim); *Evans v. Kansas City, Mo. Sch. Dist.*, 65 F.3d 98 (8th Cir.1995) (holding that only students or parents, not a teacher, have standing to challenge segregation order). *But cf. Watts v. Boyd Props.*, 758 F.2d 1482 (11th Cir. 1985) and *Meyers v. Pennypack Woods Home Ownership Ass'n*, 559 F.2d 894 (3d Cir.1977) (according fair-housing testers standing to sue under §§ 1982 and 1981, respectively, although not squarely addressing question whether the testers had suffered legal injury within the meaning of those statutes).

29. 222 F.3d at 303.

30. *Id.* The court distinguished Title VII, finding that a tester can sue for employment discrimination because Congress created in Title VII "a broad substantive right that extends far beyond the simple refusal or failure to hire." *Id.* at 298.

31. *The Guides, Ltd. v. Yarmouth Group Property Management, Inc.*, 295 F.3d 1065 (10th Cir.2002) (sole shareholder and president denied standing).

32. *See Hudson Valley Freedom Theater, Inc. v. Heimbach*, 671 F.2d 702, 708 (2d Cir.1982).

33. *See, e.g., Alizadeh v. Safeway Stores, Inc.*, 802 F.2d 111, 114 (5th Cir. 1986) and *Parr v. Woodmen of the World Life Ins. Co.*, 791 F.2d 888, 890 (11th Cir. 1986) (upholding § 1981 claims where defendant employer allegedly fired (*Alizadeh*) or refused to hire (*Parr*) the plaintiff because of a spouse's race); *Fiedler v. Marumsco Christian Sch.*, 631 F.2d 1144, 1149 (4th Cir.1980) (§ 1981 claim stated on claim by white students that private school expelled them because they had associated with blacks). Similarly, courts have allowed § 1981 claims even where the plaintiff is not a member of the race discriminated against, but advocates their rights and is punished for it. *See, e.g., Johnson v. University of Cincinnati*, 215 F.3d 561 (6th Cir.), *cert. denied*, 531 U.S. 1052, 121 S.Ct. 657, 148 L.Ed.2d 560 (2000) (but rejecting the claim on Eleventh Amendment immunity grounds). Also holding that § 1981 litigation against a state, state agency or sub-

question is whether the defendant must be the party with whom the plaintiff contracts or seeks to contract. Courts have answered this question in the negative, holding § 1981 is violated by a racially motivated interference with a plaintiff's right to enter into contracts with nonwhites[34] and by third parties' attempts to punish the plaintiff for making such contracts.[35]

When a customer complains of racial discrimination by an employee of a retailer, the employer can be held vicariously liable for the acts of the employee if the employee was acting within the scope of the employment.[36] Unlike sexual harassment employment cases, in these public accommodation § 1981 cases, it is no defense to respondeat superior liability that the customer suffered the discrimination at the hands of a low-level clerk. "[A] rule that only actions by supervisors are imputed to the employer would result, in most cases, in a no liability rule."[37]

A plaintiff makes out a prima facie case under § 1981 of discrimination in hotel accommodations when she demonstrates that (1) she is a member of a protected class, (2) she sought to enter into or had a contract with a hotel for accommodations, (3) she met the hotel's standard requirements for occupancy, and (4) she was denied accommodations that were available to guests outside of the protected class.[38]

Recent additional restrictions on the use of § 1981 in actions against government defendants, and a short-lived restriction on the availability of § 1981 to attack post-hire conditions of employment, are described below.

state entity functioning on behalf of the state may be barred by the Eleventh Amendment is *Sessions v. Rusk State Hosp*, 648 F.2d 1066, 1069 (5th Cir.1981). *See also Fincher v. Florida Dep't of Labor & Employment Sec. Unemployment Appeals Comm'n*, 798 F.2d 1371, 1372 (11th Cir. 1986), *cert. denied*, 479 U.S. 1072, 107 S.Ct. 1262, 94 L.Ed.2d 124 (1987) (no express congressional abrogation of the state's Eleventh Amendment immunity with respect to claims under 42 U.S.C.A. § 1985).

34. *See, e.g., Des Vergnes v. Seekonk Water Dist.*, 601 F.2d 9 (1st Cir.1979).

35. *See, e.g., Winston v. Lear–Siegler, Inc.*, 558 F.2d 1266, 1270 (6th Cir.1977); *DeMatteis v. Eastman Kodak Co.*, 511 F.2d 306, 312, *modified*, 520 F.2d 409 (2d Cir. 1975); *cf. Sullivan v. Little Hunting Park*, 396 U.S. 229, 237, 90 S.Ct. 400, 404, 24 L.Ed.2d 386 (1969) (same result under § 1982).

36. *See, e.g., Arguello v. Conoco, Inc.*, 207 F.3d 803, 809–12 (5th Cir.), *cert. denied sub nom. Escobedo v. Conoco, Inc.*, 531 U.S. 874, 121 S.Ct. 177, 148 L.Ed.2d 121 (2000). *Cf. City of Chicago v. Matchmaker Real Estate Sales Ctr., Inc.*, 982 F.2d 1086, 1089 (7th Cir.1992) (arising under the Fair Housing Act and § 1982).

37. *Arguello*, 207 F.3d at 810.

38. *See Murrell v. Ocean Mecca Motel, Inc.*, 262 F.3d 253 (4th Cir.2001) (reversing a grant of summary judgment to the defendant-hotel); *Rutstein v. Avis Rent–A–Car Systems, Inc.*, 211 F.3d 1228 (11th Cir. 2000) (denying class certification to group of Jewish plaintiffs alleging that defendant denied their right to make and enforce contracts under § 1981); *Evans v. Holiday Inns, Inc.*, 951 F.Supp. 85, 88 (D.Md.1997) (stating similar test for establishing a prima facie case of race discrimination in denying hotel accommodations); *cf. Christian v. Wal–Mart Stores, Inc.*, 252 F.3d 862, 872 (6th Cir.2001), *supplemented on denial of reh'g*, 266 F.3d 407 (6th Cir.2001) (adopting similar test when an African-American customer was evicted from a store); *Callwood v. Dave & Buster's, Inc.*, 98 F.Supp.2d 694, 707 (D.Md.2000) (applying similar formulation to claim that restaurant provided inferior service to African-American patrons).

The Supreme Court has directed the lower federal courts to borrow analogous state statutes of limitations in actions under § 1981,[39] and has held that pursuing Title VII administrative procedures does not toll the § 1981 statute of limitations.[40] The Court has explained that in actions under the Reconstruction Civil Rights Acts, the forum state's "personal injury" statute of limitations should apply;[41] and the particular period the court should borrow is the state's general or residual statute on personal injury claims rather than, for example, a statute geared specifically to intentional torts.[42]

But subsequently Congress enacted 28 U.S.C. § 1658(a), a 4–year "catchall" statute of limitations governing claims "arising under an Act of Congress enacted after [December 1, 1990]." One such post-December 1, 1990 statute is the Civil Rights Act of 1991, which, as discussed later in this subsection, amended § 1981 by overruling the Supreme Court's decision in *Patterson v. McLean Credit Union*[43] and thus restoring the application of § 1981 to terms and conditions of employment–like on-the-job harassment, failure to promote, demotion, and discharge—arising after initial contract formation. The question that then divided five circuit courts of appeals was whether a § 1981 claim asserting racial discrimination respecting a post-hire term of employment—that is, a claim made possible only by the Civil Rights Act of 1991's overruling of *Patterson*—was eligible for § 1658's 4–year statute of limitations even though the underlying statute that the 1991 Act amended, Section 1981, pre-dated December 1, 1990 by 124 years. In *Jones v. R.R. Donnelley & Sons Company*,[44] the Court held that it is. The Court concluded that a cause of action "aris[es] under an Act of Congress enacted after" December 1, 1990—and is therefore governed by § 1658's 4–year limitations period—if the particular plaintiff's claims were made possible by a post–1990 enactment. Because the *Jones* petitioners' hostile work environment, wrongful termination, and failure-to-transfer claims alleged § 1981 violations that, under *Patterson*, would not have stated a claim before December 1, 1990, but were actionable by virtue of the Civil Rights Act of 1991 amendments, they "ar[ose] under" the 1991 amendments to § 1981 and accordingly fit within the terms of § 1658. Because the vast majority of claims under Section 1981, indeed virtually all such claims other than alleged racially discriminatory refusals to hire, depend on the 1991 amendments to § 1981 that overruled *Patterson*, almost all Section 1981 claims will now be eligible for § 1658's generous 4–year

39. The Eleventh Circuit refused to borrow a state statute of repose, reasoning that it was an unnecessary, distinct state statute. *Moore v. Liberty Nat'l Life Ins. Co.*, 267 F.3d 1209, 1216 (11th Cir.2001) (noting that the court found no federal case in which a state statute of repose was borrowed to fill the gaps in a federal civil rights statute).

40. *Johnson v. Railway Express Agency*, 421 U.S. 454, 95 S.Ct. 1716, 44 L.Ed.2d 295 (1975).

41. *See Wilson v. Garcia*, 471 U.S. 261, 105 S.Ct. 1938, 85 L.Ed.2d 254 (1985) (§ 1983); *Goodman v. Lukens Steel Co.*, 482 U.S. 656, 107 S.Ct. 2617, 96 L.Ed.2d 572 (1987) (§ 1981).

42. *Owens v. Okure*, 488 U.S. 235, 109 S.Ct. 573, 102 L.Ed.2d 594 (1989).

43. 491 U.S. 164, 109 S.Ct. 2363, 105 L.Ed.2d 132 (1989).

44. ___ U.S. ___, 124 S.Ct. 1836, ___ L.Ed.2d ___ (2004).

limitations period, regardless of shorter limitations periods of the forum state. By contrast, claims under the other Reconstruction Acts, principally claims under Sections 1982, 1983, and 1985, will remain subject to the forum state's general or residual limitations period governing claims of personal injury, because the rights created by those statutes have not been substantively amended after § 1658's cutoff of December 1, 1990.

It appears likely that the liberal approach to claim accrual embraced by the Supreme Court in *National Railroad Passenger Corporation v. Morgan*[45] for "hostile environment" claims of racial or sexual harassment under Title VII will be extended to similar § 1981 claims as well.[46] A more detailed discussion of the selection and application of statutes of limitations under the Reconstruction Civil Rights Acts may be found in § 5.72.

Title 42 U.S.C.A. § 1977A(a)(1), added by § 102 of the Civil Rights Act of 1991, provides that damages under Title VII are recoverable only if the complainant "cannot recover" under § 1981. But the EEOC, relying on the Sponsors' Interpretive Memorandum,[47] has interpreted that language to bar only double recovery for the same injury, not parallel proceedings under the two statutes. Putative plaintiffs with intentional race discrimination claims against employers large enough to be covered by and not exempt from Title VII can therefore apparently choose whether to proceed under Title VII or § 1981 or both.

That choice will be heavily influenced by the availability of unlimited compensatory and punitive damages under § 1981, free of Title VII's variable caps, and by the immediate access to court under § 1981, free of the Title VII state and federal administrative prerequisite requirements with their rather early filing deadlines. Some such claimants, however, who, despite the availability of attorneys' fees, are unable to attract counsel might nevertheless prefer the Title VII route, because by statute the EEOC is expected to assist with investigation and conciliation.

In practice, however, § 1981 will usually look more attractive. Procedurally and remedially, the Reconstruction Civil Rights Acts, § 1981 in particular, may hold several attractions over Title VII. For one, no administrative exhaustion is required.[48] Second, the applicable

45. 536 U.S. 101, 122 S.Ct. 2061, 153 L.Ed.2d 106 (2002).

46. *See Madison v. IBP, Inc.,* 330 F.3d 1051 (8th Cir.2003) (even punitive damages recoverable with respect to events pre-dating the Title VII or § 1981 limitations period provided one act in the hostile environment pattern occurred within the period); *Shields v. Fort James Corporation*, 305 F.3d 1280 (11th Cir.2002) (*Morgan* standard, which allows courts to view such allegations as a single employment practice and deems all component parts of the harassment as timely charged if even the smallest portion occurred within the limitations period, applies to § 1981 claim, but employer should be allowed to plead laches as defense on remand). *But see Felton v. Polles,* 315 F.3d 470, 484–486 (5th Cir.2002) (citing *Morgan* but appearing not to apply it to § 1981 claim and instead adhering to "continuing violation" theory *Morgan* discarded).

47. 137 Cong. Rec. S15484 (Oct. 30, 1991).

48. *See Patsy v. Board of Regents*, 457 U.S. 496, 102 S.Ct. 2557, 73 L.Ed.2d 172 (1982) (§ 1983). *But see* § 5.121 *infra* on newer, more stringent administrative exhaustion requirements applicable to state and federal prisoners under the Prison Litigation Reform Act of 1996.

limitation periods borrowed from state law are normally longer than the usual 180–day or 240/300–day Title VII deadline for filing charges with federal or state agencies. Third, although jury trials are now available under either statute with respect to claims of intentional discrimination, the nineteenth-century statutes offer compensatory and punitive damages unlimited in amount;[49] while, even after the Civil Rights Act of 1991, Title VII plaintiffs who prove intentional discrimination are subject to caps on those damages that vary with the number of employees working for the defendant employer.[50] In one respect, Title VII lines up precisely with § 1983 and § 1981: punitive damages are not available against a defendant government entity.[51]

But what if the § 1981 defendant is able to prove something akin to what the Supreme Court's *Mt. Healthy City School Dist. Bd. of Educ. v. Doyle*[52] decision encourages § 1983 defendants to prove: that the challenged employment action would have been taken for lawful reasons independent of the racial component of the employer's overall motivation? The effect of this showing under § 1983 appears to be (except with respect to procedural due process and certain express or facial equal protection violations) that no federal law violation is established and the defendant may not be mulcted in damages. Under Title VII, as amended in 1991, however, the defendant who makes this "same-decision" showing is relieved only of retroactive, monetary relief; she is still considered to have violated the law and is therefore subject to prospective relief and attorneys' fees. The 1991 amendments to Title VII did not, however, make the same amendment to § 1981 or the ADEA, although it amended those statutes in other respects. Consequently, the post–*Mt. Healthy*, pre–1991 regime governing § 1981 defendants who carry the showing—a complete defense to liability—is therefore likely to prevail in most circuits.[53] And under that regime the § 1981 defendant may escape

49. The Eleventh Circuit has held that a punitive damage award under § 1981 is available only when the plaintiff proves that the defendant acted with "malice or reckless disregard" of the plaintiff's rights. *Ferrill v. Parker Group, Inc.*, 168 F.3d 468, 476 (11th Cir.1999). The court vacated an award of punitive damages because the lower court had specifically found no evidence of animus or malice.

50. *See Olmsted v. Taco Bell Corp.*, 141 F.3d 1457 (11th Cir.1998) (affirming lower court's decision to reduce damage awards of $450,000 in compensatory and $3 million in punitive damages to Title VII's cap of $300,000 because plaintiff had abandoned his § 1981 claim in a pre-trial stipulation).

51. Section 1981(b)(1) authorizes punitive damages when intentional Title VII discrimination is proved (and other, traditional requirements for punitive damages are satisfied) except against "a government, government agency, or political subdivision." The Supreme Court has held punitive damages generally unavailable in § 1983 actions against government in *City of Newport v. Fact Concerts, Inc.*, 453 U.S. 247, 101 S.Ct. 2748, 69 L.Ed.2d 616 (1981). And lower courts have extended the *City of Newport* ruling to actions under § 1981. *See Walters v. City of Atlanta*, 803 F.2d 1135 (11th Cir.1986) and cases there cited.

52. 429 U.S. 274, 97 S.Ct. 568, 50 L.Ed.2d 471 (1977).

53. *Ballard v. Muskogee Reg'l Med. Ctr.*, 238 F.3d 1250 (10th Cir.2001) (First Amendment case under Section 1983); *Pulliam v. Tallapoosa County Jail,* 185 F.3d 1182, 1184 (11th Cir.1999); *Mabra v. United Food & Commercial Workers Local Union,* 176 F.3d 1357 (11th Cir.1999) (cases under Section 1981). The Eighth Circuit, purporting to distinguish § 1981 from Section 1983 in this respect, upheld a jury award of damages for a violation of Section 1981 even though the defendant had carried the showing described (for § 1983

without liability, whereas the Title VII discrimination plaintiff (although perhaps not the Title VII retaliation plaintiff) will establish a violation and thereby have an opportunity to receive declaratory and injunctive relief and, in turn, attorney's fees as a "prevailing party."[54] Indeed, even if the Section 1981 defendant fails to plead the defense affirmatively, it may be preserved if mentioned in the pretrial order.[55]

A potential plaintiff with an intentional race discrimination claim actionable under both statutes may prefer Title VII if she cannot afford counsel and believes that state or federal agency administrative processing of her charge will induce her employer to settle. In addition, it remains possible, to an as yet uncertain extent, for a plaintiff who cannot prove intentional discrimination and would therefore fail under § 1981 to succeed under Title VII by establishing that an employer's neutral practice had a disproportionate adverse impact on her group and that the employer cannot justify the practice as a matter of job relatedness and business necessity.

In actions against state and local government employers, it appears increasingly likely, as discussed in detail in the "*Jett*" sections that follow[56], that § 1981 is not available on its own terms and instead the plaintiff must surmount the additional proof requirements and defenses available under § 1983. If this is so, then Title VII may once again become a more attractive option for asserting intentional race discrimination claims against state or local government employers. And Title VII would appear to be the *only* remedy for race discrimination in federal employment, which has been held outside the reach of § 1981.[57]

In its 1988 Term, the Court held in *Patterson v. McLean Credit Union*[58] that discriminatory conduct directed against an employee after her initial hiring falls outside the right granted by § 1981 to "make" a

cases) by *Mt. Healthy*. *See Edwards v. Jewish Hosp.*, 855 F.2d 1345 (8th Cir.1988). The court asserted that § 1981 aims to deter as well as compensate, while § 1983 has only a compensation rationale. Some support may have been drawn for the proposition that § 1983 seeks only to compensate from the Supreme Court's decisions in *Mt. Healthy* and *Carey v. Piphus*, 435 U.S. 247, 98 S.Ct. 1042, 55 L.Ed.2d 252 (1978). But well before *Edwards* was decided, the Court had made clear that § 1983 has a distinct deterrent rationale, and that punitive damages are sometimes necessary to fulfill it. *Smith v. Wade*, 461 U.S. 30, 103 S.Ct. 1625, 75 L.Ed.2d 632 (1983). *But see* § 2.26, *infra*. This section discusses recent authority to the effect that the § 1983 defendant found to have violated *equal protection* is liable, and subject to declaratory and injunctive relief and attorneys' fees, and possibly also emotional distress and punitive damages (but not to a hiring or promotion order or economic compensation like back or front pay), even when he carries the "same decision" showing that ordinarily negates any liability altogether.

54. *See* Chapter 4, *infra*, on Attorney's Fees under § 706(k) of Title VII and 42 U.S.C.A. § 1988 with respect to actions under all of the Reconstruction Civil Rights Acts.

55. *Pulliam v. Tallapoosa County Jail*, 185 F.3d at 1185, n.4.

56. §§ 1.8, 1.10–1.13.

57. *Lee v. Hughes*, No. 5:96–CV–316–3 (M.D.Ga.1997), *aff'd on other grounds*, 145 F.3d 1272 (11th Cir.1998), *cert. denied*, 525 U.S. 1138, 119 S.Ct. 1026, 143 L.Ed.2d 37 (1999); *Williams v. Glickman*, 936 F.Supp. 1, 5 (D.D.C.1996); *Gallardo v. Board of County Comm'rs*, 857 F.Supp. 783 (D.Kan. 1994). *See Martin v. Heckler*, 773 F.2d 1145, 1152 (11th Cir.1985).

58. 491 U.S. 164, 109 S.Ct. 2363, 105 L.Ed.2d 132 (1989).

contract free from racial discrimination. The 1991 legislation overturns this decision and thereby restores 42 U.S.C.A. § 1981 as a forceful supplementary vehicle for redressing race or ancestry discrimination in contracting, although only when the defendant's conduct is shown, by direct or indirect evidence, to be *intentional*.[59] The legislation provides that the right to "make" a contract extends beyond initial formation to include "performance, modification and termination" and thus reaches not only dismissal but also ongoing terms and conditions of employment, probably including retaliation and race-based harassment.[60]

The 1991 legislation likely restores § 1981 post-hiring retaliation claims by overturning *Patterson*.[61] The contours of such a claim, however, remain unclear.[62] The Eleventh Circuit, for example, revived a § 1981 post-hiring retaliation claim by a black plaintiff alleging that she was terminated for filing an EEOC charge for race discrimination,[63] but rejected a claim by a white plaintiff fired for complaining of racial slurs about blacks.[64] In general, the retaliatory conduct, to be actionable, must respond to an employee's assertion of rights protected by Section 1981.[65] Thus the claim would fail if the underlying discrimination were based on religion, a ground that per se is probably not protected by § 1981.[66] The Seventh Circuit requires a type of double causation: in order for retaliation to be actionable under § 1981, the plaintiff must show that the defendant interfered with his right to enforce the contract on account of race, and the plaintiff must then show that the retaliation itself had a racial motivation.[67] However, this double causation requirement is sus-

59. *See General Bldg. Contractors Ass'n. v. Pennsylvania*, 458 U.S. 375, 102 S.Ct. 3141, 73 L.Ed.2d 835 (1982).

60. Section 101(b) (amending 42 U.S.C.A. § 1981 (1988)). *See, e.g., Foley v. University of Houston System*, 324 F.3d 310 (5th Cir.2003) (1991 Act restored a claim of retaliation under § 1981); *Hawkins v. 1115 Legal Service Care*, 163 F.3d 684 (2d Cir. 1998) (§ 1981 as amended in 1991 reaches claims of unlawful retaliation, harassment and discrimination in hiring, discharge, demotion, promotion, and transfer); *Carney v. The American University*, 151 F.3d 1090, 1094 (D.C.Cir.1998) (assuming without deciding that retaliation is actionable under § 1981); *Andrews v. Lakeshore Rehab. Hosp.*, 140 F.3d 1405, 1412–13 (11th Cir. 1998) (same); *Kim v. Nash Finch Co.*, 123 F.3d 1046, 1059 (8th Cir.1997); *Barge v. Anheuser–Busch, Inc.*, 87 F.3d 256, 259 (8th Cir.1996) (same). *But cf. Felton v. Polles*, 315 F.3d 470, 483–486 (5th Cir.2002) (stating that while Fifth Circuit decisions recognize a post–1991 Act § 1981 harassment claim against individual private-sector defendants, the court has not specified the requisite prima facie elements and hence individual § 1981 government official defendants facing harassment charges may be eligible for qualified immunity, because the applicable law as to them is not clearly established).

61. *Cf.* EEOC Guidance on Investigating, Analyzing Retaliation Claims, EEOC Compliance Manual § 8–1 (1998).

62. *See Bass v. Board of County Comm'rs, Orange County, Fla.*, 242 F.3d 996, 1016 (11th Cir.2001) (whether § 1981 retaliation claim elements are identical to those under Title VII an open question); *Olmsted v. Taco Bell Corp.*, 141 F.3d 1457 (11th Cir.1998).

63. *Andrews v. Lakeshore Rehab. Hosp.*, 140 F.3d 1405 (11th Cir.1998).

64. *Little v. United Tech.*, 103 F.3d 956 (11th Cir.1997). *But cf. Jackson v. Motel 6*, 130 F.3d 999 (11th Cir.1997) (allowing plaintiff to proceed with § 1981 retaliation claim).

65. *See Foley v. University of Houston System*, 355 F.3d 333, 339 (5th Cir.2003); *Hawkins v. 1115 Legal Service Care*, 163 F.3d 684 (2d Cir.1998).

66. *Pennington v. City of Huntsville*, 261 F.3d 1262 (11th Cir.2001).

67. *Daniels v. Pipefitters' Ass'n Local Union No. 597*, 945 F.2d 906 (7th Cir.1991)

pect; the party complaining of retaliation need not also be a member of a protected group.[68]

Another emerging Title VII proof requirement—that the plaintiff show a substantial or material adverse impact on terms and conditions of employment—has sometimes been held inapplicable to Reconstruction Act claims.[69] And the Eleventh Circuit has held that neither the BFOQ nor business necessity defenses, available in some circumstances under Title VII, will defeat a § 1981 claim.[70] The court stated that the business necessity defense is available only to claims of disparate impact, a claim not cognizable under § 1981, which requires proof of intentional discrimination. And a BFOQ defense, the court noted, is not available to a charge of racial discrimination.[71]

Section 1981 contains no threshold numerical requirement for employer coverage. In the course of considering the amendments, Congress observed that § 1981 constitutes the only protection against race or ancestry discrimination for those millions of applicants or employees whose employers are too small to be covered by Title VII. Despite this understanding, the amendments make no attempt to protect those applicants or employees against the other forms of discrimination prohibited by Title VII, that is, sex, religion, or national origin, or against race discrimination resulting solely from the effects of a neutral practice.[72] Indeed, by capping Title VII damages, while leaving uncapped the compensatory and punitive damages recoverable under § 1981, Congress rather pointedly expresses greater concern with intentional race discrim-

(for retaliation to be actionable under § 1981, the retaliation itself must be racially motivated). *See also Kim v. Nash Finch Co.*, 123 F.3d 1046 (8th Cir.1997) (allowing § 1981 claim by Korean plaintiff retaliated against because he filed EEOC complaint).

68. *See, e.g., Anderson v. Phillips Petroleum Co.*, 722 F.Supp. 668, 671–72 (D.Kan.1989).

69. *Power v. Summers*, 226 F.3d 815 (7th Cir.2000) (case under § 1983). *But cf. Felton v. Polles*, 315 F.3d 470, 486 (5th Cir.2002) (applying the Title VII requirement that plaintiff must complain of an "ultimate employment decision" to claim under § 1981).

70. *See Ferrill v. Parker Group, Inc.*, 168 F.3d 468, 473–74 (11th Cir.1999).

71. *Id.* This holding by the Eleventh Circuit arguably conflicts with a Seventh Circuit case, *Wittmer v. Peters*, 87 F.3d 916 (7th Cir.1996), in which the court crafted a narrow racial BFOQ.

72. It is well settled that § 1981 affords no protection against discrimination based on gender. *See McDonald v. Santa Fe Trail Transp. Co.*, 427 U.S. 273, 96 S.Ct. 2574, 49 L.Ed.2d 493 (1976). *See also Runyon v. McCrary*, 427 U.S. 160, 96 S.Ct. 2586, 49 L.Ed.2d 415 (1976) (applying § 1981 to purely private conduct and affirmed in that respect by *Patterson v. McLean Credit Union*, 491 U.S. 164, 109 S.Ct. 2363, 105 L.Ed.2d 132 (1989)). While it is also clear that § 1981 does prohibit discrimination based on ancestry (ethnic or physiognomic characteristic), *St. Francis Coll. v. Al–Khazraji*, 481 U.S. 604, 107 S.Ct. 2022, 95 L.Ed.2d 582 (1987); *Shaare Tefila Congregation v. Cobb*, 481 U.S. 615, 107 S.Ct. 2019, 95 L.Ed.2d 594 (1987), those opinions also suggest that it provides no protection against religious discrimination as such. The circuits are split on whether § 1981 reaches private sector discrimination because of alienage. *See Anderson v. Conboy*, 156 F.3d 167 (2d Cir.1998) (holding yes; relying especially on 1991 amendments' confirmation that the statute reaches private interference with contracting); *Duane v. GEICO*, 37 F.3d 1036 (4th Cir. 1994) (holding yes); *Bhandari v. First Nat'l Bank of Commerce*, 829 F.2d 1343 (5th Cir. 1987) (holding no). Appellate decisions are in accord that *governmental* alienage discrimination is actionable under § 1981.

ination than with unintentional discrimination or intentional discrimination based on Title VII's other prohibited grounds.

In § 1981 disparate treatment discrimination cases, courts commonly permit the showing of intent requisite under the Reconstruction Acts to be made inferentially, that is, through the *McDonnell Douglas/Burdine/St. Mary's* formula of shifting evidentiary burdens that is paradigmatic under Title VII.[73] Similarly, once a plaintiff has established a prima face case of retaliation under § 1981, most circuits will consider *McDonnell Douglas* inferential evidence to discredit any neutral employer reason for the adverse action at issue.[74] Nevertheless, there have been rumblings of discontent with the dominant view that treats such inferential evidence as an adequate foundation not only for liability but also for punitive damages.[75] The Supreme Court's decision in *Kolstad v. American Dental Association,*[76] should put an end to these rumblings, while at

73. *See, e.g., St. Mary's Honor Ctr. v. Hicks*, 509 U.S. 502, 506 n. 1, 113 S.Ct. 2742, 2746, 125 L.Ed.2d 407 (1993), *Patterson v. McLean Credit Union,* 491 U.S. 164, 109 S.Ct. 2363, 105 L.Ed.2d 132 (1989); *Williams v. Lindenwood Univ.*, 288 F.3d 349, 356–57 (8th Cir.2002) (and noting that "injecting racial language at all into the decision-making process creates the inference that race had something to do with the decision-making process"); *Sledge v. Goodyear Dunlop Tires North Am., Ltd.*, 275 F.3d 1014, 1015 (11th Cir.2001); *Perry v. Woodward*, 199 F.3d 1126, 1135–41 (10th Cir.1999), *cert. denied*, 529 U.S. 1110, 120 S.Ct. 1964, 146 L.Ed.2d 796 (2000); *Barbour v. Merrill,* 48 F.3d 1270 (D.C.Cir.1995).

74. The plaintiff's prima facie case of retaliation consists of showing (1) statutorily protected activity, which in § 1981 cases would typically be evidence of the plaintiff's opposition to a race-or ancestry-based denial of the right to make or enforce a contract; (2) an adverse consequence, for example termination of employment; and (3) a causal connection between the two. Some courts require more or less direct evidence that the protest or opposition was the "but for" cause of the adverse consequence; others permit the fact finder to infer the causal connection from evidence of the defendant's knowledge of the plaintiff's protected activity and a close degree of temporal proximity between the protected activity and the adverse consequence. *See, e.g., Hysten v. Burlington Northern and Santa Fe Ry. Co.*, 296 F.3d 1177 (10th Cir.2002) (three months elapsing between plaintiff's filing of race discrimination suit and employer reprimand insufficient standing alone to establish causal connection); *O'Neal v. Ferguson Construction Co.*, 237 F.3d 1248 (10th Cir. 2001) (observing that 3–month lapse between protected activity and adverse action had been held insufficient to show causal connection, but that 1–1/2–month lapse had sufficed). *See also Dunn v. Nordstrom*, 260 F.3d 778 (7th Cir.2001) (evidence of close timing between protected activity and adverse employment consequence may be considered in determining if plaintiff has established the "but for" relationship between the two).

In any event the defendant may rebut evidence suggesting the adverse action was taken because of the plaintiff's protected activity by proffering neutral reasons for the adverse action. At that point the plaintiff, a la *McDonnell Douglas*, has the opportunity, and bears the burden of persuasion to demonstrate, that the defendant's neutral reason or reasons are mere "pretexts." One way a plaintiff may carry that burden is through cross-examination of defendant's witnesses that, coupled with plaintiff's prima facie evidence, is sufficient to persuade the fact finder those reasons are false and were offered to mask a retaliatory motive. *See generally Alexander v. Wisconsin Dep't of Health and Family Services*, 263 F.3d 673 (7th Cir.2001); *Roberts v. Roadway Express*, 149 F.3d 1098 (10th Cir.1998); *Barge v. Anheuser–Busch, Inc.*, 87 F.3d 256 (8th Cir.1996) (employing *McDonnell Douglas* inferential proof mode). *See also Foley v. University of Houston System*, 355 F.3d 333, 340 n. 8 (5th Cir. 2003) (equating the elements required to show retaliation under § 1981 and Title VII).

75. On the general Reconstruction Act standard for punitive damages, *see Smith v. Wade,* 461 U.S. 30, 103 S.Ct. 1625, 75 L.Ed.2d 632 (1983). For the more recent rumblings, see the petition for writ of certiorari in *Barbour v. Merrill,* 48 F.3d 1270 (D.C.Cir.1995).

76. 527 U.S. 526, 119 S.Ct. 2118, 144 L.Ed.2d 494 (1999).

the same time reaffirming that punitive damages do depend on a showing of either malice or reckless disregard of legal obligations, in addition to evidence of intentional discrimination. While proof requirements for § 1981 discrimination or retaliation claims are rather stringent, and in all cases require evidence of intentional conduct, all such claims in federal court enjoy the benefit of liberal Federal Rules notice pleading.[77]

As observed above, while the damages caps in 42 U.S.C.A. § 1981a limit the recovery of compensatory and punitive damages available under Title VII,[78] they do not limit the recovery available to plaintiffs who prevail under the amended § 1981.[79] For this reason, plaintiffs complaining under both Title VII and § 1981 of underlying intentional race or ancestry discrimination may be well advised to pursue a related retaliation claim under § 1981, as well as Title VII. But to prevail under § 1981, the retaliation plaintiff must show that the defendant took action against him in reprisal for plaintiff's assertion of one of the rights protected by § 1981—i.e., the right to be free of interference in the making or enforcement of contracts because of race or ancestry, and not, for example, gender, a prohibited ground only under Title VII.[80] And the plaintiff who has tried primary discrimination or retaliation claims under both Title VII and § 1981 and receives a favorable jury verdict may bear the additional burden of demonstrating to the court that the jury accepted her § 1981 claim if she hopes to avoid the Title VII cap on damages.[81]

Section 1981, in sum, is ordinarily superior to Title VII as a remedy for intentional, race-based discrimination in employment. Nevertheless, there are at least five situations, two of them relatively common, in which the advocate contemplating a race-based employment discrimination claim should endure Title VII's procedural prerequisites and limitations on damages rather than proceed under Section 1981 alone. The first of these, relatively rare, is where Section 1981 is unavailable because the plaintiff alleges unintentional discrimination—that is, where the plaintiff's sole complaint is that the employer utilized one or more neutral employment practices (tests, height-weight requirements, no-spouse rule) that had a disproportionate adverse impact on a group defined by race. That claim is actionable under Title VII, although it is subject to the elaborate and notoriously vague affirmative defense described by the 1991 amendments to that statute.

A second situation is quite common. Plaintiff has an intentional race-based employment discrimination claim actionable under Section

77. *See Phillip v. University of Rochester*, 316 F.3d 291, 293–294 (2d Cir.2003) (applying to Section 1981 "equal benefit" clause claim the liberal pleading standard that the Supreme Court, in *Swierkiewicz v. Sorema, N.A.*, 534 U.S. 506, 122 S.Ct. 992, 152 L.Ed.2d 1 (2002), recently reaffirmed also applies to claims under Title VII).

78. *See* 42 U.S.C.A. § 1981a(b)(3).

79. 42 U.S.C.A. § 1981a(b)(4).

80. *Hawkins*, 163 F.3d 684; *Manning v. Metropolitan Life Ins. Co.*, 127 F.3d 686, 689 n. 1 (8th Cir.1997) (retaliation for opposing gender discrimination not actionable under § 1981).

81. *See Hawkins*, 163 F.3d 684.

1981 but fears that the finder of fact will determine that the employer acted with mixed lawful and unlawful motives and would have taken action against the plaintiff (not hired, not promoted, disciplined, or fired her) based on the lawful ground alone. As observed above, the circuit authority under Section 1981, drawing on comparable Supreme Court rulings under Section 1983, treats this "same-decision" affirmative defense as a complete defense to liability, not merely a limitation on remedy. By contrast, as explained above, the mixed-motive Title VII plaintiff alleging intentional discrimination (and perhaps retaliation) remains eligible for prospective (mainly injunctive) relief and, in turn, attorney's fees even if the defense succeeds. Accordingly, she and, especially, her attorney, have some incentive to mount a Title VII, instead of or in addition to a § 1981 challenge, to intentional, race-based employment discrimination despite the possibility of a successful mixed-motive defense. This incentive is strengthened by a 2003 Supreme Court decision that a Title VII plaintiff is eligible for an instruction placing the burden of persuasion on the defendant concerning the "same-decision" issue regardless of whether the plaintiff used "direct" or inferential evidence to establish that the employer, at least in part, relied on an unlawful factor in making the challenged employment decision.[82]

Third, another relatively common circumstance, is the plaintiff who sues state or local governments for intentional, race-based employment discrimination under Section 1981. He may have to show that the adverse action was taken against him by a final policymaking official or otherwise as a matter of agency "policy"—a difficult proof hurdle imported into Section 1981 from Section 1983 cases by the Supreme Court's *Jett* decision, which appears to have survived the 1991 amendments to Section 1981.[83] The difficulty is that the typical employment discrimination claim alleges adverse action inflicted ad hoc by a lower-ranking government agent rather than through an official agency policy or by a top policymaker. When asserted against a state or local government employer, therefore, such a claim will fare far better under Title VII: except for hostile environment harassment, that statute imposes respondeat superior liability on the employer for the acts of low-ranking supervisors and managers, with no additional required proof of "policy." If, as seems likely, *Jett* survives the 1991 amendments, there can be no respondeat superior liability against units of local or state government arising from claims asserting liability based on violations of § 1981.[84]

Fourth, the unrepresented plaintiff, or plaintiff of low means, may choose to pursue a Title VII claim, at least initially, to capitalize on any free assistance in investigation or settlement that may be provided by the regional office of the Equal Employment Opportunity Commission. Pre-suit resort to the EEOC is mandated in actions under Title VII, but

82. *Desert Palace, Inc. v. Costa,* 539 U.S. 90, 123 S.Ct. 2148, 156 L.Ed.2d 84, (2003).

83. *See* §§ 1.8 and 1.10–1.13, *infra.*

84. *Felton v. Polles,* 315 F.3d 470, 482 (5th Cir.2002).

EEOC is not available for the processing of claims under the Reconstruction Civil Rights Acts.

Fifth, where the claim is brought by someone other than the injured employee, so that the plaintiff is asserting the right of a third party, broader standing has been recognized under Title VII than under Section 1981.

The vast majority of § 1981 claims, including those arising from employment, assert violations of the "same right ... to make and enforce contracts" clause. A few, however, are brought under the "equal benefit" clause, which provides a claim where a plaintiff can demonstrate that a defendant, motivated by racial animosity, has deprived or attempted to deprive him of "the full and equal benefit" of a law or proceedings "for the security of persons and property."[85] It is well established, of course, that the *contracts* clause applies to purely private conduct;[86] indeed, ironically, the private § 1981 defendant, definitively held subject to § 1981 claims only in 1976, may be worse off than his public counterpart, for he does not enjoy the qualified immunity defense enjoyed by individual § 1981 state actor defendants sued for damages in their individual capacities[87] or the *Jett* advantages that may accrue to state actor defendants sued in their official capacities.[88] The circuit decisions disagree, however, whether the *equal benefit* reaches private defendants. Section 1981(c), added in 1991, provides: "The rights protected by this section are protected against impairment *by nongovernmental discrimination* and impairment under color of State law," and that language refers to rights protected by the section as a whole, without excepting the equal benefit clause. Despite the seeming clarity of that language, the few circuits to have addressed the question are divided as to whether state action is required for an equal benefit clause claim governed by the amended statute.[89]

§ 1.3 Section 1982

This statute, enacted pursuant to Congress' Thirteenth Amendment authority, traces from the earliest Reconstruction era and secures to all citizens the right, enforceable against private as well as public defendants, to "inherit, purchase, lease, sell, hold and convey real and personal property." Beginning in the 1940's § 1982 was used mostly to challenge racially restrictive covenants in housing subdivisions. Today it

85. 42 U.S.C.A. § 1981(a), as amended in 1991.

86. *Runyon v. McCrary*, 427 U.S. 160, 96 S.Ct. 2586, 49 L.Ed.2d 415 (1976).

87. *See Foley v. University of Houston System*, 355 F.3d 333, 338 (5th Cir. 2003).

88. *See Felton v. Polles*, 315 F.3d 470 (5th Cir.2002), discussed above.

89. *Compare Chapman v. Higbee Co.*, 319 F.3d 825 (6th Cir.2003) (en banc), *cert. denied* ___ U.S. ___, 124 S.Ct. 2902, ___ L.Ed.2d ___ (2004) and *Phillip v. Univ. of Rochester*, 316 F.3d 291 (2d Cir.2003) (holding no state action required) *with Youngblood v. Hy-Vee Food Stores, Inc.*, 266 F.3d 851 (8th Cir.2001), *cert. denied*, 535 U.S. 1017, 122 S.Ct. 1606, 152 L.Ed.2d 621 (2002) and *Brown v. Philip Morris, Inc.*, 250 F.3d 789 (3d Cir.2001) (requiring state action).

also serves to fill the gaps in coverage and supplement the potential remedies of the Fair Housing Act of 1968, as amended.

§ 1.4 Section 1983

Section 1983 authorizes actions at law or suits in equity against any "person" for the deprivation of rights, privileges or immunities secured by the federal Constitution or laws, so long as the defendant acted "under color of" state law, custom or usage.

For many race discrimination claimants, § 1983 is of less utility than § 1981, for four principal reasons. First, § 1983 provides remedies for deprivations only of rights independently secured by the U.S. Constitution or federal statutes. Second, even those deprivations are actionable only if imposed "under color of" state law. Third, while the Supreme Court has held that municipalities and other local governments are "persons," and hence appropriate defendants, for purposes of § 1983,[1] it simultaneously concluded that municipalities are not subject to liability merely vicariously, for example through *respondeat superior*.[2] Instead, the Court has repeatedly insisted that local government entities are responsible only for official policies or the acts of those employees with "policy making authority," and determining this is a question of law to be decided by reference to local laws, customs, and usages.[3] In recent years, claims against state and local governments but not private defendants have been subjected to this restriction in actions under § 1981, too.[4] Fourth, the § 1983 liability of individual government employees has been sharply circumscribed by a series of Supreme Court rulings elaborating absolute immunity for legislative, judicial and prosecutorial conduct and an increasingly expansive brand of qualified immunity for the discretionary acts of officials performing executive or administrative functions.[5] (Some circuit opinions have transplanted the qualified immunity defense to § 1981 actions against government official defendants.)[6]

A comprehensive discussion of the prima facie proof elements, defenses, remedies, and related procedural intricacies of may be found in Chapters 2 and 5.

§ 1.4

1. *Monell v. Department of Soc. Servs.*, 436 U.S. 658, 98 S.Ct. 2018, 56 L.Ed.2d 611 (1978).

2. *Id.*

3. *Pembaur v. City of Cincinnati*, 475 U.S. 469, 106 S.Ct. 1292, 89 L.Ed.2d 452 (1986) (plurality opinion); *St. Louis v. Praprotnik*, 485 U.S. 112, 108 S.Ct. 915, 99 L.Ed.2d 107 (1988) (plurality opinion); and *Jett v. Dallas Indep. Sch. Dist.*, 491 U.S. 701, 109 S.Ct. 2702, 105 L.Ed.2d 598 (1989) (5–member majority opinion).

4. See §§ 1.8 and 1.10–1.13, *infra*.

5. *See generally Forrester v. White*, 484 U.S. 219, 108 S.Ct. 538, 98 L.Ed.2d 555 (1988) (absolute judicial immunity); *Burns v. Reed*, 500 U.S. 478, 111 S.Ct. 1934, 114 L.Ed.2d 547 (1991) (absolute prosecutorial immunity); and *Harlow v. Fitzgerald*, 457 U.S. 800, 102 S.Ct. 2727, 73 L.Ed.2d 396 (1982) and *Anderson v. Creighton*, 483 U.S. 635, 107 S.Ct. 3034, 97 L.Ed.2d 523 (1987) (easing the standards and procedures for defending on the ground of qualified immunity).

6. See *Bishop v. Avera*, 177 F.3d 1233 (11th Cir.1999).

§ 1.5 Sections 1985(1) and (2)

The dearth of reported cases concerning section 1985(1) is a reflection of the changed historical and social circumstances since its narrow prohibition was enacted. As its text makes clear, a § 1985(1) private right of action for damages attaches only when two or more persons conspire to impede a *federal* officer from discharging his official duties, or to injure his person or property for trying to lawfully discharge or for having lawfully discharged those duties, and only then when the means of conspiracy includes "force, intimidation, or threat."[1]

The first part of section 1985(2) is almost as narrow, for it proscribes the intimidation, by forceful or threatening conspiratorial means, of *federal court* witnesses and parties.[2] The second part, however, while also creating a damage claim only against conspirators, has a somewhat wider scope. For one thing, its text does not specify any particular unlawful means. Further, it affords the claim to redress conspiracies that have the purpose of hindering or impeding "in any manner, the due course of justice in any State or Territory," if undertaken with the "intent to deny to any citizen the equal protection of the laws, or to injure him or his property for lawfully enforcing ... the right of any person, or class of persons, to the equal protection of the laws." But several circuits[3] have added to these bare-bones allegations the same gloss that the Supreme Court subsequently placed[4] on the similar "equal protection" language of a companion section, § 1985(3): the plaintiff must also prove that the conspiracy was motivated by invidious racial, or perhaps other, class-based animus. Accordingly, because the Supreme Court has never upheld a § 1985(3) claim based on a conspiracy directed against any class other than African–Americans,[5] only such claims and

§ 1.5

1. *See Morast v. Lance*, 807 F.2d 926, 929 (11th Cir.1987), *disapproved on other grounds, Haddle v. Garrison*, 525 U.S. 121, 119 S.Ct. 489, 142 L.Ed.2d 502 (1998); *Congress of Racial Equality v. Clemmons*, 323 F.2d 54, 63 (5th Cir.1963).

2. *See Blankenship v. McDonald*, 176 F.3d 1192, 1196 (9th Cir.1999), *cert. denied*, 528 U.S. 1153, 120 S.Ct. 1157, 145 L.Ed.2d 1069 (2000) (§ 1985(2) protects parties to a federal court proceeding and cannot be utilized for witness tampering or intimidation claim unless the tampering effectively denies the party from presenting an effective case); *Kush v. Rutledge*, 460 U.S. 719, 103 S.Ct. 1483, 75 L.Ed.2d 413 (1983); *Rode v. Dellarciprete*, 845 F.2d 1195 (3d Cir.1988); *Morast*, 807 F.2d at 929 (testimony before a federal agency insufficient to invoke § 1985(2) protection).

Because conduct violative of § 1985(2) is, in most circumstances, also criminal, *see* 18 U.S.C.A. § 1512 and 18 U.S.C.A. § 371, the intracorporate conspiracy doctrine is not available as a defense under § 1985(2). *See McAndrew v. Lockheed Martin*, 206 F.3d 1031 (11th Cir.2000).

3. *See, e.g., Harrison v. Springdale Water & Sewer Comm'n*, 780 F.2d 1422, 1430 (8th Cir.1986); *Bretz v. Kelman*, 773 F.2d 1026, 1030 (9th Cir.1985); *Bradt v. Smith*, 634 F.2d 796, 801 (5th Cir.1981); *Williams v. St. Joseph Hosp.*, 629 F.2d 448, 451 (7th Cir.1980); *Dacey v. Dorsey*, 568 F.2d 275, 277 (2d Cir.1978); *Brawer v. Horowitz*, 535 F.2d 830, 840 (3d Cir.1976); *Hahn v. Sargent*, 523 F.2d 461, 469 (1st Cir.1975).

4. *Griffin v. Breckenridge*, 403 U.S. 88, 102, 91 S.Ct. 1790, 1798, 29 L.Ed.2d 338 (1971), discussed in § 1.6 immediately following.

5. *See Bray v. Alexandria Women's Health Clinic*, 506 U.S. 263, 269, 113 S.Ct. 753, 759, 122 L.Ed.2d 34 (1993). Several circuit courts allow § 1985(3) claims by at least some nonrace-based classes. See § 1.6, *infra*.

those by any other target group the Court may recognize would lie in those circuits under § 1985(2). Still, because equal protection is a two way street racially, and the Supreme Court applies strict scrutiny to classifications burdening whites as well as blacks, a black witness was held to state a § 1985(2) claim against black school officials who allegedly retaliated against him for state court testimony favorable to a white teacher and supportive of her equal protection rights that they sought to hinder.[6]

§ 1.6 Section 1985(3)

a. *The "Deprivation" Clause*

Section 1985(3) is a purely remedial statute that, like § 1983 but unlike § 1981, creates no substantive rights itself.[1] Its first clause, by far the most frequently litigated, provides a federal cause of action for damages[2] for the redress of conspiracies that have the purpose and result of "depriving either directly or indirectly, any person or class of persons of the equal protection of the laws, or of equal privileges and immunities under the laws."[3] A plaintiff under this "deprivation" clause must allege and prove (1) the elements of a conspiracy that (2) deprived the plaintiff of rights rather vaguely described with reference to unspecified "laws" providing for "equal protection" or "equal privileges and immunities." The conspiracy elements are standard, requiring principally an agreement by two or more distinct persons[4] or entities[5] to engage in conduct

6. *Chavis v. Clayton County Sch. Dist.*, 300 F.3d 1288 (11th Cir.2002).

§ 1.6

1. *Great Am. Fed. Savings & Loan Ass'n v. Novotny*, 442 U.S. 366, 372, 99 S.Ct. 2345, 2349, 60 L.Ed.2d 957 (1979).

2. The Supreme Court has not decided if § 1985(3) supports a prayer for injunctive relief. *Bray v. Alexandria Women's Health Clinic*, 506 U.S. 263, 285 n. 16, 113 S.Ct. 753, 767 n. 16, 122 L.Ed.2d 34 (1993).

3. 42 U.S.C.A. § 1985(3) (1988).

4. Foreign governments are not "persons" under the statute. *Sturdza v. United Arab Emirates*, 281 F.3d 1287 (D.C.Cir. 2002), *petition for cert. filed* (July 06, 2002), *relying on Breard v. Greene*, 523 U.S. 371, 378, 118 S.Ct. 1352, 1356, 140 L.Ed.2d 529 (1998) (holding that a foreign government is not a "person" as that term is used in § 1983).

5. In general, § 1985(3) is not violated by discussions, agreements, or actions taken between two or more individuals who serve the same corporation or other entity. *See, e.g., Dickerson v. Alachua County Comm'n*, 200 F.3d 761, 768 (11th Cir.2000); *Benningfield v. City of Houston*, 157 F.3d 369, 378 (5th Cir.1998), *cert. denied*, 526 U.S. 1065, 119 S.Ct. 1457, 143 L.Ed.2d 543 (1999) (applying the intracorporate conspiracy doctrine to plaintiffs' § 1985(3) claims alleging defendant supervisors conspired to deprive plaintiffs of their First Amendment and equal protection rights but finding the claims fell within an exception to the doctrine which arises when corporate employees act for their own personal purposes); *Wright v. Illinois Dep't of Children & Family Servs.*, 40 F.3d 1492 (7th Cir.1994); *Johnson v. Hills & Dales Gen. Hosp.*, 40 F.3d 837 (6th Cir.1994); *Hartman v. Board of Trustees*, 4 F.3d 465, 469–71 (7th Cir. 1993); *Hull v. Cuyahoga Valley Joint Vocational Sch. Dist. Bd. of Educ.*, 926 F.2d 505, 509–10 (6th Cir.1991) (affirming district court's judgment that plaintiff's § 1985(3) claims were barred by the intracorporate conspiracy doctrine and reaffirming the circuit's extension of the doctrine from the context of antitrust litigation to allegations of conspiracy under the Civil Rights Act); *Robison v. Canterbury Village, Inc.*, 848 F.2d 424, 430–31 (3d Cir.1988); *Buschi v. Kirven*, 775 F.2d 1240, 1252 (4th Cir.1985); *Cross v. General Motors Corp.*, 721 F.2d 1152, 1156 (8th Cir.1983); *Rice v. President & Fellows of Harvard Coll.*, 663 F.2d 336, 338 (1st Cir.1981); *Herrmann v. Moore*, 576 F.2d 453 (2d Cir.1978); *Girard v. 94th*

that resulted in the deprivation of the requisite rights, plus some overt act in furtherance of that agreement. The protected "rights" question has proven more difficult. Section 1985(3) undoubtedly applies to conspiracies aimed at infringing certain fundamental constitutional rights. But the Court has struggled with elucidating which federal constitutional provisions secure the kind of "equal" rights § 1983 protects. It was forced to come to grips with that question when it considered whether the deprivation clause reaches only conspiracies involving government actors or also those where private defendants act alone.

Paving the way for damage actions against purely private actors, the Court in *Griffin v. Breckenridge*[6] held that state action is a required element if, as is almost always the case, the particular right plaintiff invokes is itself dependent on state action. (Virtually all rights protected by the U.S. Constitution, other than the rights to interstate travel and freedom from involuntary servitude, do depend on state action.) Thus, for example, *United Brotherhood of Carpenters and Joiners v. Scott*[7] later held that because the First Amendment prohibits infringements only by government, a § 1985(3) claim against union members for conspiracy to deprive plaintiffs of rights to free speech and association failed for lack of evidence of state involvement.[8]

But in holding in *Grifffin* that § 1985(3) could reach certain purely private conspiracies, the Court expressed concern (much as it did when it stretched § 1983 in *Monell* to reach government entity defendants) that the deprivation clause might become a "general federal tort law."[9] To avoid the resulting "constitutional shoals," the Court crafted a distinct element of the claim, one not apparent from statutory text: there must be a class-based motivation behind the defendants' conspiracy to deprive the plaintiff of those equal rights.[10] Specifically, the Court extracted from the textually covered "*equal*" protection, privileges and immunities a requirement that the plaintiff must show "some racial, or perhaps otherwise class-based, invidiously discriminatory animus behind the conspirators' action."[11] Although the Court devised this new requirement to counter the problems it anticipated in applying the deprivation clause to purely private conspiracies, it fastened the requirement on the "equal protection" and "equal privileges" language that must be met to state a

Street & Fifth Ave. Corp., 530 F.2d 66, 70–72 (2d Cir.1976). *But see McAndrew v. Lockheed Martin Corp.*,206 F.3d 1031 (11th Cir.2000) (doctrine does not apply to alleged criminal conspiracy to violate civil rights); *Brever v. Rockwell Int'l Corp.*, 40 F.3d 1119, 1127 (10th Cir.1994) (declining to apply the intracorporate conspiracy doctrine to a § 1985(2) claim because the intracorporate conspiracy doctrine, "designed to allow one corporation to take actions that two corporations could not agree to do, should not be construed to permit the same corporation and its employees to engage in civil rights violations"); *but cf. Quinn v. Nassau County Police Dep't,* 53 F.Supp.2d 347 (E.D.N.Y. 1999) (finding exception to doctrine where alleged conspirator pursues purely private interests, as with sexual harassment).

6. 403 U.S. 88, 99, 91 S.Ct. 1790, 1797, 29 L.Ed.2d 338 (1971).

7. 463 U.S. 825, 103 S.Ct. 3352, 77 L.Ed.2d 1049 (1983).

8. *Carpenters v. Scott*, 463 U.S. 825, at 832, 103 S.Ct. 3352, at 3358, 77 L.Ed.2d 1049.

9. 403 U.S. at 102.

10. *Id.* at 88.

11. *Id.* at 102.

claim concerning *any* conspiracy, public or private. The "animus" requirement has accordingly been read as applicable to claims against conspiracies under color of state law as well as those against purely private conspiracies.[12]

By contrast, in a decision that brings the public-private constitutional "rights" question of *Griffin* full circle, the Court in *Bray v. Alexandria Women's Health Clinic* has described *Carpenters* as holding that § 1985(3) reaches only those private conspiracies that are aimed at constitutional rights "protected against private, *as well as* official, encroachment."[13] Section § 1985(3) accordingly provides redress against private conspiratorial invasion only for the Thirteenth Amendment right to be free from involuntary servitude and a limited right to interstate travel—the lone constitutional provisions recognized as affording affirmative protection against private as well as public invasion.[14]

The contours of the requisite class-based motivation or animus have not been fully drawn, but there are now some definite demarcations. Conspiracies directed against groups defined by race or racial advocacy are most clearly within the ambit of § 1985(3).[15] As under § 1981, however, the kind of "race" qualifying for protection is not always apparent. For example a circuit court has ruled that a target religious group containing both Jewish and non-Jewish members could not constitute a racial class for § 1985(3) purposes because of its racial diversity.[16] In *Griffin* the Court intimated with its "perhaps" language that certain non-racial but group-based motivations might also sustain a 1985(3) claim. But it held that conspiratorial conduct "motivated by economic or commercial animus" is outside the statute's reach.[17]

It remains uncertain whether gender-based motivation qualifies as an actionable animus, even after the Court's recent decision in *Bray*. In *Bray*, a women's clinic that provided pregnancy and abortion services alleged that defendant pro-life protesters, all acting without government encouragement or support, conspired to deny women the right to travel

12. *See Aulson v. Blanchard*, 83 F.3d 1, 3 (1st Cir.1996) (citing cases); *Gagliardi v. Village of Pawling*, 18 F.3d 188, 194 (2d Cir.1994).

13. *Bray v. Alexandria Women's Health Clinic*, 506 U.S. 263, 278, 113 S.Ct. 753, 764, 122 L.Ed.2d 34 (1993) (emphasis supplied) (quoting *United Bhd. of Carpenters and Joiners v. Scott*, 463 U.S. 825, 833, 103 S.Ct. 3352, 3358, 77 L.Ed.2d 1049 (1983)).

14. *Id.*

15. *Griffin*, 403 U.S. at 102, 91 S.Ct. at 1798.

16. *Jews for Jesus, Inc. v. Jewish Cmty. Relations Council of N.Y., Inc.*, 968 F.2d 286 (2d Cir.1992).

17. *Carpenters*, 463 U.S. at 834, 103 S.Ct. at 3359 ("antinonunion" motivation). While there is no consensus whether conduct motivated by purely political animus is actionable, it has been held that claims of a target class are cognizable only when that class "is comprised of a distinctive and identifiable group" whose members could be ascertained "by means of objective criteria." *Aulson v. Blanchard,* 83 F.3d 1 (1st Cir.1996). Circuit courts are divided whether a conspiracy aimed at handicapped or mentally retarded persons suggests the requisite class-based discriminatory animus. *Compare Lake v. Arnold*, 112 F.3d 682 (3d Cir.1997) and *People by Abrams v. 11 Cornwell Co.*, 695 F.2d 34 (2d Cir.1982) (finding § 1985(3) protection) *with D'Amato v. Wisconsin Gas Co.*, 760 F.2d 1474 (7th Cir. 1985) and *Wilhelm v. Continental Title Co.*, 720 F.2d 1173 (10th Cir.1983) (no § 1985(3) protection).

in interstate commerce to receive those services. The alleged overt act in furtherance of this conspiracy was the attempt to block the entrance to the clinic, and the conspiracy was said to have been motivated by an invidiously discriminatory class-based animus—a desire to deny women the equal protection of the laws.

Plaintiffs argued before the Court that the protesters' animus was directed at the class of all women, because all women have a right to seek an abortion. Defendants, however, argued that their protests were targeted not at a class defined by gender but rather at all persons, women or men, who sought or provided abortion services. The defendants maintained in the alternative that their blockades did not obstruct a right to interstate travel protected by § 1985(3).

The Court did not decide whether gender-based animus is actionable,[18] because it found the "deprivation" claim foundered for two independent reasons. For one, the Court found no actionable right. The right to abortion did not qualify in an action against purely private conspirators because it is protected only against official and not also private encroachment. The right to interstate travel, although enforceable against private conduct, did not qualify either; it protected interstate travelers only against discriminatory treatment vis-a-vis local intrastate abortion seekers, and there was no such disparity in *Bray*.

By analogy to the construction of § 1985(3)'s criminal counterpart,[19] the Court has also insisted, in *United States v. Guest*,[20] that to be actionable under § 1985(3) a conspiracy must have the specific purpose, and not merely the effect, of interfering with a protected right. The defendants' conduct must be "aimed at" that right.[21] Since, on the record before the Court in *Bray*, the defendants conspired to and opposed and interfered with abortions whether or not they were performed after interstate travel, that right was neither implicated nor purposefully targeted within the meaning of § 1985(3).[22] In an accompanying footnote the majority vehemently disagreed with the dissent's suggestion that its requirement of a conscious purpose to impair a

18. Most circuits courts have extended § 1985(3) protection to gender-based classes. *See, e.g. Libertad v. Welch*, 53 F.3d 428 (1st Cir.1995); *Novotny v. Great Amer. Fed. Sav. & Loan Ass'n*, 584 F.2d 1235 (3d Cir.1978), *vacated in part*, 442 U.S. 366, 99 S.Ct. 2345, 60 L.Ed.2d 957 (1979); *National Org. for Women v. Operation Rescue,* 914 F.2d 582 (4th Cir.1990), *aff'd in part, rev'd in part, sub nom. Bray v. Alexandria Women's Health Clinic*, 506 U.S. 263, 113 S.Ct. 753, 122 L.Ed.2d 34 (1993); *Southard v. Texas Bd. of Criminal Justice,* 114 F.3d 539 (5th Cir.1997); *Haverstick Enters., Inc. v. Financial Fed. Credit, Inc.*, 32 F.3d 989 (6th Cir.1994); *Hicks v. Resolution Trust Corp.*, 970 F.2d 378 (7th Cir.1992); *Shortbull v. Looking Elk*, 677 F.2d 645 (8th Cir. 1982); *Sever v. Alaska Pulp Corp.*, 978 F.2d 1529 (9th Cir.1992); *Lyes v. City of Riviera Beach*, 166 F.3d 1332 (11th Cir.1999).

19. 18 U.S.C.A. § 241.

20. 383 U.S. 745, 86 S.Ct. 1170, 16 L.Ed.2d 239 (1966).

21. *Bray,* 506 U.S. at 275, 113 S.Ct. at 762 (quoting *Carpenters*, 463 U.S. at 833, 103 S.Ct. at 3358).

22. *Bray* has been read in this respect as limited to the record before the Court, with the suggestion that if the private defendants' animus were directed against a right to travel protected against private as well as public interference, a § 1985(3) claim against private defendants might be stated. *Town of West Hartford v. Operation Rescue*, 991 F.2d 1039, 1048 (2d Cir.1993).

protected right was tantamount to the criminal element of "wilfulness," which the Court distinguished as requiring knowledge that the right is federally protected.[23]

A court of appeals decision illustrates the interplay between the "rights" and "intent" requirements as explicated in *Bray* and underscores how they operate as separate barriers to a deprivation clause claim. The plaintiff asserted claims against private conspirators based on interference with his rights under the First, Fifth, and Fourteenth Amendments. In an attempt to satisfy the § 1985(3) requirement of a right enforceable against private as well as public action, he also alleged that the private conspiracy was aimed at and intended to influence state conduct. Relying on *Bray*, the court nevertheless held the claims insufficient because each constitutional provision the plaintiff relied on creates rights only against the government.[24] The "private rights" and "aimed at" requirements in an action against privately acting defendants must also be independently satisfied even if it is proven that the defendants acted with the requisite racial animus—these are three distinct elements of proof.[25]

Similarly, it was an independent ground for rejection of the plaintiffs' deprivation claim in *Bray* that, even assuming the requisite "class" targeted by the defendants' animus could be stretched beyond race to include, for example, gender—something the court found it unnecessary to decide—the concept "connotes something more than a group of individuals who share a desire to engage in conduct that the § 1985(3) defendant disfavors." Thus to the extent that the *Bray* plaintiffs attempted to show that the conspiracy was aimed at women seeking abortions, rather than women as such, their claim failed to satisfy the animus requirement.[26] The Court viewed this requirement as demanding evidence not merely that defendants' conduct had a disproportionate adverse impact (in this case, 100%) on women but that they shared a purpose to injure the class by virtue of a uniform class characteristic—for instance, "women *by reason of their sex*."[27] On the record the Court was unwilling to presume that defendants' opposition to abortion reflected such a sex-based intent, concluding that the goal of preventing abortion was a sufficiently "proper and reasonable" value judgment, to

23. 506 U.S. at 276 n.6, 113 S.Ct. at 763 n.6.

24. *Tilton v. Richardson*, 6 F.3d 683 (10th Cir.1993) (repeatedly stating that the *Carpenters/Bray* "rights" limitations applies only to "private" conspiracies). Similarly, in *Trautz v. Weisman*, 819 F.Supp. 282, 290 (S.D.N.Y.1993), the court implied that the "private rights" requirement applied only to private conspiracies. But the racial *animus* requirement applies to conspiracies under color of state law as well as those that are purely private. *See Aulson v. Blanchard*, 83 F.3d 1 (1st Cir.1996) (class-based discriminatory animus requirement applies to purely public actor conspiracy).

25. *See, e.g., Spencer v. Casavilla*, 839 F.Supp. 1014, 1016–1017 (S.D.N.Y.1993), *aff'd in part, vacated in part*, 44 F.3d 74 (2d Cir.1994) (plaintiff's verdict vacated because, although defendants acted with the requisite racial animus, there was no evidence from which jury could have concluded that they assaulted the plaintiff with the intent of depriving him of an intrastate or interstate right to travel).

26. *See* discussion of *Bray, supra*.

27. 113 S.Ct. at 759 (emphasis in original).

some degree recurrently supported by Congress, to escape the *Griffin* description of "invidiously discriminatory animus."[28]

In two major respects, then, the Court has sharply circumscribed the scope and utility of § 1985(3)'s "deprivation" clause. First, although the statute's "equal rights" language was written only three years after the Fourteenth Amendment was ratified, *Griffin*'s extratextual gloss on the protected "class" and the related required "animus," as confirmed by *Carpenters*, denies protection on many of the grounds embraced by the Fourteenth Amendment. In his separate opinion in *Bray*, for example, Justice Souter argues that certain class categories clearly eligible for heightened scrutiny under the Equal Protection Clause as analogous to race should probably also be covered by § 1985(3)—he lists national origin, alienage, gender, and illegitimacy.[29] But he adds that under the majority's restrictive view of animus, § 1985(3) probably does not provide protection for all these legislative classifications, even though the Clause itself, at least to some degree, clearly does.

Second, the Court has severely curtailed the rights which, when violated, can serve as the springboard to a deprivation clause claim. It began in *Griffin* by expanding, within the racial animus sphere, the rights protected by § 1985(3) beyond those protected by the Fourteenth Amendment—that is, it swept purely private conspiracies within the reach of the statute so that the statute, unlike the Amendment, does not always hinge on state action. Yet the Court ended up in *Carpenters* and *Bray* by *limiting* the statute's ambit of protection in the private realm to the constitutional rights, currently numbered at just two, protected against private interference.

It might appear that joint public-private alleged conspirators who with racial animus interfere on racial grounds with First Amendment rights cannot be reached by § 1985(3) because First Amendment rights are not protected against private invasion. But a closer look at *Bray* suggests that the "private rights" limitation applies only to conspiracies by defendants acting purely privately. The facts at bar as well as the textual setting of this requirement within the *Bray* opinion[30] support this conclusion.[31]

28. More recently, the Court has held that similar interference with plaintiffs' access to abortion services may constitute a conspiracy prohibited by the Racketeering–Influenced and Corrupt Organizations Act, finding in RICO no requirement that the defendants have an economic motivation. *National Org. for Women v. Scheidler*, 510 U.S. 1215, 114 S.Ct. 1340, 127 L.Ed.2d 688 (1994).

29. Similarly, Justice O'Connor stated that § 1985(3) protects those classes that merit heightened scrutiny under the Equal Protection Clause. *Bray*, 506 U.S. at 350 (O'Connor, J., dissenting). Several circuits have adopted an Equal Protection Clause framework for deciding § 1985(3) cases. *See, e.g., Aulson v. Blanchard*, 83 F.3d 1 (1st Cir.1996); *Haverstick Enters. v. Financial Fed. Credit, Inc.*, 32 F.3d 989 (6th Cir.1994).

30. The part of the opinion that elaborates the requirement that the right violated be protected against private, and not just official encroachment begins with a paragraph that describes the requirement as pertaining to a § 1985(3) "*private* conspiracy." 506 U.S. at 274, 113 S.Ct. at 762 (emphasis added).

31. *See Tilton v. Richardson*, 6 F.3d 683, 686–687 (10th Cir.1993) (repeatedly stating that the *Carpenters/Bray* "rights"

Still, Section 1985(3)'s deprivation clause, as a source of protection for constitutional rights, is sorely wounded. As long as the protected target "class" extends little beyond race or the advocacy of racial views, the clause will be seldom needed when the conspirators include state actors: it is rarely popular or prudent today for government officials to conspire on such grounds. And the clause is largely disabled as applied to the potentially far more numerous category of purely private conspiracies. *Bray* insists that such conspiracies are actionable only when aimed at the two constitutional rights that affirmatively prohibit private as well as public abridgements, but conspiracies to enslave or to infringe the right to interstate travel do not abound.[32]

The Court has left open whether conspiratorial deprivation of equal rights protected by federal or state *statutes* might also trigger § 1985(3) liability.[33] But if, as appears to be the case,[34] the recently refined "animus" requirement (in contrast to the "private rights" requirement) applies to all § 1985(3) deprivation clause conspiracies, public or private, there would appear to be relatively little scope for actions based on violations of federal or state statutes. Consider, for example, the legal status of a conspiracy directed against the disabled. It is doubtful that disability is a suspect or quasi-suspect equal protection classification.[35] Even if it were, the *Bray* take on "animus" strongly suggests that freedom from discrimination on that ground is not a right protected against conspiratorial invasion by the deprivation clause. Can a federal statutory violation serve as an end run around this requirement? For example, because disability discrimination in employment by larger employers is now prohibited by the Americans With Disabilities Act, is a conspiracy to deprive a person of rights protected by that federal statute also actionable under § 1985(3)?

Probably not. Most lower courts that have addressed the issue concluded, well before *Bray*, that the disabled do not constitute the kind of "class" that § 1985(3) protects, again because Congress' main concern in enacting the Ku Klux Klan Act of 1871 was to combat racial discrimination during Reconstruction against African–Americans.[36] Although

limitations applies only to "private" conspiracies). In *Trautz v. Weisman*, 819 F.Supp. 282, 290 (S.D.N.Y.1993), the court wrote that the racial animus requirement applies to conspiracies under color of state law as well as those that are purely private. It implied that the "private rights" requirement applied only to the latter.

32. An example of a successful plaintiff in a purely private conspiracy case is *Scott v. Ross*, 140 F.3d 1275 (9th Cir.1998), *cert. denied sub nom. Cult Awareness Network v. Scott*, 526 U.S. 1033, 119 S.Ct. 1285, 143 L.Ed.2d 378 (1999). There, a cult de-programming group was found vicariously liable under agency theory for the acts of a member who kidnaped and held the plaintiff, at the request of plaintiff's family, in an attempt to de-program him.

33. *Carpenters v. Scott*, 463 U.S. at 57, 103 S.Ct. at 2874.

34. *See* text *supra*, this section.

35. *See Story v. Green*, 978 F.2d 60, 64 (2d Cir.1992).

36. *See, e.g., D'Amato v. Wisconsin Gas Co.*, 760 F.2d 1474, 1476–87 (7th Cir.1985); *Wilhelm v. Continental Title Co.*, 720 F.2d 1173, 1176–77 (10th Cir.1983); *Downs v. Sawtelle*, 574 F.2d 1, 16 (1st Cir.1978). *But see Trautz v. Weisman*, 819 F.Supp. 282, 291–294 (S.D.N.Y.1993) (reasoning that disability is an "inherent personal characteristic," even when it is not visible to the naked eye, and therefore shares attributes

Bray did not decide if women as such, or other non-African Americans or their political advocates, could constitute a target "class" for the required deprivation clause animus, the tenor of Justice Scalia's opinion points to a negative answer to this question.[37] Thus even if a disabled plaintiff might surmount the "rights" problem by using the ADA or another federal statute as the source of protection, her claim might founder on the separate requirement of a race-based or "perhaps" otherwise invidiously discriminatory animus.

Although it has not decided whether violations of federal equal rights statutes may serve as the predicate for § 1985(3) liability, the Court has set one firm outer limit. Section 1985(3) is ousted if the particular federal statute on which plaintiff relies has its own elaborate remedial and procedural scheme. The Court in *Great American Federal Savings & Loan Association v. Novotny*[38] held that § 1985(3) is unavailable as an alternative remedy for employment discrimination prohibited by Title VII, expressing the fear that it might be used to bypass the detailed state and local administrative procedures, conciliation mechanisms and judicial remedies that Congress specified in the modern statute. At least one circuit has read *Novotny* narrowly to allow a constitutional § 1985(3) conspiracy claim for employment discrimination.[39] There, the Eleventh Circuit allowed a § 1985(3) claim despite the availability of Title VII because the court found the plaintiff claimed a violation of his Constitutional rights, and not rights protected only by Title VII. In *Carpenters* the Court found it unnecessary to decide whether rights guaranteed by state law are protected under § 1985(3), because it concluded that the plaintiff had failed to demonstrate the requisite class-based animus to support the claim.[40]

While the converse is certainly not true, virtually any conspiratorial activity that could meet the multiple stringent requirements of § 1985(3) could also be cast as a conspiracy under § 1983.[41] If the prospective plaintiff could in such a case meet § 1985's higher demands, she may be well advised to assert the § 1985(3) claim, either alone or as

similar to those of race-based classifications that have supported claims under § 1985(3)); *Shortbull v. Looking Elk*, 677 F.2d 645, 649 (8th Cir.1982) (allowing 1985(3) claims for both gender-and disability-based conspiracies); *Lake v. Arnold*, 112 F.3d 682, 686–88 (3d Cir.1997) (holding that mentally retarded are entitled to § 1985(3) protection, in part based on the purpose of the ADA).

37. Several circuits have allowed § 1985(3) claims based on animus toward other nonrace-based classes. *See, e.g. LeBlanc–Sternberg v. Fletcher*, 67 F.3d 412 (2d Cir.1995) (religion); *Sherwin Manor Nursing Ctr. v. McAuliffe*, 37 F.3d 1216 (7th Cir.1994) (religion); *Park v. City of Atlanta*, 120 F.3d 1157 (11th Cir.1997) (national origin).

38. 442 U.S. 366, 99 S.Ct. 2345, 60 L.Ed.2d 957 (1979).

39. *Dickerson v. Alachua County Comm'n*, 200 F.3d 761, 765 (11th Cir.2000). The Eleventh Circuit has also held that a constitutional cause of action under § 1983 is not preempted by Title VII. *See Johnson v. City of Fort Lauderdale*, 148 F.3d 1228 (11th Cir.1998).

40. 463 U.S. at 833, 103 S.Ct. at 3358.

41. For examples of § 1983 claims alleging that the predicate constitutional right was deprived as the result of conspiracy, see *Burrell v. Board of Trustees of Ga. Military Coll.*, 970 F.2d 785 (11th Cir.1992); *Bell v. City of Milwaukee*, 746 F.2d 1205 (7th Cir.1984); and *Ryland v. Shapiro*, 708 F.2d 967 (5th Cir.1983).

an alternative to the § 1983–conspiracy claim, in an effort to avoid the qualified immunity defense. There is divergent opinion among the federal circuit courts as to whether a public official sued under § 1985(3) may claim a variant of the qualified immunity defense that is available to an individual defendant under § 1983. A decision denying that defense reasoned that the § 1985(3) requirement of intentional, race-based animus protects against imposition of liability for actions taken in good faith; the additional protection of qualified immunity is not necessary, in other words, to assure that a public official will vigorously discharge the duties of his office.[42] A decision upholding the defense asserts that despite the ultimate protection on the merits that the animus element affords public officials sued under § 1985(3), the same basic rationale warranting qualified immunity under § 1983 obtains: the necessity to defend such actions will discourage persons from holding public office, divert public officials' energies from official business, and chill them in the exercise of their duties.[43]

b. The "Hindrance" Clause

Section 1985(3) has a second clause that punishes conspiracies for the purpose of "preventing or hindering the constituted authorities of any State or Territory from giving or securing ... the equal protection of the laws." Liability under this "hindrance" clause requires at a minimum a conspiracy of sufficient force to overwhelm the capacity of government to administer law evenhandedly. Five members of the Court in *Bray* concluded that a hindrance claim was not properly presented for review. Nevertheless, they suggested that both the private-rights and animus requirements that the Court had elaborated for "deprivation" claims would apply to hindrance claims as well.

The dissenters, by contrast, argued that the hindrance clause is available where overwhelming conspiratorial force disables duly constituted authorities from affording equal protection, even when private defendants target a right dependent on state action and even when they are not animated by race or like class characteristic. Some of the dissenters relied on, and the majority distinguished, the Court's approach to the first clause of § 1985(2), which provides a cause of action against conspirators who seek to intimidate or injure federal court parties or witnesses. The Court had held the *Griffin* animus requirement inapplicable to actions under that clause in *Kush v. Rutledge*.[44] The *Bray* majority noted that the first clause of § 1985(2)—unlike the second clause of that subsection (affording a cause of action against conspirators seeking to obstruct justice within a State or Territory), and unlike both the deprivation and hindrance clauses of § 1985(3)—did not contain the equal protection limitation on protected rights from which the Court had derived the *Griffin* requirement of race-based animus.

42. *Burrell v. Board of Trustees of Ga. Military Coll.*, 970 F.2d 785, 793–794 (11th Cir.1992). *Accord Johnson v. City of Fort Lauderdale, Fla.*, 126 F.3d 1372 (11th Cir. 1997).

43. *Bisbee v. Bey*, 39 F.3d 1096 (10th Cir.1994).

44. 460 U.S. 719, 103 S.Ct. 1483, 75 L.Ed.2d 413 (1983).

But with the resignation of Justice White, lower courts are left in a quandary about applying the deprivation clause restrictions to the hindrance clause. With his vote excluded, the justices split 4–4 on those questions in the extended dictum on the subject in *Bray*. A court of appeals has drawn the following composite picture of the views of the four dissenters on the hindrance clause, as expressed in three dissenting opinions: (1) The conspirators' purpose must be to hinder law enforcement authorities from providing normal police protection to a (2) protected class of persons that may include a class of women, where (3) the class is attempting to exercise any constitutional right (not limited to rights protected against private interference) and (4) the defendants harbor a class-based animus which, however, unlike the animus required for the deprivation clause as construed in *Bray*, is inferable from defendants' activities aimed at conduct engaged in exclusively by members of the plaintiff class. The court of appeals accepted the dissent's composite as adequate to state a hindrance clause claim. It reasoned that the main impetus for the "rights" and "animus" requirements that the Court has read into the deprivation clause—avoiding the federalization of state tort law—is absent in the context of the hindrance clause, because the foundation of the latter is an allegation that the defendants conspired to interfere with state law enforcement. Further, the textual handle for those requirements—the equal protection language of the deprivation clause—is missing from the hindrance clause. The court concluded that the hindrance clause is violated by a conspiracy to hinder state law enforcement officials from securing to plaintiffs their constitutional right to an abortion.[45]

How the hindrance clause of Section 1985(3) is ultimately interpreted may prove to be less important if abortion seekers can challenge such conspiracies under other statutory vehicles. For example, the Supreme Court has upheld the legal sufficiency of a complaint alleging that the conduct of abortion protesters violated RICO.[46] And a number of circuit courts have upheld against First Amendment attack the constitutional validity of the Freedom of Access to Clinic Entrances Act, 18 U.S.C.A. § 248.[47]

§ 1.7 Section 1986: Negligent Failure to Prevent a Section 1985 Conspiracy

42 U.S.C.A. § 1986 creates a claim against any person who, "having knowledge that any of the wrongs conspired to be done, and mentioned in § 1985 of this title, are about to be committed, and having power to prevent or aid in preventing the commission of the same, neglects or

45. *National Abortions Fed'n v. Operation Rescue,* 8 F.3d 680 (9th Cir.1993). *See also Libertad v. Welch,* 53 F.3d 428 (1st Cir.1995) (upholding hindrance clause claim even if infringed constitutional right is enforceable only against official misconduct, provided conspiracy's purpose is to impede state officials in securing equal protection).

46. *National Org. for Women v. Scheidler,* 510 U.S. 249, 114 S.Ct. 798, 127 L.Ed.2d 99 (1994).

47. *See, e.g., American Life League, Inc. v. Reno,* 47 F.3d 642 (4th Cir.1995).

refuses so to do." The defendant "shall be liable to the party injured ... for all damages caused by such wrongful act, which such person by reasonable diligence could have prevented." The elements of the claim include a violation of § 1985; a defendant's actual knowledge of a conspiracy under that section; the defendant's neglect or refusal to prevent it, despite the power to prevent or aid in its prevention; and damages caused by such a wrongful act.[1] Note, however, that the plaintiff does not need to prove that the defendants themselves participated in the conspiracy.[2]

The "power to prevent" element virtually assures that § 1986 defendants will be limited to law enforcement authorities and other public officials.[3] The actual knowledge requirement, however, has been relaxed far below the standard the Supreme Court has set for Eighth Amendment violations by prison officials;[4] indeed that requirement has been held met by "rumors" of a § 1985(3) conspiracy sufficiently alarming to local officials that they took some precautionary measures to prevent it.[5] And the "neglects or refuses" language has been read to mean that liability does not depend on a showing that the defendant shares the kind of racially discriminatory animus prerequisite to liability for the underlying § 1985(3) conspiracy.[6]

§ 1.8 The Partial Legislative Overruling of Recent Supreme Court Restrictions on the Use of Section 1981, and the Resulting Relationship Between Section 1981 as Amended and Section 1983

Although *Patterson* reaffirmed the *Runyon* ruling that extended § 1981's application to the private sector, it also sharply restricted the scope of § 1981 claims. The Court recognized that § 1981 protects the right to "enforce" contracts; an employer is therefore prohibited from discriminating on the basis of race or national origin so as to impede the enforcement of contract rights. But five justices also ruled that the statutory prohibition on racial or ethnic discrimination in the "making" of private employment contracts does not extend to conduct occurring after the employment relation is established. Thus the Court held employer racial "harassment," fostering or tolerating a discriminatory work environment, outside the ambit of the statute.

§ 1.7

1. *Clark v. Clabaugh*, 20 F.3d 1290 (3d Cir.1994). In particular, courts have carefully scrutinized whether all the elements of a valid claim under § 1985 are in place. *Hamilton v. Chaffin*, 506 F.2d 904, 913–914 (5th Cir.1975); *Bradt v. Smith*, 634 F.2d 796, 801–02 (5th Cir.1981). The elements of the two kinds of § 1985 violations are discussed in § 1.6, *supra*.

2. *See Park v. City of Atlanta*, 120 F.3d 1157 (11th Cir.1997).

3. *See id.* (alleging that the city, the mayor, and the chief of police failed to prevent the acts of rioters).

4. *See* discussion of *Farmer v. Brennan*, 511 U.S. 825, 114 S.Ct. 1970, 128 L.Ed.2d 811 (1994) in Chapter 2 (no constitutional violation merely because prison official "should have known" of conditions constituting cruel and unusual punishment, absent actual knowledge thereof).

5. *Park v. City of Atlanta,* 120 F.3d 1157.

6. *Id.*

The majority opinion's broad language classified as non-actionable "postformation conduct" any "conditions of continuing employment." It buttressed its textual construction with the argument that the immediate opportunity to litigate afforded by § 1981 would undermine the policies of conciliation and cooperative federalism embedded in Title VII, a parallel avenue of redress against larger employers for conduct that would violate § 1981. Yet the opinion also suggests that one species of "postformation conduct"—a promotion decision which "rises to the level of an opportunity for a new and distinct relation"—may still be actionable. The Court cited the example of a law firm's refusal to admit an associate attorney to partnership, but lower courts have since had difficulty applying the "new and distinct relation" exception to other in-house opportunities for advancement.

It is also somewhat unclear whether *Patterson* precluded a claim of discriminatory discharge, for two reasons. First, discharge arguably goes to the very existence of a contract and not just the way it is performed. Second, after discharge the relationship sought to be preserved by Title VII is at an end anyway and so there is no good reason to construe § 1981 narrowly in order to avoid interference with Title VII conciliation. Nevertheless, federal circuit courts after *Patterson* generally held discharge to be outside the reach of § 1981.[1]

The extreme to which the *Patterson* definition of contract formation was taken is illustrated by *Perry v. Command Performance*.[2] The Court first decided that the limiting construction of *Patterson* applied outside employment contexts and extended to general contracting situations. But the Court conditioned the claim of a black customer, who was denied beauticians' services when she appeared for an appointment, on whether she could prove that contract formation occurred only at the time she appeared, rather than when the services had been scheduled on the telephone. Otherwise, her complaint about being denied services when she appeared in person would be related to a "post-formation" contract. Clearly § 1981 is of little use to a purchaser of services if it secures her only the right to contract for an appointment over the telephone, when her race might not be apparent to a would-be supplier of services, but then permits an outright denial of the services when she appears in person to seek performance.

The Civil Rights Act of 1991 overrules the *Patterson* limitation on the scope of the right to "make and enforce" contracts, although only prospectively.[3] Section 101 of the Civil Rights Act of 1991 adds to § 1981 the following new subsection:

§ 1.8

1. *See Taggart v. Jefferson County Child Support Enforcement Unit*, 935 F.2d 947 (8th Cir.1991); *McKnight v. General Motors Corp.*, 908 F.2d 104 (7th Cir.1990); *Courtney v. Canyon Television & Appliance Rental, Inc.*, 899 F.2d 845 (9th Cir.1990); *Lavender v. V & B Transmissions & Auto Repair*, 897 F.2d 805 (5th Cir.1990); *Carroll v. General Accident Ins. Co.*, 891 F.2d 1174 (5th Cir.1990). *But see Hicks v. Brown Group, Inc.*, 902 F.2d 630 (8th Cir.1990), *vacated by*, 499 U.S. 914, 111 S.Ct. 1299, 113 L.Ed.2d 234 (1991) (distinguishing *Patterson* to uphold discharge claim).

2. 913 F.2d 99 (3d Cir.1990).

3. *Felton v. Polles,* 315 F.3d 470, 484–485 (5th Cir.2002) ("conduct prior to the 21 November 1991 amendment of § 1981 is

(b) For purposes of this section, the term "make and enforce contracts" includes the making, performance, modification, and termination of contracts, and the enjoyment of all benefits, privileges, terms, and conditions of the contractual relationship.

The sweeping text of this addition appears to equate the sphere in which contract discrimination is forbidden by § 1981 with the wide ambit of the terms and conditions of employment protected under Title VII. In particular, it is now clear that claims of race-based harassment and discharge are once again actionable under § 1981.

On its face, § 1981 appears to reach any governmental entity, including federal, state and local governments, but a series of Supreme Court employment discrimination decisions has rendered the use of § 1981 problematic in actions against at least federal and state governmental entities. In *Brown v. General Services Administration*,[4] the Court held that the detailed procedural provisions of § 717 of Title VII, which pertain to federal employees, impliedly repealed § 1981 with respect to employment discrimination actions against the federal government. A lower court has expanded this result to preclude federal employment claims under §§ 1983 and 1985(3) as well as 1981 when Title VII is available and the employee relies on common facts in setting out each of the claims.[5]

More recently, in *Jett v. Dallas Independent School District*,[6] the Court reigned in § 1981 as an independent, free-standing source of redress in actions against local and almost surely also state governments as well. Plaintiffs sometimes bring race discrimination claims against state and local government entities under § 1981 in the hope of skirting the rigors of the § 1983 "official policy" limitation declared by *Monell* and thus prevailing with *respondeat superior*-type vicarious liability. But the Court held in *Jett* that municipalities are liable under § 1981 only if they would be liable under the more stringent standards of § 1983. The five-member majority considered it unlikely that Congress intended for § 1981, enacted in 1866 and re-enacted in 1870, to subject state instrumentalities to liability on laxer terms than those which Congress would expressly mandate for them only a year later, in 1871, with the enactment of § 1983.

The Court's reasoning in *Jett* appears in part anachronistic and in part disingenuous. First, it was far from clear when § 1983 was enacted that it reached municipalities, the kind of state unit defending in *Jett*. It was not until more than a century later, with *Monell*, that local govern-

not actionable in a § 1981 harassment claim.") *See Landgraf v. USI Film Prods.*, 511 U.S. 244, 114 S.Ct. 1483, 128 L.Ed.2d 229 (1994); *Rivers v. Roadway Express*, 511 U.S. 298, 114 S.Ct. 1510, 128 L.Ed.2d 274 (1994) (1991 Act Amendments generally nonretroactive).

4. 425 U.S. 820, 96 S.Ct. 1961, 48 L.Ed.2d 402 (1976).

5. *Rowe v. Sullivan*, 967 F.2d 186 (5th Cir.1992). *But cf. La Compania Ocho, Inc. v. United States Forest Serv.*, 874 F.Supp. 1242, 1250–51 (D.N.M.1995) (§ 1981 is available to assert nonemployment discrimination claims against the Federal government, despite negative textual inference of new Section 1981(c)).

6. 491 U.S. 701, 109 S.Ct. 2702, 105 L.Ed.2d 598 (1989).

ment entities were declared to be among the "persons" subject to § 1983 liability on any terms; and only in *Monell* itself did the Court hold that liability contingent on the presence of "policy," a term not found in the statute's text and therefore presumably absent from the minds of its framers in 1871.

Second, in the very same week that it decided *Jett*, the Court had held in *Will v. Michigan Dep't of State Police*[7] that states *eo nominee* are *not* liable under *§ 1983*, in either state or federal court; instead the federal law violations of states were held redressable under that statute only indirectly, through actions against individual state officials for prospective relief. Thus at the time the Court issued its decision in *Jett*, it should have understood that damages, as distinguished from prospective relief, were available under § 1983 only against *local* government, not against the states. Yet *Jett*'s broad language apparently extended to states the benefits of its limitation on the § 1981 liability of local governments: they are liable only for conduct for which they could be held responsible in an action brought pursuant to § 1983. It is at least curious that the Court in *Jett* would rely on the existence of a § 1983 remedy against states as a reason for restricting the § 1981 liability of local governments when it had just disclaimed that the states are liable under § 1983 in *Will*. It is stranger still that the Court now evidently restricts the states' amenability to damages under § 1981 in reliance on their nonexistent liability under § 1983.

In any event, in an apparent attempt to overrule *Jett*, Congress in § 101 of the Civil Rights Act of 1991 appended to § 1981 the following paragraph:

> (c) The rights protected by this section are protected against impairment by nongovernmental discrimination and impairment under color of State law.

The protection against impairment by nongovernmental discrimination simply codifies the *Runyon* holding, reaffirmed by *Patterson*, that § 1981 extends to purely private, as well as governmental, discrimination. Indeed the Sponsors' Interpretive Memorandum,[8] identifies *only* this purpose for the entire new paragraph (c). Does the paragraph's last clause, then, asserting that the rights protected by § 1981 are protected from "impairment under color of State law," overrule *Jett*? Perhaps not, for that decision never denied that the § 1981 right to be free of race discrimination in contracting was enforceable to some degree against state and local government. It held only that in actions against those entities the § 1981 plaintiff must establish the "policy" element of the § 1983 prima facie case. On this reading, and a "plain text" approach to statutory interpretation, the Supreme Court might find that the final clause of section (c) actually codifies rather than overrules *Jett*!

7. 491 U.S. 58, 109 S.Ct. 2304, 105 L.Ed.2d 45 (1989).

8. Cong. Rec. S15483 (Oct. 30, 1991).

Jett, if it has not been legislatively overruled, could have far-reaching restrictive implications. Suppose the *Jett* limitation of § 1981 claims to Section 1983 proof survives judicial construction of new § 1981(c) and the limitation is definitively held applicable to cases against state as well as local government defendants. Would *Jett* then entirely preclude § 1981 claims against states *eo nominee* because after *Will* those claims now fail under § 1983? If so, states could not be subjected to damages for violations of federal rights under either § 1983 or § 1981. Per *Will*, plaintiffs would instead be remitted to § 1983 claims against individual state officials for prospective relief, and then would prevail only if they could prove that the officials were implementing established state policy or custom. Let us now consider such possibilities in more detail.

§ 1.9 [Reserved]

B. *JETT, WILL,* AND THE CIVIL RIGHTS ACT OF 1991: THE PROOF REQUIREMENTS OF SECTION 1981 IN ACTIONS AGAINST STATE OR LOCAL GOVERNMENTS

§ 1.10 In General

With its decisions in *Will v. Michigan Department of State Police*,[1] and *Jett v. Dallas Independent School Dist.*,[2] the Supreme Court imposed significant restrictions on plaintiffs alleging intentional race discrimination and seeking redress against state and local governments under, respectively, 42 U.S.C.A. § 1983 and 42 U.S.C.A. § 1981. The Civil Rights Act of 1991 casts some doubt on the continued vitality of *Jett*. How the federal courts interpret the 1991 Act as applied to *Jett* will determine whether and to what degree such a plaintiff can pursue remedies against government under § 1981, or only under § 1983.

§ 1.11 Claims Arising From Acts of Discrimination on or Before Nov. 21, 1991

The Supreme Court has held that the Civil Rights Act of 1991 does not apply retroactively.[1] It prohibits acts of discrimination that occur after its enactment on November 21, 1991.[2] As a result, our analysis

§ 1.10

1. 491 U.S. 58, 109 S.Ct. 2304, 105 L.Ed.2d 45 (1989).

2. 491 U.S. 701, 109 S.Ct. 2702, 105 L.Ed.2d 598 (1989).

§ 1.11

1. *Landgraf v. USI Film Prods.*, 511 U.S. 244, 114 S.Ct. 1483, 128 L.Ed.2d 229 (1994); *Rivers v. Roadway Express*, 511 U.S. 298, 114 S.Ct. 1510, 128 L.Ed.2d 274 (1994).

2. *Landgraf v. USI Film Prods.*, 511 U.S. 244, 114 S.Ct. 1483, 128 L.Ed.2d 229 (1994); *Rivers v. Roadway Express*, 511 U.S. 298, 114 S.Ct. 1510, 128 L.Ed.2d 274 (1994).

begins with the interplay of §§ 1981 and 1983 after *Will* and *Jett*, but before Nov. 21, 1991, and without regard to the 1991 Civil Rights Act.

In *Will v. Michigan Department of State Police*,[3] the Supreme Court held that "neither a state or its officials acting in their official capacities are 'persons' under Section 1983."[4] Hence, the Court concluded that under § 1983 states are not suable at all in their own name and state officials sued in their official capacities are subject only to prospective relief.[5]

In that same term, the Court also decided *Jett v. Dallas Independent School Dist.*[6] In *Jett,* the Court severely limited the applicability of § 1981. The Court stated,

> We think the history of the 1866 Act and the 1871 Act . . . indicates that Congress intended that the explicit remedial provisions of Section 1983 be controlling in the context of damages actions brought against state actors alleging violation of the rights declared in Section 1981.[7]

Consequently, "the express 'action at law' provided by Section *1983* . . . provides the exclusive federal damages *remedy* for the violation of the *rights* guaranteed by Section 1981 when the claim is pressed against a state actor."[8] The Court explained the effect of this holding:

> [T]o prevail on his [Section 1981] claim for damages against the school district, [plaintiff] must show that the violation of his 'right to make contracts' protected by Section 1981 was caused by a custom or policy within the meaning of Monell and subsequent [Section 1983] cases.[9]

The language of the *Jett* opinion broadly applies the § 1983 limitations to any § 1981 claim against a "state actor." This has led one court to conclude that its restriction extends to suits against individual state officials, not just the state itself—despite one statement by the Court that "§ 1983 constitutes the exclusive federal remedy for violation of the rights guaranteed in § 1981 by state governmental *units*."[10] A plaintiff seeking redress for deprivations of the rights guaranteed by § 1981 must therefore also satisfy the additional prima facie proof element of § 1983—a showing of official policy or custom.

3. 491 U.S. 58, 109 S.Ct. 2304, 105 L.Ed.2d 45, (1989).

4. *Id.* at 71, 109 S.Ct. at 2312.

5. *Id.* at 63, 109 S.Ct. at 2308.

6. 491 U.S. 701, 109 S.Ct. 2702, 105 L.Ed.2d 598 (1989).

7. *Id.* at 731, 109 S.Ct. at 2720.

8. *Id.* at 735, 109 S.Ct. at 2723 (emphasis added).

9. *Id.* at 735–736, 109 S.Ct. at 2723.

10. *Felton v. Polles,* 315 F.3d 470, 481–483 (5th Cir.2002). Of course the question whether § 1981 claims against individual government defendants must be asserted through the remedy vehicle of § 1983 need not even be reached if, as the Fifth Circuit has suggested, no § 1981 claim lies in the first place against individual municipal, *Oden v. Oktibbeha County, Miss.*, 246 F.3d 458 (5th Cir.), *cert. denied*, 534 U.S. 949, 122 S.Ct. 342, 151 L.Ed.2d 258 (2001), or state, *Felton v. Polles,* 315 F.3d at 481, employees, only against the municipal or state employer who allegedly denied the plaintiff the right to make or enforce a contract.

Accordingly, after *Will* and *Jett* but before the 1991 Act, a plaintiff with a claim of intentional discrimination faced several potential roadblocks to redress under §§ 1981 and 1983. Under *Jett*, the plaintiff clearly couldn't win a suit under § 1981 against a *municipality* or *local* government unless he could show a policy or custom as required by § 1983. Because of *Will*, she couldn't sue the *state* as such, under § 1983. And perhaps her § 1981 claim against a *state* would falter as well. After all, the language of *Jett* apparently required the plaintiff to meet all § 1983 requirements in order to perfect a § 1981 claim against a state actor, and under *Will* a state was no longer a § 1983 "person."

On the other hand, under the logic of *Jett*, a plaintiff possibly *could* recover against a state under § 1981. The Court in *Jett* was primarily concerned with preventing a plaintiff from using § 1981 as an "end-around" § 1983's requirements for bringing suit against a state or local governmental actor. But, since the Court had just held in *Will* that states could *not* be sued under § 1983, § 1981 claims against states could no longer be viewed as circumventing § 1983 requirements. That is, allowing a plaintiff to proceed against a state under the less rigorous standards of § 1981 would not have been circumventing the stricter standards of § 1983, since states were no longer suable under § 1983 at all. On this reasoning, a plaintiff could still sue a state under § 1981 without meeting the "policy" hurdle of § 1983.

The Civil Rights Act of 1991 added a new paragraph to § 1981. In § 101(c) of the 1991 Act, Congress provided:

> (c) The rights protected by this section are protected against impairment by nongovernmental discrimination *and impairment under color of state law*.[11]

The crucial inquiry raised by this text is whether Congress intended to overrule *Jett*.

§ 1.12 Claims Arising From Intentional Race Discrimination After the Effective Date of the 1991 Act

The early reported *district court* cases held or implied that the 1991 Act overrules *Jett*. For example, in *Arnett v. Davis County School District*,[1] the court explained,

> In the Civil Rights Act of 1991, however, Congress amended §1981 to make clear its intent that §1981's protections be extended to impairment of that section's rights "under color of State law."[2]

Similarly, in *Morris v. State of Kansas Department of Revenue*,[3] a United States District Court observed,

11. Pub.L. 102–166, § 101 (1991) (codified at 42 U.S.C.A. § 1981(c)) (emphasis added).

§ 1.12

1. 1993 WL 434053 at *5 & n. 8 (D.Utah 1993).

2. Codified at 42 U.S.C.A. § 1981(c) (*overruling Jett v. Dallas Indep. Sch. Dist.*, 491 U.S. 701, 109 S.Ct. 2702, 105 L.Ed.2d 598 (1989)).

3. 849 F.Supp. 1421 (D.Kan.1994).

The Civil Rights Act of 1991 amended § 1981 to clarify that "[t]he rights protected by this section are protected against ... impairment under color of State law." 42 U.S.C.A. § 1981(c). In effect, this amendment overrules *Jett.* (emphasis added).[4]

In *Ford v. City of Rockford,*[5] another district court concluded that *Jett* had been overruled. The district court stated, "Congress ... *overruled* the Jett holding in its enactment of the Civil Rights Act of 1991,[6] by extending the ambit of Section 1981 to state action."[7]

Vakharia v. Swedish Covenant Hospital,[8] implicitly reached the same conclusion. The district court stated,

> [W]hen a municipal agency is involved, the municipal employee's isolated acts will not subject the municipal employer to liability under Section 1981—*at least as Section 1981* existed prior to the Civil Rights Act of 1991—unless the employee was following established policy.[9]

By emphasizing that its decision was based on the law before the 1991 Act, the district court suggested that the 1991 Act had overruled *Jett.*

Nevertheless, some more recent circuit court decisions hold that the 1991 Act did *not* overrule *Jett.* For example, the Act nowhere expressly addresses the *Jett* holding, e.g., by authorizing the § 1981 claim against a state or local government entity to proceed without regard to the limitations of § 1983. Further, the simple statement in new § 1981(c) that § 1981 protects against "impairment under color of state law" does not contradict the holding in *Jett.* In fact, the whole premise of *Jett* was that a plaintiff suing a state or local government entity was not limited to a claim under § 1983 but could assert a claim, albeit a peculiarly limited one, under § 1981 as well. *Jett* only demanded that the plaintiff bringing a § 1981 claim against a government entity satisfy the requirements of § 1983 for entity liability. Viewed this way, the language of new § 1981(c) arguably codifies, rather than overrules, *Jett.*

These conclusions are fortified by the way a Supreme Court that takes a "plain-text" approach to statutory interpretation is likely to view subsection (c). Even if the Court resorts to legislative history it would find only a congressional determination to codify *Runyon.* There is no stated intention to overrule *Jett,* despite the express stated intention found elsewhere in the 1991 legislation to overrule other specifically named Supreme Court decisions. Thus, although the decisions do not always articulate all these reasons, the Fourth, Fifth, Eighth and Elev-

4. *Morris,* 849 F.Supp. at 1426 (citing *Arnett,* 1993 WL 434053 at *5).

5. 1992 WL 309603 at *2 (N.D.Ill. 1992).

6. 42 U.S.C.A. § 1981(c)(2).

7. 1992 WL 309603 at *2 (emphasis added).

8. 824 F.Supp. 769 (N.D.Ill.1993). *See also La Compania Ocho, Inc. v. United States Forest Serv.,* 874 F.Supp. 1242, 1251 (D.N.M.1995) (same conclusion in dictum).

9. *Id.* at 785 & n. 1 (emphasis added).

enth Circuits have assumed or concluded that *Jett* enjoys continuing vitality notwithstanding § 1981(c).[10]

Some decisions have suggested an intermediate position. These courts treat § 1981(c) as overruling what they take to be the *Jett* holding that § 1981 violations can be remedied only under § 1983. Thus § 1981 stands on its own as the source of a right and a remedy. Nevertheless, these courts also observe that nothing about the 1991 amendment implies that local governments should be liable vicariously under § 1981, any more than they are under § 1983. Rather, "municipal liability for public officials' violations of sec. 1981" must be determined by reference to the principles applicable "under sec. 1983 using the *Monell* analysis."[11] The difference in these judicial approaches appears solely one of pleading; plaintiff still must prove "policy" to prevail.

§ 1.13 The Practical Significance of the *Jett*-Related Language in the Civil Rights Act of 1991

If the 1991 Act is construed to overrule *Jett*, a plaintiff with an intentional race discrimination claim against a state or local government employer can make a claim under § 1981, unencumbered by the "policy" proof demanded by § 1983. This § 1981 claim could be against all "state action" defendants, local governmental entities as well as the states themselves.

But if, as is more likely, *Jett* is held not overruled by the 1991 Act and extended to claims against state entities, a plaintiff with an intentional race discrimination claim against any state or local government defendant will be somewhat hamstrung.[1] She can still pursue a claim

10. *Felton v. Polles* 315 F.3d 470, 482–483 (5th Cir. 2002); *Oden v. Oktibbeha County, Miss.*, 246 F.3d 458 (5th Cir.2001), *cert. denied*, 534 U.S. 948, 122 S.Ct. 341, 151 L.Ed.2d 258 (2001); *Butts v. County of Volusia*, 222 F.3d 891 (11th Cir.2000); *Dennis v. County of Fairfax*, 55 F.3d 151, 156 n. 1 (4th Cir.1995); *Williams v. Little Rock Mun. Water Works*, 21 F.3d 218 (8th Cir. 1994); *Cotterell v. New York City Transit Police Dep't*, 1995 WL 604700 (E.D.N.Y. 1995).

11. *Philippeaux v. North Central Bronx Hosp.*, 871 F.Supp. 640, 655 (S.D.N.Y.1994). *See also Gallardo v. Board of County Comm'rs*, 857 F.Supp. 783, 786 (D.Kan. 1994). This reasoning has been endorsed by a circuit court opinion. *Federation of African American Contractors v. City of Oakland*, 96 F.3d 1204 (9th Cir.1996). *See also Smith v. Chicago Sch. Reform Bd. of Trustees*, 165 F.3d 1142, 1148–49 (7th Cir.1999) (reversing plaintiff's verdict where the only defendant was a municipal government agency, explaining that respondeat superior was not available even if a high-ranking official committed the discrimination, and remanding to allow plaintiff to try to prove that the agency's official policy or custom was discriminatory); *Hopp v. City of Pittsburgh*, 194 F.3d 434 (3d Cir.1999) (§ 1981 claim lies against local government entity, but plaintiff must prove the "policy" element required to establish a § 1983 claim). For a discussion of vicarious governmental entity liability under § 1983 as elaborated in *Monell v. Department of Soc. Servs.*, 436 U.S. 658, 98 S.Ct. 2018, 56 L.Ed.2d 611 (1978), see Chapter 2.

§ 1.13

1. See, for example, *Butts v. County of Volusia*, 222 F.3d 891 (11th Cir.2000). In *Butts*, a county employee sued the county, a political subdivision of the state, for race discrimination under § 1981. Subsequently, plaintiff filed a second suit pursuant to Title VII, but the lower court dismissed that suit because it alleged the same factual allegations as the § 1981 suit. Plaintiff then attempted to amend the first suit to add Title VII, but the motion to amend was denied because it was filed after the scheduling deadline. The circuit court affirmed

under § 1981, probably even against the state.[2] At a minimum, the 1991 Act confirms that § 1981 furnishes a *right* to be free of racial discrimination in contracting that may not be impaired "under color of state law," including presumably by the state itself. But to recover the plaintiff would have to meet the proof requirements of § 1983 by showing that her injury was inflicted by a formal government policy, a local policymaking official, or through "deliberate indifference."[3] And state defendants sued in their individual capacity for § 1981 violations asserted through § 1983 of course have available the defense of qualified immunity.

A third possible scenario will result if *Jett* is held not to have been overruled by the 1991 Act, but is held to apply only to local government defendants. Because *Will*, decided earlier in the same week as *Jett*, clearly precluded § 1983 claims against states, *Jett's* broad language may be subordinated to *Jett*'s logic, and its holding would then likely impinge only on § 1981 claims against local governments. Under this interpretation, an employee with an intentional race discrimination claim could use § 1981 "neat" in actions against *state* governments but would remain obliged to meet § 1983's "policy" requirement when seeking redress under § 1981 from *local* government defendants.

Unless Congress acts to overrule *Will* or to clarify that it intended to overrule *Jett*, only plaintiffs challenging the conduct of municipal or other local, as opposed to state or federal, governments may now be able to take advantage of the immediate court access and generous remedies afforded by the Reconstruction Civil Rights Acts; and even those plaintiffs may have to meet the formidable new requirements of § 1983. Yet when a *private* defendant intentionally refuses, because of race or ancestry, to execute or perform a contract, the unsuccessful applicant will still clearly have a claim under § 1981, in accordance with new paragraph (c); and after the overruling of *Patterson* by new paragraph (b), that claim will once again secure the right to make and enforce contracts without discrimination across the entire spectrum of the contractual relationship. The ironic residue is that § 1981 claims against government defendants are less clearly (in the case of states) or simply

the lower court's entry of summary judgment against the plaintiff, finding that § 1981 provided no cause of action against a state actor.

2. But it is unclear whether a § 1981–guaranteed right, pursued through a § 1983 claim, can even lie against the state since, per *Will*, the state is not a § 1983 "person."

3. See, for example, *Gant v. Wallingford Bd. of Educ.*, 195 F.3d 134, 140–41 (2d Cir.1999), where the court adopted the deliberate indifference standard enunciated in *Davis v. Monroe County Bd. of Educ.*, 526 U.S. 629, 119 S.Ct. 1661, 143 L.Ed.2d 839 (1999) in its analysis of an African–American student's § 1981 claim against the school board and school officials for failing to rectify racial harassment. In *Davis*, the Court held that under Title IX of the Education Amendments of 1972, 20 U.S.C.A. § 1681 *et seq.*, a school that receives federal funds may be liable to a student for money damages if it is deliberately indifferent to sufficiently severe student-on-student sexual harassment. *See also Murrell v. School Dist. No. 1*, 186 F.3d 1238, 1249–51 (10th Cir.1999) (holding that schoolteachers, administrators, and school boards violate equal protection principles through deliberate indifference to sexual harassment of a student by another student). See the discussion of Title IX and *Davis* in Chapter 3, especially § 3.20.

not (in the case of the federal government) actionable, and may (in the case of local governments) succeed only on stricter (i.e., § 1983) proof terms, than claims against private sector defendants—this despite that fact that, until *Runyon* was decided in 1976, private defendants were not thought subject to suit under § 1981 at all!

§§ 1.14–1.19 [Reserved]

C. RECENT PROCEDURAL LIMITATIONS ON THE RECONSTRUCTION CIVIL RIGHTS ACTS

§ 1.20 In General

The federal courts' role in enforcing the Reconstruction Civil Rights Acts has also been diminished by liberal application of the doctrines of *res judicata* and collateral estoppel. The Supreme Court has found no policy of § 1983 that warrants denying state judgments their normal preclusive effect in federal court under the Full Faith and Credit Statute.[1] These judgments now therefore bar civil rights claims from relitigation to the same extent as in the forum state's courts.[2] Indeed, relying on federal common law, the Supreme Court has even approved the preclusion of Civil Rights Acts claims by unreviewed quasi-judicial determinations of state administrative agencies.[3] These developments are discussed more fully in Chapter 5.

§ 1.21 Expansion and Contraction: The Supreme Court's Dialectic Approach to Interpreting the Reconstruction Civil Rights Acts

The Supreme Court has in the past several decades both breathed new life into the civil rights legislation enacted after the Civil War and then taken steps to curtail the resulting claims. After expanding the §§ 1981 and 1982 concept of "race" in *McDonald*, *Al-Kharazi*, and *Shaare Tefila*, and bringing purely private conduct within the reach of those statutes in *Jones*, *Runyon*, and *Patterson*, the Court demanded proof of intent in *General Building Contractors,* and in *Jett* imported restrictive § 1983 liability requirements into § 1981 claims against government defendants. Only Congress' overruling of the restrictive *Patterson* reading of the incidents of contract reached by § 1981 saved that statute from falling into virtual desuetude.

Meanwhile, after its pioneering extension of § 1983 liability to the unauthorized as well as sanctioned acts of government employees in

§ 1.20

1. 28 U.S.C.A. § 1738.

2. *Allen v. McCurry*, 449 U.S. 90, 101 S.Ct. 411, 66 L.Ed.2d 308 (1980) (collateral estoppel effect accorded prior state criminal proceeding); *Migra v. Warren City Sch. Dist. Bd. of Educ.*, 465 U.S. 75, 104 S.Ct. 892, 79 L.Ed.2d 56 (1984) (res judicata effect accorded prior state civil action).

3. *University of Tenn. v. Elliott*, 478 U.S. 788, 106 S.Ct. 3220, 92 L.Ed.2d 635 (1986).

Monroe, the Court clamped down on claims against individual defendants by affording them an ever more generous defense of qualified immunity in such cases as *Harlow, Creighton*, *Mitchell*, and *Siegert v. Gilley*. The Court apparently learned from *Monroe* the lesson that expansive terms of liability under § 1983 will invite large numbers of federal court lawsuits. For this time, when it subjected government entities to § 1983 liability in *Monell*, it simultaneously instituted restrictive checks in the latter part of the same opinion. The prima facie "policy" requirement announced by *Monell* has since been even more strictly reformulated in subsequent cases—*Pembaur* and *Praprotnik* for constitutional violations stemming from affirmative misconduct, and *City of Canton* and *Board of County Commissioners of Bryan County v. Brown*[1] for violations occasioned by flagrant failures to act. And the Court has found it necessary to temper the *Maine v. Thiboutot* construction of the "and laws" language of § 1983, which authorized claims based on the violation of any federal statute, by announcing the "rights" and "comprehensive remedies" limitations exemplified by, respectively, *Suter v. Artist* and *National Sea Clammers*.

As with *Monell*'s holding on the § 1983 liability of government entities, so with the Court's decision in *Griffin* that § 1985(3) could impose liability on private as well as public conspirators: the Court, anticipating that otherwise many ordinary multi-defendant torts could be transmuted into federal constitutional conspiracy cases, found in the statute's protection of "equal rights" a requirement that the plaintiff must show invidious racial or otherwise class-based animus. Later decisions would clarify that the "otherwise" does not extend beyond race to include economic motivation (*Scott v. Carpenters*) and that conspiracies limited to private actors violate § 1985(3) only if they invade the two constitutional rights protected against purely private interference, the interstate right to travel and freedom from involuntary servitude (*Bray*). And while the Court has not clarified whether § 1985(3) remedies the conspiratorial deprivation of rights secured by federal statutes, it has precluded the use of § 1985(3) if the right in question is redressable under another federal statute. (*Novotny*). Finally, it is wise to assume that actions against a state, state agency or sub-state entity functioning on behalf of the state that are brought under § 1985, like those under § 1981, are subject to the defense of Eleventh Amendment immunity.[2]

We now turn to these developments under § 1983.

§ 1.21

1. 520 U.S. 397, 117 S.Ct. 1382, 137 L.Ed.2d 626 (1997).

2. *Fincher v. Florida Dep't of Labor & Employment Sec. Unemployment Appeals Comm'n*, 798 F.2d 1371, 1372 (11th Cir. 1986), *cert. denied*, 479 U.S. 1072, 107 S.Ct. 1262, 94 L.Ed.2d 124 (1987).

Chapter Two

SECTION 1983

Analysis

A. INTRODUCTION

§ 2.1 In General

Section 42 U.S.C.A. § 1983 (1988) is easily the most important of the Reconstruction Civil Rights Acts, as measured both by the importance of its primarily constitutional workload and by the sheer number of federal cases brought under its auspices. The statute was originally passed as § 1 of the Ku Klux Klan Act of April 20, 1871,[1] and titled "An Act to enforce the Provisions of the Fourteenth Amendment to the Constitution of the United States, and for other Purposes." It provides as follows:

> Every person who, under color of any statute, ordinance, regulation, custom, or usage, of any State or Territory or the District of Columbia, subjects, or causes to be subjected, any citizen of the United States or other person within the jurisdiction thereof to the deprivation of any rights, privileges, or immunities secured by the Constitution and laws, shall be liable to the party injured in an action at law, suit in equity, or other proper proceeding for redress,

§ 2.1

1. Ch. 22, § 1, 17 Stat. 13 (1871).

except that in any action brought against a judicial officer for an act or omission taken in such officer's judicial capacity, injunctive relief shall not be granted unless a declaratory decree was violated or declaratory relief was unavailable. For the purposes of this section, any Act of Congress applicable exclusively to the District of Columbia shall be considered to be a statute of the District of Columbia.[2]

Section 1983 therefore creates a claim for legal or equitable relief against (1) every "person" who (2) "under color of" state legislation, custom, or usage (3) "subjects, or causes [another] to be subjected" (4) to the deprivation of rights secured by the federal "Constitution and laws." The causation requirement, as we shall see, is not pro forma, and is particularly rigid in cases where the defendant is a government entity.[3] A closely related, standard tort element that is also required to state a § 1983 claim is that defendant's act caused plaintiff some recognized constitutional harm or injury.[4]

Section 1983 as interpreted today takes a strikingly asymmetrical shape. The statute's text simply provides for the liability of defendants who "cause [a plaintiff] to be subjected" to the loss of a federally secured right. In adumbrating this causation requirement, however, the Supreme Court places an additional obstacle in the path of a plaintiff who sues a government entity. An entity's liability is restricted to conduct of its agents that implements entity "policy," defined as "a deliberate choice to follow a course of action . . . from among various alternatives."[5] In the typical case, the agent who inflicts the injury does not act pursuant to a formal ordinance or written administrative directive; yet the liability of his entity demands a showing that an official with "final" discretionary authority under positive state law specifically authorized or ratified the agent's injury-producing act.[6] Alternatively, if injury results from an

2. 42 U.S.C.A. § 1983 (1988).

3. *See generally Phillips ex rel. Phillips v. Monroe County*, 311 F.3d 369 (5th Cir. 2002) (alleged failure to provide inmate medical care, even if violative of Eighth Amendment, not the cause of inmate's death and hence not actionable); *Estate of Brooks ex. rel. Brooks v. United States*, 197 F.3d 1245, 1247–48 (9th Cir.1999) (causation a required element of § 1983 claim, and defendant county not a legal cause of plaintiff's extended detention because it lacked authority either to bring plaintiff before a judicial officer or to release him absent direction from the United States); *Morris v. Lindau*, 196 F.3d 102, 113–114 (2d Cir.1999) (in First Amendment retaliation case, plaintiff fails causation element for lack of evidence that defendants responsible for his discharge were aware of his protected speech). The issue can arise in the same way as in ordinary tort cases, too. *Compare Henderson v. Sheahan*, 196 F.3d 839 (7th Cir.1999), *cert. denied*, 530 U.S. 1244, 120 S.Ct. 2691, 147 L.Ed.2d 962 (2000) (claim that jail officials violated due process by exposing plaintiff to second-hand smoke fails for want of sufficient evidence that the exposure would subject plaintiff to an increased risk of serious future medical harm) with *Warren v. Keane*, 196 F.3d 330 (2d Cir.1999) (material fact issue precludes summary judgment on same claim).

4. *See, e.g., Smith ex rel. Smith v. Siegelman*, 322 F.3d 1290 (11th Cir.2003) (no deprivation of liberty interest that could violate due process absent allegation or evidence that plaintiff had been discharged, demoted, denied promotion as a result of defendants' conduct).

5. *Pembaur v. City of Cincinnati*, 475 U.S. 469, 483, 106 S.Ct. 1292, 1300, 89 L.Ed.2d 452 (1986) (plurality opinion).

6. *See City of St. Louis v. Praprotnik*, 485 U.S. 112, 127, 108 S.Ct. 915, 926, 99 L.Ed.2d 107 (1988) (plurality opinion). *Praprotnik* commanded a majority of the Court in *Jett v. Dallas Indep. Sch. Dist.*, 491 U.S. 701, 737–38, 109 S.Ct. 2702, 2724, 105

agent's omission, policy may be found in the entity's "deliberate indifference" to a frequently recurring circumstance.[7] Still, if the plaintiff can satisfy any of these formidable policy hurdles, she recovers from an entity defendant even if the federal right violated had not been judicially recognized before the incident that caused the harm.[8] The case against the entity can therefore still serve as a staging ground for dialogue about the creation of new constitutional protections.

Measured against the statute's overriding purpose of restraining federally unlawful state sponsored conduct,[9] current entity defendant doctrine makes formal sense but in practice falls short of its animating ideal. In the abstract, the Court's reaffirmation of the statute's federal lawmaking potential has intuitive appeal. If, as the Court writes, "the public as a whole has an interest" that is served by government conduct in conformity with federal law,[10] and if constraining local government conduct within federal norms is the statute's signal aim, then preserving entity litigation as a crucible for the vindication of evolving constitutional standards seems appropriate and necessary. In the concrete world of litigation, however, the "policy" barrier principally protects local government and its fisc.

By contrast, the prima facie case against a government official is far less exacting. Whenever an individual agent causes a recognized constitutional harm, she is prima facie liable even if the entity approved her conduct and she had a blameless state of mind.[11] Nevertheless, the Court, prompted by concerns about litigation floodgates, federalism, and judicial interference with discretionary government decisions,[12] has craft-

L.Ed.2d 598 (1989). Alternatively, the policy element may be met by evidence that the agent's act was consistent with a settled entity custom. *See Monell v. Department of Soc. Servs.*, 436 U.S. 658, 690–91, 98 S.Ct. 2018, 2035–2036, 56 L.Ed.2d 611 (1978).

7. *See City of Canton v. Harris*, 489 U.S. 378, 388, 109 S.Ct. 1197, 1205, 103 L.Ed.2d 412 (1989).

8. See Sections D and E infra this chapter.

9. The language of the statute and the congressional goals identified by Justice Douglas in *Monroe v. Pape*, 365 U.S. 167, 173–74, 81 S.Ct. 473, 477, 5 L.Ed.2d 492 (1961), overruled on a different issue by *Monell v. Department of Soc. Servs.*, 436 U.S. 658, 98 S.Ct. 2018, 56 L.Ed.2d 611 (1978), reflect this purpose. *See also* Marshall S. Shapo, *Constitutional Tort: Monroe v. Pape and the Frontiers Beyond*, 60 N.W.U.L.Rev. 277, 280 (1965) (determining that legislative history reveals the intent to create a federal remedy where state remedies are unavailable or inadequate).

10. *Hensley v. Eckerhart*, 461 U.S. 424, 444 n. 4, 103 S.Ct. 1933, 1945 n. 4, 76 L.Ed.2d 40 (1983) (Brennan, J., concurring in part and dissenting in part).

11. *Monroe* is still good law on this point. *See Daniels v. Williams*, 474 U.S. 327, 330–331, 106 S.Ct. 662, 664–665, 88 L.Ed.2d 662 (1986) (overruling *Parratt v. Taylor*, 451 U.S. 527, 101 S.Ct. 1908, 68 L.Ed.2d 420 (1981), to the extent that *Parratt* held that negligence was sufficient to state a claim for a state-caused "deprivation," but otherwise leaving undisturbed the conclusion that § 1983 contains no independent state-of-mind requirement). But where the predicate violation requires proof of defendant's state of mind, the plaintiff must adduce this evidence. *See, e.g., Hayden v. Grayson*, 134 F.3d 449 (1st Cir.1998), *cert. denied*, 524 U.S. 953, 118 S.Ct. 2370, 141 L.Ed.2d 738 (1998) (equal protection claim).

12. Beginning in 1976, the Court began to take seriously its concern that absent significant restraints § 1983 would become "a font of tort law." *Paul v. Davis*, 424 U.S. 693, 701, 96 S.Ct. 1155, 1160, 47 L.Ed.2d 405 (1976); *see also* Theodore Eisenberg & Stewart Schwab, *The Reality of Constitutional Tort Litigation*, 72 Cornell

ed an expansive affirmative defense that more than offsets the laxity of the prima facie requirements. Executive or administrative government agents, including those whose positions make them most likely to inflict injury on ordinary citizens, escape liability for damages by grace of qualified immunity unless the right violated was previously recognized by judicial precedent of unmistakable application and clarity.[13]

§ 2.2 "Absolute" Immunities

Certain legislative, judicial, and prosecutorial functions cut so close to the core of representative democracy or the justice system that the common law has created "absolute" immunity to protect these officials' freedom of action. "Absolute," as we shall see, does not necessarily free all these officials from all liability; injunctive relief may still lie, and in that case the immunity will not free the official from the necessity of defending her conduct in court.[1] Rather, "absolute" refers to the fact that within the immunized sphere, such conduct will not give rise to damages (or, in the case of legislators, any liability) even if motivated by personal gain, retribution or bias and even if undertaken as part of a conspiracy.[2] As with the qualified immunity of officials performing executive or administrative functions, defendants asserting absolute immunity enjoy the procedural protection of an immediate interlocutory appeal from the denial of a motion asserting the immunity.[3] This is necessary so that the person who claims the immunity shall not have to "answer for his conduct in a civil damages action."[4]

Thus, with respect to their primary functions, individual judges and prosecutors are accorded an even broader form of immunity from damages than executive or administrative officials. They, and other officials who exercise judicial or prosecutorial functions,[5] are accorded "absolute"

L.Rev. 641, 646–47 (1987) (arguing that the Court's efforts to curb procedural due process litigation are rooted in a desire to stem a flood of litigation). Eisenberg and Schwab conclude, however, that the growth in civil rights litigation has not been as explosive as commonly assumed. See *Paul* at 693–95, 96 S.Ct. at 1157–1158. *Paul* also evinces the fear that § 1983 litigation will become a mechanism for federal trenching on state prerogatives. *See Paul* at 700–01, 96 S.Ct. at 1160–1161; *see also infra* text, § 2.41 (discussing *Paul*).

13. *See Anderson v. Creighton*, 483 U.S. 635, 646 n. 6, 107 S.Ct. 3034, 3042 n. 6, 97 L.Ed.2d 523 (1987); *Harlow v. Fitzgerald*, 457 U.S. 800, 817–819, 102 S.Ct. 2727, 2738–2739, 73 L.Ed.2d 396 (1982).

§ 2.2

1. Note, however, that a 1998 amendment to § 1983 prohibits injunctive relief against a judicial officer for an act or omission taken in such officer's judicial capacity unless a declaratory decree was violated or declaratory relief was unavailable.

2. *See, e.g., Tenney v. Brandhove*, 341 U.S. 367, 377, 71 S.Ct. 783, 788, 95 L.Ed. 1019 (1951); *Wood v. Strickland*, 420 U.S. 308, 317, 95 S.Ct. 992, 998, 43 L.Ed.2d 214 (1975). Political motive also does not defeat the immunity. *Bernard v. County of Suffolk*, 356 F.3d 495 (2d Cir. 2004).

3. *Nixon v. Fitzgerald*, 457 U.S. 731, 742, 102 S.Ct. 2690, 2697, 73 L.Ed.2d 349 (1982).

4. *Mitchell v. Forsyth*, 472 U.S. 511, 525, 105 S.Ct. 2806, 2814, 86 L.Ed.2d 411 (1985).

5. *See Supreme Court of Va. v. Consumers Union*, 446 U.S. 719, 100 S.Ct. 1967, 64 L.Ed.2d 641 (1980) (Virginia Supreme Court justices acted in a legislative capacity in promulgating bar disciplinary rules); *Eldridge v. Gibson*, 332 F.3d 1019 (6th Cir.2003) (private lawyers serving as appointed special prosecutors in criminal

immunity with respect to all truly "judicial" or "prosecutorial" conduct. Absolute immunity is an affirmative defense that may be waived in federal court if defendant fails to assert it in an answer or pre-answer motion to dismiss;[6] consequently, the burden of proof in establishing eligibility for absolute immunity lies with the individual asserting it.[7] Eligibility for the immunity depends on a functional characterization of the challenged conduct.[8] This means not only that persons other than judges or prosecutors are entitled to a "quasi" version of absolute immunity to the extent that they undertake functions that a court agrees are "judicial" or "prosecutorial" in character;[9] it also means that

trial accorded absolute prosecutorial immunity); *Brown v. Newberger*, 291 F.3d 89, 94 (1st Cir.2002) (court-ordered sexual abuse evaluators implicitly held to be acting under color of law because of their "close association with the judicial process," but accorded absolute, quasi-judicial immunity); *Rippy ex rel. Rippy v. Hattaway*, 270 F.3d 416 (6th Cir.2001) (social workers receive absolute immunity with respect to quasi-prosecutorial role of petitioning for custody of child and alleged failures to ensure guardian ad litem representation); *Beck v. Texas State Bd. Of Dental Examiners*, 204 F.3d 629 (5th Cir.2000), *cert. denied*, 531 U.S. 871, 121 S.Ct. 171, 148 L.Ed.2d 117 (2000) (board members performed adjudicative function entailing quasi-judicial immunity in revoking dentist's license; their investigator, in conducting a warrantless search of dentist's office, eligible only for qualified immunity since he neither initiated disciplinary proceedings nor prosecuted complaint); *Dunham v. Wadley*, 195 F.3d 1007 (8th Cir.1999), *cert. denied*, 531 U.S. 819, 121 S.Ct. 60, 148 L.Ed.2d 26 (2000) (veterinary examining board members receive absolute quasi-judicial immunity respecting their determination that plaintiff practiced without a license, since they performed duties comparable to those of courts); *Romano v. Bible*, 169 F.3d 1182 (9th Cir.1999), *cert. denied*, 528 U.S. 816, 120 S.Ct. 55, 145 L.Ed.2d 48 (1999) (gaming board accorded absolute immunity when acting as prosecutors in investigating and filing complaint against plaintiff); *Montero v. Travis*, 171 F.3d 757 (2d Cir. 1999) (per curiam) (parole board officials afforded absolute quasi-judicial immunity for adjudicative functions in parole revocation hearings); *Martin v. Hendren*, 127 F.3d 720 (8th Cir.1997) (derivative absolute immunity is available for police officer who carried out a judge's order to handcuff litigant and remove her from the courtroom); *Ernst v. Child and Youth Servs. of Chester County*, 108 F.3d 486 (3d Cir. 1997), *cert. denied*, 522 U.S. 850, 118 S.Ct. 139, 139 L.Ed.2d 87 (1997) (child welfare caseworkers perform essentially prosecutorial function warranting absolute immunity in preparing and initiating dependency proceedings, including the formulation and presentation of recommendations to the court). *But cf. Scotto v. Almenas*, 143 F.3d 105 (2d Cir.1998) (parole officer who prepared false parole violation report not entitled to absolute immunity because act was not a judicial or prosecutorial function). See also cases cited immediately supra.

6. *Cozzo v. Tangipahoa Parish Council–President Government*, 279 F.3d 273, 283 (5th Cir. 2002) (waiver of absolute immunity where defendants pleaded only qualified immunity.)

7. *Hafer v. Melo*, 502 U.S. 21, 27, 112 S.Ct. 358, 363, 116 L.Ed.2d 301 (1991) (citing *Burns v. Reed*, 500 U.S. 478, 111 S.Ct. 1934, 114 L.Ed.2d 547 (1991)).

8. *See Forrester v. White*, 484 U.S. 219, 227–29, 108 S.Ct. 538, 544–545, 98 L.Ed.2d 555 (1988).

9. *See, e.g., Whitesel v. Sengenberger*, 222 F.3d 861 (10th Cir.2000) (pretrial services officers designated by state judges receive quasi-judicial immunity for issuance of defective temporary restraining order); *Crenshaw v. Baynerd*, 180 F.3d 866 (7th Cir.1999), *cert. denied*, 528 U.S. 952, 120 S.Ct. 374, 145 L.Ed.2d 292 (1999) (state civil rights commission members acted in quasi-judicial capacity in determining they lacked jurisdiction to review complaint against state judge); *Bush v. Rauch*, 38 F.3d 842 (6th Cir.1994) (probate court administrator eligible for quasi-judicial absolute immunity in connection with preparation of an assessment of a juvenile pursuant to order of a judicial referee); *White v. Armontrout*, 29 F.3d 357 (8th Cir.1994) (extradition officer performed duties of a quasi-judicial nature in administering extradition requests and issuing rendition warrants, and therefore entitled to absolute immunity with respect to those activities). *But see Cleavinger v. Saxner*, 474 U.S. 193, 206,

judges and prosecutors do not receive absolute immunity with respect to their administrative, executive, investigative or other functions not deemed "judicial" or "prosecutorial."[10]

The absolute immunity of a judge extends to any conduct that may be considered a "judicial act" performed in the exercise of an arguably judicial function.[11] The immunity insulates the judge from damages liability not only for erroneous or malicious conduct, but also for acting "in excess of his authority," even where his "commission of grave procedural errors" denied a party fundamental fairness.[12] Only when the judge acts in the "clear absence of all jurisdiction" does she forfeit the immunity. The Court has cited with approval an example intended to distinguish immunized judicial acts—these that are merely "in excess of" authority—and unprotected conduct undertaken without even colorable jurisdiction. Falling in the former category would be a criminal court judge's conviction of a defendant for a non-existent crime; falling in the latter would be the trying of a criminal case by a probate judge.[13] Egregiousness of error, in other words, does not suffice to forfeit the

106 S.Ct. 496, 503, 88 L.Ed.2d 507 (1985) (members of a prison disciplinary committee entitled only to qualified immunity even though they informally adjudicate. The Court observed that the committee members are prison employees rather than professional hearing officers and often make credibility determinations between inmates and fellow employees, "a relationship hardly ... conducive to a truly adjudicatory performance." *Id.* at 203–04.) *See also Moore v. Gunnison Valley Hosp.*, 310 F.3d 1315 (10th Cir.2002) (hospital peer-review members who disciplined physician not accorded absolute judicial immunity because committee they served lacked important attributes of judicial body); *Gray v. Poole,* 275 F.3d 1113 (D.C.Cir.2002) (social worker who recommended initiation of child neglect proceeding acted in investigatory and advisory role to local prosecutor and so eligible only for qualified immunity); *Tulloch v. Coughlin*, 50 F.3d 114 (2d Cir.1995) (prison disciplinary officer eligible only for qualified immunity where hearing informal and thus not classically "adjudicative").

10. *See, e.g., Supreme Court of Va. v. Consumers Union*, 446 U.S. 719, 100 S.Ct. 1967, 64 L.Ed.2d 641 (1980) (judges do not enjoy judicial immunity respecting legislative or administrative functions); *Zarcone v. Perry*, 572 F.2d 52 (2d Cir.1978) (judge who ordered the handcuffing of a courthouse sandwich seller for purveying "putrid" coffee enjoyed no immunity from damages liability since the conduct fell outside any aspect of the process of judging); *Blouin ex rel. Estate of Pouliot v. Spitzer*, 356 F.3d 348 (2d. Cir. 2004) (attorneys generally receive qualified immunity respecting alleged interference with patient's medical care); *Morley v. Walker*, 175 F.3d 756 (9th Cir. 1999) (deputy district attorney who allegedly knew he lacked probable cause when he signed an affidavit to arrest plaintiff eligible only for qualified immunity, although probably eligible for absolute immunity respecting his subsequent conduct in the ensuing judicial proceedings).

11. *See, e.g., Barrett v. Harrington*, 130 F.3d 246 (6th Cir.1997), cert. denied, 523 U.S. 1075, 118 S.Ct. 1517, 140 L.Ed.2d 670 (1998) (judge who instigated a criminal investigation against a litigant for making threats against the judge and thereby obstructing the judicial process was immune; act was taken to protect the integrity of judiciary and was therefore a "judicial act").

12. *Stump v. Sparkman*, 435 U.S. 349, 98 S.Ct. 1099, 55 L.Ed.2d 331 (1978) (judge immune from liability for having approved a parent's petition seeking the sterilization of a child without affording the child's constitutionally required minimum rights of representation and hearing).

13. *Id.* (quoting *Bradley v. Fisher*, 80 U.S. (13 Wall.) 335, 351, 20 L.Ed. 646 (1871)). Similarly, a municipal judge who lacked the authority to issue an arrest warrant in an effort to enforce a judgment of conviction issued by a circuit court was found to have acted only in excess of jurisdiction, not in its complete absence. *Duty v. City of Springdale, Ark.*, 42 F.3d 460 (8th Cir.1994).

immunity.[14] That requires an act not even arguably falling within the formal description of the bounds of office. A 1998 amendment to § 1983 extends judicial immunity to injunctive relief as well, unless a declaratory decree was violated or declaratory relief was unavailable.

As decisions of the Supreme Court attest, the functional characterization process for prosecutors proceeds case by case. Prosecutors' decisions to initiate, not initiate, or delay the initiation of criminal or civil commitment or child neglect proceedings, or to seek or advocate for warrants, are prototypically eligible for the immunity; their personal involvement as witnesses or affiants in support of those proceedings is not.[15] Prosecutors are absolutely immune with respect to initiating proceedings to obtain a search warrant and advocating positions to

14. *Stump v. Sparkman*, 435 U.S. 349, 357, 98 S.Ct. 1099, 1105, 55 L.Ed.2d 331 (1978) (citing *Bradley v. Fisher*); *Tucker v. Outwater*, 118 F.3d 930 (2d Cir.1997), *cert. denied*, 522 U.S. 997, 118 S.Ct. 562, 139 L.Ed.2d 402 (1997) (judge was not acting in clear absence of all jurisdiction when she arraigned, set bail for and remanded the accused despite clear noncompliance with requirement that arrest warrant be endorsed by another court and accused be informed of right to appear in that other court).

15. *See Burns v. Reed*, 500 U.S. at 492–498, 111 S.Ct. at 1942–45 (holding that the prosecutor's advice to police that they could interview a suspect under hypnosis relates to the prosecutor's investigative role and is not sufficiently connected to the judicial process to warrant absolute immunity); *Buckley v. Fitzsimmons*, 509 U.S. 259, 113 S.Ct. 2606, 125 L.Ed.2d 209 (1993) (prosecutor cannot claim absolute immunity concerning his alleged fabrication of evidence during preliminary criminal investigation or his allegedly false statements at press conference announcing indictment, since neither function concerned his role as an advocate; these "investigative" activities were more analogous to police work and accordingly eligible at most only for qualified immunity). In *Burns* the prosecutor was held absolutely immune with respect to his initiating proceedings to obtain a search warrant and advocating positions to secure that warrant during a probable cause hearing. *Accord Gray v.* Poole, 243 F.3d 572 (D.C.Cir.2001); *Dababnah v. Keller-Burnside*, 208 F.3d 467 (4th Cir.2000) (prosecutor absolutely immune for seeking, in defendant's presence in court, order securing defendant's property after defendant's arrest); *Lomaz v. Hennosy*, 151 F.3d 493 (6th Cir.1998) (prosecutors absolutely immune for conduct related to obtaining and executing search warrant). Decisions on whether to charge *Spiegel v. Rabinovitz,* 121 F.3d 251 (7th Cir.1997), or to delay in charging, *Anderson v. Simon,* 217 F.3d 472 (7th Cir. 2000), qualify for the immunity. So does an erroneous or incomplete evaluation of matters referred for prosecution, including drafting papers that rely on the affirmations of others and submitting them in support of civil or administrative enforcement proceedings. *Scott v. Hern,* 216 F.3d 897, 908–910 (10th Cir.2000); *Springmen v. Williams*, 122 F.3d 211 (4th Cir.1997) (prosecutor absolutely immune for deciding to initiate criminal prosecution even though he did not sign the charging papers; immunity attaches to the decision-maker). On the other hand, a prosecutor received only qualified immunity with respect to his investigation of a child's sexual abuse charges and his advice to police that probable cause existed to arrest the parent. These acts were treated as investigatory, and hence ineligible for the defense, rather than as immunized advocacy. *See Hill v. City of New York*, 45 F.3d 653 (2d Cir.1995). And a state prosecutor who countermanded a judge's direction that a court reporter prepare a criminal trial transcript for use in a habeas proceeding was similarly held unprotected by absolute immunity, the challenged conduct being regarded as far removed from the core prosecutorial functions of bringing charges and presenting evidence. *See Gagan v. Norton*, 35 F.3d 1473 (10th Cir.1994), *cert. denied*, 513 U.S. 1183, 115 S.Ct. 1175, 130 L.Ed.2d 1128 (1995). Similarly, state district attorneys who allegedly delayed a prisoner's retransfer to federal custody for several weeks after the formal conclusion of state criminal proceedings could claim only qualified, not absolute immunity. *See Pinaud v. County of Suffolk*, 52 F.3d 1139 (2d Cir.1995). But post-conviction prosecutorial activity in aid of appeal, including retention of evidence pending final decision, is absolutely protected. *Par-*

secure that warrant during a probable cause hearing,[16] but not if they give false sworn testimony establishing the grounds for issuing a warrant.[17] Certainly the immunity includes a prosecutor's decisions about which witnesses to call or evidence to present,[18] as well as out-of-court efforts to control how testimony will be presented.[19] Witnesses, including police officers enjoy absolute immunity from liability for their testimony in adversarial hearings, even when the testimony is allegedly perjured.[20] The great weight of intermediate appellate authority extends this immunity beyond testimony during trial to embrace even a pretrial conspiracy to commit perjury. These courts reason that otherwise most actions against witness defendants, the majority of whom do not prepare their testimony alone, could be restyled as conspiracy claims, thereby undermining the policies supporting witness immunity.[21] Of course conduct

kinson v. Cozzolino, 238 F.3d 145 (2d Cir. 2001).

16. *See Burns v. Reed*, 500 U.S. 478, 111 S.Ct. 1934, 114 L.Ed.2d 547.

17. *Kalina v. Fletcher*, 522 U.S. 118, 118 S.Ct. 502, 139 L.Ed.2d 471 (1997). *See Morley v. Walker*, 175 F.3d 756 (9th Cir. 1999) (deputy district attorney who allegedly knew he lacked probable cause when he signed an affidavit to arrest plaintiff eligible only for qualified, not absolute immunity). *See also Milstein v. Cooley*, 257 F.3d 1004 (9th Cir.2001) (no absolute immunity for district attorneys who fabricated evidence, before empaneling of grand jury by acquiring known false statements to prosecute a defense lawyer).

18. *Imbler v. Pachtman*, 424 U.S. 409, 431 n. 33, 96 S.Ct. 984, 47 L.Ed.2d 128 (1976). This rule has been applied even where a prosecutor allegedly instructed a witness falsely to implicate the § 1983 plaintiff in a murder trial, because the instruction took place during an interview intended to secure testimony against an identified suspect, rather than as part of an investigatory effort to identify a suspect or establish probable cause. *Rivera v. Leal*, 359 F.3d 1350 (11th Cir. 2004) (absolute immunity attached to prosecutor's assertion of opinion about evidence during court proceeding); *Cousin v. Small*, 325 F.3d 627 (5th Cir.2003) (per curiam). *Accord, Spurlock v. Thompson*, 330 F.3d 791 (6th Cir. 2003) (prosecutor's decision knowingly to have witnesses testify falsely at criminal trial insulated by absolute immunity).

19. *Buckley v. Fitzsimmons,* 509 U.S. 259, 272–73, 113 S.Ct. 2606, 125 L.Ed.2d 209 (1993) (quoting *Imbler*); *Mowbray v. Cameron County, Tex.*, 274 F.3d 269, 276–277 (5th Cir.2001).

20. *Briscoe v. LaHue*, 460 U.S. 325, 103 S.Ct. 1108, 75 L.Ed.2d 96 (1983); *Moore v. McDonald*, 30 F.3d 616 (5th Cir. 1994). *But see Keko v. Hingle*, 318 F.3d 639 (5th Cir.2003) (physician's pre-testimonial activities of examining murder victim's body, examining criminal defendant's dental impressions, and writing report implicating § 1983 plaintiff not protected by absolute immunity); *Hammond v. Kunard*, 148 F.3d 692 (7th Cir.1998), *appeal after remand* 234 F.3d 1273 (7th Cir.2000) (absolute immunity not available to law enforcement officers who testified falsely in criminal proceeding because the complaint focused on conduct committed prior to prosecutor's decision to present case to grand jury). There are decisions both ways on whether a law enforcement officer enjoys derivative witness immunity when accused of inducing or coercing a witness to testify falsely. Compare *Jones v. Cannon*, 174 F.3d 1271 (11th Cir.1999) (officer receives absolute immunity for allegedly suborning perjured testimony from arrestee's cell mate) with *Paine v. City of Lompoc*, 265 F.3d 975 (9th Cir.2001) (police officers absolutely immune respecting their prior testimony against plaintiff but not respecting their conspiracy to suppress and fabricate evidence in that proceeding); *Spurlock v. Satterfield*, 167 F.3d 995 (6th Cir.1999) (deputy sheriff absolutely immune respecting own testimony in plaintiff's prior criminal trial, but not for allegedly fabricating probable cause or for coercing or inducing informant into testifying falsely).

21. *See, e.g., Mowbray v. Cameron County, Tex.*, 274 F.3d 269, 277–278 (5th Cir.2001) (citing authority from seven other circuits subscribing to the expanded scope of witness immunity and one contrary circuit decision).

ineligible for absolute immunity may nevertheless warrant qualified immunity.[22]

22. This is vividly illustrated by the decision of the Seventh Circuit on remand from *Burns v. Reed*. Although the Supreme Court had denied absolute immunity, the Seventh Circuit granted a prosecutor qualified immunity for asking a suspect to submit to hypnosis because courts were then divided about the admissibility of confessions from hypnotized suspects. See *Burns v. Reed*, 44 F.3d 524 (7th Cir.1995), *cert. denied*, 515 U.S. 1145, 115 S.Ct. 2583, 132 L.Ed.2d 832 (1995). *See also Beck v. Texas State Bd. Of Dental Examiners*, 204 F.3d 629, 637–639 (5th Cir.2000), *cert. denied*, 531 U.S. 871, 121 S.Ct. 171, 148 L.Ed.2d 117 (2000) (investigator not eligible for absolute immunity for warrantless search of dental office because he neither initiated disciplinary proceedings nor pursued prosecution nevertheless receives qualified immunity from damages because administrative search violated no clearly established federal right of plaintiff); *Smith v. Garretto*, 147 F.3d 91 (2d Cir.1998) (prosecutor's retaliatory action in orchestrating sting to catch government employee accepting bribe was investigatory and not entitled to absolute immunity, but qualified immunity was available as it was not clearly established that such retaliatory entrapment violated any constitutionally protected right).

The circuits have generally hewed to the *Burns* distinctions, extending absolute immunity to the acts of prosecutors or their subordinates that are integrally related to the initiation or pressing of prosecution (e.g., seeking an indictment), while conferring only qualified immunity to advice or conduct that is part and parcel of preliminary investigation. See *Ross Yordy Constr. Co. v. Naylor*, 55 F.3d 285 (7th Cir.1995), *cert. denied*, 516 U.S. 931, 116 S.Ct. 338, 133 L.Ed.2d 236 (1995); *Hill v. City of New York*, 45 F.3d 653 (2d Cir.1995). But the line is thin and wavering. Compare *Ireland v. Tunis*, 113 F.3d 1435 (6th Cir.1997), *cert. denied*, 522 U.S. 996, 118 S.Ct. 560, 139 L.Ed.2d 401 (1997) (absolute immunity in filing criminal complaint and seeking arrest warrant against mayor, despite improper political motivations), and *Pena v. Mattox*, 84 F.3d 894, 896 (7th Cir.1996) (prosecutor entitled to absolute immunity with respect to procuring erroneous arrest warrant) with *Kalina v. Fletcher*, 522 U.S. 118, 118 S.Ct. 502, 139 L.Ed.2d 471 (1997) (prosecutor denied absolute immunity respecting her alleged false statements made to procure arrest warrant, on theory that this function is merely investigative, even though warrant was sought to compel criminal defendant, the § 1983 plaintiff, to respond to formal criminal charges prosecutor had previously instituted); *Goldstein v. Moatz*, 364 F.3d 205 (4th Cir. 2004) (patent officials ineligible for absolute immunity concerning investigation in attorney disciplinary proceeding, at least before probable cause assessment). *Spurlock v. Thompson*, 330 F.3d 791 (6th Cir.2003) (prosecutorial conduct designed to hinder rather than further investigation and to cover up prosecutor's own misconduct, by threatening or coercing witnesses long after § 1983 plaintiff's criminal trial had concluded, deemed "investigatory" and hence ineligible for absolute immunity); *Prince v. Hicks*, 198 F.3d 607 (6th Cir.1999) (prosecutor's alleged improper or inadequate investigation of criminal charges against arrestee, and giving of legal advice to police officer before prosecutor had found probable cause or decided to initiate criminal proceedings, held preliminary conduct not part of her advocate's role and thus ineligible for absolute immunity). Cf. *R.S. (Linda) v. D. (Richard)*, 410 U.S. 614, 619, 93 S.Ct. 1146, 1149, 35 L.Ed.2d 536 (1973) (private citizen lacks standing to complain that prosecutor exercised discretion not to prosecute another).

The Second Circuit has pioneered what will probably prove a rare, alternative circumstance that forfeits absolute immunity. It held that conduct otherwise "prosecutorial" in function is not eligible for absolute immunity if manifestly beyond the outer bounds of a prosecutor's authority or jurisdiction, by analogy to *Stump v. Sparkman*, 435 U.S. 349, 98 S.Ct. 1099, 55 L.Ed.2d 331 (1978). *Doe v. Phillips*, 81 F.3d 1204 (2d Cir.1996), *cert. denied*, 520 U.S. 1115, 117 S.Ct. 1244, 137 L.Ed.2d 326 (1997) (prosecutor compelled suspect to swear to her innocence on a bible in church as a condition of dismissal of charges against her). In fact, it appears that the court here may simply have concluded that an act so obviously unconstitutional must be outside those outer bounds, contrary to the reasoning and facts of *Stump* itself.

This kind of obvious or egregious violation exception to absolute immunity is echoed by a similar emerging exception to qualified immunity. *See LaBounty v. Coughlin*, 137 F.3d 68 (2d Cir.1998) (taking judicial notice that facts regarding dangers of friable asbestos were well enough known so that a reasonable person would have understood that exposing inmate to friable asbestos would violate Eighth Amendment); *Jenkins v. Talladega City Bd. of Educ.*, 95 F.3d 1036, 1040–1041 (11th Cir.1996), *cert. denied*, 522 U.S. 966, 118 S.Ct. 412, 139

Legislators enjoy the broadest generally available immunity of all: an absolute immunity not only from damages but also from declaratory and injunctive relief.[23] This immunity extends to state,[24] regional,[25] and local[26] legislators. As with the absolute immunity of judges and prosecutors, this immunity shields only the "legislative functions" of legislators[27] or, occasionally, others.[28] The Supreme Court has ruled that voting for proposed legislation,[29] investigating committee topics,[30] preparing

L.Ed.2d 315 (1997) (where defendant's conduct is more egregious than conduct of the same general type that has been condemned by prior cases, law is clearly established absent factual similar controlling precedent); *McMillian v. Johnson*, 88 F.3d 1554, 1556 (11th Cir.1996), *cert. denied*, 521 U.S. 1121, 117 S.Ct. 2514, 138 L.Ed.2d 1016 (1997) (prior case law categorically banned any pretrial punishment, so unlawfulness of placing detainee on death row should have been apparent given "the extraordinary allegations in this case," even absent authoritative precedent finding that identical conduct unlawful); *Dolihite v. Maughon*, 74 F.3d 1027, 1028 (11th Cir.1996), *cert. denied*, 519 U.S. 870, 117 S.Ct. 185, 136 L.Ed.2d 123 (1996) (law clearly established if defendant's alleged conduct is as egregious as or more egregious than similar conduct in prior case); *K.H. v. Morgan*, 914 F.2d 846, 851 (7th Cir.1990) ("conduct y" is clearly established to be unlawful if it is "worse than" conduct x with respect to the reason x was earlier held to be unconstitutional); cf. *United States v. Lanier*, 520 U.S. 259, 117 S.Ct. 1219, 137 L.Ed.2d 432 (1997) (dictum to same effect concerning § 1983 qualified immunity in prosecution of judge under 18 U.S.C.A. § 242 for sexually assaulting in his chambers a litigant, court employees and a federal official with judicial liaison duties). Yet the Court has all but rejected a comparable egregiousness exception to the "policy" requirement for imposing liability on government entities. *Board of County Comm'rs of Bryan County, Oklahoma v. Brown*, 520 U.S. 397, 117 S.Ct. 1382, 137 L.Ed.2d 626 (1997) (county not liable for a one-time flagrant failure by a final policymaking official to use even ordinary diligence in checking the background of a law enforcement candidate because the prior conduct that would have been discovered involved at worst an improper or unlawful use of force not identical to the particular unconstitutional use of official force challenged in the § 1983 action).

23. *See Supreme Court of Va. v. Consumers Union, Inc.*, 446 U.S. at 730–34, 100 S.Ct. at 1973–1976.

24. *Tenney v. Brandhove*, 341 U.S. 367, 71 S.Ct. 783, 95 L.Ed. 1019 (1951).

25. *Lake Country Estates, Inc. v. Tahoe Reg'l Planning Agency*, 440 U.S. 391, 99 S.Ct. 1171, 59 L.Ed.2d 401 (1979).

26. *Bogan v. Scott–Harris*, 523 U.S. 44, 118 S.Ct. 966, 140 L.Ed.2d 79 (1998). For circuit authority, see *Carlos v. Santos*, 123 F.3d 61 (2d Cir.1997); *Trevino v. Gates*, 23 F.3d 1480 (9th Cir.1994), *cert. denied*, 513 U.S. 932, 115 S.Ct. 327, 130 L.Ed.2d 286 (1994); *Executive 100, Inc. v. Martin County*, 922 F.2d 1536, 1539 (11th Cir.1991), *cert. denied*, 502 U.S. 810, 112 S.Ct. 55, 116 L.Ed.2d 32 (1991); *Cutting v. Muzzey*, 724 F.2d 259 (1st Cir.1984); *Kuzinich v. Santa Clara County*, 689 F.2d 1345, 1349 (9th Cir.1982); *Hernandez v. City of Lafayette*, 643 F.2d 1188, 1193 (5th Cir.1981), *cert. denied*, 455 U.S. 907, 102 S.Ct. 1251, 71 L.Ed.2d 444 (1982); *Gorman Towers, Inc. v. Bogoslavsky*, 626 F.2d 607 (8th Cir.1980).

27. *See Hafer v. Melo*, 502 U.S. at 27–31, 112 S.Ct. at 363–64; *Burns v. Reed*, 500 U.S. 478, 111 S.Ct. 1934, 114 L.Ed.2d 547; *Harlow v. Fitzgerald*, 457 U.S. at 807, 102 S.Ct. at 2732. *Cf. Tower v. Glover*, 467 U.S. 914, 920, 104 S.Ct. 2820, 2824, 81 L.Ed.2d 758 (1984) ("The Court has recognized absolute § 1983 immunity for legislators acting within their legislative roles....") (citations omitted).

28. *Supreme Court of Va. v. Consumers Union, Inc.*, 446 U.S. at 731, 100 S.Ct. at 1974 (judges enjoy legislative immunity with respect to their role in promulgating rules of conduct for lawyers); *Romero–Barcelo v. Hernandez–Agosto*, 75 F.3d 23 (1st Cir.1996) (legislative committee counsel entitled to absolute immunity concerning conduct during committee hearings); *Redwood Village Partnership v. Graham*, 26 F.3d 839 (8th Cir.1994), cert. denied, 513 U.S. 962, 115 S.Ct. 423, 130 L.Ed.2d 337 (1994) (state agency employees enjoy legislative immunity with respect to promulgation of health care rules). *See Acevedo–Garcia v. Vera–Monroig*, 204 F.3d 1, 8 (1st Cir.2000) (recognizing that absolute legislative immunity might apply to local executive officials with respect to legislative functions).

29. *Kilbourn v. Thompson*, 103 U.S. (13 Otto) 168, 26 L.Ed. 377 (1880).

30. *Tenney v. Brandhove*, 341 U.S. 367, 71 S.Ct. 783, 95 L.Ed. 1019 (1951).

committee reports,[31] and speaking before a legislative assembly[32] are legislative functions. Activities outside the scope of legislative functions are the taking of bribes[33] and disseminating press releases to the public.[34]

The circuits have had difficulty applying the required functional analysis for "legislative" acts falling somewhere between these extremes. For example, at least one circuit appears to hold that legislators perform legislative functions whenever the form of their conduct replicates the traditional way in which legislative bodies act: "voting, debate and reacting to public opinion are manifestly in furtherance of legislative duties."[35] Others look more searchingly at the substance of the particular challenged act, distinguishing "legislative" decisions that implicate policy and have general application from merely "ad hoc," "administrative" or "enforcement" decisions that target one or a few citizens or apply policy previously promulgated.[36] Ancillary, preliminary tasks necessary to

31. *Doe v. McMillan*, 412 U.S. 306, 93 S.Ct. 2018, 36 L.Ed.2d 912 (1973).

32. *United States v. Johnson*, 383 U.S. 169, 86 S.Ct. 749, 15 L.Ed.2d 681 (1966).

33. *United States v. Brewster*, 408 U.S. 501, 92 S.Ct. 2531, 33 L.Ed.2d 507 (1972).

34. *Hutchinson v. Proxmire*, 443 U.S. 111, 99 S.Ct. 2675, 61 L.Ed.2d 411 (1979).

35. *DeSisto College, Inc. v. Line*, 888 F.2d 755, 765 (11th Cir.1989), cert. denied, 495 U.S. 952, 110 S.Ct. 2219, 109 L.Ed.2d 544 (1990) (quoted in *Brown v. Crawford County*, 960 F.2d 1002, 1011 (11th Cir. 1992)). However in *Smith v. Lomax*, 45 F.3d 402 (11th Cir.1995), the same court treated a county governing body's decision to replace its clerk, allegedly for racial reasons, as "administrative" rather than legislative. The court rejected the argument that this personnel issue acquired a protected, legislative character merely because the decision was reached as the result of a formal vote by the legislative body. See *Wright v. Montgomery County,* 215 F.3d 367 (3d Cir. 2000), *cert. denied,* 531 U.S. 1126, 121 S.Ct. 881, 148 L.Ed.2d 790 (2001) (county officials not eligible for absolute immunity for discharge of single employee, as decision did not implicate general policy); *Canary v. Osborn,* 211 F.3d 324 (6th Cir.2000), *cert. denied,* 531 U.S. 927, 121 S.Ct. 304, 148 L.Ed.2d 244 (2000) (board of education members not eligible for absolute quasi-legislative immunity for voting not to renew assistant principal's contract, where vote allegedly in retaliation for his whistleblowing about cheating on student achievement tests). Yet a vote to reorganize an entire department is legislative in nature and warrants the immunity, despite the resulting elimination of personnel. *Macuba v. Deboer*, 193 F.3d 1316 (11th Cir.1999). And staging a town meeting is a legislative function, even if the local legislators planned and executed the meeting as a forum for personal attacks on the town's chief of police. *Carlos v. Santos*, 123 F.3d 61 (2d Cir.1997).

36. *See Maitland v. University of Minnesota*, 260 F.3d 959 (8th Cir.2001) (in approving a consent decree authorizing pay increases to female but not male faculty members, board's regents acted in administrative, not legislative capacity). *Acevedo–Garcia v. Vera–Monroig*, 204 F.3d 1, 8 (1st Cir.2000) (court employs presumption that employment decisions are generally administrative, and not eligible for the immunity, except when accomplished through policymaking or budget restructuring that has prospective application and reaches beyond particular incumbent occupants of office rather than merely targeting specific individuals); *Canary v. Osborn*, 211 F.3d 324 (6th Cir.2000), cert. denied, 531 U.S. 927, 121 S.Ct. 304, 148 L.Ed.2d 244 (2000) (board of education members not eligible for absolute quasi-legislative immunity for voting not to renew assistant principal's contract, where vote allegedly in retaliation for his whistleblowing about cheating on student achievement tests); *Macuba v. Deboer*, 193 F.3d 1316 (11th Cir.1999) (vote to reorganize an entire department is legislative in nature and warrants the immunity, despite the resulting elimination of personnel); *Jessen v. Town of Eastchester*, 114 F.3d 7 (2d Cir.1997) (termination of town employee mere administrative act outside legislative immunity); *Carver v. Foerster*, 102 F.3d 96 (3d Cir.1996) (abolition of local government positions of particular employees, allegedly as act of political reprisal, is not generally applicable discretionary policymaking about use of county funds that

the exercise of legislative functions have also served to confer immunity on legislative officials;[37] and that immunity may extend derivatively to subordinate officials whose work is related to the legislative task.[38]

This problem of characterizing acts as within the legislative function has proved particularly vexing with respect to the land-use decisions of local governments and zoning boards. Several circuit courts characterize zoning or building permit decisions as mere executive enforcement activity that warrants only qualified, not absolute immunity whenever the local legislature or board (1) violates its own procedures[39] or applicable zoning ordinance provisions;[40] (2) enforces existing zoning rules in a way that relates specifically to particular individuals or has an impact that singles them out for different treatment;[41] or (3) makes even traditional "legislative" decisions of general application in bad faith, corruptly, or in furtherance of personal rather than public interests.[42]

would warrant absolute immunity but only an executive decision concerning implementation of cutback or administrative decision as to which employees to fire); *Billingsley v. St. Louis County*, 70 F.3d 61 (8th Cir.1995) (council member receives only qualified immunity in connection with termination of employee); *Roberson v. Mullins*, 29 F.3d 132 (4th Cir.1994) (no absolute legislative immunity respecting county board members' discharge of employee). *But see Bogan v. Scott–Harris*, 523 U.S. 44, 118 S.Ct. 966, 140 L.Ed.2d 79 (1998) (finding that the elimination of a city job via a budget bill has prospective implications beyond the current holder of the position and granting absolute immunity to council members who voted in favor of the elimination of the position and to the mayor who presented the bill and signed it into law); *Trevino By and Through Cruz v. Gates*, 23 F.3d 1480 (9th Cir.1994) (council members who voted to pay a punitive damages award pursuant to statutory authority perform an administrative, not a legislative function, and hence are eligible only for qualified immunity); *Haskell v. Washington Township*, 864 F.2d 1266 (6th Cir.1988); *Cinevision Corp. v. City of Burbank*, 745 F.2d 560, 580 (9th Cir.1984), *cert. denied*, 471 U.S. 1054, 105 S.Ct. 2115, 85 L.Ed.2d 480 (1985); *Cutting v. Muzzey*, 724 F.2d 259; *Scott v. Greenville County*, 716 F.2d 1409 (4th Cir.1983). *But cf. Whitener v. McWatters*, 112 F.3d 740 (4th Cir.1997) (absolute immunity shields county board of supervisors' discipline of one of their own members as legislative act).

37. *Ellis v. Coffee County Bd. of Registrars*, 981 F.2d 1185 (11th Cir.1993) (county commissioners performed legislative function in investigating the eligibility vel non of listed electors, because they needed that information to perform the concededly legislative function of delineating precinct lines); *National Ass'n of Soc. Workers v. Harwood*, 69 F.3d 622 (1st Cir.1995) (state representatives absolutely immune concerning rule excluding certain lobbyists from vicinity of legislative deliberations).

38. *Ellis*, 981 F.2d at 1193–94 (conferring legislative immunity on county attorney who served as legal advisor to legislators performing legislative function, because the efficient operation of contemporary government necessitates adjuncts performing responsibilities traditionally executed by the legislators).

39. *Donivan v. Dallastown Borough*, 835 F.2d 486, 488–89 (3d Cir.1987), cert. denied sub nom. *McKinsey v. Donivan*, 485 U.S. 1035, 108 S.Ct. 1596, 99 L.Ed.2d 910 (1988).

40. *Scott v. Greenville County*, 716 F.2d 1409 (4th Cir.1983).

41. *Bateson v. Geisse*, 857 F.2d 1300, 1304 (9th Cir.1988) (no absolute immunity for denying building permits because those do not apply to the general community or involve formulation of public policy); *Cutting v. Muzzey*, 724 F.2d 259 (plaintiff's subdivision approval conditioned on his completing a road); *Scott v. Greenville County, supra,* 716 F.2d 1409 (county council placed moratorium on building permit in response to citizens' protests over plaintiff's planned multi-family dwellings).

42. *Haskell v. Washington Tp.*, 864 F.2d 1266 (6th Cir.1988). *See also Scott*, 716 F.2d at 1423 (court concurred with plaintiff's allegation that council treated his application with a "lack of impartiality" and a "departure from established practice and applicable law.")

A decision of the Supreme Court provides some guidance for deciding whether an act falls within the legislative function. In *Bogan v. Scott–Harris*,[43] the Court explained that courts must focus on the nature of the act, rather than the motive of the actor. The plaintiff was a city employee whose position was eliminated via a budget bill. She alleged the city eliminated her job in retaliation for her speech regarding the job performance of another, and presumably well connected, city employee. The Court focused on three factors to be considered when characterizing an act as legislative in function. First, whether the act itself, regardless of the actor, is integral to the legislative process. In *Bogan*, the Court held that the mayor's acts in presenting a budget and subsequently signing the budget bill into law are legislative acts, despite the mayor's position as chief executive. His actions were integral to the legislative process, and thus, were shielded by absolute legislative immunity, even if done with a retaliatory motive. Second, the Court asked whether the acts "bore all the hallmarks of traditional legislation."[44] The budget bill represented a "discretionary, policy-making decision implicating the budgetary priorities of the city and the services the city provides,"[45] and the acts taken in relation to the budget were traditionally legislative in function. Finally, because the budget bill eliminated only one position, the Court inquired whether the act had prospective implications. The Court found that the complete elimination of a city job is an act that reaches beyond the person currently occupying the position and had prospective implications. Thus, all actors—the mayor and the city council members—were entitled to absolute legislative immunity.

The first criterion examined by the Court in *Bogan*, that is, whether the act is integral to the legislative process, seems to support the approach taken by the Eleventh Circuit in *Brown v. Crawford County, Ga.*[46] In *Brown*, the circuit court held that any kind of zoning or land use decision, including action that voids a prior approval of a development plan, is "normally ... a legislative function,"[47] despite its acknowledgment that an act can properly be characterized as legislative only when it has "a policymaking function and general application."[48]

The key to the Eleventh Circuit's approach appears to be its heavy reliance on the form of the local government's decision: a vote.[49] This approach garners much support from the *Bogan* Court's emphasis on the legislative process. But at least one other circuit has specifically concluded that the fact that the decision is in the form of a vote does not necessarily make that decision "legislative" for purposes of absolute immunity.[50] The Court in *Bogan* specifically declined to decide whether

43. 523 U.S. 44, 118 S.Ct. 966, 140 L.Ed.2d 79 (1998).

44. *Id.* at 54, 118 S.Ct. at 973.

45. *Id.*

46. 960 F.2d 1002 (11th Cir.1992).

47. *Brown*, 960 F.2d at 1012 (citing *Baytree of Inverrary Realty Partners v. City of Lauderhill*, 873 F.2d 1407, 1409 (11th Cir.1989)).

48. *Brown*, 960 F.2d at 1011 (citing *Crymes v. DeKalb County*, 923 F.2d 1482, 1485 (11th Cir.1991)).

49. *Brown*, 960 F.2d at 1011, 1012.

50. *Cinevision*, 745 F.2d at 580. The Eleventh Circuit, too, outside the zoning context, has subsequently disclaimed that the mere fact that a county government's decision is reached as the result of a vote

an act was legislative solely because it was part of the legislative process. Thus, this apparent conflict between the circuits remains unresolved.

Certainly absolute immunity is not available merely because the action taken was within the scope of the legislators' authority and involved the exercise of a necessary governmental function.[51] On the other hand, the Eleventh Circuit's refusal to deny immunity by reference to the motivations of the defendants[52] seems consistent with the traditional purposes of any absolute immunity,[53] and is certainly congruent with the subsequent *Bogan* decision. Looking at the motivations of the defendants would require preliminary fact-based proceedings the burden of which would defeat the objective of relieving the official from the rigors of litigation. But the court's refusal in *Brown* to examine the exceptional and perhaps unique impact of a building permit moratorium on a single citizen or the alleged irregularity of the county's proceedings gives excessive weight to its presumption that a vote signifies a "legislative" act.[54]

A decision of another circuit seems to point the other way. Although county council members were absolutely immune with respect to a commercial rezoning that the court considered legislative in character, they were accorded only qualified immunity with respect to enactment of an ordinance that voided a previously approved plan of development.[55] And because the ordinance had no prospective implications, this holding is consonant with the Supreme Court's third criterion in *Bogan*: an act is legislative in function if it has prospective implications. The Court did not indicate whether all three of its criteria must be satisfied to find an act legislative in function. Nor did it say whether a finding that an act is integral to the legislative process is alone sufficient to characterize the act as legislative. The act at issue in Brown lacked prospective implications, but was arguably legislative in that it was integral to the legislative process and bore the hallmarks of traditional legislation.

Post–*Bogan* circuit decisions focus on whether the legislative act involved the formulation of policy. In *San Pedro Hotel Co., Inc. v. City of Los Angeles,*[56] the Ninth Circuit held that a city council member who voted against giving a redevelopment loan to a group developing housing for the mentally disabled was protected by legislative immunity, despite

renders that decision "legislative" in character for purposes of absolute immunity. *Smith v. Lomax*, 45 F.3d 402 (11th Cir. 1995).

51. *Hafer v. Melo*, 502 U.S. at 27, 112 S.Ct. at 363.

52. "Even if Brown could prove conspiracy or bad faith, an unworthy purpose does not preclude absolute immunity to legislators acting in their legislative capacity." *Brown*, 960 F.2d at 1012.

53. *See, e.g., Tenney*, 341 U.S. at 377, 71 S.Ct. at 788; *Wood v. Strickland*, 420 U.S. 308, 317, 95 S.Ct. 992, 998, 43 L.Ed.2d 214 (1975) (discussion of absolute immunity in a decision raising the issue of qualified immunity).

54. In appraising this criticism of the opinion in Brown, the reader should understand that one of the authors was co-counsel on appeal for the unsuccessful developer plaintiff.

55. *Acierno v. Cloutier*, 1994 WL 319783 (3d Cir.1994), reh'g granted en banc and vacated on other grounds, 40 F.3d 597 (3d Cir.1994).

56. 159 F.3d 470 (9th Cir.1998).

the apparent limited impact of the loan. The court found that council's actions regarding the proposed loan both involved the formation of policy and applied to the public at large because the disbursement of public funds in support of one project necessarily meant that other projects were not being funded. Similarly, in a suit brought by prisoners in a county jail alleging overcrowded conditions, the Eleventh Circuit conferred absolute immunity on county commissioners who voted to approve a county budget.[57] The court held that voting on a budget was an act of policymaking with general application. An instructive contrast is furnished by a Tenth Circuit decision,[58] where a county commission voted to prohibit a meeting attendee from participating in or speaking before commission meetings. The court held that the commissioners' actions were administrative, and thus not legislatively immune from attendee's claims, despite the arguably legislative process of the vote. The court said that the legislative function involves determining, formulating, and making policy: voting on an issue, in and of itself, does not determine that the act is legislative in nature. Because the vote to ban the plaintiff's participation did not concern the enactment or promulgation of public policy, the censure vote was not related to any legislation or legislative function. Similarly, a First Circuit decision denied legislative immunity to executive municipal officials in connection with their imposing restrictions on and selectively laying off employees belonging to an opposing political party. The Court presumed that employment decisions are generally administrative, except when accomplished through traditional legislative policymaking means like budget restructuring. *Bogan* was distinguished because the replacement of discharged employees and acts of political harassment were not accomplished by means of an ordinance and targeted specific individuals with no prospective impact reaching beyond the persons affected.[59]

Absolute legislative immunity, and judicial immunity received by judicial officers,[60] relieve the defendant of liability for prospective relief

57. *Woods v. Gamel*, 132 F.3d 1417 (11th Cir.1998).

58. *Kamplain v. Curry County Bd. of Comm'rs*, 159 F.3d 1248 (10th Cir.1998).

59. *Acevedo–Garcia v. Vera–Monroig*, 204 F.3d 1, 8 (1st Cir.2000).

60. A 1996 amendment to § 1983 in effect overruled *Pulliam v. Allen*, 466 U.S. 522, 541–44, 104 S.Ct. 1970, 1980–1983, 80 L.Ed.2d 565 (1984) (holding that judges, absolutely immune from damages, are subject to injunctive relief and attorneys' fees). Under the amendment, a judicial officer eligible for absolute judicial immunity will face injunctive relief, the sole remaining springboard for attorneys' fees, only in the unlikely event that she violates a prior declaratory decree or "declaratory relief was unavailable." Thus even when a judge is acting in the clear excess of jurisdiction, she will ordinarily be insulated from injunctive relief as well as damages—leaving no predicate for attorney's fees.

It is hard to see what additional protections judicial officers receive from a companion amendment, made to 42 U.S.C.A. § 1988(b). It provides that "in any action brought against a judicial officer for an act or omission taken in such officer's judicial capacity, such officer shall not be held liable for any costs, including attorney's fees, unless such action was clearly in excess of such officer's jurisdiction." This appears merely to relieve judicial officers of liability for costs and fees where their conduct is not clearly in excess of jurisdiction—put otherwise, when absolute judicial immunity attaches. But if the immunity does attach, judicial officers will now, under the amendment to § 1983, almost always be relieved of liability for injunctive relief as well as as well as damages. The other immunities, qualified or absolute, ordinarily insulate only against damages. Thus prospective relief should be available not only for executive and administrative conduct shielded from damages by qualified immunity, but also for conduct within the scope of "absolute" prosecutorial, though not legislative or judicial, immunity. Yet relatively few plaintiffs who sue individual government officials will attain full or even meaningful relief from prospective remedies alone. And the attempt to secure injunctive or declaratory relief is likely to encounter special standing, abstention, or comity-driven obstacles to federal intervention that may preclude litigation in federal court.[61]

One consequence of the combined broad sweep of absolute and qualified immunity for government agents is a distinctly diluted role for claims against individual defendants. In contrast to actions against government entities, there is somewhat less potential for dynamic law-making in § 1983 actions against individuals.

The Court's wide blanket of immunity for individual defendants has a second serious consequence. The vicious official who intends to harm a citizen may be absolved of any § 1983 liability. This happens either if the right the plaintiff asserts is not judicially recognized to the requisite degree of specificity, or if, despite the settled nature of the right, the factfinder concludes that the defendant could not reasonably have realized that her contemplated conduct would violate it.

damages. The plaintiff in such a case would ordinarily not then be a "prevailing party" and would therefore not be eligible for attorney's fees under the clause of § 1988(b) that immediately precedes the amendment. Perhaps the amendment to § 1988(b) does have some independent significance, relieving judicial officers whose conduct is covered by the immunity from liability for costs or attorney's fees in cases where the plaintiff recovers purely declaratory relief. But if that relief does not require any significant change in defendant's position, plaintiff would again probably not be a prevailing party eligible for attorney's fees even in the absence of § 1988(b). *See Farrar v. Hobby*, 506 U.S. 103, 113 S.Ct. 566, 121 L.Ed.2d 494 (1992), discussed in Chapter 4.

Plaintiffs seeking a way around these amendments might note that they give special protection not to any defendant asserting judicial immunity, only to "a judicial officer for an act or omission taken in such officer's judicial capacity." By its terms, then, the amendments do not limit injunctive relief or consequent costs or fees in cases against executive or administrative officers who receive absolute immunity for functions deemed "judicial" or "quasi-judicial."

61. *See, e.g., City of Los Angeles v. Lyons*, 461 U.S. 95, 111, 103 S.Ct. 1660, 1670, 75 L.Ed.2d 675 (1983) (holding that an individual had no standing to request injunctive relief from police use of chokeholds because he was not in immediate danger of sustaining another direct injury); *Rizzo v. Goode*, 423 U.S. 362, 371–73, 96 S.Ct. 598, 604–605, 46 L.Ed.2d 561 (1976) (stating that individuals had no standing to request an injunction compelling the police to adopt new procedures where their alleged injury was too speculative to satisfy Article III's "case or controversy" requirement); *Younger v. Harris*, 401 U.S. 37, 49, 54, 91 S.Ct. 746, 753, 755, 27 L.Ed.2d 669 (1971) (holding that federal court in § 1983 action may not enjoin pending state criminal proceeding in which the federal issue could be raised as a defense, and should dismiss); *Railroad Comm'n of Tex. v. Pullman Co.*, 312 U.S. 496, 501, 61 S.Ct. 643, 645, 85 L.Ed. 971 (1941) (holding that federal court § 1983 action for injunction against state-sanctioned conduct should be stayed to enable a state tribunal to interpret unsettled state law if a narrowing in-

There is some foundation for the Court's oft-stated concern about chilling the initiative of individual government agents by saddling them with damage liability when they are guilty only of failing to predict the vagaries of constitutional doctrine.[62] Additionally, it is unfair for that individual to face liability, as she does under the Court's regime, when she acts without some degree of certainty that her conduct may cause harm or when she attempts, however clumsily, to serve the best interests of her employer. The Court's immunity doctrines, first announced at a time when only the individual agent, and not the entity, was a cognizable "person" subject to § 1983 damages liability, are at once too generous and too stingy. If the agent acts with intent to harm, the deterrence and compensation goals of § 1983 are ill-served by letting her escape liability merely because a court later concludes that the particular federal right at issue was only dimly established at the time of the violation. If, in contrast, an individual agent acting without an intent to harm impairs a right that has been "recognized" to the Court's satisfaction, there is little need to use the agent as an incremental source of remedy. The goals of facilitating government restraint, deterrence, compensation, and dynamic lawmaking would be better served by restricting liability to the government unit.

Section 1983 today is almost entirely a judicial construct. Its open-textured language is as immune to self-definition as that of the Fourteenth Amendment, whose enforcement it was passed to ensure.[63] As discussed in the balance of this Part A., the Court has radically reconstructed § 1983 beginning with its landmark 1961 decision in *Monroe v. Pape*.[64]

Part B. then addresses the interplay between the statutory element "under color of law" and the Fourteenth and Fifth Amendments' "state action" requirement. Because most § 1983 actions are predicated on violations of the Due Process Clause of one of these Amendments, the plaintiff must often prove both that the defendant acted "under color of law" and that the action constituted "state action." When the defendant is a private party, proof of "state action" satisfies the "under color of law" requirement, but the reverse is not necessarily true; while actions may qualify as "under color of law" somewhat easily, they qualify as "state action" only when they are "fairly attributable" to the state. When the defendant is a public entity, the "under color of law" and "state action" requirements are less distinct.

Parts C., D., and E. turn to the substance of the judicially constructed doctrine in the individual and entity cases, respectively. After the Court's most recent ministrations, this historic statute of sweeping

terpretation might obviate the need to decide a federal question).

62. *See Scheuer v. Rhodes*, 416 U.S. 232, 240, 94 S.Ct. 1683, 1688, 40 L.Ed.2d 90 (1974).

63. The title to the original Klan Act went beyond enforcement of the Fourteenth Amendment to include "other Purposes." *See supra* § 2.1.

64. 365 U.S. 167, 81 S.Ct. 473, 5 L.Ed.2d 492 (1961), *overruled on a different issue by Monell v. Department of Soc. Servs.*, 436 U.S. 658, 98 S.Ct. 2018, 56 L.Ed.2d 611 (1978).

potential application yields an odd and desiccated residue. On the one hand, there are yawning gaps in both entity and individual defendant liability. Only in a formal sense does the entity suit serve the original Reconstructors' goal of bringing local governments to heel; in practice, the difficulty of demonstrating "policy" or "custom" provides the entity an expansive exemption from liability. At the same time, the individual defendant's qualified immunity absolves him from liability for even an intentionally inflicted constitutional harm, so long as his conduct was not clearly and specifically prohibited by a prior decision.

Yet the Court has also shown a remarkable willingness to expand the scope of § 1983 to redress the deprivation of rights created by federal statute.[65] This stands as a pointed and puzzling contrast to the Court's crabbed approach to the definition and enforcement of the fundamental constitutional rights that lie at § 1983's core.

Part F. considers the consequences of this asymmetry between cases against individual government agents and those against their entities. The Court's intuition in treating the entity case as a vessel for the development of constitutional law is consonant with history and apparent congressional purpose. But the particularized rules it has devised to govern those actions erode § 1983's force as a bulwark against state-sponsored conduct that lacks the formal approval of law. The current asymmetry cannot be explained either as a device to achieve mirror-image parity between entity and individual actions or as an expedient crafted to reduce federal calendar congestion.

Part G. discusses *Bivens* actions, the judicially created counterpart to § 1983 that applies when the defendant is, or acts in concert with, a federal official. As we will see, much of the § 1983 jurisprudence has been applied to *Bivens* actions, including the concepts of absolute and qualified immunity.

Part H. examines the use of § 1983 as a tool for redressing state actions' violations of rights conferred by federal statutes.

Part I. explores new liability configurations for actions involving each type of defendant. It begins by assaying scholarly proposals that posit a unitary legislative goal of compensation or deterrence. But the statute in fact has multiple objectives. The suggestions that end this part would foster not only entity accountability but also the subsidiary goals of compensating victims and facilitating the dynamic declaration of federal rights.

In particular, there is need for a modified species of respondeat superior to govern the liability of local government entities. This, it is true, would create liability without fault and therefore faces the criticism that money damages for constitutional violations should be confined to the restrictive, Aristotelian concept of "corrective justice." But a fault-

65. *See* Henry P. Monaghan, *Federal Statutory Review Under Section 1983 and the APA*, 91 Colum.L.Rev. 233, 234 (1991).

based approach unduly sacrifices entity accountability for federal law violations, particularly given the existing limits on standing to secure injunctive relief.

In contrast, it is proposed here that fault should control the liability of § 1983 individual defendants. An individual defendant who acts with intent to harm and with the express, implied, or apparent authorization of his governing entity should be liable for all federally unlawful conduct. The settledness of the constitutional right on the eve of injury, currently the key to qualified immunity for the individual, should be irrelevant.[66] But the individual should not be liable for innocent violations. Thus under the proposal the entity would be liable when the individual is, but also, frequently, when the individual is not. Such a reshaped asymmetry would assure that § 1983 serves the signal aim of guaranteeing local government restraint against all federally unlawful conduct, whatever the legal vintage of the violation it would also create a reliable source of victim compensation and recapture the statute's potential as a vehicle for the dynamic declaration of federal rights.

§ 2.3 The Tradition of Judicial Dynamism in Elaborating Section 1983

A preliminary word about the judicial tradition of supplying § 1983's missing links. The text and legislative history are remarkably opaque on the standards governing the critical liability and defense issues with which the Court has grappled during the last thirty years. Despite the Court's fondness for historical answers to questions about § 1983's new applications, the statute is impervious to determinate historical analysis.[1] The question therefore is not whether the legislative history demands, but simply whether it forecloses, one or another approach.

The Court's contemporary reworkings of § 1983 liability standards and defenses cannot be readily squared with transparent legislative history or some static notion of the common law. Despite occasional protestations to the contrary,[2] the Court has regularly resorted to a dynamic lawmaking methodology in devising the qualified immunity

66. The status of the right may be relevant, however, to the amount of damages. *See infra* § 2.62.

§ 2.3

1. *See, e.g.*, Peter W. Low & John C. Jeffries, Jr., Federal Courts and the Law of Federal–State Relations 940 (2d ed. 1989) ("[T]he legislative history reveals no occasion for ... focused and collective consideration of the issue. Instead, inferences must be drawn from scattered statements of individual legislators...."); Gene R. Shreve, *Symmetries of Access in Civil Rights Litigation: Politics, Pragmatism, and Will*, 66 Ind. L.J. 1, 18 (1990) ("Evidence from congressional debates preceding the enactment of § 1983 reveals little or no interest in the subject of state liability."); Cass R. Sunstein, *Section 1983 and the Private Enforcement of Federal Law*, 49 U.Chi.L.Rev. 394, 396–97 (1982) ("[A]lthough courts and commentators have devoted much attention to the legislative history of section 1983, there remains considerable dispute about the intended scope of that provision." (footnotes omitted)).

2. *See* Larry Kramer & Alan O. Sykes, *Municipal Liability Under § 1983: A Legal & Economic Analysis*, 1987 Sup.Ct.Rev. 249, 265 nn. 62–63 (1987) (citing cases).

doctrine, the major limitation on the liability of individuals.[3] The Court tells us that § 1983 should be "read against the background of tort liability."[4]

Until recently, it seemed doubtful that the Court believed the 1871 Congress intended to freeze in place the then-prevailing common law rules. For then it would be hard to account for the Court's dramatic expansion in the past decade of qualified immunity.[5] The Court launched that effort without even purporting to locate the new rules in the common law tradition, fashioning them instead out of whole cloth in order to relieve discretion-wielding officials of the burdens of discovery and trial.[6] Yet in one case the Court has reemphasized the primacy of common law doctrine circa 1871 as the basis for fashioning § 1981 principles of liability and remedy.[7]

3. Although the Court has stated flatly that "[t]here is no federal general common law," *Erie R.R. v. Tompkins*, 304 U.S. 64, 78, 58 S.Ct. 817, 822, 82 L.Ed. 1188 (1938), and that it would create common law in suits between individuals only when there existed "a significant conflict between some federal policy . . . and the use of state law," *Wallis v. Pan Am. Petroleum Corp.*, 384 U.S. 63, 68, 86 S.Ct. 1301, 1304, 16 L.Ed.2d 369 (1966) (refusing to resolve a contract dispute between claimants subject to the Mineral Leasing Act of 1920 by recourse to federal common law), in fact the Court has at times created federal common law, and done so in statutory actions sounding in tort. *See Dice v. Akron, C. & Y. R.R. Co.*, 342 U.S. 359, 361, 72 S.Ct. 312, 314, 96 L.Ed. 398 (1952) (holding that the validity of a release under the Federal Employers' Liability Act was a question of federal law); *see also* Kramer & Sykes, 1987 Sup.Ct.Rev. at 265–67 (citing other cases in which the Court betrayed its willingness to make federal common law).

4. *Monroe*, 365 U.S. at 187, 81 S.Ct. at 484; *see also Carey v. Piphus*, 435 U.S. 247, 258 n. 13, 98 S.Ct. 1042, 1049 n. 13, 55 L.Ed.2d 252 (1978) (noting that the Court has employed tort law principles "in constructing immunities under § 1983"); *Imbler v. Pachtman*, 424 U.S. 409, 418, 96 S.Ct. 984, 989, 47 L.Ed.2d 128 (1976) (explaining that "§ 1983 is to be read in harmony with general principles of tort immunities and defenses"). *See generally* Sheldon H. Nahmod, *Section 1983 and the "Background" of Tort Liability*, 50 Ind. L. J. 5, 32 (1974) (arguing that general tort principles are relevant "by analogy" but not determinative in § 1983 cases); Charles A. Rothfeld, Comment, *Section 1983 Municipal Liability and the Doctrine of Respondeat Superior*, 46 U.Chi.L.Rev. 935, 955–62 (1979) (suggesting that common law tort concepts support a theory of respondeat superior liability for municipalities under § 1983); Peter M. Van Zante, Comment, *Choice of Law Under Section 1983*, 37 U.Chi.L.Rev. 494, 507–08 (1970) (indicating that the language from *Monroe* has been construed to enable courts to fashion a federal common law of § 1983 liability based on various sources of tort law), cited in Kramer & Sykes, 1987 Sup. Ct.Rev. at 257 n.30.

5. Laura Oren has traced the Court's departures from the nineteenth century common law of government officials' qualified immunity. She also notes how the Court, on the entity—defendant side of the equation, has overlooked the evolving relaxation of state sovereign immunity. *See* Oren, *Immunity and Accountability in Civil Rights Litigation: Who Should Pay?*, 50 U.Pitt.L.Rev. 935, 947–62 (1989). David Rudovsky reminds us that the Court has several times asserted that only the common law as it stood in 1871, when § 1983's forerunner was enacted, should guide the interpretation of the statute. *See* David Rudovsky, *The Qualified Immunity Doctrine in the Supreme Court: Judicial Activism and the Restriction of Constitutional Rights*, 138 U.Pa.L.Rev. 23, 36–37 (1989) (citing cases). Among other occasions the Court made this point in *Owen v. City of Independence*, 445 U.S. 622, 635–637, 100 S.Ct. 1398, 1407–1409, 63 L.Ed.2d 673 (1980), just two years before it undertook wholesale revisions of common law qualified immunity in *Harlow v. Fitzgerald*, 457 U.S. 800, 102 S.Ct. 2727, 73 L.Ed.2d 396 (1982).

6. *See infra* § 2.22.

7. *Compare Heck v. Humphrey*, 512 U.S. 477, 482, 114 S.Ct. 2364, 2370, 129 L.Ed.2d 383 (1994) (re-affirming that the common law of torts provides the "starting point" for fashioning the legal standards

Similarly, neither the language nor legislative history of § 1983 supports the Court's "policy" barrier to the liability of local entities. Rather, the requirement has its origin in a raw ipse dixit announced in dictum.[8] And the justices divided sharply on the existence and nature of the nineteenth century understanding about the amenability of those entities on any terms.[9] When, for instance, in *Smith v. Wade*[10] the Court was forced to fill a gap in text, it expressly disclaimed that the common law of 1871 "is absolutely controlling, or that current law is irrelevant. On the contrary, if the prevailing view on some point of general tort law had changed substantially in the intervening century ... we might be highly reluctant to assume that Congress intended to perpetuate now-obsolete doctrine."[11] The Court specifically rejected the idea "that Congress necessarily intended to freeze into permanent law whatever principles were current in 1871, rather than to incorporate applicable general legal principles as they evolve."[12]

The proponents of the statute were apparently content to establish a general federal remedy for injuries resulting from the denial of federally protected rights under color of state law.[13] Congress conferred on the federal courts the power not only to develop such interstitial procedural matters as prerequisites to suit,[14] limitations,[15] and remedies,[16] but also

that define violations and remedies) (quoting *Carey v. Piphus*, 435 U.S. 247, 257–58, 98 S.Ct. 1042, 1049, 55 L.Ed.2d 252 (1978)) *with Wyatt v. Cole*, 504 U.S. 158, 112 S.Ct. 1827, 118 L.Ed.2d 504 (1992) (re-acknowledging that in *Harlow v. Fitzgerald*, 457 U.S. 800, 102 S.Ct. 2727, 73 L.Ed.2d 396 (1982), the Court "completely reformulated qualified immunity along principles not at all embodied in the common law") (quoting *Anderson v. Creighton*, 483 U.S. 635, 645, 107 S.Ct. 3034, 3042, 97 L.Ed.2d 523 (1987)). Further, even in *Wyatt*, where the Court held qualified immunity unavailable to private creditors charged with liability for invoking unconstitutional means of recovering on a debt, five justices wrote that the result should be dictated by their (differing) understandings of the nineteenth-century common law. See opinions of Kennedy, J., concurring and Rehnquist, C.J., dissenting. Similarly, some justices have questioned the extension of absolute immunity to prosecutors, *see Buckley v. Fitzsimmons*, 509 U.S. 259, 113 S.Ct. 2606, 125 L.Ed.2d 209 (1993) (Justices Scalia and Thomas), and social workers, see *Hoffman v. Harris*, 511 U.S. 1060, 114 S.Ct. 1631, 128 L.Ed.2d 354 (1994) (Thomas, J., dissenting from denial of certiorari), who did not enjoy immunity in 1871.

8. *See infra* § 2.31.

9. *See Monell v. Department of Soc. Servs.*, 436 U.S. 658, 98 S.Ct. 2018, 56 L.Ed.2d 611 (1978).

10. 461 U.S. 30, 103 S.Ct. 1625, 75 L.Ed.2d 632 (1983).

11. *Id.* at 34 n.2, 103 S.Ct. at 1629 n.2.

12. *Id.*

13. *See* Kramer & Sykes, 1987 Sup.Ct. Rev. at 257–59.

14. *See, e.g., Felder v. Casey*, 487 U.S. 131, 153, 108 S.Ct. 2302, 2314, 101 L.Ed.2d 123 (1988) (holding that state court may not apply state notice of claim requirement in a § 1983 action); *Patsy v. Board of Regents*, 457 U.S. 496, 516, 102 S.Ct. 2557, 2568, 73 L.Ed.2d 172 (1982) (holding that, except for prisoners governed by 42 U.S.C.A. § 1997e, no mandatory exhaustion of state administrative remedies is required); *Harris v. Hegmann*, 198 F.3d 153, 157 (5th Cir.1999) § 1997e, as amended by the Prison Litigation Reform Act (PLRA) of 1996, requires state (and federal) prisoners to exhaust available administrative remedies before filing suit under (Section 1983). *But see Knight v. Kenai Peninsula Borough Sch. Dist.*, 131 F.3d 807 (9th Cir.1997), *cert. denied sub nom. Anchorage Educ. Ass'n v. Patterson*, 524 U.S. 904, 118 S.Ct. 2060, 141 L.Ed.2d 138 (1998) (only prisoner plaintiffs are required to exhaust administrative remedies under § 1983; nonunion school teachers were not required to exhaust union remedies to which they never agreed). *See* § 5.7 for a fuller discussion of the exhaustion and other requirements of the PLRA.

15. *See, e.g., Owens v. Okure*, 488 U.S. 235, 249–251, 109 S.Ct. 573, 581–582, 102 L.Ed.2d 594 (1989) (selecting an applicable statute of limitations).

16. *See, e.g.*, 42 U.S.C.A. § 1988 (1988) (stating that "the court, in its discretion,

to fence off the basic boundaries of individual and entity liability.[17] The statute was passed during the heyday of *Swift v. Tyson,*[18] when "the existence of an evolving common law and of federal judicial power to share in its development was a given."[19] The strident disagreement among today's Justices about the scope of entity liability, even as they enlarge beyond recognition the common law immunity of individual officials, offers powerful testimony that on these fundamental issues the common law of 1871 provides no real guidance.[20]

The only sound alternative is to "turn to the policies underlying Section 1983 to determine which rule best accords" with them.[21] Indeed, even when the Court has examined the common law and discovered a reasonably determinate answer, it has sometimes asked the further question "whether considerations of public policy dictate a [result] contrary" to the original common law.[22] Such a question would be superfluous unless the Court had reserved for itself the power to shape rules of liability and defense as a matter of federal common law.[23]

Section 1983 fits Professor Eskridge's description of some statutes: "original legislative expectations have been overtaken by subsequent changes in society and law."[24] The judicial evolution of the statute underscores the societal transformations that have necessitated the dynamic tradition. For example in the *Slaughter–House Cases,*[25] decided in 1873, two years after the Klan Act was passed, the Court then "doubt[ed] very much whether any action of a State not directed by way of discrimination against the negroes ... [would] ever be held to come

may allow ... a reasonable attorney's fee as part of the costs"); *Smith,* 461 U.S. at 56, 103 S.Ct. at 1640 (approving punitive damages against a state officer); *City of Newport v. Fact Concerts, Inc.,* 453 U.S. 247, 271, 101 S.Ct. 2748, 2762, 69 L.Ed.2d 616 (1981) (disapproving punitive damages against municipalities absent highly unusual circumstances); *see infra* § 2.34.

17. *See* Kramer & Sykes, 1987 Sup.Ct. Rev. at 264–65.

18. 41 U.S. (16 Pet.) 1, 10 L.Ed. 865 (1842).

19. *See* Kramer & Sykes, 1987 Sup.Ct. Rev. at 264.

20. *See id.* at 266. *See generally* Jack M. Beermann, *A Critical Approach to Section 1983 with Special Attention to Sources of Law,* 42 Stan.L.Rev. 51 (1989) (arguing that when the Court purports to use the common law of 1871, it typically uses modern principles of tort law and effectively creates new federal common law).

21. *Smith,* 461 U.S. at 93, 103 S.Ct. at 1659 (O'Connor, J., dissenting).

22. *City of Newport,* 453 U.S. at 266, 101 S.Ct. at 2759; *see also* Kramer & Sykes, 1987 Sup.Ct.Rev. at 266 (characterizing the Court's questioning as "whether the considerations supporting the common law rule likewise warrant immunity under § 1983").

23. If we are wrong about this—if, for example, entity liability must be shaped as the common law had it in 1871—our argument for respondeat superior is seriously undermined. Although the doctrine was then current and applied to municipal corporations, courts carved out a notable exception for the corporation's "governmental," as distinct from "proprietary," functions. The "vast majority of § 1983 claims" concern functions of a type that courts then considered "governmental." Kramer & Sykes, 1987 Sup.Ct. Rev. at 262–63 (citing Ronald M. Levin, *The Section 1983 Municipal Immunity Doctrine,* 65 Geo. L.J. 1483, 1521 n.156 (1977)).

24. William N. Eskridge, Jr., *Dynamic Statutory Interpretation,* 135 U.Pa.L.Rev. 1479, 1484 (1987).

25. 83 U.S. (16 Wall.) 36, 21 L.Ed. 394 (1872).

within the purview'' of the Equal Protection Clause.[26] By 1978, however, in *Monell v. Department of Social Services*,[27] the Court, in holding explicitly for the first time that § 1983 reaches government entities,[28] sustained an equal protection challenge to a municipal employment rule requiring pregnant women to take a predetermined period of pregnancy leave.[29]

Roe v. Wade,[30] brought in part under Section 1983,[31] illustrates the problem more distinctly. The very constitutional right the action was brought to enforce, the newly emerging right of privacy, was one of which the Fourteenth Amendment's framers could scarcely have conceived. Similarly, *Maine v. Thiboutot*,[32] which held that the statute's "and laws" language[33] permits actions for the unlawful denial of federal statutory entitlements, arose in a welfare state society that the framers simply would not recognize.

§ 2.4 *Monroe* as the Basis for Modern Section 1983 Actions

This judicial dynamism has produced the asymmetric shape of § 1983 actions against individuals and entities. In the past thirty years, in particular, there have been bursts of expansion, followed by equally striking contractions.

By its terms, § 1983 liability attaches to "[e]very person" who causes the loss of rights secured by the Constitution and laws of the United States. Thus an individual state actor is unexceptionably within the statute's reach. It is not altogether surprising, therefore, that the Court in *Monroe v. Pape*[1] would carve out an expansive prima facie case in actions against such defendants. *Monroe* marks the modern reemergence of § 1983 from 90 years of relative slumber. It is also the progenitor of the subsequent torrent of § 1983 litigation and as such the ultimate source of the Court's reactive retrenchment.

The invasion of the Monroes' home by Chicago's finest in violation of the Fourth Amendment and the laws of Illinois furnished the occasion for the Court to construe the § 1983 requirement that the defendant inflict the injury "under color of" state law. The Court linked the

26. 83 U.S. at 80.

27. 436 U.S. 658, 98 S.Ct. 2018, 56 L.Ed.2d 611 (1978).

28. *Monell* also required though that the § 1983 plaintiff who sues such an entity must prove the existence of a "policy" that caused the federal right deprivation. That requirement is discussed *infra* this Chapter, Part D.

29. *See Monell*, 436 U.S. at 660–661, 98 S.Ct. at 2020, 2021.

30. 410 U.S. 113, 93 S.Ct. 705, 35 L.Ed.2d 147 (1973).

31. See *Roe v. Wade*, 314 F.Supp. 1217, 1219 n. 1 (N.D.Tex.1970), *aff'd in part and rev'd in part*, 410 U.S. 113, 93 S.Ct. 705, 35 L.Ed.2d 147 (1973).

32. 448 U.S. 1, 100 S.Ct. 2502, 65 L.Ed.2d 555 (1980).

33. For the full statute, see *supra* § 2.1 (stating that the statute provides redress for the loss of rights guaranteed by the "Constitution and laws" of the United States).

§ 2.4

1. 365 U.S. 167, 81 S.Ct. 473, 5 L.Ed.2d 492 (1961), *overruled on a different issue by Monell v. Department of Soc. Servs.*, 436 U.S. 658, 98 S.Ct. 2018, 56 L.Ed.2d 611 (1978).

"under color of" requirement to the long-settled interpretation of state action under the Fourteenth Amendment,[2] which § 1983 was passed to enforce.[3] Justice Douglas' opinion for the Court concluded that § 1983 reaches federally unlawful conduct carried out by individual defendants under the badge of or clothed in state authority, irrespective of state approval.[4] The Court so decided despite indications that state law could provide relief at least as complete as federal law and absent any allegation that the state had discriminatorily denied such relief on other occasions.[5] The special nature of the violation also had implications for remedy and forum. "It is no answer," Justice Douglas wrote, "that the State has a law which if enforced would give relief. The federal remedy is supplementary to the state remedy, and the latter need not be first sought and refused before the federal one is invoked."[6]

The apparent availability of a remedy under Illinois law, however, casts doubt on whether any of the purposes of § 1983 identified by the majority supports the *Monroe* result. Justice Douglas wrote that the legislation had "three main aims": to override certain state laws; to provide a federal remedy not provided by state law; and to provide such a remedy "where the state remedy, though adequate in theory, was not available in practice."[7] None of these purposes would have been advanced by upholding the legal sufficiency of Monroe's claim.

The better rationale appears in Justice Harlan's concurrence, drawn from the "flavor of the legislative history." He wrote that Congress

2. *See Home Tel. & Tel. Co. v. City of Los Angeles*, 227 U.S. 278, 287–94, 33 S.Ct. 312, 315–317, 57 L.Ed. 510 (1913). The municipal defendant argued in *Home Tel.* that a claim alleging it had imposed confiscatory telephone rates in violation of due process failed for want of state action because no state court had yet sustained the rate under the state's own due process clause. Only when a state court so ruled, defendant's counsel urged, would state authorization occur, and only then would there be the state action requisite for a Fourteenth Amendment violation. *See id.* at 282; *see also The Civil Rights Cases*, 109 U.S. 3, 3 S.Ct. 18, 27 L.Ed. 835 (1883) (restricting the reach of the Fourteenth Amendment to acts under state authority). The Court held to the contrary that the Fourteenth Amendment could be violated either when the state in its sovereign capacity commits acts that conflict with the amendment, or simply when "state powers [are] abused by those who possessed them." *Home Tel.*, 227 U.S. at 288, 33 S.Ct. at 315. It is now settled that Fourteenth Amendment constructions of "state action" are authoritative of § 1983's "under color of" language as well. *See Lugar v. Edmondson Oil Co.*, 457 U.S. 922, 935, 102 S.Ct. 2744, 2752, 73 L.Ed.2d 482 (1982). See fuller discussion of the Constitution's "state action" and statutory "under color of" requirements *infra* this chapter Part B.

3. *See Monroe*, 365 U.S. at 171, 81 S.Ct. at 475 (holding that the purpose of the statute is, as its title states, "to enforce the Provisions of the Fourteenth Amendment").

4. *See id.* at 183–85, 81 S.Ct. at 482–483.

5. Justice Frankfurter pointed out that Illinois decisions had found similar police intrusions unlawful and that the complaint lacked concrete allegations of Illinois's unwillingness to enforce those decisions. *See id.* at 224–25 & n.33–34 (Frankfurter, J., dissenting in part).

6. *Id.* at 183, 81 S.Ct. at 482. The Court found support for its decision in two opinions that had examined the criminal counterpart to § 1983. *See Screws v. United States*, 325 U.S. 91, 108, 65 S.Ct. 1031, 1038, 89 L.Ed. 1495 (1945); *United States v. Classic*, 313 U.S. 299, 326–27 & n. 10, 61 S.Ct. 1031, 1043 & n. 10, 85 L.Ed. 1368 (1941). In both cases, individuals were held criminally liable for conduct that violated not only federal law, but state law as well.

7. *Monroe*, 365 U.S. at 173–74, 81 S.Ct. at 477.

sought to provide a supplementary remedy because "deprivation of a constitutional right is significantly different from and more serious than a violation of a state right and therefore deserves a different remedy even though the same act may constitute both a state tort and the deprivation of a constitutional right."[8]

Justice Harlan, an ardent proponent of federalism, viewed the State and its law as the dominant regulators of "primary private activity."[9] He fervently believed that state courts are ordinarily as competent and trustworthy as federal courts to uphold federally guaranteed constitutional rights.[10] Moreover, he located the support for this claim directly in the Constitution.[11] Nevertheless, he would not subscribe to the view of dissenting Justice Frankfurter that conduct could be considered under color of state law only upon proof that the state authorized or approved its agent's act.[12] For Justice Harlan, the mere allegation that a federal right was violated created an entitlement to a federal remedy in a federal court.[13]

8. *Id.* at 196, 81 S.Ct. at 488 (Harlan, J., concurring).

9. *Hanna v. Plumer*, 380 U.S. 460, 475, 85 S.Ct. 1136, 1146, 14 L.Ed.2d 8 (1965) (Harlan, J., concurring). Justice Harlan began his *Monroe* concurrence by noting that the issue was "very close indeed," but that he felt constrained, in part, by precedent construing § 1983's criminal counterpart statute. *Monroe*, 365 U.S. at 192, 81 S.Ct. at 486 (Harlan, J., concurring).

10. For example, Justice Harlan did not insist on an independent federal forum if providing one threatened to undermine the state's ability to enforce its criminal laws. In his dissent in *Dombrowski v. Pfister*, 380 U.S. 479, 85 S.Ct. 1116, 14 L.Ed.2d 22 (1965), Harlan argued that no independent federal forum is necessary if a § 1983 plaintiff can raise a claim as a defendant in an ongoing state criminal proceeding. *See id.* at 498–99 (Harlan, J., dissenting). By joining Justice Stewart's concurring opinion in *Younger v. Harris*, 401 U.S. 37, 54–56, 91 S.Ct. 746, 755, 27 L.Ed.2d 669 (1971), rather than subscribing to Justice Black's far broader opinion for the majority, Justice Harlan in effect reiterated that his support for a judicially crafted ban on federal injunctive interference with state judicial proceedings was limited to the case of criminal prosecutions. In Justice Stewart's words, the offense to state interests arising from a federal injunction "is likely to be less in a civil proceeding." *Id.* at 55 n.2 (Stewart, J., concurring).

11. *See Hanna*, 380 U.S. at 474–75, 85 S.Ct. at 1145–1146 (Harlan, J., concurring) (noting that the Court had already "recognized that the scheme of our Constitution envisions an allocation ... between state and federal legislative processes which is undercut if the federal judiciary can make substantive law affecting state affairs beyond the bounds of congressional legislative powers").

12. *See Monroe*, 365 U.S. at 193–94, 81 S.Ct. at 487–488 (Harlan, J., concurring). Frankfurter questioned whether the enacting Congress had intended to replace state tort law whenever a state actor committed a tort. *See id.* at 238–45, 81 S.Ct. at 511–516 (Frankfurter, J., dissenting). *See generally* Melvin R. Durchslag, *Federalism and Constitutional Liberties: Varying the Remedy to Save the Right*, 54 N.Y.U.L.Rev. 723, 736 (1979) (noting that Justice Frankfurter used federalism principles as a guide to congressional intent). Support for the Frankfurter position is provided by Eric H. Zagrans, *"Under Color of" What Law: A Reconstructed Model of Section 1983 Liability*, 71 Va.L.Rev. 499 (1985). *But see* Gene R. Nichol, Jr., *Federalism, State Courts, and Section 1983*, 73 Va.L.Rev. 959, 985 (1987) (concluding that § 1983 was intended to be a highly intrusive remedy for violations of limited scope).

13. *See Monroe*, 365 U.S. at 194–98, 81 S.Ct. at 488–90 (Harlan, J., concurring). According to Justice Frankfurter, if the state actor's behavior was authorized by the state a § 1983 action would lie; if unauthorized, a remedy lay in state law or not at all. As interpreted by Justice Frankfurter, the state approval requirement was a device for allocating jurisdiction between federal and state trial courts. *See id.* at 236–37, 81 S.Ct. at 510–511 (Frankfurter, J., dissenting). Although he could hypothesize two legislative reasons to support Justice

Justice Harlan's reminder that government-perpetrated harms are different is central, not only to the *Monroe* result but also conceptually. Organic theories describing the formation and maintenance of government characteristically posit mutual defense and protection as bedrock moving causes.[14] Laying aside the contemporary events that inspired the original Klan Act,[15] citizens have the right to expect and demand that the entity to which they turn for defense will not itself become the villain. Constraining government actors who violate that basic understanding, and providing meaningful redress for the victims of such activity, vindicate the very purpose of government, symbolically[16] as well as in practice. Complaints that § 1983 actions intrude too often or too deeply into local government decision-making ring rather hollow if the statute's purpose

Frankfurter's interpretation of the statute's state action requirement, Justice Harlan found the hypotheticals unpersuasive. *See id.* at 193–94, 81 S.Ct. at 487–488 (Harlan, J., concurring).

The first hypothesis rested on Congress's fear that state courts would be unwilling to find that a state official had state authority to violate an individual's constitutional rights. Justice Harlan found no support in the legislative history, however, for "congressional concern about the burdens of litigation placed upon the victims of 'authorized' ... contrasted to the victims of unauthorized violations." *Id.* at 195–96, 81 S.Ct. at 488.

A second hypothesis fared no better. Justice Harlan suggested that the Reconstruction Congress might have concluded that state approved violations of constitutional rights were more offensive than unauthorized violations. *See id.* at 198, 81 S.Ct. at 489. This potential explanation failed for a number of reasons. Perhaps most important, virtually no deprivation of due process could ever receive ultimate state approval because all states had their own due process clauses. One Senator speaking in the debates "indicated a complete overlap in every State." *Id.* (quoting Senator Trumbull). Justice Harlan found it impossible to believe that Congress would enact § 1983, given self-executing Fourteenth Amendment protections, but then limit its availability when states had constitutional counterparts similar to the amendment.

One could imagine, he continued, that despite the state law counterpart, state courts would still find the conduct unauthorized, *see id.* at 198–99, 81 S.Ct. at 489–90, thus funneling the case into state court under Justice Frankfurter's reading. Such speculation created its own anomaly. If the state actor is denied a federal forum for defense through removal because the state court would find his conduct unauthorized, thereby undermining the need for a federal § 1983 forum altogether, "it is difficult to contend that it is the added harmfulness of state approval that justifies a different remedy for authorized than for unauthorized actions of state officers." *Id.* at 199, 81 S.Ct. at 490. The states could be counted on to redress constitutional rights without the need for § 1983 relief. In the end, there was no legislative history to support this potential explanation. *See id.*

14. *See, e.g.*, John Locke, *The Second Treatise of Government* 54 (Thomas P. Peordon ed., 1952) (1690); John Stuart Mill, On Liberty 68–69 (Gertrude Himmelfarb ed., 1982) (1859); Michael J. Perry, *Morality, Politics, and Law* 97–98 (1988).

15. *See supra* §§ 2.1 and 2.4.

16. On the symbolic importance of a federal remedy, *see* Christina Whitman, *Constitutional Torts*, 79 Mich.L.Rev. 5, 21–25 (1980). Justice Harlan's recognition of this symbolism is also evident from his concurring opinion in *Bivens v. Six Unknown Named Agents of Federal Bureau of Narcotics*, 403 U.S. 388, 91 S.Ct. 1999, 29 L.Ed.2d 619 (1971), a context analogous to § 1983 where the defendants are federal agents. *see infra* this chapter Part G. There he wrote that it would be "at least anomalous" to conclude that the federal judiciary was "powerless to accord a damages remedy to vindicate social policies which, by virtue of their inclusion in the Constitution, are aimed predominantly at restraining the Government as an instrument of the popular will." 403 U.S. at 403–04, 91 S.Ct. at 2008–09 (Harlan, J., concurring). Accordingly, he found no impediment to the Court's implying a private right of action against federal agents for constitutional violations despite Congress's silence on the subject, a silence sharply contrasting with its express § 1983 remedy for similar viola-

is to assure that such entities abide by the organic law. As the Supreme Court has sometimes recalled, the Union did not fight the Civil War to vindicate state sovereignty.[17]

The *Monroe* Court's willingness to expose individual defendants to federal damages liability for conduct punishable under, rather than authorized by, state law is all the more remarkable because § 1983 claims were then available only against individual state actors, not against their employing entities. The amenability of states to damages at that time was merely assumed.[18] And in *Monroe* itself, the Court rejected the imposition of liability on municipalities,[19] a holding later understood to shield other local government entities as well.[20] Furthermore, except for those cases in which the defendant was a legislative or judicial official,[21] individual defendants then enjoyed only the mildest form of common law qualified immunity, defeasible either by objectively unreasonable conduct or malicious intent.[22] Restraint of government misconduct was therefore achieved entirely through the liability of individual state actors, whom the Court placed substantially at risk for acts their government principals had authorized or ordained. Yet individual liability seemed to a majority of the *Monroe* Court the necessary price of effectuating Justice Harlan's insight: constitutional violations are qualitatively different.[23]

§§ 2.5–2.9 [Reserved]

tions under color of state law. *See id.* at 405, 91 S.Ct. at 2009.

17. Justice Stewart had this point firmly within his grasp when he wrote for a majority of the Court that § 1983 was an expressly authorized exception to the Anti–Injunction Act, 22 U.S.C.A. § 2283 (1988). Following a discussion of changes in American society wrought by the Civil War, he wrote:

> Section 1983 was . . . a product of a vast transformation from the concepts of federalism that had prevailed in the late 18th century when the anti-injunction statute was enacted. The very purpose of § 1983 was to interpose the federal courts between the States and the people . . . to protect the people from unconstitutional action under color of state law.

Mitchum v. Foster, 407 U.S. 225, 242, 92 S.Ct. 2151, 2162, 32 L.Ed.2d 705 (1972). *But see Younger v. Harris*, 401 U.S. 37, 44, 91 S.Ct. 746, 750, 27 L.Ed.2d 669 (1971) (cautioning against undue interference "with the legitimate activities of the state" by the federal government even when the federal government seeks to "vindicate and protect federal rights and federal interests"). *Younger* is also discussed in Chapter 5 *infra*.

18. Later the Court would hold that the state qua state is not a "person" for purposes of civil liability under § 1983. *See Will v. Michigan Dep't of State Police*, 491 U.S. 58, 71, 109 S.Ct. 2304, 2312, 105 L.Ed.2d 45 (1989).

19. *See Monroe*, 365 U.S. at 187, 81 S.Ct. at 484.

20. *See, e.g., Moor v. Alameda County*, 411 U.S. 693, 710, 93 S.Ct. 1785, 1796, 36 L.Ed.2d 596 (1973) (exempting counties from the scope of § 1983); *Cullen v. New York State Civil Serv. Comm'n*, 435 F.Supp. 546, 557 (E.D.N.Y.1977) (exempting state, county, and local civil service commissions from § 1983 jurisdiction as departments of the sponsoring government).

21. *See, e.g., Tenney v. Brandhove*, 341 U.S. 367, 379, 71 S.Ct. 783, 789, 95 L.Ed. 1019 (1951) (granting absolute immunity to state legislative activities).

22. *See infra* § 2.22.

23. This is not to suggest that the Court, then or since, has ever fully realized Justice Harlan's companion suggestion that § 1983 violations warrant not just an alternative forum but also more generous remedies than a state affords at common law. *See Monroe*, 365 U.S. at 196 n.5, 81 S.Ct. at 488 n.5. (Harlan, J., concurring).

B. SECTION 1983 CONDUCT "UNDER COLOR OF STATE LAW" VERSUS CONSTITUTIONAL "STATE ACTION"

§ 2.10 In General

42 U.S.C.A. § 1983 provides in material part:

> The district courts shall have original jurisdiction of any civil action authorized by law to be commenced by any person: To redress the deprivation, *under color of any State law*, statute, ordinance, regulation, custom or usage, of any right, privilege or immunity *secured by the Constitution* of the United States or by any Act of Congress providing for equal rights of citizens or of all persons within the jurisdiction of the United States (emphasis added).

Section 1983 requires, independent of the "under color of" requirement, a predicate violation of a federal statute or a constitutional violation.[1] In turn, most § 1983 claims are predicated on violations of the federal constitution, rather than statutory rights; and almost all constitutional violations (save Thirteenth Amendment freedom from involuntary servitude[2] and the right to interstate travel,[3] both of which are enforceable against purely private actors) depend on Fourteenth Amendment "state action." The plaintiff must therefore usually prove not only that the defendant's conduct is "under color of state law" but also that it represents Fourteenth Amendment "state action."[4] Are these requirements identical, or merely substantially overlapping?

§ 2.11 "Under Color of State Law" and "State Action" Compared

The Fourteenth Amendment of the United States Constitution provides:

> All persons born or naturalized in the United States, and subject to the jurisdiction thereof, are citizens of the United States and of the

§ 2.10

1. *Siegert v. Gilley*, 500 U.S. 226, 232–233, 111 S.Ct. 1789, 1793–1794, 114 L.Ed.2d 277 (1991); *Brass v. County of Los Angeles*, 328 F.3d 1192 (9th Cir.2003) (county not liable under § 1983, even assuming its challenged practice constituted a policy or custom, where practice did not violate any U.S. constitutional right of arrestee); *Sonkowsky ex rel. Sonkowsky v. Board of Educ. for Ind. Sch. Dist.*, 327 F.3d 675 (8th Cir.2003) (§ 1983 claim fails for want of essential element of underlying First Amendment violation); *Penn v. Harris*, 296 F.3d 573 (7th Cir.2002) (allegation of violation of constitutional rights prerequisite to § 1983 liability). *Cf. Wood v. Kesler*, 323 F.3d 872, 881, 883 (11th Cir.2003) (defendant qualifiedly immune for lack of a predicate federal law violation); *Cook v. Tadros*, 312 F.3d 386 (8th Cir.2002) (§ 1983 conspiracy claim fails where jury found no underlying constitutional injury).

2. *Bray v. Alexandria Women's Health Clinic*, 506 U.S. 263, 278, 113 S.Ct. 753, 764, 122 L.Ed.2d 34 (1993) (*citing United States v. Kozminski*, 487 U.S. 931, 942, 108 S.Ct. 2751, 2759, 101 L.Ed.2d 788 (1988)).

3. *Id.* (*citing United States v. Guest*, 383 U.S. 745, 759 n. 17, 86 S.Ct. 1170, 1179 n. 17, 16 L.Ed.2d 239 (1966)).

4. *See Burch v. Apalachee Community Mental Health Servs., Inc.*, 840 F.2d 797, 802–803 (11th Cir.1988), *aff'd sub nom. Zinermon v. Burch*, 494 U.S. 113, 110 S.Ct. 975, 108 L.Ed.2d 100 (1990).

> State wherein they reside. No State shall make or enforce any law which shall abridge the privileges or immunities of citizens of the United states; nor shall any State deprive any person of life, liberty, or property, without due process of law; nor deny to any person within its jurisdiction the equal protection of the laws (emphasis added).

This text and the Amendment's primary focus on halting state-sanctioned suppression of newly-freed slaves during Reconstruction has long been read to mean that the Fourteenth Amendment reaches only action fairly attributable to government rather than purely private conduct.[1]

When the defendant is a state, county or municipality itself, there is little doubt about state action. Similarly, federal courts, usually relying on the state's statutory and administrative characterizations, have held a wide variety of boards, authorities, and other public or quasi-public entities to be Fourteenth Amendment state actors.[2] But ultimately the characterization is a matter for federal law,[3] so state law, while often persuasive, is not controlling.[4] Thus a federal court has held that a hospital authority is a Fourteenth Amendment state actor subject to § 1983 despite a state supreme court decision denying the authority sovereign immunity under state law because it was not "an agency or department of the state."[5] But the decision by a private physician acting at the behest of purely private actors to admit a patient to a private hospital does not become state action even when the authority to admit derives from the state's involuntary commitment statute.[6] On the other hand, it has been held that private physicians furnishing contract services to municipal government in detaining and examining arrestees brought into treatment facilities as possible mental patients may be state actors if they act in close concert with and reliance upon government officials, including their medical evaluations.[7]

§ 2.11

1. *The Civil Rights Cases*, 109 U.S. 3, 3 S.Ct. 18, 27 L.Ed. 835 (1883). But "state action" is not required for violations of the Thirteenth Amendment. *Id.* at 20–21, 3 S.Ct. at 28–29.

2. *See, e.g., Krynicky v. University of Pittsburgh*, 742 F.2d 94 (3d Cir.1984), *cert. denied*, 471 U.S. 1015, 105 S.Ct. 2018, 85 L.Ed.2d 300 (1985); *Braden v. University of Pittsburgh*, 552 F.2d 948 (3d Cir.1977). This question is closely related to questions concerning the status of subordinate entities as organs of a state for purposes of Eleventh Amendment immunity from damages claims in federal courts. See Chapter 5 *infra* for more detail concerning the factors used in characterizing these entities.

3. *See Miller–Davis Co. v. Illinois State Toll Highway Auth.*, 567 F.2d 323, 330 (7th Cir.1977).

4. *Tuveson v. Florida Governor's Council on Indian Affairs*, 734 F.2d 730, 732 (11th Cir.1984).

5. *Montene Burgess et al. v. Jay Marchwinski*, et al., No. 93–95–3 (M.D.Ga. 1994). The state supreme court decision did acknowledge, however, that the authority was "an instrumentality" of state government, obviously a critical factor in the federal law evaluation of state actor status.

6. *Ellison v. Garbarino*, 48 F.3d 192 (6th Cir.1995). Moreover, not even all state employees are state actors. *See Montano v. Hedgepeth*, 120 F.3d 844 (8th Cir.1997) (state prison chaplain, even though an employee of the state, was not state actor for purposes of § 1983 when he excommunicated an inmate from Protestant services because inmate practiced Messianic Judaism).

7. *Jensen v. Lane County*, 222 F.3d 570, 574–75 (9th Cir.2000).

Beginning with *Home Telephone & Telegraph Co. v. City of Los Angeles*,[8] the Supreme Court made plain that Fourteenth Amendment "state action" can be found even when its immediate agent acts in violation of state law—that is, when the defendant acts contrary to state policy.[9] Much later, in *Shelley v. Kraemer*,[10] the Court held that "state action" under the Fourteenth Amendment may (in limited circumstances) exist in cases where a private individual enlists the "coercive power" of the State to further private actions.

The Court has defined the § 1983 "under color of state law" requirement even more leniently. Construing a criminal counterpart to § 1983, the Supreme Court held that a person acts "under color" of state law when he exercises power "possessed by virtue of state law and made possible only because the wrongdoer is clothed with the authority of state law."[11] Then, in *Monroe v. Pape*[12], the Court exponentially expanded the class of potential defendants liable under § 1983. *Monroe* established, and it is now settled,[13] that even the defendant who abuses the power or position he receives from the state is acting "under color of" state law.

Moreover, the statutory authority to punish state agents' unconstitutional conduct even when that conduct transgresses the state's own rules or policies is itself constitutional: "There can be no doubt ... that Congress has the power to enforce provisions of the Fourteenth Amendment against those who carry a badge of authority of a State and represent it in some capacity...."[14] Combined with *Shelley, Monroe* led to an almost immediate dramatic increase in the number of § 1983 cases on the federal docket.

Since *Monroe*, the Court has further clarified, in *United States v. Price*[15] and *Lugar v. Edmondson Oil Co.*,[16] that if the plaintiff can show Fourteenth Amendment "state action," she will at the same time satisfy

8. 227 U.S. 278, 33 S.Ct. 312, 57 L.Ed. 510 (1913).

9. *Id.* at 287–294, 33 S.Ct. at 315–317.

10. 334 U.S. 1, 68 S.Ct. 836, 92 L.Ed. 1161 (1948).

11. *United States v. Classic*, 313 U.S. 299, 61 S.Ct. 1031, 85 L.Ed. 1368 (1941) construing § 20 of the Criminal Code, now 18 U.S.C.A. § 242 (as amended, 1988). *See, e.g., Monsky v. Moraghan*, 127 F.3d 243 (2d Cir.1997), *cert. denied*, 525 U.S. 823, 119 S.Ct. 66, 142 L.Ed.2d 52 (1998) (allegations in complaint that a state court judge violated plaintiff's constitutional right of access to the courts by bringing his dog into court clerk's office and allowing dog aggressively and offensively to nuzzle plaintiff were sufficient to describe conduct under color of state law where clerk's office policy barred animals but judge was permitted to ignore this policy because of his position); *Walker v. Taylorville Correctional Ctr.*, 129 F.3d 410 (7th Cir.1997) (sexual assault complaint against prison counselor sufficiently alleges state action; plaintiff alleged counselor was able to take actions solely due to position of authority).

12. 365 U.S. 167, 81 S.Ct. 473, 5 L.Ed.2d 492 (1961), *overruled on a different issue by Monell v. Department of Soc. Servs.*, 436 U.S. 658, 98 S.Ct. 2018, 56 L.Ed.2d 611 (1978).

13. *West v. Atkins*, 487 U.S. 42, 108 S.Ct. 2250, 101 L.Ed.2d 40 (1988).

14. *Monroe*, 365 U.S. at 171, 81 S.Ct. at 475.

15. 383 U.S. 787, 86 S.Ct. 1152, 16 L.Ed.2d 267 (1966).

16. 457 U.S. 922, 102 S.Ct. 2744, 73 L.Ed.2d 482 (1982).

the "under color of" requirement of § 1983. But the reverse is not necessarily true, as the following discussion illustrates.

§ 2.12 Fourteenth Amendment "State Action" by Private Party Defendants

Most Section 1983 actions assert that federal constitutional rights were violated by state or local government; and those entities are subject to constitutional obligations only by virtue of the Fourteenth Amendment.[1] In turn, when the conduct of a private party allegedly violates constitutional rights secured by the Fourteenth Amendment, the plaintiff must be able to show some kind of government involvement in the violation, notwithstanding the defendant's nominally private status. That is, there must be "state action" to recover under the Fourteenth Amendment.[2] The typical state action issue is presented when "a private party has taken the decisive step" that caused the plaintiff's harm "and the question is whether the state was sufficiently involved to treat that decisive conduct as state action."[3] From the modern cases at least[4] three umbrella Fourteenth Amendment "state action" tests may be distilled.[5]

a. The Exclusive, Traditional Public Function Test

First, the plaintiff might be able to show that the private entity, in connection with the allegedly unconstitutional conduct, carried out an exclusive public function. The "public function" test is quite narrow and rarely satisfied. It applies only where a private actor undertakes a function "traditionally the exclusive prerogative of the state."[6] The mere performance of a public function by a private entity will not suffice; the function must be one reserved exclusively to the government.[7] The

§ 2.12

1. A very few constitutional provisions are enforceable against purely private persons, but not for rights guaranteed by the Fourteenth Amendment. This small list includes freedom from slavery or involuntary servitude and the right to interstate travel. *See Bray v. Alexandria Women's Health Clinic*, 506 U.S. 263, 113 S.Ct. 753, 122 L.Ed.2d 34 (1993), discussed in Chapter 1, above.

2. *See Cohn v. National Board of Trial Advocacy*, 238 F.3d 702 (6th Cir.2000) (per curiam) (purely private entity not suable for alleged constitutional violations).

3. *National Collegiate Athletic Ass'n v. Tarkanian*, 488 U.S. 179, 192, 109 S.Ct. 454, 462, 102 L.Ed.2d 469 (1988).

4. Another circuit divides one of the tests, nexus/joint participant, into two separate tests, but does not refer separately to a government compulsion test. *See, e.g., McKeesport Hosp. v. Accreditation Council for Graduate Medical Educ.*, 24 F.3d 519 (3d Cir.1994). Conceivably a court might separately distinguish as many as ten alternative tests for state action: exclusive, traditional governmental function, governmental compulsion, joint participant, "aided by judicial coercion," "nexus/joint action," "symbiotic relationship," extensive state regulation, extensive funding, state delegation, and "entwinement."

5. *See, e.g., National Broadcasting Co., Inc. v. Communications Workers of Am., AFL–CIO*, 860 F.2d 1022, 1026 (11th Cir. 1988) (identifying the public function, state compulsion, and nexus/joint action tests).

6. *Jackson v. Metropolitan Edison Co.*, 419 U.S. 345, 353, 95 S.Ct. 449, 455, 42 L.Ed.2d 477 (1974). It has been argued that a more recent reference to this test eliminated the requirement of exclusivity. *See McKeesport Hosp. v. Accreditation Council for Graduate Medical Educ.*, 24 F.3d 519 (3d Cir.1994) (Becker, J., concurring in judgment) (quoting *Edmonson v. Leesville Concrete Co., Inc.*, 500 U.S. 614, 640, 111 S.Ct. 2077, 2093, 114 L.Ed.2d 660 (1991)).

7. *See, e.g., Kirtley v. Rainey*, 326 F.3d 1088 (9th Cir.2003) (under Washington law, court appointed guardian ad litem did not

handful of cases that have met the test involve such activities as conducting an election,[8] running a company-operated town,[9] and providing fire protection or operating a municipal park.[10] Operating a private hospital does not fall within this test even if defendants involuntarily admit mentally disturbed patients pursuant to a state statute.[11] Nor does providing private security services for city-owned property or holding an annual festival on public property, even pursuant to a city's permit.[12] While an organization composed of many private as well as public college members that administers an amateur sports program is neither a traditional nor an exclusive public function,[13] a different organization

perform a traditional or exclusive public function); *Logiodice v. Trustees of Maine Cent. Institute*, 296 F.3d 22 (1st Cir.2002) (private school operating under contract with public school district not state actor because schooling in Maine not historically provided exclusively by government).

8. *Nixon v. Condon*, 286 U.S. 73, 52 S.Ct. 484, 76 L.Ed. 984 (1932); *Terry v. Adams*, 345 U.S. 461, 73 S.Ct. 809, 97 L.Ed. 1152 (1953).

9. *Marsh v. Alabama*, 326 U.S. 501, 66 S.Ct. 276, 90 L.Ed. 265 (1946).

10. *Evans v. Newton*, 382 U.S. 296, 86 S.Ct. 486, 15 L.Ed.2d 373 (1966) (private estate ran public park). *Lee v. Katz*, 276 F.3d 550 (9th Cir.2002) (private lessee of traditional public forum owned by city and adjacent to city buildings performed public function by exclusively regulating free speech); *Buckner v. Toro*, 116 F.3d 450 (11th Cir.1997) (applying *Monell* policy or custom bases of liability in suits against private corporations performing traditional public functions); *Mark v. Borough of Hatboro*, 51 F.3d 1137 (3d Cir.1995), *cert. denied*, 516 U.S. 858, 116 S.Ct. 165, 133 L.Ed.2d 107 (1995) (volunteer fire company that received government funds). *Cf. Marsh v. Alabama*, 326 U.S. 501, 505–06, 66 S.Ct. 276, 90 L.Ed. 265 (1946) (private company exclusively regulating speech in shopping district accessible to and freely used by general public). Eminent domain and the exercise of peremptory jury selection challenges have been mentioned as other instances of 14th Amendment state action. *See Perkins v. Londonderry Basketball Club*, 196 F.3d 13, 19 (1st Cir.1999).

11. *Rockwell v. Cape Cod Hosp.*, 26 F.3d 254 (1st Cir.1994).

12. *Wade v. Byles*, 83 F.3d 902 (7th Cir.1996), *cert. denied*, 519 U.S. 935, 117 S.Ct. 311, 136 L.Ed.2d 227 (1996) (private security guard at city housing authority not performing traditionally exclusive public function); *United Auto Workers, Local No. 5285 v. Gaston Festivals, Inc.*, 43 F.3d 902 (4th Cir.1995) (festival case). The court in *Gaston* pointed out that fairs and festivals have been traditionally carried out mostly by private organizations, and that even the ordinary operation of a park for recreation purposes has been held by the Supreme Court not to represent an exclusively public function. *Gaston*, citing *Flagg Brothers, Inc. v. Brooks*, 436 U.S. 149, 98 S.Ct. 1729, 56 L.Ed.2d 185 (1978). Only when a city is shown to retain actual involvement in the daily operations of a park that it transferred to private hands would there be "state action," resting more on a joint participation rather than an exclusive public function rationale. *See Evans v. Newton*, 382 U.S. 296, 86 S.Ct. 486, 15 L.Ed.2d 373 (1966). *See also Brentwood Academy v. Tennessee Secondary School Athletic Ass'n*, 531 U.S. 288, 121 S.Ct. 924, 148 L.Ed.2d 807 (2001) (nominally private state athletic association overwhelmingly composed of government officials who exercise their own public schools' authority through the organization with the schools' direct and indirect financial support so "entwined" with constituent public schools as to be state actor). Merely permitting a festival committee to adopt and enforce its own rules during a festival does not make a municipality liable for the policies or actions of that committee. *Reinhart v. City of Brookings*, 84 F.3d 1071 (8th Cir.1996). *See also Lansing v. City of Memphis*, 202 F.3d 821 (6th Cir.2000) (private festival organizer not state actor and hence not liable under nexus, public function, or state compulsion tests, even though city cooperated with and derived financial benefit from festival).

13. *National Collegiate Athletic Ass'n v. Tarkanian*, 488 U.S. at 197, 109 S.Ct. at 465; *San Francisco Arts and Athletics, Inc. v. United States Olympic Comm.*, 483 U.S. 522, 545, 107 S.Ct. 2971, 2985, 97 L.Ed.2d 427 (1987); *Perkins v. Londonderry Basketball Club*, 196 F.3d 13, 19 (1st Cir.1999). Nor does state provision of recreational fora convert a private entity's conduct into state action. Id. at 21 (citing cases).

specifically sanctioned by a state, composed overwhelmingly of public members and directly or indirectly funded by them, may be inextricably "entwined" with the government and as such a state actor.[14] On occasion, a court will conclude that the absence of a delegation of a sovereign function not only defeats constitutional state action but even negates the Section 1983 requirement of action "under color of" state law.[15]

Lower federal courts are split as to whether private firms that operate correctional facilities under contract are performing an exclusive public function and subject to § 1983 liability because they are functioning "under color of" state law.[16] But if they are, a 5–member majority of the Supreme Court has now decided that the employees of such private firms who serve as prison guards will not enjoy the expansive contemporary version of qualified immunity accorded similarly situated public correctional officers, at least if the firm is systematically organized for private competition and functions with relatively little ongoing direct state supervision.[17] On the other hand, a circuit court has held that a

14. *Brentwood Academy v. Tennessee Secondary School Athletic Ass'n,* 531 U.S. 288, 121 S.Ct. 924, 148 L.Ed.2d 807, (state interscholastic athletic association exercising member schools' authority to regulate and consisting of almost all state's public high schools, 290 in total and of only 55 private schools, state actor).

15. *Mentavlos v. Anderson*, 249 F.3d 301 (4th Cir.), *cert. denied* 534 U.S. 952, 122 S.Ct. 349, 151 L.Ed.2d 264 (2001).

16. *Compare Blumel v. Mylander*, 919 F.Supp. 423 (M.D.Fla.1996), *Citrano v. Allen Correctional Ctr.*, 891 F.Supp. 312 (W.D.La.1995), *Manis v. Corrections Corp. of Am.*, 859 F.Supp. 302 (M.D.Tenn.1994), *Smith v. United States*, 850 F.Supp. 984 (M.D.Fla.1994) *and Tinnen v. Corrections Corp. of Am.*, 1993 WL 738121 (W.D.Tenn. 1993) (finding state action) *with Lloyd v. Corrections Corp. of Am.*, 855 F.Supp. 221 (W.D.Tenn.1994) (finding no state action). The Sixth Circuit assumed without deciding that a private firm providing correctional services was acting under color of state law, and was directed to address that question on remand by the U.S. Supreme Court. *McKnight v. Rees*, 88 F.3d 417 (6th Cir. 1996). *McKnight* was affirmed on the separate ground that the contractor, if otherwise subject to § 1983 liability, does not enjoy the full measure of qualified immunity enjoyed by government official defendants. *Richardson v. McKnight*, 521 U.S. 399, 117 S.Ct. 2100, 138 L.Ed.2d 540 (1997). *See also Malinowski v. DeLuca*, 177 F.3d 623 (7th Cir.1999) (employees of a private agency hired by municipality to conduct building inspections could not claim qualified immunity). The Court has decided, however, that private companies performing traditional federal functions under contract are not subject to *Bivens* liability even when they do act under color of federal law. *Correctional Services Corporation v. Malesko,* 534 U.S. 61, 122 S.Ct. 515, 151 L.Ed.2d 456 (2001).

17. *Richardson v. McKnight*, 521 U.S. 399, 117 S.Ct. 2100, 138 L.Ed.2d 540 (1997). The Court reasoned that "marketplace pressures provide the private firm with strong incentives to avoid overly timid, insufficiently vigorous, unduly fearful, or 'non-arduous' employee job performance" and that "insurance increases the likelihood of [private] employee indemnification and to that extent reduces the employment-discouraging fear of unwarranted liability potential applications face." Accordingly, a principal policy justification for the contemporary *Harlow v. Fitzgerald* brand of qualified immunity afforded individual government employees is considerably weaker in the private, competitive arena. Moreover, the Court found "no conclusive evidence of an historical tradition of immunity" for the 19th century contractors who performed the equivalent function of private prison management. Nevertheless, the Court suggested that ordinary qualified immunity would be available to private individuals performing government functions but associated only briefly with or closely supervised by government agents. Further, as in *Wyatt v. Cole*, 504 U.S. 158, 112 S.Ct. 1827, 118 L.Ed.2d 504 (1992), the Court did not foreclose the possibility that individual private defendants might be eligible for a lesser form of immunity based on the pre-Harlow elements of "good faith and/or probable cause" or that plaintiffs suing them might be required "to carry additional

firm performing a traditionally exclusive public function is protected by the *Monell* decision, and so is liable only if the federal constitutional or statutory injury is inflicted pursuant to a governmental policy or custom.[18]

b. The State Compulsion or Overwhelming Encouragement Test

This test, which overlaps with the "nexus" test discussed immediately following, is also rarely met. It subjects the private actor to liability if the government has coerced the allegedly unconstitutional conduct, or at least provided overwhelming encouragement tantamount to coercion.[19] This test was found not satisfied by the relationship between a state board of medicine and the private accreditation council with which it conducted joint inspections of a hospital's graduate residency program. Although Pennsylvania statutes contemplated that the state Board would rely on the accrediting judgments of the accreditation council, the relationship was defined in regulations as one of "comity";[20] and since the Board did not dictate or influence the council's accreditation judgments, no state action was found.[21] Even when a private party acts under regulatory pressure[22] or to resolve litigation asserting noncompliance with state law,[23] its conduct typically falls short of state action unless it is "dictated" or "compelled" by the government.

c. The "Aided By Judicial Coercion," "Nexus/Joint Action," "Symbiotic Relationship," Extensive State Regulation, Extensive Funding, State Delegation, and "Entwinement" Tests

This most commonly satisfied test for Fourteenth Amendment "state action" applies when "the state has so far insinuated itself into a position of interdependence" with a private party as to become a "joint participant in the enterprise."[24] A nexus sufficient for state action demands more than the government's mere acquiescence in, or even approval of the challenged conduct; it requires evidence that the state has coerced or significantly encouraged the private party to engage in that conduct.[25] It covers a wide variety of public-private interconnections

burdens." *See also Malinowski v. DeLuca*, 177 F.3d 623 (7th Cir.1999).

18. *Buckner v. Toro*, 116 F.3d 450 (11th Cir.1997), *cert. denied*, 522 U.S. 1018, 118 S.Ct. 608, 139 L.Ed.2d 495 (1997). The *Monell* doctrine is discussed in §§ 2.30 et seq., *infra.*

19. *San Francisco Arts and Athletics, Inc. v. U.S. Olympic Committee*, 483 U.S. 522, 107 S.Ct. 2971, 97 L.Ed.2d 427 (1987) (citing *Blum v. Yaretsky*, 457 U.S. 991, 1004, 102 S.Ct. 2777, 2785, 73 L.Ed.2d 534 (1982)).

20. *McKeesport Hosp., supra* (Becker, J., concurring in judgment).

21. *Id.*

22. *Cf. Mathis v. Pacific Gas and Elec. Co.*, 75 F.3d 498 (9th Cir.1996) (pressure from federal administrative agency). *But see Kia P. v. McIntyre*, 235 F.3d 749 (2d Cir. 2000), *cert. denied* 534 U.S. 820, 122 S.Ct. 51, 151 L.Ed.2d 21 (2001) (private hospital state actor to extent it held child after medical clearance pending release approval from state child welfare authorities).

23. *Logan v. Bennington College Corp.*, 72 F.3d 1017 (2d Cir.1995), cert. denied, 519 U.S. 822, 117 S.Ct. 79, 136 L.Ed.2d 37 (1996).

24. *Burton v. Wilmington Parking Auth.*, 365 U.S. 715, 725, 81 S.Ct. 856, 862, 6 L.Ed.2d 45 (1961).

25. *American Mfrs. Mutual Ins. Co. v. Sullivan*, 526 U.S. 40, 51, 119 S.Ct. 977, 986, 143 L.Ed.2d 130 (1999) (private insurers authorized, but not required, by state to

that range from the state providing the means for or accepting the benefits of the private defendant's actions, substantially financing or regulating (but not compelling) the private party's unconstitutional conduct, or simply delegating to the private party significant state power.[26]

1. *State Provides Private Parties Coercive Judicial Means*

The cases involving state-provided means begin with *Shelley v. Kraemer*.[27] In *Shelley*, the Supreme Court expounded on the modern conception of Fourteenth Amendment "state action":

> [T]he principle has become firmly embedded in our constitutional law that the action inhibited by the first section of the Fourteenth Amendment is only such action as may fairly be said to be that of the States. That Amendment erects no shield against merely private conduct, however discriminatory or wrongful.[28]

Although the covenant at issue (one that prevented residents of a Missouri neighborhood from selling property to black citizens)[29] would have clearly violated the Fourteenth Amendment's Equal Protection Clause if enacted by the Missouri legislature, it was lawful as an agreement created and involving only private citizens, at least until enforcement was sought.

Some of the private parties who created the restrictive covenant did not voluntarily abide by it. When a resident attempted to sell property to a black citizen, other residents asked the courts of Missouri to block the transaction. The State of Missouri became involved through its court system.

> That the action of state courts and of judicial officers in their official capacities is to be regarded as action of the State within the meaning of the Fourteenth Amendment, is a proposition which has long been established by decisions of this Court.[30]

Private defendants may be liable as state actors when the state makes "available to such individuals the full coercive power of government."[31] The Court found a "nexus" between Missouri and the private defendants because Missouri provided the private defendants with the state's coercive judicial power.

withhold payments for disputed medical treatment, and that make the final determination themselves, not state actors under nexus test); *Blum v. Yaretsky*, 457 U.S. 991, 1004, 102 S.Ct. 2777, 2785, 73 L.Ed.2d 534 (1982). *See also Flagg Brothers, Inc. v. Brooks,* 436 U.S. 149, 164–65, 98 S.Ct. 1729, 1737–38, 56 L.Ed.2d 185 (1978); *Rayburn ex rel. Rayburn v. Hogue*, 241 F.3d 1341 (11th Cir.2001) (degree of insinuation in state's management of foster parent-foster child relationship insufficient to meet nexus/joint action test where state prohibited the challenged child abuse conduct).

26. *Jackson v. Metropolitan Edison Co.*, 419 U.S. 345, 353, 95 S.Ct. 449, 455, 42 L.Ed.2d 477 (1974).

27. 334 U.S. 1, 68 S.Ct. 836, 92 L.Ed. 1161 (1948).

28. *Id.* at 13, 68 S.Ct. at 842.

29. *Id.* at 4, 68 S.Ct. at 838.

30. *Id.* at 14, 68 S.Ct. at 842.

31. *Id.* at 19, 68 S.Ct. at 845.

State action, as that phrase is understood for the purposes of the Fourteenth Amendment, refers to exertions of state power in all forms. And when the effect of that action is to deny rights subject to the protection of the Fourteenth Amendment, it is the obligation of this Court to enforce the constitutional commands.[32]

The Court has since found a "nexus" in several cases where the private defendant uses state judicial mechanisms to cause a constitutional injury to the plaintiff. In *Sniadach v. Family Finance Corp.*,[33] the Court assumed state action where a finance company instituted a garnishment action against Sniadach pursuant to a Wisconsin state statute.[34] The Court similarly assumed state action and therefore addressed the plaintiff's due process claims in *Mitchell v. W.T. Grant Company*[35] (involving Louisiana sequestration procedure instituted by a private lien holder); *North Georgia Finishing, Inc. v. Di–Chem, Inc.*[36] (private defendant initiated garnishment under Georgia statute); *Lugar v. Edmondson Oil Co.*[37] (use of Virginia prejudgment attachment procedure); and *Connecticut v. Doehr*[38] (individual enlisted State's aid through prejudgment attachment procedure).

However, the Eleventh Circuit has held that state action does not exist where a civil rights defendant invoked state law, but affirmatively misled the state into exercising its coercive power.[39] And private hospital officials who involuntarily admitted mentally disturbed patients pursuant to authority conferred by a state statute have been held not to be acting even "under color of" state law within the meaning of § 1983.[40] Even a public university's delegation of security functions to a rock concert promoter that hired a security firm that conducted allegedly unconstitutional pat-down searches did not render the university or the promoter state actors, absent a link between university policy and the type of searches conducted.[41] And recent circuit decisions have declined to find state action merely because the defendant initiated normal civil judicial machinery as noted in § 2.16 below.

32. *Id.* at 20, 68 S.Ct. at 845.

33. 395 U.S. 337, 89 S.Ct. 1820, 23 L.Ed.2d 349 (1969).

34. *Id.* at 338, 89 S.Ct. at 1821.

35. 416 U.S. 600, 94 S.Ct. 1895, 40 L.Ed.2d 406 (1974).

36. 419 U.S. 601, 95 S.Ct. 719, 42 L.Ed.2d 751 (1975).

37. 457 U.S. 922, 102 S.Ct. 2744, 73 L.Ed.2d 482 (1982).

38. 501 U.S. 1, 111 S.Ct. 2105, 115 L.Ed.2d 1 (1991) (citing *Tulsa Professional Collection Servs., Inc. v. Pope*, 485 U.S. 478, 486, 108 S.Ct. 1340, 1345, 99 L.Ed.2d 565 (1988)). *But see Barrett v. Harwood*, 189 F.3d 297 (2d Cir.1999), *cert. denied*, 530 U.S. 1262, 120 S.Ct. 2719, 147 L.Ed.2d 984 (2000) (police officer who merely prevented violence during private repossession of property did not engage in state action because he did not affirmatively assist creditor or intimidate debtor from exercising legal right to object).

39. *Gene Thompson Lumber Co. v. Davis Parmer Lumber, Co.*, 984 F.2d 401 (11th Cir.1993) (no state action exists when the defendant gave false information that induced the state authorities to seize property pursuant to a prejudgment attachment and garnishment).

40. *Rockwell v. Cape Cod Hosp.*, 26 F.3d 254 (1st Cir.1994).

41. *Gallagher v. Neil Young Freedom Concert*, 49 F.3d 1442 (10th Cir.1995).

2. *State Acceptance of Benefits From Private Party: Herein of "Symbiosis"*

Sometimes the state action requirement is satisfied by evidence that the State knowingly accepted the benefits of unconstitutional behavior.[42] In *Burton,* a restaurant that practiced racial discrimination leased space from the state parking authority in a publicly owned building. The Court held that the State was a joint participant in the restaurant.[43] The touchstone for finding this "symbiosis" was a combination of interdependence between the private and public entities and joint participation in the challenged activity. Yet, in contrast to the nexus inquiry, which centers on the state's involvement in the challenged activity, symbiosis concentrates on their overall relationship, with emphasis on such factors as the private entity's independence vel non in conducting its daily affairs and the extent to which the public entity knowingly shared in profits generated by the private entity's unlawful conduct. Thus lower courts wrestling with similar lease arrangements have sometimes distinguished *Burton* on the ground that the government there benefited lessor not just from the restaurant's proceeds but specifically from the allegedly unconstitutional race discrimination targeted by plaintiff's claim, which boosted the restaurant's profits. Lease terms are another key factor, with the courts looking to whether the government lessor retains control over the particular conduct or activity alleged to be unconstitutional.[44]

The "benefits" route to showing joint action is rarely successful because the plaintiff has to show that the state "so far insinuated itself into a position of interdependence with the [private defendant] that it was a joint participant in the enterprise"[45]—and one that controlled either all facets of management or at a minimum the assertedly unconstitutional conduct in question. Put otherwise, the closeness of the relationship required to subject the private defendant to liability is captured in the phrase "symbiotic relationship."[46] Even where a state agency had a stake in video lotteries conducted on racetrack premises, it

42. *See Burton v. Wilmington Parking Auth.*, 365 U.S. 715, 81 S.Ct. 856, 6 L.Ed.2d 45 (1961).

43. *Id.* at 725.

44. *Willis v. University Health Servs., Inc.*, 993 F.2d 837, 840–41 (11th Cir.1993), *cert. denied*, 510 U.S. 976, 114 S.Ct. 468, 126 L.Ed.2d 420 (1993); *National Broadcasting Co., Inc.*, 860 F.2d at 1027–28; *Greco v. Orange Mem'l Hosp.*, 513 F.2d 873 (5th Cir.1975), *cert. denied*, 423 U.S. 1000, 96 S.Ct. 433, 46 L.Ed.2d 376 (1975). *Burton* has been so regularly distinguished by the Supreme Court, *see American Mfrs. Mut. Ins. Co. v. Sullivan*, 526 U.S. 40, 55–58, 119 S.Ct. 977, 988–989, 143 L.Ed.2d 130 (1999); *San Francisco Arts and Athletics, Inc. v. United States Olympic Comm.*, 483 U.S. at 547, 107 S.Ct. at 2971; *Blum v. Yaretsky*, 457 U.S. 991, 1011, 102 S.Ct. 2777, 2789, 73 L.Ed.2d 534 (1982), that its vitality, even on its own stringent terms, has recently been questioned. *Perkins v. Londonderry Basketball Club*, 196 F.3d 13, 20–21 (1st Cir.1999). Still, an occasional decision will find at least arguable symbiosis, as where the state extensively regulates and participates in the care of foster children. *Rayburn ex rel. Rayburn v. Hogue*, 241 F.3d 1341 (11th Cir.2001) (holding, however, that the State was not liable because in regulating the relationship it forbade rather than encouraged the conduct underlying the complaint, child abuse).

45. *Jackson*, 419 U.S. at 357–58, 95 S.Ct. at 457–58.

46. *Willis*, 993 F.2d at 840.

did not have a symbiotic relationship with the track owner sufficient to sustain a Section 1983 action.[47]

On occasion it appears that an arm of the state actually participates with the private party in the challenged action. State action may certainly be found if the private party acted in concert or conspired with state officials.[48] But a state medical board's reliance on the judgments of a private accrediting council's judgments did not create a sufficiently interdependent relationship to meet this test because the council was self-governed and financed and set its own standards uninfluenced by the state.[49]

3. *Extensive State Regulation*

Plaintiffs have had less success convincing courts that Fourteenth Amendment "state action" inevitably follows from extensive state regulation of a private defendant. The defendant in *Jackson v. Metropolitan Edison Company*[50] was a privately owned and operated Pennsylvania corporation, the Metropolitan Edison Company, that delivered electricity to Pennsylvania residents, including the plaintiff, Ms. Jackson. The Pennsylvania Public Utility Commission issued a certificate of public convenience to the corporation empowering it to sell electricity to the service area in which Ms. Jackson lived. The certificate subjected the company to extensive public regulation by the Commission. The company filed a general tariff with the Commission that gave the company the right to discontinue service to any customer after reasonable notice of nonpayment of bills.[51]

Jackson received electricity from the company, but the Metropolitan Edison Company terminated her service because she failed to pay her electric bill. She filed suit against Metropolitan under § 1983 alleging deprivation of her property in violation of the Fourteenth Amendment's guarantee of due process of law.[52]

47. *Crissman v. Dover Downs Entertainment Inc.*, 289 F.3d 231 (3d Cir.2002) (flow of state funds combined with heavy regulation of private harness racing facility not sufficient to make facility state actor with respect to Section 1983 action by trainer excluded from facility).

48. *See, e.g., Edmonson v. Leesville Concrete Co., Inc.*, 500 U.S. 614, 111 S.Ct. 2077, 114 L.Ed.2d 660 (1991), and *Adickes v. S.H. Kress & Co.*, 398 U.S. 144, 90 S.Ct. 1598, 26 L.Ed.2d 142 (1970); *Berger v. Hanlon*, 129 F.3d 505 (9th Cir.1997), *vacated on other grounds*, 526 U.S. 808, 119 S.Ct. 1706, 143 L.Ed.2d 978, *cert. denied*, 526 U.S. 1154, 119 S.Ct. 2039, 143 L.Ed.2d 1047 (1999) (media and police department acted in concert when police contracted to allow media to film execution of search warrant for broadcast). But it has been held that implicating state officials in a conspiracy with private defendants to show the required "state action" still demands heightened, nonconclusory pleading, despite the general acceptance of "notice pleading" in § 1983 actions. *Tahfs v. Proctor*, 316 F.3d 584 (6th Cir.2003); *Scott v. Hern*, 216 F.3d 897, 907–08 (10th Cir.2000). *See generally* § 5.80 *infra*.

49. *McKeesport Hosp. v. Accreditation Council*, 24 F.3d 519 (3d Cir.1994). Other accreditation decisions have similarly found no state action. *See, e.g., Medical Inst. of Minn. v. National Ass'n of Trade & Technical Sch.*, 817 F.2d 1310, 1312–14 (8th Cir. 1987).

50. 419 U.S. 345, 95 S.Ct. 449, 42 L.Ed.2d 477 (1974).

51. *Id.* at 346, 95 S.Ct. at 451.

52. *Id.* at 347, 95 S.Ct. at 451.

The Court observed that the utility was privately owned and operated although subject to extensive state regulation. "[T]he mere fact that a business is subject to state regulation does not by itself convert its action into that of the State for purposes of the Fourteenth Amendment."[53] Even "extensive and detailed" regulation is not necessarily enough.

Jackson argued that "state action" was evidenced by the Utility Commission's granting of a monopoly to Metropolitan. The Court doubted that a monopoly had been granted, but stated that even if Metropolitan had a monopoly, the company's termination of service was not sufficiently related to its monopoly status to infer state action.[54] Jackson argued that Metropolitan's termination represented state action because the Commission impliedly approved the termination practice by renewing the utility's license. The Court found that the State had not approved the challenged termination of service by Metropolitan. Rather, the Commission, by not changing the procedure, at most indicated that it believed the company was authorized to employ such a practice if it so desired.[55]

The Court considered another extensively regulated private defendant in *Blum v. Yaretsky*.[56] Medicaid patients brought a class action suit against their nursing home after its utilization review committee decided that the plaintiff group should be transferred to a home with a lower level of care.[57] The plaintiffs alleged a violation of the Due Process Clause of the Fourteenth Amendment based on the review committee's failure to give adequate notice of the decision to move them and denial of a hearing to challenge the decision. Before addressing the merits of the due process claim, the Court turned to the issue whether the private nursing home's decision was "state action."[58]

The Court noted, as it had in *Jackson*, that New York's extensive regulation of the nursing home was not enough to transmute the actions of the home into "state action."[59] The Court explained that

> [t]he purpose of [the nexus] requirement is to assure that constitutional standards are invoked only when it can be said that the State is responsible for the specific conduct of which the plaintiff complains. The importance of this assurance is evident when, as in this case, the complaining party seeks to hold the State liable for the actions of private parties.[60]

Citing *Jackson*, the *Blum* Court repeated that government "acquiescence" in the private defendant's conduct is not enough. Rather, a State may be held liable only "when it has exercised coercive power or has

53. *Id.* at 350, 95 S.Ct. at 453.

54. *Id.* at 351–352, 95 S.Ct. at 454.

55. *Id.* at 354–357, 95 S.Ct. at 455–457.

56. 457 U.S. 991, 102 S.Ct. 2777, 73 L.Ed.2d 534 (1982).

57. *Id.*

58. *Id.* at 993–999, 1002, 102 S.Ct. at 2780–2783, 2785.

59. *Id.* at 1004, 102 S.Ct. at 2785.

60. *Id.*

provided such significant encouragement"[61] to the private decisionmaker that it is fair to call the action "that of the State."[62]

4. *Extensive Funding*

In *Rendell–Baker v. Kohn*,[63] the Court explained that regulation and funding without state compulsion of the defendant's particular injury-inflicting conduct do not suffice for Fourteenth Amendment "state action." *Rendell–Baker* involved a § 1983 suit brought by a former vocational counselor and former teachers against their employer, a privately operated school for maladjusted high school students in Massachusetts. The plaintiffs alleged that the school had discharged them in violation of their First, Fifth and Fourteenth Amendment rights. The question for the Court was whether the decision of the private high school could be attributed to Massachusetts.

The school, although "privately" operated, received funds from both state and federal agencies that accounted for at least 90% of the school's operating budget. None of the school's fifty students paid tuition. Additionally, Massachusetts generally regulated the school's functions, including "personnel matters."[64] Nevertheless, the Court found no Fourteenth Amendment "state action" because even "extreme regulation" by the state was insufficient. "Acts of . . . private contractors do not become acts of the government by reason of their significant or even total engagement in performing public contracts."[65] The Court found "the decisions to discharge the petitioners were not compelled or even influenced by any state regulation."[66] The Court also rejected the plaintiff's argument that the school's fiscal relationship with the State was sufficiently close to deem its functions melded with those of the State.[67]

5. *State Delegation of Governmental Authority*

This route to state action is closely related to and sometimes analyzed as the "traditional governmental function" approach discussed

61. *Id. See Single Moms, Inc. v. Montana Power Co.*, 331 F.3d 743 (9th Cir.2003) (electric and gas utility did not become state actor through its lobbying efforts and efforts could not be deemed state action where state did not exercise coercive power or offer significant encouragement to utility respecting those efforts, did not control the utility or participate in running it as a joint activity, and did not delegate to it a public function). *See also George v. Pacific–CSC Work Furlough*, 91 F.3d 1227 (9th Cir. 1996), *cert. denied*, 519 U.S. 1081, 117 S.Ct. 746, 136 L.Ed.2d 684 (1997) (insufficient nexus between county and defendant private employer's decision to fire employee, where contract empowering employer to operate correctional facility did not reserve to county regulatory authority respecting termination decisions).

62. *Id. But see Payton v. Rush–Presbyterian–St. Luke's Medical Center*, 184 F.3d 623 (7th Cir.1999), *on remand*, 82 F.Supp.2d 901 (N.D.Ill.2000) (special officers endowed with full police powers under city ordinance licensing and subjecting them to all regulations governing city officers engage in state action despite being privately employed).

63. 457 U.S. 830, 102 S.Ct. 2764, 73 L.Ed.2d 418 (1982).

64. *Id.* at 831–835, 102 S.Ct. at 2766–2768.

65. *Id.* at 841, 102 S.Ct. at 2771. *See Robert S. v. Stetson School, Inc.*, 256 F.3d 159 (3d Cir.2001) (private school not state action cited by return of funding from city or detailed contract requirements pertinent to plaintiff).

66. *Id.*

67. *Id.*

above. The Supreme Court has observed that a state may officially delegate such functions to nominally private entities.[68] It has also been argued that a delegation to nominally private hands of state authority may meet the nexus or joint participant tests even if the function in question is not a traditional or exclusive state function.[69] That is one way to understand cases that have held hospital authorities to be state actors even though running a hospital is not considered a traditional governmental function.[70] On the other hand, a state medical board that retained all formal authority to make final decisions concerning the accreditation of hospital programs but deemed its function fulfilled by following the decisions of a private accrediting council was held not to have made a delegation of this kind even though it adopted wholesale or indeed "rubber stamped" the council's conclusions. The state board "remains the state actor" because it "remains ultimately responsible for approving medical training facilities. . . ."[71]

6. *"Entwinement"*

Two Supreme Court decisions find state action where, despite the failure of the foregoing tests, the nominally private defendant is pervasively "entwined with government policies" or government is pervasively "entwined in [its] management or control."[72] In the Court's most recent application of this rare test, it held a nominally private state athletic association, overwhelmingly composed of government officials who exercised their own public schools' authority through the organization by using the schools' direct and indirect financial support, so "entwined" with the constituent public schools as to be a state actor.[73] When this test is met, it suffices for state action even if no other test is.[74]

68. *West v. Atkins,* 487 U.S. 42, 56, 108 S.Ct. 2250, 2259, 101 L.Ed.2d 40 (1988).

69. *McKeesport Hosp., supra* (Becker, J. concurring in judgment). Indeed a statewide high school athletic association has been held a state actor on a similar rationale of excessive "entwinement" with the state in the organization's membership, funding, and regulatory authority. *Brentwood Academy v. Tennessee Secondary School Athletic Ass.n.,* 531 U.S. 288, 121 S.Ct. 924, 148 L.Ed.2d 807.

70. *See Stern v. Tarrant County Hosp. Dist.,* 755 F.2d 430, 433 (5th Cir.1985), *vacated on other grounds,* 778 F.2d 1052 (5th Cir.1985), *cert. denied,* 476 U.S. 1108, 106 S.Ct. 1957, 90 L.Ed.2d 365 (1986) (cited by Becker, J., concurring in judgment in *McKeesport Hosp., supra*).

71. *McKeesport Hosp., supra.*

72. *Evans v. Newton,* 382 U.S. 296, 299, 301, 86 S.Ct. 486, 488, 489, 15 L.Ed.2d 373 (1966) (city remained entwined in management and control of park it had transferred to private trustees, at least where park continued to serve public functions); *Brentwood Academy v. Tennessee Secondary School Association,* 531 U.S. 288, 121 S.Ct. 924, 148 L.Ed.2d 807 (2001) (state pervasively entwined with composition, operation and funding of statewide, interscholastic high school athletic association). On the other hand, where state action fails on an entwinement basis, it may still rest on a symbiotic relationship between government and a private defendant. *Crissman v. Dover Downs Entertainment,* 2001 WL 617503 (3d Cir.), *rehearing en banc granted,* 254 F.3d 467 (3d Cir.2001).

73. *Brentwood Academy v. Tennessee Secondary School Association,* 531 U.S. 288, 121 S.Ct. 924, 148 L.Ed.2d 807 (2001).

74. *Id. at 304.*

§ 2.13 Does a Private Actor Become Subject to the Fourteenth Amendment by Compelling a State Actor to Violate a Constitutional Right?

An interesting case presenting the flip side of Fourteenth Amendment "state action" arose from a claim by former University of Nevada–Las Vegas (UNLV) basketball coach Jerry Tarkanian against the formally private National Collegiate Athletic Association (NCAA).[1] UNLV, concededly a state actor, suspended Tarkanian after an investigation by the NCAA that found a series of possible violations of NCAA rules. The NCAA ordered UNLV to show cause why, under those rules, UNLV should not suspend Coach Tarkanian. UNLV suspended the coach rather than face suspension from the NCAA and thus exclusion from athletic competitions involving other NCAA schools.

The coach brought a § 1983 action against the NCAA alleging a violation of the Fourteenth Amendment's Due Process Clause.[2] Tarkanian claimed that UNLV had delegated its state functions to the NCAA, giving the NCAA the authority to govern UNLV's athletic program and to enforce those rules.[3] In particular he alleged that the NCAA was a state actor because it conducted the investigation and made a final decision that UNLV only "rubber-stamped." The United States Supreme Court found that these contentions fundamentally misconstrued the facts of the case.[4] Although the NCAA rules and recommendations obviously influenced the decision of UNLV, the Court viewed the injury inflicting decision as having been made by the State itself, i.e. UNLV, rather than the defendant NCAA.

The Court held that the NCAA might be a state actor had it been created by Nevada legislation.[5] However, the NCAA has hundreds of other members, both private and public, and it was the combination of those members that created and composed the entity.[6] Alternatively, UNLV could have transformed the NCAA's actions into state action if it had made the rules of the NCAA its own. The Court stated that because UNLV retained the authority to withdraw from the organization and establish its own standards or to work through the NCAA's procedures to change the rules, UNLV had not adopted the rules of the NCAA.[7]

§ 2.13

1. *National Collegiate Athletic Ass'n v. Tarkanian*, 488 U.S. 179, 109 S.Ct. 454, 102 L.Ed.2d 469 (1988).

2. *Id.* at 180–82, 109 S.Ct. at 456–57.

3. *Id.* at 192, 109 S.Ct. at 462.

4. *Id.*

5. *Id.*

6. *Id.* at 193, 109 S.Ct. at 462. *Cf. Brentwood Academy v. Tennessee Secondary School Athletic Association*, 531 U.S. 288, 121 S.Ct. 924, 148 L.Ed.2d 807 (2001) (state-sanctioned high school athletic association composed overwhelmingly of public school members a state actor).

7. *Id.* at 194–95, 109 S.Ct. at 463–64. *Cf. NCAA v. Smith*, 525 U.S. 459, 119 S.Ct. 924, 142 L.Ed.2d 929 (1999), *on remand*, 266 F.3d 152 (3d Cir.2001) (NCAA's receipt of dues from member institutions who receive federal funds does not by itself make NCAA a recipient of federal financial assistance so as to subject it to Title IX of the Education Amendments of 1972, which prohibit sex discrimination in federally funded education programs). See Chapter 3 for a district court decision distinguishing *Smith* and deeming NCAA a recipient of federal funds for purposes of a cognate statute, Title VI.

Finally, Nevada had not empowered the NCAA to investigate the actions of the coach through subpoena or contempt sanctions or given it the ability to assert sovereign power.[8]

§ 2.14 Corporate Chartering as "State Action"

The Supreme Court held that the actions of a private defendant were not attributable to the federal government under the Fifth Amendment in *San Francisco Arts & Athletics, Inc. v. United States Olympic Committee*.[1]

The plaintiff group was an organization based in San Francisco that sponsored the "Gay Olympic Games." The United States Olympic Committee (USOC) has the right to prohibit the use of the word "Olympic" and the use of Olympic symbols for commercial or promotional uses under § 110 of the Amateur Sports Act.[2] The USOC exercised this power and ordered the plaintiff organization to stop using the word "Olympic" in association with their event. The San Francisco Arts & Athletics group brought suit alleging among other claims, that the USOC enforced its rights under § 110 in a discriminatory manner in violation of the Fifth Amendment.[3] The question before the Court was whether the USOC was a Fifth Amendment state actor because Congress had granted the Committee its corporate status.[4]

That Congress granted the USOC corporate status did not suffice for "state action"; all corporations act under charters granted by some government, the Court explained.[5] Nor did congressional grant of the power to organize amateur sports transform USOC into a state actor: "neither the conduct nor the coordination of amateur sports has been a traditional governmental function."[6] Most important, Congress did not "significantly encourage" the particular challenged decision of the USOC, and therefore the action of the private entity could not be attributed to the government.[7]

§ 2.15 Public Defendants and the "Under Color of State Law" Requirement

A related, invariable, but less stringent, requirement of any § 1983 action—even one alleging a violation only of federal statutory, not constitutional rights—is a showing that the defendant acted "under color of state law." *Monroe v. Pape*,[1] as observed above, held that state

8. *Id.* at 197, 109 S.Ct. at 465.

§ 2.14

1. 483 U.S. 522, 107 S.Ct. 2971, 97 L.Ed.2d 427 (1987).

2. 92 Stat. 3048, 36 U.S.C.A. § 380.

3. "This Court's approach to Fifth Amendment equal protection claims has been ... precisely the same as to equal protection claims under the Fourteenth Amendment." *Weinberger v. Wiesenfeld*, 420 U.S. 636, 638 n. 2, 95 S.Ct. 1225, 1228 n. 2, 43 L.Ed.2d 514 (1975).

4. 483 U.S. at 524–529, 107 S.Ct. at 2975–2977.

5. *Id.* at 543–44, 107 S.Ct. at 2985.

6. *Id.* at 545, 107 S.Ct. at 2985.

7. *Id.* at 546–547, 107 S.Ct. at 2986–2987.

§ 2.15

1. 365 U.S. 167, 81 S.Ct. 473, 5 L.Ed.2d 492 (1961), overruled on a different issue by *Monell v. Department of Soc.*

officials act "under color" of state law if they are clothed with the trappings of state authority regardless of whether state law approves or disapproves the particular conduct that triggers the federal constitutional or statutory claim.[2] The Court so held by analogy to its decision in *Home Telephone* more than five decades earlier that conduct by a person generally authorized to act under state law is "state action" for purposes of the Fourteenth Amendment, even if the particular conduct at issue was not state authorized.[3] After *Monroe*, any act carried out by an individual (in an action against that individual, rather than her employing government entity) who is clothed with the authority of the state is similarly actionable under § 1983, even if the state affirmatively forbade the specific acts of the individual defendant.

> It is no answer that the State has a law which if enforced would give relief [for the conduct unauthorized or forbidden by state law]. The federal remedy is supplementary to the state remedy, and the latter need not be first sought and refused before the federal one is invoked.[4]

After *Monroe*, the courthouse doors may be open in four situations. (1) Most clearly, a state official acting within the scope of her authority and commensurately with affirmative state authorization may be sued under § 1983 for conduct allegedly violating the federal constitution or laws.[5] (2) *Monroe* added that an official acting within the scope of her employment, but whose actions are affirmatively *contrary* to the rules of the state, also acts "under color of state law." (3) *A fortiori* the official acting within the scope of her employment and whose challenged conduct is simply unaddressed by any state policy—i.e., is not prohibited but simply unauthorized—ordinarily acts "under color of state law," too. But some decisions have placed a caveat on, or perhaps only defined, these three "scope of authority" situations by insisting that the agent's conduct in question be at least arguably connected to her assigned work.[6]

Servs., 436 U.S. 658, 98 S.Ct. 2018, 56 L.Ed.2d 611 (1978).

2. *Id.* at 183–186, 81 S.Ct. at 482–484.

3. *See Home Tel. & Tel. Co. v. City of Los Angeles*, 227 U.S. at 287–94, 33 S.Ct. at 315–17.

4. 365 U.S. at 183, 81 S.Ct. at 482.

5. *Cf. Bonenberger v. Plymouth Township*, 132 F.3d 20 (3d Cir.1997) (police sergeant acted under color of state law when he sexually harassed a police dispatcher; even though he lacked actual authority to hire, fire, or demote plaintiff, as a state employee he could exert considerable control over her because he regularly supervised her).

6. *See Federer v. Gephardt*, 363 F.3d 754 (8th Cir. 2004) (challenged activity engaged in by defendant as private political candidate, although he happened to be a member of Congress). Indeed a public officer was held not to be acting under color of law in threatening a defamation action against a private citizen, even though the threat arose from the officer's detention of plaintiff during a traffic stop made by the officer in the course of his official duties. *See, Gritchen v. Collier*, 254 F.3d 807 (9th Cir.2001). *See also Townsend v. Moya,* 291 F.3d 859 (5th Cir.2002) (prison guard not acting under color of state law in cutting inmate with knife during "horseplay" on the job for lack of nexus between improper conduct and performance of defendant's official duties in that he was pursuing personal objectives without exercising the authority or weapons he possessed by virtue of his position); *Roe v. Humke*, 128 F.3d 1213 (8th Cir.1997) (police officer who took a minor to his farm and sexually assaulted her was not acting under color of state law; police officer was not acting, nor purporting to act, in an official capacity as he was off duty, out

Thus acts committed by a police officer even while on duty and in uniform are not under color of state law unless they are in some way "related to the performance of police duties."[7]

(4) What of the fourth situation, where a state official's conduct is entirely outside the scope of her employment, but she carries the badges or emblems of state authority when she comes into contact with the plaintiff? Several circuits have indicated that there are situations when the state official, although clearly outside the scope of employment, nevertheless acts "under color of state law" for the purposes of § 1983. In *Davis v. Murphy*,[8] two Milwaukee police officers were sued for shouting racial epithets and provoking a fight with five black citizens who were driving in a car behind the officers. The defendants identified themselves as police officers and were carrying their guns and badges. Milwaukee Police Department regulations stated that officers were "to be always subject to duty."[9] The Seventh Circuit found that the officers were acting "under color of state law" even though acting outside the scope of their employment.

Similarly, in *Traver v. Meshriy*[10] the Ninth Circuit held that an off-duty police officer who detained a bank customer could be sued under § 1983. Here the off-duty officer was working pursuant to the police

of uniform, unarmed, and driving his personal vehicle); *Harris v. Rhodes*, 94 F.3d 196 (5th Cir.1996) (jail maintenance worker not acting under color of state law in punching inmate in course of mutual teasing about their physical attributes where he did not use his authority to sign inmate out for work detail in order to facilitate altercation). *But cf. Griffin v. City of Opa–Locka*, 261 F.3d 1295, 1303–1307 (11th Cir.2001) (distinguishing *Almand, infra* note 7, and finding city manager acted under color of state law because he used his authority as plaintiff's supervisor to harass and humiliate her both during—as well as after–hours and at—as well as outside of—workplace); *United States v. Causey*, 185 F.3d 407 (5th Cir.1999) (police officer acted under color of state law because he used police station, patrol car and radio to plan, execute, and cover up murder of citizen who had filed complaint against him) (criminal prosecution under 18 U.S.C.A. § 242).

7. *Gibson v. City of Chicago*, 910 F.2d 1510, 1516 (7th Cir.1990) quoting *Briscoe v. LaHue*, 663 F.2d 713, 721, n. 4 (7th Cir. 1981), *aff'd*, 460 U.S. 325, 103 S.Ct. 1108, 75 L.Ed.2d 96, *cert. denied*, 460 U.S. 1037, 103 S.Ct. 1426, 75 L.Ed.2d 787 (1983) (quoting *Johnson v. Hackett*, 284 F.Supp. 933, 937 (E.D.Pa.1968)). *See Almand v. DeKalb County*, 103 F.3d 1510 (11th Cir.), *cert. denied*, 522 U.S. 966, 118 S.Ct. 411, 139 L.Ed.2d 314 (1997) (police officer who initially entered woman's apartment allegedly to discuss police business assumed to be acting in furtherance of police business, but after leaving apartment at her request, his forcible opening of front door and raping her held not "under color" of state law); *Martinez v. Colon*, 54 F.3d 980 (1st Cir.), *cert. denied*, 516 U.S. 987, 116 S.Ct. 515, 133 L.Ed.2d 423 (1995) (on–duty harassment of fellow officer a purely personal pursuit and hence not actionable although carried out with service revolver). *See also Tierney v. Vahle*, 304 F.3d 734 (7th Cir.2002) (teacher not acting under color of state law by allowing use of her private telephone to make alleged retaliatory call when caller did not mention teacher or use her public position to leverage the influence of caller's private conduct); *Becerra v. Asher*, 105 F.3d 1042 (5th Cir.), *cert. denied*, 522 U.S. 824, 118 S.Ct. 82, 139 L.Ed.2d 40 (1997) (teacher's sexual assaults on former student not linked to his duties and obligations as a teacher and therefore not "under color" of state law); *Jojola v. Chavez*, 55 F.3d 488 (10th Cir.1995) (school custodian who molested student not exercising state authority). *But see Seltzer–Bey v. Delo*, 66 F.3d 961 (8th Cir.1995) (corrections officer's sexual assault of inmate was under color of state law even though defendant's motivation was self-gratification).

8. 559 F.2d 1098 (7th Cir.1977).

9. *Id.* at 1100–1101.

10. 627 F.2d 934 (9th Cir.1980).

department's secondary hiring program as a "security teller" in a bank. The court held that although the officer was working outside the scope of his employment as a police officer, he had acted "under color of state law" because his primary duty was to contact the police department if a crime occurred.[11]

The Third Circuit also assumed that the action of an official outside the scope of his employment was nevertheless "under color" of state law.[12] Plaintiffs, members of the Accident Investigation Division of the Philadelphia Police Department, brought a claim of sexual harassment against their fellow workers and supervisors under Title VII and § 1983. One of the plaintiffs alleged harassment that included, among other things, obscene phone calls at her unlisted home phone number. The court did not discuss whether calls made by employees of the police department to the plaintiff's home during non-work hours were made "under color of state law."[13] Rather it assumed that the off-duty harassment constituted action "under color of state law" for purposes of § 1983, for it went on to address the elements of an equal protection claim for sexual discrimination under § 1983. In another case, the conduct of sheriff's deputies in supporting the sheriff's candidacy on the night before a local election was held state action, even though they were off duty, because of the nexus between the purpose of their electioneering and their official public responsibilities.[14] And an off-duty police officer working at a fast food restaurant as a private security guard acted under color of state law by wearing his uniform, displaying his badge, wearing his gun, and charging a patron with resisting a peace officer, all in proximity to his parked squad car. These trappings of office can thus transform what would otherwise be a purely private function into action "under color of" state law.[15]

Clearly, however, much off-duty conduct of state agents is not under color of state law. The Second Circuit so held in the case of an off-duty policeman who used his own weapon to shoot a guest in his own home. The Court observed that in using the weapon the defendant, intoxicated, was not invoking the authority of his department.[16] That same conclusion was reached when one of the defendant officers was the brother-in-law of the alleged victim of an assault.[17] A police officer who took a minor to his farm and sexually assaulted her was not acting under color of state law because the police officer was not acting, nor purporting to act, in an official capacity: he was off duty, out of uniform, unarmed, and driving

11. *Id.* at 937–38.

12. *Andrews v. City of Philadelphia*, 895 F.2d 1469 (3d Cir.1990).

13. *Id.* at 1475.

14. *Rossignol v. Voorhaar*, 316 F.3d 516 (4th Cir.2003).

15. *Pickrel v. City of Springfield, Illinois*, 45 F.3d 1115 (7th Cir.1995). *But cf. Chapman v. Higbee Co.*, 256 F.3d 416 (6th Cir.), *judgment vacated*, 270 F.3d 297 (6th Cir.2001) (off-duty officer employed as security guard was wearing official garb and carrying sidearm but held not state actor because stop and search was brief and he neither generated nor threatened arrest).

16. *Pitchell v. Callan*, 13 F.3d 545 (2d Cir.1994).

17. *Barna v. City of Perth Amboy*, 42 F.3d 809 (3d Cir.1994).

his personal vehicle.[18] A drunk, off-duty officer who struck and killed a pedestrian while driving his own vehicle outside his jurisdiction, who displayed no indicia of his office, who exercised no police power and was not pursuing any police activity did not act under color of state law.[19] Nor did a policewoman who, from her boyfriend's home, called 911 to report threatening conduct by his ex-girlfriend, since she did not restrain or otherwise exercise any police power.[20]

Some statuses are even more "off" than off-duty. A police officer shot the plaintiff's father after the officer had been stripped of his authority to perform any police duties because of a pending psychological examination. The Seventh Circuit held that while a state official may misuse powers he has the authority to use, if the official has no powers, then no powers exist to misuse.[21] In holding that the officer had not acted "under color" of state law, the court stated:

> While it is no doubt true that an officer who, motivated by personal animus, misuses his lawfully possessed authority to injure the plaintiff may be found to be acting under color or "pretense" of law, we have found no authority for expanding this concept of "pretense" of law to encompass the actions of an official who possessed absolutely no authority to act but nonetheless assumed the position of an imposter in pretending that he did.[22]

Apparent authority, for this court, is no substitute for a manifest lack of actual authority. Yet another court found that a government employee acting absent even apparent authority on a personal vendetta against her husband's ex-wife was acting "under color" of state law in accessing confidential information through a government-owned database at her place of employment merely because the state afforded her the means to do so![23]

In sum, the decisions in the "off-duty" cases sprawl untidily across three loose categories. There is the "without actual authority" approach, which rules out the possibility that an off-duty official is acting "under color of state law" if there is some crisp indicator that in fact he lacked authority to act despite having cloaked himself in a mantle of authority.[24] In the limited setting of off-duty officials, this approach echoes the more general position, repudiated by *Monroe v. Pape*, that conduct is "under

18. *Roe v. Humke*, 128 F.3d 1213 (8th Cir.1997).

19. *Latuszkin v. City of Chicago*, 250 F.3d 502 (7th Cir.2001).

20. *Redding v. St. Eward*, 241 F.3d 530 (6th Cir.2001).

21. *Gibson v. City of Chicago*, 910 F.2d at 1517.

22. *Id.* at 1518 (citation omitted). The same distinction between acting under "pretense" of law and in fact acting under law's "color" has been used to reject a claim against a police officer who, while on medical leave, shot and killed a bar patron who invited the officer to brawl outside the bar after the officer displayed his police identification to patrons, told them he was there to keep the peace, and asserted that his status as an officer entitled him to "look dirty" at the patron. *Parrilla–Burgos v. Hernandez–Rivera*, 108 F.3d 445 (1st Cir. 1997).

23. *McDade v. West*, 223 F.3d 1135 (9th Cir.2000).

24. *See, e.g., Barna; Searcy v. City of Dayton*, 38 F.3d 282 (6th Cir.1994); *Pitchell v. Callan*, 13 F.3d 545 (2d Cir.1994); and *Gibson v. City of Chicago*, 910 F.2d at 1517.

color of" state law only when it enjoys state authorization and approval. Second, there is the "indicia of authority" approach, far friendlier to a finding that the defendant has acted "under color of" state law. This approach answers the question affirmatively if the defendant displays sufficient trappings of state authority to lead a reasonable third-party observer to believe that the defendant is acting with government authorization.[25] And there is understandably scant authority for a third approach, which turns resolution of the question on the victim's or the defendant's own subjective perception that the defendant was acting under color of state law, even when there is no objective reason to believe that he was.[26] Related decisions governing undercover police informants have held them not to be acting under color of state law, more because the conduct in question was outside the scope of their assigned duties than because the necessity that they act in disguise precludes them from creating the reasonable impression that they are acting under color of state law.[27] And of course even a defendant who in one capacity is unarguably a public official does not act "under color of" state law when he is alleged to have violated federal law solely in another, purely private capacity.[28]

§ 2.16 Private Defendants and the "Under Color of State Law" Requirement

a. *Lugar v. Edmondson Oil Co.*[1]

In *Edmondson*, the Court analyzed the interplay between the Fourteenth Amendment requirement of "state action," needed to establish most constitutional claims brought under § 1983, and the statute's own requirement of action "under color of state law."

25. *See, e.g., Barreto–Rivera v. Medina–Vargas*, 168 F.3d 42 (1st Cir.1999) (although some evidence supported a conclusion that the officer was acting for personal motivation, evidence that the officer used his police baton, called for police backup, and shot his service revolver was sufficient to deny summary judgment on issue of acting under color of state law); *Pickrel v. City of Springfield, Illinois*, 45 F.3d 1115 (7th Cir.1995); *Gentry v. Lee's Summit*, 10 F.3d 1340 (8th Cir.1993); *Revene v. Charles County Commissioners*, 882 F.2d 870 (4th Cir.1989); *Lusby v. T.G. & Y. Stores, Inc.*, 749 F.2d 1423 (10th Cir.1984), *cert. denied*, 474 U.S. 818, 106 S.Ct. 65, 88 L.Ed.2d 53 (1985). *But see Colombo v. O'Connell*, 310 F.3d 115 (2d Cir.2002) (school superintendent did not act under color of state law but for personal motives by privately retaining lawyer to write letter to plaintiff recall petitioner threatening to sue her, when superintendent alleged recall petition libelled him) (alternative holding).

26. *See, e.g., Layne v. Sampley*, 627 F.2d 12 (6th Cir.1980); *Keller v. District of Columbia*, 809 F.Supp. 432 (E.D.Va.1993); *Manning v. Jones*, 696 F.Supp. 1231 (S.D.Ind.1988).

27. *See, e.g., Hiser v. City of Bowling Green*, 42 F.3d 382 (6th Cir.1994), *cert. denied*, 514 U.S. 1120, 115 S.Ct. 1984, 131 L.Ed.2d 871 (1995); *Ghandi v. Police Dep't of City of Detroit*, 823 F.2d 959 (6th Cir. 1987), *cert. denied*, 484 U.S. 1042, 108 S.Ct. 774, 98 L.Ed.2d 861 (1988).

28. *See Gritchen v. Collier*, 254 F.3d 807 (9th Cir.2001) (police officer not acting "under color" in threatening defamation action); *Waters v. City of Morristown, TN*, 242 F.3d 353 (6th Cir.2001) (defendant alleged to have acted as plaintiff's employer, a veterinarian, and not as city alderman).

§ 2.16

1. 457 U.S. 922, 102 S.Ct. 2744, 73 L.Ed.2d 482 (1982).

A debtor brought an action under § 1983 against a corporate creditor and its president alleging that, in attaching his property pursuant to the law of Virginia, the defendants acted jointly with the state to deprive him of his right to due process under the Fourteenth Amendment.[2] In overruling the Court of Appeals, the Court stated that "[w]hether they are identical or not, the state-action and the under-color-of-state-law requirements are obviously related. Indeed, until recently this Court did not distinguish between the two at all."[3]

The first question was whether the creditor's invocation of the state's prejudgment attachment procedure represented "state action" for purposes of the Fourteenth Amendment. The Court cited the *Sniadach* and *North Georgia Finishing* cases as authority for the finding that the present attachment procedure involves "state action" that satisfies the Fourteenth Amendment requirement. "[T]he Court has consistently held that constitutional requirements of due process apply to garnishment and prejudgment attachment procedures whenever officers of the State act jointly with a creditor in securing the property in dispute."[4]

The Court then considered whether the creditor's actions were also "under color of state law" within the meaning of § 1983. The Court stated that:

> If a defendant debtor in state-court collection proceedings can successfully challenge, on federal due process grounds, the plaintiff creditor's resort to the procedures authorized by state statute, it is difficult to understand why that same behavior by the state-court

2. *Id.* at 924–925, 102 S.Ct. at 2747.

3. *Id.* at 928, 102 S.Ct. at 2749. *See also United States v. Price*, 383 U.S. 787, 86 S.Ct. 1152, 16 L.Ed.2d 267 (1966).

4. 457 U.S. at 932–33, 102 S.Ct. at 2751–52. Carefully to be distinguished are situations in which a private party exercises authority conferred by the state but is not jointly participating with the state in implementing an unconstitutional, state-devised procedure. Thus in general "[p]rivate use of state-sanctioned private remedies or procedures does not rise to the level of state action." *Tulsa Professional Collection Services, Inc. v. Pope*, 485 U.S. 478, 485, 108 S.Ct. 1340, 1344, 99 L.Ed.2d 565 (1988). For example, an insurer that merely took advantage of state law provisions authorizing conversion from mutual to stock form was not a state actor, even when it obtained permission to do so from the state's insurance commissioner. *Gayman v. Principal Financial Services, Inc.*, 311 F.3d 851 (7th Cir.2002). A non-judicial private foreclosure sale did not make the creditor availing itself of that state procedure a state actor where the statute did not confer the power to make the sale but merely authorized the parties to contract for such foreclosure upon default. *Apao v. Bank of New York,* 324 F.3d 1091 (9th Cir.2003). A tax sale purchaser who initiated a quiet title action and allegedly violated the property owner's rights by failing to provide notice of the action did not function as a state actor because the state itself was not required by Michigan law to provide notice to the owner if the state took title to the property prior to the sale and the purchaser's relationship to the state was too distant to attribute the attribute conduct of the former to the latter. *Wittstock v. Mark A. Van Sile, Inc.*, 330 F.3d 899 (6th Cir.2003). And private attorneys, when they act independently of court employees, do not act under color of state law, or as Fourteenth Amendment state actors, merely because they are officers of the court. Thus it is widely agreed that a private lawyer does not become a state actor by issuing a subpoena. *Hahn v. Star Bank*, 190 F.3d 708, 717 (6th Cir.1999), *cert. denied*, 529 U.S. 1020, 120 S.Ct. 1423, 146 L.Ed.2d 314 (2000); *Barnard v. Young*, 720 F.2d 1188, 1189 (10th Cir.1983) (citing cases). This is true of a public defender as well; in representing an indigent defendant, the defender is performing a lawyer's traditional duties and is not acting under color of state law. *Miranda v. Clark County, Nev.*, 279 F.3d 1102 (9th Cir.2002).

> plaintiff should not provide a [federal or state court] cause of action under Section 1983. If the creditor-plaintiff violates the debtor-defendant's due process rights by seizing his property in accordance with statutory procedures, there is little or no reason to deny to the latter a cause of action under the federal statute, Section 1983, designed to provide judicial redress for just such constitutional violations.[5]

The Court made clear that "[i]f the challenged conduct of respondents constitutes [Fourteenth Amendment] state action . . . then that conduct was also action under color of state law and will support a suit under Section 1983."[6] However, the reverse is not necessarily true:

> First, although we hold that conduct satisfying the state-action requirement of the Fourteenth Amendment satisfies the [Section 1983] statutory requirement of action under color of state law, it does not follow that all conduct that satisfies the under-color-of-state-law requirement would satisfy the Fourteenth Amendment requirement of state action. If action under color of state law means nothing more than that the individual act "with knowledge of and pursuant to that statute"[7] then clearly under *Flagg Brothers* that would not, in itself, satisfy the state-action requirement of the Fourteenth Amendment. Second, although we hold in this case that the under-color-of-state-law requirement does not add anything not already included within the state-action requirement of the Fourteenth Amendment, § 1983 is applicable to other constitutional provisions and statutory provisions that contain no state-action requirement. Where such a federal right is at issue, the statutory concept of action under color of state law would be a distinct element of the case not satisfied implicitly by a finding of a violation of the particular right.[8]

In *Burrell v. Board of Trustees of Georgia Military College*,[9] the Eleventh Circuit repeated that the § 1983 "under color of state law"

5. *Lugar,* 457 U.S. at 934, 102 S.Ct. at 2752.

6. *Id.* at 935, 102 S.Ct. at 2752. *Accord, Brentwood Academy v. Tennessee Secondary School Athletic Ass'n*, 531 U.S. 288, 121 S.Ct. 924, 148 L.Ed.2d 807, n. 2 (2001). See the somewhat different statement of the First Circuit that the § 1983 "under color of" requirement "is coextensive with" the Fourteenth Amendment's "state action" requirement. *Perkins v. Londonderry Basketball Club*, 196 F.3d 13, 17 n. 1 (1st Cir. 1999). But in context this statement makes sense, because the court simply observed that a finding of no Fourteenth Amendment state action made unnecessary a separate analysis of the § 1983 "under color of" requirement.

7. *Id.* at 935 n.18, 102 S.Ct. at 2752 n.18 (*citing Adickes v. S. H. Kress & Co.*, 398 U.S. 144, 162 n. 23, 90 S.Ct. 1598, 1611 n. 23, 26 L.Ed.2d 142 (1970)).

8. *Id.* at 935 n.18, 102 S.Ct. at 2752 n.18 (emphasis added). However, the Supreme Court has indicated that two constitutional rights—freedom from involuntary servitude under the Thirteenth Amendment and a limited right to interstate travel—are affirmatively protected against any invasion, even by a private actor. *See Bray v. Alexandria Women's Health Clinic*, 506 U.S. 263, 113 S.Ct. 753, 122 L.Ed.2d 34 (1993).

9. 970 F.2d 785 (11th Cir.1992), *cert. denied*, 507 U.S. 1018, 113 S.Ct. 1814, 123 L.Ed.2d 445 (1993). Author Lewis was co-counsel for the government defendants in *Burrell*.

requirement does not necessarily satisfy the Fourteenth Amendment's "state action" requirement. The Eleventh Circuit stated that although misuse of state power may amount to conduct "under color of state law" for purposes of § 1983, the plaintiff must independently show Fourteenth Amendment "state action" by showing that the defendant's challenged actions were taken with the power granted by the state.[10] In other words, the defendant may have worn the state's clothing but not used the state's "night stick" to inflict the plaintiff's injury. Thus while private persons undoubtedly act "under color of" state law when they agree or conspire with government officials to deprive the plaintiff of federally protected rights,[11] the violation may not reflect the required "state action" if implemented through purely private means.[12] The

10. *Id.* at 790, n.12. *Cf. S.J. v. Kansas City Missouri Public School Dist.*, 294 F.3d 1025 (8th Cir.2002) (school volunteer who abused student living at his home not acting "under color of" state law because student's mother had privately made the living arrangement, even though volunteer met student at school and mother asserted his status as school volunteer induced her to let her daughter live with him and his family).

11. *See, e.g., Adickes v. S.H. Kress & Co.*, 398 U.S. 144, 90 S.Ct. 1598, 26 L.Ed.2d 142 (1970); *DuBose v. Kelly*, 187 F.3d 999 (8th Cir.1999), *appeal after remand,* 12 Fed. Appx. 428 (8th Cir.2001) (alleged conspiracy among trial court, defendant and defendant's counsel to "fix" trial made defendant and counsel state actors); *Davis v. Union Nat'l Bank*, 46 F.3d 24 (7th Cir.1994), *cert. denied*, 514 U.S. 1065, 115 S.Ct. 1696, 131 L.Ed.2d 560 (1995); *Burrell v. Board of Trustees of Georgia Military College*, 970 F.2d 785 (11th Cir.1992), *cert. denied*, 507 U.S. 1018, 113 S.Ct. 1814, 123 L.Ed.2d 445 (1993). For examples of § 1983 claims alleging conspiratorial deprivation of a predicate right, see *Pendleton v. St. Louis County*, 178 F.3d 1007 (8th Cir.1999); *Burrell v. Board of Trustees of Ga. Military College*, 970 F.2d 785 (11th Cir.1992), *cert. denied*, 507 U.S. 1018, 113 S.Ct. 1814, 123 L.Ed.2d 445 (1993); *Bell v. City of Milwaukee*, 746 F.2d 1205 (7th Cir.1984); and *Ryland v. Shapiro*, 708 F.2d 967 (5th Cir.1983). Courts commonly require heightened standards of pleading and evidence of such conspiracies. *See* § 2.12, *supra* and 5.80, infra. Moreover, the standard conspiracy elements of an agreement and overt act in furtherance thereof are required to subject a private actor to § 1983 on the theory that he was a joint actor with a state or local government. *See Brunette v. Humane Society of Ventura County*, 294 F.3d 1205 (9th Cir. 2002) (newspaper and reporters were not state actors even though unit of California government notified them, pursuant to long-standing practice, of alleged animal cruelty practices at plaintiff's ranch). And of course plaintiff's theory fails if the ostensible state actor with which it acted in concert is itself found not to be acting under color of state law. *E.F.W. v. St. Stephen's Indian High School*, 264 F.3d 1297 (10th Cir.2001).

12. Thus, for example, private attorneys, when they act independently of court employees, do not act under color of state law, or as 14th Amendment state actors, merely because they are officers of the court. Thus it is widely agreed that a private lawyer does not become a state actor by issuing a subpoena. *Hahn v. Star Bank*, 190 F.3d 708, 717 (6th Cir.1999), *cert. denied,* 529 U.S. 1020, 120 S.Ct. 1423, 146 L.Ed.2d 314 (2000); *Barnard v. Young*, 720 F.2d 1188, 1189 (10th Cir.1983) (citing cases). See note 4, *supra.* Nor does a private citizen become a state actor by initiating civil commitment procedures. *Bass v. Parkwood Hosp.*, 180 F.3d 234, 242 (5th Cir. 1999). *Pino v. Higgs*, 75 F.3d 1461, 1463–1466 (private therapist's advice to police that plaintiff be hospitalized, including report of noncriminal activities, does not constitute state action). Similarly, a licensed physician who submitted an affidavit to law enforcement officials that recommended involuntary commitment did not become a state actor by participating in a statutory scheme that any private citizen could invoke. *Scott v. Hern,* 216 F.3d 897, 906–907 (10th Cir.2000). And a privately engaged sexual abuse evaluator was not a state actor merely by virtue of knowledge that his reports would likely be used by the court. *Brown v. Newberger,* 291 F.3d 89, 93 (1st Cir.2002). Similarly, neither voluntary furnishing of information to police, *see Morris v. Dillard Dept. Stores*, 277 F.3d 743 (5th Cir.2001) (merchant not state actor based on report of store employee of suspected shoplifting) and *Rivera-Ramos v. Roman*,

Edmondson and *Burrell* opinions illustrate why in most § 1983 actions—indeed for deprivations of all constitutional rights other than the rights to interstate travel and freedom from slavery which are enforceable against private pensions—the plaintiff must first make sure that the defendant's action can be characterized as "state action" under the Fourteenth Amendment. If so, the path has been paved for proving a predicate violation of federal constitutional law; at the same time, the plaintiff will be assured that the defendant's conduct is also "under color of" state law.

b. Circuit Decisions

Unsurprisingly, given the low bar erected by the Section 1983 "under color of" requirement, the circuit decisions more commonly dismiss for failure to meet the Fourteenth Amendment "state action" requirement. In *Willis v. University Health Servs.*,[13] the Eleventh Circuit affirmed a grant of summary judgment in favor of a defendant hospital based on the plaintiff's inability to show that the hospital was a state actor with respect to the challenged conduct.[14] The Court rejected plaintiff's arguments that the hospital was a state actor under the "public function," "joint action/symbiotic relationship," or "nexus/state compulsion" tests.

The Eighth Circuit reviewed allegations that Tops Bar violated § 1983 by regularly offering female, but not male, patrons free drinks and occasionally denying male patrons entry until 10 p.m.[15] The plaintiff charged that the practices of Tops Bar discriminated against him on the basis of gender, violating the Equal Protection Clause of Fourteenth Amendment. The court concluded that the complaint failed to state a § 1983 claim for want of Fourteenth Amendment "state action" Whatever its regulatory involvement and authority over the bar, "[t]he State of Missouri did not play any part in establishing or in enforcing the alleged discriminatory policy."[16] On the other hand, a city escaped liability on

156 F.3d 276, 282 (1st Cir.1998), nor mandatory reporting of suspected child abuse to a government enforcement agency, *see Brown v. Newberger*, 291 F.3d at 93, transforms the reporter into a state actor. *But see Jensen v. Lane County*, 222 F.3d 570, 574–75 (9th Cir.2000) (private physician serving under contract with government officials to evaluate potential mental patients brought to treatment facilities by police held state actor when physician had significant consultation and interaction with county mental health workers). *See also Brown v. Newberger*, 291 F.3d at 94 (court-ordered sexual abuse evaluators implicitly held to be acting under color of law because of their "close association with the judicial process," but accorded absolute, quasi-judicial immunity.)

13. 993 F.2d 837 (11th Cir.1993), *cert. denied*, 510 U.S. 976, 114 S.Ct. 468, 126 L.Ed.2d 420 (1993).

14. *Id.* at 838. *See also Morris v. Dillard Dept. Stores*, 277 F.3d 743 (5th Cir. 2001) (merchant not state actor based on report of store employee of suspected shoplifting where officer then conducted independent investigation); *Roche v. John Hancock Mut. Life Ins. Co.*, 81 F.3d 249 (1st Cir.1996) (where police exercised independent judgment in applying for arrest warrant, employer who investigated threatening phone calls and forwarded information to police not state actor in connection with employee's arrest).

15. *Comiskey v. JFTJ Corp.*, 989 F.2d 1007 (8th Cir.1993).

16. *Id.* at 1011. Cf. *Johnson v. Knowles*, 113 F.3d 1114 (9th Cir.), *cert. denied*, 522 U.S. 996, 118 S.Ct. 559, 139 L.Ed.2d 401 (1997) (although political party committees were regulated by state, they are private actors and so party committee

the "color of state law" ground when one of its police department informants stole a check from and then killed his apartment mate. Neither of these acts fell within the scope of the activities for which the informant was working for the police; accordingly, the injuries he inflicted were not performed under color of state law.[17] And a private citizen's ad hoc assistance rendered to law enforcement officials at their request does not make the citizen a state actor, absent any agreement appointing the citizen a government agent.[18]

§§ 2.17–2.19 [Reserved]

C. THE CASE AGAINST INDIVIDUAL DEFENDANTS

§ 2.20 In General

The case against an individual agent appears to be surprisingly straightforward. But the Court has constructed the comprehensive affirmative defense of immunity that, if applicable, more than offsets the loose prima facie requirements. These two characteristics stand in antithesis from the stringent prima facie case and non-existing immunity intrinsic to the case against an entity. If the plaintiff establishes liability in an individual defendant, he is eligible for compensatory damages and, in a proper case, punitive damages.

§ 2.21 The Prima Facie Case

The prima facie case against the defendant sued in her individual capacity remains, somewhat remarkably, judicially unembellished. The plaintiff's evidence simply tracks the statute in a straight forward fashion. He must first allege that the defendant is a "person" as that term is used in the text of the statute.[1] Second, there must have been a deprivation of some right of the plaintiff that is protected under the

members did not act "under color" of state law in ousting other members).

17. *Hiser v. City of Bowling Green*, 42 F.3d 382 (6th Cir.1994), *cert. denied*, 514 U.S. 1120, 115 S.Ct. 1984, 131 L.Ed.2d 871 (1995). *See also Rodriguez v. Weprin*, 116 F.3d 62 (2d Cir.1997) (court-appointed lawyers serving as counsel to defendant do not act "under color of" state law); *Edwards v. Wallace Community College*, 49 F.3d 1517 (11th Cir.1995) (because defendant co-employees lacked supervisory authority over plaintiff, they did not act pursuant to power possessed by virtue of state authority and thus were not acting "under color of" state law even though they allegedly harassed plaintiff on the job during working hours).

18. *Muick v. Glenayre Electronics*, 280 F.3d 741 (7th Cir.2002) (employer seized plaintiff's laptop computer at behest of federal agents) (*Bivens* action); *Proffitt v. Ridgway*, 279 F.3d 503 (7th Cir.2002) (bystander who assisted police in subduing arrestee in response to police request not state actor).

§ 2.21

1. 42 U.S.C.A. § 1983 (1988). Although this requirement was until *Monell v. Dep't of Social Services, infra* § 2.31, a significant hurdle in suits against local entities, and today is an absolute obstacle to § 1983 actions against states sued eo nominee, *see Will v. Michigan Dep't of Police, infra* §§ 2.35 & 2.42, it will always be met in regard to private persons.

Constitution[2] or by *federal* law.[3] Third, the private defendant must have acted "under color of" state law in effecting the deprivation. Finally, the plaintiff must show that the deprivation caused some harm remediable by injunction or damages.[4] And *Monroe*, of course, dramatically widened the field for individual liability by making it immaterial whether the defendant acted pursuant or contrary to local government authorization.[5] It should be noted that § 1983 contains no general requirement that the plaintiff prove the defendant acted with any particular state of mind.[6] Some predicate constitutional violations may require such proof-examples include Eighth Amendment deliberate indifference, First Amendment intent to retaliate for the exercise of protected rights, and Due Process violations, which the Court has insisted are established only if the defendant acted with a more than negligent, probably reckless or intentional, state of mind.[7] Otherwise, simple negligence may serve as a basis for § 1983 liability. Not only in general need plaintiff not prove defendant's state of mind, but proof of a bad state of mind will not alone result in liability.[8]

2. Rather than, say, an ancillary subconstitutional evidentiary protection, like the rights protected by *Miranda v. Arizona*, 384 U.S. 436, 86 S.Ct. 1602, 16 L.Ed.2d 694 (1966). *See Jones v. Cannon*, 174 F.3d 1271 (11th Cir.1999) and circuit authority cited therein; *Neighbour v. Covert*, 68 F.3d 1508 (2d Cir.1995), *cert. denied*, 516 U.S. 1174, 116 S.Ct. 1267, 134 L.Ed.2d 214 (1996) (violations of *Miranda* rights not actionable under § 1983). *But cf. California Attorneys for Criminal Justice v. Butts*, 195 F.3d 1039, 1046–47 (9th Cir.1999), *cert. denied sub nom. Butts v. McNally*, 530 U.S. 1261, 120 S.Ct. 2717, 147 L.Ed.2d 983 (2000) and *Cooper v. Dupnik*, 963 F.2d 1220, 1243–44 (9th Cir.1992), *cert. denied*, 506 U.S. 953, 113 S.Ct. 407, 121 L.Ed.2d 332 (1992) (holding claim stated for violation of *Miranda* safeguards if violation accompanied by coercive tactics that, in combination, violated plaintiff's Fifth Amendment right against self-incrimination).

3. Not state law. *See Knight v. Jacobson*, 300 F.3d 1272 (11th Cir.2002) (arrest arguably violating Florida law could not support § 1983 action because it did not violate Fourth Amendment); *Ove v. Gwinn*, 264 F.3d 817 (9th Cir.2001) (complaint focusing on state statutory violation fails to assert potentially available Fourth Amendment claims and is accordingly insufficient); *Case v. Kitsap Co. Sheriff's Dep't*, 249 F.3d 921, 929 (9th Cir.2001) (violation of state law requiring arrestee to be brought before judge promptly cannot be predicate of Section 1983 claim or defeat defendant's right to qualified immunity from damages under that statute); *Wilson v. Meeks*, 52 F.3d 1547, 1554 (10th Cir.1995) (1983 claim cannot be founded on violation of police department's own regulation); *Podgurski v. Suffolk County*, unpublished opinion, (2d Cir. 1995), *cert. denied*, 516 U.S. 1048, 116 S.Ct. 711, 133 L.Ed.2d 666 (1996) (mem.) (boundary dispute against county not actionable as federal law violation). *See also Ghana v. Pearce*, 159 F.3d 1206 (9th Cir.1998) (alleged violation of Interstate Corrections Compact not predicate for § 1983 claim because not "federal" law).

4. Qualified immunity, as it now stands, insulates defendants from monetary damages only. An injunction may still be issued constraining the defendant in some way, and thus § 1988 would still provide for an award of attorney fees, despite a finding of qualified immunity. Plaintiffs' attorneys are thus not wholly without inducement for accepting cases where a grant of qualified immunity is likely.

A fifth element, i.e., that a policy or practice be shown, is only applicable in § 1983 actions against entity defendants.

5. 365 U.S. at 183–85, 81 S.Ct. at 482–83. *See* § 2.4, *supra*.

6. The *Parratt* Court, citing *Monroe*, asserted that neither the language nor legislative history of § 1983 has "been found by this Court to contain a state-of-mind requirement." *See Parratt v. Taylor*, 451 U.S. 527, 534, 101 S.Ct. 1908, 1912, 68 L.Ed.2d 420 (1981), *overruled in part by Daniels v. Williams*, 474 U.S. 327, 106 S.Ct. 662, 88 L.Ed.2d 662 (1986). *See, e.g., Hudson v. New York City*, 271 F.3d 62 (2d Cir.2001) (jury instructions erroneously suggested that plaintiff, to prevail under Section 1983, had to prove defendants' intent to violate constitutional rights where predicate Fourth Amendment violation required no such intent).

7. *Daniels v. Williams*, 474 U.S. 327, 106 S.Ct. 662, 88 L.Ed.2d 662 (1986) (Due Process).

8. *See Bethesda Lutheran Homes and Servs., Inc. v. Leean*, 154 F.3d 716 (7th Cir.1998).

D. INDIVIDUAL DEFENDANTS AND THEIR QUALIFIED IMMUNITY

§ 2.22 A Brief History of Individual Defendant Immunity[1]

Not long after *Monroe's* expansive statement of individual liability, the Court began to embrace a doctrine that defendants sued in their individual capacity[2] with respect to discretionary, as opposed to merely ministerial, functions would enjoy qualified immunity from damages[3] calculated to counter its generous prima facie case. The early history of immunity reflects the Court's effort to apply a transplanted common law doctrine to the particular circumstances of § 1983 defendants. This approach found support in the language of 42 U.S.C.A. § 1988,[4] which counsels courts to fill § 1983 cracks with spackle from state common law.[5] The Court's early grapplings with qualified immunity for individual defendants—*Tenney v. Brandhove*,[6] *Pierson v. Ray*,[7] *Imbler v. Pachtman*,[8] and *Scheuer v. Rhodes*[9]—were obedient to this task of infusing a general statutory liability standard with common law learning.[10]

§ 2.22

1. A comprehensive history of § 1983 immunities is well beyond the scope of this work. As a starting point, *see* Peter H. Schuck, *Suing Government: Citizen Remedies for Official Wrongs* 89–93, 203–05 (1983). A brief survey of the history of judicial immunity is contained in Peter H. Schuck, *The Civil Liability of Judges in the United States*, 37 Am. J. Comp. L. 655, 662–65 (1989).

2. It is settled that when officials are sued in their official capacities they are not eligible for either absolute or qualified immunity, *see, e.g., Alkire v. Irving*, 330 F.3d 802 (6th Cir.2003), and that such official-capacity suits are functionally indistinguishable from suits that name as defendant the entity the official serves. *See, e.g., Alexander v. Fulton County*, 207 F.3d 1303, 1322 n. 14 (11th Cir.2000).

3. The defense does not shield the officials who claim it from liability for equitable remedies, including reinstatement. *See, e.g., Pace v. Moriarty*, 83 F.3d 261 (8th Cir.1996). Nevertheless, the "damages" from which individual defendants are exempt when qualified immunity attaches may include costs, attorneys' fees and related expenses, even when the plaintiff seeks only injunctive or other equitable substantive relief. *D'Aguanno v. Gallagher*, 50 F.3d 877 (11th Cir.1995).

4. 42 U.S.C.A. § 1988 (1988).

5. Section 1988 directs in part that state common law, to the extent that it is not inconsistent with federal law, shall apply "in all cases [for the protection of civil rights] where [federal laws] are not adapted to the object, or are deficient in the provisions necessary to furnish suitable remedies." *Id.* Some of the interpretive difficulties with this provision are explored by Beermann, 42 Stan.L.Rev. at 58–75. He also concludes that the common law to which § 1988 directs the courts is not the common law the courts have followed. See *id.* at 61–63. Section 1988 is examined in more detail in Chapter 4, *infra*.

6. 341 U.S. 367, 379, 71 S.Ct. 783, 789, 95 L.Ed. 1019 (1951) (creating absolute immunity for state legislators' activity).

7. 386 U.S. 547, 554, 557, 87 S.Ct. 1213, 1218, 1219, 18 L.Ed.2d 288 (1967) (establishing a "qualified" defense of "good faith and probable cause" for police officers and absolute immunity for judicial officers).

8. 424 U.S. 409, 427, 96 S.Ct. 984, 993, 47 L.Ed.2d 128 (1976) (declaring absolute immunity for prosecutorial activity).

9. 416 U.S. 232, 238–49, 94 S.Ct. 1683, 1687–93, 40 L.Ed.2d 90 (1974) (containing Chief Justice Burger's full explanation of the "reasonable grounds" and "good-faith belief" version of qualified immunity for executive officers); *see also* Jerry L. Mashaw, *Civil Liability of Government Officers: Property Rights and Official Accountability*, 42 Law & Contemp. Probs. 8, 14–21 (1978) (providing a useful overview of executive immunity and its rationales).

10. *See* Mashaw, 42 Law & Contemp. Probs. at 14–16 (arguing that executive im-

In *Scheuer*, for example, the Court relied on two customary rationales for executive immunity: a "fairness" concern stemming from the injustice of holding an official liable in the absence of bad faith, and the fear of deterring and interfering with the functions of state government ("federalism").[11] Objective "reasonableness" and subjective "good faith" elements of qualified immunity were to be measured by the totality of the circumstances confronting the official at the time of the challenged conduct, considered in light of the scope of the officer's discretion.[12] A year later, however, in *Wood v. Strickland*,[13] the Court departed from this traditional approach, the first step on a march to the avowedly policy-based test it would announce in *Harlow v. Fitzgerald*[14] and *Anderson v. Creighton*[15]—the test that still prevails.

munity, as distinguished from sovereign and probably judicial immunity, is a relatively recent development).

11. *See Scheuer v. Rhodes*, 416 U.S. 232, 240, 94 S.Ct. 1683, 1688, 40 L.Ed.2d 90 (1974). In a rare category of cases where the executive or administrative official's challenged conduct is mandated by law, a key reason for immunity—encouraging the fearless exercise of discretion—disappears and the defense will not lie. *See McCullough v. Horton*, 69 F.3d 918 (8th Cir.1995) (state court clerk could not claim immunity for failing to provide transcript to inmate as required by court order). On the other hand, if a court deems the defendant's conduct clearly beyond the scope of his official authority, he enjoys no immunity because on that view the challenged act could not have been mandatory or discretionary! *In re Allen*, 106 F.3d 582 (4th Cir.1997), *cert. denied sub nom. McGraw v. Better Gov't Bureau, Inc.*, 522 U.S. 1047, 118 S.Ct. 689, 139 L.Ed.2d 635 (1998) (official must defend § 1983 claim challenging his establishment of a government agency corporation with personal funds). Ironically, the latter circumstance might lead to decisions favoring a defendant, on the ground that the challenged conduct could not be "under color of" state law or constitute unconstitutional "state action."

12. *See Scheuer*, 416 U.S. at 247–48, 94 S.Ct. at 1692. While the Court did not purport to premise its search for the existence of immunities on § 1988, it clearly did rest its finding on common law understandings. *See id.* at 238–48 & n.4, 94 S.Ct. at 1687–93 & n.4. Moreover, the Court's result was consistent with contemporary common law understanding. *See* Restatement (Second) of Torts § 895D (1979).

13. 420 U.S. 308, 95 S.Ct. 992, 43 L.Ed.2d 214 (1975), *overruled by Harlow v. Fitzgerald*, 457 U.S. 800, 102 S.Ct. 2727, 73 L.Ed.2d 396 (1982).

14. 457 U.S. 800, 818, 102 S.Ct. 2727, 2738, 73 L.Ed.2d 396 (1982) (holding that discovery should not be permitted until the court answers the threshold question "whether [the] law was clearly established at the time an action occurred").

15. 483 U.S. 635, 639–41, 107 S.Ct. 3034, 3038–40, 97 L.Ed.2d 523 (1987) (applying the qualified immunity doctrine to the execution of a search warrant, and holding that *Harlow* eliminated an inquiry into the subjective intent of the official and that the trial court should test the "objective legal reasonableness" of the challenged conduct against "clearly established" law). This departure from the immunity formula received from the common law rested "solely on the basis of policy considerations such as whether liability would have an undue chilling effect on decisionmaking." Kramer & Sykes, 1987 Sup.Ct.Rev. at 266. *But cf.* John C. Jeffries, *Compensation for Constitutional Torts: Reflections on the Significance of Fault*, 88 Mich.L.Rev. 82, 86 n.22 (1989) (suggesting that there may be some vitality left in the subjective prong if plaintiff "makes concrete and detailed allegations fairly suggestive of official bad faith"). The Court of Appeals for the District of Columbia recognizes such a remnant of the subjective test. It permits the plaintiff to defeat immunity by pleading malice with specificity and offering noncircumstantial proof of that state of mind. *See Siegert v. Gilley*, 895 F.2d 797, 800–02 (D.C.Cir.1990) (finding that "the invalidating motivation [must be] pleaded with the offer of noncircumstantial proof required to satisfy our heightened pleading standard"), aff'd on other grounds, 500 U.S. 226, 111 S.Ct. 1789, 114 L.Ed.2d 277 (1991). *But see Crawford–El v. Britton*,

Wood[16] introduced a new variable into the qualified immunity calculus by specifying that the "objective" prong of immunity identified in *Scheuer* required the defendant to demonstrate the reasonableness of her conduct in relation to the content of "settled, indisputable law." Immunity attached only if defendants proved two conditions: (1) that the challenged act was objectively reasonable in light of settled law establishing a violation of a federal[17] right and (2) that the conduct was motivated by subjective good faith.[18]

Justices Powell and Rehnquist, two of the four dissenters from this part of the opinion, would later take leading roles in forging more generous immunities. They referred to the majority's description of the objective branch as a "harsh standard, requiring [defendants to have] knowledge of what is characterized as 'settled, indisputable law' [and accordingly leaving] little substance to the doctrine of qualified immunity."[19] That standard, they argued, would impose damage liability even if the administrator, acting in good faith, was ignorant of the law. Under such conditions, liability would rest on "an unwarranted assumption as to what school officials know or can know about the law and constitutional rights."[20] The problem, Justice Powell predicted, was that "[t]hese officials [would] now act at the peril of some judge or jury subsequently finding that a good-faith belief as to the applicable law was mistaken."[21]

523 U.S. 574, 118 S.Ct. 1584, 140 L.Ed.2d 759 (1998), (overruling *Siegert*, and holding that there is no heightened pleading requirement in individual defendant cases.) *Crawford–El* is discussed more fully *infra*.

16. The case arose when school board members expelled several high school students, arguably without sufficient procedural safeguards. Although acknowledging that under existing precedent some process was required before school children could be expelled, *see* 420 U.S. at 323 n.15, 95 S.Ct. at 1001, n.15, the Court did not reach the procedural due process question because it had not been decided by the Court of Appeals. See id. at 323, 95 S.Ct. at 1001. Thus, the cause was remanded. Cf. id. at 327, 95 S.Ct. at 1003 (Powell, J., concurring in part and dissenting in part) (noting that a second school board hearing may have cured defects at a prior hearing). On this point there was unanimity. *See id.*

The more difficult issue was whether the school board members were entitled to some form of immunity. Justice White treated the general question of immunity for school administrators as one of first impression. He began by noting the split in the lower courts concerning the proper standard for the context, *see id.* at 315 & n.7, 95 S.Ct. at 997 & n.7. He then surveyed *Tenney v. Brandhove; Pierson v. Ray*; and *Scheuer v. Rhodes*, resolving the issue in favor of qualified, good faith immunity for school board members from liability for damages in § 1983 actions, *see id.* at 316–322.

17. Not a state law violation. *See Case v. Kitsap Co. Sheriff's Dep't,* 249 F.3d 921, 929 (9th Cir.2001) (violation of state law requiring arrestee to be brought before judge promptly cannot be predicate of Section 1983 claim or defeat defendant's right to qualified immunity from damages under that statute); *Wilson v. Meeks,* 52 F.3d 1547, 1554 (10th Cir.1995) (granting qualified immunity despite violation of police department's internal regulation); *Gagne v. City of Galveston*, 805 F.2d 558, 560 (5th cir.1986) (violations of local law irrelevant to official's entitlement to qualified immunity); *Backlund v. Barnhart*, 778 F.2d 1386, 1390 n. 5 (9th Cir.1985) (same).

18. *See id.* at 321–22, 95 S.Ct. at 1000–1001.

19. *Id.* at 329 (Powell, J., concurring in part and dissenting in part).

20. *Id.*

21. *Id.* Justice Powell rightly doubted that school officials would have knowledge of any but the most settled constitutional law. As a predictor of the future development of the immunity defense, however, he proved wrong in two respects.

His prediction proved ironic in *Harlow*[22] when those same dissenters, now joining a majority, confined the inquiry to the factor they had

First, it was uncertain in 1975 that doctrinal "settledness" or the reasonableness of the official's conduct would be questions for a jury. Not until *Harlow* and *Anderson*, respectively, were these questions addressed, and they were held generally to be questions for the Court. Second, as Justice Powell later realized, requiring the defendant to have knowledge of "settled, indisputable law" before subjecting her to liability in practice imposes a litigation hardship on the plaintiff rather than the defendant.

Proving that law is indisputably settled appears to be a formidable task. In Wood itself, for example, the district court had made a specific finding, unchallenged on appeal, that the officials bore no ill will toward the students. *See Wood*, 420 U.S. at 314, 95 S.Ct. at 997. Accordingly, defendants surmounted the subjective prong of the new test. The debate centered on the objective prong of the test and whether it was fair to charge the defendants with knowledge of the local status of the right to process before expulsion, or with knowledge of what constituted "settledness." The right to process as a necessary procedural incident to a ten-day suspension from public school had been decided in *Goss v. Lopez*, 419 U.S. 565, 95 S.Ct. 729, 42 L.Ed.2d 725 (1975), earlier in the same term. In arguing against the majority's "standard of required knowledge" in *Wood*, Justice Powell questioned whether school administrators could be expected to know that *Goss* was settled law. *See Wood*, 420 U.S. at 329, 95 S.Ct. at 1004 (Powell, J., concurring in part and dissenting in part).

Justice Powell's doubt, in the specific context, is problematic for a number of reasons. First, the *Wood* majority did not purport to decide whether the law was "settled," but simply remanded. Because it was not then clear whether the "settledness" issue raised a legal or factual question, the dissent's concern was somewhat premature. Second, despite Powell's claim that "most lawyers would have thought, prior to [*Goss*], that the law to the *contrary* was settled, indisputable and unquestioned," id., the majority noted that the courts of appeals had uniformly held that process was due before dismissal from public school. *See id.* at 323 n.15, 95 S.Ct. at 1002 n.15. Perhaps more important, in *Goss* itself the Court listed ten lower court cases that had required process before expulsion and dozens of others requiring process before dismissals. *See Goss*, 419 U.S. at 576–78 n.8, 95 S.Ct. at 737–38 n.8. Included within that list were district and appellate court decisions from the Eighth Circuit, which decided *Wood*.

Moreover, Justice Powell's lament was somewhat disingenuous. He dissented in *Goss*, but he went to great lengths in that opinion to distinguish the need for procedural safeguards that would accompany an expulsion—the situation in *Wood*—from the absence of need in the context of a relatively short suspension—the context of *Goss*. *See id.* at 585, 589, 590, 591, 595, 95 S.Ct. at 741, 743, 744, 745, 746 (Powell, J., dissenting) (distinguishing between relatively "routine" forms of discipline and more severe forms of school dismissals and punishment). He specifically noted that both historically and under the laws of the state where *Goss* arose, a hearing was required for the "incomparably more serious matter" of expulsion. *Id.* at 585 n.2, 95 S.Ct. at 741 n.2; see also id. at 595 & n.14, 95 S.Ct. at 746 & n.14 (suggesting that the Court should not and need not interfere with traditional disciplinary schemes used in public schools, which included no hearing for "routine" suspensions). Finally, he agreed with the majority's suggestion that any " 'fair-minded school principal' " would impose upon himself some minimum procedural safeguards prior to expulsion. *Id.* at 596 n.15, 95 S.Ct. at 747 n.15 (quoting majority opinion). In short, there was clear legal and historical precedent for the majority's position; it was "indisputably settled" in this context, and there was no "harshness" involved.

22. *Harlow v. Fitzgerald* and its successor, *Anderson v. Creighton* were not actions under § 1983 but actions against federal agents that arose directly under the Constitution. The Court first recognized an implied private right of action against individual federal agents for Constitutional violations in *Bivens v. Six Unknown Named Agents of Fed. Bureau of Narcotics*, 403 U.S. 388, 91 S.Ct. 1999, 29 L.Ed.2d 619 (1971) (permitting damages action against federal narcotics agents for arrest and search violative of 4th Amendment). *See also Davis v. Passman*, 442 U.S. 228, 99 S.Ct. 2264, 60 L.Ed.2d 846 (1979) (permitting employment discrimination claim against member of Congress under the equal protection component of the 5th amendment's due process clause). But the

once found illegitimate, the state of constitutional precedent on the eve of the challenged conduct.[23] The new majority discarded the subjective prong and in the process affected a dramatic expansion of the affirmative defense. By declaring the new immunity forfeitable solely by reference to the state of the law, the Court turned its back on the common law tradition that tied immunity to lack of culpability and, in turn, the absence of a need to deter. Instead, *Harlow*'s majority justified abandoning the good faith requirement largely as a response to the practical litigation burdens encountered by government officials accused of federal law violations when they attempted to establish their immunity.[24] The Court summarized its purely objective test as follows: Government officials "are shielded from liability for civil damages insofar as their conduct does not violate clearly established statutory or constitutional rights (the 'law prong') of which a reasonable person would have known (the 'fact prong')."[25]

The new majority must have realized on reflection that, from the defendant's perspective, the troublesome aspect of common law qualified immunity was the subjective prong, which entailed "broad-ranging discovery and the deposing of numerous persons, including an official's professional colleagues. Inquiries of this kind can be peculiarly disruptive of effective government."[26] To avoid such disruptions, the Court simply jettisoned the subjective standard, relying entirely on an inquiry into the official defendant's "presumptive knowledge of and respect for 'basic, unquestioned constitutional rights.' "[27]Arguably, even if plaintiff produces evidence of defendant's malicious state of mind, the immunity would not be defeated.[28] If, *as a matter of law*, the official could not have known about the existence of the right allegedly infringed, he escaped

qualified immunity principles developed in § 1983 and *Bivens* actions are interchangeable. *See infra*, this Chapter, Part G., for a fuller discussion of *Bivens* claims and the numerous exceptions thereto.

23. *See Harlow*, 457 U.S. at 818, 102 S.Ct. at 2738 (holding that objective reasonableness of an official's conduct is to be "measured by reference to clearly established law ... at the time an action occurred").

24. *See id.* at 806, 814–19, 102 S.Ct. at 2732, 2736–39. The new test was foreshadowed by the Court's decision in *Procunier v. Navarette*, 434 U.S. 555, 564 & n. 11, 98 S.Ct. 855, 861 & n. 11, 55 L.Ed.2d 24 (1978) (requiring a closeness between precedent and the right asserted). *See also* Oren, 50 U.Pitt.L.Rev. at 980–81 & n.195 (discussing *Procunier* and the fine distinctions that could make a precedent inadequate to establish an asserted right).

25. *Harlow*, 457 U.S. at 818, 102 S.Ct. at 2738.

26. *Harlow*, 457 U.S. at 817, 102 S.Ct. at 2738 (footnotes omitted).

27. *Id.* at 815, 102 S.Ct. at 2736 (quoting *Wood*, 420 U.S. at 322, 95 S.Ct. at 1001).

28. One passage in *Malley v. Briggs*, 475 U.S. 335, 106 S.Ct. 1092, 89 L.Ed.2d 271 (1986) seems to render the defendant's state of mind irrelevant: "Under the *Harlow* standard, ... an allegation of malice is not sufficient to defeat immunity if the defendant acted in an objectively reasonable manner." Yet in the same opinion Justice White wrote: "As the qualified immunity defense has evolved, it provides ample protection to all but the plainly incompetent *or* those who *knowingly violate the law*." (emphasis supplied). Whether qualified immunity is available at all or restricted where the plaintiff can show an unlawful or malicious state of mind element as part of the predicate right is explored more fully infra. The Supreme Court's decision in *Crawford–El v. Britton* suggests that a defendant's retaliatory or otherwise unlawful state of mind will not defeat qualified immunity, which prevails either if the challenged right was not clearly established when defendant acted or if the violation of such a right was not objectively unreasonable.

accountability. "Democracy in the jury box"[29] was abandoned. As a result, the individual defendant action seemed to have lost its utility as a medium for expounding new constitutional rights, because only rights well settled by earlier decisions would be actionable. But Supreme Court decisions in the late 1990's, *Conn v. Gabbert and Wilson v. Layne*, both discussed below, have since restored the potential of the § 1983 action against individual officials as a vehicle for declaring constitutional rights, by directing trial courts ordinarily not to reach the "clearly established law" question unless they have first determined that the claimed right currently states a cognizable violation of federal law.

Anderson extended *Harlow's* immunity standard to a lower-level official and expanded it in substance by conferring immunity unless the alleged federal law violation was established in a highly "particularized" way. Under this formulation, a right is clearly established only if it was announced in circumstances so closely analogous that a reasonable official in the defendant's position should realize the applicability of the settled precedent. Further, the officer does not forfeit the immunity merely because it was clearly settled that his conduct was in violation of state (or, in a *Bivens* action, federal) law; rather, it must be settled that the federal right plaintiff relies on was then definitively declared by an authoritative decision closely on point.[30]

Deciding on the degree of particularity by which prior decisions must condemn the defendant's currently challenged conduct is often a litigation-breeding enterprise. For example, in *Mendoza v. Block*,[31] a Ninth Circuit panel considered it clearly established that police officers' excessive force in making an arrest violates the Fourth Amendment rights of the arrestee, adding that this conclusion holds in "any arrest situation where force is used, whether it involves physical restraint, use of a baton, use of a gun, or use of a dog. We do not believe that a more particularized expression of the law is necessary for law enforcement officials using police dogs to understand that under some circumstances the use of such a 'weapon' might become unlawful." But a subsequent panel of the same circuit later limited the quoted statement to "the proposition that some uses of dogs will in particular instances violate clearly established law." The panel went on to hold that at the time defendant police officers acted, it was not "clearly established that it was unlawful to use police dogs to search for and apprehend concealed suspects by biting and seizing them."[32] Nevertheless this *Chew* decision

29. The phrase is borrowed from Aviam Soifer, *Moral Ambition, Formalism, and the "Free World" of DeShaney*, 57 Geo. Wash.L.Rev. 1513, 1528 (1989).

30. *See, e.g., Russell v. Selsky*, 35 F.3d 55 (2d Cir.1994) (prison regulation prohibited defendant from serving as both review officer and hearing officer in disciplinary proceeding, but court conferred immunity on defendant who did so because clear precedent did not then accord inmates a due process right to fair hearing).

31. 27 F.3d 1357, 1361–62 (9th Cir. 1994).

32. *Chew v. Gates*, 27 F.3d 1432, 1448–49 (9th Cir.1994), *cert. denied*, 513 U.S. 1148, 115 S.Ct. 1097, 130 L.Ed.2d 1065 (1995). The panel relied on the fact that the only reported decision passing on the constitutionality of using dogs to apprehend fleeing or concealed suspects by biting and seizing them had upheld the practice, even though the Ninth Circuit judges "seriously

cleared the way for a subsequent determination that the law now is established that an excessively long dog bite facilitated by the police violates the Constitution,[33] although dogs themselves are not suable "persons" within the meaning of Section 1983.[34]

Anderson, an FBI agent, participated in an illegal search of the Creightons' home in an effort to find Mrs. Creighton's brother, a bank robbery suspect. The agents, pleading qualified immunity, admitted knowing that warrantless searches generally violated the Fourth Amendment but asserted that they could not have realized from analogous authority the illegality of their particular conduct on the facts in question.[35] Justice Scalia, speaking for the majority, ruled that an officer could not be said to have unreasonably disregarded "clearly established" law unless authoritative constitutional precedent closely on point existed at the time of the alleged violation.[36] This standard subtly alters the *Harlow* settledness requirement, in two ways. First, it intensifies the burden on plaintiff, when faced with a motion to dismiss or summary judgment motion based on the "clearly established" prong of qualified immunity, to cite authoritative precedent on distinctly related facts in which the claimed right had been previously declared. Second, whereas *Harlow* appeared to strip the official of immunity whenever a court determined by an objective test that he should have been aware of such clearly established law declaring the plaintiff's right,[37] *Creighton* does

doubt[ed] whether we would ever have reached a similar result." *Id.* at 1447.

33. *Watkins v. City of Oakland, Cal.*, 145 F.3d 1087 (9th Cir.1998) (finding law now clearly established that excessive duration of a dog bite with police encouragement was violative of plaintiff's constitutional rights).

34. *Dye v. Wargo,* 253 F.3d 296, 299–300 (7th Cir.2001) (observing that dogs not listed in Dictionary Act, 1 U.S.C.A. § 1, in the definition of "person").

35. *See Anderson*, 483 U.S. at 638–41, 107 S.Ct. at 3037–39. The Fourth Amendment setting brings to mind the Court's refusal to apply "new rules" of law in most federal habeas cases, further stifling the development of constitutional law in the realm of criminal procedure. *See Teague v. Lane*, 489 U.S. 288, 330, 109 S.Ct. 1060, 1086, 103 L.Ed.2d 334 (1989) (Brennan, J., dissenting) (objecting to the plurality's "formidable new barrier to relief" in cases in which "a federal habeas petitioner's claim, if successful, would result in the announcement of a new rule of law"); Rudovsky, 138 U.Pa.L.Rev. at 56 ("[T]he court has placed significant limits on the power of a federal habeas corpus court to articulate new constitutional law."). Professor Arkin believes that the potential of *Teague* to restrict the development of new rules may be overstated, principally because the majority of such claims already faced one or more of the procedural bars to habeas that the Court had erected in earlier decisions. *See* Marc M. Arkin, *The Prisoner's Dilemma: Life In the Lower Federal Courts After Teague v. Lane*, 69 N.C.L.Rev. 371, 392 & n.166 (1991). Professor Rudovsky argues further that another potential arena for the development of criminal constitutional law, suppression hearings, has been largely closed off because the unlawful police conduct does not eventuate in arrest and prosecution or because of the operation of the good faith exception to the exclusionary rule. *See* Rudovsky, 138 U.Pa.L.Rev. at 55–56 (citing *United States v. Leon*, 468 U.S. 897, 104 S.Ct. 3405, 82 L.Ed.2d 677 (1984)).

36. *See Anderson*, 483 U.S. at 641, 107 S.Ct. at 3039.

37. Government officials "are shielded from liability for civil damages insofar as their conduct does not violate clearly established statutory or constitutional rights of which a reasonable person would have known." *Harlow*, 457 U.S. at 818, 102 S.Ct. at 2738.

not unless the Court finds in addition that the official should have reasonably understood that "what he is doing violates that right."[38]

This latter, factual aspect of qualified immunity provoked a "double reasonableness" criticism by the justices who joined Justice Stevens dissent in *Creighton*: that if a particular predicate right—e.g., the Fourth Amendment rights to be free of unreasonable searches and seizures—turns on objective reasonableness, then qualified immunity confers immunity on the officer even when, despite the unreasonableness of his conduct, a jury finds that he reasonably failed to realize in the circumstances the unreasonableness of his challenged conduct. In this way, the dissenters objected, the defendant enjoys the protection of the Fourth Amendment's reasonableness standard plus "an even more generous standard that protects any officer who reasonably could have believed that his conduct was constitutionally reasonable." The Court later likened this "two bites at the apple" approach to the *United States v. Leon* good-faith exception to the exclusionary rule in cases where a reasonably well-trained officer would not have realized the unlawfulness of an arrest or search pursuant to a warrant.[39] Thus in § 1983 Fourth Amendment cases challenging unreasonable arrests, searches and seizures, lower courts have frequently granted individual officers qualified immunity pursuant to *Harlow* and *Creighton* even when finding or assuming that the arrest, search or seizure in question was in fact unreasonable.[40]

38. *Anderson*, 483 U.S. at 640, 107 S.Ct. at 3039. Thus the immunity is not forfeited unless it is "apparent" that "an official action" is unlawful when measured against pre-existing law. *See id.*

39. *Malley v. Briggs*, 475 U.S. 335, 106 S.Ct. 1092, 89 L.Ed.2d 271 (1986).

40. *See, e.g., Koch v. Town of Brattleboro*, 287 F.3d 162 (2d Cir.2002) (primary occupant of premises entered by police pursuant to apparent consent of third party with lesser authority respecting premises had no clearly established right to eject police after initial entry); *Williams v. Jaglowski*, 269 F.3d 778 (7th Cir.2001) (upholding qualified immunity despite lack of probable cause because officers had "arguable probable cause"); *Sparing v. Village of Olympia Fields*, 266 F.3d 684 (7th Cir.2001) (qualified immunity for arresting officer due to unsettled state of the law governing warrantless arrest of person in or near closed door, the uncertainty focussing on whether arrestee could be considered in public view); *Leveto v. Lapina*, 258 F.3d 156 (3d Cir.2001) (federal agents executing valid search warrant could reasonably if mistakenly have believed warrant carried authority to detain occupants during search for long periods of time) (*Bivens* action); *Case v. Kitsap Co. Sheriff's Dep't*, 249 F.3d 921, 929 (9th Cir.2001) (immunity granted because reasonable officer could believe that arrest on out-of-state warrant did not violate federal constitutional right of arrestee); *Young v. City of Little Rock*, 249 F.3d 730, 735 (assuming Fourth Amendment violation in officers' misidentifying subject of arrest warrant and in arresting wrong person in reliance on it, error sufficiently reasonable to absolve defendants of liability); *Abreu–Guzman v. Ford*, 241 F.3d 69 (1st Cir.2001) (reasonable officer who arrested wrong person could have believed there was probable cause that arrestee was the individual named in indictment); *Smithson v. Aldrich*, 235 F.3d 1058 (8th Cir.2000) (arguable probable cause to arrest suffices for immunity); *Marks v. Carmody*, 234 F.3d 1006, 1009 (7th Cir.2000), *cert. denied*, 533 U.S. 903, 121 S.Ct. 2243, 150 L.Ed.2d 232 (2001) (relying on *Creighton* in false arrest case); *Wollin v. Gondert*, 192 F.3d 616, 622–25 (7th Cir.1999) (immunity granted in arrest case because there was "arguable probable cause," i.e., despite the lack of probable cause, the officer's belief that such cause existed was objectively reasonable); *Edwards v. Giles*, 51 F.3d 155, 156–157 (8th Cir.1995) (plaintiff had burden of showing that officers' actions in effecting his arrest were objectively unreasonable). *But see Cozzo v. Tangipahoa Parish Council–President Government*, 279 F.3d 273 (5th Cir. 2002) (deputy sheriffs acted objectively unreasonably in evicting plaintiff

The Supreme Court has squarely reaffirmed that, even in excessive force cases where several courts of appeals had held to the contrary, the officer who "reasonably acted unreasonably" is entitled to qualified immunity. In *Saucier v. Katz,*[41] the Court rejected the Ninth Circuit's view that qualified immunity provided no additional insulation for an officer than already inheres in the *Graham v. Connor*[42] objective reasonableness test for excessive force. Rather, the Supreme Court decided, the officer enjoys two layers of protection. The *Graham* test examines several factors (severity of the crime, whether the suspect poses an immediate threat to the safety of officers or others, whether he is resisting arrest or attempting flight) designed to assess the reasonableness of an exercise of force from a *factual* or "on-scene perspective." And the Court evidently agreed that *Graham* affords officers considerable latitude for mistaken beliefs about the amount of force necessary in particular factual circumstances. Nevertheless, the majority insisted that qualified immunity remains as an independent backstop to protect the officer from liability where he makes a reasonable mistake "as to what the *law* requires." The Court in *Saucier* thus extended to the excessive force context the reasoning of *Anderson v. Creighton*, writing "even if a court were to hold that the officer violated the Fourth Amendment by conducting an unreasonable, warrantless search, *Anderson* still operates to grant officers immunity for reasonable mistakes as to the legality of their actions."[43]

Accordingly, the *Saucier* majority, assuming (although believing it "doubtful") that the defendant there used excessive force, declared that he was nevertheless entitled to immunity because plaintiff had failed to cite dispositive or highly persuasive case law condemning the force used under closely analogous circumstances.[44] The residue of *Saucier* is that

from her home in purported reliance on temporary restraining order which they did not and would not read and which did not authorize and even impliedly negated propriety of eviction.)

41. 533 U.S. 194, 121 S.Ct. 2151, 150 L.Ed.2d 272 (2001).

42. 490 U.S. 386, 109 S.Ct. 1865, 104 L.Ed.2d 443 (1989) (holding that excessive force claims arising from arrests or investigatory stops should be appraised under the Fourth Amendment's multi-factor "objective reasonableness" test rather than under Fourteenth Amendment substantive due process principles).

43. *See, e.g., Cruz v. City of Laramie, Wyo.,* 239 F.3d 1183 (10th Cir.2001) (declaring "hog-tie" restraint excessive force but conferring qualified immunity on officer because the excessiveness not apparent from authoritative case law decided prior to the events in question).

44. Of course if a court concludes that an officer's stop, search, arrest, or other use of force is objectively reasonable as a factual matter, it should also grant qualified immunity, if that motion has been made, because the plaintiff will have failed to show the violation of a predicate constitutional right. *See Wilson v. Layne*, 526 U.S. 603, 609, 119 S.Ct. 1692, 1697, 143 L.Ed.2d 818 (1999); *Conn v. Gabbert*, 526 U.S. 286, 290, 119 S.Ct. 1292, 1295, 143 L.Ed.2d 399 (1999); *County of Sacramento v. Lewis*, 523 U.S. 833, 841 n. 5, 118 S.Ct. 1708, 1714 n. 5, 140 L.Ed.2d 1043 (1998), and *Siegert v. Gilley*, 500 U.S. 226, 232–34, 111 S.Ct. 1789, 114 L.Ed.2d 277 (1991), discussed below, which direct a trial court deciding a qualified immunity motion first to decide if plaintiff has stated a cognizable claim for relief; only if such a claim lies should the court go on to decide whether the right in question was clearly established when violated and, if so, whether a reasonable officer in defendant's circumstances would have realized he was violating that right. *See, e.g., Nelson v. Kline*, 242 F.3d 33 (1st Cir.2001) (qualified immunity granted because stop, although perhaps violating Fourth Amendment's reasonableness standard, was not objectively

"double reasonableness," both factual and legal, is the rule in all Fourth Amendment[45] cases, not just in the probable cause setting addressed by *Anderson*.[46] Nevertheless, even in excessive force situations, the immunity will still be denied where the right in question is clearly established by Supreme Court decision, case law of the circuit in question, or, in the view of some circuit courts, a consensus of decisions from other circuits, and where the surrounding facts should have made it apparent to the

unreasonable as a factual matter in sense intended by *Anderson v. Creighton*). On first reading it may appear that the *Saucier* opinion violated the issue sequencing that the Court itself had prescribed in *Conn*, *Wilson* and *Lewis*, because it decided that an assumed constitutional violation was not clearly established without first having decided if the defendants' conduct amounted to unconstitutional excessive force. Yet the Court appeared to distinguish between the role of a trial and an appellate court in addressing these issues; its opinion stressed that the certiorari review in *Saucier* was limited to the "clearly established right" question, and so it simply assumed favorably to plaintiff that the allegations showed the violation of a recognized, underlying constitutional right. 121 S.Ct. at 2156, 2159. *See McNair v. Coffey*, 279 F.3d 463, 465 (7th Cir.2002) (discussing *Saucier*). And subsequent circuit opinions have relied on *Saucier*, in addition to *Hope v. Pelzer*, 536 U.S. 730, 122 S.Ct. 2508, 2513, 153 L.Ed.2d 666 (2002), *Wilson, Lewis, Conn* and *Siegert* for the proposition that lower courts should decide first whether plaintiff has asserted a cognizable constitutional violation under current law and only if so then decide whether the alleged violation was clearly established when defendant acted and if a reasonable officer in defendant's position would have understood that what he was doing violated that clearly established right. *See e.g., Martin v. City of Oceanside*, 360 F.3d 1078 (9th Cir. 2004) (officers receive qualified immunity because the emergency aid exception to the general prohibition against warrantless, unconsented entries into homes meant plaintiff failed to prove an underlying Fourth Amendment violation); *Roe v. Texas Dep't of Protective and Regulatory Services*, 299 F.3d 395, 401–402, 403n.6 (5th Cir. 2002).

45. There lingers even after *Saucier* authority that qualified immunity is not available to officers found to have engaged in excessive force violating the Eighth Amendment, on the ground that excessive force applied maliciously and sadistically for the purpose of causing harm is categorically a clearly established constitutional violation. *See Skrtich v. Thornton*, 280 F.3d 1295 (11th Cir.2002); *Johnson v. Breeden*, 280 F.3d 1308 (11th Cir.2002). *See also McMillian v. Johnson*, 88 F.3d 1554, 1556 (11th Cir.1996), *cert. denied*, 521 U.S. 1121, 117 S.Ct. 2514, 138 L.Ed.2d 1016 (1997) (prior case law categorically banned any pretrial punishment as an Eighth Amendment violation), so unlawfulness of placing detainee on death row should have been apparent given "the extraordinary allegations in this case," even absent authoritative precedent finding that identical conduct unlawful. *But see Marquez v. Gutierrez*, 322 F.3d 689, 692–693 (9th Cir.2003) (applying *Saucier* to accord qualified immunity to prison guard for Eighth Amendment violation consisting of intentional infliction of unnecessary and wanton pain, reasoning that guard may in fact act maliciously and sadistically yet reasonably believe his actions conform to clearly established law). Qualified immunity continues to be recognized as a defense to damages for violations of other Eighth Amendment rights, for example the right to be free of official deliberate indifference with respect to an inmate's need to be protected from harm by fellow inmates. *See Tucker v. Evans*, 276 F.3d 999 (8th Cir.2002).

46. *Pace v. Capobianco*, 283 F.3d 1275 (11th Cir.2002) (police officer defendants accorded qualified immunity respecting use of deadly force against fleeing suspect who appeared to be dangerous); *Bennett v. Murphy*, 274 F.3d 133, 136 (3d Cir.2002) (trial court on remand should determine whether reasonable officer in defendant's position should have realized from pertinent case law that his conduct constituted excessive force); *Billingsley v. City of Omaha*, 277 F.3d 990 (8th Cir.2002). *See McNair v. Coffey*, 279 F.3d 463, 471 (7th Cir.2002) (Coffey, J., concurring) (describing majority's decision upholding qualified immunity as based on conclusion that defendant did use excessive force but that a reasonable officer in defendant's position would not have so understood).

defendant officer that the force in question was excessive under the applicable legal rule.[47]

The Court justified the more expansive version of *Harlow* immunity expounded in *Anderson* and reaffirmed in *Saucier* as necessary to ward off the disruptiveness attendant upon litigation. *Harlow*, the Court eventually realized, would not sufficiently enable individual defendants to escape discovery unless the trial court applied the new doctrine with reference to a narrowly drawn conception of analogous precedent. Further, *Anderson* and its progeny reflect the Supreme Court's determination to afford defendants an early resolution of that defense.[48] Chief Justice Burger's common law approach in *Scheuer*—the scope of the qualified immunity available to executive officers should vary with the "scope of discretion and responsibilities of the office and all the circumstances as they reasonably appeared . . . at the time and in light of all

47. See *Kijonka v. Seitzinger*, 363 F.3d 645 (7th Cir. 2004)(officer who consulted county prosecutor before arresting plaintiff had a reasonable, even if mistaken, basis to believe that he had probable cause to make arrest); *Storck v. City of Coral Springs*, 354 F.3d 1307 (11th Cir. 2003)(officer's arguable probable cause to arrest plaintiff entitles him to qualified immunity); *Vaughan v. Cox*, 343 F.3d 1323 (11th Cir.2003) (a second, and sua sponte, panel decision on remand for reconsideration in light of *Hope v. Pelzer*, reaffirming principle of "arguable probable cause"; extending it to use of deadly force by officer confronting fleeing motorists who may have posed threat of serious harm to defendant officer; denying summary judgment on qualified immunity because, on facts alleged by plaintiff, objectively reasonable officer could not have found he was entitled to use deadly force to apprehend automobile passenger; but observing that officer might still receive qualified immunity at trial if jury were to accept officer's version of facts); *Herzog v. Village of Winnetka, Illinois*, 309 F.3d 1041, 1044 (7th Cir.2002) (reversing summary grant of qualified immunity, without citing *Saucier*, where facts admitted on appeal excluded possibility that reasonable officer could have believed his actions did not amount to unconstitutional excessive force); *Santos v. Gates*, 287 F.3d 846 (9th Cir.2002) (leaving for jury whether excessive force used against detainee); *Phelps v. Coy*, 286 F.3d 295 (6th Cir.2002) (unreasonableness of continuing to beat arrestee during booking and after he had been neutralized and posed no threat to officers clearly established); *Clem v. Corbeau*, 284 F.3d 543 (4th Cir.2002) (reasonable officer could not have believed that mentally ill suspect posed threat of serious injury justifying deadly force, so qualified immunity denied); *Lee v. Ferraro*, 284 F.3d 1188 (11th Cir.2002) (no reasonable officer could have believed that physical abuse of motorist after arrest fully effected was lawful); *Headwaters Forest Defense v. County of Humboldt*, 276 F.3d 1125 (9th Cir.2002) (reasonable officer should have realized that repeated use of pepper spray against nonviolent protesters and refusal to wash out their eyes thereafter was excessive force); *Holland ex rel. Overdorff v. Harrington*, 268 F.3d 1179 (10th Cir.2001) (children found in residence and held there at gunpoint after SWAT team had secured premises had clearly established Fourth Amendment right to be free of excessive force). *Cf. Mickle v. Morin*, 297 F.3d 114, 122 (2d Cir.2002) (seeming to ignore *Saucier* by reversing judgment as a matter of law for police officers based on qualified immunity simply because the general prohibition on use of excessive force during arrest had been established by *Graham v. Connor* and facts were in dispute as to objective reasonableness of arrest). *But cf. Rogers v. City of Amsterdam*, 303 F.3d 155, 158–159 (2d Cir. 2002) (same circuit, again without citing *Saucier*, appears to follow its approach by upholding qualified immunity for defendants because "officers of reasonable competence could disagree on whether the probable cause test was met.")

48. See *Anderson v. Creighton* at 638–41, 107 S.Ct. at 3038–40; *see also Crawford–El v. Britton*, 523 U.S. 574, 118 S.Ct. 1584, 140 L.Ed.2d 759 (1998) and *Mitchell v. Forsyth*, 472 U.S. 511, 526, 105 S.Ct. 2806, 2815, 86 L.Ed.2d 411 (1985) (authorizing immediate appeals from denials of qualified immunity and stating that *Harlow* is designed to enable defendants who meet its minimum requirements to be dismissed from the action "before the commencement of discovery").

the circumstances"[49]—was overridden by the desire of the emerging Rehnquist Court to relieve public officials of the burden of litigation.

The resolution of the "settledness" question, which the Court advertises as part of an objective test, in fact turns on an early,[50] subjective[51] characterization by trial and appellate judges. Indeed, when *Harlow/Anderson* immunity is timely pleaded and moved on, the § 1983 plaintiff must prove in response almost exactly what the government must prove in a criminal civil rights prosecution: the deprivation of a

49. *Scheuer v. Rhodes*, 416 U.S. 232, 247–48, 94 S.Ct. 1683, 1692, 40 L.Ed.2d 90 (1974). *See also* Gary S. Gildin, *Immunizing Intentional Violations of Constitutional Rights Through Judicial Legislation: The Extension of Harlow v. Fitzgerald To Section 1983 Actions*, 38 Emory L.J. 369, 374–79 (1989) (describing the traditional common law approach to qualified immunity and criticizing the Harlow Court's departure from it because "[a]fter Harlow, even if a federal officer intended to harm the plaintiff, he is immune [from damages] if the constitutional interest in issue was not clearly established at the time of the violation"). This assertion may be slightly overstated.

50. See *Crawford–El v. Britton*, 523 U.S. 574, 118 S.Ct. 1584, 140 L.Ed.2d 759 (1998) (directing trial judges to decide qualified immunity issue before discovery) *Siegert v. Gilley*, 500 U.S. 226, 231, 111 S.Ct. 1789, 1793, 114 L.Ed.2d 277 (1991) (holding on immediate "collateral order" appeal that "whether the constitutional right asserted is 'clearly established' at the time the defendant acted" should be decided before plaintiff is permitted to conduct discovery of the underlying claim); *Gaines v. Davis*, 928 F.2d 705, 707 (5th Cir.1991) (holding on immediate "collateral order" appeal that district court's order was overly broad because it failed to limit the scope of depositions to the issue of qualified immunity). The lower courts have been moving to this position, treating the issue of qualified immunity as a threshold issue to be resolved in the early stages of a case. *See, e.g., Finnegan v. Fountain*, 915 F.2d 817, 820 (2d Cir.1990) (stating that the application of qualified immunity is a question of law for the court and not the jury to decide); *Bennett v. Parker*, 898 F.2d 1530, 1534 (11th Cir.1990), *cert. denied*, 498 U.S. 1103, 111 S.Ct. 1003, 112 L.Ed.2d 1085 (1991) (stating that, when "faced with a motion for summary judgment based on a defense of qualified immunity, the district courts should first focus on whether the plaintiff has established a constitutional violation before determining whether material issues of fact are present"); *Krause v. Bennett*, 887 F.2d 362, 369 (2d Cir.1989) (holding that when qualified immunity can be shown as a matter of law, defendants motion for judgment notwithstanding the verdict should be granted); *Eng v. Coughlin*, 858 F.2d 889, 895 (2d Cir.1988) (remanding case to district court to rule on claims of qualified immunity that were not considered when ruling on motion for summary judgment). See also *Tatro v. Kervin*, 41 F.3d 9 (1st Cir.1994) (jury instructions could not insist that § 1983 plaintiff had to prove that an arrest was "clearly" lacking probable cause or "clearly" effected with excessive force, for that would constitute a disguised, belated assertion of the qualified immunity defense that should have been determined at the outset of the action by the court as a matter of law). But if plaintiff alleges a clearly established federal law violation, discovery may proceed on the fact question whether a reasonable person in defendant's position should have realized that her conduct would violate that law. *See Largent v. Dallas*, 44 F.3d 1004 (5th Cir.1995) (unpublished), *cert. denied*, 514 U.S. 1128, 115 S.Ct. 2002, 131 L.Ed.2d 1003 (1995).

51. The initial characterization process is termed "subjective" for the following reason. The FBI agent who committed the alleged violation in *Anderson* knew that the provision in question, the Fourth Amendment, demanded a warrant. *See Anderson*, 483 U.S. at 641, 107 S.Ct. at 3039. The right was not clearly established, however, because the Court concluded that a question remained as to whether a reasonable police officer, despite the lack of probable cause, could have believed probable cause existed. *See id.* This determination, in turn, required the trial court to make an appraisal of existing precedent on the eve of the alleged injury to determine its "closeness" to the circumstances the defendant confronted. *See id.* at 646 n.6. The last step in the trial or reviewing court's determination, like the initial decision made by the police, is inherently subjective; it requires appraisal of the similarity between the conduct under scrutiny and the conduct described in prior constitutional cases.

"federal right made definite by decision or other rule of law."[52] The court in *Elder v. Holloway*,[53] held among other things that a federal circuit court of appeals might refer to its "own and other relevant precedents," not just to decisions of the Supreme Court, in determining whether the law allegedly violated was "clearly established" at the time defendant acted. The Court was similarly vague in *United States v. Lanier*.[54] This ambiguous approach leaves room for such decisions as *Jean v. Collins*,[55] in which the Fourth Circuit held that only cases from the Supreme Court, the Fourth Circuit, and the highest court of the state in which the case arose should be considered when determining if the law was clearly established. Similarly, in *Badia v. City of Miami*[56] the Eleventh Circuit found that the law regarding retaliatory discharge was not clearly established because the Eleventh Circuit itself had not decided the issue and a circuit split existed among the courts which had.

Elder did not present the question whether these "other relevant precedents" include district court decisions from the same or other circuits, or only decisions by other federal courts of appeals. Still, while the Court has directed judges merely to take circuit authority "into account" in deciding whether precedent provided a reasonable defendant fair warning that his contemplated conduct violated federal law, it has explicitly declined to hold that "decisions of the Courts of Appeals and other courts are inadequate as a matter of law" to afford that warning.[57] In context, it appears that the Supreme Court also rejects the per se rule

52. *Screws v. United States*, 325 U.S. 91, 103, 65 S.Ct. 1031, 1036, 89 L.Ed. 1495 (1945) (construing 18 U.S.C.A. § 52 (codified as amended at 18 U.S.C.A. § 242 (1988)), the criminal counterpart to § 1983, as requiring proof of scienter, but noting that "bad purpose or evil intent alone may not be sufficient"). The "requisite bad purpose" of Screws has been held satisfied if the evidence shows that the criminal defendant had the purpose to deprive the citizen of the "interests protected" by the violated federal right, even absent any consciousness of the unlawfulness of his conduct. See *United States v. Ehrlichman*, 546 F.2d 910, 921 (D.C.Cir.1976), *cert. denied*, 429 U.S. 1120, 97 S.Ct. 1155, 51 L.Ed.2d 570 (1977). The § 1983 plaintiff, therefore, must demonstrate little less against an individual immunity-claiming government official than the government must show in a criminal prosecution for a violation of the same rights. By equating the requirement of fair notice in a criminal prosecution under 18 U.S.C.A. § 242 with the corresponding clearly established component of the qualified immunity defense in actions under § 1983, the Court in *Lanier v. United States* in effect confirmed that *Anderson* holds § 1983 plaintiffs to the same general requirement of showing settledness or obviousness that the federal government must meet in a criminal prosecution for a violation of the same right! See discussion of *Lanier, infra*.

53. 510 U.S. 510, 114 S.Ct. 1019, 127 L.Ed.2d 344 (1994). One circuit applies this standard by insisting that there be a decision of the Supreme Court or its own circuit on point, "or the clearly established weight of authority from other courts must have found the law to be as the plaintiff maintains." *Seamons v. Snow*, 84 F.3d 1226, 1238 (10th Cir.1996), *on remand*, 15 F.Supp.2d 1150 (D.Utah 1998), *affirmed in part, reversed in part*, 206 F.3d 1021 (10th Cir.2000) (quoting *Medina v. City and County of Denver*, 960 F.2d 1493, 1498 (10th Cir.1992)).

54. 520 U.S. 259, 117 S.Ct. 1219, 137 L.Ed.2d 432 (1997).

55. 155 F.3d 701 (4th Cir.1998), *judgment vacated*, 526 U.S. 1142, 119 S.Ct. 2016, 143 L.Ed.2d 1029 (1999).

56. 133 F.3d 1443 (11th Cir.1998).

57. *United States v. Lanier*, 520 U.S. 259, 117 S.Ct. 1219, 137 L.Ed.2d 432 (1997) (case under § 1983's criminal counterpart, 18 U.S.C.A. § 242) (emphasis added).

of an earlier Eleventh Circuit decision[58] that only precedent of the circuit in which the allegedly unconstitutional conduct occurred can establish law clearly.[59]

As applied by the *Anderson* majority, the category of "settled" law may shrink significantly for want of sufficiently similar prior cases.[60] At

58. *McMillian v. Johnson*, 88 F.3d 1554, 1569 n. 17, 19 (11th Cir.1996), *cert. denied*, 521 U.S. 1121, 117 S.Ct. 2514, 138 L.Ed.2d 1016 (1997).

59. *United States v. Lanier*, 520 U.S. 259, 117 S.Ct. 1219, 137 L.Ed.2d 432.

60. *See* cases collected *infra* this section. The lower courts differ on just how closely the facts of the instant case must correspond to those of a previously decided circuit or Supreme Court decision for the immunity to be forfeited. At one extreme is the presumption that the immunity prevails unless prior decisions "truly compel the conclusion that the defendant's actions violated federal law," *Lassiter v. Alabama A & M Univ.*, 28 F.3d 1146, 1149 (11th Cir. 1994), by reference to law "developed in such a concrete and factually defined context [as] to make it obvious to every reasonable person" that defendant's conduct would have been unlawful. *Beauregard v. Olson*, 84 F.3d 1402, 1404 (11th Cir.1996). The Supreme Court implicitly criticized *Lassiter* in *Hope v. Pelzer*, 536 U.S. 730, 122 S.Ct. 2508, 153 L.Ed.2d 666 (2002), where it held that sometimes the law gives a defendant fair notice that the conduct in question is unconstitutional even absent a materially similar prior case in the jurisdiction. Yet other courts, often citing *Anderson* itself, observe that the precise conduct at issue need not have been held unlawful by a previous case. *See, e.g., Gruenke v. Seip*, 225 F.3d 290, 300–01 (3d Cir.2000) (despite limited expectation of privacy enjoyed by student athletes, and plaintiff's inability to cite case dealing with same intrusion, swim coach who forced student to take pregnancy test as condition of competing in meet denied qualified immunity from damages for unlawful Fourth Amendment search because a reasonable coach would have realized that student swimmer's condition not suitable for public speculation and defendant offered no explanation for breaching that boundary of reasonableness); *Markham v. White*, 172 F.3d 486 (7th Cir.1999) (equal protection right to be free from sexual harassment settled even though no prior case concerned short seminar for narcotics officers); *McMillian v. Johnson*, 88 F.3d 1554, 1556 (11th Cir.1996), *cert. denied*, 521 U.S. 1121, 117 S.Ct. 2514, 138 L.Ed.2d 1016 (1997) (prior case law categorically banned any pretrial punishment, so unlawfulness of placing detainee on death row should have been apparent, at least in light of "the extraordinary allegations in this case," even absent authoritative precedent finding that identical conduct unlawful); *Ayeni v. Mottola*, 35 F.3d 680, 686 (2d Cir.1994), *cert. denied*, 514 U.S. 1062, 115 S.Ct. 1689, 131 L.Ed.2d 554 (1995). *Accord Jones v. City of Jackson*, 203 F.3d 875, 880–881 (5th Cir. 2000) (qualified immunity unavailable for alleged nine-month detention, court finding 14th Amendment liberty interest apparently violated without citing applicable precedent); *Reitz v. Bucks County*, 125 F.3d 139 (3d Cir.1997) (denying qualified immunity despite absence of prior case on point; defendant should have known conduct was unlawful). Still another, echoing the Supreme Court's language in *Harlow* and *Creighton*, writes that the "plaintiff need not show that the specific action at issue has previously been held unlawful," only that the unlawfulness be "apparent" in light of preexisting law. *Hilliard v. City and County of Denver*, 930 F.2d 1516, 1518 (10th Cir.1991), *cert. denied*, 502 U.S. 1013, 112 S.Ct. 656, 116 L.Ed.2d 748 (1991). See also *Northen v. City of Chicago*, 126 F.3d 1024 (7th Cir.1997), *cert. denied*, 523 U.S. 1023, 118 S.Ct. 1306, 140 L.Ed.2d 471 (1998) (denying qualified immunity to police officers who arrested suspect based on their own "cockeyed" interpretation of statute; normally, a "plaintiff cannot rebut the defense of immunity without showing that the argument has been authoritatively resolved, but when the proposed interpretation is cockeyed, no such showing is required."). *See Sonoda v. Cabrera*, 255 F.3d 1035 (9th Cir.2001) (defendant officials could not reasonably have believed in the constitutionality of the executive order they relied on, given case law holding to the contrary). *But cf. Campbell v. Peters*, 256 F.3d 695 (7th Cir.2001), *cert. denied*, 535 U.S. 957, 122 S.Ct. 1363, 152 L.Ed.2d 358 (2002) (immunity granted prison officials whose revocation of inmate's good time credits based on reasonable statutory interpretation); *Spiegel v. City of Chicago*, 106 F.3d 209 (7th Cir.1997), *cert. denied*, 522 U.S. 816, 118 S.Ct. 65, 139 L.Ed.2d 27 (1997). (according qualified immunity, but only because the conduct in question was neither condemned by on-point precedent

the extreme advocated by *Anderson*'s dissenters, on the other hand, a right is clearly established if it fits within a broad generic description of any federal Constitutional or statutory right. The upshot is that the settledness concept, as viewed by the several justices in *Anderson*, is zero-sum, scarcely ever satisfied or so easily satisfied as to be meaningless. A majority adopted the strict view and as a consequence qualified immunity is now routinely invoked and very frequently upheld.[61]

In *United States v. Lanier*,[62] the Court itself re-cited the quoted phrases from *Anderson* but appeared to relax its application. There the Court upheld a criminal prosecution against a state court judge under 18 U.S.C.A. § 242 for violating the due process liberty rights of court employees and a litigant by sexually assaulting them. The judge argued that there was no Supreme Court decision on point that clearly established the violation, and hence that prosecution under § 242 violated his own due process right to fair warning of the criminal violation. The Court responded that even in this criminal setting, due process required only that the statute, as construed or standing alone, made it reasonably clear that the conduct in question was criminal. The Court, in considering a case where a judge used his judicial authority to coerce sexual favors from unwilling litigants and court employees in his chambers, observed in passing that the easiest cases often never arise, and hence never generate authoritative precedent. Ironically, then, a complete absence of case law can occasionally assist a plaintiff in showing that a right is clearly established![63] Borrowing from its "clearly established" jurisprudence under § 1983, and explicitly holding that § 242 required no more than the § 1983 "clearly established" requirement, the Court wrote that "general statements of the law are not inherently incapable of giving fair and clear warning." Further, "a general constitutional rule already identified in the decisional law may apply with obvious clarity to the specific conduct in question, even though 'the very action in question has [not] previously been held unlawful.' " The *Lanier* holding that a specific case is not invariably required to make law "clearly established" facilitates decisions permitting law to be settled for qualified immunity purposes by statutes and interpretive regulations.[64]

nor so shocking that such precedent could be dispensed with).

61. See, e.g., *Sanders v. Howze*, 177 F.3d 1245 (11th Cir.1999) (plaintiff's right to jail suicide prevention measures not clearly established by a circuit decision requiring the particular measures asserted as necessary); *Johnson v. Moore*, 948 F.2d 517, 520 (9th Cir.1991) (holding qualified immunity applies when the right alleged to have been violated is not sufficiently clear to the state official concerned); *Johnson v. Boreani*, 946 F.2d 67, 71 (8th Cir.1991) (concluding that, under the facts, summary judgment is appropriate and necessary to achieve purposes of qualified immunity defense established in *Anderson*); *Vaughan v. Ricketts*, 859 F.2d 736, 739 (9th Cir.1988) (entitling defendant to summary judgment and granting him qualified immunity if he can establish that it was reasonable to believe his act comported with the Constitution), *cert. denied*, 490 U.S. 1012, 109 S.Ct. 1655, 104 L.Ed.2d 169 (1989).

62. 520 U.S. 259, 117 S.Ct. 1219, 137 L.Ed.2d 432 (1997).

63. See, e.g., *Johnson v. Newburgh Enlarged Sch. Dist.*, 239 F.3d 246 (2d Cir. 2001) (finding clearly established a student's substantive due process right to be free of excessive force absent case on point).

64. See *Kelly v. City of Oakland*, 198 F.3d 779 (9th Cir.1999) (quid pro quo same-sex variety of sexual harassment violates clearly established law without specific

The *Lanier* "obvious clarity" mode of showing that a particular federally guaranteed right was clearly established was employed by the Court again in *Wilson v. Layne* in 1999.[65] The *Wilson* Court made three separate inquiries into whether in April 1992 it was clearly established that bringing media observers along during the execution of an arrest warrant was unlawful. The Court first asked the *Lanier* "obvious clarity" question: whether it was obvious from the general principles of the Fourth Amendment that allowing media to be present during the execution of a search warrant was unlawful.[66] The defendants in *Wilson* had argued that legitimate public and law enforcement interests were served by allowing media to observe the execution of search warrants. These interests were apparently sufficient to allow the Court to find that the officers' conduct was not obviously in violation of the Fourth Amendment. The Court then asked whether specific precedent established the violation.[67]

Without specifying which kinds of cases might suffice as precedent, the Court also rejected the plaintiff's argument that a five-week-old Sixth Circuit case that was similar but factually distinct was sufficient precedent to clearly establish a right. Although the Sixth Circuit case, *Bills v. Aseltine*,[68] correctly anticipated the holding in *Wilson* that police may not bring along third parties during an entry into a private home pursuant to a warrant for purposes unrelated to those justifying the warrant, the case was out-of-jurisdiction and merely denied summary judgment because fact issues remained. At least implicitly, then, the Court suggested that a plaintiff could "clearly establish" law by pointing to an authoritative, on-point decision from the defendant's own circuit. The third inquiry by the Court was whether "a consensus of cases of persuasive authority" existed to give a reasonable officer sufficient notice that his actions were lawful.[69] Finding none, the Court held that the right was not clearly established at the time of the events in question. is *Wilson* may be read to mean that even absent obviously violated general principles a la *Lanier*, a closely analogous U.S. Supreme Court case, and on-point authority from defendant's own circuit, a plaintiff could still show the law clearly established by a consensus of circuit decisions from other jurisdictions sufficient to alert a reasonable officer that his actions would not be lawful.[70]

holding so declaring because Title VII gave "fair warning"); *Gonzalez v. Lee County Hous. Auth.*, 161 F.3d 1290 (11th Cir.1998) (relying on Fair Housing Act and interpretative regulations).

65. 526 U.S. 603, 119 S.Ct. 1692, 143 L.Ed.2d 818 (1999).

66. *Id.* at 1700.

67. *Id.*

68. 958 F.2d 697 (6th Cir.1992).

69. *Wilson*, 119 S.Ct. at 1700. After *Wilson*, the Tenth Circuit put it this way: "In order for the law to be clearly established, 'there must be a Supreme Court or other Tenth Circuit decision on point, or the clearly established weight of authority from other circuits must have found the law to be as the plaintiff maintains.' "*Murrell v. School Dist. No. 1*, 186 F.3d 1238, 1251 (10th Cir.1999) (citing *Wilson*).

70. See, e.g., *Savard v. Rhode Island*, 320 F.3d 34, 38 (1st Cir.2003); *Murrell v. Sch. Dist. No. 1*, 186 F.3d 1238, 1251 (10th Cir.1999). *But see Thomas ex rel Thomas v. Roberts*, 323 F.3d 950, 955 (11th Cir.2003) (adhering to view that in the Eleventh Circuit, only caselaw of the Supreme Court, the Eleventh Circuit, or the highest court of a state within the circuit can clearly estab-

In *Hope v. Pelzer*,[71] the Court sought to reinforce and clarify the message of *Lanier*. The Eleventh Circuit Court of Appeals had accorded qualified immunity to prison guards who had handcuffed a prisoner at a work site to a hitching post for seven hours without regular water or bathroom breaks after the prisoner had refused to work. Its opinion had reasoned that the facts of previous cases in that circuit were not "materially similar" to the facts at bar and accordingly provided insufficient notice to impose Eighth Amendment damages liability for cruel and unusual punishment. But the Supreme Court observed that in *Lanier* it had already rejected, as a "rigid gloss on the qualified immunity standard," any requirement that previous cases be "fundamentally similar." Instead, it wrote, the touchstone is more general: "whether the state of the law" when defendants acted gave them "fair warning" that their conduct was unconstitutional.

Although the conduct in question occurred in Alabama in 1995, the Supreme Court held that fair warning was afforded by a 1974 decision of the Eleventh Circuit's predecessor court, the Fifth Circuit Court of Appeals, that had condemned as contrary to the Eighth Amendment several forms of punishment of Mississippi prisoners, including handcuffing them to a fence and to cells for long periods of time. This warning was fortified, according to the Supreme Court, by the "reasoning, though not the holding," of a 1987 Eleventh Circuit opinion suggesting that temporary denials of drinking water as punishment for a refusal to work would also amount to cruel and unusual punishment. And further warning, the Supreme Court observed, was provided by an Alabama Department of Corrections regulation promulgated in 1993 that purported to *authorize* tying an inmate to the hitching post when he refused to work or was disruptive. The Court noted that the regulation also provided the inmate should immediately be untied, and allowed to join his work detail, when he tells an officer he is ready to go to work, and that a 1994 U.S. Department of Justice study had found that Alabama's officers had not complied with the immediate-release policy.

The Supreme Court's conclusion that the Alabama guards had fair warning in 1995 from the 1974 Fifth Circuit decision condemning fence handcuffing in Mississippi for an unspecified "long period of time," coupled with the dictum of a 1987 Eleventh Circuit opinion that also reaffirmed the authority of prison guards, nonmaliciously and nonsadistically, to use force or coercive measures reasonably necessary to enforce an inmate's compliance with valid prison rules, is particularly striking given the pre–1995 trend in the district courts in Alabama. As Justice Thomas recounted in dissent, five Alabama district court decisions in 1994, one in 1993, and one in 1986 had rejected Eighth Amendment claims based on handcuffing a prisoner to a restraining bar or stationery

lish law) (citing *Marsh v. Butler County*, 268 F.3d 1014 (11th Cir.2001) (en banc)). *See also Roe v. Texas Dep't of Protective and Regulatory Services*, 299 F.3d 395, 409–410 (5th Cir.2002) (declining to decide the question where the circuit decisions were inconsistent regarding the rights at issue).

71. 536 U.S. 730, 122 S.Ct. 2508, 153 L.Ed.2d 666 (2002).

object, and no Alabama decision issued before defendants acted had found an Eighth Amendment violation based on that conduct alone.[72]

So it appears that at least on harsh facts like those in *Hope* and *Lanier*, the Supreme Court majority in reality is willing to impute to individual defendant correctional officers knowledge that only a reasonable Alabama corrections department official, or perhaps even only that department's counsel, might have gleaned from a particular reading of elderly circuit precedents—precedents that were not being applied to the precise practice in question by the district courts of the state in which the claim arose! How then to synthesize *Hope* and *Lanier* with the Court's assertion in *Anderson v. Creighton*[73] that the right violated by the defendant must have been clearly established in a "particularized" sense, and its recognition in *Saucier v. Katz*[74] that a police officer will often be entitled to qualified immunity in Fourth Amendment cases even for objectively unreasonable uses of force absent binding precedent or a case law consensus condemning such force under closely similar circumstances? Perhaps the best one can interpolate is that when state actors apply physical force that is bodily invasive, as did Judge Lanier, or when prison guards and by extension police apply physical force by means the Court deems unusual because they are not widely used nationally, as did the prison guards in *Hope*, the requirement of a case closely on point will be relaxed.

Circuit courts have understandably struggled to articulate a more universal formulation of the *Lanier and Hope* messages. The Eleventh Circuit, in the wake of its rebuke by the Supreme Court in *Hope*, initially insisted that *Hope* "did not change the preexisting law of the Eleventh Circuit much."[75] It cited a series of its pre-*Hope* decisions implementing the *Lanier* premise that even absent authoritative case law on point, "a general statement of the law might provide adequate notice of unlawfulness in the right circumstances," which it described as the "occasional 'obvious clarity' cases per *Lanier.*"[76] That court has elsewhere characterized these circumstances as "the slender category of cases in which the unlawfulness of the conduct is so obviously at the core of what ... [federal law] prohibits that clarifying caselaw is unnecessary."[77] The

72. The majority sought to distinguish one such decision on the ground that the prisoners there, unlike the plaintiff in *Hope*, were offered regular water and bathroom breaks during the time they were restrained. Justice Thomas dismissed the distinction as without significance, observing that the individual *Hope* defendants were not alleged to have denied the plaintiff water.

73. 483 U.S. 635, 640, 107 S.Ct. 3034, 97 L.Ed.2d 523 (1987).

74. 533 U.S. 194, 121 S.Ct. 2151, 150 L.Ed.2d 272 (2001).

75. *Willingham v. Loughnan*, 321 F.3d 1299, 1302–03 (11th Cir.2003) (on remand from the Supreme Court for reconsideration in light of *Hope*) (citing *Lee v. Ferraro*, 284 F.3d 1188, 1199 (11th Cir.2002)); *Rodriguez v. Farrell*, 280 F.3d 1341, 1350 n.18 (11th Cir. 2002); *Skrtich v. Thornton*, 280 F.3d 1295, 1304 n.9 (11th Cir. 2002); *Marsh v. Butler County*, 268 F.3d 1014 (11th Cir. 2001) (en banc). *Priester v. City of Riviera Beach, Florida*, 208 F.3d 919, 926 (11th Cir.2000); *Smith v. Mattox*, 127 F.3d 1416, 1419 (11th Cir.1997); *Jenkins v. Talladega City Bd. of Educ.*, 115 F.3d 821, 825 n.3 (11th Cir. 1997) (en banc).

76. *Id.* at 1302.

77. *Thomas v. Roberts*, 323 F.3d 950, 953 (11th Cir.2003).

circuit acknowledges that it encounters such circumstances only "very occasionally."[78] Still, in some situations involving official use of gratuitous, nontrivial force, the circuit does find those circumstances and deny qualified immunity.[79] On the other hand, even when the force used is deadly, the Eleventh Circuit will not dispense with factually similar precedent of the Supreme Court, its own court, or the highest court of the state in question unless it concludes there was a "clearly egregious shooting that was far beyond the hazy border of acceptable force."[80] At the opposing extreme, the Ninth Circuit reads *Hope* expansively as dispensing not just with identical but even materially similar precedent if preexisting law developed in a very different real-life setting give the defendants fair warning of a general constitutional principle.[81] The First[82] and Sixth[83] Circuits have also construed *Hope* to relieve the plaintiff of citing factually similar authority to overcome qualified immunity, but in situations where the circumstances spawning prior authority more closely resembled the cases at hand.

When the facts at bar do not fit the *Lanier/Hope* exception, the circuits do take substantially varying approaches in assessing whether a prior case *is* on point. To what degree, in other words, must the circumstances at bar correspond to the particular facts of a prior authoritative precedent? In part the answer turns not just on the predilections of a circuit's justices, but on the nature of the predicate federal law violation. Where the constitutional or statutory standard is dependent on multi-factor balancing or a determination of overall reasonableness, one panel of the Eleventh Circuit concludes, "preexisting caselaw that has applied general law to specific circumstances will

78. *Rodriguez v. Farrell*, 280 F.3d 1341, 1350 n.18 (11th Cir. 2002).

79. See *Vinyard v. Wilson*, 311 F.3d 1340 (11th Cir.2002) (pepper spraying arrestee while she was handcuffed and secured in back of patrol car); *Lee v. Ferraro*, 284 F.3d 1188, 1199 (11th Cir.2002) (officer slammed arrestee's head on car trunk although she was handcuffed and secured); *Slicker v. Jackson*, 215 F.3d 1225, 1232–33 (11th Cir.2000) (officers slammed handcuffed arrestee's head into pavement); *Priester v. City of Riviera Beach, Florida*, 208 F.3d 919, 926 (11th Cir.2000) (officer unleashed unprovoked attack by police dog for at least two minutes); *Smith v. Mattox*, 127 F.3d 1416, 1420 (11th Cir.1997) (officer broke arm of unresisting arrestee).

80. *Willingham v. Loughnan*, 321 F.3d 1299, 1304 (11th Cir.2003) (on remand from the Supreme Court for reconsideration in light of *Hope* and adhering to previous granting of immunity). In *Willingham* the panel insisted on prior authority from the Supreme Court, the Eleventh Circuit, or the Supreme Court of Florida holding unconstitutional the use of deadly force on a plaintiff "(1) who had just attempted to murder one police officer and assaulted another, (2) who was not under police control, and (3) was close by a source of weapons...."

81. *Flores v. Morgan Hill Unified School Dist.*, 324 F.3d 1130, 1136–1138 (9th Cir.2003) (finding a 14th amendment equal protection right of students to be protected by school administrators from peer sexual orientation harassment, based on circuit's prior holding subjecting sexual orientation discrimination against state employees to rational basis scrutiny, coupled with one other circuit's holding that school administrators are potentially liable to students for peer sexual orientation harassment).

82. *Savard v. Rhode Island*, 320 F.3d 34, 37–38 (1st Cir.2003) (reading *Hope* to say that requiring authority with materially similar facts is a "rigid gloss" inconsistent behind the rationale for qualified immunity).

83. *Feathers v. Aey*, 319 F.3d 843, 850 (6th Cir.2003) (even absent materially similar case law authority, officers should have known that their search on plaintiff's porch violated *Terry* principles).

almost always be necessary to draw a line that is capable of giving fair and clear notice than an official's conduct will violate federal law." It accordingly declined to transplant precedent governing a strip search of two high school students once they were in police custody to a case involving the parameters of a permissible strip-search of elementary school students by school personnel.[84] Still, the circuit remembers that it was cautioned by the Supreme Court in *Hope* not to be "unduly rigid in requiring factual similarity between prior cases and the case under consideration."[85] Perhaps with this caution in mind, a panel in that circuit has recently found sufficient notice in extant case law to deny qualified immunity on summary judgment even where the underlying constitutional question, probable cause to arrest, implicated the typical reasonableness assessment and the correlative flexible immunity concept of "arguable probable cause."[86] And another Eleventh Circuit panel, reviewing the evidence more deferentially than the Circuit typically had before *Hope*, reversed qualified immunity to a prison dentist upon concluding that a reasonable jury could find that the dentist, who had delayed 18 months before providing dentures to the inmate plaintiff, was aware of plaintiff's serious medical need as required to establish an Eighth Amendment deliberate indifference claim.[87]

A recent Tenth Circuit decision provides an interesting contrast. The case involved a teacher's alleged molesting of two students. The court found authority clearly establishing the general principle that abusing governmental authority for personal sexual gratification violates equal protection. That principle had been declared in a case arising from a government workplace. The court also found cases that had relied on government employment decisions to clearly establish law in other settings. It accordingly denied qualified immunity to the defendant teacher despite the absence of circuit-authoritative case law addressing whether sexual harassment in the schoolroom can violate equal protection.[88]

Wilson provides a kind of omnibus blueprint for plaintiffs seeking to establish that a particular right is clearly established. First, argue the *Lanier* "any fool can see" prong—that is, it is obvious from the general principles of the statute or Constitutional provision at issue that a particular right exists such that a reasonable governmental officer would be on sufficient notice that the conduct at issue was unlawful. Failing that, argue that specific precedent from defendant's circuit establishes the right, or, if such precedent is lacking, that a consensus of persuasive authority from other jurisdictions exists such that a reasonable officer could not have believed that his actions were lawful.

84. *Thomas v. Roberts*, 323 F.3d 950, 955 (11th Cir.2003).

85. *Vaughan v. Cox,* 343 F.3d 1323 (11th Cir.2003).

86. *Holmes v. Kucynda*, 321 F.3d 1069 (11th Cir.2003).

87. *Farrow v. West,* 320 F.3d 1235 (11th Cir.2003).

88. *Sh.A. ex rel. J.A. v. Tucumcari Mun. Schools,* 321 F.3d 1285 (10th Cir. 2003).

In practical litigation terms, the plaintiff must now surmount two distinct barriers to state a sufficient § 1983 claim when the individual defendant timely pleads the defense of qualified immunity. First, aided by the Supreme Court's reaffirmation of liberal pleading standards with respect to elements of the prima facie civil rights case,[89] but limited by the Court's restrictions on the scope of particular constitutional claims,[90] the plaintiff must state a claim currently deemed legally sufficient. The defendant must raise the qualified immunity defense affirmatively, or risk waiving it in accordance with Federal Rule of Civil Procedure 8(c).[91] Second, if the defendant asserts the defense, the plaintiff will bear the burden of responding to the defendant's affirmative defense of qualified immunity by satisfying the court, well before trial and usually even before discovery, that the claim in question was well settled in law at the time the defendant acted. Only if plaintiff succeeds on these two questions of law will the defendant be required to engage in discovery and ultimately establish that, on the facts as she faced them at the time, a reasonable official in her position would not have known that what she did would cross the boundaries of that clearly settled law. Where the underlying constitutional violation requires evidence of improper motivation, it has been held that circumstantial as well as direct evidence of the prohibited state of mind will suffice to withstand summary judgment on the ground of qualified immunity.[92]

Beginning with *Siegert v. Gilley*,[93] the Supreme Court has exhorted and ultimately directed trial courts to turn first to the question of current legal sufficiency. In 1998, the Supreme Court cited *Siegert* with approval, stating that the better approach to resolving cases where

89. See the discussion of *Leatherman v. Tarrant County Narcotics Intelligence and Coordination Unit*, 507 U.S. 163, 113 S.Ct. 1160, 122 L.Ed.2d 517 (1993), in Chapter 5 on Procedure (reaffirming a liberal pleading standard for testing the legal sufficiency of allegations about the "failure to train" variant on "custom" in an entity action). *See also Crawford–El v. Britton*, 523 U.S. 574, 118 S.Ct. 1584, 140 L.Ed.2d 759 (1998) (applying the same general notice pleading standards to § 1983 actions against individual defendants even when the predicate claim requires proof of defendant's state of mind.) *Accord Halstead v. Motorcycle Safety Foundation, Inc.*, 71 F.Supp.2d 464, 473 (E.D.Pa.1999). *But see Goad v. Mitchell*, 297 F.3d 497 (6th Cir. 2002); *Brown v. Cochran*, 171 F.3d 1329, 1332–33 (11th Cir.1999); *Judge v. City of Lowell*, 160 F.3d 67, 74–75 (1st Cir.1998); *Kain v. Nesbitt*, 156 F.3d 669, 673 (6th Cir.1998) (interpreting *Crawford–El* as authorizing district judges to require heightened pleading by plaintiff in a Reply following a defendant's Answer in order for plaintiff to survive qualified immunity defense, at least respecting claims requiring proof of improper motive). *But cf. Kyle K. v. Chapman*, 208 F.3d 940, 943–44 (11th Cir.2000) (rejecting heightened pleading argument, without citation to *Crawford–El*, simply by noting that initial Complaint met modest "short and plain statement of the claim" requirement of F.R.C.P. 8(a)).

90. *See* §§ 2.32 and 2.41, *infra*.

91. *Gomez v. Toledo*, 446 U.S. 635, 100 S.Ct. 1920, 64 L.Ed.2d 572 (1980); *Moore v. Morgan*, 922 F.2d 1553 (11th Cir.1991) (defendant has the burden of pleading qualified immunity because it is an affirmative defense that avoids liability even assuming plaintiff establishes all the prima facie elements of a § 1983 claim).

92. *Tompkins v. Vickers*, 26 F.3d 603 (5th Cir.1994). The broader question whether qualified immunity is defeated or altered where the predicate right contains a state of mind element is explored more fully at text *infra*.

93. 500 U.S. 226, 111 S.Ct. 1789, 114 L.Ed.2d 277 (1991). *Siegert* is also discussed in § 2.41 below and in Chapter 5 on Procedure.

qualified immunity is raised is first to determine whether the plaintiff states a legally cognizable claim at all; only if so should the trial judge address the "clearly established" prong of the defense.[94] The Court reasoned that if courts regularly avoid deciding if the right is legally cognizable by jumping straight to the clearly established prong, standards of official conduct would tend to remain uncertain. "An immunity determination, with nothing more, provides no clear standard, constitutional or non-constitutional. In practical terms, escape from uncertainty would require the issue to arise in [yet another] suit."[95] Finally, in 1999, the Court restated the *Siegert* and *County of Sacramento* suggestion in mandatory terms: when evaluating a claim of qualified immunity, "a court must first determine whether the plaintiff has alleged a deprivation of an actual constitutional right."[96]

If judges, obedient to this command, address the current cognizability of the claimed right first,[97] asking whether that right was clearly established when defendant acted only after finding the claimed right currently cognizable, § 1983 individual defendant cases will again serve as vehicles for the elaboration of constitutional rights, thus complementing that function which is uniformly served by § 1983 actions against defendant entities. A determination favorable to the plaintiff on the current cognizability questions will aid future plaintiffs, even if the instant plaintiff ultimately fails because she cannot show that the right in question was clearly established when the defendant acted. On the other hand, a determination favorable to the defendant on current

94. *County of Sacramento v. Lewis*, 523 U.S. 833, 841 n. 5, 118 S.Ct. 1708, 1714 n. 5, 140 L.Ed.2d 1043 (1998).

95. *Id.*

96. *Conn v. Gabbert*, 526 U.S. 286, 290, 119 S.Ct. 1292, 1295, 143 L.Ed.2d 399 (1999) and *Wilson v. Layne*, 526 U.S. 603, 609, 119 S.Ct. 1692, 1697, 143 L.Ed.2d 818 (1999). *See also Saucier v. Katz,* 533 U.S. 194, 201, 121 S.Ct. 2151, 150 L.Ed.2d 272 (2001) and *Hope v. Pelzer*, 536 U.S. 730, 122 S.Ct. 2508, 2513, 153 L.Ed.2d 666 (2002).

97. One circuit that had viewed *Siegert* and *County of Sacramento* as merely encouraging, not requiring it to decide current cognizability before addressing any "clearly established" questions recognizes that the Supreme Court in *Conn* and *Wilson* "has instructed us that we must first decide the merits issue, and only if we decide that in favor of the plaintiff, i.e., conclude that the violation of a bona fide federal right has been alleged or evidenced, should we reach the issue of whether that right was clearly established at the time of the violation." *Hartley v. Parnell*, 193 F.3d 1263, 1270–71 (11th Cir.1999). It should be noted, however, that even after the Supreme Court decided *Conn v. Gabbert*, though a few days before it decided *Wilson v. Layne*, another circuit decision continued to refer to the high Court's approach as "better" rather than necessary, and declined to follow it where the immunity issue was easier to decide than the question of current cognizability; judicial resources might therefore be conserved by deciding the "clearly established" issue first; and the challenged prison regulation was not likely to perpetually escape judicial scrutiny. *Horne v. Coughlin*, 178 F.3d 603 (2d Cir.1999). The opinion in *Horne* was subsequently amended, 191 F.3d 244. The court explained that it would not reach the constitutional issue despite *Siegert* and *County of Sacramento's* suggestion and *Conn* and *Wilson's* apparent mandate, because "where there is qualified immunity, a court's assertion that a constitutional right exists would be pure dictum." *Id.* at 247. The opinion observed that because the Supreme Court rejected the putative right asserted in *Conn*, its decision on the merits there was not dictum. And while the Supreme Court upheld on the merits the right in question in *Wilson*, the Second Circuit noted that the merits decision was "straightforward and unanimous"; further, the situation there was one in which injunctive relief—which is not subject to the defense of qualified immunity—would not be available for lack of prior notice.

cognizability yields that defendant an outright dismissal for failure to state a claim, rather than merely a qualified immunity dismissal that would relieve him of damages, but leave him exposed to the possibility of injunctive relief and attorney's fee liability.

Most circuits with reported decisions on the question construed *Siegert* the same way: district courts (or the circuit courts on an appeal from the denial of qualified immunity) should first determine whether the plaintiff has alleged a cognizable federal law violation under current law before considering the twin "clearly established law" and "objective reasonableness" elements of the qualified immunity defense.[98] These courts accordingly turn to the question whether the defendant's alleged conduct violated clearly established law as of the time of the events in question only if and after they have determined that the plaintiff's allegations state a currently cognizable claim. Where both of these qualified immunity legal issues are presented, *Siegert* shows at a minimum that the defendant who first asserts the defense by moving for summary judgment does not waive the question of current legal sufficiency just because that issue could have been earlier presented by a motion under F.R.C.P. 12(b)(6). Moreover, the Court's subsequent recommendation in *County of Sacramento v. Lewis*[99] and its apparent mandate in *Conn v. Gabbert*[100] and *Wilson v. Layne*,[101] strongly suggest that even if it would be easier to decide the clearly established law issue first, the trial court should ordinarily initially decide the question of current legal sufficiency. In that way, the Court observed, cases against individual defendants can retain at least some potential for determining one way or the other the contours of evolving federal constitutional and statutory rights.[102]

98. See, e.g., *Boyd v. Knox*, 47 F.3d 966, 968 (8th Cir.1995); *Wilson v. Formigoni*, 42 F.3d 1060, 1064 (7th Cir.1994); *LeRoy v. Illinois Racing Bd.*, 39 F.3d 711, 713 (7th Cir.1994), *cert. denied*, 515 U.S. 1131, 115 S.Ct. 2555, 132 L.Ed.2d 809 (1995); *Brown v. Nix*, 33 F.3d 951, 953–55 (8th Cir.1994); *Buckley v. Fitzsimmons*, 20 F.3d 789, 792 (7th Cir.1994), *cert. denied*, 513 U.S. 1085, 115 S.Ct. 740, 130 L.Ed.2d 642 (1995) (on remand); *Calhoun v. New York State Division of Parole Officers*, 999 F.2d 647 (2d Cir.1993); *Hinton v. City of Elwood*, 997 F.2d 774 (10th Cir.1993); *Grady v. El Paso Community College*, 979 F.2d 1111, 1113, 1114 (5th Cir.1992); *Silver v. Franklin Township Bd. of Zoning Appeals*, 966 F.2d 1031, 1034–36 (6th Cir.1992); and *Hunter v. District of Columbia*, 943 F.2d 69, 76 (D.C.Cir.1991). These courts view the "current cognizability" question as equivalent to the question raised by a motion to dismiss for failure to state a claim under Federal Rule of Civil Procedure 12(b) (6). Some understand the *Siegert* marching orders to require them to decide the current cognizability question as antecedent to a two-part "clearly established law" and "objective reasonableness" inquiry that composes the affirmative defense of qualified immunity under *Harlow* and *Creighton*. Others expand the qualified immunity defense to include three parts, with the issue of current legal cognizability preceding the determination whether the law was clearly established at the time the defendant acted, which in turn precedes the fact-based question of the defendant's objective reasonableness. However phrased, these decisions require determining whether the plaintiff's allegations state a claim as of the time the motion is decided before addressing whether the asserted federal law violation was clearly established at the time of the alleged wrongful acts.

99. 523 U.S. 833, 118 S.Ct. 1708, 140 L.Ed.2d 1043 (1998).

100. 526 U.S. 286, 290, 119 S.Ct. 1292, 1295, 143 L.Ed.2d 399 (1999).

101. 526 U.S. 603, 609, 119 S.Ct. 1692, 1697, 143 L.Ed.2d 818 (1999).

102. This dynamic is at work in the circuit cases following *Wilson, Conn, Saucier,* and *Hope. See, e.g., Gean v. Hattaway,*

For the most part, after *Wilson, Saucier,* and *Hope*, the circuits now take it as a mandate to decide, sequentially: (1) do the allegations state a currently cognizable constitutional claim; (2) if so, was that claim clearly established by general principles of obvious clarity or by materially similar authoritative precedent; and (3) if so, would a reasonable hypothetical officer in the circumstances that confronted the defendant have realized that what (s)he was doing would violate that clearly established right?[103]

330 F.3d 758 (6th Cir.2003) (no clearly established federal right of minors to have state conserve their social security benefits without using those funds for their maintenance when state officials did the contrary); *Martin v. Snyder*, 329 F.3d 919 (7th Cir. 2003) (when prison officials acted, not clearly established that it violated due process for them to delay by 12 months marriage of inmate and his fiancé); *Batten v. Gomez*, 324 F.3d 288 (4th Cir.2003) (no authoritative decision had held state officials to violate procedural due process by seizing minor child pursuant to another state court's order in custody proceedings without affording prior notice and hearing); *Hill v. McKinley*, 311 F.3d 899 (8th Cir. 2002) (guards who permitted restraint of female inmate nude in presence of male guards for substantial time absent threat to security or safety did not violate Fourth Amendment rights then clearly established); *Jarrett v. Town of Yarmouth*, 309 F.3d 54 (1st Cir.2002) (officer who released police dog trained to bite and hold for apprehending suspecting fleeing from traffic accident did not violate clearly established law); *Thomas v. Cohen*, 304 F.3d 563 (6th Cir.2002) (women's shelter residents had no clearly established right to be free from property seizure incident to officers' unlawful eviction of them from their rooms); *Roe v. Texas Dep't of Protective and Regulatory Services*, 299 F.3d 395, 408–410 (5th Cir. 2002) (even though social worker may have violated child's Fourth Amendment right to be free of physically intrusive strip search in connection with child abuse allegations, that right had not been clearly established by decision of Supreme Court, circuit in question, or a consensus of decisions in other circuits); *Sheets v. Mullins*, 287 F.3d 581 (6th Cir.2002) (law not clearly established that officer could violate infant victim's substantive due process rights by telling mother to wait before removing victim from proximity of father, thereby rendering victim more vulnerable to danger from father); *Higgason v. Stephens*, 288 F.3d 868 (6th Cir.2002) (qualified immunity for state police commissioner and investigating detective because son had no constitutionally protected right to be free of indictment for murdering his mother); *Inmon v. Arkansas Dep't of Correction*, 245 F.3d 1030 (8th Cir. 2001) (qualified immunity ordered because complaint failed adequately to plead an underlying predicate constitutional violation); *Gruenke v. Seip*, 225 F.3d 290, 304–07 (3d Cir.2000) (court recognizes unconstitutional interference with familial relations but accords qualified immunity because the application of the relevant general principles "to the unique circumstances of this case" cannot be said to have been clearly established); *B.C. v. Plumas Unified Sch. Dist.*, 192 F.3d 1260 (9th Cir.1999) (for future cases, court adopts on the constitutional merits the view of the Fifth Circuit that subjecting students to sniffing by law-enforcement dogs is a "search" within the meaning of the Fourth Amendment, but it absolves the individual defendants in the instant case because that view was not clearly established in the Ninth Circuit when they acted and the Seventh Circuit had held to the contrary). *See also Harrell v. Cook*, 169 F.3d 428 (7th Cir.1999) (police officers violated a constitutional right of access to the courts if they disposed of evidence relating to a theft from plaintiffs' home to prevent plaintiffs from suing alleged thief, but that right was not clearly established when officers acted).

103. See *Wilkerson v. Stalder*, 329 F.3d 431, 434–435 (5th Cir.2003); *Flores v. Morgan Hill Unified School Dist.*, 324 F.3d 1130, 1134 (9th Cir.2003); *Wood v. Kesler*, 323 F.3d 872, 877–78 (11th Cir.2003); *Schieber v. City of Philadelphia*, 320 F.3d 409, 416 (3d Cir.2003); *Roe v. Texas Dep't of Protective and Regulatory Services*, 299 F.3d 395, 401–402, 403 n.6 (5th Cir. 2002); *McClendon v. City of Columbia*, 305 F.3d 314 (5th Cir.2002) (per curiam); *Wilson v. Jones*, 251 F.3d 1340 (11th Cir.2001); *Butera v. District of Columbia,* 235 F.3d 637 (D.C.Cir.2001) (recognizing Due Process right before holding it not clearly established when defendants asked); *Scull v. New Mexico,* 236 F.3d 588 (10th Cir.2000) (deciding no current right before holding alternatively that any such right was not clearly established); *Devereaux v. Perez,* 218 F.3d 1045, 1051 (9th Cir.), *rehearing en*

An entity's liability is in part derivative of that of its agent, because it is a minimum condition of the entity's liability that the agent's conduct violates federal law. Accordingly, an entity co-defendant cannot be liable by virtue of the conduct of an individual agent if that agent is granted qualified immunity on the ground that her conduct does not violate a currently cognizable federal constitutional or statutory right.[104] By contrast, if qualified immunity is granted to the individual defendant only because the law was not clearly established at the time she acted, or it was clearly established but a reasonable person in her position would not have realized that her conduct would violate that right, a companion entity defendant would not for either such reason be relieved of liability.[105] In these latter cases the plaintiff would nevertheless still have to prove causation, damages, and the required applicable governmental "policy"—that is, that the entity had commanded or ratified the agent's federally unlawful act or with deliberate indifference had acquiesced in a pattern or custom of strikingly similar failures to act.[106] After *Siegert, County of Sacramento, Conn* and *Wilson*, one may anticipate that courts granting qualified immunity will more frequently do so on the ground that there is no currently cognizable federal law violation. If that is so, there should accordingly be more cases in which a determination of the agent's nonliability will also terminate the lawsuit in favor of the entity.

banc granted, 235 F.3d 1206 (9th Cir.2000); *Jones v. Shields,* 207 F.3d 491, 494 (8th Cir.2000); *Kitzman–Kelley v. Warner,* 203 F.3d 454, 457 (7th Cir.2000); *Suarez Corp. Indus. v. McGraw,* 202 F.3d 676, 685 (4th Cir.2000); *Hartley v. Parnell,* 193 F.3d 1263, 1270–71 (11th Cir.1999); *B.C. v. Plumas Unified Sch. Dist.,* 192 F.3d 1260, 1265–66 (9th Cir.1999); *Crosby v. Paulk,* 187 F.3d 1339, 1345 (11th Cir.1999). *See Harhay v. Town of Ellington Bd. of Educ.*, 323 F.3d 206, 211–212 (2d Cir.2003) (the three-step inquiry "should typically" be done in sequential order). *But see Kalka v. Hawk*, 215 F.3d 90, 94–98 (D.C.Cir.2000) (rejecting a reading of the U.S. Supreme Court decisions that always requires federal courts to decide whether the allegations state a constitutional claim before granting qualified immunity, reasoning: (1) if the underlying constitutional claim is upheld but immunity granted by the lower court, the government defendant would have no opportunity for interlocutory appeal of the newly declared right; (2) the sequence violates the long-standing tradition counseling judicial restraint before tackling constitutional questions; (3) the Supreme Court's rationale for directing initial decision on the constitutional question, to settle uncertain standards of official conduct, is inapplicable where plaintiff challenges an ongoing practice by injunction, since individual defendants have no qualified immunity with respect to injunctive relief; and (4) in particular civil rights actions, it cannot be determined whether plaintiff has a constitutional right in the abstract, but only after discovery or trial, yet qualified immunity, where it applies, is intended to be an immunity from suit, not just damages); *Horne v. Coughlin*, 191 F.3d 244, 247–248 (2d Cir. 1999) (also refusing always to decide current constitutional cognizability first, because (1) the sequence prescription of *Sacramento* (if not of *Conn* or *Wilson*) was "tentatively worded"; (2) a decision finding a constitutional right would become "pure dictum" in cases where qualified immunity was nevertheless upheld for lack of a clearly established right or where the defendant was not objectively unreasonable; and (3) government defendants who prevailed on immunity, and therefore had no interlocutory appeal, might have no opportunity to appeal the district court's antecedent decision declaring a constitutional right).

104. *See Heller v. City of Los Angeles*, discussed *infra* § 5.106. *But cf. Speer v. Wynne*, 276 F.3d 980, 985–987 (8th Cir. 2002) (holding *Heller* does not preclude municipal liability unless a municipal employee is found liable in individual capacity where theory of municipal liability not dependent on municipality's responsibility for officer's alleged unconstitutional acts, as where plaintiff proves a governmental policy or custom).

105. *See* § 5.108, *infra*.

106. *See* §§ 5.106–107.

This is because the ruling, even if nominally grounded in the defense of qualified immunity, will effectively have decided that the complaint fails to state a claim on which relief can be granted—a ground that defeats liability altogether, unlike qualified immunity, which precludes only damages.

Only one reported federal appellate decision since *Siegert* expressed the view that the court hearing a summary judgment motion based on qualified immunity "is concerned only with the law at the time of the defendant's actions"—that is, with whether the law was then "clearly established."[107] Putting aside the questionable soundness of this construction of *Siegert*, in context this discussion was needless.[108] There is virtue, however, in the debate, for it suggests a more flexible, third way of reading *Siegert*: on summary judgment the trial court might have discretion to turn first to the current or the past legal settledness of the asserted federal right, depending upon which question is easier to resolve or entails less burden for the court. And at least one circuit has sometimes taken this approach, turning to the "clearly established" issue first where doing so will avoid the additional analysis and needless precedent-setting involved in determining constitutional questions of first impression.[109]

If, for example, it appears a close or difficult question whether the allegation states a currently cognizable claim, it may make sense from an efficiency standpoint for the court to address the *Harlow–Creighton* "clearly settled" inquiry at the outset. Nevertheless, *Hope, Saucier, Wilson, Conn, Sacramento,* and *Siegert* seem to have foreclosed that approach. If, on the other hand, the right allegedly violated seems to have been clearly established at the time of the events in question but

107. *DiMeglio v. Haines*, 45 F.3d 790 (4th Cir.1995) (emphasis supplied). This panel opinion denigrates the timing distinction made by the Supreme Court in *Siegert* as a "tautology" that merely makes "the self-evident point that a plaintiff has not alleged the violation of a right clearly established at the time of the conduct, if he has not alleged the violation of a right that exist[s] when the motion is decided."

108. The court starts by explaining for thirteen pages why the eight other circuits had misread *Siegert* to require a preliminary inquiry into whether the plaintiff's predicate claim is currently cognizable, instead of immediately and only asking whether defendant's conduct was actionable at the time it occurred. In the next three pages, however, the panel observes four times that the claim before it was not clearly recognized either when defendant acted or currently. Thus the extended discussion setting forth the panel's unique interpretation of *Siegert* appears to have made no difference to resolution of the legal sufficiency of the complaint at hand.

109. See *Spivey v. Elliott*, 41 F.3d 1497, 1499 (11th Cir.1995). But this reasoning does not comport with the Supreme Court's policy based rationale for preferring the *Siegert* approach: § 1983 should be available as a mechanism for testing new constitutional claims because standards for official conduct can be clarified. *County of Sacramento v. Lewis*, 523 U.S. 833, 118 S.Ct. 1708, 140 L.Ed.2d 1043. And while a subsequent Eleventh Circuit panel described *Spivey* as showing that "we have not considered the *Siegert* approach mandatory," the court did in fact follow the *Siegert* direction to decide the current legal cognizability of the claim first. *Cottrell v. Caldwell*, 85 F.3d 1480, 1490 (11th Cir. 1996). *Accord Johnson v. City of Fort Lauderdale, Fla.*, 126 F.3d 1372, 1378 (11th Cir. 1997) (court must first determine whether plaintiff presents a violation of a constitutional or statutory right). The Supreme Court has subsequently held that the *Siegert/Sacramento* sequencing is mandatory. *Conn* and *Wilson*.

has subsequently been limited or overruled by a restrictive constitutional interpretation issued before the motion is decided, the court can resolve the legal aspect of qualified immunity *only* by addressing the "current cognizability" question presented by an ordinary motion to dismiss for failure to state a claim upon which relief may be granted.

Thus under the *Hope/Saucier/Siegert/Sacramento/Conn/Wilson* approach, the plaintiff's damages claim may fail on either of two legal hurdles. First, if the claim has never been recognized, or the law has moved in a pro-defense direction after the events in question, current legal insufficiency may alone lead to dismissal, either on a motion to dismiss for failure to state a claim or on summary judgment.[110] In such a case qualified immunity is granted essentially because the complaint fails to state a claim on which relief may be granted. Second, the plaintiff also loses—indeed this is where the "clearly established" rule has its bite—where a court recognizes or assumes the claimed right as of the time of decision but concludes that the right was not well established, by the Supreme Court, the relevant circuit court, or a circuit consensus, when the alleged injury was inflicted.[111]

110. See, e.g., *Cottrell v. Caldwell*, 85 F.3d 1480, 1490–1491 (11th Cir.1996); *Burrell v. Board of Trustees of Ga. Military College*, 970 F.2d 785 (11th Cir.1992), *cert. denied*, 507 U.S. 1018, 113 S.Ct. 1814, 123 L.Ed.2d 445 (1993) (facts, viewed through evolving summary judgment standards, were insufficient to show alleged conspiracy between defendant public officials and the private employer that inflicted plaintiff's actual injury, and therefore claim failed to meet § 1983's "under color of" requirement or the state action requirement of the First Amendment). *Wooten v. Campbell*, 49 F.3d 696, 699 (11th Cir.1995), *cert. denied*, 516 U.S. 943, 116 S.Ct. 379, 133 L.Ed.2d 302 (1995).

111. See, e.g., *Luna v. Pico*, 356 F.3d 481 (2d Cir. 2004)(no controlling decisions on the quantum of evidence binding prison disciplinary officials in finding inmate guilty of particular violations, so that claimed right not to be convicted except upon such evidence not clearly established); *African Trade & Information Center, Inc. v. Abromaitis*, 294 F.3d 355 (2d Cir.2002) (no clearly established right not to be denied state contract in retaliation for protected speech); *Sorrels v. McKee*, 290 F.3d 965 (9th Cir.2002) (inmate's First Amendment right to receive publications paid for other than through his prison account not clearly established when policy interfering with receipt enforced); *Cruz v. Kauai County*, 279 F.3d 1064 (9th Cir.2002) (arrestee's Fourth Amendment right not to have prosecutor personally attest to false allegations by a biased informant in order to revoke arrestee's bail not clearly established); *Virgili v. Gilbert*, 272 F.3d 391 (6th Cir.2001) (prison employee's Fourth Amendment right against strip search without reasonable suspicion not clearly established when search conducted); *Vega v. Miller*, 273 F.3d 460 (2d Cir.2001) (college administrators qualifiedly immune because they could reasonably believe there were not violating professor's assumed First Amendment right to freedom from discipline for continuing with a pedagogically motivated classroom exercise even after students called out vulgar, sexually explicit language); *McLaughlin v. Watson*, 271 F.3d 566 (3d Cir.2001) (case law holding no constitutional violation to use influence short of coercion to cause third party to take adverse action because of plaintiff's speech entitled U.S. attorney to qualified immunity for allegedly influencing state attorney general's office to take such adverse action against state agents) (*Bivens* claim); *Starlight Sugar, Inc. v. Soto*, 253 F.3d 137 (1st Cir.), *cert. denied*, 534 U.S. 1021, 122 S.Ct. 548, 151 L.Ed.2d 424 (2001) (officials receive immunity for enforcing Puerto Rico regulation violating dormant Commerce Clause in light of legal uncertainty as to Clause's applicability to Puerto Rico); *Wilson v. Jones*, 251 F.3d 1340 (11th Cir.2001) (no prior case clearly established unlawfulness of policy requiring strip searches of arrestees before admittance to jail); *Currier v. Doran*, 242 F.3d 905 (10th Cir.), *cert. denied*, 534 U.S. 1019, 122 S.Ct. 543, 151 L.Ed.2d 421 (2001) (not clearly established when state social worker instructed mother to cease alleging child abuse against father that conduct violated state-created danger theory of due process); *Flagner v. Wilkinson*, 241 F.3d 475 (6th Cir.2001) (right of prisoner, Hasidic Jew, to grow beard and sidelocks contrary to state grooming regulation not clearly established when he was compelled to cut his hair); *Hudson v. Hall*, 231 F.3d 1289 (11th Cir.2000) (no clearly established law governing application of state law on turn signals to turn from private to public roadway); *Cunningham v. Gates*, 229 F.3d 1271 (9th Cir.2000) (suggestion of *Trevino v. Gates*, 99 F.3d 911, 918 (9th Cir.1996), *cert. denied,* 520 U.S. 1117, 117 S.Ct. 1249, 137 L.Ed.2d 330 (1997) that routine, wholesale city grant of indemnification to police officers against punitive damages may violate constitutional rights, did not represent clearly established law when city counsel members so voted in instant case); *Lauro v. Charles*, 219 F.3d 202 (2d Cir.2000) (police staging a "perp walk" for media outside precinct not sufficiently analogous to giving media permission to videotape execution of search warrant, which circuit law had condemned); *Denno v. School Bd. of Volusia County*, 218 F.3d 1267, 1270–1275 (11th Cir.2000) (because one of two applicable Supreme Court decisions gave school administrators more flexibility in balancing rights in First Amendment case concerning discipline of students for displaying confederate flag, individual administrators afforded immunity). *Kyle K. v. Chapman*, 208 F.3d 940 (11th Cir.2000) (mentally retarded child committed to state hospital had no clearly established right to be protected from self-abusive behavior by nonprofessional, as distinct from professional, health service employee); *Kelly v. City of Oakland*, 198 F.3d 779 (9th Cir.1999) (right to be free of same-sex harassment of the quid pro quo variety clearly established, but right to be free of same-sex hostile environment harassment not); *Sanders v. Howze*, 177 F.3d 1245 (11th Cir.1999) (plaintiff's right to jail suicide prevention measures not clearly established by a circuit decision requiring the particular measures asserted as necessary); *Powell v. Schriver*, 175 F.3d 107 (2d Cir. 1999) (although it was clearly established that prison guards had some responsibility to respond to threat of physical harm to plaintiff posed by fellow inmates, it was not clearly established that they had an obligation to safeguard confidentiality of prisoner's medical records); *Harrell v. Cook*, 169 F.3d 428 (7th Cir.1999) (police officers violated a constitutional right of access to the courts if they disposed of evidence relating to a theft from plaintiffs' home to prevent plaintiffs from suing alleged thief, but that right was not clearly established when officers acted); *Lewis v. Cowen*, 165 F.3d 154, 166 (2d Cir.1999), *cert. denied*, 528 U.S. 823, 120 S.Ct. 70, 145 L.Ed.2d 60 (1999) (no clearly established First Amendment right on part of policymaking public employee to avoid termination for refusing to promote agency policy as directed by employer); *Moniz v. City of Ft. Lauderdale*, 145 F.3d 1278, 1282–83 (11th Cir.1998) (individual local officials implementing the requirements of a federal court consent decree entitled to qualified immunity where constitutionality of its requirements had not been challenged in court); *Greer v. Shoop*, 141 F.3d 824 (8th Cir.1998) (parole officers who failed to tell girlfriend that boyfriend, who was paroled to the girlfriend's home, was HIV+ were entitled to qualified immunity; not clearly established that this was violative of girlfriend's constitutional rights); *Wilson v. Layne*, 141 F.3d 111 (4th Cir.1998), *aff'd*, 526 U.S. 603, 119 S.Ct. 1692, 143 L.Ed.2d 818 (1999) (not clearly established at the time that police could not permit media into private residence while police were executing an arrest warrant); *Wolfe v. City of Pittsburgh*, 140 F.3d 236, 240 (3d Cir.1998) (individual local officials implementing the requirements of a federal court-ordered affirmative action plan entitled to both qualified and absolute immunity where constitutionality of order's requirements had not been challenged in court); *Petta v. Rivera*, 133 F.3d 330 (5th Cir.1998), *vacated and superseded on denial of rehearing*, 143 F.3d 895 (5th Cir.1998) (right to be free from excessive force resulting in purely emotional harm not clearly established at time); *Humphrey v. Staszak*, 148 F.3d 719 (7th Cir.1998) (not clearly established at time that actions of a bystander in following police who were making arrest, and arguing with police during arrest, did not provide probable cause for arrest of bystander for disorderly conduct under Illinois state law).

Aponte Matos v. Toledo Davila, 135 F.3d 182 (1st Cir.1998) (not clearly established that residents had a constitutional right to have police knock and announce their presence before breaking down the house's door with an axe to execute a search warrant); *Snyder v. Trepagnier*, 142 F.3d 791 (5th Cir.1998), *cert. dismissed*, 526 U.S. 1083, 119 S.Ct. 1493, 143 L.Ed.2d 575 (1999) (jury's findings that officer used excessive force and also that the officer acted reasonably are reconcilable, and thus, qualified immunity was granted; jury could have found that plaintiff did not have weapon but officer reasonably believed the plaintiff did have a gun); *Picray v. Sealock*, 138 F.3d 767 (9th Cir.1998) (not clearly established that barring someone from area around polling place for unlawfully wearing political buttons was violative of the plaintiff's constitutional rights); *Jones v. Collins*, 132 F.3d 1048, 1055 (5th Cir.1998) (retaliation for speech that plaintiff denied uttering cannot violate any clearly established right); *Friedman v. South*, 92 F.3d 989 (9th Cir.1996) (an inmate's right to kosher food not clearly established when dependent upon retroactive application of Religious Freedom Restoration Act); *Erwin v. Daley*, 92 F.3d 521 (7th Cir.1996), *cert. denied*, 519 U.S. 1116, 117 S.Ct. 958, 136 L.Ed.2d 845 (1997) (local officials granted qualified immunity for reverse-discriminatory employment decisions exceeding scope of court-ordered affirmative action program because constitutional principles suggesting the unlawfulness of their decisions were too confusing and recent for defendants to be expected to have conformed to them); *Beauregard v. Olson*, 84 F.3d 1402 (11th Cir.1996) (even assuming tax collector's deputized employees had ministerial rather than sensitive political duties so that their termination for political reasons violated First Amendment, that right not established at the time). *Hogan v. Carter*, 85 F.3d 1113 (4th Cir.), *cert. denied*, 519 U.S. 974, 117 S.Ct. 408, 136 L.Ed.2d 321 (1996) (administering psychotropic medication to prison inmate before conducting predeprivation hearing not violative of a right that was clearly established when the prison physician acted); *Suissa v. Fulton County*, 74 F.3d 266 (11th Cir.1996) (supervisor's attempt to impinge on deputy's free speech concerning contents of grievance report did not amount to clearly established prohibition on retaliation for exercising First Amendment rights); *Anderson v. Romero*, 72 F.3d 518 (7th Cir.1995) (inmate's right to confidentiality of HIV-positive status not clearly established); *Sparks v. Stutler*, 71 F.3d 259 (7th Cir.1995), *cert. denied*, 519 U.S. 948, 117 S.Ct. 357, 136 L.Ed.2d 249 (1996) (when inmate had catheter forcibly inserted into urinary tract, his right to be free from such procedure not clearly established); *St. Hilaire v. City of Laconia*, 71 F.3d 20 (1st Cir.1995), *cert. denied*, 518 U.S. 1017, 116 S.Ct. 2548, 135 L.Ed.2d 1068 (1996) (no clearly established duty to announce identity and purpose before use of deadly force); *Haney v. City of Cumming*, 69 F.3d 1098 (11th Cir.1995), *cert. denied*, 517 U.S. 1209, 116 S.Ct. 1826, 134 L.Ed.2d 931 (1996) (as non-physicians, county investigator and prison guard violated no clearly established right to psychiatric or medical need of suicidal prisoner); *Price v. Sasser*, 65 F.3d 342 (4th Cir.1995) (at time of assault, sheriff had no clearly established duty to protect inmate from other inmates); *Gunaca v. Texas*, 65 F.3d 467 (5th Cir.1995) (despite settled right of certain public officials to be free from political retaliation, no Supreme Court or Fifth Circuit decision had applied that right to the employment of a district attorney's investigator); *Trigalet v. Young*, 54 F.3d 645 (10th Cir.), *cert. denied sub nom. Trigalet v. Warrick*, 516 U.S. 932, 116 S.Ct. 340, 133 L.Ed.2d 238 (1995) (police liability for injury inflicted by third party suspect during chase was clearly established by circuit law only after events in question). *Singer v. Maine*, 49 F.3d 837 (1st Cir.1995) (predicate violation of employee's Fifth Amendment right against self incrimination not clearly established when she refused to answer questions during investigation); *Hale v. Townley*, 45 F.3d 914 (5th Cir.1995) (constitutional prohibition on retaliating against an individual for filing and winning a lawsuit not sufficiently clearly established to pin damages liability on a police officer who rammed his fist into the testicles of a night club operator with such retaliatory intent); *Rodgers v. Jabe*, 43 F.3d 1082 (6th Cir.1995) (when prison officials limited inmates' outdoor exercise, the amount of exercise to which prisoners were entitled had not been clearly established according to the law of the circuit); *Cummins v. Campbell*, 44 F.3d 847 (10th Cir.1994) (university officials who apparently prima facie violated students' First Amendment rights by delaying approval for the showing of a film celebrating Christ entitled to qualified immunity because the law then did not preclude the countervailing argument that even the university's indirect sponsorship of the film might be viewed as excessive entanglement with religion); *See, e.g., Kernats v. O'Sullivan*, 35 F.3d 1171 (7th Cir. 1994) (police officer's ejection of tenant, although an abuse of power, was not a clearly unlawful Fourth Amendment "seizure" at time it took place); *Foster v. Lake Jackson*, 28 F.3d 425 (5th Cir.1994) (constitutional right of access to the courts had been held violated, when defendants acted, to right to file suit, so alleged right to proceed in litigation free of discovery abuse after filing was not then clearly established); *Chew v. Gates*, 27 F.3d 1432, 1446–1449 (9th Cir.1994), *cert. denied*, 513 U.S. 1148, 115 S.Ct. 1097, 130 L.Ed.2d 1065 (1995); (when police officers acted it was not clearly established that unleashing police dogs on concealed suspects by biting and seizing them constituted deadly force or that any such force was unreasonable); *Prue v. City of Syracuse*, 26 F.3d 14 (2d Cir.1994) (although policeman's right to a pretermination hearing was established when he was denied reinstatement, it was not then established that his particular property interest was sufficient to trigger the protections of due process); *Harper v.*

Of course a right may have become clearly established before the defendant acted; and if so, and the right is still recognized when the qualified immunity motion is decided, and, if the defendant's conduct was objectively unreasonable, qualified immunity will be denied.[112] But

Harris County, 21 F.3d 597 (5th Cir.1994) (law at time of arrest required arrestee claiming excessive force to prove injury, so defense upheld even though significant injury is not a current requirement).

Doe v. Louisiana, 2 F.3d 1412 (5th Cir. 1993), *cert. denied sub nom. Doe v. Bennett*, 510 U.S. 1164, 114 S.Ct. 1189, 127 L.Ed.2d 539 (1994) (social worker who allegedly violated father's liberty interest in care and custody of his children did not violate a right sufficiently particularized at the time of her behavior that she would have understood that her conduct—including procuring false evidence, withholding other evidence, and making misrepresentations to judges and prosecutor—violated that right); *Wu v. University of Alabama Bd. of Trustees*, 996 F.2d 271 (11th Cir.1993) *cert. denied*, 511 U.S. 1033, 114 S.Ct. 1543, 128 L.Ed.2d 195 (1994) (in § 1983 claim based on violation of the 1964 Civil Rights Act, university officials qualifiedly immune because it was not clearly established when they acted that their retaliation against an employee for filing civil rights complaint violated Title VII when it took the form of creating a hostile environment rather than exacting a monetary or other tangible reprisal); *Woodward v. City of Worland*, 977 F.2d 1392 (10th Cir.1992), *cert. denied sub nom. Woodard v. Seghetti*, 509 U.S. 923, 113 S.Ct. 3038, 125 L.Ed.2d 724 (1993) (qualified immunity sustained because it was unclear, under law of the circuit at the time police officers and supervisors acted, that sexual harassment violated Equal Protection Clause); *Mouille v. City of Live Oak*, 977 F.2d 924 (5th Cir.1992), *cert. denied sub nom. Liberda v. City of Live Oak*, 508 U.S. 951, 113 S.Ct. 2443, 124 L.Ed.2d 660 (1993) (qualified immunity to be assessed under circuit authority in effect at time of alleged injury that established a substantive due process test for excessive force that was more congenial to defendant than the stricter, Fourth Amendment standard subsequently announced by Supreme Court); *Wilson v. Bailey*, 934 F.2d 301, 304 (11th Cir.1991) (personnel board members acting pursuant to federal court consent decree in making race-conscious employment decisions eligible for qualified immunity). *But cf. Maitland v. University of Minnesota*, 155 F.3d 1013, 1019 (8th Cir.1998) (in case where plaintiff challenged lawfulness of consent decree ordering preference for female academic employees in salaries, university officials denied qualified immunity for agreeing to and implementing that plan because it was not objectively reasonable under established law for them to agree to plan given uncertainty whether there had been a conspicuous prior gender-based salary imbalance favoring men that would justify the decree's female preference).

112. *See, e.g., Lee v. Gregory*, 363 F.3d 931 (9th Cir. 2004)(right not to be arrested where officer executing warrant knows arrestee is not person named clearly established); *Kopec v. Tate*, 361 F.3d 772 (3d Cir. 2004)(plaintiff had clearly established right to be free from excessive force in course of being handcuffed during arrest for disorderly conduct); *Wall v. County of Orange*, 364 F.3d 1107 (9th Cir. 2004)(clearly established right not to be illegally arrested and subjected to excessive force); *Kinney v. Weaver*, 367 F.3d 337 (5th Cir. 2004)(if defendant law enforcement officers retaliated against plaintiff police academy instructors because plaintiffs had offered expert testimony against another officer in an excessive force case, officers' actions violated plaintiffs' clearly established rights under the First Amendment); *Moran v. Clark*, 359 F.3d 1058 (8th Cir. 2004) (police officials and officers who allegedly manufactured evidence against an innocent officer violated officer's clearly established substantive due process rights could not have reasonably believed such actions were lawful); *Beier v. City of Lewiston*, 354 F.3d 1058 (9th Cir. 2004)(officers violated clearly established law in arresting husband in reliance on wife's unsubstantiated claim that her husband had violated domestic protection order the requirements of which the officers did not ascertain); *Cherrington v. Skeeter*, 344 F.3d 631 (6th Cir. 2003)(clearly established law violation to fail to afford arrestee judicial determination within 48 hours of arrest); *Barrow v. Greenville Ind. Sch. Dist.*, 332 F.3d 844 (5th Cir.2003) (clearly established right to educate children in private school); *Evett v. DETNTFF*, 330 F.3d 681 (5th Cir.2003) (officer objectively unreasonable in arresting person present at drug raid); *Finsel v. Cruppenink*, 326 F.3d 903 (7th Cir.2003) (deputy objectively unreasonable in kicking open motel guest's door); *Cottone v. Jenne*, 326 F.3d 1352 (11th Cir.2003) (inmate had clearly established right to have guards monitor known violent mentally ill fellow inmate); *Hosty v.*

Carter, 325 F.3d 945 (7th Cir.2003) (state university student editors had clearly established First Amendment right to print newspaper without prior university official review and approval, even though Supreme Court precedent, respecting high school students, limited that right); *Sh.A. ex rel. J.A. v. Tucumcari Mun. Schools*, 321 F.3d 1285 (10th Cir.2003) (students had clearly established right to protection from sexual molestation by teacher); *Foley v. University of Houston System*, 324 F.3d 310 (5th Cir. 2003) (state university professor had clearly established right not to be retaliated against for filing complaint of racial discrimination) (case under § 1981); *Cavalieri v. Shepard*, 321 F.3d 616 (7th Cir.2003) (pretrial detainee had clearly established right not to be subjected to deliberate indifference if defendant knew of the risk detainee would commit suicide); *Atkinson v. Taylor*, 316 F.3d 257 (3d Cir.2003) (clearly established right of inmate not to be subjected to environmental tobacco smoke that posed unreasonable risk, known by defendants, of future harm); *Hawkins v. Holloway*, 316 F.3d 777 (8th Cir.2003) (sheriff objectively unreasonable in threatening his employees with deadly force); *Anderson v. Recore*, 317 F.3d 194 (2d Cir.2003) (inmate had clearly established right to hearing before revocation of his temporary release); *Rivero v. City and County of San Francisco*, 316 F.3d 857 (9th Cir.2002) (circuit precedents gave fair notice that mortuary contract was a valuable government benefit, and so termination of contract in retaliation for mortuary president's exercise of First Amendment rights was a clearly established violation); *Kearse v. Moffett*, 311 F.3d 891 (8th Cir.2002) (per curiam) (investigator objectively unreasonable in filing arrest warrant affidavit asserting plaintiff a convicted felon when investigator's only information was that plaintiff had been arrested); *Herzog v. Village of Winnetka, Illinois*, 309 F.3d 1041, 1044 (7th Cir.2002) (reversing summary grant of qualified immunity, where officer was objectively unreasonable with respect to use of unconstitutional excessive force); *Bell v. Johnson*, 308 F.3d 594 (6th Cir.2002) (inmate had clearly established right not to be retaliated against for filing civil rights lawsuit against guards); *Patel v. Searles*, 305 F.3d 130 (2d Cir.2002) (even absent Supreme Court or circuit precedent on point, police officers denied qualified immunity for engaging in extended public and private campaign of misinformation to destroy murder suspect's family in hope of producing incriminating leads); *Loria v. Gorman*, 306 F.3d 1271 (2d Cir.2002) (officer objectively unreasonable in entering plaintiff's house and seizing him without warrant or exigent circumstances); *Bass v. Richards*, 308 F.3d 1081 (10th Cir.2002) (sheriff's deputy had clearly established right not to be retaliated against for supporting sheriff's opponent in election); *Farmer v. Perrill*, 288 F.3d 1254 (10th Cir.2002) (prisoner had clearly established right at relevant time not to be strip searched in view of others absent legitimate penological interest); *Carey v. Nevada Gaming Control Bd.*, 279 F.3d 873 (9th Cir. 2002) (prior cases unambiguously established that casino patron had Fourth Amendment right not to identify himself during a *Terry* stop); *Skrtich v. Thornton*, 280 F.3d 1295 (11th Cir.2002) (beating prisoner after incapacitating him with shock from electronic shield violates clearly established law); *Burton v. Richmond*, 276 F.3d 973 (8th Cir.2002) (social workers denied qualified immunity in view of clearly established right of children in state custody to adequate protection and supervision in foster home to which state had removed them from their natural parents); *Bishop Paiute Tribe v. County of Inyo*, 291 F.3d 549 (9th Cir.2002) (law clearly established in circuit that county officers had no jurisdiction to search and seize tribal property during criminal prosecution of individual Indian); *Martinez v. City of Oxnard*, 270 F.3d 852 (9th Cir.2001), *rev'd sub nom. Chavez v. Martinez*, 538 U.S. 760, 123 S.Ct. 1994, 155 L.Ed.2d 984 (2003) *on ground plaintiff showed no currently cognizable constitution violations*, (qualified immunity denied police sergeant who interrogated suspect being treated for life-threatening injuries in emergency room because Fifth and Fourteenth Amendment right to be free from coercion as police seek confession clearly established); *Shain v. Ellison*, 273 F.3d 56 (2d Cir.2001) (clearly established law banning post-arraignment strip searches of misdemeanor arrestees in local jail absent reasonable suspicion of possession of contraband or weapons precluded qualified immunity for county sheriff); *Trulock v. Freeh*, 275 F.3d 391 (4th Cir.2001) (search allegedly designed to retaliate against government official for publishing article critical of defendants' government agency violated clearly established right to voice such criticism, as a reasonable officer should have known) (*Bivens* claim); *LeMarbe v. Wisneski*, 266 F.3d 429 (6th Cir. 2001), *cert. denied*, 535 U.S. 1056, 122 S.Ct. 1914, 152 L.Ed.2d 824 (2002) (prisoner had clearly established Eighth Amendment right not to have prison officials act with deliberate indifference to his health and safety by delaying medical referral or treatment after making diagnosis); *Rogers v. Pendleton*, 249 F.3d 279 (4th Cir.2001) (homeowner had clearly established right to

the more the right in question is highly dependent on varying facts or subject to a test of reasonableness or balancing—examples are alleged violations of procedural due process or the Fourth or First Amendments—the greater the likelihood that the qualified immunity defense will succeed on this law prong. In these cases, in other words, it is less likely that a particular set of pleaded facts will correspond as closely as *Anderson v. Creighton* demands to the facts of an authoritative decided case.[113] And of course even if the plaintiff meets the "clearly established

be free from a search, based only on reasonable suspicion, of the curtilage of his home); *Amaechi v. West,* 237 F.3d 356 (4th Cir.2001) (arrestee had clearly established right to avoid public view of invasive body search incident to misdemeanor arrest); *Feist v. Simonson,* 222 F.3d 455 (8th Cir. 2000) (officers' possible liability for due process violation resulting from high-speed chase established by multi-circuit precedent when they acted); *Zahrey v. Coffey,* 221 F.3d 342 (2d Cir.2000) (clearly established right to avoid deprivation of liberty interest by government investigator's fabricating evidence); *Robinson v. Solano County,* 218 F.3d 1030 (9th Cir.2000) (law clear when officers stated that holding gun to suspect's head could constitute excessive force). *Priester v. City of Riviera Beach, Fla.,* 208 F.3d 919 (11th Cir.2000) (clearly established duty on part of defendant police officer to intervene to prevent another officer from continuing to use excessive force, when defendant in a position to intervene and fails to do so); *Duckworth v. Ford,* 995 F.2d 858 (8th Cir.1993) (retaliation against public employee for opposing defendant official's successful candidacy was a clearly established First Amendment violation by the time defendant acted, although it may not have been one previously); cf. *Valencia v. Wiggins,* 981 F.2d 1440 (5th Cir.1993), *cert. denied,* 509 U.S. 905, 113 S.Ct. 2998, 125 L.Ed.2d 691 (1993) (defendant inflicted injuries on pretrial detainee wantonly and sufficiently severely to disqualify defendant from claiming immunity under both Fourteenth Amendment standard currently applicable to excessive force claim and even under the test in effect in circuit at the time of events in question).

113. See, e.g., *Waters v. Churchill,* 511 U.S. 661, 114 S.Ct. 1878, 128 L.Ed.2d 686 (1994) (to be protected, speech of public employee must be of public concern and her interest not outweighed by injury to employer's efficiency interest as employer assessed that injury based on facts about the plaintiff's conduct that it reasonably believed to be true); *Fales v. Garst,* 235 F.3d 1122 (8th Cir.2001) (school's interest in efficient administration outweighs teachers' concerns about students); *Weicherding v. Riegel,* 160 F.3d 1139 (7th Cir.1998) (relying on facts as employer reasonably perceived them to uphold qualified immunity); *Baxter by Baxter v. Vigo County Sch. Corp.,* 26 F.3d 728 (7th Cir.1994); *Dartland v. Metropolitan Dade County,* 866 F.2d 1321, 1323 (11th Cir.1989) (absence of "bright line" determining when public employer may punish employee's speech leads to conclusion that any right violated was not clearly established); *Compare Sims v. Metropolitan Dade County,* 972 F.2d 1230 (11th Cir.1992) (courts should use their own knowledge of the law to determine settledness, not just cases cited by plaintiffs); *cf. Harden v. Adams,* 760 F.2d 1158 (11th Cir. 1985), *cert. denied sub nom. Grimmer v. Harden,* 474 U.S. 1007, 106 S.Ct. 530, 88 L.Ed.2d 462 (1985) (expressing reluctance to resolve complex First Amendment issues on summary judgment). *Cf. Wasson v. Sonoma County Junior College,* 203 F.3d 659 (9th Cir.2000), *cert. denied,* 531 U.S. 927, 121 S.Ct. 305, 148 L.Ed.2d 245 (2000) (even unreasonable investigation excused when employer's mistake was not about the content of plaintiff's speech, as in *Waters,* but consisted of misidentifying plaintiff as the writer of letters accusing employer of misconduct). *See also* Wells, "*Three Arguments Against Mt. Healthy: Tort Theory, Constitutional Torts, and Freedom of Speech,*" 51 Mercer L.Rev. 583, 598–99, text accompanying notes 78–81 (2000). *See also Marsh v. Butler County,* 268 F.3d 1014, 1031 n. 9 (11th Cir.2001) (en banc) (observing that when constitutional standard requires balancing or assessment of reasonableness, preexisting caselaw applying those tests in specific, closely analogous circumstances will usually be necessary to afford the individual defendant the requisite fair notice of what conduct is unlawful).

Before *Churchill,* some circuits showed substantial solicitude to plaintiffs in overcoming the qualified immunity barrier to First Amendment claims. *See, e.g., Marshall v. Allen,* 984 F.2d 787 (7th Cir.1993); *Buzek v. County of Saunders,* 972 F.2d 992 (8th Cir.1992); *Patrick v. Miller,* 953 F.2d 1240 (10th Cir.1992); *Thompson v. City of*

Starkville, 901 F.2d 456 (5th Cir.1990); *Dube v. State Univ. of New York*, 900 F.2d 587 (2d Cir.1990), *cert. denied sub nom. Wharton v. Dube*, 501 U.S. 1211, 111 S.Ct. 2814, 115 L.Ed.2d 986 (1991). In these cases qualified immunity was denied despite the prevailing test of *Connick v. Myers*, 461 U.S. 138, 103 S.Ct. 1684, 75 L.Ed.2d 708 (1983), which held that a public employee's speech is protected only if it is addressed to a matter of public concern, *see Paradis v. Montrose Mem'l Hosp.*, 157 F.3d 815 (10th Cir.1998), and if it outweighs the government's interest in effectively and efficiently fulfilling its responsibilities. After *Churchill*, it seems likely that fewer First Amendment cases involving the government as employer will even reach the "clearly established" issue, because more complaints will be dismissed for failure to state a claim upon which relief can be granted, the preliminary "current cognizability" inquiry recommended by *Siegert*, strongly recommended by *County of Sacramento v. Lewis* and finally mandated by *Conn v. Gabbert* and *Wilson v. Layne*. This is because *Churchill* defers to the government employer's own assessment of the factors in the *Connick* balance. *See, e.g., Duriex–Gauthier v. Lopez–Nieves*, 274 F.3d 4 (1st Cir.2001) (agency director responsible for political firing entitled to qualified immunity because reasonable person in director's position could have concluded that the plaintiff's job concerned partisan political interest and involved some policymaking responsibility or access to confidential information); *Shahar v. Bowers*, 120 F.3d 211 (11th Cir.1997) (no First Amendment violation because attorney general could reasonably, if uncertainly, have believed that public confidence in his office would be undermined by its hiring woman who participated in same-sex wedding and marriage, given office's responsibility to enforce state laws that prohibit sodomy and limit certain benefits to persons contracting traditional, heterosexual marriages). *See also Brewster v. Board of Educ. of Lynwood Unified Sch. Dist.*, 149 F.3d 971 (9th Cir.1998), *cert. denied*, 526 U.S. 1018, 119 S.Ct. 1252, 143 L.Ed.2d 349 (1999) (First Amendment does not protect teacher who complained about school record-keeping, even though it was a matter of public concern, because, inter alia, the statements were directed only at school officials and disrupted staff harmony and damaged trust); *David v. City & County of Denver*, 101 F.3d 1344, 1356 (10th Cir.1996), *cert. denied*, 522 U.S. 858, 118 S.Ct. 157, 139 L.Ed.2d 102 (1997) and *Morgan v. Ford*, 6 F.3d 750, 754 (11th Cir.1993), *cert. denied*, 512 U.S. 1221, 114 S.Ct. 2708, 129 L.Ed.2d 836 (1994) (public employees' complaints about non-systemic sexual harassment raise only private concerns and are motivated by purely private interests and are therefore not deserving of First Amendment protection). *But see Azzaro v. County of Allegheny*, 110 F.3d 968 (3d Cir.1997) (holding to the contrary). Another substantive law element that may cause a First Amendment retaliation claim to founder for failure to state a claim is allegation and proof that the retaliation subjected plaintiff to a materially adverse term and condition of employment. *See Jones v. Fitzgerald*, 285 F.3d 705 (8th Cir.2002) (negative memoranda placed in plaintiff's personnel file but not used to discipline her, and involuntary transfer, not materially adverse); *Duffy v. McPhillips*, 276 F.3d 988 (8th Cir.2002) (minor shifts in responsibility do not suffice).

Moreover, even those First Amendment claims by public employees that are legally cognizable may run afoul of either the clearly established law or the fact prong of qualified immunity. After *Churchill*, a court will less often find that a defendant who has weighed the employer's efficiency needs more heavily than the public value of the speech violated law that was clearly established or should have realized by reference to analogous precedent that he struck the wrong balance. *See Johnson v. Clifton*, 74 F.3d 1087 (11th Cir.1996) *cert. denied*, 519 U.S. 808, 117 S.Ct. 51, 136 L.Ed.2d 15 (1996) (police chief who allegedly retaliated against officers for testifying about him to a grand jury receives qualified immunity because no clearly established law explained to him that their testimony was a matter of public rather than personal concern to the officers). Even if the defendant violated clearly established First Amendment rights, he may still receive immunity if his actions were objectively reasonable. *See, e.g., Dirrane v. Brookline Police Dep't*, 315 F.3d 65 (1st Cir.2002) (reasonable person in position of police chief or captain would not necessarily have known that transferring officer who had charged others with criminal misconduct unlawfully retaliated against him in violation of First Amendment). *But see Washington v. Normandy Fire Protection District*, 272 F.3d 522 (8th Cir.2001) (denying qualified immunity where plaintiff's speech on matter of public concern not shown to have caused actual workplace disruption); *Keyser v. Sacramento City Unified School Dist.*, 265 F.3d 741 (9th Cir.2001) (denying qualified immunity where plaintiffs' interest in speaking on a matter of unarguably public concern held clearly to outweigh defendant employer's interest in workplace efficiency and avoiding disruption); *Hufford v. McEnaney*, 249 F.3d 1142 (9th Cir.2001) (supervisors who

law" prong of qualified immunity in such a fact-sensitive case, the defendant may well receive immunity if a reasonable person in his position would not have realized that what he was doing violated that law—that is, receive immunity under the "objective reasonableness," fact-based prong.[114] This third, independent route to qualified immunity has been reinvigorated by the Supreme Court's reminder in *Saucier* that even if the defendant's conduct continues to be unlawful as of the date of

allegedly retaliated against fire department captain for expressing concerns about co-workers' downloading pornographic material on department's computers ineligible for immunity because it was clearly established when captain spoke that the interests his expression furthered outweighed departmental interests in avoiding workplace disruption); *Hall v. Missouri Highway & Transp. Comm'n*, 235 F.3d 1065 (8th Cir. 2000) (no qualified immunity for retaliating against public employee who complained about age discrimination); *Hyland v. Wonder*, 117 F.3d 405 (9th Cir.1997), *cert. denied*, 522 U.S. 1148, 118 S.Ct. 1166, 140 L.Ed.2d 177 (1998) (judicial officials denied qualified immunity for allegedly discharging volunteer probation officer in retaliation for having criticized conditions at juvenile hall, because retaliation against persons for speaking on a matter of public concern was a clearly established violation when defendants acted). Of course cases outside the public employment sphere may center on more categorical First Amendment rights that accordingly enjoy better prospects of surviving an assertion of qualified immunity. *See Levitan v. Ashcroft*, 281 F.3d 1313 (D.C.Cir.2002) (prison officials denied qualified immunity because fact issue remained as to whether federal prison rule prohibiting Catholic inmates from consuming small amounts of communion wine substantially burdened their free exercise rights); *McBride v. Village of Michiana*, 100 F.3d 457 (6th Cir.1996), *on remand* 1998 WL 276139 (W.D.Mich.1998) (journalist had well established right not to endure retaliation by village officials for reporting on political matters); *Newell v. Sauser*, 64 F.3d 1416 (9th Cir.1995), *withdrawn*, 72 F.3d 110 (9th Cir.1995), *superseded*, 79 F.3d 115 (9th Cir.1996) (confiscating legal materials from cell of "jailhouse lawyer" violated clearly established First Amendment right). *Cf. Davis v. Norris*, 249 F.3d 800 (8th Cir. 2001) (per curiam) (denying qualified immunity respecting prison policy limiting inmates to five personal photographs even though test balanced prisoner's rights against legitimate penological objective). *But see Denno v. School Bd. of Volusia County*, 218 F.3d 1267, 1270–1275 (11th Cir.2000) (because one of two applicable Supreme Court decisions gave school administrators more flexibility in balancing rights in First Amendment case concerning discipline of students for displaying confederate flag, individual administrators afforded immunity). And although Fourth Amendment rights are balanced, or subject to a reasonableness test, qualified immunity has sometimes been denied in these cases, too. *See Gruenke v. Seip*, 225 F.3d 290 (3d Cir.2000) (sustaining claim of student coerced into taking pregnancy test by coach). *But see Saucier v. Katz*, 533 U.S. 194, 121 S.Ct. 2151, 150 L.Ed.2d 272 (2001), *on remand*, 262 F.3d 897 (9th Cir. 2001) (insisting, in Fourth Amendment excessive force case, that officers receive qualified immunity for reasonable mistakes of law even when they have used unreasonable amount of force measured by surrounding factual circumstances under test of *Graham v. Connor*). For the sometimes inconsistent authority concerning the "unsettledness" of various Fourth Amendment rights, *see infra* this section.

114. See, e.g., *Kijonka v. Seitzinger*, 363 F.3d 645 (7th Cir. 2004)(officer who consulted county prosecutor before arresting plaintiff had a reasonable, even if mistaken, basis to believe that he had probable cause to make arrest); *Storck v. City of Coral Springs*, 2003 WL 23024573 (11th Cir. 2003)(officer's arguable probable cause to arrest plaintiff entitles him to qualified immunity); *Ramirez v. Butte–Silver Bow County*, 283 F.3d 985 (9th Cir.2002) (warrant so facially deficient for lack of particularization of place to be searched and things to be seized that officer could not reasonably have believed it to be valid); *Nelson v. Heiss*, 271 F.3d 891 (9th Cir.2001) (prison officials could reasonably believe they were not violating federal statute providing for exemption of veterans' benefits against claims of creditors by placing holds on inmate's trust account, although they did violate that statute); *Kipps v. Caillier*, 205 F.3d 203, 206 (5th Cir.2000) (defendant granted immunity because his violation of plaintiff's clearly established First Amendment right to familial association with his son was not objectively unreasonable under the circumstances surrounding plaintiff's termination).

decision on his qualified immunity motion, and even if the law (s)he violated was clearly established when (s)he acted, (s)he should still receive immunity if a hypothetical reasonable officer, faced with the same circumstances, would not have realized or understood—or as some circuits formulate the inquiry, "necessarily" or "clearly" realized or understood—that what (s)he was doing violated that clearly established law.[115] A negative answer to either of the first two questions obviates the inquiry into any subsequent question.[116]

Nevertheless, the defendant's summary judgment motion may be denied if there is a triable issue whether he knew or should have known that his conduct would violate clearly established law; he must therefore endure discovery and trial on that issue.[117] Because qualified immunity is an affirmative defense,[118] one might assume that the reasonableness

115. See, e.g., *Feathers v. Aey*, 319 F.3d 843, 851 (6th Cir.2003) (even absent materially similar case law authority, officers should have known that their search on plaintiff's porch violated *Terry* principles, yet according them qualified immunity because they had a reasonable factual basis for believing they were acting consistently with *Terry*); *Kind v. Frank*, 329 F.3d 979 (8th Cir.2003) (county officials had objectively reasonable, even if mistaken, belief that offering Muslim inmate pork-free but nonvegetarian diet would not violate his rights); *Marquez v. Gutierrez*, 322 F.3d 689, 692–693 (9th Cir.2003) (guard may in fact have acted maliciously and sadistically in violation of inmates clearly established Eighth Amendment rights yet have reasonably believed his actions conformed to law); *Rudebusch v. Hughes*, 313 F.3d 506 (9th Cir.2002) (university president violated professors' equal protection rights by granting pay adjustment only to minority male faculty members, but reasonable official in president's position would not have understood that adjustments violated those rights); *Robles v. Prince George's County*, 302 F.3d 262 (4th Cir.2002) (police officer's tying detainee to metal pole unrelated to any legitimate law enforcement purpose and violated his due process rights, but it was not apparent that officers, when they acted, should have known that their conduct would violate those rights); *Estate of Ford v. Ramirez–Palmer*, 301 F.3d 1043 (9th Cir.2002) (double celling inmate violated Eighth Amendment but reasonable correctional officer in the circumstances would not have "clearly" appreciated that authorizing the double celling was impermissible); *Rogers v. City of Amsterdam*, 303 F.3d 155, 158–159 (2d Cir. 2002) (but no citation to *Saucier*); *Suboh v. District Attorney's Office of Suffolk Dist.*, 298 F.3d 81 (1st Cir.2002) (assistant district attorney who advised police officer to relinquish custody of mother's daughter to grandparents was unaware of existing custody dispute, so objectively reasonable official in attorney's position would not have understood that his advice violated mother's rights); *Franklin v. Fox*, 312 F.3d 423 (9th Cir.2002) (reasonable official in position of assistant district attorney could have believed he was not violating detainees' rights by assisting daughter to visit him even though he knew daughter's intention was to convince detainee to confess to murder of her longtime friend); *Gomez v. Atkins*, 296 F.3d 253 (4th Cir.2002) (even if sergeant filed arrest warrant application without reasonable cause, circumstances warranted reasonable belief that there was reasonable cause); *Dirrane v. Brookline Police Dep't*, 315 F.3d 65 (1st Cir.2002) (reasonable person in position of police chief or captain would not necessarily have known that transferring officer who had charged others with criminal misconduct unlawfully retaliated against him in violation of First Amendment).

116. See *Harhay v. Town of Ellington Bd. of Educ.*, 323 F.3d 206, 211–212 (2d Cir.2003).

117. *Largent v. Dallas*, 44 F.3d 1004 (5th Cir.1995) (unpublished), cert. denied, 514 U.S. 1128, 115 S.Ct. 2002, 131 L.Ed.2d 1003 (1995).

118. See *Schultea v. Wood*, 47 F.3d 1427 (5th Cir.1995) (en banc) (encouraging trial judges to order plaintiffs to serve a reply to the defendant's assertions concerning any qualified immunity defense raised in the answer). The practice recommended by *Schultea* provides trial courts a way of complying with the Supreme Court's subsequent indication in *Crawford–El v. Britton*, 523 U.S. 574, 118 S.Ct. 1584, 140 L.Ed.2d 759 (1998) that a plaintiff's Complaint need not anticipate the qualified immunity de-

issue is one on which the defendant risks the persuasion burden at trial. We might therefore expect that summary judgment on this issue would seldom be granted—only when every reasonable jury, from the evidence adduced on the motion, would have to find by a preponderance of the evidence that a hypothetical reasonable officer in the circumstances would not have realized that his conduct would violate settled law.[119] In practice, however, summary judgment is often granted on this second prong of the immunity, even where the defendant has less than overwhelming evidence about the reasonableness, in context, of his challenged action. This is because the Supreme Court has not clarified whether the defendant bears the burden of persuasion on the objective reasonableness of his actions.[120]

Application of summary judgment to the objective reasonableness issue is even more troublesome, and may be conceptually impossible, where the predicate constitutional violation includes its own subjective or "state of mind" element. An example is the wrongful intent that is prerequisite to a violation of the Equal Protection Clause.[121] How, if at all, should the ordinary qualified immunity showing, which requires no evidence by the defendant about his state of mind, be modified to take into account a state-of-mind element in the underlying predicate right? This is particularly vexing because the second prong of the defense refers to the reasonableness of a hypothetical reasonable officer, while the subjective element in the predicate right refers to the state of mind of the defendant himself. The incongruity logically leads to the following, apparently nonsensical formulation of the second-prong, summary judgment question in a case alleging denial of equal protection: "Would a reasonable jury, from the evidence on the motion, have to find by a preponderance of the evidence that a *hypothetical reasonable official* in the defendant's position would not have realized that the *defendant himself* acted with an intent to discriminate because of race or gender?" A jury could hardly determine what an objectively reasonable third party should have realized about the defendant's own subjective state of mind![122] Still less can a court, on summary judgment, predict from the

fense, while nevertheless imposing a delayed heightened pleading burden on the plaintiff respecting that defense once the individual defendant asserts it in the Answer. Although the *Schultea* reply must to some degree satisfy a heightened pleading requirement, it need not meet a clear and convincing standard, because *Crawford–El* held no such standard of proof must be met to survive summary judgment. *Shipp v. McMahon*, 199 F.3d 256, 261 (5th Cir.2000), *vacated and superseded*, 199 F.3d 256 (5th Cir.2000). *Schultea* is discussed in § 5.80, *infra*.

119. See *Anderson v. Liberty Lobby*, 477 U.S. 242, 106 S.Ct. 2505, 91 L.Ed.2d 202 (1986) (equating the ultimate burden on summary judgment with that prevailing at trial, including the relevant burden of proof).

120. *See text infra.*

121. See, e.g., *Village of Arlington Heights v. Metropolitan Hous. Development Corp.*, 429 U.S. 252, 97 S.Ct. 555, 50 L.Ed.2d 450 (1977); *Washington v. Davis*, 426 U.S. 229, 96 S.Ct. 2040, 48 L.Ed.2d 597 (1976); *Hayden v. Grayson*, 134 F.3d 449 (1st Cir.), *cert. denied*, 524 U.S. 953, 118 S.Ct. 2370, 141 L.Ed.2d 738 (1998). Disciplining an employee for racist reasons violates a clearly established right to equal protection. *See Bishop v. Avera*, 177 F.3d 1233 (11th Cir.1999).

122. The same problem may even arise where the underlying predicate right ulti-

evidence offered on the motion whether a jury determination either way on such a question could be reasonable.

What are the qualified immunity implications of cases where an intentional violation, purpose to punish, or evil or malicious state of mind is either a required element of the underlying claim or is gratuitously pleaded and proven by the plaintiff? The Supreme Court's decision in *Crawford–El v. Britton*[123] attempts to clarify the relationship between the plaintiff's prima facie showing in such cases and the qualified immunity defense. The government official defendant had argued that in cases where the predicate claim requires plaintiff to prove the defendant's subjective knowledge, intent or motive,[124] the discovery-avoidance purpose of *Harlow* could be meaningfully fulfilled only by raising the plaintiff's required prima facie quantum of proof beyond the normal preponderance of the evidence. A 5–member majority explicitly rejected this position. The majority reiterated that qualified immunity is an affirmative defense to be pleaded and proven by defendant; and it concluded that assertion of the defense does not add to the plaintiff's prima facie burden for any particular category of constitutional or federal statutory[125] claim. It held accordingly that a § 1983 plaintiff need

mately turns on an officer's objectively reasonable conduct, rather than his state of mind. For example, in *Graham v. Connor*, 490 U.S. 386, 109 S.Ct. 1865, 104 L.Ed.2d 443 (1989), the court held that the Fourth Amendment, rather than substantive due process, furnished the constitutional yardstick for measuring whether a police officer uses excessive force in making an arrest; and it reaffirmed that the Fourth Amendment issue turns on the objective reasonableness of the officer's actions, not his "evil intentions." Yet in a footnote the court observed that "in assessing the credibility of an officer's account of the circumstances that prompted the use of force a factfinder may consider ... evidence that the officer may have harbored ill-will toward the citizen." That suggested that decision on the qualified immunity defense in such a case, which in *Graham* itself the court agreed was limited to a test of objective reasonableness, will involve an evaluation of the officer's state of mind in order to conclude whether there has been a violation of the nominally objective predicate right. But after *Crawford–El v. Britton*, 523 U.S. 574, 118 S.Ct. 1584, 140 L.Ed.2d 759 (1998), it is less likely that any evidence of unlawful or even malicious intent can defeat an otherwise sound qualified immunity defense, regardless of the motive or elements of the underlying claim. See text accompanying notes 102–109, *infra*.

123. 523 U.S. 574, 118 S.Ct. 1584, 140 L.Ed.2d 759 (1998).

124. The Court's catalogue of such cases includes race and gender equal protection claims, citing *Washington v. Davis*, 426 U.S. 229, 96 S.Ct. 2040, 48 L.Ed.2d 597 (1976) and *Personnel Administrator of Mass. v. Feeney*, 442 U.S. 256, 99 S.Ct. 2282, 60 L.Ed.2d 870 (1979); cruel and unusual punishment Eighth Amendment claims, citing *Farmer v. Brennan*, 511 U.S. 825, 114 S.Ct. 1970, 128 L.Ed.2d 811 (1994); First Amendment claims alleging employment termination because of political affiliation, citing *Branti v. Finkel*, 445 U.S. 507, 100 S.Ct. 1287, 63 L.Ed.2d 574 (1980); and, as in *Crawford–El* itself, claims alleging retaliation against the plaintiff's protected speech or for exercising other constitutional rights, citing *Pickering v. Board of Ed. of Township High Sch. Dist. 205*, 391 U.S. 563, 88 S.Ct. 1731, 20 L.Ed.2d 811 (1968). Another example is a claim alleging a denial of due process based on the imposition of punishment on a pretrial detainee. In such cases the condition of which plaintiff complains is deemed prohibited punishment if it is imposed with a purpose to punish rather than incidental to a legitimate governmental purpose. *Bell v. Wolfish*, 441 U.S. 520, 99 S.Ct. 1861, 60 L.Ed.2d 447 (1979).

125. It has been held that public officials may assert qualified immunity to be relieved of damages liability for violations of federal statutory, as well as constitutional rights. *Blake v. Wright*, 179 F.3d 1003 (6th Cir.1999), *cert. denied*, 528 U.S. 1136, 120 S.Ct. 980, 145 L.Ed.2d 930 (2000).

not meet heightened pleading standards in alleging a First Amendment retaliation claim against an individual defendant official; *Crawford–El* thus applies ordinary Federal Rule 8 "notice pleading" standards in most[126] cases against individual officials, just as it held in *Leatherman* that the plaintiff has no heightened pleading burden respecting the prima facie element of "policy" in an action against a government entity. And the Court also held that the plaintiff may prove allegations of unlawful motive by the ordinary preponderance quantum, rejecting the proposed requirement of clear and convincing evidence.

The majority identified three purposes underlying the *Harlow* version of immunity and its focus on the objective legal reasonableness of defendant's challenged conduct: First, to protect public officials from the costs associated with defending damage actions; second, to permit early disposition of official—defendant claims despite allegations of subjective wrongful motivation that are not ordinarily resolvable on summary judgment; and third, to avoid the unfairness of expecting the defendant to anticipate developments in the law that might bear on his discharge of official duties. It concluded that these purposes were adequately fulfilled by the arsenal already at the defendant's disposal to bring individual—capacity litigation to a rapid close, and did not require encumbering the plaintiff's claim with heightened, claim—specific standards of pleading or proof.

Prominent among the defendant-friendly devices the Court surveyed were the *Harlow* standard itself; the requirement that the plaintiff allege not just the defendant's animus towards plaintiff himself, but "an intent to disadvantage all members of a class that includes the plaintiff ... or to deter public comment on a specific issue of public importance"; the ready availability, after *Anderson v. Liberty Lobby*,[127] of summary judgment to dispose of all § 1983 claims, including those overlaid with evidence of knowledge, intent, or motive; additional obstacles the plaintiff must confront to establish particular constitutional claims, like First Amendment claims subject to the *Mt. Healthy* defense; the restrictions of the Prison Litigation Reform Act, 110 Stat. 1321 (1996), on suits brought by inmates; the district court's power under the Federal Rules of Civil Procedure to order the plaintiff to serve a particularized reply to the qualified immunity defense once defendant asserts it in an answer, and to sequence and limit discovery on the issues raised by that defense; and the procedures previously endorsed by the Court that afford most defendants multiple interlocutory appeals from adverse district court rulings on their noting under Rule 12(b)(6) or for summary judgment.

The Court even offered individual-capacity defendants an extensive blueprint designed to minimize their litigation costs. Defendants were invited to pursue two tactics even before the plaintiff would be permitted to conduct any discovery. First, the district judge may order plaintiff to

126. But some courts require heightened pleading of a conspiracy between public and private defendants to allege the element of "state action." *See* § 2.12, *supra.*

127. 477 U.S. 242, 106 S.Ct. 2505, 91 L.Ed.2d 202 (1986).

reply to the answer asserting the qualified immunity defense, or grant a defendant's motion for a more definite statement. Second, once the defense is pleaded, the court might grant a motion to dismiss for failure to state a claim, or a summary judgment motion, on the "essentially legal" questions whether the defendant's conduct violates, and when he acted whether it violated, clearly established law. If that motion is denied, the Court noted, the defendant could take an initial interlocutory appeal. The Court continued that even if the plaintiff overcame these hurdles, the trial court could postpone discovery about the official's subjective motive until discovery is completed on factual questions concerning the defendant's conduct, its objective reasonableness, and whether the plaintiff suffered injury or engaged in constitutionally protected conduct. And even such discovery as to motive that is permitted might be limited under Federal Rules authorizing the district court to limit the number of depositions and interrogatories, the length of depositions, and the number of requests for admission.

At that point "summary judgment serves as the ultimate screen to weed out truly insubstantial lawsuits prior to trial." The Court added that to survive any summary judgment motion, the plaintiff would have to "identify affirmative evidence from which a jury could find that the plaintiff has carried his or her burden [by the ordinary preponderance of the evidence] of proving the pertinent motive." Moreover, if summary judgment should be denied on a ground related to the immunity defense, the defendant could take a second immediate interlocutory appeal.[128]

In the end, therefore, "the improper intent element of various causes of action should not ordinarily preclude summary disposition of insubstantial claims." The Court acknowledged that the first two *Harlow* purposes—avoiding or reducing defense costs and facilitating summary dismissals—would be more completely served by ratcheting upwards the proof plaintiffs must offer to survive summary judgment on particular constitutional claims. But it concluded that doing so would impose serious costs on the effectiveness of § 1983 as a means of vindicating constitutional rights, and that those costs outweigh the burdens some defendants may incur as the result of limited, deferred and contingent discovery on the question of motive.

The *Crawford–El* majority also rejected, at least implicitly, an attempted enlargement of the qualified immunity defense for those cases where the plaintiff can meet the burden of proving unlawful knowledge, intent, or motive. The proposal, raised by the second certified question, would have defeated liability in such cases whenever the defendant asserts a lawful, reasonable justification for the challenged conduct. In contrast to the *Mt. Healthy* defense to First Amendment claims, which

128. Citing *Behrens v. Pelletier*, 516 U.S. 299, 116 S.Ct. 834, 133 L.Ed.2d 773 (1996). More precisely, under *Behrens* and *Johnson v. Jones*, 515 U.S. 304, 115 S.Ct. 2151, 132 L.Ed.2d 238 (1995), the defendant could take such an interlocutory appeal from the denial of summary judgment on all issues pertaining to the immunity defense except purely factual ones like whether defendant did what plaintiff asserts she did.

requires the defendant to show that he would have taken the same action against the plaintiff for independent, lawful reasons that he in fact relied on or at least knew about at the time, the proposed expansion of qualified immunity in "motive" cases would have enabled the defendant to prevail on the basis of a reason thought up after the fact.

But the majority also strongly implied that the individual § 1983 defendant can still avoid damages liability by prevailing on the ordinary *Harlow* version of qualified immunity, even in cases where the plaintiff does establish the defendant's unlawful knowledge, intent, or animus. It wrote that under *Harlow*, "a defense of qualified immunity may not be rebutted by evidence that the defendant's conduct was malicious or otherwise improperly motivated. Evidence concerning the defendant's subjective intent is simply irrelevant to that defense." Similarly, the opinion observes that were it not for *Harlow*, an official would be unfairly held liable if he were expected to anticipate subsequent legal developments, "even when the official conduct is motivated, in part, by hostility to the plaintiff." Even more pointedly the majority observes, "The immunity standard in Harlow itself eliminates all motive-based claims in which the official's conduct did not violate clearly established law." It should follow more clearly still that the defense may override a showing of defendant's state of mind in cases where the plaintiff offers that evidence gratuitously—for example to support a prayer for punitive damages when pressing an ordinary constitutional claim that does not require proof about defendant's knowledge or state of mind.[129]

It remains difficult to predict when the lower courts will grant summary judgment where state of mind is at issue, despite the *Crawford–El* statements endorsing the defense in those cases. Before *Crawford–El*, a few circuit court opinions had suggested that proof of defendant's wrongful state of mind as part of plaintiff's prima facie case simply swept aside the qualified immunity defense or at least precluded summary judgment.[130] *Crawford–El* would seem to reject that approach. At the other extreme was the view that prima facie state of mind evidence is simply irrelevant to the normal application of the defense.[131] Most of the opinions, however, steered a middle course. They implicitly recognized that qualified immunity remained available but asserted somewhat vaguely that the state of mind evidence should be "considered" in determining whether the defense should be upheld.[132] In prac-

129. But the common sense notion that qualified immunity ought not be available when officers act in bad faith dies hard. See *Navarro v. Block*, 250 F.3d 729 (9th Cir.2001) (local legislators who in bad faith indemnify county sheriffs from punitive damage awards not eligible for qualified immunity).

130. See, e.g., *Weyant v. Okst*, 101 F.3d 845, 858 (2d Cir.1996) (8th Amendment medical deliberate indifference claim); *Jackson v. McIntosh*, 90 F.3d 330, 332 (9th Cir.1996), *cert. denied*, 519 U.S. 1029, 117 S.Ct. 584, 136 L.Ed.2d 514 (1996) (same); *McMillian v. Johnson*, 88 F.3d 1554, 1564–66 (11th Cir.1996), *cert. denied*, 521 U.S. 1121, 117 S.Ct. 2514, 138 L.Ed.2d 1016 (1997) (proof of defendant's purpose to punish a pretrial detainee, a categorical violation of Eighth Amendment, renders defense unavailable).

131. See, e.g., *Hansen v. Soldenwagner*, 19 F.3d 573, 578 (11th Cir.1994).

132. See, e.g., *Foy v. Holston*, 94 F.3d 1528, 1534–36 (11th Cir.1996) (1st Amendment religious discrimination case); *Ratliff*

tice this usually meant that if the intent- or motive-based predicate law violation were clearly established, qualified immunity could not be upheld on summary judgment because the prima facie evidence raised a question of fact as to whether a reasonable defendant in the circumstances might have realized that his conduct violated that law. Even after *Crawford–El*, the Supreme Court declined to review a circuit decision that had staked out this same middle ground.[133] Perhaps the Court is simply saying that even in motive-based cases the defendant should receive qualified immunity as a matter of law if the targeted conduct did not violate clearly established law; but that if it did violate that law, the defendant may have to go to trial to establish "objective reasonableness." Defendant, in other words, still bears the burden on the "fact prong" of qualified immunity to show that a reasonable person in her position would not have realized that her conduct would violate that law.

Significantly, most of the decisions that treat unlawful motive as relevant to objective reasonableness, presented, as did *Crawford–El*, allegations of retaliation prohibited by the First Amendment. By contrast, decisions ruling out the possibility of summary judgment typically involved per se Eighth Amendment violations based on the imposition of pretrial punishment or on medical deliberate indifference. Yet First Amendment claims may be more vulnerable to summary judgment on two grounds distinct from qualified immunity. Many First Amendment rights are not categorical, but depend on balancing a prohibited motivation (like retaliation against protected speech or political participation) against a government interest (like maintaining discipline in government employment or preserving management's ability to insist on loyal lieutenants in policymaking positions). And even where the balance on the prima facie case is struck in favor of the plaintiff, the *Mt. Healthy* defense avoids liability where the defendant proves that it would have reached the same decision for independent, lawful reasons, including those that have nothing to do with the First Amendment balancing factors. So in First Amendment cases, summary judgment may remain appropriate (even where the law in question was clearly established when defendant acted) either where no reasonable jury could find that the plaintiff's interest in pursuing protected activity outweighs the

v. DeKalb County, Ga., 62 F.3d 338, 341 (11th Cir.1995); *Tompkins v. Vickers*, 26 F.3d 603, 608 (5th Cir.1994); *Branch v. Tunnell*, 937 F.2d 1382 (9th Cir.1991); *Siegert v. Gilley*, 895 F.2d 797 (D.C.Cir.1990), *aff'd on other grounds*, 500 U.S. 226, 111 S.Ct. 1789, 114 L.Ed.2d 277 (1991); *Pueblo Neighborhood Health Ctrs. v. Losavio*, 847 F.2d 642 (10th Cir.1988); *Poe v. Haydon*, 853 F.2d 418 (6th Cir.1988), cert. denied, 488 U.S. 1007, 109 S.Ct. 788, 102 L.Ed.2d 780 (1989); *Musso v. Hourigan*, 836 F.2d 736 (2d Cir.1988).

133. *Walker v. Schwalbe*, 112 F.3d 1127 (11th Cir.1997), *cert. denied*, 523 U.S. 1117, 118 S.Ct. 1794, 140 L.Ed.2d 935 (1998) (First Amendment government employee whistleblower case). *But see McCullough v. Wyandanch Union Free Sch. Dist.*, 187 F.3d 272 (2d Cir.1999), *on remand*, 132 F.Supp.2d 87 (E.D.N.Y.2001) (assuming school superintendent violated clearly established law by terminating administrator for protected expression on matter of public concern, superintendent qualifiedly immune because it was objectively reasonable for him to believe he could recommend termination for plaintiff's disruptive speech).

government defendant's countervailing interest; or, more rarely, where every reasonable jury would have to uphold the *Mt. Healthy* defense by finding that the defendant would have reached the same decision independent of its unlawful component.

There is a serious question whether a real-life, flesh and blood jury would find that a hypothetical reasonable person in defendant's position might not have appreciated that the action taken against the plaintiff violated clearly established law, where the jury has also found that the actual defendant harmed the plaintiff with unconstitutional intent or motive. The positions may not be inconsistent as a matter of abstract logic, but few juries are likely to make both findings. Unlawful state of mind claims will more commonly be derailed by the *Harlow/Creighton* objective reasonableness prong of qualified immunity on motions for summary judgment. But deciding when to grant summary judgment is complicated by the fact that the pertinent standards are tied to the burden and quantum of persuasion at trial.[134] And the Supreme Court has not explicitly decided whether, as is usually the case with affirmative defenses, the defendant bears the burden of persuasion concerning the objective reasonableness prong of qualified immunity,[135] or, as some circuit courts have held, that burden falls on the plaintiff.[136]

We can now see more globally how evidence that a defendant's conduct shocks the conscience or was undertaken with a constitutionally prohibited state of mind affects the availability of qualified immunity. If, as in *United States v. Lanier*, a plaintiff offers convincing evidence that the defendant engaged in criminal or conscience-shocking conduct, a court may consider the violation sufficiently "obvious" or "egregious"[137] to overcome the immunity even absent on-point, authoritative precedent. On the other hand, language in *Crawford–El* suggests that evidence of the defendant's intent to harm the plaintiff or violate the plaintiff's federal rights is insufficient standing alone to undermine the defense.

134. *Anderson v. Liberty Lobby, Inc.*, 477 U.S. 242, 248, 106 S.Ct. 2505, 2510, 91 L.Ed.2d 202 (1986).

135. See., e.g., *Nelson v. McMullen*, 207 F.3d 1202 (10th Cir.2000); *DiRuzza v. County of Tehama*, 206 F.3d 1304 (9th Cir.), *cert. denied*, 531 U.S. 1035, 121 S.Ct. 624, 148 L.Ed.2d 533 (2000); *Black v. Coughlin*, 76 F.3d 72, 75 (2d Cir.1996); *Guffey v. Wyatt*, 18 F.3d 869, 871 (10th Cir.1994); *Elder v. Holloway*, 975 F.2d 1388, 1392 (9th Cir.1991), *rev'd on other grounds*, 510 U.S. 510, 114 S.Ct. 1019, 127 L.Ed.2d 344 (1994); *Benigni v. City of Hemet*, 879 F.2d 473, 479–80 (9th Cir.1988).

136. See, e.g., *Gardenhire v. Schubert*, 205 F.3d 303, 311 (6th Cir.2000); *Spiegel v. Cortese*, 196 F.3d 717, 723 (7th Cir.1999), *cert. denied*, 530 U.S. 1243, 120 S.Ct. 2688, 147 L.Ed.2d 961 (2000); *Hoard v. Sizemore*, 198 F.3d 205, 211 (6th Cir.1999); *Crawford–El v. Britton*, 93 F.3d 813, 821–23 (D.C.Cir.1996) (en banc), *vacated and remanded on other grounds*, 523 U.S. 574, 118 S.Ct. 1584, 140 L.Ed.2d 759 (1998); *Shaw v. Stroud*, 13 F.3d 791, 801 (4th Cir.), *cert. denied*, 513 U.S. 813, 115 S.Ct. 67, 130 L.Ed.2d 24 (1994); *Ellis v. Wynalda*, 999 F.2d 243, 246 (7th Cir.1993); *Pfannstiel v. City of Marion*, 918 F.2d 1178, 1183–84 (5th Cir.1990), *abrogated on other grounds sub nom. Martin v. Thomas*, 973 F.2d 449 (5th Cir.1992). An excellent discussion of both the burden of persuasion question and its implications for summary judgment may be found in Chen, "*The Burdens of Qualified Immunity: Summary Judgment and the Role of Facts in Constitutional Tort Law,*" 47 Am. Univ. L.Rev. 1 (1997).

137. *See* discussion *supra*.

One decision imaginatively expands the defense to conduct that followed the conduct to which qualified immunity attached—even though it was clearly established that the subsequent conduct, standing alone, was unconstitutional. In a pro-police reverse twist on the fruit of the poisonous tree doctrine, the Second Circuit held state troopers entitled to derivative qualified immunity for falsely arresting the plaintiff homeowner because the arrest resulted from a seizure of stolen property as to which the troopers were qualifiedly immune under the standard *Harlow/Anderson* test.[138]

Another court, arguably illegitimately, extends the clearly established requirement to the *state* law definition of the kind of "property" interests protected against unreasonable deprivation by Fourteenth Amendment due process.[139] Of course qualified immunity should attach where a federal due process right, whether or not contingent on an interest created by state law, was itself not clearly established by federal decisions when the defendant acted.[140] It is quite another thing, however, to require the plaintiff to point to state law decisions clearly establishing the kind of property or contract rights that the Supreme Court has long held protected against arbitrary deprivation by the federal due process clause. By hypothesis, it is only federal rights that the plaintiff need show were clearly established, because Section 1983 redresses the violation of those rights alone. The counterargument, flowing from *Anderson v. Creighton*, is that qualified immunity is designed to enable a reasonable government actor in defendant's situation to know that her contemplated conduct would violate federal law; and where a predicate federal right, like procedural due process, turns on the existence of an underlying state property or liberty interest, the official can confidently conclude that she will violate federal law if she denies notice or hearing only if she also has reason to know that the prospective plaintiff is entitled to notice or hearing by virtue of well developed state law.

Finally, at least one court seems to confer qualified immunity if the predicate constitutional right, whether or not clearly established, is in some sense less than "fundamental."[141]

138. *Bradway v. Gonzales*, 26 F.3d 313 (2d Cir.1994).

139. *Lassiter v. Alabama A & M Univ., Bd. of Trustees*, 28 F.3d 1146 (11th Cir. 1994) (plaintiff's property right in employment not unambiguously established by words of his employment contract or by Alabama decisions, which only after his firing recognized implied employment rights based on personnel manual). This decision is questionable not only because it requires that a state law component of a clearly established § 1983 predicate right also be clearly established, but because it answers that question in part by reference to contract terms, rather than to U.S. Supreme Court or federal circuit authority. *See Elder v. Holloway*, 510 U.S. 510, 114 S.Ct. 1019, 127 L.Ed.2d 344 (1994) (directing lower courts to assess whether a federal predicate right is clearly established by looking to their "own and other relevant precedents").

140. *Soliday v. Miami County, Ohio*, 55 F.3d 1158 (6th Cir.1995) (at time coroner ordered cremation of deceased arrestee without contacting any relatives, federal decisions had not yet established that Ohio laws conferring rights on decedents' spouses created a constitutionally cognizable "liberty" interest).

141. *Jarvis v. Wellman*, 52 F.3d 125 (6th Cir.1995).

§ 2.23 Interlocutory Appeal From Denial of the Motion: Classifying the "Law" and "Fact" Prongs

Ironically, given the justifications for its creation, the new qualified immunity regime has proven difficult to administer. An increasingly complex jurisprudence of appellate jurisdiction consumes much of the same time and funds of officials that the doctrine sought to spare. It is clear that the review on interlocutory appeal of orders denying qualified immunity is de novo.[1] But circuit courts are understandably uncertain whether to accept jurisdiction over all such appeals, or only those that raise issues of law.[2]

Immediate appeal makes sense only with respect to the qualified immunity issues that may be decided as a matter of law. As the Supreme Court wrote in *Mitchell v. Forsyth*,[3] the denial of a claim of qualified immunity is an appealable "final decision"[4] within the meaning of 28 U.S.C.A. § 1291, despite the absence of a final judgment, "to the extent that it turns on an issue of law...."[5] And *Mitchell* quite properly characterizes the qualified immunity question—whether the conduct in question violated clearly established law—as an "essentially legal question."[6] Indeed, "law" seems a fair characterization of both questions encompassed by the "clearly established" inquiry: the issue the Court in *Siegert v. Gilley, County of Sacramento v. Lewis, Conn v. Gabbert* and *Wilson v. Layne* declares should be decided first (whether the plaintiff has stated a claim for violation of what is currently cognizable as a

§ 2.23

1. *Elder v. Holloway*, 510 U.S. 510, 114 S.Ct. 1019, 127 L.Ed.2d 344 (1994).

2. Compare *Krohn v. United States*, 742 F.2d 24, 28 (1st Cir.1984) ("[T]he inhospitality [*Harlow*] evidenced towards groundless suits against officials, would best be effected by making denials of [qualified] immunity immediately appealable....") and *McSurely v. McClellan*, 697 F.2d 309, 316 (D.C.Cir.1982) ("[A]ppellate review of a denial of a motion for summary disposition must be available to ensure that government officials are fully protected against unnecessary trials under qualified immunity on the same basis as for absolute immunity.") with *Peppers v. Coates*, 887 F.2d 1493, 1496–97 (11th Cir.1989) (citing prior Eleventh Circuit authority and stating that the denial of summary judgment on the basis of qualified immunity "is reviewable after final adjudication of the case, and the collateral order doctrine cannot be invoked prematurely to confer immediate jurisdiction upon this court"). But see *Hudgins v. City of Ashburn*, 890 F.2d 396, 402–03 (11th Cir.1989) (describing the "clearly established" test as an issue of law eligible for interlocutory decision). For that end, a panel decision of the Eleventh Circuit concluded that immediate appeal is available from the denial of summary judgment on the qualified immunity defense regardless of whether the decision below turns on the "legal" determination that the right at issue is clearly established or on the "factual" determination that a reasonable person in the defendant official's position should have understood that her conduct would violate that right. See *Howell v. Evans*, 922 F.2d 712, 716–18 (11th Cir.1991), *vacated pursuant to settlement*, 931 F.2d 711 (11th Cir.1991).

3. 472 U.S. 511, 105 S.Ct. 2806, 86 L.Ed.2d 411 (1985).

4. Of course the Court was assuming, as is necessary for any truly "final decision," that the lower court's order rejected the qualified immunity defense conclusively. *See Bradford v. Huckabee*, 330 F.3d 1038 (8th Cir.2003) (rejecting interlocutory appeal where district court was not explicit that order denying defendant's motion was based on qualified immunity rather than another ground); *Krein v. Norris*, 250 F.3d 1184 (8th Cir.2001) (rejecting interlocutory appeal from qualified immunity decision that did not specifically and conclusively deny the defense).

5. *Id.* at 530, 105 S.Ct. at 2817.

6. *Id.* at 526, 105 S.Ct. at 2816.

constitutional right), and the issue identified by *Harlow/Anderson* (whether that right was clearly established by closely analogous circuit or Supreme Court decisions at the time the defendant acted).[7]

But what of the remaining, ultimate issue the court must face in ruling on the defense if it concludes that the law was clearly established? Even Justice Scalia, who wrote *Creighton*, described as "fact-specific" the objective question whether a reasonable official in the defendant's position could have believed his conduct to be lawful given the information known to him at the time and the requirements of established law.[8] Yet he nevertheless asserts that the ultimate determination of immunity must be decided "as a matter of law."[9] Subsequently, the Court in *Hunter v. Bryant*[10] admonished the lower federal courts that immunity "ordinarily should be decided by the court long before trial," and should therefore not be "routinely" placed in the hands of the jury (or, in a bench trial, decided by the judge as trier of fact).[11]

The Supreme Court has resolved a circuit dispute over whether the defendant should be granted an immediate appeal when it is apparent that qualified immunity is denied solely on the objective reasonableness issue—that is, after it has been determined or conceded that the right allegedly violated by the individual was clearly established (and is currently cognizable). The Court held in *Johnson v. Jones*[12] that no interlocutory appeal lies from an order denying summary judgment based on the qualified immunity defense when it is clear from the record that the decision turned solely on a determination that there was sufficient evidence about a question of fact to warrant a trial.[13] In doing

7. *Elder v. Holloway*, 510 U.S. 510, 114 S.Ct. 1019, 127 L.Ed.2d 344 (1994) (whether a federal right was clearly established when the defendant acted is a question of law, not "legal facts"). *See Kinzer v. Jackson*, 316 F.3d 139 (2d Cir.2003) (exercising appellate interlocutory jurisdiction where clearly established law issue could be adjudicated without reference to disputed facts).

8. *Anderson v. Creighton*, 483 U.S. 635, 641, 107 S.Ct. 3034, 3039, 97 L.Ed.2d 523 (1987).

9. *Id.* at 641, 107 S.Ct. at 3039.

10. 502 U.S. 224, 112 S.Ct. 534, 116 L.Ed.2d 589 (1991).

11. *Id.* at 226–230, 112 S.Ct. at 536–537.

12. 515 U.S. 304, 115 S.Ct. 2151, 132 L.Ed.2d 238 (1995).

13. *See Krein v. Norris*, 309 F.3d 487 (8th Cir.2002) (no interlocutory review where denial of qualified immunity turned on district court's conclusion that genuine issues of material fact remained as to whether defendant official was objectively unreasonable in violating clearly established law); *Hensley v. Horne*, 297 F.3d 344 (4th Cir.2002) (purported interlocutory appeal fails where it challenged the correctness, as opposed to the existence, of genuine issue of material fact); *Thomas v. Talley*, 251 F.3d 743 (8th Cir.2001) (no jurisdiction over interlocutory appeal of denial of qualified immunity summary judgment motion where appeal predicated on challenge of lower court's finding about sufficiency of evidence regarding discriminatory intent); *Catone v. Spielmann*, 149 F.3d 156 (2d Cir.1998) (immediate interlocutory appeal not available after district court's denial of summary judgment based on qualified immunity where denial rested on an assessment of the sufficiency of the evidence); *Berryman v. Rieger*, 150 F.3d 561 (6th Cir.1998) (no interlocutory appeal available where denial of summary judgment on qualified immunity defense is based on existence of material factual issues); *White v. Balderama*, 153 F.3d 237 (5th Cir.1998) (district court's failure to specify what factual issues led it to conclude that genuine issues of material fact precluded a determination that the defendant did not violate clearly established law required a remand; appellate court could not determine whether defendant was

so the Court recognized that appellate courts might still have to grapple with such "evidence sufficiency" questions when they are integrally related to other qualified immunity issues that are eligible for interlocutory review—for example, whether the applicable law was "clearly established." For example, a district judge may offer no reason for denying summary judgment after a defendant argues first, that there is no genuine fact issue about the nature of his conduct (a "pure" fact question that is not immediately reviewable) and second, that his proven or admitted conduct is objectively reasonable (a mixed question of law and fact that apparently is immediately reviewable). In such circumstances, the Supreme Court acknowledged, the appellate court may have to "undertake a cumbersome review of the record to determine what facts the district court ... likely assumed" when it found the law "clearly established."[14] The quoted language leaves circuit courts somewhat unclear as to the scope of their review where a district court has failed explicitly to state fact findings consistent with its ultimate conclusion. Does the Supreme Court's concern in *Johnson* against "cumbersome review" require circuit courts to ignore specific factual findings by the district judge that are at variance with its legal conclusions, or, put otherwise, does it require acceptance by the circuit courts of the facts the district court "likely assumed," however erroneous? Or may circuit courts engage in factual review when the trial court fails to articulate the facts underpinning its conclusion or sets forth contradictory findings of fact?[15]

The problem of labeling a district court's determination of the qualified immunity issue as resting on "fact" or "law" gains heightened significance from the Court's subsequent decision in *Behrens v. Pelletier*.[16] *Behrens* arose from a *Bivens* action against a federal official. The Supreme Court explicitly permitted the individual defendant to take successive interlocutory appeals. The Court affirmed the defendant's right to appeal from the denial of summary judgment, after an initial unsuccessful appeal from the denial of a motion to dismiss for failure to

bringing a reviewable challenge to the materiality of factual issues or an unreviewable challenge to their genuineness); *Naylor v. Louisiana Dept. of Corrections*, 123 F.3d 855 (5th Cir.1997) (no interlocutory appeal of denial of qualified immunity when denial was based on the existence of material fact issues); *Tang v. Rhode Island*, 120 F.3d 325 (1st Cir.1997) (district court's denial of summary judgment on qualified immunity defense not subject to interlocutory appeal where denial is based on district court's statement that fact issues remained); *Rambo v. Daley*, 68 F.3d 203 (7th Cir.1995); *Winfield v. Bass*, 67 F.3d 529 (4th Cir.1995) (applying *Johnson* by denying interlocutory appeals on pure evidence sufficiency issues).

14. *Johnson v. Jones*, 515 U.S. 304, 319, 115 S.Ct. 2151, 2159, 132 L.Ed.2d 238 (1995). See *Moniz v. City of Ft. Lauderdale*, 145 F.3d 1278, 1280–1282 (11th Cir.1998) (district court recital in order denying summary judgment that there are genuine disputed material facts does not render order unappealable if defendant grounds appeal on the assertion that, even on plaintiff's view of facts, defendant is entitled to immunity because defendant could not reasonably have known, based on clearly established law, that his challenged conduct would violate that law).

15. The dissenting judge in *Schieber v. City of Philadelphia*, 320 F.3d 409 (3d Cir. 2003) takes the latter view, attributing the former view to the two other justices on the panel.

16. 516 U.S. 299, 116 S.Ct. 834, 133 L.Ed.2d 773 (1996).

state a claim, repeating the *Mitchell v. Forsyth* rationale that the collateral order exception is designed to afford government officials the right not merely to avoid standing trial but also to avoid pre-trial discovery.[17]

On the peculiar facts of *Behrens*, the defendant presented an unusually appealing case for successive appeals. Its contention that it had not violated any clearly established federal rights was never reached by either the district or circuit court on the first interlocutory appeal. But the Supreme Court went out of its way to add that even

> in a case proceeding in a more normal fashion[,] resolution of the immunity question may "require more than one judiciously timed appeal" because the legally relevant factors bearing upon the *Harlow* question will be different on summary judgment than on an earlier motion to dismiss. At that earlier stage, it is the defendant's conduct as alleged in the complaint that is scrutinized for "objective reasonableness." On summary judgment, however, the plaintiff can no longer rest on the pleadings . . . and the Court looks to all of the evidence before it. . . .[18]

The quoted statement is confusing if read to suggest, contrary to the apparent meaning of *Johnson v. Jones*, that the *Mitchell* interlocutory appeal lies from summary judgment denials that turn solely on the sufficiency of the evidence. It is probably better read to mean that when summary judgment turns on the objective legal reasonableness of the official's conduct, that mixed question of law and fact is distinct from the purely legal "clearly established law" issues (i.e., do the allegations state a currently cognizable federal law violation, and if so did they under authoritative circuit or Supreme Court decisions extant at the time of defendant's conduct) previously decided against the official on motion to dismiss, and as such may be eligible for a successive interlocutory appeal.

The Court in *Behrens* did recognize that there might be "abuse" in successive pre-trial assertions of immunity. But it expressed confidence that the courts of appeals would exercise their supervisory powers to reject frivolous claims, for example by the use of summary procedures.[19]

17. *Id.* at 308, 116 S.Ct. at 839.

18. *Id.* at 309, 116 S.Ct. at 840.

19. *Behrens*, 116 S.Ct. at 840–41. See, e.g., *Knox v. Southwest Airlines*, 124 F.3d 1103 (9th Cir.1997) (allowing successive summary judgment motions and an interlocutory appeal just from the denial of the second motion). Another defense tactic that might be considered abuse of the availability of successive appeals has been rebuffed by a circuit court's application of the "law of the case" doctrine. In *Kimberlin v. Quinlan*, 199 F.3d 496, 501–02 (D.C.Cir.1999), *rehearing en banc denied* 207 F.3d 667 (D.C.Cir.2000), a circuit court held that there is no exception to the "law of the case" doctrine pertaining to a defendant's interlocutory appeal of an order denying qualified immunity. The defendant there lost in the trial court on the "clearly established law" prong of the defense, but appealed only a separate ruling rejecting his argument that the complaint was insufficiently pleaded. After this initial appeal failed, the defendant was held bound by "law of the case" in both the trial court on remand and on his successive appeal (concerning the objective reasonableness prong) by the ruling on the unappealed, "clearly established" issue. Cf. *Bakalis v. Golembeski*, 125 F.3d 576 (7th Cir.1997) (waiver will bar the raising of a purely legal ground for qualified immunity in a successive appeal if the ground was not raised in the first ap-

At a minimum, the Court must have had in mind that, under *Johnson v. Jones*, a successive appeal should be summarily dismissed to the extent it turns solely on the trial court's resolution of the facts (that principle should apply on any interlocutory appeal, initial or successive). But would it also be abusive for the defendant to make a second qualified immunity motion on a pure "law" ground distinct from a law ground raised by the initial motion? For example, suppose the defendant makes a motion to dismiss for failure to state a claim based on the qualified immunity issue that *County of Sacramento, Conn*, and *Wilson* instruct trial courts to consider first: whether the plaintiff's allegations state a currently cognizable violation of federal law. Suppose further that this motion is denied, and the denial is affirmed on interlocutory appeal. Would it be "abusive" for the defendant then to make a second motion based on the ultimate qualified immunity question posed by *Harlow* and *Creighton*—whether the rights in question were "clearly established" by authoritative Supreme Court or circuit precedent at the time the defendant acted? Or would it be "abusive" for the defendant to take a second interlocutory appeal if this second motion is denied? The argument that it would be "abusive" is that the defendant could have presented both "law" grounds at the time of the initial pretrial motion, either to dismiss or for summary judgment.

The intersection of *Johnson/Behrens* interlocutory appeal doctrine, and the *Sacramento/Conn/Wilson* instruction that the preliminary qualified immunity question must be whether the plaintiff has stated a currently cognizable claim, has generated some exquisite appellate hair-splitting. The problem arises when on interlocutory appeal from a denial of qualified immunity the appellate court reverses not because the law wasn't clearly established when defendant acted, or because it was but defendant couldn't have reasonably known that, but because the plaintiff has failed to state a currently cognizable claim. The *Sacramento/Conn/Wilson* sequence tell us that this "failure to state a claim" ground of decision is a legal question and an aspect of, indeed the threshold determination, at least for a trial court, in assessing qualified immunity. Presumably then interlocutory appeal should lie under *Johnson/Behrens* even if the district court denied qualified immunity on that

peal). Compare *Crocker v. Piedmont Aviation, Inc.*, 49 F.3d 735 (D.C.Cir.1995) ("law of the case" not applicable where party failed to appeal appealable issue on first appeal or present it on remand to district court but raised it for first time on second appeal, so only possible bar to appellate court's consideration of issue on second appeal would be a species of equitable waiver). Cf. *Bakalis v. Golembeski*, 125 F.3d 576 (7th Cir.1997) (waiver will bar the raising of a purely legal ground for qualified immunity in a successive appeal if the ground was not raised in the first appeal.)

The defendant's tactic there is quite different from that of a defendant who, in the trial court, withholds a fact-based summary judgment motion on qualified immunity, raises and loses only a rule 12(b)(6) motion challenging whether the complaint adequately pleads a violation of clearly established law, and appeals on the latter issue only. On remand after that unsuccessful appeal, defendant should still be able to move, on the authority of *Behrens*, for summary judgment on the mixed legal-factual ground that no reasonable person in his position would have realized he was violating clearly established law, as well as take a second interlocutory appeal if that motion is denied.

law ground alone, without reaching the distinct legal question whether the applicable law was "clearly established" when defendant acted.[20] On the other hand, language in *Johnson* suggests that interlocutory appeal does not lie to review summary judgment denials that go only to the "merits" of a claim; and at least for res judicata or claim preclusion purposes, a dismissal for failure to state a claim is under the modern Restatement (2d) of Judgment approach "on the merits" and thus bars a plaintiff from reasserting the same allegations in subsequent litigation.

So should an appellate court that reverses a denial of the defendant's qualified immunity summary judgment motion solely because it concludes the plaintiff has failed to state a currently cognizable constitutional violation direct the lower court to enter summary judgment for the defendant on the merits—thereby terminating the claim immediately—or merely reverse the denial of the defendant's summary judgment motion based on qualified immunity and remand for further proceedings? The answer should not matter if there is only one defendant facing one claim. For even though the granting of qualified immunity because the law was not clearly established, or because a reasonable person in defendant's position could not have realized that his conduct would violate clearly established law, insulates a defendant only from damages, and not from prospective declaratory or injunctive relief and therefore not from attorneys' fees, a granting of qualified immunity because plaintiff fails to state any currently recognized claim at all would relieve defendant of all liability.

But what if there is a companion official capacity claim against the same defendant, or (what amounts to the same thing), a claim against the defendant's employing local government entity? Qualified immunity is not available as a defense to those claims. Yet if the basis of the appellate court's granting qualified immunity on the individual capacity claim is that the plaintiff has stated no actionable federal constitutional or statutory violation, the same logic should also logically defeat the official capacity claims against an officer or the entity she serves.[21] Shouldn't the appellate court just say so, and direct entry of judgment for all defendants, rather than remand to an understandably confused trial judge for whatever "further proceedings" might be appropriate?

One appellate court has declined to do so, feeling bound by the *Johnson* "merits" language to reverse only the denial of qualified

20. Implicitly the majority in *Pace v. Capobianco*, 283 F.3d 1275 (11th Cir.2002) took such a position when, after *Saucier v. Katz*, 533 U.S. 194, 121 S.Ct. 2151, 150 L.Ed.2d 272 (2001), it accepted interlocutory jurisdiction to review the denial of qualified immunity in an excessive force case. Over the objection of a panel member who concurred in the judgment, the majority reversed not only on the ground that the applicable law was not clearly established, but alternatively because it found no predicate Fourth Amendment violation. The concurring judge read *Saucier* as limiting appellate jurisdiction to the question whether the law was clearly established, which it termed a "qualified immunity" issue, as distinct from the separate legal question on the "merits," that is whether plaintiff's case sketched a Fourth Amendment excessive force claim upon which relief could be granted.

21. See *Los Angeles v. Heller*, 475 U.S. 796, 106 S.Ct. 1571, 89 L.Ed.2d 806 (1986).

immunity without directing entry of judgment.[22] The Court did offer the hint that "it may be appropriate for the district court to re-visit its decision [upholding] the official capacity claim in light of this opinion." You bet the district court should "re-visit its decision"! If no claim is stated against the individual defendant, and if the entity's liability (against itself directly or via an official capacity claim) is wholly derivative of and dependent on a constitutional violation having been committed by him, no claim is stated in these circumstances against the entity either.[23] It too is entitled to dismissal for failure to state a claim. Yet the panel majority didn't feel free to say so because it believed that a judgment squarely bottomed on failure to state a claim would, as a judgment on the "merits," no longer be based on qualified immunity, as it would have to be to sustain the court's exercise of interlocutory appellate jurisdiction under *Johnson*. With respect, it is submitted that the panel misunderstood the Supreme Court's concern in *Johnson*. A case has legal as well as factual merits. It is only when a trial court denies qualified immunity for purely factual reasons that the Supreme Court believed the rationale was undermined for permitting an interlocutory appeal from a denial of qualified immunity. The High Court's understanding that a dismissal on the legal ground of failure to state a claim is part and parcel of the qualified immunity defense is apparent from *Sacramento, Conn*, and *Wilson*.

Of course not every municipal or county entity sued together with its qualified immunity-seeking officer deserves dismissal just because the officer is awarded qualified immunity. The municipality may not be disputing that its officer violated federal law, but arguing instead that it cannot be liable under § 1983 unless that violation was part of a pattern or custom of unconstitutional conduct to which it was deliberately indifferent.[24] In that situation, resolution of the officer's interlocutory appeal from an order denying him qualified immunity would not necessarily resolve a companion appeal by the entity concerning its responsibility for the violation, and accordingly an appellate court may decline jurisdiction over the entity's parallel interlocutory appeal.[25]

It is clear in any event that in some circuits defendants contemplating an interlocutory appeal must at least carefully heed the fact-law distinction. The Sixth Circuit awarded the plaintiff double costs and attorney's fees after the defendants brought an interlocutory appeal on purely factual issues. In *Berryman v. Rieger*,[26] the court stated "[b]ecause the defendants' appeal attempts to persuade us to believe their version of the facts, we must dismiss the appeal. Where it clearly appears, as here, that the defendant is unnecessarily protracting the litigation, the court should consider imposing double costs and attorney's

22. *Hartley v. Parnell*, 193 F.3d 1263, 1270–72 (11th Cir.1999).

23. See text in § 5.106, *infra*, concerning *Los Angeles v. Heller*, 475 U.S. 796, 106 S.Ct. 1571, 89 L.Ed.2d 806 (1986).

24. See § 2.32, *infra*.

25. *Crockett v. Cumberland College*, 316 F.3d 571 (6th Cir.2003).

26. See 150 F.3d 561 (6th Cir.1998).

fees as a deterrent."[27] In their brief, the defendants disputed plaintiff's version of nearly every relevant fact, yet represented to the court that the appeal turned on a purely legal question. At oral argument, the exasperated court was finally able to conclusively determine that it lacked jurisdiction over the appeal. Defendants should be cautious therefore about taking interlocutory appeals from orders that deny qualified immunity solely on the "fact" ground that there is a genuine dispute of fact about whether plaintiff engaged in protected conduct, whether plaintiff suffered an injury, what defendant did, the defendant's motives in doing it, or whether defendant's conduct was the cause of plaintiff's injury.[28]

On the other hand, *Behrens* sheds some defendant-favoring light on how to characterize the ultimate qualified immunity question—whether a reasonable person in defendant's position should have realized that her contemplated comment would violate clearly established law. Is that a question of "fact" ineligible for interlocutory review under *Johnson*, or a question sufficiently infused with "law" to be eligible for interlocutory review either initially or, under *Behrens*, after a second unsuccessful motion? The Court writes that "*Johnson* permits petitioner to claim on appeal that all of the conduct which the District Court deems sufficiently supported for purposes of summary judgment met the *Harlow* standard of 'objective legal reasonableness.' "[29] The implication is that if the defendant below relied at all in moving for summary judgment on the ultimate "legal" issue of objective legal reasonableness, a denial of the motion may be eligible for interlocutory review even if that denial is premised on disputed facts about the defendant's conduct. That "legal" issue remains: whether, given the circumstances confronting the defendant (determined most favorably to the plaintiff resisting the motion), a reasonable person in defendant's position should have realized that his act or omission would violate established, closely analogous precedent.[30] So *Behrens* reads *Johnson* narrowly, to preclude interlocutory appeal only when, as presumably would seldom be the case, the summary judgment evidentiary dispute is limited to the question of what actually happened in real life. Despite *Johnson*, then, the appellate court's

27. *Id.* at 565.

28. *See Bazan v. Hidalgo County*, 246 F.3d 481 (5th Cir.2001) (dismissing officer's interlocutory appeal from denial of summary judgment predicated solely on discrepancies between testimony of defendant officer and a witness).

29. *Behrens*, 116 S.Ct. at 842.

30. See *Beauregard v. Olson*, 84 F.3d 1402, 1403–04 (11th Cir.1996); *Heidemann v. Rother*, 84 F.3d 1021, 1026–1028 (8th Cir.1996). Cf. *Kimberlin v. Quinlan*, 199 F.3d 496, 502–03 (D.C.Cir.1999), *rehearing en banc denied,* 207 F.3d 667 (D.C.Cir.2000) (whether reasonable prison official could have believed that interfering with inmate's access to press because of content of inmate's speech was lawful was mixed law-fact question defendant could have appealed on denial of initial motion, but whether plaintiff raises genuine fact issue as to defendants' unlawful motivation, a distinct element of First Amendment retaliation claim, is a "separable" fact issue not eligible for subsequent interlocutory appeal) (dictum); *Moniz v. City of Ft. Lauderdale*, 145 F.3d 1278, 1280–1282 (11th Cir.1998) (initial interlocutory appeal permitted where appeal grounded on assertion that, even on plaintiff's view of facts, defendant is entitled to immunity because defendant could not reasonably have known, based on clearly established law, that his challenged conduct would violate that law).

interlocutory jurisdiction is intact "where the denial [of qualified immunity] is based even in part on a disputed issue of law."[31] Nevertheless, the circuit courts, perhaps fearful of being flooded with interlocutory appeals, regularly conclude that defendants' qualified immunity appeals are governed by *Johnson* rather than *Behrens* because they raise pure fact issues ineligible for interlocutory review.[32]

Behrens decides another frequently recurring issue at the fringes of qualified immunity: whether to grant immediate review where the defendant also faces a § 1983 claim for equitable relief, or any other claim not barred by the immunity doctrine. In that situation the defen-

31. *See Doe v. Gooden*, 214 F.3d 952 (8th Cir.2000) which illustrates the shadowy line between *Johnson* and *Behrens*. The court maintains that its review is limited to what the record shows the defendant knew when he acted, yet encompasses the question "of what was known" to that person. *See also Cottrell v. Caldwell*, 85 F.3d 1480, 1485 (11th Cir.1996). The Eleventh Circuit elaborated on this approach, however, in *McMillian v. Johnson*, 88 F.3d 1554, 1563 (11th Cir.1996), *cert. denied*, 521 U.S. 1121, 117 S.Ct. 2514, 138 L.Ed.2d 1016 (1997). It observed that after assuming jurisdiction on the basis outlined by *Cottrell*, the appellate court may limit the scope of its review to the pure or mixed legal issues raised and decline to review the lower court's resolution of the facts for purposes of summary judgment. In *McMillian* it conducted such a review on one issue, but not on others.

32. *See, e.g., Walker v. Horn*, 286 F.3d 705 (3d Cir.2002) (no interlocutory appellate jurisdiction where prison officials' qualified immunity summary judgment motion was denied based on existence of genuine fact issues); *Reyes v. City of Richmond*, 287 F.3d 346 (5th Cir.2002) (appeal in substance, if not in form, challenged only the genuineness, not the legal materiality, of factual disputes, so interlocutory jurisdiction lacking); *Mabrey v. Farthing*, 280 F.3d 400 (4th Cir.2002) (fact disputes about involvement of physicians and nurses in care of inmate who died of dehydration precluded appellate jurisdiction over denial of summary judgment motion based on qualified immunity); *Kimberlin v. Quinlan*, 199 F.3d 496, 502–03 (D.C.Cir.1999), *rehearing en banc denied,* 207 F.3d 667 (D.C.Cir.2000) (whether reasonable prison official could have believed that interfering with inmate's access to press because of content of inmate's speech was lawful was mixed law-fact question defendant could have appealed on denial of initial motion, but whether plaintiff raises genuine fact issue as to defendants' unlawful motivation, a distinct element of First Amendment retaliation claim, is a "separable" fact issue not eligible for subsequent interlocutory appeal) (dictum); *Ellis v. Washington County*, 198 F.3d 225, 229 (6th Cir.1999), *cert. denied*, 529 U.S. 1087, 120 S.Ct. 1720, 146 L.Ed.2d 642 (2000) (under *Johnson v. Jones*, no interlocutory review of trial court's summary judgment denial predicated on alleged genuine fact issue, even though plaintiff created that fact issue solely through what appellate court termed "the rankest type of inadmissible hearsay"); *Hoard v. Sizemore*, 198 F.3d 205, 219–220 (6th Cir.1999) (*Behrens* confirmed *Johnson v. Jones* holding that summary judgment denials not grounded on any "abstract issue of law" are not interlocutorily appealable, and a fact dispute about defendant's motivation raises no such legal issue); *Guilloty–Perez v. Fuentes–Agostini*, 196 F.3d 293 (1st Cir. 1999) (no interlocutory appeal of summary judgment denial based on material fact issues about defendants' involvement in retaliatory conduct arguably violating First Amendment and defendants' motivations); *Reynolds v. Brown*, 521 U.S. 1122, 117 S.Ct. 2516, 138 L.Ed.2d 1018 (1997), *cert. denied*, 521 U.S. 1122, 117 S.Ct. 2516, 138 L.Ed.2d 1018 (appellate court lacks jurisdiction to review denial of summary judgment based on qualified immunity because sole apparent question of law is whether facts concerning defendants' use of wrist locks on prisoner-plaintiff violated Eighth Amendment's cruel and unusual punishment prohibition); and *Jackson v. McIntosh*, 90 F.3d 330 (9th Cir.1996), *cert. denied*, 519 U.S. 1029, 117 S.Ct. 584, 136 L.Ed.2d 514 (1996) (fact dispute over defendants' motive in denying prisoner kidney transplant operation insufficient to warrant interlocutory review, regardless of objective legal reasonableness under *Harlow* and *Anderson* of that decision). *Cf. Szwedo v. Arkansas*, 284 F.3d 826 (8th Cir.2002) (district court's failure to address qualified immunity issue precluded appellate jurisdiction after denial of summary judgment motion).

dant will have to go to trial—and suffer the demands of discovery—to resist injunctive relief even if the immunity defense to the damages claim is sustained on interlocutory appeal. Confirming the predominant opinion of the circuit courts, *Behrens* holds that the individual defendant may proceed with an otherwise available interlocutory appeal even though he will almost certainly face trial on other claims as to which no qualified immunity lies.[33] The Court considered this conclusion necessary to implement the qualified immunity objective of relieving the individual defendant from the burdens of discovery and trial respecting damages liability, not just from litigation as an entirety. Were it to hold otherwise, the Court observed, the plaintiff could unilaterally subvert the government official's interlocutory appeal by seeking injunctive relief in addition to damages on a § 1983 claim, or by asserting one or more non-immune claims in the same action.

In a separate development, the Supreme Court has upheld a state's rules that deny a § 1983 defendant the same interlocutory review of a trial court's denial of his motion for qualified immunity that would be available under the *Mitchell v. Forsyth* doctrine in federal court.[34]

When both damages and prospective relief are sought, perhaps the defendant should sometimes be entitled to an interlocutory appeal under the *Mitchell* rationale even when his summary judgment motion is granted. Suppose the defendant had sought qualified immunity on the broad ground, which *Siegert*, *County of Sacramento, Conn* and *Wilson* direct lower courts to decide first, that the plaintiff's allegations are currently legally deficient. If the motion prevails on that ground, defendant will avoid liability altogether. By contrast, if his motion succeeds only on the other "law" prong identified by *Harlow* and *Creighton* (namely that the violation was not clearly established by closely analogous precedent when the defendant acted), the defendant is absolved only of damages liability and will still face trial with respect to prospective relief. The considerations underlying *Mitchell*—that the qualified immunity defense is intended as an immunity from suit—might suggest in this situation that an immediate appeal should lie, even though the defendant has prevailed, on a narrower ground, on summary judgment. But it probably does not, because the defense protects the defendant only from damages. Certainly a plaintiff, by contrast, cannot secure interlocutory relief from an order granting qualified immunity to fewer than all defendants; the collateral order exception to the final decision rule, as exemplified by *Mitchell*, does not apply here because the plaintiff is said

33. It will be remembered that qualified immunity protects only individual defendants, not government entities, and that it shields individual defendants only from damages, not injunctive or other prospective relief. *See Holmes v. Marion County Office of Family and Children*, 349 F.3d 914, 917 (7th Cir.2003) (entertaining interlocutory jurisdiction on Eleventh Amendment immunity even though state defendant conceded related claim had to be litigated).

34. *Johnson v. Fankell*, 520 U.S. 911, 117 S.Ct. 1800, 138 L.Ed.2d 108 (1997). The implications of *Fankell* for the plaintiff's decision to file a § 1983 action against individual defendants in state court, and for the defendant sued in state court to remove to federal court, are discussed in § 5.45, *infra*.

to be able to obtain effective review of such an order on appeal after a final judgment.[35]

Pendent Jurisdiction On Qualified Immunity Appeal

A related difficulty is presented when, on an individual defendant's interlocutory appeal from the denial of qualified immunity, a co-defendant invokes the circuit court's appellate jurisdiction to consider a different defense.[36] The Supreme Court has held, in *Swint v. Chambers County Comm'n*,[37] that the exceptional interlocutory jurisdiction conferred on a federal circuit court by *Mitchell v. Forsyth* to review the denial of qualified immunity does not carry with it "pendent" or "supplemental" appellate jurisdiction to review at the same time an order denying an entity co-defendant's motion asserting that its agent was not carrying out official "policy."[38]

The Court first held that the denial of the defendant county's motion could not be independently appealed on an interlocutory basis as a "collateral order" comparable to an order denying the individual defendant's assertion of qualified immunity. The Court reemphasized that there is only a small category of district court decisions prior to final judgment that constitute immediately appealable final "collateral orders" consistent with 28 U.S.C.A. § 1291. That category includes only "decisions that are conclusive, that resolve important questions separate from the merits, and that are effectively unreviewable on appeal from the final judgment in the underlying action." The Court then explained that in *Swint* the district court had reached only a tentative, incomplete determination that the county's sheriff may have been a "final policymaker" for whose decisions the county could be liable. But even had that decision been final, the Court suggested, it would not have been an immediately appealable collateral order because it could have been reviewable on appeal after final judgment. Unlike the individual defendant's qualified immunity defense—"an immunity from suit"[39] that is effectively lost if a case is erroneously permitted to go to trial—the plaintiff's failure to carry the prima facie element of *Monell* "policy" on

35. *LaTrieste Restaurant and Cabaret v. Port Chester*, 96 F.3d 598 (2d Cir.1996); *Winfrey v. School Bd. of Dade County*, 59 F.3d 155 (11th Cir.1995).

36. The issue can also arise if the plaintiff asserts a cross-appeal. It seems clear that if the issues asserted by the plaintiff's cross-appeal are not intertwined with the immunity defense raised by the defendant on interlocutory appeal, the appellate court lacks jurisdiction. See *Murphy v. Arkansas*, 127 F.3d 750 (8th Cir.1997).

37. 514 U.S. 35, 115 S.Ct. 1203, 131 L.Ed.2d 60 (1995).

38. *But cf. Sheth v. Webster*, 145 F.3d 1231 (11th Cir.1998) (appellate court had pendent appellate jurisdiction to review on interlocutory appeal the denial of "discretionary function" immunity provided by Alabama law to state officers facing pendent state tort law claims); *Morin v. Caire*, 77 F.3d 116 (5th Cir.1996) (exercising pendent appellate jurisdiction at defendant's request to decide closely related state law claims against officer who otherwise would have been forced to trial); *Gros v. City of Grand Prairie, Texas*, 209 F.3d 431, 436–437 (5th Cir.2000) (declining to exercise pendent appellate jurisdiction at plaintiffs' request to decide state law claims on which officer had prevailed below and on which he therefore would not face trial if appellate review denied).

39. 514 U.S. at 36, 115 S.Ct. at 1205 (citing *Mitchell v. Forsyth*, 472 U.S. 511, 526, 105 S.Ct. 2806, 2815, 86 L.Ed.2d 411 (1985)).

a claim against an entity defendant gives the entity a "mere defense to liability." Consequently, even in a case where a trial court rules definitively against an entity's motion based on an asserted deficiency in the plaintiff's showing of "policy," that decision would not be an independently appealable collateral order.

Alternatively, defendant county, joined by the plaintiffs, argued for "pendent appellate jurisdiction" that would enable it to piggyback on the appellate court's interlocutory "collateral order" jurisdiction over the denial of the individual defendants' qualified immunity motions. The parties are correct, the Court acknowledged, "that we have not universally required courts of appeals to confine review to the precise decision independently subject to appeal."[40] Nevertheless, judicial approval of pendent appellate jurisdiction would "drift away from the statutory instructions Congress has given to control the timing of appellate proceedings."[41]

In this regard the Court observed first that 28 U.S.C.A. Section 1292(a) specifies only three types of immediately appealable interlocutory decisions that are not appealable as "final" under Section 1291 or its "collateral order" accretion. These specifically approved cases, the Court concluded, did not include the "pendent" situation at hand. Section 1292, the Court added, authorizes district courts (with circuit court agreement) to "certify for immediate appeal interlocutory orders deemed pivotal and debatable." But pendent appellate jurisdiction, invoked by the parties with the concurrence of only the circuit court, would circumvent this "first line discretion" that Congress conferred on the district courts. In addition, the Supreme Court expressed doubt about its continuing authority to expand appellate jurisdiction by judicial decision in the face of amendments to the Rules Enabling Act[42] that authorize the Court to define finality for purposes of section 1291[43] and to provide for interlocutory appeals of nonfinal decisions not otherwise permitted under section 1292.[44] The statute calls on the Court, in exercising these powers, to proceed by formal rulemaking after consultation with and input from committees of the bench and bar after public comment or participation.[45]

Given these doubts about its own power to expand interlocutory appellate review by judicial decision after these statutory amendments, but noting its earlier decisions that had flirted with pendent appellate jurisdiction, the Court concluded that it "need not definitively or preemptively settle here whether or when it may be proper for a court of appeals with jurisdiction over one ruling to review, conjunctively, related rulings that are not themselves independently appealable."[46] Even were

40. 514 U.S. at 50, 115 S.Ct. at 1211.

41. *Id.* at 45, 115 S.Ct. at 1209.

42. 28 U.S.C.A. § 2071.

43. See 28 U.S.C.A. § 2072(c), added in 1990.

44. See 28 U.S.C.A. § 1292(e), added in 1992.

45. *Swint*, 115 U.S. at 49, 115 S.Ct. at 1210.

46. *Id.* at 50–51, 115 S.Ct. at 1212 (emphasis supplied).

the Court to approve pendent appellate jurisdiction as a general proposition, the parties in *Swint* did not contend that the decision denying the county's motion based on deficiencies in the "policy" element "was inextricably intertwined with that court's decision to deny the individual defendants' qualified immunity motions, or that review of the former decision was necessary to ensure meaningful review of the latter."[47] Any such argument would have been baseless: "The individual defendants' qualified immunity turns on whether they violated clearly established federal laws; the County Commission's liability turns on the allocation of law enforcement power in Alabama." The latter was simply an "unrelated question."[48]

The unrelatedness of the putative pendent claim in *Swint* means that the Court's willingness to approve pendent appellate jurisdiction absent formal rulemaking will not be fully tested unless it considers the question where the issues surrounding the piggy-backed claim are more closely linked to the issues involved in resolving an interlocutory appeal based on qualified immunity. The relatedness difficulty goes beyond the fact that in *Swint* the parties contended not just for pendent claim but for pendent party appellate jurisdiction.[49] An individual defendant's statute of limitations defense, for example, would not be "related" to even her own defense of qualified immunity. On the other hand, suppose the ruling below denying an individual defendant's qualified immunity motion focused on the issue that *Siegert v. Gilley, County of Sacramento v. Lewis, Conn v. Gabbert* and *Wilson v. Layne* have encouraged trial courts to determine at the threshold, namely, the current legal sufficiency of the alleged federal constitutional or statutory violation. If that issue is resolved favorably to the individual defendant, the determination also exonerates a co-defendant entity who employed her.[50]

Relatedness, in short, is not necessarily absent where a different party seeks to join an individual defendant's appeal from a qualified immunity denial;[51] and it is not necessarily present when the would-be

47. *Id. See Crockett v. Cumberland College*, 316 F.3d 571 (6th Cir.2003) (defendant municipality's *Monell* "policy or custom" argument not inextricably intertwined with police officer's interlocutory appeal challenging denial of qualified immunity, so no jurisdiction over city's interlocutory appeal).

48. *Id.* The role played by state law in determining which officials are "final policymakers," for whose decisions an entity defendant may be held liable, is discussed in § 2.31 below.

49. Pendent party interlocutory appellate jurisdiction to review denial of an individual defendant's qualified immunity motion has also been denied when the putative pendent party seek companion review is a plaintiff. *See O'Bert ex rel. Estate of O'Bert v. Vargo*, 331 F.3d 29 (2d Cir.2003) (defendant officer's assertion that he lawfully used deadly force after entering trailer not inextricably intertwined with question raised by plaintiff's assertion on appeal that officer's initial entry into trailer unlawful, so court of appeals lacked pendent jurisdiction over unlawful entry claim).

50. See discussion of *City of Los Angeles v. Heller*, 475 U.S. 796, 106 S.Ct. 1571, 89 L.Ed.2d 806 (1986) in § 5.106 on Procedure. *But cf. Barrett v. Orange County Human Rights Comm'n*, 194 F.3d 341 (2d Cir. 1999) (exoneration of commissioner defendants as individuals not preclusive of liability of county or commission, because multimember commission reach decisions as a group and plaintiff complained of decisions made by commission as a whole).

51. See *Hill v. Dekalb Reg'l Youth Detention Ctr.*, 40 F.3d 1176, 1183–84 (11th Cir.1994) (qualified immunity raised by codefendant).

pendent issue is raised by the same individual defendant who is entitled to appeal under the *Mitchell* "collateral order" doctrine.[52] Moreover, the parties' own view that pendent appellate jurisdiction serves judicial economy will not substitute for the required relatedness. All parties in *Swint*—even the plaintiffs who in the trial court had defeated the county's motion based on "policy"—sought immediate review of that decision, to no avail.

Finally, it should be remembered that even if the Supreme Court, either by rule or decision, ultimately approves the doctrine of pendent appellate jurisdiction in the qualified immunity context, the relatedness requirement, while necessary, should not suffice. Notwithstanding an appellate court's power to assume pendent jurisdiction over an issue that overlaps with the immunity question, the exercise of that power, under standard "pendent" or "supplemental" jurisdiction doctrine, remains discretionary.[53] *Id.* The discretionary factors take into account not only judicial economy but "injudicious intermeddling, and justice in the disposition."[54]

In the final analysis, the threshold test for individual immunity in § 1983 actions—was the right in question well "settled" when allegedly violated—rests on a fiction. This purportedly "objective" standard for determining qualified immunity rests on the fragile assumption that the relatively low-level employee most likely to have actual citizen contact, the cop on the beat,[55] for example, appreciates the current state of constitutional law. The dubiousness of that premise has been remarked many times.[56] In any event, after *Anderson, Monroe*'s broad sphere of

52. See *Hinson v. Edmond*, 205 F.3d 1264 (11th Cir.2000) (no jurisdiction over defendant's interlocutory appeal related to the merits, because those issues not "inextricably interwoven" with the appealable issues concerning qualified immunity); *Moniz v. City of Ft. Lauderdale*, 145 F.3d 1278, 1281 (11th Cir.1998) (because qualified immunity issue could be resolved without reaching the merits of appellants' challenge to plaintiff's standing, the jurisdictional standing issue not within pendent appellate jurisdiction).

53. See, e.g., 28 U.S.C.A. § 1367(c).

54. *Hartley v. Parnell*, 193 F.3d 1263, 1272 (11th Cir.1999) (declining in court's discretion to exercise pendent appellate jurisdiction over claim against defendant in his official capacity even though those issues may have been intertwined with issues raised by his individual capacity qualified immunity appeal over which court did have jurisdiction); *Pickens v. Hollowell*, 59 F.3d 1203, 1208 (11th Cir.1995); *O'Bar v. Pinion*, 953 F.2d 74, 80 (4th Cir.1991), applied in *DiMeglio v. Haines*, 45 F.3d 790 (4th Cir.1995).

55. Chief Justice Burger compared the discretionary decision-making of executive officials with that of cops on the beat. See *Scheuer v. Rhodes*, 416 U.S. 232, 246–47, 94 S.Ct. 1683, 1691–92, 40 L.Ed.2d 90 (1974).

56. Ironically, Justice Powell, dissenting in *Wood*, made this same objection to the "settled" standard, a standard that he later helped enlarge. See *supra* § 2.22. An acute example of the problems related to the counterfactual premise of "settledness" is furnished by *V–1 Oil Co. v. Wyoming*, 902 F.2d 1482 (10th Cir.1990), *cert. denied*, 498 U.S. 920, 111 S.Ct. 295, 112 L.Ed.2d 249 (1990). A state environmental official conducted a warrantless search of a gas station under circumstances which, the Court acknowledged, violated a "clearly established" right of the station owner. See id. at 1488. Nevertheless, the Tenth Circuit concluded that the defendant deserved immunity under an "extraordinary circumstances" exception mentioned in *Harlow v. Fitzgerald*, 457 U.S. 800, 818–19, 102 S.Ct. 2727, 2738–39, 73 L.Ed.2d 396 (1982), available to defendants who "neither knew nor should have known of the relevant legal standard." *V–1 Oil Co.*, 902 F.2d at 1488. The Court of Appeals explained that the defendant's reliance on the contemporaneous advice of a fully briefed senior state

individual defendant liability is now largely offset by a highly solicitous definition of official immunity.

§ 2.24 Private Party Qualified Immunity

As we have seen, § 1983 is aimed at deterring "state actors from using the badge of their authority to deprive individuals of their federally guaranteed rights and to provide relief to victims if such deterrence fails."[1] Although at first blush it would seem inapposite to apply to private persons a statute aimed at deterring state actors, the necessary link to government emerges where private persons conspire or act in concert with state actors to effect a deprivation of a plaintiff's constitutional or federally protected rights.[2] An understanding of the elements of the plaintiff's prima facie § 1983 case against a "private" defendant is an essential prelude to the question whether that defendant enjoys any immunity.[3] For a plaintiff suing a private party under § 1983 to withstand a motion to dismiss under Federal Rule of Civil Procedure ("F.R.C.P.") 12(b)(6),[4] the plaintiff must first allege that the defendant is a "person" as that term is used in the text of the statute.[5] Second,

assistant attorney general made the circumstances "extraordinary" even though, as a general rule, there is nothing "inherently extraordinary" about reliance on the advice of counsel. See *id.*

There is of course a long tradition of assuming, for purposes of civil as well as criminal liability, that litigants are aware of the requirements of prior decisions. See, e.g., *Burnham v. Superior Court*, 495 U.S. 604, 110 S.Ct. 2105, 109 L.Ed.2d 631 (1990) (holding that defendants will be subject to a constitutionally adequate basis of personal jurisdiction if they are served with process in any state in which they are even transiently present). According to the Supreme Court, knowledge of the transient service rule was fairly imputable to potential civil defendants by virtue of a "continuing tradition," see id. at 624, 110 S.Ct. at 2118 (plurality opinion by Scalia, J.), or a "century of judicial practice," see id. at 635, 110 S.Ct. at 2124 (Brennan, J., concurring). Even granting that assumption, however, it may be a far greater stretch to assume that a low-level government official can identify which prior constitutional law decisions are sufficiently analogous to a real-life event to furnish "clearly established" precedent within the meaning of *Anderson*.

§ 2.24

1. *Wyatt v. Cole*, 504 U.S. 158, 161, 112 S.Ct. 1827, 1830, 118 L.Ed.2d 504 (1992) (emphasis supplied) (*citing Carey v. Piphus*, 435 U.S. 247, 253–258, 98 S.Ct. 1042, 1047–1049, 55 L.Ed.2d 252 (1978)). The reliance on *Carey* for this proposition seems peculiar, since there the Court placed priority on the compensation goal, writing: "To the extent that congress intended awards under § 1983 should deter the deprivation of constitutional rights, there is no evidence that it meant to establish a deterrent more formidable than that inherent in the award of compensatory damages." *Carey*, 435 U.S. at 256, 98 S.Ct. at 1049.

2. *Adickes v. S.H. Kress & Co.*, 398 U.S. 144, 90 S.Ct. 1598, 26 L.Ed.2d 142 (1970); *Burrell v. Board of Trustees of Ga. Military College*, 970 F.2d 785 (11th Cir. 1992), *cert. denied*, 507 U.S. 1018, 113 S.Ct. 1814, 123 L.Ed.2d 445 (1993); *Berger v. Hanlon*, 129 F.3d 505 (9th Cir.1997), *vacated on other grounds*, 526 U.S. 808, 119 S.Ct. 1706, 143 L.Ed.2d 978 (1999) (media and police department acted in concert when police contracted to allow media to film execution of search warrant for broadcast). The plaintiff bears the burden of pleading and proving the elements of conspiracy between the public and private actors. *Davis v. Union Nat'l Bank*, 46 F.3d 24 (7th Cir. 1994), *cert. denied*, 514 U.S. 1065, 115 S.Ct. 1696, 131 L.Ed.2d 560 (1995).

3. Private defendants in the context of § 1983 litigation are to be distinguished from "public official" defendants. In the latter category the requirement that there be "state action" is in most cases a foregone conclusion, whereas in the former the inquiry into whether "state action" exists may often prove to be the foundation on which the plaintiff's case stands or falls.

4. Fed.R.Civ.P. 12(b)(6).

5. 42 U.S.C.A. § 1983 (1988). Although this requirement is a significant hurdle in

there must have been a deprivation of some right of the plaintiff that is protected under the Constitution or by federal law. Third, the private defendant must have acted "under color of" state law in effecting the deprivation. Finally, the plaintiff must show that the deprivation caused some harm remediable by injunction or damages.[6]

Prior to 1970, it was assumed that private actors were not subject to liability under § 1983 because of their inability to act "under color of" state law. However, *Adickes v. S.H. Kress & Co.*[7] removed this absolute impediment to suit against private persons by finding that such persons could be liable under § 1983 for "wilfully conspiring" with a state actor to deprive the plaintiff of rights protected by § 1983.

The inquiry into whether a private defendant had acted under color of state law was reformulated more expansively in *Lugar v. Edmondson Oil Co.*[8] The Court there held that a private defendant acts "under color of" if, whether or not he has conspired with a state agent, his actions are "fairly attributable" to the state.[9] This "fair attribution" test consists of two elements: (1) "the deprivation must be caused by the exercise of some right or privilege created by the State or by a rule of conduct imposed by the State or by a person for whom the State is responsible," and (2) the private defendant must have "acted together with or ... obtained significant aid from state officials" or engaged in conduct "otherwise chargeable to the State."[10] The defendants in Lugar were found to fall within the test simply because they invoked unconstitutional prejudgment property seizure devices. While the Court was thus willing to bring certain private conduct within the boundaries of § 1983 protections, it refrained from addressing whether private defendants who act concertedly with public officials are entitled to the same immunity from suit as public officials or whether in actions against private defendants plaintiffs would be required "to carry additional burdens."

In the late 1960s, the Supreme Court stated that it would accord absolute or qualified immunity from damages to certain government officials if the "tradition of immunity was so firmly rooted in the common law and was supported by such strong policy reasons that 'Congress would have specifically so provided had it wished to abolish

suits against local entities and states, it will always be met in regard to private persons.

6. Qualified immunity, as it now stands, insulates defendants from monetary damages only. An injunction may still be issued constraining the defendant in some way, and thus § 1988 would still provide for an award of attorney fees, despite a finding of qualified immunity. Plaintiffs' attorneys are thus not wholly without inducement for accepting cases where a grant of qualified immunity is likely.

A fifth element, i.e., that a policy or practice be shown, is only applicable in § 1983 actions against entity defendants.

7. 398 U.S. 144, 152, 90 S.Ct. 1598, 1605, 26 L.Ed.2d 142 (1970).

8. 457 U.S. 922, 102 S.Ct. 2744, 73 L.Ed.2d 482 (1982). *See* Section B(6)(a) *supra*.

9. 457 U.S. at 937, 102 S.Ct. at 2754. Note that this inquiry into whether a private defendant acts "under color of" state law is distinct from whether "state action" exists for purposes of the Fourteenth Amendment.

10. *Wyatt*, 504 U.S. at 161, 112 S.Ct. at 1830.

the [immunity] doctrine.' "[11] The landmark decision establishing an immunity from damages in § 1983 actions was *Pierson v. Ray*,[12] which held that police officers were entitled to a defense of good faith and probable cause. This defense was later clarified so that the public official avoided damages only if he could show both an objectively reasonable belief in the necessity of the challenged conduct and a subjective good faith belief that the conduct was necessary.[13]

Under this formulation of common law qualified immunity for public officials, many such defendants were required to proceed to trial to prove the subjective element of the immunity. The then prevalent summary judgment doctrine often failed to relieve the individual defendant of the burden of trial, even when the defendant was ultimately adjudged entitled to qualified immunity.[14] For this reason, and also to avoid chilling public officials from vigorously performing their duties, the Supreme Court in *Harlow v. Fitzgerald*[15] "completely reformulated qualified immunity along principles not at all embodied in the common law."[16]

The inquiry into the defendant's subjective beliefs was entirely eliminated, with two apparent consequences: the defendant no longer had to prove anything about his state of mind in order to claim the immunity, and plaintiff's evidence of defendant's malicious state of mind would not defeat immunity. Further, the remaining prong, focused on the objective reasonableness of the defendant's conduct, was bifurcated: for a defendant to forfeit the immunity, the violation complained of must have been one of "clearly established law" *and* a reasonable person under the circumstances the defendant confronted should have realized that the challenged conduct violated that law. The defendant enjoys the immunity if *either* proposition is untrue—if the law was "unsettled" or only "dimly", rather than "clearly", established, *or* if, although the law was clearly established, a reasonable person in the circumstances that confronted the defendant would not have realized that acting as the defendant did would violate that law. *Harlow* thus represents a marked

11. *Owen v. City of Independence*, 445 U.S. 622, 637, 100 S.Ct. 1398, 1408, 63 L.Ed.2d 673 (1980) (*quoting Pierson v. Ray*, 386 U.S. 547, 555, 87 S.Ct. 1213, 1218, 18 L.Ed.2d 288 (1967)).

12. 386 U.S. 547, 87 S.Ct. 1213, 18 L.Ed.2d 288 (1967). Although what *Pierson* established is here referred to as an "immunity" from suit, some would debate the usage of this term to describe the escape from liability that *Pierson* afforded public official defendants. For example, Justice O'Connor, writing for the Court in *Wyatt*, 504 U.S. at 165, 112 S.Ct. at 1832, referred to Pierson as establishing a "defense" for public officials sued under § 1983 rather than an immunity. Despite the fact that the end result may be the same under the two appellations, the difference between the two manifests itself in defining the plaintiff's prima facie case. The difference also assumes importance in light of *Celotex Corp. v. Catrett*, 477 U.S. 317, 106 S.Ct. 2548, 91 L.Ed.2d 265 (1986), and *Anderson v. Liberty Lobby, Inc.*, 477 U.S. 242, 106 S.Ct. 2505, 91 L.Ed.2d 202 (1986), which reformulated summary judgment law to require the plaintiff to bring forth evidence to defeat a summary judgment motion on the elements for which *he would bear the burden* at trial.

13. *Wood v. Strickland*, 420 U.S. 308, 321–22, 95 S.Ct. 992, 1000–01, 43 L.Ed.2d 214 (1975).

14. *Wyatt*, 504 U.S. at 170, 112 S.Ct. at 1835 (Kennedy, J., concurring).

15. 457 U.S. 800, 102 S.Ct. 2727, 73 L.Ed.2d 396 (1982).

16. *Anderson v. Creighton*, 483 U.S. 635, 645, 107 S.Ct. 3034, 3042, 97 L.Ed.2d 523 (1987).

departure from the Court's precedents defining the "historical" contours of common law tort immunities and defenses; henceforth policy-based considerations would determine the grant or denial of qualified immunity.[17]

The Supreme Court has inconsistently applied the burdens of pleading and proof applicable to the two elements of *Harlow*-type immunity. The Court has labeled qualified immunity an "affirmative defense."[18] As such, F.R.C.P. 8(c)[19] would ordinarily require the defendant to plead and then prove both its prongs by a preponderance of the evidence. However, *Mitchell v. Forsyth*[20] and *Siegert v. Gilley*[21] make it apparent that on at least the first, or "law", element, it is the plaintiff (once the defendant pleads qualified immunity) that bears the initial burden of finding and citing a closely analogous case.[22] Then, even if the plaintiff satisfies the district court that the cited case meets the "closely analogous" standard for clearly established law demanded by *Anderson v. Creighton*,[23] a defendant may ultimately prevail on that issue without trial and even before discovery on an immediate, interlocutory appeal.[24] In this way, *Harlow* provides a public defendant potential immunity from suit (respecting damages), and not merely a trial defense.

Whereas this first, "clearly established" prong of *Harlow*-type immunity has been characterized as a question of "law," the second level of the current qualified immunity calculus—whether the "contours of the right [were] sufficiently clear [so] that a reasonable official [in defendant's position] would understand that what he was doing would violate that right"[25]—is "fact specific."[26] Thus a defendant whose motion for summary judgment is denied not because the law was unsettled but because there is a triable issue whether he knew or should have known that his conduct would violate that clearly established law must endure discovery and trial on that issue.[27]

The somewhat labyrinthine development of qualified immunity as applied to public officials set the stage for the question left unresolved in *Lugar*—whether private defendants invoking state replevin, attachment, or garnishment statutes are entitled to the same revised, expansive

17. *Wyatt*, 504 U.S. at 170, 112 S.Ct. at 1835 (Kennedy, J., concurring).

18. *Leatherman v. Tarrant County Narcotics Intelligence and Coordination Unit*, 507 U.S. 163, 113 S.Ct. 1160, 122 L.Ed.2d 517 (1993).

19. Fed. R. Civ. P. 8(c).

20. 472 U.S. 511, 526, 105 S.Ct. 2806, 2815, 86 L.Ed.2d 411 (1985).

21. 500 U.S. 226, 231–232, 111 S.Ct. 1789, 1793, 114 L.Ed.2d 277 (1991).

22. *Cf. Elder v. Holloway*, 510 U.S. 510, 114 S.Ct. 1019, 127 L.Ed.2d 344 (1994) (holding nevertheless that appellate courts must use their own knowledge of all relevant precedents in deciding whether a right has been clearly established, "not simply those cited to or discovered by the district court").

23. 483 U.S. 635, 107 S.Ct. 3034, 97 L.Ed.2d 523 (1987).

24. *Mitchell*, 472 U.S. at 526, 105 S.Ct. at 2815.

25. *Feagley v. Waddill*, 868 F.2d 1437, 1439 (5th Cir.1989) (*citing Anderson v. Creighton*, 483 U.S. 635, 641, 107 S.Ct. 3034, 3040, 97 L.Ed.2d 523 (1987)).

26. *Id.*

27. *Hale v. Townley*, 19 F.3d 1068, 1072 (5th Cir.1994) (*citing Feagley*, 868 F.2d at 1439), *withdrawn on reconsideration*, 45 F.3d 914 (5th Cir.1995).

qualified immunity enunciated by *Harlow* and *Creighton* as their public counterparts.[28] The majority in *Wyatt v. Cole*, writing through Justice O'Connor, held they are not. Because the *Wyatt* defendants had been granted this enlarged kind of "objectively determined, immediately appealable immunity," the Court refused to analyze whether the defendants could claim the older "common law" defense conferred by *Pierson*.[29] The Court found that one of the key policy reasons favoring the *Harlow* brand of qualified immunity—the need for government officials to make discretionary decisions without undue fear of suit or liability—was absent in *Wyatt*, where a private creditor, acting purely for personal gain, set in motion the state's property-seizure machinery.[30] It remained to be seen, however, on remand, whether the defendants were entitled to an "affirmative defense [like that approved in *Pierson*] based on good faith and/or probable cause" or whether plaintiffs could be required "to carry additional burdens" in actions against private, as distinct from governmental, defendants.[31]

Although *Wyatt* produced a majority opinion, five justices either dissented or concurred. These opinions must therefore be closely parsed for clues about the future of qualified immunity for private, noncreditor defendants and of lesser defenses for the private creditor defendants. *Wyatt* provides three separate models for defining the defense available to private parties who are sued because of their use of state replevin, garnishment, or attachment statutes. The majority implies that *Pierson* may supply their only applicable defense;[32] on this view, these defendants

28. This was the issue as framed in *Wyatt,* and the majority there emphasized that their holding was limited to that precise issue. At least one appellate court, *Burrell v. Board of Trustees of Ga. Military College*, 970 F.2d 785, 795 (11th Cir.1992), *cert. denied*, 507 U.S. 1018, 113 S.Ct. 1814, 123 L.Ed.2d 445 (1993), has, however, seized upon the generality of the Court's statement in *Wyatt* concerning what had been left unresolved—"we do not foreclose the possibility that private defendants faced with § 1983 liability under *Lugar* . . . could be entitled to an affirmative defense"—by reading *Wyatt* as not limited to attachment cases. 504 U.S. at 169, 112 S.Ct. at 1834 (emphasis added).

29. See discussion of *Pierson v. Ray*, 386 U.S. 547, 87 S.Ct. 1213, 18 L.Ed.2d 288 (1967).

30. Specifically, the majority in *Wyatt* found that the type of private defendant to whom they were denying qualified immunity held "no office requiring them to exercise discretion; nor [were] they principally concerned with enhancing the public good." 504 U.S. at 168, 112 S.Ct. at 1833. Denying qualified immunity here, in short, would not "unduly impair[ ]" the public interest. *Id.*

31. 504 U.S. at 169, 112 S.Ct. at 1834. The majority thus implies that defenses for private defendants, acting with personal motives, should be determined under the pre-*Harlow* law of defenses as defined by *Pierson, Wood,* and *Scheuer*.

32. Justice O'Connor stated that *Pierson* was "of no avail" to the defendants in this case because what they had received below was a grant of *Harlow*-type immunity, thus acknowledging the difference between these two versions of the defense. 504 U.S. at 165, 112 S.Ct. at 1832. However, Justice O'Connor did label *Pierson* as the proper model for determining the availability of a "good-faith defense." *Id.* The majority left open whether the defendants in this case would be entitled to an "affirmative defense based on good faith and/or probable cause." *Id.* at 1834 (emphasis supplied). As is the case with any true affirmative defense, *Pierson, Wood,* and *Scheuer* placed the burden of establishing the defense on the defendant. *Id.*

Justice O'Connor's opinion also allows for the possibility that lower courts will apply *Pierson* to private defendants in other contexts where a private party invokes state prejudgment property seizure mechanisms. At least one court of appeals has read the

would bear the significant compound objective and subjective burdens announced by *Pierson, Wood,* and *Scheuer*. Justice Kennedy, however, would have reached back even further into § 1983 jurisprudence to the "historical" common law in effect when the statute was enacted. Finally, the Chief Justice would have adopted his own version of the "historical" common law, one significantly modified by *Harlow*.

Justice Kennedy, joined by Justice Scalia, concurred in the majority opinion, but wrote separately to elaborate on the defense available to the private defendants on remand. His baseline was formed by the common law torts of malicious prosecution and abuse of process, which he found most closely analogous to the case of a creditor misusing state prejudgment seizure laws. At common law, a defendant was liable for these torts if plaintiff could prove that defendant (a) possessed a generalized, subjectively malicious intent for filing suit, and (b) lacked probable cause for initiating suit. Lack of probable cause, in turn, could be shown in one of two ways: by demonstrating either that defendant's belief in the existence of probable cause was held in subjective bad faith (a mental element distinct from the malice that prompted filing of suit) or that defendant acted objectively unreasonably. Justice Kennedy found that at common law a private defendant could be liable if he in fact knew of the suit's invalidity, notwithstanding his objectively reasonable reliance on a state statute. Specifically, in Kennedy's view, a private defendant whose actions were objectively reasonable nevertheless remained liable if the plaintiff could prove that the defendant acted with (a) a subjectively malicious intent in bringing suit, and (b) more specifically, a subjective bad faith belief about the existence of probable cause.[33]

Thus under Justice Kennedy's faithful transplantation of the "historical" common law, the plaintiff shouldered two burdens in establishing the prima facie case. These burdens compose a mirror image of the objective "probable cause" and "subjective good faith" prongs of the § 1983 version of the "common law" compound defense announced during the 1960s and 1970s in *Pierson, Wood,* and *Scheuer*.[34] But his probable cause showing could be made disjunctively, and only the objective portion of the probable cause question was deemed a question of law. Thus what was described in *Stewart v. Sonneborn*,[35] a decision in

majority opinion in *Wyatt* as not being restricted to private defendants utilizing state replevin, garnishment, or attachment statutes. *Burrell v. Board of Trustees of Ga. Military College*, 970 F.2d at 795 ("Instead of restricting its holding to attachment cases, the Court merely left open 'the possibility that private defendants faced with [section] 1983 liability under Lugar ... could be entitled to an affirmative defense.' "). Yet the Eleventh Circuit did express serious doubt that privately acting private defendants of any kind would be able to assert qualified immunity in the wake of *Wyatt*. 970 F.2d at 795; *see infra* discussion of *Burrell*.

33. *Wyatt*, at 172, 112 S.Ct. at 1836 (Kennedy, J., concurring).

34. Indeed, under Justice Kennedy's analytic, future determinations regarding the parameters of defenses and immunities in § 1983 actions would be made according to immunity/defense law as it existed prior to *Wood, Scheuer*, and *Pierson*. Although he concurs with the result, Justice Kennedy's method in this regard is at odds with the majority's.

35. 98 U.S. (8 Otto) 187, 194, 25 L.Ed. 116 (1879), cited by *Wyatt*, 504 U.S. at 173, 112 S.Ct. at 1836 (Kennedy, J., concurring).

the same decade § 1983 was enacted, as the "exceptional" case-plaintiff shows prima facie a creditor defendant's subjective bad faith belief in probable cause—may really have been the plaintiff's principal path to overcoming immunity. This is because a creditor defendant would often emerge victorious on the question of objective reasonableness, for there was "support in the common law for the proposition" that it is objectively reasonable, as a matter of law, to rely on a statute not previously adjudged unconstitutional.[36] And the two remaining showings—malicious subjective intent in filing suit and subjective bad faith belief in probable cause—were questions of fact to be resolved by the jury.

Chief Justice Rehnquist, in a dissent joined by Justices Souter and Thomas, took issue with the majority, arguing that the contemporary *Harlow* version of § 1983 qualified immunity should have been granted on the record before the Court. The Chief Justice reached this conclusion by virtually equating the "historical" common law defense that the majority left open for consideration on remand with the modern *Harlow* version of qualified immunity. Under the Chief Justice's reading of the common law, as under Justice Kennedy's, a defendant would be liable if plaintiff made a conjunctive showing of subjective malice and lack of probable cause.[37] However, viewing the historical inquiry into probable cause through the anachronistic lens of *Harlow*, decided more than a century later, the Chief Justice found that it "principally" focused on objective reasonableness;[38] lack of probable cause should therefore no longer be demonstrable through defendant's subjectively held bad faith belief in its existence.

There was thus this difference between the Chief Justice's *Harlow*—driven view of common law probable cause and Justice Kennedy's wholesale adherence to the common law: Kennedy would allow lack of probable cause to be shown by evidence of the creditor's subjective bad faith. For the Chief Justice, this difference provided an insufficient basis on which to deny the extension of the contemporary version of qualified immunity, one geared to objective reasonableness.[39] The Chief Justice argued that the results would be the same under either *Harlow*-type immunity or the common law good faith defense. Because the plaintiff must make a conjunctive showing, her claim is defeasible when there is probable cause; and since that question, as reformulated by *Harlow*, is (despite being objective) a question of law,[40] a moving defendant should win before trial merely by showing reasonableness—"precisely the showing that entitles a public official to [*Harlow*] immunity."[41] The Chief Justice's rule allows a private defendant who acted with a subjective bad

36. *Wyatt*, 504 U.S. at 174, 112 S.Ct. at 1837 (Kennedy, J., concurring).

37. *Id.* at 176 n.1, 112 S.Ct. at 1838 n.1 (Rehnquist, C.J., dissenting).

38. *Id.* at 178, 112 S.Ct. at 1839 (Rehnquist, C.J., dissenting) (emphasis supplied).

39. *Id.* at 178 n.2, 112 S.Ct. at 1839 n.2 (Rehnquist, C.J., dissenting).

40. *Id.* at 178, 112 S.Ct. at 1839 (Rehnquist, C.J., dissenting) ("presence or absence of probable cause has long been acknowledged to be a question of law").

41. *Id.* at 179, 112 S.Ct. at 1839 (Rehnquist, C.J., dissenting) (citing *Harlow v. Fitzgerald*, 457 U.S. 800, 818, 102 S.Ct. 2727, 2738, 73 L.Ed.2d 396 (1982)).

faith belief in the existence of probable cause to be exonerated, as a matter of law, so long as his actions were objectively reasonable. Justice Kennedy, by contrast, would allow the probable cause question to be either a question of law or a question of fact, depending upon whether plaintiff chooses the "objective" or "subjective" mode of proof. The plaintiff, in other words, might still get to the jury.

The circuit courts of appeals have begun to wrestle with the questions left open by *Wyatt*: Is there a defense (short of modern § 1983 qualified immunity) available to private creditors sued for invoking a state's prejudgment property seizure devices, and may the more generous modern qualified immunity a la *Harlow* be granted to other, i.e., noncreditor defendants?[42] The Fifth Circuit Court of Appeals, on remand from *Wyatt*, observed that the five justices who concurred or dissented agreed that plaintiff bore the burden of showing in some fashion both malice and lack of probable cause, and that a private defendant could avoid damages if either of these showings failed. The Fifth Circuit accordingly held that "private defendants, at least those invoking ex parte prejudgment statutes," would not be liable unless plaintiff proved that defendant acted with malice and without probable cause.

As for proving lack of probable cause, the Fifth Circuit followed Justice Kennedy's "historical" view of the common law, as opposed to the Chief Justice's *Harlow*-driven view. That is, one way a plaintiff may establish lack of probable cause is by showing that defendant knew or should have known of the statute's constitutional infirmity. In permitting plaintiff to prevail on this subjective prong, the Fifth Circuit was influenced by the ease with which creditor defendants could meet the common law's objective prong. The creditor defendant, at least, would almost always satisfy the objective element of probable cause, given the common law authority that held it reasonable as a matter of law to rely on a state statute not previously adjudged unconstitutional. Referring to *Professional Real Estate Investors v. Columbia Pictures*,[43] the Fifth Circuit found that the creditor's objectively reasonable probable cause requires "no more than a 'reasonabl[e] belie[f] that there is a chance that [a] claim may be held valid upon adjudication.' "[44] Under that test, the court held that the *Wyatt* defendant's actions were objectively reasonable as a matter of law.

The court proceeded to the subjective probable cause question, i.e., whether the defendants knew or should have known of the statute's constitutional infirmity. The inquiry into a defendant's bad faith belief in the existence of probable cause is narrow, to be distinguished from the

42. The Court left open whether other, noncreditor private parties could be granted modern qualified immunity, since the precise question on which certiorari was granted in *Wyatt* was limited to the context of prejudgment property seizure devices. See *Sherman v. Four County Counseling Ctr.*, 987 F.2d 397, 405 (7th Cir.1993) ("[*Wyatt*] left open other immunity issues....."); *but cf. Burrell v. Board of Trustees*, 970 F.2d 785 (11th Cir.1992).

43. 508 U.S. 49, 61, 113 S.Ct. 1920, 1929, 123 L.Ed.2d 611 (1993).

44. *Wyatt*, 994 F.2d at 1113, n.285 (*quoting Hubbard v. Beatty & Hyde, Inc.*, 343 Mass. 258, 178 N.E.2d 485, 488 (1961)).

more general, separate inquiry into "malice."[45] The defendant's motives for initiating suit are irrelevant; the question is simply whether he knew that the statute he invoked was in fact unconstitutional. Because the plaintiff in *Wyatt* alleged only a violation of state law, there could have been no subjective bad faith belief in the existence of probable cause—defendant's knowledge of a federal law (due process) deficiency could not be inferred from allegation or even proof that he had violated state law. Having so held, the Fifth Circuit never reached the question whether the defendants had acted with subjective malice. The court indicated that in future suits plaintiffs seeking to travel the subjective probable cause path would be required to plead and prove that the creditor defendant knew the state statute to be unconstitutional.

Another circuit court,[46] while in basic agreement with the Fifth Circuit's approval on remand in *Wyatt* of alternative ways of showing lack of probable cause, concentrated on defining the other subjective element: malice in instituting suit. Concerned that a significant extension of § 1983 liability to private defendants would obliterate the state action requirement of the Fourteenth Amendment, the court of appeals instructed the district court on remand to consider that question in relation to the degree of latitude afforded creditors under state decisional law.[47]

Wyatt has been read for the proposition that private litigants, even if acting sufficiently in concert with government actors to be acting "under color of" state law, are generally not eligible for qualified immunity in actions under § 1983.[48] The Supreme Court has since cited *Wyatt* as leaving open the possibility that individual private defendants not entitled to the full *Harlow*esque version of the qualified immunity accorded government employee defendants might be eligible for a lesser form of immunity based on the pre-*Harlow* elements of "good faith and/or probable cause." In addition, or alternatively, the Court observed that plaintiffs in such cases might be required "to carry additional burdens."[49]

45. The specter of subjective bad faith raises it head twice in the probable cause inquiry: it is the sole question in regard to the general question of whether defendant exhibited malice in instituting civil proceedings, and it constitutes half of the probable cause inquiry. Whereas the former question looks to generalized bad intent, the latter is a more focused inquiry, searching for evidence that the defendant actually knew a specific fact, i.e., that the statute invoked by him was unconstitutional.

46. *Jordan v. Fox, Rothschild, O'Brien & Frankel*, 20 F.3d 1250 (3d Cir.1994), *on remand*, 1995 WL 141465 (E.D.Pa.1995). A remand on this issue was necessary because the court in Jordan would not rule out the possibility that the plaintiff could prove lack of probable cause. The Second Circuit similarly accords private defendants facing claims akin to malicious prosecution the affirmative defense of good faith, placing on the plaintiff the burden of proving lack of probable cause and malice. *Pinsky v. Duncan*, 79 F.3d 306 (2d Cir.1996).

47. The court in *Jordan* decided that a remand to the district court was in order because they could not do what the appeals court did on remand in *Wyatt*: find subjective bad faith belief in probable cause entirely lacking.

48. *Cooper v. Parrish*, 203 F.3d 937, 952 (6th Cir.), *cert. denied*, 523 U.S. 1094, 118 S.Ct. 1560, 140 L.Ed.2d 792 (1998), citing *Wyatt*, 504 U.S. at 168–69.

49. *Richardson v. McKnight*, 521 U.S. 399, 117 S.Ct. 2100, 138 L.Ed.2d 540 (1997).

Several circuits have addressed the other issue left unresolved by *Wyatt*—whether qualified immunity might be available to private defendants in non-creditor cases. Most broadly, the Ninth Circuit has asserted that after *Wyatt* "the law is settled that private parties are not entitled to qualified immunity in actions brought pursuant to 42 U.S.C.A. § 1983."[50] In *Burrell v. Board of Trustees of Georgia Military College*,[51] the Eleventh Circuit Court of Appeals expressed grave reservations about "the current vitality of [some] court [sic] of appeals decisions allowing [privately acting] private defendants to assert qualified immunity in non-attachment cases."[52] The Eleventh Circuit described the decisions granting qualified immunity to private non-creditor defendants as limited to situations where the private defendants had functioned as public actors—either pursuant to a government imposed contractual duty[53] or in the public interest.[54] In contrast, qualified immunity had been (and, the court thought, should continue to be) denied to all private defendants, creditors or not, when they were acting purely in furtherance of their private interests.[55] But the Eleventh Circuit also intimated

50. *Penman v. Korper*, 977 F.2d 590 (9th Cir.1992).

51. 970 F.2d 785 (11th Cir.1992), *cert. denied*, 507 U.S. 1018, 113 S.Ct. 1814, 123 L.Ed.2d 445 (1993).

52. *Id.* at 795. The court felt no compunction to address the effect *Wyatt* had on cases granting qualified immunity in the non-attachment context, however, since those cases were all distinguishable from the case before the court. *Id.*

53. *See, e.g., Cullinan v. Abramson*, 128 F.3d 301 (6th Cir.1997), *cert. denied*, 523 U.S. 1094, 118 S.Ct. 1560, 140 L.Ed.2d 792 (1998) (granting qualified immunity to city's outside counsel in RICO case brought by investment managers of the city's police pension fund).

54. Although the facts of the cases granting qualified immunity to private defendants were not entirely commensurate, they shared the common thread that the private defendant in each was under some government-imposed obligation to act or acted in furtherance of the public interest.

The court in *Burrell* analyzed three immunity-granting cases. In *DeVargas v. Mason & Hanger–Silas Mason Co.*, 844 F.2d 714 (10th Cir.1988), the Tenth Circuit granted qualified immunity to private persons who are sued on the basis of actions taken pursuant to a government contract to perform a governmental function. *Frazier v. Bailey*, 957 F.2d 920 (1st Cir.1992), specified that the duties to be performed under the government contract by the private party must be such that the private actor is deemed the functional equivalent of a government employee. In the non-contract context, *Rodriques v. Furtado*, 950 F.2d 805 (1st Cir.1991), found a physician under court order to be entitled to qualified immunity because she was cloaked with "the responsibilities of a public official [acting] in the public interest." Thus to fall within the rationale of these decisions, the private defendant must demonstrate that she was acting pursuant to a government contract or that her primary motivation was the public welfare.

55. The actions taken by the private defendants in the immunity-denying cases cited in *Burrell* may best be described as personally, as opposed to publicly, motivated. The defendants who acted in concert with government actors in these cases to evict a plaintiff, *Howerton v. Gabica*, 708 F.2d 380 (9th Cir.1983), indict a plaintiff for perjury, *Felix de Santana v. Velez*, 956 F.2d 16 (1st Cir.1992), *cert. denied*, 506 U.S. 817, 113 S.Ct. 59, 121 L.Ed.2d 28 (1992), or, as plaintiff's sibling or guardian, sterilize a plaintiff against her will, *Downs v. Sawtelle*, 574 F.2d 1 (1st Cir.1978), *cert. denied*, 439 U.S. 910, 99 S.Ct. 278, 58 L.Ed.2d 255 (1978), were considered to have acted on the basis of personal motives.

But then what motivations would fit the "governmental purpose" category? Courts are willing to grant qualified immunity where a private defendant's actions are motivated by a concern for the public welfare. See *Wyatt*, 504 U.S. at 167, 112 S.Ct. at 1833 ("principally concerned with enhancing the public good"), and *Rodriques*, 950 F.2d at 815 (acting "in the public interest"). Many actions that arguably fit the description of "personally motivated" may also be characterized as an attempt to en-

that qualified immunity might be available to private defendants in a mixed motive case—where the private defendant's acts in concert with public officials are not "solely" for the purpose of depriving plaintiff of rights protected by § 1983.[56]

Applying the distinction drawn in *Burrell*, the Seventh Circuit in *Sherman v. Four County Counseling Center*[57] found that the defendant, a private hospital, had acted pursuant to a court order and in accordance with procedures mandated by state law. Moreover, plaintiff had failed to allege that defendant had acted with improper motive or to further its own pecuniary interest, and defendant's exercise of discretion had been in discharge of government imposed duties. These facts placed the case, the Seventh Circuit thought, within the category identified by *Burrell* as warranting qualified immunity.[58] The court in *Sherman* therefore proceeded to apply *Harlow's* defendant-friendly tests in determining whether a grant of qualified immunity was appropriate.

Together, *Burrell* and *Sherman* seem to stand for the proposition that a non-creditor private defendant may be eligible for modern qualified immunity a la *Harlow* if its conduct is to some degree dictated by public norms or designed to serve a public end.[59] The future of qualified immunity for private defendants will apparently turn on how courts delineate the requisite governmental functional equivalence and public purpose. The ever increasing government inclination to privatize, and the public's desire to achieve efficiency in government, suggest that courts expressing policy-based concerns similar to the rationale of *Harlow* will be increasingly receptive to assertions of "private qualified immunity" by government contractors.[60] Indeed, without a grant of

hance the public good. For example, the defendant—spendthrift guardian in *Downs* might have argued that his attempt to exercise dominion over the plaintiff was motivated by a duty to the public at large. The success of such an argument will, however, depend on the latitude allowed defendants in asserting that their actions in fact served the public welfare. *See generally Sherman v. Four County Counseling Ctr.*, 987 F.2d 397, 406 (7th Cir.1993) (referring to the detrimental impact on the public welfare by denying qualified immunity to private hospitals that accept state mental patients for treatment).

56. The Eleventh Circuit stated that "private defendants cannot claim the protection of qualified immunity" where they are "alleged to have acted in concert with public officials for the sole purpose of depriving another of her constitutional rights." 970 F.2d at 796.

57. 987 F.2d 397 (7th Cir.1993).

58. The court rejected plaintiff's argument that the corporate form of this private defendant likened that defendant to a public entity and thus served to deny qualified immunity. That argument has been tentatively accepted elsewhere. *See, e.g., Moore v. Wyoming Medical Ctr.*, 825 F.Supp. 1531, 1542 (D.Wyo.1993).

59. *See, e.g., Warner v. Grand County*, 57 F.3d 962 (10th Cir.1995) (director of a private crisis center who conducted a strip search at a police station at the request of the arresting officer held entitled to qualified immunity because acting as public officer's agent). *Cf. Ace Beverage Co. v. Lockheed Info. Management Servs.*, 144 F.3d 1218 (9th Cir.1998) (private contractor not eligible for qualified immunity because city had limited direct supervision of contractor).

60. *See Williams v. O'Leary*, 55 F.3d 320 (7th Cir.1995) (granting qualified immunity to contract physician serving state prison). *But see Jensen v. Lane County*, 222 F.3d 570, 576–580 (9th Cir.2000) and *Halvorsen v. Baird*, 146 F.3d 680, 685–86 (9th Cir.1998) (denying, after the Supreme Court's decision in *Richardson v. McKnight*, 521 U.S. 399, 117 S.Ct. 2100, 138 L.Ed.2d 540 (1997), qualified immunity

qualified immunity, or contractual indemnity in lieu, the private sector may be less disposed to accept governmental contracts.

A 5–member majority of the Supreme Court has since decided, in *Richardson v. McKnight*,[61] that the employees of private firms who serve as prison guards do not enjoy the expansive contemporary version of qualified immunity accorded similarly situated public correctional officers, at least if the firm is systematically organized for private competition and functions with relatively little ongoing direct state supervision. The Court reasoned that "marketplace pressures provide the private firm with strong incentives to avoid overly timid, insufficiently vigorous, unduly fearful, or 'non-arduous' employee job performance" and that "insurance increases the likelihood of [private] employee indemnification and to that extent reduces the employment-discouraging fear of unwarranted liability potential applications face." Accordingly, a principal policy justification for the contemporary *Harlow v. Fitzgerald* brand of qualified immunity afforded individual government employees is considerably weaker in the private, competitive arena. Further, the Court found "no conclusive evidence of an historical tradition of immunity" for the 19th century contractors who performed the equivalent function of private prison management.[62]

Many other private defendants, even though not under contract with the government, nevertheless act in concert with public officials. Whether these private defendants will receive qualified immunity hinges upon, in *Wyatt's* terms, whether "the public interest will be . . . unduly impaired if immunity is denied."[63] *Sherman* puts some flesh on the bare bones of the requisite "public interest." The court there found that the defendant private hospital was fulfilling a public duty when it treated the plaintiff. Extending qualified immunity in this situation would encourage public service, the Court concluded, and thereby benefit not only individuals, but the community as a whole. Mental patients would be able to remain closer to home and family, rather than being taken away to some distant state-operated facility. If private hospitals refused to accept state mental patients, greater loads would be imposed on an already over-burdened state system. Thus the "public interest in maximizing the number of facilities available for the detention and treatment

to, respectively, contract physician evaluating arrestees as possible mental patients for involuntary commitment and to employees of center performing involuntary detoxification services under contract with state, reasoning that unwarranted timidity in performing public services, a justification for immunity, would be overcome by the threat of market competition and the private defendants' ability to insure or obtain indemnity against liability).

61. 521 U.S. 399, 117 S.Ct. 2100, 138 L.Ed.2d 540 (1997).

62. *Richardson v. McKnight*, 521 U.S. 399, 117 S.Ct. 2100, 138 L.Ed.2d 540 (1997). *See also Malinowski v. DeLuca*, 177 F.3d 623 (7th Cir.1999) (private building inspectors hired by municipality cannot claim qualified immunity where they carried out their duties largely without governmental supervision or direction).

63. 504 U.S. at 167–68, 112 S.Ct. at 1833–34. One court has extended the narrower "good faith" brand of immunity to private actors who, although executing a judicial search and seizure order in a federal civil lawsuit, were acting to further private interests. *Vector Research, Inc. v. Howard & Howard*, 76 F.3d 692 (6th Cir.1996) (*Bivens* action).

of the mentally ill" was best served by a grant of qualified immunity to the private defendant.[64]

In the wake of *Richardson*, circuit courts that find enough cooperation between a private contractor defendant and local government to brand the defendant a "state actor" acting "under color of" state law have usually nevertheless not found those defendants subject to sufficient government supervision to be eligible for qualified immunity.[65] Alternatively, they have denied the private defendant immunity on the ground that the market forces identified in *Richardson* would offset unwarranted timidity in their performance of public services.[66]

§ 2.25 Compensatory and Punitive Damages

If the judge or jury finds liability—if the plaintiff establishes all elements of the prima facie case and surmounts the immunity defense—compensatory damages may be awarded in any appropriate proved amount[1] for actual economic loss (medical expenses or lost income, for example), pain and suffering, humiliation, embarrassment, emotional distress, and, at least in some circuits,[2] harm to reputation. Compensatory damages are not presumed, however, and the plaintiff must plead and prove them.[3] Thus damages based on the jury's assessment of the value

64. *Sherman*, 987 F.2d at 406.

65. *See, e.g., Cooper v. Parrish*, 203 F.3d 937, 952–53 (6th Cir.), *cert. denied*, 531 U.S. 877, 121 S.Ct. 185, 148 L.Ed.2d 128 (2000) (private attorney who assisted prosecutors on unofficial, unpaid basis was not acting at "behest" of government and therefore not eligible for qualified immunity); *Malinowski v. DeLuca*, 177 F.3d 623 (7th Cir.1999) (immunity denied due to lack of historical precedent for immunizing private building inspectors, and because they carried out their duties largely without government supervision); *Hinson v. Edmond*, 192 F.3d 1342 (11th Cir.1999), as amended, 205 F.3d 1264 (11th Cir.2000) (privately employed prison physicians had no "firmly rooted" historical tradition of immunity, and functioned on profit-making basis subject to market discipline with relatively little governmental supervision); *Ace Beverage Co. v. Lockheed Information Management*, 144 F.3d 1218 (9th Cir.1998) (information management corporation that processed parking tickets for government denied immunity because it assumed extended administrative task for a local government that set only general policy, leaving private defendant responsible for daily implementation and oversight). *But cf. Cullinan v. Abramson*, 128 F.3d 301, 310 (6th Cir. 1997), *cert. denied*, 523 U.S. 1094, 118 S.Ct. 1560, 140 L.Ed.2d 792 (1998) (law firm hired as outside counsel for city served at its "behest," as the term was used in *Richardson*, and therefore was eligible for qualified immunity).

66. *See Jensen v. Lane County*, 222 F.3d 570, 576–580 (9th Cir.2000) and *Halvorsen v. Baird*, 146 F.3d 680, 685–86 (9th Cir.1998) (denying qualified immunity to, respectively, contract physician evaluating arrestees as possible mental patients for involuntary commitment and to employees of center performing involuntary detoxification services under contract with state).

§ 2.25

1. See *Memphis Community Sch. Dist. v. Stachura*, 477 U.S. 299, 106 S.Ct. 2537, 91 L.Ed.2d 249 (1986).

2. *See, e.g., Fraternal Order of Police v. Tucker*, 868 F.2d 74 (3d Cir.1989); *Anderson v. Central Point Sch. Dist.*, 746 F.2d 505 (9th Cir.1984); *Marrero v. City of Hialeah*, 625 F.2d 499 (5th Cir.1980), *cert. denied sub nom. Rashkind v. Marrero*, 450 U.S. 913, 101 S.Ct. 1353, 67 L.Ed.2d 337 (1981).

3. *Memphis Community Sch. Dist. v. Stachura*, 477 U.S. 299, 106 S.Ct. 2537, 91 L.Ed.2d 249 (1986); *Carey v. Piphus*, 435 U.S. 247, 263, 98 S.Ct. 1042, 1052, 55 L.Ed.2d 252 (1978) (in particular cases, a plaintiff who has proved a violation of procedural due process may be able to establish "mental and emotional distress actually . . . caused by the denial of procedural due process itself"). A related but distinct question

or importance of the particular right violated are unauthorized by Section 1983, because they are not compensatory in that they do not redress harm to the plaintiff suffered as a result of the deprivation.[4] Moreover, where the defendant counters the plaintiff's prima facie showing of a constitutional violation by demonstrating that it would have reached the same decision for independent, lawful reasons, a recent Supreme Court decision, *Texas v. Lesage*,[5] strongly suggests that no retroactive relief is available.

In general, juries enjoy wide leeway in computing compensatory damages, including damages for emotional distress, and their awards will usually be upheld on appeal unless clearly erroneous or without any evidentiary support.[6] Punitive damages are more stringently reviewed, and in Reconstruction Act cases require evidence of malice or willful or reckless disregard of plaintiff's rights above and beyond the evidence of an intentional violation that may be required to establish liability under Sections 1981 and 1982, and, for certain constitutional violations, Section 1983.[7] Further, in a series of recent cases, the Supreme Court has subjected large punitive awards to Due Process standards of proportionality.

As the following section discusses, nominal damages are appropriate and may even be required for the violation of certain important "absolute" constitutional rights like procedural due process.[8] The plaintiff may often be unable to prove that economic loss was caused by the mere denial of notice or hearing; so the provision of nominal damages, with the consequent possibility of attorneys' fees, is designed to ensure a practical incentive to vindicate that right.[9] But damages that do not

concerns the type of evidence courts will deem adequate to support a finding that the defendant's violation caused plaintiff economic or emotional harm. *See Malloy v. Monahan*, 73 F.3d 1012 (10th Cir.1996) (plaintiff's own testimony provided an adequate foundation for recovering lost profits from home rehabilitation business). And only certain damages are deemed to flow from certain constitutional violations. *See Hector v. Watt,* 235 F.3d 154 (3d Cir.2000) (damages flowing from unreasonable searches or seizures include privacy-related physical injuries, property loss, or injury to reputation, but exclude compensation for injuries resulting from the unlawfully-aided discovery of incriminating evidence and any resulting prosecution).

4. *Memphis*, 477 U.S. at 310, 106 S.Ct. at 2544–45.

5. 528 U.S. 18, 120 S.Ct. 467, 145 L.Ed.2d 347 (1999), discussed in detail in § 2.26, *infra*.

6. *See, e.g., The Guides, Ltd. v. Yarmouth Group Property Management, Inc.*, 295 F.3d 1065, 1075–76 (8th Cir. 2002) (upholding all lost profits supported by testimony of plaintiff's expert, but ordering remittitur striking additional damages based entirely on speculation).

7. *Id.* at 1076–77.

8. *Carey v. Piphus*, 435 U.S. 247, 98 S.Ct. 1042, 55 L.Ed.2d 252 (1978). The prevailing plaintiff in a Reconstruction Civil Rights Act case may be entitled to an instruction permitting the jury to award nominal damages even if she cannot prove actual injury. *See Hicks v. Brown Group, Inc.*, 902 F.2d 630, 652–54 (8th Cir.1990). *See also Campos–Orrego v. Rivera*, 175 F.3d 89 (1st Cir.1999) (nominal damages are so fundamental to procedural due process claims that plaintiff allowed to seek them for the first time after verdict). The subject is discussed more fully in the following subsection, 2.26.

9. However, nominal damages are plain error when parties stipulate some actual damages. *See Westcott v. Crinklaw*, 133 F.3d 658 (8th Cir.1998) (holding jury's finding of excessive force coupled with evidence of plaintiff's injuries incompatible with nominal award). But nominal damages may

compensate for harm to the plaintiff must remain truly minimal: the Court has rejected the notion of substantial damages for the "inherent value" of the invaded constitutional right.[10] Nevertheless, there is a shadowy subcategory of cases in which substantial "presumed damages" are allowed. The damages in those cases are said to compensate for nonmonetary harms that the plaintiff actually proves he suffered but cannot readily quantify—harms resulting, for example, from denial of the right to vote. The Supreme Court asserts that in such cases the jury does not indulge the prohibited presumption that plaintiff was harmed by defendant's constitutional violation, but instead permissibly presumes the amount of that harm from its personal knowledge of the value of that loss.[11] The availability of presumed damages in certain voting cases, however, does not preclude the award of compensatory damages where they are supported by the evidence.[12] On the other hand, no jury instruction on presumed damages is required when the jury is authorized to or does render a compensatory damages award.[13]

Where appropriate, punitive damages may also be awarded against § 1983 individual defendants. (Government entity defendants are immune from punitive damages in all but extraordinary circumstances virtually impossible to prove. See § 2.34, *infra.*) Compensatory damages are not a prerequisite for punitives, which may be awarded when plaintiff recovers any relief on the merits—declaratory or injunctive relief, nominal damages, or actual or presumed compensatory damages.[14] But if ordinary compensatory damages (say for emotional distress, pain and suffering, out of pocket medical and psychiatric expenses) are awarded, there is authority that punitives must bear a "reasonable relationship" to them.[15] If, on the other hand, the only merits relief is nominal damages, there is no fixed limit on the punitives.[16] A plaintiff

be appropriate where the use of excessive force does not result in any credible injury to the plaintiff, or where both justified and unjustified force were used and the jury could reasonably conclude that any injuries resulted from the justified use of force. *See, e.g., Amato v. City of Saratoga Springs, N.Y.*, 170 F.3d 311, 314 (2d Cir.1999); *Briggs v. Marshall*, 93 F.3d 355, 360 (7th Cir.1996); *Haywood v. Koehler*, 78 F.3d 101, 104 (2d Cir.1996); *Gibeau v. Nellis*, 18 F.3d 107, 110 (2d Cir.1994).

10. *Memphis Community Sch. Dist. v. Stachura*, 477 U.S. 299, 106 S.Ct. 2537, 91 L.Ed.2d 249 (1986).

11. *Memphis*, 477 U.S. at 312, n.14, 106 S.Ct. at 2545, n.14 (discussing *Nixon v. Herndon*, 273 U.S. 536, 47 S.Ct. 446, 71 L.Ed. 759 (1927)).

12. *See Taylor v. Howe*, 280 F.3d 1210 (8th Cir.2002) (approving compensatory awards of $500 to $2000 to black voters).

13. *Memphis*, 477 U.S. at 312, 106 S.Ct. at 2545; *Trevino v. Gates*, 99 F.3d 911, 921–922 (9th Cir.1996), *cert. denied,* 520 U.S. 1117, 117 S.Ct. 1249, 137 L.Ed.2d 330 (1997).

14. *See generally Smith v. Wade*, 461 U.S. 30, 55 n. 21, 103 S.Ct. 1625, 1639 n. 21, 75 L.Ed.2d 632 (1983); *Campos–Orrego v. Rivera*, 175 F.3d 89 (1st Cir.1999) (punitive damages for a constitutional violation permissible even absent any award of compensatory damages). *Davis v. Mason County*, 927 F.2d 1473 (9th Cir.1991), *cert. denied*, 502 U.S. 899, 112 S.Ct. 275, 116 L.Ed.2d 227 (1991). See § 2.26.

15. *See Edwards v. Jewish Hosp.*, 855 F.2d 1345 (8th Cir.1988).

16. *Id.; Lee v. Edwards*, 101 F.3d 805 (2d Cir.1996) (dictum that $200,000 punitive award, if compliant with other Due Process requirements, not excessive in relation to nominal damages award of $1). Federal courts place the burden on the defendant of proving that its precarious financial condition renders a punitive award excessive. *Chavez v. Keat*, 34 Cal.App.4th 1406, 41 Cal.Rptr.2d 72 (1995) (citing federal

with particularly appealing prospects for an outsize punitive award may therefore ironically be somewhat better off if she recovers only nominal damages and not the other, more standard species of compensatory damages—provided of course that the expected punitives are large enough to offset those compensatories.

The central question in imposing punitive damages is determining what level of culpability warrants their imposition: should damages designed to punish an actor be awarded for negligent behavior, or should they be reserved for conduct exhibiting a more culpable state of mind, such as recklessness or purposefulness? The Supreme Court set the currently prevailing standard in *Smith v. Wade*.[17]

Wade was assigned to a reformatory for youthful offenders where the defendant worked as a guard. After other inmates acted violently toward him, he voluntarily checked into the institution's protective custody unit and was placed in a cell with one other inmate. Defendant Smith placed in the cell a third inmate who had been segregated for fighting. Another cell was available in the same area with only one occupant, but Smith made no effort to discover this fact. Further, another inmate had been beaten to death in the same area, while Smith was on duty, only a few weeks earlier. Wade alleged that his cellmates beat and sexually assaulted him and that Smith violated Wade's Eighth Amendment rights because Smith knew or should have known that such an incident was likely. The jury found Smith liable and awarded Wade $5,000 in punitive damages, under instructions allowing punitive damages if the defendant's conduct displayed a "reckless or callous disregard of, or indifference to, the rights or safety of others."[18] Smith appealed that award.

Before the Supreme Court, Smith argued that the test for a punitive damages award under § 1983 should be one of "actual malicious intent—ill will, spite, or intent to injure,"[19] particularly because, in the Eighth Amendment context, any lesser standard would permit punitive damages with no greater evidence of culpability than that necessary to establish liability. The Court discussed the historical variations among the standards states had applied in awarding punitive damages under the common law at the time § 1983 was adopted, concluding that the majority allowed punitive damages without a showing of intent. The most important difference among the states was "over the degree of negligence, recklessness, carelessness, or culpable indifference that should be required—not over whether actual intent was essential."[20]

The district judge had instructed the jury that Smith could be liable for violating the Eighth Amendment only if his conduct evidenced "a

cases). But the Supreme Court indicated in *BMW of N. Am. v. Gore*, 517 U.S. 559, 116 S.Ct. 1589, 134 L.Ed.2d 809 (1996) that Due Process would be offended by a punitive award that exceeded 10% of a defendant's net worth.

17. 461 U.S. 30, 51, 103 S.Ct. 1625, 1637, 75 L.Ed.2d 632 (1983).

18. *Id.* at 33, 103 S.Ct. at 1628.

19. *Id.* at 37, 103 S.Ct. at 1630 (internal quotation omitted).

20. *Id.* at 40, 103 S.Ct. at 1632.

callous indifference or a thoughtless disregard"[21] for Wade's rights. Smith argued that the standard for punitive damages should be even higher, because punitive awards are meant to redress "extraordinary misconduct."[22] Otherwise, Smith maintained, prison guards could not avoid punitive damage assessments because the standard for punitive damages was so close to the standard for the underlying constitutional violation. The Court rejected that contention, reasoning that "the need for exceptional clarity in the standard for punitive damages arises only if one assumes that there are substantial numbers of officers who will not be deterred by ..." the threat of personal liability for other damages.[23] The Court held that punitive damages may be awarded "when the defendant's conduct is shown to be motivated by evil motive or intent, or when it involves reckless or callous indifference to the federally protected rights of others, as well as intentional violations of federal law."[24]

Although § 1983 contains no state of mind requirement, many of the predicate constitutional violations do depend on a showing of intent. As a practical matter, therefore, plaintiffs must often prove an intentional violation of a federally protected right in order to establish § 1983 liability. Yet that intent may and often is proved inferentially, as where Reconstruction Act plaintiffs borrow the *McDonnell Douglas/Burdine/St.Mary's* formulation so common in actions under Title VII.[25] Against this background what did the Court in *Wade* really mean, by its "as well as" language? Did it mean, as its words would suggest, that in addition to the showing of intent often required for liability the defendant must have exhibited either evil motive or a callous disregard for federally protected rights, or did it mean simply that punitive damages are appropriate whenever there is evidence of an intentional violation of law? The latter interpretation, although textually problematic, seems to rest on the premise that a showing of the state of mind necessary for an intentional violation of federal rights may include a showing of callous disregard for those rights. A few circuit opinions on the issue have adopted that interpretation, construing the quoted language from *Wade* to mean that a showing of intent sufficient to establish liability also authorizes punitive damages.[26]

21. *Id.* at 33, 103 S.Ct. at 1628.

22. *Id.*

23. *Id.* at 50, 103 S.Ct. at 1637. The Court in *Smith* thus takes a step beyond its observation several years earlier in *Carey v. Piphus*, 435 U.S. 247, 256, 98 S.Ct. 1042, 1049, 55 L.Ed.2d 252 (1978) that Congress may not have intended any "deterrent more formidable than that inherent in the award of compensatory damages."

24. *Id.* at 56, 103 S.Ct. at 1637 (emphasis added).

25. *See St. Mary's Honor Center v. Hicks*, 509 U.S. 502, 506 n. 1, 113 S.Ct. 2742, 2747 n. 1, 125 L.Ed.2d 407 (1993) (noting the interchangeable use of the inferential mode of proving intent in actions under the Reconstruction Acts and Title VII).

26. *See Rowlett v. Anheuser–Busch, Inc.*, 832 F.2d 194, 205 (1st Cir.1987) (§ 1981 case discussing *Smith v. Wade*; "the state of mind necessary to trigger liability [in most § 1983 cases] is at least as culpable as that required to make punitive damages applicable"). *See also Barbour v. Merrill*, 48 F.3d 1270 (D.C.Cir.1995), *cert. dismissed*, 516 U.S. 1155, 116 S.Ct. 1037, 134 L.Ed.2d 113 (1996) (holding in § 1981 case that evidence of an intentional civil rights violation is sufficient to permit a jury to award punitive damages).

But the Seventh Circuit has interpreted *Wade* to mean that punitive damages are available only when, in addition to any showing of intent that may be necessary for underlying liability, the defendant demonstrates "a specific intent to violate a knowable right."[27] This language, in turn, requires that "the application of the law to the facts at hand" must be "so clear at the time of the act that reasonably competent people would have agreed on its application."[28] In effect, this may place on the plaintiff a "clearly established law" requirement for punitive damages against an individual defendant that corresponds to a key element of the qualified immunity defense. But most individual defendants assert that defense routinely; so under this formulation, when the plaintiff overcomes that defense and demonstrates liability, she will likely also be eligible for punitive damages. (Of course the significant expansion and relaxation of the requirements for establishing the qualified immunity defense since *Wade* will make fewer individual defendants subject to *any* damages.) Several other circuits, too, have plainly declined to permit a jury to award punitive damages based solely on the evidence that establishes an intentional violation; they have required a variety of additional showings respecting defendant's state of mind.[29]

This latter, somewhat stricter view is supported by the Supreme Court's decision in *Kolstad v. American Dental Association.*[30] There the Court held that the elements of "malice" or "reckless indifference" essential to punitive damages in Title VII actions under the language of

27. *Williamson v. Handy Button Machine Co.*, 817 F.2d 1290, 1296 (7th Cir. 1987) (Section 1981 case) (citing *Soderbeck v. Burnett County*, 752 F.2d 285, 289–91 (7th Cir.1985)).

28. *Id.*

29. *See, e.g., Iacobucci v. Boulter*, 193 F.3d 14 (1st Cir.1999) (applying Supreme Court decision in *Kolstad, infra*, to deny punitive damages in false arrest case absent evidence that the defendant knew he lacked probable cause or was consciously indifferent to its presence); *Coleman v. Rahija*, 114 F.3d 778 (8th Cir.1997) (egregiousness required); *Cornell v. Woods*, 69 F.3d 1383 (8th Cir.1995) (same); *Jackson v. Pool Mortgage Co.*, 868 F.2d 1178, 1182 (10th Cir.1989) (personal animosity and malice required); *Stephens v. South Atlantic Canners, Inc.*, 848 F.2d 484, 489 (4th Cir.1988); *Beauford v. Sisters of Mercy*, 816 F.2d 1104, 1109 (6th Cir.1987) (egregiousness, willfulness, or malice required); *Walters v. City of Atlanta*, 803 F.2d 1135, 1147 (11th Cir.1986) (all requiring, in addition to intentional violations of § 1981, ill will or callous disregard). *See also Wulf v. City of Wichita*, 883 F.2d 842, 867 (10th Cir.1989) (upholding § 1983 liability based upon a First Amendment violation, but noting that "not every intentional violation of a plaintiff's constitutional rights subjects a defendant to punitive damages" and vacating punitive damage award); *Hernandez–Tirado v. Artau*, 874 F.2d 866, 869 (1st Cir.1989) (upholding § 1983 liability based upon a First Amendment violation, but holding that "[i]f one accepts the proposition that not every case involving an intentional tort calls for punitive damages, that punitive damages are reserved for instances where the defendant's conduct is of the sort that calls for deterrence and punishment over and above that provided by compensatory awards, then punitive damages cannot be assessed in this case"); *Ivey v. Wilson*, 832 F.2d 950, 958 (6th Cir.1987) (upholding § 1983 liability based upon a due process violation, but vacating award of punitive damages); *Lavicky v. Burnett*, 758 F.2d 468, 477 (10th Cir.1985) (upholding both the district court's finding of liability under § 1983 for due process and Fourth Amendment violations, and its denial of punitive damages as a matter of law); *Soderbeck v. Burnett County*, 752 F.2d 285, 289–90 (7th Cir.1985) (upholding both the district court's finding of § 1983 liability based upon a First Amendment violation, and its denial of punitive damages as a matter of law).

30. 527 U.S. 526, 119 S.Ct. 2118, 144 L.Ed.2d 494 (1999).

the Civil Rights Act of 1991, while not requiring proof of "egregious" or "outrageous" defendant conduct, do require evidence concerning the defendant's state of mind that goes beyond showing mere intentional discrimination. The *Kolstad* view of punitive damages under Title VII is likely to be influential in resolving the uncertainty in the circuit decisions on punitive damages under the Reconstruction statutes. The "malice or ... reckless indifference" required by § 1981a(b)(1) of the 1991 Act is in substance indistinguishable from the "evil motive or intent" or "reckless of callous indifference" standards the Supreme Court announced in *Smith v. Wade*. Indeed the Report of the House Judiciary Committee on the 1991 Act explained that the Title VII punitive damages standard is "taken directly from civil rights law," and it quoted and cited with approval the page in the Smith opinion that announced the "evil motive or intent" or "reckless or callous indifference" formulations.[31] And the *Kolstad* majority relied heavily on *Smith* for its conclusion that eligibility for punitive damages depends on evidence reflecting the defendant's subjective consciousness of the risk of illegality: "Applying this standard in the context of § 1981a [that is, in Title VII actions], an employer must at least discriminate in the face of a perceived risk that its actions will violate federal law to be liable in punitive damages."

Nevertheless, the Court wrote in *Kolstad*, where the intentional violation is founded on egregious or outrageous conduct, the fact finder may infer the requisite "evil motive" from that evidence alone. Alternatively, a punitive award may rest on evidence showing the "employer's knowledge that it may be acting in violation of federal law." Justice Stevens, writing for four members of the Court who concurred on this point, observed that while the majority's standard does not require employer knowledge of the law, "he must know that his acts violate the law or must 'carelessly disregard whether or not one has the right so to act.' " He suggested that a jury might find a willful violation authorizing punitive damages from evidence that an employer expressed "hostility toward employment discrimination laws" or concealed its actual selection procedures "because it knows they violate federal law."

In any event, the *Kolstad* majority insists that an employer's mere awareness "that it is engaging in discrimination" will not, standing alone, support the award. It identified a number of circumstances in which a violation, while intentional in the sense that the defendant intends to harm the plaintiff, or to discriminate in a generic sense, or to subject the plaintiff to "disparate treatment" within the meaning of Title VII or ADA, should not expose the defendant to punitive damages. "[T]he employer may simply be unaware of the relevant federal prohibition. There will be cases, moreover, in which the employer discriminates with the distinct belief that its discrimination is lawful. The underlying theory of discrimination may be novel or otherwise poorly recognized, or an employer may reasonably believe that its discrimination satisfies a bona fide occupational qualification defense or other statutory exception

31. H.R.Rep.No. 102–40, pt. 2., p. 29 (1991). The Report of the House Education and Labor Committee echoes this approach. H.R.Rep.No. 102–40, p. 74 (1991).

to liability." Evidence that an employer knowingly relied on a ground prohibited by statute, in short, does not in itself translate into evidence that the employer knew it was acting in violation of federal law.

Over the past decade, the Supreme Court has several times revisited the issue of alleged violations of the Eighth Amendment in the prisoner context, the very setting that gave rise to the decision in *Wade*.[32] Those decisions may further alter the debate over the test for punitive damages in prisoner-plaintiff Reconstruction Act cases in a direction favorable to defendants. In *Farmer v. Brennan*,[33] the Court held that a prison official does not violate the Eighth Amendment, even where the risk of substantial harm to inmates was obvious and a reasonable person would have noticed it, if he was not actually aware of the risk. In light of this higher, "subjective recklessness" threshold for the predicate Eighth Amendment liability of prison caretakers, the Supreme Court may now more likely agree with the "plain text," stricter reading of *Wade*. Punitive damages may be available only if the plaintiff shows knowledge or state of mind more acute or focused than that prerequisite for primary liability, because punitive awards are meant to punish aggravated forms of wrongdoing. In *Farmer*, the Court qualified its holding by observing that so long as the defendant knew of the risk posed to prisoners in general by a given practice, he could be liable, even without knowing that the risk in question would befall the particular plaintiff.[34] Perhaps that knowledge may become the "plus" factor required before prison caretakers become subject to punitive damages. The permissible amount of punitive damages available against defendants in any kind of action is subject to amorphous due process limitations crafted by the Supreme Court in 1996.[35]

§ 2.26 "Mixed Motive" Cases: Are Damages Available if Defendant Carries the "Same–Decision" Showing?

In the famous *Mt. Healthy* decision,[1] the Supreme Court held that once the plaintiff shows that constitutionally protected speech was a "substantial" or "motivating" factor[2] in the adverse action he suffered, a government employer may avoid liability for those damages that flow

32. *See* § 2.32 *infra*.

33. 511 U.S. 825, 835, 114 S.Ct. 1970, 1978, 128 L.Ed.2d 811 (1994).

34. *Id.*

35. See *BMW of N. Am. v. Gore*, 517 U.S. 559, 116 S.Ct. 1589, 134 L.Ed.2d 809 (1996), which measures the excessiveness of punitive damage awards by the guideposts of (1) degree of reprehensiveness; (2) ratio of punitive to compensatory damages; and (3) relation between damages in the instant and comparable cases. Gore was applied in *Lee v. Edwards*, 101 F.3d 805 (2d Cir.1996) (reducing $200,000 punitive award to $75,000 in § 1983 police misconduct action, not because ratio to nominal damages excessive, but because amount was excessive in relation to awards in comparable cases).

§ 2.26

1. *Mt. Healthy City Sch. Dist. Bd. of Educ. v. Doyle*, 429 U.S. 274, 97 S.Ct. 568, 50 L.Ed.2d 471 (1977).

2. *Id.* The Court has since interpreted *Mt. Healthy* to mean that the defendant, to avoid or minimize liability, must undertake the required "same-decision" showing whenever the plaintiff has shown that an unconstitutional motive was a "but-for cause" of the adverse action. *Givhan v. Western Line Consol. Sch. Dist.*, 439 U.S. 410, 417, 99 S.Ct. 693, 697, 58 L.Ed.2d 619

from an unconstitutional suppression of speech if it can prove "by a preponderance of the evidence that it would have reached the same decision ... even in the absence of the [employee's] protected conduct." There is widespread agreement that where the defendant carries the *Mt. Healthy* showing in these "mixed-motive" cases, the § 1983 plaintiff may not receive compensatory damages for injuries caused by the tangible detriment, for example employment discharge, of which she complains. This is because the defendant has in substance defeated causation by showing that those injuries would have been inflicted for independent, lawful reasons.[3]

But that leaves two possibilities for the "*Mount Healthy*-ed plaintiff" to recover substantial damages. First, she might be eligible for any compensatory damages that she can prove followed from the unconstitutional conduct itself, apart from those related to the imposition of the tangible detriment. Second, she might be entitled to nominal damages. The Supreme Court has indicated that punitive damages (i.e., those otherwise warranted under *Smith v. Wade*) are available if the § 1983 plaintiff obtains any relief on the merits, including nominal damages or

(1979). See also *Regents of Univ. of California v. Bakke*, 438 U.S. 265, note 54, 98 S.Ct. 2733, 57 L.Ed.2d 750 and accompanying text (1978) (Supreme Court plurality refers to defendant's "burden of proving that, but for the existence of its unconstitutional special admissions program, [plaintiff] ... would not have been admitted.") Circuit authority is divided as to whether the reverse discrimination plaintiff who demonstrates the unlawfulness of a race-preferential policy under the Equal Protection Clause enjoys the usual *Mt. Healthy* burden shift that requires the defendant to prove that the plaintiff would not have prevailed even absent the unlawful preference. *Compare Pulliam v. Tallapoosa County Jail*, 185 F.3d 1182, 1188–89 (11th Cir.1999) (defendant has burden of persuasion, but failure to so instruct is harmless error where plaintiff failed to object or show substantial likelihood that jury would have found for him after a proper instruction); *Price v. City of Charlotte, N.C.*, 93 F.3d 1241 (4th Cir. 1996), *cert. denied*, 520 U.S. 1116, 117 S.Ct. 1246, 137 L.Ed.2d 328 (1997), and *Hopwood v. Texas*, 78 F.3d 932, 956 (5th Cir.1996) (holding yes), *cert. denied sub nom. Thurgood Marshall Legal Soc'y v. Hopwood*, 518 U.S. 1033, 116 S.Ct. 2580, 135 L.Ed.2d 1094 (1996) with *Henson v. University of Arkansas*, 519 F.2d 576, 577–78 (8th Cir.1975) (per curiam) (holding no). In jurisdictions that do impose the "same decision" burden of persuasion on the defendant, it is error prejudicial to plaintiff to instruct that an unconstitutional reason must be "the" rather than "a" mitigating factor underlying the defendant's actions. *Reynolds v. Green*, 184 F.3d 589 (6th Cir.1999), *appeal after remand*, 25 Fed.Appx. 256 (6th Cir. 2001).

3. *Carey v. Piphus*, 435 U.S. 247, 260, 98 S.Ct. 1042, 1050, 55 L.Ed.2d 252 (citing *Mt. Healthy*, 429 U.S. at 285–286, 97 S.Ct. at 575–576). *See* Nahmod, *Civil Rights and Civil Liberties Litigation: The Law of Section 1983* (3d ed. 1991) 281–283. It should be remembered that a causal link between defendant's violation of a cognizable constitutional right and the particular injury claimed by plaintiff is a required element of any § 1983 claim. *See Estate of Brooks v. United States*, 197 F.3d 1245, 1247–48 (9th Cir.1999) (causation a required element of § 1983 claim, and defendant county not a legal cause of plaintiff's extended detention because it lacked authority either to bring plaintiff before a judicial officer or to release him absent direction from the United States); *Morris v. Lindau*, 196 F.3d 102, 113–14 (2d Cir.1999) (in First Amendment retaliation case, plaintiff fails causation element for lack of evidence that defendants responsible for his discharge were aware of his protected speech). The issue can arise in the same way as in ordinary tort cases, too. Compare *Henderson v. Sheahan*, 196 F.3d 839 (7th Cir.1999), *cert. denied*, 530 U.S. 1244, 120 S.Ct. 2691, 147 L.Ed.2d 962 (2000) (claim that jail officials violated due process by exposing plaintiff to second-hand smoke fails for want of sufficient evidence that the exposure would subject plaintiff to an increased risk of serious future medical harm) *with Warren v. Keane*, 196 F.3d 330 (2d Cir.1999) (material fact issue precludes summary judgment on same claim).

an injunction or declaratory judgment; actual compensatory damages, in other words, are not a prerequisite.[4] And there is authority for the proposition that, while punitive damages must bear a proportional relationship to any compensatory damages awarded, they need not be proportional to nominal damages.[5]

These possibilities acquire larger significance because nominal damages, punitive damages or both constitute relief on the merits that would make these plaintiffs "prevailing parties" eligible for a substantial award of attorney's fees under the Civil Rights Attorney's Fees Awards Act of 1976.[6] It is settled that these awards need not be proportional to the component of the judgment representing recovery for economic or emotional damages. The prospect of such a fee recovery attracts counsel to represent potential plaintiffs who were victimized by unconstitutional conduct but whose consequent tangible loss can be independently, lawfully explained by the defendant. But in *Farrar v. Hobby*[7], a Supreme Court majority held that while recovery of nominal damages alone makes plaintiff a "prevailing party" eligible for fees under § 1988, the amount of the fee award that is "reasonable" where those damages represent an insignificant portion of the relief originally sought is ordinarily nothing. Faithfully applied, then, *Farrar* could make fee awards a rarity in cases where § 1983 plaintiffs recover only nominal damages. The lower courts have resisted strict enforcement of *Farrar*, however, relying on Justice O'Connor's concurring opinion to find several factors that in practice make substantial fee awards readily recoverable even when the plaintiff recovers only nominal damages.[8]

In *Carey v. Piphus*,[9] the Supreme Court held that the plaintiff who proves a violation of the special, "absolute" right to procedural due

4. *Smith v. Wade*, 461 U.S. 30, 55 n. 21, 103 S.Ct. 1625, 1639, n. 21, 75 L.Ed.2d 632 (1983). *See also Carey v. Piphus*, 435 U.S. 247, 256 n. 11, 98 S.Ct. 1042, 1049 n. 11, 55 L.Ed.2d 252 (1978) (noting without approval or disapproval decisions that awarded punitive damages for the sole purpose of deterring or punishing constitutional violations). There is authority that the prevailing plaintiff in a Reconstruction Civil Rights Act case is entitled to nominal damages whether or not she can prove actual injury, *Hicks v. Brown Group, Inc.*, 902 F.2d 630, 652–54 (8th Cir.1990), but only if the request for nominal damages is timely. For this purpose "timely" means making the request for nominal damages in a request to charge the jury, see *Kerr–Selgas v. American Airlines, Inc.*, 69 F.3d 1205 (1st Cir.1995) and *Cooper Distrib. Co. v. Amana Refrigeration, Inc.*, 63 F.3d 262 (3d Cir. 1995), or even as early as the pretrial order, *Walker v. Anderson Elec. Connectors*, 944 F.2d 841 (11th Cir.1991). *But see Campos–Orrego v. Rivera*, 175 F.3d 89 (1st Cir.1999) (nominal damages are so fundamental to procedural due process claims that plaintiff allowed to seek them for the first time after verdict).

5. *See Edwards v. Jewish Hosp. of St. Louis*, 855 F.2d 1345, 1352 (8th Cir.1988) (case under § 1981). *But cf. Campos–Orrego v. Rivera*, 175 F.3d 89 (1st Cir.1999) (punitive damage award for a constitutional violation permissible even absent any award of compensatory damages).

6. Amending 42 U.S.C.A. § 1988. *See Carey v. Piphus*, 435 U.S. 247, 256–57, 98 S.Ct. 1042, 1049, 55 L.Ed.2d 252 n. 11–12 (1978).

7. 506 U.S. 103, 113 S.Ct. 566, 121 L.Ed.2d 494 (1992). *Farrar* is discussed in more detail in Chapter 4, *infra*.

8. *See, e.g., Brandau v. Kansas*, 168 F.3d 1179 (10th Cir.1999), *cert. denied*, 526 U.S. 1133, 119 S.Ct. 1808, 143 L.Ed.2d 1012 (1999) and cases cited therein. Decisions relaxing *Farrar* are discussed in more detail in Chapter 4.

9. 435 U.S. 247, 98 S.Ct. 1042, 55 L.Ed.2d 252 (1978).

process is eligible to receive certain forms of damages even though the defendant, by prevailing on the *Mt. Healthy* showing, has broken the chain of causation between unconstitutional conduct and loss of job or consequent emotional distress.[10] Specifically, that plaintiff is entitled to nominal damages of no more than $1 and may recover any damages for emotional distress (mental suffering or emotional anguish) that he can prove were caused by the denial of notice or hearing, as distinct from those damages caused by the loss of job or other adverse action taken by the defendant.[11] But *Carey* doesn't answer whether the § 1983 plaintiff who proves that a violation of a right other than procedural due process was a "motivating factor" in the adverse action taken against her can obtain any damages where the defendant, per *Mt. Healthy*, proves that the plaintiff would have suffered the adverse action in any event. And the Supreme Court's more recent decision in *Texas v. Lesage*,[12] discussed in detail below, precludes any damages award where the defendant carries the same—decision showing—at least in equal protection and First Amendment retaliation cases and perhaps even in any § 1983 case, including those involving procedural due process challenges like the one in *Carey*.

Scholarly commentary has suggested[13] or argued[14] in the affirmative, reasoning that while the adverse consequence of employment loss cannot be attributed to unconstitutional conduct when the employer makes the *Mt. Healthy* showing, plaintiffs should forfeit only those elements of damage attributable to that loss.[15] Accordingly, the contention is that while backpay and other compensatory damages attributable to the defendant's challenged action (e.g., discharge) must be denied, compensatory damages resulting from the defendant's reliance on another, unconstitutional motive are available, as are nominal and therefore punitive damages.[16] Where malice is present and plaintiff's counsel

10. *Id.* at 266, 98 S.Ct. at 1054.

11. Such compensatory damages, however, require proof and may not be presumed to follow upon every denial of procedural due process. *See Carey, supra.*

12. 528 U.S. 18, 120 S.Ct. 467, 145 L.Ed.2d 347 (1999).

13. Sullivan, Richards, Zimmer & Calloway, *Cases and Materials on Employment Discrimination* 1097 (Little Brown 3d ed. 1994) (citing *Edwards v. Jewish Hosp.*, 855 F.2d 1345 (8th Cir.1988)). Edwards supports awarding damages to the mixed-motive plaintiff in an action under § 1981, but not § 1983. In fact the *Edwards* opinion specifically distinguishes the statutes, acknowledging that a prior Eighth Circuit panel had concluded in *Hervey v. City of Little Rock*, 787 F.2d 1223 (8th Cir.1986), that the mixed-motive plaintiff *cannot* receive damages in actions under § 1983. The authors nevertheless write that the "more sensible" approach outlined in Edwards "may emerge" in cases under § 1983 as well as § 1981. *Texas v. Lesage*, discussed herein, seems to doom that approach, for *Lesage* appears to deny all retroactive relief in any § 1983 action in which the defendant carries the "same-decision" burden of persuasion.

14. *See* Nahmod, *Civil Rights and Civil Liberties Litigation: The Law of Section 1983* (3d ed. 1994) 281–283 and 1993 Cumulative Supplement, at 95 (arguing that the "proper interpretation of *Mount Healthy*" calls for the defendant who carries the "same-decision" burden to remain liable, but only for the reduced remedies that can fairly be said to have been caused by the constitutional violation). *See also* Nahmod, *Mt. Healthy and Causation-in-Fact: The Court Still Doesn't Get It!*, 51 Mercer Law Rev. 603 (2000).

15. *See, e.g., Merritt v. Mackey*, 932 F.2d 1317 (9th Cir.1991).

16. Cf. *Edwards v. Jewish Hosp.*, 855 F.2d 1345 (8th Cir.1988) (while awarding nominal and punitive damages in § 1981

therefore anticipates the possibility of recovering punitive as well as nominal damages concerning the unlawful, "motivating" factor, this approach, should it prevail, would provide an incentive to prosecute a § 1983 action notwithstanding the anticipation that defendant can make a successful *Mt. Healthy* showing.[17]

This view derives some support from the language of the *Mount Healthy* opinion, which, however, also may be read to mean that the "same-decision" showing does not merely limit available remedies but defeats liability for a constitutional violation. The Court answered in the negative an issue it defined as follows: whether, despite the defendant's showing, plaintiff's demonstration that First and Fourteenth Amendment violations had figured substantially in the challenged employment decision "would necessarily amount to a constitutional violation *justifying remedial action*."[18] If the quoted phrase is truncated after "constitutional violation," it would seem that the Court intended to hold that no violation may be found if the defendant makes the required showing. On the other hand, the "necessarily" qualification leaves the door open for a plaintiff to argue that liability may lie despite a defendant's "same-decision" showing. Likewise "justifying remedial action" may be viewed as a critical modifier of "constitutional violation," suggesting that defendant's showing doesn't defeat the formal finding of a violation but, depending on the circumstances, limits or eliminates remedies. This view is somewhat fortified by the Court's statement in *Mount Healthy* that its specific concern was with the trial court's "conclusion that Doyle is entitled to reinstatement with backpay,"[19] and with its insistence on a "test of causation which distinguishes between a result caused by a constitutional violation and one not so caused."[20] The problem for the Court was that *even if* a violation had been shown, there had not yet been proof of a loss attributable to that violation. It remanded for application of the "same-decision" test, but provided no specific direction for further proceedings.

The Court's references to *Mount Healthy* a year later in *Carey* are consistent with that reading. It stressed that § 1983 damages are appropriate only when the defendant's conduct is "found ... to have been violative of ... constitutional rights and to have caused compensable injury."[21] Citing *Mount Healthy*, the Court agreed that the *Carey* defendant's "same-decision" showing meant that the *Carey* plaintiffs' suspen-

action, court denied compensatory damages after the defendant's "*Mount Healthy*" showing, but only because the evidence showed that emotional distress resulted from plaintiff's discharge, rather than from employer's reliance on his race). *See also* Nahmod, *supra*, 3d ed. at 283 (compensatory damages caused by defendant's reliance on unconstitutional motive recoverable despite defendant's *Mount Healthy* showing).

17. The prospect of punitives is important. A Supreme Court decision would usually award $0 in attorney's fees under § 1988 to plaintiffs who recover only nominal damages in actions under § 1983, at least when they had sought more substantial relief. *See* discussion of *Farrar v. Hobby* in Chapter 4 on Attorney's Fees, below.

18. *Mount Healthy*, 429 U.S. at 285, 97 S.Ct. at 575 (emphasis supplied).

19. *Id.* at 284, 97 S.Ct. at 574.

20. *Id.* at 286, 97 S.Ct. at 575.

21. 435 U.S. at 254, 98 S.Ct. at 1047 (quoting *Wood v. Strickland*, 420 U.S. 308, 319, 95 S.Ct. 992, 999, 43 L.Ed.2d 214 (1975)) (emphasis supplied in *Wood*).

sions could not be considered caused by defendant's failure to accord them procedural due process; and in turn damages for those suspensions would represent a "windfall" rather than the required "compensation."[22] But it added that the "interests protected by a particular constitutional right may not also be protected by" the ordinary principles of damages derived from the common law of torts;[23] and it recognized that some, but not necessarily all, victims of procedural due process might suffer emotional distress from the denial of process itself. That distress would be compensable, the Court held, even though the distress related to a "justified deprivation"—e.g. a loss of employment that the employer has proven would have come about for independent, lawful reasons—is not.

Can either or both of the *Carey* conclusions—procedural due process denials entitle plaintiffs to $1 in nominal damages and make them eligible for provable compensatory damages caused by the denial itself—be generalized to all constitutional violations that might be vindicated through § 1983? The nominal damages holding was restricted quite clearly to the Court's recognition that deprivations of that particular "absolute" right is of "importance to organized society" and must be "scrupulously observed."[24] The compensatory damages holding, however, was not expressly so limited, for it was premised on general § 1983 principles of damages. Nevertheless, most post-*Mount Healthy* authority outside the procedural due process arena suggests that carrying the "same-decision" burden defeats a finding of constitutional violation and accordingly relieves the defendant of all monetary remedies.

For example, circuit courts have specifically applied *Mount Healthy* to find that the defendant's "same-decision" showing defeats liability altogether.[25] Professor Nahmod, the chief exponent of the view that notwithstanding a defendant's *Mount Healthy* showing, a § 1983 plaintiff may recover compensatory damages directly caused by any unconstitutional behavior, cites a number of circuit decisions as applications of *Mount Healthy*.[26] In only one of the cited cases, however, does the court discuss the possibility of the plaintiff recovering damages of any kind after the defendant carried the *Mt. Healthy* "same-decision" burden. That was a case[27] where the particular violation was of procedural due process, and the court, relying specifically on *Carey*, held that plaintiff

22. 435 U.S. at 260, 98 S.Ct. at 1050.

23. *Id.* at 258, 98 S.Ct. at 1049.

24. 435 U.S. at 266, 98 S.Ct. at 1054. *Accord, Farrar v. Hobby*, 506 U.S. 103, 113 S.Ct. 566, 121 L.Ed.2d 494 (1992). See *Campos–Orrego v. Rivera*, 175 F.3d 89 (1st Cir.1999) (nominal damages for due process violation).

25. *See, e.g., Harris v. Shelby County Bd. of Educ.*, 99 F.3d 1078 (11th Cir.1996) (contrasting the complete affirmative defense of *Mt. Healthy* with the comparable "same-decision" defense of §§ 703(m) and 706(g)(2)(B), added to Title VII by the Civil Rights Act of 1991, which merely limit defendant's liability to prospective relief and attorney's fees); *Foy v. Holston*, 94 F.3d 1528, 1534–1536 (11th Cir.1996); *O'Day v. McDonnell Douglas Helicopter Co.*, 79 F.3d 756 (9th Cir.1996); and *Hervey v. City of Little Rock*, 787 F.2d 1223 (8th Cir.1986), reaffirmed with respect to § 1983, though distinguished with respect to § 1981, in *Edwards v. Jewish Hosp.*, 855 F.2d 1345.

26. *Nahmod, supra* note 14.

27. *Burt v. Abel*, 585 F.2d 613 (4th Cir.1978).

was entitled to nominal damages and might recover any damages for emotional distress that could be traced to the unlawful denial of process. The remaining decisions cited by Professor Nahmod concerned alleged substantive violations other than procedural due process. In many of these the defendant was not required to carry the "same-decision" showing because plaintiff had failed in the first instance to demonstrate an unlawful substantial factor[28] to the satisfaction of the reviewing court.[29] In others the defendant was held not to have succeeded with the "same-decision" showing.[30] Only the remaining category—cases where defendant carried the "same-decision" showing with respect to a violation other than procedural due process—pertains to Professor Nahmod's point. Neither decision in that category, however, approved or even alluded to the possibility that the plaintiff could recover damages of any kind—nominal, compensatory, or punitive.[31] In one the court wrote that because the defendant sustained the *Mt. Healthy* burden, "[the plaintiff] cannot have incurred any damages from deprivation of a job to which he was not entitled. His only relief would be declaratory."[32] In the other, the court went even further. Although it observed that the plaintiff sought monetary damages, it simply affirmed the directed verdict for defendant with no remand to consider remedy.[33]

28. Sometimes the court reached this conclusion because it found that the impermissible motivation was not a "but-for" causative factor, relying on *Givhan v. Western Line Consol. Sch. Dist.*, 439 U.S. 410, 99 S.Ct. 693, 58 L.Ed.2d 619 (1979). *Fisher v. Flynn*, 598 F.2d 663, 665 (1st Cir.1979). Other courts arrived at the same conclusion based on the view that prima facie proof of unlawfulness that followed the inferential method of demonstrating intent approved for Title VII cases by *McDonnell Douglas* and *Burdine* did not suffice to require the defendant to discharge the same-decision burden. *Tanner v. McCall*, 625 F.2d 1183, 1194 (5th Cir.1980), *cert. denied*, 451 U.S. 907, 101 S.Ct. 1975, 68 L.Ed.2d 295 (1981). Similarly, one circuit has written that while the "same-decision" escape from liability is an affirmative defense the defendant may not have to plead it affirmatively in the answer but need only raise it through evidence at trial or in a pretrial order. *Pulliam v. Tallapoosa County Jail*, 185 F.3d 1182, 1185 (11th Cir.1999).

29. *Best v. Boswell*, 696 F.2d 1282 (11th Cir.1983), *cert. denied*, 464 U.S. 828, 104 S.Ct. 103, 78 L.Ed.2d 107 (1983); *White v. South Park Indep. Sch. Dist.*, 693 F.2d 1163 (5th Cir.1982); *Tanner v. McCall*, 625 F.2d 1183 (5th Cir.1980), *cert. denied*, 451 U.S. 907, 101 S.Ct. 1975, 68 L.Ed.2d 295 (1981); *Correa v. Nampa Sch. Dist.*, 645 F.2d 814 (9th Cir.1981); *Nekolny v. Painter*, 653 F.2d 1164 (7th Cir.1981) (remanded for jury determination of motivating factor question), *cert. denied*, 455 U.S. 1021, 102 S.Ct. 1719, 72 L.Ed.2d 139 (1982); *Fisher v. Flynn*, 598 F.2d 663 (1st Cir.1979); *Skehan v. Bd. of Trustees of Bloomsburg State College*, 590 F.2d 470 (3d Cir.1978).

30. *Barnes v. Bosley*, 745 F.2d 501 (8th Cir.1984), *cert. denied*, 471 U.S. 1017, 105 S.Ct. 2022, 85 L.Ed.2d 303 (1985); *Berry v. Battey*, 666 F.2d 1183 (8th Cir.1981); *Zoll v. Eastern Allamakee Community Sch. Dist.*, 588 F.2d 246 (8th Cir.1978); *Allen v. Autauga County Bd. of Educ.*, 685 F.2d 1302 (11th Cir.1982); *Williams v. City of Valdosta*, 689 F.2d 964 (11th Cir.1982); *Trotman v. Board of Trustees of Lincoln Univ.*, 635 F.2d 216 (3d Cir.1980) (remanded for determination of "same decision" question), *cert. denied*, 451 U.S. 986, 101 S.Ct. 2320, 68 L.Ed.2d 844 (1981); *Goss v. San Jacinto Junior College*, 588 F.2d 96 (5th Cir.1979) modified by 595 F.2d 1119 (5th Cir.1979) (concerning attorney's fees).

31. *Neal v. Howell*, 689 F.2d 473 (4th Cir.1982); *Ledford v. Delancey*, 612 F.2d 883 (4th Cir.1980).

32. *Ledford*, 612 F.2d at 886.

33. *Neal v. Howell*, 689 F.2d 473 (4th Cir.1982). In the Fourth Edition of his treatise, Professor Nahmod updates his view of the post-*Mt. Healthy* circuit decisions, reading most of them as defeating liability and not just limiting remedies. 1 Nahmod, *Civil Rights and Civil Liberties Litigation: The Law of Section 1983*, § 4:10, at 4–34 n.13 (4th ed.1997).

Nor does the somewhat different handling of the problem in Title VII actions suggest that § 1983 defendants (other than those charged with procedural due process violations) who meet *Mount Healthy's* burden remain liable for nominal or compensatory damages. The 1991 Civil Rights Act provides that the Title VII plaintiff who has shown discrimination to be a "motivating" factor in an employment decision has established a law violation—and as such is eligible for declaratory or injunctive relief and, consequently, attorney's fees—even if the defendant carries a "same-decision" burden comparable to the one *Mount Healthy* authorizes in actions under § 1983.[34] Professor Nahmod asserts that this amendment "brings Title VII in line with" his position, that *Mount Healthy* "goes to [i.e., limits only] remedy and [does] not [defeat] liability, and that consequently a § 1983 defendant who carries ... [the 'same-decision' showing] has *not* prevailed on the merits."[35] This assertion is curious in two respects.

First, Professor Nahmod's position concerning the § 1983 defendant who carries the *Mount Healthy* burden is that she may remain liable for compensatory damages for emotional distress attributable to the employer's resort to unconstitutional conduct (i.e., reliance on an impermissible motive) even though, as he acknowledges, the plaintiff cannot recover for such damages attributable to an employment discharge the defendant has independently justified.[36] By contrast, the counterpart Title VII defendant after the 1991 amendment is relieved of all retrospective liability—compensatory and punitive damages, back pay, and probably nominal damages as well. She is subject only to prospective relief and attorney's fees.[37] So even the 1991 Amendments do not bring that statute "in line" with Professor Nahmod's view about § 1983 under *Mount Healthy*. Second, every justice participating in *Price Waterhouse* explicitly referred to *Mount Healthy* as the model for then unamended Title VII; agreed that discharge of defendant's "same-decision" burden in a Title VII action prevented a finding of statutory violation;[38] and therefore apparently understood *Mount Healthy* to relieve the § 1983 defendant who discharges the "same-decision" showing of all liability. It therefore took a Congressional decision to treat Title VII differently from § 1983: to subject the Title VII "mixed-motive" defendant to prospective relief and attorney's fees.

A reference by the Court to *Mt. Healthy* fortifies the conclusion that the employer who carries the same-decision burden is probably relieved of all liability, not merely of damages. The Court described *Mt. Healthy* as holding "that if the lawful reason alone would have sufficed to justify

34. *See* § 703(m) of Title VII, added by the 1991 Civil Rights Act.

35. *Nahmod, supra* note 14, 1993 Cumulative Supplement at 95.

36. *Nahmod, supra* note 14, 3d ed. at 283.

37. *See* § 706(g)(2)(B), the companion provision to § 703(m), added by the 1991 Civil Rights Act.

38. *Price Waterhouse v. Hopkins*, 490 U.S. 228, 258, 109 S.Ct. 1775, 1794, 104 L.Ed.2d 268 (1989) [last paragraph of decision](defendant avoids a "finding of liability" when it carries the same-decision burden).

the firing, the employee could not prevail in a suit against an employer." The rule, wrote the Court, was prompted by a desire to relieve the employer of the burden of disentangling an independently sufficient lawful motive from an unlawful one where both played a part in the challenged action.[39] In context, the Court distinguished *Mt. Healthy* from situations where it is assumed or proven that the employer's sole motive in imposing an employment detriment is unlawful, but the employer subsequently happens upon evidence that it claims would have then led it to take the same action lawfully. The Court held that in the latter situation, an employer is liable for the economic damage caused by its initial, unlawful conduct only until it discovers the separate, "after-acquired" evidence. Although the question was not directly presented, the Court's clear implication in placing *Mt. Healthy* in the "mixed-motives" rather than the "after-acquired evidence" category was that the employee whose demonstration of discrimination is trumped by the "same-decision" showing has not proven any cognizable violation.

In sum, although a careful reading of *Mt. Healthy*, as amplified by *Carey*, leaves room for damage awards against defendants who demonstrate independent, lawful reasons for conduct challenged under § 1983, the lower federal courts, now joined by the Supreme Court in *Price Waterhouse*, have generally read the decision differently. Apart from § 1983 plaintiffs praying for relief from denials of procedural due process, most other plaintiffs may expect that all monetary relief will be denied if the defendant can show it would have taken the same action for reasons that do not violate federal law.

But in recent years the impact of a defendant's "same-decision" showing has been limited in equal protection cases, in part because the Supreme Court has reconceptualized what constitutes an equal protection violation. In *Northeastern Florida Chapter of Associated General Contractors v. City of Jacksonville*,[40] the Court declared that an equal protection violation is complete if the plaintiff proves a race-based denial of the right to compete.[41] Accordingly, the Court held, a defendant's

39. *McKennon v. Nashville Banner Publishing Co.*, 513 U.S. 352, 115 S.Ct. 879, 130 L.Ed.2d 852 (1995). This discussion in McKennon has thus been read to assert in dictum that the *Mt. Healthy* approach where it applies, defeats liability "outright". *O'Day v. McDonnell Douglas Helicopter Co.*, 79 F.3d 756 (9th Cir.1996).

40. 508 U.S. 656, 113 S.Ct. 2297, 124 L.Ed.2d 586 (1993). The Court has adhered to this understanding of equal protection standing in subsequent voting rights cases. *See, e.g., United States v. Hays*, 515 U.S. 737, 115 S.Ct. 2431, 132 L.Ed.2d 635 (1995). For a discussion illustrating that the defendant's usual *Mt. Healthy* showing no longer defeats equal protection standing, see § 5.55, *infra*.

41. The seeds of this approach are visible in *Regents of Univ. of California v. Bakke*, 438 U.S. 265, 98 S.Ct. 2733, 57 L.Ed.2d 750 (1978). There a plurality of the Supreme Court observed that a race-preferential admissions program not narrowly tailored to meet a goal of educational "diversity" violated the white plaintiff's "individual" right to equal protection. It explicitly distinguished *Mt. Healthy* because the defendant in *Bakke* had "conceded that it could not carry its burden of proving that, but for the existence of its unlawful special admissions program, [plaintiff] ... would not have been admitted." *Id.* at note 54 and accompanying text. It also agreed with the trial court that the unconstitutional injury was suffered at the moment the plaintiff was prohibited, because of a racial classification, from competing for each place in the medical school class. Accordingly, the plurality wrote in dictum that, even

showing that it would have reached the same challenged decision in awarding a government benefit even absent any unlawful consideration of race will not defeat the plaintiff's standing, but is relevant only to the question of appropriate remedy. A growing number of lower federal courts have therefore concluded that the plaintiff who proves that the defendant's express consideration of race prevented him from being further considered for a contract, as in *Jacksonville*, or a state university admission, or a government job or promotion, has established the constitutional violation.[42] That equal protection plaintiff is therefore eligible, at a minimum, for declaratory and injunctive relief prohibiting the future use of race and, if otherwise appropriate, for attorney's fees. (Some courts would apparently go further and allow damages for emotional distress.)

The circuits have wrestled with two subsidiary questions raised by this relaxed application of the *Mt. Healthy* principle to equal protection claims. First, does the equal protection defendant carry the burden of persuasion on the same-decision showing once the plaintiff establishes liability by proving that he was denied a race-free right to compete, as the defendant would in the *Mt. Healthy* First Amendment setting?[43] Or must the plaintiff, to be eligible for affirmative relief—e.g., the contract,

if *Bakke* would not have been admitted in the absence of the unconstitutional affirmative action program, he would have had standing to redress a constitutional injury, with the question of his "admission *vel non* ... merely one of relief." *Id.* at note 14.

42. *See, e.g., Thigpen v. Bibb County, Georgia*, 223 F.3d 1231 (11th Cir.2000) (promotion denial in county employment); *W.H. Scott Construction Co., Inc. v. City of Jackson, Miss.*, 199 F.3d 206, 212–213 (5th Cir.1999) (contracting); *Price v. City of Charlotte, N.C.*, 93 F.3d 1241 (4th Cir. 1996), *cert. denied*, 520 U.S. 1116, 117 S.Ct. 1246, 137 L.Ed.2d 328 (1997) (promotion denial in city employment; plaintiff denied promotion but accorded standing, prevailed on liability, and held eligible for all monetary remedies despite city's showing that even absent its reliance on race it would not have promoted plaintiff); *Hopwood v. Texas*, 78 F.3d 932 (5th Cir.1996), *cert. denied* sub nom. *Thurgood Marshall Legal Soc'y v. Hopwood*, 518 U.S. 1033, 116 S.Ct. 2580, 135 L.Ed.2d 1094 (1996) (white law school applicant eligible for remedies upon proof that she was denied equal right to compete because of her race, even if university ignored its burden of persuasion that she would have been denied admission in any event); *cf. Salter v. Douglas MacArthur State Technical College*, 929 F.Supp. 1470, 1477–78 (employer liable for reverse discrimination under Title VII, because white plaintiff was denied an equal right to compete, although he would not have been hired in any event). In these courts, the defendant found to have violated equal protection is liable, and subject to declaratory and injunctive relief and attorney's fees, and possibly also emotional distress and punitive damages (but not to a hiring or promotion order or economic compensation like back or front pay), even when he carries the "same decision" showing that ordinarily negates any liability altogether.

43. The same-decision issue has become a standard feature of First Amendment employment retaliation cases. See, e.g., *Walker v. Schwalbe*, 112 F.3d 1127, 1131 (11th Cir.1997), *cert. denied*, 523 U.S. 1117, 118 S.Ct. 1794, 140 L.Ed.2d 935 (1998) (First Amendment government employee whistleblower case). The Supreme Court's opinion in *Mt. Healthy* treated the issue as an affirmative defense, not, as Walker implies, as an element of plaintiff's claim. The lower courts, however, have not always shared the same conception of what the Supreme Court meant in *Mt. Healthy* when it referred to the First Amendment plaintiff's burden of showing that the retaliatory factor was "motivating" or "substantial." Most courts read this language as imposing a de facto "but for" requirement on the plaintiff. *See* Wells, *Three Arguments Against Mt. Healthy: Tort Theory, Constitutional Torts, and Freedom of Speech*, 51 Mercer L.Rev. 583, 584–87 (2000). But every now and then a court decides otherwise. *See Suppan v. Dadonna*, 203 F.3d 228, 236 (3d Cir.2000).

the university admission, the job or promotion, and compensatory and punitive damages—persuade that absent the defendant's reliance on race, the plaintiff would have been selected? Second, if the defendant carries, or the plaintiff fails to refute, the same-decision showing, to what extent if any is the plaintiff nevertheless eligible for emotional distress and punitive damages to vindicate the dignitary interests injured as the result of the equal protection violation?[44]

Moreover, plaintiffs with Fourth Amendment claims, which are also subject to de facto "same decision" rules of the sort approved in *Mt. Healthy*, may nevertheless be able to establish liability and achieve limited relief. The "independent source" and "inevitable discovery" doctrines render harmless the admission of evidence obtained through an unlawful search or seizure. When a criminal conviction is sustained in reliance on those rules, the prosecutor has effectively demonstrated that the same decision would have been reached notwithstanding a constitutional violation. The Supreme Court held in *Heck v. Humphrey*[45] that a convicted person's claim under Section 1983 is barred—unless and until that conviction has been reversed on appeal or impugned by a writ of habeas corpus—if, assuming the claim were successful, it would inevitably undermine the conviction's validity. Citing the ever-present possibility that a conviction in which unconstitutionally obtained evidence was admitted may be upheld pursuant to the independent source or inevitable discovery rules, one circuit holds that § 1983 Fourth Amendment claims are not barred by *Heck* because, even assuming the plaintiff prevails, they do not inevitably taint his prior conviction.[46] But the same reasoning means that the § 1983 plaintiff may recover only those damages he proves to have been immediately caused by the unlawful search or seizure, and not damages caused by its consequences. In other words, until a conviction is overturned on the ground that evidence produced by an illegal search or seizure was inadmissible, the plaintiff cannot prove that the Fourth Amendment violation caused the additional damages attendant upon imprisonment. Thus in this setting the possibility that the prosecution might make a "same decision" showing in a criminal appeal actually keeps alive § 1983 claims that *Heck* would otherwise bar, but also serves to limit the plaintiff's available relief. Of

44. On the burdens and remedies issues, respectively, *see* § 2.26, *supra*. Post–*City of Jacksonville* decisions nevertheless refer to the "same decision" showing of *Mt. Healthy* as a complete affirmative defense even to an equal protection claim. See, e.g., *Harris v. Shelby County Bd. of Educ.*, 99 F.3d 1078 (11th Cir.1996). *See also Whitaker v. Wallace*, 170 F.3d 541, 544–45 (6th Cir.1999) and *Heil v. Santoro*, 147 F.3d 103, 110 (2d Cir.1998). But those decisions do not consider the effect of *City of Jacksonville* on the Supreme Court's current conception of an equal protection violation. Yet the Supreme Court's decision in *Texas v. Lesage*, discussed in detail below, reinforces the view of these courts that a same-decision showing defeats liability altogether in equal protection cases under § 1983.

45. 512 U.S. 477, 114 S.Ct. 2364, 129 L.Ed.2d 383 (1994). See the fuller discussion of *Heck* in Chapter 5.

46. See *Gonzalez v. Entress*, 133 F.3d 551, 553–54 (7th Cir.1998). *But see Schilling v. White*, 58 F.3d 1081 (6th Cir.1995) (holding that a § 1983 action alleging an unconstitutional search or seizure is premature and must be dismissed without prejudice, if brought while the plaintiff still faces criminal punishment).

course a same-decision showing made during a Fourth Amendment case may also play its more traditional role of defeating liability altogether.[47]

If the claim is of the kind, e.g., equal protection, on which plaintiff may prevail despite a defendant's successful "same decision" showing, attorney's fees will be potentially recoverable. But what if, as will be true in many such cases, the plaintiff recovers only a small percentage of what she originally sought? Then the Supreme Court's decision in *Farrar v. Hobby*,[48] discussed in detail in Chapter 4, may make fees unavailable in practice. There the Court held that a plaintiff seeking substantial damages who recovers only nominal damages is a "prevailing party" eligible for fees under § 1988, but that ordinarily the only reasonable fee award for that recovery is $0. Where *Farrar* is applied, therefore, a *Mt. Healthy*-ed plaintiff who does not recover compensatory damages will also fail to obtain the most significant remaining element of monetary relief: fees. Yet the circuits have mounted a rear-guard resistance to the literal enforcement of *Farrar* that affords prevailing plaintiffs attorney's fees more readily than the *Farrar* majority opinion suggests.[49]

The conclusion that the *Mt. Healthy* "same-decision" showing, even when it is a complete defense, is a defense only to particular constitutional claims, and perhaps only to First Amendment claims, seemed to have been strengthened by the reference to its operation in *Crawford–El v. Britton*,[50] also a case involving alleged retaliation for the exercise of protected speech. There the Court wrote that "with certain types of claims, proof of an improper motive is not sufficient to establish a constitutional violation—there must also be evidence of causation. Accordingly, when a public employee shows that protected speech was a 'motivating factor' in an adverse employment decision, the employer still prevails by showing that it would have reached the same decision in the absence of the protected conduct."[51] In context, the reference to "certain types of claims" seemed particularly significant by way of contrast to the uniform approach the majority there demanded respecting the prima facie elements of constitutional torts. The Court in *Crawford–El* rejected the argument of individual government official defendants that the policies underlying the affirmative defense of qualified immunity warrant imposing on the plaintiff heightened pleading or proof burdens in the subset of constitutional claims requiring proof about defendant's state of mind.[52]

But despite the promise of *Carey*, and despite the Court's recognition that an equal protection violation is complete upon proof of a race-

47. *See Smith v. Edwards*, 175 F.3d 99 (2d Cir.1999).

48. 506 U.S. 103, 113 S.Ct. 566, 121 L.Ed.2d 494 (1992).

49. *See, e.g., Brandau v. Kansas*, 168 F.3d 1179 (10th Cir.1999), *cert. denied*, 526 U.S. 1133, 119 S.Ct. 1808, 143 L.Ed.2d 1012 (1999), discussed in Chapter 4, *infra*.

50. 523 U.S. 574, 118 S.Ct. 1584, 140 L.Ed.2d 759 (1998).

51. *Crawford–El v. Britton*, 523 U.S. 574, 593, 118 S.Ct. 1584, 1594, 140 L.Ed.2d 759 (1998) (emphasis added) (citing *Mt. Healthy*).

52. *Crawford–El* is discussed more fully in § 2.22 *supra*.

based denial of the right to compete, the *Mt. Healthy* "complete defense" view, developed in First Amendment retaliation cases, has now triumphed. In a unanimous, per curiam decision in *Texas v. Lesage*,[53] reached without briefing or oral argument, the Supreme Court held in a reverse discrimination equal protection case brought by a white plaintiff who was denied consideration for admission to a state university's graduate program that despite defendants' impermissible reliance on race, they had "defeat[ed] liability" by proving that plaintiff would have also been denied admission under a race-neutral policy. In so ruling the Court rejected any distinction between the First Amendment claim in *Mt. Healthy* and the Equal Protection claim at hand, and generalized the result to all § 1983 claims: "Simply put, where a plaintiff challenges a discrete governmental decision as being based on an impermissible criterion and it is undisputed that the government would have made the same decision regardless, there is no cognizable injury warranting relief under § 1983."[54]

Taken at face, this sweeping language not only confirms the no-damages approach of *Mt. Healthy* in First Amendment cases, and extends that approach to all equal protection claims (including the far more numerous standard discrimination claims brought by African–American plaintiffs), but also applies it to any claim brought under § 1983. Arguably *Lesage* even overrules *Carey*, albeit sub silentio, so that "nominal" damages (and therefore attorney's fees) may no longer remain available for a deprivation of even the "absolute" right of procedural due process. Nevertheless, the cryptic opinion leaves doubts about its depth and reach.

For one thing, even in the Equal Protection setting presented by *Lesage* itself, there remains the possibility of some relief even when the "same-decision" showing is made. The Court observes that the "*Mt. Healthied*" Equal Protection plaintiff may receive prospective, injunctive relief against "an ongoing race-conscious program."[55] As support for this proposition the Court cited its affirmative action decisions holding that an Equal Protection violation is complete as soon as government denies a race-free opportunity to compete; thus a white plaintiff whose race knocked him out of consideration has standing and may receive injunctive relief even if the government defendant can prove that it would have denied him a contract, educational admission or job for another, lawful reason or reasons. But this means of course that in such a case the plaintiff, in order to be granted an injunction, must have shown some "cognizable injury warranting relief under § 1983"; and the government defendant, which must change its program to obey that injunction, has not in fact altogether defeated "liability."

53. 528 U.S. 18, 120 S.Ct. 467, 145 L.Ed.2d 347 (1999) (per curiam).

54. A recent appellate opinion applies this principle, without citing *Lesage*, by denying all relief to those white plaintiffs denied consideration for promotion because of their race whom the government defendant proved it would not have promoted anyway for independent, lawful reasons. *Alexander v. Fulton County, Ga.*, 207 F.3d 1303 (11th Cir.2000).

55. *Id.* at 468.

The *Lesage* opinion fails to explain why the continuing effects of a race-conscious program constitute in effect a cognizable injury but provable emotional distress attributable to the stigma of being denied consideration for a government benefit because of one's race is not. Presumably the sting of the stigmatism is at least as great when government officials make a discrete decision to deny an African–American applicant a job, a contract, or a place in a public university because of his race. Yet the government would not be foolish enough to maintain an "ongoing race-conscious program" preferential to whites. As a result, 45 years after *Brown v. Board of Education*,[56] we are left with the irony, at least if *Lesage* is taken literally and applied to standard Equal Protection race discrimination cases brought by African–Americans,[57] that in the rather common "same-decision" situation the Supreme Court now affords any relief only to plaintiffs who are white (or male).

It is also possible that *Lesage* does not implicitly overrule the *Carey* allowance of nominal damages (and therefore the possibility of attorney's fees) to the plaintiff who is "*Mt. Healthied*" after having proven a violation of procedural due process. After all, the Court in *Carey* observed that there may be varying prerequisites for recovering damages for different kinds of constitutional violations, and it labeled the procedural due process right as "absolute" and not dependent on the "merits" of the plaintiff's substantive allegations. It has similarly been held that there is also a right to nominal damages upon proof of an infringement of a First Amendment right of free speech.[58] Yet it seems "perverse" to permit the procedural due process or First Amendment plaintiff to recover nominal damages and yet deny those damages, as well as actual emotional distress damages, to African–American plaintiffs denied consideration because of their race.[59]

Another possibility is that the harsh rule emerging from the per curiam opinion in *Lesage* is the result of the failure of Mr. Lesage sufficiently to alert the Court that he sought nominal damages, or damages for emotional distress occasioned by the race-conscious admis-

56. 347 U.S. 483, 74 S.Ct. 686, 98 L.Ed. 873 (1954).

57. If read to apply equally to "discrete" employment, contract, or educational admission claims of African–Americans, *Lesage* will simply confirm the view of earlier circuit opinions that a "same-decision" showing by the government defendant defeats a § 1983 Equal Protection claim as completely as *Mt. Healthy* holds that such a showing defeats First Amendment claims. *See, e.g., Harris v. Shelby County Bd. of Educ.*, 99 F.3d 1078 (11th Cir.1996). Professor Christina Whitman suggests that formal, race-conscious programs benefitting members of historically excluded minority races may outrage white plaintiffs about the procedures the government employs, but they do not result in stigmatic personal injury flowing from any adverse societal judgment about the inherent worth or capacities of whites or males. Whitman, *An Essay on Texas v. Lesage*, 51 Mercer L.Rev. 621, 635 (2000). She acknowledges, however, that the Court's opinions take the discrimination against whites seriously and offer no basis for a precedent—grounded way of distinguishing the *Lesage* ban on all retroactive relief in a standard race-discrimination case brought by an African–American plaintiff.

58. *Risdal v. Halford*, 209 F.3d 1071 (8th Cir.2000).

59. *See Whitman*, 51 Mercer L.Rev. at 634.

sions program. That is, the Court may have understood his general prayer for monetary relief to refer only to the kind of damages that *Mt. Healthy* has unequivocally, and less controversially,[60] rejected, namely economic loss resulting from denial of the unconstitutionally motivated job loss, contract loss, or educational rejection.[61]

In any event, *Lesage* itself illustrates that the *Jacksonville* principle applies outside government contracting programs to educational affirmative action plans as well.[62] Indeed it appears to apply to government affirmative action programs awarding any kind of benefit, including terms and conditions of employment.[63] Still, there remains some doubt how to characterize *Lesage*. For example, even though the Supreme Court's opinion made no explicit reference to standing, *Lesage* has been construed as dealing with that issue alone, and not about the merits. In particular, *Lesage* has been described as specifying how the reverse discrimination plaintiff challenging a government affirmative action program may satisfy the "injury in fact" component of standing under Article III.[64]

But what satisfies the standing requirement—when, in other words, is a plaintiff "unable to compete on an equal footing," as the Supreme Court put it in *Jacksonville, Adarand, and Lesage*? Is it enough that the plaintiff-candidate participated in a process at one stage or component of which some white candidate (herself or another) was ruled out of consideration because of race? Or, at the other extreme, must the plaintiff show that, but for the consideration of race, she would have attained the government benefit (contract, educational admission, or job) for which she applied? One circuit adopts a third, intermediate position. To gain standing, the plaintiff must show that her own application was in fact treated differently at some stage of the process because of her race. That is, the plaintiff's personal subjection to actual, race-based dissimilar treatment suffices for standing even if she cannot show that, but for the consideration of race, her candidacy would have succeeded.[65] The opinion then suggests that on the merits, even if the defendant proffers the *Mt. Healthy* same-decision defense, the plaintiff might be

60. *See* Nahmod, 51 Mercer L.Rev. at 605 ("plaintiff should be entitled to whatever compensatory damages that he can prove are attributable to the First Amendment violation itself, excluding any damages attributable to the job loss").

61. Whitman, 51 Mercer L.Rev. at 634.

62. *Wooden v. Board of Regents of Univ. System of Georgia*, 247 F.3d 1262 (11th Cir.2001).

63. *Thigpen v. Bibb County, Georgia*, 223 F.3d 1231 (11th Cir.2000) (promotion denial in county employment) (author Lewis served as co-counsel for Plaintiffs in *Thigpen*).

64. *Wooden, supra.*

65. *Id. But see Aiken v. Hackett*, 281 F.3d 516 (6th Cir.2002) (white police officers lacked standing where they could not show they would have received promotions absent racial preference program and where they did not allege that program continued to disadvantage them in competing for promotions). *But cf. Yeager v. General Motors Corp.*, 265 F.3d 389 (6th Cir.2001) (white applicants to apprenticeship program challenging racial preference lacked standing, despite allegation of ongoing injury; court deemed injury speculative because not imminent, in that employer might terminate apprenticeship program or future white applicants, the court itself speculated, might achieve higher scores so that plaintiffs would fail to obtain apprenticeship without regard to the racial preference).

entitled to declaratory or injunctive relief directing the defendant to reconsider plaintiff's application in an entirely race-neutral process, despite the possibility that the outcome would be precisely the same as under the original, race-conscious process.[66]

§§ 2.27–2.29 [Reserved]

E. THE CASE AGAINST ENTITY DEFENDANTS

§ 2.30 In General

The case against an entity defendant fundamentally differs from the case against an individual. The prima facie case against an entity requires, in addition to the elements of the case against an individual, a showing that an entity "policy" caused the injury. It seems clear from the Supreme Court's opinions that "policy" is not a defense that the entity defendant must carry; rather, it is incumbent on the plaintiff to plead this additional element of the prima facie case[1] and to prove it by a preponderance of the evidence.[2] This showing is made by demonstrating either established policy or deliberate indifference to a protected right. The entity has no affirmative defense of immunity. And even after the burdensome "policy" hurdle has been cleared, the plaintiff is entitled only to compensatory damages.

§ 2.31 The Origins and Evolution of the "Policy" Requirement

Monroe approved a wide variety of claims against individual defendants for federal law violations their entity principals had not authorized. At the same time, however, it declared that local government entities lie wholly outside the ambit of § 1983. Although from a plain-meaning perspective everything such an entity does is surely "under color of" state law,[1] the Court concluded that it simply was not a "person" civilly liable for that conduct.

This conclusion was premised upon the significance the Court attached to the rejection of an amendment to the original statute, proposed by Senator Sherman, that would have made government entities liable to citizens injured by specific acts of violence committed by private citi-

66. *Wooden, supra* note 64.

§ 2.30

1. *See Leatherman v. Tarrant County Narcotics Intelligence and Coordination Unit*, 507 U.S. 163, 113 S.Ct. 1160, 122 L.Ed.2d 517 (1993).

2. *See generally Monell v. Department of Soc. Servs.*, 436 U.S. 658, 98 S.Ct. 2018, 56 L.Ed.2d 611 (1978); *Owen v. City of Independence*, 445 U.S. 622, 100 S.Ct. 1398, 63 L.Ed.2d 673 (1980). *See also Jeffes v. Barnes*, 208 F.3d 49,57–58 (2d Cir.2000), *cert. denied*, 531 U.S. 813, 121 S.Ct. 47, 148 L.Ed.2d 16 (2000). *But see Kelly v. City of Oakland*, 198 F.3d 779 (9th Cir.1999) (city defendant waived the *Monell* "defense" by failing to raise it until a reply brief in connection with its motion for new trial).

§ 2.31

1. *See Monell v. Department of Soc. Servs.*, 436 U.S. 658, 707, 98 S.Ct. 2018, 2044, 56 L.Ed.2d 611 (1978) (Powell, J., concurring) ("No conduct of government comes more clearly within the 'under color of' state law language of § 1983.").

zens.[2] The federal compulsion to monitor citizen conduct that would have been imposed on state entities under the amendment seemed to offend the prevailing theory of dual sovereignty, which forbade the national government from imposing duties or obligations on officers of the state or state instrumentalities.[3]

Seventeen years later, the Court gave a very different reading to that same history. Justice Brennan's opinion in *Monell v. Department of Social Services*[4] agreed that the 1871 Congress, in rejecting the Sherman Amendment, doubted its " 'constitutional power to impose ... [civil liability] upon county and town organizations.' "[5]But the real vice of the Amendment, according to the revisionist view, was that the duty imposed on state policies was new; it was the federal imposition on the states of a fresh obligation that aroused the ire of the Amendment's victorious opponents. Section 1983, the *Monell* Court observed, imposed no such new obligation on any state or local government. Instead, it merely subjected local government to civil liability for violating federal constitutional obligations already a part of the organic law of the land.[6] This explains why several opponents of the Amendment nevertheless voted to enact § 1983 into law.[7]

Having cleared away the constitutional objection *Monroe* had raised, the *Monell* majority turned to the statutory question: whether the 1871 Congress intended to include local government entities within the definition of "person" suable under § 1983. The Court answered affirmatively, relying principally on the Dictionary Act of 1871, passed only two months before the law that became § 1983. The Dictionary Act provided that " 'in all acts hereafter passed ... the word "person" may extend ... to bodies politic and corporate.' "[8] The majority concluded in sum-

2. *See Monroe v. Pape*, 365 U.S. 167, 188–92, 81 S.Ct. 473, 485–86, 5 L.Ed.2d 492 (1961), *overruled in part by Monell v. Department of Social Services*, 436 U.S. 658, 98 S.Ct. 2018, 56 L.Ed.2d 611 (1978).

3. *See id.* at 190, 81 S.Ct. at 485; *see also Monell*, 436 U.S. at 669–83, 98 S.Ct. at 2025–32 (surveying the drafting Congress's debate over potential dual sovereignty limitations on their authority).

4. 436 U.S. 658, 98 S.Ct. 2018, 56 L.Ed.2d 611 (1978).

5. *Id.* at 664, 98 S.Ct. at 2022 (quoting *Monroe*, 365 U.S. at 190, 81 S.Ct. at 485).

6. *See id.* at 669–83, 98 S.Ct. at 2025–32. The *Monell* majority relied on history that illustrated how such preexisting constitutional duties were enforced civilly against municipalities during the reign of dual sovereignty. In effect, then, it drew a distinction between the legislative imposition of new obligations and the judicial declaration of rights discovered in extant text, with only the former offending dual sovereignty. The Court's attempt to reconcile opposition to the Sherman Amendment based on dual sovereignty with its application of § 1983 to local government entities encounters an additional difficulty after passage of § 1983. The statute's framers might well regard expansive constitutional constructions first announced after the statute's enactment, as well as the federal statutory obligations that now may be enforced against local government through § 1983 actions, *see infra* Part F, as fresh obligations offensive to dual sovereignty. Mitigating this difficulty is the fairly rapid waning of dual sovereignty after enactment of § 1983, and the use of § 1983 to impose liability for violations of federal statutory rights is a fairly recent development. *See Maine v. Thiboutot*, 448 U.S. 1, 6–8, 100 S.Ct. 2502, 2505–2506, 65 L.Ed.2d 555 (1980) (defining the "and laws" language of § 1983 to apply to the deprivation of statutory benefits).

7. *See* Kramer & Sykes, 1987 Sup.Ct. Rev. at 260.

8. *Monell*, 436 U.S. at 688, 98 S.Ct. at 2034 (quoting Act of Feb. 25, 1871, ch. 71, § 2, 16 Stat. 431 (1871)).

mary fashion that corporations, including municipal corporations, were customarily treated identically with natural persons for purposes of constitutional and statutory construction.[9]

The *Monell* retrospective on the 1871 Congress's doubt about its constitutional power to subject local governments to civil liability is not controversial on its merits. Even Justice Rehnquist in dissent acknowledged the probable correctness of the majority's conclusion on that point.[10] What is remarkable is that the Court would return to that issue only seventeen years after *Monroe's* excursion through the same history, and in the same year the Senate was considering overturning the *Monroe* exclusion of municipal governments from the reach of § 1983.[11] The majority itself recognized the awkwardness of the rapid overruling.[12]

Still, it is not surprising that the Court would strain so hard to sweep government entities within § 1983. The extant qualified immunity doctrine, while not yet overwhelmingly tilted in favor of the defendant, was tied to the concept of reasonableness and therefore made recovery against individual officers uncertain. Further, even if the plaintiff prevailed the officer was likely to be judgment-proof, and the practice of indemnification, although widespread, was equally uncertain and uneven. Some governments would not indemnify at all, and others only for conduct comporting with varying definitions of scope of authority.[13]

9. *See id.* at 688–89.

10. *See id.* at 723 (Rehnquist, J., dissenting) (stating that "it may well be that on the basis of this closer analysis ... a conclusion contrary to ... Monroe ... could have been reached ... 17 years ago"); see also *id.* at 722 (granting that the Court was "probably correct" in its analysis of the Sherman Amendment debates).

11. *See id.* at 719.

12. The majority labored to explain why stare decisis should not preclude it from overruling this portion of *Monroe*. The *Monell* overruling of the *Monroe* entity immunity holding in such a short time span is a striking early instance of the demise of statutory stare decisis, so decisively reaffirmed as late as 1938 in Justice Brandeis's celebrated opinion in *Erie R.R. v. Tompkins*, 304 U.S. 64, 79–80, 58 S.Ct. 817, 823, 82 L.Ed. 1188 (1938). That demise is catalogued, almost defiantly, in the per curiam opinion of the Court that sua sponte called for rebriefing and reargument in *Patterson v. McLean Credit Union*, 485 U.S. 617, 618, 108 S.Ct. 1419, 1420, 99 L.Ed.2d 879 (1988) (citing cases).

13. The availability of indemnification then, as today, is not entirely clear. The Yale Project, sampling Connecticut district court filings from 1970–77, found that no costs were borne by police officers sued under federal statutes. *See* Project, *Suing the Police in Federal Court*, 88 Yale L. J. 781, 810–11 (1979) (noting that Connecticut required indemnification under Conn. Gen. Stat. § 7–465 (1977)). By the same token, one commentator writes that other municipalities were experiencing difficulty purchasing comprehensive liability insurance for employees and elected officials. *See* Martin J. Jaron, Jr., *The Threat of Personal Liability Under the Federal Civil Rights Act: Does It Interfere with the Performance of State and Local Government?*, 13 Urb. Law. 1 (1981), *reprinted in Section 1983: Sword and Shield* 309, 327–29 (Robert H. Freilich & Richard G. Carlisle eds., 1983); *see also* Schuck, 37 Am. J. Comp. L. at 85 (discussing self-insurance and the purchase of insurance by states, localities, and public officials). Most observers seem to agree that some form of indemnification was and is available, although the scope varies from jurisdiction to jurisdiction. *See, e.g., id.* at 86 (explaining that "[m]ost states provide some form of indemnification or other protection against adverse judgments or settlements, but some apparently provide it only in narrowly circumscribed situations" (citation omitted)); Low & Jeffries, *Federal Courts and the Law of Federal–State Relations* at 924 (pointing out that although most government employers choose to protect their employees against damage liability, the availability of such protection often depends on statutes, ordinances, and prac-

Indemnification thus did not assure the satisfaction of judgments in many cases embraced by *Monroe's* broad "under color of" umbrella.

The Court was also influenced by the fundamental structural consideration that § 1983, itself constitutionally dependent upon state action, was specifically aimed at state-sponsored conduct. If local government officials and low-level employees could be reached precisely because they carried the badge of government authority, is it reasonable to suppose that the 1871 Congress intended to absolve the very governments who handed out the badges?[14]

But *Monell* announced an equally important restriction on the scope of the new liability of entities. Having stretched jurisprudential convention to arrive at a result on the "person" definition that was consonant with constitutional history and pre-*Monroe* precedent, the Court in *Monell* strained every bit as hard to narrow the terms of local government liability.[15] The Court held that local government entities can be liable under § 1983 only if the conduct causing the constitutional violation is carried out "pursuant to official municipal policy of some nature."[16]

How Justice Brennan for the majority derived the "policy" limitation is a source of wonder. He began the journey with the statute's text, noting that the defendant, to be liable, must " 'subject[ ], or cause [a plaintiff] to be subjected' "to the deprivation of federally secured rights.[17] That sparse language, he concluded, "cannot be easily read to impose

tices in each jurisdiction). Professor Jeffries now believes that "the state or local government officer who is acting within the scope of his or her employment in something other than extreme bad faith can count on government defense and indemnification." Jeffries, *In Praise of the Eleventh Amendment and Section 1983*, 84 Va.L.Rev. 47 (1998). *See also Wilson v. Town of Mendon*, 294 F.3d 1 (1st Cir.2002) (asserting, also without empirical support, that "a verdict against the municipal employee will almost always result in satisfaction of the judgment by the municipality because of the indemnification provisions typically found in bargaining agreements between municipalities and their employee unions.")

14. Indeed, Justice Powell noted the "oddness" of imposing liability on the agent but not the principal for whom the agent worked. *See Monell*, 436 U.S. at 705, 98 S.Ct. at 2043 (Powell, J., concurring). There is admittedly a similar oddness in the proposal here to impose liability on the entity principal in circumstances where the agent would be absolved. *see infra* § 2.62.

15. *Monell*, 436 U.S. at 714, 98 S.Ct. at 2047 (Stevens, J., concurring in part). The narrowing construction is contained in a separate discussion that one justice termed "merely advisory" and "not necessary to explain the Court's decision." The city's pregnancy leave requirement was adopted "as a matter of official policy," and the majority admitted that "this case unquestionably involve[d] official policy as a moving force of the constitutional violation." 436 U.S. at 694, 98 S.Ct. at 2037. *Monell*, therefore, furnished no occasion to consider the circumstances under which local governments should be liable for *unauthorized* federal law violations.

16. *Id.* at 691, 98 S.Ct. at 2036. Subsequently, lower courts have held the requirements of *Monell* and its progeny fully applicable to private corporations subject to § 1983 claims because their challenged actions occurred "under color of" state law. The issue has arisen primarily in the case of companies employing special police officers or security guards. Thus such a company is not liable for the acts of its agents on the theory of respondeat superior, but only when it has an official policy or custom that causes the deprivation of federal rights. *Austin v. Paramount Parks, Inc.*, 195 F.3d 715, 727–28 (4th Cir.1999); *Sanders v. Sears, Roebuck & Co.*, 984 F.2d 972, 975–76 (8th Cir.1993); *Rojas v. Alexander's Dep't Store, Inc.*, 924 F.2d 406 (2d Cir.1990).

17. *Id.* at 691–92, 98 S.Ct. at 2036–37 (quoting § 1983).

liability vicariously on governing bodies." Because Congress provided "that A's tort became B's liability if B 'caused' A to subject another to a tort suggests that Congress did not intend Section 1983 liability to attach where such causation was absent."[18] And only some deliberate act labeled "official policy" or an unconstitutional act committed by a final policymaker for the entity, or, alternatively, a widespread and settled local government "custom"[19] would show causation by a government entity.

18. *Id.* at 692, 98 S.Ct. at 2037 (emphasis added).

19. The *Monell* opinion provides that the entity may be liable for constitutional violations inflicted through settled practice or "custom" even when governmental officials have not approved that practice formally, i.e. through "policy" or through an unconstitutional act committed or approved by a final policymaking official. The Court is explicit about this in *Board of County Commrs. of Bryan County, Oklahoma v. Brown*, 520 U.S. 397, 404, 117 S.Ct. 1382, 1388, 137 L.Ed.2d 626 (1997). Generally, one incident, or even a small number of scattered incidents, will not suffice to show a custom. *See Gable v. City of Chicago*, 296 F.3d 531 (7th Cir.2002) (3 incidents during four-year period fails); *Pardue v. Ashe*,36 Fed. appx. (6th Cir. 2002) (one incident fails); *Novack v. County of Wood*, 226 F.3d 525 (7th Cir.2000) (same). While the case of "custom" is difficult, it can be made. *See Griffin v. City of Opa–Locka*, 261 F.3d 1295, 1308–1312 (11th Cir.2001) (upholding jury finding of "custom" of sexual harassment); *McCormick v. City of Chicago,* 230 F.3d 319 (7th Cir.2000) (finding claim that city had custom of permitting white police officers to discriminate with impunity against African–American citizens adequately alleged); *Jeffes v. Barnes*, 208 F.3d 49, 61 (2d Cir.), *cert. denied*, 531 U.S. 813, 121 S.Ct. 47, 148 L.Ed.2d 16 (2000) (final policymaker's acquiescence in a longstanding unconstitutional practice or custom of subordinates can entail entity liability if the relevant practice becomes the local government's "standard operating procedure" or "is so widespread as to have the force of law.") (citing, respectively, *Jett v. Dallas Ind. Sch. Dist.*, 491 U.S. 701, 737, 109 S.Ct. 2702, 2723, 105 L.Ed.2d 598 (1989) and *Bryan County*, 520 U.S. at 404); *Navarro v. Block*, 72 F.3d 712 (9th Cir.1995); *Greensboro Professional Fire Fighters Ass'n Local 3157 v. City of Greensboro*, 64 F.3d 962 (4th Cir. 1995) (treating custom or practice as an alternative predicate for municipal liability, even absent "policy"); *Sorlucco v. New York City Police Dep't*, 971 F.2d 864, 870 (2d Cir.1992) (entity liability may be based on unwritten custom); *Brown v. City of Fort Lauderdale*, 923 F.2d 1474 (11th Cir.1991) (custom through widespread, settled practice a distinct alternative route to establish policy—i.e., an alternative to finding that a final policymaker inflicted or approved the unconstitutional conduct); *Matthias v. Bingley*, 906 F.2d 1047 (5th Cir.1990) (police department's unlawful custom of failing to notifying property claimants about property seized in criminal investigations); *Andrews v. City of Philadelphia*, 895 F.2d 1469, 1480 (3d Cir.1990) (custom is established by practices that are "so permanent and well settled as to virtually constitute law"); *Fletcher v. O'Donnell*, 867 F.2d 791, 793–94 (3d Cir.1989) (plaintiff may establish custom with evidence of supervisors' knowledge and acquiescence); *Jones v. City of Chicago*, 856 F.2d 985 (7th Cir.1988) (unconstitutional police custom of withholding "street files" from state's attorney, leading to indirect *Brady* violations); *Spell v. McDaniel*, 824 F.2d 1380, 1387 (4th Cir. 1987) (custom may be established either through "actual" knowledge of subordinates' unconstitutional conduct, as evidenced by recorded reports to or discussions by the governing municipal body, or by constructive knowledge resulting from widespread, flagrant practices of which governing body should have known); *Garza v. City of Omaha*, 814 F.2d 553 (8th Cir.1987) (city liable for pattern of disparate treatment against Mexican–Americans that was instigated and ratified by subordinate supervisory personnel); *Bohen v. City of East Chicago, Ind.*, 799 F.2d 1180 (7th Cir.1986) (sexual harassment in municipal fire department was "on-going and accepted practice"); *White-Ruiz v. City of New York*, 1996 WL 603983 (S.D.N.Y.1996) (whether police department's "code of silence" about unlawful police misconduct constituted a custom or usage sufficiently widespread as to imply entity acquiescence held a jury question precluding summary judgment). *See* Gilles, *Breaking The Code of Silence: Rediscovering "Custom" in Section 1983 Municipal Liability*, 80 *Boston Univ. L.Rev.* 17 (2000). *But see Navarro Pineda v. City of*

Ascribing such independent, greater-than-boilerplate significance to causation language in a statute remediating constitutional torts is somewhat surprising, since causation is an invariable prerequisite of liability for civil harms. The language Justice Brennan construed is susceptible to equally plausible alternative interpretations. One way an entity may "cause" a person to be subjected to a constitutional injury, for example, is simply to charge its agents to meet specified objectives without taking reasonable steps to prevent them from trampling on federally protected rights. No deliberative act on the part of the employer is required to "cause" deprivations in this fashion. Although this interpretation is perhaps dubious as applied to those predicate violations dependent upon an element of wrongful intent,[20] no textual imperative extends such a limitation to the deprivation of other constitutional or statutory rights, or to the interpretation of § 1983 itself. And it is not apparent why the Court deems an injury to be caused by the entity when its agent acts pursuant to official policy, but not otherwise.[21] Perhaps "subjects, or causes to be subjected" refer not to a government authorization requirement but simply to the differing degrees of proximity between the depriver and the deprived that varying circumstances may present.[22]

Houston, *291 F.3d 325 (5th Cir.2002) (11 warrantless residence searches by gang task force did not establish custom in view of large size of city and police force);* Gregory v. Shelby County, Tn., *220 F.3d 433, 442 (6th Cir.2000) (lapse in enforcement of written jail policy "on more than one occasion" not sufficient);* Abbott v. Village of Winthrop Harbor, *205 F.3d 976 (7th Cir. 2000) (no "widespread practice" amounting to custom);* Carter v. Morris, *164 F.3d 215 (4th Cir.1999) (multiple informal complaints or § 1983 claims insufficient to show custom);* Trevino v. Gates, *99 F.3d 911, 918–920 (9th Cir.1996) (city's "varied and inconsistent* ad hoc *practice" of indemnifying individual defendant officers for punitive damage judgments not a standard operating procedure of long standing and hence did not establish "custom" as an alternative to a formal policy or policy based on delegation or ratification);* Sargi v. Kent City Bd. of Educ., *70 F.3d 907 (6th Cir.1995) (no violation where driver failed to intervene after child had seizure on school bus). The elements of custom claims are contrasted with those of "policy" claims in § 2.32,* infra.

20. *See, e.g., Personnel Adm'r v. Feeney*, 442 U.S. 256, 279, 99 S.Ct. 2282, 2296, 60 L.Ed.2d 870 (1979) (holding that the "intent" necessary to state a claim for denial of equal protection of the laws requires plaintiff to show that the decision was made "because of, 'not merely in spite of' its adverse effects"); *Estelle v. Gamble*, 429 U.S. 97, 106, 97 S.Ct. 285, 292, 50 L.Ed.2d 251 (1976) (holding that "deliberate indifference" is demanded to state an Eighth Amendment claim for deprivation of medical attention).

21. *See Kramer & Sykes*, 1987 Sup.Ct. Rev. at 256.

22. Virtually the same phrase first appears in § 2 of the Act of April 9, 1866, ch. 31, 14 Stat. 27 (1866) (codified in scattered sections of 42 U.S.C.A.). Section 1 of that Act declared rights to contract and dispose of property free from racial discrimination. Section 2, described by Senator Trumbull, a sponsor, as "the valuable section of the bill so far as protecting the rights of freedmen is concerned," prescribes criminal punishments for any person who, under color of state law, "shall subject or cause to be subjected" any "inhabitant" to the deprivation of § 1 rights. 1 *Statutory History of the United States* 112 (Bernard Schwartz ed., 1970). Senator Trumbull explains that ensuring the freedom of newly freed slaves requires criminal sanctions for "any person who [ ] shall deprive another of any right or subject him to any punishment in consequence of his ... race." *Id.* Provided he acts under color of law, therefore, a putative defendant could himself immediately "subject" an inhabitant to the deprivation of a § 1 right, or could accomplish the same end by "causing" another to "subject" the inhabitant to the deprivation. Thus, a deputy sheriff could deny a § 1 right directly or prevail upon a fellow deputy or a private citizen to do so. Significantly, in none of these examples would the initiator-defen-

Justice Brennan bolstered his government authorization interpretation by arguing that failure to require official policy behind the challenged conduct would create a federal law of respondeat superior that "would have raised all the constitutional problems" that caused the rejection of the Sherman Amendment.[23] He reasoned that encumbering local governments with civil liability whenever their agents violate constitutional norms would be tantamount to federal imposition of an "obligation to keep the peace, an obligation Congress chose not to impose because it thought imposition of such an obligation unconstitutional."[24]

Many federal constitutional and statutory duties, however, are not tantamount to a "new" obligation to keep the peace. For example, the challenged requirement in *Monell*—that pregnant city employees take unpaid leaves of absence while still medically able to work[25]—violated either equal protection or the then current "irrebuttable presumption" variation of due process.[26] Even if an individual supervisor had imposed this requirement in an ad hoc manner, rather than pursuant to city policy or custom, imposing liability on the city would certainly not have burdened it with an obligation to keep the peace or with any other "new" obligation not already mandated by the Constitution.[27]

dant be implementing any "policy" in the sense of a deliberative decision of his entity.

23. *Monell*, 436 U.S. at 693, 98 S.Ct. at 2037.

24. *Id.* The Court has continued to eschew efforts that would, in effect, obligate local governments or governmental units to keep the peace among civilians. *Cf. DeShaney v. Winnebago County Dep't of Soc. Servs.*, 489 U.S. 189, 198–203, 109 S.Ct. 998, 1005–1007, 103 L.Ed.2d 249 (1989) (holding that the failure of a county department of social services to provide a minor with adequate protection against his father's violence did not violate that minor's due process rights). *But see S.S. v. McMullen*, 186 F.3d 1066 (8th Cir.1999) (upheld substantive due process claim where state employee placed child back in father's custody knowing of his association with convicted pedophile). *DeShaney* has been read more generally to mean that members of the public have no actionable constitutional claim against government for failing to protect them from harm inflicted by third parties. *See L.W. v. Grubbs*, 974 F.2d 119 (9th Cir.1992), *cert. denied*, 508 U.S. 951, 113 S.Ct. 2442, 124 L.Ed.2d 660 (1993). The Court has subsequently clarified that *DeShaney* does not limit the liability of state officials for their own violations of a plaintiff's bodily integrity, even outside a custodial setting. *See United States v. Lanier*, 520 U.S. 259 n. 7, 117 S.Ct. 1219, 137 L.Ed.2d 432 (1997) (case under 18 U.S.C.A. § 242). For a discussion of the "special relationship" and "state-created danger" exceptions to this prevailing general principle of substantive due process doctrine, see text *infra* § 2.32. An unusual and provocative discussion of the interface between "private action" and the requirement of state action may be found in Laurence H. Tribe, *The Curvature of Constitutional Space: What Lawyers Can Learn From Modern Physics*, 103 Harv.L.Rev. 1, 8–13 (1989) (discussing *DeShaney*). See also Blumoff, *Some Moral Implications of Finding No State Action*, 70 Notre Dame L.Rev. 95 (1994) (viewing the Court's approach in *DeShaney* as abdicating its role to shape public values).

25. *See Monell*, 436 U.S. at 660–61, 98 S.Ct. at 2020–21.

26. *See, e.g., Cleveland Bd. of Educ. v. LaFleur*, 414 U.S. 632, 643–48, 94 S.Ct. 791, 798–800, 39 L.Ed.2d 52 (1974) (stating that a school board's presumption that a woman five or more months pregnant is physically unfit to teach in a classroom is an "irrebuttable presumption" and thus suspect under the Due Process Clause); *Stanley v. Illinois*, 405 U.S. 645, 654, 92 S.Ct. 1208, 1214, 31 L.Ed.2d 551 (1972) (ruling that an Illinois statute containing an irrebuttable presumption that unmarried fathers are incompetent to raise their children violated the Due Process Clause).

27. The obligation of state officials to obey the Constitution was not a "new" one offensive to the dual sovereignty conception of the Sherman Amendment opponents,

Why would the Court blithely take away, with its "policy" requirement, so much of what it had labored mightily to give by overruling the restrictive *Monroe* definition of "person"? Despite authoring *Monell's* majority opinion, Justice Brennan's subsequent enthusiasm for the dictum is doubtful. Seeking to contain his Frankenstein, he later described the "policy" requirement as intended merely to distinguish the municipality's acts from those of its employees.[28] Eventually he would take sharp issue with decisions that found policy only in positive local legislation or in a pattern so regular it amounted to "custom." Only two years after *Monell*, in the course of rejecting entity immunity, he endorsed the very "loss-spreading" principle that *Monell* had found inadequate to justify subjecting entities to respondeat superior.[29] In short, the policy dictum may simply have been the price that some justices paid for their brethren's agreement to override stare decisis—the volte face from *Monroe*—that made it possible to reach entities at all.

Since first invented in *Monell*, "policy" can be established not only through conduct formally adopted by the entity or enshrined in settled custom but also through decisions of a final policy-making official who commits the federal law violation herself or ratifies the unlawful act of a delegate. The "policy" barrier thus echoes dissenting Justice Frankfurter's argument in *Monroe* that an agent's actions must have state authorization to occur "under color of" state law.[30] In fact, "policy" circumscribes the scope of entity liability even more sharply than Justice Frankfurter would have curbed the liability of individual defendants in *Monroe*. Not only do entities, like their agents under Justice Frankfurter's view, escape liability for conduct undertaken without "authority"; under *Monell* and its progeny, the agents' authorized acts cannot be attributed to the entity unless the authorization stems from sources sufficiently high or formal to qualify as an aspect of official policy.

The requirement of a "final" policymaker emerged, again as dictum, in a plurality opinion in *Pembaur v. City of Cincinnati*.[31] A county prosecutor and subordinate law enforcement officials authorized and executed, respectively, the service of capiases by breaking down the door of a private physician's office. All of the Justices agreed that the conduct

who recognized as much in enacting § 1983. In principle, vicarious municipal liability for the constitutional torts of a municipality's agents simply holds the municipality to the same preexisting constitutional standards incumbent on state officers. The distinction that the individual state officer need only answer for his own behavior, while the municipality must answer for that of its employee, is irrelevant to the "new obligation" objection that animated opposition to the Sherman Amendment. *See Kramer & Sykes*, 1987 Sup.Ct. Rev. at 259–60. Indeed respondeat superior was a well-established common law rule at the time. *See City of Oklahoma City v. Tuttle*, 471 U.S. 808, 835–39, 105 S.Ct. 2427, 2442–45, 85 L.Ed.2d 791 (1985) (Stevens, J., dissenting).

28. *See Pembaur v. City of Cincinnati*, 475 U.S. 469, 479–81, 106 S.Ct. 1292, 1298–99, 89 L.Ed.2d 452 (1986).

29. *See Owen v. City of Independence*, 445 U.S. 622, 655, 100 S.Ct. 1398, 1417, 63 L.Ed.2d 673 (1980).

30. *See Monroe v. Pape*, 365 U.S. 167, 257, 81 S.Ct. 473, 522, 5 L.Ed.2d 492 (1961) (Frankfurter, J., concurring in part and dissenting in part), *overruled in part by Monell v. Department of Soc. Servs.*, 436 U.S. 658, 98 S.Ct. 2018, 56 L.Ed.2d 611 (1978).

31. 475 U.S. 469, 106 S.Ct. 1292, 89 L.Ed.2d 452 (1986).

that gave rise to the action violated the Constitution only if a Fourth Amendment precedent, *Steagald v. United States*,[32] were to apply retroactively. The plurality allowed the action to proceed against the county because a state statute specifically authorized the county prosecutor to advise the local police on such matters as the lawfulness of entry.[33] It has become conventional for the definition of a "final policymaker" to be dictated by the provisions of state law.[34]

The "final policymaker" requirement appears in response to dissenting Justice Powell's charge in *Pembaur* that the plurality had reopened the door to respondeat superior.[35] Justice Powell argues convincingly that the off-hand, hasty decision of a harried assistant prosecutor (made during a telephone conversation while a horde of municipal police officers, axes poised, awaited his direction) does not amount to policy[36]—at least not if, as the plurality insisted, "policy" requires "a deliberate choice to follow a course of action ... made from among various alternatives."[37] Generally speaking, Justice Powell would have found "policy" only when a legislative body adopts a rule of universal applicability like the pregnancy policy at issue in *Monell*.[38] Justice Brennan, for the *Pembaur* plurality, pushed the liability potential somewhat further, so that even individual decisions may represent the entity's policy, but only if "the decisionmaker possesses final authority to establish policy with respect to the action ordered."[39]

The individual *Pembaur* defendants were absolved by *Harlow's* version of "clearly established" qualified immunity.[40] Because their liability was premised on applying Steagald retroactively, the legal question was not resolved at the time the capias was served. These defendants did not, therefore, act in violation of clearly established law. Thus if Justice Powell's analysis, exonerating the county, had carried the day, no one would have been liable to the plaintiff for what the Court agreed was a constitutional violation.

32. 451 U.S. 204, 101 S.Ct. 1642, 68 L.Ed.2d 38 (1981).

33. *See Pembaur*, 375 U.S. at 484–85, 106 S.Ct. at 1300–01.

34. *See, e.g., Brown v. Neumann*, 188 F.3d 1289 (11th Cir.1999) (per curiam) (interpreting Florida statute to determine if it directly conferred final policy making authority on deputy sheriff); *Swint v. Wadley*, 5 F.3d 1435 (11th Cir.1993), rev'd on other grounds sub nom. *Swint v. Chambers County Comm'n*, 514 U.S. 35, 115 S.Ct. 1203, 131 L.Ed.2d 60 (1995) (state law defines Alabama county sheriffs as state officials respecting law enforcement functions, so county is not responsible under § 1983 county sheriffs' conduct).

35. *See id.* at 499–502, 106 S.Ct. at 1308–1309 (Powell, J., dissenting). Within two years, Brennan attempted to disown, at least in part, the same requirement of finality. *See City of St. Louis v. Praprotnik*, 485 U.S. 112, 144–46, 108 S.Ct. 915, 935–36, 99 L.Ed.2d 107 (1988) (Brennan, J., concurring).

36. *See Pembaur*, 475 U.S. at 501 (Powell, J., dissenting).

37. *Id.* at 483, 106 S.Ct. at 1300 (plurality opinion).

38. *See id.* at 499–502, 106 S.Ct. at 1308–1309 (Powell, J., dissenting).

39. *Id.* at 481, 106 S.Ct. at 1299.

40. *See id.* at 475 (plurality opinion). Whether the prosecutor, in contrast to the subordinate officers, would have been eligible for absolute immunity per *Imbler v. Pachtman*, 424 U.S. 409, 96 S.Ct. 984, 47 L.Ed.2d 128 (1976), turns on whether his advice concerning the capias service would be classified as intimately related to the prosecutor's role as an advocate for the public in the judicial system. *See supra* § 2.2.

But suppose the precedent on which the individual defendants' liability turned had been decided before the *Pembaur* events and was deemed sufficiently clearly established to satisfy *Harlow* and *Anderson*. There could still be no actionable entity policy as defined by Justice Powell, because no positive legislation or government pronouncement gave the prosecutor final authority to make policy about the service on Dr. Pembaur. In such a case, the Court would likely visit liability not upon the entity but upon the police officers alone,[41] even though they had followed standard departmental operating procedure by calling the assistant prosecutor for instructions. The result works at cross-purposes with one of the traditional rationales for individual immunity, fairness to the government agent.

The finality requirement, borne of the floodgates fear, eventually evolved so stringently that it frequently forecloses the accountability of a solvent entity. In *City of St. Louis v. Praprotnik*,[42] the Court tightened the finality qualification by demanding ratification of delegates' decisions and rationales.[43] After reiterating that "the authority to make municipal policy is necessarily the authority to make final policy,"[44] the Court explained that the act of an individual that departs from the *final* policymaker's instructions is not the act of the municipality. Accordingly, when a policymaker delegates policymaking responsibility, entity liability attaches only if "the authorized policymakers approve a subordinate's decision and the basis for it."[45]

This demand, articulated without accompanying justification, creates a prima facie burden of Herculean proportions. First, it promises to have widespread application. Few citizens deal with "final policymakers" on a day-to-day basis; they deal more commonly with subordinates whose decisions require clearance. Second, the injury is seldom related to the "basis" of, or intent behind, the subordinate's policy choice, but more often results from the implementation of an earlier choice. Relatively few plaintiffs have been able to negotiate these shoals.

The facts of *Praprotnik* illustrate the problem. Plaintiff complained that he was laid off from city employment in violation of the First Amendment because he was a whistle-blower. He was subjected to retaliation, the jury found, for appealing an adverse personnel decision

41. The Court expressed no opinion on the availability of qualified immunity for the *Pembaur* prosecutor. See 475 U.S. at 474 n.2, 106 S.Ct. at 1295 n.2. It is now apparent that the prosecutor, if not eligible for absolute immunity with respect to the giving of advice concerning service of the capias would be eligible for qualified immunity under *Harlow*. See *Burns v. Reed*, 500 U.S. 478, 495, 111 S.Ct. 1934, 1944, 114 L.Ed.2d 547 (1991).

42. 485 U.S. 112, 108 S.Ct. 915, 99 L.Ed.2d 107 (1988).

43. Only a plurality reached this conclusion, but their views commanded a majority in *Jett v. Dallas Indep. Sch. Dist.*, 491 U.S. 701, 737–38, 109 S.Ct. 2702, 2724, 105 L.Ed.2d 598 (1989).

44. *Praprotnik*, 485 U.S. at 127, 108 S.Ct. at 926 (citing *Pembaur*, 475 U.S. at 481–84, 106 S.Ct. at 1299–1301).

45. *Id.* The Court hastened to distinguish the case where "a particular decision by a subordinate was cast in the form of a policy statement and expressly approved by the supervising policymaker." *Id.* at 130, 108 S.Ct. at 928. One wonders how often that really happens.

that, in turn, was the result of his public opposition to a controversial decision to purchase an expensive piece of sculpture.[46] A majority of the Court agreed that the supervisor who discharged plaintiff lacked final personnel policymaking authority and therefore absolved the entity.[47] A plurality offered several interrelated reasons for its conclusion: the superior who made the decision to lay off the plaintiff possessed only discretionary implementation authority under the policymaking aegis of the city's civil service commission; the superior's control fell short of full-fledged delegated authority with respect to personnel policy; and, the possibility that an official could make a personnel decision based on a retaliatory motive was at odds with the city charter provision that specified "merit and fitness" as the sole criteria.[48] The Court concluded that the city had "enacted no ordinance designed to retaliate against respondent"[49] and that the only "final" decisions were those of the Civil Service Commission.[50]

The circuits have struggled to identify the characteristics that render an individual official or collective body a "final policymaker" whose actions may be attributed to the entity. Formally they recognize that state law "will always direct a court to some official or body that has responsibility for making law or setting policy in any given area of a local government's business,"[51] and that local officials may implement government policy through their decisions in the field even in the absence of formal legislation. In some cases, local legislation points to the injury-inflictor as a final policymaker. For example, in one early post-*Praprotnik* decision, a municipal court judge was held a final policymaker with respect to the discharge of his court clerk, because it was clear from a personnel manual that the city had absolutely delegated to the judge the authority to make final personnel decisions.[52] Similarly, a city manager was held a final policymaker with respect to employment decisions because the city's charter prohibited the county commissioners from reviewing the manager's decisions.[53] Also, a deputy district attorney

46. *See id.* at 150–55, 108 S.Ct. at 938–40 (Stevens, J., dissenting).

47. *See id.* at 131, 108 S.Ct. at 928 (O'Connor, J., plurality opinion); *id.* at 137, 108 S.Ct. at 931 (Brennan, J., concurring in judgment, writing for three Justices).

48. *See id.* at 124–30, 108 S.Ct. at 924–28.

49. *Id.* at 128, 108 S.Ct. at 926.

50. *See id.* at 129, 108 S.Ct. at 927 (quoting St. Louis City Charter, art. XVIII, § 2(a)).

51. *Flores v. Cameron County, Texas*, 92 F.3d 258 (5th Cir.1996) (quoting *Praprotnik* and *Pembauer*). In *Brown v. City of Fort Lauderdale*, 923 F.2d 1474 (11th Cir. 1991), for example, the court noted a "rich variety of ways in which the power of government is distributed among a host of different officials and official bodies" that may share policymaking authority. It therefore directed the district court to examine not just state law "but also the relevant customs and practices" of the defendant government entity to determine if individual officials were permitted in fact to wield policymaking authority respecting personnel decisions.

52. *Williams v. Butler*, 863 F.2d 1398 (8th Cir.1988) (en banc), *cert. denied*, 492 U.S. 906, 109 S.Ct. 3215, 106 L.Ed.2d 565 (1989).

53. *Martinez v. City of Opa–Locka*, 971 F.2d 708 (11th Cir.1992) (where city charter expressly denied city commission authority to interfere with personnel decisions by city manager, thus insulating his decisions from review, commission had delegated final policymaking authority to city manager and city could be liable for manager's decisions). *See Jeffes v. Barnes*, 208 F.3d 49, 57–61 (2d Cir.), *cert. denied*, 531 U.S. 813,

was held a final policymaker regarding a decision to prosecute because the deputy's authority under state law was coextensive with that of the principal district attorney and there was no evidence that the principal attorney had in fact constrained the deputy's authority.[54] But more commonly lower courts have concluded that local law, and the entity's practice under that law, do not point to the injury inflictor as a "final policymaker" in the strict sense described by *Praprotnik*.[55]

Alternatively, a consistent pattern by policymakers of permitting subordinate's decisions to stand unreviewed may establish a "custom" of delegation notwithstanding the formal arrangements declared by local law.[56] By contrast, delegation followed by the delegator's complete inattention to the delegee's decisions has in other cases been held to insulate

121 S.Ct. 47, 148 L.Ed.2d 16 (2000) (state law and actual practice under that law showed sheriff was final policymaking official concerning his staff members' duties toward each other to respect their exercise of First Amendment rights, where sheriff functioned autonomously on that subject without supervision by county's chief executive officer). *But cf. Manor Healthcare Corp. v. Lomelo*, 929 F.2d 633 (11th Cir.1991) (mayor not final policymaker where city council could override decisions and plaintiff failed to seek override).

54. *Webb v. Sloan*, 330 F.3d 1158 (9th Cir.2003).

55. *See, e.g. Quinn v. Monroe County*, 330 F.3d 1320 (11th Cir.2003) (council, not county administrator who made challenged decision, was final policymaker, and council had not approved any alleged unconstitutional motive of administrator); *Tharling v. City of Port Lavaca*, 329 F.3d 422 (5th Cir. 2003) (city council, not city manager who made decision to terminate plaintiff, was final policymaker, and information received by council, through notice to one of its members, did not apprise it of conduct of plaintiff that might have warranted First Amendment protection); *Beattie v. Madison County Sch. Dist.*, 254 F.3d 595 (5th Cir. 2001) (only school board, not principal or superintendent, was final policymaker, and it had no knowledge of plaintiff's constitutionally protected activity); *Cozzo v. Tangipahoa Parish Council–President Government*, 279 F.3d 273, 289 (5th Cir. 2002) (injury inflictor had not been delegated policymaking authority, so as to create supervisory liability for single incident per *Praprotnik*); *Bechtel v. City of Belton, MO*, 250 F.3d 1157 (8th Cir.2001) (municipal fire chief's alleged order directing captain to spy on plaintiff did not bind municipality because his actions were potentially reviewable by city administrator and thus administrator, not chief, was final policymaker); *Brown v. Lyford*, 243 F.3d 185 (5th Cir.), *cert. denied* 534 U.S. 817, 122 S.Ct. 46, 151 L.Ed.2d 17 (2001) (special prosecutor accused of civil rights violations in connection with prosecution not final policymaker); *Riddick v. School Bd. of City of Portsmouth*, 238 F.3d 518 (4th Cir.2000) (city school board, not superintendent or high school principal, had final policymaking authority over disciplinary matters under Virginia law, and school officials' decision respecting nonretention of coach could not bind board because it had not approved their decision and the allegedly unconstitutional basis for it); *Abbott v. Village of Winthrop Harbor*, 205 F.3d 976, 981–983 (7th Cir.2000) (Illinois law confided final policymaking authority to connect police department line to emergency telephone system not in defendant village's police chief but in an emergency telephone system board); *Austin v. Paramount Parks, Inc.*, 195 F.3d 715, 728–31 (4th Cir. 1999) (loss prevention manager who acquiesced in arrests by special police officers not final policymaker, because neither Virginia nor county law gave defendant private park or its employees authority over law enforcement functions of special police officers, nor as a matter of custom or usage had manager directed or prevented such officers from effecting an arrest); *Murrell v. School Dist. No. 1*, 186 F.3d 1238, 1249 (10th Cir.1999) (principal and teachers not final policymakers whose inaction can bind defendant school district even though court finds or assumes they had the authority to end student-on-student harassment and could therefore bind the district for purposes of liability under Title IX).

56. *Mandel v. Doe*, 888 F.2d 783, 791 (11th Cir.1989) (county board of commissioners' repeated deference to medical care decisions for prisoners made by physician's assistant constituted custom or policy of delegation or ratification for which county could be held liable).

the entity from liability, since the delegator cannot approve the basis for decisions of which it has chosen to remain unaware![57] And where local government entities or high officials retain under state law the authority to review the decisions of subordinates, the entities have been held not liable for the subordinates' decisions on the theory that putative delegations of authority are incomplete, even where review rarely if ever occurs or is exercised only pro forma.[58] On the other hand, some circuit decisions scrutinize the reality of the review. These courts find a valid delegation, and hence impose responsibility on local governments for the decisions of subordinate injury-inflictors, unless those decisions are subject to meaningful review.[59]

In the absence of express or implicit delegation, liability may be predicated on "the ratification of a subordinate's actions by a final policymaker."[60] The circuit decisions insist that the final policymaker authorize, acquiesce in, or otherwise ratify the conduct of a subordinate that unconstitutionally inflicts injury on the plaintiff. But they illustrate

57. *See Flores v. Cameron County, Texas*, 92 F.3d 258 (5th Cir.1996) (where supervisor of juvenile detention center was de facto policymaker, but Juvenile Board retained actual final policymaking authority, Board was insulated from liability for juvenile's death).

58. *See. e.g., Matthews v. Columbia County*, 294 F.3d 1294 (11th Cir.2002) (person allegedly given power to select positions to be eliminated in reduction in force was subject to review by government board and therefore had not been delegated final policymaking authority); *Bechtel v. City of Belton, MO*, 250 F.3d 1157 (8th Cir.2001) (municipal fire chief's alleged order directing captain to spy on plaintiff did not bind municipality because his actions were potentially reviewable by city administrator and thus administrator, not chief, was final policymaker); *Riddick v. School Bd. of City of Portsmouth,* 238 F.3d 518 (4th Cir.2000) (city not liable for employment decision of school superintendent and principal because city school board retained final disciplinary authority under Virginia law); *Eugene v. Alief Indep. Sch. Dist.*, 65 F.3d 1299 (5th Cir.1995) (citing Texas law, principal was not delegated policymaking authority in area of security, even though he had decision-making authority in that area); *Jantz v. Muci*, 976 F.2d 623, 630–31 (10th Cir.1992), *cert. denied*, 508 U.S. 952, 113 S.Ct. 2445, 124 L.Ed.2d 662 (1993) (citing Kansas law, delegation by school board to principal incomplete event though board rarely altered principal's decisions); *Worsham v. City of Pasadena*, 881 F.2d 1336 (5th Cir.1989) (mayor's indefinite suspension of city employees not fairly attributable to city because city council was empowered to review decision); *Williams v. Butler*, 863 F.2d 1398 (8th Cir.1988) (en banc), *cert. denied*, 492 U.S. 906, 109 S.Ct. 3215, 106 L.Ed.2d 565 (1989) (delegation is incomplete when a superior body within defendant entity retains right to review even though it does not exercise that right or investigate the basis of the decision at hand) (dictum).

59. *Quinn v. Monroe County,* 330 F.3d 1320 (11th Cir.2003) (county administrator was not final policymaker with respect to plaintiff's termination where Florida law made administrator's decision subject to review by council and council in fact afforded her full hearing); *Morro v. City of Birmingham,* 117 F.3d 508 (11th Cir.1997) (police chief not final policymaker where evidence showed that a personnel board in fact reviewed his decisions); *Scala v. City of Winter Park,* 116 F.3d 1396 (11th Cir.1997) (city not liable for termination decision of city manager and public safety director where decision was subject to meaningful, and not merely rubber-stamp review by city civil service board, and plaintiff had failed to seek such review). *But cf. Todd v. Kelley,* 783 So.2d 31 (Ala.Civ.App.2000) (even where review of mayor's decision to dismiss police officer was purely advisory and nonbinding, mayor was final policymaking official).

60. *Mandel v. Doe*, 888 F.2d 783, 791 (11th Cir.1989). See, e.g., *Christie v. Iopa*, 176 F.3d 1231 (9th Cir.), *cert. denied,* 528 U.S. 928, 120 S.Ct. 324, 145 L.Ed.2d 253 (1999) (county might be liable for prosecutor's ratification of act of deputy prosecutor, even though deputy did not have delegated final policymaking authority, ab initio under Hawaii law).

the difficulty of defining ratification consistently in terms of requisite degree of formality and specificity.[61] The decisions do consistently stress the insistence of the Supreme Court in *Praprotnik* that the final policymaker, to bind the entity through ratification, must approve not only the subordinate's decision, but also the (allegedly unconstitutional) basis for it.[62] These decisions therefore in effect put pressure on a potential § 1983 plaintiff desirous of suing the local governmental entity to pursue administrative review up to and including the official or reviewing board that a court might deem to be the "final" policymaker; otherwise the final policymaker remains free to deny that it knew the basis of the

61. *Monfils v. Taylor*, 165 F.3d 511 (7th Cir.1998), *cert. denied,* 528 U.S. 810, 120 S.Ct. 43, 145 L.Ed.2d 39 (1999) (city not liable for police chief's failure to discipline subordinate, because a mere failure to discipline a subordinate injury-inflictor cannot constitute ratification of that person's conduct); *Gattis v. Brice*, 136 F.3d 724 (11th Cir.1998) (to ratify subordinate's injury-inflicting decision, final policymaker must know of and ratify the subordinate's improper motives, not just his recommendation); *Hyland v. Wonder*, 117 F.3d 405 (9th Cir.1997), *cert. denied*, 522 U.S. 1148, 118 S.Ct. 1166, 140 L.Ed.2d 177 (1998) (ratification does not require a formal act); *Trevino v. Gates*, 99 F.3d 911 (9th Cir. 1996), cert. denied, 520 U.S. 1117, 117 S.Ct. 1249, 137 L.Ed.2d 330 (1997) (formal city council vote to pay punitive damages judgments against police officers does not amount to ratification of their unconstitutional conduct); *Hill v. Clifton*, 74 F.3d 1150 (11th Cir.1996) (police chief lacked final policymaking authority to demote officer, and city manager with policymaking authority approved only chief's demotion of plaintiff, not the allegedly improper motive); *Hall v. Marion School District No. 2*, 31 F.3d 183 (4th Cir.1994) (school board, the final policymaker, was fully aware of injury inflictor's retaliation and ratified his decisions by failing to intervene despite knowledge of injury inflictor's plan to terminate plaintiff for improper reasons); *Meyers v. City of Cincinnati*, 14 F.3d 1115 (6th Cir.1994) (on internal administrative appeal from decision of city manager forcing plaintiff's retirement, civil service commission, the final policymaking authority, substantively determined that plaintiff was not unconstitutionally coerced, thereby ratifying decision); *Cornfield v. Consolidated High School District No. 230*, 991 F.2d 1316 (7th Cir.1993) (insufficient evidence that school board president endorsed any specific policy of strip searches); *Feliciano v. City of Cleveland*, 988 F.2d 649 (6th Cir.1993) (director of public safety's acquiescence in a single discretionary decision by police chief insufficient to show ratification, where no evidence that director knew of allegedly unconstitutional administration of drug tests on which decision was based); *Gillette v. Delmore*, 979 F.2d 1342 (9th Cir.1992) (final policymaker's mere upholding of disciplinary decision upon review of plaintiff's employment record and brief hearing conducted by subordinate not a deliberate choice to endorse subordinate's unconstitutional action and therefore not ratification); *Wright v. Sheppard*, 919 F.2d 665 (11th Cir.1990) (plaintiff-citizen's oral complaint to secretary of sheriff, county's final policymaker, insufficient to show that sheriff knew the unconstitutional basis of deputy's harassment of plaintiff); *Andrews v. City of Philadelphia*, 895 F.2d 1469 (3d Cir.1990) (final policymaker neither delegated authority to injury inflictor nor approved the basis of his decisions).

62. Accordingly, a county could not be bound by alleged false statements of one of three county commissioners, even though the board of commissioners was its final policymaker, where only a majority of 3–member board was authorized to establish policy and board had not delegated to commissioner in question authority to speak for it. *LaVerdure v. County of Montgomery*, 324 F.3d 123 (3d Cir.2003). Similarly, where only one, or less than a majority, of the members of a final policymaking commission was proven to hold an actionable unconstitutional motive, the other members could not be deemed to have ratified the unlawful basis by voting as he did, absent evidence that they were acting on the basis of, and not merely with knowledge of, that motive. *Matthews v. Columbia County*, 294 F.3d 1294 (11th Cir.2002). And where a city agreed to indemnify officers for a Section 1983 punitive damages judgment, it was held not to have ratified "the basis for" the unconstitutional police conduct that resulted in the judgment, but rather only to have decided to compensate the victims of that deprivation. *Trevino v. Gates*, 99 F.3d 911, 920–921 (9th Cir.1996).

challenged decision.[63] Moreover, a plaintiff cannot safely refrain from pursuing and exhausting internal review in the hope that a court will find a delegation of final policymaking authority to the subordinate injury-inflictor; such a delegation will be found only if there is no theoretical or actual meaningful opportunity for review, something the potential plaintiff cannot know in advance.

Of course in "benign neglect" scenarios insufficient to establish policy through ratification plaintiffs may attempt to fasten liability on the entity through the alternative to "policy", namely "custom": "a series of decisions by a subordinate official ... of which the supervisor must have been aware."[64]

It will be the rare plaintiff suing a government entity who will be able to show that her injury was inflicted directly by a final policymaking official, or was the result of a formal entity policy, or even was caused by a practice so widespread as to rise to the level of "custom." The only avenue remaining for entity liability under *Praprotnik* is proof that the final policymaker designated by state law approved or ratified not only the decision of the injury-inflicting subordinate, but also the basis for that decision. That approval may be shown if the decision was made by someone to whom the final policymaker delegated the final decision without reserving the right to review. Or it may be shown by evidence that the final policymaker reviewed a subordinate's decision and ratified both the decision and its unconstitutional rationale. To show the final policymaker's knowledge of the basis for the subordinate's decision, however, the prospective plaintiff cannot just hope that the final policymaker will have learned of the decision and its rationale fortuitously. By in effect forcing the prospective plaintiff to utilize any available internal grievance process within the government entity, and to pursue permissible appeals all the way up to the level of the final policymaker, *Praprotnik* creates a de facto exhaustion of administrative remedies requirement. Such a requirement is sharply at variance with the Court's formal

63. *But see Pearson v. Macon–Bibb County Hospital Authority*, 952 F.2d 1274 (11th Cir.1992) (even where plaintiff failed to exhaust formal, available review procedures, entity may be bound if final policymaker informally learns of unconstitutional basis for subordinate's decision and then approves it).

64. *Praprotnik*, 485 U.S. at 130, 108 S.Ct. at 927. *See also Beck v. Pittsburgh*, 89 F.3d 966 (3d Cir.1996), *cert. denied*, 519 U.S. 1151, 117 S.Ct. 1086, 137 L.Ed.2d 219 (1997) (entity liability grounded on tacit custom of authorizing use of excessive force; identification of final policymaker not required). Absent a finding of policy formed through "custom" based on a pattern of similar alleged unconstitutional acts, plaintiff must of course identify a specific final policymaker for the particular entity defendant and secure district court findings that those policymakers violated the plaintiff's rights. *See Speer v. City of Wynne*, 276 F.3d 980 (8th Cir.2002) (remanding for such findings). On occasion a court will blend evidence about the conduct of a final policymaker with evidence of custom to conclude that the entity defendant maintained a "policy" actionable under Section 1983. *See Fairley v. Luman*, 281 F.3d 913 (9th Cir. 2002) (per curiam) (evidence that police chief, final policymaker for city, was aware that allegedly unconstitutional warrant procedures were not uncommon yet failed to act to remedy the problem sufficed for "policy"). Such cases suggest that policy may be found where a final policymaker is aware of but fails to deal with a pattern of unconstitutional conduct that is not as well established as would be required for finding policy through "custom" alone.

doctrine that a judicial forum is immediately available for claims under Section 1983, without the requirement of exhaustion of administrative remedies.[65]

Some government entities have benefited from an apparent extension of *Praprotnik*: an entity escapes liability if legislation recites that the ultimate governing body either retains the authority to prohibit or in fact prohibits the allegedly unlawful conduct. Thus in cases involving alleged discriminatory or retaliatory terminations by a sheriff and police chief who had final, unreviewable authority to make the challenged decisions, the government entities nevertheless avoided liability because local ordinances prohibited the kind of discrimination involved.[66] These decisions reason that as an abstract matter a person who otherwise perfectly fits the description of a "final policymaker" could not have been authorized to engage in conduct formally prohibited by the entity's positive law. Another court took the doctrine a step further. A county was not liable for the medical decisions of a jailer with unreviewable final authority because a state statute reserved to the county legislature the authority to enact ordinances and issue regulations regarding medical care, even though it had never, in fact, done so![67] In effect, these doctrines revive, in favor of entity defendants challenging the prima facie showing of "policy," the "under color of state law" argument, rejected in *Monroe*, that there can be no Section 1983 liability where an agent of government acts in violation of local law.

65. *See Patsy v. Board of Regents*, 457 U.S. 496, 516, 102 S.Ct. 2557, 2568, 73 L.Ed.2d 172 (1982). There are limited exceptions to the non-exhaustion rule. The Prison Litigation Reform Act contains an express exception that requires prisoners to exhaust available administrative remedies, even when they appear futile, before filing claims challenging prison conditions. See 42 U.S.C.A. § 1997e ("No action shall be brought with respect to prison conditions under section 1983 of this title, or any other Federal law, by a prisoner confined in any jail, prison, or other correctional facility until such administrative remedies as are available are exhausted.") A Supreme Court decision, *Heck v. Humphrey*, 512 U.S. 477, 114 S.Ct. 2364, 129 L.Ed.2d 383 (1994), in effect requires exhaustion of judicial remedies by persons convicted of a crime, including prisoners, before asserting any claim under Section 1983 that if successful would necessarily undermine the validity of a conviction. *See also Frazier v. Fairhaven School Committee*, 276 F.3d 52, 57–63 (1st Cir.2002) (assuming that despite comprehensive remedy under Individuals With Disabilities Education Act, § 1983 "and laws" claim based on IDEA is available, but holding that plaintiff bringing such a claim must first exhaust administrative remedies provided by IDEA even though only money damages sought and despite general non-exhaustion rule for Section 1983; and citing two circuit decisions reaching same conclusion and three others permitting the IDEA-based Section 1983 damages-only claim without requiring exhaustion). *Accord, Robb v. Bethel School Dist. No. 403,* 308 F.3d 1047 (9th Cir.2002). Also, occasionally the underlying constitutional right sought to be vindicated by the action under Section 1983 in effect also requires preliminary exhaustion of administrative or state-court remedies. *See Sandy Creek Investors, Ltd. v. City of Jonestown, Tex.*, 325 F.3d 623 (5th Cir.2003) (landowner's § 1983 14th Amendment takings claim not ripe where plaintiff failed first to seek compensation administratively or in state court).

66. *Lankford v. City of Hobart*, 73 F.3d 283 (10th Cir.1996) (even assuming police chief accused of sexually harassing employees had final policymaking authority, no municipal liability where city had written policy expressly forbidding sexual harassment); *Auriemma v. Rice*, 957 F.2d 397 (7th Cir.1992); *Crowley v. Prince George's Co.*, 890 F.2d 683 (4th Cir.1989), *cert. denied*, 506 U.S. 833, 113 S.Ct. 101, 121 L.Ed.2d 61 (1992).

67. *Johnson v. Hardin County*, 908 F.2d 1280 (6th Cir.1990).

In a 5–4 decision, the Supreme Court has endorsed this deference to state law in determining whether to attribute the unconstitutional conduct of an admitted final policymaker to a particular government entity defendant. Plaintiff's § 1983 claim against an Alabama county asserted that the defendant sheriff intimidated the plaintiff's co-defendant into falsely inculpating him and also suppressed exculpatory evidence. The sheriff was elected by county voters, was the chief law enforcement officer within the county, and was funded by the county, and the parties agreed he was the "final policymaker" with respect to the allegedly unconstitutional conduct. But the Court, after canvassing Alabama constitutional provisions and statutes, ruled that under Alabama law he could act only on behalf of the state, rather than the county, with respect to matters of criminal investigation and law enforcement. So it concluded that the sheriff could represent the state alone when acting in a law enforcement capacity, and hence that the state is the sole entity defendant that could be liable, under *Monell* and *Praprotnik*, for his final policymaking in the law enforcement sphere.[68] But of course a state as such is not a "person" suable under § 1983 in either state or federal court;[69] so that the practical effect of holding that a county or city defendant was acting on behalf of a state is to preclude § 1983 liability in either state or federal court. Putting *Pembauer, Praprotnik* and *McMillian* together, the Court confides to state law two distinct questions. First, whether an individual defendant's conduct was engaged in or approved by a final policymaker. Second, whether the final policymaker, when he engaged in the allegedly unconstitutional conduct,

68. *McMillian v. Monroe Co., Ala.*, 520 U.S. 781, 117 S.Ct. 1734, 138 L.Ed.2d 1 (1997). *See also Carter v. City of Philadelphia*, 181 F.3d 339 (3d Cir.1999) (local law enforcement officers may act for state when prosecuting crimes, but serve as local policy makers with respect to managing or administering their own offices, including training, supervision and discipline); *Brotherton v. Cleveland*, 173 F.3d 552 (6th Cir.1999), *on remand,* 141 F.Supp.2d 894 (S.D.Ohio 2001) (in implementing cornea removal policy, coroner acted for the county, rather than state because county would satisfy money judgment and coroner was elected county official who acted autonomously and was not compelled to devise the policy at issue by state law); *Turquitt v. Jefferson County, Ala.*, 137 F.3d 1285 (11th Cir.1998) (Alabama county could not be held liable for death of pretrial detainee in county jail because the sheriff, a state official, is responsible for operation of jail); *Graves v. Lowery*, 117 F.3d 723 (3d Cir.1997), *on remand,* 98 F.Supp.2d 613 (M.D.Pa.2000) (county a de facto coemployer of court clerks where it maintained and communicated personnel policies to plaintiffs that led them to believe that county had hiring, termination, and reinstatement authority); *Esteves v. Brock*, 106 F.3d 674 (5th Cir. 1997) (because a prosecutor under Texas law acts for the state in serving as an advocate in court, a defendant county could not be liable for his allegedly unconstitutional use of peremptory strikes). Under Title VII, by contrast, function trumps form in determining whether a county may be liable for discrimination against employees formally considered employees of the state.

69. *See Will v. Michigan Dep't of State Police*, 491 U.S. 58, 109 S.Ct. 2304, 105 L.Ed.2d 45, especially at p. 71, text accompanying n.10 (1989), discussed in detail in § 2.35 and § 2.42. And under the analysis in *Will*, a sub-state entity that enjoys immunity from damages suit in federal court for purposes of the Eleventh Amendment is not a "person" within the meaning of Section 1983 and will therefore also be immune from suit under that statute in either state or federal court. *Kirchmann v. Lake Elsinore Unified School District,* 83 Cal.App.4th 1098, 1103–1104, 100 Cal.Rptr.2d 289, 293–294 (4th Dist.2000), *cert. denied*, 533 U.S. 902, 121 S.Ct. 2242, 150 L.Ed.2d 231 (2001) (collecting citations).

was performing a function on behalf of a local government entity or the state.

The Court acknowledged a practical consequence of its decision. Under Alabama's sovereign immunity law, the plaintiff did not have the option to repair to state court to hold the state liable for the sheriff's final policymaking on its behalf, because a sheriff is absolutely immune from all damage suits stemming from official acts. So the plaintiff's only evident alternatives, in a state like Alabama, are likely to be legally or practically deficient. If she insists on damages, she can sue the sheriff under § 1983 in federal court in his individual capacity only,[70] subject to the qualified immunity defense and in the devout hope that the sheriff is solvent or entitled to indemnity. Or she can bring the § 1983 action in federal court against the sheriff in his official state capacity, but then will be limited, under the Court's interpretations of the Eleventh Amendment, to prospective relief and attorney's fees.[71]

The Court's decision does not disturb the rulings of federal appellate courts that for the most part have concluded that sheriffs in other states act on behalf of their counties in executing their principal functions.[72] The majority acknowledged that to some degree the question whether a sheriff acts on behalf of a county or state with respect to a particular function is thus left to the vagaries of varying state laws. But it denied that a state, on behalf of its local governments, could capitalize on the decision by simply amending constitutional provisions and statutes to reclassify local government functions as its own. If such manipulation were attempted, the Court wrote, the plaintiff could pierce the form by proving a "widespread practice" established by "custom or usage" that would demonstrate that the function in question was carried out in the name of the local government entity.

The dominant influence of local law in determining whether an entity may be liable by virtue of the conduct of a "final policymaking official" is illustrated by two Eleventh Circuit decisions respecting the

70. *See Hafer v. Melo*, 502 U.S. 21, 112 S.Ct. 358, 116 L.Ed.2d 301 (1991), discussed in § 2.35, *infra*.

71. *See Will v. Michigan Dep't of State Police*, 491 U.S. 58, 109 S.Ct. 2304, 105 L.Ed.2d 45, especially at p. 71 n.10 (1989), discussed in § 2.35, *infra*. A suit naming a public official defendant in his official capacity is treated as brought against his government entity in all respects other than name. *Kentucky v. Graham*, 473 U.S. 159, 105 S.Ct. 3099, 87 L.Ed.2d 114 (1985). According to *Will*, the state could not be sued under § 1983 in its own name in any court, because the state as such is not a "person" within the meaning of § 1983. *See also McMillian v. Johnson*, 88 F.3d 1573, 1576 n. 2 (11th Cir.1996), aff'd, 520 U.S. 781, 785 n. 2, 117 S.Ct. 1734, 1737 n. 2, 138 L.Ed.2d 1 (1997).

72. *See e.g., Cozzo v. Tangipahoa Parish Council–President Government*, 279 F.3d 273 (5th Cir. 2002) (under Louisiana law). *But cf. Manders v. Lee*, 338 F.3d 1304 (11th Cir. 2003)(en banc), *cert. denied*, ___ U.S. ___, 124 S.Ct. 1061, 157 L.Ed.2d 892 (2004) (even though state law uncertain as to whether State would be liable to pay judgment against sheriff's office, Georgia sheriffs act on behalf of the state, not the counties that employ them, with respect to implementation of policies respecting use of force, and therefore enjoy Eleventh Amendment immunity; dissent would have defined the relevant function at issue in case not as policymaking relating to force but as maintenance of county jail, in which case sheriff would have been acting for the county).

duties of Alabama sheriffs. In *Turquitt v. Jefferson County, Alabama,*[73] county liability concerning a sheriff's hiring decisions at a county jail was rejected because under Alabama law the county's only responsibilities were to fund and provide jail facilities, not to hire for or operate those facilities. Similarly, in *Swint v. City of Wadley,*[74] the county could not be held liable for the sheriff's authorization of a raid on criminal suspects because the state's statutes bestowed law enforcement duties on the sheriffs. Seventh Circuit decisions similarly show that whether a sheriff acts on behalf of a county or state depends upon state law allocations of authority for particular decisions.[75] Typically, sheriffs are viewed by the law of other states as final policy makers for the counties, not the states, they serve in overseeing local jails and employment policies therein.[76] The opinions diverge in identifying the sovereigns served by prosecuting attorneys.[77] Also, a Kansas municipal judge has been held not to be a final policymaker for his city with respect to his procedures for issuing arrest warrants because his authority to issue warrants was constrained by his general duty to follow state law.[78]

Praprotnik's requirements pay excessive respect to federalism and raise a substantial question about fairness to individual defendants. Federalism concerns were actually implicated only tangentially, since imposing liability on the entity would not have intruded on the legitimate exercise of discretionary government authority: prohibiting retaliation for exercising First Amendment rights is not meddlesome interfer-

73. 137 F.3d 1285 (11th Cir.), *cert. denied,* 525 U.S. 874, 119 S.Ct. 174, 142 L.Ed.2d 142 (1998).

74. 5 F.3d 1435, 1450–1451 (11th Cir. 1993), *rev'd on other grounds sub nom. Swint v. Chambers County Comm'n,* 514 U.S. 35, 115 S.Ct. 1203, 131 L.Ed.2d 60 (1995).

75. *Compare DeGenova v. Sheriff of DuPage County,* 209 F.3d 973 (7th Cir. 2000) (Illinois sheriffs are county officials in managing local jails, precluding any Eleventh Amendment defense); *Franklin v. Zaruba,* 150 F.3d 682 (7th Cir.1998), *cert. denied,* 525 U.S. 1141, 119 S.Ct. 1033, 143 L.Ed.2d 42 (1999) (Illinois sheriffs are also county, not state officials, in executing general law enforcement duties); and *Scott v. O'Grady,* 975 F.2d 366, 368 (7th Cir.1992), *cert. denied,* 508 U.S. 942, 113 S.Ct. 2421, 124 L.Ed.2d 643 (1993) (Illinois sheriffs act on behalf of State when executing judicial writs of assistance).

76. *See Streit v. County of Los Angeles,* 236 F.3d 552 (9th Cir.2001) (applying California law); *Jeffes v. Barnes,* 208 F.3d 49 (2d Cir.), *cert. denied,* 531 U.S. 813, 121 S.Ct. 47, 148 L.Ed.2d 16 (2000) (under New York law).

77. *See Mowbray v. Cameron County, Tex.,* 274 F.3d 269, 278 (5th Cir.2001) (district attorney in prosecutorial capacity in criminal matters acts for the state, not county, precluding liability of defendant county for prosecutor's acts; sheriff was relevant final policymaker for county, but unconstitutional acts were alleged not against sheriff but only against lower-level officers and prosecutors); *Weiner v. San Diego County,* 210 F.3d 1025 (9th Cir.2000) (under California law, district attorney made decision to re-prosecute as a state, not a county, official, so that state could not be liable for that decision); *Owens v. Fulton County,* 877 F.2d 947 (11th Cir.1989) (prosecutorial decisions of a Georgia district attorney represent an exercise of state, rather than county power, for which the state alone is responsible). *Cf. Carter v. City of Philadelphia,* 181 F.3d 339 (3d Cir.1999) (district attorney's office not an arm of the state for Eleventh Amendment purposes because the state would not pay judgments against the office and it was funded by defendant city, not treated as surrogate for the state under state law, and enjoyed considerable autonomy in its operations).

78. *Ledbetter v. City of Topeka,* 318 F.3d 1183 (10th Cir.2003).

ence and requires no wholesale reordering of personnel decisionmaking.[79] From the fairness perspective, *Praprotnik* sacrifices the subordinate who in good faith inadvertently violates a clearly established constitutional right. Liability is possible only for the underling, despite the superior's approval of the injurious decision, so long as the superior does not also approve its "basis."

The Court's insistence on entity "policy," and the finality and ratification refinements in particular, are theoretically and practically suspect. Theoretically, any liability imposed upon government is necessarily vicarious: governments operate only through human agency. Thus the Court's insistence that the "entity" act advertently (either through deliberative policy, or, where the injury is caused by omission, through the somewhat oxymoronic "deliberate indifference" demanded by *City of Canton v. Harris*)[80] is hard to understand. Practically, from the viewpoints of both the state actor who commits and the person who suffers the violation, the actor's authority appears complete. *Pembaur's* prosecutor and *Praprotnik's* perpetrator both assumed they had authority to do what they did, their relevant subordinates assumed the same, and the victims suffered as a result.

§ 2.32 "Deliberate Indifference": Showing *Monell* "Policy" Where an Entity Unconstitutionally Fails to Train or Otherwise Act

"Deliberate indifference" is the Court's surrogate test for "policy" where the constitutional violation allegedly results from government inaction or omission. In the seminal case *City of Canton v. Harris*,[1] the plaintiff had been detained by the police and manifested symptoms of emotional or mental distress. She asserted that the police failed to provide her medical care or attention and that this failure to act caused her further injury. She claimed that the city's failure to train its personnel to cope with emotional distress violated a constitutional right[2] comparable to the right to medical care enjoyed by a detainee or arrestee who manifests symptoms of physical illness.

79. Today at least it appears settled that retaliation for exercising free speech rights protected by the First Amendment is actionable under § 1983. See *Maynard v. City of San Jose*, 37 F.3d 1396 (9th Cir. 1994).

80. 489 U.S. 378, 392, 109 S.Ct. 1197, 1206, 103 L.Ed.2d 412 (1989) (remanding the question whether a city's failure adequately to train police officers to assess a detainee's need for medical assistance stemmed from "deliberate indifference"). *See* § 2.32 following.

§ 2.32

1. 489 U.S. 378, 109 S.Ct. 1197, 103 L.Ed.2d 412 (1989).

2. It should be stressed that a local government's failure to train or screen that results in injury to plaintiff is not actionable under Section 1983 unless the failure led to a recognized federal constitutional violation that in turn caused plaintiff's injuries. *Trigalet v. City of Tulsa*, 239 F.3d 1150 (10th Cir.), *cert. denied,* 534 U.S. 814, 122 S.Ct. 40, 151 L.Ed.2d 13 (2001) (even assuming city's training and supervision respecting limits on vehicular pursuits were deliberately indifferent, city not responsible for death of motorists killed in collision with fleeing suspect if the city's police officers did not exceed constitutional limits in conducting chase).

The Supreme Court held that in order to show that a failure to train or similar failure to act amounts to advertent "policy" fairly attributable to the entity, a plaintiff must demonstrate that the need for such training was "obvious" from "usual and recurring situations."[3] A government entity therefore usually cannot be liable to a suspect on the basis of a detective's single mistaken identification of her, because an isolated incident does not tend to show the persistent or repeated violation essential to show "custom" or "policy" under *City of Canton*.[4] That kind of obviousness is required to demonstrate that "the inadequacy [of training was] so likely to result in the violation of constitutional rights, that the policymakers ... can reasonably be said to have been deliberately indifferent to the need."[5] Speaking through Justice White, the Court also insisted on a clear causal link between an unconstitutional omission and harm suffered by the plaintiff. For example, if an entity provides appropriate training but the injury is inflicted by an agent who, having received that instruction, disregards it, only the agent could be liable.[6] In general, this "causation" prerequisite to § 1983 entity liability

3. *Id.* at 391, 109 S.Ct. at 1206. Hence a failure to train police on how to conduct internal investigations held not a predicate for municipal liability absent evidence of department awareness from prior instances that a failure to train would violate constitutional rights. *Williams v. Heavener,* 217 F.3d 529, 532 (7th Cir.2000).

4. *Campbell v. City of San Antonio*, 43 F.3d 973 (5th Cir.1995). *See Williams v. Heavener*, 217 F.3d 529, 532 (7th Cir.2000) (single deviation from police order requiring subjects of internal investigations to be read rights insufficient to amount to custom); *Carter v. Morris,* 164 F.3d 215 (4th Cir.1999) (evidence of two incidents over previous ten years that were similar to those complained of by plaintiff insufficient to demonstrate policy). *See also West v. Waymire,* 114 F.3d 646 (7th Cir.), *cert. denied*, 522 U.S. 932, 118 S.Ct. 337, 139 L.Ed.2d 261 (1997) (town had no obligation to take measures to prevent officer from using his law enforcement status to intimidate minor into engaging in sex with him because no information or prior episodes had made that danger obvious); *Robles v. City of Fort Wayne,* 113 F.3d 732 (7th Cir. 1997) (absent pattern of similar violations by police performing off-duty security work, city not responsible for failure to train respecting excessive force in that setting). *Cf. Sewell v. Town of Lake Hamilton,* 117 F.3d 488 (11th Cir.1997), *cert. denied,* 522 U.S. 1075, 118 S.Ct. 852, 139 L.Ed.2d 753 (1998) (town not deliberately indifferent for failing to train or supervise officer who allegedly sexually molested arrestee because obviousness of the violation meant failure to train or supervise was not the cause of the constitutional injury). *See also Church v. City of Huntsville,* 30 F.3d 1332, 1345 (11th Cir. 1994). Nevertheless, summary judgment has been denied upon a determination that a city's practice of using only one jailer amounted to official custom or policy, *Scott v. Moore,* 85 F.3d 230 (5th Cir.1996); and at least one circuit turns over to a jury the question whether local government acquiesced in an alleged custom of tolerating excessive force by police. *Beck v. City of Pittsburgh,* 89 F.3d 966 (3d Cir.1996), *cert. denied,* 519 U.S. 1151, 117 S.Ct. 1086, 137 L.Ed.2d 219 (1997).

5. *City of Canton*, 489 U.S. at 390, 109 S.Ct. at 1205. *See, e.g., Miranda v. Clark County,* 279 F.3d 1102 (9th Cir.2002) (per curiam) (county's alleged failure to train deputy public defenders did not evince deliberate indifference and so could not subject it to Section 1983 liability).

6. *Id.* at 391, 109 S.Ct. at 1206. *See Dye v. Wargo,* 253 F.3d 296, 299 (7th Cir. 2001) (inadequate training finding may generate liability only if it shows municipality has policy of improper conduct "that training could extirpate.") *Piotrowski v. City of Houston,* 237 F.3d 567 (5th Cir.2001) (police department's moonlighting policy not moving force behind attempted contract killing of plaintiff); *Ellis v. Washington County,* 198 F.3d 225, 226–227 (6th Cir. 1999), *cert. denied,* 529 U.S. 1087, 120 S.Ct. 1720, 146 L.Ed.2d 642 (2000) (county not liable for allegedly deficient failure to train jailors to prevent inmate suicides; that failure could not have been a cause of the particular suicide at bar, which even plaintiff's witnesses could not have predicted).

contrasts with the respondeat superior basis of employer liability for most violations under Title VII.[7]

The Court has shed light on the ways in which "deliberate indifference" for § 1983 purposes may be shown. It has distinguished the *Canton* requirement from the element a prisoner must show to demonstrate that the government's infliction of pain upon him violates the Eighth Amendment's cruel and unusual punishment clause. For Eighth Amendment liability, the prison official must unnecessarily and wantonly inflict injury upon the prisoner either intentionally or with a state of mind characterized at a minimum by "deliberate indifference"[8] to a substantial and serious risk of harm to the inmate.[9] Federal intermediate appellate courts had equated this Eighth Amendment "deliberate indifference" with one or another form of recklessness.[10] In *Farmer v. Brennan*[11] the Supreme Court clarified that the Amendment is violated only if the prison official is "subjectively" reckless in the criminal sense, that is, consciously disregards a substantial risk of serious harm despite his actual knowledge of that risk.[12] Specifically distinguishing the "delib-

Cf. Jeffes v. Barnes, 208 F.3d 49, 57, 61–64 (2d Cir.), *cert. denied*, 531 U.S. 813, 121 S.Ct. 47, 148 L.Ed.2d 16 (2000) (jury question whether municipal policy was the cause of retaliation against plaintiffs in violation of their First Amendment rights). Similarly, if the individual government officer's violation is deemed obvious even without any training, the lack of training cannot be considered the cause of the constitutional injury. *See Sewell v. Town of Lake Hamilton*, 117 F.3d 488 (11th Cir.1997), *cert. denied*, 522 U.S. 1075, 118 S.Ct. 852, 139 L.Ed.2d 753 (1998) (town not deliberately indifferent for failing to train or supervise officer who allegedly sexually molested arrestee). That is why plaintiffs complaining about clearly unconstitutional conduct may be better advised to explore a "custom" route, where they need not make the perhaps impossible showing that the entity's failure to train was the cause of plaintiff's injuries. *See also Gold v. City of Miami*, 151 F.3d 1346 (11th Cir.1998) (on false arrest claim, plaintiff failed to adduce evidence there was a policy of inadequate training; therefore, no entity liability could lie, even though city conceded arrest was unlawful).

7. Occasionally, an echo of the § 1983 "causation" requirement will relieve a Title VII defendant of liability, where the ultimate challenged decision is made lawfully by the person who speaks for the employer. *See Willis v. Marion County Auditor's Office*, 118 F.3d 542 (7th Cir.1997) (county not liable for supervisor's alleged racial animosity where decision to terminate plaintiff made by higher-level, reviewing authority for lawful reasons).

8. *See, e.g., Wilson v. Seiter*, 501 U.S. 294, 302–03, 111 S.Ct. 2321, 2326–27, 115 L.Ed.2d 271 (1991); *Moore v. Jackson*, 123 F.3d 1082 (8th Cir.1997), *appeal after remand,* 16 Fed.Appx. 517 (8th Cir.2001) (prison officials could not be held liable for deliberate indifference to an inmate's serious medical needs without proof they knew of the serious medical needs).

9. *See Helling v. McKinney*, 509 U.S. 25, 113 S.Ct. 2475, 125 L.Ed.2d 22 (1993).

10. *See, e.g.*, cases cited by the Court in *Farmer v. Brennan*, 511 U.S. 825 n. 4, 114 S.Ct. 1970 n. 4, 128 L.Ed.2d 811 (1994).

11. 511 U.S. 825, 114 S.Ct. 1970, 128 L.Ed.2d 811 (1994).

12. *Id.* at 1978. *See also Dunigan v. Winnebago County*, 165 F.3d 587 (7th Cir. 1999) (state official is deliberately indifferent if he knows of and disregards an excessive risk to inmate health or safety; the official must both be aware of facts from which the inference could be drawn that a substantial risk of serious harm exists, and he must also draw the inference). It is not necessary for the plaintiff to show that the known harm would befall any particular inmate, let alone the plaintiff, or to show that it would be inflicted by any particular inmate. And the factfinder may, but need not, conclude that the defendant official knew of the substantial risk from the very fact of its obviousness. Further, the official would not escape liability if, strongly suspecting the existence of such a risk, she failed to verify the underlying facts. *Id.* at 1980–82. But if the factfinder concludes that the defendant was in fact unaware of

erate indifference" concept declared by *Canton*, the Court held that a prison official does not violate the Eighth Amendment, even where the risk of substantial harm to inmates was obvious and a reasonable prison official would have noticed it, if she was not actually aware of that risk.[13]

The Court emphasized that § 1983, unlike the Amendment, contains no state of mind requirement. Rather, "deliberate indifference" was "used in the Canton case [not to define a predicate constitutional violation but] for the quite different purpose of identifying the threshold for holding a city responsible for the constitutional torts committed by its ... agents."[14] Unlike the Eighth Amendment requirement, entity liability for omissions under § 1983 does not depend on actual notice; "constructive notice of the need for preventative action can form the basis of a showing of deliberate indifference."[15] Thus as far as § 1983 is concerned, the entity faces liability, even for a single failure to train, when it either knows or *should know* of a recurring situation within its bailiwick that threatens a constitutional deprivation and the entity nevertheless fails to take appropriate responsive measures.[16] The § 1983

such a substantial risk of harm, she may not be held liable even if the risk was obvious and a reasonable official in the defendant's position would have been aware of it. And because the defendant's knowledge of substantial risk of harm must be subjective and actual, it has been held in a case involving allegedly inadequate care to a pretrial detainee in a psychiatric ward that the factfinder may not infer the requisite knowledge from expert testimony showing a mere difference of opinion among medical personnel as to appropriate patient treatment. *Estate of Cole v. Fromm*, 94 F.3d 254 (7th Cir.1996), *cert. denied*, 519 U.S. 1109, 117 S.Ct. 945, 136 L.Ed.2d 834 (1997). An additional requirement is evidence of improper medical treatment of the inmate. *Mays v. Rhodes*, 255 F.3d 644 (8th Cir.2001).

13. *Id.* at 1980. *See also Ruark v. Drury*, 21 F.3d 213 (8th Cir.), *cert. denied*, 513 U.S. 813, 115 S.Ct. 66, 130 L.Ed.2d 23 (1994) (jail officials must not only be aware of risk of substantial harm to inmate but their failure to respond must be prompted by "obduracy" or "wantonness").

14. *Id.* at 1981 (quoting *Collins v. City of Harker Heights*, 503 U.S. 115, 124, 112 S.Ct. 1061, 1068, 117 L.Ed.2d 261 (1992)). Still, as in any other § 1983 case, the plaintiff attempting to hold a government entity liable for an omission characterized by deliberate indifference must also show that he was deprived of a cognizable federal right. *See Hernandez v. City of Goshen, IN*, 324 F.3d 535 (7th Cir.2003) (despite inadequate training, city not liable for police department policy of failing to come to aid of persons facing foreseeable risk of harm absent allegations that policy created or increased danger to victims and therefore violated due process).

15. *Reynolds v. Borough of Avalon*, 799 F.Supp. 442, 446 (D.N.J.1992) (citing *Canton*).

16. *See Simmons v. City of Philadelphia*, 947 F.2d 1042, 1061 n. 14 (3d Cir. 1991), *cert. denied*, 503 U.S. 985, 112 S.Ct. 1671, 118 L.Ed.2d 391 (1992). The Supreme Court left open this possibility of liability for a single incident of failing to train in *Board of County Comm'rs Bryan County v. Brown*, 520 U.S. 397, 409, 117 S.Ct. 1382, 1391, 137 L.Ed.2d 626 (1997) (citing *City of Canton*). Examples include a government's failure to inform police officers about the constitutional limitations on the use of deadly force, *see City of Canton*, 489 U.S. at 390 n.10, 109 S.Ct. at 1205 n.10, or a failure to institute a policy against, or procedures to report sexual harassment, or to advise employees of their rights and obligations under such a policy. *Reynolds*, 799 F.Supp. at 446. These omissions could rise to the level of § 1983 "deliberate indifference" even if the policymakers lacked actual knowledge about prior incidents, provided the circumstances had recurred frequently enough to make the need for action obvious. *City of Canton*, 489 U.S. at 390 n.10, 109 S.Ct. at 1205 n.10. *See also Brown v. Bryan County, OK*, 219 F.3d 450, 462 (5th Cir.2000) (county liable for failure to train single deputy in arrest procedures where jury could reasonably have concluded that it was obvious to final policymaker that fail-

plaintiff bears the burden of demonstrating the entity agent's actual knowledge only when, as with Eighth Amendment claims, a violation of the particular predicate right depends upon the defendant's acting with that state of mind.

Justice O'Connor, writing for three Justices in *Canton*, seemed to perceive that there are two issues, one factual and one legal, necessarily embedded in the element of obviousness. The factual issue is whether the situation confronting the entity was sufficiently recurrent that a constitutional harm resulting from inaction was apparent. But knowledge or reasonably imputable knowledge that a failure to act would obviously violate a constitutional right may also assume that the right in question had been previously determined, a distinct legal question. Justice O'Connor concluded that this legal component "ha[d] not and could not" be met in *City of Canton*.[17] After all, she argued, the Court had "not yet addressed the precise nature of the obligations that . . . Due Process . . . places upon the police to seek medical care for pretrial detainees who have been *physically* injured."[18] A fortiori, she seemed to argue, there was no clear legal obligation with respect to the duty to prevent emotional or mental harms. There were, consequently, "no clear constitutional guideposts for the municipalities."[19] Absent such guideposts, the need for training could not, as a matter of simple logic, be obvious.

The majority did not confront the issue directly, noting only that "we must assume that [plaintiff's] constitutional right . . . was denied by city employees—whatever the nature of that right might be."[20] We are thus left to speculate whether the majority, in remanding, was authorizing the court of appeals on remand to recognize a new constitutional duty on the part of municipalities to provide adequate training for the treatment of mentally disabled pretrial detainees. The majority's failure to dispel Justice O'Connor's suspicions on this point permits the inference that the city would face potential liability for what was at best a dimly sketched right.

Some support for this conclusion may be drawn from Justice White's repeated generalized references to the denial of "medical attention" or "care," shorn of Justice O'Connor's distinction between care for physical and psychiatric conditions.[21] Liability would then be fastened on a municipality for a violation of rights that, at the very least, does not meet the highly particularized version of the "clearly established" requirement adumbrated in *Anderson v. Creighton*,[22] for the liability of individual defendants.[23]

ure to do so would result in deprivations of rights and cause plaintiff's injuries).

17. *Id.* at 394, 109 S.Ct. at 1207 (O'Connor, J., concurring in part and dissenting in part).

18. *Id.* at 397, 109 S.Ct. at 1209.

19. *Id.*

20. *Id.* at 389 n.8, 109 S.Ct. at 1205 n.8.

21. *See id.* at 381–82, 389 n.8, 109 S.Ct. at 1201, 1205 n.8.

22. 483 U.S. 635, 107 S.Ct. 3034, 97 L.Ed.2d 523 (1987).

23. *See supra* § 2.22.

Of course neither the disposition nor the discussion in *City of Canton* compels this interpretation. The Court did not purport to highlight the contours of the right.[24] It was apparently open on remand for the city to argue that there was no or little circuit authority supporting a right of pretrial detainees to psychiatric care and, even if there was, that it was not sufficiently settled when they acted that failure to furnish such care would "obviously" violate that constitutional right. The Court's "whatever the nature of the right" statement can be read to suggest that it was simply dealing with the § 1983 issue (whether the *Monell* "policy" requirement could ever be satisfied by entity omission) and that it did not undertake to decide whether the particular predicate right alleged was constitutionally cognizable.

Accordingly, should a reconstituted Court (Justices Souter, Thomas, Ginsburg and Breyer having replaced Justices Brennan, Marshall, White, and Blackmun) address the issue squarely, it may agree with Justice O'Connor that the § 1983 predicate right must to some degree be settled before an entity may be held liable on the basis of an agent's omission. If so, the entity in such cases would enjoy a prima facie escape from liability that in substance mirrors the immunity from damages enjoyed by individual officials via an affirmative defense.[25] An implicit settledness requirement, even if it is less stringent than the clearly established law necessary to overcome the qualified immunity defense of individual defendants, would lessen the significance of the Court's refusal in *Owen v. City of Independence*[26] to accord entities a formal immunity. Indeed, if the predicate right is unsettled enough to prevent the plaintiff from satisfying the "obviousness" facet of "deliberate indifference," the entity in an omission case may be somewhat better off than the individual defendant; it would be spared liability not only from damages but also from injunctive or declaratory relief and therefore from attorney's fees incident thereto.[27]

Subsequent decisions have pointed up some of the ambiguities implicit in the *Canton* standard for the liability of government entities based on the omissions of their agents. Despite some occasional loose language to the contrary,[28] the circuits seem to be in accord that under *Canton* entity liability may be predicated either on actual or constructive notice of the risks posed by a failure to act. Indeed the word "obvious" itself implies that the conclusion that the "entity" reasonably should have drawn (about a risk of constitutional injury if action is not taken) is based on events or data that fall short of giving certain knowledge. But

24. *See City of Canton*, 489 U.S. at 389 n.8, 109 S.Ct. at 1205 n.8.

25. *See supra* § 2.22.

26. 445 U.S. 622, 100 S.Ct. 1398, 63 L.Ed.2d 673 (1980).

27. The Court in *Supreme Court of Va. v. Consumers Union, Inc.*, 446 U.S. 719, 100 S.Ct. 1967, 64 L.Ed.2d 641 (1980), authorized attorney's fees even where only injunctive relief was obtained.

28. *See Mateyko v. Felix*, 924 F.2d 824 (9th Cir.1990), *cert. denied*, 502 U.S. 814, 112 S.Ct. 65, 116 L.Ed.2d 40 (1991) (finding no municipal liability absent evidence that a city had actual knowledge that failing to provide a lengthier, more detailed training program on tazer guns would create an unjustifiable risk to the citizenry).

what is it that the entity must know, or reasonably should have known, before the entity can be liable? Is it that a failure to take action is likely, or "substantially certain," to result in a violation of constitutional rights?[29] Or is it knowledge that the wrong decision by the entity's employee will frequently result in the deprivation of a citizen's constitutional rights?[30] And while the facts giving rise to *Canton* itself, and most of its progeny, involve a pattern or history of prior, similar constitutional violations,[31] from time to time entity liability is grounded on a single failure to act, i.e., on a unique, previously unencountered situation, where that failure would result in a constitutional violation deemed obvious because the facts are flagrant or the law violation well settled.[32]

These uncertainties have spawned varying formulations in the circuits of the required elements of a claim for failure to train. In cases alleging failure to train about excessive force, for example, one circuit requires evidence of "a pattern of similar incidents in which citizens were injured or endangered by intentional or negligent policy, misconduct and/or that serious incompetence or misbehavior was general or widespread throughout the police force."[33] Under that standard, mere failure to discipline a single officer for a single incident cannot give rise to the custom or policy requisite for entity liability.[34] Another requires proof that (1) officers breached constitutional limitations on the use of force; (2) force was occasioned by circumstances that are usual and recurring for police officers; (3) inadequate training on the use of force reflects deliberate indifference of the entity toward those with whom the officers will predictably interact; and (4) the inadequate training caused the plaintiff's constitutional deprivation.[35]

Still another circuit extracts from *City of Canton* three requirements applicable in any attempt to fasten liability on an entity for failure to

29. *See Popham v. City of Talladega*, 742 F.Supp. 1504, (N.D.Ala.1989), aff'd, 908 F.2d 1561 (11th Cir.1990).

30. *See Walker v. City of New York*, 974 F.2d 293 (2d Cir.1992), *cert. denied*, 507 U.S. 961, 113 S.Ct. 1387, 122 L.Ed.2d 762 (1993).

31. *See, e.g., Young v. City of Augusta*, 59 F.3d 1160 (11th Cir.1995); *Walker v. City of New York*, 974 F.2d 293 (2d Cir.1992); *Dorman v. District of Columbia*, 888 F.2d 159 (D.C.Cir.1989).

32. *See Atchinson v. District of Columbia*, 73 F.3d 418 (D.C.Cir.1996) (improper training claim legally sufficient although based on single episode of officer shooting plaintiff in broad daylight after ordering him to freeze); *Oviatt v. Pearce*, 954 F.2d 1470 (9th Cir.1992). This phenomenon is also at work in the closely related setting of the liability of supervisors, discussed in § 2.36, *infra*. *But see Larkin v. St. Louis Housing Authority*, 355 F.3d 1114 (8th Cir. 2004) (need for additional training of armed security guard who shot and killed plaintiff's decedent not obvious from mere fact of its brevity). *But cf. Board of County Commr's of Bryan County, Oklahoma v. Brown*, 520 U.S. 397, 117 S.Ct. 1382, 137 L.Ed.2d 626 (1997) (county not liable for a one-time flagrant failure by a final policymaking official to use even ordinary diligence in checking the background of a law enforcement candidate, because the prior conduct that would have been discovered involved at worst an improper or unlawful use of private force not identical to the particular unconstitutional use of official force challenged in the § 1983 action). *Bryan County* is discussed *infra*.

33. *Fraire v. City of Arlington*, 957 F.2d 1268, 1278 (5th Cir.), *cert. denied*, 506 U.S. 973, 113 S.Ct. 462, 121 L.Ed.2d 371 (1992).

34. *Id.* at 1278–79.

35. *Allen v. Muskogee, Okl.*, 119 F.3d 837, 841–42 (10th Cir.1997), *cert. denied*, 522 U.S. 1148, 118 S.Ct. 1165, 140 L.Ed.2d 176 (1998).

train or supervise.[36] First, that a policymaker for the defendant knows to a moral certainty that subordinate employees will confront the circumstances giving rise to the claim. Second, that there is a history of entity employees mishandling that situation or the situation presented the employee in question with a difficult choice of a kind that training or supervision would have made less difficult.[37] And third, that a wrong choice by the employee will frequently cause the deprivation of constitutional rights.

Another circuit outlines two more general ways that an entity may be said to have made the kind of deliberate choice about training among alternative courses of action that *City of Canton* treats as essential to entity liability.[38] First, where the need for a particular kind of training is obvious because officers recurrently face "clear constitutional duties."[39] This would be met, for example, in the case of training officers on the use of excessive or deadly force—a single failure to train about such force might therefore be actionable—but not by the need to train jailers to recognize the symptoms of emotional illness. Alternatively, there may be a longstanding and widespread practice, pattern or custom of constitutional violations so well settled that the entity knows or should know that corrective measures are needed—a theory the court held could render the defendant entity liable under the Eighth Amendment for failure to train jailers to recognize and act in the face of symptoms of serious emotional illness.

Owen v. City of Independence,[40] in the course of denying any sort of across-the-board, generally available Section 1983 immunity to local government entities, suggests another rationale, not mentioned in the *City of Canton* opinion, for treating "omissions" claims more skeptically than those alleging affirmatively unlawful conduct. In *Owen*, Justice Brennan for the majority labored mightily to minimize the scope of the common law tort immunity that extended to "discretionary" (but not "ministerial") government functions. He explained that the immunity excused the local government entity from "acting in one manner or another," but "once any particular decision was made, the city was fully liable for injuries incurred in the [tortious] execution of its judgment." Yet if this was so, what would be the consequences of carrying forward

36. *Walker v. City of New York*, 974 F.2d at 297–98.

37. The court observed that this requirement could be met even in the standard scenario in which the officer must decide to use deadly force in apprehending a fleeing suspect. It agreed that the plaintiff could also meet this element where, even though the proper course is clear, "the employee has powerful incentives to make the wrong choice." 974 F.2d at 297. On the other hand, where the proper response—for example, not to commit perjury—is obvious even without training or supervision, the failure to train or supervise will generally not be the cause of a wrong decision and therefore cannot support an inference of deliberate indifference. A plaintiff could avoid this last pitfall, however, if she can show that the entity's policymakers were aware of a pattern of obviously improper conduct but nevertheless failed to provide appropriate training or supervision. *Id.* at 299–300.

38. *Young v. City of Augusta*, 59 F.3d 1160, 1172 (11th Cir.1995).

39. *Id.* at 1172.

40. 445 U.S. 622, 100 S.Ct. 1398, 63 L.Ed.2d 673 (1980).

that common law immunity to Section 1983? Might it not be plausibly maintained, for example, that while local government has a duty to execute in a constitutional manner those functions it ventures to undertake, the constitution cannot prescribe what those functions are? Put otherwise, isn't it constitutional for the entity to fail to act at all? Had that argument been presented and prevailed in *City of Canton*, the Court might have extended the common law's version of "good faith" immunity to local government defendants in any Section 1983 action predicated on the entity's federally unlawful failure to act. And because such an immunity defense is rooted in Section 1983 itself, not tied to a particular predicate right, it might even avail the government defendant in circumstances where a failure to act is prima facie unlawful under the Constitution.[41]

Thus while the prima facie elements of "policy" that *City of Canton* imposes on the plaintiff in a failure-to-act case are undoubtedly formidable, many plaintiffs would fare still worse if the court had transported to Section 1983 the common law's good-faith defense for discretionary functions.

It is an irony of *City of Canton* that "deliberate indifference" is at once the most substantively difficult and procedurally favorable for the plaintiff. In contrast to the other entity—defendant opinions that refined the *Monell* notion of "policy," Justice White's opinion in *City of Canton* does not assert that the "deliberate indifference" issue is a preliminary question of law for the court. Unless, as suggested above, there is a "settled law" aspect to "deliberate indifference", the Court's description of the test—whether the need for entity action was "so obvious, and the inadequacy so likely to result in the violation of constitutional rights, that the policymakers ... can reasonably be said to have been deliberately indifferent"—[42] reveals that its satisfaction is a question of degree and the ultimate inquiry is inherently one of fact and hence for a jury.

Justice White alludes to the jury function respecting the related aspect of the prima facie omissions case, causation. Deciding whether more or better training would have avoided the particular plaintiff's injury "may not be an easy task," he writes, but "judge and jury, doing their respective jobs, will be adequate to the task."[43] Justice O'Connor dissented from this point, stating that "[a]llowing an inadequate training claim such as this one to go to the jury based upon a single incident would only invite jury nullification of *Monell*."[44] Circuit authority after *Canton* also recognizes the role of the jury in resolving the "policy" issue

41. A failure to act may become actionable, for example, as a violation of due process under the "custody" and "special relationship" exceptions to the general rule of *DeShaney* that government is not obliged to offer protection against harm inflicted by private third parties. See *infra* this Section.

42. *Id.* at 390, 109 S.Ct. at 1205.

43. *City of Canton*, 489 U.S. at 391, 109 S.Ct. at 1206 (adopting a strict causation standard to avoid the possibility of the city realizing "unprecedented liability").

44. *Id.* at 399, 109 S.Ct. at 1210 (O'Connor, J., concurring in part and dissenting in part).

in an omissions setting.[45] And the availability of jury trial in § 1983 cases generally has been confirmed by the Supreme Court's decision in *City of Monterey v. Del Monte Dunes at Monterey, Ltd.*[46] There the Court held that whenever the plaintiff seeks legal relief—which will be the vast majority of the time, especially given the severe limitations the Court has placed on injunctive relief[47]—all § 1983 claims implicate the Seventh Amendment right to jury trial, even if the underlying substantive claim is of the kind that would have been brought in equity before 1791.[48]

Plaintiffs' lawyers might, therefore, be tempted to frame their complaints against entities, when possible, as omission rather than action cases. Although complaints of omission are substantively more difficult to prove, requiring as they do a showing of deliberate indifference,[49] the prospect of a jury to determine the "policy" issue may entice

45. *See Griffin v. City of Opa–Locka*, 261 F.3d 1295, 1312 (11th Cir.2001), *cert. denied,* 535 U.S. 1033, 122 S.Ct. 1789, 152 L.Ed.2d 648 (2002) (jury could reasonably have found that city had policy or custom of ignoring or tolerating sexual harassment); *Young v. City of Little Rock*, 249 F.3d 730, 736 (8th Cir.2001), *cert. denied,* 534 U.S. 1129, 122 S.Ct. 1067, 151 L.Ed.2d 970 (2002) (jury could decide whether defendant city knew of unconstitutional strip-search policy followed in county jail to which city surrendered prisoners); *Brown v. Bryan County*, 219 F.3d 450 (5th Cir.2000) (jury verdict for plaintiff upheld in failure to train case); *Jeffes v. Barnes*, 208 F.3d 49, 61 (2d Cir.), *cert. denied*, 531 U.S. 813, 121 S.Ct. 47, 148 L.Ed.2d 16 (2000); *Beck v. City of Pittsburgh*, 89 F.3d 966 (3d Cir.1996), *cert. denied*, 519 U.S. 1151, 117 S.Ct. 1086, 137 L.Ed.2d 219 (1997); *Oviatt v. Pearce*, 954 F.2d 1470 (9th Cir.1992). It is not entirely surprising that the Supreme Court confides this question to the jury, since causation is classically within the jury's province. *See Gattis v. Brice*, 136 F.3d 724, 726 (11th Cir.1998); *Gardetto v. Mason*, 100 F.3d 803, 811–18 (10th Cir.1996); *Shands v. City of Kennett*, 993 F.2d 1337, 1343 (8th Cir.1993), *cert. denied*, 510 U.S. 1072, 114 S.Ct. 880, 127 L.Ed.2d 75 (1994). Cf. *Trevino v. Gates*, 99 F.3d 911, 920 (9th Cir.1996) (acknowledging that "Normally, the question of whether a policy or custom exists would be a jury question," but deciding that plaintiff had failed to show custom or policy as a matter of law so that summary judgment appropriate). The jury function in *City of Canton* "deliberate indifference" cases involving local government entity omissions or failures that produce constitutional violations stands in stark contrast to the Supreme Court's direction that judges, and judges alone, must decide "final policymaker" status under local law per *Praprotnik* in cases where entities are charged with liability based on their agents' affirmative acts.

46. 526 U.S. 687, 119 S.Ct. 1624, 143 L.Ed.2d 882 (1999).

47. See the discussion of *City of Los Angeles v. Lyons*, 461 U.S. 95, 103 S.Ct. 1660, 75 L.Ed.2d 675 (1983), in §§ 2.2, 2.61, and 5.55.

48. See Part IVA–1 of the opinion of Justice Kennedy for a majority of the Court. The Court also held that no jury trial right is conferred by the statute itself, but the Seventh Amendment right suffices on its own to entitle either party to demand trial by jury respecting any § 1983 claim seeking legal relief.

49. *See, e.g., Grazier ex rel. White v. City of Philadelphia*, 328 F.3d 120 (3d Cir. 2003) (police training program not deliberately indifferent in case involving deadly force against motorists where city implemented directives reflecting constitutional police procedure and instructed officers on proper techniques for vehicle investigations and stops); *Serafin v. City of Johnstown*, 53 Fed. Appx. 211 (3d Cir.2002) (absence of formal suicide prevention training did not create obvious risk of constitutionally cognizable harm or manifest city's deliberate indifference in light of other safeguards taken); *Frake v. City of Chicago*, 210 F.3d 779 (7th Cir.2000) (no deliberate indifference to suicide risk, despite use of horizontal bars that had facilitated past detainee suicides, where city took other precautions including training, monitoring and removal of personal items that detainees could use to commit suicide); *Liebe v. Norton*, 157 F.3d 574, 578–579 (8th Cir.1998) (no deliberate indifference where county took affirmative steps to prevent inmate suicides and had not experienced previous suicide at jail, even though

some plaintiffs' lawyers to brave the risks of an omissions theory. Casting the grievance in terms of an ongoing policy may also help overcome what otherwise might be a limitations problem by enabling the plaintiff to invoke the "continuing violation" doctrine.[50]

But Justice O'Connor has succeeded in circumscribing the jury's role in one type of "omission" case, a failure to screen in hiring. Writing for five members of the Court in *Board of County Commr's of Bryan County, Oklahoma v. Brown*,[51] she observed that a jury could not find a county liable for a policymaking sheriff's highly negligent, deliberate indifference to the prior record of an applicant he hired as a deputy. As a matter of law, she wrote, a jury could find county liability only if the sheriff had shown deliberate indifference to a constitutional right of a subsequent victim of the carelessly hired deputy; and such deliberate indifference is proven only where the deprivation of the third party's constitutional right would have been the "plainly obvious consequence" of more adequate scrutiny. Proving that, in turn, seems to require evidence of a tightly tailored fit between the particular culpable trait that more careful screening of the applicant would have uncovered, and the particular conduct of the deputy that constituted a violation of the victim's constitutional rights.

The Court ostensibly distinguished *Canton* on the ground that the risk flowing from a particular glaring omission in a training regimen is in some sense more obvious than the risk flowing from inadequate screening of an applicant's background. (Ironically, if the government agent's conduct is deemed self-evidently unconstitutional, even a failure to train claim may collapse because any lack of training would not be the "cause" of the unconstitutional conduct).[52] It is not clear, however, if what the Court claims to be more predictable about failures to train than failures to screen is the particular future conduct of an agent that would

it placed inexperienced jailer in charge and its conduct may have amounted to negligence); *Rellergert v. Cape Girardeau County*, 924 F.2d 794, 797 (8th Cir.1991) (holding that a prison guard's actions, including letting a suicidal prisoner out of his sight, did not amount to deliberate indifference); *Mateyko v. Felix*, 924 F.2d 824, 826 (9th Cir.1990), *cert. denied*, 502 U.S. 814, 112 S.Ct. 65, 116 L.Ed.2d 40 (1991) (stating that municipality's failure to train officer thoroughly enough to use tazer gun safely and properly, at best establishes mere negligence).

50. *See Gutowsky v. County of Placer*, 108 F.3d 256 (9th Cir.), *cert. denied*, 522 U.S. 914, 118 S.Ct. 298, 139 L.Ed.2d 229 (1997) (material fact question about actionable county custom or policy triggers continuing violations doctrine, thereby precluding summary judgment on limitations).

51. 520 U.S. 397, 117 S.Ct. 1382, 137 L.Ed.2d 626 (1997).

52. *See Boncher v. Brown*, 272 F.3d 484, 488 (7th Cir.2001) (better training probably would not have prevented decedent's suicide because intake officers still had to rely on basic judgment skills); *Ellis v. Washington County*, 198 F.3d 225 (6th Cir.1999), *cert. denied*, 529 U.S. 1087, 120 S.Ct. 1720, 146 L.Ed.2d 642 (2000); *Criswell v. Wayne County*, 165 F.3d 26 (Table, Text in Westlaw), Unpublished Disposition, 1998 WL 598739 (6th Cir.1998) (no causal link between county's training program and death of detainee, since even well trained jail official would not have realized that decedent would attempt suicide); *Sewell v. Town of Lake Hamilton*, 117 F.3d 488 (11th Cir.1997), *cert. denied*, 522 U.S. 1075, 118 S.Ct. 852, 139 L.Ed.2d 753 (1998) (town not deliberately indifferent for failing to train or supervise officer who allegedly sexually molested arrestee; the obviousness of the violation meant failure to train or supervise was not the cause of the constitutional injury).

be attributable to inadequate training, or the constitutional right of a victim that may be transgressed as a result. It therefore also remains unclear whether, in a failure to screen case, the plaintiff must prove that the "plainly obvious consequence" of negligent or even highly negligent screening is the particular conduct that the agent—applicant will consequently commit, or the particular constitutional injury that he will inflict.[53]

A plaintiff may alternatively attempt to show "policy" either by proving *Praprotnik*-type approval by a final policymaker or by framing the case in *Canton* terms as involving a deliberately indifferent failure to act. In *Chew v. Gates*,[54] for example, a city defendant attempted to avoid liability for a police practice of using dogs to bite, maul, and thereby apprehend concealed suspects, arguing that such a "policy was attributable only to the officers responsible for training the canine units." The Court rejected this argument, however, citing *Praprotnik* for the proposition that a government entity "cannot escape liability for the consequences of established and ongoing departmental policy ... simply by permitting such basic policy decisions to be made by lower level officials who are not ordinarily considered policymakers."[55] The court added that "even if we were to accept the city's argument that no jury could find that departmental canine policy was officially sanctioned, municipal liability could be found under the 'deliberate indifference' formulation of *Monell* liability." Citing *City of Canton*, the panel explained that the entity's failure to adopt a departmental policy governing police use of animals that were shown to have bitten suspects more than 40% of the time those animals were used reflected "deliberate indifference" to constitutional rights.[56]

The careful reader will have observed that the opinion in *Chew* refers to a jury function in deciding "deliberate indifference." It should be recalled, by contrast, that the Supreme Court has insisted that determining the other variants of "policy"—namely legislation, a governing body's official pronouncement, or a "final policymaking official"—is a question of law for the court. Justice O'Connor's *City of*

53. This confusion is at work in footnote 1 of the Supreme Court's decision in *Bryan County*, where the majority denies that the *Bryan County* opinion demands a higher degree of obviousness than does *City of Canton*. There the Court refers interchangeably to, on one hand, a policymaker's disregard of the "known and obvious consequences" of hiring a particular officer—a reference to conduct—and, on the other, to its requirement of a link between the officer's background and "the particular constitutional violation" suffered by the victim—a reference to law. Post-*Bryan County* appellate decisions read the Court as requiring a nexus between inadequate checking of an applicant's criminal background and the particular subsequent conduct that constituted the constitutional violation. *Gros v. City of Grand Prairie, Texas*, 209 F.3d 431, 433–436 (5th Cir.2000) (evidence in pre-employment file that applicant was too aggressive may show that hiring was negligent, but hiring was not deliberately indifferent as required by *Bryan County* absent evidence that he had sexually assaulted or harassed, falsely arrested, improperly searched or seized, or used excessive force against a third party); *Doe v. Hillsboro Indep. Sch. Dist.*, 113 F.3d 1412 (5th Cir.1997) (en banc).

54. 27 F.3d 1432 (9th Cir.1994), *cert. denied*, 513 U.S. 1148, 115 S.Ct. 1097, 130 L.Ed.2d 1065 (1995).

55. *Id.* at 1445.

56. *Id.*

Canton *opinion criticizes Justice White's references in the majority's opinion to a jury role in deciding "deliberate indifference." This provides support for the conclusion that the* Canton *majority did contemplate that juries would decide at least the fact-laden issues of whether the need for entity action was "so obvious" that failure to act would amount to deliberate indifference, and of whether a failure to train was the cause of the plaintiff's particular harm. But a "failure to train" case is more likely to reach a jury than a "failure to screen" case, after the Court's decision last Term in* Board of County Commissioners of Bryan County, Oklahoma v. Brown.[57] Bryan County *in effect holds that juries, as a matter of law, cannot reasonably find that a one-time negligent screening of the record of a law enforcement applicant amounts to a local government's actionable "policy" unless the subsequent unconstitutional conduct of the officer is virtually identical to the past deficiency or dereliction that more careful screening would have unearthed*[58]*. By contrast, the fact that failure to train allegations, as in* Canton, *target conduct that typically recurs enhances the plaintiff's ability to show that a particular, even a single failure to train caused his injuries.*[59]

For the same reason, the more stringent *Bryan County* standard should not defeat cases in which the plaintiff attempts to show entity responsibility through custom, as opposed to policy. That is, custom claims—even more certainly than failure to train claims, and wholly unlike claims of isolated, inadequate screening—by definition entail recurring, widespread instances of constitutional misconduct.[60] Custom claims remain an important alternative to a showing of municipal "policy." For instance, when a municipality has a valid "policy" on the books and has taken measures to train its employees about a particular type of conduct with unconstitutional potential, the only recourse for a plaintiff harmed by a lower level municipal employee (provided she is not a delegated final policymaker and that her unconstitutional act, and underlying rationale for it, have not been ratified by a final policymaker) is to establish that the lower level employee's actions were part of a widespread municipal "custom."

57. 520 U.S. 397, 117 S.Ct. 1382, 137 L.Ed.2d 626 (1997), discussed *supra.*

58. *See, e.g., Morris v. Crawford County,* 299 F.3d 919 (8th Cir.2002) (where deputy sheriff's sole violent pre-hire act was slapping of an inmate, and the instant allegations concerned excessive force by utilizing a knee drop that severed the detainee's intestine, the requisite causal connection between county's failure to screen and the resulting constitutional harm was absent).

59. *Id.* at 409–410. In fact the Fifth Circuit so held on remand in *Brown v. Bryan County,* 219 F.3d 450, 462 (5th Cir. 2000). But it deems this "single incident exception" rare. *Cozzo v. Tangipahoa Parish Council–President Government,* 262 F.3d 501, 515 (5th Cir.2001), *opinion withdrawn and superseded,* 279 F.3d 273 (5th Cir. 2002). *See also, Graham v. County of Washtenaw,* 358 F.3d 377 (6th Cir. 2004) (county's policy of delegating authority to contract provider to make medical care decisions respecting prisoners not the cause or "moving force" of inmate's death).

60. *See* cases collected at § 2.31, footnote 19, *supra; Cozzo v. Tangipahoa Parish Council–President Government,* 279 F.3d 273, 290 (5th Cir. 2002); *Griffin v. City of Opa–Locka,* 261 F.3d 1295, 1311, 1313–1314 (11th Cir.2001), *cert. denied,* 535 U.S. 1033, 122 S.Ct. 1789, 152 L.Ed.2d 648 (2002) (upholding city liability based on, respectively, custom evidence and evidence of inadequate screening violating *Bryan County*).

Apart from some confusion in decisions of the Seventh and Eighth Circuits, the lower federal courts, in the absence of definitive Supreme Court guidance, appear to have developed a rough consensus on what plaintiffs must prove to show a "custom."[61] First, a plaintiff must establish that a municipal "custom" exists. While the number of unconstitutional actions necessary to establish a "custom" is essentially a question of fact, the "custom" usually must occur with sufficient frequency and duration to be attributed to the municipality; it cannot be based on isolated or sporadic incidents of conduct.

Second, a final policymaker (or delegated final policymaker with nonreviewable decision-making authority) must have actual or constructive knowledge of the "custom." While actual knowledge is a fortiori sufficient to establish this element, liability is usually imputed to the municipality via constructive knowledge—the unconstitutional practice is so widespread or flagrant the final policymaking officials should have known about it. The Ninth and Tenth Circuits have abandoned this second element because it is somewhat duplicative.[62] If an unconstitutional practice is found to be so pervasive and widespread as to constitute a municipal "custom," it will necessarily be sufficient to impute constructive knowledge to the municipality. The Seventh and Eighth Circuits have strayed from their sister circuits on this second element, requiring plaintiffs to establish the municipality's deliberate indifference to the custom.[63] Seemingly contrary to recurrent Supreme Court indications that deliberate indifference is a requirement only of the "policy" mode of entity liability, those circuits characterize deliberate indifference as an element of "custom" as well.

61. *Bordanaro v. McLeod*, 871 F.2d 1151 (1st Cir. 1989); *Miller v. Kennebec County*, 219 F.3d 8, 12–13 (1st Cir. 2000); *Sorlucco v. New York City Police Department*, 971 F.2d 864, 873 (2nd Cir. 1992); *Jeffes v. Barnes*, 208 F.3d 49 (2nd Cir. 2000); *Andrews v. City of Philadelphia*, 895 F.2d 1469 (3rd Cir. 1990); *Bielevicz v. Dubinon*, 915 F.2d 845 (3rd Cir. 1990); *Spell v. McDaniel*, 824 F.2d 1380 (4th Cir. 1987); *Carter v. Morris*, 164 F.3d 215 (4th Cir. 1999); *Pineda v. City of Houston*, 291 F.3d 325 (5th Cir. 2002); *Gregory v. Shelby County, Tennessee*, 220 F.3d 433, 442 (6th Cir. 2000); *Alkire v. Irving*, 330 F.3d 802, 815 (6th Cir. 2003); *Jones v. City of Chicago*, 856 F.2d 985, 996 (7th Cir. 1988); *Gable v. City of Chicago*, 296 F.3d 531, 537 (7th Cir. 2002); *Harris v. City of Pagedale*, 821 F.2d 499, 504 (8th Cir. 1987); *Ware v. Jackson County, Missouri*, 150 F.3d 873, 880 (8th Cir. 1998); *Thompson v. City of Los Angeles*, 885 F.2d 1439, 1443–44 (9th Cir. 1989); *Navarro v. Block*, 72 F.3d 712, 715 (9th Cir. 1995); *Trevino v. Gates*, 99 F.3d 911, 918–20 (9th Cir. 1996); *Starrett v. Wadley* , 876 F.2d 808, 820 (10th Cir. 1989); *Lankford v. City of Hobart*, 73 F.3d 283, 286 (10th Cir. 1996); *Anaya v. Crossroads Managed Care Sys.*, 195 F.3d 584, 592 (10th Cir. 1999); *Brown v. City of Fort Lauderdale*, 923 F.2d 1474, 1481 (11th Cir. 1991); *Griffin v. City of Opa–Locka*, 261 F.3d 1295, 1308 (11th Cir. 2001); *Cuesta v. School Bd. of Miami–Dade County, Florida*, 285 F.3d 962, 967 (11th Cir. 2002); *Carter v. District of Columbia*, 795 F.2d 116, 122 (D.C. Cir. 1986); *Warren v. District of Columbia*, 353 F.3d 36, 38 (D.C. Cir. 2004).

62. *Thompson v. City of Los Angeles*, 885 F.2d 1439, 1443–44 (9th Cir. 1989); *Navarro v. Block*, 73 F.3d 712, 715 (9th Cir. 1995); *Trevino v. Gates*, 99 F.3d 911, 918–20 (9th Cir. 1996); *Starrett v. Wadley* , 876 F.2d 808, 820 (10th Cir. 1989); *Lankford v. City of Hobart*, 72 F.3d 283, 286 (10th Cir. 1996); *Anaya v. Crossroads Managed Care Sys.*, 195 F.3d 584, 592 (10th Cir. 1999).

63. *Jones v. City of Chicago*, 856 F.2d 985, 996 (7th Cir. 1988); *Gable v. City of Chicago*, 296 F.3d 531, 537 (7th Cir. 2002); *Harris v. City of Pagedale*, 821 F.2d 499, 504 (8th Cir. 1987); *Ware v. Jackson County, Missouri*, 150 F.3d 873, 880 (8th Cir. 1998).

The third and final element required to establish 'custom' is causation. The municipal 'custom' must cause the plaintiff's constitutional deprivation and does so when either an affirmative or other fairly direct casual link is established between the plaintiff's injury and the municipality's unconstitutional 'custom.'

A separate procedural development somewhat diminishes the practical utility of the *Canton* "omissions" approach, despite its potential access to trial by jury. Under the Supreme Court's solicitous treatment of summary judgment, entities can achieve dismissal before trial by convincing the judge that no reasonable jury could find each of the distinct, demanding elements of deliberate indifference by a preponderance of the evidence.[64] But the Court's June 2000 decision in *Reeves v. Sanderson Plumbing Products*[65] directs federal trial judges, in ruling on motions for judgment as a matter of law, and, by extension, summary judgment, to refrain from invading the jury's province by making credibility determinations, and specifically to credit only the unimpeached and uncontradicted evidence favoring the moving party.

In any event liability of the government itself now lingers only in the relatively rare situations where the entity broadcasts the unconstitutionality of its practice in a formal pronouncement;[66] acts pursuant to its legislative body,[67] positive state legislation,[68] or through an acknowledged final policymaking official; manifestly endorses subordinates' discrete decisions through delegation or ratification at the highest administrative level;[69] or inflicts the federal injury through an omission characterized by "deliberate indifference"[70] or through a long-standing, routine practice amounting to "custom." Further, in all but the last two situations, the question will be one of state law to be decided before trial by the court rather than by a jury.[71] All of these paths to "policy," and hence to an

64. *See Anderson v. Liberty Lobby, Inc.*, 477 U.S. 242, 252, 106 S.Ct. 2505, 2512, 91 L.Ed.2d 202 (1986) (noting in a First Amendment action that, in ruling on summary judgment under Federal Rule of Civil Procedure 56, a trial judge should consider "whether a reasonable factfinder could conclude ... the plaintiff had shown actual malice with convincing clarity"). *Trevino v. Gates*, 99 F.3d 911, 920 (9th Cir.1996) (rejecting plaintiff's attempted showing of custom on summary judgment). These ramifications of *Canton* are discussed in more detail in Chapter 5.

65. 530 U.S. 133, 120 S.Ct. 2097, 147 L.Ed.2d 105 (2000).

66. *See Monell v. Department of Soc. Servs.*, 436 U.S. 658, 98 S.Ct. 2018, 56 L.Ed.2d 611 (1978).

67. *See Owen v. City of Independence*, 445 U.S. 622, 100 S.Ct. 1398, 63 L.Ed.2d 673 (1980).

68. *See Pembaur v. City of Cincinnati*, 475 U.S. 469, 106 S.Ct. 1292, 89 L.Ed.2d 452 (1986).

69. *See City of St. Louis v. Praprotnik*, 485 U.S. 112, 108 S.Ct. 915, 99 L.Ed.2d 107 (1988).

70. *See City of Canton v. Harris*, 489 U.S. 378, 109 S.Ct. 1197, 103 L.Ed.2d 412 (1989). *See also Plumeau v. School Dist. No. 40 County of Yamhill*, 130 F.3d 432 (9th Cir.1997) (student had due process right to be free from state-imposed violations of bodily integrity but failure to raise sufficient evidence of school district's custom or policy of ignoring complaints of unconstitutional conduct barred entity liability).

71. See discussion of *Canton, supra. Accord, Jeffes v. Barnes*, 208 F.3d 49, 57–61 (2d Cir.), *cert. denied*, 531 U.S. 813, 121 S.Ct. 47, 148 L.Ed.2d 16 (2000) (whether official is final policymaker in the relevant area of municipality's business is to be determined by state and local positive law, supplemented by custom or usage that has the force of law). *See also infra* § 5.105. For an opinion that canvasses all these alternative routes to "policy," see *Trevino v. Gates*,

actionable prima facie claim, are strewn with obstacles not presented by respondeat superior.[72]

Recent restrictions on the substantive reach of due process contribute to the decreasing utility of the Reconstruction Statutes in actions complaining about the ordinary, daily employment decisions of government employers. Citing its concern that the Due Process Clause not become a font of tort law, the Supreme Court held in *Collins v. City of Harker Heights, Texas*[73] that Due Process, far from assuring relief against mistaken or demonstrably erroneous personnel decisions, does not even guarantee municipal (or, presumably, state or county) government employees "a workplace that is free of unreasonable risks of harm."[74]

The case was brought by the widow of a city employee who died of asphyxia after entering a manhole over a sewer line in the course of his employment duties. The complaint alleged that the city was on notice from a prior incident of the general risks of entering its sewer lines and that it had a custom and policy of failing to train about those dangers. But there was no allegation that plaintiff's decedent's supervisor inflicted any deliberate harm or, in the Court's words, that he "knew or should have known that there was a significant risk" that the decedent would be injured when the supervisor directed him to enter the sewer.

The Court accepted for purposes of the motion to dismiss that the complaint alleged deliberate indifference arising from the city's failure to train sufficiently to satisfy the *City of Canton* variant on *Monell's* custom or policy prerequisite to § 1983 liability. Further, the Court rejected two blanket bars on the use of § 1983 that had been erected by the court of appeals below: plaintiff was not per se precluded from proceeding either because the injury was inflicted against a government employee or because she failed to allege an "abuse of governmental power separate and apart from . . . proof of a constitutional violation."

Nevertheless, the Court found no predicate Due Process violation and hence no violation of § 1983. It acknowledged that in certain unusual situations—it referred to the retaliation for political speech at issue in *Praprotnik*, the gender discrimination asserted in *Monell*, and arbitrary conduct that shocks the conscience—government employees could state First Amendment, Equal Protection, or Due Process claims. But it wrote that the Due Process Clause has principally been applied to deliberate decisions by governmental officials. The Court implied that a government employee who voluntarily accepted an offer of employment and hence is not in custody could state a due process claim with respect

99 F.3d 911, esp. at 918 and 918 n.2. (9th Cir.1996).

72. *See* Kramer & Sykes, 1987 Sup.Ct. Rev. at 254.

73. 503 U.S. 115, 112 S.Ct. 1061, 117 L.Ed.2d 261 (1992).

74. The Court has reemphasized this point by recognizing that the government has a freer hand in regulating its employees' speech than those of ordinary citizens because of the enhanced efficiency concern it has as employer and not simply as sovereign. *Waters v. Churchill*, 511 U.S. 661, 114 S.Ct. 1878, 128 L.Ed.2d 686 (1994).

to the regular duties of that employment only by alleging conduct evincing some level of culpability greater than mere negligence. The Court distinguished conditions of custody or confinement that implicate liberty and trigger some minimal substantive due process standards of care for arrestees because the state has placed them in peril, increased their risk of harm, or acted to render them more vulnerable to danger.[75] In brief, the government employer and employee do not stand in the kind of "special relationship" characterized by official physical restraint or custody that on occasion has warranted an exception to the general rule that the state has no constitutional duty to protect persons from negligence or third-person private violence.[76]

75. Citing *Revere v. Massachusetts General Hosp.*, 463 U.S. 239, 103 S.Ct. 2979, 77 L.Ed.2d 605 (1983); pretrial detainees, *Bell v. Wolfish*, 441 U.S. 520, 99 S.Ct. 1861, 60 L.Ed.2d 447 (1979); convicts, *Turner v. Safley*, 482 U.S. 78, 107 S.Ct. 2254, 96 L.Ed.2d 64 (1987); mental patients, *Youngberg v. Romeo*, 457 U.S. 307, 102 S.Ct. 2452, 73 L.Ed.2d 28 (1982); *Penilla v. Huntington Park*, 115 F.3d 707 (9th Cir.1997) (per curiam), *cert. denied*, 524 U.S. 904, 118 S.Ct. 2059, 141 L.Ed.2d 137 (1998) (plaintiff stated due process claim against officers who increased his medical risk by canceling a 911 call and removing him from public view, thereby rendering it impossible for him to receive emergency aid). But the proof requirements for this "state-created danger" theory are high. *See Ewolski v. City of Brunswick*, 287 F.3d 492 (6th Cir.2002) (because police faced limited and risky alternatives in attempting to deal with deranged man who had barricaded his family inside their home, they did not violate due process by unsuccessfully assaulting him with armored vehicle, even though he had then already retreated and did not pose immediate threat). *But cf. Albright v. Oliver*, 510 U.S. 266, 114 S.Ct. 807, 127 L.Ed.2d 114 (1994) (criminal defendant apparently still in custody has no substantive due process right to be free from baseless initiation of prosecution because his injury was potentially redressable under an amendment, the Fourth, more explicitly addressed to the type of government conduct at issue) (plurality opinion). *Cf. McCullah v. Gadert*, 344 F.3d 655 (7th Cir. 2003) (availability of state law malicious prosecution claim does not displace Fourth Amendment claim asserting wrongful arrest and detention).

76. Courts have found such a relationship where state agencies have removed children from their home and assumed guardianship, then exposed them knowingly or recklessly to placements posing serious risks of physical harm. *See Camp v. Gregory*, 67 F.3d 1286 (7th Cir.1995), *cert. denied*, 517 U.S. 1244, 116 S.Ct. 2498, 135 L.Ed.2d 190 (1996). But for the most part, this "special relationship" exception has not extended a duty of care enforceable under due process beyond involuntarily committed mental patients and incarcerated prisoners. *See, e.g., J.O. v. Alton Community Unit Sch. Dist. 11*, 909 F.2d 267, 272 (7th Cir.1990), *cert. denied*, 506 U.S. 1087, 113 S.Ct. 1066, 122 L.Ed.2d 371 (1993). For example, the relationship between a student and his school district usually falls outside the "special relationship" exception, for want of the physical custody element stressed by the Supreme Court in *DeShaney*. *See, e.g., Doe v. Hillsboro Indep. Sch. Dist.*, 113 F.3d 1412 (5th Cir.1997) (en banc) (compulsory school attendance creates neither a "special" or "custodial" relationship within the meaning of *DeShaney* adequate to hold a school board or upper-level school officials liable for a custodian's rape of student) (alternative holding); *Sargi v. Kent City Bd. of Educ.*, 70 F.3d 907 (6th Cir.1995) (no violation where driver failed to intervene after child had seizure on school bus); *Walton v. Alexander*, 44 F.3d 1297 (5th Cir. 1995) (en banc) ("special relationship" exception unavailable to student who voluntarily enrolled in residential special education program, defeating student's right to protection from sexual molestation by fellow student at a school for the deaf); *Stevens v. Umsted*, 131 F.3d 697, 700 (7th Cir.1997) (limiting "special relationship" to prisoners and involuntarily institutionalized individuals); *Johnson v. Dallas Indep. Sch. Dist.*, 38 F.3d 198 (5th Cir.1994), *cert. denied*, 514 U.S. 1017, 115 S.Ct. 1361, 131 L.Ed.2d 218 (1995); *Leffall v. Dallas Indep. Sch. Dist.*, 28 F.3d 521 (5th Cir.1994); *Graham v. Independent Sch. Dist. No. I–89*, 22 F.3d 991 (10th Cir.1994) (no § 1983 liability of school for independent conduct of its students); *D.R. v. Middle Bucks Area Vocational Tech. Sch.*, 972 F.2d 1364 (3d Cir. 1992), *cert. denied*, 506 U.S. 1079, 113 S.Ct. 1045, 122 L.Ed.2d 354 (1993); *J.O. v. Alton*

Despite *Collins*, it appears that a government employee may state a Due Process claim against her employing entity where the government has engaged in affirmative conduct that places the plaintiff in special danger. In *L.W. v. Grubbs*,[77] a registered nurse employed by a state correctional institution alleged that she was directed to work alone in a clinic with a particular inmate who "was a violent sex offender who had failed all treatment programs at the institution."[78] Purporting to distinguish *Collins* on this point, the Ninth Circuit observed that the government defendants thereby "took affirmative steps to place her at significant risk, and ... they knew of the risks." The court noted instances where this "danger creation" exception to the government's general exemption from liability for third-party acts[79] warranted upholding a due

Community Unit Sch. Dist. 11, 909 F.2d 267 (7th Cir.1990), *cert. denied*, 506 U.S. 1087, 113 S.Ct. 1066, 122 L.Ed.2d 371 (1993). *But cf. Doe v. Taylor Indep. Sch. Dist.*, 15 F.3d 443 (5th Cir.1994), *cert. denied*, 513 U.S. 815, 115 S.Ct. 70, 130 L.Ed.2d 25 (1994) (principal potentially liable for deliberate indifference to teacher's repeated and notorious sexual harassment of student). *Cf. Spivey v. Elliott*, 41 F.3d 1497 (11th Cir.1995) (no "clearly established" constitutional right of student at a residential school for the hearing impaired to protection from a classmate's sexual assault). Given the tilt of these decisions, it is not surprising that an appellate court has ruled that university officials enjoyed qualified immunity from liability for failing to protect a student from another student's threats, because it was not "clearly established" that they had a federal duty to protect him. *Alexander v. University of N. Fla.*, 39 F.3d 290 (11th Cir.1994), *cert. denied*, 514 U.S. 1067, 115 S.Ct. 1699, 131 L.Ed.2d 561 (1995). *See also Santamorena v. Georgia Military College*, 147 F.3d 1337 (11th Cir.1998) (school officials granted qualified immunity; not clearly established at the time that a voluntary custodial relationship between a residential military school and a resident student gave rise to constitutional right of protection from a private third party's rape of student on campus). School districts may be liable for failure to protect students from gender based harassment by fellow students under Title IX of the Education Amendments of 1972. *See* discussion in § 3.20 *infra*.

77. 974 F.2d 119 (9th Cir.1992), *cert. denied*, 508 U.S. 951, 113 S.Ct. 2442, 124 L.Ed.2d 660 (1993).

78. *Id.* at 120.

79. *DeShaney v. Winnebago County Dep't of Soc. Servs.*, 489 U.S. 189, 109 S.Ct. 998, 103 L.Ed.2d 249 (1989). The danger-creation exception has been summarized as follows: "If the state puts a man in a position of danger from private persons and then fails to protect him, it will not be heard to say that is role was merely passive...." *Bowers v. DeVito*, 686 F.2d 616 (7th Cir.1982). *See also Kallstrom v. Columbus, Ohio*, 136 F.3d 1055 (6th Cir.1998) (city could be liable under government-created danger exception for disclosing identifying information about undercover officers and their families to defense attorneys representing violent gang members). It is recognized in some circumstances by all the federal circuits. *See Butera v. District of Columbia*, 235 F.3d 637 (D.C.Cir.2001); *Frances–Colon v. Ramirez,* 107 F.3d 62, 64 (1st Cir.1997); *Dwares v. City of New York,* 985 F.2d 94, 99 (2d Cir.1993); *Kneipp v. Tedder,* 95 F.3d 1199, 1201 (3d Cir.1996); *Pinder v. Johnson* 54 F.3d 1169, 1175–77 (4th Cir.1995) (*en banc*), *cert. denied*, 516 U.S. 994, 116 S.Ct. 530, 133 L.Ed.2d 436 (1995); *McClendon v. City of Columbia*, 258 F.3d 432 (5th Cir.2001) (police officer's loan of gun to confidential informant increased danger to shooting victim who stated due process claim for injury inflicted by third-party informant); *Johnson v. Dallas Indep. Sch. Distr.* 38 F.3d 198, 200–01 (5th Cir. 1994), *cert. denied,* 514 U.S. 1017, 115 S.Ct. 1361, 131 L.Ed.2d 218 (1995); *Kallstrom v. City of Columbus,* 136 F.3d 1055, 1066–67 (6th Cir.1998); *Reed v. Gardner,* 986 F.2d 1122, 1125 (7th Cir.1993), *cert. denied*, 510 U.S. 947, 114 S.Ct. 389, 126 L.Ed.2d 337 (1993); *Gregory v. City of Rogers*, 974 F.2d 1006, 1010 (8th Cir.1992) (*en banc*), *cert. denied* 507 U.S. 913, 113 S.Ct. 1265, 122 L.Ed.2d 661 (1993); *Wood v. Ostrander*, 879 F.2d 583, 589–90 (9th Cir.1989), *cert. denied*, 498 U.S. 938, 111 S.Ct. 341, 112 L.Ed.2d 305 (1990); *Uhlrig v. Harder*, 64 F.3d 567, 572 & n. 7 (10th Cir.1995), *cert. denied*, 516 U.S. 1118, 116 S.Ct. 924, 133 L.Ed.2d 853 (1996); *Wyke v. Polk County Sch. Bd.*, 129 F.3d 560, 567 (11th Cir.1997). If, however, the court concludes that an

process claim on behalf of persons other than governmental employees,[80] and concluded that *Collins* did not preclude use of this exception by the plaintiff because of her employee status.[81]

officer failed to enhance the preexisting danger confronting the plaintiff, *see, e.g., Windle v. City of Marion*, 321 F.3d 658 (7th Cir.2003), *Jones v. Union, County, TN*, 296 F.3d 417 (6th Cir.2002), or did not due so through an "affirmative act," *Schieber v. City of Philadelphia*, 320 F.3d 409, 424 (3d Cir.2003) (Nygaard, J., concurring), *DeShaney* applies and there is no due process violation. *See also Schieber v. City of Philadelphia*, 320 F.3d 409, 417 (3d Cir.2003) (Stapleton, J.) (adding to the danger-creation exception to *DeShaney* the additional requirement, derived from *County of Sacramento v. Lewis*, 523 U.S. 833, 118 S.Ct. 1708, 140 L.Ed.2d 1043 (1998), that the officer's conduct must be shocking to the conscience to violate Due Process in this setting). *See Ruiz v. McDonnell*, 299 F.3d 1173 (10th Cir.2002) (danger-creation exception fails because state actors did not commit affirmative act increasing child's danger and state's conduct did not shock the conscience). And of course the danger-creation exception cannot apply if the evidence reveals that government officials lacked knowledge of the danger to which the plaintiff was exposed. *See Lewis v. Anderson*, 308 F.3d 768 (7th Cir.2002); *Morin v. Moore*, 309 F.3d 316 (5th Cir.2002).

80. *Sutton v. Utah State Sch. for the Deaf and Blind*, 173 F.3d 1226 (10th Cir. 1999) (allowing § 1983 individual failure to train/deliberate indifference substantive due process claim where state-controlled school principal, on notice of previous complaints, failed to train staff and institute measures to prevent another incident of sexual assault on child resident); *Cornelius v. Town of Highland Lake*, 880 F.2d 348 (11th Cir.1989), *cert. denied sub nom. Spears v. Cornelius*, 494 U.S. 1066, 110 S.Ct. 1784, 108 L.Ed.2d 785 (1990); *Wood v. Ostrander*, 879 F.2d 583 (9th Cir.1989), *cert. denied*, 498 U.S. 938, 111 S.Ct. 341, 112 L.Ed.2d 305 (1990). *But see Doe v. Hillsboro Indep. Sch. Dist.*, 113 F.3d 1412 (5th Cir.1997) (en banc) (danger-creation theory fails to impose liability on school district for placing student in same area as school custodian who raped her where officials had no knowledge of his criminal background); *Leffall v. Dallas Indep. Sch. Dist.*, 28 F.3d 521 (5th Cir.1994) (even a negligent failure to provide adequate security at a school dance would not fit within the state-created danger exception, because a substantive due process claim also requires showing that defendants' acted with a culpable state of mind akin to "deliberate indifference"). It remains clear that an ordinary citizen cannot state a due process claim against local government simply because its police fail to rescue her from the criminal depredations of another private actor unless there is a special relationship or the government created the peril in which she found herself. *Gazette v. City of Pontiac*, 41 F.3d 1061 (6th Cir.1994) (plaintiff's due process rights not violated where she was abducted by employee of private car wash). *See also Scott v. Moore*, 114 F.3d 51 (5th Cir.1997) (absent actual knowledge that its existing jail staffing policy created a substantial additional risk of harm to female detainees, a city had no due process duty to increase staffing). *But see Doe v. Washington County*, 150 F.3d 920 (8th Cir.1998) (county liable where sufficient evidence existed that county's policy of housing juvenile detainees in overcrowded conditions caused violation of constitutional rights of juvenile who was raped and tortured by cellmates).

81. The *Harker Heights* refusal to apply the "special relationship" or "danger creation" exceptions to due process claims by local government employees has been adhered to in *Martinez v. Uphoff*, 265 F.3d 1130 (10th Cir.2001) (rejecting "danger creation" substantive due process claim of prison guard's widow alleging failure to segregate certain inmates, inmate overcrowding, improper guard training, and inadequate staffing as insufficient to meet circuit's "conscience-shocking" gloss on theory); *Lewellen v. Metropolitan Gov't of Nashville and Davidson Co., Tenn.*, 34 F.3d 345 (6th Cir.1994), *cert. denied*, 513 U.S. 1112, 115 S.Ct. 903, 130 L.Ed.2d 787 (1995) (gross recklessness in exposing employee to high voltage lines not arbitrary because not intended to punish or retaliate) and *Henderson v. Gunther*, 931 P.2d 1150 (Colo. 1997). *Cf. Wallace v. Adkins*, 115 F.3d 427 (7th Cir.1997) (prison guard's claim that higher officials violated his substantive due process rights by assigning him to work in proximity to a prisoner who had threatened to kill him failed for want of evidence that the assignment presented greater-than-usual danger).

The Ninth Circuit has carved out yet another exception to *Collins*. In *Jensen v. City of Oxnard*,[82] the court allowed a suit by the widow of a police officer fatally shot on the job. The court found that the decedent retained his right to be free of unreasonable seizures by fellow officers, thus further limiting *Collins* to its facts.

But an argument could be made in such situations that even if there is a predicate due process violation, liability would in any event exceed the permissible scope of Section 1983. In *Monell*, Justice Brennan, writing for the majority, distinguished between the kinds of obligations that, consistent with the "dual sovereignty" theory prevailing in 1871 when the statute was enacted, could and could not constitutionally be imposed on local government entities by means of liability under Section 1983. Congress, he concluded, acted with the understanding that it could constitutionally enforce obligations already incumbent on local government by virtue of the constitution—for instance, to refrain from conducting unlawful searches and seizures, inflicting excessive force, or trampling first amendment freedoms. But Congress also believed that it could not, without unduly intruding on state sovereignty, saddle local government with fresh, affirmative obligations, like the duty to protect citizens from violence at the hands of other citizens that the rejected Sherman Amendment would indirectly have created. Yet in substance it is obligations of the latter sort that are sought to be enforced by "*DeShaney*" claims—those that would hold schools responsible for student-on-student violence or, more generally, would attribute the acts or omissions of third parties to local government entities. Section 1983 claims based on such rights might therefore ultimately be held subject to a good-faith immunity, even if cognizable constitutionally. This possibility is enhanced by a resurgence of dual sovereignty rhetoric in the opinions of the Court.[83]

Of course there are many other constitutional rights that were first declared, or applied as against the states, since 1871, and their enforcement through Section 1983 has therefore effectively imposed "new" constitutional obligations on local government. Indeed the same could be said of virtually all federal statutory rights enforced through Section 1983, the vast majority of which originated after 1871. Viewed this way, the third-party liability situations are merely a small subset of a huge number of "new" federal rights. And Section 1983 judgments have routinely vindicated these new rights, notwithstanding the *Monell* majority's conclusion that the 1871 Congress would have doubted its power to enforce them against local government.

Too, governmental employees frequently advance § 1983 claims alleging that race, sex, age or alienage discrimination on the job violates equal protection.[84] But these claims are also rather restricted. Presum-

82. 145 F.3d 1078 (9th Cir.), *cert. denied*, 525 U.S. 1016, 119 S.Ct. 540, 142 L.Ed.2d 449 (1998).

83. *See, e.g., New York v. United States*, 505 U.S. 144, 112 S.Ct. 2408, 120 L.Ed.2d 120 (1992); *Gregory v. Ashcroft*, 501 U.S. 452, 111 S.Ct. 2395, 115 L.Ed.2d 410 (1991).

84. The potential for equal protection claims is enlarged by the Supreme Court's recent decision in *Village of Willowbrook v. Olech*, 528 U.S. 562, 120 S.Ct. 1073, 145

ably because of the purposeful discrimination requirement inherent in the Equal Protection Clause itself, courts entertaining employment discrimination claims under § 1983 have eschewed Title VII's somewhat more easily proven "neutral practice/disproportionate adverse impact" theory in favor of the elements, defenses, allocation and order of proof developed in Title VII cases asserting intentional, individual disparate treatment.[85] In general, when § 1983 is used as a parallel remedy for employment discrimination—that is, when the defendant government entity has acted under "color of state law" and has injured the plaintiff through the application of "policy"—courts have equated the protection

L.Ed.2d 1060 (2000) (per curiam). Until that decision, it had generally been considered that an equal protection plaintiff had to show that he was a member of a suspect or semi-suspect class, had been deprived of a fundamental right, had been treated adversely relative to others similarly situated, or that the government's classification of him was not rationally related to a legitimate government interest. *See DeMuria v. Hawkes*, 328 F.3d 704 (2d Cir.2003) (class of one equal protection claim stated by residents alleging defendant police officer provided them a lesser degree of protection than typically afforded other residents and that officer acted arbitrarily and with malice because plaintiffs had dispute with his friend); *Shehee v. Luttrell*, 199 F.3d 295, 301 (6th Cir.1999) (*Bivens* claim). But in *Olech* the Court upheld as sufficient to state a claim allegations that the defendant village had singled plaintiff out for discriminatory treatment, by delaying and imposing special restrictions on plaintiff's application to connect their property to the local water supply, in retaliation for plaintiff's prior suit against the village. The allegation that the village's requirements were "irrational and wholly arbitrary" sufficed to state a "class of one" equal protection claim, even absent comparison with any other group more favorably treated, and without regard to plaintiffs' additional allegations of retaliatory motivation. *But cf. Nevel v. Village of Schaumburg*, 297 F.3d 673 (7th Cir.2002) (property owners whose request to improve historic landmark was denied failed to state claim where defendants had legitimate interest in upholding their rules and their animus towards plaintiffs was not sole cause for denial); *Purze v. Village of Winthrop Harbor*, 286 F.3d 452 (7th Cir.2002) (claim of property developer plaintiffs relying on traditional equal protection disparate treatment theory failed in view of evidence that there were relevant differences between them and allegedly comparable individuals); *Hilton v. City of Wheeling*, 209 F.3d 1005 (7th Cir.2000), *cert. denied*, 531 U.S. 1080, 121 S.Ct. 781, 148 L.Ed.2d 678 (2001) (no equal protection violation where plaintiff alleged adverse police treatment in comparison to treatment of neighbors, absent allegations of improper motive). And it is settled that the equal protection plaintiff, unlike his counterpart claiming under the Due Process Clause, need not allege a legally cognizable property right or liberty interest, only that the state disparately treated similarly situated persons or acted irrationally and arbitrarily. *Thigpen v. Bibb County, Georgia*, 223 F.3d 1231 (11th Cir.2000).

There is, however, a separate § 1983 pleading limitation on equal protection claims by government employees. The government employment applicant or incumbent plaintiff does not state an Equal Protection claim if she merely alleges race, sex, religious or national origin discrimination that violates Title VII of the Civil Rights Act of 1964. *See Day v. Wayne County Bd. of Auditors*, 749 F.2d 1199, 1204–05 (6th Cir.1984) (no constitutional claim, and hence no claim under § 1983, where plaintiff alleged retaliation violating only Title VII). Nevertheless, the evidence required to establish a properly alleged equal protection claim mirrors the evidence required to recover under Title VII. *See Morris v. Oldham County Fiscal Court*, 201 F.3d 784 (6th Cir.2000) (dismissing sexual harassment claim under § 1983 because parallel claim under Title VII failed). Governmental employees also bring § 1981 claims alleging racial discrimination in the right to make and enforce contracts. The Supreme Court has required use of Title VII's intentional discrimination proof mode in these actions (against private as well as public employers), *Patterson v. McLean Credit Union*, 491 U.S. 164, 186, 109 S.Ct. 2363, 2377, 105 L.Ed.2d 132 (1989), because the Court has construed § 1981 itself to be violated only upon proof of intentional discrimination. *General Bldg. Contractors Ass'n, Inc. v. Pennsylvania*, 458 U.S. 375, 102 S.Ct. 3141, 73 L.Ed.2d 835 (1982).

85. *See St. Mary's Honor Ctr. v. Hicks*, 509 U.S. 502, 506 n. 1, 113 S.Ct. 2742, 2747 n. 1, 125 L.Ed.2d 407 (1993).

afforded by the two statutes and hence accepted for § 1983 purposes the same proof modes that establish intentional discrimination under Title VII.[86] Harassment on the basis of national origin has thus been held actionable on the same terms under § 1983 as under Title VII.[87] But reliance on § 1983 as a separate remedy for violation of Title VII also submits the plaintiff to the additional requirements of § 1983: the policy element against entity employers, and the qualified immunity defense to claims against individual superiors.[88]

§ 2.33 No Affirmative Defense of Immunity for Entity Defendants

Despite the limits on government employee suits against their entities, and the increasingly difficult "policy" barrier facing all § 1983 plaintiffs who sue government entities, the Court has held that entity defendants enjoy no affirmative defense comparable to the immunity enjoyed by defendant individuals. In *Owen v. City of Independence*,[1] the Court denied municipalities a good faith immunity from suit under § 1983, discounting the likelihood that entity liability would chill the vigorous execution of government function. The majority questioned whether "the hazard of municipal loss will deter a public officer from the conscientious exercise of his duties."[2] Denying entities immunity appears to recognize the protection they enjoy from the restrictions that *Monell* places upon the prima facie claim; seldom will an isolated entity act meet the rigors of "policy."[3] (The Court has protected public funds to some

86. *See Wu v. Thomas*, 863 F.2d 1543, 1549 n. 9 (11th Cir.1989); *Alexander v. Chicago Park Dist.*, 773 F.2d 850, 856 (7th Cir.1985), *cert. denied*, 475 U.S. 1095, 106 S.Ct. 1492, 89 L.Ed.2d 894 (1986); *Carrion v. Yeshiva Univ.*, 535 F.2d 722, 729 (2d Cir.1976); *Duffy v. Wolle*, 123 F.3d 1026, 1037 (8th Cir.1997), *cert. denied*, 523 U.S. 1137, 118 S.Ct. 1839, 140 L.Ed.2d 1090 (1998) (recognizing that the *McDonnell–Douglas* framework is applicable in § 1983 cases, and allowing the same for *Bivens* claims). Most circuits have held or implied that a government employee plaintiff may bring a § 1983 claim based on an equal protection violation without asserting an available companion claim under Title VII. *See Thigpen v. Bibb County, Georgia*, 223 F.3d 1231 (11th Cir.2000); *Annis v. County of Westchester*, 36 F.3d 251, 254–55 (2d Cir.1994) (listing cases). A § 1983 claim by a government employee might be displaced by Title VII only if the § 1983 claim were based solely on a violation of Title VII itself, rather than on an equal protection or other constitutional violation. *See Day v. Wayne County Bd. of Auditors*, 749 F.2d 1199, 1204–05 (6th Cir.1984). All circuits seem to agree that the government employee plaintiff may bring the Title VII claim and a constitutionally-based § 1983 claim together. In sharp contrast, the availability of Title VII displaces rather than supplements relief under 42 U.S.C.A. § 1985(3) and, for federal employees, under § 1981. *See* § 1.6.

87. *Boutros v. Canton Reg'l Transit Auth.*, 997 F.2d 198 (6th Cir.1993).

88. *See Wu v. Thomas*, 996 F.2d 271 (11th Cir.1993), *cert. denied sub nom. Wu v. Board of Trustees*, 511 U.S. 1033, 114 S.Ct. 1543, 128 L.Ed.2d 195 (1994) (upholding qualified immunity defense to liability or conduct arguably but not clearly violating Title VII).

§ 2.33

1. 445 U.S. 622, 100 S.Ct. 1398, 63 L.Ed.2d 673 (1980).

2. *Id.* at 656, 100 S.Ct. at 1418.

3. *Compare Pembaur*, 475 U.S. at 484–85 (noting that the assistant prosecutor's advice to deputies to break down door to serve capiases constituted policy in violation of Fourth Amendment when state law specifically sanctioned the advice-giving function) and *City of Newport v. Fact Concerts, Inc.*, 453 U.S. 247, 253, 101 S.Ct. 2748, 2752, 69 L.Ed.2d 616 (1981) (recognizing that a vote by the City Council itself

degree by precluding punitive damages even when an entity action lies).[4]

Owen denied the municipality only the *qualified* or "good faith" immunity enjoyed by its agents for executive or administrative acts; it did not explicitly address whether an entity could derivatively claim absolute immunity when called to account for the legislative or judicial functions of its agents. The concept of absolute immunity for entities is somewhat peculiar on its face because, at least in the context of legislative acts, it seeks immunity for prototypical, officially authorized government policies—the kind of conduct for which *Monell* subjected entities to liability in the first place. Until recently, the circuit courts uniformly acknowledged this incongruity, rejecting assertions of absolute legislative immunity by local government entities and individual legislators sued in their official capacity.[5] Further, in *Lake Country Estates, Inc. v. Tahoe Regional Planning Agency*,[6] the Supreme Court, in extending legislative immunity to regional legislators, did not confer it on the agency they served. And in *Spallone v. United States*,[7] the Supreme Court, presented with claims of absolute immunity by local legislators, noted without criticism the lower courts' decisions finding liability on the part of the legislators' entity, the city.

But two pronouncements by circuit court judges at least suggest that an entity may claim the absolute immunity of its individual legislators.[8] This development would appear to be stillborn in light of the latest observations on the subject by the Supreme Court in *Leatherman v. Tarrant County Narcotics Intelligence and Coordination Unit*,[9] where the Court rejected the Fifth Circuit's heightened pleading rule for § 1983 actions against municipalities.[10] Writing for a unanimous Court, Chief Justice Rehnquist dismissed the argument that the standard, more relaxed, requirements of notice pleading would improperly subject local government to expensive and time consuming discovery, thereby "eviscerating their immunity from suit...." That argument, he wrote, "wrongly equates freedom from liability [which the municipality would enjoy if the plaintiff cannot show the 'policy' required by *Monell* and its progeny] with immunity from suit...." *Monell* and *Owen*, he continued,

to cancel contract, based on content of group's music, violated First Amendment) with *Praprotnik*, 485 U.S. at 123, 108 S.Ct. at 924 (holding that a plaintiff's allegation that he was fired because he was a whistle-blower did not constitute policy if, inter alia, city employee who discharged plaintiff did not have final policy-making authority).

4. *See infra* § 2.34.

5. *See Reed v. Village of Shorewood*, 704 F.2d 943, 953 (7th Cir.1983) (municipality denied the absolute legislative immunity of its policymakers); *W.D.D., Inc. v. Thornbury Township*, 839 F.2d 151, 154 n. 3 (3d Cir.1988), vacated on other grounds, 850 F.2d 170 (3d Cir.1988), *cert. denied*, 488 U.S. 892, 109 S.Ct. 228, 102 L.Ed.2d 218 (1988); *Goldberg v. Town of Rocky Hill*, 973 F.2d 70 (2d Cir.1992).

6. 440 U.S. 391, 99 S.Ct. 1171, 59 L.Ed.2d 401 (1979).

7. 493 U.S. 265, 110 S.Ct. 625, 107 L.Ed.2d 644 (1990).

8. *Hollyday v. Rainey*, 964 F.2d 1441, 1443 (4th Cir.1992), *cert. denied*, 506 U.S. 1014, 113 S.Ct. 636, 121 L.Ed.2d 567 (1992) (opinion of Judge Hall); *Brown v. Crawford County*, 960 F.2d 1002, 1012 n. 17 (11th Cir.1992).

9. 507 U.S. 163, 113 S.Ct. 1160, 122 L.Ed.2d 517 (1993).

10. *See* discussion of *Leatherman* in Chapter 5, *infra*.

"make it quite clear that, unlike various government officials, municipalities do not enjoy immunity from suit—*either absolute or qualified*—under § 1983." Nevertheless, the requirement of deliberate indifference in failure to act or omission cases against entities, like the *Praprotnik* requirement that a final entity policymaking official approved or ratified the unconstitutional conduct, builds a fault or culpability showing into the plaintiff's own prima facie case.

§ 2.34 Punitive Damages Not Available

The menu of damages available to a plaintiff suing an individual and to a plaintiff suing an entity lays bare another asymmetry between the two cases. The case against an individual offers both compensatory and punitive damages, but, barring scarcely imaginable circumstances, the case against an entity defendant offers only compensatory damages.[1] In *City of Newport v. Fact Concerts, Inc.*,[2] the Court held that municipalities are ordinarily immune from punitive damages under § 1983. This is true even though establishing a violation by a municipality in effect requires proof of intentional discrimination—via established "policy"[3] or "deliberate indifference."[4]

The city of Newport, R.I., licensed plaintiff Fact Concerts, Inc. to present a jazz concert near the city. Shortly before the date of the concert, Fact Concerts hired a band city council members believed to be a rock and roll band. Although Fact Concerts explained that the band was in fact a jazz band, the council did not investigate that assertion, instead focusing on the fact that the band might attract a rowdy crowd. The facts indicate that the council was actually more concerned with the idea of avoiding rock and roll music than with the claimed public safety issues.[5] The potential revocation received considerable attention in the media, and although the band performed and the concert took place without incident, fewer than half the available tickets were sold. Fact Concerts brought suit against the city and its officials, alleging a violation of First Amendment rights and due process under color of state law, seeking both compensatory and punitive damages.

The Court noted two primary remedial goals of § 1983; deterring misconduct and compensating the injured.[6] Further, it observed that punitive damages are designed specifically to punish wrongdoers as well

§ 2.34

1. *See Memphis Community Sch. Dist. v. Stachura*, 477 U.S. 299, 106 S.Ct. 2537, 91 L.Ed.2d 249 (1986) (authorizing compensatory damages).

2. 453 U.S. 247, 271, 101 S.Ct. 2748, 2762, 69 L.Ed.2d 616 (1981). *Accord, Chestnut v. City of Lowell*, 305 F.3d 18 (1st Cir.2002) (in light of *City of Newport*, jury instruction permitting punitive damages against city in excessive force case was plain error).

3. *St. Louis v. Praprotnik*, 485 U.S. 112, 108 S.Ct. 915, 99 L.Ed.2d 107 (1988). *See supra* § 2.31.

4. *City of Canton v. Harris*, 489 U.S. 378, 109 S.Ct. 1197, 103 L.Ed.2d 412 (1989). *See supra* § 2.32.

5. *See* 453 U.S. at 250 n.3, 101 S.Ct. at 2751 n.3 (council members concerned with attracting "long-haired hangers-on").

6. *Id.* at 266–67, 101 S.Ct. at 2759–60.

as prevent future misconduct.[7] In light of these objectives, the Court concluded that punitive damages are not "sensibly" assessed against a government entity.[8] First, a municipality cannot act on its own, and a judgment assessing punitive damages against it would actually punish the taxpayers, rather than the wrongdoer.[9] Second, the Court reasoned that compensatory damages adequately deter § 1983 violations because (1) an official would not be deterred by the threat of damages assessed against his employer, (2) compensatory damages are just as likely as punitives to induce the public to vote a law-violating official out of office, and (3) large punitive damages are likely to endanger the financial integrity of governmental entities.[10]

Despite its concern to protect blameless taxpayers, the *Newport* Court did not foreclose completely the possibility of visiting punitive damages on entities in cases where its taxpayers could fairly be considered directly responsible for "an outrageous abuse of constitutional rights."[11] But such a case is scarcely imaginable. After one decision that rejected the possible exception, *Webster v. City of Houston*,[12] commentators asked, "If the[se] facts [...] do not attain the necessary level of outrageousness, what facts would?"[13]

In *Webster*, seventeen-year-old Randy Webster stole a van from a dealership, and three police officers gave chase. Randy eventually lost control of the van. The police removed him from the vehicle, subdued him, and *then* shot and killed him. Afterwards, they planted a weapon in his hand. At trial, the long-standing police department "policy" allowing the use of "throw down" weapons to cover-up police misconduct was revealed. The jury found that the City of Houston and the officers violated Randy Webster's constitutional rights and assessed punitive damages of $1 million against the officers and $200,000 against the city.

The Court of Appeals, relying on *City of Newport*, reversed the verdict as to punitive damages against the city. The majority noted that "the plight of Randy Webster, however reprehensible, however tragic, does not rise to the level of outrageous conduct" contemplated by *Newport*[14] because the Congress that drafted the original 1871 version of § 1983 lived in a time of terrible violence, too.

Circuit Judge Goldberg disagreed with the majority on this point. He argued that *Webster* fit the exception imagined by the *Newport* court. While the entire costs of the city's discrimination reached the *Newport* court in the form of lost revenue, the entire costs of the widely accepted

7. *Id.* at 268, 101 S.Ct. at 2760.

8. *Id.* at 267, 101 S.Ct. at 2760.

9. *Id.*

10. *Id.* at 268–70, 101 S.Ct. at 2760–61.

11. *Id.* at 267 n.29, 101 S.Ct. at 2760 n.29.

12. 689 F.2d 1220 (5th Cir.1982), *reh'g granted*, 711 F.2d 35 (5th Cir.1983). *See Webster v. City of Houston*, 739 F.2d 993 (5th Cir.1984), where the Court of Appeals reversed in part, on the issue that jury could have found municipal liability under the instructions.

13. *See* Low & Jeffries, *Civil Rights Actions*, 2d ed. (Foundation 1994) at 299 n.2.

14. 689 F.2d at 1229.

"throw down weapon" policy revealed in Webster did not reach the court. "It is only by threat of punitive damages that we can arouse policymakers from their dozing to eradicate policies such as this."[15] Goldberg's comments received considerable attention but have had little impact. Despite the escape hatch left by the Supreme Court in *City of Newport*, municipalities—local and state governments and their agencies—have remained immune from punitive damages. No reported case has been discovered that has found the kind of outrageous taxpayer—directed discrimination *Newport* requires for the imposition of punitive damages on entities.[16]

§ 2.35 A Hybrid: Suits Against State Officers in Their Official and Individual Capacities

Sharply to be distinguished from § 1983 claims against a state, and from "official-capacity" actions against an individual state officer, are "personal-capacity" suits intended to establish the officer's individual liability.

Will v. Michigan Department of State Police[1] teaches that the state itself is not a "person" liable under Section 1983; and neither, at least with respect to damages, is a state officer sued in his official capacity, since to that extent he is functionally only a stand-in for the state. But does the logic of *Will* also preclude damages from state officers named in their personal capacities for conduct undertaken in their official capacities? That is, since any defendant must have acted "under color of" state law to be liable under Section 1983, does this mean that the individual defendant has necessarily also acted "officially" and as such acquires the state's own immunity from Section 1983 liability?

The Supreme Court rejected this argument in *Hafer v. Melo*,[2] holding state officials named in their personal capacities fully responsible in damages for federal law violations, even though their injury-inflicting conduct took place under color of state law. The Court explained that "officers sued in their personal capacity come to court as individuals," even when the conduct for which they are sought to be held accountable was undertaken in their official capacities.[3] In a reverse spin on the argument rejected in *Monroe v. Pape*,[4] *Hafer* asserted alternatively that she could only be personally liable for those acts that were outside her authority or inessential to the performance of her official functions;

15. *Id.* at 1238.

16. For a recent example, see *Daskalea v. District of Columbia*, 227 F.3d 433 (D.C.Cir.2000) (taxpayers not directly responsible for the negligent supervision of jail employees that caused plaintiff's injuries).

§ 2.35

1. 491 U.S. 58, 109 S.Ct. 2304, 105 L.Ed.2d 45 (1989). See *infra* this section and § 2.42 for fuller discussion of *Will*.

2. 502 U.S. 21, 112 S.Ct. 358, 116 L.Ed.2d 301 (1991).

3. *Id.* at 26, 112 S.Ct. at 362.

4. There the individual defendants argued that they could only be acting "under color of" state law if their conduct were authorized and approved by their employing entities. *See* § 2.4, above.

essential, authorized conduct should be attributable to the state and therefore beyond the ambit of Section 1983. The Court rejected this position, too, observing that the statute typically reaches state executive and administrative conduct that violates federal law, subject only to qualified immunity, even when that conduct is official and necessary.

Hafer thus clarifies that a plaintiff may recover damages under Section 1983 against an individual state official sued in her *personal* capacity even though, per *Will*, the state itself is not suable in its own name. Of course in such personal-capacity actions, as in similar suits against city or county officials, the plaintiff need not show that the officer defendant acted pursuant to governmental policy or custom; on the other hand, such defendants, unlike those sued in an official capacity, may invoke the defense of qualified immunity.[5] At the same time, *Hafer* reaffirms that the Section 1983 plaintiff may still recover prospective relief (of a kind not forbidden by the Eleventh Amendment)[6] from a state official named as a defendant in her official capacity—in suits for prospective relief, in other words, the official—capacity defendant sued for prospective relief only is a "person."[7] Indeed because *Will* found the state not suable eo nominee under Section 1983, naming the state agent in her official capacity is the only route to injunctive or declaratory relief against federally unlawful state conduct.

When the plaintiff takes pains in drafting the complaint to indicate that he intends to sue the public official in her individual capacity, therefore, the official remains a full-fledged § 1983 "person" subject to all appropriate relief, including damages.[8] We thus have a variegated

5. *Hafer*, 502 U.S. at 25, 112 S.Ct. at 361.

6. In general, the Eleventh Amendment would forbid even prospective relief to the extent that the costs of future state compliance with federal law would include compensation to victims for past federal law violations. *See* discussion of *Edelman v. Jordan*, 415 U.S. 651, 94 S.Ct. 1347, 39 L.Ed.2d 662 (1974), *Milliken v. Bradley (II)*, 433 U.S. 267, 97 S.Ct. 2749, 53 L.Ed.2d 745 (1977), in § 5.35, and *Anderson v. Branen*, 17 F.3d 552 (2d Cir.1994) (supervisor held to same reasonableness standard as his subordinate officer).

7. *Will v. Michigan Dept. of State Police*, 491 U.S. 58, 71 n. 10, 109 S.Ct. 2304, 2312 n. 10, 105 L.Ed.2d 45 (1989). By analogy to the jurisprudence that had grown up under the Eleventh Amendment, the Court wrote that "official-capacity actions for prospective relief are not treated as actions against the State." *See Hinkle v. City of Clarksburg*, 81 F.3d 416 (4th Cir.1996); *Scott v. Henrich*, 39 F.3d 912 (9th Cir. 1994), *cert. denied*, 515 U.S. 1159, 115 S.Ct. 2612, 132 L.Ed.2d 855 (1995); *Thompson v. Boggs*, 33 F.3d 847 (7th Cir.1994), *cert. denied*, 514 U.S. 1063, 115 S.Ct. 1692, 131 L.Ed.2d 556 (1995); *Spears v. City of Louisville*, 27 F.3d 567 (6th Cir.1994).

8. *See Hafer v. Melo*, 502 U.S. 21, 112 S.Ct. 358, 116 L.Ed.2d 301 (1991). Failure to specify in the caption that the individual defendant is being sued in an individual capacity may result in a dismissal on Eleventh Amendment grounds if the official defendant is a state, *Shepherd v. Wellman*, 313 F.3d 963 (6th Cir.2002), or forfeit the plaintiff's right to damages. *Colvin v. McDougall*, 62 F.3d 1316 (11th Cir.1995). But where the caption is clear in naming a defendant individually, it provides that defendant adequate notice, even if the complaint names him only in his official capacity. *Marsh v. Butler County*, 225 F.3d 1243, 1251 n. 4 (11th Cir.2000). The Sixth Circuit has held that even if a plaintiff fails explicitly to allege that a defendant is sued in his individual capacity, if the "course of proceedings" subsequently informs Section 1983 defendants that they were so named, the complaint will not be deemed deficient. *Moore v. City of Harriman*, 272 F.3d 769 (6th Cir.2001). And the Seventh Circuit has adopted a rule that where the plaintiff alleges tortious conduct by individual officers

meaning for the word "person," depending on whether a state official is sued in her official or her individual capacities; and under the *Will* decision we also have a dual definition even within the category of official-capacity defendant: she is a § 1983 "person," and hence suable, only to the extent that the relief sought against her is the kind the Eleventh Amendment would permit against a state—that is, prospective relief.

The remaining question, then, is whether, where the plaintiff seeks prospective relief for a federal law violation against a local governmental entity, there is any utility in the common practice of joining the government agent as a companion "official capacity" defendant. If in fact the agent is deemed to serve a city, county or other local government or government agency that is truly distinct from the state, naming that agent in her official capacity appears to be a redundancy with no operative litigation significance: for both Eleventh Amendment and Section 1983 purposes, naming the official capacity defendant is simply another way of naming the entity itself,[9] and the local entity is suable directly as a "person." But on occasion there is room for genuine doubt about the entity's status as a "local" or "state" instrumentality. Although such determinations are ultimately a matter of federal law, they are sometimes highly unpredictable. The federal characterization may decide the question by analogy to factors used in Eleventh Amendment analysis; and it borrows heavily from a welter of potentially applicable state law provisions governing the organic relationship between the state and its subsidiaries, the allocation of functions between them, program funding, and financial responsibility.[10] Given this uncertainty, if there is any chance that the target government entity may be adjudged a tentacle of the state, the plaintiff's lawyer in search of prospective relief may find that the apparent redundancy of adding an official-capacity defendant agent represents salvation. Under *Hafer* and *Will*, the presence of the official-capacity defendant would preserve the possibility of obtaining prospective relief, and in turn attorney's fees,[11] although not

(as opposed to merely seeking injunctive relief against an official policy or custom), the defendants will be presumed sued in their individual capacities, even if the plaintiff fails to so specify. *Miller v. Smith*, 220 F.3d 491 (7th Cir.2000).

9. *See, e.g., Hafer*, discussing *Kentucky v. Graham*, 473 U.S. 159, 105 S.Ct. 3099, 87 L.Ed.2d 114 (1985). *See also Liebe v. Norton*, 157 F.3d 574, 578 (8th Cir.1998).

10. *See Callahan v. City of Philadelphia*, 207 F.3d 668 (3d Cir.2000). There the court used three Eleventh Amendment factors—whether the money that would be used to pay a judgment would come from the state treasury, the status of defendants under state law as state or county agents, and the degree of state supervisory and administrative authority over the defendants—to determine if the defendants, Philadelphia judges, were "persons" within the meaning of § 1983 as interpreted by *Will*. But while the court considered the first of those factors the most important in an Eleventh Amendment analysis, it deemed that factor less important in a § 1983 "person" analysis. Accordingly, it held the defendant judges not to be "persons" for § 1983 purposes even though their courts were largely funded locally, rather than by the Commonwealth of Pennsylvania. *See also* § 5.35, concerning the use of state law to characterize defendants as "the state" *vel non* for Eleventh Amendment purposes.

11. Fees to the prevailing party under the Civil Rights Attorney's Fees Awards Act of 1976, which was codified as the last sentence in 42 U.S.C.A. § 1988, would be available, notwithstanding the Eleventh Amendment, even if the Section 1983 action

damages. Naming a state official-capacity defendant out of prudence gains heightened importance after the Supreme Court's decision in *McMillian v. Monroe Co., Ala.*,[12] which somewhat increases the chance that a local final policymaking official may, with respect to specific functions, be deemed to be acting solely on behalf of the state, rather than a county or city, if state law so provides or suggests.

§ 2.36 Personal Liability of Supervisors Compared

The preceding sections have explored the prerequisites for liability of government entities and the alternative of suit against an entity official in her official capacity where the entity cannot be sued directly. The prima facie cases against both are identical, and neither enjoys any general immunity. Indeed where it is necessary to sue the official in her official capacity (as in the case of a state official whose entity cannot be reached directly under Section 1983), the actions differ only in the sphere of damages. An entity suable under the statute would be exposed to compensatory (though not punitive) damages, but its official sued officially is subject only to prospective relief and attorney's fees.

It is often advantageous, however, for the victim of a federal law violation to join a higher-ranking official as a defendant in her *personal* capacity, even when a claim does lie against the official's entity. The supervisor, manager, or high-ranking policymaking official may be liable under some circumstances where the entity would not be; and if adjudged liable, she may in appropriate cases have to respond in punitive damages, unavailable against the entity itself. In the discussion that follows, the word "supervisor" will denote such a superior official, sued in an "individual" or "personal" capacity for damages.

A plaintiff may seek to hold the supervisor defendant personally liable in a wide range of situations. A police chief, for example, might personally accompany subordinate officers who conduct a raid on the plaintiff's establishment. By so participating, she is probably subjecting herself to prima facie liability on the same terms as those pertaining to her subordinate officers. Alternatively, the plaintiff might seek to hold the supervisor responsible even absent such participation. For example, the chief might have pre-approved the raid despite information from which she knew or should have known that the raid might violate federal rights. Or she may have failed adequately to train or supervise the subordinate officers conducting the raid, a failure the plaintiff may try to

were heard in federal court. *Hutto v. Finney*, 437 U.S. 678, 98 S.Ct. 2565, 57 L.Ed.2d 522 (1978). Obviously, the arena in which the abrogation of Eleventh Amendment immunity declared by the 1976 Fees Act, and approved in *Hutto*, will operate is substantially narrowed by the Court's holding in *Will* that states sued in their own name under Section 1983 are entitled to dismissal for failure to state a claim on which relief can be granted. Nevertheless, *Hutto* should still have force in permitting fees in actions where the plaintiff seeks prospective relief against named state officials or where, for whatever reason, the state itself consents to a judgment or waives the defense available to it under *Will*.

12. 520 U.S. 781, 117 S.Ct. 1734, 138 L.Ed.2d 1 (1997). *McMillian* is discussed *supra*.

causally link to a deprivation of federal rights.[1] More generally, supervisory liability is imposed in the supervisor's individual capacity for his own culpable action or inaction in supervising, training, or controlling subordinates;[2] for acquiescing, condoning or fostering constitutional violations;[3] or for tolerating dangerous reckless conduct by subordinates in a way that tends to prove the supervisor's pre-existing disposition and policy;[4] and even for failing to reprimand or discharge.[5] Finally the chief, even if she had no knowledge that the raid in question was going to occur, may have promulgated a departmental policy that permitted or encouraged an unconstitutional raid.[6]

In the first, "participation" variant, there is no reason to differentiate the standards under which the chief should be liable from those applicable to the subordinates. In the terms of Section 1983, each is a "person" who through personal involvement has "subject[ed]" the plaintiff to a deprivation of federal rights. Absent evidence that the supervisory defendant personally participated in a federal law violation, either alone or with subordinates, this "participation" route to supervisory liability will fail.[7]

In all the latter, non-participation situations, however, the chief's conduct may be reached by the immediately following, disjunctive phrase of the statute: she is then a "person" who has "cause[d the plaintiff] to be subjected" to the federal law violation. In outlining the terms of an entity's liability in *Monell*, the Supreme Court addressed this language in a way that also seems peculiarly appropriate to these "non-participation" situations involving a supervisor:

§ 2.36

1. *See, e.g., Sutton v. Utah State Sch. for the Deaf and Blind*, 173 F.3d 1226 (10th Cir.1999) (allowing § 1983 individual failure to train substantive due process claim where state-controlled school principal, on notice of previous complaints, failed to train staff and institute measures to prevent another incident of sexual assault on child resident). Contrast *Burge v. Parish of St. Tammany*, 187 F.3d 452 (5th Cir.1999), *on remand,* 2000 WL 815879 (E.D.La.2000) (prosecution's failure to disclose material, exculpatory evidence so obviously violated *Brady* rule that violation could not be attributed to supervising district attorney's failure to train).

2. *See, e.g., Clay v. Conlee*, 815 F.2d 1164, 1170 (8th Cir.1987).

3. *See, e.g., Larez v. City of Los Angeles*, 946 F.2d 630, 646–47 (9th Cir.1991) (Los Angeles Police Chief Daryl Gates allegedly "set a tone which condoned and encouraged the use of excessive force"); *Meade v. Grubbs*, 841 F.2d 1512, 1528 (10th Cir.1988) (supervisor's mere acquiescence in constitutional deprivations).

4. *See, e.g., Grandstaff v. City of Borger*, 767 F.2d 161, 171 (5th Cir.1985), *cert. denied*, 480 U.S. 916, 107 S.Ct. 1369, 94 L.Ed.2d 686 (1987).

5. *McRorie v. Shimoda*, 795 F.2d 780, 784 (9th Cir.1986).

6. The authors are indebted to Michael Rafter, Mercer Law School Class of 1995, for suggesting these variations, which he elaborated from the facts of *Swint v. Wadley*, 5 F.3d 1435 (11th Cir.1993), modified on reh'g, 11 F.3d 1030 (11th Cir.1994), *cert. denied*, 514 U.S. 1003, 115 S.Ct. 1312, 131 L.Ed.2d 194 (1995).

7. *See, e.g., Palmer v. Marion County*, 327 F.3d 588 (7th Cir.2003) (no showing sheriff was personally involved in beating of pretrial detainee by other jail inmates); *Meloy v. Bachmeier*, 302 F.3d 845 (8th Cir. 2002) (prison medical director did not personally treat inmate and functioned only in administrative role); *Doe ex rel. Doe v. City of Roseville*, 296 F.3d 431 (6th Cir.2002) (school superintendents and principals did not participate in (or encourage, authorize, approve or knowingly acquiesce in) sexual abuse of student by teacher and accordingly did not bear supervisory liability).

> Indeed, the fact that Congress did specifically provide that A's [that is, the subordinate's] tort became B's [that is, the supervisor's] liability if B "caused" A to subject another [that is, the plaintiff] to a tort suggests that Congress did not intend § 1983 liability to attach where such causation was absent.[8]

To observe that supervisors may be liable under the "caused to be subjected" branch of the statute, however, does not supply the precise elements of such liability. Outside the direct participation situation, after all, the supervisor and the subordinate are differently situated, for only the subordinate has inflicted the ultimate injury on the plaintiff on the sense of the traditional tort concept of proximate cause. Yet the supervisor, like the subordinate, is an individual defendant sued in her personal capacity, who therefore may assert the defense of qualified immunity[9]. On the other hand, it is that same humanness of the supervisor that sets her apart from the entity she serves. The supervisor can therefore be liable where the entity sometimes cannot, for "causing" the subordinate to inflict an injury or by failing to take precautions (or taking the wrong precautions) against a risk of constitutional harm that should have been apparent from a pattern of prior similar events.[10] And perhaps because the supervisor, unlike her entity, can fall back on the generous qualified immunity defense, there is rough justice in holding her prima facie responsible for failing to avoid harm even in the unprecedented situations in which *City of Canton* always absolves the entity. There are thus two key distinguishing characteristics of supervisory liability in non-participation contexts: the supervisor faces civil liability because of constitutional injury inflicted by a subordinate, yet sometimes is in a better position to know about and prevent the injury than her employing entity.

This odd situation of the "man in the middle" gives rise to incongruous possibilities. It would seem reasonable to assert, for example, in line with the conventional wisdom that Section 1983 simply provides remedies for violations declared elsewhere in federal law, that the supervisor may only be liable when she has violated all the elements of the same predicate right infringed by her subordinate. As we have seen, however, some predicate rights—notably those protected by Equal Protection and the Eighth Amendment—are violated only when the defendant is shown to have acted with a highly culpable state of mind.[11] In the

8. *Monell v. Department of Soc. Servs.*, 436 U.S. 658, 98 S.Ct. 2018, 56 L.Ed.2d 611 (1978).

9. *See, e.g., Cottone v. Jenne*, 326 F.3d 1352 (11th Cir.2003) (prison supervisory officials who had complied with consent decree entitled to qualified immunity).

10. *See, e.g., Quinn v. Monroe County*, 330 F.3d 1320 (11th Cir.2003) (official who was not "final policymaker" for purposes of attributing his actions to defendant county was nevertheless an "official decisionmaker" with respect to the plaintiff's termination and hence subject to individual liability).

11. The requisite scienter is described in Equal Protection decisions as involving an "intent" to discriminate. In most Eighth Amendment situations involving prisoners, it takes the form of "deliberate indifference" defined as a failure to prevent substantial bodily harm despite actual knowledge of the particular risk that will produce it.

failure to train or failure to supervise variations, the plaintiff will often be unable to prove that the supervisor failed to act with any such culpable state of mind. Yet in some such cases—those where a pattern of recurring situations should have made the risk of constitutional injury created by a failure to train or supervise "obvious"—the supervisor's entity would be liable under the standard of *City of Canton*. The supervisor might then escape liability for which both his subordinate and entity might be responsible.[12]

An alternative approach overcomes this incongruity but generates others. The "causation interpretation" holds that a defendant (e.g., a supervisor) who acts or fails to act under color of state law in such a way as to require, encourage, or permit another (e.g., a subordinate), also acting under color of state law, to violate the plaintiff's federally guaranteed rights, has herself violated Section 1983. It is of course prerequisite that the *subordinate* committed all the elements composing the predicate violation, including any requisite state of mind; but does it suffice for the liability of the supervisor that she violated some separate duty, deriving from Section 1983, federal common law, or even state law, to prevent the subordinate from inflicting injury? Under this interpretation, a defendant supervisor whose failure to forestall a subordinate from infringing a federal right is merely negligent or reckless might be liable even though she did not possess the more culpable state of mind that the subordinate must have had in order to violate that right.[13]

The foregoing interpretation solves the incongruity of absolving a supervisor from liability for an intent-based predicate violation by the subordinate even where the entity would be liable under the standard of *City of Canton*. But if the requisite state of mind for supervisory liability is mere negligence, the supervisor under this approach might be liable in cases where the entity, under *City of Canton*, is not. And even if the prerequisite mental state for supervisory liability is brought into line with the kind of "deliberate indifference" described in *Canton*, this approach violates the understanding that Section 1983 itself (as distinguished from some of the predicate rights for which it provides a remedy) has no uniform state of mind requirement. Even if, for example, as is the case with most First and Fourth Amendment violations, the plaintiff need not prove any scienter on the part of the *subordinate*, the supervisor could be liable only upon proof of a reckless state of mind mandated by Section 1983 itself. Further, as is true of the entity's own

12. Professor Nahmod has favored this "Fourteenth Amendment" interpretation of Section 1983 that imposes liability only on defendants who can be found to have violated each of the elements of a predicate constitutional or statutory standard, including any requisite scienter. *See* Nahmod, *Constitutional Accountability in Section 1983 Litigation*, 68 Iowa L.Rev. 1 (1982).

13. *Id.* An approach like this is endorsed by Professor Brown, in *Accountability in Government and Section 1983*, 25 U. Mich. J.L. Reform 53 (1991). *See Lockridge v. Board of Trustees, Univ. of Arkansas*, 294 F.3d 1010 (8th Cir.2002) (reasonable jury could find university chancellor liable based on personal involvement in failing to promote plaintiff where record indicates his discretion to determine appointment process, his ultimate authority concerning hiring decisions, and background promotion policy, while "ambiguous," might be direct evidence of race discrimination).

liability under *Canton*, the ultimate source of the supervisor's duty is Section 1983, contrary to the convention that the statute creates no rights or duties of its own.

The courts have had little difficulty with two small pieces of this puzzle. First, in the situation where the supervisor actively participates in the subordinate's violation, the supervisor is liable on the same terms as the subordinate for "subjecting" the plaintiff to a federal law deprivation. Indeed a minority view is that only active participation in the violation suffices for a supervisor's liability.[14] Second, where the plaintiff seeks to hold the supervisor liable by reference to the conduct of a subordinate, the supervisor is not liable unless the subordinate has in fact breached a constitutional obligation, with whatever required scienter the predicate violation entails.[15]

Confusion abounds, however, concerning the terms of supervisor liability in non-participation cases. The Supreme Court's only reference to supervisory liability, made in the course of restricting injunctive relief, rejects automatic, "course of employment" or respondeat superior-type vicarious liability for supervisors.[16] At a minimum, then, it appears that some degree of culpability on the part of the supervisor must be shown—at least negligence.[17] But the circuit opinions are deeply divided over the appropriate standard for supervisory culpability. They range from requiring only grossly negligent conduct;[18] to a compromise approach requiring recklessly or deliberately indifferent conduct;[19] to requiring actual knowledge of and acquiescence in a subordinate's constitutional violation.[20] Consequently, they also differ over whether the supervisor

14. *See, e.g., Shehee v. Luttrell*, 199 F.3d 295, 300 (6th Cir.1999), *cert. denied*, 528 U.S. 562, 120 S.Ct. 1073, 145 L.Ed.2d 1060 (2000) (*Bivens* claim) (supervisor's liability depends on his encouragement of or active participation in a failure to supervise, control, or train; mere awareness of unconstitutional activity, coupled with failure to take appropriate action, will not suffice); *Tilson v. Forrest City Police Dep't*, 28 F.3d 802 (8th Cir.1994), *cert. denied*, 514 U.S. 1004, 115 S.Ct. 1315, 131 L.Ed.2d 196 (1995); *Sample v. Dieckss*, 885 F.2d 1099 (3d Cir.1989).

15. *See Danese v. Asman*, 875 F.2d 1239 (6th Cir.1989), *cert. denied*, 494 U.S. 1027, 110 S.Ct. 1473, 108 L.Ed.2d 610 (1990). *See also Tilson*, 28 F.3d 802 (police chief could not be liable for failing to promulgate adequate written procedures governing a criminal investigation where his subordinate officers were not shown to have followed unlawful procedures in taking the plaintiff into custody).

16. *Rizzo v. Goode*, 423 U.S. 362, 371, 96 S.Ct. 598, 604, 46 L.Ed.2d 561 (1976)

17. *See* Kinports, *The Buck Does Not Stop Here: Supervisory Liability In Section 1983 Cases*, 1997 Univ. of Ill.L.Rev. 147, 188 (1997). This article contains an excellent summary of the conflicting standards reflected in the opinions of the federal circuit courts. Although no circuit currently supports supervisory liability based on simple negligence, the article contends for such a uniform standard.

18. *Black v. Coughlin*, 76 F.3d 72, 74 (2d Cir.1996); *cf. Maldonado–Denis v. Castillo–Rodriguez*, 23 F.3d 576, 582 (1st Cir. 1994) (gross negligence may "signify" the requisite "deliberate indifference").

19. *See Hill v. Dekalb Reg'l Youth Detention Ctr.*, 40 F.3d 1176 (11th Cir.1994); *Gaudreault v. Municipality of Salem*, 923 F.2d 203 (1st Cir.1990), *cert. denied*, 500 U.S. 956, 111 S.Ct. 2266, 114 L.Ed.2d 718 (1991).

20. *See, e.g. International Action Center v. U.S.*, 365 F.3d 20 (D.C.Cir. 2004) (concluding that supervisors had no actual constructive knowledge of past constitutional violations, hence no liability for failure to supervise); *Gentry v. Duckworth*, 65 F.3d 555, 561 (7th Cir.1995); *Jojola v. Chavez*, 55 F.3d 488, 490 (10th Cir.1995); *Baker v. Monroe Township*, 50 F.3d 1186, 1194 (3d Cir.1995); *Ripson v. Alles*, 21 F.3d 805, 809

can be liable for failing to reign in a subordinate when she should have been aware of the subordinate's unconstitutional conduct; or only when she was aware of a risk of such conduct; or, most stringently, only when she was actually aware of the violation.[21]

For the most part, the courts have opted for the "causation" approach. The decisions that take this tack rely heavily both on the causation language of Section 1983 and the analogy from precedent furnished by *City of Canton*. The "deliberate indifference" that these courts prescribe for supervisory liability is equated with the *Canton* standard for entity liability. This means that ordinarily the plaintiff cannot prevail, when seeking to hold the supervisor liable for an omission, by pointing only to one or even several isolated prior incidents posing a risk of constitutional harm. Instead, plaintiff must show continued supervisor inaction despite documented widespread occurrences.[22]

(8th Cir.1994); *Walton v. City of Southfield*, 995 F.2d 1331, 1340 (6th Cir.1993); *Sanders v. English*, 950 F.2d 1152, 1159–60 (5th Cir.1992); *Larez v. City of Los Angeles*, 946 F.2d 630, 646 (9th Cir.1991).

21. *See, e.g., Hinkle v. City of Clarksburg*, 81 F.3d 416 (4th Cir.1996); *Scott v. Henrich*, 39 F.3d 912 (9th Cir.1994), *cert. denied*, 515 U.S. 1159, 115 S.Ct. 2612, 132 L.Ed.2d 855 (1995); *Thompson v. Boggs*, 33 F.3d 847 (7th Cir.1994), *cert. denied*, 514 U.S. 1063, 115 S.Ct. 1692, 131 L.Ed.2d 556 (1995); *Spears v. City of Louisville*, 27 F.3d 567 (6th Cir.1994).

22. *See Cozzo v. Tangipahoa Parish Council–President Government*, 279 F.3d 273, 289–290 (5th Cir. 2002) (requiring multiple prior complaints about the conduct at issue to show that a failure à la *City of Canton* to train amounted to deliberate indifference to plaintiff's constitutional right); *Pena v. Leombruni*, 200 F.3d 1031, 1033–34 (7th Cir.1999), *cert. denied*, 530 U.S. 1208, 120 S.Ct. 2207, 147 L.Ed.2d 240 (2000) (sheriff's failure to instruct subordinates on the use of force against people who appear to be crazed not equivalent to the general failure to instruct on the use of deadly force that *Canton* mentioned as an instance of deliberate indifference; the failure to instruct would be deliberately indifferent only if county had "seen a rash of police killings of crazy people" that clearly "could have been avoided by the adoption of" particular measures) (citing *Allen v. Muskogee*, 119 F.3d 837, 845 (10th Cir.1997), *cert. denied*, 522 U.S. 1148, 118 S.Ct. 1165, 140 L.Ed.2d 176 (1998)); *Hartley v. Parnell*, 193 F.3d 1263, 1269 (11th Cir.1999); *Liebe v. Norton*, 157 F.3d 574, 579–580 (8th Cir.1998) (equating the *Canton* "deliberate indifference" standard governing entity liability for a failure to train with the standard for supervisory liability, requiring at least tacit authorization of unconstitutional conduct); *Love v. Haigler*, 47 F.3d 1165 (4th Cir. 1995); *Maldonado–Denis v. Castillo–Rodriguez*, 23 F.3d 576, 582 (1st Cir.1994); *Shaw v. Stroud*, 13 F.3d 791 (4th Cir.), *cert. denied*, 513 U.S. 814, 115 S.Ct. 68, 130 L.Ed.2d 24 (1994) (3 prior similar incidents in year ending more than 1½ years before shooting at issue a sufficient pattern for supervisory liability in excessive force situation); *Sanders v. Brewer*, 972 F.2d 920, 923 (8th Cir.1992). *But cf. Butera v. Cottey*, 285 F.3d 601 (7th Cir.2002) (sheriff did not receive the actual notice of specific risk of serious harm to pretrial detainee requisite for deliberate indifference); *Sealey v. Giltner*, 116 F.3d 47 (2d Cir.1997), *on remand*, 997 F.Supp. 316 (N.D.N.Y.1998) (corrections commissioner who received two letters about prisoner's appeal concerning administrative segregation not liable absent some personal involvement in underlying alleged due process violations); *Lillard v. Shelby County Bd. of Ed.*, 76 F.3d 716, 728 (6th Cir.1996) (high school principal and superintendent defendants not liable for teacher's sexual harassment where only "some incidents" brought to their attention and they neither "encouraged ... or directly participated"); *Jojola v. Chavez*, 55 F.3d 488, 490–491 (10th Cir.1995) (high school principal and superintendent not liable for custodian's sexual assault of student because four incidents and several rumors over 19 years of custodian's employment not a sufficient pattern to show supervisors' knowledge of and acquiescence in misconduct); *Manarite v. City of Springfield*, 957 F.2d 953 (1st Cir.1992), *cert. denied*, 506 U.S. 837, 113 S.Ct. 113, 121 L.Ed.2d 70 (1992) (sheriff merely negligent, and not deliberately indifferent, in failing to take steps to prevent pretrial detainee's suicide

But the analogy to *Canton* also means that the supervisor need only have constructive rather than actual knowledge of the subordinate's involvement in conduct that threatens a substantial risk of constitutional injury to citizens in the plaintiff's position.[23] Unfortunately, the elements of constructive knowledge are phrased variously in the circuit decisions. There are statements in the cases that the supervisor is liable if she either knew "or reasonably should have known" of the situation in which the subordinate would likely subject the plaintiff to a deprivation of federal rights;[24] or if she failed to take action that is "obviously necessary" to prevent the harm to persons in plaintiff's position.[25] Other courts impose the same prima facie requirement in substance, using different words. For example, several circuits require what they call "reckless" or "callous" indifference, "gross negligence," or "deliberate indifference."[26] The Eleventh Circuit implements that standard by bor-

despite 16 similar incidents in 3 prior years). *But see Swint v. Wadley*, 51 F.3d 988 (11th Cir.1995) (on remand) (sheriff's authorization of second raid after receiving information that alerted him that prior raid violated Fourth Amendment might show deliberate indifference). *Cf. Febus–Rodriguez v. Betancourt–Lebron*, 14 F.3d 87 (1st Cir.1994) (for supervisor to be liable, subordinate's prior incidents of misconduct must be related to conduct currently challenged). *But cf. Atchinson v. District of Columbia*, 73 F.3d 418 (D.C.Cir.1996) (supervisory liability can attach to even isolated misconduct of subordinate if violation sufficiently serious or flagrant). And in some circuits a supervisor's complete inaction in the face of one or a small number of complaints can offset the lack of a pattern. *See Hale v. Tallapoosa County*, 50 F.3d 1579 (11th Cir.1995) (sheriff who disregarded any means of dealing with regular inmate violence other than fund-raising to build a new jail may have been deliberately indifferent); *Bator v. Hawaii*, 39 F.3d 1021, 1029 (9th Cir.1994) and *Lipsett v. University of Puerto Rico*, 864 F.2d 881, 902 (1st Cir.1988) (even plaintiff's own complaints of harassment can serve as foundation of deliberate indifference where supervisor ignores complaints and refuses even to investigate). *See Gros v. City of Grand Prairie, Texas*, 209 F.3d 431, 433–34 (5th Cir.2000) (the particularly exacting brand of "deliberate indifference" required to establish a negligent hiring or "failure to screen" claim against a government entity under *Board of County Commissioners of Bryan County, Oklahoma v. Brown*, discussed above, is also required to establish individual supervisory liability in that situation; thus plaintiff must show that adequate scrutiny of an applicant's background would have led a reasonable supervisor to conclude that a deprivation of a third party's rights, in the particular way plaintiff was injured, would be a plainly obvious consequence of the decision to hire).

23. *Id.*

24. *See e.g., Taylor v. Michigan Dep't of Corrections*, 69 F.3d 76 (6th Cir.1995); *Snell v. Tunnell*, 920 F.2d 673 (10th Cir. 1990), *cert. denied sub nom. Sweptson v. Snell*, 499 U.S. 976, 111 S.Ct. 1622, 113 L.Ed.2d 719 (1991); *Howard v. Adkison*, 887 F.2d 134 (8th Cir.1989). *See generally Doe v. Taylor Indep. Sch. Dist.*, 15 F.3d 443 (5th Cir.), *cert. denied*, 513 U.S. 815, 115 S.Ct. 70, 130 L.Ed.2d 25 (1994) (equating individual supervisor's liability with the standard used to assess the liability of a new municipality under *Canton*).

25. *Doe v. Taylor Independent School Dist.*, 15 F.3d 443 (5th Cir.1994).

26. *Doe v. Bowles*, 254 F.3d 617 (6th Cir.2001) (supervisor not deliberately indifferent in allegedly failing to protect inmate from assault violating plaintiff's Eighth Amendment rights); *Jones v. Wellham*, 104 F.3d 620 (4th Cir.1997) (finding no "deliberate indifference" where police chief disciplined, but did not discharge officer accused of rape who ten years later raped another woman); *Starzenski v. City of Elkhart*, 87 F.3d 872, 880 (7th Cir.1996), *cert. denied*, 519 U.S. 1055, 117 S.Ct. 683, 136 L.Ed.2d 608 (1997); *Baker v. Putnal*, 75 F.3d 190 (5th Cir.1996) (requiring deliberate indifference or gross negligence); *Hill v. Dekalb Reg'l Youth Detention Ctr.*, 40 F.3d 1176 (11th Cir.1994); *Maldonado–Denis v. Castillo–Rodriguez*, 23 F.3d 576, 582 (1st Cir. 1994) (gross negligence may "signify" the requisite "deliberate indifference"); *White v. Holmes*, 21 F.3d 277, 280 (8th Cir.1994); *Febus–Rodriguez v. Betancourt–Lebron*, 14 F.3d 87, 92 (1st Cir.1994); *Shaw v. Stroud*, 13 F.3d 791, 799 (4th Cir.1994), cert. de-

rowing the phraseology of the qualified immunity defense, transplanting it to the prima facie case against the supervisor.[27] This circuit assimilates the usual qualified immunity defense into the plaintiff's case against the supervisor by giving her the burden of showing that a reasonable person similarly situated to defendant would have understood that a failure to train or supervise, or to correct a pattern of violations by subordinates, constituted deliberate indifference.[28] Of course, where the supervisor, with actual knowledge of the peril, nevertheless affirmatively approves the subordinate's conduct that endangers the plaintiff's rights, the supervisor's liability is even clearer.[29]

Still other appellate decisions, however, including even some in the same circuits, articulate a more stringent version of the "causation" approach that limits supervisors' liability to situations where they are personally involved in inflicting the violation or had actual knowledge of the conduct of the subordinate who committed the federal law violation. These courts find that "deliberate indifference" in the *City of Canton* sense requires a conscious acceptance of a known and serious risk; the supervisor therefore lacks the scienter required by Section 1983 unless he knowingly acquiesces in unconstitutional behavior.[30] This approach is

nied, 513 U.S. 813, 115 S.Ct. 67, 130 L.Ed.2d 24 (1994); *Gates v. Unified Sch. Dist. No. 449*, 996 F.2d 1035, 1041 (10th Cir.1993); *Black by Black v. Indiana Area Sch. Dist.*, 985 F.2d 707, 712 (3d Cir.1993); *Gaudreault v. Municipality of Salem*, 923 F.2d 203 (1st Cir.1990), *cert. denied*, 500 U.S. 956, 111 S.Ct. 2266, 114 L.Ed.2d 718 (1991); *Howard v. Adkison*, 887 F.2d 134 (8th Cir.1989); *Gutierrez–Rodriguez v. Cartagena*, 882 F.2d 553 (1st Cir.1989); *Meriwether v. Coughlin*, 879 F.2d 1037 (2d Cir. 1989). The court in *Gutierrez–Rodriguez* observed that there is no significant difference between a "gross negligence amounting to deliberate indifference" and a "reckless and callous indifference" standard.

27. *Greason v. Kemp*, 891 F.2d 829 (11th Cir.1990) (supervisor is liable "when a reasonable person in the supervisor's position would have known that his conduct infringed the constitutional rights of the plaintiff ... and his conduct was causally related to the constitutional violation committed by his subordinate"). *Accord Belcher v. City of Foley*, 30 F.3d 1390, 1397 (11th Cir.1994). The Eleventh Circuit has elaborated that supervisory officials cannot be liable on the basis of respondeat superior, but only in three situations. (1), where the supervisor "personally participates" in the alleged constitutional violation; (2) where his actions cause that deprivation, as where a history of widespread, flagrant, rampant, continued abuse puts him on notice of the need to correct the alleged deprivation, and he fails to do so; or (3) where he causes that deprivation through an unconstitutional policy or custom of his own that reflects deliberate indifference to federally protected rights. *Hartley v. Parnell*, 193 F.3d 1263, 1269 (11th Cir.1999). *See also Marsh v. Butler County, Alabama*, 225 F.3d 1243, 1251–2 (11th Cir.2000) (an official may be liable for establishing or utilizing a policy or custom that amounts to deliberate indifference to the plaintiff's rights).

28. *Adams v. Poag*, 61 F.3d 1537 (11th Cir.1995). The Court has described the degree of notice required to trigger supervisory liability in stringent terms: "the deprivations that constitute widespread abuse sufficient to notify the supervising official must be obvious, flagrant, rampant, and of continued duration." *Braddy v. Florida Dep't of Labor and Emp. Security*, 133 F.3d 797, 802 (11th Cir.1998).

29. *Swint v. Wadley*, 5 F.3d 1435 (11th Cir.1993), *modified on reh'g*, 11 F.3d 1030 (11th Cir.1994), *cert. denied*, 514 U.S. 1003, 115 S.Ct. 1312, 131 L.Ed.2d 194 (1995) (sheriff who approved a raid by subordinate officers that violated established law, and did so with knowledge of the defective manner in which an earlier raid had been conducted, potentially liable for improper supervision).

30. *Shehee v. Luttrell*, 199 F.3d 295, 300 (6th Cir.1999), *cert. denied*, 528 U.S. 562, 120 S.Ct. 1073, 145 L.Ed.2d 1060 (2000) (*Bivens* claim) (supervisor's liability depends on his encouragement of or active participation in a failure to supervise, control, or train; mere awareness of unconsti-

echoed by language in another opinion that hinged supervisory liability for devising an unconstitutional policy about the use of deadly canine force, or for failing adequately to train or supervise a subordinate in the use of that force, on whether the supervisor "authorized, approved, or acquiesced" in such a policy.[31] Interestingly, however, the court that announced this test also indicated that if such involvement could be shown, those supervisors might be liable even though the subordinate officer who unleashed the force had been found nonliable because he acted reasonably given the procedures established by his superiors.[32] Perhaps it is fair to generalize that courts are more likely to impute constructive knowledge to a supervisor in a "failure to train" case, where recurrent situations make obvious the need for training subordinates in a particular task. By contrast, courts will more likely require the plaintiff to show the supervisor's actual knowledge of subordinate misconduct in cases alleging a failure to supervise or discipline.

The residue of these decisions is that a supervisor may be liable either because of her personal involvement in the constitutional injury inflicted on the plaintiff or because of her "deliberate indifference." But there remains continuing uncertainty whether this "deliberate indifference" demands evidence of a more culpable state of mind than is reflected in a city's simple failure to take precautionary measures in the

tutional activity, coupled with failure to take appropriate action, will not suffice); *Murrell v. School Dist. No. 1*, 186 F.3d 1238, 1250 (10th Cir.1999) (finding claim stated against teacher and principal by allegations that they actually knew of and acquiesced in student-on-student sexual harassment); *Green v. Branson*, 108 F.3d 1296 (10th Cir.1997) (using "deliberate indifference" standard but writing that it requires the supervisor to "know" that his failure to guide or control the subordinate is creating a substantial risk of bodily harm); *Doe v. Claiborne County*, 103 F.3d 495, 513 (6th Cir.1996) (requiring sufficient knowledge of subordinate's unconstitutional conduct to amount to "tacit authorization"); *Williams v. Neal*, 99 F.3d 1151 (10th Cir.1996); *Von Funderburk v. Block*, 68 F.3d 482 (9th Cir.1995); *Larson v. Miller*, 55 F.3d 1343, 1349 (8th Cir.1995); *Jojola v. Chavez*, 55 F.3d 488, 490 (10th Cir.1995); *Baker v. Monroe Township*, 50 F.3d 1186 (3d Cir.1995); *Woodward v. City of Worland*, 977 F.2d 1392 (10th Cir.1992), *cert. denied sub nom. Woodard v. Seghetti*, 509 U.S. 923, 113 S.Ct. 3038, 125 L.Ed.2d 724 (1993); *Andrews v. City of Philadelphia*, 895 F.2d 1469 (3d Cir.1990). *See Boyd v. Knox*, 47 F.3d 966 (8th Cir.1995) (where the predicate violation involved a prison official's alleged indifference to a prisoner's medical needs, the official must actually know of and disregard a particular, serious potential harm). The *Boyd* standard seems dictated more by the particular Eighth Amendment violation in question than by the panel's view of a general Section 1983 requirement for supervisor liability. The opinion relies on the Supreme Court's opinion in *Farmer v. Brennan*, 511 U.S. 825, 837, 114 S.Ct. 1970, 1979, 128 L.Ed.2d 811 (1994), which holds that a prison official must have actual knowledge of a substantial risk of harm before his failure to take steps to safeguard an inmate violates that Amendment. *See also Rascon v. Hardiman*, 803 F.2d 269 (7th Cir.1986) (supervisor must have knowingly, wilfully, or recklessly caused the alleged deprivation by failing to act); *Johnson v. Quinones*, 145 F.3d 164 (4th Cir.1998). *But cf. Stoneking v. Bradford Area Sch. Dist.*, 882 F.2d 720, 725–26 (3d Cir.1989), *cert. denied sub nom. Smith v. Stoneking*, 493 U.S. 1044, 110 S.Ct. 840, 107 L.Ed.2d 835 (1990) (articulating a condonation requirement but permitting it to be satisfied by evidence that defendants encouraged a climate that allowed unconstitutional conduct).

31. *Chew v. Gates*, 27 F.3d 1432, 1438–1439 (9th Cir.1994), *cert. denied*, 513 U.S. 1148, 115 S.Ct. 1097, 130 L.Ed.2d 1065 (1995). *See also Neely v. Feinstein*, 50 F.3d 1502 (9th Cir.1995) (supervisor's conscious indifference to risk that aide would sexually abuse psychiatric patient defeats qualified immunity).

32. *Chew v. Gates*, 27 F.3d 1432 (9th Cir.1994).

face of persistent evidence of the need to do so. One structural argument against the higher standard is that the "actual knowledge" test effectively eliminates the individual supervisor's defense of qualified immunity: how could a supervisor show that she reasonably failed to appreciate that inaction would likely violate the plaintiff's settled right where plaintiff has already shown that she knowingly acquiesced in the unconstitutional behavior? On the other hand, even the more lenient version of supervisory "deliberate indifference" alters the qualified immunity defense procedurally: in effect plaintiff has to show the supervisor's unreasonable failure to act as part of the prima facie case. Accordingly, the burden of persuading that a supervisor unreasonably failed to act falls on the plaintiff, while the same burden, if part of the qualified immunity defense of a subordinate, is the defendant's.

§§ 2.37–2.39 [Reserved]

F. THE PRACTICAL CONSEQUENCES OF ASYMMETRICAL PRIMA FACIE CASES AND DEFENSES IN INDIVIDUAL AND ENTITY ACTIONS: OF *PAUL* AND *PARRATT*, *ZINERMON* AND *SIEGERT*

§ 2.40 In General

The divergence of the prima facie elements and defenses in § 1983 actions against individuals and entities may be viewed as responses by the Court to three perceived problems: unfairness to individual defendants, the opening of litigation floodgates, and threats to federalism resulting from intrusive interference with vigorous state administration of public functions. This Section explores the varying techniques the Court has employed to address these issues, the resulting differentiation of the individual and entity cases, and the consequences for dynamic lawmaking. Broadly speaking, the case against an individual includes a somewhat easily established prima facie case countered by an extensive immunity and offers no opportunity for development in constitutional doctrine. On the other hand, although the case against an entity begins with a formidable prima facie case, it is unchecked by a general immunity defense and therefore still holds out the possibility of doctrinal development.

§ 2.41 Individual Defendant Cases

In suits against individual defendants the Court has responded to the swelling of § 1983 litigation after *Monroe*, and the consequent constraints on government decisionmaking, not only by fortifying the qualified immunity defense but also by defining more restrictively certain predicate constitutional violations.

a. Recapping the Prima Facie Case

The plaintiff's prima facie case is judicially unembellished and tracks the language of the statute in a straightforward manner. The plaintiff must allege and persuade the factfinder by a preponderance of the evidence that the defendant, (1) under color of state law, (2) deprived or caused the plaintiff to be deprived (3) of a federally protected right and (4) with resulting harm to the plaintiff. While the plaintiff may encounter difficulty in establishing these elements she need not make the formidable additional showing of "policy" required for the prima facie case against an entity.

b. The Enlargement of Qualified Immunity

As we have seen, the early common law immunity doctrine typified by cases like *Scheuer v. Rhodes*[1] demanded a fact-based inquiry that sought to unfetter discretionary administration of the law. This qualified immunity insulated individual public officials, ineligible for absolute immunity, from liability without fault through the general defense of good faith and probable cause.[2] *Scheuer* identified two bases for this qualified immunity: the injustice of punishing the officer who, in good faith, exercises discretion as a requirement of his job, and the fear that the threat of liability would chill the officer's execution of his duties "with the decisiveness and judgment required by the public good."[3]

Yet in *Harlow v. Fitzgerald*[4] and again in *Anderson v. Creighton*,[5] the Court jettisoned this heavily fact-laden version of common law immunity. It substituted a two-part inquiry that begins and usually ends with a legal question, the settledness of the specific right at issue. More rarely, if the right is deemed well-settled, the test of immunity unfolds into a factual inquiry about the reasonableness of official conduct in light of that highly particularized precedent. These decisions were avowedly designed to enable defendants to obtain early dismissals before extensive (and preferably, before any) discovery. Substantively, they broaden immunity so that it is generally no longer defeasible by evidence of subjective bad faith. What had traditionally been a jury question aimed at determining the justice of excusing the officer in light of all the circumstances she confronted in the course of discretionary decision-making is now usually a question of law for the trial judge.

Although qualified immunity may protect the defendant from monetary damages, the doctrine cannot shield him from injunctive relief. And a grant of an injunction would authorize an award of attorney's fees under § 1988. Thus an attorney may still find incentive to take a case where a grant of qualified immunity is likely.

§ 2.41

1. 416 U.S. 232, 94 S.Ct. 1683, 40 L.Ed.2d 90 (1974).

2. *See supra* § 2.22.

3. 416 U.S. at 240, 94 S.Ct. at 1688.

4. 457 U.S. 800, 102 S.Ct. 2727, 73 L.Ed.2d 396 (1982).

5. 483 U.S. 635, 107 S.Ct. 3034, 97 L.Ed.2d 523 (1987).

c. *Paring Down the Predicate Constitutional Violations and Restricting Constitutional Development*

At the same time, the Court was further closing the floodgates[6] on individual actions by narrowing certain predicate constitutional protections. In *Paul v. Davis*,[7] the Court announced its determination to prevent the Fourteenth Amendment from becoming "a font of tort law"[8] through the medium of actions under § 1983. Justice Rehnquist, following a course laid out in *Board of Regents of State Colleges v. Roth*,[9] contracted the circumstances under which any process is due to avoid " 'alter[ing] the basic relations between the States and the national government.' "[10]

The plaintiff in *Paul* alleged that police had deprived him of his liberty by posting his name as an "active shoplifter" before any adjudication on the charge. Laboring to avoid finding a predicate liberty interest, the Court distinguished *Wisconsin v. Constantineau*,[11] where the Court had held that "[w]here a person's good name ... is at stake because of what the government is doing to him, notice and an opportunity to be heard are essential." In *Paul*, by contrast, the Court refused to recognize a generalized constitutional liberty interest to be free from state-perpetrated defamation and it found "no specific constitutional guarantee" safeguarding reputation. Moreover, plaintiff could cite no source of a liberty interest in state law.[12]

6. *See Eisenberg & Schwab*, 72 Cornell L.Rev. at 646–47 (arguing that the *Paul* and *Parratt* lines of authority, discussed below, had their impetus in a desire to control the flood of litigation).

7. 424 U.S. 693, 96 S.Ct. 1155, 47 L.Ed.2d 405 (1976).

8. *Id.* at 701, 96 S.Ct. at 1160.

9. 408 U.S. 564, 569–79, 92 S.Ct. 2701, 2705–10, 33 L.Ed.2d 548 (1972) (holding that untenured teacher had no property right and was not deprived of liberty upon nonrenewal of his contract). The significance of *Roth* in the development of Fourteenth Amendment jurisprudence occupies a central role in Henry P. Monaghan, *Of "Liberty" and "Property,"* 62 Cornell L.Rev. 405, 409 (1977) (concluding that after *Roth*, "life, liberty and property" no longer "embrace the full range of state conduct having serious impact upon individual interests").

10. *Paul*, 424 U.S. at 700, 96 S.Ct. at 1160 (*quoting Screws v. United States*, 325 U.S. 91, 109, 65 S.Ct. 1031, 1039, 89 L.Ed. 1495 (1945) (plurality opinion)). For a blistering critique of *Paul* that remains as convincing today as when it was written, *see* Monaghan, *id.* On Justice Rehnquist's federalism concerns see Durchslag, 54 N.Y.U.L.Rev. at 739–41. *See generally* Sheldon H. Nahmod, *Due Process, State Remedies, and Section 1983*, 34 Kan.L.Rev. 217, 217–18 (1985) (discussing the several policies that drove the Burger Court's § 1983 jurisprudence).

11. 400 U.S. 433, 91 S.Ct. 507, 27 L.Ed.2d 515 (1971).

12. For a brief time, however, some residual constitutional interest in reputation appeared to survive *Paul*. *See Paul* 424 U.S. at 700, 96 S.Ct. at 1160 and *Owen v. City of Independence*, 445 U.S. 622, 100 S.Ct. 1398, 63 L.Ed.2d 673 (1980). Such hope was largely dashed by *Siegert v. Gilley*, 500 U.S. 226, 231, 111 S.Ct. 1789, 1793, 114 L.Ed.2d 277 (1991), which held that the Fourteenth Amendment provides no redress even when the defamation occurs roughly contemporaneously with permanent termination from government employment. But some circuit courts have staged something of a rear-guard action, finding ways to interpret or distinguish *Siegert* so as to uphold liberty-interest claims even where the statements in question take place soon after, rather than exactly contemporaneous with, the plaintiff's termination. *See Campanelli v. Bockrath*, 100 F.3d 1476, 1482–83 (9th Cir.1996); *Mertik v. Blalock*, 983 F.2d 1353, 1363 (6th Cir.1993). Nevertheless, the defendant's allegedly actionable statements must occur in the course of and be related to the reasons for the plaintiff's termination or "significant alteration of some other legal right or status." *Von Stein v. Brescher*, 904 F.2d 572, 582 (11th Cir.1990). Thus while roughly contemporaneous statements about the reasons for or possibly the

Concurrently, in the *Parratt*[13] line of cases, the Court sharply curtailed the procedural "deprivations" redressable by due process, thereby affording state actors an escape from federal liability for otherwise actionable conduct. In *Parratt*, prison officials negligently deprived an inmate of his property without due process of law. The Court, recognizing that property deprivations ordinarily require predeprivation process,[14] held that a postdeprivation state tort law remedy satisfies the obligation to provide process whenever the deprivation is effected by the "random and unauthorized" conduct of government officials. This result obtains, the Court wrote, even if the state remedy is more restrictive and affords lesser relief than § 1983. It reasoned that the random and unauthorized nature of the deprivation made it impracticable for the state to provide predeprivation process because the state official could not predict precisely when the deprivation would occur.

The *Parratt* doctrine reached its apogee three years later in *Hudson v. Palmer*,[15] where the Court ruled that the rationale of *Parratt* extended to intentional conduct. The Court in Hudson could "discern no logical distinction between negligent and intentional deprivations of property insofar as the 'practicality' of affording pre-deprivation process is concerned." The State could no more predict its agents' random and unauthorized intentional conduct than it could anticipate similar negligent conduct. Postdeprivation state tort law remedies, therefore, provided all the process that was due.

Parratt has turned out to have had a shorter reach than was generally thought when it was decided. For one thing, the Court has whittled away at the kinds of conduct that constitute a deprivation of due process; and if there is no "deprivation," the *Parratt* exception for "random and unauthorized" situations where there is a "postdeprivation remedy" never comes into play.

For example, it is now clear that the defendant must hold a "more than negligent" state of mind before his conduct can rise to the level of a "deprivation" actionable as a denial of due process. Thus in *Daniels v. Williams*,[16] and *Davidson v. Cannon*,[17] the Court concluded that negli-

manner of termination can be the basis of a defamation-based constitutional claim, statements only about plaintiff's conduct in the aftermath of termination cannot. *Renaud v. Wyoming Dep't of Family Servs.*, 203 F.3d 723, 727–28 (10th Cir.2000). And at least one circuit concludes that the allegedly defamatory statement must take place in connection with a "discharge or more"–a transfer or denied promotion will not suffice. *Cannon v. City of West Palm Beach*, 250 F.3d 1299 (11th Cir.2001) (denying name-clearing hearing to plaintiff denied a promotion in connection with the stigmatizing injury to reputation).

13. *See Parratt v. Taylor*, 451 U.S. 527, 536–42, 101 S.Ct. 1908, 1913–16, 68 L.Ed.2d 420 (1981), *overruled in part by Daniels v. Williams*, 474 U.S. 327, 106 S.Ct. 662, 88 L.Ed.2d 662 (1986).

14. *But see City of West Covina v. Perkins*, 525 U.S. 234, 119 S.Ct. 678, 142 L.Ed.2d 636, *on remand,* 167 F.3d 1286 (9th Cir.1999) (due process does not require police who seize property for criminal investigation purposes to advise the owner of the state law remedies for recovering the property, where publicly available statutes and case law provide that information).

15. 468 U.S. 517, 104 S.Ct. 3194, 82 L.Ed.2d 393 (1984).

16. 474 U.S. 327, 106 S.Ct. 662, 88 L.Ed.2d 662 (1986).

17. 474 U.S. 344, 106 S.Ct. 668, 88 L.Ed.2d 677 (1986).

gent acts do not provide an adequate predicate for due process violations. In *Davidson*, the Court found no liberty deprivation, and therefore no violation of due process, when prison officials negligently failed to protect an inmate from a beating at the hands of another inmate, despite evidence that the officials had some foreknowledge of the possibility.[18] And in *Daniels*, a companion case that in this respect overruled *Parratt*, the Court explained that some degree of fault greater than "mere lack of care" is prerequisite to an actionable "deprivation of Due Process."[19]

Further, the Court has declared two sorts of limitations on the applicability of *Parratt* as an escape from liability even in the dwindling number of "more than negligent" settings in which the Court still finds due process "deprivations." First, in *Logan v. Zimmerman Brush Co.*,[20] the Court limited *Parratt* to instances of random and unauthorized conduct by government officials, as distinct from established procedures declared by state law.[21] Plaintiff in *Logan* challenged his firing in the proper state administrative agency, but the agency negligently failed to hold a hearing within the time limit mandated by statute. Rejecting *Parratt's* applicability, the Court stated that "[u]nlike the complainant in *Parratt, Logan* is challenging not the [commission's] error, but the 'established state procedure' that destroys his entitlement without according him proper procedural safeguards." Because the state system itself rather than the random and unauthorized conduct of state officials destroyed plaintiff's inchoate property interest in their discrimination claims, the Court concluded that predeprivation process was required, despite the existence of an adequate state remedy.

Second, in *Zinermon v. Burch*,[22] the Court limited *Parratt/Hudson's* "random and unauthorized" exception to cases where it would be impossible or at least extremely difficult for the government officials on the scene to provide process before a deprivation. In *Zinermon,* plaintiff claimed that state officials wilfully and recklessly disregarded his rights to due process by admitting him "voluntarily" to a state mental hospital when the staff knew or should have known that he was incompetent to give the informed consent required by statute. Distinguishing *Parratt* and *Hudson*, the Court determined that defendants' conduct was something other than "random and unauthorized."

18. *See id.* at 347–48, 106 S.Ct. at 670.

19. 474 U.S. at 330–31, 106 S.Ct. at 664–65. *See Lemoine v. New Horizons Ranch and Center, Inc.*, 174 F.3d 629 (5th Cir.1999) (mere negligence of state employee could not violate due process). *Compare Rooney v. Watson*, 101 F.3d 1378 (11th Cir. 1996), *cert. denied*, 522 U.S. 966, 118 S.Ct. 412, 139 L.Ed.2d 315 (1997) (even grossly negligent conduct states no constitutional violation) and *Trigalet v. Young*, 54 F.3d 645 (10th Cir.), *cert. denied sub nom. Trigalet v. Warrick*, 516 U.S. 932, 116 S.Ct. 340, 133 L.Ed.2d 238 (1995) (recklessness suffices).

20. 455 U.S. 422, 102 S.Ct. 1148, 71 L.Ed.2d 265 (1982).

21. *See, e.g., Alexandre v. Cortes*, 140 F.3d 406 (2d Cir.1998) (finding police officer's release of impounded automobile to lien holder actionable under due process clause; city's established procedure did not provide notice to owner of post-deprivation procedures or provide for resolution of ownership disputes).

22. 494 U.S. 113, 110 S.Ct. 975, 108 L.Ed.2d 100 (1990). *Zinermon* is discussed in more detail *infra*.

The moment of deprivation and the fact that some prospective patients might lack capacity were predictable, the Court wrote. Therefore the state, before taking plaintiff's liberty, could have accorded him a predeprivation hearing that would have guarded against an admission in violation of the statute. Moreover, the Court concluded, the conduct in question could not be considered "unauthorized" in the *Parratt/Hudson* sense, because the State had delegated to the hospital staff the authority to make admissions decisions even if it had not prescribed any particular procedure to determine the competence to consent requisite to a voluntary admission. The Court thus held *Parratt/Hudson* inapplicable when identified government personnel with evident statutory discretion to provide appropriate process can feasibly provide a predeprivation hearing that will reduce the risk of an erroneous deprivation.

The Court in *Zinermon* also assuaged the fear that *Parratt* would excuse violations of substantive due process. It placed *Parratt* squarely within the procedural due process context created by *Mathews v. Eldridge.*[23] *Parratt,* stressed the Court, was simply a special application of the *Mathews* balancing test for determining what procedural safeguards are constitutionally required—an application that tilted the scales against the provision of predeprivation process. In so saying, the Court folded *Parratt* into a line of cases bracketed by *Zinermon* and *Logan. Parratt* does not control either when, as in *Logan,* the state formally creates established procedure but as a practical matter makes it unavailable, or when, as in *Zinermon,* the state fails to provide predeprivation process that it readily could have provided. Viewed with the hindsight of *Zinermon, Parratt* accordingly leaves unaffected the *Monroe* holding that individual defendants may still be accountable under § 1983 for violations of most (clearly established) constitutional rights (other than random and unauthorized procedural due process violations for which state law allows a post-deprivation remedy) even when their conduct is entirely unauthorized by their governing principal.[24]

23. 424 U.S. 319, 96 S.Ct. 893, 47 L.Ed.2d 18 (1976).

24. At least four members of the current Court are on record as being uncomfortable with the reach of *Parratt.* Justices Kennedy and Thomas, concurring in the judgment only in *Albright v. Oliver,* 510 U.S. 266, 114 S.Ct. 807, 127 L.Ed.2d 114 (1994), complain that the Court has not given the doctrine its full sway. In *Albright,* a plurality of the court wrote that a criminal defendant apparently still in custody has no substantive due process right to be free from baseless initiation of prosecution because his injury was potentially redressable under an amendment, the Fourth, more explicitly addressed to the type of government conduct at issue. As those Justices saw it, *Parratt* is designed to further the resolve expressed in *Paul* to prevent § 1983 from becoming an open-ended font of tort law. To that end they regard *Parratt* not merely as a limit on the scope of procedural due process but as a prohibition of relief under § 1983—for any due process claim, procedural or substantive—where the state actor's challenged conduct is random and unauthorized and state law provides an adequate postdeprivation remedy. Given Illinois' malicious prosecution civil remedy, and their characterization of the defendant's conduct as random and unauthorized, they would have denied the *Albright* plaintiff any remedy under § 1983 even assuming, contrary to the plurality's conclusion, that a substantive due process claim was stated. None of the five opinions in *Albright* commanded a majority, leading to widespread disagreement in the lower courts as to the viability of a constitutionally-based claim of malicious prosecution. Compare *Frantz v. Village of* Bradford, 245 F.3d 869 (6th Cir.2001) (malicious prosecution actionable only through Fourth

But *Parratt* does block relief for at least procedural due process claims even when the defendant's conduct reflects the required level of due process culpability the Court now requires (i.e., recklessness or intent) and even when, notwithstanding *Paul/Roth/Siegert*, the complaint in other respects states a cognizable deprivation of liberty or property. As such, *Parratt* still constitutes a separate limitation on the process that is due whenever a conduct is random and unauthorized; in such cases, almost any state post-deprivation remedy supplants federal relief. *Parratt* thus stands as a striking counterpoint to Justice Harlan's observation in *Monroe* that Congress apparently contemplated fuller relief under § 1983 than the states might afford for the same misconduct.[25]

Amendment claims for unreasonable seizure, arrest absent probable cause, and false imprisonment); *Reed v. City of Chicago*, 77 F.3d 1049 (7th Cir.1996) (rejecting the "continuing seizure" theory endorsed by Justice Ginsburg, concurring in *Albright*, under which plaintiff could state a Fourth Amendment claim by alleging that post-arrest he was released on bond and obliged to respond to charges); *Murphy v. Lynn*, 118 F.3d 938 (2d Cir.1997), *cert. denied*, 522 U.S. 1115, 118 S.Ct. 1051, 140 L.Ed.2d 114 (1998); *Whiting v. Traylor*, 85 F.3d 581 (11th Cir.1996) and *Taylor v. Meacham*, 82 F.3d 1556 (10th Cir.), *cert. denied*, 519 U.S. 871, 117 S.Ct. 186, 136 L.Ed.2d 125 (1996) (malicious prosecution gives rise to a claim under the Fourth Amendment, and that Amendment only); *Torres v. McLaughlin*, 163 F.3d 169 (3d Cir.1998), *cert. denied*, 528 U.S. 1079, 120 S.Ct. 797, 145 L.Ed.2d 672 (2000) (dismissing on merits a Fourth Amendment claim based on post-conviction incarceration, but leaving open possibility of malicious prosecution claim based on Fourth and possibly other Amendments, excluding only substantive due process); *Perez–Ruiz v. Crespo–Guillen*, 25 F.3d 40 (1st Cir.1994) (no § 1983 claim grounded in malicious prosecution lies if state tort law furnishes adequate remedy).

At the other end of the spectrum, dissenting Justice Stevens (who lamented in his opinion that he was the author, while a judge on the Seventh Circuit Court of Appeals, of a forerunner of *Parratt*) joined by Justice Blackmun, began by describing *Parratt* as "categorically inapplicable" to substantive due process claims, on the authority of *Zinermon*. See *Cozzo v. Tangipahoa Parish Council–President Government*, 262 F.3d 501, 517–518 (5th Cir.2001) (*Parratt/Hudson* doctrine is an exception solely to procedural due process violations, and therefore does not excuse a substantive due process claim grounded in a violation of the Fourth Amendment's right to be free of unreasonable seizures). Issue was clearly joined on this point with Justices Kennedy and Thomas, who had objected that *Zinermon* itself was an evasion of *Parratt* achieved by mischaracterizing the *Zinermon* claim as based on substantive, rather than procedural, due process. Indeed Justices Stevens and Blackmun deem *Parratt* "reconcilable with § 1983" in only a handful of "situations in which no constitutional violation [apparently of procedural due process] occurs." They virtually limit *Parratt* to its facts—a negligent, rather than reckless or intentional loss of property—and in particular find it inapplicable to most deprivations of liberty. In the process, they implicitly call into question the *Parratt* progeny like *Daniels, Davidson*, and *Hudson* that denied § 1983 remedies for random and unauthorized government agent conduct, more culpable than negligence, that resulted in deprivations of liberty.

If either of these polar positions commands a majority on the Court, the aggregate effect of *Parratt* on § 1983 would be altered. Should the *Kennedy/Thomas* view prevail, *Parratt* would become a broad-spectrum limitation on remedies under § 1983 within the entire sphere of due process, even without narrowing the formal scope of due process itself. Should the Stevens/Blackmun view prevail, it would be considerably more clear than it appears today that *Parratt*, far from limiting § 1983 remedies generally, is merely a declaration about the scope of procedural due process that would logically exist in its absence. To them the decision simply affirms that the only process that is due when a government agent acts negligently—by definition, an act the government entity cannot anticipate and for which it accordingly cannot provide process beforehand—is a subsequent state law remedy for damages.

25. *See Monroe v. Pape*, 365 U.S. 167, 196 n. 5, 81 S.Ct. 473, 488 n. 5, 5 L.Ed.2d

As the foregoing discussion reveals, the Court, concerned about calendar congestion, fairness to government officers, and intrusion on state prerogatives, has constricted the scope of due process and equal protection principally in the course of deciding § 1983 suits against individual defendants. True, the pattern is wavy. For example, the Court has, at least formally, eschewed de minimis exceptions to claims based on liberty[26] as well as property.[27] Nevertheless, constitutional claims rooted in the protection of property seemingly stand on a surer footing with the current Court than claims based on liberty. As we have seen, the Court has excluded whole categories of losses from the "liberty" protected by substantive (*Paul; Siegert; DeShaney; Collins*) and procedural (*Parratt; Zinermon*) due process. It also excludes any substantive due process claim based on allegations that the Court construes as implicating a more specific Bill of Rights provision—the Fourth Amendment, as in *Albright v. Oliver*, or the Eighth, as in *Graham v. Connor*—apparently regardless of whether the more specific guarantee favors or undermines the plaintiff's case. Yet at the same time the Court has extended the embrace of the Fourth Amendment's unlawful seizure protection to reach invasions of the defendant's property as well as his person.[28]

Still, neither the newly shrunken circumference of these important predicate constitutional rights nor the "clearly established" approach to individual defendant immunity represents a broad-spectrum restriction on the scope of § 1983 itself. Instead, the doctrinal accretions simply reduce the plaintiff's chances of success in stating a claim—of procedural due process violations, for example, under the *Parratt* line of cases, or of substantive due process violations, as evidenced by *Roth/Paul/Siegert*

492 (1961) (Harlan, J., concurring), *overruled in part by Monell v. Department of Soc. Servs.*, 436 U.S. 658, 98 S.Ct. 2018, 56 L.Ed.2d 611 (1978). *See Myers v. Klevenhagen*, 97 F.3d 91 (5th Cir.1996) (per curiam) and *Hamlin v. Vaudenberg*, 95 F.3d 580 (7th Cir.1996) (*Parratt* precludes procedural due process claims by prisoners where there were "adequate" state post-deprivation remedies). At least one court has placed the burden of alleging and proving the inadequacy of state post-deprivation remedies on the plaintiff. *Strasburger v. Board of Educ.*, 143 F.3d 351 (7th Cir.1998), *cert. denied*, 525 U.S. 1069, 119 S.Ct. 800, 142 L.Ed.2d 661 (1999).

26. *Albright v. Oliver*, 510 U.S. 266, 114 S.Ct. 807, 127 L.Ed.2d 114 (1994).

27. *Connecticut v. Doehr*, 501 U.S. 1, 12, 111 S.Ct. 2105, 2113, 115 L.Ed.2d 1 (1991); *Peralta v. Heights Medical Ctr., Inc.*, 485 U.S. 80, 85, 108 S.Ct. 896, 899, 99 L.Ed.2d 75 (1988) (temporary or partial impairments of property trigger procedural due process protection); *Rush v. Savchuk*, 444 U.S. 320, 100 S.Ct. 571, 62 L.Ed.2d 516 (1980) (the slight and speculative jeopardy to an insured's property where he is indemnified and defended by his insurer nevertheless qualifies for the full protections of the personal jurisdiction branch of substantive due process).

28. *Soldal v. Cook County, Ill.*, 506 U.S. 56, 113 S.Ct. 538, 121 L.Ed.2d 450 (1992). *Accord, Bonds v. Cox*, 20 F.3d 697 (6th Cir.1994) . *See also Sams v. City of Milwaukee*, 117 F.3d 991 (7th Cir.1997) (confirming that due process gives the lienholder of an abandoned vehicle the right to notice prior to public sale). *Cf. Putman v. Unknown Smith*, 98 F.3d 1093 (8th Cir. 1996) (deprivation of car owners' due process rights not "random and unauthorized" within meaning of *Parratt* where seizure made under "zero-tolerance" policy whereby county seized all vehicles from which suspected drugs had been recovered). *But cf. City of West Covina v. Perkins*, 525 U.S. 234, 119 S.Ct. 678, 142 L.Ed.2d 636, *on remand,* 167 F.3d 1286 (9th Cir.1999) (due process does not require police who seize property for criminal investigation purposes to advise the owner of the state law remedies for recovering the property, where publicly available statutes and case law provide that information).

and *Albright, Collins,* and *Graham.* Similarly, the qualified immunity decisions, *Harlow* and *Anderson v. Creighton,* while they doom all constitutional claims against individual defendants when the right asserted was not judicially articulated with clarity at the time of the challenged conduct, do not by themselves increase the plaintiff's prima facie burden under § 1983. Nevertheless, the combination of sharply curtailed predicate protections and the greatly expanded qualified immunity defense does as a practical matter significantly disable § 1983 individual—defendant litigation from pushing the frontiers of federally protected rights.[29]

d. Tactics in Individual Defendant Litigation After Zinermon and Siegert

Ironically, it is in a procedural due process case—the least fruitful category of predicate constitutional claim after *Parratt, Hudson,* and *Davidson*[30]—that the Court allows room for the individual action to facilitate substantive doctrinal evolution. A close look at this decision, *Zinermon v. Burch,*[31] and its aftermath is necessary to appreciate this possibility.

Burch attempted to have himself "voluntarily" admitted to a state mental hospital at a time he claimed he was disoriented and psychologically incompetent to give informed consent. He alleged that the staff knew or should have known that he was incompetent and, by admitting him nevertheless, wilfully or recklessly disregarded his rights to due process. The Eleventh Circuit reversed the district court's ruling that because the staff's conduct was random and unauthorized *Burch* had failed to state a claim under *Parratt* and *Hudson.* As framed by the Supreme Court majority, the issue was whether Florida, in delegating to mid-level state hospital employees the voluntary admission decision, owed admittees some pre-admission process to determine whether consent was in fact informed.[32]

29. More ominously still, the "clearly established" barrier may affirmatively encourage officials who otherwise would be probable civil defendants to take a chance on constitutionally questionable conduct. Government agents know their decisions are largely free from constitutional scrutiny to the extent that no specific precedent unequivocally prohibits them. *See* Rudovsky, 138 U.Pa.L.Rev. at 54. For example, Professor Rudovsky foresees the possibility that *Anderson's* double bite at reasonableness might reduce the Fourth Amendment's own probable cause requirement into a subconstitutional inquiry into the reasonableness of the officer's belief about the reasonableness of an arrest or search, despite the absence in fact of probable cause. See id. at 52–53. This result would freeze the state of constitutional law. See *id.* at 53. *But see Katz v. United States* and the cases cited in § 2.22, for the dominant view of the circuits that the individual defendant accused of excessive force enjoys only a one-layer reasonable defense, under which an unreasonable use of force under the circumstances will also preclude qualified immunity.

30. *See* subpart c. immediately preceding.

31. 494 U.S. 113, 110 S.Ct. 975, 108 L.Ed.2d 100 (1990).

32. *See id.* at 114–15, 132, 110 S.Ct. at 977–78, 987. Florida had a complex series of procedures for use in determining the propriety of involuntary psychiatric admissions. *See id.* at 121–22, 110 S.Ct. at 981. Those procedures, however, did not cover the case in which a person attempted to admit himself as a voluntary patient when there was reason to doubt his capacity to give informed consent. The statute governing voluntary admissions required "express and informed consent" to be given "volun-

A five-member Supreme Court majority affirmed, distinguishing *Parratt* and *Hudson* on the ground that the defendants' conduct was something other than "random and unauthorized." For one thing, the Court found that because the moment of deprivation and the fact that some prospective patients might lack capacity were predictable, the State, before taking *Burch's* liberty, could have accorded him a pre-deprivation hearing that would have guarded against an admission in violation of the statute.[33] Moreover, the conduct could not be considered "unauthorized" in the *Parratt/Hudson* sense because the state had delegated authority to the hospital staff to make admissions decisions, without prescribing any particular procedure to determine the competence to consent requisite to a voluntary admission.[34]

Zinermon thus renders *Parratt* and *Hudson* inapplicable when identified government personnel with evident statutory discretion to provide appropriate process can feasibly provide a pre-deprivation hearing that will reduce the risk of an erroneous deprivation of liberty.[35] In general,

tarily [and] in writing," but provided no process for determining voluntariness. *Id.* at 122, 110 S.Ct. at 981 (quoting Fla. Stat. §§ 394.465(1)(a), 394.455(22) (1990)).

33. *See id.* at 132–33, 110 S.Ct. at 987. Among the important aspects of the decision was the majority's statement that liberty as well as property interests are subject to the *Parratt/Hudson* doctrine. *See id.* at 131–32, 110 S.Ct. at 986–87.

34. *See id.* at 137, 110 S.Ct. at 989. Justice Blackmun articulated the distinction somewhat differently and perhaps less clearly. He stated that *Parratt* does not apply because (a) the state could foresee that mental patients might lack capacity, (b) providing pre-deprivation process was not literally impossible in view of the established procedure for determining involuntary admissions, and (c) the conduct was not "unauthorized," since the State had delegated admissions decisions to the hospital staff. *See id.* at 136–37, 110 S.Ct. at 989–90. Points (a) and (c) seem to be reasons that support point (b), rather than independent criteria that distinguish *Parratt* and *Hudson*.

35. The case has cleared up several questions concerning the reach of the *Parratt* doctrine. It can now be said with confidence that the holdings of *Parratt* and *Hudson* regarding "random and unauthorized" avoidance of liability are limited to procedural due process claims involving situations in which pre-deprivation process is literally impossible. The Court has assuaged the fear, identified by Henry P. Monaghan, *State Law Wrongs, State Law Remedies, and the Fourteenth Amendment*, 86 Colum.L.Rev. 979, 985–86 (1986), that *Parratt* also restricted substantive due process claims. The *Zinermon* condition that the process plaintiff demands must have "value," see *Zinermon*, 494 U.S. at 134, 110 S.Ct. at 988, would not even be an issue if the subject were fundamental, substantive rights. This conclusion is fortified by the lengths to which the majority and dissent went to place *Parratt* squarely within the procedural due process context created by *Mathews v. Eldridge*, 424 U.S. 319, 96 S.Ct. 893, 47 L.Ed.2d 18 (1976). *See Zinermon*, 494 U.S. at 127–129, 110 S.Ct. at 984–985; *id.* at 147–48, 110 S.Ct. at 994–95 (O'Connor, J., dissenting). *See generally* Laura Oren, *Signing Into Heaven: Zinermon v. Burch, Federal Rights, and State Remedies Thirty Years After Monroe v. Pape*, 40 Emory L.J. 1, 67 (1991) (concluding that *Parratt* is now a narrow doctrine). But the *Zinermon* end-run of *Parratt* may ultimately be limited to situations where the discretion of the entity's actors to design pre-deprivation procedures is "uncircumscribed" and results from "statutory oversight." *See Easter House v. Felder*, 910 F.2d 1387, 1401 (7th Cir.1990) (en banc), *cert. denied*, 498 U.S. 1067, 111 S.Ct. 783, 112 L.Ed.2d 846 (1991). See also *Alexander v. Ieyoub*, 62 F.3d 709 (5th Cir.1995). *But cf. Cushing v. City of Chicago*, 3 F.3d 1156, 1165–66 (7th Cir.1993) (distinguishing *Easter House*). And rumblings suggest that some justices are eager to extend (or restore) *Parratt* to preclude substantive due process claims. *See Albright v. Oliver*, 510 U.S. 266, 114 S.Ct. 807, 127 L.Ed.2d 114 (1994), discussed *supra*. *See also Cathey v. Guenther*, 47 F.3d 162 (5th Cir.1995) (applying doctrine to destruction of property case).

when the moment of deprivation is predictable and accordingly predeprivation process is possible, *Parratt* will not doom a claim of procedural due process.[36] By declaring new doctrine, *Zinermon* appears to refute the argument that the state of constitutional law is frozen in § 1983 damage actions against individual defendants. Even if *Burch* himself loses on qualified immunity, in any subsequent action the law declared by *Zinermon* will be settled, and local governments put on notice that in the mental health context they must adopt appropriate procedures to determine voluntariness.

It appeared, however, after *Zinermon* that tactically shrewd defense counsel could thwart the law-evolution potential of the individual defendant action. The practical lesson of the case may simply have been that defendants should press for a decision on the affirmative defense of immunity rather than move to dismiss the complaint for legal insufficiency under *Parratt*.[37] For example, had defense counsel in *Zinermon*

36. *See, e.g., Armendariz v. Penman*, 31 F.3d 860 (9th Cir.1994), *vacated in part on reh'g en banc*, 75 F.3d 1311 (9th Cir. 1996); *Alexander v. Ieyoub*, 62 F.3d 709 (5th Cir.1995); *Gentry v. City of Lee's Summit*, 10 F.3d 1340 (8th Cir.1993); *Mertik v. Blalock*, 983 F.2d 1353 (6th Cir.1993); *Ezekwo v. New York City Health & Hosp. Corp.*, 940 F.2d 775 (2d Cir.1991), *cert. denied*, 502 U.S. 1013, 112 S.Ct. 657, 116 L.Ed.2d 749 (1991); *Plumer v. State of Maryland*, 915 F.2d 927 (4th Cir.1990); and *Fields v. Durham*, 909 F.2d 94 (4th Cir.1990), *cert. denied*, 498 U.S. 1068, 111 S.Ct. 786, 112 L.Ed.2d 849 (1991). Of course, rejection of the *Parratt* defense merely indicates that some process is due; the due process claim may still fail if for some other reason the court finds that the plaintiff received all the process that was due in the particular circumstances. *See, e.g., Caine v. Hardy*, 943 F.2d 1406, 1412 (5th Cir.1991), *cert. denied*, 503 U.S. 936, 112 S.Ct. 1474, 117 L.Ed.2d 618 (1992); *Plumer*, 915 F.2d at 931; *Fields*, 909 F.2d at 97–98. And *Parratt* will also continue to be applied where the court concludes that the moment of deprivation was unpredictable, unauthorized, or unforeseeable. *See Lowe v. Scott*, 959 F.2d 323 (1st Cir.1992). Last, courts have devised an "emergency circumstances" exception that permits application of *Parratt*, despite *Zinermon*, when the circumstances surrounding a particular, predictable deprivation necessitate prompt action by the government actor. *See Harris v. City of Akron*, 20 F.3d 1396 (6th Cir.), *cert. denied*, 513 U.S. 1001, 115 S.Ct. 512, 130 L.Ed.2d 419 (1994). The cases are not clear, however, whether *Zinermon* trumps *Parratt* when the moment of deprivation is predictable but the official is not authorized to effect the deprivation.

37. *See Danese v. Asman*, 875 F.2d 1239, 1240 (6th Cir.1989), *cert. denied*, 494 U.S. 1027, 110 S.Ct. 1473, 108 L.Ed.2d 610 (1990). The plaintiff in *Danese* might well have succeeded with a procedural due process claim that could have skirted *Parratt* via *Zinermon* had not the defendant successfully pressed the qualified immunity defense first. *See id.* at 1242–44.

As a purely procedural matter, defendants are entitled to move separately on the defenses of legal insufficiency and qualified immunity, provided both defenses are properly preserved in the responsive pleading. See Fed. R. Civ. P. 12(b), 8(c), 7(b). The former defense attacks the legal adequacy of the plaintiff's claim and is resolved solely by reference to the allegations of the complaint, while the latter asserts an affirmative defense, which, if legally sufficient and factually supported, avoids liability for damages even if the elements of the claim are adequately pleaded and proven. Given the ease of deciding the legal insufficiency issue, and its ripeness at the threshold of a lawsuit, a defendant would ordinarily make that motion first.

Substantively, however, the current version of qualified immunity subsumes the question of legal sufficiency that is normally raised by a motion to dismiss for failure to state a claim. While it remains unclear how settled a right must be to meet the Court's requirements, a determination that a particular right is well settled must mean at a minimum that the right has been recognized by a court of some dignity and does state a legally sufficient claim. Rejection of the qualified immunity defense on its first, legal prong would thus doom a follow-up motion to dismiss for failure to state a claim. By the same token, however, a plaintiff's claim, although adequate to survive a

followed that tack, the *Parratt* question would probably never have arisen: even assuming *Burch* had a right to the procedural protections he claimed, that right was not clearly settled at the time he was admitted. Damage actions against entities accordingly seemed the only sure vehicle for the creation of new constitutional protections, so long as counsel for individual defendants raised the qualified immunity defense initially.[38] This conclusion seemed buttressed by the extreme latitude appellate courts have granted the *Harlow/Anderson* immunity defense—insisting on its resolution before discovery,[39] permitting immediate appeals from the denial of qualified immunity motions,[40] and applying zealously the "clearly established" concept.[41]

But these tactics should now be of little moment after *Siegert v. Gilley*[42] and *County of Sacramento v. Lewis*.[43] In *Siegert*, the plaintiff, a former government psychiatrist, brought a defamation action, presumably under what he perceived to be the residue of *Paul v. Davis*.[44] The Court of Appeals for the District of Columbia assumed, without deciding, that plaintiff stated a claim under *Paul*, but remanded the case with instructions to dismiss because, among other things, the right was not clearly established.[45]

The Supreme Court majority affirmed, but rejected the sequencing of issues implicit in the circuit court's analysis. Concluding that "[a] necessary concomitant to the determination of whether the constitutional right asserted ... is 'clearly established' ... is the determination of

motion to dismiss for legal insufficiency, may not implicate a right that is settled to the degree necessary to avoid the defense of qualified immunity. From an efficiency standpoint it seemed after *Zinermon* that the individual defendant was better advised to move on qualified immunity at the outset, even though the ultimate denial of that motion would spell the defeat of the legal insufficiency defense as well.

38. *See, e.g., P.C. v. McLaughlin*, 913 F.2d 1033, 1039–41 (2d Cir.1990) (determining that the issue of whether officials complied with federally incorporated state statutory requirements for admitting plaintiff to residential school for retarded individuals, and thus with requirements of the Education of the Handicapped Act of 1975, 20 U.S.C.A. §§ 1401, 1415(b)(1)(C), (b)(2) (1988), was pretermitted by a grant of qualified immunity through the application of *Harlow*).

39. *See* § 2.22.

40. *See* § 2.23.

41. See generally § 2.22. *See also Auriemma v. Rice*, 895 F.2d 338, 340, 344 (7th Cir.1990), *aff'd in part and rev'd in part*, 910 F.2d 1449 (7th Cir.1990), *cert. denied*, 501 U.S. 1204, 111 S.Ct. 2796, 115 L.Ed.2d 970 (1991) (holding that police superintendent qualifies for immunity when prior decisions failed to establish clearly that he could not reasonably have relied on race as a factor in reorganizing his department, even though he did not purport to be implementing an affirmative action plan when he promoted black officers and demoted only white officers); *Danese v. Asman*, 875 F.2d at 1244 (stating that a pretrial detainee's generalized right to medical care does not clearly establish a correlative right to be screened to determine if such care is needed). The divergence of approaches to § 1983 entity and individual actions becomes evident upon comparison of *Danese and City of Canton v. Harris*, 489 U.S. 378, 109 S.Ct. 1197, 103 L.Ed.2d 412 (1989). *Danese* provides immunity although the right is arguably clearly established, but in *City of Canton*, an entity action, a majority refused to foreclose an almost identical claim despite its novelty. See § 2.32.

42. 500 U.S. 226, 111 S.Ct. 1789, 114 L.Ed.2d 277 (1991).

43. 523 U.S. 833, 118 S.Ct. 1708, 140 L.Ed.2d 1043 (1998).

44. 424 U.S. 693, 96 S.Ct. 1155, 47 L.Ed.2d 405 (1976).

45. *See Siegert v. Gilley*, 895 F.2d 797, 803 (D.C.Cir.1990), aff'd, 500 U.S. 226, 111 S.Ct. 1789, 114 L.Ed.2d 277 (1991).

whether [there is] ... a constitutional right at all,"[46] the Court found no such right, despite *Paul*.[47] This approach, by scrutinizing a component of the defense that is identical to the "rights" element of a § 1983 plaintiff's prima facie claim, has the potential to absolve the defendant from any liability, including prospective relief and attorney's fees; by contrast, the qualified immunity defense as such relieves the individual defendant from liability for damages alone.[48] In this way the *Siegert* prescription for sequencing these issues promises some government officials even greater freedom from the expense and time demands of litigation than they enjoyed when trial courts turned immediately to the question whether an assumed right was clearly established.[49] *County of Sacramento* commends the *Siegert* sequencing for the additional reason that it in effect requires trial judges ruling on § 1983 qualified immunity motions to determine the current contours of constitutional rights even in actions against individual defendants alone. And in 1999, the Court finally mandated this sequence.[50]

Thus the approach mandated by *Siegert, County of Sacramento, Conn v. Gabbert* and *Wilson v. Layne* also renders doubtful the conclusion that § 1983 damage actions against individuals are dead-ends for the development of new constitutional rights. A trial court, directed to

46. *Siegert*, 500 U.S. at 232, 111 S.Ct. at 1793.

47. *See* discussion of *Paul supra*.

48. *See Siegert*, 500 U.S. at 233, 111 S.Ct. at 1794. The "damages" shielded by qualified immunity may, however, include costs, attorney's fees, and related expenses, even in purely equitable suits. *D'Aguanno v. Gallagher*, 50 F.3d 877 (11th Cir.1995).

49. *See Siegert*, 500 U.S. at 232, 111 S.Ct. at 1793; *Burrell v. Board of Trustees of Ga. Military College*, 970 F.2d 785 (11th Cir.1992), *cert. denied*, 507 U.S. 1018, 113 S.Ct. 1814, 123 L.Ed.2d 445 (1993). One of the authors participated as co-counsel to the government defendants in *Burrell*. The court of appeals, on interlocutory review of an order denying motions to dismiss and summary judgment based on qualified immunity, never decided whether the particular First Amendment right plaintiff claimed had been clearly established at the time of her termination from private employment. Instead, it found no genuine issue of fact as to a conspiracy between the government defendants and the private defendants who actually effected that termination. Without such a conspiracy there was wanting the "state action" necessary to establish a predicate § 1983 claim under the First Amendment, and the complaint failed to target conduct "under color of" state law. On this point, *see also Fries v. Helsper*, 146 F.3d 452 (7th Cir.1998), *cert. denied*, 525 U.S. 930, 119 S.Ct. 337, 142 L.Ed.2d 278 (1998).

Burrell thus illustrates the flexibility the *Siegert* sequencing affords individual defendants who assert qualified immunity (as well as courts desirous of granting them pretrial dismissal). Although the court of appeals repeatedly emphasized that it viewed its interlocutory jurisdiction as limited to the question of qualified immunity, its decision did not turn on an evaluation of the core constitutional right in question or its settledness when the defendants acted. Rather, in substance the court treated the complaint, after the factual development generated by a motion for summary judgment, as failing to state a claim because of a deficiency in the "under color of" element essential to any § 1983 action. And dismissal on that ground proved to be a more comprehensive victory for the defendants than if they had merely been relieved of trial on damages because of qualified immunity. Because the court of appeals had found in essence that no § 1983 claim could be stated, for want of state action or action under color of state law, the trial court dismissed all the § 1983 claims against them in their entirety when the case returned to the district court after the Supreme Court's denial of certiorari.

50. *Conn v. Gabbert*, 526 U.S. 286, 290, 119 S.Ct. 1292, 1295, 143 L.Ed.2d 399 (1999); *Wilson v. Layne*, 526 U.S. 603, 609, 119 S.Ct. 1692, 1697, 143 L.Ed.2d 818 (1999).

decide whether there is a right before determining whether that right is clearly established, may generate precedent declaring new rights.[51] In many cases, of course, the trial court will find for the defendant and no new rights will arise. There is a possibility, however, that in resolving the legal insufficiency claim first, the trial court will find for the plaintiff. In that event, the *Siegert/County of Sacramento/Conn v. Gabbert/Wilson v. Layne* marching orders for trial courts—do not decide whether a right was well settled at the time the defendant acted until you have first decided that such a right is currently cognizable—may, as in *Zinermon*, work to the disadvantage of future defendants. That is, even if, in the rights—deciding case (Case 1), the qualified immunity defense ultimately prevails, the right may have been sufficiently declared there to be deemed clearly established, and thus defeat a claim of immunity in a subsequent action (Case 2).

Thus a defendant's attorney, after *Siegert, County of Sacramento, Conn, and Wilson* no longer gain any advantage by pressing for qualified immunity before moving to dismiss for the plaintiff's failure to allege the violation of a federal right. Instructed by *Siegert, County of Sacramento, Conn*, and *Wilson*, trial courts should usually refuse to decide how settled a right was before deciding if any such right now is.[52] Moreover, counsel for the instant defendant may conclude that her interests (unlike those of potential future defendants) are better served by litigating the "rights" issue first. After all, a determination that there is no predicate right avoids all liability, not just liability for damages.[53] A threshold determination of the rights issue, if it is favorable to defendant, therefore fully implements the Supreme Court's resolve to provide a complete immunity from suit, not just from liability.[54] Under previous practice, where trial courts usually ruled first on the "clearly established" ques-

51. The Supreme Court in *County of Sacramento v. Lewis*, 523 U.S. 833, 118 S.Ct. 1708, 140 L.Ed.2d 1043 (1998) recognized this point: the generally sound rule of avoiding determination of constitutional issues stands in the way of using § 1983 suits against individuals as a crucible for testing constitutional claims. "An immunity determination, with nothing more, provides no clear standard ... [S]tandards of official conduct would tend to remain uncertain." *Id.* at 1714 n.5. *See also Conn v. Gabbert*, 526 U.S. 286, 290, 119 S.Ct. 1292, 1295, 143 L.Ed.2d 399 (1999); *Wilson v. Layne*, 526 U.S. 603, 609, 119 S.Ct. 1692, 1697, 143 L.Ed.2d 818 (1999) (mandating that courts determine whether the plaintiff has alleged the deprivation of an actual constitutional right first).

52. Some lower courts had viewed the *Siegert* discussion on this point not as a command but as a description of the sequence for deciding the two legal aspects of qualified immunity that would usually be most efficient. See § 2.22, *supra*. That approach has been eclipsed by the Supreme Court's approving reference to *Siegert* in *County of Sacramento v. Lewis*, and the mandate in *Conn v. Gabbert* and *Wilson v. Layne*.

53. *See County of Sacramento*, supra (if courts address the clearly established issue first and resolve it favorably to defendant, only actions in which the defendant is ineligible for qualified immunity—e.g., those seeking solely injunctive relief and those against entities—could serve as vehicles for testing new constitutional claims). *See* the discussion of *Behrens v. Pelletier* in § 2.23, *supra*.

54. *See Siegert*, 500 U.S. at 232–33, 111 S.Ct. at 1793–94 (concluding that qualified immunity creates "an immunity from suit rather than a mere defense to liability") (quoting *Mitchell v. Forsyth*, 472 U.S. 511, 526, 105 S.Ct. 2806, 2815, 86 L.Ed.2d 411 (1985)).

tion, a defendant who prevailed on the qualified immunity defense would be relieved of liability for damages only.[55]

Still, the post-*Siegert/County of Sacramento/Conn/Wilson* use of § 1983 individual damage actions to achieve a declaration of new rights may prove limited. First, if Case 1 fails to move beyond the district court, Case 2 may not accord a great deal of weight to the part of the Case 1 opinion that declares a right; perhaps only authority of the Supreme Court or the pertinent circuit is of sufficient dignity to generate clearly established law.[56] Second, even an appellate opinion in Case 1 may have little precedential value if, after declaring a right, it nevertheless finds the defendant qualifiedly immune because the right was not well established. A court in Case 2 may reason that the Case 1 court did not need to consider the "rights" issue carefully because declaration of the right had no effect on the Case 1 result.[57]

Today, if the trial court rules against the defendant on the "current rights" question when it is posed as an aspect of qualified immunity, the defendant will have a preliminary interlocutory appeal. If that appeal fails, the defendant may then move the trial court to dismiss or enter summary judgment on the second "law" ground, namely that the right in question was not clearly established when the defendant acted. (Alternatively, or in addition, this second motion might rest on the "fact" ground that a reasonable person in the circumstances would not have realized that acting or failing to act would violate that right). If the second motion is denied, defendant may then pursue a second interlocutory appeal.[58]

§ 2.42 Entity Defendant Cases

a. The Prima Facie Element of "Policy"

In actions against entity defendants the Court has for the most part addressed the same problems of fairness, federalism, and floodgates not by eroding selected predicate federal rights or enlarging immunities (as it did in actions against individual defendants), but by heightening the plaintiff's prima facie showing necessary to state any claim under § 1983. In *Monell*, the Court appeared to conclude that it would be unfair to encumber entities with liability on the same terms as it had exposed individual defendants under *Monroe*—that is, liability for any conduct carried out under the emblem of government authority, whether

55. *See Harlow* and *Anderson, supra.* On the possibilities and perils of using suits for injunctive relief against individual officials as a vehicle for creating new procedural rights, *see supra* § 2.2 and *infra*, Chapter 5 (concerning *Lyons v. City of Los Angeles*).

56. *Cf. Davis v. Scherer*, 468 U.S. 183, 192, 104 S.Ct. 3012, 3018, 82 L.Ed.2d 139 (1984) (citing circuit authority as evidence of precedent that is "clearly established"). *But see* § 2.22, *supra.*

57. *Cf. Restatement (Second) of Judgments* §§ 17(3), 28 (1982) (stating that issue preclusion is appropriate only when determination of the common issue was essential to the earlier judgment); § 27, comment o (where trial court judgment in first action rests on independent, alternate grounds, neither ground has preclusive effect unless one or both are affirmed on appeal).

58. *See* the discussion of *Behrens v. Pelletier* in § 2.23, *supra.*

or not authorized in fact or enshrined in official policy. The *Monell* court addressed this concern by adding the "policy" element to a plaintiff's prima facie claim against an entity defendant and thereby generically reducing the scope of the § 1983 claim against an entity.[1]

The Court's policy-impelled changes on the entity side reflect more than modest tinkering with particular species of claims such as due process. Rather, in § 1983 entity litigation the Court has placed wholesale limitations on the nature of claims assertable against the government. The original architect of these restrictions, Justice Brennan, would only two years later consider it " 'uniquely amiss' "if the government entity, " 'to which all in our society look for the ... setting of worthy norms and goals for social conduct,' "was to enjoy a qualified immunity to backstop the stringent prima facie case set out in *Monell*.[2] In effect, the majority he spoke for in Owen found that *Monell* already provided an adequate response to fears about fairness. "Policy" ensures that the government can be held responsible only for conduct unequivocally attributable to its advertent decisions.

b. The Missing Immunity Defense

Given the formidable, even forbidding, requirements of *Monell's* prima facie policy element and its even more rigorous subsequent fortification, it is tempting to conclude that the Court's decision in *Owen* to eschew developing a common law of immunity for entity defendants is largely an empty gesture. Who needs immunity from a case so hard to build? But there is operative and symbolic significance in the Court's refusal to confer on government entity defendants an immunity parallel to the one that it would soon confer unrestrainedly on their agents.

The *Owen* dissenters may have overstated their case by asserting that the majority's rejection of immunity imposes "strict liability" on local government entities.[3] It is clear hyperbole, for example, to suggest that strict liability operates in a "failure to act" case like *City of Canton*, in which entity liability attaches only upon a showing of "deliberate indifference." The *Owen* dissenters were on target, however, when they lamented that denying entities immunity sometimes ends up subjecting them to civil liability for constitutional violations announced for the first time in the instant litigation.

By denying entities an immunity defense parallel to that enjoyed by their agents, *Owen* preserves the possibility that § 1983 entity cases may continue to serve as a crucible for the development of federal constitutional law, provided the plaintiff can thread the prima facie policy needle

§ 2.42

1. *See Monell v. Department of Soc. Servs.*, 436 U.S. 658, 691, 98 S.Ct. 2018, 2036, 56 L.Ed.2d 611 (1978) and its progeny, discussed in detail above in §§ 2.31 and 2.32.

2. *Owen v. City of Independence*, 445 U.S. 622, 651, 100 S.Ct. 1398, 1415, 63 L.Ed.2d 673 (1980) (*quoting Adickes v. S.H. Kress & Co.*, 398 U.S. 144, 190, 90 S.Ct. 1598, 1620, 26 L.Ed.2d 142 (1970) (Brennan, J., concurring in part and dissenting in part)).

3. *See Owen v. City of Independence*, 445 U.S. 622, 658, 100 S.Ct. 1398, 1419, 63 L.Ed.2d 673 (1980) (Powell, J., dissenting).

of *Monell* and its progeny.[4] The dissenters saw this clearly. Inveighing against what they foresaw as "strict liability on municipalities for constitutional violations," they accused the majority of ignoring "the vast weight of common-law precedent as well as the current state law of municipal immunity."[5] The result, according to the dissent, was that the government entity, unlike its agent, would be liable if it "incorrectly—though reasonably and in good faith—forecasts the course of constitutional law."[6]

Justice Brennan, for the majority, responded that by compounding the qualified immunity for individuals with a "good faith" immunity for the entity the Court might completely "freez[e]" constitutional development.[7] Second, he declared that if officials prove unable to forecast some doctrinal development, "it is fairer to allocate any resulting financial loss to the inevitable costs of government borne by all the taxpayers, than to

4. This statement may be somewhat overbroad. Two situations come to mind in which the entity, like its individual agents, may enjoy additional protection just because the predicate right allegedly violated is not well settled.

First, the entity may enjoy immunity from damages when the decision declaring its liability breaks sharply with past precedent. *See infra* text discussing the potential impact of *American Trucking Ass'ns, Inc. v. Smith*, 496 U.S. 167, 110 S.Ct. 2323, 110 L.Ed.2d 148 (1990), and *Dennis v. Higgins*, 498 U.S. 439, 111 S.Ct. 865, 112 L.Ed.2d 969 (1991), on entity immunity. Second, when the plaintiff asserts that entity "policy" takes the form of an omission, plaintiff is required to demonstrate that it should have been obvious to the entity's agent that failure to act would violate a constitutional right. That, in turn, implies that the right in question must have been somewhat settled before the events at issue in the action. *See supra* § 2.32 (discussing *City of Canton v. Harris*, 489 U.S. 378, 109 S.Ct. 1197, 103 L.Ed.2d 412 (1989)). If the Court comes to recognize this legal requirement explicitly, entities in these omission cases would escape all liability for newly declared rights. They would be better off than similarly situated individual defendants, who are shielded only from damages liability under the "clearly established" version of qualified immunity.

Nevertheless, in other contexts the entity action remains the primary vehicle for creating new constitutional rights. An instructive example of this progenerative potential is glimpsed by comparing *Owen*, an entity action, with *Paul v. Davis*, 424 U.S. 693, 96 S.Ct. 1155, 47 L.Ed.2d 405 (1976), an action against an individual. In *Owen*, the majority strained the record to find that the defamatory statements about the plaintiff police chief were made in the course of his discharge from public employment and thus implicated a liberty interest protected by due process under the decision in *Wisconsin v. Constantineau*, 400 U.S. 433, 91 S.Ct. 507, 27 L.Ed.2d 515 (1971), *see supra* § 2.41 and *Board of Regents of State Colleges v. Roth*, 408 U.S. 564, 92 S.Ct. 2701, 33 L.Ed.2d 548 (1972). See *Owen*, 445 U.S. at 633–34 n.13, 100 S.Ct. at 1406–07 n.13. In *Paul*, by contrast, the Court labored to avoid finding a predicate liberty interest by conjuring up the thinnest imaginable distinctions to distinguish Constantineau. *See* Monaghan, 62 Cornell L.Rev. at 423–29; David L. Shapiro, *Mr. Justice Rehnquist: A Preliminary View*, 90 Harv.L.Rev. 293, 324–28 (1976). It may not be a coincidence that in *Owen*, unlike *Paul*, the defendant was an entity. *Cf. supra* § 2.41 (comparing *City of Canton* with *Danese v. Asman*, 875 F.2d 1239 (6th Cir.1989), *cert. denied*, 494 U.S. 1027, 110 S.Ct. 1473, 108 L.Ed.2d 610 (1990)).

5. *Owen*, 445 U.S. at 658, 100 S.Ct. at 1419 (Powell, J., dissenting). Beginning only two years later with *Harlow v. Fitzgerald*, 457 U.S. 800, 102 S.Ct. 2727, 73 L.Ed.2d 396 (1982), the Court superseded the common law approach to individual immunity with its more expansive version driven by concerns for calendar congestion and effective government administration. *See supra* § 2.22.

6. *Owen*, 445 U.S. at 668, 100 S.Ct. at 1424 (Powell, J., dissenting).

7. *See id.* at 651 n.33, 100 S.Ct. at 1415 n.33.

allow its impact to be felt solely by those whose rights, albeit newly recognized, have been violated."[8]

A plurality of the Court, in *American Trucking Associations, Inc. v. Smith*,[9] reiterated in dictum its understanding that Owen allows for doctrinal development in actions against entities, but it did so in circumstances that paradoxically also hint at *Owen's* demise.[10] *Smith* expressly endorsed *Owen*, and its understanding that suits against municipalities will continue to stage the recognition of at least some new constitutional guarantees. But skeptics might see *Smith* as spade work for overruling or qualifying *Owen's* rejection of entity immunity.

Smith reviewed a dormant commerce clause challenge to Arkansas's flat rate highway equalization tax. The Arkansas Supreme Court initially affirmed the trial court's ruling upholding application of the tax to nonresident motorists. During the pendency of the petitioner's appeal to the United States Supreme Court, the Court struck down a similar statute in *American Trucking Ass'ns., Inc. v. Scheiner*,[11] in a decision that the Smith Court described as "a clear break from" established precedent.[12] The *Smith* Court thereafter vacated the judgment of the Arkansas Supreme Court and remanded. The Arkansas Supreme Court subsequently held the state act unconstitutional, but concluded that, under *Chevron Oil Co. v. Huson*,[13] *Scheiner* could not be applied retroactively. Accordingly, petitioners were denied a full refund. They appealed again to the United States Supreme Court.

The Supreme Court upheld the Arkansas high court in pertinent part. First, the Court held that, in light of the pre-*Scheiner* precedent that reasonably supported the state's belief that its tax was permissible, "the purpose of the Commerce Clause does not dictate retroactive application of *Scheiner*," since retroactive application would not deter future state efforts to erect trade barriers.[14] The Court also found that equitable considerations, which constitute one prong of the retroactivity analysis required by *Chevron Oil*, supported the decision to forego retroactive application. The state legislature had relied in good faith on past precedent in passing the tax and "had good reason" to believe it was constitutional.[15]

In discussing whether the equities favored retroactive application, the Court addressed petitioner's analogy to *Owen*, namely, that an entity could not " 'disavow liability for the injury it has begotten.' "[16] Petitioner

8. *Id.* at 655, 100 S.Ct. at 1417.

9. 496 U.S. 167, 183, 110 S.Ct. 2323, 2334, 110 L.Ed.2d 148 (1990) (O'Connor, J., plurality opinion).

10. Although *Smith* and *Dennis v. Higgins*, 498 U.S. 439, 111 S.Ct. 865, 112 L.Ed.2d 969 (1991), discussed below, were brought nominally against individuals, they may be regarded functionally as actions against the entities for whom the named defendants worked.

11. 483 U.S. 266, 107 S.Ct. 2829, 97 L.Ed.2d 226 (1987).

12. *Smith*, 496 U.S, at 183, 110 S.Ct. at 2334.

13. 404 U.S. 97, 92 S.Ct. 349, 30 L.Ed.2d 296 (1971).

14. *Smith*, 496 U.S. at 180, 110 S.Ct. at 2332.

15. *Id.* at 182, 110 S.Ct. at 2333.

16. *Id.* at 183, 110 S.Ct. at 2334 (*quoting Owen*, 445 U.S. at 651, 100 S.Ct. at 1415).

argued that the state was not entitled to what was in effect a good faith immunity. The Court, however, distinguished *Owen*. Unlike the constitutional issue at bar, Justice O'Connor stated, *Owen* involved a determination of congressional intent, and thus "provide[d] little guidance for determining the fairest way to apply our own decisions."[17] The Court then suggested that the policy issues underlying *Owen* were distinct. *Owen* determined that a "special [municipal] immunity for violations of constitutional rights would not best serve the goals of § 1983, even if those rights had not been clearly established when the violation occurred."[18] *Owen*, the plurality explained, rested in some measure on a deterrence rationale; entity liability would cause the municipal official to " 'consider whether his decision comports with constitutional mandates and ... weigh the risk that a violation might result in an award of damages from the public treasury.' "[19] By contrast, Justice O'Connor wrote, when Supreme Court constitutional determinations "clearly break[ ] with precedent ... which ... public officials could not anticipate," a different analysis applies.[20] Thus in *Smith* the Court's refusal to require the state to provide a full refund had the effect of conferring a partial, one-time immunity from damages only, and then only in a "clearly breaks" context.

Smith's rhetorical support for *Owen* is offset in some measure by the questionable nature of the plurality's distinctions.[21] The claim that *Owen*-generated damages might deter a government official from violating the law, whereas the prospect of a state tax refund would not, is highly debatable. A break with clear precedent would a priori be no more foreseeable in one case than in the other. The Court's distinction between sources of violation—statutory versus constitutional—is not wholly convincing either. Section 1983 individual defendant immunity doctrine, after all, has sometimes been imported from the realm of "*Bivens*" actions that arise directly under the Constitution.[22]

Smith could therefore be viewed as providing an opening for subsequent reappraisal of *Owen* on the good faith immunity issue. One could contend that the Court is preparing to limit *Owen* by citing to *Smith* as a basis for reconsideration. In *Owen* itself the plaintiff's claim did not clearly break with, but merely took a step beyond, existing precedent.[23] So the Court has room to invoke the *Smith* immunity in a Section 1983 entity case where the decision or rule contended for by the plaintiff does chart unarguably virgin territory. That this possibility is not far-fetched is suggested by the Court's adoption of standards friendly to non-retroactive application of new rules in a cognate civil rights context, federal habeas corpus law. There the Court precludes retroactive applica-

17. *Id.*

18. *Id.*

19. *Id.* (quoting *Owen*, 445 U.S. at 656, 100 S.Ct. at 1418).

20. *Id.*

21. *See* Peter W. Low & John C. Jeffries, Jr., *Civil Rights Actions* (Foundation 1988) 6–7 (Supp. 1991) (asking whether the plurality is sub silentio creating an exception to *Owen*, and if so, how such an exception differs from affording municipal government a good faith immunity).

22. See *supra*, Chapter 2, Part G.

23. *See infra* text this section.

tion of "new constitutional rules of criminal procedure," with new rules broadly defined in that setting to include those that merely break new ground.[24] The Court has since applied this approach to validate state court criminal law interpretations that failed to forecast constitutional developments, provided that they represented "reasonable, good-faith interpretations of existing precedents."[25]

The Court's decision in *Dennis v. Higgins*,[26] by finding alleged state tax violations of the Commerce Clause actionable under § 1983, suggests that in such cases an even broader immunity than Smith affords is separately accomplished by a distinct § 1983 doctrinal development. Before *Dennis*, such actions were sui generis; it was unclear what source of law spawned them.[27] *Dennis*, however, clarifies that Section 1983 is the remedial vehicle; and under *Will v. Michigan Department of State Police*,[28] which held that a state is not a "person" for purposes of Section 1983,[29] neither a tax nor any other Section 1983 claim lies against the state as such. As applied to states sued eo nomine, *Smith's* limited, partial immunity pales by comparison. *Will* shields the state as a named defendant from all § 1983 liability, even where there is no clear break with existing precedent. By analogy to Eleventh Amendment jurisprudence,[30] *Will* did continue the fiction that permits claimants to obtain prospective (but not retroactive) relief against unconstitutional state conduct by the device of naming individual state officers in their official capacities.[31] But where state officials are sued under Section 1983 in their official capacities, *Will* now precludes retroactive relief[32]—and it

24. *Teague v. Lane*, 489 U.S. 288, 301, 310, 109 S.Ct. 1060, 1070, 1075, 103 L.Ed.2d 334 (1989).

25. *Butler v. McKellar*, 494 U.S. 407, 414, 110 S.Ct. 1212, 1217, 108 L.Ed.2d 347 (1990) (refusing to apply a "new rule" barring certain police-initiated interrogations to the defendant's murder conviction). *But see Griffith v. Kentucky*, 479 U.S. 314, 107 S.Ct. 708, 93 L.Ed.2d 649 (1987) (ordering retroactive application of even newly declared rules in all criminal cases pending on direct review).

26. 498 U.S. 439, 111 S.Ct. 865, 112 L.Ed.2d 969 (1991).

27. *See, e.g., McKesson Corp. v. Division of Alcoholic Beverages & Tobacco*, 496 U.S. 18, 49 n. 34, 110 S.Ct. 2238, 2257 n. 34, 110 L.Ed.2d 17 (1990) (suggesting that authority for the action arose because Florida had waived sovereign immunity in its own courts); *Ward v. Board of County Comm'rs*, 253 U.S. 17, 24, 40 S.Ct. 419, 422, 64 L.Ed. 751 (1920) (explaining that " 'the law, independent of any statute,' "provided the substantive grounds for the litigation (*quoting Marsh v. Fulton County*, 77 U.S. (10 Wall.) 676, 684, 19 L.Ed. 1040 (1870))).

28. 491 U.S. 58, 109 S.Ct. 2304, 105 L.Ed.2d 45 (1989).

29. *See supra* § 2.35. Neither is a dog a "person," even when the dog is proximately responsible for plaintiff's injuries. *Dye v. Wargo*, 253 F.3d 296, 299–300 (7th Cir.2001) (relying on absence of dogs from list of "persons" in Dictionary Act, 1 U.S.C § 1).

30. *See generally Ex parte Young*, 209 U.S. 123, 28 S.Ct. 441, 52 L.Ed. 714 (1908), discussed infra this section.

31. *See Will*, 491 U.S. at 71 n.10, 109 S.Ct. at 2312 n.10.

32. *See Will*, 491 U.S. at 71 n.10, 109 S.Ct. at 2312 n.10, and *Hafer v. Melo*, 502 U.S. 21, 112 S.Ct. 358, 116 L.Ed.2d 301 (1991). *Cf. Edelman v. Jordan*, 415 U.S. 651, 663, 94 S.Ct. 1347, 1356, 39 L.Ed.2d 662 (1974) (noting that "even though a State is not named a party, ... the suit may [if the state pays] nonetheless be barred by the Eleventh Amendment"). (Of some potential import is the fact that *Edelman* relied on *Ford Motor Co. v. Department of Treasury*, 323 U.S. 459, 65 S.Ct. 347, 89 L.Ed. 389 (1945); there the Court held that a non-resident's challenge to a state income tax could not be maintained in

does so even where, as seems not to have been the case in *Smith*, the state officials could reasonably have anticipated the unconstitutionality of their conduct.

The situation is somewhat different with respect to a tax refund (or other) claim against a political subdivision of the state that does not look to the state to satisfy an adverse judgment. Unlike the State itself, the local government entity is a "person" suable under Section 1983. Where a decision against that subdivision sharply breaks with existing precedent, the *Smith* remedial limitation could be extended to that entity, undermining the *Owen* rejection of entity immunity. But there is substantial reason to doubt that the Smith limitation on *Owen* will extend downward to benefit cities and counties. For one thing, *Owen* itself involved a municipal defendant. For another, *Owen* now has no direct application even to the states, having been eclipsed by *Will*; to mean anything at all it must apply to state subdivisions. Finally, the *Smith* plurality opinion falls in line with the tradition of deference to the choices of states, not their creatures. An across-the-board overruling of *Owen* premised on the decision in *Smith* (which the Court partly justified by distinguishing it from *Owen*) seems most unlikely.

Moreover, the very vitality of *Smith* is challenged by the opinion of the court in *Harper v. Virginia Department of Taxation*. Broad dictum in Part II of the opinion, subscribed to by five justices, comes close to overruling *sub silentio Chevron Oil*, the precedential foundation of *Smith*.[33]

federal court, regardless of the identity of the party formally named.) If tax refunds are deemed a "retroactive" remedy, *Will*—with its analogy to Eleventh Amendment learning like *Edelman*—would limit the § 1983 plaintiff, in state or federal court, to injunctive relief. Whether tax refunds are always precluded as "retroactive" is undecided. *But cf. Ford Motor Co. v. Department of Treasury*, 323 U.S. 459, 65 S.Ct. 347, 89 L.Ed. 389 (1945). In *Edelman*, the Court had denied federal welfare beneficiaries, suing in federal court, recovery of benefits wrongfully withheld by state officials. The Court held that under the aegis of the Eleventh Amendment and *Ex parte Young*, a federal court could award only prospective relief against a state employee sued in her official capacity, and that "equitable restitution" of benefits was a species of nonrecoverable, retroactive relief. *Edelman*, 415 U.S. at 666–69, 94 S.Ct. at 1357–59.

To avoid the retroactive label, one could perhaps distinguish the payment coerced from taxpayers' pockets, as in *Smith*, from the statutory benefits withheld through wrongful computation in *Edelman*. But it is not altogether clear why taxpayers injured by state laws are more deserving of full recovery than impecunious plaintiffs for whom Congress has created an entitlement. The equities are especially obscure because the underlying substantive constitutional law gives states special options to remedy Commerce Clause taxing violations. Subject to very niggardly due process protections, they may decline to refund entirely and instead eliminate the discriminatory trade barrier by increasing the taxes of those who benefited under the invalid act. See Part III of *Harper v. Virginia Dept. of Taxation*, 509 U.S. 86, 113 S.Ct. 2510, 125 L.Ed.2d 74 (1993); *McKesson*, 496 U.S. at 40, 110 S.Ct. at 2252. Thus the ultimate violation in the Commerce Clause context is not reflected in taxes wrongfully levied, but simply in the inequality of the taxing mechanism. By contrast, the problem in the entitlement context is the loss of funds that can never be recovered. The taxpayer, in short, may stand on shakier equitable footing than the welfare recipient. If state law itself provides a refund, that legal remedy, if deemed adequate, forecloses injunctive relief under § 1983; hence no attorney's fees under § 1988 may be awarded. *National Private Truck Council v. Oklahoma Tax Comm'n*, 515 U.S. 582, 115 S.Ct. 2351, 132 L.Ed.2d 509 (1995).

33. 509 U.S. 86, 113 S.Ct. 2510, 125 L.Ed.2d 74 (1993).

The *Harper* holding is limited to the proposition that "this Court's application of a rule of federal law to the parties before the Court requires every [subsequent] court to give retroactive effect to that decision"—even as to events that predate the announcement of the rule. Because the majority concluded that the Court had retroactively applied an earlier decision invalidating Michigan's taxation of federal retirement benefits, while exempting state or local retirement benefits, it had only to condemn "selective" prospective application to Virginia's similar taxing scheme held unlawful in *Harper*. Yet several justices were convinced that the Michigan precedent had not in fact been applied retroactively to the state taxing authorities there, and those justices were therefore prepared to argue for "pure" prospective application to Virginia, under the authority of *Chevron* and *Smith*.

Justice Scalia, one of the five justices who joined the dictum against such pure prospectivity in Part II of the Court's opinion, concurred separately to condemn all forms of prospective judicial decisionmaking. He strongly suggested that the majority was abandoning *Chevron*, just as the Court had concluded in *Griffith v. Kentucky*[34] that any "newly declared ... rule" must be applied retroactively in all "criminal cases pending on direct review." In his view, any form of prospective decisionmaking in civil cases violates the "traditional" or pre-*Chevron* norm of constitutional adjudication that calls for full retrospective application, even of newly declared rules of law.

Chevron and *Smith* may not in fact be dead. Perhaps the majority strained to find that *Harper* involved only "selective" rather than "pure" prospectivity in order to avoid condemning the possibility of prospective application in any civil case. Second, not all justices were convinced that the Virginia tax scheme was condemned under a "new rule" and was therefore eligible for prospective application in the first place.[35] Finally, one of the justices who concurred in Part II, Justice Blackmun, is no longer on the Court, leaving some doubt whether a majority of the current Court would overrule *Chevron*. Nevertheless, the opinions as a whole suggest that *Chevron* and, in turn, *Smith*, are living on borrowed time. Indeed, as this book went to press, the Court in a tort case described *Harper* as having overruled *Chevron* insofar as that decision "permitted the prospective—only application of a new rule of law."[36]

Owen therefore seems unimpaired, and the liability of cities and counties under Section 1983 for the violation of even strikingly "new rules" of constitutional law remains open ended, notwithstanding *Smith's* remedial limitation. In any event, the Court, after citing *Smith*, has now held that, in general, remedial lenity is available only when an independent principle of law like qualified immunity trumps the usual

34. 479 U.S. 314, 322, 107 S.Ct. 708, 713, 93 L.Ed.2d 649 (1987).

35. *See, e.g.*, Kennedy, J., concurring.

36. *Reynoldsville Casket Co. v. Hyde*, 514 U.S. 749, 115 S.Ct. 1745, 131 L.Ed.2d 820 (1995). *See* Fisch, *Retroactivity And Legal Change: an Equilibrium Approach*, 110 Harv.L.Rev. 1055 (1997).

policy favoring retroactivity, not simply where there is *Chevron*-esque justifiable reliance on an old rule.[37] Finally, even if *Smith* should survive, its limitation on remedies in "clear break" cases is unlikely to portend an end to incremental, as distinct from dramatic, doctrinal development. After all, the one-time immunity that *Smith* created from the new constitutional restriction announced by *Scheiner* was limited to state taxes received before the *Scheiner* decision.[38] The tax condemned in *Smith* could no longer be collected, even though full refunds were unavailable. Thus there remains ample incentive for local taxpayers to bring suit based on a "new rule" to obtain injunctive relief and, consequently, attorney's fees.

A separate development, however, does raise the possibility that the Court might depart from *Owen* directly and carve out some degree of governmental immunity across the board under Section 1983. A growing number of Justices have expressed support for the proposition that the common law of 1871 should take primacy over judicial declarations of statutory policy in shaping § 1983 doctrine concerning elements of liability, damages, and even immunities.[39] The dissenters in *Owen* took sharp issue with the majority's conclusion that there was no municipal immunity at common law. They observed that municipalities were generally not held liable for conduct undertaken in a "governmental" rather than "proprietary" capacity, and stressed that local governments enjoyed a good-faith immunity respecting the manner in which they discharged their "discretionary," as opposed to "ministerial" duties. Should the Court come to accept the *Owen* dissenters' reading of the 19th-century common law, it might feel impelled to exalt that reading over the statutory policies of compensation and deterrence that figured so heavily in the Owen decision to deny local government immunity. Nevertheless, lower courts continue to adhere to *Owen's* flat denial of entity immunity.[40]

c. *An Open Door for Constitutional Development*

Plaintiffs suing local government entities may proceed to trial even if the particular federal right allegedly invaded by that policy lacked prior judicial recognition—a circumstance that would establish immunity for an individual defendant.[41] Still, even those plaintiffs who can demonstrate that the violation of a constitutional right took place under the aegis of an entity's official policy must allege at the threshold the

37. *Id.*

38. *Smith*, 496 U.S. at 185–89, 110 S.Ct. at 2335–36.

39. See § 2.2, *supra*. Lower courts, however, are adhering to *Owen*'s flat denial of entity immunity. *Berkley v. Common Council of Charleston*, 63 F.3d 295 (4th Cir.1995) (en banc), *cert. denied*, 516 U.S. 1073, 116 S.Ct. 775, 133 L.Ed.2d 727 (1996).

40. *See Berkley*, 63 F.3d 295.

41. With respect to entity omissions, and thus the "deliberate indifference" standard, it may be difficult for the plaintiff to show that the need for entity action was "obvious" in the absence of settled law. *See City of Canton v. Harris*, 489 U.S. 378, 390 n. 10, 109 S.Ct. 1197, 1205 n. 10, 103 L.Ed.2d 412 (1989) (citing Tennessee v. Garner, 471 U.S. 1, 105 S.Ct. 1694, 85 L.Ed.2d 1 (1985)); Mark R. Brown, *Correlating Municipal Liability and Official Immunity Under Section 1983*, 1989 U.Ill. L.Rev. 625, 656 (1989).

violation of a constitutional right that the court is currently willing to recognize.[42] And in that connection it should be borne in mind that the Court has given increasingly restrictive readings to the liberty component of the Eighth Amendment and the Fourteenth Amendment's Due Process Clause.[43]

42. *See* discussion of *Siegert v. Gilley* in § 5.108, *infra.*

43. *See, e.g., Farmer v. Brennan,* 511 U.S. 825, 114 S.Ct. 1970, 128 L.Ed.2d 811 (1994) (prison official violates Eighth Amendment by failing to protect inmate health or safety only when defendant is deliberately indifferent in the sense of "subjective recklessness": plaintiff must prove that defendant in fact knew that inmates faced a substantial risk of serious harm and disregarded that risk by failing to take reasonable precautions); *Tucker v. Evans,* 276 F.3d 999, 1001–03 (8th Cir.2002) (qualified immunity for prison officials when Eighth Amendment claim predicated on surprise attack on plaintiff by another inmate, and even gross negligence insufficient to prove Eighth Amendment violation); *Smith v. Gray,* 259 F.3d 933 (8th Cir.2001) (Eighth Amendment claim failed because defendant officers lacked actual knowledge that possible future assault by another inmate was likely to present a significant risk of serious bodily harm to plaintiff); *McElligott v. Foley,* 182 F.3d 1248, 1254–55 (11th Cir.1999) (medical mistreatment claim under Eighth Amendment requires proof that defendant (1) knew of a risk of serious harm (harm diagnosed by a physician or so obvious that a lay person would perceive the need for physician's attention); (2) disregarded that risk through delay or inaction; and (3) the "disregard" came about through conduct more serious than mere negligence or medical malpractice); *Hill v. Dekalb Regional Youth Detention Center,* 40 F.3d 1176 (11th Cir.1994) (neither inadvertent failure to provide adequate medical care nor physician's negligence or malpractice states Eighth Amendment medical mistreatment claim); *Johnson v. Quinones,* 145 F.3d 164 (4th Cir.1998) (no Eighth Amendment claim where plaintiff fails to adduce evidence that defendant knew of serious medical needs); *but cf. Smith v. Mensinger,* 293 F.3d 641 (3d Cir. 2002) (officer's failure to intervene in inmate beating can violate Eighth Amendment if officer knew that fellow officers were using excessive force and nevertheless refused to intervene despite an opportunity to do so); *Lawson v. Dallas County,* 286 F.3d 257 (5th Cir.2002) (jail medical personnel displayed deliberate indifference to paraplegic inmate's medical condition by ignoring medical instructions about regular dressing changes and medication); *Comstock v. McCrary,* 273 F.3d 693 (6th Cir. 2001) (prison psychologist deliberately indifferent in releasing prisoner from suicide watch without making "reasoned" evaluation of suicide risk after having placed him on that watch one day before); *Sanville v. McCaughtry,* 266 F.3d 724 (7th Cir.2001), (inmate's mother stated Eighth Amendment claim after his suicide when she alleged his history of mental illness, loss of a third of his body weight, express statements to guards of his intent to kill himself, and other evidence of suicidal intent); *McElligott v. Foley, supra,* 182 F.3d at 1256–57 (deliberate failure to further diagnose and treat prisoner's severe pain of deteriorating condition states Eighth Amendment claim). *See also Albright v. Oliver,* 510 U.S. 266, 114 S.Ct. 807, 127 L.Ed.2d 114 (1994) (criminal suspect has no substantive due process right to be free from baseless initiation of prosecution because Fourth Amendment is explicitly addressed to the type of government conduct at issue) (plurality opinion) *Albright* has since been read "virtually to foreclose" converting a malicious prosecution claim into a § 1983 claim asserting a violation of substantive due process. *Perez–Ruiz v. Crespo–Guillen,* 25 F.3d 40 (1st Cir.1994). *But cf. Gallo v. City of Philadelphia,* 161 F.3d 217 (3d Cir.1998) and *Singer v. Fulton County Sheriff,* 63 F.3d 110 (2d Cir.1995), *cert. denied,* 517 U.S. 1189, 116 S.Ct. 1676, 134 L.Ed.2d 779 (1996) (both holding that Fourth Amendment malicious prosecution claim may be based on liberty deprivations amounting to "seizure"); *Collins v. City of Harker Heights,* 503 U.S. 115, 112 S.Ct. 1061, 117 L.Ed.2d 261 (1992) (government employer has no duty enforceable as an aspect of substantive due process to provide safe working environment to its employees); *Siegert v. Gilley,* 500 U.S. 226, 111 S.Ct. 1789, 114 L.Ed.2d 277 (1991) (defamation attributable to federal agency and uttered shortly after employee's termination from the agency's employment implicates no liberty interest protected by due process); *Graham v. Connor,* 490 U.S. 386, 109 S.Ct. 1865, 104 L.Ed.2d 443 (1989) (excessive force claims analyzed under Fourth Amendment rather than due process standards because that amendment was an explicit textual source of protection against the alleged police mis-

Entity liability under § 1983 for newly declared constitutional rights, reaffirmed in dictum by a plurality in *American Trucking Associations, Inc. v. Smith*,[44] was realized in *Owen* itself. The plaintiff, a former police chief, was discharged under stigmatizing circumstances and denied an opportunity publicly to clear his name. The majority agreed that a due process hearing was required and held that local governments enjoyed no § 1983 immunity.[45] The dissenters argued vehemently that the Court had not previously accorded employees at will a "name clearing" hearing after their discharge. Consequently, no protectable species of property or liberty existed, at least if there was no public disclosure of the reasons for discharge; the majority's denial of immunity thus cleared the way for the Court to declare a theretofore unsettled constitutional right.[46]

This same dynamic was also at work in *St. Louis v. Praprotnik*,[47] in which the plaintiff lost not because the entity was relieved of the duty to anticipate developments in constitutional law but because the Court found the alleged retaliatory conduct not fairly attributable to the entity.[48]

Finally, *City of Canton* graphically underscores how entities may be accountable for merely nascent constitutional violations. Explaining why they would have denied the plaintiff a remand to establish "deliberate indifference," the dissenters, speaking through Justice O'Connor, complained that the predicate right of a pretrial detainee to medical attention for emotional injury had not been definitively established. She confronted the majority with what she deemed to be a legal requirement

conduct at issue). But *Graham* does not suggest that all constitutional claims challenging physically abusive conduct must be brought under the Fourth or the Eighth Amendments, only that if such a particular constitutional protection applies the claim does not lie under substantive due process. *United States v. Lanier*, 520 U.S. 259 n. 7, 117 S.Ct. 1219, 137 L.Ed.2d 432 (1997) (case under 18 U.S.C.A. § 242).

44. 496 U.S. 167, 183, 110 S.Ct. 2323, 2334, 110 L.Ed.2d 148 (1990) (O'Connor, J., plurality opinion) (rejecting retroactive application of *American Trucking Ass'ns, Inc. v. Scheiner*, 483 U.S. 266, 107 S.Ct. 2829, 97 L.Ed.2d 226 (1987), against a state as a matter of judicial policy, while adhering to the view that § 1983 confers no general immunity on municipalities). Notwithstanding its apparent endorsement of *Owen*, the *Smith* decision, in tandem with *Dennis v. Higgins*, 498 U.S. 439, 446–51, 111 S.Ct. 865, 870–73, 112 L.Ed.2d 969 (1991) (allowing suits for violation of the Commerce Clause to proceed under § 1983), contains some potential for stimulating a limited, partial entity immunity, a prospect discussed *supra*.

45. *See Owen*, 445 U.S. at 635–38, 100 S.Ct. at 1407–09.

46. *See id.* at 661–64, 100 S.Ct. at 1420–23 (Powell, J., dissenting). The durability of expanded constitutional rights declared in § 1983 actions is another matter. For example, the *Owen* dissenters' position on the predicate "name-clearing" claim now apparently commands a majority of the Court. *See Siegert v. Gilley*, 500 U.S. 226, 231, 111 S.Ct. 1789, 1793, 114 L.Ed.2d 277 (1991) (holding insufficient to state a claim plaintiff's allegation that his former supervisor's defamatory statements violated due process by causing the loss of current and future government employment). But *Siegert's* negative reprise on the type of liberty interest in reputation that Owen recognized does not alter the fact that the § 1983 action against the entity in *Owen* did generate new doctrine at the time, or that entity actions still serve that function. *See County of Sacramento v. Lewis*, 523 U.S. 833, 118 S.Ct. 1708, 140 L.Ed.2d 1043 (1998).

47. 485 U.S. 112, 108 S.Ct. 915, 99 L.Ed.2d 107 (1988).

48. *See Praprotnik*, 485 U.S. at 128–30, 108 S.Ct. at 926–28.

implicit in the "deliberate indifference" formulation—a reasonably well-settled constitutional right.[49] Notwithstanding these protests, the majority ordered a remand perhaps permitting the plaintiff to convince the lower courts that the police officers had committed a constitutional predicate violation and that the city could fairly be responsible for it.[50]

§ 2.43 The Residue: A Mixed Picture

No unitary explanation of these divergent developments has proven entirely satisfactory. Why would the Court start by easing the plaintiff's prima facie burden against individual defendants, only to end up by cutting back on key predicate constitutional protections and insulating many of the remaining federal law violations with a defendant-friendly form of qualified immunity? Why on the other hand would the Court erect such a formidable barrier as "policy" to the liability of government entities?

Professors Low and Jeffries have suggested, for example, that the latest formulations of *Monell* "policy" in cases such as *Praprotnik* and *City of Canton* confer a de facto qualified immunity on entities, and hence wreak the revenge of the *Owen* dissenters.[1] If this were correct, the current asymmetry in form would really bring about a symmetry in substance, with immunity being the bridge between the two types of actions. But the *Monell* "policy" stricture, even as rigidly applied, is still only an effort to identify liability—conducive conduct that the factfinder can fairly impute to the entity; it does not categorically preclude novel federal claims. If the plaintiff demonstrates "policy" or its "deliberate indifference" surrogate,[2] the entity may face liability for unsettled federal constitutional or statutory violations, despite its agents' reasonable behavior. For individual defendants, either of these characteristics—the unsettled nature of the predicate right or the objective reasonableness of the state actor's conduct—would provide immunity, at least from damages. There is no symmetry in substance.

It has similarly been suspected that the *Parratt* doctrine is the individual defendant's counterpart to the *Monell* requirement of a policy or custom.[3] But *Parratt* is simply not the comprehensive barrier to

49. *See City of Canton v. Harris*, 489 U.S. 378, 396–97, 109 S.Ct. 1197, 1208–09, 103 L.Ed.2d 412 (1989) (O'Connor, J., concurring in part and dissenting in part).

50. To a lesser degree the phenomenon was also at work in *Pembaur*. The new law on which the liability of all *Pembaur* defendants turned had been declared by *Steagald*. Yet the Supreme Court noted that three circuits, including the one in which the defendants' conduct took place, had reached conclusions contrary to *Steagald* as of the events in question. See *Pembaur*, 475 U.S. at 486, 106 S.Ct. at 1301 (White, J., concurring); id. at 492–93 (Powell, J. dissenting); *supra* § 2.31. Since the relevant law had not then been firmly established, the individual defendants were entitled to exoneration by virtue of qualified immunity even if *Steagald* were given retroactive effect. The Court in *Pembaur* did expose the entity to liability on the basis of a retroactive application of *Steagald*, subject only to the prima facie showing of "policy."

§ 2.43

1. *See* Low & Jeffries, *Civil Rights Action* at 39.

2. *See supra* § 2.32.

3. *See* Susan Bandes, *Monell, Parratt, Daniels, and Davidson: Distinguishing a*

claims against individuals that the evolved version of "policy" raises to claims against entities. The circuitous logic of *Parratt*, in which the state provision of remedial process after the deprivation of constitutionally protected liberty or property transforms a denial of property without due process into a denial with due process,[4] pertains only to constitutional violations that turn on the denial of some sort of process.[5] Indeed, the *Parratt* opinion itself stressed that the reason certain forms of post-deprivation process sanitized apparently unlawful conduct was to prevent the Fourteenth Amendment, and that amendment only, from becoming the dreaded " 'font of tort law.' "[6]

Thus the *Parratt* opinion cited as support *Paul v. Davis*,[7] in which the same fear had driven it to limit the scope of constitutionally protected liberty to deprivations that included the loss of a state-defined right. Justice Rehnquist, also the author of *Parratt*, stated explicitly that the holding did not affect enforcement of interests that have their origin directly in the Bill of Rights. On the authority of *Monroe*, Rehnquist wrote that those interests may be redressed under § 1983 "independently of state law."[8] Consequently, and especially in light of *Zinermon*,[9] it is apparent that *Parratt* leaves unaffected the *Monroe* holding that individual defendants may be liable under § 1983 for violations of constitutional rights other than procedural due process. Potential liability per *Monroe* holds even when the individual defendant's conduct is entirely unauthorized by her governing principal and when her conduct, authorized or not, is random in the sense that it was not dictated or endorsed by the kind of entity policy that *Monell* requires for the liability of an entity.

Nor does expediency fully account for these developments. The Court has, of course, noted and apparently acted upon concerns about calendar congestion. Its responses have ranged from broadening the immunities available to individual defendants, paring down the scope of constitutionally protected "property" and "liberty," restrictively redefining "deprivations," and hinging the obligation to provide process on the subsequent availability of doubtfully efficacious state remedies. And in service of efficiency the Court has employed a common technique to dam the flow of entity and individual litigation: early disposition by the court. On the entity side, it has delegated to trial judges the function of deciding whether an entity's official has final policymaking authority,

Custom or Policy from a Random, Unauthorized Act, 72 Iowa L.Rev. 101 (1986).

4. *See* Monaghan, 86 Colum.L.Rev. at 985–86.

5. *See supra* § 2.41 discussing *Zinermon v. Burch*, 494 U.S. 113, 110 S.Ct. 975, 108 L.Ed.2d 100 (1990), which strongly suggests that *Parratt* now will be confined to procedural due process claims alone, as a special application of the formulation of *Mathews v. Eldridge*, 424 U.S. 319, 348–49, 96 S.Ct. 893, 909–10, 47 L.Ed.2d 18 (1976).

6. *Parratt v. Taylor*, 451 U.S. 527, 544, 101 S.Ct. 1908, 1917, 68 L.Ed.2d 420 (1981) (*quoting Paul v. Davis*, 424 U.S. 693, 701, 96 S.Ct. 1155, 1160, 47 L.Ed.2d 405 (1976)), *overruled in part by Daniels v. Williams*, 474 U.S. 327, 106 S.Ct. 662, 88 L.Ed.2d 662 (1986).

7. 424 U.S. 693, 96 S.Ct. 1155, 47 L.Ed.2d 405 (1976).

8. *Id.* at 711 n.5, 96 S.Ct. at 1165 n.5.

9. *See supra* § 2.41.

characterizing this as a question of state law.[10] Similarly, an individual official's assertion of qualified immunity turns initially, and usually ultimately, on the legal question whether plaintiff's claimed right is clearly established as a matter of federal law. In both instances liability is determinable in the first instance by the judge and offers a potentially quick escape from the litigation. Still, if a desire to stanch the dikes has spurred the Court to sap § 1983's strength as a vehicle for vindicating federal constitutional rights, what explains the Court's generally indulgent approach to § 1983 as a remedy for violations of federal statutory rights?[11] That story follows.

§§ 2.44–2.46 [Reserved]

G. *BIVENS* ACTIONS

§ 2.47 In General

Section 1983 does not provide a remedy for deprivations of Constitutionally protected rights at the hands of federal, as opposed to state, officials. Nor has Congress passed a federal counterpart to § 1983 to provide such relief. Instead, in *Bivens v. Six Unknown Named Agents of the Federal Bureau of Narcotics*,[1] the Supreme Court implied a private right of action for Fourth Amendment violations by federal officials.[2] The Court has since extended *Bivens* to cover violations of the Fifth and Eighth Amendments.[3] Lower courts have also invoked *Bivens* to remedy violations of the First and Sixth Amendments.[4]

10. This was a major point of contention in *City of St. Louis v. Praprotnik*, 485 U.S. 112, 108 S.Ct. 915, 99 L.Ed.2d 107 (1988). Justice O'Connor, for the plurality, opined that federal courts are "not . . . justified in assuming that municipal policymaking authority lies somewhere other than where the applicable [state or local] law purports to put it." *Id.* at 126, 108 S.Ct. at 925. In contrast, Justice Brennan would have treated the issue as a question of fact; he argued unsuccessfully that denominating the issue as one of state law permitted the municipalities to escape liability "for the acts of all but a small minority of actual city policymakers" named in a statute. *Id.* at 132, 108 S.Ct. at 928 (Brennan, J., concurring). Justice O'Connor's position has carried the day. *See Jett v. Dallas Indep. Sch. Dist.*, 491 U.S. 701, 737–38, 109 S.Ct. 2702, 2724, 105 L.Ed.2d 598 (1989) (remanding for a determination whether a school superintendent, who approved an allegedly racially motivated reassignment, had "final policymaking authority" over employee transfers under state law).

11. This trend is manifest in, for example, *Wilder v. Virginia Hosp. Ass'n*, 496 U.S. 498, 509, 110 S.Ct. 2510, 2517, 110 L.Ed.2d 455 (1990); *Golden State Transit Corp. v. City of Los Angeles*, 493 U.S. 103, 105, 110 S.Ct. 444, 448, 107 L.Ed.2d 420 (1989); and *Wright v. Roanoke Redev. and Hous. Auth.*, 479 U.S. 418, 107 S.Ct. 766, 93 L.Ed.2d 781 (1987). *See* Monaghan, 91 Colum.L.Rev. at 247 (concluding that "section 1983's availability turns only on whether federal statutory law creates a 'primary' right, even though the federal law does not otherwise establish a 'remedial' right").

§ 2.47

1. 403 U.S. 388, 91 S.Ct. 1999, 29 L.Ed.2d 619 (1971).

2. *Id.* at 389.

3. *See Davis v. Passman*, 442 U.S. 228, 99 S.Ct. 2264, 60 L.Ed.2d 846 (1979) (Fifth Amendment); *Carlson v. Green*, 446 U.S. 14, 100 S.Ct. 1468, 64 L.Ed.2d 15 (1980) (Eighth Amendment).

4. *See, e.g., Milhouse v. Carlson*, 652 F.2d 371 (3d Cir.1981) (First Amendment); *Berlin Democratic Club v. Rumsfeld*, 410 F.Supp. 144 (D.D.C.1976) (First and Sixth Amendments).

To state a *Bivens* claim, the plaintiff must allege a compensable injury to a legally protected interest by a deprivation of a right secured by the Constitution and the laws of the United States at the hands of a federal official acting under color of federal law. Yet in distinct contrast to similar situations involving state contractors, who are considered acting "under color of" state law and so are subject to Section 1983 liability, the Supreme Court has held that a plaintiff fails to state a *Bivens* claim against a privately owned corporation even when it is performing an exclusive federal governmental function.[5] And the United States and its agencies cannot be held liable absent an express waiver of sovereign immunity;[6] rather, the Federal Torts Claim Act[7] is the only vehicle for such suits, assuming the action does not fall within one of the statutory exceptions.[8] So the only proper *Bivens* defendants are federal employees in their individual capacities. Derivative liability is not available in a *Bivens* action for the conduct of others; the liability of *Bivens* defendants can be predicated only on their own actual and knowing participation in the allegedly unconstitutional conduct.[9] *Bivens* plaintiffs can, however, utilize the Title VII *McDonnell-Douglas* circumstantial mode of proof.[10] Generally, the only remedies available in a *Bivens* action are compensatory and punitive damages.[11]

§ 2.48 Limitations on the Availability of *Bivens* Actions

The principal rationale for implying a *Bivens* claim rests on the imperative of providing redress for constitutional violations committed by federal agents even absent a Congressionally granted remedy. Nevertheless, the Court has placed several substantial limitations on the availability of *Bivens* actions. First, *Bivens* actions are not available where there are "special factors counseling hesitation in the absence of affirmative action by Congress."[1] Second, the Court has refused to imply *Bivens* actions where there is "a textually demonstrable constitutional commitment of [an] issue to a coordinate political department."[2] Third, certain government officials might "enjoy such independent status in

5. Private corporations acting under color of federal law, for example as government contractors, are immune from *Bivens* claims. *Correctional Services Corporation v. Malesko*, 534 U.S. 61, 122 S.Ct. 515, 151 L.Ed.2d 456 (2001).

6. *See, e.g., Federal Deposit Ins. Corp. v. Meyer*, 510 U.S. 471, 114 S.Ct. 996, 127 L.Ed.2d 308 (1994).

7. 28 U.S.C.A. § 1346 et seq.

8. *See, e.g.*, 28 U.S.C.A. § 2680(a), the discretionary function exception. *See also* § 2.49, *infra*.

9. *See, e.g., Risley v. Hawk*, 108 F.3d 1396, 1396 (D.C.Cir.1997); *Abate v. Southern Pacific Transp. Co.*, 993 F.2d 107, 110 (5th Cir.1993).

10. *See, e.g., Risley v. Hawk*, 108 F.3d 1396, 1396 (D.C.Cir.1997); *Abate v. Southern Pacific Transp. Co.*, 993 F.2d 107, 110 (5th Cir.1993). *See Duffy v. Wolle*, 123 F.3d 1026, 1037 (8th Cir.1997), *cert. denied*, 523 U.S. 1137, 118 S.Ct. 1839, 140 L.Ed.2d 1090 (1998) (accepting that the *McDonnell-Douglas* framework is used in Section 1983 cases and that Section 1983 principles in turn are frequently imported into *Bivens* actions).

11. *See, e.g., Butz v. Economou*, 438 U.S. 478, 504–05, 98 S.Ct. 2894, 2909–10, 57 L.Ed.2d 895 (1978).

§ 2.48

1. *Bivens*, 403 U.S. at 396.

2. *Davis v. Passman*, 442 U.S. 228, 242, 99 S.Ct. 2264, 2275, 60 L.Ed.2d 846 (1979) (quoting *Baker v. Carr*, 369 U.S. 186, 217, 82 S.Ct. 691, 710, 7 L.Ed.2d 663 (1962)).

our constitutional scheme as to suggest that judicially created remedies against them might be inappropriate."[3] Finally, a *Bivens* remedy is barred "when defendants show that Congress has provided an alternative remedy which it explicitly declared to be a substitute for recovery directly under the Constitution and viewed as equally effective."[4]

These limitations have resulted in the rejection of a variety of claims. For example, in *Bush v. Lucas*,[5] the Court held that Congress's complete occupation of the federal personnel field was a "special factor" of the kind foreshadowed in *Bivens* that counseled against fashioning a *Bivens* remedy in matters related to federal personnel policy, even though the civil service laws of the time failed to provide the plaintiff with full relief. Similarly, in *Schweiker v. Chilicky*,[6] the Court rejected a claim asserting due process violations in the denial of Social Security disability benefits. The Court has also held that the unique disciplinary structure of the military constitutes a "special factor" warranting preclusion of a *Bivens* claim by enlisted military personnel.[7] And in *United States v. Stanley*,[8] the Court denied relief under the Constitution to a former serviceman precisely because the Federal Tort Claims Act gave none—that is, because the claimed injury arose out of activity "incident to service." In effect, the *Stanley* decision gives Congress the last word on the appropriate measure of compensation for Constitutional violations.[9]

After enactment of the Civil Service Reform Act ("CSRA"), the Court has used this same approach to preclude federal employees from using most alternative statutory routes to obtain administrative or judicial review of adverse personnel action. In *United States v. Fausto*, 484 U.S. 439, 108 S.Ct. 668, 98 L.Ed.2d 830 (1988), it rejected a claim under the Back Pay Act that would have indirectly provided for review of adverse federal personnel action by a court that was not an "appropriate authority" to review that action under CSRA. The Court concluded that Congress had intended to withhold such review by failing to provide for it in the CSRA, which it treated as a comprehensive and exhaustive scheme of protections and remedies for federal employees.

Following the Court's lead, the circuits have routinely denied federal employees review of adverse agency action except to the extent and

3. *Nixon v. Fitzgerald*, 457 U.S. 731, 749–752, 102 S.Ct. 2690, 2701–02, 73 L.Ed.2d 349 (1982) (President of United States cannot be a proper defendant in a *Bivens* action because of the President's unique position in the constitutional scheme).

4. *Carlson v. Green*, 446 U.S. at 18–19, 100 S.Ct. at 1472. *See, e.g., Bennett v. Barnett,* 210 F.3d 272 (5th Cir.), *cert. denied* 531 U.S. 875, 121 S.Ct. 181, 148 L.Ed.2d 125 (2000) (Postal Reorganization Act's grievance procedure displaces *Bivens* civil action); *Fishburn v. Brown*, 125 F.3d 979 (6th Cir.1997) (no *Bivens* action available for alleged due process violations against IRS agents; other remedial scheme available).

5. 462 U.S. 367, 380–381, 103 S.Ct. 2404, 2413, 76 L.Ed.2d 648 (1983).

6. 487 U.S. 412, 108 S.Ct. 2460, 101 L.Ed.2d 370 (1988).

7. *Chappell v. Wallace*, 462 U.S. 296, 103 S.Ct. 2362, 76 L.Ed.2d 586 (1983).

8. 483 U.S. 669, 107 S.Ct. 3054, 97 L.Ed.2d 550 (1987).

9. *See generally* Bandes, *Reinventing Bivens! The Self–Executing Constitution*, 68 S.Ca.L.Rev. 289 (1995).

before the administrative and judicial fora, and subject to the remedies, if any, authorized by CSRA. In the great majority of such cases the agency's action is not challenged on grounds of discrimination made actionable by other statutes, but rather on grounds of unfair, arbitrary or otherwise unconstitutional treatment. Such mine-run claims are routinely rejected regardless of whether they are cast under *Bivens*, the Back Pay Act, the Administrative Procedure Act or other statutory remedies available before CSRA was enacted, and regardless of whether they seek relief against U.S. agencies or individual federal officers.[10]

A federal employee whose employing agency is a covered "employer" and whose job classification is within the ambit of § 717 of Title VII, 42 U.S.C.A. § 2000e–16, does enjoy the protection against discrimination afforded by that statute.[11] But what if § 717 is unavailable? Can the plaintiff then assert a discrimination-based constitutional claim via *Bivens*? In *Davis v. Passman*, the Court held that a federal employee who complained of discrimination of a kind otherwise actionable under Title VII but who could not invoke its protection because her job classification was "expressly unprotected by the statute" could pursue the *Bivens* constitutional remedy, because "§ 717 leaves undisturbed whatever remedies petitioner might otherwise possess." But the CSRA was not in effect at the time of the personnel actions challenged in *Davis*, and *Davis* antedated the Court's decisions in *Bush, Schweiker*, and *Fausto*. There is accordingly room for the federal defendant to argue that a *Bivens* claim of unconstitutional discrimination by a federal employee not protected by Title VII is ousted today not by Title VII, but because that conduct either is *or is not* redressed under CSRA, which now occupies the federal personnel field.[12] Yet there are also indications that the *Davis* holding,

10. *See, e.g., Hall v. Clinton*, 235 F.3d 202 (4th Cir.2000), *cert. denied*, 532 U.S. 995, 121 S.Ct. 1656, 149 L.Ed.2d 639 (2001) (plaintiff's coverage under CSRA impliedly precludes *Bivens* claim against First Lady under 42 U.S.C.A. § 1985(1) as well as companion claim alleging due process violations against plaintiff's co-workers, even though no defendant supervised plaintiff); *Massey v. Helman*, 196 F.3d 727, 736–738 (7th Cir. 1999), *cert. denied*, 532 U.S. 1065, 121 S.Ct. 2214, 150 L.Ed.2d 208 (2001) (*Bivens* claim of federal prison physician who could have invoked CSRA procedures to complain about alleged retaliation violating his First Amendment rights is precluded as failing to state claim on which relief can be granted); *Golt v. United States*, 186 F.3d 1158 (9th Cir.1999); *Ayrault v. Pena*, 60 F.3d 346, 348 (7th Cir.1995); *LeBlanc v. United States*, 50 F.3d 1025, 1030 (Fed.Cir.1995); *McAuliffe v. Rice*, 966 F.2d 979, 981 (5th Cir.1992); *Jones v. Tennessee Valley Auth.*, 948 F.2d 258, 264 (6th Cir.1991); *Saul v. United States*, 928 F.2d 829, 840 (9th Cir.1991) (extending preclusion to warrantless search conducted by plaintiff's supervisor, notwithstanding footnote in *Bush v. Lucas* suggesting that such *Bivens* claims would not be precluded because searches are outside the "personnel actions" covered by CSRA); *Stephens v. Department of Health and Human Servs.*, 901 F.2d 1571, 1576–77 (11th Cir. 1990), *cert. denied*, 498 U.S. 998, 111 S.Ct. 555, 112 L.Ed.2d 562 (1990); *Lombardi v. Small Business Admin.*, 889 F.2d 959, 961 (10th Cir.1989); *Yokum v. United States*, 877 F.2d 276, 280–81 (4th Cir.1989); *McIntosh v. Turner*, 861 F.2d 524, 526–27 (8th Cir.1988); *Diaz v. United States Postal Serv.*, 853 F.2d 5, 9 (1st Cir.1988). *But see Stewart v. Evans*, 275 F.3d 1126 (D.C.Cir. 2002) (disagreeing with *Saul* and relying on *Bush v. Lucas* footnote in upholding *Bivens* claim based on supervisor's warrantless search).

11. *See Brown v. General Servs. Admin.*, 425 U.S. 820, 96 S.Ct. 1961, 48 L.Ed.2d 402 (1976).

12. See *Hall v. Clinton*, 235 F.3d 202 (4th Cir.2000), *cert. denied,* 532 U.S. 995, 121 S.Ct. 1656, 149 L.Ed.2d 639 (2001) (CSRA remedy exclusive because alleged

which preserves discrimination-based *Bivens* constitutional claims even though they are not cognizable under Title VII, may survive the *Schweiker* principle that preempts *Bivens* claims not provided for in other comprehensive, remedial statutory schemes like the CSRA.[13] In any event, even if a *Bivens* claim is precluded when it seeks to challenge "prohibited personnel practices," including a "personnel action" covered but not redressable under CSRA, the challenged conduct must in fact be within CSRA's general scope. While the quoted terms have been defined quite broadly, so as to preclude a *Bivens* claim,[14] there are limits.[15]

Recent circuit decisions also preclude *Bivens* claims under other federal statutory regulatory and remedial schemes, even when those statutes provide lesser remedies than the unlimited damages available for a constitutional violation via a successful *Bivens* lawsuit.[16] And even though federal prisoners are not eligible to pursue alternative federal statutory schemes to seek vindication of constitutional violations arising

wrongful act arose out of federal employment, even though claim was against fellow employee and hence not actionable under CSRA); *Blankenship v. McDonald*, 176 F.3d 1192, 1195 (9th Cir.1999), *cert. denied,* 528 U.S. 1153, 120 S.Ct. 1157, 145 L.Ed.2d 1069 (2000) (*Bivens* claim of judicial employee in "excepted service," who is therefore covered under CSRA, precluded even though CSRA afforded her no administrative or judicial remedies); *Lee v. Hughes*, 145 F.3d 1272 (11th Cir.1998), *cert. denied*, 525 U.S. 1138, 119 S.Ct. 1026, 143 L.Ed.2d 37 (1999) (probation officer in excepted service not eligible for Title VII or CSRA remedies is also precluded from using *Bivens* to assert race discrimination claim because conduct in question covered, although not protected, by CSRA). *See Collins v. Bender*, 195 F.3d 1076, 1078 (9th Cir.1999) (observing in dictum that if the challenged conduct that is the subject of plaintiff's *Bivens* claim can be considered a "personnel action" violating merit principles, then "CSRA procedures, not the federal courts, will determine what remedy, if any, is available"). *But see Duffy v. Wolle*, 123 F.3d 1026 (8th Cir.1997), *cert. denied*, 523 U.S. 1137, 118 S.Ct. 1839, 140 L.Ed.2d 1090 (1998) (probation officer who had no CSRA remedy may pursue *Bivens* claim for unconstitutional employment discrimination).

13. *See Federal Deposit Ins. Corp. v. Meyer*, 510 U.S. 471, 484 n. 9, 114 S.Ct. 996, 1005 n. 9, 127 L.Ed.2d 308 (1994) (in dictum, observing that *Davis* and *Schweiker* operate in different "contexts").

14. *See, e.g., Saul v. United States*, 928 F.2d 829, 834 (9th Cir.1991) (the CSRA-covered "personnel action," including its subconcept of "corrective action," broad enough to embrace supervisors' seizing and opening plaintiff's personal mail, addressed to him at the office).

15. *See Stewart v. Evans*, 275 F.3d 1126 (D.C.Cir.2002) (relying on *Bush v. Lucas* footnote in upholding *Bivens* claim based on supervisor's warrantless search even on work premises). *See also Collins v. Bender*, 195 F.3d 1076, 1078–1080 (9th Cir. 1999) (government supervisors' search of plaintiff's private property at his home based on their belief that he was dangerous was too attenuated from the workplace to be considered a "personnel action" within the ambit of CSRA, so *Bivens* claim lies).

16. *Libas Ltd. v. Carillo*, 329 F.3d 1128 (9th Cir.2003) (statutory remedial scheme authorizing importer to challenge customs duty precluded *Bivens* claim); *Bennett v. Barnett*, 210 F.3d 272 (5th Cir.2000), *cert. denied*, 531 U.S. 875, 121 S.Ct. 181, 148 L.Ed.2d 125 (2000) (*Bivens* claim preempted by Postal Reorganization Act) (postal worker alleging his rights were violated by internal investigation could proceed under Postal Reorganization Act, which provided him collective bargaining rights but not damages for constitutional violations); *Carpenter's Produce v. Arnold*, 189 F.3d 686 (8th Cir.1999) (federal disaster relief claimants alleging race discrimination in their quest for benefits could pursue extensive administrative process followed by judicial review, although at most they could receive reinstatement of benefits, not damages for the alleged constitutional violation) . *But see Robbins v. Wilkie*, 300 F.3d 1208 (10th Cir.2002) (ranch owner stated *Bivens* claim against Bureau of Land Management employees for alleged extortion in effort to force owner to grant the Bureau an easement).

from prison conditions, the Prison Litigation Reform Act[17] has been held to require them to exhaust any available remedies before they may proceed with a *Bivens* action.[18]

§ 2.49 Immunities and Other Defenses in *Bivens* Actions

Where a *Bivens* action does lie, the Court has held that § 1983 and *Bivens* immunities are interchangeable.[1] In *Butz*, this interchangeability worked to narrow the federal officials' immunity from the absolute immunity they were then afforded from liability for ordinary, nonconstitutional torts under *Barr v. Matteo*,[2] to the modest version of common law qualified immunity then prevalent under § 1983.[3] Only a few years

17. 42 U.S.C.A. § 1197e(a).

18. Before the PLRA was enacted in 1996 to amend § 1997e, that section was held to apply only to state prisoners. *McCarthy v. Madigan*, 503 U.S. 140, 112 S.Ct. 1081, 117 L.Ed.2d 291 (1992). But as amended by PLRA, § 1997e(a) provides that no prison conditions action shall be brought under "any ... federal law" "by a prisoner confined in any jail, prison or other correctional facility until such administrative remedies as are available are exhausted." This language requires federal, like state prisoners to exhaust available administrative remedies before commencing an action under *Bivens*. *See Porter v. Nussle*, 534 U.S. 516, 122 S.Ct. 983, 988, 152 L.Ed.2d 12 (2002). For more detail on the PLRA, *see* § 5.7, *infra*.

§ 2.49

1. *See, e.g., Wilson v. Layne*, 526 U.S. 603, 609, 119 S.Ct. 1692, 1696–97, 143 L.Ed.2d 818 (1999); *Graham v. Connor*, 490 U.S. 386, 394 n. 9, 109 S.Ct. 1865, 1870 n. 9, 104 L.Ed.2d 443 (1989) *Harlow*, 457 U.S. at 818 n.30, 102 S.Ct. at 2738 n.30; *Butz v. Economou*, 438 U.S. 478, 496–504, 98 S.Ct. 2894, 2905–2910, 57 L.Ed.2d 895 (1978). Circuit opinions now apply the *Harlow/Creighton* § 1983 qualified immunity to federal *Bivens* defendants as a matter of course. *See Kalka v. Hawk,* 215 F.3d 90 (D.C.Cir.2000).

2. 360 U.S. 564, 79 S.Ct. 1335, 3 L.Ed.2d 1434 (1959). Language in Justice Harlan's opinion for a plurality in *Barr v. Matteo*, 360 U.S. 564, 79 S.Ct. 1335, 3 L.Ed.2d 1434 (1959), conferred immunity on federal officials from common law tort liability whenever the challenged act took place "within the outer perimeter" of their duties, or within the scope of their employment. *Id.* at 575. The Court later retreated from that stark position. *See Westfall v. Erwin*, 484 U.S. 292, 298 n. 4, 108 S.Ct. 580, 584 n. 4, 98 L.Ed.2d 619 (1988) (holding that the conduct must also represent an exercise of discretion to qualify for the immunity). *Westfall* itself has in pertinent part been legislatively overruled. *See* Federal Employees Liability Reform and Tort Compensation Act of 1988, Pub.L.No. 100–694, § 5, 102 Stat. 4563, 4564 (1988) (codified at 28 U.S.C.A. § 2679(b)(1) (1988)); *Lunsford v. Price*, 885 F.2d 236, 237 n. 5 (5th Cir.1989) (stating that law "in essence" overrules *Westfall*); *Jordan v. Hudson*, 879 F.2d 98, 99 (4th Cir.1989) (stating that law "expressly displaces *Westfall*"); *Newman v. Soballe*, 871 F.2d 969, 971 (11th Cir.1989) (stating that law was "enacted to negate ... *Westfall*"). This statute, while preserving tort claims against the United States, precludes any damages action against the individual federal employee for any "negligent or wrongful act or omission" undertaken "while acting within the scope of his office or employment." 28 U.S.C.A. § 2679(b)(1) (1988). See, e.g., *Garrett v. Hawk*, 127 F.3d 1263 (10th Cir.1997). "Wrongful" act as used in the federal employee context has long been understood to include conduct more egregious than simple negligence but not rising to the level of intentional harms. See *Hatahley v. United States*, 351 U.S. 173, 181, 76 S.Ct. 745, 751, 100 L.Ed. 1065 (1956) (stating that " 'wrongful' ... [is] intended to include situations ... which might not be considered strictly negligent"); *Dalehite v. United States*, 346 U.S. 15, 45, 73 S.Ct. 956, 972, 97 L.Ed. 1427 (1953) (same); *In re Bomb Disaster at Roseville, Cal., on Apr. 28, 1973*, 438 F.Supp. 769, 778 & n. 2 (E.D.Cal.1977) ("Congress intended to include more than negligence and trespass in the word 'wrongful.' "). This approach appears similar to the one proposed for state actors under § 1983: the entity is accountable under modified respondeat superior, the individual agent only for intentionally harmful acts.

3. *See* Oren, 50 U.Pitt.L.Rev. at 970–72.

later, however, in *Harlow*, the Court relied on the interchangeability of immunities to extend the generous qualified immunity the Court subsequently had granted federal officials in *Bivens* actions to defendants under § 1983. One commentator has written that the linkage of immunity doctrine developed in § 1983 and *Bivens* actions may be threatened by the Court's recent assertions (see § 2.2 supra) that the common law as understood in 1871 is the paramount guidepost for fashioning § 1983 rules of liability, remedy and immunity—a principle that does not pertain to the judge-made cause of action declared in *Bivens*.[4]

The Court has unanimously declined to extend the *Bivens* principle to claims against federal government agencies, as distinct from their agents.[5] Noting that the *Bivens* remedy is an effective deterrent against the commission of constitutional violations by federal agents, the Court reasoned that affording a parallel claim against their employing entity would undermine that deterrence. The Court also expressed particular concern that affording a remedy against the agency would allow the plaintiff to circumvent the individual agent's official qualified immunity. These conclusions are curious given the Court's equation of the purposes and scope of § 1983 and *Bivens* immunity. If affording a remedy against a state or local employing entity under § 1983, as the Court did in *Monell*, does not unduly undermine the desired deterrence of the agent or unwisely circumvent the agent's qualified immunity, why should the result be different in the federal *Bivens* setting?

§§ 2.50–2.54 [Reserved]

H. SECTION 1983 AS A REMEDY FOR FEDERAL STATUTORY VIOLATIONS

§ 2.55 In General

In *Maine v. Thiboutot*,[1] the Court, fully cognizant of the enormous resulting potential increase of § 1983 "filings in our already overburdened courts,"[2] nevertheless charted a course conspicuously hospitable to the assertion of these historically tangential claims.

Section 1983 got off to an uncertain start as a remedy for federal statutory violations. In *Pennhurst State School and Hospital v. Halderman*,[3] Justice Rehnquist articulated two related but distinct potential limitations on the use of § 1983 to remedy violations of other federal

4. See Steinglass, *Section 1983 Litigation In State Courts* (Clark Boardman) § 2.5(c), p. 2–47 and § 5.2(b), p. 5–7 (12/94).

5. *Federal Deposit Ins. Corp. v. Meyer*, 510 U.S. 471, 114 S.Ct. 996, 127 L.Ed.2d 308 (1994).

§ 2.55

1. 448 U.S. 1, 100 S.Ct. 2502, 65 L.Ed.2d 555 (1980).

2. *Id.* at 23, 100 S.Ct. at 2514 (Powell, J., dissenting).

3. 451 U.S. 1, 101 S.Ct. 1531, 67 L.Ed.2d 694 (1981) [hereinafter *Pennhurst* I].

statutes. The first was a substantive rights restriction, corresponding to the *Paul* or *Parratt* restrictions in due process cases, that inquires whether the particular § 1983 plaintiff has a private right of action to enforce the predicate statute. The second was a more general limitation that would oust § 1983 even when the plaintiff has standing to enforce the underlying federal statutory guarantee if that statute could be read to provide the " 'exclusive remedy for violations of its terms.' "[4] In *Golden State Transit Corp. v. City of Los Angeles*,[5] the Court clarified that the plaintiff has the burden of proving that her claim under Section 1983 involves the violation of a federal right of action, of which she is the beneficiary, as opposed to a mere violation of federal law. By contrast, respecting the second limitation sketched in *Pennhurst*, it is the defendant who bears the burden of demonstrating that Congress, by providing a comprehensive, detailed remedial scheme for enforcement of the predicate statute, has expressly or impliedly foreclosed the possibility of enforcement under Section 1983.

a. The Substantive Rights Restriction

The first limitation Justice Rehnquist articulated in *Pennhurst*, a narrow definition of the "rights secured by" a predicate federal statute, at first also garnered little support.[6] After *Golden State*, it appeared that a § 1983 plaintiff would ordinarily be recognized as having an enforceable "right" of action for local governmental violations of other federal

4. *Id.* at 28, 101 S.Ct. at 1545 (quoting *Thiboutot*, 448 U.S. at 22 n.11, 100 S.Ct. at 2514 n.11 (Powell, J., dissenting)).

The second limitation was applied soon thereafter, but has since waned. Justice Powell found the "exclusive remedy" standard met in *Middlesex County Sewerage Auth. v. National Sea Clammers Ass'n*, 453 U.S. 1, 13, 101 S.Ct. 2615, 2622, 69 L.Ed.2d 435 (1981) (finding that Congress had provided "unusually elaborate [judicial] enforcement provisions" in two environmental statutes that should oust § 1983). Similarly, in *Smith v. Robinson*, 468 U.S. 992, 1009, 104 S.Ct. 3457, 3467, 82 L.Ed.2d 746 (1984), the Court held that the remedy formulated by Congress for the violation of the Education of the Handicapped Act was exclusive avenue of redress.

5. 493 U.S. 103, 106, 110 S.Ct. 444, 448, 107 L.Ed.2d 420 (1989).

6. In *Wright v. City of Roanoke*, 479 U.S. 418, 107 S.Ct. 766, 93 L.Ed.2d 781 (1987), the Court held that low-income tenants had a right, enforceable through § 1983, to sue a housing authority for utility charges that allegedly exceeded ceilings established by administrative regulations issued under federal housing legislation, where the regulations defined the "reasonable amount" allowed. Justice Kennedy raised the "rights" objection again in *Golden State Transit Corp. v. City of Los Angeles*, 493 U.S. 103, 110 S.Ct. 444, 107 L.Ed.2d 420 (1989), but was joined only by Chief Justice Rehnquist and Justice O'Connor. See id. at 114–19, 110 S.Ct. at 452–55 (Kennedy, J., dissenting). The Court permitted a private cab company in *Golden State* to maintain a § 1983 damages action against Los Angeles after the city conditioned renewal of its franchise on the company's reaching agreement with a union on a new labor contract. The Court viewed the company as having an enforceable "right" to a remedy for conduct by the city that the National Labor Relations Act in terms prohibited only as between employers and unions.

The Court continued to reject the "rights" argument in its 1990 term. In *Wilder*, the Court permitted Medicaid providers to sue under § 1983 for reimbursement at rates that federal law demanded be "reasonable and adequate," where the predicate statute and implementing regulations at least identified the "factors to be considered" in determining the required rates. See *Suter v. Artist M.*, 503 U.S. 347, 355, 112 S.Ct. 1360, 1366, 118 L.Ed.2d 1 (1992) (citing Wilder); *cf. Dennis v. Higgins*, 498 U.S. 439, 111 S.Ct. 865, 112 L.Ed.2d 969 (1991) (giving similar broad meaning to the constitutional "rights" enforceable through § 1983).

statutes whenever the statutory provision in question was intended to benefit that plaintiff. The § 1983 right of action would be defeasible only if the predicate provision reflected a mere "congressional preference" rather than a binding governmental obligation or if the plaintiff's interest was so "vague and amorphous" that the judiciary could not enforce it.[7]

But since *Pennhurst* the Court has thrice found a federal statutory mandate too generalized to give rise to a "right" enforceable through § 1983. In *Suter v. Artist M.*,[8] the Court considered a claim based on alleged violations of a statutory provision that conditioned federal funding for state child welfare, foster care and adoption programs upon a state's submission of a plan approved by the Secretary of Health and Human Services. To be approved the plan had to contain assurances that the state would make "reasonable efforts" to avoid removing children from their homes and reasonable efforts, if they were removed, to reunify their families. The Court observed that, in contrast to the provisions at issue in *Wright* and *Wilder*, neither the statute nor its implementing regulations offered the states concrete guidance about the required "reasonable efforts," other than that they must be described in a plan to be approved by the Secretary. It concluded that the term therefore imposed a mere "generalized duty" unenforceable through an action under § 1983 action or, for the same reason, through a private right of action implied directly under the adoption statute.[9] But whenever Congress does specify the state's duties in a regulatory statute, a plaintiff who is an intended beneficiary of the statute will have a "right" to enforce it against local governments and officials and state officials.[10]

In *Blessing v. Freestone*,[11] the Court held that § 1983 could not be used to enforce Title IV–D of the Social Security Act against a state's child support services program and achieve substantial compliance with the statute's requirements. In a narrow holding, the Court stated that the plaintiffs failed to "identify with particularity the rights they claimed, since it is impossible to determine whether Title IV–D, as an undifferentiated whole, gives rise to undefined rights."[12] It is not

7. *Wilder*, 496 U.S. at 509, 110 S.Ct. at 2517 (quoting, respectively, *Pennhurst* and *Golden State*).

8. 503 U.S. 347, 112 S.Ct. 1360, 118 L.Ed.2d 1 (1992).

9. In turn, an authoritative judicial determination that there is no implied private right of action under a particular statute may mean that federal courts will lack subject matter jurisdiction to revisit that issue in a subsequent case, at least for a period of time sufficiently long to respect a later court's conception of stare decisis. *See Bell v. Hood*, 327 U.S. 678, 682, 66 S.Ct. 773, 776, 90 L.Ed. 939 (1946).

10. Because of *Will v. Michigan Dep't of State Police*, 491 U.S. 58, 109 S.Ct. 2304, 105 L.Ed.2d 45 (1989), and the vapors of the Eleventh Amendment, see *supra* §§ 2.35 and 2.42 and *infra* § 5.35, the entitlement suit must take the form of an action against an individual state official. Yet in substance, it is a suit against a state entity charged with a violation in implementing a federal statute or regulation. Thus, there is no "settled law" defense; in any case the settled nature of the right exists a priori in the federal enactment. Additionally, there is no doubt about the existence of state "policy" for purposes of entity liability, because the policy resides in the challenged regulation.

11. 520 U.S. 329, 117 S.Ct. 1353, 137 L.Ed.2d 569 (1997).

12. *Id.* at 1360.

enough, the Court wrote, that plaintiff assert a violation of federal law; rather plaintiff must show that Congress gave her a federal right to enforce such violations through a civil action. The three-part "enforceable right" test that emerged from *Blessing* requires the plaintiff to show (1) that Congress intended the provision in question to benefit her; (2) that the right is sufficiently definite (not so "vague and amorphous") that its enforcement would not unduly strain judicial competence; and (3) that the statute unambiguously imposes a binding obligation on local government, meaning that its requirements are asserted in mandatory, not merely hortatory or precatory terms.[13] (A successful demonstration of these factors creates a rebuttable presumption that plaintiff has alleged the violation of a right enforceable through Section 1983. To overcome this showing a defendant must demonstrate that Congress either expressly foreclosed a Section 1983 remedy in the terms of the predicate statute or did so impliedly by creating a comprehensive enforcement scheme incompatible with individual judicial actions under Section 1983.[14])

Justices Scalia and Kennedy concurred, stating that it was unnecessary for the Court to decide whether third party beneficiaries to a spending clause statute could ever be successful in pressing a right to sue to enforce such statutes.[15] This concurrence cast some doubt on the Court's holdings in *Wilder* and *Wright*, two other spending clause "and laws" cases, and highlights the change in the Court's composition since those cases. What remains unclear is whether the statutes in *Suter* and *Blessing* simply failed the vagueness test, or whether "and laws" claims must be pleaded with particularity, or whether the decision represents a fundamental change in the availability of § 1983 to enforce federal statutes.

A number of federal circuit courts mounted a rear-guard action against *Suter* and *Blessing*, distinguishing them with some regularity. Decision has usually turned on element (2) from the *Blessing* formula, whether the predicate statute, alone or as fleshed out by its implementing regulations, creates a right sufficiently definite to be susceptible of judicial enforcement. These courts have sometimes noted that the court in *Suter* did not reverse *Golden State*, *Wilder*, or *Wright*; still, they have been forced to acknowledge that the Court in *Suter* and *Blessing* also did not adhere to the two-part, plaintiff-favorable paradigm set out in *Golden State*.[16] So these courts read *Suter* as simply reemphasizing the point made in *Pennhurst* that conditions imposed on the grant of federal monies under the Congressional spending power "must be imposed

13. *Id.* at 1359. See *Groten v. California*, 251 F.3d 844 (9th Cir.2001) (§ 1983 "and laws" claim may be founded on violation of federal statute allowing out-of-state real estate enterprises to operate temporarily in state).

14. *Golden State, supra,* 493 U.S. at 106. *See also Wilder*, 496 U.S. at 520–21, 110 S.Ct. at 2523–24.

15. *Blessing, supra,* 117 S.Ct. at 1364.

16. *Miller v. Whitburn*, 10 F.3d 1315, 1319 (7th Cir.1993); *Arkansas Medical Society, Inc. v. Reynolds*, 6 F.3d 519, 524 (8th Cir.1993).

unambiguously."[17] In finding that Section 1983 may be used to vindicate other relatively vague, statutory provisions—not all that different from the "reasonable efforts" requirement of the Child Welfare Act that *Suter* held too vague to be enforced under Section 1983–these courts stressed that in *Wilder* the court authorized the use of Section 1983 to enforce the "reasonable and adequate" reimbursement rates standard in the Boren Amendment to the Medicaid Act. What distinguishes cases like *Wilder* from cases like *Suter* and *Blessing*, these courts concluded, is a detailed specification, either in the predicate statute alone or in its implementing regulations, of factors that aid judges in determining whether the state has complied with a federal mandate or followed specific directions for executing a generalized state plan.[18]

17. *Arkansas Medical Soc., Inc.*, 6 F.3d 519, citing *Suter*, 112 S.Ct. at 1366.

18. *See, e.g., Doe, 1–13 v. Chiles,* 136 F.3d 709, 716–718, 718 n.17 (11th Cir. 1998) (requirement of Section 1396(a)(8) of Medicaid Act that medical assistance be furnished with "reasonable promptness" sufficiently definite because, as with the "reasonable and adequate" rate question at issue in *Wilder*, the statute together with its implementing regulations identified factors permitting judicial determination of a range of reasonableness; further, addressing *Blessing* factor (3), and unlike the merely "procedural" requirement at issue in *Suter* that state plans provide that states make "reasonable efforts" to keep families together when considering adoption, the "reasonable promptness" provision of Medicaid Act Section 1396(a)(8) was written in mandatory, substantive terms). *But see City of Chicago v. Lindley*, 66 F.3d 819 (7th Cir. 1995) (Older Americans Act provision that agencies "take into account" geographical and social factors in erecting formula for distributing funds too amorphous to create rights enforceable under § 1983).

The circuits have taken at least three approaches to the question whether an administrative regulation may be taken into account in resolving the ultimate question whether a predicate statute creates a sufficiently definite, mandatory, and judicially enforceable right. The first is that a Section 1983 "and laws" claim must be founded on the terms or clear implications of the statute itself; thus a claim fails if it is based even in part on a distinctive feature of a regulation promulgated under authority of that statute, even assuming the regulation is otherwise valid. *See Smith v. Kirk*, 821 F.2d 980, 984 (4th Cir.1987). This approach is consistent with the views of Justices O'Connor, Powell, Scalia and Chief Justice Rehnquist, dissenting in *Wright*, who opined that the federal rights enforceable under Section 1983 cannot derive from regulations alone or even from valid administrative interpretations of right-creating federal statutes. 479 U.S. at 437–38.

An intermediate approach takes cues from the position apparently taken by the Supreme Court majority in *Wright*, 479 U.S. at 430–32, and *Suter*, 503 U.S. at 357–362. If the statute itself confers on the plaintiff a specific, mandatory, and judicially enforceable right, "and a valid regulation merely further defines or fleshes out the content of that right, then the statute–'in conjunction with the regulation'–may create a federal right as further defined by the regulation." *Harris v. James,* 127 F.3d 993, 1008–1009 (11th Cir.1997) (concluding that a Medicaid transportation regulation did not merely define the content of a specific right but purported to confer one under statutory provisions that conferred none); *Kissimmee River Valley Sportsman Ass'n v. City of Lakeland*, 250 F.3d 1324 (11th Cir. 2001) (same view of a regulation under Federal Aid in Sportfish Recreation Act affording access to waterways for personal watercraft with common horsepower ratings). *See Farley v. Philadelphia Housing Authority*, 102 F.3d 697, 699 (3d Cir.1996) (relying in part on a regulation but observing that the plaintiff's Section 1983 claim "arises strictly under" the predicate statute); *Albiston v. Maine Comm'r of Human Servs.*, 7 F.3d 258, 263 (1st Cir.1993) (enforcing provisions of regulation that fleshed out statutory duty).

A less nuanced approach simply approves Section 1983 claims based on the violation of valid regulations standing alone, even if the regulations describe obligations or rights not expressly or impliedly found in the statute under which they are promulgated. *See Boatman v. Hammons* 164 F.3d 286 (6th Cir.1998) (disagreeing with *Harris v. James* and upholding a Section 1983 claim based on the Medicaid transportation regulation); *Buckley v. City*

Thus in *Lampkin v. District of Columbia*,[19] the court held the right to educate homeless children, created by the McKinney Homeless Assistance Act, enforceable through Section 1983. While its description of the contents of the required state plan was no more elaborate than that contained in the adoption statute at issue in *Suter*, "the McKinney Act provides specific directions for the plan's execution," as well as "obligations that are independent of the plan." Similarly, in *Miller v. Whit-*

of Redding, California, 66 F.3d 188 (9th Cir.1995) (concluding, contrary to the Eleventh Circuit's subsequent decision in *Kissimmee*, that a Section 1983 claim could be based on the waterways access regulation); *Loschiavo v. City of Dearborn*, 33 F.3d 548, 551 (6th Cir.1994), *cert. denied*, 513 U.S. 1150, 115 S.Ct. 1099, 130 L.Ed.2d 1067 (1995); *West Virginia Univ. Hospitals v. Casey*, 885 F.2d 11, 18 (3d. Cir.1989), *cert. denied*, 496 U.S. 936, 110 S.Ct. 3213, 110 L.Ed.2d 661 (1990); *Samuels v. District of Columbia*, 770 F.2d 184, 199 (D.C.Cir. 1985). This approach is in line with the view of Justices Stevens, Brennan and Blackmun in *Guardians Ass'n v. Civil Serv. Comm'n of New York*, 463 U.S. 582, 638, 103 S.Ct. 3221, 3251, 77 L.Ed.2d 866 (1983) that the Section 1983 "remedy is intended to redress the deprivation of all valid federal laws, including statutes and regulations having the force of law." *See also Mallett v. Wisconsin Division of Vocational Rehabilitation*, 130 F.3d 1245, 1252–53 (7th Cir. 1997) and *Clifton v. Schafer* 969 F.2d 278, 285 (7th Cir.1992) (approving in principle Section 1983 claims asserting the right to a state plan complying with requirements of a federal regulation, but denying the claims at hand because they asserted only isolated violations of concededly legal plans).

The Supreme Court's recent decision in *Alexander v. Sandoval*, 532 U.S. 275, 121 S.Ct. 1511, 149 L.Ed.2d 517 (2001), discussed in Chapter 3, *infra*, points up the potential importance of this question. The Court held that no implied right of action lies under Section 602 of Title VI of the Civil Rights Act of 1964, 42 U.S.C.A. § 2000d–1, which authorizes federal agencies to promulgate regulations to "effectuate" Title VI rights. Accordingly, the Court, assuming the validity of Justice Department disparate-impact regulations plaintiffs sought to enforce, nevertheless rejected their claim to enforce them by an action brought directly under Section 602. The four dissenters specifically suggested, however, that future plaintiffs could circumvent the ruling simply by asserting claims to enforce those regulations under the "and laws" clause of Section 1983. A Third Circuit alternative holding before *Sandoval*, *Powell v. Ridge*, 189 F.3d 387 (3d Cir.1999), seemed to agree. But after *Sandoval*, the Third Circuit has held that EPA disparate-impact regulations promulgated to implement Title VI could not be enforced under Section 1983. The court reasoned that Title VI Section 602 empowers agencies to adopt regulations solely to enforce the Title VI ban on intentional discrimination, and no other explicit Title VI language prohibits disparate-impact discrimination. *South Camden Citizens In Action v. New Jersey Department of Environmental Protection*, 274 F.3d 771 (3d Cir.2001). This decision seems consistent with the content of Title VI, which the Supreme Court has said prohibits only intentional discrimination. See Chapter 3, *infra*. Thus the future viability of Section 1983 actions as a way around the *Sandoval* holding may depend on the Supreme Court's ultimate determination as to whether "and laws" claims may be based on any valid regulation, or only on those that merely refine duties that are express or clearly implied in the statute under which a regulation is issued. But if the Court's recent strict approach to "and laws" claims founded directly on predicate statutes is any guide, *see Gonzaga University v. Doe*, 536 U.S. 273, 122 S.Ct. 2268, 153 L.Ed.2d 309 (2002), *infra*, it seems unlikely that the Court would uphold a Section 1983 claim based soley on valid federal regulations absent a "right" firmly rooted in statutory text. Because an "and laws" claim, after *Gonzaga*, must be founded on explicit statutory text and not legislative history, it seems doubtful that it may rest solely on rights described by an administrative regulation implementing a federal statute, even if the regulation is within the ambit of the promulgating agency's statutory authority and otherwise valid. *But see Bosscher v. Township of Algoma*, 246 F.Supp.2d 791, 796-799 (W.D.Mich.2003) (§ 1983 actions may be founded on federal agency regulations and interpretive rulings, but, in assessing whether regulations and rulings create a right enforceable by a particular plaintiff, courts may not use the *Blessing* test but must find explicit rights creating terms in the text of the regulation).

19. 27 F.3d 605, 610–612 (D.C.Cir. 1994), *cert. denied*, 513 U.S. 1016, 115 S.Ct. 578, 130 L.Ed.2d 493 (1994).

burn,[20] a child was permitted to enforce a right to "necessary ... treatment" under the Medicaid Act because the statute, together with its implementing regulations, specified "in copious detail, those services for which a Medicaid-participating state must provide payment in order to discharge its obligation to make ... services available to all qualified individuals." Although the state agency administering the program had substantial discretion to choose how to comply with the federal mandate to pay for necessary treatment, and in particular could exclude "experimental" treatment, federal courts could review under Section 1983 whether the agency's definitions of "experimental" comported with relevant federal definitions of that term.[21] And in *Arkansas Medical Society v. Reynolds*,[22] a Medicaid Act provision requiring a state plan to provide for care and services "to the extent that such care and services are available to the general population in the geographic area" was held sufficiently definite to be enforceable under Section 1983. The court found this "equal access" provision arguably more specific than the language of the Boren Amendment found enforceable in *Wilder*, because its legislative history and implementing regulations in effect defined "general population" to require a comparison of Medicaid recipients' access with that of the insured population, rather than the entire population of the surrounding geographic area. To one court evaluating what constitutes "reasonable promptness" in providing medical assistance under the Medicaid Act was "less onerous" and "inherently more circumscribed and judicially ascertainable" than fixing the limits of "reasonable efforts" in the placement of foster children under the Adoption Assistance and Child welfare Act.[23]

Sometimes these same or other circuits, however, have not been so willing to circumvent *Suter*. The Eleventh Circuit, for example, discounted the significance of a regulation under the Federal Aid in Sportfish Recreation Act specifying that funded launch facilities accommodate power boats with common horsepower ratings, deeming it too far removed from the statute's principal aims to create an enforceable right to equal access for such boats at those facilities.[24] The First Circuit, in *Stowell v. Ives*[25] rejected plaintiff's attempt to enforce a provision of the Medicare Catastrophic Coverage Act that required the Secretary of Health and Human Services to disapprove any state plan for medical assistance if payment levels were less than payment levels in effect under plan on May 1, 1988. The court held that this spending clause statute did not impose any direct obligation on the state so as to give rise to cause of action cognizable under § 1983. Similarly, in *City of Chicago v. Lindley*,[26] the Seventh Circuit held that the Older Americans Act, which required states to use "the best available data" to develop a

20. 10 F.3d 1315, 1319–1320 (7th Cir. 1993).

21. *Id.* at 1320.

22. 6 F.3d 519 (8th Cir.1993).

23. *Doe, 1–13 v. Chiles,* 136 F.3d 709, 717–718 (11th Cir.1998).

24. *Kissimmee River Valley Sportsman Ass'n v. City of Lakeland*, 250 F.3d 1324 (11th Cir.), *cert. denied,* 534 U.S. 1040, 122 S.Ct. 613, 151 L.Ed.2d 537 (2001).

25. 976 F.2d 65 (1st Cir.1992).

26. 66 F.3d 819 (7th Cir.1995).

funds—distribution formula "that takes into account" the geographical distribution of older individuals within the state with "particular attention" to low-income minority older individuals, did not create any rights enforceable under § 1983. The court found that this statute was too vague and imposed no specific obligations on the state, thus precluding the plaintiff's claim.[27]

The Sixth Circuit offered an approach that tried to reconcile these cases. In *Tony L. v. Childers*,[28] the court proposed that there are two kinds of "and laws" cases—those like *Wilder* in which the statutes or implementing regulations provide certain and enforceable criteria and those like *Suter* that lack the specificity needed for judicial enforcement. Statutes that require the payment of specified sums of money,[29] that require the recognition of tribal adoptions,[30] that mandate the institution of individualized rehabilitation programs,[31] or that require a public agency to comply with a grievance award[32] can be enforced through a § 1983 claim because the courts can have confidence in crafting a judicial remedy.[33] Statutes that fail specifically to define the content of a right cannot be judicially enforced through § 1983.[34]

It now appears that the Court has endorsed *Suter*, and a strict reading of *Blessing*, in preference to the more permissive approach taken in *Wright* and *Wilder*. The issue in *Gonzaga University v. Doe*[35] was whether nondisclosure provisions of the Family Educational Rights and Privacy Act of 1974 ("FERPA") were enforceable through a private Section 1983 action for damages. The Court acknowledged that in *Wright* and *Wilder*, other cases involving Spending Clause legislation, it had identified individual rights that are enforceable through Section 1983. It further acknowledged that language in those opinions, as well as in *Blessing*, had suggested that a plaintiff could enforce a federal statute

27. *See also King v. Town of Hempstead*, 161 F.3d 112 (2d Cir.1998) (no § 1983 cause of action for town's allegedly negligent administration of Housing and Community Development Act); *White v. Chambliss*, 112 F.3d 731 (4th Cir.1997), cert. denied, 522 U.S. 913, 118 S.Ct. 296, 139 L.Ed.2d 228 (1997) (rejecting plaintiff's § 1983 claim to enforce the Adoption Assistance and Child Welfare Act); *Clifton v. Schafer*, 969 F.2d 278 (7th Cir.1992) (AFDC program not enforceable by § 1983 private right of action).

28. 71 F.3d 1182 (6th Cir.1995), *cert. denied*, 517 U.S. 1212, 116 S.Ct. 1834, 134 L.Ed.2d 938 (1996).

29. *Buckley v. City of Redding*, 66 F.3d 188 (9th Cir.1995) (allowing § 1983 claim to enforce a statute requiring a certain sum of money to be spent on recreational boating); *Albiston v. Maine Comm'r of Human Servs.*, 7 F.3d 258 (1st Cir.1993).

30. *Native Village of Venetie IRA Council v. State of Alaska*, 155 F.3d 1150 (9th Cir.1998) (Indian Child Welfare Act created an enforceable right and contained no specific enforcement scheme).

31. *Mallett v. Wisconsin Div. of Vocational Rehabilitation*, 130 F.3d 1245 (7th Cir.1997), *appeal after remand*, 248 F.3d 1158 (7th Cir.2000); *Marshall v. Switzer*, 10 F.3d 925 (2d Cir.1993).

32. *Farley v. Philadelphia Hous. Auth.*, 102 F.3d 697 (3d Cir.1996).

33. *See also Doe v. Chiles*, 136 F.3d 709 (11th Cir.1998) (statute requiring state Medicaid plan to provide medical assistance with reasonable promptness created federal right enforceable under § 1983 by developmentally disabled persons who had been placed on a waiting list for entry into intermediate care facility).

34. *See, e.g., Harris v. James*, 127 F.3d 993 (11th Cir.1997).

35. 536 U.S. 273, 122 S.Ct. 2268, 153 L.Ed.2d 309 (2002).

through a Section 1983 action so long as she was within the general zone of interest the statute was intended to protect or an intended beneficiary of the statutory provision in question.

But the Court added that in both *Wright* and *Wilder*, the statutory provisions at issue defined a mandatory benefit focused on the individual through a more or less "objective" monetary entitlement. Moreover, the Court continued, its more recent spending statute decisions, *Suter* and *Blessing*, had denied enforceability through Section 1983 because the text of the provisions at issue failed to focus on the needs or entitlements of particular persons but instead elaborated only aggregate or system-wide yardsticks for the respective state agencies charged with spending federal money. Accordingly, the Court asserted, these later decisions stand for the proposition that statutory text must unambiguously sketch individual "*rights*, not the broader or vaguer [concept of] 'benefits' or 'interests,' "in order to be enforced through an action under Section 1983. Correlatively, the Court equated the test for statutory rights enforceable via the Section 1983 "and laws" clause with the first required element of its increasingly strict test[36] for implying a private right of action directly from a predicate statute. In each case, the initial inquiry is whether Congress intended to create a federal right, an inquiry the Court says is guided exclusively, or almost exclusively, by the text or phrasing of the statutory provision in question. Subsequent lower court decisions relying on *Gonzaga* have declined to supplement express statutory text with legislative history or other indications of congressional intent on the issue whether a particular statutory provision confers an individually enforceable right on the plaintiff.[37] It would seem to follow a fortiori that an "and laws" claim, after *Gonzaga*, may not be founded solely on rights described by an administrative regulation implementing a federal statute, even if the regulation is within the ambit of the promulgating agency's statutory authority and otherwise valid.[38] That topic is discussed above in this section and in greater detail in Chapter 3.

In "and laws" cases, however, the devil is truly in the details. Just which language in a statute as a whole will suffice to suggest that a particular provision of the statute was intended to afford individual, rather than merely aggregate rights? Here it may be helpful to contrast the approach of the *Gonzaga* majority and dissenting opinions. The

36. See the discussion of the Supreme Court's "private right of action" cases *infra*.

37. *See, e.g., Taylor v. Vermont Dep't of Educ.*, 313 F.3d 768, 785–786 (2d Cir.2002) (even though FERPA's record-access provision, to greater degree than the FERPA nondisclosure provisions at issue in *Gonzaga*, had text suggesting individual right, that implication was not unambiguous and FERPA as a whole had aggregate focus prohibiting institutional practices or policies); *Almendares v. Palmer*, 2002 WL 31730963 at *5–6 (N.D.Ohio 2002) (after *Gonzaga*, legislative history cannot cure deficiencies in a statute's text in clearly and unambiguously giving the particular plaintiff an enforceable right and cannot be used to create a private right of action).

38. *But see Bosscher v. Township of Algoma*, 246 F.Supp.2d 791, 796-799 (W.D.Mich.2003) (§ 1983 actions may be founded on federal agency regulations and interpretive rulings, but, in assessing whether regulations and rulings create a right enforceable by a particular plaintiff, courts may not use the *Blessing* test but must find explicit rights creating terms in the text of the regulation).

majority zeroes in on the language of the FERPA subsections at issue, observing that they lack the individually focused terminology of two statutes, Titles VI and IX, from which the Court had implied private rights of action. Instead, the FERPA subsections reflect what the majority considers an aggregate as opposed to personal focus, as they ban the funding of educational institutions that have a prohibited "policy or practice" of releasing education records without expressing concern for individual students or parents.[39]

None of the Court's prior "and laws" decisions had required the kind of explicit, rights-creating statutory text (e.g., the "no person shall" language of Titles VI and IX), in the particular provision the plaintiff relies on, that the *Gonzaga* majority deems prerequisite to enforcement via § 1983. Indeed, in dissent Justice Stevens opined that the new textual standard overruled *Wilder sub silentio*.[40] In a footnote the majority specifically rejects the dissent's reliance on other FERPA provisions that use the term "rights," suggesting that in context the term is used simply as a shorthand for standards and procedures that must be adhered to by funding recipients rather than as a specification of individual entitlements. But this abrupt dismissal leaves unresolved whether in future cases a court may look to a provision elsewhere in a statute that does in fact contain individual rights-conferring language to aid its determination whether the particular provision at issue also confers such rights.

To buttress its conclusion that Congress in enacting FERPA did not intend to confer individual rights enforceable through private judicial actions, the Court considered it important that FERPA established an administrative enforcement scheme, in contrast to the absence of any federal review mechanism in the statutes at issue in *Wright* and *Wilder*. While expressly declining to decide if those procedures were sufficiently comprehensive to impliedly preclude a separate "and laws" remedy under Section 1983—the "remedial preclusion" barrier to "and laws" claim considered immediately below—the Court deemed the provision of administrative enforcement an additional indication that Congress did not intend to create individually enforceable private rights.[41] But the "personal rights" and "no remedial preclusion through specification of

39. One commentator has suggested that the *Gonzaga* strict insistence on statutory text conferring a personal, individually enforceable right may be limited to statutes enacted pursuant to Congress' spending clause authority. Chemerinsky, "Limiting suits to Enforce Federal Laws," 39 TRIAL 70, 71 (2003). But much of the Court's reasoning was not geared to the fact that FERPA was enacted pursuant to the spending clause. In any event, the proposed limitation has limited force because so many of the statutes that have been held enforceable under § 1983's "and laws" clause have been grounded in Congress' spending clause authority.

40. 536 U.S. at 300 n.8.

41. Also significant for the *Gonzaga* Court was that FERPA centralized enforcement in the Department of Education to avoid the multiple interpretations that might have been expected if enforcement had been regionalized. The Court concluded that it was implausible to presume that Congress nonetheless would have intended private lawsuits to be brought throughout the nation, as they could only result in the same multiple interpretations that the national administrative enforcement scheme was intended to avoid.

alternative enforcement mechanisms" issues remain independent barriers to § 1983 "and laws" claims; even though a statute contains *no* enforcement mechanism, the claim will fail if the specific provision plaintiff relies on lacks specific, personal, individual rights-creating language.[42]

Perhaps for that reason the dissent faulted the majority for blurring the issues by considering congressional intent about enforcement as part of its discussion about congressional intent to create an individually enforceable federal right.[43] In pre-*Gonzaga* decisions, the enforcement/alternative remedies/implied preclusion issue was considered only if and after a determination that the provision in question afforded plaintiff an individual right. The burden of persuasion on the threshold individual right question was on the plaintiff, while the burden of persuasion on the remedial preclusion issue was squarely on the defendant. Thus after *Gonzaga's* melding of these issues, plaintiffs will now bear a burden of persuasion on the threshold individual right issue that is increasingly difficult to meet, with the consequence that defendants may never have to bear a burden of persuasion about remedial preclusion.

b. The Remedies Restriction

On this second issue, Justice White dissenting in *Pennhurst*, argued that the Court should read *Thiboutot* as erecting the "presumption that a federal statute creating federal rights may be enforced in a Section 1983 action," rebuttable only by an express indication in the underlying statute that Congress considered its stated remedies to be exclusive.[44]

In three subsequent decisions, that presumption has apparently carried the day.[45] The Court has found § 1983 available if the predicate statute provides either no remedy, as in *Golden State Transit Corp.*, or only an administrative remedy, as in *Wilder* and *Wright*, for the kind of violation alleged. Only when the entitlement statute created its own judicial remedy[46] or a "carefully tailored administrative and judicial mechanism"[47] has the Supreme Court held § 1983 displaced as a matter

42. *See 31 Foster Children v. Bush*, 329 F.3d 1255 (11th Cir.2003) (provision of Adoption Assistance and Child Welfare Act requiring provision of child's health and education record to foster parents did not confer rights enforceable by foster children, so "and laws" claim fails despite absence of any alternative enforcement mechanism).

43. 536 U.S. at 300 (Stevens, J., dissenting).

44. *Pennhurst I*, 451 U.S. at 51, 101 S.Ct. at 1557 (White, J., dissenting in part); cf. *Bush v. Lucas*, 462 U.S. 367, 390, 103 S.Ct. 2404, 2417, 76 L.Ed.2d 648 (1983) (Marshall, J., concurring in unanimous decision) (precluding *Bivens* recovery for a government employee if Congress provided a comprehensive administrative and judicial remedy that was "substantially as effective as a damages action").

45. *See* text following this section.

46. *See Middlesex County Sewerage Auth. v. National Sea Clammers*, 453 U.S. 1, 101 S.Ct. 2615, 69 L.Ed.2d 435 (1981).

47. *Smith v. Robinson*, 468 U.S. 992, 1009, 104 S.Ct. 3457, 3467, 82 L.Ed.2d 746 (1984). *But see* Handicapped Children's Protection Act of 1986, 20 U.S.C.A. § 1415 (1988) (overruling *Smith* and authorizing attorney's fees pursuant to 42 U.S.C.A. § 1988 in connection with successful constitutional or federal statutory claims even when the same relief, with an express fee authorization, is available under the Education of the Handicapped Act, 20 U.S.C.A. §§ 1401–1485 (1988)).

Thus in *Golden State*, 493 U.S. at 106, and *Blessing*, 520 U.S. at 347, the Supreme Court distinguished *Sea Clammers* and

of congressional intent. The Court's decisions on this issue therefore seem to hold that § 1983 is supplanted only when Congress has provided a carefully considered federal[48] judicial remedy for the predicate statutory violation. The circuit decisions reach varying conclusions as to when such a remedy is sufficiently comprehensive to preclude the action under § 1983.[49]

Smith v. Robinson, observing that the availability only of *administrative* mechanisms for enforcement of the right in question will not foreclose the Section 1983 claim. *See Mallett v. Wisconsin Div. of Vocational Rehabilitation*, 130 F.3d 1245, 1255–56 (7th Cir.1997), *appeal after remand,* 248 F.3d 1158 (7th Cir.2000) (Rehabilitation Act).

48. *Wilder* provided support for a "federal" qualification by rejecting the argument that the availability of state judicial review of Virginia's implementation of the Medicaid amendment was relevant to the availability of relief under § 1983. *See Wilder v. Virginia Hosp. Ass'n*, 496 U.S. at 524 n.20, 110 S.Ct. at 2525 n.20.

49. *See e.g. Abrams v. City of Rancho Palos Verdes*, 354 F.3d 1094 (9th Cir. 2004) (no comprehensive remedial scheme in Telecommunications Act to foreclose § 1983 claim based on violation of that statute); *National Home Equity Mortg. Ass'n v. E. Joseph Face, Jr.*, 283 F.3d 220 (4th Cir. 2002) (assuming that Mortgage Transaction Parity Act may be enforced through Section 1983 claim); *Frazier v. Fairhaven School Committee*, 276 F.3d 52, 57–63 (1st Cir. 2002) (assuming that despite comprehensive remedy under Individuals With Disabilities Education Act, § 1983 "and laws" claim based on IDEA is available, but holding that plaintiff bringing such a claim must first exhaust administrative remedies provided by IDEA even though only money damages sought and despite general non-exhaustion rule for Section 1983; and citing two circuit decisions reaching same conclusion and three others permitting the IDEA-based Section 1983 damages-only claim without requiring exhaustion); *accord, Robb v. Bethel School Dist. No. 403,* 308 F.3d 1047 (9th Cir.2002); *Vinson v. Thomas*, 288 F.3d 1145 (9th Cir.2002) (detailed remedial schemes of Title II of Americans with Disabilities Act and Section 504 of Rehabilitation Act impliedly preclude Section 1983 "and laws" claims against state official based on violations of those statutes); *Grey v. Wilburn*, 270 F.3d 607 (8th Cir.2001) (remedial frameworks under the Rehabilitation Act and the Americans with Disabilities Act sufficiently extensive and comprehensive to displace separate judicial remedy under § 1983, but plaintiff may per *Ex Parte Young* exception to Eleventh Amendment seek injunctive relief against state officials directly under those statutes); *Padilla v. School Dist. No. 1,* 233 F.3d 1268 (10th Cir.2000) (comprehensive remedy under Individuals With Disabilities Education Act impliedly precludes § 1983 "and laws" claim based on IDEA); *Murrell v. School Dist. No. 1*, 186 F.3d 1238, 1249 (10th Cir. 1999); *Seamons v. Snow*, 84 F.3d 1226, 1233 (10th Cir.1996); *Doe v. Petaluma City Sch. Dist.*, 54 F.3d 1447 (9th Cir.1995) (holding or assuming that Title IX claim gives rise to § 1983 "and laws" claim); and *Lillard v. Shelby County Bd. of Educ.*, 76 F.3d 716 (6th Cir.1996) (Title IX enforcement scheme, even including implied judicial cause of action, insufficiently comprehensive to foreclose § 1983 action based on independent due process rights) with *Lollar v. Baker*, 196 F.3d 603, 608–610 (5th Cir. 1999) (available Rehabilitation Act claim against employing agency, but not individual state actor, forecloses § 1983 claim against individual state actor where only alleged deprivation of rights is under Rehabilitation Act); *Alsbrook v. City of Maumelle*, 184 F.3d 999, 1010–11 (8th Cir.1999), *cert. dismissed sub nom. Alsbrook v. Arkansas*, 529 U.S. 1001, 120 S.Ct. 1265, 146 L.Ed.2d 215 (2000) (Americans With Disabilities Act judicial remedial scheme providing monetary compensation against entity sufficiently comprehensive to bar § 1983 individual capacity claims); *Kendall v. City of Chesapeake, Va.*, 174 F.3d 437 (4th Cir. 1999) (detailed criminal penalties, private right of action for unpaid wages, overtime, liquidated damages and ancillary relief impliedly preclude relief based on FLSA rights under § 1983); *Holbrook v. City of Alpharetta, Ga.*, 112 F.3d 1522 (11th Cir.1997) (the remedial frameworks under the Rehabilitation Act and the Americans with Disabilities Act sufficiently extensive and comprehensive to displace separate judicial remedy under § 1983); *Pfeiffer by Pfeiffer v. Marion Center Area School Dist.*, 917 F.2d 779 (3d Cir.1990) (Title IX administrative enforcement scheme, coupled with implied judicial cause of action, comprehensive enough to foreclose all § 1983 claims); *Hobbs v. Hawkins*, 968 F.2d 471 (5th Cir.1992) (civil rights claim for damages for a violation of

When there is an express judicial remedy provided in the predicate statute, the circuit courts have uniformly disallowed § 1983 claims to enforce the statute.[50] At the other extreme, where only state administrative grievance procedures (or less) are available, the courts permit § 1983 enforcement.[51] There is less agreement when the statute provides only for federal administrative procedures[52] or when there exists an implied private right of action to enforce the predicate statute.[53] But if the predicate statute expressly saves other federal laws from impairment, the § 1983 "and laws" claim lies regardless of the comprehensiveness of its remedy scheme.[54] On the other hand, where it has been held that a statute affords no private civil action against particular kinds of defendants,[55] a Section 1983 "and laws" claim may lie to fill the gap.[56]

Why would the Court assiduously nick away at § 1983 jurisdiction in its primary sphere, the vindication of constitutional rights, yet in *Maine v. Thiboutot* open the doors to an acknowledged potential onslaught of litigation whenever any of a multitude of federal statutes, mostly not providing for civil rights, is violated under color of state law? Particularly inexplicable was the Court's embrace of federal statutory claims under § 1983 after the Court had just announced a notably more restrictive approach to implying judicial rights of action directly under

right to a free election under Labor Management Relations Act held preempted by a comprehensive administrative enforcement mechanism); and *Mennone v. Gordon*, 889 F.Supp. 53 (D.Conn.1995) (rejecting use of § 1983 as vehicle for Title IX claim). *Cf. Grey v. Wilburn*, 270 F.3d 607 (8th Cir. 2001) (comprehensive judicial remedial schemes of the Americans With Disabilities Act and Rehabilitation Act preclude Section 1983 claim allegedly based on an Equal Protection violation, where plaintiff alleged no facts to support the constitutional claim other than those supporting his statutory claims). For the possibility that remedial preclusion of "and laws" claims may be found more frequently in the wake of *Seminole Tribe of Florida v. Florida*, 517 U.S. 44, 116 S.Ct. 1114, 134 L.Ed.2d 252 (1996) (overruling *Pennsylvania v. Union Gas Co.*, 491 U.S. 1, 109 S.Ct. 2273, 105 L.Ed.2d 1 (1989)), see the discussion in § 5.35, *infra*.

50. *See, e.g., Sellers v. School Bd. of Mannassas, Va.*, 141 F.3d 524 (4th Cir. 1998), *cert. denied*, 525 U.S. 871, 119 S.Ct. 168, 142 L.Ed.2d 137 (1998) (Individuals with Disabilities Education Act); *Mattoon v. City of Pittsfield*, 980 F.2d 1 (1st Cir.1992) (Safe Water Drinking Act included administrative fines and allowed private right of action to establish drinking water regulations and obtain injunctions); *Garcia v. Cecos Internat'l, Inc.*, 761 F.2d 76 (1st Cir. 1985) (Resource Conservation and Recovery Act).

51. *See, e.g., Native Village of Venetie IRA Council v. State of Alaska*, 155 F.3d 1150 (9th Cir.1998) (Indian Child Welfare Act); *Wright v. Roanoke*, 479 U.S. 418, 107 S.Ct. 766, 93 L.Ed.2d 781 (1987) (Brooke Amendment to the Fair Housing Act); *Victorian v. Miller*, 813 F.2d 718 (5th Cir.1987) (Food Stamp Act).

52. *See, e.g., Chan v. New York*, 1 F.3d 96 (2d Cir.1993), *cert. denied*, 510 U.S. 978, 114 S.Ct. 472, 126 L.Ed.2d 423 (1993) (allowing a § 1983 suit to enforce the Housing and Community Development Act).

53. *Compare Lakoski v. James*, 66 F.3d 751 (5th Cir.1995), *cert. denied* sub nom. *Lakoski v. University of Tex.*, 519 U.S. 947, 117 S.Ct. 357, 136 L.Ed.2d 249 (1996) (§ 1983 unavailable in Title IX) with *Crawford v. Davis*, 109 F.3d 1281 (8th Cir.1997) (allowing § 1983 claim to enforce Title IX).

54. *AT&T Wireless PCS, Inc. v. Atlanta, Ga.*, 210 F.3d 1322 (11th Cir.2000).

55. See *Butts v. County of Volusia*, 222 F.3d 891, 894 (11th Cir.2000) (Section 1981) rights against state actors may not be enforced directly under Section 1981, but only through Section 1983 with all the restrictions of the latter, per U.S. Supreme Court's decision in *Jett v. Dallas Ind. School Dist.*, 491 U.S. 701, 109 S.Ct. 2702, 105 L.Ed.2d 598 (1989).

56. *Butts, supra*, 222 F.3d at 894; *Webster v. Fulton County*, 283 F.3d 1254 (11th Cir.2002).

other federal statutes.[57] The Court's relative receptiveness to § 1983 statutory claims has been even more baffling because this result is not compelled. For example, there is a more than respectable historical argument that the addition in 1874 of the words "and laws" to § 1983 was intended merely to parallel the subject matter jurisdiction conferred

57. *See, e.g., Transamerica Mortgage Advisors, Inc. v. Lewis*, 444 U.S. 11, 24, 100 S.Ct. 242, 249, 62 L.Ed.2d 146 (1979) (holding that there is "a limited private remedy under the Investment Advisors Act of 1940" despite no express provision for a private cause of action); *Touche Ross & Co. v. Redington*, 442 U.S. 560, 576–77, 99 S.Ct. 2479, 2489–90, 61 L.Ed.2d 82 (1979) (refusing to find a private cause of action under § 17(a) of the Securities Exchange Act of 1934, 15 U.S.C.A. § 78g(a) (1988), despite having previously found one under § 14(a), 15 U.S.C.A. § 78n(a) (1988)). This curiosity is elaborated by Monaghan, 91 Colum.L.Rev. 233.

The central, initial inquiry in deciding whether to imply a private right of action directly under a federal statute (i.e., without use of Section 1983) is whether Congress intended, expressly or impliedly, to afford persons injured by the statute's violation a private cause of action, i.e., remedy. *See Touche Ross, supra,* 442 U.S. at 575, denying that the four factors previously described by *Cort v. Ash*, 422 U.S. 66, 95 S.Ct. 2080, 45 L.Ed.2d 26 (1975) should be weighted equally and placing ultimate emphasis on indications of Congressional intent to afford a private judicial remedy. By contrast, the three-part *Blessing* test to determine whether a plaintiff might vindicate rights conferred by that statute through an action under *Section 1983* asked simply whether that statute creates a federal *right* in favor of the particular plaintiff. Put otherwise, on the Section 1983 "and laws" issue it is really beside the point whether the predicate statute expresses or implies the availability of a cause of action, because Section 1983 itself provides the remedy. *Gonzaga University v. Doe,* 536 U.S. 273, 122 S.Ct. 2268, 2273–2276, 153 L.Ed.2d 309 (2002).

It is therefore not surprising that *pre-Gonzaga* circuit decisions not infrequently concluded that the plaintiff may proceed with a Section 1983 "and laws" claim based on a violation of a predicate federal statute even after concluding that no private right of action may fairly be implied under that statute directly. *See, e.g., Mallett v. Wisconsin Div. of Vocational Rehabilitation*, 130 F.3d 1245, 1248–57 (7th Cir.1997), *appeal after remand,* 248 F.3d 1158 (7th Cir.2000) (Rehabilitation Act); *Chan v. City of New York*, 1 F.3d 96 (2d Cir.1993) (Housing and Community Development Act); *Fay v. South Colonie Cent. School District*, 802 F.2d 21, 33 (2d Cir.1986), *overruled* in light of *Gonzaga* by *Taylor v. Vermont Dep't of Educ.*, 313 F.3d 768, 786 (2d Cir.2002) (Family Educational Rights and Privacy Act); *Keaukaha-Panaewa Comm. Ass'n v. Hawaiian Homes Comm'n*, 739 F.2d 1467, 1470–71 (9th Cir.1984). But *Gonzaga, supra,* moves away from expansive language in *Blessing* and other decisions that had found enforceable rights, and therefore upheld "and laws" claims, merely because the Section 1983 plaintiff was within the ambit of a predicate statute's "interests" or "benefits." With *Gonzaga* the Court strictly insists on clear statutory textual indications of a "right" privately enforceable through Section 1983 and equates that inquiry with its increasingly restrictive approach in direct implied private rights of action cases. Application of this "rights" standard, newly enunciated for "and laws" cases, may cause many future "and laws" claims to founder despite the general recognition that Section 1983 provides a remedy for the vindication of individual rights that are expressly, or virtually expressly, declared by federal statutes.

Just as some circuits resisted a broad interpretation of the *Suter* and *Blessing* holdings in order to sustain "and laws" claims, some lower courts cling to the expansive language of *Blessing* or the holding of *Wilder* to avoid the even more restrictive test of *Gonzaga. Compare Bosscher v. Township of Algoma*, 246 F.Supp.2d 791 (W.D.Mich.2003) and *Almendares v. Palmer*, 2002 WL 31730963 (N.D.Ohio 2002) (*Blessing* 3–factor test supplanted by *Gonzaga) with Missouri Child Care Ass'n v. Martin*, 241 F.Supp.2d 1032, 1041 (W.D.Mo. 2003) (applying *Wilder* and *Blessing* with the observation that if the Supreme Court had intended to overrule *Wilder,* it should have done so explicitly); *Arrington v. Fuller*, 237 F.Supp.2d 1307, 1314 (M.D.Ala.2002) (holding *Blessing* rationale still applicable). *Cf. Henry's Wrecker Service Co.of Fairfax County, Inc. v. Prince George's County*, 214 F.Supp.2d 541, 543–44 (D.Md. 2002)(*Gonzaga* called *Blessing* 3–factor test into serious doubt, or "tightened" it, but did not flatly reject it).

by the forerunner of 28 U.S.C.A. § 1343(3), a section limited to claims arising under "any law providing for equal rights."[58] On that reading, the Court might have restricted "and laws" claims to statutes forbidding discrimination, rather than embracing violations of all manner of ordinary federal commerce and welfare laws. The Court's decision in *Gonzaga*, however, partially closes the door to statute-based Section 1983 claims by realigning the requirement of an individual "right" with the restrictive initial element for establishing an implied private right of action.

Most § 1983 "and laws" claims are brought against local governmental entities for alleged failures to implement faithfully welfare or benefits programs as prescribed by federal law. On occasion, however, an "and laws" damages claim will be brought against an individual state or local official. And it has been held in such cases that public officials may assert qualified immunity against damages liability for violations of federal statutory rights, just as they may claim that immunity in cases alleging violations of federal constitutional rights.[59]

58. *See Maine v. Thiboutot*, 448 U.S. 1, 14–19, 100 S.Ct. 2502, 2509–2512, 65 L.Ed.2d 555 (1980) (Powell, J., dissenting) (reviewing the historical argument); *cf.* John C. Jeffries, Jr., *Damages for Constitutional Violations: The Relation of Risk to Injury in Constitutional Torts*, 75 Va.L.Rev. 1461, 1485 n.60 (1989) (discussing the Supreme Court's efforts to except particular statutes from its general rule that § 1983 provides a private damages action for all federal statutes).

59. *Blake v. Wright*, 179 F.3d 1003 (6th Cir.1999), *cert. denied*, 528 U.S. 1136, 120 S.Ct. 980, 145 L.Ed.2d 930 (2000).

SUMMARY OF THE "AND LAWS" BRANCH OF § 1983

Section 1983 claim can be predicated on violation of *any* federal statute (*Thiboutot*), subject to the following "rights" and "remedies" caveats:

IF	*UNLESS*
Plaintiff shows she is an intended beneficiary of the federal statutory standard and thus has an enforceable "*right*";	*Defendant shows* that comprehensive *remedies* provided by the predicate statute impliedly preclude a civil claim under Section 1983.
and	x *National Sea Clammers* x *Smith v. Robinson* (predicate statutes provided limited *judicial* remedies).
That right, as elaborated by the statute, its legislative history, and federal implementing regulations, is sufficiently definite for judicial enforcement (with *Gonzaga* virtually requiring that the right be explicit from statutory text).	√ *Wright v. Roanoke* (predicate statute provided only *administrative* remedies)
That right is binding and mandatory, not predictory √ *Wilder* x *Suter* x *Blessing* x *Gonzaga University* Post-*Suter* circuit decisions mostly distinguish *Suter*, follow *Wilder*, on this point	

√ = Claim recognized
x = Claim rejected

§§ 2.56–2.59 [Reserved]

I. SECTION 1983 REMEDIES AND DETERRENCE OF FEDERAL LAW VIOLATIONS BY ENTITY AND INDIVIDUAL DEFENDANTS: A NEW ASYMMETRY

§ 2.60 In General

It makes little sense to redesign liability standards around compensation or deterrence alone. Each should be taken into account. Even more important is recognition that a dynamic federal common law of § 1983 should be informed by the dominant congressional goal underlying provision of a private right of action against any "person" to redress federal injuries inflicted "under color of any statute, ordinance, regulation, custom, or usage, of any State or Territory."[1] The implicit purpose

§ 2.60

1. 42 U.S.C.A. § 1983 (1988).

of § 1983 is the restraint of governmental conduct violative of any federal right, not just conduct that is the subject of distinct, unexceptionable judicial articulation. All such conduct should be restrained independent of the value of private compensation.[2]

Exalting government restraint as the dominant concern of the enacting Reconstruction Congress does not denigrate victim compensation, which remains an important supplementary mechanism for achieving deterrence. An emphasis on restraint need not ignore either the common law's concern for fairness in subjecting individual defendants to damages or the new federalists' concern that local government be permitted to function free of needless national intrusion. These related values are accommodated to varying degrees in the proposal set forth in this part.

Each of the historical reasons offered by Justice Douglas for the enactment of § 1983 touches issues of governmental structure: the need to "override certain kinds of state laws," to "provide[ ] a remedy where state law was inadequate," and to "provide a federal remedy where the state remedy, though adequate in theory, was not available in practice."[3] Justice Harlan's views similarly point to the paramount importance of government restraint, whether directly through deterrence or indirectly through victim compensation.[4] For the statute to have significant prophylactic effect, it must enforce all constitutional norms, not just those fortuitously enmeshed in government policy. The culpability requirement embedded in both the Court's qualified immunity and "policy" doctrines, however, is calculated to confound that end.

The Court has tacitly recognized the signal importance of the entity as a defendant by denying local governments the immunity it conferred on individual defendants charged with transgressing emerging constitutional rights. Indeed, the particular defendant in the action in which the Court first explicitly extended § 1983 to federal statutory violations was an entity.[5] Consequently, a local government is now liable for federal statutory violations, which by their nature implicate policy, as soon as federal law is declared; an individual is liable for a constitutional violation only after some uncertain hiatus during which the judiciary establishes a right with clarity.

Admittedly, the central premise of government restraint is virtually irreconcilable with the principal holding of *Will v. Michigan Department*

2. The Court has recognized the overriding public nature of the interests served by civil rights legislation: the "public as a whole has an interest in the vindication of the rights conferred by the statutes enumerated in § 1988, over and above the value of a civil rights remedy to a particular plaintiff." *Hensley v. Eckerhart*, 461 U.S. 424, 444 n. 4, 103 S.Ct. 1933, 1945 n. 4, 76 L.Ed.2d 40 (1983) (Brennan, J., concurring in part and dissenting in part).

3. *Monroe*, 365 U.S. at 173–74, 81 S.Ct. at 477; see *supra* § 2.4. *See also* Shapo, 60 N.W.U.L.Rev. at 280 (stating that the enacting Congress was concerned about "a widespread outbreak of violence" exacerbated by "the relative inaction of state and local governments . . . [creating a situation] which bordered on anarchy").

4. *See supra* § 2.4.

5. *See Maine v. Thiboutot*, 448 U.S. 1, 2, 100 S.Ct. 2502, 2503, 65 L.Ed.2d 555 (1980).

of State Police:[6] that the states in their own name are not § 1983 "persons" subject to any liability at all. The *Will* result is countertextual; by its terms the statute mentions only states and territories, not cities or counties, and it was enacted to implement Fourteenth Amendment restrictions on state action.[7] *Will* is also heedless of Justice Powell's complaint in *Owen* that the Court imposed strict damages liability on a level of government, a municipality, "least able to bear it."[8] By extending comprehensive damage immunity in all courts, state and federal, to the entity best able to offer relief, the state, the Court in *Will* left the state's poorer subdivisions to fend for themselves.

Yet even within *Will* there is indirect support for the government restraint thesis. By reaffirming that an individual state agent named in her official capacity remains a § 1983 "person" for purposes of prospective relief,[9] the Court continues to nurture the root concept of the statute. Conduct fairly attributable to government that causes the deprivation of federally secured rights should be subject to judicial oversight and a federal remedy in a proceeding under federal law, and generally in a forum of the plaintiff's choice.[10]

6. 491 U.S. 58, 109 S.Ct. 2304, 105 L.Ed.2d 45 (1989). The Court has since extended that holding to exclude territories from § 1983's coverage. *See Ngiraingas v. Sanchez*, 495 U.S. 182, 192, 110 S.Ct. 1737, 1743, 109 L.Ed.2d 163 (1990).

7. The *Will* opinion glossed over an important interpretive difficulty foreseen by Justice Powell. In *Monell v. Department of Soc. Servs.*, 436 U.S. 658, 98 S.Ct. 2018, 56 L.Ed.2d 611 (1978), Justice Powell described the awkwardness of importing the Eleventh Amendment fiction of *Ex parte Young*, 209 U.S. 123, 28 S.Ct. 441, 52 L.Ed. 714 (1908), into § 1983. The consequence is that a public official sued in his official capacity is a "person" only to the extent the plaintiff prays for prospective relief. See *Monell*, 436 U.S. at 712, 98 S.Ct. at 2047 (Powell, J., concurring). As Justice Powell observed, the decision in *Monell* to subject local government entities to liability as § 1983 "persons" avoided this bifurcation, which had no support in the text of the statute. See id. at 711–12, 98 S.Ct. at 2046–47. *Will* resurrects the bifurcation at the level of state government on the authority of *Ex parte Young*, making no mention of the problem Justice Powell had identified. See *Will*, 491 U.S. at 71 n.10, 109 S.Ct. at 2312 n.10. Nevertheless, *Will* continues to be relied on for the proposition that a substate entity enjoying immunity from damages suit in federal court for purposes of the Eleventh Amendment is not a "person" within the meaning of Section 1983 and will therefore also be immune from suit under that statute in either state or federal court. *See Kirchmann v. Lake Elsinore Unified School District*, 83 Cal.App.4th 1098, 1103–1104, 100 Cal.Rptr.2d 289, 293–294 (4th Dist.2000), *cert.* denied 533 U.S. 902, 121 S.Ct. 2242, 150 L.Ed.2d 231 (2001) (collecting citations).

8. *Owen v. City of Independence*, 445 U.S. 622, 670, 100 S.Ct. 1398, 1425, 63 L.Ed.2d 673 (1980) (Powell, J., dissenting). Justice Powell's lament increases in poignancy after *City of St. Louis v. Praprotnik*, 485 U.S. 112, 108 S.Ct. 915, 99 L.Ed.2d 107 (1988), restricted ad hoc "policy" to decisions by final policymakers. See id. at 127, 108 S.Ct. at 926. Because of *Praprotnik*, the lowest levels of state government and the smallest government entities are most vulnerable to § 1983 liability. In a county or town with a one-or two-member constabulary or executive department, virtually every decision affecting a citizen may be made by a final policymaking official. *See Alkire v. Irving*, 305 F.3d 456, 467 (6th Cir.2002) (where Sheriff established policy of detaining persons in county jail for more than 48 hours before their initial court appearance, "any policy of county employee Sheriff Zimmerly on holding detainees until trial was also a county policy.... It is not necessary that Holmes County officially endorsed this policy through legislative action for it to carry its imprimatur.")

9. *See Will*, 491 U.S. at 71 n.10, 109 S.Ct. at 2312 n.10.

10. Special circumstances that fetter the plaintiff's choice of forum or require prior presentation of the facts underlying a § 1983 claim to a state tribunal are discussed at length in Chapter 5 *infra*.

Identifying the statute's objectives in these terms leads to several related prescriptive tenets. First, although a government acts through individuals,[11] it is ultimately the government's conduct with which we are concerned. Moreover, for the compensatory goal to be met, limitations on the liability of the agent, driven by concerns about fairness and untoward stifling of initiative, demand correlative enlargement of the liability of the entity.[12] Consequently, if the plaintiff can demonstrate a violation of her federal rights, the only remaining question we should ask before attaching liability to the entity is whether it can fairly be charged with the conduct. This conclusion is bolstered by the widespread availability of government employee indemnification.[13] In the common situation in which the employee meets the entity's indemnification requirements, it is the entity that pays even if only the individual defendant formally suffers the adverse judgment.

The overriding need for restraint of government misconduct, the concern for fairness to individual defendants, and the need to avoid undue chilling of government initiative counsel a dual course. Entity accountability should be enhanced by discarding the *Monell* "policy" limitation; and the scope of individual liability under *Monroe* requires both widening and narrowing, with local government agents presumptively responsible for all federal law violations, settled or unsettled, but only if they intended to harm their victims.

§ 2.61 Entity Liability: Respondeat Superior Redux

The "policy" dictum in *Monell* reflected the concern, prompted by one of several available interpretations of statutory text, that an entity's liability should be limited to conduct fairly attributable to it. As shown above,[1] however, the "policy" stricture, especially as elaborated through *Pembaur* and *Praprotnik*, goes beyond what is necessary to attribute fairly the actor's conduct to the entity. That concern could be largely satisfied under traditional notions of respondeat superior, which the Court has sedulously resisted.[2] Proposed here is a modified version of common law respondeat superior as the basis for the liability of the government entity principal. The government would be responsible for the conduct of its agent who acts with the principal's authority, either

11. *See, e.g., Brown*, 1989 U.Ill.L.Rev. at 654 (stating that the problem with applying a fault standard to determine entity liability "is simple: [the entity] cannot think"); *Kramer & Sykes*, 1987 Sup.Ct.Rev. at 253 ("The problem is that municipal action is always—can only be—carried out by persons employed by the municipality").

12. *See Oren*, 50 U.Pitt.L.Rev. at 1000–03 (supporting municipal liability based on respondeat superior, the inclusion of state and federal governments in the scope of the money damages remedy, and the exclusion of an action against an individual official in light of the available governmental remedy).

13. *See supra* § 2.31.

§ 2.61

1. *See supra* §§ 2.31 and 2.32.

2. *See, e.g., City of Canton v. Harris*, 489 U.S. 378, 385, 392, 109 S.Ct. 1197, 1203, 1206, 103 L.Ed.2d 412 (1989); *City of St. Louis v. Praprotnik*, 485 U.S. 112, 124, 125, 108 S.Ct. 915, 925, 99 L.Ed.2d 107 n. 1, 2 (1988); *Monell v. Department of Soc. Servs.*, 436 U.S. 658, 692–95, 98 S.Ct. 2018, 2037–38, 56 L.Ed.2d 611 (1978).

express or implied[3] or, at the edge, apparent.[4] Asking if the injury-producing decision or conduct occurred within the actual, implied, or apparent scope of the state actor's duties[5] should assure fair attribution to the entity. At a minimum, a positive answer to the question means that the entity is responsible for a representation to a third person, the plaintiff, that the state actor had authority to act.[6]

In most cases an effective remedy lies against the entity and not its agents. Respondeat superior generally provides a remedy against entities even if the challenged act does not rise to the level of "policy" as defined by state law. The proposed version of respondeat superior would modify the common law by reaching the entity principal under some circumstances in which its agent would be absolved.[7] Respondeat superior has

3. "Authority is the power of the agent to affect the legal relations of the principal by acts done in accordance with the principal's manifestations of consent to him." *Restatement (Second) of Agency* § 7 (1957). This manifestation of consent can be either express or implied. *See id.* cmt. c.

The *Restatement*'s drafters include "implied" authority as simply a subspecies of express authority, recognizing that no principal can describe all the details of the tasks she wants performed. The scope of consent, therefore, rests on the familiar notion of "reasonable inference." *See id.* cmt. b. As that comment indicates, "[t]he agent's conduct is authorized if he is reasonable in drawing an inference that the principal intended him so to act although that was not the principal's intent." *Id.*

4. Again this prescription rests on noncontroversial, routinely applied principles in agency law. When "it is reasonable for the third person," or by extension, an injured plaintiff in a § 1983 action, "to believe that the agent is authorized" to undertake a certain act, such conduct has the trappings of apparent authority. *See id.* § 8 cmt. c. Under these circumstances vicarious liability is premised on conduct of the principal that permits the third party reasonably to believe that the authority exists, such as giving the agent a badge. *See id.* cmt. b (stating that manifestations of the principal sufficient to create apparent authority include those made "directly to a third person, or . . . to the community, by signs, . . . by authorizing the agent to state that he is authorized"); *see also id.* § 27 cmt. a (stating that the creation of apparent authority occurs through the "indicia of authority given by the principal to the agent"). A latent lesson of *Monroe v. Pape*, 365 U.S. 167, 81 S.Ct. 473, 5 L.Ed.2d 492 (1961), *overruled in part by Monell v. Department of Soc. Servs.*, 436 U.S. 658, 98 S.Ct. 2018, 56 L.Ed.2d 611 (1978), is that apparent authority is a sufficient condition for liability, although *Monroe* involved an individual defendant, not an entity. The individual actors in *Monroe*, carrying and no doubt displaying badges or other indicators of entity approval, were liable even though their conduct violated state law.

5. No entity liability exists when an official acts wholly outside any colorable actual, implied, or apparent authority. First, if the defendant is not clothed with government authority, it is hard to see how his acts can be "under color of" state law. Second, consider Professor Brown's observation, derived from Justice White's position in *Pembaur v. City of Cincinnati*, 475 U.S. 469, 106 S.Ct. 1292, 89 L.Ed.2d 452 (1986), that entities may not properly be held responsible for conduct that their officials could not reasonably believe to have been authorized. Brown explains that courts define respondeat superior broadly so that "persons who act beyond their authority are necessarily acting unreasonably." *Brown*, 1989 U.Ill.L.Rev. at 683 & n.365.

6. Liability for intentional torts undertaken with apparent authority is covered generally in *Restatement (Second) of Agency* §§ 245, 254, 257, 266 (1957) (describing conditions of liability for use of force, defamation, misrepresentation, and physical harms, respectively).

7. The version of respondeat superior advocated here is "modified" because, under familiar principles of respondeat superior, both the agent who originally causes the harm and his principal are liable, the latter vicariously. See W. Page Keeton et al., *Prosser and Keeton on the Law of Torts* 499 (5th ed. 1984). Moreover, the principal is liable not only for the agent's ordinary negligence, but also for intentional torts committed in furtherance of the employer's busi-

the added virtue of affording whatever meaningful restraint is possible against "good faith" torts by compelling higher-level officials to weigh the risk that their agents' conduct could result in an award of damages from the public treasury.[8] At the same time, if reasonably enforced, respondeat superior should serve to ensure that entities are held responsible only for conduct they actually or apparently authorize.[9]

By relaxing the § 1983 notion of "policy," the proposed standard would lead to a different result in a case like *Praprotnik*, in which the supervisor who affected the plaintiff's retaliatory discharge had apparent authority to make that personnel decision. Yet it would not alter the results of cases in which the Court has circumscribed § 1983 by redefining predicate constitutional violations. For example, this approach would not disturb the result in *DeShaney v. Winnebago County Department of Social Services*,[10] because the predicate "liberty" interest would still be wanting.[11]

ness, *see id.* at 505. The proposals advanced here for individuals, however, would free individuals from liability unless they act with intent to harm. *See infra* § 2.62. This leads to the result, jarring from a traditional perspective, of "vicarious" liability for a principal predicated on acts for which the agent is absolved.

Two reasons justify this departure from standard doctrine. First, retaining entity liability even under circumstances that in fairness should relieve agents from liability is essential for fulfilling § 1983's fundamental purpose of restraining governmental misconduct. Second, there may be only negligible differences in practice between the operation of ordinary principles of respondeat superior and the suggested modification. The need for vicarious liability stems from the judgment-proof status of many employees. *See, e.g.*, Clarence Morris & C. Robert Morris, Jr., *Morris on Torts* 252 (2d ed. 1980); *see also* Schuck, *Suing Government* at 33 (noting that the doctrine was originally conceived as a surety device that was called upon if the employee was unable to pay). For satisfaction of a judgment the injured plaintiff looks to the employer, the deep pocket to whom the risk is allocated. See Keeton et al., *supra*, at 500; Morris & Morris, *supra*, at 252. In theory, the employer then has a claim for subrogation against the employee. The fact that the latter is judgment-proof, added to the potential problems an employer would face in recruiting and retaining employees so threatened, however, has meant that the employer generally foregoes prosecution of this claim and instead seeks to deter employee misconduct indirectly, through discipline and discharge. *See id.* at 252; Schuck, *supra* at 105.

The modifications proposed are designed in part to encourage precisely such deterrence. At the same time, to the extent they deprive government entities of their common law subrogation rights as principals, the forfeiture is not grievous in practice and may be necessary to stimulate internal checks on employee misconduct.

8. *See Owen v. City of Independence*, 445 U.S. 622, 656, 100 S.Ct. 1398, 1418, 63 L.Ed.2d 673 (1980) (making the same observation on the narrower assumption that entity liability would attach only for acts of policy).

9. The doctrine of respondeat superior has, at times, known no apparent limitations, *see, e.g., Fruit v. Schreiner*, 502 P.2d 133, 142 (Alaska 1972) (holding employer liable where employee at a convention was involved in an automobile accident en route to a tavern in the early morning), a fact attributable in part to the absence of a uniform rationale. *See Riviello v. Waldron*, 47 N.Y.2d 297, 418 N.Y.S.2d 300, 303, 391 N.E.2d 1278, 1281 (1979) (discussing the evolution of the rationales underlying respondeat superior).

In the § 1983 context, *Monell* discussed two justifications, deterrence and loss-spreading. *See Monell*, 436 U.S. at 693–94, 98 S.Ct. at 2037–38. *Owen* accepted the equitable "loss-spreading" purpose. *See Owen*, 445 U.S. at 655 & n.39, 100 S.Ct. at 1417 & n.39. The proposal here ties liability to scope of authority—what conduct did the agent have the actual, apparent, or implied authority to undertake?

10. 489 U.S. 189, 109 S.Ct. 998, 103 L.Ed.2d 249 (1989).

11. *See id.* at 195–96, 109 S.Ct. at 1003–04.

Similarly, the floodgates concern would continue to be substantially ameliorated even if respondeat superior were recognized as the appropriate standard for entity liability. The *Roth/Paul* and *Parratt*[12] lines of authority, involving individual defendants, have eliminated the greatest potential "font" of tort law by redefining restrictively the property or liberty protected by procedural due process and the nature of actionable deprivations.[13] These limitations on liability that follow from the paring down of particular predicate constitutional violations would still exculpate entities even if, as here proposed, they were held generally accountable via respondeat superior for "random and unauthorized" federal law violations of their agents that did not implicate the loss of procedural protections.[14]

In the proposed redesign, actions against entities arising from "random and unauthorized" conduct would no longer be flatly precluded, since liability would no longer hinge on the existence of formal "policy." Nevertheless, if a particular challenge to such conduct were brought on procedural due process grounds the plaintiff would likely still encounter the restrictions raised by *Parratt. Parratt* reconceptualizes when process is due, as *Paul* and *Roth* reconceptualize whether it is due at all. Although *Paul* was an individual defendant action, *Roth* was brought against an entity. Thus, the doctrinal origins of the "random and unauthorized" restriction on procedural due process claims suggest that it should be available to entity defendants.

The proposal would remove the "policy" barrier that applies to all § 1983 entity actions regardless of the nature of the predicate right. *Parratt*, by contrast, narrows the scope of a particular federal right, procedural due process. Thus, even though § 1983 would reach an entity despite the absence of entity policy, a plaintiff who sues an entity complaining that the agent's "random and unauthorized" conduct violated her procedural due process rights could still lose by virtue of *Parratt*. In the end, the plaintiff would fail to state a sufficient § 1983 claim, because no recognized predicate constitutional violation occurred. Further, except in highly unusual circumstances pointing to direct taxpayer involvement in a violation, entities would continue to be exempt from punitive damages.[15] Proof requirements surrounding causation and damages would furnish further protection of entity coffers.[16]

12. *See supra* § 2.41.

13. "*Parratt* cases" involve individual defendants because the *Parratt* predicate for absolution from conduct that would otherwise violate procedural due process is that the conduct be "random and unauthorized." *Parratt v. Taylor*, 451 U.S. 527, 541, 101 S.Ct. 1908, 1916, 68 L.Ed.2d 420 (1981), *overruled in part by Daniels v. Williams*, 474 U.S. 327, 106 S.Ct. 662, 88 L.Ed.2d 662 (1986); see also *supra* § 2.41 (discussing "*Parratt* cases"). To conclude that a defendant's conduct is random and unauthorized is to define a situation in which the defendant is an individual. Under current law an entity defendant would escape liability in the same circumstances on the broader ground, pertinent to all § 1983 claims, that such conduct could not represent an implementation of *Monell* "policy."

14. *See e.g., Albright v. Oliver*, 510 U.S. 266, 114 S.Ct. 807, 127 L.Ed.2d 114 (1994).

15. *See City of Newport v. Fact Concerts, Inc.*, 453 U.S. 247, 271, 101 S.Ct. 2748, 2762, 69 L.Ed.2d 616 (1981).

16. The courts do not simply give away an entity's funds. Many decisions indicate that entities may avoid liability for conduct

Respondeat superior does impose a species of liability without fault. Application of the doctrine assumes that compensation to victims of unconstitutional conduct is not only an important objective of § 1983, but an invariable consequence of a judgment of entity liability. But the Court's current framework, that at least in the prima facie case leaves individual government employees rather than government itself primarily responsible for constitutional violations, puts the "focus on individual responsibility [and thereby] tends to divert attention from problems of government structure and organization, as distinct from the specific acts of individual officials."[17]

The importance of this point is reflected in the current asymmetric shape of the prima facie and defensive cases of individual and entity defendants. The Court has chosen to preserve the entity action as the primary stage for dialogue over the definition of constitutional rights. Emerging issues stemming from "government structure and organization," such as property taxation to finance public education, across-the-board practices respecting zoning and public employment, and police department decisions on the use of force, are often best contested in the entity suit.[18] Neither the text nor history of § 1983 suggests that judges who decide these vital constitutional questions should restrict compensation to those violations that, in some uncertain way, reflect entity "fault."

The Court's skewed emphasis on individual rather than entity responsibility also undermines efforts to challenge systemically caused constitutional harms, perhaps the most important and least accessible area of government conduct.[19] Individual defendants, and in turn their indemnifying entities, are frequently absolved from liability under the *Harlow/Creighton* version of qualified immunity. Further, when "policy" cannot be shown, the entity has no direct liability at all; and when policy

that clearly constitutes "policy" if the plaintiff is unable to bear the burden of proving that her federal injury was proximately caused by the implementation of that policy. *See Liggins v. Morris*, 749 F.Supp. 967, 972 (D.Minn.1990); *Pembaur v. City of Cincinnati*, 745 F.Supp. 446, 457 (S.D.Ohio 1990), aff'd, 947 F.2d 945 (6th Cir.1991); *see also Memphis Community Sch. Dist. v. Stachura*, 477 U.S. 299, 308, 106 S.Ct. 2537, 2543, 91 L.Ed.2d 249 (1986) (rejecting a jury instruction that permitted the jury to assess the significance of the right violated in measuring damages); *Carey v. Piphus*, 435 U.S. 247, 266, 98 S.Ct. 1042, 1054, 55 L.Ed.2d 252 (1978) (rejecting an award of substantial damages without proof of injury).

17. *Jeffries*, 88 Mich.L.Rev. at 85.

18. *See Oren*, 50 U.Pitt.L.Rev. at 1005 (remarking that the Court's decisions allowing landowners to challenge takings in § 1983 actions, coupled with *Harlow* immunity for the individual zoning board members, means that "only in the land use area is responsibility likely to be allocated to the government rather than to the official").

19. Justice Douglas's historical exegesis in *Monroe* on the factors animating the enactment of § 1983 highlights systemic governing problems in the Reconstruction South. *See Monroe v. Pape*, 365 U.S. 167, 173–74, 81 S.Ct. 473, 477, 5 L.Ed.2d 492 (1961), *overruled in part by Monell v. Department of Soc. Servs.*, 436 U.S. 658, 98 S.Ct. 2018, 56 L.Ed.2d 611 (1978); *see also* Shapo, 60 N.W.U.L.Rev. at 280 (noting that, in the eyes of the legislators who proposed § 1983, the relative inaction of state and local governments exacerbated the widespread outbreak of violence the statute was meant to address). Professor Jeffries would preclude a damage remedy for systemic harms because, he argues, they fall outside the risk that ordinarily makes such injuries compensable in tort. *See* Jeffries, 75 Va.L.Rev. at 1480.

is shown, the city is liable only for compensatory damages.[20] Thus, the overall design appears to presuppose that injunctive relief will be awarded and will sufficiently deter. Yet *City of Los Angeles v. Lyons*[21] critically subverts that assumption with its standing requirement that a plaintiff who seeks injunctive relief demonstrate "a sufficient likelihood" that he will suffer the same injury in the future.[22]

In denying injunctive relief against the entity the *Lyons* Court comforted itself that if the plaintiff suffers constitutional injury he will at least obtain recompense in the form of damages from the individual government defendants.[23] That assumption rings almost cynically hollow, however, because only a year earlier, in *Harlow*, the Court had crafted the "clearly established" feature of the qualified immunity defense that barred many damages claims at the threshold. That bar extended to the case at hand, as the *Lyons* majority itself appeared to recognize![24]

In fact, the Court has argued just the other way around: damages against an entity are essential to eradicate institutional government misconduct precisely because of the difficulty of securing injunctive relief. In *City of Riverside v. Rivera*,[25] a damages action against thirty members of the Riverside Police Department, the Court quoted approvingly from the trial judge's opinion that the " 'institutional behavior involved here ... [harassing Chicanos because of their national origin] had to be stopped.' "[26]Alluding to *Lyons*-like limitations, the Court wrote that damages relief was critical to deterrence because "injunctive relief generally is unavailable."[27]

§ 2.62 Individual Liability and the Controlling Role of Fault

Proof of fault is in essence, although not formally, required for individual defendants to be liable under § 1983. This is because the plaintiff must overcome the routinely asserted defense of qualified immunity, and by doing so has effectively shown the defendant officer negligent in not having conformed his conduct to that of a hypothetical reasonable officer faced with the same circumstances. In entity defendant cases, proof of fault or other culpability is not formally required, as

20. *City of Newport v. Fact Concerts, Inc.*, 453 U.S. 247, 101 S.Ct. 2748, 69 L.Ed.2d 616 (1981), discussed *supra* § 2.34.

21. 461 U.S. 95, 105–10, 103 S.Ct. 1660, 1667–70, 75 L.Ed.2d 675 (1983) (denying injunctive relief to the victim of an unlawful police chokehold because the victim could not show that he personally was likely to be subject to a future chokehold).

22. *See id.* at 111, 103 S.Ct. at 1670. Standing is discussed in more detail in Chapter 5 below.

23. *Id.*

24. *See id.* at 111, 103 S.Ct. at 1670 ("The legality of the violence to which *Lyons* claims he was once subjected is at issue in his suit for damages and can be determined there."). Justice Marshall pointed out in dissent that there had been no prior occasion to test the contours of Los Angeles's chokehold practice. *See id.* at 118, 103 S.Ct. at 1673 (Marshall, J., dissenting). The violation, if any, was therefore probably not "clearly established" under the test *Harlow* had laid down; individual police defendants would therefore likely receive qualified immunity.

25. 477 U.S. 561, 106 S.Ct. 2686, 91 L.Ed.2d 466 (1986).

26. *Id.* at 574, 106 S.Ct. at 2694.

27. *Id.* at 575, 106 S.Ct. at 2694.

Owen v. City of Independence denies entity defendants any good faith or qualified immunity defense. Yet as a practical matter, the prima facie "policy" element of *Monell* that the plaintiff must prove for entity liability comes close to reintroducing an element of fault. This can be seen in decisions like *Praprotnik*, which demands evidence that the entity's highest policymakers approved or ratified their agent's unconstitutional conduct; or like *City of Canton v. Harris* and *Brown v. Bryan County*, which demand evidence of a pattern of entity behavior from which it may be found that its agents were deliberately indifferent in their failure to act.[1]

Preferably application of fault concepts should be limited to government officials, as distinct from their employers. Because entities act through their agents[2] and are therefore liable only vicariously, deterrence has its most immediate impact in relation to the conduct of individuals.[3] For example, suppose that the individual defendant were to face liability when, but only when, her conduct was committed with the intent to harm, or a state of mind approaching a desire to produce harmful consequences.[4] This standard assures direct deterrence when it

§ 2.62

1. Jeffries, *In Praise of the Eleventh Amendment and Section* 1983, 84 Va.L.Rev. 55, 58 (1998). In this article Professor Jeffries supports the Court's insistence on proof of a functional equivalent of fault in § 1983 actions against individual defendants as well as entities. A principal reason he advances in support of qualified immunity is that its effective fault requirement is necessary to prevent the chilling or overdeterrence that he believes would likely infect the performance of government employees if they were more readily subject to liability. He observes that unlike private sector employees, who may be motivated by the prospect of salary increases or other forms of compensation, government employees are less able to appropriate for themselves the benefits of vigorous job performance. He also observes that government employees must be concerned that enthusiastic exercise of their discretion may subject their entities to large judgments and in turn subject themselves to discipline. The discussion in *Richardson v. McKnight*, 521 U.S. 399, 117 S.Ct. 2100, 138 L.Ed.2d 540 (1997), reflects that the Supreme Court continues to share Professor Jeffries' concerns. In denying qualified immunity to prison personnel working for private companies under contract with state government, the Court reasoned that "marketplace pressures provide the private firm with strong incentives to avoid overly timid, insufficiently vigorous, unduly fearful, or 'non-arduous' employee job performance." Similarly, the Court viewed the availability of insurance as increasing "the likelihood of [private] employee indemnification and to that extent reduces the employment—discouraging fear of unwarranted liability...." The Court specifically contrasted the situation of government employees, who it believed need qualified immunity precisely because they are more likely to succumb to lax execution of their duties for fear of individual liability.

2. *See* Brown, 1989 U.Ill.L.Rev. at 653–54.

3. *Cf. Owen v. City of Independence*, 445 U.S. 622, 655–66, 100 S.Ct. 1398, 1417–18, 63 L.Ed.2d 673 (1980) (arguing that the risk of inhibiting an agent's decisiveness, a symptom of overdeterrence, is reduced when threat of personal liability is removed).

4. (The terms "intentional" and "intent" sound as if they represent a unitary, determinate conception. In fact, in the ordinary parlance of tort law, the conclusion that an actor's conduct was "intentional" may reflect relatively distinct levels of culpability.) *See, e.g., Garratt v. Dailey*, 46 Wash.2d 197, 279 P.2d 1091, 1093–94 (1955) (holding actor liable for the tort of battery if he intended to bring about contact with the plaintiff, even if he did not intend the contact to cause the ensuing harm). Provisionally, as it is used in this Treatise, "intent" conforms with two routinely used criteria: one is stated by the *Restatement (Second) of Torts* § 8A (1965) (describing "intent" as either "[(a)] the actor desires to cause [the] consequences of his act, or [(b)] ... believes that the conse-

is most needed: when the state actor decides to inflict harm that amounts to a constitutional injury or tort. Absent an intent to harm, this suggestion would still relieve the individual of liability for all acts that the entity directed or authorized[5] (a situation in which individual liability seems unfair)[6] as well as for conduct that is entirely unauthorized and as such is not under color of state law.

Under traditional tort law, conduct as low on the culpability scale as mere negligence implicates deterrence and warrants damages. The "reasonable person" fiction presupposes that the defendant did not act as a reasonable person ought to have acted under the same or similar circumstances.[7] The Court's transplant of a negligence standard to the § 1983 prima facie case against individual officials engenders wide-ranging potential liability with little appreciable deterrence and with large potential for chilling officials in the execution of their duties. In fact that's at least a major reason why the Court has felt compelled to offset the likelihood of damages by inventing the whole series of trouble-some immunities for these defendants.

It is difficult to achieve a significant deterrent effect when a government official causes an unintended constitutional harm. An employee engaged unwittingly in an actually or apparently authorized function will not even be calculating whether the federal right he might negligently[8] or recklessly[9] violate will be deemed "clearly established." The

quences are substantially certain to result from it"); the other is used in suits under 42 U.S.C.A. § 1985(3) (1988) (attaching liability for a conspiracy depriving persons of rights or privileges). *See, e.g., Griffin v. Breckenridge*, 403 U.S. 88, 102 n. 10, 91 S.Ct. 1790, 1798 n. 10, 29 L.Ed.2d 338 (1971) ("The motivation aspect of § 1985(3) focuses not on scienter in relation to deprivation of rights but on invidiously discriminatory animus.").

5. Or apparently authorized. *See infra.*

6. *See infra.*

7. *See, e.g., Restatement (Second) of Torts* § 283 (1965) ("[T]he standard of conduct to which he must conform to avoid being negligent is that of a reasonable man under like circumstances."). The classic description of the interface between the negligence standard and deterrence remains that of Justice Holmes. *See* Oliver W. Holmes, *The Common Law* 76–78 (Mark D. Howe ed., 1963) (1881).

8. Although the Court has rendered mere negligence largely obsolete for constitutional torts, simple negligence may serve as a basis for § 1983 liability outside the procedural due process arena from which it was excluded by *Daniels v. Williams*, 474 U.S. 327, 106 S.Ct. 662, 88 L.Ed.2d 662 (1986). The *Parratt* Court, citing *Monroe*, asserted that neither the language nor legislative history of § 1983 has "been found by this Court to contain a state-of-mind requirement." *See Parratt v. Taylor*, 451 U.S. 527, 534, 101 S.Ct. 1908, 1912, 68 L.Ed.2d 420 (1981), *overruled in part by Daniels v. Williams*, 474 U.S. 327, 106 S.Ct. 662, 88 L.Ed.2d 662 (1986). In *Daniels*, an action predicated on an alleged due process violation, the Court held that "the Due Process Clause is simply not implicated by a negligent act," since a negligent loss does not amount to a "deprivation" within the meaning of the Fourteenth Amendment. *Daniels*, 474 U.S. at 328, 106 S.Ct. at 663. Accordingly, the Court overruled *Parratt* but only "to the extent that it states that mere lack of due care by a state official may 'deprive' an individual of life, liberty, or property under the Fourteenth Amendment." *Id.* at 330–31, 106 S.Ct. at 664 (emphasis added).

It is true that the predecessor to § 1983 was enacted to enforce the Fourteenth Amendment, see supra § 2.1, by contemporaries of the amendment's drafters, and both statute and amendment include the similar requirement of a "deprivation." One might therefore conclude that § 1983, like the due process clause, is violated only when the defendant acts with more than a negligent state of mind. Nevertheless, it is apparent that the Court was at some pains

9. See note 9 on page 305.

reasonable person standard of general tort law may be justified on the basis of wealth transfer, but it is unlikely that personal liability will significantly deter the individual defendant who acts carelessly, but in good faith. By contrast, subjecting the entity to liability for all federal rights deprivations attributable to its agents' acts within the scope of their agency should spur renewed internal checks and constraints on reckless or negligent conduct by government employees.[10]

Even the Court's expansive version of individual immunity, reflected in the "clearly established" rule as refined by *Anderson*, does not fully avoid chilling the employee who is aware that he is acting within the scope of his duties. The chilling potential disappears only if liability is limited to deliberately caused harms, those rooted in intentional misconduct.[11]

Limiting the occasions for individual liability is tolerable in compensatory terms only if coupled with an expansion of entity liability. Vicarious entity liability would relieve the claim against individual officers from having to fill the gaps left by *Monell's* conception of "policy." Put bluntly, emphasis on entity liability for damages will more

in *Daniels* not to overturn the more general conclusion of *Monroe* and *Parratt* that § 1983, as distinct from certain predicate constitutional rights that might be vindicated in § 1983 actions (such as procedural due process), contains no general state of mind requirement. *See, e.g.*, the following cases all decided under § 1983: *Graham v. Connor*, 490 U.S. 386, 396–97, 109 S.Ct. 1865, 1872–73, 104 L.Ed.2d 443 (1989) (holding that claims of excessive force in connection with arrest by police should be assessed under objective Fourth Amendment reasonableness standard); *First English Evangelical Lutheran Church v. County of Los Angeles*, 482 U.S. 304, 316 n. 9, 107 S.Ct. 2378, 2386 n. 9, 96 L.Ed.2d 250 (1987) (stating that even unintentional interference with property rights can constitute an unconstitutional taking); *Kolender v. Lawson*, 461 U.S. 352, 103 S.Ct. 1855, 75 L.Ed.2d 903 (1983) (determining an ordinance to be violative of the First Amendment when it is "objectively" vague).

9. It is assumed here that reckless conduct continues to be a staple source of § 1983 liability, even in the procedural due process realm. *See Collins v. City of Harker Heights*, 503 U.S. 115, 112 S.Ct. 1061, 117 L.Ed.2d 261 (1992); *Zinermon v. Burch*, 494 U.S. 113, 137, 110 S.Ct. 975, 989, 108 L.Ed.2d 100 (1990) (holding that a claim of " 'willful, wanton and reckless disregard of' ... constitutional rights" is sufficient to state a claim under § 1983 (quoting appendix to petition for certiorari)); *see also Redman v. County of San Diego*, 942 F.2d 1435, 1440 (9th Cir.1991), *cert. denied*, 502 U.S. 1074, 112 S.Ct. 972, 117 L.Ed.2d 137 (1992) (gross negligence or recklessness sufficient for due process liability under Daniels); *Archie v. City of Racine*, 847 F.2d 1211, 1220 (7th Cir.1988) (*en banc*) *cert. denied*, 489 U.S. 1065, 109 S.Ct. 1338, 103 L.Ed.2d 809 (1989) (recklessness sufficient for liability); *Harris v. Maynard*, 843 F.2d 414, 416 (10th Cir.1988) (wanton or obdurate disregard or deliberate indifference sufficient for liability); *Morales v. New York State Dep't of Corrections*, 842 F.2d 27, 30 (2d Cir.1988) (deliberate indifference sufficient for liability); *Colburn v. Upper Darby Township*, 838 F.2d 663, 669 (3d Cir.1988), *cert. denied*, 489 U.S. 1065, 109 S.Ct. 1338, 103 L.Ed.2d 808 (1989) (reckless indifference sufficient for liability); *Taylor v. Ledbetter*, 818 F.2d 791, 793 (11th Cir.1987) (*en banc*), *cert. denied*, 489 U.S. 1065, 109 S.Ct. 1337, 103 L.Ed.2d 808 (1989) (deliberate indifference sufficient for liability); *Nishiyama v. Dickson County*, 814 F.2d 277, 281–83 (6th Cir. 1987) (en banc) (reckless indifference sufficient for liability). *But see Washington v. District of Columbia*, 802 F.2d 1478, 1481 (D.C.Cir.1986) (reckless failure to act insufficient to create § 1983 liability).

10. *See* Kramer & Sykes, 1987 Sup.Ct. Rev. at 290–91.

11. "Because the [individual] employee need only refrain from deliberate misconduct to avoid liability, he or she has no incentive to become over cautious." *Id.* at 275 n.92.

often assure a solvent defendant.[12] It should foster deterrence, too, if, as is widely believed, damages deter more effectively than injunctive relief alone.[13]

The suggested framework for individual defendant cases also renders irrelevant for liability purposes the degree to which the allegedly violated right was "settled" on the eve of injury.[14] Consequently, the framework obviates the nettlesome and subjective analogizing to prior cases that in the current judicial climate reveals a "settled" right as a highly prized rarity. Whether trammeling a settled or unsettled federal right, intentional conduct is deterrable and accordingly should be subject to the penalties of the statute.[15]

12. *But see* Oren, *Section 1983 and Sex Abuse In Schools: Making a Federal Case Out of It*, 72 Chi.Kent L.Rev. 747 (1997) (urging easier proof requirements in cases against individual supervisors to offset the difficulties of recovering against entities generated by *Monell* and its progeny).

13. When an injunction is not obeyed, the courts customarily resort to a monetary sanction for civil contempt. *See, e.g., Spallone v. United States*, 487 U.S. 1251, 1260, 109 S.Ct. 14, 20, 101 L.Ed.2d 964 (1988) (mem.) (rejecting City of Yonkers's request to stay imposition of monetary sanctions for contempt in refusing to carry out district court's housing desegregation mandate). *See generally*, Dan B. Dobbs, *Handbook of the Law of Remedies* 96–98 (1973).

14. The "settledness" of a right may help the factfinder assess the degree of wrongful intent and, therefore, may bear on the appropriateness and measure of punitive damages. *See, e.g., Restatement (Second) of Torts* §§ 908(2), 501 cmt. b (1965).

15. One permutation of "settledness" requires additional explanation. When an agent with apparent, but neither express nor implied authority, acts without wrongful intent, liability should extend to the entity alone. The argument for holding the officer liable as well is that under such circumstances the imposition of individual liability serves a deterrence function, especially if the violated right is settled. Liability may discourage state actors from disregarding their government principal's actual or reasonably inferable instructions even if they believe, although unreasonably, that they serve its interest by violating the principal's instructions. The fear of chilling is minimal because the assumption that the government does not wish to encourage such conduct is probably accurate. Further, employees on a frolic and detour would not be eligible for qualified immunity as it is currently conceived, because conduct wholly outside the scope of one's actual or implied authority would be neither ministerial nor discretionary. See § 2.22, *supra*.

Nevertheless, individual defendants should not be subject to liability when they act with no more than apparent authority, regardless of the status of the violated right. If the right is not well settled, the deterrent effect of liability is simply too attenuated. First, it taxes the imagination to hypothesize many contexts in which an agent, acting without intent to harm, will violate newly declared rights while working with only apparent authority. More importantly, it strains credulity to assume that an agent, unreasonably departing from what she herself understands her duties to be, will be deterred by the threat of liability that may arise if a judge, acting after the conduct in question, comes to one but not another subjective conclusion about the status of the legal right. Alternatively, a government employee who acts outside the bounds of any reasonable description of her job will probably not fear a potential judgment for damages contingent on the creation of later-declared rights.

Given the apparently marginal deterrence achieved by imposing liability in this situation, coupled with the fact that the compensation goal could be fulfilled by an action against the entity, it is doubtful whether liability should be recognized for this conduct at the farthest frontiers of state action. One might respond that damages may be an appropriate remedy for dealing with such a loose cannon. The context, however, is still unintentionally harmful conduct, for which a punishment rationale is usually out of place.

A more difficult case is when this apparently authorized agent violates a settled right. The case for liability is arguably stronger, but so is the reason for rejecting it. First, deterrence is unlikely for all the reasons advanced above. Second, and more important, in light of the very few contexts

In this respect the proposal squares partially with *Monroe*. It conforms fully with the general proposition for which *Monroe* is best known—that individuals may be liable for "unauthorized" conduct, defined as conduct that violates or is not affirmatively warranted under state law. For several reasons, though, it makes sense to restrict individual liability, for authorized or unauthorized acts, to intentionally harmful conduct. First, in light of *Monell*, it is no longer necessary for individual defendants to carry the weight of the entity on their shoulders; compensation—and its accompanying deterrence—should now be available directly from the entity. Second, in all but intentional harm situations,[16] the modest or negligible gain to deterrence from individual liability will often be outweighed by the unfairness visited upon an individual whose only failure was to follow instructions or not predict nascent rights.

Finally, the troublesome aspects of the "clearly established" version of qualified immunity,[17] especially its potential for pinching off § 1983's potential as a crucible for developing constitutional standards, make that game worth far less than its candle. With the significantly expanded basis of entity liability proposed, it would no longer be necessary to impose liability on individuals for unintended harms. With the scope of potential claims against individual defendants substantially reduced both by the Court's contractions in the predicate constitutional law and by the exclusion proposed here of liability for most authorized acts, the cost of taking aggravated, intentionally caused constitutional torts to trial seems worth the concomitant potential for deterrence. The latter-day, policy-driven version of qualified immunity announced by *Harlow* and expanded in *Anderson*[18] becomes unnecessary when the primary factor that drove it, the fear of chill, is satisfied by an intent prerequisite for individual liability.

Excising the individual defendant's qualified immunity defense from § 1983's calculus as the tradeoff for making intent to harm an element of the plaintiff's case-in-chief will have variable effects on the policies the Court has cited in crafting that defense. Government officials would no longer have to guess, at their own potential risk, whether contemplated conduct would be deemed within their discretion or whether the constitutional right the conduct might violate would be deemed well settled. Officials could instead work within the scope of their authority without fear of § 1983 damage liability so long as they refrain from inflicting injury intentionally. Coincidentally, this would bring § 1983 in line with Congress's revised rules respecting the liability of federal employees for common law torts.

It is true that increased entity liability would occupy the time of officials as witnesses. Further, individuals named as defendants would

in which such an injury may occur, the costs of applying the clearly established test are excessive.

16. *See supra* for the definition of intentional harm as used here.

17. *See supra* § 2.22.

18. *Anderson v. Creighton*, 483 U.S. 635, 107 S.Ct. 3034, 97 L.Ed.2d 523 (1987). *See supra* § 2.22.

forfeit the possibility of early dismissal held out by *Harlow/Anderson* immunity; in the vast majority of such cases the official would have to submit to trial, because the key question of intent to harm would be for the jury.

In the aggregate, however, fewer officials may be expected to spend significant time in court. Far fewer cases would likely be brought against them, for in most potential liability situations, the entity, with its usually deeper pocket, would also be liable, and on easier proof terms.

Although, in an intentional harm regime, punitive damages would be potentially available in all remaining cases of individual liability,[19] the number of actions brought against individual officials should sharply decline. The difficulty of satisfying the intent to harm standard should give considerable pause to counsel who contemplate naming individual defendants, even apart from the tactical issue of jury sympathy for an individual sued with an entity co-defendant. To avoid Rule 11 sanctions, plaintiffs' allegations must be fairly well founded,[20] and their lawyers can receive statutory attorney's fees only if the allegations are so well founded that the client prevails.[21] For the plaintiff, securing the individual official as a less hostile witness in a claim against the entity will often be worth sacrificing the doubtful possibility of collecting punitive damages against the official himself.[22]

Saddling the entity with liability for all federal law violations its agents commit within the scope of their authority, and at the same time relieving agents of liability for all but egregious harms, admittedly takes an asymmetrical approach to state of mind. The Court's own framework suffers from the same flaw, but in reverse. The Court reaches individuals regardless of state of mind and entities if they are acting with the degree of advertence reflected in the several variations of official policy.[23] The

19. For a discussion of the present approach to punitive damages, *see supra* § 2.25. The "intent to harm" standard suggested here for any individual liability demands a somewhat greater showing of fault than *Smith v. Wade*, 461 U.S. 30, 103 S.Ct. 1625, 75 L.Ed.2d 632 (1983), does even for punitive damages. But the additional chilling of initiative entailed by the relative lenity of *Smith* is a disadvantage that more than offsets its potential for an incremental gain in deterrence. If entities were liable for actual damages whenever the individual would be liable, as proposed here, compensation and hence indirect deterrence would be promoted. Moreover, it is difficult to imagine that the Court's scheme deters an individual defendant unaware of a risk that an ordinarily reasonable and prudent person should recognize.

20. *See* Fed. R. Civ. P. 11; Edward J. Imwinkelried & Theodore Y. Blumoff, *Pretrial Discovery: Strategy & Tactics* § 13:10 n.26 (Supp. 1994). See Chapter 5 *infra*.

21. *See* 42 U.S.C.A. § 1988. *See* Civil Rights Attorneys Fees Act, Chapter 4, *infra*.

22. These proposals *will* in all likelihood increase filings against *entities*, but probably not unduly. The due process sphere would remain narrowly defined under the *Roth/Paul/Siegert, Davidson/Daniels* and *Parratt/Hudson* lines of authority. *See supra* Part E. Additionally, the proposals are interrelated and inseparable. Thus, one could anticipate a substantial reduction in the number of filings against individuals. Finally, if voters find their local government units frequently sued, it may be because the conduct of those units is questionable. As a result, voters or supervising officials have the option of removing chronic or egregious constitutional tortfeasors from office. *See City of Newport v. Fact Concerts, Inc.*, 453 U.S. 247, 269, 101 S.Ct. 2748, 2761, 69 L.Ed.2d 616 (1981) (suggesting that municipal liability for compensatory damages "may ... induce the public to vote the wrongdoers out of office").

23. *See supra* §§ 2.31 and 2.32 (discussing the Court's several formulations of "official policy" as the prerequisite for enti-

difference is that the aesthetic flaw of the proposal here may be better calculated to serve the statute's paramount purpose of restraining governmental misconduct.[24]

ty liability). Of these official policy formulations, the "deliberate indifference" element of *City of Canton v. Harris*, 489 U.S. 378, 109 S.Ct. 1197, 103 L.Ed.2d 412 (1989), applicable in cases where the plaintiff seeks to hold the entity liable for an omission, most clearly reflects the requirement of advertence. Some degree of advertence is also evinced in the Court's other approved variations: the official policy statement (*Monell*), legislation (*Pembaur*), vote of highest legislative authority (*Owen*), settled custom (*Praprotnik* and *Jett*), or delegation of final policymaking authority to an individual official (*Praprotnik* and *Jett*).

24. *See supra* § 2.4. For a powerful contrary position that contends strict liability of government entities would lead to unintended overdeterrence of desirable law enforcement activity, *see* Jeffries, *supra* note 1, this section.

Chapter Three

PROHIBITIONS ON RACE DISCRIMINATION IN FEDERALLY FUNDED PROGRAMS AND SEX DISCRIMINATION IN FEDERALLY FUNDED EDUCATION PROGRAMS: TITLES VI AND IX

Analysis

A. INTRODUCTION

§ 3.1 Titles VI and IX Generally

Title VI of the Civil Rights Act of 1964 prohibits discrimination based on race, color, or national origin in federally funded programs or activities.[1] Notwithstanding this broad provision, the Title does not reach employment practices except where a primary objective of the federal assistance is to provide employment.[2] Thus, except for federally funded employment programs, Title VI is unavailable to supplement Title VII of the 1964 Civil Rights Act as a remedy for race or national origin discrimination in employment.

Although in important respects Title IX of the Education Amendments of 1972 is modeled after Title VI as a ban on discrimination in federally funded programs,[3] Title IX is a prohibition only on sex discrimination and only with respect to education. In one critical respect, Title IX is broader than Title VI: it contains no counterpart to Title VI's general disclaimer of applicability to employment practices. Accordingly, to some degree Title IX redresses sex discrimination in employment, as well as in admissions and general educational activities, by federally funded education programs.[4]

Despite these differences, the statutes are mostly of similar design, and many of the issues arising under Title VI also arise under Title IX. Accordingly, in *Grove City College v. Bell*, the Supreme Court recognized the practice of looking to the substantial body of law developed under Title VI when examining Title IX questions.[5]

§§ 3.2–3.4 [Reserved]

B. TITLE VI

§ 3.5 In General

The primary prohibition of Title VI provides that:

> No person in the United States shall, on the ground of race, color or national origin, be excluded from participation in, be denied the benefits of, or be subjected to discrimination under any program or activity receiving Federal financial assistance.[1]

Programs or activities that receive federal financial support by way of grants, loans, or contracts (other than those of insurance or guaranty) are subject to Title VI sanctions.[2] The Title prohibits discrimination based on race, color or national origin, but not sex or religion. At least one circuit has allowed a retaliation claim under Title VI.[3]

§ 3.1

1. Title VI of the Civil Rights Act of 1964 is codified in 42 U.S.C.A. §§ 2000d—2000d–4a.

2. 42 U.S.C.A. § 2000d–3.

3. Title IX is codified at 20 U.S.C.A. §§ 1681–1688.

4. *North Haven Bd. of Educ. v. Bell*, 456 U.S. 512, 520–35, 102 S.Ct. 1912, 1917–26, 72 L.Ed.2d 299 (1982).

5. 465 U.S. 555, 566, 104 S.Ct. 1211, 1218, 79 L.Ed.2d 516 (1984), overruled in another respect by the Civil Rights Restoration Act of 1987, discussed below (interpreting Education Amendments of 1972, Title IX, 20 U.S.C.A. §§ 1681–1693).

§ 3.5

1. 42 U.S.C.A. § 2000d.

2. 42 U.S.C.A. § 2000d, d–1.

3. *Peters v. Jenney*, 327 F.3d 307, 318–19 (4th Cir.2003) (relying on case law developed under 42 U.S.C.A. §§ 1981 and 1982 to hold that a retaliation claim can proceed under Title VI despite the lack of such a provision in the statute). The court in *Pe-*

§ 3.6 Covered Programs or Activities

The scope of the "program or activity" language in Title VI has been a source of debate. In *Grove City College*, the Supreme Court interpreted the phrase "program or activity" narrowly.[1] The Court held that Title IX, and presumably, by extension, Title VI after which Title IX was modeled, prohibited discrimination only in the *particular* program or activity receiving the federal assistance, not in all the programs and activities conducted by the institution receiving such assistance.[2]

The Civil Rights Restoration Act of 1987,[3] returned to earlier judicial interpretations by defining the programs or activities covered by Title VI to include "all" of a recipient's operations.[4] More particularly, the Restoration Act provides that where federal aid is extended to any program within a college, university or other public system of elementary, secondary or higher education, the entire institution or system is covered by the prohibitions of Title VI.[5] For state and local governments, only the department or agency that receives the aid is covered;[6] logically, however, when one entity of a state or local government receives federal aid and distributes it to another, both entities are covered. Finally, for private corporations, the entire corporation would fall under Title VI only if the aid is extended to the corporation as a whole, or if the corporation provides a public service. The entire corporation may also

ters made clear that while there is no Title VI cause of action for disparate impact claims, *Alexander v. Sandoval,* 532 U.S. 275, 291, 121 S.Ct. 1511, 149 L.Ed.2d 517 (2001), a private right of action exists for intentional discrimination under Title VI and the regulations applying its ban on intentional discrimination. While Title VI does not specifically prohibit retaliation, the court found that the prohibition of retaliation was part of the "core anti-discrimination mandate" of Title VI. The court recited a federal regulation promulgated by the U.S. Department of Education at 34 CFR Part 100.7(e), targeting conduct that related to the section's core prohibition of racial discrimination by addressing "intimidatory, coercive or discriminatory conduct engaged in 'for the purpose of interfering with any right' "secured by § 601 of Title VI. The court held that this anti-retaliation regulation was enforceable through a private cause of action, to the extent that it forbade retaliation for opposing practices that were unlawful discrimination. *But cf. Jackson v. Birmingham Bd. of Educ.*, 309 F.3d 1333 (11th Cir.2002), *petition for cert. filed*, 71 USLW 3736 (May 13, 2003) (while declining to resolve whether a private right of action for retaliation exists under Title IX, holding that neither Title IX itself nor 34 CFR Part 100.7(e) implies a private right of action for retaliation in favor of individuals who, although not themselves the victims of gender discrimination, suffer retaliation because they have complained about gender discrimination suffered by others).

§ 3.6

1. 465 U.S. at 570, 104 S.Ct. at 1220.

2. *See* discussion under Title IX in § 3.16.

3. Pub.L. No. 100–259 (1988), § 7, 102 Stat. 31.

4. 42 U.S.C.A. § 2000d–4a. *But see Cureton v. National Collegiate Athletic Ass'n*, 198 F.3d 107, 115–16 (3d Cir.1999) (despite Congressional restoration of Title VI to define the programs or activities covered by Title VI to include all of a recipient's operations, holding that the implementing regulations which include language referring to "parts or programs of an institution" do not preclude recipients of federal funds from discriminating with respect to a program not receiving federal funds). Thus, at least in the Third Circuit, a federally funded institution may discriminate by using criteria or methods of administrative which have merely a disparate impact on racial minorities because, under the *Cureton* interpretation, the regulations which bar such discrimination apply only to those programs operated by the institution which directly receive the federal funds.

5. 42 U.S.C.A. § 2000d–4a(2).

6. 42 U.S.C.A. § 2000d–4a(1).

not be covered if the federal assistance is extended to only one geographically separate facility.[7]

The Restoration Act provides government funding agencies power to review all of an institution's programs for discrimination. This should be carefully distinguished from the scope of the allowable administrative sanction if unlawful discrimination is found. Denial or termination of funds is limited to the "particular program, or part thereof" in which the noncompliance was found.[8]

§ 3.7 Exemptions

Title VI permits no agency action with respect to "any employment practice of any employer ... except where a primary objective of the Federal financial assistance is to provide employment." Thus only federally funded employment programs are subject to Title VI penalties for the kind of race or national origin discrimination in employment prohibited by Title VII of the Civil Rights Act of 1964.

§ 3.8 Administrative Enforcement

Federal funding agencies must issue regulations designed to effectuate Title VI.[1] Applicants for and recipients of federal financial assistance must comply with those regulations to qualify for or maintain levels of federal funding. The agencies may take action to enforce the regulations by refusing to grant or by terminating funds upon an administrative determination of non-compliance with the regulations.[2] Federal agencies are required to engage in coordinated enforcement efforts with the U.S. Attorney General. They may, for example, refuse to grant or continue assistance only after notice to the offending party and the failure of attempts to secure voluntary compliance.[3]

§ 3.9 The Elements of a Private Action Under Title VI

Although Title VI provides expressly only for administrative enforcement, the Supreme Court has implied a private cause of action for individuals to enforce both the statute and implementing regulations that prohibit intentional discrimination.[1] Title VI has been held to reach claims of reverse discrimination as well.[2] And there is authority that funds recipients may be reached for third-party intentional race discrimination carried out in their programs, for example in cases of peer racial

7. 42 U.S.C.A. § 2000d–4a(3).

8. 42 U.S.C.A. § 2000d–1.

§ 3.8

1. 42 U.S.C.A. § 2000d–1.

2. *Id.*

3. *Id.*

§ 3.9

1. *Guardians Ass'n v. Civil Serv. Comm'n*, 463 U.S. 582, 103 S.Ct. 3221, 77 L.Ed.2d 866 (1983). *But see Alexander v. Sandoval*, 532 U.S. 275, 121 S.Ct. 1511, 149 L.Ed.2d 517 (2001), discussed *infra* this section.

2. *Regents of Univ. of Calif. v. Bakke*, 438 U.S. 265, 98 S.Ct. 2733, 57 L.Ed.2d 750 (1978); *Baker v. Board of Regents*, 991 F.2d 628 (10th Cir.1993).

harassment by students in a federally funded school.[3] Like Title XI, most courts have held that individual supervisors and managers, as distinct from institutional educational federal funds recipients, are not separately subject to Title VI liability.[4]

The fractionated opinions in *Guardians Association v. Civil Service Commission*[5] suggest that proof of a violation of the statute itself, as opposed to its implementing regulations, requires evidence in some form of discriminatory intent.[6] Long before *Guardians* the Court had held that Title VI would be violated by conduct that violates the Fourteenth Amendment's equal protection clause,[7] which in turn is violated only by evidence of intentional discrimination.[8] The opinions in *Guardians* had subsequently been consistently read to uphold the regulations of the administrative agencies charged with enforcing Title VI; and those regulations prohibit not just intentional race or national origin discrimination but also policies and practices that have disproportionate adverse effect or impact on those grounds.[9] But the Supreme Court has rejected a private right of action to enforce these regulations that prohibit disparate impact. In *Alexander v. Sandoval,*[10] the Court found no evidence that Congress intended to create such a private right of action, and hence overturned the long line of circuit court cases allowing such a claim.

At issue in *Alexander v. Sandoval* was the Alabama Department of Public Safety's decision to administer state driver's license examinations

3. *See Bryant v. Independent School Dist. No. I–38 of Garvin County, OK,* 334 F.3d 928 (10th Cir.2003) (applying Title IX peer harassment deliberate indifference standard to racial harassment claim under Title VI); *Monteiro v. Tempe Union High Sch. Dist.,* 158 F.3d 1022, 1034 (9th Cir. 1998).

4. *See, e.g., Boulahanis v. Board of Regents,* 198 F.3d 633, 641 (7th Cir.1999), *cert. denied,* 530 U.S. 1284, 120 S.Ct. 2762, 147 L.Ed.2d 1022 (2000). Resort to § 1983 has also been rejected by courts. *See id.*; *Alexander v. Chicago Park Dist.,* 773 F.2d 850, 856 (7th Cir.1985). See § 3.19 for a discussion of this topic as it relates to claims under Title IX.

5. 463 U.S. 582, 103 S.Ct. 3221, 77 L.Ed.2d 866 (1983).

6. Seven justices agreed that a violation of the statute itself required discriminatory intent. *See id.* at 608, 103 S.Ct. at 3235 (Powell, J., and Burger, C.J., concurring); *id.* at 612, 103 S.Ct. at 3237 (Rehnquist, J., concurring); *id.* at 612, 103 S.Ct. at 3237 (O'Connor, J., concurring); and *id.* at 642, 103 S.Ct. at 3253 (Stevens, Brennan, and Blackmun, JJ., dissenting).

7. *Bakke,* 438 U.S. at 286–287, 98 S.Ct. at 2746.

8. *See Washington v. Davis,* 426 U.S. 229, 96 S.Ct. 2040, 48 L.Ed.2d 597 (1976). *See also United States v. Fordice,* 505 U.S. 717, 732 n. 7, 112 S.Ct. 2727, 2737 n. 7, 120 L.Ed.2d 575 (1992).

9. *See Sandoval v. Hagan,* 197 F.3d 484, 502–508 (11th Cir.1999), *rev'd, Alexander v. Sandoval,* 532 U.S. 275, 121 S.Ct. 1511, 149 L.Ed.2d 517 (2001); *Burton v. City of Belle Glade,* 178 F.3d 1175, 1202–03 (11th Cir.1999); *Chester Residents Concerned for Quality Living v. Seif,* 132 F.3d 925, 936–37 (3d Cir.1997), *vacated as moot,* 524 U.S. 974, 119 S.Ct. 22, 141 L.Ed.2d 783 (1998); *Buchanan v. City of Bolivar, Tenn.,* 99 F.3d 1352, 1356 n. 5 (6th Cir.1996); *Villanueva v. Carere,* 85 F.3d 481, 486 (10th Cir.1996); *New York Urban League, Inc. v. New York,* 71 F.3d 1031, 1036 (2d Cir. 1995); *Elston v. Talladega County Bd. of Educ.,* 997 F.2d 1394, 1407 (11th Cir.1993); *David K. v. Lane,* 839 F.2d 1265, 1274 (7th Cir.1988); *Castaneda v. Pickard,* 781 F.2d 456, 465 n. 11 (5th Cir.1986); *Latinos Unidos De Chelsea v. Secretary of Hous. & Urban Dev.,* 799 F.2d 774, 785 n. 20 (1st Cir.1986); *Larry P. v. Riles,* 793 F.2d 969, 981–82 (9th Cir.1984); *Georgia State Conference of Branches of NAACP v. Georgia,* 775 F.2d 1403, 1417 (11th Cir.1985).

10. 532 U.S. 275, 121 S.Ct. 1511, 149 L.Ed.2d 517 (2001).

only in English. Plaintiffs challenged the English-only rule as violative of a Department of Justice regulation forbidding funding recipients to "utilize criteria or methods of administration which have the effect of subjecting individuals to discrimination because of their race, color, or national origin."[11] DOJ is authorized to promulgate such a regulation pursuant to § 602 of Title VI.[12] Although it was clear from *Cannon v. University of Chicago*[13] that a private right of action exists to enforce both Titles VI and IX, prior Supreme Court precedent established that only intentional discrimination is proscribed under § 601.[14] The issue facing the Court, then, was whether a private cause of action exists to enforce the DOJ regulation prohibiting disparate impact.

But the *Sandoval* majority avoided what appears to be the logical first step in the analysis—whether the regulations were themselves a valid proscription against activities that have a disparate impact on racial groups. Instead, the Court *assumed* the validity of the regulations and read the certiorari petition narrowly as limiting the controversy to just this latter question of whether a private cause of action exists which the Court answered in the negative. *Sandoval* leaves unanswered at least two questions: first, whether there might be administrative enforcement of the disparate impact regulations; and second, whether plaintiffs intent on a private right of action might end-run the *Sandoval* holding and avail themselves of § 1983's "and laws" clause to enforce the regulations.[15] Several courts have rejected this end-run approach.[16]

Title VI courts have adopted the approach to "mixed-motive" disparate treatment cases that the Court has prescribed for cases of constitutional violations under the Reconstruction Civil Rights Acts: if the plaintiff establishes that the challenged action was taken in part for a prohibited racial reason, the burden is on the defendant to establish that it would have reached the same decision independent of the unlawful component of its overall conduct or motivation.[17] But unlike the approach taken in constitutional cases, and similar to the approach under

11. 28 CFR § 42.104(b)(2) (1999). *See also* 49 CFR § 21.5(b)(2) (2000) (similar DOT regulation).

12. 42 U.S.C.A. § 2000d–1.

13. 441 U.S. 677, 99 S.Ct. 1946, 60 L.Ed.2d 560 (1979).

14. *Regents of Univ. of Cal. v. Bakke,* 438 U.S. 265, 98 S.Ct. 2733, 57 L.Ed.2d 750 (1978); *Guardians Assn. v. Civil Serv. Comm'n of New York City,* 463 U.S. 582, 103 S.Ct. 3221, 77 L.Ed.2d 866 (1983).

15. *See* § 2.55 *supra* for a discussion of the "and laws" clause of § 1983 and the more general question of whether regulations are among the "laws" that the "and laws" clause can be used to enforce.

16. *South Camden Citizens In Action v. New Jersey Department of Environmental Protection,* 274 F.3d 771 (3d Cir.2001) (reasoning that Title VI § 602 empowers agencies to adopt regulations solely to enforce the Title VI ban on intentional discrimination, and no other explicit Title VI language prohibits disparate-impact discrimination); *Ceaser v. Pataki,* 2002 WL 472271 (S.D.N.Y. 2002). *But see White v. Engler,* 188 F.Supp.2d 730 (E.D.Mich.2001) (allowing § 1983 claim to enforce the regulations).

17. *See Bakke,* 438 U.S. 265, 98 S.Ct. 2733, 57 L.Ed.2d 750 (opinion of Powell, J.); *Hopwood v. Texas,* 861 F.Supp. 551 (W.D.Tex.1994), *rev'd,* 78 F.3d 932 (5th Cir. 1996), *cert. denied sub nom. Thurgood Marshall Legal Soc. v. Hopwood,* 518 U.S. 1033, 116 S.Ct. 2580, 135 L.Ed.2d 1094 (1996) (citing *Carey v. Piphus,* 435 U.S. 247, 98 S.Ct. 1042, 55 L.Ed.2d 252 (1978) and *Mt. Healthy City Sch. Dist. Bd. of Educ. v. Doyle,* 429 U.S. 274, 97 S.Ct. 568, 50 L.Ed.2d 471 (1977)).

Title VII of the 1964 Civil Rights Act as amended in 1991, the Title VI plaintiff has standing and is eligible for limited relief even when the defendant carries that burden.[18]

For statute of limitations purposes, the Title VI claim has been characterized as an action for injury to personal rights.[19] Following the practice under the Reconstruction Acts of borrowing the forum state's general limitations period on personal injury claims to measure timeliness,[20] a federal appeals court held a Title VI claim barred for having been filed outside California's one-year statute.[21]

§ 3.10 Damages

There remains some question about the menu of Title VI monetary remedies. Just as the opinions differed on the "intent" question in *Guardians*, they diverged on the remedies available to a plaintiff as well. Of course, because the Court found no violation of Title VI itself, it found no liability; the discussion of remedies in the opinions is therefore dictum, however helpful.

The conflict centered on the presence or absence of intentional discrimination. Justices White and Rehnquist held that in "the absence of discriminatory intent," the court should fashion only injunctive, noncompensatory relief, but they did not specify what remedies were available if intentional discrimination was proven.[1] In a joint concurrence, Justice Powell and Chief Justice Burger concluded, first, that the only appropriate remedy for a violation of the statute was termination of federal funding and, second, that there could be no relief awarded to private litigants because there was no private right of action under Title VI.[2] The remaining five justices agreed that the plaintiff might be entitled to prospective and retroactive legal and equitable relief. Justices Marshall, Stevens, Brennan and Blackmun held that such remedies were available to Title VI plaintiffs in general.[3] But Justice O'Connor clearly delineated a difference between the remedies she would approve for victims of intentional and unintentional discrimination. She reiterated her view, subsequently adopted in *Alexander v. Sandoval,* that intent is required to show a violation of Title VI and that conduct causing a

18. *See Bakke*, 438 U.S. at 281 n.14, 98 S.Ct. at 2743 n.14 and 438 U.S. at 320 n.54, 98 S.Ct. 2764 n. 54; *Hopwood*, 78 F.3d at 956–57.

19. *Baker*, 991 F.2d 628.

20. *See* Chapter 5 on Procedure Under the Reconstruction Acts.

21. *Taylor v. Regents of Univ. of Calif.*, 993 F.2d 710 (9th Cir.1993).

§ 3.10

1. *Guardians Assoc. v. Civil Serv. Comm'n*, 463 U.S. 582, 592 n. 20, 103 S.Ct. 3221, 3230 n. 20, 77 L.Ed.2d 866 (1983) ("... it *may* be that the victim of intentional discrimination *should* be entitled to a compensatory award.") (emphasis added). *See Powell v. Ridge*, 189 F.3d 387 (3d Cir.), *cert. denied*, 528 U.S. 1046, 120 S.Ct. 579, 145 L.Ed.2d 482 (1999) (a discriminatory "effects" violation of an implementing regulation gave rise to a private right of action, at least to secure injunctive relief).

2. *Id.* at 609, 103 S.Ct. at 3236. *Cf.* 42 U.S.C.A. § 2000d–1 (Title VI language recognizes termination of funds as sole administrative sanction for violation of the statute).

3. *Id.* at 624–34, 103 S.Ct. at 3244–50 (Marshall, J., dissenting); *id.* at 635–39, 103 S.Ct. at 3250–52 (Stevens, Brennan, and Blackmun, JJ., dissenting).

discriminatory impact, in violation of agency regulations, cannot serve as a basis for civil liability. But she agreed that plaintiffs who prove discriminatory intent are entitled to awards of prospective and retrospective relief.[4]

A year later, in *Conrail v. Darrone*, Justice Powell sought to bring coherence to the welter of *Guardians* opinions by reasoning that "[a] majority of the Court [in *Guardians*] agreed that retrospective relief is available to private plaintiffs for [intentional] discrimination."[5] A unanimous Supreme Court held that backpay is an appropriate remedy for intentional violations of federally funded employment programs.[6]

The Civil Rights Remedies Equalization Amendment of 1986 permits federal courts to award retrospective relief under Title IX against a state or state agency, expressly abrogating what would otherwise be their immunity under the Eleventh Amendment.[7] Even more recently, in *Franklin*, a Title IX case alleging intentional sex discrimination, the Court ruled that "a cognizable cause of action brought pursuant to a federal statute" is remediable by all appropriate relief, including damages, back pay and prospective relief.[8] Writing for the court in *Franklin*, Justice White intimates that both *Guardians* and *Conrail* support this conclusion,[9] and given the courts' regular transportation of precedent from one field to the other,[10] intentional Title VI violations may now be so remediable. So the significance of *Franklin* for Title VI cases is that it may add compensatory damages to back pay as remedies for a violations of Title VI itself, i.e., intentional discriminatory violations.

The Supreme Court held, however, that punitive damages are not available in a private right of action under Title VI. In *Barnes v. Gorman*,[11] the Court wrote that Title VI's funding is of a contractual nature; in return for federal funds, the recipients agree to comply with federally imposed conditions.[12] This contractual nature of Spending Clause legislation dictates among other things the scope of the remedies available for violation of these federal conditions: compensatory damages and injunctive relief are available as in any breach of contract case, but

4. *Id.* at 615, 103 S.Ct. at 3239 (O'Connor, J., concurring).

5. *Consolidated Rail Corp. v. Darrone*, 465 U.S. 624, 631 n. 9, 104 S.Ct. 1248, 1253 n. 9, 79 L.Ed.2d 568 (1984). And now that the Court has closed the doors to disparate impact claims by private plaintiffs, Justice Powell's discussion of unintentional discrimination is irrelevant. *See Alexander v. Sandoval*, 532 U.S. 275, 121 S.Ct. 1511, 149 L.Ed.2d 517 (2001), discussed in § 3.9.

6. *Id.*

7. 42 U.S.C.A. § 2000d–7(a)(1) provides that: "[a] State shall not be immune under the Eleventh Amendment of the Constitution of the United States from suit in Federal court for a violation of ... title VI of the Civil Rights Act of 1964."

8. *Franklin v. Gwinnett County Pub. Sch.*, 503 U.S. 60, 112 S.Ct. 1028, 117 L.Ed.2d 208 (1992).

9. *Id.*

10. *See, e.g., Sharif v. New York State Educ. Dep't*, 709 F.Supp. 345, 360 (S.D.N.Y. 1989) (courts examining Title IX questions look to the law developed under Title VI). *See also Grove City College*, 465 U.S. at 566, 104 S.Ct. at 1218 (Title IX was patterned after Title VI and same Congressional underlies both statutes).

11. 536 U.S. 181, 122 S.Ct. 2097, 153 L.Ed.2d 230 (2002).

12. *Id.* at 185–186, 122 S.Ct. at 2100–01 (citing *inter alia Pennhurst State School and Hospital v. Halderman,* 451 U.S. 1, 17, 101 S.Ct. 1531, 67 L.Ed.2d 694 (1981)).

punitive damages are extra-contractual and are not available for Title VI, or Title IX, violations.[13]

§§ 3.11–3.14 [Reserved]

C. TITLE IX

§ 3.15 In General

Title IX's primary prohibition provides that

> No person in the United States shall, on the basis of *sex*, be excluded from participation in, be denied the benefit of, or be subjected to discrimination under any *education* program or activity receiving Federal financial assistance.... [1]

Federal assistance includes grants, loans, or contracts other than those of insurance or guaranty.[2] The *Grove City College* holding that federal assistance funnelled directly to students constitutes "assistance" to the students' educational institutions, thus triggering Title IX regulation of programs or of the institution itself, appears undisturbed either by subsequent decisions[3] or by the 1987 Restoration Act.

§ 3.16 Covered Programs or Activities

The "program or activity" language in Title IX has followed the same interpretive evolution as the same language in Title VI. Lower courts held that discrimination in any program within an institution receiving federal assistance was a violation of Title IX even though the particular discriminatory program was not the subject of the assistance. But in *Grove City College*, the Supreme Court interpreted the phrase "program or activity" narrowly, holding that Title IX prohibited discrimination only in the *particular* educational program or activity receiving the federal assistance, not in all the educational programs and activities conducted by the institution receiving such assistance.[1] The Civil Rights Restoration Act of 1987[2] overturned this holding by defining the "program or activity" covered by Title IX to include "all" of a recipient's operations.[3] So where federal aid is extended to any program within a college, university or other public system of elementary, secondary or higher education, the entire institution or system is covered by the prohibitions of Title IX.[4] Where a state and local government department

13. *Id.*

§ 3.15

1. 20 U.S.C.A. § 1681. *See also* 20 U.S.C.A. § 1684 (prohibiting discrimination because of blindness or severe visual impairment).

2. 20 U.S.C.A. § 1682. *See* 20 U.S.C.A. § 1685 (contracts of insurance or guaranty).

3. *Cf. United States Dep't of Transp. v. Paralyzed Veterans of America*, 477 U.S. 597, 106 S.Ct. 2705, 91 L.Ed.2d 494 (1986).

§ 3.16

1. *Grove City College*, 465 U.S. at 566, 104 S.Ct. at 1218.

2. Pub.L.No. 100–259 (1988).

3. 20 U.S.C.A. § 1687.

4. 42 U.S.C.A. § 1687(2)(B). *See Yusuf v. Vassar College*, 35 F.3d 709 (2d Cir.1994) (because Vassar was an institution that re-

(or agency) other than schools receives federal aid for an educational program or activity and the funds stay within that particular department, only that department is subject to Title IX sanctions; but if the aid is distributed to other departments or agencies, all entities that receive it are covered.[5] Finally, a private corporation that receives aid as a whole or that provides a public service would fall under Title VI. But the entire corporation may not be covered if the federal funds are extended to only a geographically separate facility.[6]

As under Title VI, a government agency that provides funding has power to review all of a recipient's programs for discrimination. But denial or termination of funds is limited to the "particular program, or part thereof" in which the noncompliance is found.[7]

Are indirect beneficiaries of federal funds covered by Title IX? For example, the National Collegiate Athletic Association is funded by dues paid by federally-funded colleges and universities. Can it be sued pursuant to Title IX? In *NCAA v. Smith*,[8] the Court said no. A female graduate student athlete sued the NCAA under, inter alia, Title IX seeking a waiver of the rule that prohibits a graduate student from participating in intercollegiate athletics at any school except the student's undergraduate institution. The NCAA filed a motion to dismiss alleging that it could not be liable under Title IX because it did not receive federal funds. The plaintiff argued that it was an indirect recipient of federal funds under 34 C.F.R. § 106.2(h), which defines "recipient" as any entity "to whom Federal financial assistance is extended directly or through another recipient." The Court, however, interpreted this regulation to mean that only those entities that actually receive federal monies, either directly or through an intermediary, are covered by Title IX; those entities that merely benefit economically are not. The Court distinguished *Grove City College*, where the schools received federal funds through its students who receive federal grants and loans: those monies were earmarked for education and the money flowed directly from the federal government to the schools through the students. The NCAA merely benefitted by its members' receipt of the money.

The Court, however, noted that two other theories advanced by the plaintiff may bring the NCAA within Title IX. The first theory, termed the "controlling authority" theory, posits that when a federal funds recipient, such as a university, cedes controlling authority over a federally funded program, the controlling entity is covered by Title IX.[9] The second theory is that the NCAA directly and indirectly received federal funds through the National Youth Sports Program (NYSP) and the National Youth Sports Program Fund,[10] which are administered by the

ceives Federal financial assistance, a claim for damages from sexual harassment could be made under Title IX).

5. 42 U.S.C.A. § 1687(1)(B).

6. 42 U.S.C.A. § 1687(3)(B).

7. 42 U.S.C.A. § 1682.

8. 525 U.S. 459, 119 S.Ct. 924, 142 L.Ed.2d 929 (1999).

9. *NCAA v. Smith*, 525 U.S. at 469–70, 119 S.Ct. at 930.

10. The NYSP is a community service program administered by the NCAA.

NCAA.[11] The Court left both of these theories to the court below on remand. The case came back to the Third Circuit after the trial court granted defendant's motion to dismiss and denied plaintiff's motion to amend her complaint to add these two alternative theories. The Third Circuit rejected the first theory on remand, finding that the NCAA was not the controlling authority over the intercollegiate athletic programs of its member institutions.[12] Citing its opinion in *Cureton v. NCAA*,[13] which in turn relied on the Supreme Court's precedent in *NCAA v. Tarkanian*,[14] the Third Circuit reasoned that the NCAA does not control its members; although the NCAA can impose sanctions on its members, the member universities do exercise choices regarding complying with the NCAA and remaining a member of the NCAA.[15] As it did in *Cureton* vis-a-vis Title VI, the court found that the NCAA was not a controlling authority such that it was covered by Title IX.[16] On the second theory, however, the court found that, if proven, allegations that the NCAA indirectly received federal funds through the youth sports programs would suffice to bring the NCAA with the scope of Title IX.[17] The court therefore reversed the trial court's dismissal, and remanded for further proceedings.

§ 3.17 Exemptions

Title IX contains no counterpart to Title VI's general disclaimer on applicability to employment practices. Thus, Title IX redresses sex discrimination in employment by federally funded education institutions.[1] The Restoration Act exempts entities controlled by religious organizations from Title IX coverage if the application of Title IX's provisions would conflict with the organization's religious tenets.[2]

§ 3.18 Administrative Enforcement

Provision for administrative enforcement under Title IX is the same as under Title VI. Federal agencies must issue regulations designed to effectuate Title IX's goals.[1] Applicants for and recipients of federal financial assistance must comply with those regulations. The agencies may enforce the regulations by refusing to grant or by terminating funds upon an administrative determination of non-compliance with the regu-

11. *NCAA v. Smith*, 525 U.S. at 469–70, 119 S.Ct. at 930.

12. *Smith v. NCAA*, 266 F.3d 152 (3d Cir.2001).

13. 198 F.3d 107 (3d Cir.1999) (African–American student athletes challenging the NCAA's scholastic aptitude test requirements for incoming freshman athletes as having a disparate impact on blacks and violative of Title VI).

14. 488 U.S. 179, 109 S.Ct. 454, 102 L.Ed.2d 469 (1988) (holding that the University of Nevada–Las Vegas had not ceded its authority over its coaching personnel and therefore the NCAA was not a state actor under § 1983).

15. *See Tarkanian*, 488 U.S. at 198 n.19, 109 S.Ct. at 465 n.19.

16. 266 F.3d 152 (3d Cir.2001).

17. *Id.*

§ 3.17

1. *See North Haven Bd. of Educ.*, 456 U.S. 512, 102 S.Ct. 1912, 72 L.Ed.2d 299.

2. 20 U.S.C.A. § 1687(4).

§ 3.18

1. 20 U.S.C.A. § 1682.

lations.[2] Federal agencies are required to engage in coordinated enforcement efforts with the U.S. Attorney General. They may, for example, refuse to grant or continue assistance only after notice to the offending party and failure of attempts to secure voluntary compliance.[3]

§ 3.19 Elements of the Private Action Under Title IX

The Supreme Court has implied a private right of action under Title IX.[1] The right of action appears to extend to claims of sex discrimination in employment,[2] but it is unclear whether a plaintiff can bring a retaliation claim under Title IX.[3] The preceding statement must be qualified, however, because the Supreme Court's decision holding Title IX applicable to employment practices did not specifically consider the private right of action question.[4] Thus a debate is emerging in the circuit decisions over whether the existence of a detailed judicial remedy for employment discrimination under Title VII of the 1964 Civil Rights Act (amended as of 1991 to permit compensatory and punitive damages subject to statutory caps) forecloses a judicially implied remedy under Title IX (which has no cap on such relief) with respect to gender discriminatory practices that are actionable under Title VII and committed by federally funded education institutions or their agents.[5]

2. *Id.*

3. *Id.*

§ 3.19

1. *Cannon v. Univ. of Chicago,* 441 U.S. 677, 688, 99 S.Ct. 1946, 1953, 60 L.Ed.2d 560 (1979).

2. *Preston v. Virginia,* 31 F.3d 203 (4th Cir.1994); *Bowers v. Baylor Univ.,* 862 F.Supp. 142 (W.D.Tex.1994); *Henschke v. New York Hosp.-Cornell Med. Ctr.,* 821 F.Supp. 166 (S.D.N.Y.1993). Interestingly, education programs conducted by the federal government itself are not included.

3. *See Jackson v. Birmingham Bd. of Educ.,* 309 F.3d 1333 (11th Cir.2002), *petition for cert. filed,* 71 USLW 3736 (May 13, 2003) (while declining to resolve whether a private right of action for retaliation exists under Title IX, holding that neither Title IX itself nor 34 CFR Part 100.7(e) implies a private right of action for retaliation in favor of individuals who, although not themselves the victims of gender discrimination, suffer retaliation because they have complained about gender discrimination suffered by others). See also *Atkinson v. Lafayette Coll.,* 2002 WL 123449, at *11 (E.D.Pa.2002) ("[I]n the wake of *Sandoval,* there is no private right of action under Title IX to enforce the anti-retaliation regulation. . . ."); *Litman v. George Mason Univ.,* 156 F.Supp.2d 579, 584–85 (E.D.Va. 2001) ("Congress was aware that it could create a right of action for retaliatory treatment, and it did so in Title VII; it did not do so in Title IX."). The Fourth Circuit held, pre-*Sandoval,* that such a claim could be brought. *See Preston v. Commonwealth of Va. ex rel. New River Cmty. Coll.,* 31 F.3d 203, 206 (4th Cir.1994) ("Retaliation . . . for filing a claim of gender discrimination is prohibited under Title IX.").

4. *See North Haven Bd. of Educ. v. Bell,* 456 U.S. 512, 102 S.Ct. 1912, 72 L.Ed.2d 299 (1982).

5. *Compare Lakoski v. James,* 66 F.3d 751 (5th Cir.1995) (Title IX claim foreclosed) *and Holt v. Lewis,* 955 F.Supp. 1385, 1388–89 (N.D.Ala.1995), *aff'd without opinion,* 109 F.3d 771 (11th Cir.1997) (no Title IX private right of action for retaliatory discharge) *with Lipsett v. University of Puerto Rico,* 864 F.2d 881, 896–97 (1st Cir. 1988); *O'Connor v. Peru State College,* 781 F.2d 632, 642 n. 8 (8th Cir.1986) (no foreclosure of Title IX claim) *and Mabry v. State Bd. of Community Colleges* and *Occupational Educ.,* 813 F.2d 311, 316–18 (10th Cir.1987) (assuming no foreclosure). *Cf. Lowrey v. Texas A & M Univ. Sys.,* 117 F.3d 242 (5th Cir.1997) (distinguishing *Lakoski* to permit Title IX retaliation claim based on employer reaction to plaintiff's participation in Title IX administrative investigation, reasoning that such a retaliation claim lies exclusively under Title IX).

Even if a federal education funds recipient may be subject to a private damages claim under Title IX for gender discrimination in employment, the scope of the liability is unclear. The Supreme Court held that a student claiming sexual harassment by a teacher has no claim unless an official with authority to end the discrimination had actual knowledge of the discrimination and failed to act such that the failure amounted to deliberate indifference.[6] Presumably a small number of teachers with gender-based employment discrimination claims could meet this strict standard if the harassment was committed by or came to the attention of a principal or other high ranking administrative official. Liability would be considerably broader, and could more easily reach co-worker sexual harassment of teachers, if *Gebser* is limited to the student-plaintiff context and entity liability standards in employment cases are borrowed from those the Court has declared under Title VII.

The administrative regulations promulgated under Title IX, like those under Title VI, purport to prohibit discrimination resulting from facially neutral policies that have gender-discriminatory effect as well as intentional discrimination based on gender.[7] Lower courts have applied the impact principle to Title IX actions when the plaintiff distinctly pleads a violation of the applicable implementing regulations, as distinct from the statute alone.[8] Use of the impact theory is fortified by the growing judicial receptiveness to transplanting Title VII liability principles to claims under Title IX.[9] The Court's decision in *Alexander v. Sandoval*,[10] however, casts significant doubt on any private right of action for enforcing regulations that bar disproportionate adverse impact.

A related uncertain question is whether individual supervisors and managers, as distinct from institutional educational federal funds recipients, are separately subject to Title IX liability. A majority of the few decisions on point hold that they are not,[11] thus reaching a result

6. *Gebser v. Lago Vista Ind. Sch. Dist.*, 524 U.S. 274, 118 S.Ct. 1989, 141 L.Ed.2d 277 (1998).

7. One regulation, for example, bans "administer[ing] or operat[ing] any test or other criteria for admission which has a disproportionately adverse effect on persons on the basis of sex unless the use of such test is shown to predict validly success in the education program or activity in question and alternative tests or criteria which do not have such a disproportionate adverse effect are shown to be unavailable." 34 C.F.R. § 106.21(b)(2).

8. *See, e.g., Mabry*, 813 F.2d at 317 n.6; *Sharif v. New York State Educ. Dep't*, 709 F.Supp. at 361.

9. *See Murray v. New York Univ. College of Dentistry*, 57 F.3d 243 (2d Cir.1995); *Brown v. Hot, Sexy and Safer Productions, Inc.*, 68 F.3d 525 (1st Cir.1995) (applying Title VII hostile sexual environment standards to Title IX settings).

10. 532 U.S. 275, 121 S.Ct. 1511, 149 L.Ed.2d 517 (2001) (holding that no private right of action exists for plaintiffs advancing a disparate impact claim). *Alexander* is discussed in § 3.9 *supra*.

11. *Boulahanis v. Board of Regents*, 198 F.3d 633, 640 (7th Cir.1999), *cert. denied*, 530 U.S. 1284, 120 S.Ct. 2762, 147 L.Ed.2d 1022 (2000); *Hartley v. Parnell*, 193 F.3d 1263, 1270 (11th Cir.1999); *Kinman v. Omaha Pub. Sch. Dist.*, 171 F.3d 607, 611 (8th Cir.1999); *Smith v. Metropolitan Sch. Dist. Perry Tp.*, 128 F.3d 1014, 1019 (7th Cir.1997); *Lillard v. Shelby County Bd. of Educ.*, 76 F.3d 716, 730 (6th Cir.1996) (Nelson, J., concurring) (stating that only educational institutions may be found liable for Title IX violations); *Lipsett v. University of Puerto Rico*, 864 F.2d 881, 896–97 (1st Cir.

consistent with the weight of recent authority under Title VII. Creative plaintiffs' counsel have attempted to skirt this obstacle by suing educational officials individually for Title IX statutory violations under the "and laws" branch of § 1983, with mixed success.[12] Section 1983 claims alleging that teachers and other individuals have committed constitutional violations, as opposed to Title IX violations, have enjoyed somewhat greater success.[13]

§ 3.20 Sexual Harassment of Students Under Title IX

Because Title IX is Spending Clause legislation which is constitutional only if the funds recipient has clear notice of the strings attached to funding, and because Title IX liability requires that an "appropriate person" have notice and an opportunity to rectify any violation,[1] the Supreme Court held in *Gebser v. Lago Vista Independent School District*[2]

1988); *Nelson v. Temple Univ.*, 920 F.Supp. 633 (E.D.Pa.1996). *But see Murrell v. School Dist. No. 1*, 186 F.3d 1238 (10th Cir.1999) (implicitly accepting the notion of individual liability); *Mennone v. Gordon*, 889 F.Supp. 53 (D.Conn.1995) (holding individual defendant potentially liable under Title IX but according him a purported "qualified immunity" defense under that statute). *See also Oona R. v. McCaffrey*, 143 F.3d 473 (9th Cir.1998), *cert. denied*, 526 U.S. 1154, 119 S.Ct. 2039, 143 L.Ed.2d 1047 (1999); *Doe v. Petaluma City Sch. Dist.*, 54 F.3d 1447 (9th Cir.1995) (on a motion to dismiss, discussing qualified immunity defense without deciding if individuals are subject to suit under Title IX).

12. *Compare Crawford v. Davis*, 109 F.3d 1281, 1284 (8th Cir.1997) (finding no preclusion) *and Lillard v. Shelby County Bd. of Educ.*, 76 F.3d 716, 722–24 (6th Cir.1996) (same) *with Boulahanis v. Board of Regents*, 198 F.3d 633, 639–40 (7th Cir. 1999), *cert. denied*, 530 U.S. 1284, 120 S.Ct. 2762, 147 L.Ed.2d 1022 (2000) (finding preclusion); *Bruneau v. South Kortright Central Sch. Dist.*, 163 F.3d 749 (2d Cir.1998), *cert. denied*, 526 U.S. 1145, 119 S.Ct. 2020, 143 L.Ed.2d 1032 (1999) (Title IX precludes § 1983 suit to enforce rights arising under both Title IX and the equal protection clause); *Waid v. Merrill Area Pub. Schs.*, 91 F.3d 857, 862–63 (7th Cir.1996) (dicta); *Seamons v. Snow*, 84 F.3d 1226, 1234 n. 8 (10th Cir.1996) (allowing § 1983 claim for constitutional violations but not for Title IX statutory violations) *and Lakoski v. James*, 66 F.3d 751, 755 (5th Cir.1995), *cert. denied*, 519 U.S. 947, 117 S.Ct. 357, 136 L.Ed.2d 249 (1996). *See also supra* § 2.55.

13. *See Baynard v. Malone*, 268 F.3d 228 (4th Cir.2001) (affirming jury verdict against school principal, finding deliberate indifference to risk that teacher was abusing a student); *Kinman v. Omaha Pub. Sch. Dist.*, 171 F.3d 607, 611 (8th Cir.1999); *Crawford v. Davis*, 109 F.3d 1281, 1284 (8th Cir.1997); *Seamons v. Snow*, 84 F.3d 1226, 1234 n. 8 (10th Cir.1996); *Lillard v. Shelby County Bd. of Educ.*, 76 F.3d 716, 722–24 (6th Cir.1996). *But see Bruneau v. South Kortright Central Sch. Dist.*, 163 F.3d 749 (2d Cir.1998), *cert. denied*, 526 U.S. 1145, 119 S.Ct. 2020, 143 L.Ed.2d 1032 (1999) (Title IX precludes § 1983 suit to enforce rights arising under both Title IX and the equal protection clause); *Waid v. Merrill Area Pub. Schs.*, 91 F.3d 857, 863 (7th Cir.1996) (Congress effectively superseded a cause of action under § 1983 that was based on constitutional principles of equal protection); *Williams v. School Dist. of Bethlehem, Pa.*, 998 F.2d 168, 176 (3d Cir.1993); *Pfeiffer v. Marion Center Area Sch. Dist.*, 917 F.2d 779, 789 (3d Cir.1990).

§ 3.20

1. Title IX authorizes agencies who disburse education funding to enforce Title IX's non-discrimination by suspending or terminating the flow of funds only after notice is given to "the appropriate person or persons of the failure to comply with the requirement." 20 U.S.C.A. § 1682. *See also* 34 C.F.R. § 100.8.

2. 524 U.S. 274, 118 S.Ct. 1989, 141 L.Ed.2d 277 (1998). *See also Floyd v. Waiters*, 171 F.3d 1264 (11th Cir.1999), *cert. denied*,528 U.S. 891, 120 S.Ct. 215, 145 L.Ed.2d 181 (1999) (finding no liability under *Gebser* absent evidence that person with authority had knowledge of the misconduct and failed to act); *Morse v. Regents of Univ. of Colo.*, 154 F.3d 1124 (10th Cir. 1998) (reinstating complaint alleging sexual harassment by ROTC instructor after

that a school district is liable in damages for the sexual harassment of a student by a teacher only when an official with authority to end the discrimination had actual knowledge of the discrimination and failed to act, such that the failure amounted to deliberate indifference. Under this formulation, the Court avoided a perceived "risk that the [federal funds] recipient would be liable in damages not for its own official decision, but instead for its employees' independent action."[3] It is unclear whether *Gebser*'s strict notice and deliberate indifference requirements apply when the plaintiff seeks prospective relief only.[4]

The Court has applied the *Gebser* actual knowledge/deliberate indifference standard to peer or student-on-student sexual harassment in *Davis v. Monroe County Board of Education*.[5] As in *Gebser*, the Court grounded a school district's potential liability on the district's own acts of discrimination by failing to respond (after actual notice through a high-level official) to known incidents of sexual harassment.[6] So in peer harassment cases, the plaintiff must allege and show, as in a teacher-student case governed by *Gebser*, that (1) officials authorized to respond on behalf of the defendant school district (probably including a school principal, and certainly a superintendent or board member)[7] received (2)

12(b)(6) dismissal in light of *Gebser*); *Smith v. Metropolitan Sch. Dist. Perry Tp.*, 128 F.3d 1014 (7th Cir.1997), *cert. denied*, 524 U.S. 951, 118 S.Ct. 2367, 141 L.Ed.2d 736 (1998) (proper standard for Title IX liability was whether school board or district had actual knowledge of discrimination but failed to take action); *Rosa H. v. San Elizario Ind. Sch. Dist.*, 106 F.3d 648 (5th Cir. 1997) (school must have "actual knowledge" and fail to respond in order to be liable under Title IX for teacher harassment of student; this means that an employee vested by the board with supervisory power over offending employee must have received knowledge of the abuse and failed to exercise delegated power to take corrective); *Canutillo Indep. Sch. Dist. v. Leija*, 101 F.3d 393 (5th Cir.1996).

3. *Id.* at 290–91, 118 S.Ct. at 1999.

4. *See* Department of Education, Office for Civil Rights; *Sexual Harassment Guidance: Harassment of Students by School Employees, Other Students, or Third Parties*, 62 Fed.Reg. 12,034 (1997) (equitable relief available upon showing that recipient knew or should have known of the harassment).

5. 526 U.S. 629, 119 S.Ct. 1661, 143 L.Ed.2d 839 (1999). *See also Morse v. Regents of Univ. of Colo.*, 154 F.3d 1124 (10th Cir.1998) (pre-*Davis*, but applying the standard prescribed in *Davis* to reinstate peer sexual harassment complaint after 12(b)(6) dismissal).

6. *See, e.g., Doe v. University of Illinois*, 138 F.3d 653, 662 (7th Cir.1998), *vacated and remanded for further consideration in light of Davis v. Monroe County Bd. of Educ.*, 526 U.S. 629, 119 S.Ct. 1661, 143 L.Ed.2d 839 (1999) (recipients liable for "its own actions and inaction in the face of its knowledge that the harassment was occurring"). *Compare Murrell v. School Dist. No. 1, Denver, Colo.*, 186 F.3d 1238 (10th Cir. 1999) (mother's direct contact with school principal advising him of specific incidents involving her daughter and the particular student who had assaulted her gave principal actual notice attributable to school district) *with Ostrander v. Duggan*, 341 F.3d 745 (8th Cir. 2003)(university lacked sufficient knowledge of sexual assault by a particular member of fraternity because prior reports to university officials of assaults by members of that fraternity did not involve the same member or the same location). Alternatively, the court in *Ostrander* reasoned that the university could not be liable because it lacked substantial ownership, possession or control of the fraternity house in which plaintiff was attacked and accordingly plaintiff could not meet the statutory requirement that the harassment occurred "under" and "operation of" a federal funds recipient.

7. And notice to teachers may suffice where the harasser is a student and is therefore subordinate to teachers. *See Murrell v. School Dist. No. 1, Denver, Colo.*, 186 F.3d 1238 (10th Cir.1999) (district liable through notice to principal and teachers because they exercised substantial control over the student-harasser and the school

actual notice of sexual harassment[8] and then (3) failed to respond at all, or responded in a way that evidenced deliberate indifference. This means, at least in the peer harassment context that a school board, through its high officials, either failed to respond at all to the victim's complaints, or responded in a "clearly unreasonable," not a merely unreasonable fashion.[9] Thus, where a school district persisted in taking obviously ineffective actions in light of actual notice of sexual harassment, the district acted with the requisite deliberate indifference.[10]

environment and had authority to halt his sexual assaults). *But see Floyd v. Waiters,* 171 F.3d 1264 (11th Cir.), *cert. denied,* 528 U.S. 891, 120 S.Ct. 215, 145 L.Ed.2d 181 (1999) (limiting the group of officials to school superintendents and school board members; "For liability in Georgia, the superintendent or the board must have actual knowledge of the sexual harassment and then fail to take reasonable steps to end the abuse."). *But cf. Warren v. Reading Sch. Dist.*, 278 F.3d 163, 170–71 (3d Cir.2002) (refusing to limit the pool of appropriate persons to school board and finding school principal, but not guidance counselor, sufficiently high enough to affix liability despite state law limiting principal's authority to fire a teacher). Subsequent to *Davis*, a guidance issued by the Office for Civil Rights of the U.S. Department of Education takes the position that a school has actionable knowledge if a "responsible employee" knew of the harassment. Revised Sexual Harassment Guidance: Sexual Harassment of Students by School Employees, Other Students, or Third Parties, 66 Fed.Reg. 5, 512 (January 19, 2001). The quoted term includes "any employee who has the authority to take action to redress the harassment, ... the duty to report to appropriate school officials sexual harassment or any other misconduct by students or employees, or an individual who a student could reasonably believe has this authority or responsibility." In OCR's view, that concept in turn could in specific circumstances include "a principal, campus security, bus driver, teacher, affirmative action officer, or staff in the office of student affairs." *Id.*

8. *See, e.g., Davis v. DeKalb County Sch. Dist.*, 233 F.3d 1367, 1371 (11th Cir. 2000) (affirming trial court's grant of summary judgment to defendant school district upon finding that district had no actual notice where school children who were molested by teacher did not tell anyone at the time of the molestations, and finding that Defendants were not deliberately indifferent to information that should have put them on notice). Thus, where a school district did not have actual knowledge of harassment, molestation and rape of a female mentally impaired student by a male mentally impaired student until after the alleged incidents, and took quick and effective corrective and preventative steps after it received notice, liability cannot lie under Title IX. *Soper v. Hoben*, 195 F.3d 845, 855 (6th Cir.1999). *See also P.H. v. School Dist. of Kansas City,* 265 F.3d 653, 662–63 (8th Cir.2001) (school district did not have sufficient actual knowledge of high school teacher's sexual abuse of student to impose Title IX liability for alleged deliberate indifference to acts of teacher-student harassment, where, although other teachers complained that the teacher was spending too much time with the student who was excessively absent and tardy and that it was causing the student's grades to suffer, and there were concerns that the teacher might be showing favoritism to the student and other students, none of the complaints voiced any suspicions of sexual abuse); *Baynard v. Malone,* 268 F.3d 228 (4th Cir.2001) (adopting strict "actual notice" requirement such that liability can only be imposed on district when school district officials possessed actual knowledge of the discriminatory conduct in question; actual notice of a *substantial risk* of ongoing sexual abuse is insufficient as a matter of law); *Reese v. Jefferson Sch. Dist. No. 14J*, 208 F.3d 736, 740 (9th Cir. 2000) (no liability absent evidence that harassment occurred after the school district learned of the plaintiffs' allegations).

9. *Davis*, 119 S.Ct. at 1674; *Gabrielle M. v. Park Forest–Chicago Heights, Ill. Sch. Dist. 163*, 315 F.3d 817 (7th Cir.2003) (district's response to classmate's inappropriate conduct was not clearly unreasonable where after each alleged incident, classmate was disciplined and steps were taken to prevent future inappropriate conduct, namely, suspending classmate from recess, placing classmate in timeout, giving classmate detention, suspending classmate, sending classmate and other students to school's psychologist, and calling parents).

10. *Vance v. Spencer County Pub. Sch. Dist.*, 231 F.3d 253, 259 (6th Cir.2000) (district's actions of "talking" to the offending students was ineffective as demonstrated by the continuing harassment). The Sixth Cir-

In addition, under *Davis*, peer harassment must be (4) so severe and pervasive as to deprive the victim of educational opportunities or benefits.[11] While this requirement could be met by evidence that after a sexual advance or attack the victim could not attend school at all, or suffered a marked decline in her achievement or ability to learn, it is not clear how else the plaintiff may establish educational detriment.[12] Finally, the majority writes somewhat delphically that peer harassment to be actionable must have the potential for a "systemic effect on a program or activity"; this requirement makes it "unlikely" that liability could be based on "a single instance of one-on-one peer harassment."[13] Several courts have, however, stated that a single instance of sexual harassment is not per se incapable of supporting a Title IX claim.[14] Several circuits have applied *Gebser* and *Davis* to uphold Title VI actions alleging peer racial harassment.[15] Same-sex peer sexual harassment is also actionable.[16]

The lower courts have had numerous opportunities since *Gebser* and *Davis* to flesh out what constitutes deliberate indifference. The Eighth Circuit has held that school officials who investigated reported allega-

cuit noted that "[s]uch minimalist response is not within the contemplation of a reasonable response." *Id.* at 260.

11. *Id.* at 1675. A complaint alleging that school officials remained idle despite actual knowledge of a fellow student's assaults of the plaintiff, and that their deliberate indifference deprived plaintiff of access to the school's educational opportunities stated a Title IX claim against the school district. *Murrell v. School District No. 1*, 186 F.3d 1238 (10th Cir.1999). *See also Vance v. Spencer County Pub. Sch. Dist.*, 231 F.3d 253, 259 (6th Cir.2000) (holding that where a student is stabbed in the hand with a pen and is physically assaulted by peers, the plaintiff has shown circumstances that effectively denied her educational opportunities).

12. *See, e.g., Hawkins v. Sarasota County Sch. Bd.*, 322 F.3d 1279 (11th Cir. 2003) (second grade boy's alleged persistent making of sexually explicit and vulgar remarks to, and objectively offensive touching of, three girls in his class was not severe enough to have a systemic effect of denying the girls equal access to an educational program or activity as required to support a Title IX claim against the school district, where, although two of the girls said they faked being sick several times in order not to go to school, none of the girls told their parents until months after the alleged harassment began, none suffered a decline in grades, none of their teachers observed any change in their demeanor or classroom participation, and there was no physical exclusion or denial of access to facilities).

13. *Id.* at 1676.

14. *See, e.g., Vance v. Spencer County Pub. Sch. Dist.*, 231 F.3d 253, 259 (6th Cir.2000); *Doe v. School Admin. Dist. No. 19*, 66 F.Supp.2d 57, 62 (D.Me.1999) ("Within the context of Title IX, a student's claim of hostile environment can arise from a single incident") (citing *Brown v. Hot, Sexy & Safer Prods.*, 68 F.3d 525, 541 n. 13 (1st Cir.1995) (noting that "[w]e do not hold that a one-time episode is not *per se* incapable of sustaining a hostile environment claim")).

15. *See Monteiro v. Tempe Union High Sch. Dist.*, 158 F.3d 1022, 1034 (9th Cir. 1998) (allowing claim to proceed upon evidence that school officials were aware of peer racial harassment but failed to act). Although *Montiero* was decided before the Supreme Court applied the *Gebser* standard to peer sexual harassment in *Davis v. Monroe County Bd. of Educ.*, 526 U.S. 629, 119 S.Ct. 1661, 143 L.Ed.2d 839 (1999), the Ninth Circuit correctly anticipated the holding in *Davis*. The deliberate indifference standard was also adopted by the Second Circuit in a § 1981 student-on-student racial harassment case. *See Gant v. Wallingford Bd. of Educ.*, 195 F.3d 134 (2d Cir.1999).

16. *See Doe v. Dallas Indep. Sch. Dist.*, 153 F.3d 211, 219 (5th Cir.1998); *Kinman v. Omaha Pub. Sch. Dist.*, 94 F.3d 463, 468 (8th Cir.1996). *See also Oncale v. Sundowner Offshore Servs., Inc.*, 523 U.S. 75, 118 S.Ct. 998, 140 L.Ed.2d 201 (1998) (allowing a same sex sexual harassment claim under Title VII).

tions of sexual harassment and initiated termination proceedings once they obtained conclusive proof could not be held liable.[17] So long as school officials do not "turn a blind eye and do nothing," liability cannot lie.[18] In an unpublished opinion, the Fourth Circuit also found no basis for school district liability where the school board was promptly notified of a student's sexual harassment allegations and the board immediately removed the student from the teacher's class and placed the teacher on a "plan of assistance," which represented the second step of the board's three step progressive discipline policy.[19] Although a school district is not required to remedy or ensure against harassment, it can be held liable if it continues to use the same anti-harassment measures that had already proven ineffective in curtailing the harassing behavior.[20]

As examples of what satisfies the deliberate indifference standard, consider the following cases: In *Davis,* a male student fondled a female student's breasts; spoke in vulgar language to her; engaged in sexually suggestive behavior toward her; told her "I want to get into bed with you" and "I want to feel your boobs"; and placed a door stop in his pants and acted in a suggestive manner toward her.[21] In addition, other girls, who the male student harassed, sought an audience with the principal, which a teacher denied. When plaintiff's mother asked the principal what disciplinary action he planned to take against the student, he responded "I guess I'll have to threaten him a little bit harder."[22] Although both plaintiff and her mother informed plaintiff's teacher about the incidents, the school took none of the following actions: disciplining the student, separating plaintiff from the student, or establishing a sexual harassment policy or procedure.[23] The Supreme Court stated that this lack of response could suggest "deliberate indifference on the part of the Board, which made no effort whatsoever either to investigate or to put an end to the harassment."[24]

In *Murrell v. School District No. 1,*[25] a male student sexually assaulted plaintiff, a physically impaired special education student, on several occasions. On one occasion, upon discovering the two students, a janitor told them to clean up and returned them to class. Although the teachers allegedly knew about the assault, they did not inform plaintiff's

17. *See Kinman v. Omaha Pub. Sch. Dist.*, 171 F.3d 607, 610 (8th Cir.1999).

18. *Id. See also Oden v. Northern Marianas College*, 284 F.3d 1058, 1061 (9th Cir.2002), *judgment vac'd* and *remanded for further consideration,* 539 U.S. 924, 123 S.Ct. 2600, 156 L.Ed.2d 601 (2003) (finding that college was not deliberately indifferent where upon receiving actual knowledge of the alleged sexual harassment, the college took action by (1) providing counselors to assist plaintiff in documenting and presenting her case before the college's committee on sexual harassment; (2) providing plaintiff with one-on-one counseling sessions; (3) instructing the alleged harasser to avoid contact with plaintiff; (4) conducting a hearing; (5) concluding that the plaintiff had been sexually harassed; and (6) imposing a number of disciplinary sanctions upon the harasser).

19. *Littleton v. Board of Educ. of County of Ohio*, 172 F.3d 43 (4th Cir.1999).

20. *See Vance v. Spencer County Pub. Sch. Dist.*, 231 F.3d 253 (6th Cir.2000).

21. 526 U.S. at 633–636.

22. *Id.* at 635.

23. *Id.* at 634–635.

24. *Id.* at 654.

25. 186 F.3d 1238, 1243 (10th Cir. 1999).

parent.[26] After another sexual assault, plaintiff's teachers allegedly told her not to tell her mother about the incident and to forget that it happened.[27] At no time did the school ever inform law enforcement, investigate, or discipline the offending student.[28] In upholding plaintiff's claim, the Tenth Circuit found defendant school district deliberately indifferent under Title IX.[29]

In *Wills v. Brown University*,[30] the First Circuit further elaborated the deliberate indifference standard: If the institution takes timely and reasonable measures to end the harassment, it is not liable under Title IX for prior harassment. Of course, if it learns that its measures have proved inadequate, it may be required to take further steps to avoid new liability.

In *Doe v. School Admin. Dist. No. 19*,[31] the court held that a jury could find that the following amounted to unreasonable responses in light of known circumstances: (1) after various school personnel complained to the principal that a female teacher was having sex with male students, the principal did not investigate nor confront the female teacher with the specific allegations; (2) the principal warned a substitute teacher that she could be sued for slander for telling him that the female teacher was having sex with a male student and made no effort to investigate the matter; and (3) rather than investigate, the superintendent told the principal to question some of the male students about the allegations.

In *Canty v. Old Rochester Regional School District*,[32] a coach in the defendant school district raped a student on school property.[33] In response, defendant school district issued the coach a reprimand letter. Later, the school district issued two more reprimand letters in response to further inappropriate contact between the student and the coach. The court held that it was disingenuous for the defendant district to conclude that written reprimands and restricting the coach from contact with plaintiff were " 'timely and reasonable measures to end the harassment.' "[34] The court further reasoned that once the defendant district had knowledge that the reprimand letters were "inadequate," the district was required to "take further steps to avoid new liability."[35]

§ 3.21 Damages

In *Franklin v. Gwinnett County Public Schools*, the Supreme Court held that a successful Title IX plaintiff is eligible for all traditional legal and equitable relief that may be appropriate, damages as well as back

26. *See id.* at 1244.

27. *See id.*

28. *See id.*

29. *See id.* at 1248.

30. 184 F.3d 20, 25 (1st Cir.1999)

31. 66 F.Supp.2d 57, 60–64 (D.Me. 1999).

32. 66 F.Supp.2d 114, 115 (D.Mass. 1999).

33. *See id.* at 115.

34. *Id.* at 116 (quoting *Wills,* 184 F.3d at 25).

35. *Id.* at 117.

pay and prospective relief.[1] However, because Title IX is Spending Clause legislation that is analogous to a contract, punitive damages are not available.[2] The Civil Rights Remedies Equalization Amendment of 1986 ("CRREA")[3] permits federal courts to award retrospective relief under, among other statutes, Titles VI and IX, against a state or state agency, expressly abrogating what would otherwise be their immunity under the Eleventh Amendment.[4]

§ 3.22 College Athletic Programs Under Title IX

Title IX was enacted in 1972. Pursuant to 20 U.S.C.A. § 1682, which requires that federal funding agencies establish regulations regarding use of their funds, in 1975, the Department of Health, Education and Welfare (HEW) first promulgated agency regulations concerning federal funding and athletics programs.[1] In 1979, the HEW Office for Civil Rights published a policy interpretation of the athletic provisions of the agency's regulations.[2] That same year, Congress split HEW into the Departments of Education (DOE) and Health and Human Services (HHS), and each agency adopted substantially identical agency regulations.[3] Although the policy interpretation purports to address the HHS version of the regulations, all education functions were transferred to

§ 3.21

1. 503 U.S. 60, 112 S.Ct. 1028, 117 L.Ed.2d 208 (1992) (when Title IX was passed there was a presumption in favor of all available remedies, and Congress made no effort to alter that presumption).

2. *Barnes v. Gorman*, 536 U.S. 181, 122 S.Ct. 2097, 153 L.Ed.2d 230 (2002). Ths decision is discussed more fully *supra* § 3.10.

3. 42 U.S.C.A. § 2000d–7(b).

4. *See also Cherry v. University of Wisc. Sys. Bd. of Regents*, 265 F.3d 541 (7th Cir.2001) (finding that in the CRREA, Congress clearly and unambiguously manifested its intent to condition a state receipt's of Title IX funds on its waiver of immunity); *Fuller v. Rayburn*, 161 F.3d 516, 518 (8th Cir.1998) (valid abrogation regarding Title VI); *Lesage v. Texas*, 158 F.3d 213, 219 (5th Cir.1998), *rev'd on other grounds*, 528 U.S. 18, 120 S.Ct. 467, 145 L.Ed.2d 347 (1999) (holding that Congress has validly abrogated states' immunity to Title VI suits for damages); *Franks v. Kentucky Sch. for the Deaf*, 142 F.3d 360, 363 (6th Cir.1998) (Congress validly abrogated states' Eleventh Amendment immunity in actions brought under Title IX); *Doe v. University of Ill.*, 138 F.3d 653, 660 (7th Cir.1998), *vacated and remanded for further consideration in light of Davis v. Monroe County Bd. of Educ.*, 526 U.S. 629, 119 S.Ct. 1661, 143 L.Ed.2d 839 (1999) (abrogation valid with respect to Title IX); *Crawford v. Davis*, 109 F.3d 1281, 1283 (8th Cir.1997) (valid abrogation regarding Title IX). Alternatively, both the Fourth and Fifth Circuits have expressly held that the states waive their Eleventh Amendment immunity pursuant to Congressional sending clause power by accepting federal funds under Title IX. *Pederson v. Louisiana State Univ.*, 213 F.3d 858, 875–877 (5th Cir.2000); *Litman v. George Mason Univ.*, 186 F.3d 544, 555 (4th Cir.1999), *cert. denied*, 528 U.S. 1181, 120 S.Ct. 1220, 145 L.Ed.2d 1120 (2000). *Cf. Davis v. Monroe County Bd. of Ed.*, 526 U.S. 629, 119 S.Ct. 1661, 1669, 143 L.Ed.2d 839 (1999) (stating that "we have repeatedly treated Title IX as legislation enacted pursuant to Congress authority under the Spending Clause").

§ 3.22

1. 45 C.F.R. § 86.41 (1992).

2. 45 C.F.R. Part 86: Title IX of the Education Amendments of 1972; a Policy Interpretation; Title IX and Intercollegiate Athletics, 44 Fed. Reg. 71,413 (1979).

3. *Compare* 34 C.F.R. § 106.41 (1992) (DOE regulations) *with* 45 C.F.R. § 86.41 (1992) (HHS regulations).

DOE,[4] and, since then, lower courts have applied the policy interpretation to the DOE regulations.[5]

When the policy interpretation was published in 1979, the "program or activity" language in Title IX was construed to reach "any" program at an institution receiving federal funds.[6] Apparently, DOE initiated many cases. But in 1984, the Supreme Court's holding in *Grove City College*, that Title IX was violated only if the "particular" program receiving federal funds was discriminatory, put an end to at least seventy such cases before any of them was decided.[7] The Civil Rights Restoration Act of 1987 reinstated the institution-wide definition of "program or activity." The legislative history suggests that one goal of the 1987 Restoration Act was to foster the development of women's athletics.[8] After the 1987 Act, college athletic programs became a focal point of Title IX litigation.[9]

a. The Regulatory Framework

The Department of Education regulations identify ten factors to be used in examining a claim that an athletic program provides unequal opportunities to members of one sex. The list includes:

> 1. Whether the selection of sports and levels of competition effectively accommodate the interests and abilities of members of both sexes;
> 2. The provision of equipment and supplies;
> 3. Scheduling of games and practices time;
> 4. Travel and per diem allowances;
> 5. Opportunity to receive coaching and academic tutoring;
> 6. Assignment and compensation of coaches and tutors;
> 7. Provision of locker rooms, practice and competitive facilities;
> 8. Provision of medical and training facilities and services;
> 9. Provision of housing and dining facilities and services;
> 10. Publicity.[10]

Even as fleshed out by DOE, these multiple unweighted factors have spawned the inevitable progeny: inconsistent, contradictory and largely ad hoc judicial decisions. Sometimes, for reasons no more compelling

4. 20 U.S.C.A. § 3441(a).

5. *See, e.g., Roberts v. Colorado State Bd. of Agriculture*, 998 F.2d 824, 828 (10th Cir.1993).

6. *See, e.g., Haffer v. Temple Univ.*, 524 F.Supp. 531 (E.D.Pa.1981) (entire University subject to Title IX even though the received federal funds were not "earmarked" for athletics), *aff'd*, 688 F.2d 14 (3d Cir. 1982).

7. *See Statements on Civil Rights Restoration Act*, Daily Lab.Rep. (BNA) No. 53 at D1 (Mar. 20, 1981).

8. *See* 130 Cong. Rec. S11,253 (daily ed. Sept. 17 1984) (statement of Sen. Hatch).

9. *See e.g.*, Jennifer L. Henderson, *Gender Equity in Intercollegiate Athletics: A Commitment to Fairness*, 5 Seton Hall J. Sports L. 133 (1995); Janet Judge et al., *Perspective, Gender Equity in the 1990s: An Athletic Administrator's Survival Guide to Title IX and Gender Equity Compliance*, 5 Seton Hall J. Sports L. 313 (1995).

10. 34 C.F.R. § 106.41 (1992).

than convenience, a decision will turn solely on factor one. For the same reason, factors two through ten may be lumped together as solely a question of money spent. And sometimes a factor not even listed will control.

b. The Policy Interpretation

The policy interpretation separately divides Title IX coverage into three areas, including athletic scholarships, equivalence in other athletic benefits and opportunities, and "effective accommodation" of the interests and abilities of athletes of both sexes.[11] Scholarships represent a new area not listed in the DOE regulations. Equivalence in other athletic benefits and opportunities represents a composite or summation of factors two through ten of the regulations. "Effective accommodation" is formed from factor one of the regulations. The OCR Policy Interpretation in effect elevates one factor in the agency regulations to a complete compliance section on its own. Because Congress explicitly delegated to the agency the task of prescribing standards for athletic programs under Title IX, courts defer substantially to the umbrella policy interpretation and evaluate claims of discrimination according to its detailed guidelines.[12]

1. Policy Interpretation Compliance Area 1: Equal Opportunity in Athletic Scholarships

According to the policy interpretation, equal opportunity to receive athletic scholarships requires that proportionately equal amounts of financial assistance be available to men's and women's athletic programs as a whole.[13] The amount available for men is divided by the total number of participants in each of the men's athletic programs. A similar calculation will be made for the women's programs. If the two resulting figures are "substantially proportionate to their participation rates," the institution will be found to be in compliance with the regulations. If the figures are disparate, the institution may still be in compliance if it can offer legitimate non-discriminatory factors to explain the difference.[14]

In *Gonyo v. Drake University*,[15] members of a discontinued men's wrestling team petitioned for an injunction requiring reinstatement of the program. Drake University allotted 8.57 scholarships to the wres-

11. 44 Fed.Reg. at 71,415.

12. *See, e.g., Boulahanis v. Board of Regents*, 198 F.3d 633, 637–38 (7th Cir. 1999), *cert. denied*, 530 U.S. 1284, 120 S.Ct. 2762, 147 L.Ed.2d 1022 (2000) (holding the policy interpretations to be a reasonable exercise of the agencies' congressionally-delegated discretion to interpret the law); *Kelley v. Board of Trustees*, 35 F.3d 265, 270–71 (7th Cir.1994) (holding that the policy guidelines are entitled to deference because they are neither arbitrary or capricious, nor manifestly contrary to the statute); *Roberts*, 998 F.2d 824; *Cohen v. Brown Univ.*, 991 F.2d 888, 895 (1st Cir.1993) (stating that "the degree of deference [given to agency interpretations] is particularly high in Title IX cases because Congress explicitly delegated to the agency the task of prescribing standards for athletic programs under Title IX"), *on remand*, 879 F.Supp. 185 (D.R.I. 1995), *aff'd in part, rev'd in part*, 101 F.3d 155 (1st Cir.1996), *cert. denied*, 520 U.S. 1186, 117 S.Ct. 1469, 137 L.Ed.2d 682 (1997).

13. 44 Fed.Reg. at 71,415.

14. *Id.* at 71,415.

15. 837 F.Supp. 989 (S.D.Iowa 1993).

tling team, and the petitioners argued that the decrease in athletic scholarship awards amounted to discrimination against them. In the 1992–93 year, women were awarded 6% more scholarships than men, but there was a 17.8% disparity in participation by women. Discontinuing the wrestling program would decrease the participation disparity to 16.9%. Drake argued that the former wrestling scholarships would be used to attract more women to its athletic programs in an attempt to correct historical discrimination against them in those programs. The court denied the petition and advanced two grounds for its decision. First, the court implied that it accepted Drake's affirmative action argument as legitimate justification for discontinuing the program.[16] Second, and, perhaps in the long run, more importantly, it concluded that decreasing the participation disparity, an "effective accommodation" evaluation, predominates the examination of alleged discrimination in athletic programs because Title IX was enacted to encourage athletic participation by women.[17] Thus, the district court agreed with other courts that the "effective accommodation" consideration may, in the end, be the more important factor.[18]

The Second Circuit has held that only varsity, and not club, athletes have standing to challenge unequal allocation of benefits and scholarships between varsity men's and women's teams because nonvarsity athletes plaintiffs cannot claim they have suffered individualized or personal injury from the alleged discriminatory treatment of female varsity athletes with regards to athletic benefits.[19]

2. *Policy Interpretation Compliance Area 2: Equivalence in Other Athletic Benefits and Opportunities*

The second area identified in the policy interpretation, equivalence in other athletic benefits and opportunities, involves measurements of factors two through ten listed in the regulations.[20] If comparison reveals that both sexes are treated equally in other athletic benefits and opportunities, viewed from the perspective of aggregate participation in all sports, the institution will be found to be in compliance with the regulations. If the comparison reveals an inequality, the institution may still be compliance if it can show that the disparity is the result of legitimate non-discriminatory factors—the unique aspects of particular sports, an affirmative action program to overcome historical discrimination, or temporary sex-neutral factors related special circumstances, such as fluctuations in recruitment of first-year athletes.[21]

In *Favia v. Indiana University of Pennsylvania*,[22] after Indiana University of Pennsylvania (IUP) dropped two men's teams and two women's teams, members of the canceled women's gymnastics team

16. *Id.* at 995.

17. *Id.* at 996.

18. *See* cases cited *infra*.

19. *See Boucher v. Syracuse University*, 164 F.3d 113, 116 (2d Cir.1999).

20. 44 Fed.Reg. 71,416.

21. *Id.*

22. 7 F.3d 332 (3d Cir.1993).

were granted a preliminary injunction requiring reinstatement of the program based on allegations that elimination of the team created unequal athletic opportunities for women. The school sought a modification of the injunction allowing it instead to replace the fifteen-member gymnastics team with a fifty-member soccer team. IUP argued that doing so would decrease a disparity in women's participation by 4.05%. The court denied IUP's request for modification.

After first announcing that equivalence in other athletic benefits and opportunities may be assessed by comparing aggregate expenditures for male and female teams,[23] the court concluded that the modification would increase a funding disparity in IUP's program. Before the original spending reduction, IUP allocated more than 65% of its total athletics budget to men's programs. The proposed soccer team would cost only one-third of what the gymnastics team had cost, further increasing the gap in funding levels. But regardless of the funding issue, the court wrote, "in the absence of a continuing program expansion," a 4.05% reduction in an existing 15.6% participation disparity fell short of a school's obligation to "provide athletic opportunities in proportion to gender composition of [the] student body."[24] Here again, a lower court indicated that the "effective accommodation" consideration may be the determinate factor.[25]

3. Policy Interpretation Compliance Area 3: "Effective Accommodation" of the Interests of Both Sexes

Even if an institution provides equal athletic scholarships and equivalence in other athletic benefits and opportunities, it may violate Title IX if it fails effectively to accommodate the interests and abilities of athletes of both sexes.[26] Indeed, most courts say they decide Title IX claims by reference to the vague factor of "ineffective accommodation." The policy interpretation recognizes disparity in opportunities[27] within an individual segment of the athletic program if the disparity is "substantial enough in and of [it]self to deny equality of athletic opportunity;" otherwise, the policy interpretation prescribes measuring the "institution's program as a whole."[28] In all cases to date, where a court addresses "effective accommodation," it considers the athletic program as a whole.

Three sub-factors are examined in evaluating a claim of "ineffective accommodation:" the determination of students' interests and abilities; the selection of sports offered; and the levels of competition available.[29] Just as "effective accommodation" turns out to be the most important of the three broad areas identified by the policy interpretation, the "levels

23. *Id.* at 343.

24. *Id.* at 434–44.

25. *See* cases cited *infra*.

26. *See, e.g., Roberts*, 998 F.2d 824; *Cohen*, 991 F.2d 888; *Favia*, 7 F.3d 332.

27. When evaluating disparity in opportunities, it is the aggregate number of opportunities provided for each sex, and not the number of teams funded for each sex, that are counted. *See Boucher*, 164 F.3d at 116 n.4; *cf. Cohen*, 991 F.2d at 897.

28. 44 Fed.Reg. at 71,418.

29. *Id.* at 71,417.

of competition'' sub-factor is the most frequently applied measure of ''effective accommodation.''

(a) Determinations of Students' Interests

The first sub-factor focuses on the process an institution uses to determine its students' athletic interests and abilities. The process must reflect the increasing levels of women's interests and abilities; must not disadvantage the underrepresented sex; must consider historical team performance; and must be responsive to the expressed interests of members of the underrepresented sex who are capable of intercollegiate competition.[30]

The process of determining students' interests, however, cannot be tainted with archaic stereotypes. In *Pederson v. Louisiana State University*,[31] the Fifth Circuit sharply criticized Louisiana State University which argued that it was in compliance with Title IX because its female students did not want to participate in athletics.[32] Finding that the school intentionally discriminated in violation of Title IX, the court stated that the university brazenly ''perpetuated antiquated stereotypes'' and made ''a decision not to provide equal athletic opportunities for its female students because of paternalism and stereotypical assumptions about their interests and abilities.''[33]

(b) The Selection of Sports Offered

The second sub-factor focuses on equal opportunity for members of both sexes to participate in the teams an institution chooses to sponsor. This may require that the institution allow both sexes to try out for an integrated team or sponsor separate teams for each sex. If the sport is a contact sport, an institution must sponsor separate teams if: first, there is historical discrimination against the excluded sex; and, second, members of that sex possess sufficient interest and ability to maintain a viable team and a reasonable expectation of intercollegiate competition for it. If the sport is a non-contact sport, an institution must sponsor a separate team for the members of the excluded sex only if, in addition to historical exclusion and sufficient interest and ability, they possess insufficient skill to be selected for or compete actively on an integrated team.[34]

The DOE regulations further state that if a school ''operates or sponsors a team in a particular sport for members of one sex but operates or sponsors no such team for members of the other sex, . . . members of the excluded sex must be allowed to try out for the team offered unless the sport involved is a contact sport.''[35] Courts have, however, broadly interpreted the contact sport exception to mean that a school cannot be liable for a Title IX violation for any type of gender

30. *Id.*

31. 213 F.3d 858 (5th Cir.2000).

32. *Id.* at 877.

33. *Id.* at 877–881.

34. 44 Fed.Reg. at 71,417–8.

35. 34 C.F.R. § 106.41(b).

discrimination in a contact sport. For example, in *Williams v. School District of Bethlehem*,[36] the Third Circuit rejected Title IX liability when a school district removed a boy from a girl's high school field hockey team. The court stated that the contact sport exception is "the broadest exception recognized to the overarching goal of equal athletic opportunity."[37]

When faced with similar circumstances, however, the Fourth Circuit came to a different conclusion. In *Mercer v. Duke University*,[38] Heather Mercer, an all-state place kicker in high school, had been allowed to try out for the Duke football team as a walk-on kicker and had been made a member of the team. Once she was a member of the team, however, Duke University subjected her to disparate treatment compared to other walk-on kickers, and eventually removed her from the team. The Fourth Circuit held that even though Duke was never under any obligation to allow Mercer to try out for the team, once she tried out and was made a member of the team, Duke was obligated to provide her with equal benefits and opportunities.[39]

(c) The Levels of Competition Available

The final sub-factor, levels of competition, is the most important because it addresses an institution's obligation to allow both sexes equal opportunity to participate in intercollegiate competition.[40] The Policy Interpretation allows schools to demonstrate effective accommodation in three ways: (1) by showing that the participation opportunities in athletic programs for both sexes is substantially proportional to their respective enrollments; (2) by producing evidence of a history and continuing practice of developing participation opportunities for the under-represented sex; or (3) by showing that existing programs fully and effectively accommodate the interests and abilities of both sexes.[41] The institution will be found to be in compliance with Title IX if it can demonstrate compliance with any of the three prongs.[42]

36. 998 F.2d 168 (3d Cir.1993)

37. *Id.* at 171. *See also Barnett v. Texas Wrestling Ass'n*, 16 F.Supp.2d 690 (N.D.Tex.1998) (no Title IX liability where a state wrestling association refused to allow two female members of an otherwise all-male high school wrestling team to compete in state tournament).

38. 190 F.3d 643 (4th Cir.1999).

39. *Id.* at 647–48. After remand, the case went to trial and the jury awarded plaintiff $2 million.

40. 44 Fed.Reg. at 71,418.

41. *Id.* at 71,415–17. *See Boucher v. Syracuse University*, 1998 WL 167296 at *3 (N.D.N.Y.1998), *aff'd in part and rev'd in part on other grounds*, 164 F.3d 113 (2d Cir.1999) ("Where a university has a practice of expanding its athletic program, approaching proportionality and meeting the needs of the under-represented gender; and continues to expand in response to its student body's interest and abilities, as well as that of secondary feeder schools; symmetry in athletic programs is not required under Title IX, and liability may be avoided. Under this 'safe harbor' of a continuing practice of program expansion, courts look to the institution's past and continuing remedial efforts to provide nondiscriminatory participation opportunities through program expansion") (citing *Cohen*, 991 F.2d at 898).

42. In 1996, the DOE's Office for Civil Rights issued the *Clarification of Intercollegiate Athletics Policy Guidance: The Three–Part Test*. The Clarification makes clear that an institution can comply with Title IX by demonstrating satisfaction of any of the three prongs. The Clarification is available at *http://www.ed.gov.offices/OCR/clarif-*

Cases usually turn on the third factor: the "substantial proportion" question.[43] The policy interpretation asks "[w]hether intercollegiate level participation opportunities for male and female students in all sports are provided in numbers substantially proportionate to their respective enrollments."[44] The *Title IX Athletics Investigator's Manual* suggests that "[i]f the enrollment is 52% male and 48% female, then, ideally, about 52% of the participants in the athletics program should be male and 48% female."[45] There is no brightline test for acceptable levels of disparity from the norm, and the decisions illustrate the difficulty courts confront in deciding what degree of underrepresentation in participation percentages amounts to "ineffective accommodation."[46]

In *Cohen v. Brown University*,[47] the court placed on the plaintiff the burden of demonstrating both disparity and unmet interest, concluding that a Title IX plaintiff does not enjoy the shift of burden to the defendant that inures to the benefit of a Title VII plaintiff attempting to demonstrate the disproportionate adverse impact of a neutral practice. It nevertheless found that the defendant's dropping of two men's and two women's teams violated Title IX because the cut resulted in an 11.4% underrepresentation participation by women.[48] In *Roberts v. Colorado State Bd. of Agriculture*,[49] the court found that Colorado State University violated Title IX by eliminating a fast pitch softball team because the resulting 10.5% disparity in women's participation was excessive. In

ic.html. See also Pederson, 213 F.3d at 879; *Neal v. Board of Trustees*, 198 F.3d 763, 767 (9th Cir.1999); *Boulahanis*, 198 F.3d at 635.

43. The United States Court of Appeals for the First Circuit identified reasons for de-emphasizing the second and third sub-factors. As far as showing a continuing expansion of programs for the underrepresented, the court noted that "in an era of fiscal austerity, few universities are prone to expand athletic opportunities." *Cohen*, 991 F.2d at 989. And the full-and-effective accommodation "benchmark sets a high standard: it demands not merely some accommodation, but full and effective accommodation. If there is sufficient interest and ability among members of the statistically underrepresented gender, not slaked by existing programs, an institution necessarily fails this prong of the test." *Id.*

44. 44 Fed.Reg. at 71,418.

45. Office for Civil Rights, Dep't. of Educ., *Title IX Athletics Investigator's Manual*, at 24 (1990).

46. *Cohen v. Brown Univ.*, 879 F.Supp. 185 (D.R.I.1995) (substantially proportionate must be stringent enough to effectuate the purposes of Title IX defined to mean that gender balance of university's intercollegiate athletic program, as a whole, must mirror the gender balance of its student enrollment). *But cf. Cohen v. Brown Univ.*, 101 F.3d 155 (1st Cir.1996), *cert. denied*, 520 U.S. 1186, 117 S.Ct. 1469, 137 L.Ed.2d 682 (1997) (excluding from the calculation of participation opportunities by gender varsity teams funded by donors, as distinct from the defendant university itself).

47. 991 F.2d 888 (1st Cir.1993), *on remand*, 879 F.Supp. 185 (D.R.I.1995), *aff'd in part, rev'd in part*, 101 F.3d 155 (1st Cir.1996), *cert. denied*, 520 U.S. 1186, 117 S.Ct. 1469, 137 L.Ed.2d 682 (1997). In the second appeal, the First Circuit upheld the regulations as interpreted by OCR. It rejected the University's argument that OCR's three-part test was satisfied if athletic resources were allocated in accordance with genders' "relative interests" in various sports, if the school nevertheless failed fully and effectively to accommodate the interests and abilities of women, the underrepresented gender. The court also upheld as against an equal protection challenge the university's challenge to the district court's "full accommodation" order, employing intermediate scrutiny.

48. The First Circuit distinguished Title VII by asserting, among other reasons, that Title IX's goals are largely aspirational rather than mandatory. *Id.* at 902.

49. 998 F.2d 824 (10th Cir.1993).

Favia v. Indiana University of Pennsylvania,[50] the court rejected an athletic program change that would have decreased the disparity from 15.6% to 12.6%, because even the lower figure would not have alleviated the Title IX violation.

Every circuit to address the issue agrees that an institution can achieve substantial proportionality by decreasing participation of an overrepresented group while maintaining the level of participation of the underrepresented group.[51] In *Kelley*, for example, men were overrepresented in the institution's varsity programs by about 20%. The court held that dropping the men's swimming team without dropping the women's team did not violate Title IX because apparently men would continue to be at least proportionately represented even without the swimming team. Similarly, in *Chalenor v. University of North Dakota*,[52] the court upheld a university's decision to cancel the men's wrestling team in an effort to reduce spending and reduce the disproportionality between men's and women's athletic participation while leaving all women's teams intact.

50. 7 F.3d 332 (3d Cir.1993).

51. *See, e.g., Neal v. Board of Trustees*, 198 F.3d 763, 769–770 (9th Cir.1999); *Boulahanis*, 198 F.3d at 638–39 (dropping men's wrestling and soccer did not violate Title IX because men's participation in athletics continued to be substantially proportionate to their enrollment); *Horner v. Kentucky High Sch. Athletic Ass'n*, 43 F.3d 265, 275 (6th Cir.1994); *Kelley*, 35 F.3d at 269; *Roberts*, 998 F.2d at 830; *Cohen*, 991 F.2d at 898 n.15.

52. 291 F.3d 1042, 1048–49 (8th Cir. 2002). Every court to address the issue has allowed a college or university to reduce men's athletic opportunities to achieve substantial proportionality. *See Miami University Wrestling Club v. Miami Univ.*, 302 F.3d 608 (6th Cir.2002) (university's equalization of athletic opportunities for men and women by eliminating men's team sports was not violation of Title IX); *Neal*, 198 F.3d at 771 (allowing university to make gender-conscious decisions and noting that "the plain meaning of the nondiscrimination principle set forth in 20 U.S.C.A. §§ 1681(a) does not bar remedial actions designed to achieve substantial proportionality between athletic rosters and student bodies"); *Boulahanis v. Bd. of Regents*, 198 F.3d 633, 638 (7th Cir.1999) (holding that university's elimination of men's soccer and men's wrestling teams "is not a violation of Title IX as long as men's participation in athletics continues to be 'substantially proportionate' to their enrollment") (citation omitted), *cert. denied*, 530 U.S. 1284, 120 S.Ct. 2762, 147 L.Ed.2d 1022 (2000); *Horner v. Ky. High Sch. Athletic Ass'n*, 43 F.3d 265, 275 (6th Cir.1994) (noting that "[a]n institution need not pour ever-increasing sums into its athletic programs in order to bring itself into compliance, but has the option of reducing opportunities for the overrepresented gender while keeping opportunities for the underrepresented gender stable") (citation omitted); *Kelley v. Bd. of Trustees.*, 35 F.3d 265, 270 (7th Cir.1994) (allowing university to eliminate men's swimming team while retaining women's swimming team because male athletes on the whole "would continue to be more than substantially proportionate to their presence in the University's student body"), *cert. denied*, 513 U.S. 1128, 115 S.Ct. 938, 130 L.Ed.2d 883 (1995); *Roberts v. Colo. State Bd. of Agric.*, 998 F.2d 824, 830 (10th Cir.) ("Financially strapped institutions may still comply with Title IX by cutting athletic programs such that men's and women's athletic participation rates become substantially proportionate to their representation in the undergraduate population."), *cert. denied*, 510 U.S. 1004, 114 S.Ct. 580, 126 L.Ed.2d 478 (1993); *Cohen*, 991 F.2d at 898 n. 15 (noting that university can "bring itself into compliance" with Title IX "by reducing opportunities for the overrepresented gender while keeping opportunities stable for the underrepresented gender (or reducing them to a much lesser extent)"). *Cf. National Wrestling Coaches Ass'n v. Dept. of Educ.*, 366 F.3d 930 (D.C. Cir. 2004) (associations advancing men's wrestling lacked standing to challenge Title IX enforcement because alleged injury, elimination or reduction of men's wrestling, speculative, so they failed to show that injury would be redressed by their challenge).

Fourteenth Amendment equal protection clauses challenges brought by males where male athletic opportunities were cut have also been rejected by the courts.[53] The Seventh Circuit's opinion in *Cohen II* addresses this issue at length. Adopting an intermediate level of scrutiny, the court found that Title IX and its accompanying regulations and policy interpretations furthered the "clearly important" governmental objective of avoiding the use of federal funds to support discriminatory practices, and that the statute and regulations were "clearly substantially related" to this objective.[54]

53. *See, e.g., Neal,* 198 F.3d at 772–773; *Kelley,* 35 F.3d at 272.

54. *Cohen,* 101 F.3d at 184.

Chapter Four

COSTS AND FEES: FEDERAL RULE OF CIVIL PROCEDURE 54(d), THE CIVIL RIGHTS ATTORNEY'S FEES AWARDS ACT, AND FEDERAL RULE 68

Analysis

A. RULE 54(d) COSTS TO PREVAILING PLAINTIFFS OR DEFENDANTS

§ 4.1 In General

Unlike attorney's fees under Title VII or § 1988, which as we shall see are ordinarily awardable only to prevailing plaintiffs, either side that prevails is presumptively entitled to costs under Fed.R.Civ.P. 54(d).[1]

§ 4.1

1. *See Bass v. E.I.DuPont de Nemours & Co.*, 324 F.3d 761 (4th Cir. 2003) (affirming award of costs under FRCP 54(d) to prevailing defendant even though plaintiff impecunious).

Indeed the argument has been rejected that a losing Title VII plaintiff may be assessed costs only on the same terms as she should be assessed fees—that is, when the claim was frivolous, unreasonable, or without foundation.[2]

The awarding of costs lies within the sound discretion of the district court and may be denied where the award would be inequitable.[3] Citing that discretion, a district court has cut in half a large award of costs to a defendant law firm that prevailed after lengthy litigation involving its alleged unlawful denial of partnership on the basis of gender. The court took into account that the case was "close"; that it presented important issues of public concern and had been pursued by the plaintiff at great financial cost; and that the plaintiff was of modest means while the defendant was a large corporate firm.[4] A defendant state that achieved a dismissal without prejudice on grounds of Eleventh Amendment immunity was held to have prevailed within the meaning of FRCP 54(d), and to be eligible for an award of costs; the circuit viewed Rule 54(d) costs unavailable for dismissals based on lack of subject matter jurisdiction, but deemed the Eleventh Amendment ground as a nonjurisdictional affirmative defense.[5]

The "costs" recoverable by any prevailing party are limited, however, to items specified by a separate federal statute, 28 U.S.C.A. § 1920. These include clerk and marshal fees, fees by court reporters for transcripts "necessarily obtained for use in the case;"[6] printing disbursements and witness fees; specified docket fees; and fees for court-appointed experts and certain interpreters. Most important, "costs" as used in Rule 54(d) do *not* include the prevailing party's attorney's fees. This is consistent with the ordinary "American rule" which, as explained by the Supreme Court, calls for each side to pay its own lawyer, win or lose, unless there is specific statutory authority for fee "shifting."[7] It is to such fee-shifting statutes that we now turn.

2. *See, e.g., Cosgrove v. Sears, Roebuck & Co.*, 191 F.3d 98 (2d Cir.1999); *Croker v. Boeing Co.*, 662 F.2d 975 (3d Cir.1981). And plaintiff's modest means do not suffice to overcome the presumption that costs are to be awarded to the prevailing party, although misconduct by the prevailing party or plaintiff's clear inability to pay might. *Cherry v. Champion International Corp.*, 186 F.3d 442 (4th Cir.1999).

3. *Friedman v. Ganassi*, 853 F.2d 207 (3d Cir.1988), *cert. denied*, 488 U.S. 1042, 109 S.Ct. 867, 102 L.Ed.2d 991 (1989).

4. *Ezold v. Wolf, Block, Schorr and Solis-Cohen*, 758 F.Supp. 303 (E.D.Pa. 1991). *See also White & White, Inc. v. American Hosp. Supply Corp.*, 786 F.2d 728, 732–33 (6th Cir.1986) (denial of costs may be proper in close and difficult cases; "the closeness of a case is judged ... by the refinement of perception required to recognize, sift through and organize relevant evidence, and by the difficulty of discerning the law of the case").

5. *Miles v. State of California*, 320 F.3d 986 (9th Cir.2003).

6. Some courts have taxed at least part of the costs associated with videotaping a deposition, *see Morrison v. Reichhold Chems., Inc.*, 97 F.3d 460 (11th Cir.1996), *Barber v. Ruth*, 7 F.3d 636 (7th Cir.1993), *Echostar Satellite Corp. v. Advanced Communications Corp.*, 902 F.Supp. 213 (D.Colo.1995), despite the argument that those costs are not the fees of a "court reporter" for a "stenographic transcript." Depositions are also compensable as costs where court finds they were reasonably necessary. *Zotos v. Lindbergh Sch. Dist.*, 121 F.3d 356 (8th Cir.1997).

7. *Alyeska Pipeline Serv. Co. v. Wilderness Society*, 421 U.S. 240, 95 S.Ct. 1612, 44 L.Ed.2d 141 (1975).

§§ 4.2–4.4 [Reserved]

B. INTRODUCTION TO THE CIVIL RIGHTS ATTORNEY'S FEES AWARDS ACT

§ 4.5 In General

The Civil Rights Attorney's Fees Awards Act (the "Act"), a 1976 amendment to 42 U.S.C.A. § 1988, permits a discretionary award of attorney's fees, in a "reasonable" amount, as part of the costs recoverable by prevailing parties, other than the United States,[1] in any action or proceeding pursuant to 42 U.S.C.A. §§ 1981, 1982, 1983, 1985, and 1986, as well as Titles VI and IX.[2] The purpose of the award is to enable plaintiffs to attract competent legal counsel; perhaps that is why fees have been denied for lawyers' public relations efforts on behalf of their clients.[3] The Act parallels separate statutory authority to award attorney's fees to prevailing parties in actions under the Rehabilitation Act of 1973,[4] the Age Discrimination in Employment Act,[5] the Equal Pay Act,[6] the Clean Water Act,[7] the Fair Labor Standards Act,[8] and under Title VII.[9] In fact, over a hundred separate statutes allow for court awarded attorney's fees. The principles governing eligibility for and computation of awards are largely interchangeable among these statutes.

Although a plaintiff must receive at least some relief on the merits in order to become a "prevailing party" eligible for fees, success on a "significant issue," even if it is not a "central" one, will suffice.[10] But

§ 4.5

1. So the United States as prevailing plaintiff cannot recover fees under § 1988, while the United States as losing plaintiff may be assessed fees per the Equal Access to Justice Act, § 5.15, *infra*, in circumstances where private defendants would not be subject to fee liability under § 1988.

2. 42 U.S.C.A. § 1988(b). But not state law discrimination claims where no federal claims are advanced. *See Paz v. Long Island R. Co.*, 128 F.3d 121 (2d Cir.1997). And an important exception to fee awards under § 1988 is created by the Prison Litigation Reform Act, which restricts such awards in "any action brought by a prisoner," not just those related to prison conditions. *Jackson v. State Bd. of Pardons and Paroles*, 331 F.3d 790 (11th Cir.2003).

3. *Halderman v. Pennhurst State Sch. & Hosp.*, 49 F.3d 939 (3d Cir.1995).

4. 29 U.S.C.A. § 794(a).

5. 29 U.S.C.A. § 626(b) (incorporating standards from the Fair Labor Standards Act, 29 U.S.C.A. § 216(b)). Textually, the ADEA and the FLSA differ from the other statutes in that they require fees to be shifted as the result of "any judgment" awarded to a plaintiff, with no reference to the concept of "prevailing party." See 29 U.S.C.A. § 626(b) of the ADEA, incorporating 29 U.S.C.A. § 216(b) of the FLSA. Nevertheless, a circuit has imported all the restrictions surrounding the "prevailing party" showing into fee disputes arising from judgments under the ADEA. *See Salvatori v. Westinghouse Electric Corp.*, 190 F.3d 1244 (11th Cir.1999), *cert. denied*, 528 U.S. 1160, 120 S.Ct. 1172, 145 L.Ed.2d 1081 (2000) (plaintiff who obtained judgment on merits of ADEA claim but no monetary or punitive relief denied fees); *Nance v. Maxwell Federal Credit Union*, 186 F.3d 1338 (11th Cir.1999) (fees denied when plaintiff proved defendant's conduct violated ADEA but could not prove consequent injury and accordingly received no relief).

6. 29 U.S.C.A. § 206(d) (incorporating standards from the Fair Labor Standards Act, 29 U.S.C.A. § 216(b)).

7. 33 U.S.C.A. § 1365.

8. 29 U.S.C.A. § 216(b).

9. 42 U.S.C.A. § 2000e–5(k).

10. *See Texas State Teachers Ass'n v. Garland Indep. Sch. Dist.*, 489 U.S. 782, 109 S.Ct. 1486, 103 L.Ed.2d 866 (1989); *Wal–Mart Stores, Inc. v. Barton*, 223 F.3d 770 (8th Cir.2000) (attorney's fees properly

opinion is divided as to whether fee eligibility depends upon the plaintiff's having prevailed on a claim under one of the § 1988–referenced federal statutes, rather than a related claim under state law.[11] A plaintiff adjudged to be a prevailing party should ordinarily receive a fee award absent "special circumstances," such as the plaintiff's egregious misconduct.[12] These circumstances are rarely found.[13] But *pro se* plaintiffs who also happen to be attorneys have been ruled ineligible for a fee award.[14]

awarded where plaintiff succeeded on the claim "at the heart of her case" and obtained a substantial judgment that served to vindicate important personal rights); *Shrader v. OMC Aluminum Boat Group, Inc.*, 128 F.3d 1218 (8th Cir.1997); *District of Columbia v. Patterson*, 667 A.2d 1338 (D.C.App.1995), *cert. denied*, 519 U.S. 1058, 117 S.Ct. 688, 136 L.Ed.2d 612 (1997) (remanding to determine if plaintiff could establish prevailing party status with respect to claims other than the 4th Amendment claim as to which the appellate court held she had not prevailed).

11. *Contrast Williams v. Hanover Hous. Auth.*, 113 F.3d 1294 (1st Cir.1997) and *Exeter–West Greenwich Reg'l Sch. v. Pontarelli*, 788 F.2d 47 (1st Cir.1986) (attorney's fees recoverable even where plaintiff technically prevails only on state law claim, provided dispositive state law question is closely connected with the federal claim) *with National Private Truck Council, Inc. v. Oklahoma Tax Comm'n*, 515 U.S. 582, 115 S.Ct. 2351, 132 L.Ed.2d 509 (1995) (plaintiff not prevailing party). *Cf. Bridges v. Eastman Kodak Co.*, 102 F.3d 56 (2d Cir.1996), *cert. denied sub nom. Yourdon, Inc. v. Bridges*, 520 U.S. 1274, 117 S.Ct. 2453, 138 L.Ed.2d 211 (1997) (plaintiff who prevailed on merits but recovered no back pay under Title VII, yet who obtained $20,000 compensatory damages on related state law claim, is "prevailing party" eligible for attorney's fees and costs under Title VII).

12. *See, e.g., Patricia P. v. Board of Educ. of Oak Park*, 203 F.3d 462 (7th Cir. 2000) (under IDEA, even if the private school placement is appropriate, plaintiff can be denied fees where she did not cooperate in making the child available for evaluation)*; Lee v. American Eagle Airlines, Inc.*, 93 F.Supp.2d 1322 (S.D.Fla.2000) (denying prevailing plaintiff attorney's fees due to egregious misconduct of counsel during trial); *Christiansburg Garment Co. v. EEOC*, 434 U.S. 412, 98 S.Ct. 694, 54 L.Ed.2d 648 (1978). *Cf. Chaney v. New Orleans Pub. Facility Management, Inc.*, 1998 WL 87617 (E.D.La.1998) (denying prevailing party attorneys' fees in Title VII action, finding performance of plaintiff's attorneys did not merit attorneys' fees). Failure to mitigate damages is not sufficient misconduct to forfeit fees. *Bridges v. Eastman Kodak Co.*, 102 F.3d 56 (2d Cir.1996), *cert. denied sub nom. Yourdon, Inc. v. Bridges*, 520 U.S. 1274, 117 S.Ct. 2453, 138 L.Ed.2d 211 (1997). But a state court denied fees under § 1988 to plaintiffs who successfully attacked the Federal constitutionality of a state law enforced but not enacted by defendant municipality, on the ground that plaintiffs should have known that the municipality could not be independently liable for the unconstitutional state statute. *Minnesota Council of Dog Clubs v. Minneapolis,* 540 N.W.2d 903 (Minn.App.1995), *cert. denied,* 518 U.S. 1005, 116 S.Ct. 2524, 135 L.Ed.2d 1048 (1996). In the class action context, a plaintiff who had opted out of a class settlement and then litigated the claim and received exactly the same damages had the plaintiff remained in the class, was deemed not a prevailing and was denied attorney's fees. *See Rivera–Rosario v. United States Dep't of Agriculture*, 202 F.3d 35, 36 (1st Cir.2000). *But see Raishevich v. Foster*, 247 F.3d 337 (2d Cir.2001) (reversing district court's finding of special circumstances where plaintiff rejected a court-proposed settlement offer that was less than her eventual recovery).

13. *See, e.g., N.A.A.C.P. v. Town of East Haven,* 259 F.3d 113 (2d Cir.2001), *cert. denied* 534 U.S. 1129, 122 S.Ct. 1068, 151 L.Ed.2d 971 (2002) (plaintiff did not act in bad faith that would forfeit fee award by declining to settle on terms that failed to meet its substantive demands). *Gumbhir v. Curators of Univ. of Mo.*, 157 F.3d 1141, 1146 (8th Cir.1998), *cert. denied* 526 U.S. 1005, 119 S.Ct. 1143, 143 L.Ed.2d 210 (1999) (declining to deny an award because of litigation conduct). *See also* Zimmer, Sullivan & Richards, *Cases and Materials on Employment Discrimination* 663–64 (2d ed. 1988).

14. *Kay v. Ehrler*, 499 U.S. 432, 111 S.Ct. 1435, 113 L.Ed.2d 486 (1991). *See also Doe v. Board of Educ. of Baltimore County*, 165 F.3d 260 (4th Cir.1998), *cert. denied*, 526 U.S. 1159, 119 S.Ct. 2049, 144 L.Ed.2d 216 (1999) (legal representation of disabled child by attorney-parent a "special circum-

And a plaintiff who recovers only nominal damages, although a prevailing party, may be entitled to no fee award if those damages represent only a slight degree of success achieved in the litigation.[15]

To achieve success on a "significant issue" and thus "prevail" so as to be eligible for fees, the plaintiff need only obtain some relief which changes his legal relationship with the defendant and is more than merely technical or *de minimis*.[16] In general, if the relief plaintiff initially seeks is "of the same general type" as the relief eventually obtained, plaintiff may be considered a prevailing party.[17] An injunction requiring a company to correct a racially intimidating work atmosphere, for example, has sufficed as the predicate for a fee award to a plaintiff who lost on most of his individual claims of race discrimination.[18] But in

stance" disqualifying child, an IDEA plaintiff, from award of fees).

15. *Farrar v. Hobby*, 506 U.S. 103, 113 S.Ct. 566, 121 L.Ed.2d 494 (1992). *See also Johnson v. City of Aiken*, 278 F.3d 333 (4th Cir.2002) (recovery of 35 cents on Fourth Amendment claim was insignificant, resulting in no fee award); *Tyler v. Corner Const. Corp., Inc.*, 167 F.3d 1202 (8th Cir.1999) (treating a "nuisance settlement" as a special circumstance rendering unjust a fee award to prevailing party).

The Seventh Circuit defined a "nuisance settlement" as having a value less than the costs of the defense at the time of the settlement. *Kitchen v. TTX Co.*, 284 F.3d 688, 691–92 (7th Cir.2002). Thus, if the value of a settlement exceeds the cost of defense, thus acknowledging risk in continuing the litigation, plaintiff is a prevailing party and is entitled to fees. *Id.*

16. *See Hewitt v. Helms*, 482 U.S. 755, 107 S.Ct. 2672, 96 L.Ed.2d 654 (1987) (declaration that prison authority violated due process with no finding of liability because qualified immunity defense sustained, did not enable plaintiff to prevail; nor did the change of policy resulting from his suit because he did not benefit from change, having been earlier released from prison); *Rhodes v. Stewart*, 488 U.S. 1, 109 S.Ct. 202, 102 L.Ed.2d 1 (1988) (even judgment ordering prison to modify magazine policy respecting inmates did not make plaintiffs prevailing parties, because one was dead and the other released when policy change was made, so neither personally benefited from judgment). *Compare Barnes v. Broward County Sheriff's Office*, 190 F.3d 1274 (11th Cir.1999) (applicant who obtained injunction against pre-employment medical examination as violating ADA did not prevail because he did not directly benefit from judgment at time of its entry, despite possibility he might benefit from it in the future should he reapply for employment) *with Ensley Branch N.A.A.C.P. v. Seibels*, 31 F.3d 1548 (11th Cir.1994) (current employees prevailed by eliminating race-conscious personnel decisions through judgment striking down affirmative action policies). *See also Jacobson v. City of Coates*, 171 F.3d 1162 (8th Cir.1999) (determination that one of two challenged ordinances was unconstitutional changed legal relationship between parties sufficient to entitle plaintiffs to attorney's fees under § 1988 despite trial court's characterization of victory as "technical" and "insignificant"); *LeBlanc-Sternberg v. Fletcher*, 143 F.3d 748, 759 (2d Cir. 1998) (plaintiffs directly benefitted from and prevailed by obtaining injunction against zoning regulations that would impair their ability to conduct religious services); *Layton v. Elder*, 143 F.3d 469, 470–73 (8th Cir.1998) (injunction obtained by plaintiffs mandating county to make its services available to them despite their disability effected material change in plaintiffs' relationship with county and accordingly they were prevailing parties eligible for fees).

17. *Lyte v. Sara Lee Corp.*, 950 F.2d 101 (2d Cir.1991).

18. *Ruffin v. Great Dane Trailers*, 969 F.2d 989 (11th Cir.1992), *cert. denied*, 507 U.S. 910, 113 S.Ct. 1257, 122 L.Ed.2d 655 (1993); *LeBlanc–Sternberg v. Fletcher*, 143 F.3d 748 (2d Cir.1998) (award of injunctive relief against only one defendant sufficient where injunction materially alters legal relationship between parties by modifying defendant's behavior in way that directly benefits plaintiff).

Obtaining equitable relief does not automatically confer prevailing party status for purposes of the Fees Act. *See Tex. State Teachers Ass'n v. Garland Indep. Sch. Dist.*, 489 U.S. 782, 782–83, 109 S.Ct. 1486, 103 L.Ed.2d 866 (1989); *Rhodes v. Stewart*, 488 U.S. 1, 3–4, 109 S.Ct. 202, 203, 102 L.Ed.2d

applying this standard, courts have sometimes resorted to a highly subjective appraisal of plaintiff's original objective in bringing suit, denying fees where that objective was not obtained.[19]

A finding of a violation under § 1983 may lead to an award of nominal damages where the predicate constitutional violation is "absolute," that is not dependent upon the merits of the plaintiff's substantive assertions or the magnitude of injury resulting from a violation.[20] Such damages may now be available under Title VII, which provides for certain kinds of legal relief since its amendment by the Civil Rights Act of 1991.[21] Whether such nominal damages can serve as a springboard for § 1988 attorney's fees was the subject of conflict among the circuits.[22]

In *Farrar v. Hobby*,[23] the Supreme Court attempted to resolve this conflict, but did so somewhat oddly. It formally conferred prevailing party status on plaintiffs who recover only nominal damages, but did so under standards that fix the amount of a reasonable attorney's fee at zero when their degree of success is slight. The Court confirmed that "a plaintiff 'prevails' when actual relief on the merits of his claim materially alters the legal relationship between the parties by modifying the defendant's behavior in a way that directly benefits the plaintiff"; and it acknowledged that even a judgment for only nominal damages "modifies the defendant's behavior for the plaintiff's benefit by forcing the defendant to pay an amount of money he otherwise would not pay." But it then drained this conclusion of practical significance under most circumstances by adding that when a plaintiff, having failed to prove an essential element of a claim for monetary relief, recovers only nominal damages, "the only reasonable fee is usually no fee at all."[24]

1 (1988) (per curiam). An inquiring court always must make a qualitative inquiry into the import of the relief obtained. *Gay Officers Action League v. Puerto Rico*, 247 F.3d 288 (1st Cir.2001) (where officers achieved declaratory and injunctive relief in their challenge to a police department regulation which made "associat[ing] with ... homosexuals" violative of the code of conduct and exposed violators to official discipline, plaintiffs were prevailing parties even if the regulation was not regularly enforced).

19. *See, e.g., Cady v. City of Chicago*, 43 F.3d 326 (7th Cir.1994).

20. *Carey v. Piphus*, 435 U.S. 247, 98 S.Ct. 1042, 55 L.Ed.2d 252 (1978) (nominal damages available for denial of procedural due process).

21. *See Barber v. T. D. Williamson*, 254 F.3d 1223 (10th Cir.2001) (fees based on nominal damages, when plaintiff proved hostile work environment violating Title VII, subject to both "significant legal issue" requirement and *Farrar* "relative importance" rule discussed in text immediately below). *But cf. Walker v. Anderson Elec. Connectors*, 944 F.2d 841 (11th Cir.1991), *cert. denied*, 506 U.S. 1078, 113 S.Ct. 1043, 122 L.Ed.2d 352 (1993), which held nominal damages unavailable under, or at least not mandated by, the pre-amended Title VII.

22. *See, e.g., Romberg v. Nichols*, 953 F.2d 1152 (9th Cir.1992) (nominal damages award of $1 creates prevailing party status), *vacated by*, 506 U.S. 1075, 113 S.Ct. 1038, 122 L.Ed.2d 348 (1993); *Ruggiero v. Krzeminski*, 928 F.2d 558 (2d Cir.1991); *Scofield v. City of Hillsborough*, 862 F.2d 759 (9th Cir.1988); *Coleman v. Turner*, 838 F.2d 1004 (8th Cir.1988); *Nephew v. City of Aurora*, 830 F.2d 1547 (10th Cir.1987) (en banc), *cert. denied*, 485 U.S. 976, 108 S.Ct. 1269, 99 L.Ed.2d 481 (1988); *Garner v. Wal–Mart Stores, Inc.*, 807 F.2d 1536 (11th Cir.1987).

23. 506 U.S. 103, 113 S.Ct. 566, 121 L.Ed.2d 494 (1992).

24. *Farrar v. Hobby*, 506 U.S. 103, 113 S.Ct. 566, 121 L.Ed.2d 494; *McCardle v. Haddad*, 131 F.3d 43 (2d Cir.1997) (affirming fees award of 33 cents where only nominal damages were recovered); *Cartwright v. Stamper*, 7 F.3d 106 (7th Cir.1993) (fees

In *Carey v. Piphus*,[25] the Court had found that nominal damages must be available for deprivations of "absolute" rights like procedural due process because of "the importance to organized society that those rights be scrupulously observed." After *Farrar*, however, it is difficult to understand how, where there is little or no actual economic or emotional injury, the Court contemplates that such rights will be enforced if attorney's fees are only theoretically and not practically available to plaintiffs who successfully prosecute suits for their violation.[26] One possibility is that lower courts will limit *Farrar* to its facts: no jury specification of the constitutional right violated and no specific jury finding that the defendant's conduct caused the plaintiff's (nominal) damages. In one case, for example, a jury specifically found that a municipality's policy regarding excessive police force resulted in $1 of harm to an otherwise unsympathetic plaintiff, and the city disciplined an officer and modified its policy during the litigation. Upholding a fee award of $66,535, the appellate court distinguished *Farrar*, concluding that the finding benefitted the department and the community and might have collateral estoppel effect in subsequent litigation.[27] These distinctions, however, seem a thin evasion of *Farrar*. Plaintiffs could create them routinely by requesting special interrogatories concerning the right violated and causation, and the jury would presumably find causation whenever it awarded damages, even nominal ones. Another evasive tactic has been specifically rebuffed: if the plaintiff's lawyer first asks for nominal damages at the end of trial, when things look bleak for his client, the plaintiff who then recovers $1, while technically prevailing, will fail to recover fees by virtue of *Farrar*.[28] But a small damages award is not necessarily conclusive on the issue of fees. Because there is no federal small claims court and no amount in controversy requirement in civil rights cases, the Seventh Circuit instructs courts to determine whether the plaintiff aimed high and fell short, in which case *Farrar* may deprive the prevailing plaintiff of a fee,[29] or whether it was simply a

denied because $5 nominal damages award so "de minimis" that plaintiff's success on several claims would have little deterrent effect).

25. *See* 435 U.S. at 266, 98 S.Ct. at 1054.

26. *See Barber v. T. D. Williamson*, 254 F.3d 1223 (10th Cir.2001) (plaintiff must succeed on significant issue and that issue must be important in the *Farrar* sense, that is relative to all issues decided; fees may not be awarded based solely on the absent importance of an issue on which plaintiff succeeded (Title VII case)). Fees might fail in this situation either because an award of nominal damages may be trivial in relation to the relief originally sought or because no nominal damages may be recoverable. *See, e.g., Kerr–Selgas v. American Airlines, Inc.*, 69 F.3d 1205 (1st Cir. 1995) (nominal damages must be timely requested before a jury retires). *Cf. Walker v. Anderson Elec. Connectors*, 944 F.2d 841 (11th Cir.1991) (a finding of a Title VII violation does not mandate an award of nominal damages, and therefore, if plaintiff achieves no other relief, does not qualify the plaintiff for prevailing party status), *cert. denied*, 506 U.S. 1078, 113 S.Ct. 1043, 122 L.Ed.2d 352 (1993). *But cf. Hashimoto v. Dalton*, 118 F.3d 671 (9th Cir.1997) (distinguishing *Walker* as a case where plaintiff only technically prevailed, and awarding fees, where plaintiff recovered non-economic relief in the form of an administrative order by EEOC directing defendant to take measures to prevent future instances of retaliation).

27. *Wilcox v. City of Reno*, 42 F.3d 550 (9th Cir.1994).

28. *Romberg v. Nichols*, 48 F.3d 453 (9th Cir.1995).

29. *Cole v. Wodziak*, 169 F.3d 486 (7th Cir.1999) (approving sharp reduction of fee

small claim and was tried accordingly.[30] Other courts resist a literal adherence to *Farrar*, awarding fees even where plaintiff's monetary recovery falls many multiples short of what she sought.[31] These courts follow Justice O'Connor's *Farrar* concurrence in weighing the difference between the judgment sought and that obtained, the significance of the legal issue on which plaintiff prevailed, and the lawsuit's public purpose.[32] Other lower courts, at the opposite end of the spectrum, indulge a virtually insuperable presumption that the only reasonable fee to the prevailing party is zero where plaintiff recovers nominal damages alone after having sought compensatory and/or punitive damages initially.[33]

Another possibility, somewhat uncertain, is that the recovery of nominal damages may permit the § 1983 plaintiff to recover punitive damages otherwise warranted by a malicious or aggravated violation of procedural due process.[34] But is there a more reliable general incentive for a lawyer to pursue a § 1983 case involving an "ordinary" constitutional or federal statutory violation in what promises to be a case of "mixed motives"—that is, where she anticipates that the defendant could carry the *Mt. Healthy City School District Bd. of Education v. Doyle*[35] burden of demonstrating that it would have subjected the plaintiff to the same loss or deprivation for a lawful reason or reasons wholly independent of a substantial federally unlawful motive? In those cases there is probably[36] no constitutional or federal statutory "violation," and hence no possible monetary relief on the merits or, accordingly, attorney's fees.

On the other hand, what if the plaintiff from the outset seeks no compensatory or punitive damages, only declaratory relief or an injunc-

where plaintiffs recovered less than 10% of what they demanded).

30. *See Hyde v. Small*, 123 F.3d 583 (7th Cir.1997), *appeal after remand* 139 F.3d 901 (7th Cir.1998) ($500 compensatory damages award did not, by itself, justify denial of fees).

31. *See Brandau v. State of Kansas*, 168 F.3d 1179 (10th Cir.), *cert. denied*, 526 U.S. 1133, 119 S.Ct. 1808, 143 L.Ed.2d 1012 (1999), and cases cited therein.

32. *Id. See also Connolly v. National School Bus Serv., Inc.* 177 F.3d 593, 597 (7th Cir.1999) (employing the three factor test set forth by Justice O'Connor in *Farrar*). Under this test, the court should "look at the difference between the judgment and the recovery sought, the significance of the legal issues on which the plaintiff prevailed and finally, the public purpose served by the litigation" *Id.* (quoting *Cartwright v. Stamper*, 7 F.3d 106, 109 (7th Cir.1993)). "The standard is whether the fees are reasonable in relation to the difficulty, stakes, and outcome of the case." *Id.* (quoting *Bankston v. State of Illinois*, 60 F.3d 1249, 1256 (7th Cir.1995)). The Eighth Circuit explicitly applies the three factors outlined by Justice O'Connor: 1) the difference between amount sought and amount recovered, 2) significance of the legal issue on which plaintiff prevailed, and 3) any resulting public goal or purpose served. *Murray v. City of Onawa, Iowa*, 323 F.3d 616 (8th Cir.2003) (upholding fee award, reasoning that discrepancy between $500,000 plaintiff sought and the $1 she received was "not an outrageous split.")

33. *See, e.g., Pouillon v. Little*, 326 F.3d 713 (6th Cir.2003); *Johnson v. City of Aiken*, 278 F.3d 333, 338 (4th Cir.2002).

34. *See* discussion in Chapter 2 on remedies in § 1983 "mixed motive" cases governed by *Mt. Healthy*.

35. 429 U.S. 274, 97 S.Ct. 568, 50 L.Ed.2d 471 (1977). *Mt. Healthy* and its relation to damages is discussed in Chapter 2 on § 1983.

36. But see the contrary argument advanced in scholarly commentary that is discussed in § 2.25, *supra* concerning the effect of a *Mt. Healthy* showing on plaintiff's damages.

tion, and recovers one?[37] Has he not then achieved substantial, indeed entire success on the merits? And what if there are multiple claims? It is clear enough that a plaintiff's recovery of compensatory damages on fewer than all of the claims not only makes him technically prevailing but also entitles him to attorney's fees, although only with respect to the hours reasonably expended in pursuit of the successful claim or claims.[38] Or suppose the plaintiff prevails on several claims, obtaining only nominal damages on each? In this situation the Fifth Circuit has ruled that the plaintiff is not a prevailing party, arguably inconsistently with even the niggardly approach of *Farrar*.[39] The decisions struggle to define whether a plaintiff's "primary" goal was recovery of substantial monetary damages or merely injunctive relief to vindicate constitutional rights; if the former, then a "reasonable" fee may be nothing at all where the defendant's conduct is altered but no monetary relief is obtained.[40]

Farrar left unresolved a related question: can one become a prevailing party without having obtained, in the Supreme Court's words, a "consent decree, enforceable judgment or settlement," but simply because the filing of a lawsuit proved to be the "catalyst" that brought about some of the lawsuit's objectives? This theory would require the plaintiff to prove that the legal action is causally linked to the relief obtained by settlement or defendant's unilateral action,[41] and that the

37. *See, e.g., Phelps v. Hamilton*, 120 F.3d 1126 (10th Cir.1997) (where plaintiffs' suit resulted in the invalidation of a state statute and led to legislative action to correct the constitutional infirmity, success was not merely technical, and fees must be awarded). *See also Owner–Operator Indep. Drivers Ass'n, Inc. v. Bissell*, 210 F.3d 595, 598–99 (6th Cir.2000) (even where plaintiff gains only a declaratory judgment plaintiff can recover fees as prevailing party).

38. *See Blum v. Stenson*, 465 U.S. 886, 104 S.Ct. 1541, 79 L.Ed.2d 891 (1984); *cf. Texas State Teachers Ass'n v. Garland Indep. Sch. Dist.*, 489 U.S. 782, 790–91, 109 S.Ct. 1486, 1486–1492, 103 L.Ed.2d 866 (1989) (litigant need not prevail on all issues or even central issue, only a significant one, to prevail). *See also Morales v. San Rafael, Calif.*, 96 F.3d 359 (9th Cir.1996), *amended on denial of rehearing*, 108 F.3d 981 (9th Cir.1997) (where plaintiff suffered dismissal of § 1983 claim against municipal defendant but recovered more than $17,000 from individual police officer, *Farrar* inapplicable because those damages are not nominal, even though they were far less than plaintiff sought); *Stivers v. Pierce*, 71 F.3d 732, 751 (9th Cir.1995) (despite *Farrar*, plaintiff is prevailing party even though only partially successful in obtaining the relief or benefit sought through the litigation). See text *infra*, respecting the circumstances warranting fee reduction where plaintiff has not prevailed on all claims.

39. *Peters v. Polk County Mem'l Hosp.*, 7 F.3d 229 (5th Cir.1993) (unpublished opinion), *cert. denied*, 513 U.S. 807, 115 S.Ct. 53, 130 L.Ed.2d 13 (1994).

40. Compare *Cramblit v. Fikse*, 33 F.3d 633 (6th Cir.1994) (per curiam) (plaintiff deemed to have fallen short of ultimate monetary goals and hence is denied fees) *with Friend v. Kolodzieczak*, 72 F.3d 1386 (9th Cir.1995), *cert. denied*, 516 U.S. 1146, 116 S.Ct. 1016, 134 L.Ed.2d 96 (1996) (inmate plaintiffs awarded substantial fees after settlement expanding their access to religious services and sacraments upon court's determination that their "primary" goal was an injunction).

41. When the catalyst theory prevailed in the circuits, a defendant could not defeat a plaintiff's right to attorneys' fees by taking steps to moot the case after the plaintiff obtained the relief he sought, for in such a case mootness does not alter the plaintiff's status as a prevailing party. *See, e.g., Young v. City of Chicago*, 202 F.3d 1000 (7th Cir. 2000); *Morris v. West Palm Beach, Fla.*, 194 F.3d 1203, 1207 (11th Cir.1999); *National Black Police Ass'n v. District of Columbia Board of Elections & Ethics*, 168 F.3d 525, 528–29 (D.C.Cir.1999); *Associated General Contractors of Connecticut, Inc. v. City of*

defendant's change in position was required by law and not merely gratuitous.[42]

In a stunning 5–4 decision that caught analysts and civil rights lawyers off guard, the Supreme Court, rejecting the view of twelve of the thirteen circuit courts that had ruled on the question,[43] held in *Buckhannon Board and Care Home, Inc. v. West Virginia Dep't of Health and Human Resources*[44] that even a plaintiff who demonstrates that his suit for injunctive relief was the "catalyst" for the defendant's "voluntary" midsuit abandonment or modification of a challenged practice is not a "prevailing party" within the meaning of federal fee-shifting statutes, and so is ineligible for court-ordered attorneys' fees, unless he is awarded some *judicial* relief. Relying on a Black's Law Dictionary definition of "prevailing party" in preference to the Webster's Third New International Dictionary definition of "prevail" relied on by the dissent, the majority ruled that the plaintiff must receive a "judgment" or "some relief by the court" to fit within the statutory term "prevailing party." Although the holding technically extends only to actions under the Fair Housing Amendments Act and the Americans With Disabilities Act, circuit courts, consistent with language in *Buckhannon*, have extended the *Buckhannon* holding to actions under any of the Reconstruction Civil Rights Acts, notably Section 1983, under which prevailing parties are eligible for fees pursuant to the Civil Rights Attorneys' Fees Act of 1976, 42 U.S.C.A. § 1988,[45] as well as to the contemporary employment dis-

New Haven, 41 F.3d 62, 68 and n. 9 (2d Cir.1994); *Martinez v. Wilson*, 32 F.3d 1415, 1422 n. 8 (9th Cir.1994); *Dahlem v. Board of Education*, 901 F.2d 1508, 1512 (10th Cir.1990); *Grano v. Barry*, 783 F.2d 1104, 1108–09 (D.C.Cir.1986); *Bishop v. Committee on Professional Ethics*, 686 F.2d 1278, 1289–91 (8th Cir.1982).

42. *See, e.g., Owner–Operator Indep. Drivers Ass'n, Inc. v. Bissell*, 210 F.3d 595, 597–98 (6th Cir.2000); *Payne v. Board of Educ.*, 88 F.3d 392, 397 (6th Cir.1996); *Johnston v. Jago*, 691 F.2d 283, 286 (6th Cir.1982).

43. Compare *S–1 v. State Bd. of Educ. of North Carolina*, 21 F.3d 49 (4th Cir. 1994), *cert. denied*, 513 U.S. 876, 115 S.Ct. 205, 130 L.Ed.2d 135 (1994) (rejecting catalyst theory) *with Morris v. West Palm Beach, Fla.*, 194 F.3d 1203, 1207 (11th Cir. 1999); *Payne v. Board of Education, Cleveland City Schools*, 88 F.3d 392, 397 & n. 2 (6th Cir.1996); *Stivers v. Pierce*, 71 F.3d 732, 751–52, 753 n. 10 (9th Cir.1995); *Marbley v. Bane*, 57 F.3d 224, 234 (2d Cir. 1995); *Zinn v. Shalala*, 35 F.3d 273, 276 (7th Cir.1994); *Beard v. Teska*, 31 F.3d 942, 951 (10th Cir.1994); *Baumgartner v. Harrisburg Housing Authority*, 21 F.3d 541, 548–50 (3d Cir.1994); *Little Rock Sch. Dist. v. Pulaski County Special Sch. Dist.*, 17 F.3d 260, 263 & n. 2 (8th Cir.1994); *Craig v. Gregg County, Tex.*, 988 F.2d 18, 20–21 (5th Cir.1993); *Paris v. U.S. Dept. of Housing and Urban Dev.*, 988 F.2d 236, 238 (1st Cir.1993). *See also Wilcox v. City of Reno*, 42 F.3d 550 (9th Cir.1994) (arrestee who was punched in the face by a police officer held entitled to attorney's fees, although he received only nominal damages, because the litigation also led to the city's disciplining of the officer and modifying its policy governing the use of force); *Dunn v. The Florida Bar*, 889 F.2d 1010 (11th Cir.1989) (where defendants had the ability to change their unlawful behavior but failed to do so until faced with litigation, plaintiff can recover fees under the catalyst theory). *Cf. New Hampshire v. Adams*, 159 F.3d 680 (1st Cir.1998) (denying fees upon finding that IDEA proceedings were not the catalyst for a settlement affording plaintiff additional services).

44. 532 U.S. 598, 121 S.Ct. 1835, 149 L.Ed.2d 855 (2001).

45. *See, e.g., National Home Equity Mortgate Ass'n v. Face*, 322 F.3d 802 (4th Cir.2003) (in § 1983 "and laws" action, *Buckhannon* definition of "prevailing party" applies); *Habich v. City of Dearborn*, 331 F.3d 524 (6th Cir.2003) (remanding for determination of "prevailing party" status in action under § 1983); *Federation of Ad-*

crimination statutes,[46] and other civil rights statutes like the Individuals With Disabilities Education Act.[47] Indeed, a growing consensus has developed that *Buckhannon* applies to fee awards under any statute with "prevailing party" language,[48] but not to awards under statutes that hinge recovery of fees on other language, in particular "whenever . . . appropriate."[49]

The majority did agree that settlements enforced through consent decrees, as well as formal determinations of liability on the merits, will count as judicial relief qualifying the plaintiff for prevailing party status, because each effects a court-ordered change in the legal relationship between the parties.[50] Absent those formal judicial rulings, circuit courts are somewhat at sea as to what judicial involvement is necessary. And it suggested that the defendant's mid-litigation cessation of a practice sought to be enjoined will not moot the case by depriving the court of jurisdiction to determine the legality of the challenged practice "unless it is 'absolutely clear that the allegedly wrongful behavior could not reasonably be expected to recur.' " But the plaintiff whose suit results in the defendant's "voluntary" abandonment or modification of the practice at issue must not rest there and simply move for attorneys' fees, for

vertising Industry Representatives, Inc. v. City of Chicago, 326 F.3d 924 (7th Cir.2003) (plaintiff in § 1983 action failed to obtain enforceable judgment on merits or other court-ordered relief withstanding appeal and therefore not "prevailing party" within meaning of § 1988 as construed in *Buckhannon*); *Cody v. Hillard*, 304 F.3d 767 (8th Cir.2002) (finding that plaintiff achieved "prevailing party" status respecting § 1988 after underlying action under § 1983); *Watson v. County of Riverside*, 300 F.3d 1092 (9th Cir.2002) (same); *Richardson v. Miller,* 279 F.3d 1, 4–5 (1st Cir.2002); *Chambers v. Ohio Dep't of Human Servs.*, 273 F.3d 690, 693 (6th Cir.2001) (class plaintiffs in § 1983 action denied fees even though suit prompted state to modify regulations and notice requirements where those modifications were implemented prior to any court adjudication); *Johnson v. ITT Aerospace/Communications Div. of ITT Indus., Inc.*, 272 F.3d 498, 500 (7th Cir.2001); *N.Y. State Fed'n of Taxi Drivers, Inc. v. Westchester County Taxi and Limousine Comm'n,* 272 F.3d 154, 158 (2d Cir.2001) (§ 1983); *Griffin v. Steeltek, Inc.*, 261 F.3d 1026, 1029 (10th Cir.2001) (ADA); *Johnson v. Rodriguez,* 260 F.3d 493, 495 (5th Cir. 2001) (§ 1983); *Bennett v. Yoshina,* 259 F.3d 1097, 1100–01 (9th Cir.2001) (§ 1983).

46. *Johnson v. ITT Aerospace/Communications Div. of ITT Indus., Inc.,* 272 F.3d 498, 500 (7th Cir.2001) (Title VII).

47. *John T. ex rel. Paul T. v. Del. County Intermediate Unit*, 318 F.3d 545 (3d Cir.2003); *J.C. v. Regional Sch. Dist. 10,* 278 F.3d 119, 124–25 (2d Cir.2002) (under IDEA, where school developed IEP in response to administrative appeal by student, plaintiff was not entitled to fees as relief was not court-sanctioned).

48. *See, e.g., Thomas v. National Science Foundation*, 330 F.3d 486 (D.C.Cir. 2003) (Equal Access to Justice Act); *Perez-Arellano v. Smith*, 279 F.3d 791, 794 (9th Cir.2002) (Equal Access to Justice Act); *Smyth v. Rivero*, 282 F.3d 268, 274 (4th Cir.2002); *Crabill v. Trans Union, L.L.C.*, 259 F.3d 662, 667 (7th Cir.2001) (Fair Credit Reporting Act). *See generally "Does Buckhannon Apply? An Analysis of Judicial Application and Extension of the Supreme Court Decision Eighteen Months After and Beyond,"* 13 *Duke Environmental Law & Policy Forum* (2002).

49. *See, e.g., Sierra Club v. Environmental Protection Agency*, 322 F.3d 718 (D.C. Cir.2003) (declining to apply *Buckhannon* to Clean Air Act); *Loggerhead Turtle v. County Council of Volusia County, Florida*, 307 F.3d 1318 (11th Cir.2002) (same as to Endangered Species Act); *Center for Biological Diversity v. Norton*, 262 F.3d 1077, 1080 n. 2 (10th Cir.2001) (raising issue sua sponte and reaching same conclusion).

50. *See Cody v. Hillard*, 304 F.3d 767 (8th Cir.2002) (court-ordered consent decree is "clearly" the kind of judicially sanctioned change that qualifies plaintiff as prevailing party under *Buckhannon*).

she has not yet obtained "judicial" relief.[51] Instead she must, in the words of the dissent, "wage total law" and "litigate on and on" until she receives judicial confirmation that the practice the defendant abandoned or altered was in fact unlawful.

The ruling should have little practical consequence in damage-only cases, since no change in a defendant's challenged practices can moot such a case.[52] But the settlement posture of plaintiff's counsel is drastically affected to the extent her client seeks declaratory or injunctive relief. The ruling pressures plaintiff's counsel in such cases to negotiate for attorney fees at the same time she negotiates for relief accruing only to her client, raising the specter of conflict with the client's interests. Or she could attempt to lessen client conflicts by negotiating on behalf of her client alone but insisting as a condition of settlement that any resulting agreement be embodied in a consent decree or consent judgment[53]—which clearly qualify under *Buckhannon* for "prevailing party" status[54] and hence for court-ordered fee eligibility. But if the defendant is unwilling to have an agreement providing relief to the plaintiff memorialized in a court order or judgment, plaintiff and plaintiff's counsel run the risk of losing any statutory fee award if they reach a partial settlement not inclusive of fees. The circuits are split on the degree of judicial memorialization or enforcement of a private settlement that qualifies plaintiff as a "prevailing party" in the wake of *Buckhannon*.[55]

51. *Johnson v. Rodriguez,* 260 F.3d 493 (5th Cir.2001) (per curiam) (applying *Buckhannon*).

52. But if damages are denied by judicial order, plaintiff is not a prevailing party eligible for fees just because plaintiff sought damages at the outset of the action. *Federation of Advertising Industry Representatives, Inc. v. City of Chicago*, 326 F.3d 924, 929 (7th Cir.2003).

53. The Third Circuit lists several characteristics that can be used to distinguish between a stipulated settlement (and thus vulnerable to *Buckhannon*) and a court-sanctioned settlement: whether the agreement (1) "contains mandatory language;" (2) is entitled "Order," (3) bears the signature of the District Court judge, not the parties' counsel; and (4) allows for the right to request judicial enforcement of the settlement. *Truesdell v. Philadelphia Housing Auth.*, 290 F.3d 159, 165 (3d Cir. 2002).

54. It appears that *Buckhannon* applies only to those cases where it is disputed whether plaintiff is a prevailing party, and has no impact on the amount of fees to be awarded to a plaintiff who is clearly prevailing. *See, e.g., Villano v. City of Boynton Beach*, 254 F.3d 1302 (11th Cir.2001) (deciding only amount of fees and not mentioning *Buckhannon*).

55. Compare *Smalbein ex rel. Estate of Smalbein v. City of Daytona Beach*, 353 F.3d 901 (11th Cir. 2003) (per curiam) (settlement agreement made estate prevailing party because its terms were incorporated into a dismissal order that retained jurisdiction for enforcement purposes); *Richard S. v. Dep't of Developmental Services of State of California*, 317 F.3d 1080 (9th Cir.2003) (settlement agreement makes plaintiff "prevailing party" because it was "enforceable"); *Fish v. St. Cloud University*, 295 F.3d 849 (8th Cir.2002) (noting *Buckhannon* but relying on pre-*Buckhannon* circuit authority that relief through settlement makes plaintiffs "prevailing parties"); *American Disability Association, Inc. v. Chmielarz*, 289 F.3d 1315, 1320 (11th Cir. 2002) (either incorporation of settlement's terms into final court order, or express judicial retention of jurisdiction to enforce settlement gives necessary judicial imprimatur for "prevailing party" status); *with Christina A. v. Bloomberg* 315 F.3d 990 (8th Cir.2003) (reversing fee award even though court approved settlement agreement and retained jurisdiction); *Christina A. ex rel. Jennifer A. v. Bloomberg*, 315 F.3d 990 (8th Cir.2003) (settlement agreement in class action did not confer prevailing party status, even though settlement approved by court and court retained jurisdiction to enforce agreement, because only remedies for en-

It has been argued that the *Farrar* limitation, while applicable to all cases under the Reconstruction civil rights acts, is wholly inapplicable to "mixed-motive" cases under Title VII or the ADA. The argument is based on Section 706(g)(2)(B), added by the 1991 Civil Rights Act, which specifically authorizes an award of attorney's fees under those statutes even when the employer makes the "same-decision" showing—that is, where the plaintiff has had only partial success.[56] But an appellate court has rejected that argument, observing that both the decision to award and the amount of attorney's fees are discretionary under Section 706(g)(2)(B) just as under Section 1988, the provision construed in *Farrar*. And it wrote that plaintiff's rejection of a settlement offer is one factor the court may take into account in deciding the appropriate amount of a fee award.[57]

Recoverability of fees for services performed in a preliminary administrative proceeding depends in part on whether the proceeding is optional or mandatory. If the state or local administrative proceeding is mandated, as it is under Title VII, fees for legal services performed in that hearing can be recovered in an independent Title VII action. This is because the state or local administrative proceedings in a deferral state, and the EEOC proceedings in any state, qualify as a "proceeding under this subchapter" within the meaning of Title VII § 706(k).[58] If the prior administrative hearing is optional, however, fees are generally not awarded because such a hearing is not considered an "action or proceed-

forcement would be breach of contract action or reinstatement of lawsuit, not contempt); *J.C. v. Regional Sch. Dist. 10*, 278 F.3d 119, 124–25 (2d Cir.2002) (only consent decrees and judicial orders qualify); *Richardson v. Miller*, 279 F.3d 1, 4 (1st Cir. 2002) (district court's brokering of private agreement did not represent adjudication or approval, so plaintiff did not prevail).

56. Section 706(g)(2)(B) is codified at 42 U.S.C.A. § 2000e–5(g)(2)(B). *See Gudenkauf v. Stauffer Communications, Inc.*, 158 F.3d 1074 (10th Cir.1998) (plaintiff who prevails in a mixed motive case should ordinarily be awarded attorney's fees in all but special circumstances despite inability to recover money damages or obtain injunctive relief).

57. *Sheppard v. Riverview Nursing Ctr.*, 88 F.3d 1332 (4th Cir.1996), *cert. denied*, 519 U.S. 993, 117 S.Ct. 483, 136 L.Ed.2d 377 (1996) (also considering such factors as why other relief was not awarded, what public purposes where served, how ubiquitous and wrongful the defendant's conduct was, and the strength of the discriminatory motive and other motives—such as unsatisfactory actions of the employee—in influencing the termination decision, even though both played a part in it). *See also Norris v. Sysco Corp.*, 191 F.3d 1043, 1050–51 (9th Cir.1999), *cert. denied* 528 U.S. 1182, 120 S.Ct. 1221, 145 L.Ed.2d 1121 (2000) (affirming award of attorney's fees in failure to promote claim where defendant proved that it would not have promoted plaintiff absent the unlawful reason); *Akrabawi v. Carnes Co.*, 152 F.3d 688 (7th Cir.1998) (denying attorney's fees where jury found discrimination but employer carried same decision showing); *Canup v. Chipman–Union, Inc.*, 123 F.3d 1440 (11th Cir.1997) (disallowing attorney's fees in mixed motive case). *But see Garcia v. City of Houston*, 201 F.3d 672 (5th Cir.2000) (rejecting Fourth Circuit approach and agreeing with *Gudenkauf* that attorneys' fees be awarded in mixed-motive cases in all but special circumstances, and that the plaintiff's role in helping to end unlawful discrimination in the workplace be weighed heavily).

58. *New York Gaslight Club, Inc. v. Carey*, 447 U.S. 54, 100 S.Ct. 2024, 64 L.Ed.2d 723 (1980). *See also Jones v. American State Bank*, 857 F.2d 494 (8th Cir. 1988) (extending *Carey* to allow fees for pre-suit administrative work even where the subsequent suit seeks only that remedy and no relief on the merits). *But see Chris v. Tenet*, 221 F.3d 648 (4th Cir.2000), *cert. denied* 531 U.S. 1191, 121 S.Ct. 1189, 149 L.Ed.2d 105 (2001) (holding *contra Jones*).

ing to enforce" civil rights under the language of § 1988. For example, because a plaintiff is not required to exhaust his administrative remedies before bringing a § 1983 action,[59] services performed in administrative proceedings on § 1983 claims are not compensable under § 1988.[60] Sometimes, however, where the administrative work is "useful and of a type ordinarily necessary to advance the civil rights litigation," fees may be awarded.[61] In *Pennsylvania v. Delaware Valley Citizens' Council for Clean Air*,[62] the Court applied this exception so as to allow fees.[63] The *Delaware I* Court found that post-judgment administrative proceedings, held to enforce a consent decree, were "crucial to the vindication of [plaintiff's] rights," and concluded that the attorney's services performed for those proceedings were compensable.

But it remains unsettled whether, or under what circumstances, a plaintiff who achieves complete merits relief through settlement or decision in pre-litigation administrative proceedings may pursue a judicial action seeking only compensation for the attorney's fees she incurred in the pre-suit proceedings. After all, in the leading case upholding an action for fees incurred in prior administrative proceedings under Title VII, *New York Gaslight Club, Inc. v. Carey*,[64] the plaintiff's action for fees was coupled with a claim on the merits. Yet the Eighth Circuit subsequently extended *Carey* to encompass Title VII actions brought solely to recover fees incurred in prior administrative proceedings. In *Jones v. American State Bank*,[65] the parties settled plaintiff's pregnancy discrimination claim during the administrative proceedings, but the state deferral agency denied attorney's fees as unavailable under state law. The Eighth Circuit affirmed the federal district court's award of fees

59. *See Patsy v. Florida Bd. of Regents*, 457 U.S. 496, 102 S.Ct. 2557, 73 L.Ed.2d 172 (1982).

60. *Webb v. Dyer County Bd. of Educ.*, 471 U.S. 234, 105 S.Ct. 1923, 85 L.Ed.2d 233 (1985). *See also Duello v. University of Wisc. Bd. of Regents*, 176 Wis.2d 961, 501 N.W.2d 38 (1993) (fees incurred in connection with successful internal grievance procedure not compensable under § 706(k) of Title VII).

61. *Webb,* 471 U.S. 234, 105 S.Ct. 1923, 85 L.Ed.2d 233.

62. 478 U.S. 546, 106 S.Ct. 3088, 92 L.Ed.2d 439 (1986) ("*Delaware I*") (applying § 304(d) of the Clean Air Act).

63. *In Brooks v. Georgia State Bd. of Elections,* 997 F.2d 857 (11th Cir.1993), the court awarded a plaintiff fees with respect to his attorney's preclearance work under § 5 of the Voting Rights Act of 1965 before the United States Justice Department, where the district court conditioned plaintiff's remedy on the results of those administrative proceedings. The court considered the preclearance work "useful and ordinarily necessary to the litigation" within the meaning of *Webb* because the judicial decision turned on the preclearance outcome. 987 F.2d at 860. It also relaxed the *Delaware I* requirement that the administrative legal work be "crucial" to the vindication of adjudicated rights "to mean not much more than that it be relevant to those rights and related to terms of the judgment." *Id.* at 864. For similar reasons, post-judgment monitoring of consent decrees by means of related litigation, even in distinct actions, is compensable under § 1988. *See Delaware I,* 478 U.S. at 559–60, 106 S.Ct. at 3095; *Cody v. Hillard*, 304 F.3d 767 (8th Cir.2002); *Mills v. Freeman*, 118 F.3d 727, 733–34 (11th Cir.1997); *Eirhart v. Libbey–Owens–Ford Co.*, 996 F.2d 846 (7th Cir.1993); *Miller v. Carson,* 628 F.2d 346, 348 (5th Cir. 1980). *Cf. Armstrong v. Davis*, 318 F.3d 965 (9th Cir.2003) (prisoners who prevailed on Americans With Disabilities Act claims also received fee award for work their counsel performed in defending a judgment involving identical issues in separate litigation).

64. 447 U.S. 54, 100 S.Ct. 2024, 64 L.Ed.2d 723 (1980).

65. 857 F.2d 494 (8th Cir.1988).

under Section 706(k). It reasoned that because, as the Supreme Court stressed repeatedly in *Carey*, the state deferral agency proceeding was mandated by Title VII and complementary to the federal statutory scheme, the administrative proceeding constituted an "action or proceeding" for which fees might be awarded within the meaning of § 706(k).

In so holding, the Eighth Circuit treated *Jones* as distinguishable from a post-*Carey* Supreme Court decision, *North Carolina Department of Transportation v. Crest Street Community Council*.[66] There the Supreme Court erected a distinct barrier to recovering attorney's fees for services performed in optional administrative proceedings followed by fees-only lawsuits under any of the *civil rights* statutes for which fees are recoverable under *42 U.S.C.A. § 1988*. The plaintiffs in *Crest* objected to racially discriminatory aspects of the state's plan for a new highway, alleging that the plan violated Title VI,[67] one of the statutes listed in § 1988. The state transportation department agreed that the plan would constitute a prima facie violation of Title VI, and the parties ultimately negotiated a compromise plan. But the agreement made no provision for attorney's fees, other than to reserve plaintiff's rights to them, so the plaintiffs later instituted an action under § 1988 for fees incurred during the state proceedings and ensuing negotiations. The Court in *Crest* held that, regardless of whether negotiations following the filing of an optional administrative complaint under Title VI are themselves "proceedings to enforce" that statute, § 1988 does not authorize the recovery of fees incurred in *any* pre-suit administrative proceedings unless a judicial action is filed that also seeks relief on the merits.[68]

The Court in *Crest* relied on language in § 1988, absent from Section 706(k) of Title VII, stipulating that fees may be awarded only "in the action or proceeding to enforce" the listed civil rights laws, including Title VI. It concluded that the judicial action in which fees are sought, and not just the pre-litigation administrative agency proceedings for which they are sought, must qualify as an "action or proceeding to enforce a provision" of Title VI (or any of the other civil rights statutes listed in § 1988).[69] And it further concluded that a judicial action for fees

66. 479 U.S. 6, 107 S.Ct. 336, 93 L.Ed.2d 188 (1986).

67. Title VI of the Civil Rights Act of 1964, codified in 42 U.S.C.A. §§ 2000d—2000d–4a, prohibits discrimination based on race, color, or national origin in federally funded programs or activities.

68. In this respect *Crest* sweeps more broadly than an earlier post-*Carey* decision, *Webb v. Dyer County Board of Education*, 471 U.S. 234, 105 S.Ct. 1923, 85 L.Ed.2d 233 (1985). As observed above, in *Webb*, the court held that attorney's services performed in an optional state administrative proceeding invoked by the plaintiff before filing an action under *§ 1983* are not compensable under § 1988. The *Webb* opinion reasoned that the administrative proceeding conducted before the § 1983 judicial action was not itself a "proceeding to enforce" that statute (By contrast, *Crest* describes *Carey* as holding that "mandatory state employment discrimination proceedings *are* proceedings to enforce *Title VII*." 479 U.S. at 11 (emphasis added)). But *Webb* did not require, as *Crest* does, that the ensuing judicial action in which attorneys' fees are sought for services rendered in pre-suit administrative proceedings or negotiations must itself be a "proceeding to enforce"; nor does it require that to qualify as such a proceeding, the judicial action must invariably concern relief on the merits as well as fees.

69. *Crest*, 479 U.S. at 14, 107 S.Ct. at 341.

alone could not be considered an action "to enforce" such a provision. Accordingly, it insisted that *under § 1988*, an award of fees for pre-suit administrative agency work is authorized only if a party prevails on a *merits-based* claim under one of the referenced civil rights statutes in a *judicial action* filed concurrently with, or subsequent to, the administrative proceedings. *Crest* did, however, recognize that if the ensuing judicial action meets this definition of a "proceeding to enforce" a § 1988 statute, a court "may still award attorney's fees for time spent on administrative proceedings to enforce the civil rights claim prior to the litigation."[70] In fact, so long as the civil rights plaintiff files a judicial action seeking merits relief, she may recover in that action fees for whatever attorney's work at the administrative stage was "useful and of a type ordinarily necessary to advance the civil rights litigation to the stage it reached before settlement"—regardless of whether the underlying administrative proceeding is characterized as a "proceeding to enforce" one of the § 1988 statutes.[71]

Carey and *Crest* have distinctly variable tactical implications, recognized in those opinions. The prospective Title VII, ADEA, ADA or other employment discrimination plaintiff, operating under the *Carey* regime, may be less reluctant to reach a merits-only settlement at one or more of the mandated administrative stages, even if the parties fail to reach agreement as to fees. That is because *Carey* suggests, as *Jones* holds, that in a subsequent judicial action under those statutes she may seek fees alone. On the other hand, under the *Carey* opinion and *Jones* holding, prospective plaintiffs and their lawyers will feel less pressure to reach complete settlements in pre-suit proceedings under those statutes. By contrast, under *Crest*, prospective civil rights plaintiffs and their lawyers may bypass optional administrative proceedings entirely and resort immediately to suit unless they perceive a real possibility of advantageous and complete resolution, including fees, in a pre-suit forum. This tendency may be exacerbated by separate authority, discussed in Chapter 5, holding that adverse fact-findings by quasi-judicial administrative tribunals may have issue preclusive (collateral estoppel) effect in subsequent proceedings under § 1983.

That *Carey* survives *Crest* on *Carey*'s own facts—i.e., a Title VII judicial action combining a merits claim with the claim for fees—is supported even by a recent Fourth Circuit opinion that relies on *Crest* to reject the *Jones* extension of *Carey* to fees-only employment discrimination lawsuits. In *Chris v. Tenet,*[72] the court held that a fees-only action does not lie under § 706(k) of Title VII. The court reasoned that where a Title VII plaintiff sues for fees only, the trial court lacks subject matter jurisdiction to award fees. It explained that a special Title VII jurisdictional grant in § 706(f)(3) refers only to legal proceedings in a court of law to enforce the substantive guarantees of Title VII and does not extend to an action solely for fees incurred during Title VII administra-

70. *Id.* at 15.

71. *Id.* (quoting *Webb*, 471 U.S. at 243, 105 S.Ct. at 1928).

72. 221 F.3d 648 (4th Cir.2000).

tive proceedings. It also quoted the Supreme Court's observation in *Crest* that it is entirely reasonable to limit the award of attorney's fees to those parties who, in order to obtain relief, found it necessary to file a complaint in court.[73] But the Fourth Circuit did distinguish *Carey*, observing that the plaintiff there had originally sought merits relief in addition to attorney's fees.[74]

Indeed, there is much to be said for the Eighth Circuit view in *Jones* that *Carey* survives *Crest* even where the employment discrimination plaintiff does *not* seek relief on the merits, only fees for work done in prior proceedings. Not only does the Title VII fee provision, § 706(k), lack the "proceeding to enforce" language of § 1988; it mandates the plaintiff's prior resort to EEOC and, if available, state or local administrative proceedings. While the Supreme Court in *Crest* was critical of some of *Carey*'s policy justifications, the opinion sedulously refrains from overruling *Carey*, and for good reason: the textual and structural differences distinguishing Title VII from § 1988 with respect to fees are more fundamental and deserve greater decisional weight than *Carey*'s passing reference to policy. Further, while it is true, as the *Chris* opinion recounts, that the plaintiff in *Carey* initially presented a merits claim, the Supreme Court's opinion made little of that. Instead it stressed the permissive language of § 706(k)—allowing courts to award fees in "any action or proceeding under this subchapter"—and the Title VII mandate that putative plaintiffs initiate such proceedings in state or local antidiscrimination agencies and the EEOC.

Fees may be awarded *pendente lite* when a plaintiff achieves some durable interim relief on the merits,[75] for example an injunction that works some permanent change in the legal relations between the parties.[76] More generally the Supreme Court has approved the award of fees

73. *Id.* at 654 (quoting *Crest*, 479 U.S. at 14, 107 S.Ct. at 341).

74. *Chris*, 221 F.3d at 653–54.

75. But the award of interim fees is immediately appealable as a collateral order where the fees might not be recoverable by the defendant from the plaintiff if the award were reversed at the end of the litigation, so that refusal of an immediate appeal might inflict irreparable harm on the defendant. *People Who Care v. Rockford Board of Education*, 272 F.3d 936, 937 (7th Cir.2001); *Construction Industry Retirement Fund v. Kasper Trucking, Inc.*, 10 F.3d 465, 468 (7th Cir.1993); *Richardson v. Penfold*, 900 F.2d 116 (7th Cir.1990); *Palmer v. City of Chicago*, 806 F.2d 1316 (7th Cir.1986); *Law v. National Collegiate Athletic Ass'n*, 134 F.3d 1025, 1027 (10th Cir.1998); *Riverhead Savings Bank v. National Mortgage Equity Corp.*, 893 F.2d 1109, 1113–15 (9th Cir.1990); *Webster v. Sowders*, 846 F.2d 1032, 1035 (6th Cir.1988).

76. *See Hanrahan v. Hampton*, 446 U.S. 754, 100 S.Ct. 1987, 64 L.Ed.2d 670 (1980); *Murphy v. Fort Worth Ind. Sch. Dist.*, 334 F.3d 470 (5th Cir.2003) (per curiam) (high school student prevailed who obtained injunction against procedural due process violation). *Cf. Walker v. City of Mesquite, TX*, 313 F.3d 246 (5th Cir.2002) (plaintiffs who persuaded court to vacate central provision of remedial order they challenged held prevailing parties in action governed by fee provisions of § 1988); *Utility Automation 2000, Inc. v. Choctawhatchee Electric Cooperative, Inc.*, 298 F.3d 1238, 1248 (11th Cir.2002) (judgment pursuant to FRCP 68 has "necessary judicial *imprimatur*" to confer prevailing party status on plaintiff); *Gotro v. R & B Realty Group*, 69 F.3d 1485 (9th Cir.1995) (even contingent fee litigant who has not actually incurred the obligation to pay for his lawyer's work in obtaining remand of improperly removed case may recover those fees from the defendant as "actual expenses, including attorney's fees, incurred" within the meaning of 28 U.S.C.A. § 1447(c)).

pendente lite to a party who has obtained some relief on the merits at trial or on appeal.[77] But plaintiffs did not acquire prevailing party status by virtue of obtaining an injunction pending appeal that merely preserved the status quo in a circuit that determines the propriety of such injunctions principally by balancing the equities and harms attendant on granting or denying relief, rather than by weighing the merits.[78] And attorney's fees for preliminary injunctive relief have been denied where the injunction is ultimately reversed on appeal, the party having obtained that injunction then being regarded as not having prevailed.[79] After *Buckhannon*, there is dispute in the circuits as to whether a plaintiff who obtains only a preliminary injunction, even one that is unappealed or that survives appeal, is a "prevailing party" who has obtained some judicial relief that changes the legal relationship between the parties.[80]

Attorney's fees may be awarded for services necessary to implement or enforce a consent decree that resulted from earlier, successful litigation.[81] And a prevailing party may also recover, to the degree of her success, fees for services rendered in an unsuccessful judicial action if she ultimately prevails in a subsequent related judicial action.[82]

To calculate the amount of a "reasonable" award of attorney's fees the court must arrive first at a "lodestar" figure that represents a reasonable hourly rate[83] multiplied by the number of hours reasonably expended on matters on which the plaintiff prevailed.[84] Both the reason-

77. *Hewitt v. Helms*, 482 U.S. 755, 107 S.Ct. 2672, 96 L.Ed.2d 654 (1987). *But cf. District of Columbia v. Patterson*, 667 A.2d 1338 (D.C.App.1995), *cert. denied*, 519 U.S. 1058, 117 S.Ct. 688, 136 L.Ed.2d 612 (1997) (civil rights plaintiff who obtained hearing after seizure of property, but ultimately failed to show the unconstitutionality of the forfeiture statute that facilitated the seizure, and therefore did not recover the property or obtain any other tangible benefit of the kind she sought, not "prevailing party").

78. *LaRouche v. Kezer*, 20 F.3d 68 (2d Cir.1994).

79. *N.A.A.C.P. v. Detroit Police Officers Ass'n*, 46 F.3d 528 (6th Cir.1995). *See also Krocka v. City of Chicago*, 203 F.3d 507, 517–18 (7th Cir.2000); *Webb v. Ada County*, 195 F.3d 524 (9th Cir.1999) (denying fees despite plaintiff's victory at a preliminary stage of litigation where plaintiff ultimately lost); *Board of Educ. of Oak Park v. Nathan R.*, 199 F.3d 377, 382 (7th Cir.2000); *Hunger v. Leininger*, 15 F.3d 664, 670 (7th Cir.1994).

80. *Compare Habich v. City of Dearborn*, 331 F.3d 524 (6th Cir.2003) (concluding that a district judge's informal directive to defendant might make plaintiff "prevailing party" even though judge did not formally grant plaintiff's motion for preliminary injunction) and *Watson v. County of Riverside*, 300 F.3d 1092 (9th Cir.2002) (finding that plaintiff achieved "prevailing party" status by virtue of preliminary injunction despite failing to obtain other relief sought) *with Thomas v. National Science Foundation*, 330 F.3d 486 (D.C.Cir. 2003) (preliminary injunction that merely preserved status quo insufficient to enable plaintiff to prevail, because it was a mere "judicial pronouncement" of defendant's violation unaccompanied by "judicial relief") and *Smyth v. Rivero*, 282 F.3d 268, 274 (4th Cir.2002) (preliminary injunction not within *Buckhannon* requirement of an "enforceable judgment on the merits").

81. *Eirhart v. Libbey–Owens–Ford Co.*, 996 F.2d 846 (7th Cir.1993).

82. *Cabrales v. County of Los Angeles*, 935 F.2d 1050 (9th Cir.1991).

83. The rate employed by courts is the current market rate, not the rate at the onset of the litigation. *See, e.g., Lanni v. State of New Jersey*, 259 F.3d 146 (3d Cir. 2001).

84. *Blum v. Stenson*, 465 U.S. 886, 897, 104 S.Ct. 1541, 1548, 79 L.Ed.2d 891 (1984); *Hensley v. Eckerhart*, 461 U.S. 424, 103 S.Ct. 1933, 76 L.Ed.2d 40 (1983). *See*

able hours and reasonable rates questions are committed to the discretion of the district courts,[85] although elements of legal analysis integral to their decisions are reviewable de novo.[86] Fees sought by the plaintiff that are attributable to attorney time clearly devoted only to unsuccessful claims will be deducted from the overall request.[87] And a high number of hours in a case with a relatively modest claim for compensatory damages has been sharply reduced.[88] But where a party prevails on only one of multiple legal claims rooted in the same factual nucleus, fees should not be reduced automatically.[89] Instead, so long as the plaintiff has obtained "excellent" relief, he should recover a fully compensatory fee encompassing all hours reasonably expended on the litigation;[90] less than "excellent" but still "substantial" relief may warrant a fee reduc-

also Quaratino v. Tiffany & Co., 166 F.3d 422 (2d Cir.1999) (overturning district court's abandonment of lodestar approach); *Coutin v. Young & Rubicam Puerto Rico, Inc.*, 124 F.3d 331 (1st Cir.1997).

85. *See, e.g., Zuchel v. City and County of Denver*, 997 F.2d 730, 743 (10th Cir. 1993).

86. *See, e.g., Oviatt v. Pearce*, 954 F.2d 1470, 1481 (9th Cir.1992).

87. *See Green v. Torres*, 361 F.3d 96 (2d Cir. 2004) (per curiam) (approving 20% reduction from lodestar because claims withdrawn voluntarily shortly before trial lacked evidentiary support); *Gumbhir v. Curators of Univ. of Missouri*, 157 F.3d 1141 (8th Cir.1998) (requested attorney's fees were reduced by nearly 90% where plaintiff prevailed on only one claim with modest compensatory damages); *Daniel v. Loveridge*, 32 F.3d 1472 (10th Cir.1994).

88. *Gumbhir*, 157 F.3d at 1146.

89. *See Roberts v. Roadway Exp., Inc.*, 149 F.3d 1098 (10th Cir.1998) (fee award not subject to reduction where unsuccessful race claim was necessarily related to successful retaliation claim); *Jenkins v. Missouri*, 131 F.3d 716 (8th Cir.1997); *Shrader v. OMC Aluminum Boat Group, Inc.*, 128 F.3d 1218 (8th Cir.1997) (where successful claim is interrelated to unsuccessful claim, court should not separate hours spent on separate claims).

90. *See, e.g., Villano v. City of Boynton Beach*, 254 F.3d 1302 (11th Cir.2001) (where plaintiff succeeds on some claims, court must evaluate whether plaintiff had excellent success before deciding to reduce hours for unsuccessful claims). In *Villano*, the parties agreed that the plaintiff was a prevailing party and entitled to a reasonable award of fees and costs under 42 U.S.C.A. § 1988. The district court and magistrate reduced hours because Plaintiff had failed on a number of claims, including claims against a party that was dismissed. "The district court concluded that Appellant obtained only limited success and spent many hours on unsuccessful claims." The 11th Circuit reversed the reduction on this basis, holding that when the plaintiff has obtained "excellent results" overall, in light of what Plaintiff originally sought, "his attorney should recover a fully compensatory fee.... If the court determines that the result obtained was an excellent result, then the award of fees 'will encompass all hours reasonably expended on the litigation, and indeed in some cases of exceptional success an enhanced award may be justified.' [If] the results obtained are deemed excellent ... all hours reasonably expended are compensable. Whether hours were reasonably expended on litigation is a different question than whether hours were necessary to the litigation, the latter standard being the more exacting of the two." *Id.* at 1308 (quoting *Hensley*, 461 U.S. at 435). Further, in deciding whether the plaintiff has obtained excellent overall results, the Eleventh Circuit directs district judges to take into account "the vital role private litigation plays in the enforcement of civil rights, the difficulties involved in sustaining those lawsuits, the heightened importance of such lawsuits when the defendant is a public body, and the public benefit that occurs when those lawsuits ultimately vindicated a constitutional right." *Id.* at 1308. "Public benefit is a distinct measure of success in civil rights actions and was a central aim of Appellant's litigation." *Id.* at 1307. The Eleventh Circuit reversed the trial court's reduction of fees in part because the district judge and magistrate failed to take this special feature of civil rights actions into account. *See also Emery v. Hunt*, 272 F.3d 1042, 1047 (8th Cir.2001) (full award of fees appropriate even where plaintiff succeeded only on state law claims where both federal and state law claims rested on a common core of factual and legal issues).

tion in proportion to plaintiff's overall degree of success.[91] By not reducing the fee award simply because the plaintiff fails to prevail on every contention, this approach encourages plaintiff's counsel to advance alternative grounds for relief as authorized by F.R.C.P. 8(e). Similarly, time should not be deducted for unsuccessful but reasonable arguments made in support of a successful claim.[92]

The circuit courts appear to be in accord that time spent in establishing the prevailing party's entitlement to a fee award under § 1988 is itself compensable.[93] But such requests for "fees-on-fees" are themselves subject to reduction in proportion to the degree by which the "merits fees" award was discounted, as a percentage of merits fees claimed. For example, where plaintiffs recovered 87.2% of the fees claimed for work related to the underlying merits of the action, a reduction of 12.8%, their lodestar award for the fees incurred in petitioning for those fees was also disallowed by 12.8%.[94] The court distinguished a caution by the Supreme Court that merits fees should not be reduced simply because the trial court failed to reach or rejected alternative legal *grounds* (as opposed to *claims*) advanced by a prevailing plaintiff.[95] In fees-on-fees situations the prevailing plaintiff would have an incentive to gild the lily, and the losing defendant little incentive to challenge improper billing entries, if defendants had to pay 100% of the plaintiff's attorney's fee work in situations where one could reasonably expect only a modest trimming of the underlying award of merits fees.

Even with respect to claims on which the plaintiff prevailed, fees may not be awarded for hours that are "excessive, redundant, or

91. *Hensley v. Eckerhart,* 461 U.S. 424, 103 S.Ct. 1933, 76 L.Ed.2d 40 (1983); *Goos v. National Ass'n of Realtors,* 74 F.3d 300, 302 (D.C.Cir.1996). But the court may not calculate attorney fees by means of a purely mathematical comparison between the number of claims pressed and the number prevailed upon; rather, the appropriate inquiry concerns whether the claims on which the employee prevailed are related to those on which he or she did not. *Brodziak v. Runyon*, 145 F.3d 194 (4th Cir.1998). *See also Lanni v. State of New Jersey*, 259 F.3d 146 (3d Cir.2001) (reduction of 25% proper where plaintiff prevailed on only two of ten claims and against only two of nine defendants and the time spent pursuing the unsuccessful claims did not contribute in any way to plaintiff's success on remaining claims). *But see Sinajini v. Board of Educ. of San Juan Sch. Dist.*, 233 F.3d 1236 (10th Cir.2000) (rejecting lower court's finding that because plaintiff succeeded on only one of approximately 21 claims for relief, plaintiffs had achieved only limited success, and emphasizing that a lawsuit cannot be viewed as a series of discrete claims and lower courts should focus on the significance of the overall relief obtained by the plaintiff). Plaintiffs may be able to avoid this problem by drafting streamlined complaints.

92. *See Jaffee v. Redmond*, 142 F.3d 409 (7th Cir.1998).

93. *See, e.g., Thompson v. Pharmacy Corp. of America*, 334 F.3d 1242 (11th Cir. 2003) (abuse of discretion for district court to deny all fees for time prevailing party spent litigating fee issue, even though her attorney engaged in excessive and unnecessary work in seeking fees); *Villano v. City of Boynton Beach*, 254 F.3d 1302, 1304 (11th Cir.2001) (prevailing party entitled to reasonable compensation for litigating § 1988 award); *Jenkins v. Missouri*, 170 F.3d 846 (8th Cir.1999) (where plaintiff class prevailed on appeal and was awarded attorney's fees on appeal, class was entitled to attorney's fees for defending against defendant's petitions for rehearing of appeals); *Clark v. City of Los Angeles*, 803 F.2d 987, 992 (9th Cir.1986) (citing cases).

94. *Thompson v. Gomez,* 45 F.3d 1365 (9th Cir.1995).

95. *Id.* (citing *Hensley v. Eckerhart,* 461 U.S. 424, 103 S.Ct. 1933, 76 L.Ed.2d 40 (1983)).

otherwise unnecessary."[96] The court will carefully scrutinize plaintiff's counsel's time records in the post-judgment hearing, if any,[97] on attorney's fees to determine which hours were reasonably necessary to the outcome on successful claims.[98] Where EEOC successfully prosecuted a disparate treatment claim on behalf of the plaintiff, who joined the action to assert state law claims on which she did not prevail, a circuit court ruled that she was entitled to attorney's fees only with respect to the additional contribution, if any, by her attorney to the EEOC's successful efforts.[99] The court viewed most of the private attorney's services as redundant or unnecessary. But where, in another case, the court halved the hours for which compensation was requested to account for duplication in services rendered by plaintiff's two counsel, it was an abuse of discretion also to cut the rate of hourly compensation on the theory that "the actual rate was the combined rates" of each counsel: that "corrected twice for a single problem."[100]

The Court in *Blum v. Stenson*[101] held that the lodestar is based on market rates in the relevant community, and therefore fees awardable to nonprofit legal services organizations may not be limited to actual costs. Similarly, fee awards may compensate for the work of law clerks and paralegals, again at market rates.[102] To say that the lodestar rate is based on rates prevailing in the relevant community masks two difficult subissues: *which lawyer's* rate in a diverse legal community where lawyers of differing experience, special skills, and reputation enjoy different degrees of market power; and *which community's* rate where a lawyer from one community performs services in another with a significantly different prevailing market average. *Blum* seems to rest on the premise that the appropriate market rate for § 1988 purposes is "the opportunity cost of that time, the income foregone by [the lawyer in] representing this plaintiff."[103] It follows that an established billing rate

96. *Hensley v. Eckerhart*, 461 U.S. 424, 103 S.Ct. 1933, 76 L.Ed.2d 40 (1983). *See, e.g., Evans v. Port Auth. of N.Y. and N.J.*, 273 F.3d 346, 362 (3d Cir.2001) (fee award excessive where submissions disclosed multiple instances of duplicative billing by two partners for identical tasks); *Maldonado v. Houstoun*, (3d Cir.2001) (claims on 276.65 hours on appeal involving single, relatively uncomplicated issue reduced to 120 hours, where some attorneys had represented plaintiffs in district court).

97. Whether a hearing is held in connection with the fee application is discretionary with the district court. *See, e.g., Thompson v. Pharmacy Corp. of America*, 334 F.3d 1242 (11th Cir.2003) (hearing required only where requested, where there are disputes of fact, where the written record is insufficiently clear to allow trial court to resolve those disputes, and where the district court possesses sufficient expertise to resolve such issues as reasonableness of the fee, the hours expended, and the significance of the outcome).

98. *See Miller v. Woodharbor Molding & Millworks, Inc.*, 174 F.3d 948 (8th Cir. 1999) (per curiam) (fees were inadequately documented because they failed consistently or specifically to identify the substance or content of the billed tasks). *But cf. Kline v. City of Kansas City, Mo.*, 245 F.3d 707, 709 (8th Cir.2001) (contemporaneous time accounts are not required to support a motion for attorneys' fees as long as the trial court concludes that reconstructed records satisfactorily document the time).

99. *EEOC v. Clear Lake Dodge*, 60 F.3d 1146, 1154 (5th Cir.1995).

100. *Carter v. Sedgwick County, Kansas*, 36 F.3d 952, 956 (10th Cir.1994).

101. 465 U.S. 886, 104 S.Ct. 1541, 79 L.Ed.2d 891 (1984).

102. *Missouri v. Jenkins*, 491 U.S. 274, 109 S.Ct. 2463, 105 L.Ed.2d 229 (1989).

103. *Gusman v. Unisys Corp.*, 986 F.2d 1146 (7th Cir.1993).

of the prevailing party's lawyer deserves significant weight. Thus a district court erred in compensating the prevailing plaintiff's counsel in an excessive force case at the lower rate that the defendant city paid lawyers to defend those cases.[104]

But what if the rate of the prevailing party's lawyer, a member of a firm in a large urban city, is significantly greater than the rate of a hypothetical counterpart lawyer in the smaller city where the bulk of the legal services were rendered? Using the opportunity-cost premise, the Seventh Circuit held that the (in that case, higher) rate set by the market for the prevailing party's counsel is presumptively appropriate in calculating the lodestar.[105] No burden was placed on the prevailing party to show that she could not have obtained comparable representation at the lower rates prevailing in the smaller community. Instead, the court placed the burden on the losing party to demonstrate that a lower rate would more accurately reflect the winning lawyer's opportunity cost, for example by showing that he ordinarily commands the high rate claimed in only a small percentage of the total number of hours he "sells" in a year, devoting the balance to court-fixed contingent fee litigation. In that event, the court concluded, his true "market-clearing price" may be considerably less than the hourly fee that a few of his clients were willing to pay.[106] More commonly, courts will require the prevailing party who uses expensive non-local counsel to demonstrate her inability to obtain comparable, less expensive representation locally.[107]

Another difficult task facing a court in calculating a lodestar is to identify the issues on which plaintiff prevailed and in turn the number of hours counsel reasonably expended on those issues. In this sense degree of success is a critical component of the ultimate fee award. But a lodestar-based fee award need not be proportionate to the amount of damages a plaintiff recovers with respect to a successful issue.[108]

104. *Trevino v. Gates*, 99 F.3d 911 (9th Cir.1996), *cert. denied*, 520 U.S. 1117, 117 S.Ct. 1249, 137 L.Ed.2d 330 (1997). *See also Brooks v. Georgia State Board of Elections*, 997 F.2d 857, 869–70 (11th Cir.1993) ("the fee charged by a government attorney is simply irrelevant to the establishment of a reasonable hourly rate for a plaintiff's civil rights lawyer").

105. Thus, where a Washington, D.C. lawyer was specially retained to depose federal government witnesses in Washington, D.C., the Washington, D.C. market rate was appropriate and not the Knoxville, TN rate, the situs of the action. *Adcock–Ladd v. Sec'y of Treasury*, 227 F.3d 343, 351 (6th Cir.2000).

106. *Id.*

107. *See* § 4.10, infra.

108. *Riverside v. Rivera*, 477 U.S. 561, 106 S.Ct. 2686, 91 L.Ed.2d 466 (1986) (upholding attorney's fee award of $245,456 where recovery under federal civil rights statutes was only $13,300); *Thomas v. National Football League Players Ass'n*, 273 F.3d 1124, 1129 (D.C.Cir.2001) (after reducing fees for failed claims, approving fees nearly five times plaintiff's recovery); *McKenzie v. Cooper, Levins & Pastko, Inc.*, 990 F.2d 1183, 1185 (11th Cir.1993) (after a reduction to eliminate an enhancement for contingency, appellate court approves a fee award of over $121,000 where the back pay recovery was only $8600); *Grant v. Bethlehem Steel Corp.*, 973 F.2d 96 (2d Cir.1992) (affirming an award of over half a million dollars in attorney's fees where plaintiffs had settled for only $60,000), *cert. denied*, 506 U.S. 1053, 113 S.Ct. 978, 122 L.Ed.2d 132 (1993). *But see Migis v. Pearle Vision, Inc.*, 135 F.3d 1041 (5th Cir.1998) (reversing fees award that equaled six and on half times the compensatory award where plaintiff succeeded on only one of eight claims).

Attorney's fees may be augmented to compensate for delay in payment (as distinct from risk of nonpayment or "contingency"—to be discussed below). Risk of delay is compensated "either by basing the award on current rates or by adjusting the fee based on historical rates to reflect its present value."[109]

The Eleventh Amendment does not bar that adjustment in an action against a state. More generally, by the terms of the Civil Rights Attorneys' Fees Act of 1976, 42 U.S.C.A. § 1988(b), the Amendment does not bar fees against the state to the prevailing party, other than the United States, in any action or proceeding to enforce a provision of any of the Reconstruction Acts or Title VI of the Civil Rights Act of 1964 or Title IX .[110] Such fees constitute an item of "costs" under the language of § 1988 and may therefore be recovered from a state even in federal court, notwithstanding the Eleventh Amendment.[111] The significance of this statutory abrogation has diminished since 1989, when the Court held in *Will v. Michigan Dept. of State Police*[112] that states sued in their own name are not proper defendants under § 1983. Nevertheless, the Civil Rights Act of 1976 continues to have significance in the reduced class of § 1983 actions challenging state action that *Will* approves, i.e., official-capacity actions against named state officials for prospective or injunctive relief.[113]

Additional adjustment factors to the lodestar include the novelty and difficulty of the questions presented, the extent to which the demands of the case preclude other legal employment, the undesirability of the case, awards in similar cases, and the experience, reputation, and ability of the attorneys. Circuit courts have been reluctant to approve reduction in the amount of an award below the lodestar because of erroneous "billing judgment" by a plaintiff's lawyer in spending considerable time pursuing a claim that a district court considered relatively simple.[114] These adjustment factors may refine but cannot substitute for the basic multiplication of a reasonable billing rate by the number of hours reasonably expended on successful claims. Similarly, the attorney's fee award may not be limited by a contingent-fee arrangement that yields a lesser sum than the lodestar.[115]

109. *Missouri v. Jenkins*, 491 U.S. 274, 109 S.Ct. 2463, 105 L.Ed.2d 229.

110. *Id.*

111. The Civil Rights Attorney's Fees Awards Act of 1976, 42 U.S.C.A. § 1988, effectively abrogates the Eleventh Amendment immunity of states from awards of costs and attorney's fees in actions under § 1983, the other Reconstruction Civil Rights Acts, and Titles VI and IX. *Hutto v. Finney*, 437 U.S. 678, 98 S.Ct. 2565, 57 L.Ed.2d 522 (1978). The specific abrogation of immunity in § 1988 recognized in *Hutto* survives the Supreme Court's decision in *Seminole Tribe of Florida v. Florida*, 517 U.S. 44, 116 S.Ct. 1114, 134 L.Ed.2d 252 (1996), because Congress acted pursuant to § 5 of the Fourteenth Amendment. *See* Chapter 5 on Eleventh Amendment immunity.

112. 491 U.S. 58, 109 S.Ct. 2304, 105 L.Ed.2d 45 (1989).

113. *Id.* at note 10.

114. *Quaratino v. Tiffany & Co.*, 166 F.3d 422 (2d Cir.1999) (reversing district court's halving of lodestar through "billing judgment" approach); *Robinson v. City of Edmond*, 160 F.3d 1275 (10th Cir.1998) (reversing fee reduction because district court viewed case as "fairly" simple).

115. *Blanchard v. Bergeron*, 489 U.S. 87, 109 S.Ct. 939, 103 L.Ed.2d 67 (1989).

In *Evans v. Jeff D.*,[116] the Court approved the practice of compulsory waiver of attorney's fees by settlement. FRCP 23 requires district court approval of class action settlements. Parties are free to negotiate the terms of a settlement and may waive statutorily authorized attorney's fees.[117] The Court held that § 1988 does not interfere with that freedom. The Civil Rights Act of 1991 leaves *Evans* intact. The Court in *Evans* did, however, leave open the possibility that a defendant's insistence that the plaintiff waive an attorney's fee award under § 1988, while not violating federal law, might violate local law or ethical prohibitions; and a few jurisdictions have on occasion so held. In addition, it is undecided whether a city or county's uniform policy of insisting on waiver of § 1988 fees as a condition of settling any federal civil rights action unlawfully conflicts with the policies of § 1988.[118]

Venegas v. Mitchell,[119] treats the effect of a § 1988 fee award on the plaintiff's contractual arrangement with his own attorney. It holds that § 1988 does not invalidate a contingent fee agreement providing for payments substantially in excess of the reasonable fee recoverable from the defendant. That is, § 1988 controls only the relationship between the losing defendant and the prevailing plaintiff, not between the plaintiff and plaintiff's own attorney. Although under general § 1988 principles plaintiff's own portion of a recovery may not include amounts she has agreed to pay her attorney that exceed the "reasonable" amounts recoverable as attorney's fees from the defendant, *Venegas* also reinforces a plaintiff's capacity to secure counsel of her choice by upholding the integrity of the private fee agreement. This decision has been applied to actions under Title VII as well.[120] On the other hand, the plaintiff's attorney's fee award under § 1988 may not be absolutely limited by a contingent-fee arrangement that calls for a lesser sum than the lodestar.[121]

Previously, a prevailing plaintiff was not entitled to have its expert witnesses compensated by the losing party, absent contractual or statutory authority stating otherwise.[122] In *West Virginia Univ. Hosps. v. Casey*,[123] the Court held that § 1988 does not authorize the recovery of expert witness fees. They are limited to the amount designated for all witnesses, $30 per day. The Civil Rights Act of 1991, which includes

116. 475 U.S. 717, 106 S.Ct. 1531, 89 L.Ed.2d 747 (1986).

117. And failure to broach issue of attorney's fees during settlement negotiations can operate as a waiver of such an award. *See Wray v. Clarke*, 151 F.3d 807, 809 (8th Cir.1998).

118. *See, e.g., Bernhardt v. Los Angeles County*, 339 F.3d 920 (9th Cir. 2003)(approving preliminary injunction against such a policy).

119. 495 U.S. 82, 110 S.Ct. 1679, 109 L.Ed.2d 74 (1990).

120. *Gobert v. U.S. Dept of the Interior*, 323 F.3d 1099 (5th Cir.2003).

121. *Blanchard v. Bergeron*, 489 U.S. 87, 109 S.Ct. 939, 103 L.Ed.2d 67 (1989). *But see In Time Products, Ltd. v. Toy Biz, Inc.*, 38 F.3d 660 (2d Cir.1994) (award must be reasonably related to a hypothetical fee arrangement that the prevailing party could have made with an attorney, which the court set at a 33% contingency).

122. *Crawford Fitting Co. v. J.T. Gibbons*, 482 U.S. 437, 107 S.Ct. 2494, 96 L.Ed.2d 385 (1987).

123. 499 U.S. 83, 111 S.Ct. 1138, 113 L.Ed.2d 68 (1991).

expert fees as a part of an attorney's fee award under Title VII, reverses *West Virginia Univ. Hosps. v. Casey* in part. The Act authorizes expert witness fees in actions or proceedings to enforce provisions of § 1981 and § 1981a, but not § 1983.[124] Of course, the Supreme Court has already included certain related costs, e.g., those for law clerks and paralegals, as part of the attorney's fees recoverable under § 1988.[125]

Depending on the circuit, post-judgment interest on attorney's fees may begin to accrue either from the date of the judgment that unconditionally entitled the prevailing party to reasonable attorney's fees,[126] or from the date that the award of attorney's fees is quantified.[127]

§§ 4.6–4.9 [Reserved]

C. LODESTAR MAY NOT BE ENHANCED FOR "CONTINGENCY," OR RISK OF LOSS

§ 4.10 In General

There is a strong presumption that the lodestar represents a reasonable fee, and any upward or downward adjustments may take into account only those factors not used in arriving at the lodestar.[1] In any event the lodestar may not be adjusted upward by a "multiplier" to compensate for an attorney's risk of loss, or "contingency"—as distinct from the loss caused by delay—unless perhaps evidence is produced to show that the possibility of an enhanced fee was required in order to attract counsel.[2] The Court in *Delaware II* rendered a 4–1–4 decision on the issue of the availability of contingency multipliers. As a result of this splintered decision, lower courts are attempting to implement the views of Justice O'Connor. Justice O'Connor would allow an enhancement for risk when an applicant has shown that: (1) the relevant market[3] compen-

124. This problem can be compounded if courts conclude, as the Eleventh Circuit has, that § 1983 is the sole vehicle for asserting § 1981 claims against state actors. *See Butts v. Volusia County*, 222 F.3d 891 (11th Cir.2000). One district court finessed its way around this result by holding that where the underlying claim is based on § 1981, the action should be deemed brought under § 1981 for purposes of eligibility to recover expert witness fees, even if the vehicle for asserting the § 1981 right is § 1983. *See Webster Greenthumb Co. v. Fulton County*, 112 F.Supp.2d 1339 (N.D.Ga. 2000).

125. *Missouri v. Jenkins*, 491 U.S. 274, 109 S.Ct. 2463, 105 L.Ed.2d 229.

126. *Associated General Contractors of Ohio, Inc. v. Drabik*, 250 F.3d 482 (6th Cir.2001); *Friend v. Kolodzieczak*, 72 F.3d 1386, 1391 (9th Cir.1995); *BankAtlantic v. Blythe Eastman Paine Webber, Inc.*, 12 F.3d 1045, 1052–53 (11th Cir.1994); *Jenkins v. State of Missouri*, 931 F.2d 1273, 1275 (8th Cir.1991); *Mathis v. Spears*, 857 F.2d 749 (Fed.Cir.1988); *Copper Liquor, Inc. v. Adolph Coors Co.*, 701 F.2d 542, 543 (5th Cir.1983) (en banc) (same).

127. *Eaves v. County of Cape May*, 239 F.3d 527, 530 (3d Cir.2001); *MidAmerica Fed. Sav. & Loan Assoc. v. Shearson/American Express, Inc.*, 962 F.2d 1470, 1475–76 (10th Cir.1992).

§ 4.10

1. *See Hensley v. Eckerhart*, 461 U.S. 424, 103 S.Ct. 1933, 76 L.Ed.2d 40 (1983); *Pennsylvania v. Delaware Valley Citizens' Council for Clean Air*, 478 U.S. 546, 106 S.Ct. 3088, 92 L.Ed.2d 439 (1986) ("*Delaware I*").

2. *Pennsylvania v. Delaware Valley Citizens' Council for Clean Air*, 483 U.S. 711, 107 S.Ct. 3078, 97 L.Ed.2d 585 (1987) (O'Connor, J., concurring) ("*Delaware II*").

3. And, with one exception, it does seem to be the market that serves as the

sates for risk, and (2) but for the enhancement, he would have faced "substantial difficulties" in securing counsel in the relevant market.

The D.C. Circuit, en banc, reversed two of its prior panel decisions establishing the availability of enhancements for the D.C. market.[4] The D.C. Circuit interpreted the opinions of the plurality and Justice O'Connor in *Delaware II* as both requiring that a multiplier be made available only when a plaintiff would have encountered "substantial difficulties" in securing counsel without a risk enhancement. The plurality and Justice O'Connor disagreed, however, on "when" and "how" to apply a multiplier. Because of this disagreement, the D.C. Circuit viewed it as impossible to implement the "substantial difficulties" test. Concluding that no middle ground existed for contingency enhancements, the court held that they would not be available in Washington, D.C.

Previously, the courts in the D.C. and Ninth Circuits had looked to how the relevant market or locality treats contingency claims on an across the board, predetermined basis (instead of examining riskiness of lawsuits on a case by case basis). The Ninth Circuit still approves lodestar enhancement upon the finding of two factors: (1) the relevant legal market adds a premium for contingency (100% in *Bernardi*); and (2) absent such an enhancement the plaintiff would have encountered substantial difficulty in securing counsel.[5] Plaintiff in *Fadhl* satisfied her burden by presenting over thirty-five affidavits from local attorneys which established that a 100% contingency multiplier was necessary to ensure future contingency representation in San Francisco. A 100% enhancement must be applied to multipliers awarded in future lawsuits in the San Francisco market unless new evidence or legislation is presented warranting otherwise. This presumption in favor of a predetermined multiplier greatly eases plaintiff's evidentiary burden.

The circuit courts have taken three general approaches with contingency awards. As noted above, the D.C. Circuit completely bars contin-

nexus for the litigation, even when the particular attorney is from a more expensive market. *See, e.g., Mathur v. Bd. of Trustees of Southern Illinois University*, 317 F.3d 738 (7th Cir.2003) (plaintiff carried burden of showing he could not find local representation with sufficient expertise and no conflict of interest, and was therefore awarded hourly rates of out-of-town attorneys); *Hopwood v. Texas*, 236 F.3d 256, 281 (5th Cir. 2000) (mandating use of Austin, Texas market rates, where litigation was hosted, not Washington, D.C. rates for appellate attorneys); *Leroy v. City of Houston*, 906 F.2d 1068, 1079 (5th Cir.1990) (hourly rates are to be computed according to the prevailing market rates in the relevant legal market, not the rates that "lions at the bar may command"); *Donnell v. U. S.*, 682 F.2d 240, 251 (D.C.Cir.1982) ("the relevant community is the one in which the district court sits"); *American Civil Liberties Union of Georgia v. Barnes*, 168 F.3d 423, 437 (11th Cir.1999) (general rule is that the "relevant market" for purposes of determining the reasonable hourly rate for an attorney's services is "the place where the case is filed"). But a plaintiff may receive a fee award at the higher rate customarily received by out-of-town counsel when she can show that no local counsel could adequately perform the specialized services required. On this question the burden of persuasion is on the prevailing party seeking fees. *Id.*

4. *King v. Palmer*, 950 F.2d 771 (D.C.Cir.1991) (en banc), *reversing King v. Palmer*, 906 F.2d 762 (D.C.Cir.1990) and *overruling McKenzie v. Kennickell*, 875 F.2d 330 (D.C.Cir.1989).

5. *Bernardi v. Yeutter*, 942 F.2d 562 (9th Cir.), *amended by*, 951 F.2d 971 (9th Cir.1991); *Fadhl v. City and County of San Francisco*, 859 F.2d 649 (9th Cir.1988).

gency multipliers.[6] The Fourth, Sixth, Seventh, and Ninth Circuits have affirmed contingency awards.[7] The majority of the circuits, however, explicitly limit the availability of contingency multipliers to "exceptional cases" only.[8]

The Third Circuit has announced stringent standards for enhancing the lodestar amount by a contingency multiplier and in each of the following cases has refused to approve one.[9] Before enhancing a fee award, the Third Circuit requires a plaintiff to satisfy four evidentiary factors: (1) how the relevant market treats contingency fee cases differently from hourly fee cases; (2) the degree to which the market compensates for risk of nonpayment; (3) the multiplier cannot be more than is necessary to secure counsel in the market as well as the case; and (4) absent such an enhancement the plaintiff would have encountered substantial difficulty in securing counsel.[10] The Third Circuit will not presume such factors, but insists on expert testimony (and perhaps a costly econometric study) to demonstrate them.

A decision of the Supreme Court, *Burlington v. Dague*,[11] appears to have ended this debate in favor of flatly precluding contingency enhancement. Although the underlying claims at issue were brought under modern environmental statutes, the Court's opinion and citations to cases, including *King v. Palmer*,[12] in which fees were sought under § 1988 or Title VII, strongly suggest that the holding will apply to fee applications under the latter statutes as well.

What if, as a result of *Dague* or otherwise, a putative plaintiff cannot attract counsel? Section 706(f)(1)(B)[13] authorizes the court, upon application and under such circumstances as it deems just, to "appoint an attorney" for a complainant and authorize commencement of the action without fees, costs, or security. And what if the court is unable, after diligent effort, to locate a lawyer willing to take the case without up-front compensation? There is authority that § 706(f)(1)(B) may be read to require the coercive appointment of counsel; this reading is partly justified by the fact that the unwilling lawyer may ultimately be

6. *See King v. Palmer*, 950 F.2d 771.

7. *See Craig v. Secretary, Dep't of Health & Human Servs.*, 864 F.2d 324 (4th Cir.1989); *Fite v. First Tennessee Prod. Credit Ass'n*, 861 F.2d 884 (6th Cir.1988); *Skelton v. General Motors Corp.*, 860 F.2d 250 (7th Cir.1988), *cert. denied*, 493 U.S. 810, 110 S.Ct. 53, 107 L.Ed.2d 22 (1989); *Bernardi v. Yeutter*, 942 F.2d 562.

8. *See, e.g., Rode v. Dellarciprete*, 892 F.2d 1177 (3d Cir.1990); *Hendrickson v. Branstad*, 934 F.2d 158 (8th Cir.1991); *Smith v. Freeman*, 921 F.2d 1120 (10th Cir.1990); *Norman v. Hous. Auth.*, 836 F.2d 1292 (11th Cir.1988); *Leroy v. City of Houston*, 831 F.2d 576 (5th Cir.1987) *cert. denied*, 486 U.S. 1008, 108 S.Ct. 1735, 100 L.Ed.2d 199 (1988).

9. *E.g., Kelly v. Matlack, Inc.*, 903 F.2d 978 (3d Cir.1990); *Rode v. Dellarciprete*, 892 F.2d 1177; *Blum v. Witco Chem. Corp.*, 888 F.2d 975 (3d Cir.1989) ("*Witco II*"); *Blum v. Witco Chem. Corp.*, 829 F.2d 367 (3d Cir.1987) ("*Witco I*").

10. *Rode v. Dellarciprete*, 892 F.2d 1177.

11. 505 U.S. 557, 112 S.Ct. 2638, 120 L.Ed.2d 449 (1992).

12. 950 F.2d 771.

13. 42 U.S.C.A. § 2000e–5(f)(1)(B).

compensated as the result of a statutory award of attorney's fees if his client prevails.[14]

§§ 4.11–4.14 [Reserved]

D. PREVAILING DEFENDANTS

§ 4.15 In General

While a prevailing plaintiff is ordinarily to be awarded attorney's fees in all but special circumstances, the Supreme Court in *Christiansburg Garment Co. v. EEOC*[1] has interpreted § 706(k) to preclude attorney's fees to a prevailing defendant unless the plaintiff's action was "frivolous, unreasonable, or without foundation." This appears to mean that a fee award to a prevailing defendant is unwarranted where the plaintiff's claim, although plainly flawed, is colorable.[2] The plaintiff's failure to establish a prima facie case, the unprecedented nature of a claim, the defendant's offer of a settlement, or the dismissal of an action before trial all figure in determining whether a claim is sufficiently frivolous, unreasonable, or groundless to justify taxing attorney's fees against a plaintiff.[3] If the defendant can show that a plaintiff asserted a claim in subjective bad faith, the case for awarding the defendant his attorney's fees is stronger. But the circumstances warranting fees to a prevailing defendant must be truly exceptional, so much so that a trial court does not abuse its discretion in denying such fees even if no reason is stated for the denial.[4] And where EEOC is the plaintiff, it is not even enough for the defendant seeking attorney's fees to show that EEOC failed to present credible evidence of discrimination. In such a case the defendant has the even more difficult burden of demonstrating that EEOC should have "anticipated at the outset that none of its evidence of discriminatory conduct was credible" or unreasonably believed that it

14. *See Scott v. Tyson Foods, Inc.*, 943 F.2d 17 (8th Cir.1991); *Bradshaw v. U.S. District Court*, 742 F.2d 515 (9th Cir.1984) and *Bradshaw v. Zoological Soc. of San Diego*, 662 F.2d 1301 (9th Cir.1981). *Cf. Howard v. Military Dep't*, 5 F.3d 537 (9th Cir.1993).

§ 4.15

1. 434 U.S. 412, 98 S.Ct. 694, 54 L.Ed.2d 648 (1978).

2. *See, e.g., Barnes Foundation v. Township of Lower Merion*, 242 F.3d 151 (3d Cir.2001) (even though all claims were barred by a First Amendment immunity doctrine, the law in the Third Circuit was not settled and although claims against five of the six defendants were not colorable due to a lack of evidence, the claim against the sixth individual was colorable and while the sixth individual could not claim fees, the other five defendants could, assuming the action was not brought in bad faith); *Sayers v. Stewart Sleep Center, Inc.*, 140 F.3d 1351 (11th Cir.1998); *EEOC v. Reichhold Chems., Inc.*, 988 F.2d 1564, 1570–71 (11th Cir.1993). *See also E.E.O.C. v. L.B. Foster Co.*, 123 F.3d 746 (3d Cir.1997) (where plaintiff's proof would suffice if credited, claim cannot be considered as frivolous); *AFSCME v. County of Nassau*, 96 F.3d 644 (2d Cir.1996), *cert. denied*, 520 U.S. 1104, 117 S.Ct. 1107, 137 L.Ed.2d 309 (1997) (reversing fee award against plaintiff that prevailed on a narrow claim closely related to a broader one on which it failed).

3. *See, e.g., Bass v. E.I. DuPont de Nemours & Co.*, 324 F.3d 761 (4th Cir. 2003) (plaintiff failed to allege facts supporting a claim for relief even under the liberal pleading standards applicable to Title VII claims and was ordered to pay $21,937 in fees even though court agreed award would impose substantial financial burden).

4. *Maag v. Wessler*, 993 F.2d 718 (9th Cir.1993).

had made adequate efforts to conciliate.[5] It is difficult to imagine a situation in which the defendant could carry that showing.

If the standard for prevailing plaintiffs announced in *Farrar* were the test of whether a defendant is a "prevailing party," the defendant might qualify for fees when the plaintiff voluntarily dismisses her suit with prejudice even before a decision on the merits by motion for summary judgment or at trial.[6] Such a dismissal does, after all, alter the legal relationship between the parties to the benefit of the defendant. But a circuit court observed that the *Christiansburg* opinion reflects the Supreme Court's mandate that separate, more stringent standards govern the fee eligibility of prevailing Title VII defendants. To show the frivolousness, unreasonableness, or groundlessness demanded by *Christiansburg*, the court concluded, the defendant must ordinarily have prevailed on a motion for summary judgment on the merits.[7] On the other hand, the granting of a summary judgment motion does not ensure fees.[8] Yet it has also been held that denial of a defendant's summary judgment motion does not necessarily prevent its recovering attorney's fees under the *Christiansburg* standard if plaintiff should have realized, from subsequent pretrial discovery, that his claim was groundless.[9] The prevailing defendant eligible for fees under *Christiansburg* may, like the prevailing plaintiff, also recover the reasonable fees and expenses incurred in proceedings to collect the underlying fee award should plaintiff decline to pay it.[10]

The Equal Access to Justice Act,[11] unlike § 1988 and its Title VII counterpart,[12] provides for fee awards to prevailing defendants when the plaintiff's claim is merely groundless but not frivolous, if the unsuccessful plaintiff is the U.S. government. The circuit courts are in conflict concerning whether EAJA is available in actions under statutes (like the

5. *EEOC v. Bruno's Restaurant*, 13 F.3d 285 (9th Cir.1993). *See EEOC v. Hendrix College*, 53 F.3d 209 (8th Cir.1995) (upholding award where EEOC was found to have failed to investigate before filing action).

6. *But see Dean v. Riser*, 240 F.3d 505 (5th Cir.2001) (defendant is not prevailing party within meaning of § 1988 even when civil rights plaintiff voluntarily dismisses his claim, unless defendant can demonstrate that plaintiff withdrew to avoid disfavorable judgment on merits).

7. *See, e.g., LeBlanc–Sternberg v. Fletcher*, 143 F.3d 765 (2d Cir.1998) (where plaintiff survives a 12(b)(6) motion to dismiss, a motion for summary judgment and a post-trial motion for judgment as a matter of law, plaintiff's claim is not frivolous as a matter of law); *Marquart v. Lodge 837, Int'l Ass'n of Machinists and Aerospace Workers*, 26 F.3d 842 (8th Cir.1994). *Cf. Walker v. City of Bogalusa*, 168 F.3d 237 (5th Cir. 1999) (awarding defendant fees for plaintiff's failure to produce evidence of defendant's discriminatory purpose or adverse impact). *But see Bonner v. Mobile Energy Servs. Co.*, 246 F.3d 1303 (11th Cir.2001) (even though the plaintiff's evidence is "markedly weak" and does not survive summary judgment, where the plaintiff stated a prima facie case, and a neutral arbitrator concluded that the plaintiff was fired for no just cause, and where the employer had made an offer of $125,000 to settle the case prior to declaring bankruptcy, plaintiff's case was not frivolous or unreasonable and fees for the prevailing defendant were not warranted).

8. *Riddle v. Egensperger*, 266 F.3d 542 (6th Cir.2001) (applying test as of time complaint filed).

9. *Flowers v. Jefferson Hospital Ass'n*, 49 F.3d 391 (8th Cir.1995) (per curiam).

10. *Vukadinovich v. McCarthy*, 59 F.3d 58 (7th Cir.1995).

11. 28 U.S.C.A. § 2412(d).

12. 42 U.S.C.A. § 2000e–5(k).

Reconstruction Acts and Title VII) that have their own fee-shifting statutes.[13] The circuits that have visited the issue thus far have allowed a prevailing defendant to recover fees from the government under the ADEA which has no fee-shifting provision for prevailing defendants.[14] And even where EAJA applies, a defendant employer will not be entitled to fees if the evidence presented by EEOC as plaintiff, although seriously flawed, is supported by anecdotal evidence.[15]

The *Christiansburg* test has been applied to govern the award of attorney's fees against unsuccessful intervenors. The Supreme Court characterized as "particularly welcome" a union's intervention challenging a proposed settlement of a sex discrimination action in order to protect "the legitimate expectations of . . . [male] employees innocent of any wrongdoing."[16] The decision encouraged intervention by holding that intervenors would be liable for plaintiffs' costs of defending a settlement only when the intervention is "frivolous, unreasonable, or without foundation."[17] In effect, then, intervention becomes *per se* a "special circumstance" that warrants denial of a fee award to a prevailing plaintiff.[18] The Civil Rights Act of 1991 leaves this approach intact. In actions under the ADEA, several circuits have required prevailing defendants to show not that plaintiff's claim was objectively frivolous, but that it was brought in bad faith.[19]

13. *Compare Nowd v. Rubin,* 76 F.3d 25 (1st Cir.1996) (case under ADEA) *and Gavette v. Office of Personnel Management,* 808 F.2d 1456, 1463 (Fed.Cir.1986) (yes) *with Escobar Ruiz v. INS,* 787 F.2d 1294, 1296 (9th Cir.1986) (no).

14. *See EEOC v. O & G Spring & Wire Forms Specialty Co.*, 38 F.3d 872, 881–83 (7th Cir.1994); *EEOC v. Clay Printing Co.*, 13 F.3d 813, 815 (4th Cir.1994) (assessing attorney's fees against the EEOC in an ADEA case).

15. *EEOC v. O & G Spring and Wire Forms Specialty Co.,* 38 F.3d 872 (7th Cir. 1994), *cert. denied,* 513 U.S. 1198, 115 S.Ct. 1270, 131 L.Ed.2d 148 (1995).

16. *Independent Fed'n of Flight Attendants v. Zipes*, 491 U.S. 754, 764, 109 S.Ct. 2732, 2738, 105 L.Ed.2d 639 (1989).

17. *Id.* at 761, 109 S.Ct. at 2736–37.

18. Whether fees are available for successfully opposing an attempted intervention was addressed in *Hopwood v. Texas,* 236 F.3d 256 (5th Cir.2000). A multitude of organizations, including the NAACP Legal Defense Fund, had been unsuccessful in their attempts to intervene, but the district court denied plaintiff's motion for fees from the state of Texas expended on their opposition. In *Independent Fed'n of Flight Attendants v. Zipes*, 491 U.S. 754, 109 S.Ct. 2732, 105 L.Ed.2d 639 (1989), the plaintiff sought an award of attorney's fees from the intervenor. The Supreme Court held that recovery of fees from the intervenor cannot be had unless the intervention is "frivolous, unreasonable, or without foundation." *Id.* at 761, 491 U.S. 754, 109 S.Ct. 2732, 105 L.Ed.2d 639. The circuits have extended this holding to the award of fees to prevailing plaintiffs from the pockets of losing defendants when the fees are based on interventions by third-parties. *See, e.g., Rum Creek Coal Sales, Inc. v. Caperton*, 31 F.3d 169, 176–78 (4th Cir.1994); *Bigby v. City of Chicago*, 927 F.2d 1426, 1428–29 (7th Cir. 1991). The Fifth Circuit declined to decide the issue, because Texas had not taken a position on the attempted interventions. In addition, the potential intervenors made clear both to the trial court and to us in *Hopwood I* that the purpose of their intervention was to raise arguments and defenses that Texas itself had no interest in raising. *See Hopwood v. Texas,* 1994 WL 242362, at *1; *Hopwood I,* 21 F.3d at 605. "It would be inequitable now for us to force Texas to pay for costs associated with a failed intervention which, in our determination, would have brought nothing more to the table than did Texas." *Hopwood v. State of Texas,* 236 F.3d 256 (5th Cir. 2000).

19. *Turlington v. Atlanta Gas Light Co.*, 135 F.3d 1428 (11th Cir.1998) (citing cases).

§§ 4.16–4.19 [Reserved]

E. RULE 68 OFFERS OF JUDGMENT

§ 4.20 In General

Federal Rule 68 authorizes the defendant, at any time more than 10 days before trial, to "offer to allow judgment to be taken against [it] ... for the money or property ... specified in the offer, with costs then accrued." It then provides that, if the offer is not accepted and a judgment obtained by the plaintiff "is not more favorable than the offer, the offeree must pay the costs incurred after the making of the offer." On its face, then, Rule 68 merely relieves a defendant who makes such an offer that is not accepted by the plaintiff and equaled or exceeded by a final judgment from what would otherwise be its liability for the "costs" routinely taxable under Federal Rule of Civil Procedure 54(d) in favor of prevailing parties in any federal civil action. Such an offer is valid even when it is conditioned upon acceptance of its terms by all plaintiffs, and a settlement agreement counts as a "judgment" that triggers the cost-shifting permitted by Rule 68.[1]

Rule 54(d) costs, however, are relatively minor, as they are universally understood not to include attorney's fees. The real bite of Rule 68 in civil rights and employment discrimination actions results from the interplay of that rule with the provisions in Title VII and § 1988 that call for an award of "a reasonable attorney's fee *as part of the costs*."[2] Importing the italicized language into the word "costs" as it appears in Rule 68, the Supreme Court in *Marek v. Chesny*[3] held that a defendant's offer of judgment in a civil rights action governed by statutory provisions for attorney's fees can shift what would otherwise be the losing defendant's liability for the prevailing plaintiff's attorney's fees, as well as ordinary costs. Specifically, a Rule 68 offer that meets the requirements of that Rule relieves the losing defendant of liability for the plaintiff's post-offer attorney's fees as well as her ordinary costs of litigation. This holding greatly increases the defendant's incentive to make a Rule 68 offer, and the Civil Rights Act of 1991 leaves *Marek* intact. The *Marek* holding goes well beyond actions under the Reconstruction Civil Rights statutes governed by § 1988. In *Lyte v. Sara Lee Corp.*,[4] the court held that attorney's fees are a part of the "costs" shifted by a defendant's offer of judgment under FRCP 68 in actions under any statute that allows fee awards as a part of "costs," which would include those under Title VII, EPA, and ADEA.

The defendant's offer, to avoid liability for costs and fees to the prevailing plaintiff, must, in the words of Rule 68, include the plaintiff's "costs then accrued," that is, up until the time of the offer. The "costs"

§ 4.20

1. *See Lang v. Gates*, 36 F.3d 73 (9th Cir.1994).

2. Section 706(k) of Title VII; 42 U.S.C.A. § 1988, final sentence.

3. 473 U.S. 1, 105 S.Ct. 3012, 87 L.Ed.2d 1 (1985).

4. 950 F.2d 101 (2d Cir.1991).

that must be included in the offer—like the "costs" mentioned in the subsequent phrase of Rule 68 that shifts liability for attorney's fees if the offer is rejected—have been held to include the amount of the plaintiff's attorney's fees accrued at the time of the offer. This is because a prevailing plaintiff would, absent an offer, ordinarily be entitled by judgment to an award of attorney's fees for pre-offer work.[5] Accordingly, those fees, together with ordinary costs, must be added to the judgment to calculate the total received by judgment that the offer must equal or exceed to shift post-offer costs and fees under Rule 68. Where an offer no longer exceeded, in fact was slightly less than, the amount of plaintiff's judgment once pre-offer attorney's fees were added to the judgment, the Rule 68 requirement that the offer equal or exceed the judgment was held not met and the defendant was therefore subject to the usual assessment of costs and fees owed a prevailing plaintiff, including those incurred after the making of its offer.[6]

In another case, the offer promised not only "costs then accrued," as prescribed by Rule 68, but also "reasonable attorney fees as determined by the court."[7] The Ninth Circuit construed the language of the offer to authorize a district judge's award of attorney's fees for plaintiffs' counsel's preparation of a fee petition *after* they accepted the offer, even though under Rule 68 costs, and hence, under *Marek*, fees, are halted by a successful offer. The court indicated that if the defendant had offered to pay only plaintiff's "costs then accrued," the offer would have clearly and unambiguously limited plaintiff's fees to the full extent that *Marek* and Rule 68 permit. The decision points up the necessity for defendant's counsel to draft tightly worded offers that not only meet Rule 68's strictures but also stay within them. A majority of circuits that have confronted the question have held that any waiver of or limitation on attorney's fees in actions under statutes providing for the recovery of fees by prevailing plaintiffs must be "clear and unambiguous."[8] Similarly, a circuit court has ruled ineffective a Rule 68 offer that failed to apportion the offer among the multiple plaintiffs. By advising only that the offered sum was "to be divided among all three plaintiffs," the offer failed to give the notice each required to evaluate whether to accept.[9]

5. *See Scheeler v. Crane Co.*, 21 F.3d 791 (8th Cir.1994) (diversity case under Iowa civil rights statute).

6. *Id.*

7. *Holland v. Roeser*, 37 F.3d 501 (9th Cir.1994).

8. *See, e.g., Ellis v. University of Kansas Med. Ctr.*, 163 F.3d 1186, 1199–1201 (10th Cir.1998); *Muckleshoot Tribe v. Puget Sound Power & Light Co.*, 875 F.2d 695, 698 and n. 5 (9th Cir.1989); *Jennings v. Metropolitan Government of Nashville*, 715 F.2d 1111, 1114 (6th Cir.1983) (silence in settlement agreement does not waive plaintiff's right to pursue fees under § 1988). *See also El Club Del Barrio, Inc. v. United Community Corporations, Inc.*, 735 F.2d 98, 100 (3d Cir.1984); *cf. Valley Disposal, Inc. v. Central Vermont Solid Waste Management Dist.*, 71 F.3d 1053, 1058 (2d Cir.1995). *But see Wilson v. Nomura Securities Int'l, Inc.*, 361 F.3d 86 (2d Cir. 2004) (employee who accepted offer inclusive of "all costs available under all local, state or federal statutes accrued to date" held to have waived separate fee award under city human rights law); *Wray v. Clarke*, 151 F.3d 807, 809 (8th Cir.1998); *Elmore v. Shuler*, 787 F.2d 601, 603 (D.C.Cir.1986) (plaintiff must show that settlement agreement does not waive § 1988 fees and possibly even reserve that right affirmatively).

9. *See Gavoni v. Dobbs House, Inc.*, 164 F.3d 1071 (7th Cir.1999) (tort action).

The inclusion of attorney's fees in the Rule 68 post-offer "costs" that the plaintiff may be precluded from recovering assumes that the underlying fee statute includes "attorney's fees" within the definition of "costs." That is the case with most fee statutes, including § 1988, its counterpart under ADEA, and the principal Title VII fee provision, Section 706(k). By contrast, since the "mixed-motive" remedies section of Title VII, Section 706(g)(2)(B), refers to "costs" and "attorney's fees" distinctly and separately, attorney's fees will not be counted as part of the post-offer Rule 68 "costs" a plaintiff is barred from recovering where the entitlement to fees flows only from that section.[10]

Likewise, at least one circuit has held that attorney's fees are not shifted as part of costs in ADA actions because the text of the ADA does not define attorney's fees as part of costs.[11] In an ADA action, "the court or agency, in its discretion, may allow the prevailing party ... a reasonable attorney's fee, including litigation expenses, *and* costs."[12] Under this section, then, Congress did not define costs to include fees for the purposes of the ADA. Therefore, an offer that mentions only "costs" and is silent on the issue of fees cannot relieve the defendant of its statutory liability for fees.[13]

Can Rule 68 be used not just to relieve the defendant of cost and fee liability to a prevailing plaintiff but as the basis for an award of attorney's fees to a prevailing defendant? If so, Rule 68 could serve as the defendant's end run around the *Christiansburg Garment* test applicable to claims under the Reconstruction Acts and employment discrimination statutes. That is, a defendant would become eligible for attorney's fees simply by submitting what proves to be a shrewd offer of judgment in cases where the plaintiff has prevailed and therefore defendant has not shown the groundlessness, frivolousness, or subjective bad faith the Supreme Court has required. But the circuits to have considered the issue have all rejected this argument in civil rights and employment discrimination actions governed by *Christianburgs Garment's* plaintiff-tilted interpretation of "prevailing party." They confirm that FRCP 68, while a one-way street available only to defendants, helps them only if the plaintiff prevails,[14] and then only by relieving them of what would otherwise be their liability for plaintiff's costs and fees, not by making them eligible for a fee award themselves.[15].

10. *Sheppard v. Riverview Nursing Ctr.*, 88 F.3d 1332 (4th Cir.), *cert. denied*, 519 U.S. 993, 117 S.Ct. 483, 136 L.Ed.2d 377 (1996).

11. *See Webb v. James*, 147 F.3d 617 (7th Cir.1998).

12. 42 U.S.C.A. § 12205 (emphasis added).

13. *See Webb v. James*, 147 F.3d 617, 622–23 (7th Cir.1998).

14. *Delta Air Lines, Inc. v. August*, 450 U.S. 346, 352, 101 S.Ct. 1146, 67 L.Ed.2d 287 (1981) (Rule 68 has no application if defendant wins the underlying lawsuit).

15. *Le v. University of Pennsylvania*, 321 F.3d 403, 410–11 (3d Cir. 2003)(Title VII action); *Payne v. Milwaukee County*, 288 F.3d 1021, 1027 (7th Cir. 2002)(§ 1983 action); *E.E.O.C. v. Bailey Ford, Inc.*, 26 F.3d 570 (5th Cir. 1994)(same); *O'Brien v. City of Greers Ferry*, 873 F.2d 1115 (8th Cir. 1989)(same); *Crossman v. Marcoccio*, 806 F.2d 329 (1st Cir. 1986)(same). *Cf. Champion Produce, Inc. v. Ruby Robinson Co., Inc.*, 342 F.3d 1016, 1028–1031 (9th Cir. 2003)(applying to an underlying Idaho fee-authorizing statute the *Marek* reasoning that only fees properly awardable under

By contrast, there is also complete consensus among the circuits to have decided the issue that where plaintiff's trial recovery (plus court-ordered pre-offer costs and fees) does not exceed the defendant's rejected Rule 68 offer, the defendant is entitled to an award from plaintiff of its post-offer *costs*, i.e., excluding post-offer fees.[16] The decisions thus read the Rule 68 requirement that the offeree "pay the costs incurred after the making of the offer" to mean not just that offeree bear its own post-offer costs but that it be ordered to pay those of the offeror. These courts find no tension between FRCP 54(d), which awards presumptive but still discretionary costs only to prevailing parties, and this application of FRCP 68, which mandates costs to a non-prevailing defendant that submitted a Rule 68 offer which was successful in the sense that plaintiff, after rejecting it, could not recover more at trial.

If, however, as the circuits agree, plaintiffs who fail to surpass at trial a Rule 68 offer they rejected must pay post-offer defense costs; and if Rule 68 "costs," per *Marek*, are defined by reference to the underlying statute awarding costs and/or fees to prevailing parties; and if, as is true of Section 1988, in the case of civil rights actions, and Section 706(k), in the cases of Title VII actions, the underlying statutes do authorize the recovery of fees as part of "costs"; then shouldn't Rule 68 also require the plaintiff to pay the defendant's post-offer *fees*? The circuit decisions collected in footnote 15 above have all rejected this syllogism. They stress the statement in *Marek* that "the term 'costs' in Rule 68 was intended to refer [only] to all costs *properly awardable* under the relevant substantive statute ..."[17] And fees to a defendant where Rule 68 is triggered would not be properly awardable under Sections 1988 or 706(k) for two reasons. First, those statutes authorize fees only to prevailing parties; Rule 68 is triggered only where the plaintiff, not the defendant, has prevailed. Second, *Christiansburg Garment* interprets those statutes to mean that a defendant can be a prevailing party only where the plaintiff's claim is frivolous, unreasonable or without foundation, and that will certainly not be the case in the situation under examination, where the plaintiff has to some degree prevailed.

In brief, Rule 68 is triggered when the sum of plaintiff's trial recovery, plus her pre-offer costs and fees as awarded by the court, fails to exceed defendant's offer. When the Rule is triggered in civil rights or employment discrimination cases, the Rule denies the plaintiff eligibility for the post-offer costs or fees she would ordinarily be awarded by virtue

applicable fee statute can be imposed on Rule 68 offeree). *But cf. Jordan v. Time, Inc.*, 111 F.3d 102 (11th Cir. 1997)(awarding fees to losing defendant under Rule 68 where underlying fee award statute, the Copyright Act, defined "costs" to include fees).

16. *Pouillon v. Little*, 326 F.3d 713 (6th Cir. 2003); *Tunison v. Continental Airlines Corporation, Inc.*, 162 F.3d 1187, 1193–1194 (D.C. Cir. 1998); *O'Brien v. City of Greers Ferry*, 873 F.2d 1115 (8th Cir. 1989); *Crossman v. Marcoccio*, 806 F.2d 329 (1st Cir. 1986); *Liberty Mutual Ins. Co. v. EEOC*, 691 F.2d 438, 442 (9th Cir. 1982). *Cf. Liberty Mutual Ins. Co. v. EEOC*, 691 F.2d 438, 442 (9th Cir. 1982)(holding Rule 68 mandates that plaintiff pay defendant's post-offer costs after defendant prevailed via summary judgment on state law claim).

17. *Marek*, 473 U.S. at 9, 105 S.Ct. 3012 (emphasis added).

of the underlying applicable fee-authorizing statute; and it also requires the plaintiff-offeree to pay the defendant-offeror the latter's post-offer costs, but not fees.

Courts have generally held that Rule 68 offers of judgment may not be revoked during the 10 day period set by the Rule.[18] Moreover, recission may not be an available remedy for mutual mistakes because the mandatory language of Rule 68, requiring that the clerk "shall enter judgment" upon the filing of an offer, removes discretion from the trial court as to whether to enter judgment upon the filing of the accepted offer.[19] Relief from a judgment entered as a result of a Rule 68 offer and acceptance may be available under Rule 60. Rule 60(b) provides in relevant part that "[o]n motion and upon such terms as are just, the court may relieve a party or a party's legal representative from a final judgment order or proceeding for the following reasons: (1) mistake, inadvertence, surprise, or excusable neglect; ... (3) fraud (whether heretofore denominated intrinsic or extrinsic), misrepresentation, or other misconduct of an adverse party; (4) the judgment is void; ... or (6) any other reason justifying relief from the operation of the judgment."[20] On the other hand, a defendant who fails to renew an offer of judgment on retrial of an action remains eligible for Rule 68 costs from the plaintiff if on retrial the plaintiff's judgment is for less than the amount of the offer.[21]

18. *See Webb v. James*, 147 F.3d 617 (7th Cir.1998); *Richardson v. National R.R. Passenger Corp.*, 49 F.3d 760, 764 (D.C.Cir. 1995) (all federal courts to consider the issue have treated Rule 68 offers as generally irrevocable during the 10 day period) (citing *Colonial Penn Ins. Co. v. Coil*, 887 F.2d 1236, 1240 (4th Cir.1989); *Fisher v. Stolaruk Corp.*, 110 F.R.D. 74, 75 (E.D.Mich.1986); *Radecki v. Amoco Oil Co.*, 858 F.2d 397, 402 (8th Cir.1988) (in dicta)). *See also* Charles Alan Wright, Arthur R. Miller & Richard L. Marcus, *Federal Practice and Procedure*: Civil 2d, § 3004 (1997) (the courts have agreed with one of the drafters that Rule 68 offers cannot be withdrawn once served).

19. *See Webb v. James*, 147 F.3d 617, 621 (7th Cir.1998); *Mallory v. Eyrich*, 922 F.2d 1273, 1279 (6th Cir.1991).

20. *See Webb v. James*, 147 F.3d 617, 622 (7th Cir.1998).

21. *Pouillon v. Little*, 326 F.3d 713 (6th Cir.2003).

Chapter Five

PROCEDURAL ASPECTS OF LITIGATING UNDER THE RECONSTRUCTION STATUTES AND CONTEMPORARY CIVIL RIGHTS AND EMPLOYMENT DISCRIMINATION LEGISLATION

Analysis

P. DISCOVERY, EVIDENCE, PRE–TRIAL ORDERS, WAIVER OF OBJECTIONS, AND RELATED ISSUES

Q. SUMMARY JUDGMENT (F.R.C.P. 56), SETTLEMENT, AND JUDGMENT AS A MATTER OF LAW UNDER F.R.C.P. 50(a) ("DIRECTED VERDICT") AND 50(b) ("J.N.O.V.")

R. SECTION 1983 ACTIONS AGAINST INDIVIDUAL AND ENTITY DEFENDANTS—BIFURCATION OF CLAIMS FOR TRIAL

S. CLASS ACTIONS

T. CLAIM AND ISSUE PRECLUSION IN ACTIONS UNDER TITLE VII AND THE RECONSTRUCTION CIVIL RIGHTS ACTS

U. ARBITRATION

V. INTER–ACTION AND INTRA–ACTION PRECLUSION

W. FORECLOSURE OF RECONSTRUCTION ACT CLAIMS BY RELEASE—DISMISSAL AGREEMENTS

X. THE PRECLUSIVE EFFECT OF EMPLOYMENT DISCRIMINATION CONSENT JUDGMENTS ON NONPARTIES

A. OVERVIEW—THE NEW FEDERALISM IN CIVIL RIGHTS FORUM SELECTION: STATE PRIMACY REASSERTED

§ 5.1 In General

In keeping with § 1983's historic purposes, given new voice by *Monroe v. Pape*,[1] the Supreme Court has on occasion declared that the statute's provision of a federal judicial forum was an integral, purposeful element of the overall scheme envisioned by the Reconstruction Congress that enacted it. Yet concrete recognition of the desirability of preserving a federal forum for resolution of alleged federal law violations under color of state law is seldom reflected in the Court's actual holdings. Indeed, looking back over the past quarter century, only two such instances stand out.

In *Mitchum v. Foster*[2] the Court cited the availability of a federal forum as sufficiently important to create an express § 1983 exception to the Anti–Injunction Act, one of the earliest restrictions on the ability of federal courts to interfere with state courts.[3] As a result there is no blanket, statutory barrier arising out of the Anti–Injunction Act to a federal court's enjoining parallel state court proceedings, thereby preserving the federal courts's opportunity to render an initial decision on federal constitutional or statutory rights asserted in § 1983 litigation. As we shall see, however, the barn door was already largely shut. One year earlier, in *Younger v. Harris*[4] the Court had begun to fashion its own rules restricting federal court interference by injunction, declaratory judgment or other equitable relief, with ongoing state proceedings.[5] *Younger*, seizing on the fact that a federal court's exercise of equity jurisdiction is discretionary, ushered in a variety of abstention doctrines against interference with state proceedings that express deference not only to pending state judicial actions but sometimes also to state administrative or regulatory schemes.

A decade after *Mitchum*, the Court again paid homage to the importance of a federal forum by deciding, in *Patsy v. Board of Regents*,[6] that a § 1983 plaintiff generally need not exhaust state administrative

§ 5.1

1. *See* Chapter 2, introductory section.

2. 407 U.S. 225, 92 S.Ct. 2151, 32 L.Ed.2d 705 (1972).

3. 28 U.S.C.A. § 2283. Originally enacted as part of the Judiciary Act of 1793, the Anti–Injunction Act provides, "A court of the United States may not grant an injunction to stay proceedings in a State court except as expressly authorized by Act of Congress, or where necessary in aid of its jurisdiction, or to protect or effectuate its judgments."

4. 401 U.S. 37, 91 S.Ct. 746, 27 L.Ed.2d 669 (1971).

5. *Younger* generally requires the target of an ongoing state prosecution to raise all constitutional claims as defenses to that state action and prevents the state court defendant from filing a collateral federal action raising the same claims.

6. 457 U.S. 496, 102 S.Ct. 2557, 73 L.Ed.2d 172 (1982).

remedies before commencing a judicial lawsuit.[7] But this homage, too, has steadily dissolved into lip service. The new federalism of the *Burger* and *Rehnquist* Courts has made striking inroads into the notion that a federal judicial forum is indispensable, or even particularly important, to vindicating the federal rights actionable through the vehicle of § 1983. Without overturning, or even directly eroding *Patsy*, the Court has carved out an ever expanding domain in which would—be civil rights litigants are forced in the first instance to litigate key issues or entire claims before state administrative or judicial tribunals.

For example, the civil rights claimant who sees that she is about to be or has become entangled in state criminal or important civil litigation or even administrative proceedings and who seeks immediate relief from a federal court is usually now shunted back into the state system. For the most part the Supreme Court has accomplished this result by continually enlarging the classification of state tribunals and matters that trigger *Younger* and its progeny. Those decisions, in the name of intersystem comity, forbid federal court intervention by injunction or declaratory relief with a variety of ongoing state criminal and important civil proceedings. Indeed the policies underlying *Younger* have blossomed to such a degree that, together with its offspring, the decision now constitutes what may fairly be called the rule that swallows the *Mitchum* exception to the Anti–Injunction Act. In addition to the pure *Younger* prescription of dismissal, the Court has developed a host of "abstention" doctrines that temporarily derail federal proceedings by means of stays pending the completion of state proceedings. Chief among these is *Railroad Commission v. Pullman Co.*,[8] which authorizes the stay of federal actions, including those under § 1983,[9] where a particular resolution of an uncertain issue of state law may obviate the need for federal court resolution of a constitutional question.[10] The Court has even

7. The Prison Litigation Reform Act of 1995 which revised remedies for prison condition lawsuits does require administrative exhaustion for prisoners. See 42 U.S.C.A. § 1997e ("No action shall be brought with respect to prison conditions under section 1983 of this title, or any other Federal law, by a prisoner confined in any jail, prison, or other correctional facility until such administrative remedies as are available are exhausted.") *Patsy v. Board of Regents*, 457 U.S. 496, 516, 102 S.Ct. 2557, 2568, 73 L.Ed.2d 172 (1982). There are other limited exceptions to the non-exhaustion rule. A Supreme Court decision, *Heck v. Humphrey*, 512 U.S. 477, 114 S.Ct. 2364, 129 L.Ed.2d 383 (1994), in effect requires exhaustion of judicial remedies by persons convicted of a crime, including prisoners, before asserting any claim under Section 1983 that if successful would necessarily undermine the validity of the conviction. *See also Frazier v. Fairhaven School Committee*, 276 F.3d 52, 57–63 (1st Cir.2002), which assumes that despite available comprehensive remedy under Individuals With Disabilities Education Act, § 1983 "and laws" claim based on IDEA may proceed, but holds that plaintiff bringing such a claim must first exhaust administrative remedies provided by IDEA even though only money damages sought and despite general non-exhaustion rule for Section 1983 (citing two circuit decisions reaching same conclusion and three others permitting the IDEA-based Section 1983 damages-only claim without requiring exhaustion). *Accord, Robb v. Bethel School Dist. No. 403*, 308 F.3d 1047 (9th Cir.2002).

8. 312 U.S. 496, 61 S.Ct. 643, 85 L.Ed. 971 (1941).

9. *See Askew v. Hargrave*, 401 U.S. 476, 91 S.Ct. 856, 28 L.Ed.2d 196 (1971).

10. But see the discussion in § 5.15, *infra*, of *Arizonans for Official English v. Arizona*, 520 U.S. 43, 75–6, 117 S.Ct. 1055, 1073, 137 L.Ed.2d 170 (1997), wherein the

expanded this "wait and see" approach, accomplished by a stay rather than outright dismissal, to other kinds of federal court civil rights actions—those not likely to be mooted by state court resolution of uncertain issues of state law, a la *Pullman*—that seek only damages (and therefore may[11] escape dismissal under *Younger*) but raise issues involved in ongoing state proceedings.[12] Similarly, the Court in *Heck v. Humphrey*[13] has now required the equivalent of federal court abstention pending the conclusion of ordinary state criminal appeals and habeas proceedings even when the § 1983 plaintiff seeks only damages relief.

The award would taint the validity of the underlying state criminal trial judgment. And occasionally the underlying constitutional right sought to be vindicated by the action under Section 1983 in effect also requires preliminary exhaustion of administrative or state court remedies.[14]

The federal courthouse door, having been shut by *Younger* or temporarily closed via a variant of abstention, is often then effectively locked by the Court's companion doctrines that accord most important state judicial and administrative determinations claim or issue preclusive effect when the civil rights claimant later resorts to federal court. The Court has found no § 1983 exception to the federal Full Faith and Credit Statute,[15] which requires federal courts to accord as much preclusive effect to a state court judgment as that state's courts would under the

Court expressed a strong preference for certification of novel state law questions rather than exercising *Pullman* abstention. And the decision in *Pennhurst State School & Hosp. v. Halderman*, 465 U.S. 89, 104 S.Ct. 900, 79 L.Ed.2d 67 (1984), rejecting as a violation of the Eleventh Amendment federal court jurisdiction to adjudicate violations of state law by state officials, even when only prospective relief is sought, has significantly reduced the number of occasions suitable for *Pullman* abstention.

11. The Court wrote in the case under discussion, *Deakins v. Monaghan*, 484 U.S. 193, 108 S.Ct. 523, 98 L.Ed.2d 529 (1988), that it was not deciding whether *Younger* might apply to federal court actions in which only damages are sought. But it has since held that the strong *Younger* medicine of outright abstention—that is, dismissal or remand—is available only where equitable or other discretionary relief is sought. In pure legal damages actions the defendant may be granted only the milder relief of a stay. *Quackenbush v. Allstate Ins. Co.*, 517 U.S. 706, 116 S.Ct. 1712, 135 L.Ed.2d 1 (1996).

12. *Deakins v. Monaghan*, 484 U.S. 193, 108 S.Ct. 523, 98 L.Ed.2d 529 (1988) (authorizing stay, but not dismissal, of federal court damages action under § 1983 pending completion of state grand jury proceedings). *See also Bellotti v. Baird*, 428 U.S. 132, 146, 96 S.Ct. 2857, 2865, 49 L.Ed.2d 844 (1976) (approving abstention until state law was construed by state courts if such construction "would 'at least materially change the nature of the problem' . . ."; quoting *Harrison v. NAACP*, 360 U.S. 167, 177, 79 S.Ct. 1025, 1030, 3 L.Ed.2d 1152 (1959)) (emphasis added).

13. 512 U.S. 477, 487 n. 8, 114 S.Ct. 2364, 2373 n. 8, 129 L.Ed.2d 383 (1994) (citing *Colorado River Water Conservation Dist. v. United States*, 424 U.S. 800, 96 S.Ct. 1236, 47 L.Ed.2d 483 (1976)). *Heck* is discussed in more detail below. Technically, however, *Heck* is based not on abstention but on an exception to the scope of § 1983 itself. The Court has since held outright abstention unavailable where no equitable or otherwise discretionary relief is sought; only a stay is available if the plaintiff seeks purely legal relief, e.g., damages. *Quackenbush v. Allstate Ins. Co.*, 517 U.S. 706, 116 S.Ct. 1712, 135 L.Ed.2d 1 (1996).

14. *See, e.g., Sandy Creek Investors, Ltd. v. City of Jonestown, TX*, 325 F.3d 623 (5th Cir.2003) (landowner's § 1983 14th Amendment takings claim not ripe where plaintiff failed first to seek compensation administratively or in state court).

15. 428 U.S.C.A. § 1738.

state's own law of preclusion. Accordingly, entire "claims"—defined in broad, transactional terms—that were asserted by state court litigants may not be relitigated by them in federal court against the same adversary, at least if that state's own law of res judicata would preclude relitigation.[16] Similarly, so long as the state's law of collateral estoppel would preclude her from relitigating, a § 1983 plaintiff is ordinarily bound by adverse state court determinations on particular issues, even when the § 1983 defendant was not a party to the state action.[17] Such issue preclusion will often render a practical nullity the theoretically ameliorating feature of *Pullman* abstention—the § 1983 plaintiff's ability to return to federal court after the state court action has concluded.[18]

Last, where the state proceedings were administrative rather than judicial, and the Full Faith and Credit Statute is therefore inapplicable, the Court has fashioned a federal common law of preclusion. Here, too, the Court's former preference that federal civil rights plaintiffs have access to an unencumbered federal forum has not proven sufficiently powerful to warrant an exception to the ordinary state law rules governing res judicata and collateral estoppel. The § 1983 plaintiff will be precluded (to the same degree as she would be in the state's courts) from relitigating issues determined adversely to her in state administrative proceedings that are deemed "quasi-judicial" in their formality and fairness.[19] The moral, for putative civil rights plaintiffs desirous of a fresh federal forum, is to be both selective and lucky. Be selective in forum choice by refraining from initiating optional preliminary state court or formal agency proceedings, the results of which, if adverse, might preclude a later action under § 1983. Be lucky by avoiding becoming the target of state criminal or important civil judicial lawsuits or state administrative proceedings which, while still pending, may bar federal court interference under *Younger* or *Deakins/Quackenbush*; and by avoiding criminal conviction which, under *Heck*, may prevent a § 1983 claim that would taint that conviction from even arising unless and until the conviction is overturned on direct appeal or habeas.

It is just as dangerous to trust in state tribunals as to be trapped by them. The Supreme Court has encouraged the litigation of civil rights claims in state courts by holding that they have jurisdiction fully concurrent with that of the federal courts to entertain claims under the Reconstruction statutes[20] and Title VII[21] and other discrimination stat-

16. *Migra v. Warren City Sch. Dist.*, 465 U.S. 75, 104 S.Ct. 892, 79 L.Ed.2d 56 (1984).

17. *See Allen v. McCurry*, 449 U.S. 90, 101 S.Ct. 411, 66 L.Ed.2d 308 (1980) (section 1983 plaintiff cannot relitigate issues determined against him in state criminal trial).

18. *See England v. Louisiana State Bd. of Med. Examiners*, 375 U.S. 411, 84 S.Ct. 461, 11 L.Ed.2d 440 (1964). Upon return of the action to federal court after *England* reservation, issue preclusion applies with respect to the state law issues litigated in state court. *Instructional Sys., Inc. v. Computer Curriculum Corp.*, 35 F.3d 813 (3d Cir.1994), *cert. denied*, 513 U.S. 1183, 115 S.Ct. 1176, 130 L.Ed.2d 1128 (1995).

19. *University of Tennessee v. Elliott*, 478 U.S. 788, 106 S.Ct. 3220, 92 L.Ed.2d 635 (1986).

20. *Howlett v. Rose*, 496 U.S. 356, 110 S.Ct. 2430, 110 L.Ed.2d 332 (1990). The potential advantages of pursuing § 1983 claims in state court are discussed in Section I, below. §§ 5.45 and 5.46.

21. *Yellow Freight v. Donnelly*, 494 U.S. 820, 110 S.Ct. 1566, 108 L.Ed.2d 834

utes. In a curious decision that seemingly runs counter to the new federalism, the Court even forces state judges to relieve the § 1983 plaintiff of complying with a relatively minor procedural obstacle-filing a notice of claim with a local government entity defendant before filing suit.[22] And many potential civil rights litigants, especially state employees, will find state administrative agencies able and willing to entertain related state law causes of action.

But the apparent hospitality of state tribunals can turn into a trap. Woe betide the civil rights litigant who resorts to them voluntarily in the hope of later obtaining a de novo hearing on a Reconstruction Act claim in federal court. That course is perilous even if she asserts in the state court[23] only state law causes of action with elements of proof entirely distinct from those of, say, § 1981 or § 1983. If the federal court later concludes that the federal civil rights claim stems from the same spatial and temporal circumstances as those that gave rise to the state cause of action[24]—the test in modern preclusion law for claim identity—the federal claims will likely be extinguished by the state's law of claim preclusion or "res judicata" just as completely as the same doctrine, applied by force of the Full Faith and Credit Statute, plagues the involuntary state litigant. Even if the "claims," for preclusion purposes, are viewed as different, the federal civil rights plaintiff may be bound by (or, if she prevailed in the state tribunal, take advantage of) state court findings on discrete issues.

Similar pitfalls await the civil rights plaintiff who first submits related state law claims to a "quasi-judicial" state administrative agency.[25] A loss there may jeopardize the outcome of a subsequent federal civil rights lawsuit. Depending on the potential recoveries under state law before the agency and under the federal civil rights acts before a court, it may therefore be wiser to forego the state agency forum—even

(1990). Although Title VII itself expressly confers subject matter jurisdiction on federal courts to hear "actions brought under this title," § 706(f)(3), 42 U.S.C.A. § 2000e–5(f)(3), federal question jurisdiction does not extend to suits brought to enforce Title VII settlement agreements. Such actions are based simply on state contract law, and the jurisdiction of a federal court to hear them thus depends on meeting the requirements of 28 U.S.C.A. § 1332: the happenstance presence of complete diversity of citizenship and a claim of greater than $75,000. *Morris v. City of Hobart, Okla.*, 39 F.3d 1105 (10th Cir.1994), *cert. denied*, 514 U.S. 1109, 115 S.Ct. 1960, 131 L.Ed.2d 852 (1995). *See Kokkonen v. Guardian Life Ins. Co.*, 511 U.S. 375, 114 S.Ct. 1673, 128 L.Ed.2d 391 (1994) (rejecting the proposition that a federal court that failed to retain jurisdiction over a primary controversy has "ancillary" jurisdiction to hear a separate action to enforce a settlement agreement reached in the underlying action). Counsel desirous of enforcing such an agreement should therefore take care to incorporate it by reference in an order of dismissal or request the court explicitly to retain jurisdiction pending satisfaction of the agreement.

22. *Felder v. Casey*, 487 U.S. 131, 108 S.Ct. 2302, 101 L.Ed.2d 123 (1988).

23. The state administrative agency likely would have jurisdiction to entertain only the state, not the federal cause of action.

24. Restatement (Second) of Judgments, § 24.

25. The plaintiff in *University of Tennessee v. Elliott*, 478 U.S. 788, 106 S.Ct. 3220, 92 L.Ed.2d 635 (1986), voluntarily initiated the state administrative proceedings that later cast a shadow on his federal court action under § 1983.

if, under state law, that means abandoning the state cause of action—and proceed directly to state or federal court. In a federal court, the state cause of action could be joined to the federal claim under supplemental jurisdiction;[26] a state court, as observed above, would have concurrent jurisdiction to hear the federal claim together with the claim under state law. On the other hand, if counsel is highly confident about prevailing before such a state administrative tribunal (and also confident that the federal civil rights claim will not be precluded by res judicata), it may be tactically advantageous to pursue the state administrative remedy. In that event the agency's favorable fact findings may be accorded issue preclusive effect in the subsequent civil rights action, easing the plaintiff's burden of proof.

But what if the particular federal statute under which the plaintiff wishes to proceed *mandates* prior resort to state administrative remedies as a prerequisite to asserting the federal law claim in (state or federal) court? Although *Patsy* relieves most Reconstruction Act plaintiffs[27] of any such requirement, the major employment discrimination statutes, Title VII, ADEA and ADA (but not EPA), require the filing of charges with state or local, as well as federal, antidiscrimination agencies in the vast majority of states that have parallel laws, procedures and remedies consistent with federal standards. The Supreme Court has avoided a Catch–22 situation by holding that the employment discrimination plaintiff who resorts to a state administrative tribunal only to the extent mandated by federal law will not be claim precluded and may proceed to court for a trial de novo.[28] But even this decision had a peculiar new—federalist twist. If the plaintiff seeks review of the state antidiscrimination agency's ruling in state *court*—more resort to state process than the federal statutes demand—she runs the full risks of preclusion under the Full Faith and Credit Statute.[29]

Even the historic federal habeas writ, long a bulwark against unconstitutional state excesses, now stands, at least in relative terms, as something of an obstacle rather than an aid to the enforcement of federal constitutional rights. Current state prisoners desirous of using § 1983 to secure immediate or early release from state incarceration,[30] and current or former[31] state prisoners seeking any § 1983 relief, even damages, that depends upon showing the invalidity of their underlying state convictions,[32] are now *compelled* to repair instead to federal habeas. And because the federal habeas statute mandates prior resort to state

26. *See* 28 U.S.C.A. § 1367(a) and (c), discussed below.

27. The Prison Litigation Reform Act of 1995 does require administrative exhaustion for prisoners. See 42 U.S.C.A. § 1997e.

28. *Kremer v. Chemical Constr. Corp.*, 456 U.S. 461, 102 S.Ct. 1883, 72 L.Ed.2d 262 (1982) (Title VII).

29. *Id.*

30. *Preiser v. Rodriguez*, 411 U.S. 475, 93 S.Ct. 1827, 36 L.Ed.2d 439 (1973); *Wolff v. McDonnell*, 418 U.S. 539, 94 S.Ct. 2963, 41 L.Ed.2d 935 (1974).

31. Whether a former prisoner seeking damages under § 1983 is barred by *Heck* is not altogether clear. See § 5.7, *infra*.

32. *Heck v. Humphrey*, 512 U.S. 477, 114 S.Ct. 2364, 129 L.Ed.2d 383 (1994) (holding legally insufficient a § 1983 claim analogous to malicious prosecution because the plaintiff's proof would impugn his underlying criminal conviction).

habeas remedies,[33] the upshot of these decisions is to provide state tribunals (or possibly a federal habeas court) the first and, given the likelihood of a *Heck* bar or preclusion,[34] probably the only opportunity to review these federal constitutional claims.

Consider, then, the hardy, lucky or shrewd plaintiff who has threaded all these needles and gets to federal court. Even there, the litigation of her Reconstruction Act claims (but not claims of employment discrimination) will to some degree be impaired by the brooding omnipresence of state law. The Supreme Court has interpreted a remedial provision that pertains to all the Reconstruction Acts[35] to require the application of important quasi-substantive state rules-governing limitations periods,[36] tolling circumstances,[37] and survivorship of actions,[38] for example—in actions under those statutes in federal as well as state court. And will the federal judgment be accorded the same extensive preclusive effect that the Court insists federal courts accord state tribunals? The answer is not yet clear, but there are hints that it may be "No." The Court has raised the possibility, for example, that the diminishing class of state prisoners' claims still assertable under § 1983 rather than remitted to state and federal habeas corpus may generate judgments of doubtful potency. Federal preclusion law, the Court wrote, may take account of the policy of deference to state habeas that is embodied in the federal habeas statute, so that "preclusion [of state courts based on prior federal court findings] will not necessarily be an automatic, or even a permissible, effect."[39]

Finally, worthy of note is an incipient development parallel to the Court's reinvigoration of federalism. Should this development ripen, it promises to oust significant additional numbers of employment discrimination and perhaps even Reconstruction Act claims from the federal (and state) courts. The Court, turning aside from an ancient judicial suspicion, has begun to countenance the arbitration of claims asserting federal statutory rights pursuant to pre-dispute agreements to arbitrate. To be sure, the extant authority holds that an agreement to arbitrate, otherwise enforceable under the Federal Arbitration Act, cannot prevent

33. 28 U.S.C.A. § 2254(b). The full scope of the "exhaustion" and "procedural default" doctrines the Supreme Court has developed to flesh out the requirements of the statute is beyond the scope of this book. Nevertheless, *O'Sullivan v. Boerckel*, 526 U.S. 838, 119 S.Ct. 1728, 144 L.Ed.2d 1 (1999), provides a useful primer. There the Court construed the "default" branch of statutory deference to state criminal procedures to require a convict to pursue each level of standard, nonexceptional appellate review provided by the state criminal system. This means that the convict must seek even purely discretionary review by the state's highest court, unless the state formally provides that review is unavailable. The mere fact that such review is discretionary and even somewhat discouraged by rule or practice, however, does not make review unavailable for these purposes and accordingly does not excuse the failure to seek review.

34. *See* §§ 5.118 and 5.119.

35. 42 U.S.C.A. § 1988.

36. *Wilson v. Garcia*, 471 U.S. 261, 105 S.Ct. 1938, 85 L.Ed.2d 254 (1985).

37. *Board of Regents v. Tomanio*, 446 U.S. 478, 100 S.Ct. 1790, 64 L.Ed.2d 440 (1980).

38. *Robertson v. Wegmann*, 436 U.S. 584, 98 S.Ct. 1991, 56 L.Ed.2d 554 (1978).

39. *Heck v. Humphrey*, 512 U.S. at 488 & n.9, 114 S.Ct. at 2373 & n.9.

a Reconstruction Act claimant from having her day in court.[40] But in a noncollectively bargained setting, where the agreement to arbitrate was also not contained in an individual contract of employment, the Court has stayed litigation under the federal age discrimination statute pending arbitration,[41] a decision extended by most circuit courts to claims under Title VII as well. It remains to be seen if the Court will extend this holding to bar statutory employment discrimination litigation under ADEA or Title VII once noncollectively bargained arbitration is completed will adhere to precedent that allows de novo litigation of Title VII claims notwithstanding a completed arbitration proceeding and award where the agreement to arbitrate was collectively bargained.[42]

The value served here is not federalism, of course—at its broadest, deference to arbitral awards would preclude state as well as federal litigation—but easing calendar congestion at all levels of the nation's judiciary. In refusing to permit agreements to arbitrate to preclude access to judicial fora with respect to Reconstruction Act claims, the Court questioned the competence and legitimacy of arbitrators to provide authoritative resolutions of Congressionally declared rights.[43] Ironically, if arbitration should come to foreclose judicial litigation of most employment discrimination claims, but the authority denying that effect to collectively bargained arbitration agreements remains as an exception, the group of claimants arguably least in need of judicial protection—those represented by a union—would be the only ones to whom the judicial forum would remain open.

40. *McDonald v. City of West Branch*, 466 U.S. 284, 104 S.Ct. 1799, 80 L.Ed.2d 302 (1984).

41. *Gilmer v. Interstate/Johnson Lane Corp.*, 500 U.S. 20, 111 S.Ct. 1647, 114 L.Ed.2d 26 (1991).

42. *Alexander v. Gardner–Denver Co.*, 415 U.S. 36, 94 S.Ct. 1011, 39 L.Ed.2d 147 (1974). The variety of possible judicial resolutions of these questions is surveyed in § 7.6.

43. *McDonald v. City of West Branch*, 466 U.S. 284, 104 S.Ct. 1799, 80 L.Ed.2d 302 (1984).

When a Federal Judicial Forum for § 1983 Claims/Issues Is/Is Not So "Special" That the Plaintiff Has Access, First Access, or Unencumbered Access to It

THE FEDERAL FORUM *IS* SO SPECIAL	THE FEDERAL FORUM IS *NOT* SUFFICIENTLY SPECIAL
— that access is allowed even when defendant has acted in *violation* of *state* law and even when state courts have historically afforded a remedy for such violations: *Monroe v. Pape*, 365 U.S. 167, 81 S.Ct. 473, 5 L.Ed.2d 492 (1961)	— to escape the judge-made, comity-driven *Younger* doctrine that counsels federal court dismissal of § 1983 actions seeking to enjoin or otherwise interfere with state criminal, important civil and even administrative proceedings in which the § 1983 plaintiff can conceivably raise the federal issue. *Younger* may apply whether the state proceedings were pending before or initiated after the commencement of the federal court § 1983 action, provided that the state proceeding was not instituted in manifest bad faith: *Younger v. Harris*, 401 U.S. 37, 91 S.Ct. 746, 27 L.Ed.2d 669 (1971); *Hicks v. Miranda*, 422 U.S. 332, 95 S.Ct. 2281, 45 L.Ed.2d 223 (1975) (applying doctrine to later-filed state proceedings); *Trainor v. Hernandez*, 431 U.S. 434, 97 S.Ct. 1911, 52 L.Ed.2d 486 (1977) (applying doctrine to civil judicial proceedings); *Middlesex County Ethics Comm. v. Garden State Bar Ass'n*, 457 U.S. 423, 102 S.Ct. 2515, 73 L.Ed.2d 116 (1982) (applying doctrine to administrative proceedings); *Pennzoil Co. v. Texaco, Inc.*, 481 U.S. 1, 107 S.Ct. 1519, 95 L.Ed.2d 1 (1987) (establishing presumption that the federal issue can be raised in the state proceeding); *Samuels v. Mackell*, 401 U.S. 66, 91 S.Ct. 764, 27 L.Ed.2d 688 (1971) (extending abstention doctrine to federal actions seeking only declaratory not injunctive relief); *cf. Deakins v. Monaghan*, 484 U.S. 193, 108 S.Ct. 523, 98 L.Ed.2d 529 (1988) (approving stay of federal damages action pending conclusion of earlier commenced state grand jury proceedings); *Quackenbush v. Allstate Ins. Co.*, 517 U.S. 706, 116 S.Ct. 1712, 135 L.Ed.2d 1 (1996) (only a stay, not dismissal a la *Younger*, appropriate when plaintiff seeks only damages or other legal relief)

THE FEDERAL FORUM *IS* SO SPECIAL	THE FEDERAL FORUM IS *NOT* SUFFICIENTLY SPECIAL
— that § 1983 is an exception to the *categorical* ban of the Anti–Injunction Act against federal court interference with prior pending state judicial proceedings: *Mitchum v. Foster,* 407 U.S. 225, 92 S.Ct. 2151, 32 L.Ed.2d 705 (1972)	— to warrant an exception to collateral estoppel (*issue* preclusion) once state judicial or quasi-judicial administrative proceedings have gone to judgment or decision, in subsequent federal court actions under § 1983: *Allen v. McCurry,* 449 U.S. 90, 101 S.Ct. 411, 66 L.Ed.2d 308 (1980) (estoppel under 28 U.S.C.A. § 1738 bars prisoner's challenge in § 1983 action to underlying conviction, even when federal court habeas corpus not available); *University of Tennessee v. Elliott,* 478 U.S. 788, 106 S.Ct. 3220, 92 L.Ed.2d 635 (1986) (judge-made extension of collateral estoppel where fact finding made in quasi-judicial state administrative proceedings)
— that § 1983 plaintiffs (excluding prisoners complaining of conditions of confinement, who must exhaust available state administrative remedies under the Prison Litigation Reform Act) need not exhaust available state administrative proceedings before filing suit under § 1983: *Patsy v. Bd. of Regents,* 457 U.S. 496, 102 S.Ct. 2557, 73 L.Ed.2d 172 (1982)	— to warrant an exception to res judicata (*claim* preclusion), if plaintiff has earlier filed a state court civil action or counterclaim based on federal *or* state law and arising from the same transaction that gives rise to the § 1983 claim: *Migra v. Warren City Sch. Dist. Bd. of Educ.,* 465 U.S. 75, 104 S.Ct. 892, 79 L.Ed.2d 56 (1984)
— that the § 1983 claim may proceed notwithstanding a prior adverse arbitration award: *McDonald v. West Branch, Mi.,* 466 U.S. 284, 104 S.Ct. 1799, 80 L.Ed.2d 302 (1984)	— to permit a § 1983 claim seeking release or early release from incarceration following state court criminal conviction until and unless that conviction is first overturned on direct review in state court or collaterally through federal (and, accordingly, *prior state*) habeas corpus (*Preiser v. Rodriguez,* 411 U.S. 475, 93 S.Ct. 1827, 36 L.Ed.2d 439 (1973)), or to permit a § 1983 claim seeking only damages where that claim, if successful, would taint the validity of such a conviction, or have the effect of changing the actual duration of the criminal sentence, until and unless that conviction is first overturned (*Heck v. Humphrey,* 512 U.S. 477, 114 S.Ct. 2364, 129 L.Ed.2d 383 (1994)); *Muhammad v. Close,* ___ U.S. ___, 124 S.Ct. 1303, 158 L.Ed.2d 32 (2004)
— that after *Pullman* abstention, the plaintiff may return to federal court to pursue a § 1983 claim	— to avoid the expansion of the *Rooker-Feldman* doctrine, an expansion that effectively precludes

THE FEDERAL FORUM *IS* SO SPECIAL	THE FEDERAL FORUM IS *NOT* SUFFICIENTLY SPECIAL
first commenced there: *England v. Louisiana State Bd. of Medical Examiners,* 375 U.S. 411, 84 S.Ct. 461, 11 L.Ed.2d 440 (1964); and that *Burford* abstention is seldom if ever appropriate to sidetrack an action under § 1983, *see New Orleans Public Service, Inc. v. Council of New Orleans*, 491 U.S. 350, 109 S.Ct. 2506, 105 L.Ed.2d 298 (1989)	the assertion in federal court of a § 1983 claim that has the potential to call into question a state court judgment, even in circumstances where state law, applicable under 28 U.S.C.A. § 1738, would not require preclusion.

§§ 5.2–5.5 [Reserved]

B. FEDERAL SUBJECT MATTER JURISDICTION

§ 5.6 Original Jurisdiction

Two of the Reconstruction Act Statutes, 42 U.S.C.A. §§ 1983 and 1985, create remedies only, for claims based on independently created rights; Sections 1981 and 1982 create rights; but none of these statutes confers federal court jurisdiction. Federal court jurisdiction proceeds from 28 U.S.C.A. § 1331, the federal question jurisdictional statute. Congress also added a separate statute, 28 U.S.C.A. § 1343, which provides for original jurisdiction in "any civil action" brought to "redress the deprivation, under color of State law, ... of any right ... secured by the Constitution ... or by any *Act of Congress providing for equal rights* of citizens." (emphasis added). The Court read this language to give jurisdiction only where the right being abridged is one granted in the Constitution or in a statute intended to secure equal rights, not simply any civil right.[1] Narrow construction of § 1343 had major significance when § 1331 had a $10,000 amount in controversy requirement; since the elimination of that requirement for federal questions in December of 1980, civil rights plaintiffs have pleaded jurisdiction under § 1331 alone, or in combination with § 1343. There appears to be little advantage to invoking § 1343 as the basis for federal subject matter jurisdiction in civil rights claims.[2] Cautious civil rights lawyers nevertheless plead both § 1343 and § 1331 as distinct bases to support original and, under 28 U.S.C.A. § 1441, removal, federal court subject matter jurisdiction over Reconstruction Act claims.

Contemporary employment discrimination statutes contain their own express authorizations of federal subject matter jurisdiction, although again it is not clear what these add now that § 1331 has been shorn of its amount in controversy requirement.[3] A fine, sometimes

§ 5.6

1. *Chapman v. Houston Welfare Rights Org.*, 441 U.S. 600, 99 S.Ct. 1905, 60 L.Ed.2d 508 (1979); *Maine v. Thiboutot*, 448 U.S. 1, 100 S.Ct. 2502, 65 L.Ed.2d 555 (1980).

2. But see text immediately below.

3. *See, e.g.*, Title VII § 706(f)(3), 42 U.S.C.A. § 2000e–5(f)(3).

barely discernible line separates issues classified as going to subject matter jurisdiction under these statutes, and therefore determinable at the threshold by the court, and issues classified as part of plaintiff's claim, and therefore determinable (on demand) by a jury.[4] The outcome of this decision also affects whether the district court can exercise its supplemental jurisdiction over state law claims and whether the result is subject to collateral attack.[5]

The plaintiff should take care, however, especially when she also asserts claims under state law, to allege that her federal law claim "arises under" the predicate Reconstruction Act or employment discrimination statute. The Supreme Court has long insisted that in order to invoke federal subject matter jurisdiction under § 1331, the plaintiff's right to relief must be created by or at a minimum depend heavily on the construction of federal law.[6] The allegations of a right under federal law may not be "wholly insubstantial and frivolous" (for example, negated by recent authoritative precedent) or "immaterial" (for example, a federal claim "tail" wagging a "dog" composed of multiple state law claims of greater magnitude).[7] The Court has shown reluctance to

4. *Compare Scarfo v. Ginsberg,* 175 F.3d 957 (11th Cir.1999), *cert. denied,* 529 U.S. 1003, 120 S.Ct. 1267, 146 L.Ed.2d 217 (2000) (whether the defendants, corporations and their owner, constituted a "single employer" subject to Title VII is a quasi-jurisdictional question that determines whether Title VII applies and therefore must be decided by the court, which must answer it affirmatively before a jury may determine the related element of plaintiff's claim, i.e., whether 15 or more "employees" worked for such a "single employer") with *Garcia v. Copenhaver, Bell & Assocs.*, 104 F.3d 1256 (11th Cir.1997) (plaintiff must show that defendant is an "employer" as an element of her prima facie case under ADEA, so the issue goes to the merits and should be decided by a jury at trial).

5. *See Da Silva v. Kinsho Int'l Corp.*, 229 F.3d 358 (2d Cir.2000) (holding that the 15 employee threshold for Title VII coverage was not jurisdictional and allowing lower court to exercise its supplemental jurisdiction). *Accord Sharpe v. Jefferson Distributing Co.*, 148 F.3d 676, 677 (7th Cir. 1998) ("A plaintiff's inability to demonstrate that the defendant has 15 employees is just like any other failure to meet a statutory requirement."); *EEOC v. St. Francis Xavier Parochial School,* 117 F.3d 621, 623–25 (D.C.Cir.1997) (ADA case). *But see Scarfo v. Ginsberg,* 175 F.3d 957, 960 (11th Cir.1999); *Greenlees v. Eidenmuller Enterprises, Inc.*, 32 F.3d 197, 198 (5th Cir. 1994); *Childs v. Local 18, IBEW,* 719 F.2d 1379, 1382 (9th Cir.1983); *Armbruster v. Quinn,* 711 F.2d 1332, 1335 (6th Cir.1983); *see also Hukill v. Auto Care, Inc.*, 192 F.3d 437, 441–42 (4th Cir.1999) (same as to Family and Medical Leave Act, 29 U.S.C.A. § 2611(4)(A)(i)).

6. *See, e.g., Louisville & Nashville R.R. v. Mottley*, 211 U.S. 149, 29 S.Ct. 42, 53 L.Ed. 126 (1908).

7. *Bell v. Hood*, 327 U.S. 678, 66 S.Ct. 773, 90 L.Ed. 939 (1946). But the immateriality or insubstantiality of a purported federal law claim is an exception to the general requirement that a federal court exercise federal subject matter jurisdiction over claims that the plaintiff has squarely based on federal law. In *Bell*, the Supreme Court offered examples that in effect branded a claim "insubstantial" only if it had been ruled legally insufficient rather recently by a court of considerable authority, and "immaterial" only if the federal claim or claims were slight in number, weight, or relief sought in relation to one or more state law claims. Accordingly, a federal court that finds a claim the plaintiff pleaded under federal law to be legally insufficient should ordinarily dismiss it not for lack of federal subject matter jurisdiction but for failure to state a claim on which relief can be granted. *Id.* From time to time, however, lower courts reverse the presumption, demanding that the plaintiff's federal law claim be affirmatively substantial. *See Lovern v. Edwards*, 190 F.3d 648, 654–656 (4th Cir. 1999) (dismissing for lack of subject matter jurisdiction a claim because plaintiff's rights were not "directly and sharply" implicated by defendant's challenged conduct).

recognize federal question jurisdiction of the district courts based on allegations that a federal statutory standard defines one of the elements of a claim that exists solely by virtue of state law.[8] Similarly, a defendant may not remove an action (on the basis of a federal question) where plaintiff's state law complaint refers to Title VII merely for such definitional purposes.[9]

This authorization for federal subject matter jurisdiction does not of course dispense with the necessity of securing personal jurisdiction over each defendant both constitutionally and under Federal Rule 4(k), as amended in December 1993. Whether a district court must first decide subject matter jurisdiction before considering personal jurisdiction depends upon whether either inquiry raises difficult or novel questions. In *Ruhrgas v. Marathon Oil Co.*,[10] the district court was faced with a very difficult and arduous subject matter jurisdiction inquiry; it chose to bypass the tough issue and dismiss the removed case on personal jurisdictional grounds, an issue that was considerably more straightforward. The Fifth Circuit reversed, finding that subject matter jurisdiction was more fundamental and must in all cases be considered at the threshold. The Supreme Court reversed, acknowledging that while in most instances subject matter jurisdiction will not present difficult questions and should be the threshold inquiry, when subject matter jurisdiction presents novel or challenging questions, and the personal jurisdictional inquiry presents no complex issues of state law, a court may proceed to decide the personal jurisdiction issue first. Although *Ruhrgas* involved a removed case, the holding appears equally applicable to cases brought to federal court in the first instance.

§ 5.7 Special Situations Requiring De Facto Exhaustion of State Tribunals as Prerequisite to Asserting the Federal Claim

Unlike actions under Title VII, ADEA or ADA, there is no general requirement of exhaustion of administrative remedies before a Reconstruction Act lawsuit may be brought.[1] It is not that unusual, however, for the federal courts to conclude that the plaintiff's federal claims must exclusively, or at least initially, be presented to state *judicial* systems against the plaintiff's wishes.[2] These are now considered in detail.

8. *See Merrell Dow Pharmaceuticals Inc. v. Thompson*, 478 U.S. 804, 106 S.Ct. 3229, 92 L.Ed.2d 650 (1986).

9. *Rains v. Criterion Sys., Inc.*, 80 F.3d 339 (9th Cir.1996).

10. 526 U.S. 574, 119 S.Ct. 1563, 143 L.Ed.2d 760 (1999).

§ 5.7

1. *Patsy v. Board of Regents*, 457 U.S. 496, 516, 102 S.Ct. 2557, 2568, 73 L.Ed.2d 172 (1982) (holding that no mandatory exhaustion of state administrative remedies is required).

2. *See, e.g., Heck v. Humphrey*, 512 U.S. 477, 114 S.Ct. 2364, 129 L.Ed.2d 383 (1994) and *Preiser v. Rodriguez*, 411 U.S. 475, 93 S.Ct. 1827, 36 L.Ed.2d 439 (1973) (requiring a state prisoner who invokes § 1983 seeking immediate or earlier release from incarceration (*Preiser*) or any relief, including damages, that depends on substantively invalidating his state conviction (*Heck*), to pursue the exclusive remedy of federal habeas corpus relief under 28 U.S.C.A. § 2254 and, hence, to resort first to state court); *Younger v. Harris*, 401 U.S. 37, 54, 91 S.Ct. 746, 755, 27 L.Ed.2d 669

The Court has in effect mandated prior resort to state judicial tribunals through at least one doctrine that in form does the very different work of narrowing the scope of a particular constitutional right sought to be vindicated under § 1983. The *Parratt* decision,[3] discussed in Chapter 2, the § 1983 Chapter, is a good example. It and its progeny make the availability of a federal forum to consider a procedural due process claim challenging "random and unauthorized" action by a government official turn on whether state law provides an adequate remedy. If so, and assuming no diversity of citizenship, such a plaintiff is in effect required to proceed in the state courts under state law and will have no federal law claim to pursue elsewhere.

More commonly, though, a tangle of interrelated procedural doctrines remits putative § 1983 plaintiffs to state court, leaving them free in theory—a possibility undermined in practice by estoppel doctrines and the plaintiff's sheer weariness—to pursue a federal court § 1983 claim later. In *Preiser v. Rodriguez*,[4] for example, the Court ruled that when prisoners invoke § 1983 seeking immediate release or a shortened period of imprisonment, and not simply relief stemming from the conditions of their confinement, federal habeas corpus under 28 U.S.C.A. § 2254 is their exclusive federal remedy. Under the terms of that statute, in turn, they must first resort to state court to pursue the state's own habeas remedy. Indeed the Court so held in *Preiser* even though the conduct complained of under § 1983 related not to the underlying criminal trial but to the action of state prison officials in reducing the plaintiff's good-time credits.

In *Heck v. Humphrey*,[5] the Court has extended *Preiser* by holding § 1983 unavailable whenever, regardless of the relief sought, the claim of a prisoner or former prisoner[6], in order to succeed, must necessarily invalidate or taint an underlying state conviction that has not been reversed, expunged, or vacated. Section 1983, in other words, may be used to challenge the validity of only those criminal convictions that have been set aside by the state's appellate courts[7] or a state habeas

(1971) (banning federal injunctive relief that would impede prior pending state criminal proceedings); *Trainor v. Hernandez*, 431 U.S. 434, 97 S.Ct. 1911, 52 L.Ed.2d 486 (1977) (banning federal declaratory relief that would impede prior pending state civil proceedings); *Railroad Comm'n v. Pullman Co.*, 312 U.S. 496, 61 S.Ct. 643, 85 L.Ed. 971 (1941) (declaring a doctrine of abstention that, theoretically at least, merely postpones the exercise of federal jurisdiction when state court clarification of uncertain state law might obviate the necessity of a federal constitutional ruling).

3. *Parratt v. Taylor*, 451 U.S. 527, 101 S.Ct. 1908, 68 L.Ed.2d 420 (1981).

4. 411 U.S. 475, 93 S.Ct. 1827, 36 L.Ed.2d 439 (1973).

5. 512 U.S. 477, 114 S.Ct. 2364, 129 L.Ed.2d 383 (1994).

6. Whether a former prisoner seeking damages under § 1983 is barred by *Heck* is not altogether clear. See text § 5.7, *infra*. The Sixth Circuit has held the doctrine applicable to a potential *future* prisoner, that is, a criminal defendant not yet convicted. *Shamaeizadeh v. Cunigan*, 182 F.3d 391 (6th Cir.1999), *cert. denied*, 528 U.S. 1021, 120 S.Ct. 531, 145 L.Ed.2d 412 (1999).

7. *See O'Sullivan v. Boerckel*, 526 U.S. 838, 119 S.Ct. 1728, 144 L.Ed.2d 1 (1999), discussed in § 5.1, *supra*. *See also Clay v. Allen*, 242 F.3d 679 (5th Cir.2001) (*Heck* does not apply to bar a civil rights suit after the conviction was reversed on direct appeal even if the criminal defendant faces a retri-

tribunal or called into question on federal habeas.[8] The Court based this conclusion principally on the common law requirement prevailing when § 1983 was enacted that the tort of malicious prosecution could lie only if the underlying proceeding had terminated favorably to the plaintiff.[9] Although the court's notion is essentially one of prematurity—the § 1983 claim is not ripe unless and until the state conviction has been overturned—it took pains to describe the ground on which such an action should be dismissed as legal insufficiency. Given the confusion about characterizing the nature of the *Heck* objection, it is not surprising that lower courts are split as to whether dismissal for *Heck* reasons is with or without prejudice.[10]

Whether *Heck* applies, or will continue to apply, to former prisoners (or prisoners who were merely fined) seeking § 1983 damages is not altogether clear. Several circuit opinions have suggested that an exception to *Heck* probably exists for § 1983 damages suits when no other route is available to challenge a criminal conviction—e.g., when the claim is by a former prisoner who can no longer challenge a conviction via habeas. The suggestion has its roots in the concurring and dissenting opinions in *Spencer v. Kemna.*[11] *Spencer*, a state parolee whose parole had been revoked, filed a state habeas petition that was rejected by all state courts, including the state supreme court. He then filed a federal habeas petition, but the district court did not act on the petition before *Spencer* was again released from custody on parole and the term of his imprisonment had expired. Subsequently, the district court mooted his petition because it no longer satisfied the "in custody" requirement of the habeas statute. The Eighth Circuit affirmed, as did the Supreme Court, though on different grounds.

In an opinion by Justice Souter, the Court observed that Article III's "case or controversy" requirement must be met throughout the litiga-

al); *Davis v. Zain*, 79 F.3d 18 (5th Cir.1996) (per curiam) (pending retrial no bar to § 1983 action where state would not re-use tainted evidence that led to plaintiff's reversed conviction).

8. *See Smith v. Gonzales,* 222 F.3d 1220 (10th Cir.2000) (federal appellate habeas order vacating conviction due to prosecution's failure to disclose exculpatory evidence ended *Heck* bar; claim therefore accrued on date of that order, despite possibility of retrial); *Figueroa v. Rivera*, 147 F.3d 77 (1st Cir.1998) (damages claim for alleged unconstitutional conviction barred by *Heck*). Applying *Heck*, an appellate court has ordered a civil rights action remanded to permit the inmate—plaintiff to try to demonstrate that the conviction challenged in federal court had been invalidated. It was possible, the court wrote, that the subject conviction had been set aside but that the inmate had been convicted again upon retrial. *Bell v. Peters*, 33 F.3d 18 (7th Cir.1994).

9. *Heck*, 114 S.Ct. at 2370.

10. *Compare Arvie v. Broussard*, 42 F.3d 249 (5th Cir.1994) (per curiam) (with prejudice) with *Williams v. Schario*, 93 F.3d 527 (8th Cir.1996) and *Fottler v. United States*, 73 F.3d 1064 (10th Cir.1996) (without prejudice). As the caption of *Fottler* would suggest, the *Heck* doctrine has been extended to *Bivens* claims of unconstitutional conduct against federal officers. *See, e.g., Robinson v. Jones*, 142 F.3d 905, 907 (6th Cir.1998) and *Shamaeizadeh v. Cunigan*, 182 F.3d 391, 397 (6th Cir.1999), *cert. denied*, 528 U.S. 1021, 120 S.Ct. 531, 145 L.Ed.2d 412 (1999), applying *Heck* to the claims of a federal prisoner and federal defendant whose charges were dismissed, respectively; *Clemente v. Allen*, 120 F.3d 703 (7th Cir.1997); *Williams v. Hill*, 74 F.3d 1339 (D.C.Cir.1996) (per curiam). See § 2.48, *supra*.

11. 523 U.S. 1, 118 S.Ct. 978, 140 L.Ed.2d 43 (1998).

tion. While a currently incarcerated prisoner challenging his confinement will always satisfy that requirement, a released prisoner can satisfy it only if there are continuing collateral consequences (such as deprivation of the right to vote, to hold office, to serve on a jury, or to engage in certain businesses). Because Spencer was challenging only his revocation of parole and not his original conviction, the Court found that he was burdened by no continuing collateral consequences,[12] and hence his claim was moot and could not satisfy the Article III justiciability requirement. Spencer had argued that because *Heck* would foreclose him from pursuing a damages action under § 1983 unless and until he could establish the invalidity of his parole revocation, his action to establish that invalidity cannot be moot. The Court stated in response, that it did not believe "that a § 1983 action for damages must always and everywhere be available. It is not certain, in any event, that a § 1983 damages claim would be foreclosed. If, for example, petitioner were to seek damages for using the wrong procedures, not for reaching the wrong result, and if that procedural defect did not necessarily imply the invalidity of the revocation, then *Heck* would have no application all."[13]

In a concurrence, Justice Breyer, joined by Justices O'Connor, Ginsburg, and Breyer, wrote "[t]he better view ... is that a former prisoner, no longer" in custody, "may bring a § 1983 action establishing the unconstitutionality of a conviction or confinement without being bound to satisfy a [*Heck*-like] favorable-termination requirement that it would be impossible as a matter of law for him to satisfy.... After a prisoner's release from custody, the habeas statute and its exhaustion requirement have nothing to do with his right to any relief."[14] Justice Stevens dissented, stating that "[g]iven the Court's holding that petitioner does not have a remedy under the habeas statute, it is perfectly clear, as Justice Souter explains, that he may bring an action under § 1983."[15] These five Justices together have seriously undermined the continuing applicability of *Heck* to former prisoners and those convicted but never incarcerated, but the circuits are divided in their willingness to apply the "exception."[16]

12. *See Lane v. Williams*, 455 U.S. 624, 102 S.Ct. 1322, 71 L.Ed.2d 508 (1982) (rejecting the contention of convicted felons who had completed their sentences that their challenges to their sentences of three years' mandatory parole at the conclusion of their fixed terms of incarceration (which parole they had violated) were not moot because the revocations of parole could be used to their detriment in future parole proceedings should they ever be convicted of other crimes).

13. *Spencer*, 523 U.S. at 17, 118 S.Ct. at 988 (citing *Heck* and *Edwards v. Balisok*, discussed *infra* this section).

14. *Id.* at 21, 118 S.Ct. at 990 (Souter, J., concurring). In a separate concurrence, Justice Ginsburg wrote, "[i]ndividuals without recourse to the habeas statute because they are not 'in custody' (people merely fined or whose sentences have been fully served, for example) fit within § 1983's 'broad reach' ". *Id.* (citations omitted).

15. *Id.* at 25 n.8, 118 S.Ct. at 992 n.8 (Stevens, J., dissenting).

16. *See Randell v. Johnson,* 227 F.3d 300 (5th Cir.2000) (applying bar to former prisoner despite acknowledging his inability to obtain habeas relief after his release from custody); *Hoard v. Reddy,* 175 F.3d 531 (7th Cir.1999), *cert. denied,* 528 U.S. 970, 120 S.Ct. 411, 145 L.Ed.2d 320 (1999); *Carr v. O'Leary,* 167 F.3d 1124, 1127 (7th Cir.1999) (acknowledging what it terms "an exception" but finding the facts of the case outside the exception); *Nance v. Vieregge,* 147 F.3d 589, 591 (7th Cir.1998), *cert. de-*

The potential reach of *Heck* may turn on how directly or comprehensively a § 1983 claim must call into question an unreversed, undisturbed state criminal conviction in order to be deemed legally insufficient. At the extremes, the answers are easy. A prisoner's challenge solely to the conditions of her confinement does not implicate the validity of the underlying conviction at all.[17] Correlatively, prisoners' § 1983 claims predicated on unconstitutional conditions of confinement will not be claim precluded by a previous habeas proceeding.[18] For claim preclusion ("res judicata") purposes, that is, a claim challenging the underlying trial or administrative handling of a prisoner's good-time credits, on the one hand, and, on the other, a claim challenging unconstitutional conditions, are distinct.[19] Of course, despite the failure of claim preclusion, issue preclusion ("collateral estoppel") remains a potential impediment to the success of the subsequent action under § 1983 if previous judicial or quasi-judicial proceedings have generated factfindings on common issues.

Appellate decisions were in conflict about the application of *Heck* to conditions of confinement disputes and to prison disciplinary proceedings that lead to prisoners' loss of good time credits, as well as other determinations that effectively extend their sentences.[20] In *Edwards v.*

nied, 525 U.S. 973, 119 S.Ct. 426, 142 L.Ed.2d 347 (1998); *Sylvester v. Hanks*, 140 F.3d 713, 714 (7th Cir.1998). *Cf. Huey v. Stine,* 230 F.3d 226 (6th Cir.2000) (inmate who had served detention resulting from prison disciplinary proceeding subject to *Heck* bar although unavailable for that detention). *But cf. Sims v. Artuz,* 230 F.3d 14 (2d Cir.2000) (former inmate who challenged conditions of confinement resulting from prison disciplinary proceedings not subject to *Heck* because not challenging length of confinement). The First Circuit has also acknowledged the *Spencer* opinions, but stated that it was bound to follow the binding applicable precedent of *Heck*. *Figueroa v. Rivera*, 147 F.3d 77, 81 n. 3 (1st Cir.1998). The Ninth Circuit recognizes that the application of *Heck* to former prisoners or prisoners merely fined is in doubt after *Spencer*. *Cabrera v. City of Huntington Park*, 159 F.3d 374, 380 n. 6 (9th Cir.1998). *See also Harden v. Pataki*, 320 F.3d 1289, 1299 (11th Cir.2003) (unavailability of habeas for convict to challenge extradition once he is returned to demanding state means § 1983 claim must lie, given the view of the five justices who would limit *Heck* to situations where the plaintiff could first obtain a ruling under state law); *Nonnette v. Small*, 316 F.3d 872 (9th Cir.2002) (because parolee had fully served time resulting from revocation of his good-time credits and had been released from custody, habeas was unavailable to him and he could therefore seek § 1983 damages attacking the revocation even though success in the action would imply invalidity of prison disciplinary proceeding).

17. *See Channer v. Mitchell*, 43 F.3d 786 (2d Cir.1994) (Eighth Amendment claim); *Figueroa v. Rivera*, 147 F.3d 77 (1st Cir.1998) (Eighth Amendment deliberate indifference claim can proceed despite *Heck*).

18. See the discussion of the intersection between *Heck* and preclusion doctrines in § 5.119, infra.

19. *Rhodes v. Hannigan*, 12 F.3d 989 (10th Cir.1993).

20. Compare *Stone–Bey v. Barnes*, 120 F.3d 718 (7th Cir.1997) (procedural due process claim arising from disciplinary proceeding barred by *Heck*); *Butterfield v. Bail*, 120 F.3d 1023 (9th Cir.1997) (inmate challenging use of false testimony in prison disciplinary hearing barred by *Heck*); *Post v. Gilmore*, 111 F.3d 556 (7th Cir.1997) (per curiam) (inmate's § 1983 action should be stayed pending decision on habeas petition seeking restoration of good-time credits subtracted because of prison discipline); *Sheldon v. Hundley*, 83 F.3d 231 (8th Cir. 1996); and *Miller v. Indiana Dep't of Corr.*, 75 F.3d 330 (7th Cir.1996) (the "conviction" that would be undermined by the prisoner's claim includes, for *Heck* purposes, administrative rulings concerning prison discipline that have the effect of lengthening an inmate's sentence) with *Armento–Bey v. Harper*, 68 F.3d 215 (8th Cir.

Balisok, the Supreme Court resolved some of this uncertainty by holding *Heck* applicable to bar a § 1983 claim alleging due process violations in the conduct of a prison disciplinary hearing. Even though that claim challenged only the procedures that led to the discipline, rather than the validity of the discipline itself, *Heck* applied. The Court concluded that while the complaint sought damages only for a deprivation of good-time credits without due process, and not for the substantive deprivation of credits as such, success in plaintiff's particular § 1983 claim, which alleged bias and deceit by the prison hearing officer, would in fact impugn the underlying procedures and in turn "could be such as necessarily to imply" error in the resulting punishment.[21] Since *Balisok*, circuit courts readily apply *Heck* to bar claims that would necessarily imply the invalidity of an inmate's loss of good time credits.[22] One circuit has extended *Heck*'s reach to delay or bar § 1983 damage suits premised on the invalidity of preconviction confinement resulting from legal process, although not confinement resulting from, for example, ad hoc false imprisonment by police.[23]

But in other decisions involving challenges to prison conditions, courts distinguish *Balisok* and rely on the Court's pre-*Heck* decision in *Wolff v. McDonnell*.[24] *Wolff* held that a prisoner's § 1983 claim may lie where his particular challenge to a prison hearing or practice is "purely procedural,"[25] i.e., it seeks damages only for a procedural violation and not for the substantive consequence of the violation AND (unlike in *Balisok* where plaintiff alleged the prison hearing officer was biased) the intrinsic nature of the challenge—for example, in *Wolff* itself the absence of written notice of charges or written statement of the basis of the decision—would not in fact necessarily invalidate, directly or indirectly, an underlying conviction or period of confinement.[26] Similarly, § 1983

1995) and *Woods v. Smith*, 60 F.3d 1161 (5th Cir.1995), *cert. denied*, 516 U.S. 1084, 116 S.Ct. 800, 133 L.Ed.2d 747 (1996) (assuming or deciding that challenges to prison disciplinary procedures do not call into question the lawfulness of the underlying conviction and are therefore not barred by *Heck*). *See also Bulger v. United States Bureau of Prisons*, 65 F.3d 48 (5th Cir.1995) (losing the mere ability to accrue good-time credits automatically does not inevitably affect the duration or fundamental nature of a prisoner's sentence as required by *Sandin v. Conner*, 515 U.S. 472, 115 S.Ct. 2293, 132 L.Ed.2d 418 (1995), and thus does not deprive prisoner of a liberty interest).

21. 520 U.S. 641, 117 S.Ct. 1584, 137 L.Ed.2d 906 (1997).

22. *See Lusz v. Scott*, 126 F.3d 1018 (7th Cir.1997) (procedural due process claim); *Clarke v. Stalder*, 154 F.3d 186, 190 (5th Cir.1998), *cert. denied*, 525 U.S. 1151, 119 S.Ct. 1052, 143 L.Ed.2d 58 (1999) (prisoner was precluded from bringing claim seeking facial declaration of unconstitutionality of corrections rule inasmuch as favorable ruling on claim would necessarily imply the invalidity of his loss of good-time credits).

23. *Antonelli v. Foster*, 104 F.3d 899 (7th Cir.1997), *cert. denied*, 522 U.S. 834, 118 S.Ct. 104, 139 L.Ed.2d 58 (1997) (plaintiff detained pursuant to parole violator warrant had to successfully challenge that detention in habeas or parole revocation proceedings as precondition to accrual of § 1983 claim).

24. 418 U.S. 539, 94 S.Ct. 2963, 41 L.Ed.2d 935 (1974).

25. This terminology and the explanation in text for the divergent results in *Wolff* and *Heck*, far more cogent than any provided by the Supreme Court, have been offered by a panel of the Eleventh Circuit. *Harden v. Pataki*, 320 F.3d 1289, 1295 n. 9 (11th Cir.2003).

26. *See, e.g., Jenkins v. Haubert*, 179 F.3d 19, 21 (2d Cir.1999) (upholding despite *Heck* a prisoner's § 1983 claim that, like

suits that seek restoration or acceleration of parole eligibility have been allowed to proceed where, as is true with most purely discretionary parole systems, the challenge will not necessarily affect the duration of the plaintiff's confinement.[27] These decisions are supported by dictum in another Supreme Court decision[28] to the effect that despite *Heck* and *Balisok*, a prisoner's § 1983 claim is cognizable if he seeks relief against use of unconstitutional procedures, as distinct from relief for the result of those procedures, and if the defect of which he complains does not necessarily imply the invalidity of the conviction or sentence.

The Court has now clarified some of the uncertainty on this subject remaining after *Balisok*. In *Muhammad v. Close*[29] the Court specifically rejected Sixth circuit precedent that had held every § 1983 action challenging prison disciplinary proceedings subject to *Heck*. The Court found that the particular prison administrative determinations neither implied the invalidity of the underlying conviction nor, under applicable state laws and regulations, eliminated any of the § 1983 plaintiff's good-time credits. Accordingly, the inmate's suit challenging the prison discipline at issue could not be "construed as seeking a judgment at odds with his conviction or with the State's calculation of time to be served in accordance with the underlying sentence." Put otherwise, his claims did not seek the kind of relief for which habeas could have been granted; habeas exhaustion policy was therefore not at issue; and accordingly the favorable-termination requirement of *Heck* did not apply.[30] *Balisok* was distinguished as a case "where the [prison] administrative action taken against the plaintiff could affect credits toward release based on good-time served."[31] The Court explained that whether disciplinary proceedings could have the effect of extending the duration of confinement—thus triggering the *Heck* bar—"is a matter of state law or regulation. . . ."[32]

Suppose it is not clear whether the testimony or evidence collaterally attacked by means of the action under § 1983 was in fact necessary to the conviction? That possibility is akin to the Court's ever expanding concept in the post-conviction remedy arena of "harmless error."[33] How, after the fact, in a subsequent state or federal court proceeding under

the one in *Balisok*, alleged bias by prison hearing officer but where a favorable result would affect only the conditions, not the fact of plaintiff's confinement); *Johnson v. Litscher,* 260 F.3d 826 (7th Cir.2001); *Huang v. Johnson*, 251 F.3d 65 (2d Cir. 2001); *Sims v. Artuz,* 230 F.3d 14 (2d Cir. 2000); and *Jenkins v. Haubert*, 179 F.3d 19 (2d Cir.1999) (all holding that § 1983 plaintiffs challenging disciplinary sanctions, but in actions that if successful would not affect their convictions or the length of their confinements, may proceed free of *Heck* and *Edwards*).

27. *Dotson v. Wilkinson,* 300 F.3d 661 (6th Cir.2002); *Moran v. Sondalle,* 218 F.3d 647 (7th Cir.2000) (per curiam); *Metheny v. Hammonds*, 216 F.3d 1307 (11th Cir.2000), *cert. denied*, 531 U.S. 1196, 121 S.Ct. 1200, 149 L.Ed.2d 114 (2001); *Anyanwutaku v. Moore*, 151 F.3d 1053, 1055 (D.C.Cir.1998); *Neal v. Shimoda*, 131 F.3d 818 (9th Cir. 1997).

28. *Spencer v. Kemna*, 523 U.S. 1, 17, 118 S.Ct. 978, 140 L.Ed.2d 43 (1998).

29. ___ U.S. ___, 124 S.Ct. 1303, 158 L.Ed.2d 32 (2004).

30. *Id.* at 1306.

31. *Id.* at 1304.

32. *Id.* at 1306.

33. *See* § 5.103, *infra* on the "harmless error" concept on appeal.

§ 1983, can the plaintiff demonstrate that the federally unlawful conduct for which she seeks damages was not instrumental to her conviction, or how can the defendant moving to dismiss under *Heck* demonstrate the contrary? Lower court decisions increasingly resolve such questions in favor of *Heck* application if the challenge "undermines" an underlying conviction, even without directly challenging its validity.[34]

Would a successful § 1983 claim challenging the admission of unlawfully obtained evidence that contributed to a finding of guilt necessarily unsettle the foundation of a conviction so that *Heck* would bar the door? The "independent source," "inevitable discovery," and "harmless error" doctrines render harmless the admission of many types of evidence obtained through an unlawful arrest, search or seizure. When a criminal conviction is sustained in reliance on those rules, the prosecutor has effectively demonstrated that the same decision would have been reached notwithstanding a constitutional violation. Citing the ever-present possibility that a conviction in which unconstitutionally obtained evidence was admitted may be upheld pursuant to the independent source or inevitable discovery rules, one circuit holds that § 1983 Fourth Amendment claims as a class are not barred by *Heck* because, even assuming the plaintiff prevails, they do not inevitably taint his prior conviction.[35]

34. *See Ryan v. DuPage County Jury Comm'n*, 105 F.3d 329 (7th Cir.1996) (per curiam) (*Heck* applies to inmate's § 1983 action challenging unfair jury selection procedures in his criminal trials, because the challenge necessarily undermined those convictions even if it did not challenge their substantive validity).

35. *See Kelley v. Myler*, 149 F.3d 641 (7th Cir.1998); *Gonzalez v. Entress*, 133 F.3d 551, 553–54 (7th Cir.1998); *Washington v. Summerville*, 127 F.3d 552 (7th Cir. 1997), *cert. denied*, 523 U.S. 1073, 118 S.Ct. 1515, 140 L.Ed.2d 668 (1998); *Perez v. Sifel*, 57 F.3d 503, 505 (7th Cir.1995) (per curiam). *But see Shamaeizadeh v. Cunigan*, 182 F.3d 391 (6th Cir.1999), *cert. denied*, 528 U.S. 1021, 120 S.Ct. 531, 145 L.Ed.2d 412 (1999) (*Heck* bar extends to Fourth Amendment claim of criminal defendant, so his § 1983 claim did not accrue for limitations purposes until dismissal of criminal charges against him); *Jalili–Khiabani v. Oakland County*, 66 F.3d 326 (6th Cir.1995) and *Schilling v. White*, 58 F.3d 1081 (6th Cir.1995) (holding that § 1983 action alleging an unconstitutional search or seizure is premature, and must be dismissed without prejudice, if brought while the plaintiff still faces criminal punishment). *But cf. Townes v. City of N.Y.*, 176 F.3d 138 (2d Cir.1999), *cert. denied*, 528 U.S. 964, 120 S.Ct. 398, 145 L.Ed.2d 311 (1999) (implicitly assuming Fourth Amendment claim is not barred by *Heck* but holding claim against officer fails for lack of proof of causation because trial judge's ruling refusing to suppress unconstitutionally obtained evidence was independent, superseding cause of plaintiff's harm).

The source of the disagreement between the Seventh Circuit's near-blanket exception to *Heck* for Fourth Amendment claims (except claims for false arrest made pursuant to a warrant, which are more akin to malicious prosecution claims and therefore accrue only when the criminal charges are dismissed, see *Snodderly v. R.U.F.F. Drug Enforcement Task Force*, 239 F.3d 892 (7th Cir.2001)), and the Sixth Circuit's routine application of *Heck* to bar Fourth Amendment claims unless and until a conviction is invalidated turn on their differing readings of footnote 7 of the Supreme Court's opinion in *Heck*. The Seventh Circuit relies on the Court's assertion early in the footnote that success on a § 1983 claim for an unreasonable search does not trigger the bar because it would not necessarily imply that a resulting conviction was unlawful. This follows, the Supreme Court explained, even where evidence resulting from the allegedly unreasonable search was introduced in the criminal trial that resulted in a conviction, because the conviction would not be necessarily tainted by a finding that the search was unlawful (and the evidence resulting from it accordingly should have been excluded), because of the independent source, inevitable discovery, and harmless error doctrines. The Sixth Circuit considers those observations qualified, however, by the following further explanation in the footnote: "In order to recover compensatory damages, the § 1983 plaintiff must prove not only that the search was unlawful, but that it caused him actual compensable injury which, we hold today, does not encompass the 'injury' of being convicted and imprisoned, at least not until the conviction has been overturned." 512 U.S. at 487 n.7 (citation omitted). But the Seventh Circuit reads this latter statement merely as limiting the damages recoverable in such a case, i.e., as prohibiting damages attributable to conviction and imprisonment (but not those attributable to the unlawful search or arrest) unless the conviction has been overturned, and not as undermining the Court's conclusion earlier in the footnote that Fourth Amendment claims may proceed because the independent source, inevitable discovery, and harmless error doctrines prevent satisfaction of *Heck*'s "inevitably undermine" prerequisite. Decisions of the Eighth, *Whitmore v. Harrington*, 204 F.3d 784 (8th Cir.2000) (unlawful investigative stop) and *Moore v. Sims*, 200 F.3d 1170 (8th Cir.2000) (illegal detention and search), Tenth, *Beck v. City of Muskogee Police Dep't*, 195 F.3d 553, 558–559 (10th Cir.1999) (search and seizure leading to rape conviction), and Eleventh, *Datz v. Kilgore*, 51 F.3d 252, 253 n. 1 (11th Cir.1995) (unlawful search) Circuits subscribe to the Seventh Circuit's reading, and appear to consider the bar generally inapplicable to Fourth Amendment claims, even where evidence resulting from an unlawful arrest or search was admitted at the underlying criminal trial that resulted in the conviction. Because of the effective presumption that *Heck* does not bar Fourth Amendment claims, the § 1983 action may proceed unless a record has been developed that plainly reveals that success in the action would necessarily imply the invalidity of the underlying conviction. *Hughes v. Lott*, 350 F.3d 1157 (11th Cir. 2003). Still, that burden can be met, as where evidence on which the conviction depends could only have been obtained through the challenged search. *Ballenger v. Owens*, 352 F.3d 842 (4th Cir. 2003).

The reasoning underlying the Seventh Circuit's categorical rejection of the *Heck* bar in Fourth Amendment cases has been extended Fifth Amendment unlawful confession cases, *Simmons v. O'Brien*, 77 F.3d 1093 (8th Cir.1996), were the harmless error doctrine also applies, as well as to cases where the criminal conviction might stand on alternative grounds notwithstanding the success of plaintiff's claim under § 1983. *Beck*, 195 F.3d at 560. On the other hand, a Ninth Circuit decision appears to adhere to the Sixth Circuit approach, holding that a § 1983 search and seizure claim does not accrue until consequent criminal charges have been dismissed or a conviction overturned. *Harvey v. Waldron*, 210 F.3d 1008 (9th Cir.2000).

Yet subsequently the Sixth Circuit itself appears to have moderated its absolutist *Schilling* approach that has been read to deny any *Heck* bar exception to all Fourth Amendment claims. In *Shamaeizadeh v. Cunigan*, 182 F.3d 391, 396 (6th Cir.1999), *cert. denied*, 528 U.S. 1021, 120 S.Ct. 531, 145 L.Ed.2d 412 (1999), the panel observes that the plaintiff in *Schilling* had sought damages related to his conviction, so that success on his claim would necessarily have challenged the validity of his conviction, thereby barring that claim under *Heck*. That left open the possibility, however, that *Heck* might not apply in the case of a plaintiff seeking damages only for an unlawful search or seizure. Indeed the *Shamaeizadeh* panel, reconsidering the import of footnote 7 in *Heck*, says it "explicitly states that if evidence obtained at the allegedly unconstitutional search resulted in the § 1983 plaintiff's conviction, after being admitted under an exception to the exclusionary rule, a § 1983 action may lie [without the conviction having first been overturned], but the § 1983 plaintiff may not seek damages for the injury of being convicted and imprisoned until the conviction is overturned." *Id. See also Chatman v. Slagle*, 107 F.3d 380, 381–384 (6th Cir.1997) (affirming in dictum that *Heck* does not apply to § 1983 action for damages attributable to allegedly unreasonable search even if search produced evidence introduced in the criminal trial that led to conviction) (quoting parts of n.7 of *Heck*). Thus today the Sixth Circuit may be in a small camp that rejects both the view that *Heck* always applies to Fourth Amendment claims, as language in *Schilling* had suggested, or never does, the view of the Seventh Circuit. Rather, the Sixth Circuit now counsels federal trial courts to conduct a case by case, independent review of the state criminal trial record to see if, as a result of harmless error, independent source, inevitable discovery, or other exception to the exclusionary rule, a successful § 1983 action might not inevitably taint the state criminal conviction—in which case the claim could proceed even if that conviction had not been overturned. That approach—a limited exception to the *Heck* bar for Fourth Amendment cases—may also be subscribed to by the Fifth Circuit. *See Mackey v. Dickson*, 47 F.3d 744, 746 (5th

But the same reasoning means that the § 1983 plaintiff may recover only those damages he proves to have been specifically caused by the unlawful search or seizure, and not damages caused by its consequences like conviction and incarceration. In other words, until a conviction is overturned on the ground that evidence produced by an illegal search or seizure was inadmissible, the plaintiff cannot use § 1983 to prove that the Fourth Amendment violation caused the additional damages attendant upon imprisonment. Thus in this setting the possibility that the prosecution might make a "same decision" showing in a criminal appeal actually keeps alive § 1983 claims that *Heck* would otherwise bar, but also serves to limit the plaintiff's available relief. Moreover, under this approach the claim accrues at the moment of the unlawful arrest, search, or seizure, effectively compelling the plaintiff to bring his § 1983 claim before the criminal proceedings, or post-conviction challenges to a conviction, are concluded if he hopes to commence his action timely. (Of course a same-decision showing made during a Fourth Amendment case under § 1983 may also play its more traditional role of defeating liability altogether.)[36]

The reasoning underlying the Seventh Circuit's categorical rejection of the *Heck* bar in Fourth Amendment cases has been extended to Fifth Amendment unlawful confession cases, *Simmons v. O'Brien*, 77 F.3d 1093 (8th Cir.1996), where the harmless error doctrine also applies, as well as to cases where the criminal conviction might stand on alternative grounds notwithstanding the success of plaintiff's claim under § 1983. *Beck*, 195 F.3d at 560. On the other hand, a Ninth Circuit decision appears to adhere to the Sixth Circuit approach, holding that a § 1983 search and seizure claim does not accrue until consequent criminal

Cir.1995) (§ 1983 claim based on unlawful arrest stayed pending court's evaluation of evidence at resulting criminal trial).

The Seventh Circuit's approach—creating a general exception to the *Heck* bar for Fourth Amendment claims—is plaintiff-friendly on the surface. But in practice it requires plaintiffs to file their § 1983 claims during the course of or soon after a criminal proceeding, since their claims will accrue for limitations purposes at the time of an unconstitutional arrest or search. This, in the Sixth Circuit's view, will "misdirect" a criminal defendant, *Shamaeizadeh*, 182 F.3d at 399 (holding, in accord with *Smith v. Holtz*, 87 F.3d 108 (3d Cir. 1996), that *Heck*'s reasoning applies even before any conviction results, i.e., while state criminal proceedings are still pending, so that the applicable state limitations period on a Fourth Amendment § 1983 claim begins running only on the date criminal charges resulting from the alleged Fourth Amendment violation are dismissed). *See also Covington v. City of N.Y.*, 171 F.3d 117, 124 (2d Cir.1999), *cert. denied*, 528 U.S. 946, 120 S.Ct. 363, 145 L.Ed.2d 284 (1999) (holding *Heck* bar applies so as to delay the accrual of claims that, if successful, would necessarily imply the invalidity of a potential conviction resulting from a pending criminal proceeding). Of course the Sixth Circuit approach, while potentially more plaintiff friendly, entails administrative disadvantages, as it may require the § 1983 trial judge to scour the state criminal record for clues as to whether a judgment for plaintiff would necessarily undermine the conviction. And it requires at least some putative Fourth Amendment claimants to withhold their § 1983 actions until after reversal of habeas condemnation of a conviction, which of course may never come to pass. But if the judgment is reversed, condemned or expunged the plaintiff then enjoys the benefit of delayed accrual of the claim, so that it is far less likely to be time barred.

36. *See Smith v. Edwards*, 175 F.3d 99 (2d Cir.1999).

charges have been dismissed or a conviction overturned. *Harvey v. Waldron*, 210 F.3d 1008 (9th Cir.2000).

One may imagine, though, a situation in which the only source of the sole evidence that led to a conviction was an unconstitutional arrest, search, or seizure. In that situation, it would seem that a successful challenge to that arrest, search, or seizure in a § 1983 action would inevitably undermine the validity of the resulting conviction.[37] Perhaps anticipating that possibility, another circuit has declared a rule that, instead of delaying the § 1983 action per *Heck*, defeats it altogether. The opinion reasons that the unconstitutional underlying event can never have been the legal cause of the plaintiff's conviction, because the trial court's refusal to suppress that evidence was an intervening and superseding cause.[38] That approach treats the claim as accruing when the Fourth Amendment violation occurred, requires the plaintiff to assert the claim in a timely manner running from that event, deems it outside the *Heck* bar, and then denies it on the merits. And it is difficult to see how the plaintiff could effectively challenge what the court conceives to be the legal cause of her harm—the trial court's hypothetically erroneous ruling on a motion to suppress—because that decision would be insulated by absolute immunity.

Related uncertainties about the scope of *Heck* have surfaced in the appellate decisions. Circuits agree that if extradition is justified, a § 1983 claim will lie not for injury attributable to the extradition itself, but at most for injuries like emotional distress, or nominal or punitive damages, caused by a due process deprivation in the extradition procedures.[39] Yet they are divided as to whether damages in such a case would necessarily invalidate the underlying conviction or sentence.[40] In one case claims based on allegations that police officers committed perjury and coerced witnesses to wrongfully identify the § 1983 plaintiff (as a criminal) were held barred by *Heck* absent evidence that the conviction had been invalidated; but a claim against another officer asserting cruel and unusual punishment for placing the plaintiff in a particular holding

37. *See, e.g., Ballenger v. Owens*, 352 F.3d 842 (4th Cir. 2003); *Covington v. City of N.Y.*, 171 F.3d 117 (2d Cir.1999), cert. denied, 528 U.S. 946, 120 S.Ct. 363, 145 L.Ed.2d 284 (1999).

38. *Townes v. City of N.Y.*, 176 F.3d 138 (2d Cir.1999), *cert. denied*, 528 U.S. 964, 120 S.Ct. 398, 145 L.Ed.2d 311 (1999).

39. *Harden v. Pataki*, 320 F.3d 1289, 1300 (11th Cir.2003); *Long v. Shillinger*, 927 F.2d 525, 528 (10th Cir. 1991).

40. *Compare Harden v. Pataki*, 320 F.3d 1289, 1295–1298 (11th Cir.2003) (§ 1983 damages claim challenging validity of extradition procedures was "purely procedural" in that it had no bearing direct or indirect on plaintiff's underlying guilt or innocence) *with Knowlin v. Thompson*, 207 F.3d 907, 908 (7th Cir.2000) (plaintiff challenging procedures would have to show some injury beyond procedurally-compliant extradition, and that showing would necessarily imply the invalidity of the underlying parole revocation). The Eleventh Circuit in *Harden* took issue with the Seventh Circuit's view that plaintiff, to succeed, would have to cast doubt on whether he would have been extradited had constitutional extradition procedures been used, pointing out that plaintiff would have been eligible for distinct emotional distress, nominal, and possibly even punitive damages flowing solely from establishing a violation of procedural due process. *Harden*, 320 F.3d at 1300–1301.

cell did not implicate the conviction's validity and hence escaped the *Heck* bar.[41]

The Fifth Circuit faced a more difficult task in sorting out the claims of another § 1983 plaintiff that he had been falsely arrested (for disorderly conduct and resisting a search) in the absence of probable cause; that the arresting officers had used excessive force; and that he had been maliciously prosecuted. The court held the false arrest and malicious prosecution claims not cognizable by virtue of *Heck*, because to some degree at least both of those claims implied the invalidity of the initiation of the criminal process and in turn of the criminal conviction.[42]

41. *Channer v. Mitchell*, 43 F.3d 786 (2d Cir.1994) (per curiam). A similar split is reflected in *Perez v. Sifel*, 57 F.3d 503 (7th Cir.1995) (claims against officer for improperly procuring plaintiff's conviction barred by *Heck*; illegal search and arrest claims required further evaluation to determine whether, if successful, they would necessarily undermine plaintiff's conviction). *See also Williams v. Schario*, 93 F.3d 527 (8th Cir.1996) (claim alleging that police officer presented false testimony during plaintiff's preliminary hearing and maliciously prosecuted plaintiff dismissed without prejudice until resulting conviction reversed, expunged, or called into question by federal habeas).

42. *See Guerrero v. Gates*, 357 F.3d 911 (9th Cir. 2004) (claims alleging wrongful arrest and malicious conspiracy to bring false charges barred by *Heck*); *Wells v. Bonner,* 45 F.3d 90 (5th Cir.1995). In general, claims relating to unlawful arrest arise at the time of arrest. *Brooks v. City of Winston–Salem*, 85 F.3d 178, 182–83 (4th Cir. 1996). But *Heck* creates a logical exception to that rule for case where a plaintiff challenges the federal lawfulness of an arrest that led to a conviction for resisting arrest. 512 U.S. at 486 n.6. The circuits have reached divergent decisions on the application vel non of *Heck* to various constitutionally based claims of false arrest. *Cabrera v. City of Huntington Park*, 159 F.3d 374 (9th Cir.1998) (*Heck* applies, so false arrest accrues, if at all, only when conviction is invalidated); *Johnson v. Bax*, 63 F.3d 154 (2d Cir.1995) (§ 1983 claims alleging violation of arrested plaintiff's First Amendment rights may proceed, while false imprisonment and false arrest claims may not); *Woods v. Candela*, 47 F.3d 545, 546 (2d Cir.1995), *cert. denied*, 516 U.S. 808, 116 S.Ct. 54, 133 L.Ed.2d 18 (1995). Yet in *Hernandez v. Kenny*, 208 F.3d 226 (10th Cir.2000), the court wrote broadly that *Heck* presumptively does not apply to a wide range of police actions directed at a criminal suspect, including unlawful arrest, interrogation or search and seizure. *Cf. Leather v. Eyck*, 180 F.3d 420 (2d Cir.1999) (claim of selective prosecution in retaliation for exercising free speech rights may proceed despite unreversed conviction for D.W.I. resulting from that prosecution). *But see Beck v. City of Muskogee Police Dep't*, 195 F.3d 553, 560 (10th Cir.1999) (claim of malicious prosecution on rape charges subject to *Heck* and therefore ripe only when charges dismissed). *Heck* itself indicated that malicious prosecution claims and claims alleging violations of the prosecution-disclosure rule of *Brady v. Maryland*, 373 U.S. 83, 83 S.Ct. 1194, 10 L.Ed.2d 215 (1963) may be subject to its bar. 512 U.S. at 489–90, 114 S.Ct. at 2364. *See Smith v. Gonzales,* 222 F.3d 1220 (10th Cir.2000) (*Heck* bar applied for *Brady* violation).

Lower courts have sometimes struggled with whether to bar Section 1983 excessive force actions under *Heck* when the underlying conviction was for resisting arrest. In *Heck* itself, the Supreme Court gave the example of a § 1983 claim for unreasonable seizure, observing that the claim, if successful, might negate an element of the offense of resisting arrest. *See Heck,* 512 U.S. at 487 n. 6, 114 S.Ct. 2364. To decide if this is so, courts must look both to the claims raised under § 1983 and to the specific offenses for which the § 1983 claimant was convicted.

The outcome seems to depend on whether the use of excessive force renders the arrest unlawful under state law. In *Nelson v. Jashurek,* 109 F.3d 142 (3rd Cir. 1997), for example, Nelson was allowed to proceed on a § 1983 claim, despite having an outstanding conviction for resisting Jashureck's arrest, because in Pennsylvania "a finding that Jashureck used excessive 'substantial force' would not imply that the arrest was unlawful...." *Nelson,* 109 F.3d at 145 (internal quotation marks in original). Similarly, in *Martinez v. City of Albuquerque,* 184 F.3d 1123 (10th Cir.

By contrast, the court considered it apparent that even if the plaintiff could demonstrate that the arresting officers used excessive force, a § 1983 judgment on that ground would not demonstrate the invalidity of most criminal judgments and accordingly could proceed notwithstanding *Heck*.[43]

Twice the Fifth Circuit's opinion recites that a determination in the § 1983 action that the challenged conduct is unlawful need only "imply" the invalidity of the conviction. Yet twice the opinion recites that such a determination must "necessarily imply" the conviction's invalidity before *Heck* would stand in the way. The false arrest claim was held legally insufficient in its entirety even though the plaintiff was convicted only for resisting the search, not for disorderly conduct. The *Heck* inquiry should focus, the court reasoned, on the validity of the arrest that was challenged by the § 1983 claim, not the outcome of the charges springing from that arrest. To win his § 1983 false arrest claim, the plaintiff would have had to show no probable cause to arrest him on either charge, which in turn would have demonstrated the invalidity of his conviction for resisting search, thereby triggering *Heck*.

An even more stringent version of *Heck*—one that makes it irrelevant whether a civil action will necessarily or only possibly imply the invalidity of an outstanding criminal conviction—has been applied to federal prisoners. Under this variant, habeas corpus is the federal prisoner's sole remedy to challenge a parole eligibility date or achieve any other relief that might have a "probabilistic impact" on the duration of his custody. Any other claim that might have such an impact is barred, even though its success would not necessarily result in the prisoner's earlier release.[44]

1999), Martinez was allowed to proceed with a §§ 1983 claim "to the extent ... [it] d[id] not challenge the *lawfulness* of his arrest ... [under New Mexicol law]." *Martinez,* 184 F.3d at 1125 (emphasis in original). And in *Robinson v. Doe,* 272 F.3d 921 (7th Cir.2001), a § 1983 action asserting that Robinson was arrested with excessive force was not barred by *Heck* because, under Illinois law, "[p]olice might well use excessive force in effecting a perfectly lawful arrest." *Robinson,* 272 F.3d at 923. By contrast, because California law treats an arrest as unlawful when effected with excessive force, success in a § 1983 action alleging excessive force during an arrest necessarily implies the invalidity of the plaintiff's prior conviction for resisting arrest, and the action is thus barred under *Heck*. *Smith v. City of Hemet*, 356 F.3d 1138 (9th Cir. 2004).

43. *Wells v. Bonner*, 45 F.3d 90 (5th Cir.1995). *See also Sanford v. Motts,* 258 F.3d 1117 (9th Cir.2001) (no *Heck* bar to action alleging excessive force in arresting plaintiff, as that force may have been applied after plaintiff's resistance and obstruction for which she was convicted); *Martinez v. City of Albuquerque*, 184 F.3d 1123 (10th Cir.1999) (excessive force claim concerning arrest not *Heck*-barred by conviction for resisting arrest based on plaintiff's flight from scene before arrest); *Cabrera v. City of Huntington Park*, 159 F.3d 374 (9th Cir.1998) (*Heck* does not apply to excessive force claim, which accrues at the time of the arrest); *Jackson v. Suffolk County Homicide Bureau*, 135 F.3d 254 (2d Cir.1998) (*Heck* no bar to excessive force claim); *Washington v. Summerville*, 127 F.3d 552 (7th Cir.1997), *cert. denied*, 523 U.S. 1073, 118 S.Ct. 1515, 140 L.Ed.2d 668 (1998); *Nelson v. Jashurek*, 109 F.3d 142 (3d Cir.1997); *Smithart v. Towery*, 79 F.3d 951 (9th Cir.1996). *But see Sappington v. Bartee*, 195 F.3d 234 (5th Cir.1999) (per curiam) (§ 1983 excessive force claim *Heck*-barred because if successful it would necessarily undermine plaintiff's conviction for aggravated assault of police officer).

44. *See Bourke v. Hawk–Sawyer,* 269 F.3d 1072 (D.C.Cir.2001).

A variety of de facto state-court deferral situations are governed or inspired by the doctrine of *Younger v. Harris*,[45] which as enlarged prohibits federal courts from issuing injunctive, declaratory, or other declaratory relief that would intrude on pending criminal and other important state court proceedings. Of course, *Heck* usually stands as a bar to the § 1983 action only where there is an outstanding criminal or penal judgment. There may be related bars where state criminal or important civil proceedings are still pending at or after the commencement of the § 1983 action. Thus, as the following section describes, the *Younger* doctrine may compel dismissal of § 1983 claims seeking equitable or, as elaborated in *Samuels v. Mackell*,[46] declaratory relief that would interfere with such proceedings. Moreover, even if the § 1983 plaintiff seeks only damages, her action may be stayed pending resolution of ongoing state criminal or even important civil proceedings under the Court's decision in *Deakins v. Monaghan*[47] and *Quackenbush v. Allstate Ins. Co.*[48]

In 1995, lawsuits initiated by prisoners accounted for more than twenty-five percent of the total number of cases filed in the federal district courts.[49] In an effort to stem the perceived "flood of prisoner lawsuits in federal court,"[50] Congress enacted the Prison Litigation Reform Act of 1995[51] ("PLRA") "to curtail prisoner tort, civil rights and conditions [of confinement] litigation."[52] The PLRA, effective April 26, 1996,[53] amended Titles 11, 18, 28 and 42 of the United States Code and

45. 401 U.S. 37, 54, 91 S.Ct. 746, 755, 27 L.Ed.2d 669 (1971).

46. 401 U.S. 66, 91 S.Ct. 764, 27 L.Ed.2d 688 (1971).

47. 484 U.S. 193, 108 S.Ct. 523, 98 L.Ed.2d 529 (1988). Both *Younger* and *Deakins* principles were so applied in *Simpson v. Rowan*, 73 F.3d 134 (7th Cir.1995), *cert. denied*, 519 U.S. 833, 117 S.Ct. 104, 136 L.Ed.2d 58 (1996).

48. 517 U.S. 706, 116 S.Ct. 1712, 135 L.Ed.2d 1 (1996). *See also Shamaeizadeh v. Cunigan*, 182 F.3d 391 (6th Cir.1999), *cert. denied*, 528 U.S. 1021, 120 S.Ct. 531, 145 L.Ed.2d 412 (1999) (applying *Heck* to bar § 1983 claim by criminal defendant not yet convicted).

49. *Roller v. Gunn*, 107 F.3d 227, 230 (4th Cir.1997) (citing Administrative Office of the United States Courts, 1995 Federal Court Management Statistics 167).

50. *Harris v. Garner*, 216 F.3d 970, 971 (11th Cir.2000).

51. Pub.L. No. 104–134, 110 Stat. 1321 (1996).

52. *Anderson v. Singletary*, 111 F.3d 801, 805 (11th Cir.1997).

53. Various provisions of the PLRA have been held not to be retroactive in effect. *See, e.g., Martin v. Hadix*, 527 U.S. 343, 119 S.Ct. 1998, 144 L.Ed.2d 347 (1999) (new limitations on attorney's fees applies to post-enactment monitoring of consent decree, but not to services performed before effective date); *Altizer v. Deeds*, 191 F.3d 540 (4th Cir.1999) (three strikes provision not applicable to suits brought before effective date of PLRA); *Craig v. Eberly*, 164 F.3d 490 (10th Cir.1998) (limit on award of emotional distress damages applies only to cases filed after effective date of law); *Brown v. Toombs*, 139 F.3d 1102 (6th Cir. 1998) (PLRA exhaustion requirement applies to cases brought after effective date of law but not to cases filed before); *Winters v. Sissel*, 167 F.3d 413 (8th Cir.1999) (PLRA limits on attorney's fees applies to all hours expended after law went into effect); *Blissett v. Casey*, 147 F.3d 218 (2d Cir.1998) (PLRA provision on attorney's fees not apply to work done before Act passed); *Cooper v. Casey*, 97 F.3d 914 (7th Cir.1996) (limit on attorneys' fees not apply to cases filed prior to effective date of new law). *But see Inmates of D.C. Jail v. Jackson*, 158 F.3d 1357 (D.C.Cir.1998) (new few schedule applies to attorney's work monitoring compliance with consent decree entered before effective date of PLRA); *Alexander S. v. Boyd*, 113 F.3d 1373 (4th Cir.1997) (law limiting fees applied retroactively). In addition, the requirement of complete adminis-

is codified at several locations.[54]

The PLRA purports to accomplish several objectives. First, the PLRA contains provisions which were intended to "get the federal courts out of the business of running jails"[55] by limiting the circumstances under which courts may enter injunctions against unconstitutional prison conditions such as overcrowding.[56] Second, the PLRA contains provisions that establish new procedural requirements for prisoner[57] civil suits designed to curtail frivolous and malicious prisoner litigation.[58] The main prisoner filing provisions require indigent prisoners to pay filing fees in civil actions and appeals;[59] subject prisoner suits to sua sponte dismissal if the court determines the action is frivolous, malicious, or fails to state a claim;[60] impose a three-strike provision on prisoners who have had three actions or appeals dismissed[61] as frivolous, malicious, or failing to

trative exhaustion has been held to apply only to cases filed after the PLRA went into effect, even if the claims arose before the law became effective. *See White v. McGinnis*, 131 F.3d 593 (6th Cir.1997).

54. *See, e.g.,* 18 U.S.C.A. § 3626(b) (1994) (containing termination of relief provision); 28 U.S.C.A. § 1915(g) (1994) (containing three strikes provision); 42 U.S.C.A. § 1988(b) (1994) (containing attorney fee provision).

55. *Benjamin v. Jacobson*, 172 F.3d 144, 182 (2d Cir.1999) (Calabresi, J., concurring).

56. Prospective injunctive relief must be supported by a judicial finding that the relief is narrowly tailored to extend no further than the particular plaintiff. *See* § 3626(a); *Oluwa v. Gomez*, 133 F.3d 1237, 1239 (9th Cir.1998) (injunction invalid where requisite finding was absent). Under the PLRA, preliminary injunctions automatically expire after ninety days, *see* § 3626(a)(2), and all injunctions terminate after one or two years upon motion from a party or intervenor. To avoid the termination of injunctive relief, the court must make written findings that prospective relief remains necessary to correct an ongoing violation of a federal right. *See* § 3626(b); *Castillo v. Cameron County*, 238 F.3d 339, 354 (5th Cir.2001) (injunctive relief not available for future threat of prison overcrowding because prison was not currently overcrowded); *Hadix v. Johnson*, 228 F.3d 662, 670–671 (6th Cir.2000) (court may not continue prospective relief without issuing written findings and giving plaintiffs opportunity to submit evidence of continuous and ongoing violation); *Cason v. Seckinger*, 231 F.3d 777, 783–84 (11th Cir.2000) (current and ongoing violation refers to violation that exists right now, not potential or likely violation that will occur if relief terminates).

57. The PLRA does not apply to ex-prisoners. *See Doe v. Washington County*, 150 F.3d 920 (8th Cir.1998) (PLRA limits on attorney's fees not applicable to suits brought by former prisoners even if suit relates to prison conditions).

58. And the circuits have required strict compliance with the statute; substantial compliance is not enough. *See, e.g., Wright v. Hollingsworth*, 260 F.3d 357 (5th Cir.2001).

59. 28 U.S.C.A. § 1915(b)(1) (Supp. V 2000). The requirement that a prisoner pay filing fees arises when the complaint is delivered to the district court, *Dupree v. Palmer*, 284 F.3d 1234 (11th Cir.2002), and the subsequent dismissal of the complaint for violation of the three-strikes provision did not obviate the filing fee requirement. *In re Alea*, 286 F.3d 378 (6th Cir.2002). *See also Rowe v. Shake*, 196 F.3d 778 (7th Cir. 1999) (must pay fee regardless of prisoner's fee status); *Nicholas v. Tucker*, 114 F.3d 17 (2d Cir.1997); *Roller v. Gunn*, 107 F.3d 227 (4th Cir.1997); *Hampton v. Hobbs*, 106 F.3d 1281 (6th Cir.1997) (same). Prisoners may not join claims under the federal joinder rules to share paying the mandatory filing fee, even when the claims arise out of the same transaction or occurrence. *Hubbard v. Haley*, 262 F.3d 1194 (11th Cir.2001).

60. 28 U.S.C.A. § 1915(e)(2) (Supp. V 2000); 42 U.S.C.A. § 1997e(c)(1) (Supp. V 2000).

In addition, the PLRA requires dismissal of a frivolous case and does not allow a pro se prisoner an opportunity to amend the complaint to correct any deficiencies. *Lopez v. Smith*, 160 F.3d 567 (9th Cir.1998); *Talley-Bey v. Knebl*, 168 F.3d 884 (6th Cir. 1999).

61. An appeal of a dismissed action that is dismissed is a separate strike. *See*

state a claim unless the prisoner is in imminent danger[62] of serious physical injury;[63] severely limit or eliminate[64] actions for mental or emotional injury without a prior showing of physical injury;[65] and limit attorneys' fees.[66]

In addition, the PLRA imposes requirements to exhaust all possible administrative remedies before bringing actions "with respect to prison conditions."[67] Thus a prisoner plaintiff must allege exhaustion of all administrative remedies and submit proof, such as a document showing final disposition of grievance. The Supreme Court held in *Porter v. Nussle*[68] that the PLRA exhaustion requirement applies to all inmate suits about prison life, whether they involve general circumstances or particular episodes, and whether they allege excessive force or some other wrong. The term "prison conditions" thus applies to suit for excessive force by correction officers and exhaustion is required.[69] The Supreme Court also held in *Booth v. Churner*[70] that the prisoner must exhaust whatever administrative remedy is available even if that remedy would not accord all the relief sought. Thus, if prisoner complained about excessive force by guards and sought both injunctive and monetary relief and only the former was available in state system, prisoner must still invoke and exhaust whatever system would give him part of the relief sought.[71] The statute of limitations on

Jennings v. Natrona Co. Detention Center, 175 F.3d 775 (10th Cir.1999). Even dismissals that occurred prior to the effective date of PLRA count as strikes. *See, e.g.*, *Ibrahim v. District of Columbia*, 208 F.3d 1032 (D.C.Cir.2000); *Welch v. Galie*, 207 F.3d 130 (2d Cir.2000).

62. The imminent danger requirement refers to dangers at the time of filing suit, not to prior danger that no longer exists at time of filing. *Abdul-Akbar v. McKelvie*, 239 F.3d 307 (3d Cir.2001); *Medberry v. Butler*, 185 F.3d 1189 (11th Cir.1999); *Ashley v. Dilworth*, 147 F.3d 715 (8th Cir.1998). *Cf. Hunt v. Uphoff*, 199 F.3d 1220, 1222 (10th Cir.1999) (alleging failure to provide adequate medical care for serious conditions satisfies the imminent danger requirement).

63. 28 U.S.C.A. § 1915(g) (Supp. V 2000).

64. This provision is limited to suits for monetary relief; hence a suit for injunctive and declaratory relief was not subject to the physical injury rule. *Thompson v. Carter*, 284 F.3d 411, 418 (2d Cir.2002) (citing cases).

65. 42 U.S.C.A. § 1997e(e) (Supp. V 2000). *See Searles v. Van Bebber*, 251 F.3d 869, 877 (10th Cir.2001) (proof of physical injury required before damages for emotional injury could be awarded to Jewish prisoner who alleged prison officials denied him Kosher diet); *Herman v. Holiday*, 238 F.3d 660 (5th Cir.2001) (prisoner's claim that he was exposed to asbestos barred by PLRA if only emotional distress damages claimed); *Allah v. Al-Hafeez*, 226 F.3d 247 (3d Cir. 2000) (prisoner entitled to only nominal damages for interference with religion); *Harris v. Garner*, 216 F.3d 970 (11th Cir. 2000) (en banc) (limit on damages applies to cases brought by persons who were prisoners when suit started; later status irrelevant); *Davis v. District of Columbia*, 158 F.3d 1342 (D.C.Cir.1998) (limit applies to claims brought under ADA as well as § 1983 claims); *Cassidy v. Indiana Department of Corrections*, 199 F.3d 374 (7th Cir. 2000) (restriction on emotional distress damages applies to constitutional and statutory claims).

66. 42 U.S.C.A. § 1997e(d) (Supp. V 2000). *But see Hernandez v. Kalinowski*, 146 F.3d 196 (3d Cir.1998) ("fees on fees" can be awarded under PLRA).

67. 28 U.S.C.A. §§ 1997e(a).

68. 534 U.S. 516, 122 S.Ct. 983, 152 L.Ed.2d 12 (2002).

69. *See also Johnson v. Breeden*, 280 F.3d 1308 (11th Cir.2002).

70. 532 U.S. 731, 121 S.Ct. 1819, 149 L.Ed.2d 958 (2001).

71. *See also Carroll v. Yates*, 362 F.3d 984 (7th Cir. 2004) (where prison review board failed to inform inmate that he must

prisoners' civil rights claims is tolled pending administrative exhaustion.[72]

§ 5.8 Appellate Jurisdiction of the Federal Circuit Courts

Title 28 U.S.C.A. § 1291 in terms limits the jurisdiction of the courts of appeals to review of all "final decisions" by a federal district court. The interpretation of "final decision" is narrow and strict. For example, even a district court order dismissing a claim, but fewer than all the claims against a party,[1] or dismissing a party, but fewer than all

appear in person, inmate adequately exhausted by filing written grievance); *Neal v. Goord*, 267 F.3d 116 (2d Cir.2001) (claim that medical services in prison inadequate must be administratively exhausted prior to filing; even if claim is exhausted afterward, case must still be dismissed); *Larkin v. Galloway*, 266 F.3d 718 (7th Cir.2001) (prisoner must exhaust administrative remedies in claim against correction officers who assaulted him even if remedy not available for monetary damages; claim still relates to prison conditions within meaning of the law); *Richardson v. Spurlock*, 260 F.3d 495 (5th Cir.2001) (when prisoner filed administrative appeal instead of disciplinary appeal required by regulations, prisoner failed to exhaust and case must be dismissed); *Wright v. Hollingsworth*, 260 F.3d 357 (5th Cir.2001) (exhaustion required even if only damages sought and grievance procedure cannot award damages); *Graves v. Norris*, 218 F.3d 884 (8th Cir.2000) (even if some claims exhausted and others pending when case dismissed, federal suit must be dismissed unless all claims exhausted); *Higginbottom v. Carter*, 223 F.3d 1259 (11th Cir.2000) (exhaustion requirements apply to excessive force claims); *Massey v. Wheeler*, 221 F.3d 1030 (7th Cir.2000) (prisoner must allege in complaint that he had exhausted all administrative remedies that were available); *McAlphin v. Morgan*, 216 F.3d 680 (8th Cir.2000) (prisoner must supply documentary proof of exhaustion); *Knuckles El v. Toombs*, 215 F.3d 640 (6th Cir.2000) (prisoner must plead that he has exhausted all administrative remedies); *Castano v. Nebraska Dept. of Corrections*, 201 F.3d 1023 (8th Cir.2000) (exhaustion requirement applies to general claim that Spanish-speaking interpreters must be afforded Spanish-speaking prisoners in prison disciplinary proceedings); *Brown v. Toombs*, 139 F.3d 1102 (6th Cir.1998) (courts should invoke administrative exhaustion requirement sua sponte, even if not raised by defendants); *Brown v. Sikes*, 212 F.3d 1205 (11th Cir.2000) (prisoner exhausted administrative remedies even though he did not name warden and commissioner in earlier administrative grievance); *Massey v. Helman*, 196 F.3d 727 (7th Cir.1999) (as long as administrative remedy is available, does not have to be "effective" and exhaustion still required); *see also Nyhuis v. Reno*, 204 F.3d 65 (3d Cir.2000) (administrative exhaustion requirement applies to *Bivens* action as well as Section 1983 actions); *Snider v. Melindez*, 199 F.3d 108 (2d Cir.1999) (district court cannot dismiss prisoner case sua sponte on grounds of failure to exhaust without giving inmate chance to be heard); *Miller v. Tanner*, 196 F.3d 1190 (11th Cir. 1999) (prisoner did exhaust all administrative claims even though he failed to sign grievance form and failed to appeal denial, when regulations did not require that he take such steps); *Hartsfield v. Vidor*, 199 F.3d 305 (6th Cir.1999) (claim of use of excessive force is claim relating to "prison conditions" and exhaustion is required; inmate's failure to appeal grievance indicates no exhaustion of remedies); *Freeman v. Francis*, 196 F.3d 641 (6th Cir.1999) (must exhaust all administrative remedies even if seek only monetary damages not available in administrative proceedings); *Wendell v. Asher*, 162 F.3d 887 (5th Cir.1998) (must exhaust all remedies regardless of effectiveness); *Underwood v. Wilson*, 151 F.3d 292 (5th Cir.1998) (prisoner's suit filed before exhaustion of all remedies properly dismissed with prejudice even though exhaustion occurred after suit filed).

72. *See, e.g., Brown v. Morgan*, 209 F.3d 595 (6th Cir.2000); *Clifford v. Gibbs*, 298 F.3d 328 (5th Cir.2002); *Johnson v. Rivera*, 272 F.3d 519, 522 (7th Cir.2001) (holding that in the ordinary case, a federal court must toll the limitations period while a prisoner completes the administrative grievance process).

§ 5.8

1. *See Hill v. Henderson*, 195 F.3d 671, 674–678 (D.C.Cir.1999) (holding, on purported appeal from dismissal of one claim, that district court's subsequent transfer of remaining Title VII and ADEA claims to a

the parties,[2] is usually not a "final decision" under § 1291 and accordingly is not appealable at that time unless the district court expressly determines "that there is no just reason for delay" and accordingly enters partial judgment under Federal Rule of Civil Procedure 54(b).

district in another circuit furnished no reason for exception to general rule that a dismissal of fewer than all claims is a nonfinal and hence not immediately reviewable decision). Most circuits to have addressed the issue are in accord that reviewability of pre-transfer orders lies instead in the circuit to which transfer was made. *See Hill*, 195 F.3d at 674–678; *EEOC v. Northwest Airlines, Inc.*, 188 F.3d 695, 700 (6th Cir. 1999); *Chaiken v. VV Publishing Corp.*, 119 F.3d 1018, 1025 n. 2 (2d Cir.1997), *cert. denied*, 522 U.S. 1149, 118 S.Ct. 1169, 140 L.Ed.2d 179 (1998); *Mackensworth v. S.S.Am. Merchant*, 28 F.3d 246, 249–252 (2d Cir.1994); *Tel–Phonic Servs., Inc. v. TBS Intern., Inc.*, 975 F.2d 1134, 1138 (5th Cir.1992). The majority rule, by temporarily withholding review of the order dismissing fewer than all claims, may eliminate need for appellate review anywhere it plaintiff is satisfied by the outcome in the transferee court and avoids piecemeal appeals in two courts. *But see McGeorge v. Continental Airlines, Inc.*, 871 F.2d 952 (10th Cir.1989) (circuit court in transferee district held it lacked appellate jurisdiction to review dismissal order of district court in transferor district, citing 28 U.S.C.A. § 1294(1), which provides that "appeals from reviewable decisions of the district ... courts shall be taken to ... the court of appeals for the circuit embracing the district"). The majority approach, by contrast, would not consider a pre-transfer dismissal order a "reviewable decision" within the meaning of § 1294, and therefore would not consider review of that decision restricted to the court of appeals for the circuit where the transfer order was issued. *See, e.g., Hill*, 195 F.3d at 675.

2. *But see Reuber v. United States*, 773 F.2d 1367 (D.C.Cir.1985) (where district court dismissed one party but then transferred remaining part of action to another district in another circuit, plaintiff held able to appeal the dismissal to transferor circuit court as a final judgment, apparently on the assumption that the dismissal order would eventually become final when the transferee district court disposed of the rest of the case). The decision is in tension with the general rule that orders of one district court made before transfer are reviewable by the circuit court embracing the transferee district court, an appeal which would only ripen, however, upon the issuance of one or more final decisions (or their fungible equivalent under § 1291) by the transferee district court. *See Chapple v. Levinsky*, 961 F.2d 372, 374 (2d Cir.1992); *Carteret Sav. Bank, FA v. Shushan*, 919 F.2d 225, 228 (3d Cir.1990); *Magnetic Eng'g & Mfg. Co. v. Dings Mfg. Co.*, 178 F.2d 866, 870 (2d Cir. 1950) (Hand, J.). As for the orders granting transfer themselves, they are not, under § 1404, final appealable orders or, ordinarily, reviewable collateral orders. *See Ukiah Adventist Hosp. v. FTC*, 981 F.2d 543, 546 (D.C.Cir.1992), *cert. denied*, 510 U.S. 825, 114 S.Ct. 88, 126 L.Ed.2d 55 (1993). But those orders may usually be challenged by a petition for writ of mandamus, if only for abuse of discretion or perhaps mere legal infirmity, in the court of appeals for the circuit of origin. *See In re Scott* 709 F.2d 717, 719 (D.C.Cir.1983) and 15 Charles Alan Wright, Arthur R. Miller & Edward H. Cooper, *Federal Practice and Procedure* § 3855 (1986 & Supp. 1999) (collecting cases). Thus they are immediately "reviewable orders," within the meaning of 28 U.S.C.A. § 1294, by the court of appeals embracing the transferor district court. Perhaps for that reason transfer orders have usually been held nonreviewable in the transferee circuit. *See TEC Floor Corp. v. Wal–Mart Stores, Inc.*, 4 F.3d 599, 602 (8th Cir.1993); *In re Briscoe*, 976 F.2d 1425, 1426 (D.C.Cir.1992); *Moses v. Business Card Express, Inc.*, 929 F.2d 1131, 1136 (6th Cir.1991), *cert. denied*, 502 U.S. 821, 112 S.Ct. 81, 116 L.Ed.2d 54 (1991); *Reyes v. Supervisor of the DEA*, 834 F.2d 1093, 1095 (1st Cir.1987); *Roofing & Sheet Metal Servs. v. La Quinta Motor Inns*, 689 F.2d 982, 986–87 (11th Cir.1982); *Linnell v. Sloan*, 636 F.2d 65, 67 (4th Cir.1980); *Purex Corp. v. St. Louis Nat'l Stockyards Co.*, 374 F.2d 998, 1000 (7th Cir.1967), *cert. denied*, 389 U.S. 824, 88 S.Ct. 59, 19 L.Ed.2d 77 (1967). *But see Nascone v. Spudnuts, Inc.*, 735 F.2d 763, 773 n. 9 (3d Cir.1984) (transferee court after final judgment may determine whether it in fact has venue); *American Fid. Fire Ins. Co. v. United States Dist. Ct.*, 538 F.2d 1371, 1377 n. 4 (9th Cir.1976) (declining writ of mandamus to review transfer order on ground that transferee circuit could review transfer order after final judgment); *Magnetic Eng'g & Mfg. Co. v. Dings Mfg. Co.*, 178 F.2d 866, 868–870 (2d Cir.1950) (Hand, J.) (transfer as well as pre-transfer orders reviewable by transferee circuit).

If, however, a federal district court certifies in an order that a nonfinal or "interlocutory" decision involves a "controlling question of law as to which there is substantial ground for difference of opinion," and that immediate review "may materially advance the ultimate termination of the litigation," the appellate court may, in its discretion, permit an immediate appeal from that order.[3] In addition, 28 U.S.C.A. § 1292(a)(1) provides (except where direct review is available in the Supreme Court) for "interlocutory" review of any nonfinal decision granting, continuing, modifying, refusing or dissolving an injunction, or refusing to dissolve or modify them.[4]

Apart from those limited express statutory authorizations for immediate review of nonfinal decisions, case law stemming from *Cohen v. Beneficial Industrial Loan Corp.*[5] provides for review by the federal circuit courts of a narrow class of nonfinal "collateral orders" that are both separable from the merits of the cause and the immediate review of which is deemed important for one or more of several different reasons of policy. Sections 2.23, above, and 5.101 below, discuss one such recognized "collateral order" exception, that permits interlocutory review of many orders denying a § 1983 defendant's motion to dismiss or summary judgment motion based on the defense of qualified immunity. The immediate reviewability of an order denying Eleventh Amendment immunity, is another instance of the "collateral order" exception. See § 5.101, *infra*. There is also a nascent but discernible doctrine of pendent appellate federal subject matter jurisdiction that may, very rarely, afford interlocutory review of nonfinal decisions that are very closely related to immediately reviewable "collateral orders." The nonfinal and hence ordinarily nonappealable orders may be entertained on interlocutory review if they raise issues so "inextricably intertwined" with the appealable "collateral order" (e.g., the order denying a state's Eleventh Amendment immunity or a § 1983 defendant's motion based on qualified immunity) that "review of the former ... [is] necessary to ensure meaningful review of the latter."[6]

For considerations governing the disposition of appeals, see § 5.103, *infra*.

3. 28 U.S.C.A. § 1292(b).

4. But a district court's interlocutory order denying exclusion of certain inmates from definition of plaintiff class challenging state prison's medical care system has been held not to have the practical effect of granting or denying injunctive relief, and hence not appealable per § 1292(a)(1). *Plata v. Davis*, 329 F.3d 1101 (9th Cir.2003).

5. 337 U.S. 541, 546, 69 S.Ct. 1221, 93 L.Ed. 1528 (1949).

6. *Swint v. Chambers County Comm'n*, 514 U.S. 35, 51, 115 S.Ct. 1203, 131 L.Ed.2d 60 (1995). Applying that standard, an appellate court that rejected state officials' Eleventh Amendment defense also declined to hear their objection to plaintiff's standing, because "we may resolve the Eleventh Amendment immunity issue without reaching the merits of standing." *Summit Med. Assocs., P.C. v. Pryor*, 180 F.3d 1326, 1335 (11th Cir.1999), *cert. denied*, 529 U.S. 1012, 120 S.Ct. 1287, 146 L.Ed.2d 233 (2000). *See also Moniz v. City of Ft. Lauderdale*, 145 F.3d 1278, 1281 (11th Cir.1998) (because qualified immunity issue could be resolved without reaching the merits of appellants' challenge to plaintiff's standing, the jurisdictional standing issue not within pendent appellate jurisdiction).

§ 5.9 Venue

The Reconstruction Civil Rights Acts, most notably 42 U.S.C.A. § 1981, 1982, 1983 and 1985, make no explicit provision for venue. Venue for actions presenting even one of these federal question claims therefore lies in the first instance in the districts provided by the pertinent subsection of the general federal venue statute, 28 U.S.C.A. § 1391(b). Plaintiff's choices will include under § 1391(b)(1) any district, if any, in which all defendants "reside."[1] In most civil rights actions, even where there are multiple defendants, they are likely to all reside in the same district, so that subsection (b)(1) will afford a venue choice. Let us suppose, however, that this choice is not tactically appealing to plaintiff, or that not all defendants reside in the same district, so that subsection (b)(1) affords no choice at all. The plaintiff will always be able to fall back on the choice or choices provided by subsection (b)(2), namely, the district or districts in which "a substantial part" of the claim arises. In the typical civil rights case, where the alleged unlawful conduct is entirely within the district that embraces a local government subdivision, (b)(2) gives the venue choice of the district in which plaintiff was subjected to the alleged civil rights violation and in which it caused him injury. If there is but a single defendant, both (b)(1) and (b)(2) would typically give the same venue choice, because the district where a government entity or individual official defendant resides will also likely be the district in which all, or at least a part, of the claim arose.

Venue for employment discrimination claims under Title VII, the Age Discrimination in Employment Act, the Equal Pay Act, or the Americans With Disabilities Act is provided for expressly by the statutes creating those claims. Because the defendants in these cases are commonly far-flung corporate employers, rather than municipalities or counties existing within one district only, it is not surprising that these statutes afford broader venue choice than does the general federal venue state, 28 U.S.C.A. § 1391, applicable to civil rights claims. Venue for a Title VII claim, for example, lies "in any judicial district in the State in which the unlawful employment practice is alleged to have been committed, in the judicial district in which the employment records relevant to such practice are maintained and administered, or in the judicial district in which the aggrieved person would have worked but for the alleged unlawful employment practice, but if the respondent is not found within any such district, such an action may be brought within the judicial district in which the respondent has his principal office."[2]

§ 5.9

1. It should be kept in mind that § 1391(c), in turn, identifies each district in which a corporate defendant "resides" for purposes of subsection (b)(1). The district where an individual defendant "resides" within the meaning of subsection (b)(1) is not self-evident, either. A majority of the circuit courts to have confronted the issue have concluded that an individual's "residence" for venue purposes equates with his "domicile," a more restrictive concept used to determine a basis of constitutional personal jurisdiction and citizenship for purposes of federal subject matter jurisdiction under 28 U.S.C.A. § 1332. *See Manley v. Engram*, 755 F.2d 1463, 1466 n. 3 (11th Cir.1985) (citations omitted).

2. Title VII § 706(f)(3), 42 U.S.C.A. § 2000e–5(f)(3).

But plaintiff may have commenced either a civil rights or employment discrimination action in state court. That is possible because state courts enjoy concurrent subject matter jurisdiction over those claims.[3] Quite commonly defendants will believe it tactically advantageous to defend such claims in federal court, before a judge virtually always tenured for life and before a usually more rural jury pool distributed in a district that surrounds but is not limited to urban population centers. Defendants will be able to remove to federal court any action containing even one federal civil rights or employment discrimination claim, under the authority of 28 U.S.C.A. § 1441(a) and the first sentence of § 1441(b). In that situation, original federal venue lies in only one district: the federal district embracing the state court from which the action was removed. § 1441(a).

So far we have been speaking only of the appropriate federal venues originally selected by the plaintiff. Once plaintiff lays venue in a federal judicial district, or defendant removes an action that the plaintiff filed in state court to the federal judicial district in which that state court sits, either party may have an opportunity to move to transfer venue to another federal judicial district. 28 U.S.C.A. §§ 1404 and 1406 provide for transfer *from* a federal judicial district where both personal jurisdiction, and original venue (under § 1391, or under a special statutory venue provision like Title VII's, or after removal under § 1441(a)), are proper—transfer per § 1404[4]—or where personal jurisdiction, or venue, or both are faulty—transfer per § 1406.[5] But transfer under either § 1404 or § 1406 is possible to only those federal judicial districts in which the action might originally have been brought, which the Supreme Court has construed to mean any district that would have had good personal jurisdiction and venue at the time the plaintiff filed in the original federal district.[6] Moreover, before transferring, the district judge must find that the proposed transferee district is more convenient to parties and witnesses than the original, transferor district, and that a transfer would be in the interest of justice. See §§ 1404, 1406.

Does the specification of particular venues in Title VII preclude the district judge from exercising his usual discretion under § 1404 or § 1406 to transfer the action to another district that would be more convenient (and that also has sound personal jurisdiction and venue)? No. Even if the plaintiff has filed originally in a district specified by Title VII, the district court may transfer under the usual standards for transfer under § 1404, i.e., upon determining that the proposed transferee district also had good personal jurisdiction and venue at the time the

3. *See* § 5.1, *supra.*

4. *Ferens v. John Deere Co.*, 494 U.S. 516, 110 S.Ct. 1274, 108 L.Ed.2d 443 (1990) (§ 1404 used only where both venue and personal jurisdiction are correct).

5. *See Goldlawr v. Heiman*, 369 U.S. 463, 82 S.Ct. 913, 8 L.Ed.2d 39 (1962). (§ 1406 permits transfer from district lacking personal jurisdiction).

6. *Hoffman v. Blaski*, 363 U.S. 335, 80 S.Ct. 1084, 4 L.Ed.2d 1254 (1960).

action was filed and will be more convenient to parties and witnesses and that the transfer will be in the interest of justice.[7]

Whether transfer will be granted, however, especially on defendant's motion, is quite a different matter. The plaintiff's forum choice "should not be disturbed unless it is clearly outweighed by other considerations."[8] But neither plaintiff's forum choice, nor a possible delay attendant upon transfer, should obstruct a transfer on defendant's motion if defendant demonstrates the proposed transferee forum is significantly more convenient from the standpoint of location of employment and witnesses to the alleged violations and of pertinent books and records.[9] Once, however, transfer is ordered, it is reviewed only for "a clear abuse of discretion."[10] A more complicated question is how to obtain review of an order granting transfer. (An order denying transfer is manifestly not a "final decision" within the meaning of 28 U.S.C.A. § 1291 and hence is not reviewable by the court of appeals superintending the original federal judicial district until and unless the party who sought transfer suffers an adverse, appealable final judgment.[11]) An order granting transfer has been held to be neither a final appealable order at the time entered nor reviewable under the "collateral order" exception that would permit immediate federal appellate interlocutory review by the court of appeals for the circuit superintending the district court that ordered transfer.[12] The district court to which transfer is ordered will generally be unable to review the order that transferred the action to it because of the doctrine of "law of the case."[13] Nor, where transfer is ordered to a district in another circuit, will most transferee circuits review the transferor district court's order granting transfer.[14]

7. *Ross v. Buckeye Cellulose Corp.*, 980 F.2d 648, 655 (11th Cir.1993), *cert. denied,* 513 U.S. 814, 115 S.Ct. 69, 130 L.Ed.2d 24 (1994).

8. *Robinson v. Giarmarco & Bill*, 74 F.3d 253, 260 (11th Cir.1996); *Howell v. Tanner*, 650 F.2d 610, 616 (5th Cir.1981), *cert. denied*, 456 U.S. 918, 102 S.Ct. 1775, 72 L.Ed.2d 178 (1982).

9. *In re Horseshoe Entertainment*, 305 F.3d 354 (5th Cir.2002).

10. *Richardson v. Alabama St. Bd. of Educ.*, 935 F.2d 1240, 1248 (11th Cir.1991); Howell, 650 F.2d at 616.

11. *See supra* § 5.8 for a discussion of the "final decision" rule.

12. *See Ukiah Adventist Hosp. v. FTC*, 981 F.2d 543, 546 (D.C.Cir.1992), cert. denied, 510 U.S. 825, 114 S.Ct. 88, 126 L.Ed.2d 55 (1993); § 5.8, *supra*, on the "collateral order" exception to the "final decision" rule of 28 U.S.C.A. § 1291. Still, on rare occasion, courts of appeals for the circuit superintending the court ordering transfer will entertain petitions for writs of mandamus to review those orders. *See In re Scott* 709 F.2d 717, 719 (D.C.Cir.1983) and 15 Charles Alan Wright, Arthur R. Miller & Edward H. Cooper, Federal Practice and Procedure § 3855 (1986 & Supp. 1999) (collecting cases).

13. *See Chrysler Credit Corp. v. Country Chrysler*, 928 F.2d 1509, 1518 (10th Cir.1991).

14. *See TEC Floor Corp. v. Wal–Mart Stores, Inc.*, 4 F.3d 599, 602 (8th Cir.1993); *In re Briscoe*, 976 F.2d 1425, 1426 (D.C.Cir. 1992); *Moses v. Business Card Express, Inc.*, 929 F.2d 1131, 1136 (6th Cir.), *cert. denied*, 502 U.S. 821, 112 S.Ct. 81, 116 L.Ed.2d 54 (1991); *Reyes v. Supervisor of the DEA*, 834 F.2d 1093, 1095 (1st Cir.1987); *Roofing & Sheet Metal Serv. v. La Quinta Motor Inns*, 689 F.2d 982, 986–87 (11th Cir.1982); *Linnell v. Sloan*, 636 F.2d 65, 67 (4th Cir. 1980); *Purex Corp. v. St. Louis Nat'l Stockyards Co.*, 374 F.2d 998, 1000 (7th Cir. 1967), *cert. denied*, 389 U.S. 824, 88 S.Ct. 59, 19 L.Ed.2d 77 (1967). *But see Nascone v. Spudnuts, Inc.*, 735 F.2d 763, 773 n. 9 (3d Cir.1984) (transferee court after final judgment may determine whether it in fact has venue); *American Fid. Fire Ins. Co. v. United States Dist. Ct.*, 538 F.2d 1371, 1377 n. 4

One possibility is that the party who unsuccessfully opposed transfer will move after transfer in the transferee district for "re-transfer" back to the transferor district. The denial of that motion would be reviewable, after final judgment, by the circuit court embracing the transferee district.[15]

C. *YOUNGER* NONINTERVENTION

§ 5.10 State Proceedings

a. Criminal

In *Younger v. Harris*, the Supreme Court held that federal courts may not enjoin pending[1] state court criminal proceedings absent extraordinary circumstances; instead, the court must dismiss the federal action even though the state court criminal defendant challenges in the federal action the constitutionality of the criminal statute under which the state is proceeding and all justiciability requirements are met. Expressly declining to rest its decision on the Anti–Injunction Act,[2] to which § 1983 was found to be an exception a year later in *Mitchum v. Foster*,[3] the Court in *Younger v. Harris*[4] fashioned this noninterference policy based on considerations of equity and comity that it termed "our federalism."[5] Traditional doctrines of equity, said the Court, preclude restraint of an existing criminal prosecution "when the movant has an adequate remedy at law and will not suffer irreparable injury if denied equitable relief." Moreover, principles of federalism and comity, "that is, a proper respect for state functions," prevent "undue interference with legitimate activities of the States."

Drawing upon these principles, the Court established a firm bar to federal intervention in ongoing state criminal proceedings when the federal plaintiff has an opportunity to raise his constitutional challenges as a defense to the state prosecution. *Younger*, when considered with the Anti–Injunction Act, should be understood as a separate and independent bar to federal court injunctions; if a federal court plaintiff seeks to enjoin or award declaratory relief against ongoing state proceedings,[6] the

(9th Cir.1976) (declining writ of mandamus to review transfer order on ground that transferee circuit could review transfer order after final judgment); *Magnetic Eng'g & Mfg. Co. v. Dings Mfg. Co.*, 178 F.2d 866, 868–870 (2d Cir.1950) (Hand, J.) (transfer orders reviewable by transferee circuit). The majority rule may turn on the recognition of the transferee circuit that courts of appeals for the transferor circuit may entertain petitions for writs of mandamus to review those orders, as indicated in one of the previous footnotes.

15. *See Nascone v. Spudnuts, Inc.*, 735 F.2d 763, 765–66 (3d Cir.1984); *Purex Corp. v. St. Louis Nat'l Stockyards Co.*, 374 F.2d 998, 1000 (7th Cir.), *cert. denied*, 389 U.S. 824, 88 S.Ct. 59, 19 L.Ed.2d 77 (1967).

§ 5.10

1. For when an action is "pending," *see* § 5.11.

2. *See* § 5.1, *supra*, and § 5.45, *infra*.

3. 407 U.S. 225, 92 S.Ct. 2151, 32 L.Ed.2d 705 (1972).

4. 401 U.S. 37, 91 S.Ct. 746, 27 L.Ed.2d 669 (1971).

5. *Id.* at 43, 91 S.Ct. at 750.

6. *But see General Auto Service Station LLC v. City of Chicago*, 319 F.3d 902 (7th Cir.2003) (where plaintiff sought only a declaration of its substantive rights, not a declaratory judgment halting state court action, *Younger* inapplicable) (alternative holding).

plaintiff to avoid dismissal must satisfy both an exception to the Anti–Injunction Act (which she does if her claim is under § 1983) and fall outside the parameters of *Younger* abstention. The basic elements in support of *Younger* abstention have been summarized as follows: the federal court plaintiff seeks an order interfering with (1) ongoing state proceedings that (2) implicate important state interests (criminal, or, as discussed below, "important" civil proceedings) and (3) provide plaintiff an adequatc opportunity to litigate federal claims.[7] Recent circuit decisions have relied on the "inadequate opportunity" rationale in rejecting *Younger* dismissal in a variety of settings.[8]

The *Younger* doctrine does, however, recognize a number of exceptions. Federal interference with a pending criminal prosecution against the plaintiff would be justified if the threat of irreparable injury is "both great and immediate" and "cannot be eliminated by his defense against a single criminal prosecution."[9] But in *Younger* itself the Supreme Court denied any categorical exception for First Amendment claims, rejecting the assertion that impeding the plaintiff's path to federal court on such claims inevitably results in irreparable injury. Instead, the Court explained, the exceptions must be truly exceptional: provable prosecutorial bad faith or harassment warrants federal interference, as do other extraordinary circumstances like challenges to state statutes that are "flagrantly and patently violative of express constitutional prohibitions in every clause, sentence, and paragraph."[10] The exception for bad faith

7. *See, e.g., Nivens v. Gilchrist*, 319 F.3d 151 (4th Cir.2003) (§ 1983 plaintiffs had adequate opportunity in pending state criminal drug prosecution to raise claim that prosecution violated double jeopardy after they had paid drug taxes); *H.C. ex rel. Gordon v. Koppel*, 203 F.3d 610, 613 (9th Cir.2000). *But cf. Gerstein v. Pugh*, 420 U.S. 103, 95 S.Ct. 854, 43 L.Ed.2d 54 (1975) (where legality of pretrial detention of § 1983 plaintiff could not be raised in defense of his criminal prosecution, plaintiff lacked adequate opportunity and *Younger* abstention held inapplicable).

8. *See, e.g., Habich v. City of Dearborn*, 331 F.3d 524, 530–532 (6th Cir.2003) (noncongruence of issues before federal court and state court reviewing local administrative agency, in sense that issues in plaintiff's federal action could neither be proven as part of the state court case in chief nor raised as an affirmative defense, meant federal issues were collateral to the state proceeding and federal plaintiffs therefore lacked opportunity to raise their claim in state proceedings; moreover, § 1983 plaintiff did not have that "opportunity" for *Younger* purposes merely because she could file a new or amended state court complaint containing her federal claims); *Meredith v. State of Oregon*, 321 F.3d 807 (9th Cir. 2003) (although there were ongoing state administrative proceedings that implicated important state interests, plaintiff did not have adequate opportunity to raise First Amendment claims during those proceedings); *General Auto Service Station LLC v. City of Chicago*, 319 F.3d 902 (7th Cir.2003) (building owner could maintain § 1983 action challenging city's sign ordinance on First Amendment and due process grounds where no state forum was available to owner to raise those issues) (alternative holding).

9. *Id.* at 44, 91 S.Ct. at 751.

10. The district court should hold an evidentiary hearing to determine whether there has been sufficient prosecutorial bad faith to avoid *Younger*, rather than rely on conclusory statements in prosecutors' affidavits. *Kern v. Clark,* 331 F.3d 9 (2d Cir. 2003) (per curiam). When the § 1983 claim is presented after the conclusion of a state court trial, however, *Younger* has been construed to bar a federal court from proceeding even when the plaintiff alleges that the underlying prosecution was undertaken in bad faith. The Fifth Circuit reasoned that the § 1983 action would then impermissibly entail review of the state court's judgment. *Musslewhite v. State Bar of Texas*, 32 F.3d 942 (5th Cir.1994), *cert. denied*, 515 U.S.

state criminal prosecutions is narrow.[11]

b. *Quasi–Criminal: State a Party*

The Supreme Court first extended *Younger* to the civil setting in a quasi-criminal matter to which the State was a party. In *Huffman v. Pursue, Ltd.*,[12] the Court determined that *Younger* prohibited a federal civil rights action from interfering with a state civil nuisance proceeding. The Court characterized the proceeding as "both in aid of and closely related to criminal statutes which prohibit the dissemination of obscene materials." Federal court interference might result in duplicative proceedings, could be interpreted "as reflecting negatively upon the state court's ability to enforce constitutional principles,"[13] and would thus constitute "an offense to the State's interest . . . likely to be every bit as great as it would be were this a criminal proceeding."

c. *Civil: State a Party*

As predicted by Justice Brennan in his dissent in *Huffman*,[14] in *Trainor v. Hernandez*,[15] the Court extended *Younger* to all civil proceedings regardless of their nature so long as the State is a party.[16] The Court emphasized that "the State was a party to the suit in its role of administering its public-assistance programs" and was vindicating "important state policies such as safeguarding the fiscal integrity of those programs." Relying again on the *Younger* principles of federalism and comity, the Court reasoned that a federal injunction of a state civil enforcement suit would also result in duplicative proceedings, would disrupt suits by the State in its sovereign capacity, and would reflect negatively on the State's ability to adjudicate federal claims. Absent extraordinary circumstances warranting federal equitable relief, concluded the Court, "the principles of *Younger* and *Huffman* are broad enough to apply to interference by a federal court with an ongoing civil enforcement action such as this, brought by the State in its sovereign capacity."

But where the state is not acting in a sovereign capacity seeking to enforce a state program and in the absence of a substantial state

1103, 115 S.Ct. 2248, 132 L.Ed.2d 256 (1995).

11. The Court in *Younger* distinguished a previous case, *Dombrowski v. Pfister*, 380 U.S. 479, 85 S.Ct. 1116, 14 L.Ed.2d 22 (1965), as involving state criminal prosecution for the purpose of harassment and not conviction. Since then the Court has rejected all bad faith arguments, but some lower courts have applied the exception. *See, e.g., Nobby Lobby, Inc. v. City of Dallas*, 970 F.2d 82 (5th Cir.1992) (bad faith based on police repeated seizures of questionable constitutionality); *The Video Store, Inc. v. Holcomb*, 729 F.Supp. 579 (S.D.Ohio 1990) (existence of twelve simultaneously pending lawsuits evidences bad faith). *But see Phelps v. Hamilton*, 122 F.3d 885 (10th Cir.1997) (rejecting bad faith argument despite allegations of animus toward anti-homosexual protestors and because the number of prosecutions instituted against the protestors was small in comparison to the total number of cases prosecuted by the county).

12. 420 U.S. 592, 95 S.Ct. 1200, 43 L.Ed.2d 482 (1975).

13. *See Steffel v. Thompson*, 415 U.S. 452, 94 S.Ct. 1209, 39 L.Ed.2d 505 (1974).

14. *Huffman*, 420 U.S. at 613.

15. 431 U.S. 434, 97 S.Ct. 1911, 52 L.Ed.2d 486 (1977).

16. The Court forbade lower federal courts from issuing declaratory relief that

interest, *Younger* abstention is not applicable. For example, in a case related to the flood of tobacco litigation, the Second Circuit held that where a state is merely pressing a subrogation claim grounded in tort, *Younger* abstention is not warranted.[17]

d. Civil: State Not a Party, but Important State Interests Involved

1. Judicial Interests

The Court has also extended *Younger* to civil cases in which the State is not a party, but important state interests are present. Dismissal of the federal action is required, for example, when necessary to assure the integrity of the state's judicial system. In *Juidice v. Vail*,[18] the Court determined that the State's interest in the contempt process, though not as important as the State's interest in enforcement of its criminal laws,[19] or in the maintenance of a quasi-criminal proceeding,[20] was sufficiently important to warrant federal court nonintervention. Similarly, in *Pennzoil Co. v. Texaco, Inc.*,[21] the State's interest in ensuring that its money judgments were executed was sufficiently weighty to require noninterference. And because family relations are a traditional area of state concern,[22] circuit courts have invoked *Younger* to bar attempts to enjoin ongoing state child custody proceedings.[23]

A federal appellate court has applied these principles in upholding the dismissal under *Younger* of an action by a mobile home park owner against a municipal entity. The owner challenged the city's rent control ordinance in federal court as an unconstitutional taking, after he had initiated a prior state proceeding that he asserted he was required to initiate first to meet the ripeness requirement of the Just Compensation Clause. *Younger* required dismissal, the court concluded, because of the state's substantial interest in municipal rent control ordinances.[24] The ruling may put a plaintiff who also has other federal claims to the choice of forfeiting either her takings claims (by bypassing state court) or, as in the case at bar, a federal forum for all her federal claims.

would impede prior pending state civil proceedings.

17. *Philip Morris, Inc. v. Blumenthal*, 123 F.3d 103, 106 (2d Cir.1997), cert. denied, 524 U.S. 937, 118 S.Ct. 2340, 141 L.Ed.2d 712 (1998) (courts must look beyond the style of the state's pleading and consider the underlying nature of the state proceeding on which the federal lawsuit would impinge).

18. 430 U.S. 327, 97 S.Ct. 1211, 51 L.Ed.2d 376 (1977).

19. *See Younger*, 401 U.S. 37, 91 S.Ct. 746, 27 L.Ed.2d 669.

20. *See Huffman*, 420 U.S. 592, 95 S.Ct. 1200, 43 L.Ed.2d 482.

21. 481 U.S. 1, 107 S.Ct. 1519, 95 L.Ed.2d 1 (1987).

22. *Moore v. Sims*, 442 U.S. 415, 435, 99 S.Ct. 2371, 60 L.Ed.2d 994 (1979).

23. *H.C. ex rel. Gordon v. Koppel*, 203 F.3d 610, 613–614 (9th Cir.2000); *Mann v. Conlin*, 22 F.3d 100, 106 (6th Cir.1994), *cert. denied*, 513 U.S. 870, 115 S.Ct. 193, 130 L.Ed.2d 126 (1994).

24. *Mission Oaks Mobile Home Park v. Hollister, Calif.*, 989 F.2d 359 (9th Cir. 1993), *cert. denied*, 510 U.S. 1110, 114 S.Ct. 1052, 127 L.Ed.2d 373 (1994). *See also Armco, Inc. v. United Steelworkers of America*, 280 F.3d 669 (6th Cir.2002) (vacating lower court consent decree entered in § 1983 case as violative of *Younger* absten-

2. *Administrative Interests*

In *Middlesex County Ethics Comm. v. Garden State Bar Ass'n*,[25] the Court applied *Younger* to administrative proceedings as well. Refusing to allow federal court interference with a pending state bar investigation, conducted under the aegis of a state supreme court, the Court analogized bar disciplinary actions to judicial proceedings and emphasized their "special importance" in maintaining the professionalism of the state's practicing attorneys. In *Hawaii Hous. Auth. v. Midkiff*,[26] the Court refused to apply *Younger* to an administrative proceeding expressly declared by state law not to be part of the state's judicial system. But in *Ohio Civil Rights Comm'n v. Dayton Christian Sch.*,[27] the Court resolved any doubt concerning the applicability of *Younger* to administrative proceedings unconnected with the state judicial system. Federal courts must abstain from interfering with administrative proceedings "in which important state interests are vindicated, so long as in the course of those proceedings the federal plaintiff would have had a full and fair opportunity to litigate his constitutional claim."[28]

An exception has been declared where a prior federal administrative proceeding with facially conclusive preemptive force is pending before the state administrative proceeding commences. In that situation, it has been held that there can be no significant state interest that would be served by *Younger* abstention because the state agency would be acting in excess of its lawful authority.[29]

§ 5.11 "Pendency"

a. *Rationale*

Younger and its progeny evince a strong federal policy against most federal court interference with pending state proceedings. Critical to the doctrine is the assumption of parity between federal and state courts in deciding constitutional issues. So long as a pending state proceeding provides the putative civil rights plaintiff an adequate forum in which to present his federal claims, a federal court should avoid reaching the claim itself by dismissing the federal action.

At least initially, the Court refused to dismiss unless it was clear not only that a state proceeding was pending but also that it provided the

tion doctrine where decree addressed same issues pending in state court).

25. 457 U.S. 423, 102 S.Ct. 2515, 73 L.Ed.2d 116 (1982). *Accord Hirsh v. Justices of Supreme Court of California*, 67 F.3d 708 (9th Cir.1995) (per curiam).

26. 467 U.S. 229, 104 S.Ct. 2321, 81 L.Ed.2d 186 (1984).

27. 477 U.S. 619, 106 S.Ct. 2718, 91 L.Ed.2d 512 (1986).

28. *See also Green v. Benden*, 281 F.3d 661 (7th Cir.2002) (finding *Younger* abstention appropriate where pending state-court administrative review action provided adequate opportunity for plaintiff to raise his due process and equal protection challenges).

29. *Chaulk Servs., Inc. v. Massachusetts Comm'n Against Discrimination*, 70 F.3d 1361 (1st Cir.1995), *cert. denied* 518 U.S. 1005, 116 S.Ct. 2525, 135 L.Ed.2d 1049 (1996) (distinguishing *New Orleans Pub. Serv., Inc. v. Council of New Orleans*, 491 U.S. 350, 109 S.Ct. 2506, 105 L.Ed.2d 298 (1989), as holding that *Younger* abstention applies when plaintiff mounts a "substan-

federal plaintiff with a forum in which his federal claims could in fact be heard. In Trainor, for instance, the Court remanded with a direction to address the issue of the federal plaintiffs' opportunity to litigate their constitutional claims in state court. But beginning in *Moore v. Sims*,[1] the Court in effect reversed the presumption about that opportunity, writing that *Younger* nonintervention applies "unless state law clearly bars the interposition of the constitutional claims."[2] But at least the Court there undertook an independent examination of that question, concluding that the plaintiffs had failed to present their federal issue by way of counterclaim, as state law apparently permitted.[3] By contrast in *Pennzoil Co. v. Texaco, Inc.*,[4] the Court dismissed the federal action even though it was unclear whether state procedure would permit presentation of plaintiff's constitutional claims. The Court substituted for searching inquiry the strong presumption that a federal plaintiff can raise a constitutional claim in a pending state proceeding unless it "plainly appears" from "unambiguous authority to the contrary" that she cannot.[5]

b. Absence of Pending State Proceedings

When no state proceeding is actually pending at or after[6] the time the federal complaint is filed, *Younger* on its own terms is inapplicable.[7] Federal interference cannot then result in duplicative proceedings or reflect negatively upon the competency of state courts to resolve constitutional issues. Even though as discussed in subpart "f." following, *Younger* dismissal is available even when the state prosecution was initiated after commencement of the federal action, the state prosecution must in fact be pending, not merely predictably possible.[8] Moreover, dismissal by a federal court "may place the hapless plaintiff between the Scylla of intentionally flouting state law and the Charybdis of foregoing what he believes to be constitutionally protected activity in order to

tial," but not "facially conclusive," constitutional challenge to the state proceedings).

§ 5.11

1. 442 U.S. 415, 99 S.Ct. 2371, 60 L.Ed.2d 994 (1979).

2. *Id.* at 425–426, 99 S.Ct. at 2378–79.

3. *Id.* at n.9.

4. 481 U.S. 1, 107 S.Ct. 1519, 95 L.Ed.2d 1 (1987).

5. *Id.* at 14, 107 S.Ct. at 1527.

6. *But see Pathways, Inc. v. Dunne*, 329 F.3d 108 (2d Cir.2003) (district court dismissal when state proceedings were pending vacated when no state proceedings remained pending at time of federal appeal).

7. Purportedly to implement *Younger* and *Heck*, an appellate decision expands their holdings to bar § 1983 damages relief by former prisoners who bypassed the opportunity to challenge in state court the restrictions on their liberty while they were still confined. *Nelson v. Murphy*, 44 F.3d 497 (7th Cir.1995), *cert. denied*, 516 U.S. 1027, 116 S.Ct. 671, 133 L.Ed.2d 521 (1995).

8. *Agriesti v. MGM Grand Hotels*, 53 F.3d 1000 (9th Cir.1995). And the state proceeding must be pending against the federal civil plaintiff. Thus, *Younger* abstention was held inapplicable where the child welfare citizens' advocacy group that sued under § 1983 was never made a party to the particular state court child custody case that generated the gag orders the group challenged as unconstitutional. *FOCUS v. Allegheny County Court of Common Pleas*, 75 F.3d 834 (3d Cir.1996). In this way, the liberal approach to standing that enabled the citizens group to challenge the gag orders on free speech grounds, see section "L," below, facilitates an end-run of the *Younger* bar. *But cf. Anthony v. Council*, 316 F.3d 412 (3d Cir.2003) (*Younger* abstention appropriate even though federal plaintiffs were not currently appearing in state child support proceeding where each was subject to state court child support orders requiring state court involvement).

avoid becoming enmeshed in a criminal proceeding."[9] But even if a federal court finds *Younger* inapplicable, relief may still be denied if the federal plaintiff fails to meet justiciability requirements by not presenting a live and continuing controversy. To determine standing to sue, the Court focuses on the nature of the threat encountered by plaintiff.

c. *Actual Threats of Prosecution*

Actual threats of prosecution can provide the federal plaintiff with a claim capable of surviving both justiciability and *Younger* requirements. In *Steffel*, the Court held that relief could be provided by a federal court if plaintiff had actually been threatened with prosecution, but was not then subject to a pending state proceeding. The actual threat of prosecution provided the continuing and live controversy required for standing.

d. *Implied or Apparent Threats of Prosecution*

Federal relief is also available, despite *Younger*, in situations involving only imminent implied or apparent threats of prosecution. In *Doran v. Salem Inn, Inc.*,[10] plaintiffs sought federal relief against a newly enacted ordinance prohibiting topless dancing. Two of the three plaintiffs complied with the ordinance while seeking federal relief, but the third violated it and was subjected to state prosecution. Relying on *Steffel*, the Court held that *Younger* did not bar a grant of federal relief to the two complying plaintiffs, against whom no state prosecution was or could be pending. Furthermore, *Younger* did not require dismissal simply because the complying plaintiff's claims presented the same issue as that of the third, noncomplying plaintiff. Again, the threat of prosecution, in this case an imminent implied or apparent one, satisfied justiciability requirements.

e. *Unmatured Threats of Prosecution*

Although actual or apparent threats of prosecution can provide grounds for federal relief, claims may not be based on purely speculative threats. Such claims fall victim to the justiciability requirements of Article III.[11] In *Younger* itself, the Court dismissed the claims of three intervenors who alleged that the state law in question made them "feel inhibited" in advocating or teaching certain political ideologies. And in *Juidice*, the Court dismissed the claims of plaintiffs who had already been prosecuted under the challenged contempt statute, had paid their fines, and had not alleged a threat of further prosecution. The Court in both *Younger* and *Juidice* found the claims failed to present a live and continuing controversy.

f. *After–Filed Pending State Proceedings*

Even if the federal plaintiff meets justiciability requirements, a state prosecutor may still effectively abort the federal action by initiating a

9. *See Steffel*, 415 U.S. at 462, 94 S.Ct. at 1217.

10. 422 U.S. 922, 95 S.Ct. 2561, 45 L.Ed.2d 648 (1975).

11. *See Younger*, 401 U.S. 37, 91 S.Ct. 746, 27 L.Ed.2d 669; *Juidice, supra*, § 5.10, 430 U.S. 327, 97 S.Ct. 1211, 51 L.Ed.2d 376.

state prosecution thereafter.[12] In *Hicks and Doran*, the Court dismissed plaintiffs' federal claims when state prosecutions were initiated against plaintiffs a day after their suits were filed in federal court. Emphasizing that the initiation of state proceedings provided plaintiffs a forum in which to adjudicate their constitutional claims, the Court held that federal courts must dismiss if state proceedings are begun prior to any "proceedings of substance on the merits" on the federal claim, *Hicks*, or when "the federal litigation [is] in its embryonic stage and no contested matter [has] been decided."[13] In *Midkiff*,[14] the Court, without deciding whether the issuance of a federal restraining order was substantial in this sense, did decide that the grant of a preliminary injunction brought the federal action past the "embryonic stage" of litigation.

g. State Proceedings Pending on Appeal

A state proceeding may sometimes be found still pending even after a final state judgment has been rendered against the federal plaintiff. In *Huffman*, for instance, plaintiff sought relief in federal court, rather than appeal within the state system. The Court, recognizing the finality of the state judgment, nevertheless invoked *Younger* noninterference. Interference with the State's appellate proceedings, noted the Court, would be "even more disruptive and offensive because the State [had] already won a nisi prius determination that its valid policies are being violated in a fashion which justifies judicial abatement." In *Wooley v. Maynard*,[15] however, the Court found *Younger* inapplicable where the plaintiff, unlike *Huffman*, had not attempted "to annul the results of a state trial" by substituting federal action for a state appeal. Plaintiff in *Wooley* had been repeatedly prosecuted for violation of the same state statute, had acquiesced in previous convictions, and merely sought prospective relief from further prosecution.

§ 5.12 Kinds of Relief Barred

The Court has refused to except particular species of federal judicial equitable relief from the *Younger* bar on the basis of their lesser intrusiveness. In *Samuels v. Mackell*,[1] a companion case to *Younger*, for example, the Court held that because "a declaratory judgment will result in precisely the same interference with and disruption of state proceedings that the long-standing policy limiting injunctions was designed to avoid," federal courts may not provide a plaintiff even declaratory relief while she is subject to an ongoing state criminal prosecution. While "the practical effect of the two forms of relief will be virtually identical," the Court did, however, recognize that there may be exceptional situations

12. *Hicks v. Miranda*, 422 U.S. 332, 95 S.Ct. 2281, 45 L.Ed.2d 223 (1975); *Doran*, *supra* this section.

13. *Doran*, 422 U.S. 922, 95 S.Ct. 2561, 45 L.Ed.2d 648.

14. *Hawaii Housing Authority v. Midkiff*, 467 U.S. 229, 104 S.Ct. 2321, 81 L.Ed.2d 186 (1984).

15. 430 U.S. 705, 710, 97 S.Ct. 1428, 1433, 51 L.Ed.2d 752 (1977).

§ 5.12

1. 401 U.S. 66, 91 S.Ct. 764, 27 L.Ed.2d 688 (1971).

when declaratory relief would be allowed but injunctive relief would be too intrusive. Any exceptional circumstance sufficient to except a federal court suit for declaratory relief from the *Younger* and *Samuels* bar has yet to be found. Moreover, in *Pennzoil* and *Doran*, the Court failed to find the grant of a preliminary injunction to be any less intrusive than the imposition of a permanent injunction. When a state proceeding is pending, therefore, federal courts may not grant any form of equitable relief, absent extraordinary circumstances. *Younger* dismissal applies, that is, where the federal plaintiff seeks equitable, declaratory or other discretionary relief. But the bar applies only if the relief sought would as a practical matter interfere with the ongoing state proceeding.[2]

By contrast, it is clear that courts lack authority under *Younger* "to dismiss or remand cases based on abstention principles ... where the relief being sought is [damages rather than] equitable or otherwise discretionary" remedies.[3] Rather, the Court in *Quackenbush* suggested that where solely legal relief is sought, the court may issue an abstention-based order staying the federal action. But even under *Quackenbush*, the action may be dismissed if damages are contingent on a prior declaration that a state tax scheme is unconstitutional and may therefore no longer be enforced.[4]

§§ 5.13–5.14 [Reserved]

D. *PULLMAN* ABSTENTION

§ 5.15 The Basic Doctrine

Whereas *Younger* requires federal courts to refrain altogether from interfering by injunction with important pending state proceedings, the abstention doctrine announced in *Railroad Commission v. Pullman Co.*,[1] merely postpones the exercise of federal jurisdiction when state court clarification of uncertain state law might obviate the necessity of a federal constitutional ruling. In *Pullman*, plaintiffs challenged not only the constitutionality of a state commission's regulation, but also the commission's authority under state law to promulgate the regulation itself. The Court held that federal courts must abstain, that is, defer to pending state court resolution of the issue, when two requirements are met. First there must be an ambiguous state law touching on an area of sensitive social policy. Lower courts have sometimes applied this test restrictively, adding the gloss that abstention should be denied when

2. *Montclair Parkowners Ass'n v. City of Montclair*, 264 F.3d 829 (9th Cir.2001) (federal court action paralleling state court challenge to city ordinance could proceed despite *Younger* where no injunctive or other relief was sought that would impede state suit).

3. *Quackenbush v. Allstate Ins. Co.*, 517 U.S. 706, 730, 116 S.Ct. 1712, 1728, 135 L.Ed.2d 1 (1996).

4. *Id.* (citing *National Private Truck Council, Inc. v. Oklahoma Tax Comm'n*, 515 U.S. 582, 115 S.Ct. 2351, 132 L.Ed.2d 509 (1995)).

§ 5.15

1. 312 U.S. 496, 61 S.Ct. 643, 85 L.Ed. 971 (1941).

there is no alternative to federal adjudication.[2] Among the reasons the Supreme Court gave for the doctrine was a desire to avoid friction between federal and state courts, to reduce the likelihood of erroneous interpretations of state law, and to avoid unnecessary constitutional rulings. Hence the second requirement, whether resolution of state law issues in state court is likely to moot or narrow the federal constitutional questions. Even when both requirements are met, a federal court must stay its hand only until a definitive ruling is made in state court. If the state court upholds the validity of the state regulation or law, then plaintiff may return to federal court for a constitutional ruling.

The use of *Pullman* abstention has been seriously brought into question by the Court's decision in *Arizonans for Official English v. Arizona*.[3] There the Court strongly criticized resort to *Pullman* abstention, preferring instead certification of state law questions to state supreme courts, a procedure available in most states. Describing *Pullman* abstention as "[a]ttractive in theory," the doctrine has "proved protracted and expensive in practice" entailing "a full round of litigation in the state-court system before any resumption of proceedings in federal court."[4] Certification of novel state-law questions to state courts allows the federal judiciary to "put the question directly to the State's highest court, reducing the delay, cutting the cost, and increasing the assurance of gaining an authoritative response."[5]

The decision in *Pennhurst State School & Hosp. v. Halderman*,[6] denying as a violation of the Eleventh Amendment federal court jurisdiction to adjudicate violations of state law by state officials, even when only prospective relief is sought, has also significantly reduced the number of occasions suitable for *Pullman* abstention.

2. *See Porter v. Jones*, 319 F.3d 483, 492–494 (9th Cir.2003) (citing cases) (*Pullman* abstention inappropriate because it was "far from clear" that First Amendment issue would be resolved by state court before plaintiff would again desire to engage in allegedly protected First Amendment expression). Because federal courts are particularly well-suited to hear First Amendment challenges, this gloss has led to the further position that *Pullman* abstention is seldom appropriate in First Amendment cases. *Id.* (citing cases).

3. 520 U.S. 43, 75–6, 117 S.Ct. 1055, 1073, 137 L.Ed.2d 170 (1997). *See also Lehman Brothers v. Schein*, 416 U.S. 386, 391, 94 S.Ct. 1741, 1744, 40 L.Ed.2d 215 (1974) (through certification of novel or unsettled questions of state law for authoritative answers by a state's highest court, a federal court may save "time, energy, and resources and hel[p] build a cooperative judicial federalism"); *Bellotti v. Baird*, 428 U.S. 132, 148, 96 S.Ct. 2857, 2866–2867, 49 L.Ed.2d 844 (1976) (to warrant district court certification, "[i]t is sufficient that the statute is susceptible of . . . an interpretation [that] would avoid or substantially modify the federal constitutional challenge to the statute"). For examples of federal court certification to state courts, see *Parents Involved in Community Schools v. Seattle Sch. Dist. No. 1*, 294 F.3d 1085 (9th Cir.2002) (certifying question to state court where no state court had yet construed a new state statute); *Pittman v. Cole*, 267 F.3d 1269, 1288 (11th Cir.2001) (directing district court to certify question to state supreme court).

4. *Arizonans*, 520 U.S. at 75–76, 117 S.Ct. at 1073.

5. *Id.*

6. 465 U.S. 89, 104 S.Ct. 900, 79 L.Ed.2d 67 (1984).

§ 5.16 Applicability

To warrant *Pullman* abstention, the meaning of a state law affecting significant social policy must be substantially unclear, and there must be a reasonable probability that clarification in state court would make a federal court constitutional ruling unnecessary. Because of these two prerequisites, abstention is not required simply because a state law is challenged as unconstitutionally vague.[1] If a narrowing construction cannot save the alleged unconstitutionally vague statute from invalidation, the federal court may address the issue. Abstention also is not required when a challenged state constitutional provision is identical with a federal constitutional provision.[2] Federal courts must abstain, however, if the state court's construction of a unique provision of the state constitution might obviate the need for a constitutional ruling.[3] Case law has clarified a third requirement: that the federal court's erroneous construction of state law would disrupt important state policies.[4] In any event, even when these requirements are in place, *Pullman* abstention is discretionary with the court, to be exercised only when the vector effect of the three factors overcomes the presumption that a federal court should exercise the subject matter jurisdiction Congress has conferred on it by statute.

It appears that the presence of a mere federal question is insufficient to trigger *Pullman* abstention; the federal plaintiff must present a "substantial constitutional claim."[5] And at times the Supreme Court and commentators have suggested that the federal court should be especially wary of abstaining in actions brought under § 1983.[6]

A special species of deferral, akin to the requirement of ripeness, and significantly different from the type prescribed by *Pullman*, applies to federal actions challenging the reapportionment of state or federal election districts under the U.S. Constitution or statutes. Absent evidence that a state's legislature or courts "will fail timely" to perform their primary duty and responsibility to reapportion federal congressional or state legislative districts, "a federal court must neither affirmatively obstruct state reapportionment nor permit federal litigation to be used

§ 5.16

1. *Baggett v. Bullitt*, 377 U.S. 360, 84 S.Ct. 1316, 12 L.Ed.2d 377 (1964).

2. *Wisconsin v. Constantineau*, 400 U.S. 433, 91 S.Ct. 507, 27 L.Ed.2d 515 (1971). *Cf. Williams v. Lambert*, 46 F.3d 1275 (2d Cir.1995) (*Pullman* abstention inappropriate where the unresolved issue was one of both federal and state constitutional law).

3. *Reetz v. Bozanich*, 397 U.S. 82, 90 S.Ct. 788, 25 L.Ed.2d 68 (1970).

4. *See, e.g., Chez Sez III Corp. v. Township of Union*, 945 F.2d 628, 631 (3d Cir. 1991), *cert. denied*, 503 U.S. 907, 112 S.Ct. 1265, 117 L.Ed.2d 493 (1992).

5. *Railroad Comm'n v. Pullman, Co.*, 312 U.S. 496, 498–501, 61 S.Ct. 643, 644–45, 85 L.Ed. 971 (1941). *See also Hawaii Hous. Auth. v. Midkiff*, 467 U.S. 229, 236, 104 S.Ct. 2321, 2326, 81 L.Ed.2d 186 (1984) (referring to the presence of "a substantial federal constitutional question").

6. *See, e.g., Mayor of Phila. v. Educational Equality League*, 415 U.S. 605, 628, 94 S.Ct. 1323, 1337, 39 L.Ed.2d 630 (1974); *McNeese v. Board of Educ.*, 373 U.S. 668, 673–74, 83 S.Ct. 1433, 1436–37, 10 L.Ed.2d 622 (1963); 17A Charles A. Wright et al., *Federal Practice and Procedure* § 4242 (1988).

to impede it."[7] Thus, unlike the *Pullman* doctrine, reapportionment deferral is called for when there is pending a state legislative, and not just a judicial resolution, and includes challenges based on federal, and not just state law. Further, deferral under this doctrine is not dependent on an identity of the issues on which the reapportionment is challenged in state and federal court. Rather, this type of deferral is triggered simply by virtue of "the nature of the relief requested: reapportionment of election districts."[8]

The Seventh Circuit has crafted an abstention doctrine founded on *Pullman* principles. In *Gottfried v. Medical Planning Servs., Inc.*,[9] an anti-abortion protestor challenged in federal court a long-standing state court injunction against picketing near a physician's home and office under § 1983. No state court proceeding was pending, so neither *Younger* nor *Colorado River* abstention, see § 5.28, infra, applied; nor did any other previously formulated abstention doctrines. Under *Pullman* doctrines of comity and federalism, however, the Seventh Circuit held that federal courts should stay the challenge by a nonparty to a state court injunction until after the plaintiff seeks relief from the state court.

§ 5.17 Procedure

Once a federal court abstains, the parties need only try their state issues in state court and may reserve litigation of their constitutional issues for return to federal court.[1] If a party chooses to litigate his constitutional challenges in state court without effective reservation, she relinquishes the right to return to federal court. "[A]n explicit reservation is not indispensable; a litigant is in no event to be denied his return to [federal court] unless it clearly appears that he voluntarily ... and fully litigated his federal claims in state courts. When the reservation has been made, however, his right to return will in all events be preserved."[2]

In theory that is; in practice, doctrine and real life get in the way. For one thing, the state court in the course of rendering judgment may have made findings on facts common to both the state and federal claims. If so, the federal court may, upon reasserting jurisdiction, be compelled to accord issue preclusive effect to those findings in accordance with the Supreme Court's general interpretation of the Full Faith and Credit Statute, 28 U.S.C.A. § 1738.[3] For another, the plaintiff, or

7. *Growe v. Emison*, 507 U.S. 25, 33, 113 S.Ct. 1075, 1081, 122 L.Ed.2d 388 (1993).

8. *Id.*

9. 142 F.3d 326 (6th Cir.1998), *cert. denied*, 525 U.S. 1041, 119 S.Ct. 592, 142 L.Ed.2d 534 (1998).

§ 5.17

1. *England v. Louisiana State Bd. of Med. Examiners*, 375 U.S. 411, 84 S.Ct. 461, 11 L.Ed.2d 440 (1964).

2. *Id.* at 421, 84 S.Ct. at 468.

3. *See* text § 5.119, *infra*, discussing *Allen v. McCurry*. *But see Instructional Sys., Inc. v. Computer Curriculum Corp.*, 35 F.3d 813 (3d Cir.1994), *cert. denied*, 513 U.S. 1183, 115 S.Ct. 1176, 130 L.Ed.2d 1128 (1995) (neither claim (res judicata) nor issue (collateral estoppel) preclusion will bar litigation of the federal law issues upon return of the proceedings to federal court).

the plaintiff's lawyer, may have become literally or financially exhausted as a result of exhausting the state judicial forum, or the relief sought may have become moot before the long-awaited return-trip to federal court. *Pullman* cases take an extraordinarily long time to litigate fully. For that reason, the Supreme Court has expressed the strong preference that courts in *Pullman* situations certify novel questions of state law to the state's highest courts to avoid the delay, cost and uncertainty that plagues *Pullman* abstention.[4]

§§ 5.18–5.19 [Reserved]

E. *YOUNGER–PULLMAN* INTERACTION

§ 5.20 In General

The formerly clear line of demarcation between *Younger* nonintervention and *Pullman* abstention has been redrawn to favor the federal defendant. In *Pennzoil*, the Court infused its *Younger* analysis with *Pullman* considerations, yet refused to adopt the more lenient *Pullman* abstention procedures when confronted with ambiguity in the state's procedural framework for considering the constitutional claims. Rejecting plaintiff's inadequate procedures argument, the Court dismissed rather than stayed its hand in favor of a state court determination of whether plaintiff could in fact raise its constitutional claims in state court. The Court presumed that plaintiff could raise his federal claims in state court, despite the ambiguity.

Although *Younger* and *Pullman* may be combined to fortify the defendant's effort to achieve dismissal of the federal action, plaintiffs have had less success in arguing for the milder *Pullman* solution to a *Younger* problem. In *Temple of Lost Sheep, Inc. v. Abrams*,[1] the court ruled that the federal plaintiff may not avoid preclusion by reserving its federal claims in state court following a *Younger* dismissal.[2] These courts emphasize that reservation of federal claims in the *Younger* context is incompatible with the doctrine's central assumption of parity between federal and state courts.

§§ 5.21–5.24 [Reserved]

F. *YOUNGER* PENUMBRAS AND OTHER ABSTENTION DOCTRINES

§ 5.25 In General

When uncertain whether *Younger* applies, the Court has adopted a

4. *See Arizonans for Official English v. Arizona*, 520 U.S. 43, 117 S.Ct. 1055, 137 L.Ed.2d 170 (1997).

§ 5.20

1. 930 F.2d 178 (2d Cir.1991), *cert. denied*, 502 U.S. 866, 112 S.Ct. 193, 116 L.Ed.2d 153 (1991).

2. *Accord, Mission Oaks Mobile Home Park v. City of Hollister*, 989 F.2d 359, 362 (9th Cir.1993), *cert. denied*, 510 U.S. 1110, 114 S.Ct. 1052, 127 L.Ed.2d 373 (1994).

wait-and-see attitude. In *Deakins v. Monaghan*,[1] for example, plaintiff sought monetary damages in federal court from an allegedly unconstitutional search that lead to a state grand jury investigation. Without deciding whether a grand jury investigation amounted to a pending state proceeding for *Younger* purposes, or whether the doctrine applies to federal actions seeking only monetary relief, the Court applied *Younger* principles, but ordered only a *Pullman* remedy. It held that federal courts must "stay rather than dismiss federal claims that are not cognizable in the parallel state proceeding."[2] Where the underlying state proceeding is criminal, and damages there are accordingly unavailable, this holding is a logical extension of the requirement numbered (3), above, for *Younger* abstention, namely, that the federal plaintiff would have an opportunity to present his claims (and receive relief thereon) in the state proceeding.[3] A stay, reasoned the Court, would allow the state proceeding to go forward without federal interference while still maintaining the federal court's jurisdiction. Even where the underlying state proceeding is not criminal, and hence damages relief might be available, the Court has since held that a pure-damages federal action may be stayed, but not dismissed or remanded, in deference to state interests; wholesale abstention with dismissal of the federal action, in other words, is available only where the federal plaintiff seeks equitable, declaratory or otherwise discretionary relief.[4]

But suppose the would-be civil rights plaintiff, sensitive to the Court's deference to state policies and procedures, waits until state criminal proceedings are completed in her favor before filing under § 1983. Will the action be time barred on the theory that the claim accrued at the time of a challenged search or arrest, or will it go forward based on the theory that the claim did not accrue until a state court vacated the conviction?[5] The better and predominant view is that the claim is timely, because under the reasoning of *Heck* it was not even ripe until the plaintiff's conviction was invalidated in the state courts.[6]

The Supreme Court has not hesitated to apply the full *Younger* medicine of dismissal when convicted prisoners assert § 1983 claims in federal court in an attempt to circumvent the habeas corpus exhaustion rule. In *Preiser v. Rodriguez*,[7] discussed above, prisoners sought injunctive relief in federal court to compel restoration of good-conduct-time credits, which would result in their immediate release. In holding that the prisoners' sole remedy was through habeas corpus, the Court relied on *Younger* considerations of comity: the State's opportunity to correct

§ 5.25

1. 484 U.S. 193, 108 S.Ct. 523, 98 L.Ed.2d 529 (1988).

2. *Id.* at 202, 108 S.Ct. at 529–30.

3. *See Simpson v. Rowan*, 73 F.3d 134, 138–39 (7th Cir.1995), *cert. denied*, 519 U.S. 833, 117 S.Ct. 104, 136 L.Ed.2d 58 (1996).

4. *Quackenbush v. Allstate Ins. Co.*, 517 U.S. 706, 116 S.Ct. 1712, 135 L.Ed.2d 1 (1996).

5. See the discussion of *Heck* as it affects statute of limitations issue in § 5.74, *infra*.

6. *See, e.g, Woods v. Candela*, 47 F.3d 545 (2d Cir.1995), *cert. denied*, 516 U.S. 808, 116 S.Ct. 54, 133 L.Ed.2d 18 (1995). *See* § 5.74, *infra*.

7. 411 U.S. 475, 93 S.Ct. 1827, 36 L.Ed.2d 439 (1973).

its errors could be second guessed, if at all, through the federal habeas procedure alone. Although the Court in *Preiser* limited its holding to prisoners' § 1983 claims that sought immediate or speedier release from confinement, in *Heck v. Humphrey*[8] the doctrine was expanded to bar the § 1983 actions of all prisoners, current and perhaps also former,[9] who seek any relief, including damages, that would necessarily invalidate their underlying convictions.[10]

§ 5.26 [Reserved]

§ 5.27 *Rooker–Feldman* Doctrine

The *Rooker–Feldman* doctrine has its origins in a pair of cases decided sixty years apart. In *Rooker v. Fidelity Trust Co.*,[1] decided in 1923, the Court held that lower federal courts lack jurisdiction to entertain not only direct but even disguised appeals from state court judgments because that power is reserved to the Supreme Court. The bar was triggered if constitutional questions presented in a federal district court action "actually arose in" the previous state action. The *Rooker* opinion reasoned that under 28 U.S.C.A. § 1257, only the Supreme Court, not lower federal courts, have appellate jurisdiction to review decisions of the state courts (and only of the highest state court)—by implication, lower federal courts do not. In 1983, the Supreme Court extended the doctrine when it held in *District of Columbia Court of Appeals v. Feldman*[2] that lower federal courts cannot hear "challenges to state court decisions in particular cases arising out of judicial proceedings" or decide questions "inextricably intertwined" with state court judgments—even if those questions were not explicitly decided or addressed in an opinion accompanying the state judgment.[3] Still, *Feldman*

8. 512 U.S. 477, 114 S.Ct. 2364, 129 L.Ed.2d 383 (1994).

9. Whether a former prisoner seeking damages under § 1983 is barred by *Heck* is not altogether clear. *See* text § 5.7, *supra*.

10. *See* text § 5.7, *supra*. In *Guerro v. Mulhearn*, 498 F.2d 1249 (1st Cir.1974), the First Circuit reached a similar result, relying on *Younger* principles of comity.

§ 5.27

1. 263 U.S. 413, 416, 44 S.Ct. 149, 150, 68 L.Ed. 362 (1923).

2. 460 U.S. 462, 476, 103 S.Ct. 1303, 1311, 75 L.Ed.2d 206 (1983).

3. *See Richard v. Hoechst Celanese Chemical Group, Inc.*, 355 F.3d 345 (5th Cir. 2003) (state court class certification findings intertwined with § 1983 constitutional challenge to that court's approval of class action settlement); *Schmitt v. Schmitt*, 324 F.3d 484 (7th Cir.2003) (federal court action could not review interlocutory state court decisions in divorce-related action regarding adequacy of service of process and personal jurisdiction, because state court was capable of resolving those questions under federal standards); *Ballinger v. Culotta*, 322 F.3d 546 (8th Cir.2003) (federal court action by father against state child support officials amounted to prohibited appeal of state court award of custody to grandfather); *Kenmen Engineering v. City of Union*, 314 F.3d 468 (10th Cir.2002) (due process and takings claims relating to losses allegedly resulting from state-court order were barred by *Rooker-Feldman* because inextricably intertwined with that order and because relief sought would undo state court judgment); *Ace Const. v. City of St. Louis*, 263 F.3d 831 (8th Cir.2001) (§ 1983 claim alleging zoning changes violated procedural due process barred by state court judgment rejecting plaintiff's standing to challenge those changes); *Ahmed v. Washington*, 262 F.3d 979 (9th Cir.2001) (state court judgment denying wrongful termination claim forecloses federal court action alleging retaliation in violation of First

made clear that when the federal district court challenge implicates not a state judicial but a state administrative or legislative decision, including an administrative decision by a state court, the negative pregnant drawn from the Supreme Court's exclusive appellate jurisdiction over state court decisions is not implicated, and the doctrine does not bar.[4] And it

Amendment). *Edwards v. Illinois Bd. of Admissions to Bar,* 261 F.3d 723 (7th Cir. 2001) (Illinois Supreme Court's denial of bar certification would in essence be reviewed by federal action challenging under the Americans with Disabilities Act a bar admissions requirement that mental health records be disclosed as pre-condition of certification); *Brown & Root, Inc. v. Breckenridge,* 211 F.3d 194 (4th Cir.2000) (because state court both addressed and decided employer's Federal Arbitration Act claim later presented in federal court, plaintiff a fortiori had the "opportunity" to present the federal claim to state court; *Rooker–Feldman* therefore bars even though state court placed its ruling on different, non-federal ground); *Kridel v. Florida Pub. Employees,* 180 F.3d 269 (11th Cir.1999) (unpublished), *cert. denied,* 528 U.S. 1079, 120 S.Ct. 797, 145 L.Ed.2d 672 (2000) (federal claim challenging dismissal inextricably intertwined with state court judgment affirming administrative decision upholding plaintiff's dismissal, and plaintiff had reasonable opportunity to litigate federal claims in state proceedings). *See also Keene Corp. v. Cass,* 908 F.2d 293, 296 (8th Cir.1990) (a state claim is inextricably intertwined if the federal challenge succeeds only to the extent that the state court wrongly decided the issues before it). *But see Simes v. Huckabee,* 354 F.3d 823 (8th Cir. 2004) (no bar where state court had declined to address federal claims); *Merrill Lynch Business Financial Services, Inc. v. Nudell,* 363 F.3d 1072 (10th Cir. 2004) (state court dismissal of creditor's action against guarantor not on merits and thus not decided or intertwined with creditor's subsequent federal collection action); *Desi's Pizza, Inc. v. City of Wilkes–Barre,* 321 F.3d 411 (3d Cir.2003) (no bar because success of federal law claims based on selective prosecution would not undermine validity of state court judgment ordering closure of plaintiff's bar as a nuisance even though that judgment resulted from one of the alleged wrongful prosecutions); *Peterson Novelties, Inc. v. City of Berkley,* 305 F.3d 386 (6th Cir.2002) (doctrine does not bar federal law action against city for seizing plaintiff retailer's goods and arresting its employees because a finding that city violated plaintiff's constitutional rights would not implicitly hold that state court erred in refusing to hold city in contempt, because state court did not discuss the lawfulness of city's conduct); *Brokaw v. Weaver,* 305 F.3d 660 (7th Cir.2002) (no bar where plaintiff's allegations that defendants unconstitutionally conspired to falsely accuse her parents of child neglect was independent of, and therefore could not impugn, state court decision declaring her a ward of the state); *Goodman v. Sipos,* 259 F.3d 1327 (11th Cir.2001) (doctrine does not bar illegal search claim by parents as that claim not "inextricably intertwined" with ex parte state juvenile proceeding); *Rivers v. McLeod,* 252 F.3d 99 (2d Cir.2001) (plaintiff grandfather's § 1983 action alleging foster care institution failed to provide grandson reasonable medical care not inextricably intertwined with issues in state family court proceedings modifying grandfather's visitation rights); *Parkview Associates Partnership v. City of Lebanon,* 225 F.3d 321 (3d Cir.2000) (*Rooker-Feldman* doctrine did not bar federal district court from entertaining personal care home's suit challenging denial of zoning permit as violative of federal and state anti-discrimination statutes, even though state courts had affirmed denial of permit; home had not presented its disability-based discrimination claims to state courts, and federal district court would not have had to review state courts' determinations that denial was supported by substantial evidence in record); *Johnson v. Rodrigues,* 226 F.3d 1103 (10th Cir.2000) (plaintiff's general challenge to state's adoption laws not barred because he was not party to adoption proceeding and challenged no particular state court decision on merits); *Sheehan v. Marr,* 207 F.3d 35 (1st Cir.2000) (Americans With Disabilities Act claim not barred by doctrine because state administrative and judicial framework for contesting involuntary retirement inadequately designed to provide plaintiff an opportunity to litigate the "failure to accommodate" aspect of an ADA claim).

4. *See also Verizon Maryland, Inc. v. Public Serv. Comm'n of Maryland,* 535 U.S. 635, 122 S.Ct. 1753, 1759 n. 3, 152 L.Ed.2d 871 (2002) (doctrine has no application to state court review of executive action, including state administrative agency determinations); *Van Harken v. City of Chicago,* 103 F.3d 1346, 1349 (7th Cir.1997), *cert. denied,* 520 U.S. 1241, 117 S.Ct. 1846, 137

has been held that for the doctrine to bar, the state court proceedings cannot be ongoing, as would trigger the *Younger* nonintervention doctrine, but must have resulted in a final judgment.[5] The great expansion of the doctrine has been worked by the lower federal courts, which have relied on it more than 500 times since *Feldman*.[6]

At first glance, the doctrine appears to be redundant. The Anti–Injunction Act, 28 U.S.C.A. § 2283, prohibits federal courts from enjoining most ongoing state court proceedings. Unless, therefore, the plaintiff's suit is under § 1983, which the Supreme Court in *Mitchum v. Foster*[7] excepted from the Anti–Injunction Act, *Rooker–Feldman* adds little. Further, even in actions under § 1983, *Younger* abstention will usually counsel dismissal of the federal action in which the plaintiff seeks injunctive or declaratory relief that would interfere with an ongoing state judicial proceeding. It is true that where a federal court plaintiff seeks relief that calls into question a completed state court judgment, neither the Anti–Injunction Act nor *Younger* likely applies. Nevertheless, *Rooker–Feldman* may still be redundant if the claim asserted in federal court arises from the same real-life transaction that gave rise to the prior state case; then state common law claim preclusion ("res judicata"), made applicable to the federal courts by the Full Faith and Credit Statute,[8] will usually[9] preclude all claims that were raised or could have been raised in the state case. But where the federal plaintiff alleges that the source of his harm was the state suit itself, res judicata would not preclude the federal suit because the claim did not accrue until after the state court judgment was final and so is not transactionally related to the facts giving rise to the first suit. There *Rooker–Feldman* could lead to dismissal where preclusion law could not. Indeed one commentator has argued that it is only where the federal action targets conduct related to the actual state court proceeding that the doctrine should have any application, because only such claims could fairly be

L.Ed.2d 1049 (1997); *United States v. Illinois Pollution Control Bd.*, 17 F.Supp.2d 800 (N.D.Ill.1998) (*Rooker–Feldman* does not apply to protect state administrative determinations from subsequent federal litigation). *But cf. Manley v. City of Chicago,* 236 F.3d 392 (7th Cir.2001) (police officer's termination that was fully challenged both administratively and in state court precluded federal relief that effectively required review of state courts' rulings).

5. *H.C ex rel. Gordon v. Koppel*, 203 F.3d 610, 612–613 (9th Cir.2000).

6. Sherry, *Judicial Federalism in the Trenches: The Rooker–Feldman Doctrine in Action*, 74 Notre Dame L.Rev. 1085, 1088 (1999).

7. 407 U.S. 225, 92 S.Ct. 2151, 32 L.Ed.2d 705 (1972).

8. 28 U.S.C.A. § 1738 (1994). See *Allen v. McCurry*, 449 U.S. 90, 101 S.Ct. 411, 66 L.Ed.2d 308 (1980) and *Migra v. Warren City Sch. Dist. Bd. of Educ.*, 465 U.S. 75, 104 S.Ct. 892, 79 L.Ed.2d 56 (1984), requiring federal courts hearing claims under § 1983 to apply, respectively, issue and claim preclusion to the same extent as the law of the state that rendered the prior judgment. See § 5.117, *infra*.

9. There are of course limited exceptions to claim preclusion. If, for example, the prior action was terminated in defendant's favor because of jurisdiction, venue or a few other grounds considered not on the "merits," or if the court hearing that action lacked subject matter jurisdiction to entertain the claim advanced in the second action, the former judgment does not bar. *See* §§ 5.116 and 5.118, *infra*. But a circuit court has held that if preclusion is unfair because the first court lacked subject matter jurisdiction, neither should *Rooker–Feldman* bar the second action. *King v. State Educ. Dep't*, 182 F.3d 162 (2d Cir. 1999).

characterized as an "appeal," rather than merely an attempt to relitigate.[10]

The Full Faith and Credit Statute similarly requires federal courts to apply the state law of issue preclusion or "collateral estoppel," which often precludes a plaintiff who was a party to a prior state court action and who commences a federal action on the same or even a different transaction from relitigating an issue that was litigated in, determined by, and essential to the prior state court judgment. If the requirements of issue preclusion are met, *Rooker–Feldman* is largely redundant, but not wholly: as a jurisdictional doctrine, it admits of few if any exceptions, unlike the more flexible preclusion principles which operate only when the party being precluded had a full and fair opportunity in the prior proceeding to litigate the issue in question.

Similarly, where the plaintiff in the second, federal action was a stranger to the state proceeding, issue preclusion against her would almost surely fail, because it would deny her the basic Due Process rights to notice and opportunity to be heard. *Rooker–Feldman* could again serve as a distinctive barrier in that situation. Further, while the law of an increasing number of states permits an action 1 stranger to invoke issue preclusion in a second action (against a party who was a party to the prior, state proceeding), even though Due Process would forbid preclusion of the stranger, other states do not recognize such "nonmutual" estoppel. And federal courts are obliged by the Full Faith and Credit Statute to give as much preclusive effect to a prior state judgment as would the law of the rendering state, but no more.[11] Accordingly, on such facts, federal courts could bar an action under *Rooker–Feldman* where they could not through the state law of preclusion made applicable through the Statute.

Rooker–Feldman fills these voids by barring suits where the requested relief would effectively nullify or modify the state judgment.[12] It can reach beyond state law preclusion principles because it permits federal courts to characterize the federal action as in substance an impermissible "appeal" of the state court judgment. To the extent that it employs inflexible jurisdictional principles to extend the reach of the less rigid,

10. Beerman, *Comments on Rooker–Feldman or Let State Law be Our Guide*, 74 Notre Dame L.Rev. 1209, 1214 (1999).

11. *Marrese v. American Acad. of Orthopaedic Surgeons*, 470 U.S. 373, 384, 105 S.Ct. 1327, 1334, 84 L.Ed.2d 274 (1985); *Migra*, 465 U.S. at 88 (White, J., concurring). *See also Haring v. Prosise*, discussed *infra* § 5.119.

12. *Compare Snider v. City of Excelsior Springs, Mo.*, 154 F.3d 809 (8th Cir.1998) (where state court certified class of time share owners in a hotel, determined the relevant damages from condemnation procedures against the hotel, and extinguished the property interests of the class, *Rooker–Feldman* abstention prohibited the court from hearing a federal suit challenging the condemnation proceedings under the takings clause) with *Hachamovitch v. DeBuono*, 159 F.3d 687 (2d Cir.1998) (*Rooker–Feldman* not applicable to federal court proceeding challenging the state medical disciplinary scheme because a ruling favorable to plaintiff would not undermine the state court finding). *See generally Landers Seed Co. v. Champaign Nat'l Bank*, 15 F.3d 729, 732 (7th Cir.1994), *cert. denied*, 513 U.S. 811, 115 S.Ct. 62, 130 L.Ed.2d 20 (1994); *Charchenko v. City of Stillwater*, 47 F.3d 981, 983 (8th Cir.1995).

case-sensitive preclusion doctrines, *Rooker–Feldman* is on dubious theoretical footing—among other reasons because it upsets the Congressional judgment embodied in the Full Faith and Credit Act, 28 U.S.C.A. § 1738, that federal courts should accord state court judgments only as much preclusive effect as they would enjoy in that state's own courts.[13] Its invocation is particularly troubling when used to dismiss actions under § 1983, which, from its inception in 1871, has been designed in part to provide a federal forum for the adjudication of federal law claims, and has also been held not to require exhaustion of state remedies.[14]

§ 5.28 *Colorado River* Abstention Doctrine

Colorado River abstention is a narrow abstention doctrine that allows federal courts to avoid duplicative litigation by dismissing a suit when a parallel proceeding is ongoing in a state forum.[1] Unlike other abstention doctrines, *Colorado River* is designed to promote "wise judicial administration," but mere duplication is not sufficient.[2] As a result, *Colorado River* abstention should be used only in "exceptional" circumstances.[3] The Court has identified several factors to be considered in deciding whether to apply *Colorado River* abstention. These factors are: (1) which court first assumed jurisdiction over the property in dispute; (2) the inconvenience of the federal forum; (3) the desirability of avoiding piecemeal litigation; and (4) the order in which jurisdiction was obtained.[4] These factors are to be applied as part of a balancing process rather than as a "mechanical checklist."[5] For example, in considering the order in which jurisdiction was obtained, it is important not only to determine whether the state or the federal complaint was filed first, but

13. Beerman, 74 Notre Dame L.Rev. at 1221–23. Although the Supreme Court has upheld the application of 28 U.S.C.A. § 1738 to § 1983 actions, see §§ 5.116, 5.117, and 5.119, *infra*, it has carefully limited its scope to the degree of preclusion that would be accorded by the courts of the state that rendered the judgment. *See Haring v. Prosise*, discussed *infra* § 5.119. A line of Fifth Circuit decisions implicitly recognizes that the doctrine should not be used to expand preclusion rules, permitting its use only where the action would also be barred under state law. *See, e.g, Davis v. Bayless*, 70 F.3d 367, 376 (5th Cir.1995); *Gauthier v. Continental Diving Servs., Inc.*, 831 F.2d 559, 561 (5th Cir.1987).

14. Bandes, *The Rooker–Feldman Doctrine: Evaluating Its Jurisdictional Status*, 49 Notre Dame L.Rev. 1175, 1186–1193, 1205 (1999).

§ 5.28

1. The doctrine was first articulated in *Colorado River Water Conservation Dist. v. United States*, 424 U.S. 800, 96 S.Ct. 1236, 47 L.Ed.2d 483 (1976) and was subsequently applied in *Moses H. Cone Mem'l Hosp. v. Mercury Constr. Corp.*, 460 U.S. 1, 19, 103 S.Ct. 927, 938, 74 L.Ed.2d 765 (1983) and *Arizona v. San Carlos Apache Tribe of Ariz.*, 463 U.S. 545, 103 S.Ct. 3201, 77 L.Ed.2d 837 (1983). *See also Currie v. Group Ins. Comm'n*, 290 F.3d 1 (1st Cir.2002) (abstaining where difficult questions of state law transcend the federal law issues).

2. *Colorado River*, 424 U.S. at 817–18, 96 S.Ct. at 1246–47.

3. *Id.* at 818, 96 S.Ct. at 1246–47; Cone, 460 U.S. at 19, 103 S.Ct. at 938–39. *See also Gregory v. Daly*, 243 F.3d 687 (2d Cir.2001) (allowing federal sexual harassment suit to proceed concurrently with state sexual harassment suit where no exceptional circumstances exist); *American Disposal Servs., Inc. v. O'Brien*, 839 F.2d 84, 87 (2d Cir.1988) ("[T]he existence of concurrent federal and state proceedings regarding the same subject matter is not by itself sufficient to justify dismissal under *Colorado River*.").

4. *Colorado River*, 424 U.S. at 818, 96 S.Ct. at 1246–47.

5. *Cone*, 460 U.S. at 16, 103 S.Ct. at 937.

also to assess how much progress has been made in the two actions.[6] Moreover, as part of this flexible approach, additional factors such as the probable inadequacy of the state court proceedings may be considered.[7]

§ 5.29 [Reserved]

§ 5.30 *Burford* Abstention Doctrine

A rarely invoked doctrine, first declared in a diversity case, comes into play when a federal court concludes that exercising jurisdiction would unduly interfere with a complex state administrative—judicial regulatory scheme designed to yield uniformity of result. In such situations, at least when the federal law claims are tangential and adequately determinable by the state's courts on judicial review of the agency, the federal court should abstain.[1] Three criteria have been identified as prerequisite to *Burford* abstention: (1) the subject of state regulation must be of significant and special concern to the state; (2) that regulatory scheme must be detailed and complex; and (3) the federal issues are not resolvable unless the federal court immerses itself in the technicalities of state regulation.[2] The Court in *Quackenbush v. Allstate Ins. Co.*[3] described two situations where *Burford* abstention is warranted.[4] First, federal courts should abstain from deciding "difficult questions of state law bearing on policy problems of substantial public import whose importance transcends the result in the case then at bar."[5] Second, federal courts should abstain where federal review "would be disruptive of state efforts to establish a coherent policy with respect to a matter of substantial public concern."[6] The Seventh Circuit has stated that under

6. *Id. See also Villa Marina Yacht Sales, Inc. v. Hatteras Yachts*, 947 F.2d 529, 535 (1st Cir.1991) (holding that state case was further advanced because of development of record for preliminary injunction hearing).

7. *Id.* at 26, 103 S.Ct. at 942. The Seventh Circuit has listed ten factors to be considered. *See Caminiti & Iatarola, Ltd. v. Behnke Warehousing, Inc.*, 962 F.2d 698 (7th Cir.1992).

§ 5.30

1. *Burford v. Sun Oil Co.*, 319 U.S. 315, 63 S.Ct. 1098, 87 L.Ed. 1424 (1943).

2. *See, e.g., Chiropractic Am. v. Lavecchia*, 180 F.3d 99 (3d Cir.1999), cert. denied, 528 U.S. 930, 120 S.Ct. 327, 145 L.Ed.2d 255 (1999) (answering all three in the affirmative and upholding *Burford* abstention in case challenging on due process and equal protection grounds a state's automobile accident insurance scheme); *Izzo v. Borough of River Edge*, 843 F.2d 765, 769 (3d Cir. 1988).

3. 517 U.S. 706, 116 S.Ct. 1712, 135 L.Ed.2d 1 (1996).

4. *See also International Coll. of Surgeons v. City of Chicago*, 153 F.3d 356, 361–62 (7th Cir.1998) (on remand from Supreme Court).

5. *Quackenbush*, 517 U.S. at 726–27, 116 S.Ct. at 1725–26 (quoting *New Orleans Pub. Serv., Inc. v. Council of New Orleans*, 491 U.S. 350, 361, 109 S.Ct. 2506, 2514, 105 L.Ed.2d 298 (1989) (quoting *Colorado River Water Conservation Dist. v. United States*, 424 U.S. 800, 814, 96 S.Ct. 1236, 1244, 47 L.Ed.2d 483 (1976))). *See Habich v. City of Dearborn*, 331 F.3d 524, 532–534 (6th Cir. 2003) (*Burford* abstention inappropriate because federal action focused on events prior to events at issue in state court action and involved no state law issue).

6. *Id.* (rejecting *Burford* abstention arguments under the first prong because the state law at issue was settled, and declining to abstain on the second prong because review was available in county court, a forum not so special as to warrant abstention). *See also United States v. Illinois Pollution Control Bd.*, 17 F.Supp.2d 800 (N.D.Ill.1998) (finding first situation not applicable because at its heart the case was

this second prong, two essential elements must exist to justify abstention: first, the state must offer some forum in which the claim can be litigated, and second, that forum must be special—"it must stand in a special relationship of technical oversight or concentrated review to the evaluation of the claim."[7]

It is unclear whether *Burford* abstention sidetracks actions under § 1983. In *New Orleans Public Service, Inc. v. Council of New Orleans*,[8] the Supreme Court ruled *Burford* abstention inappropriate upon finding the federal constitutional challenge to the regulatory scheme not entangled with the construction of state law and unlikely to interfere unduly with the state's uniformity goals.[9] The Court has subsequently described this result as the outcome of a balancing process in which a strong federal interest in having certain kinds of cases, rights or interests adjudicated in federal court outweighed a state's interest in uniform treatment of, or local control over, a local problem addressed by state law.[10] Thus federal interests in resolving a preemption issue (*New Orleans Pub. Serv., Inc.*)[11] or in furthering policies that promote the enforcement of arbitration agreements involving interstate commerce (*Quackenbush*) have served to defeat *Burford* abstention. Because *Burford* abstention is founded upon the federal district court's equitable discretion, the doctrine has been held inapplicable where the plaintiff seeks legal relief alone—some injunctive, declaratory or other discretionary relief is prerequisite to dismissal or remand of the federal action, and even where such relief is sought the court may only stay, not dismiss the action.[12]

§§ 5.31–5.34 [Reserved]

about whether an Illinois law had retroactive effect—an issue that was not a difficult question of state law, and, under second prong, that *Burford* abstention was not called for because no special forum existed for technical oversight of the claim).

7. *See International Coll. v. City of Chicago*, 153 F.3d 356 (7th Cir.1998) and cases cited therein. *Cf. Habich v. City of Dearborn*, 331 F.3d 524, 533–534 (6th Cir. 2003) (federal action would not disrupt state efforts to establish coherent policy respecting substantial public concern; state law regulatory uniformity not jeopardized because plaintiff challenged only whether city should have sold a particular piece of property and provided more process before padlocking her home).

8. 491 U.S. 350, 109 S.Ct. 2506, 105 L.Ed.2d 298 (1989).

9. *But cf. Berman Enters., Inc. v. Jorling*, 3 F.3d 602 (2d Cir.1993), *cert. denied*, 510 U.S. 1073, 114 S.Ct. 883, 127 L.Ed.2d 78 (1994) (*Burford* principles offered as alternative ground for ordering abstention of § 1983 claim where the only unresolved federal claim turned on a construction of state law which might obviate the need for federal court litigation).

10. *Quackenbush v. Allstate Ins. Co.*, 517 U.S. 706, 116 S.Ct. 1712, 135 L.Ed.2d 1 (1996).

11. *See also Kentucky West Va. Gas Co. v. Pennsylvania Pub. Util. Comm'n*, 791 F.2d 1111, 1115–1116 (3d Cir.1986), aff'd, 837 F.2d 600 (3d Cir.1988), *cert. denied*, 488 U.S. 941, 109 S.Ct. 365, 102 L.Ed.2d 355 (1988); *Middle South Energy, Inc. v. Arkansas Pub. Serv. Comm'n*, 772 F.2d 404, 417 (8th Cir.1985), *cert. denied sub nom. Ratepayers Fight Back v. Middle South Energy, Inc.*, 474 U.S. 1102, 106 S.Ct. 884, 88 L.Ed.2d 919 (1986); *Baggett v. Department of Professional Regulation*, 717 F.2d 521, 524 (11th Cir.1983); *International Bhd. of Elec. Workers v. Public Serv. Comm'n of Nevada*, 614 F.2d 206, 212 n. 1 (9th Cir. 1980).

12. *Id.*

G. THE ELEVENTH AMENDMENT

§ 5.35 In General

Prior to the adoption of the Eleventh Amendment, the Supreme Court had interpreted the case and controversy language of Article III, § 2, which defined federal subject matter jurisdiction to include suits "between a State and Citizens of another state," to permit federal suits between those two parties based on pure diversity.[1] In response to that decision, Congress promptly enacted the Eleventh Amendment, ensuring some degree of state sovereign immunity in federal court.

The Eleventh Amendment provides that the "Judicial power of the United States shall not be construed to extend to any suit in law or equity, commenced or prosecuted against one of the United States by Citizens of another State, or by citizens of any foreign state." Applicable only to actions in federal court, the Eleventh Amendment bars suits against a state government by citizens of that state, other states, and foreign states.

The Supreme Court has expanded the scope of the Eleventh Amendment beyond its textual confines to apply to diversity actions involving state citizen plaintiffs, to federal questions, and to pendent claims. Coverage was extended to federal question jurisdiction in *Hans v. Louisiana*.[2] Based on the principle of sovereign immunity, the Court in *Hans* held that the Eleventh Amendment bars suits against a state government by its own citizens. Since by hypothesis original federal subject matter jurisdiction in an action against a state by one of its own citizens must be based on a federal question, one effect of *Hans* is to bar even federal question claims for damages that are asserted against a state by one of its own citizens. Further expansion occurred in *Pennhurst State Sch. & Hosp. v. Halderman*,[3] in which the Supreme Court held that the Eleventh Amendment bars federal courts from determining pendent state law claims.

The Supreme Court has limited the Eleventh Amendment to actions against the state, state officials sued in their official capacity, units of state government, or where a money judgment will be satisfied out of state funds. It does not immunize local government units as such.[4] Nor does the Eleventh Amendment bar a state court from exercising jurisdiction over another state,[5] or bar the United States government from suing

§ 5.35

1. *Chisholm v. Georgia*, 2 U.S. (2 Dall.) 419, 1 L.Ed. 440 (1793).

2. 134 U.S. 1, 10 S.Ct. 504, 33 L.Ed. 842 (1890).

3. 465 U.S. 89, 121, 104 S.Ct. 900, 919, 79 L.Ed.2d 67 (1984).

4. *See e.g., Lincoln Co. v. Luning*, 133 U.S. 529, 530, 10 S.Ct. 363, 363, 33 L.Ed. 766 (1890) (counties); *Workman v. City of N.Y.*, 179 U.S. 552, 574, 21 S.Ct. 212, 220, 45 L.Ed. 314 (1900) (cities); *Mt. Healthy City Sch. Dist. Bd. of Educ. v. Doyle*, 429 U.S. 274, 97 S.Ct. 568, 50 L.Ed.2d 471 (1977) (municipalities, school districts); *but cf. Florida Dep't of Health & Rehabilitative Servs. v. Florida Nursing Home Ass'n*, 450 U.S. 147, 101 S.Ct. 1032, 67 L.Ed.2d 132 (1981) (state agencies protected).

5. *Nevada v. Hall*, 440 U.S. 410, 421, 99 S.Ct. 1182, 1188, 59 L.Ed.2d 416 (1979).

a state in federal court.[6]

The Eleventh Amendment will generally not bar suit, even if it otherwise applies, where the relief sought is wholly prospective, or the state has consented to federal suit, or a congressional act overrides the immunity. Although the state in its own name enjoys Eleventh Amendment protection, the ability to bring suit against a state official (other than in her individual capacity) depends primarily on the type of relief sought. Under the fiction of *Ex Parte Young*,[7] the Eleventh Amendment does not act as a bar to federal question suits naming a state official as defendant so long as the relief sought is truly prospective.[8] The compromise effected by the *Ex Parte Young* exception was designed to promote the supremacy of federal law by permitting suits to enjoin state officials to conform to federal law prospectively. It rested in part on the benign fiction that to the extent the official was in fact violating the U. S. Constitution, (s)he *could* not be representing the state, which was assumed to be obedient to the Constitution. Under *Edelman v. Jordan*,[9] elaborating *Young,* the Eleventh Amendment permits official capacity actions against individual state agents for prospective relief[10] even when implementation of the judgment would adversely impact the state treasury, but bars similar actions for relief a court deems retrospective, including compensatory damages and back pay. But when a plaintiff alleges only that a state official is violating *state* law, the Supreme Court has held that the rationale underlying the *Young/Edelman* compromise

6. *United States v. Mississippi*, 380 U.S. 128, 140–41, 85 S.Ct. 808, 814–15, 13 L.Ed.2d 717 (1965). *See also EEOC v. Bd. Of Regents Of University Of Wisconsin System*, 288 F.3d 296, 299 (7th Cir.2002) (states waived immunity from suit by federal government when ratifying the Constitution).

7. 209 U.S. 123, 159–60, 28 S.Ct. 441, 454, 52 L.Ed. 714 (1908). *Seminole Tribe of Florida v. Florida*, 517 U.S. 44, 116 S.Ct. 1114, 134 L.Ed.2d 252 (1996), generally reaffirms the vitality of *Ex Parte Young* as permitting prospective injunctive relief against state officials for federal statutory, as well as constitutional, violations. But it also renders the *Young* exception unavailable where the plaintiff complains of the violation of a federal statute that contains its own detailed, administrative remedial scheme and remedies more limited than the full powers of a federal court, including contempt, that would be brought to bear in an action pursuant to *Young*. See the discussion of *Seminole* and its implications *infra* this section. Lower federal courts have also ousted *Young*-based federal court injunction suits against state officials where there is no specific threatened enforcement action by the defendants. *See, e.g., Children's Healthcare is a Legal Duty, Inc. v. Deters*, 92 F.3d 1412 (6th Cir.1996), *cert. denied*, 519 U.S. 1149, 117 S.Ct. 1082, 137 L.Ed.2d 217 (1997).

8. *See, e.g., Porter v. Jones*, 319 F.3d 483, 491 (9th Cir.2003) (rejecting argument that Eleventh Amendment bars adjudication of past conduct as confusing liability with remedy, and upholding *Ex Parte Young* claim limited to injunctive and declaratory relief); *Klingler v. Director, Dep't of Revenue*, 281 F.3d 776 (8th Cir.2002) (under *Ex parte Young*, Eleventh Amendment did not bar plaintiffs' ADA claims for declaratory and injunctive relief, but plaintiffs' claims would not support recovery of monetary damages). *But cf. Idaho v. Coeur d'Alene Tribe*, 521 U.S. 261, 281–283, 117 S.Ct. 2028, 138 L.Ed.2d 438 (1997) (barring suit couched in terms of prospective relief but that in essence was equivalent to a quiet title suit); *Papasan v. Allain*, 478 U.S. 265, 278, 106 S.Ct. 2932, 92 L.Ed.2d 209 (1986) (barring relief tantamount to an award of damages although styled otherwise by plaintiff).

9. 415 U.S. 651, 94 S.Ct. 1347, 39 L.Ed.2d 662 (1974).

10. *See Doe 1–13 v. Chiles*, 136 F.3d 709 (11th Cir.1998) (a "plaintiff's claim seeking prospective injunction relief against a state officer's ongoing violation of federal law can ordinarily proceed in federal court.").

evaporates, because subjecting the states to federal court injunctive relief would not in such a case vindicate supreme federal authority.[11]

State law, which should be borrowed as a matter of federal law so long as not inconsistent with federal policy, defines whether an official is considered an officer of the state and therefore immune from federal suit. Courts will interpret whether state law requires a state or local treasury to pay judgments rendered against its officials. In *Carr v. City of Florence, Alabama*,[12] Alabama law regarded the defendant, a county sheriff, as a state officer. The court presumed that the defendant was a state official because the plaintiff failed to present "clear evidence" that any judgment would be paid out of the local treasury rather than a state treasury. Under Florida law, however, a sheriff is considered a county official.[13] As a result, there is no presumption immunizing him. Instead, the defendant sheriff must provide evidence that the judgment would come from state funds rather than a local treasury. In some cases the characterization of the employing entity will be functionally rather than categorically defined. Thus sheriff's officials otherwise clearly county employees received Eleventh Amendment immunity from damages for actions in their official capacity when the court found that they were acting as an arm of the state;[14] but sheriffs acting as county rather than state agents could be sued for damages in federal court.[15]

The circuit courts consider a variety of factors in determining whether a state instrumentality like a local government, college or authority is entitled to Eleventh Amendment immunity. These include degree of local autonomy and control, the performance or not of central governmental functions, the instrumentality's power to sue or be sued, its separate corporate status, its ability to take property in its own name, and its capacity through bond-levy or taxing authority to raise its own

11. *Pennhurst State School & Hospital v. Halderman,* 465 U.S. 89, 104 S.Ct. 900, 79 L.Ed.2d 67 (1984) (*"Pennhurst II"*). *But cf. Bush v. Gore,* 531 U.S. 1046, 121 S.Ct. 512, 148 L.Ed.2d 553 (2000) (Supreme Court's order halting implementation of the Florida Supreme Court's interpretation of Florida law based on U.S. Supreme Court's view that Florida interpretation violated U. S. Constitution's right of Equal Protection). *Pennhurst II* was distinguished in *Frew v. Hawkins* ___ U.S. ___, 124 S.Ct. 899, 157 L.Ed.2D 855 (2004) (rejecting Eleventh Amendment objection to Federal jurisdiction in action seeking enforcement of consent decree implementing Federal statute).

12. 916 F.2d 1521 (11th Cir.1990).

13. *See Hutton v. Strickland*, 919 F.2d 1531 (11th Cir.1990).

14. *See, e.g., Scott v. O'Grady*, 975 F.2d 366 (7th Cir.1992), *cert. denied*, 508 U.S. 942, 113 S.Ct. 2421, 124 L.Ed.2d 643 (1993) (while evicting tenants ancillary to a foreclosure action). *Manders v. Lee*, 338 F.3d 1304 (11th Cir. 2003)(en banc) *cert. denied*, ___ U.S. ___, 124 S.Ct. 1061, 157 L.Ed.2d 892 (2004)(even though state law uncertain as to whether State would be liable to pay judgment against sheriff's office, Georgia sheriffs act on behalf of the state, not the counties that employ them, with respect to implementation of policies respecting use of force, and therefore enjoy Eleventh Amendment immunity; dissent would have defined the relevant function at issue in case not as policymaking relating to force but as maintenance of county jail, in which case sheriff would have been acting for the county).

15. *See, e.g., Evans v. City of Bishop*, 238 F.3d 586 (5th Cir.2000) (per curiam) (no evidence that city overwhelmingly controlled by state in employing function, so no immunity); *Franklin v. Zaruba*, 150 F.3d 682 (7th Cir.1998), *cert. denied*, 525 U.S. 1141, 119 S.Ct. 1033, 143 L.Ed.2d 42 (1999) (Illinois law); *Ruehman v. Sheahan*, 34 F.3d 525 (7th Cir.1994) (Illinois law).

operating funds.[16] The dominant factor has been whether the funds to satisfy a judgment would be derived from the state's treasury, and the Supreme Court agrees that liability for a money judgment is "of considerable importance."[17] An earlier Supreme Court decision, in denying immunity to a bi-state entity created under the Compact Clause, asserted that the touchstone is whether, under state law, a state will bear financial responsibility for an adverse judgment against the entity.[18] But the Court has subsequently clarified that a state subdivision's formal, legal responsibility for a judgment suffices to confer the immunity, even if the subdivision will be indemnified by a third party. It is the entity's "potential legal liability, rather than its ability or inability to require a third party to reimburse it, or to discharge the liability in the first instance, that is relevant."[19]

16. *See, e.g. Cozzo v. Tangipahoa Parish Council–President Government,* 262 F.3d 501, 508 (5th Cir.2001); *Carter v. City of Philadelphia*, 181 F.3d 339 (3d Cir.1999), cert. denied, 528 U.S. 1005, 120 S.Ct. 499, 145 L.Ed.2d 385 (1999) (district attorney's office not an arm of the state for Eleventh Amendment purposes because the state would not pay judgments against the office and it was funded by defendant city, not treated as surrogate for the state under state law, and enjoyed considerable autonomy in its operations).

17. *Regents of the Univ. of Cal. v. Doe*, 519 U.S. 425, 429, 117 S.Ct. 900, 904, 137 L.Ed.2d 55 (1997); *Holmes v. Marion County Office of Family and Children*, 349 F.3d 914, 918–919 (7th Cir. 2003) (dispositive question is "who pays?"); *Cozzo v. Tangipahoa Parish Council–President Government*, 279 F.3d 273, 282 (5th Cir. 2002); *Cash v. Granville County Bd. of Educ.*, 242 F.3d 219 (4th Cir.2001) (because any effect on state treasury was speculative, indirect and ancillary, local school board could be sued in federal court under FLSA for overtime pay); *Clissuras v. City University of New York*, 359 F.3d 79 (2d Cir. 2004) (city college "arm of state" where state would be liable for damage award against college and controlled college's governance and operation); *Callahan v. City of Phila.*, 207 F.3d 668, 670 (3d Cir.2000) (dictum) (describing most significant factor as whether a judgment against an agency would be paid from the state's treasury); *Becker v. University of Nebraska*, 191 F.3d 904, 908–909 (8th Cir. 1999) (conferring 11th Amendment immunity in ADEA case on state university to protect state treasury from liability that would have had "essentially the same practical consequences as a judgment against the State itself" . . .) (quoting *Doe*, 519 U.S. at 429–430). One circuit subdivides this "most important" factor, i.e., whether the State will ultimately have to fund the substate entity's liability, as follows: the substate entity is treated as an arm of the state, and hence is immune, either if the State is liable for the judgment against the local officials or locality, or if it is liable for the local agent's "general debts and obligations." *Cozzo, supra,* 279 F.3d at 282 (Finding neither true under Louisiana law). *But see Manders v. Lee*, 338 F.3d 1304 (11th Cir. 2003) (en banc), *cert. denied* ___ U.S. ___, 124 S.Ct. 1061, 157 L.Ed.2d 892 (2004) (sheriffs in Georgia act for the state in connection with all uses of force even though state may not have to pay such judgments).

18. *Hess v. Port Auth. Trans–Hudson Corp.*, 513 U.S. 30, 44–47, 115 S.Ct. 394, 403–404, 130 L.Ed.2d 245 (1994). The dissent in *Hess* would alternatively have conferred immunity if a state exercises political or governmental control over the defendant. *Id.* at 410–411 (O'Connor, J. dissenting). *See also Duke v. Grady Mun. Sch.*, 127 F.3d 972 (10th Cir.1997) (school district not an arm of the state where state would not be liable for a judgment against the district). *See Jones v. Washington Metro. Area Transit Auth.*, 205 F.3d 428, 432 (D.C.Cir. 2000) (permitting agency created by Congressional compact, and subscribed to by two states and the District of Columbia, to claim the immunity, in an ADEA case after *Kimel*, in order to protect the governments' treasuries). *See Fresenius Medical Care Cardiovascular Resources, Inc. v. Puerto Rico and Caribbean Cardiovascular Center Corp.*, 322 F.3d 56 (1st Cir.2003) (*Hess* tests asks first whether state has structured the entity defendant to share its sovereignty, but if that inquiry is unclear the vulnerability of the state's purse to an adverse judgment is critical).

19. *Regents of the Univ. of California v. Doe*, 519 U.S. 425, 429, 117 S.Ct. 900,

The line between prospective and retrospective relief is delicate, sometimes appearing to be little more than semantic. For example, in *Milliken v. Bradley*,[20] the Court characterized as prospective the spending of state funds on compensatory educational programs because the funds "were a necessary consequence of compliance in the future with [the court ordered school desegregation plan]."[21] The Court recognized that compliance with the decree would entail a "direct and substantial impact on the state treasury" and that the educational components of the decree, although operating only prospectively, were designed to eliminate continuing conditions of inequality and in that sense could be considered "compensatory." But in *Edelman's* terms, this additional spending was still only an "ancillary effect" of a plan that operated "prospectively to bring about the delayed benefits of a unitary school system." Similarly, a court ordered award of attorney's fees to be paid by a state treasury was characterized as "ancillary" to prospective relief and therefore not barred by the Eleventh Amendment.[22] By contrast, the Court in *Edelman* itself characterized as retrospective, and hence barred, the payment of wrongfully withheld federal welfare benefits, treating such funds as a form of compensation for past injustices and therefore indistinguishable from an award of money damages against the state.[23] Of course those payments might also have been characterized as "part of a plan that operates prospectively to bring about the delayed benefits" of the statutory welfare scheme.

Even when the Eleventh Amendment otherwise applies, the action is against the state itself and the relief is characterized as retrospective, the Eleventh Amendment will not bar suit if a state is held to have consented to be sued in federal court. The Court has held that Congress intended no such consent when it enacted § 1983 in 1871, apparently because it was not until the Court's decision in *Monell* in 1978 that § 1983 was held to apply to cities or counties, let alone states.[24] In any event, the status of § 1983 under the Eleventh Amendment has been mooted by the Court's ruling that a state, when sued its own name or through an official capacity action seeking damages against one of its officials, is not a "person" suable under § 1983.[25] Accordingly, regardless of the relief sought, the state as such is simply not a proper § 1983 defendant in actions brought in either state or federal court. A court of

904, 137 L.Ed.2d 55 (1997). *But cf. Champagne v. Jefferson Parish Sheriff's Office*, 188 F.3d 312 (5th Cir.1999) (state agency enjoys the immunity more because it was state funded and within the government executive branch than because it had capacity to sue and be sued).

20. 433 U.S. 267, 290, 97 S.Ct. 2749, 2762, 53 L.Ed.2d 745 (1977).

21. *Id.* at 289, 97 S.Ct. at 2762.

22. *Hutto v. Finney*, 437 U.S. 678, 692, 98 S.Ct. 2565, 2574, 57 L.Ed.2d 522 (1978). *See also Randolph v. Rodgers*, 253 F.3d 342 (8th Cir.2001) (costs of complying with ADA and Rehabilitation Act ancillary to the prospective relief).

23. *Edelman*, 415 U.S. at 668, 94 S.Ct. at 1358.

24. *See Edelman* as explained by *Fitzpatrick v. Bitzer*, 427 U.S. 445, 456, 96 S.Ct. 2666, 2671, 49 L.Ed.2d 614 (1976); *cf. Quern v. Jordan*, 440 U.S. 332, 99 S.Ct. 1139, 59 L.Ed.2d 358 (1979), reaffirming *Edelman* on a different rationale.

25. *Will v. Michigan Dep't of State Police*, 491 U.S. 58, 109 S.Ct. 2304, 105 L.Ed.2d 45 (1989).

appeals decision extends this principle by holding that a federal court may not remedy a civil rights violation by awarding a defendant county contribution against its state, notwithstanding a general right to contribution under § 1983.[26]

In *Will v. Michigan Dep't of State Police*,[27] the Supreme Court held, however, that a state official can be a defendant "person" within the meaning of § 1983, even when sued in her official capacity, to the extent that the relief sought against her is of the "prospective" kind allowed under the Eleventh Amendment jurisprudence exemplified by *Ex parte Young, Edelman, and Milliken*.[28] The *Will* bifurcated definition of the statutory term "person" as applied to the individual state official is evidently driven by and devolved from the 11th Amendment, yet in turn that definition renders the 11th Amendment largely beside the point in § 1983 actions against a state. Indeed a given defendant may not qualify for Eleventh Amendment immunity yet still be considered a non-"person" within the meaning of § 1983 and accordingly entitled to dismissal for failure to state a claim for relief.[29]

In one unusual situation where *Will* would ordinarily bar the § 1983 action of its own force, the Eleventh Amendment may still be important. A state might neglect to raise the *Will* objection until the case is on appeal. Since *Will* in essence furnishes a defense of legal insufficiency rather than lack of subject matter jurisdiction, defendant's failure to raise that defense during trial might result in its waiver.[30] Whether the Eleventh Amendment objection, in contrast, is deemed a matter of subject matter jurisdiction or a waivable, affirmative defense is unclear. The Court in *Edelman* indicated that the immunity was a jurisdictional bar that can be raised for the first time on appeal,[31] and, in a later case, that a defendant whose Eleventh Amendment dismissal motion fails may seek immediate interlocutory review.[32] However, in *Wisconsin Dep't of*

26. *Harris v. Angelina County, Tex.*, 31 F.3d 331 (5th Cir.1994).

27. 491 U.S. 58, 109 S.Ct. 2304, 105 L.Ed.2d 45 (1989).

28. *Id.* at 71 n.10, 109 S.Ct. at 2312 n.10. *Will* is discussed in detail in Chapter 2 *supra*.

29. *See Callahan v. City of Philadelphia* 207 F.3d 668, 670–673 (3d Cir.2000) (judicial defendant officials and their agency, funded both by the state and one of its cities, not "persons" under Will and therefore not suable under § 1983, even though arguably not eligible for 11th Amendment immunity, the court deeming the financial responsibility factor "less significant in a section 1983 'person' analysis than in an Eleventh Amendment jurisdictional analysis.")

30. *See* FRCP 12(h)(2).

31. *Edelman*, 415 U.S. at 677–78, 94 S.Ct. at 1362–63; see FRCP 12(h)(3).

32. *Puerto Rico Aqueduct and Sewer Auth. v. Metcalf & Eddy, Inc.*, 506 U.S. 139, 113 S.Ct. 684, 121 L.Ed.2d 605 (1993). The immediate reviewability of an order denying Eleventh Amendment immunity is an instance of the "collateral order" exception to the usual rule, under 28 U.S.C.A. § 1291, that limits the jurisdiction of the courts of appeals to "final decisions" of the federal district courts. *Thomas v. Nakatani*, 309 F.3d 1203 (9th Cir.2002); *Nanda v. Bd. of Trustees of Univ. of Illinois*, 303 F.3d 817, 821 (7th Cir.2002). See § 2.23, *supra*, on the "collateral order" exception that permits interlocutory review of many orders denying a § 1983 defendant's motion to dismiss or summary judgment motion based on the defense of qualified immunity. But under *Swint v. Chambers County Comm'n*, 514 U.S. 35, 51, 115 S.Ct. 1203, 1212, 131 L.Ed.2d 60 (1995), other, nonfinal and hence ordinarily nonappealable orders may be addressed on interlocutory review of the

Corr. v. Schacht,[33] the Court stated that the immunity was subject to waiver and that a court could exercise subject matter jurisdiction if the state does not assert it—hardly a characteristic of a defense grounded in subject matter jurisdiction.

Sharply to be distinguished from § 1983 claims against a state, and from "official-capacity" actions against an individual state officer, are "personal-capacity" suits intended to establish the officer's individual liability. To the extent she is sued personally, a state official is a § 1983 "person" liable for all otherwise appropriate relief, including damages.[34] Further, as in similar suits against city or county officials, the plaintiff need not prove that the defendant's challenged conduct was undertaken as a matter of state "policy"; it suffices to prove that, acting under color of state law, she deprived the plaintiff of a federally protected right. On the other hand, unlike the entity or entity official defendant in an "official-capacity" suit, the personal-capacity defendant may invoke the affirmative defense of qualified immunity to avoid the relief of damages.[35]

The Court has articulated increasingly strict standards for ascertaining whether Congress has abrogated the states' immunity from retrospective relief in federal court, demanding unmistakable specificity and clarity.[36] The clear statutory statement the Court now demands as evidence of an intent to abrogate must reference "either the Eleventh Amendment or the States' sovereign immunity," rather than simply a class of defendants that expressly or by construction includes the states.[37] The Civil Rights Remedies Equalization Amendment of

denial of an Eleventh Amendment motion only if they raise issues "inextricably intertwined" with the appealable (e.g., Eleventh Amendment) decision, so that "review of the former ... [is] necessary to ensure meaningful review of the latter." Applying that standard, an appellate court that rejected state officials' Eleventh Amendment defense also declined to hear their objection to plaintiff's standing, because "we may resolve the Eleventh Amendment immunity issue without reaching the merits of standing." *Summit Med. Assocs., P.C. v. Pryor*, 180 F.3d 1326, 1335 (11th Cir.1999), *cert. denied*, 529 U.S. 1012, 120 S.Ct. 1287, 146 L.Ed.2d 233 (2000).

33. 524 U.S. 381, 389, 118 S.Ct. 2047, 2052–53, 141 L.Ed.2d 364 (1998). There Justice Kennedy, concurring, opined that a state waives the immunity by removing an action to federal court, a decision that has been followed by a circuit court. *See McLaughlin v. Board of Trustees of State Colleges of Colorado*, 215 F.3d 1168, 1170–71 (10th Cir.2000). *But see Lapides v. Board of Regents of University System of Georgia*, 535 U.S. 613, 122 S.Ct. 1640, 152 L.Ed.2d 806 (2002) (state waiver of Eleventh Amendment immunity by simply removing case to federal court limited to state law claims). While the Supreme Court in *Schacht* wrote that a federal court "can ignore" the immunity if the state does not assert it, a circuit court has held that it need not ignore the unasserted immunity. *Higgins v. State of Mississippi*, 217 F.3d 951, 953–54 (7th Cir.2000). *See also Katz v. Regents of the Univ. of Calif.*, 229 F.3d 831, 834–35 (9th Cir.2000); *Hill v. Blind Ind. & Services of Maryland*, 179 F.3d 754, 760 (9th Cir.1999).

34. *Will v. Michigan Dep't of State Police*, 491 U.S. 58, 109 S.Ct. 2304, 105 L.Ed.2d 45 (1989).

35. *Hafer v. Melo*, 502 U.S. 21, 112 S.Ct. 358, 116 L.Ed.2d 301 (1991).

36. *See, e.g., Atascadero State Hosp. v. Scanlon*, 473 U.S. 234, 238, 105 S.Ct. 3142, 3145, 87 L.Ed.2d 171 (1985).

37. *See, e.g., Dellmuth v. Muth*, 491 U.S. 223, 230, 109 S.Ct. 2397, 2401, 105 L.Ed.2d 181 (1989); *Welch v. Texas Dep't of Hwys. & Pub. Transp.*, 483 U.S. 468, 478, 107 S.Ct. 2941, 2948, 97 L.Ed.2d 389 (1987) (explicitly overruling *Parden v. Terminal Railway of Ala. State Docks Dep't*, 377 U.S.

1986[38] meets this test, expressly overriding what would otherwise be state immunity so as to permit federal courts to award retroactive relief, under, among other statutes, Titles VI and IX. Similarly, after the Court held that the original Education of the Handicapped Act failed with sufficient clarity to abrogate 11th Amendment immunity,[39] Congress specifically amended it in § 1403 of the Individuals with Disabilities Education Act,[40] to authorize federal courts to award retroactive relief against states and state agencies with respect to violations occurring after October 30, 1990. And after Congress, citing its legislative authority under section five of the Fourteenth Amendment, amended Title VII in 1972 to provide expressly for the liability of state (as well as local) governments, the Court in *Fitzpatrick v. Bitzer* determined that Congress, acting under its Section 5 powers, may "provide for private suits against States or state officials which are constitutionally impermissible in other contexts."[41] Yet the Court in *Fitzpatrick* may not have addressed specifically the question whether the particular abrogation of Title VII was valid, for it observed that the state officials there did "not contend that the substantive provisions of Title VII as applied here are not a proper exercise of congressional authority under § 5 of the Fourteenth Amendment."[42]

184, 84 S.Ct. 1207, 12 L.Ed.2d 233 (1964)). The Court's insistence on an unmistakably clear statement of intent to abrogate what would otherwise be the Eleventh Amendment immunity of a state is reflected in its holding, in *Raygor v. Regents of Univ. of Minnesota,* 534 U.S. 533, 122 S.Ct. 999, 152 L.Ed.2d 27, (2002) that 28 U.S.C.A. § 1367(d), which tolls the limitations period for at least 30 days after dismissal of a claim as to which plaintiff unsuccessfully invoked a federal district court's supplemental jurisdiction, does not apply to claims against states. *But cf. Jinks v. Richland County*, 538 U.S. 456, 123 S.Ct. 1667, 155 L.Ed.2d 631 (2003) (because counties are not eligible for Eleventh Amendment immunity, no similar narrow construction of Section 1367(d) is warranted and its tolling provision does apply against a defendant county).

38. 42 U.S.C.A. § 2000d–7.

39. *See Dellmuth v. Muth*, 491 U.S. 223, 109 S.Ct. 2397, 105 L.Ed.2d 181 (1989).

40. 20 U.S.C.A. §§ 1401–1485.

41. *Fitzpatrick v. Bitzer*, 427 U.S. 445, 456, 96 S.Ct. 2666, 49 L.Ed.2d 614 (1976).

42. *Id.* at 456 n.11. Since *Fitzpatrick*, moreover, the Supreme Court has announced considerably more stringent restrictions on Congress' power to abrogate the states' Eleventh Amendment immunity, even when it does so expressly, by legislating under section five of the Fourteenth Amendment. *City of Boerne v. Flores*, 521 U.S. 507, 117 S.Ct. 2157, 138 L.Ed.2d 624 (1997). Applying a "congruence and proportionality" test, the Supreme Court in *Boerne* held that Congress lacked authority under the Fourteenth Amendment to apply the Religious Freedom Restoration Act to state or local governments. *But cf. Kikumura v. Hurley*, 242 F.3d 950, 959 (10th Cir. 2001) and *In re Young*, 141 F.3d 854, 858–59 (8th Cir.1998) (both holding that RFRA was severable and remains applicable to the federal government).

After *Boerne*, there has been considerable ferment in the lower federal courts respecting the validity of Congress' attempts to override Eleventh Amendment immunity under a number of civil rights statutes other than Title VII. The Supreme Court has resolved the circuit split concerning the 11th Amendment's application to claims against states based on the ADEA. In *Kimel v. Florida Bd. of Regents*, 528 U.S. 62, 120 S.Ct. 631, 145 L.Ed.2d 522 (2000), the Court held that Congress, while expressly purporting to overrule the states' immunity, did not do so validly. Applying the *City of Boerne* "congruence and proportionality" test for "appropriate" § 5 legislation, the Court concluded that ADEA prohibits considerable "rational" age discrimination not prohibited by the 14th Amendment as construed. Nor could ADEA be appropriate as reasonably prophylactic legislation, because viewing the legislative record of ADEA, the Court viewed its extension as "an unwarranted response to a perhaps inconsequential problem" of age discrimination by the States.

In *Board of Trustees, Univ. of Alabama v. Garrett,* 531 U.S. 356, 121 S.Ct. 955, 148 L.Ed.2d 866 (2001), the Supreme Court applied the broad approach of *Kimel* to find an invalid Congressional abrogation of the states' Eleventh Amendment immunity from private federal damages actions against unconsenting states under the employment provisions of the Americans With Disabilities Act. Congress, it held, lacked a sufficient evidentiary basis demonstrating a pattern of unconstitutional (i.e, arbitrary, irrational) employment discrimination by states when it enacted the ADA's Title I. Alternatively, the ADA's remedies—in particular its disproportionate adverse impact proof mode and its requirement that employers make reasonable accommodation to applicants' and employees' disabilities—are disproportionate to and incongruent with any arbitrary, intentional state employment discrimination that Congress did unearth. And while the plaintiffs before the Court apparently pressed only reasonable accommodation claims, the opinion leaves little doubt that no part of Title I—even the ban on discrimination—supports private money damages actions against a state. *See especially id.* at note 9. *See also Velasco v. Illinois Dept. of Human Services*, 246 F.3d 1010 (7th Cir.2001).

A negative pregnant in *Garrett* suggests that the Court might incline more favorably towards effective Congressional abrogation of the states' immunity from actions under ADA Titles II and III. The Court notes that the legislative record and resulting findings in Senate and House reports were deficient respecting a history of state *employment* (i.e., Title I) discrimination against the disabled, specifically distinguishing the more ample record and findings about public services and accommodations. 531 U.S. at 371 n.7, 121 S.Ct. at 966 n. 7 and accompanying text. The absence of clear direction from the Court has resulted in a conflict among the circuits regarding claims brought under Title II of the ADA. *Compare Hason v. Medical Bd. of Cal.,* 279 F.3d 1167, 1171 (9th Cir.) (reaffirming circuit precedent holding that Title II constitutes a valid abrogation of state immunity), *reh'g en banc denied,* 294 F.3d 1166 (9th Cir.2002) *with Angel v. Kentucky*, 314 F.3d 262 (6th Cir. 2002) (no valid abrogation of Title II claims sounding in equal protection); *Robinson v. University of Akron School of Law*, 307 F.3d 409 (6th Cir.2002) (plaintiff's only valid ADA claim, alleging failure to accommodate, sounded not in due process but in equal protection, as to which state immunity not validly abrogated); *Wessel v. Glendening*, 306 F.3d 203 (4th Cir.2002) (no valid abrogation of Title II, as congressional record of state discrimination against disabled inadequate and its remedies, particularly duty of reasonable accommodation, not proportional to underlying problem identified by Fourteenth Amendment); *Popovich v. Cuyahoga County Court of Common Pleas,* 276 F.3d 808, 812, 813–16 (6th Cir.2002) (en banc) (concluding Title II does not constitute a valid abrogation of state immunity under the Equal Protection Clause, but does constitute a valid abrogation of immunity under the Due Process Clause), *petition for cert. filed,* 70 U.S.L.W. 3656 (Apr. 8, 2002); *Thompson v. Colorado,* 278 F.3d 1020 (10th Cir.2001), *cert. denied,* 535 U.S. 1077, 122 S.Ct. 1960, 152 L.Ed.2d 1021 (2002) (same) *and Reickenbacker v. Foster,* 274 F.3d 974 (5th Cir.2001) (same). *Cf. Demshki v. Monteith*, 255 F.3d 986 (9th Cir.2001) (retaliation claim under Title V barred where claim is predicated on alleged violations of Title I). Further, several circuits have allowed *Ex Parte Young* claims for injunctive relief against state officials to enforce Title II notwithstanding that by its terms it applies only to public entities. *See, e.g., Miranda B. v. Kitzhaber*, 328 F.3d 1181 (9th Cir.2003) (per curiam) (citing similar decisions from three other circuits).

Passing references in the Court's opinion in *Garrett* give mixed signals about the future of Title [VII] "impact" actions against state employers. On one hand, the Court approvingly cites *Fitzpatrick v. Bitzer,* 427 U.S. 445, 96 S.Ct. 2666, 49 L.Ed.2d 614 (1976) for the proposition that Eleventh Amendment immunity is limited by the enforcement provisions of Section 5 of the Fourteenth Amendment. On the other, the Court observes that disparate racial impact is insufficient to establish a Fourteenth Amendment violation even though racial classifications are subjected to strict scrutiny. One circuit has reaffirmed the authority of *Fitzpatrick* notwithstanding *City of Boerne*, and even extended *Fitzpatrick* by specifically holding the disproportionate adverse *impact* (unintentional discrimination) provisions of Title VII, not just its core disparate treatment (intentional discrimination) principle, as within Congress' § 5 authority. In *In re Employment Discrimination Litigation Against the State of Ala.*, 198 F.3d 1305 (11th Cir.1999), the Eleventh Circuit acknowledged some "incongruence" between Title VII and the 14th Amendment because proving the disproportionate adverse impact of a neutral employment practice does not demand the same kind of proof of discriminatory intent that is essential to show a violation of the 14th Amendment's Equal Protection Clause. Nevertheless, the court deemed the disparate impact mode of proof, as devised by the Supreme Court in *Griggs v. Duke Power Co.*, 401 U.S. 424, 91 S.Ct. 849, 28 L.Ed.2d 158 (1971), and subsequently elaborated by case law and the 1991 Civil Rights Act amendments to Title VII, as preventative rules that target the same core injury, intentional discrimination, as the 14th Amendment. Further, the court observed that under Title VII, employers can defend practices that have disproportionate adverse impact merely by showing the practice job related and consistent with business necessity; they need not show the "compelling interest" required by the Religious Freedom Restoration Act, struck down in *Boerne*, to justify legislation adversely affecting religious free exercise. Hence the court viewed the "means" evidenced by Title VII's disparate impact proof mode as "neither incongruent with the purpose of preventing intentional discrimination in public employment, nor disproportionate to the injury to be avoided." 198 F.3d at 1323–1324. The *In re Employment Discrimination Litigation* decision, however, was issued shortly before the Supreme Court decided *Kimel v. Florida Bd. of Regents*, 528 U.S. 62, 120 S.Ct. 631, 145 L.Ed.2d 522 (2000), discussed below, and the reasoning of *Kimel*, together with its successor decision, *Garrett,* may undercut the Eleventh Circuit's conclusion upholding under § 5 the *disparate impact* provisions of Title VII that prohibit certain neutral, not intentionally discriminatory employment practices that have disproportionate adverse impact and cannot be justified under the standard of job relatedness and business necessity. *But cf. Downing v. Board of Trustees of Univ. of Alabama*, 321 F.3d 1017 (11th Cir.2003) (Title VII's anti-harassment provision replicates the kind of intentional discrimination prohibited by Equal Protection Clause, and is congruent with and proportional to it, and the statute's anti-retaliation provision is valid Section 5 abrogation legislation because even if it prohibits conduct not itself unconstitutional it deters the kind of conduct the Clause prohibits); *Nanda v. Board of Trustees of University of Illinois*, 303 F.3d 817, 832 (7th Cir.2002) (acknowledging that *Fitzpatrick* may not have definitively decided the question, but holding that even in light of *Boerne, Kimel*, and *Garrett*, Title VII's principal *disparate treatment*, i.e., intentional discrimination liability provisions and remedies are congruent with and proportional to the evil of race discrimination identified by the Fourteenth Amendment); *Okruhlik v. University of Arkansas,* 255 F.3d 615 (8th Cir.2001) (reaffirming valid Congressional abrogation of Eleventh Amendment immunity respecting Title VII intentional discrimination claims, after *Kimel*).

After *Kimel* and *Garrett*, which both insisted on a rigorous, documented and widespread pattern of, respectively, age or disability discrimination as prerequisite to valid abrogation under Section 5 of the Fourteenth Amendment, *Nevada Dept. of Human Resources v. Hibbs*, 538 U.S. 721, 123 S.Ct. 1972, 155 L.Ed.2d 953 (2003), is something of a surprise. It held that Congress validly abrogated the immunity of all the states from money damages in federal court for violations of the family-care provision of the Family and Medical Leave Act, regardless of the existence of a widespread pattern of such discrimination by the particular state defendant, Nevada. Indeed the Court, per Chief Justice Rehnquist, came close to admitting one of the cornerstones of Justice Kennedy's dissent, that the legislative record relied on when Congress enacted the provision in question had not demonstrated the type of widespread history of intentional gender discrimination that *Kimel* and *Garrett* had required. The majority explained that because gender discrimination triggers heightened scrutiny under the Fourteenth Amendment, whereas age-or disability-based distinctions are assessed under the considerably more lenient "rational basis" standard, "it was easier for Congress to show a pattern of state constitutional violations" in the form of gender discrimination against men in affording family leave. In effect the Court adopts a sliding scale: the lower the level of constitutional scrutiny applied to a particular classification, the more elaborate, detailed and widespread must be the congressional record required to justify abrogation of Eleventh Amendment immunity. The majority also found the FMLA's gender-neutral remedy—requiring state employers to adhere to a minimum standard of family leave for all eligible employees—was proportional and congruent to the targeted violation identified by the legislative record, in this case the states' history of affording family leave primarily or exclusively to women in accordance with a stereotype that women alone are responsible for family caregiving. In relying on the seminal Fourteenth Amendment, Section 5 decision of *Katzenbach v. Morgan*, 384 U.S. 641, 86 S.Ct. 1717, 16 L.Ed.2d 828 (1966), the opinion appeared to restore a bit of Congress' authority to enforce the substantive prohibitions of the Fourteenth Amendment, at least with respect to suspect or semi-suspect classifications like race and gender. The Court wrote that "Congress may en-

But no matter how specifically Congress purports to override Eleventh Amendment immunity, the Supreme Court has held, in *Seminole Tribe of Florida v. Florida*,[43] that it lacks power to do so when it is acting only pursuant to the Commerce Clause, as distinct from the Fourteenth Amendment. Thus while *Ex Parte Young* still allows federal court suits for truly prospective relief against state officials,[44] *Seminole* effectively

act so-called prophylactic legislation that proscribes facially constitutional conduct, in order to prevent and deter unconstitutional conduct." The implication is that the Court, despite *Kimel* and *Garrett*, might well uphold the Congressional abrogation of states' Eleventh Amendment immunity at least for those actions under Title VII of the Civil Rights Act of 1964 where plaintiff offers evidence of individual disparate treatment (intentional discrimination), which mirrors the type of evidence required to show an Equal Protection violation, and possibly even where plaintiff's only evidence is that a neutral practice had disproportionate racial or gender adverse impact. As observed earlier in this footnote, those have been open questions in recent circuit court decisions. By the same token, however, when states are sued under Title VII on a prohibited statutory ground, for example religion or national origin, that may not enjoy any, or as much, Fourteenth Amendment protection, *Hibbs* can be distinguished and abrogation more readily invalidated. *See Holmes v. Marion County Office of Family and Children*, 349 F.3d 914 (7th Cir.2003) (Title VII's requirement of religious reasonable accommodation—as distinct from its prohibition on religious discrimination—rests on Congress' Commerce Clause authority alone, not also its power to enforce the Fourteenth Amendment, and hence Congress ineffectively abrogated Eleventh Amendment immunity respecting that type of discrimination).

In *Tennessee v. Lane*, ___ U.S. ___, 124 S.Ct. 1978, ___ L.Ed.2d ___ (2004), the Supreme Court again upheld an express Congressional override of Eleventh Amendment immunity, this one found in Title II of the Americans With Disabilities Act, but only to the narrow extent of permitting federal court damage claims against states for violating Title II's duty to make "reasonable modifications" to the physical characteristics of courthouses to assure access by the disabled. Distinguishing *Garrett*, which invalidated the purported Congressional abrogation in ADA's Title I of state immunity from damage liability for disability discrimination in employment, the Court stressed that in Title II, as applied to this case, more than discrimination against that class was at stake; on the facts of *Lane*, Title II's reasonable modification standard was necessary and appropriately tailored to assure the distinct and fundamental constitutional right of access to the courts. Because discrimination based on disability is not subject to heightened Fourteenth Amendment scrutiny, but denial of a fundamental right is, that distinction was critical to enable the *Lane* majority to rely on *Hibbs* for the proposition that Congress has broader § 5 powers when its legislation aims at types of discrimination that are subject to heightened scrutiny. On the other hand, the majority asserted that Title II was supported by a stronger legislative record of past state discrimination in the provision of accessible physical facilities than the history of state employment discrimination relied on by Congress in enacting the Family Medical Leave Act provision at issue in *Hibbs*.

43. 517 U.S. 44, 116 S.Ct. 1114, 134 L.Ed.2d 252 (1996) (overruling *Pennsylvania v. Union Gas Co.*, 491 U.S. 1, 109 S.Ct. 2273, 105 L.Ed.2d 1 (1989)).

44. *See, e.g., Frazier v. Simmons*, 254 F.3d 1247 (10th Cir.2001) (*ex Parte Young* suit for prospective injunctive relief under the ADA). As the court in *Frazier* noted, plaintiffs must clearly seek equitable relief in the complaint: "We caution practitioners that a boilerplate recitation of 'just and equitable' relief included in one's prayer for relief is far from an exemplary request for prospective equitable relief under the *Ex parte Young* doctrine." *Cf. Lightfoot v. Union Carbide Corp.*, 110 F.3d 898, 910 (2d Cir.1997) (holding, in an ADEA action, plaintiff's 'general, ritualistic prayer for additional ["just and proper"] relief' was insufficient to defeat summary judgment because plaintiff rejected defendant's offer of reinstatement and failed to specify what activity ought to be enjoined); *Rosen v. Cascade Int'l, Inc.*, 21 F.3d 1520, 1526 n. 12 (11th Cir.1994) (rejecting, in the context of a securities fraud action, 'appellees' suggestion that they successfully invoked the district court's equitable jurisdiction through their requests for any additional relief as may appear 'just and proper' at the conclusion of each complaint. The mere incanta-

extends *Hans v. Louisiana*'s ban on federal court suits (whether brought by citizens or noncitizens of the defendant state) against the states themselves. Even when those suits are based on federal question claims, the states are immune unless Congress in creating a given claim expressly overrode Eleventh Amendment immunity in a valid exercise of its Fourteenth Amendment, § 5 authority. In the wake of *Seminole*, lower federal courts have denied jurisdiction over private actions against states in federal court when they have concluded that the underlying statute is enacted pursuant only to Congress' authority under the Commerce Clause.[45] And the Supreme Court impliedly affirmed such cases in

tion of such boilerplate language does not convert a legal cause of action into a legitimate request for equitable relief.)." *Id.* at 1254. *See also Calderon v. Kansas Dep't of Soc. and Rehab. Servs.*, 181 F.3d 1180 (10th Cir.1999) (asking whether plaintiff's "complaint gave *any indication* that she might be entitled to injunctive relief for ongoing federal ... violations by state officials"); *Andrus v. Arkansas,* 197 F.3d 953 (8th Cir. 1999) ("Fed.R.Civ.P. 9 does not create any special pleading requirements relating to requests for relief, ... and, as a general rule, requesting incorrect relief is not grounds for dismissal" and holding that where plaintiffs' complaint specifically requested injunctive relief and "such other equitable relief as is just and proper," that plaintiff was entitled to proceed under *Ex Parte Young*).

45. The Supreme Court has confirmed the judgment of every circuit that considered the question that Congress may not validly abrogate the states' immunity from private suits under the Fair Labor Standards Act brought against them in their own name, even when brought in the state's own courts. *See Alden v. Maine*, 527 U.S. 706, 712, 119 S.Ct. 2240, 2246, 144 L.Ed.2d 636 (1999). Such suits may accordingly be brought, if at all, only by the Secretary of Labor on behalf of the United States. *See Abril v. Virginia*, 145 F.3d 182, 189 (4th Cir.1998); *Mueller v. Thompson*, 133 F.3d 1063, 1064 (7th Cir.1998); *Powell v. Florida*, 132 F.3d 677, 678 (11th Cir. 1998), cert. denied, 524 U.S. 916, 118 S.Ct. 2297, 141 L.Ed.2d 158 (1998); *Quillin v. Oregon*, 127 F.3d 1136, 1138 (9th Cir.1997); *Close v. New York*, 125 F.3d 31, 36 (2d Cir.1997); *Mills v. Maine*, 118 F.3d 37, 48 (1st Cir.1997); *Aaron v. Kansas*, 115 F.3d 813, 814 (10th Cir.1997); *Raper v. Iowa*, 115 F.3d 623, 624 (8th Cir.1997); *Balgowan v. New Jersey*, 115 F.3d 214, 217 (3d Cir. 1997); *Moad v. Arkansas State Police Dep't*, 111 F.3d 585, 587 (8th Cir.1997); *and Wilson–Jones v. Caviness*, 99 F.3d 203, 211 (6th Cir.1996), *amended on denial of reh'g*, 107 F.3d 358 (6th Cir.1997). Of course a private plaintiff FLSA suit against a state official seeking prospective relief only may still lie in federal court per *Ex Parte Young*.

In *Alden*, the claim brought against Maine in its own courts was based on the Fair Labor Standards Act, validly enacted pursuant to Congressional authority under Article I of the Constitution. Thus *Alden* does not specifically address whether the immunity of states from suit on federal claims in their own courts holds even when the predicate federal law statute was enacted pursuant to Congress' 14th Amendment, § 5 authority. Yet the reasoning of the opinion—that the states enjoyed immunity from suit in state court without their consent before the founding of the nation, and nothing in the Constitution alters that immunity—admits of no exceptions. After all, Congress' 14th Amendment, § 5 ability to override what would otherwise be a state's 11th Amendment immunity from suit in federal court merely limits the force of an amendment to the Constitution, the Eleventh; it does not speak to the state's immunities predating the Constitution itself.

The circuits have held that there is no Eleventh Amendment immunity for suits brought under the Equal Pay Act, because that Act was passed pursuant to Congress's § 5 Fourteenth Amendment powers and those powers were exercised in a manner congruent with and proportionate to the prohibition on gender discrimination with which the Fourteenth Amendment is concerned. *See Cherry v. University of Wisconsin System Bd. of Regents,* 265 F.3d 541 (7th Cir.2001); *Siler–Khodr v. Univ. of Texas Health Science Center San Antonio,* 261 F.3d 542 (5th Cir.2001); *Kovacevich v. Kent State University,* 224 F.3d 806 (6th Cir. 2000); *Hundertmark v. Florida Dep't of Transp.*, 205 F.3d 1272 (11th Cir.2000) (per curiam) (declaring that EPA's legislative record reflected findings of substantial gender-based workplace wage discrimination, acknowledging that such findings did not extend to the public sector, but asserting that no such findings are necessary because

Florida Prepaid Postsecondary Educ. Expense Bd. v. College Savings Bank, holding that Congress lacked the authority to abrogate states' immunity under the patent laws.[46] Thus, any question whether private plaintiff actions based on statutes passed solely pursuant to Commerce Clause authority and providing for exclusive federal court jurisdiction—antitrust, bankruptcy,[47] copyright,[48] patent, and certain environmental

gender discrimination is a national problem). *O'Sullivan v. Minnesota*, 191 F.3d 965 (8th Cir.1999); *Anderson v. State Univ. of N.Y.*, 169 F.3d 117 (2d Cir.1999), *vacated for reconsideration after Kimel*, 528 U.S. 1111, 120 S.Ct. 929, 145 L.Ed.2d 807 (2000); *Varner v. Illinois State Univ.*, 150 F.3d 706 (7th Cir.1998), *vacated for reconsideration after Kimel*, 528 U.S. 1110, 120 S.Ct. 928, 145 L.Ed.2d 806 (2000); *Ussery v. Louisiana*, 150 F.3d 431 (5th Cir.1998); *Timmer v. Michigan Dep't of Commerce*, 104 F.3d 833, 838–40 (6th Cir.1997).

Similarly, the circuits have concluded that states are not immune from federal court suits brought to vindicate rights granted by Titles VI and IX. *See, e.g., Fuller v. Rayburn*, 161 F.3d 516, 518 (8th Cir. 1998) (Title VI); *Lesage v. Texas*, 158 F.3d 213, 217 (5th Cir.1998), *reversed on other grounds*, 528 U.S. 18, 120 S.Ct. 467, 145 L.Ed.2d 347 (1999) (Title VI); *Cherry v. Univ. of Wisconsin Bd. of Regents, supra,* (Title IX); *Pederson v. Louisiana State Univ.,* 213 F.3d 858, 876 (5th Cir.2000) (Title IX); *Litman v. George Mason Univ.*, 186 F.3d 544 (4th Cir.1999) (Title IX); *Franks v. Kentucky Sch. for the Deaf*, 142 F.3d 360, 363 (6th Cir.1998) (Title IX); *Crawford v. Davis*, 109 F.3d 1281 (8th Cir. 1997) (Title IX).

However, the Supreme Court and several circuit courts have found that states cannot assert Eleventh Amendment immunity against claims brought under the RHA as the states waive their immunity by accepting the federal funds made available through that statute. *See Lane v. Pena*, 518 U.S. 187, 200, 116 S.Ct. 2092, 135 L.Ed.2d 486 (1996) (recognizing § 504 of the RHA to be an "unambiguous waiver of the State's Eleventh Amendment immunity"); *Nihiser v. Ohio E.P.A.*, 269 F.3d 626 (6th Cir.2001); *Jim C. v. United States*, 235 F.3d 1079 (8th Cir.2000) (en banc); *Stanley v. Litscher*, 213 F.3d 340 (7th Cir.2000); *Clark v. California*, 123 F.3d 1267 (9th Cir.1997). *But see Miller v. Texas Tech Univ. Health Sciences Center*, 330 F.3d 691 (5th Cir.2003) (holding, in light of more recent Supreme Court authority including *Garrett*, that 1986 Rehabilitation Act amendments did not validly abrogate state sovereign immunity). Lower courts continue to be divided as to whether a state's mere acceptance of federal financial assistance with conditions attached qualifies as a sufficiently express and voluntary waiver of Eleventh Amendment immunity. *Compare Koslow v. Commonwealth of Pennsylvania,* 302 F.3d 161 (3d Cir.2002) (state's acceptance of funds under State Criminal Alien Assistance Program for its Department of Corrections waived its immunity from claims under section of the Rehabilitation Act, and federal conditions placed on use of those funds constitutional) *with Johnson v. Louisiana Dept. of Educ.*, 330 F.3d 362 (5th Cir.2003) (state could not have knowingly waived Eleventh Amendment immunity from claims under RHA by accepting federal funds under that statute because at time of acceptance it had not been judicially determined that RHA did not validly abrogate the immunity and therefore entities could not know that they retained any such immunity to waive).

46. 527 U.S. 627, 119 S.Ct. 2199, 144 L.Ed.2d 575 (1999). Despite Congress' unmistakably clear attempt to abrogate the immunity under the patent laws, the court held it lacked the authority to do so pursuant to the commerce clause or legislation.

47. *See In re Sacred Heart Hosp. of Norristown*, 133 F.3d 237 (3d Cir.1998) (barring a suit against a state in bankruptcy court); *In re Estate of Fernandez*, 123 F.3d 241, 243 (5th Cir.1997), *amended*, 130 F.3d 1138 (5th Cir.1997); *In re Creative Goldsmiths of Washington*, D.C., Inc., 119 F.3d 1140, 1145 (4th Cir.1997), *cert. denied sub nom. Schlossberg v. Maryland Comptroller of Treasury*, 523 U.S. 1075, 118 S.Ct. 1517, 140 L.Ed.2d 670 (1998); *In re NVR, LP*, 189 F.3d 442 (4th Cir.1999), *cert. denied sub nom NVR Homes, Inc. v. Clerks of the Circuit Courts*, 528 U.S. 1117, 120 S.Ct. 936, 145 L.Ed.2d 815 (2000); *In re Tri–City Turf Club, Inc.*, 203 B.R. 617 (Bkrtcy. E.D.Ky.1996); *In re Lush Lawns, Inc.*, 203 B.R. 418 (Bkrtcy.N.D.Ohio1996); *In re York–Hannover Devs., Inc.*, 201 B.R. 137, 140 (Bkrtcy.E.D.N.C.1996); *In re Midland Mechanical Contractors, Inc.*, 200 B.R. 453, 457–58 (Bkrtcy.N.D.Ga.1996); *In re Burke*, 200 B.R. 282, 286 (Bkrtcy.S.D.Ga.1996); *In*

48. See note 48 on page 445.

statutes among others—may proceed against states or state instrumentalities in any forum has been answered by the Court—Congressional Article I attempts to make states amenable to suit will inevitably fail.

To an as yet uncertain degree, the *Seminole* decision also curtails federal court actions against state officials, the most common vehicle for enforcing compliance with federal law. The Court subjected an *Ex Parte Young* claim against Florida officials to its more general doctrine that disfavors implied private rights of action under federal statutes.[49] It seems unlikely, however, that either *Seminole* holding will have any effect on the vast majority of actions under § 1983, namely those based on a violation of the federal constitution.[50] Even before *Seminole*, it was clear that no § 1983 claim (based on a federal constitutional violation or an "and laws" claim based on violation of a federal statute) lies in any forum against a state in its own name. Such claims failed when brought in federal court because the Fourteenth Amendment Congressional override in § 1983 is insufficiently express.[51] Subsequently, in 1989, the Court held more broadly that no § 1983 claim against a state in its own name lies in any court, state or federal, because the 1871 Congress did not intend the defined defendant "person" to include a sovereign state.[52]

So the more vital, and shaded question is whether the second *Seminole* holding—that *Ex Parte Young* claims against state officials based on predicate violations of federal statutes may be precluded if the particular predicate statute contains a detailed or comprehensive remedial scheme that omits private rights of action—will restrict § 1983 (or *Bivens*)[53] claims against state (or federal) officials. Constitutionally-based claims against those officials should not be at all impaired. Unlike the statute at issue in *Seminole,* § 1983 expressly authorizes a private judicial action for damages and equitable relief. The same 1989 decision that deemed states eo nominee as unsuable non-"persons" specifically referenced *Ex Parte Young* in noting that § 1983 does subject state officials sued in their official capacity to prospective relief to cure

re Martinez, 196 B.R. 225, 230 (D.P.R. 1996). *But cf. In re Headrick*, 200 B.R. 963 (Bkrtcy.S.D.Ga.1996), aff'd, 146 F.3d 1313 (11th Cir.1998), *cert. denied*, 527 U.S. 1043, 119 S.Ct. 2410, 144 L.Ed.2d 808 (1999) (by filing proof of bankruptcy claim, state waived immunity).

48. *See Chavez v. Arte Publico Press*, 157 F.3d 282, 291 (5th Cir.1998), *vacated for reconsideration in light of College Sav. Bank and Florida Prepaid Postsecondary Educ. Expense Bd.*, 180 F.3d 674 (5th Cir. 1999) (*Seminole* condemns Congress's effort to force unconsenting states into federal court as the price of doing business regulated by the Lanham and Copyright Acts). *See also College Sav. Bank v. Florida Prepaid Postsecondary Educ. Expense Bd.*, 527 U.S. 666, 119 S.Ct. 2219, 144 L.Ed.2d 605 (1999) (holding state immune under Lanham Act).

49. The Court found the suit displaced by the extremely limited, but specific remedial provisions of the Indian Gaming Regulatory Act, which did not include private judicial actions.

50. And at least one circuit has found that *Seminole* has no effect on claims brought under §§ 1981 and 1985 either. *See Ellis v. University of Kansas Med. Ctr.*, 163 F.3d 1186, 1195–98 (10th Cir.1998).

51. *Quern v. Jordan*, 440 U.S. 332, 99 S.Ct. 1139, 59 L.Ed.2d 358 (1979).

52. *Will v. Michigan Dep't of State Police*, 491 U.S. 58, 71, 109 S.Ct. 2304, 2312, 105 L.Ed.2d 45 (1989).

53. *Bivens v. Six Unknown Named Agents of Fed. Bureau of Narcotics*, 403 U.S. 388, 91 S.Ct. 1999, 29 L.Ed.2d 619 (1971).

constitutional violations.[54] Subsequently, the Court held state officials liable in damages under § 1983 for constitutional violations when named in their personal capacities.[55] Put otherwise, however important *Ex Parte Young* may have been in 1908 as the source of an implied private, judicially enforceable claim against state officers behaving unconstitutionally, § 1983 now stands as an independent source of that claim.

Bivens actions (for constitutional violations by federal officials) are somewhat more vulnerable to implied preclusion a la *Seminole*. First, no statute expressly provides a private judicial action for such claims. Second, it might be argued that § 1983, by providing a right of action for constitutional violations against state actors, precludes a similar claim against federal actors. But that argument, fully aired by the *Bivens* dissent, was rejected by a majority of the Court. And because the federalism/state sovereignty undertone of *Seminole* is missing in the *Bivens* context, it seems even more doubtful that *Seminole* should be read to overrule that quarter-century-old precedent sub silentio.

But what of § 1983 "and laws" claims—those that use the remedial vehicle of § 1983 to vindicate violations of other federal statutes?[56] After all, those claims, asserting an implied private right of action based on federal statutory violations, are commonly directed against state officials—just like the claim at issue in *Seminole* under the Indian Gaming Regulatory Act against the governor of Florida. Nevertheless, the effect of *Seminole* on such claims should be felt, if at all, only at the margins. Even before *Seminole*, the Court had developed a line of authority that precludes an "and laws" claim if the detail or comprehensiveness of the predicate statute's remedial scheme makes it unlikely that Congress would favorably countenance a supplementary private judicial action under § 1983. But so long as the § 1983 "and laws" claim is founded on a clear, specific, mandatory, and judicially enforceable right, and is not implicitly precluded by judicial remedies in the predicate federal statute, it remains enforceable against state officials, through injunctive relief of the sort that meets the evolved *Ex Parte Young* criteria, notwithstanding *Seminole Tribe*.[57] *Seminole*, then, may come into play more as authority

54. *Will*, 491 U.S. at 71 n.10.

55. *Hafer v. Melo*, 502 U.S. 21, 112 S.Ct. 358, 116 L.Ed.2d 301 (1991). *See Porter v. Jones*, 319 F.3d 483, 491 (9th Cir.2003) (relying on *Hafer* to reject argument that Eleventh Amendment bars damages claims against state officials named in their individual capacities).

56. These claims, and their possible preclusion if a court deems the remedial scheme of the predicate statute sufficiently detailed or comprehensive, are discussed in § 2.50. That section also addresses the requirement that the predicate statute § 1983 confers on plaintiff a specific, mandatory, and judicially enforceable right.

57. *See Frew ex rel. Frew v. Hawkins*, ___ U.S. ___, 124 S.Ct. 899, 157 L.Ed.2d 855 (2004) (enforcing federal consent decree against state officials, to implement a federal statute, even though provisions of decree implied requirements greater than those of the statute itself); *Rosie D. ex rel. John D. v. Swift*, 310 F.3d 230 (1st Cir.2002) (Medicaid Act's administrative hearing remedy not sufficiently comprehensive to foreclose beneficiaries' *Ex Parte Young* claims for prospective relief against state officials); *Missouri Child Care Ass'n v. Cross*, 294 F.3d 1034 (8th Cir.2002) (federal oversight and withholding of funds for noncompliance not sufficiently elaborated remedial scheme to preclude *Ex Parte Young* claims for declaratory and injunctive relief against state officials to enforce Adoption Assistance and Child Welfare Act); *Gibson v. Arkansas Dep't of Correction*, 265 F.3d 718 (8th Cir.

for a strict application of this implied remedial preclusion doctrine than as an independent limitation on § 1983 claims based on the violation of federal statutes.

After *Seminole*, the Court did deny access to a federal forum per the *Young* exception when another tribe claimed title, through an 1873 Presidential Executive Order, to lands submerged under a lake and prayed for declaratory and injunctive relief invalidating state statutes purporting to regulate those lands and prohibiting further regulation. All nine Justices agreed that *Seminole* did not disturb the "continuing validity" of the *Young* doctrine. Seven Justices, three concurring in and four dissenting from the judgment, even agreed that the *Young* presumption of a federal forum remains intact, and is not defeasible through case-by-case balancing, whenever the plaintiff alleges an ongoing violation of federal law for which truly prospective relief is sought. Nevertheless, five Justices voted to deny federal court jurisdiction under the "particular and special circumstances" of this "functional" title suit that if successful would abolish rather than merely diminish state regulatory authority. They considered these consequences to be more threatening to Idaho's core sovereignty than other *Young* suits that, for example, curtailed state ratemaking authority (as in *Young* itself), discretion to withhold welfare benefits, or policies regarding prisoners. Two of those Justices wrote more generally that a "case-by-case analysis" is required whenever a plaintiff invokes the *Young* exception. Yet even they would apparently permit the *Young* federal court suit, without a potentially fatal balancing process, where, as was not the case here, the state's own courts are closed to the federal law claim because of state law immunity and hence unavailable for the vindication of federal interests. These Justices, then, would subject the *Young* claim to a potentially fatal balancing process only in cases in which the defendant state's courts are open to consider the federal law claim but the plaintiff urges the necessity of a federal forum because "the case calls for the interpretation of federal law."[58]

Attorney's fees in civil rights and employment discrimination cases are wholly outside the strictures of the Eleventh Amendment as the result of Congressional abrogation that the Supreme Court has upheld. Under 42 U.S.C.A. § 1988, codifying the Civil Rights Attorneys Fees Act of 1976, such fees are considered compensation for "expenses incurred in litigation seeking only prospective relief," instead of "retroactive liability for prelitigation conduct."[59] Attorney's fees against a state are available to the prevailing party based on his degree of success on any "significant" issue that "changes the legal relationship between [the plaintiff]

2001) (ADA); *Cornforth v. University of Oklahoma*, 263 F.3d 1129 (10th Cir.2001). *cert. denied* 534 U.S. 1162, 122 S.Ct. 1172, 152 L.Ed.2d 116 (2002) (FMLA); *Randolph v. Rodgers*, 253 F.3d 342 (8th Cir.2001) (ADA).

58. *Idaho v. Coeur d'Alene Tribe*, 521 U.S. 261, 117 S.Ct. 2028, 138 L.Ed.2d 438 (1997).

59. *Hutto v. Finney*, 437 U.S. 678, 695, 98 S.Ct. 2565, 2576, 57 L.Ed.2d 522 (1978).

and the defendant.''[60] In addition, such an award can include prejudgment interest or a fee enhancement for delay in payment based on current market rates rather than those rates relevant at the time the legal services were rendered.[61]

With respect to claims under § 1983, the Eleventh Amendment is of little significance given the Supreme Court's view that claims against the state itself, or official capacity claims against individual state officers that will be satisfied out of the state's treasury, fail to state a claim for relief under that statute.[62] Nevertheless, official capacity actions against named state officials that seek only prospective relief still state a claim under Section 1983[63] and avoid the bar of the Amendment via *Ex Parte Young*. But the Eleventh Amendment defense still appears to be critical in federal court actions brought against a state or state officials under 42 U.S.C.A. §§ 1981, 1982, 1985, and other civil rights statutes.[64] However, in *Jett v. Dallas Independent Sch. Dist.*,[65] the Court imported the prima facie elements of a § 1983 claim into, and thus made significantly more stringent the required elements of, § 1981 claims against local government entities. Consequently, in a § 1981 action in federal court against a state entity or official, the Court might also import the § 1983 holding of *Will* that the state in its own name is not a proper defendant. In that event, a state defendant sued under § 1981 should succeed with a timely objection contending that the complaint fails to state a claim, and the Eleventh Amendment objection would then become merely a quasi-jurisdictional backstop to the defense of legal insufficiency. Whether *Jett* succeeds in removing § 1981 from the plaintiff's arsenal against state government is somewhat clouded by a provision of the Civil Rights Act of 1991 that reaffirms the availability of § 1981 in actions against government entities as well as individuals. But that provision has been construed merely to affirm that § 1981 is an available remedy against some government defendants, not necessarily the state. Indeed, several circuit decisions conclude that the 1991 Act failed to overrule *Jett,* so that no

60. *Texas State Teachers Ass'n v. Garland Indep. Sch. Dist.*, 489 U.S. 782, 792, 109 S.Ct. 1486, 1493, 103 L.Ed.2d 866 (1989).

61. *Missouri v. Jenkins*, 491 U.S. 274, 109 S.Ct. 2463, 105 L.Ed.2d 229 (1989). *See Jones v. Washington Metro. Area Transit Auth.*, 205 F.3d 428, 432 (D.C.Cir.2000) (Congress expressly and validly abrogated states' Eleventh Amendment immunity respecting prejudgment interest on back pay in enacting Title VII).

62. *Will v. Michigan Dep't of State Police*, 491 U.S. 58, 109 S.Ct. 2304, 105 L.Ed.2d 45 (1989). *See McLaughlin v. Board of Trustees of State Colleges of Colorado,* 215 F.3d 1168 (10th Cir.2000) (state agency waived Eleventh Amendment defense by removing, but plaintiff held not to have stated claim for relief under *Will*).

63. *Will v. Michigan Dep't of State Police*, n.10. *See Nanda v. Board of Trustees of University of Illinois*, 303 F.3d 817, 832 (7th Cir.2002) (citing *Will* for both propositions).

64. *See, e.g., Johnson v. University of Cincinnati,* 215 F.3d 561, 571 (6th Cir. 2000) (upholding defense as barring § 1981 and § 1983 claims); *Fincher v. Florida Dep't of Labor & Employment Sec. Unemployment Appeals Comm'n*, 798 F.2d 1371, 1372 (11th Cir.1986), *cert. denied*, 479 U.S. 1072, 107 S.Ct. 1262, 94 L.Ed.2d 124 (1987) (no express abrogation respecting actions under 42 U.S.C.§ 1985); *Sessions v. Rusk State Hosp.*, 648 F.2d 1066, 1069 (5th Cir. 1981) (Amendment applicable in § 1981 litigation).

65. 491 U.S. 701, 109 S.Ct. 2702, 105 L.Ed.2d 598 (1989).

independent § 1981 claim lies against *any* government defendant. This construction is plausible not only because of the awkward wording of the 1991 provision but because its other, more apparent purpose is simply to codify the Supreme Court's decisions that have applied § 1981 to purely private conduct.[66]

The Eleventh Amendment as construed in *Seminole*, then, prohibits federal courts from exercising jurisdiction over private party suits under Article I statutes against states sued in their own names. But may the states be sued on such statutes in their own courts? In *Alden v. Maine*,[67] the Court held that Congress cannot, by legislating pursuant to its Article I powers, override the immunity that a nonconsenting state enjoyed before the Constitutional Convention from suits in its own courts. Thus a nonconsenting state or state subentity may not be sued by a private party on federal claims, any more than on state claims, in its own courts.[68] Accordingly, unless a state waives its immunity from suit in its own courts or the federal courts, the judicial means of compelling a state to obey a federal statute enacted solely on Congress' Article I authority are rather limited. First, an aggrieved party may seek compensatory relief if she can prevail on the relevant federal official to bring suit against the state in federal court in the name of the United States, an option existing before and indirectly reaffirmed by *Alden*.[69] Second, a private party may bring suit herself in federal court by naming as defendant a state official and contenting herself with prospective relief under the umbrella of *Ex Parte Young*, to the extent that a *Young* claim based on a federal statute survives implied preclusion under the second holding of *Seminole Tribe*. Third, she may sue in federal court for compensatory relief against the state official in his individual capacity, although in such an action the relief must be sought from the officer personally, and not from the state treasury.[70]

§§ 5.36–5.39 [Reserved]

H. SUPPLEMENTAL (INCLUDING "PENDENT") JURISDICTION

§ 5.40 In General

Supplemental or pendent claim jurisdiction allows a plaintiff who

66. *See* the discussion of *Jett* and the 1991 Civil Rights Act in Chapter 1 on the Reconstruction statutes.

67. 527 U.S. 706, 119 S.Ct. 2240, 144 L.Ed.2d 636 (1999).

68. *Id.* at 712, 119 S.Ct. at 2246. The Court distinguished *Nevada v. Hall*, 440 U.S. 410, 99 S.Ct. 1182, 59 L.Ed.2d 416 (1979), wherein the state of Nevada was sued in a California state court. The Court explained that the Constitution did not reflect "an agreement between the states to respect" one another's sovereign immunity; only an agreement between states or the principle of comity could immunize one state from suit in another's courts. *Alden*, 527 U.S. at 738–39, 119 S.Ct. at 2259–60.

69. *See Alden*, 527 U.S. at 756, 119 S.Ct. at 2267; *U.S. v. Mississippi Dept. of Public Safety*, 321 F.3d 495 (5th Cir.2003) (U.S. as plaintiff not subject to Amendment regardless of whether it seeks to vindicate rights of an individual or to remedy a pattern of intentional discrimination violating Americans with Disabilities Act).

70. *Id.* at 757, 119 S.Ct. at 2267–68.

has a federal claim against a nondiverse defendant[1] in federal court to append a transactionally related state law claim against the same defendant. For the past half-century the Court has authorized some form of pendent jurisdiction, recognizing that in its absence the plaintiff would be forced to litigate the distinct but related federal and state claims in two fora or to abandon the federal forum. The Court fully articulated the article III criteria for pendent claim jurisdiction in *United Mine Workers of America v. Gibbs.*[2] For a federal court to have constitutional power to entertain the state law claim, that claim and the federal law claim on which jurisdiction is founded must arise from a "common nucleus of operative fact"; the claims must be such that the plaintiff would normally be expected to try both in one judicial proceeding; and the federal claim must be "substantial."

The *Gibbs* opinion did not allude to the settled understanding that federal subject matter jurisdiction requires not just a constitutional foundation—in this case, Article III—but also a Congressional authorization or acceptance of that jurisdiction as manifested in a federal statute. But the court did identify several factors that a federal trial court, having concluded that it has constitutional power to hear both claims, should take into account in deciding whether, in its discretion, to dismiss the state law claim. It observed that the doctrine's justification "lies in considerations of judicial economy, convenience and fairness to litigants"—a later case, *Carnegie–Mellon,*[3] added "comity" to the list—and if these are absent "a federal court should hesitate to exercise jurisdiction over state claims." The *Gibbs* opinion specifically mentioned two examples of situations in which the trial judge should consider declining to exercise otherwise available pendent jurisdiction: where "the state issues substantially predominate, whether in terms of proof, of the scope of the issues raised, or of the comprehensiveness of the remedy sought"; and where there are "reasons independent of jurisdictional considerations, such as the likelihood of jury confusion in treating divergent legal theories of relief," that would warrant separate trials of the state and federal claims. *Carnegie–Mellon* read *Gibbs* as conferring substantial discretion on the trial courts to assert *or decline* jurisdiction over pendent claims, guided only by the ultimate values of judicial economy, convenience and fairness to litigants, and comity.

So the *Gibbs* authorization of pendent claim jurisdiction might have remained were it not for Congressional dissatisfaction with the Court's ultimate rejection of a parallel doctrine, pendent *party* jurisdiction. The situation arises when a plaintiff tries to append to a substantial federal question claim—for example, a claim under § 1983, Title VII, ADEA, or

§ 5.40

1. If all the requirements of the diversity statute, 28 U.S.C.A. § 1332, are met, the federal district court is *required* to accept original jurisdiction over all claims, state as well as federal, whether or not they are related. *Cemer v. Marathon Oil Co.,* 583 F.2d 830 (6th Cir.1978).

2. 383 U.S. 715, 86 S.Ct. 1130, 16 L.Ed.2d 218 (1966).

3. *Carnegie–Mellon Univ. v. Cohill,* 484 U.S. 343, 108 S.Ct. 614, 98 L.Ed.2d 720 (1988).

any of the other federal statutes prohibiting civil rights deprivations or employment discrimination—a claim under state law against *another defendant*, again where the requirements of complete diversity of citizenship are lacking. The question is whether, even assuming the state law claim bears a sufficient factual nexus to the federal law claim to meet the *Gibbs* test of constitutional power, a court should exercise jurisdiction over a party "not named in any claim that is independently cognizable by the federal court."[4]

The Court first restricted pendent party jurisdiction in *Aldinger v. Howard*.[5] There a plaintiff sought to append to § 1983 claims against nondiverse individual defendants a factually related state law claim against a county. At the time, however, neither a county nor other local government entity was a suable "person" under § 1983.[6] Assuming that the *Gibbs* minimum prerequisite for Article III jurisdictional power was present—the claims arose from a common nucleus of real-life fact—and without denying the possibility of pendent party jurisdiction in principle, the Court insisted that "careful attention" also be given to the jurisdictional requirement of statutory authorization that it had ignored in *Gibbs*. It observed that 28 U.S.C.A. § 1343, the special statutory foundation for claims under § 1983, provides jurisdiction only over claims "authorized by law" and that § 1983 claims against a county were not so authorized. The Court in *Aldinger* therefore refused to uphold a "back door" version of pendent party jurisdiction over the county, that is to hear a state law claim that the federal jurisdictional statute on which the action against the individual defendants was founded would have barred.

Only two years later, however, the Court declared that a city or a county is a "person" suable under § 1983. This decision undermined the rationale relied on in *Aldinger* for refusing to append state law claims against local government entities to § 1983 claims against individual defendants. Lower courts were then forced to decide if *Aldinger* was hinting at a more broadly based ban on pendent party jurisdiction, and they divided over this question. The Court's answer came in 1989 in *Finley*, where it interpreted *Aldinger* as indicating that "the Gibbs approach would not be extended to the pendent—party field" because "a [federal statutory] grant of jurisdiction over claims involving particular parties does not itself confer jurisdiction over additional claims by or against different parties." At the same time, the Court reaffirmed pendent claim jurisdiction as declared by *Gibbs*. The burden was on Congress, in other words, to spell out its willingness to confer subject matter jurisdiction to the full extent of its constitutional power with respect to pendent parties, though not with respect to pendent claims.

In response to *Finley*, a federal courts study committee recommended that Congress enact express statutory authority for pendent and

4. *Finley v. United States*, 490 U.S. 545, 109 S.Ct. 2003, 104 L.Ed.2d 593 (1989).

5. 427 U.S. 1, 96 S.Ct. 2413, 49 L.Ed.2d 276 (1976).

6. See Chapter 2.

other forms of ancillary jurisdiction. As part of the Judicial Improvements Act of 1990 Congress adopted a new statute[7] that provides for supplemental jurisdiction. As it relates to civil rights or employment discrimination claims based on federal law, the first sentence of § 1367(a) declares that the federal district courts "shall have" supplemental jurisdiction "over all other claims that are so related" to the foundational federal law claims "that they form part of the case or controversy under Article III of the United States Constitution." Since the *Gibbs* test for constitutional power was an interpretation of Article III, this part of the new statute provides statutory confirmation for the *Gibbs* "common nucleus" approach to pendent claim jurisdiction. The second sentence of § 1367(a) changes the result of *Finley* by providing: "Such supplemental jurisdiction shall include claims that involve the joinder or intervention of additional parties." Thus there is now express statutory authorization for pendent party jurisdiction on the same relaxed "common nucleus" standard that *Gibbs* and § 1367(a)'s first sentence provide for pendent claim jurisdiction.[8]

But does this statute, the impetus for which was a desire to respond to *Finley* by providing congressional authorization for supplemental jurisdiction in pendent party situations, also, inadvertently or by design, liberalize the scope of pendent claim jurisdiction by restricting the circumstances under which federal judges may decline to exercise it? One such suggestion emerges from the first sentence of § 1367(a), which states that the district courts "shall have" supplemental jurisdiction over all state law claims that show the *Gibbs* relationship to the foundation claim based on federal law. When the Court in *Gibbs* sketched the contours of pendent jurisdiction, it carefully eschewed any such mandatory language.

A second such suggestion emerges from § 1367(c). This subdivision authorizes district courts to decline to exercise supplemental jurisdiction only in four specifically enumerated circumstances, rather than, as under *Gibbs*, for any reason not comporting with judicial economy, convenience, fairness or comity. The first three circumstances roughly track the particular examples mentioned in *Gibbs*: (1) the putative supplemental claim "raises a novel or complex issue of State law"; (2) it "substantially predominates over" the federal question claim on which federal subject matter jurisdiction is initially founded; and (3) the court has already dismissed the claims that gave it original jurisdiction—in *Gibbs* terms, the federal question claims proved insubstantial.[9]

7. 28 U.S.C.A. § 1367.

8. *See Ammerman v. Sween*, 54 F.3d 423 (7th Cir.1995) (upholding supplemental jurisdiction over state law assault claim against co-employee as sufficiently related to Title VII claim against employer).

9. *See Patel v. Penman*, 103 F.3d 868 (9th Cir.1996), *cert. denied*, 520 U.S. 1240, 117 S.Ct. 1845, 137 L.Ed.2d 1048 (1997) (district court properly exercised discretion to refuse supplemental jurisdiction over state law claim after dismissal of § 1983 claims and all Fair Housing Act claims, and state law claim substantially predominated over remaining constitutional claims).

But the fourth appears to restrict the district judges' discretion to decline supplemental jurisdiction somewhat more than the open-ended *Gibbs* reference to generalized considerations of efficiency, fairness, and federalism: the trial court may decline pendent jurisdiction only "(4) in *exceptional* circumstances, [when] there are other *compelling* reasons." (emphasis added). Taking their cue from the structure of the limited subdivision (c) exceptions to the supplemental jurisdiction that subdivision (a) says the district courts "shall have," lower courts have ruled that § 1367 creates a presumption in favor of supplemental jurisdiction unless one of the specific subdivision (c) exceptions applies.[10] On this reading of the statute the range of a district judge's discretion to decline to exercise supplemental jurisdiction has been so narrowed that a decision to do so may be overturned by mandamus.[11] But the pertinent House Report seems to deny this result. It states that § 1367 merely "codifies" the *Gibbs* factors, overrules *Finley* and allows for pendent party jurisdiction.[12]

§§ 5.41–5.44 [Reserved]

I. STATE COURT JURISDICTION

§ 5.45 In General

Under the Supremacy Clause of the U.S. Constitution, state courts have a duty to enforce federal rights unless Congress, by declaring federal court jurisdiction to be original *and exclusive*, affirmatively divests state courts of their competence to hear such claims. None of the Reconstruction Civil Rights Acts, or the modern employment discrimination statutes, asserts that the original jurisdiction of the federal courts is exclusive. Accordingly, the Supreme Court has held that state courts have full concurrent jurisdiction over federal civil rights and Title VII claims.[1] And they must exercise that jurisdiction without discrimination when it is properly invoked. The only "valid excuse" for refusing to do so is reliance on a neutral procedural policy that the state court applies to all kinds of claims, including those under state law—and occasionally even such a reason may be overridden if deemed inconsistent with a policy of federal law.[2]

10. *Executive Software North Am., Inc. v. United States Dist. Court for Central Dist. of Cal.*, 24 F.3d 1545 (9th Cir.1994); *Growth Horizons, Inc. v. Delaware County*, 983 F.2d 1277 (3d Cir.1993).

11. *See Executive Software*, 24 F.3d at 1562.

12. H.R.Rep.No. 713, 101st Cong., 2d Sess. 29 (1990) reprinted in 1990 U.S.C.A.C.A.N. 6802, 6875.

§ 5.45

1. *Howlett v. Rose*, 496 U.S. 356, 110 S.Ct. 2430, 110 L.Ed.2d 332 (1990) (§ 1983). Similarly, the Court has upheld concurrent jurisdiction in Title VII cases. Nothing in the legislative history indicating Congress' anticipation that most Title VII cases would be brought in federal court overcomes the presumptive jurisdiction of the state courts. Nor does the fact that a Title VII right to sue arises only after review by both state administrative agencies *and* the federal EEOC affect the question of what judicial forum should entertain the action. *Yellow Freight v. Donnelly*, 494 U.S. 820, 110 S.Ct. 1566, 108 L.Ed.2d 834 (1990).

2. *Howlett*, 496 U.S. at 369–70, 110 S.Ct. at 2439.

Because of this concurrent jurisdiction, a plaintiff may choose to bring her civil rights or employment discrimination claim in state or federal court.[3] The reasons for filing in state court are varied and depend on the environment of the state system under consideration.[4] For example, the assumed sympathies of a particular state court judge or jury pool, relative to predictions about the counterpart federal judge or jury, may attract the plaintiff; an elected state judge's potentially greater susceptibility to public opinion may be particularly important here. Other factors in deciding between state and federal court fall into three general categories: choice of law considerations, procedural or administrative differences, and doctrinal limitations on the federal courts.

The choice of law considerations are two-fold. First, a plaintiff who has not conclusively determined to bring suit under § 1983 may find that state law provides rights of action more congenial from the standpoint of proof or remedies.[5] Federal courts would only be able to entertain such state law claims (assuming they were not accompanied by claims under federal law and accordingly eligible for federal "supplemental" jurisdiction under 28 U.S.C.A. § 1367) if all plaintiffs and defendants happen to be of diverse citizenship and the sum of the claims against each defendant exceeds $75,000, thereby satisfying 28 U.S.C.A. § 1332(a)(1). Second, where a plaintiff is determined to pursue a § 1983

3. To capitalize on eased claim requirements, a plaintiff may wish to sue under a state civil rights statute, in either state or federal court. For example, the Minnesota Supreme Court has held that the Minnesota Human Rights Act's definitions of "discriminate" and "sexual harassment" relieve a plaintiff of the burden of making the *Oncale* showing, mandatory to prove a claim under Title VII, that same-sex sexual harassment was "because of sex." *Cummings v. Koehnen*, 568 N.W.2d 418, 424 (Minn.1997).

4. For an excellent comprehensive discussion of the factors involved in choosing between state and federal court, see Steven H. Steinglass, *Section 1983 Litigation in State Courts*, Part B (1994).

5. A few examples will illustrate such substantive differences in state versus federal civil rights and employment discrimination claims. *See Vielma v. Eureka Co.*, 218 F.3d 458 (5th Cir.2000) (receipt of EEOC right to sue notice does not trigger time limits for filing suit under Texas discrimination statute); *Mitchem v. Counts*, 259 Va. 179, 523 S.E.2d 246 (Va.2000) (state human rights act applicable to employers who do not meet the 15 employee jurisdictional threshold); *Downey v. Crowley*, 236 F.3d 1019 (9th Cir.2001) (Washington law, unlike Americans With Disabilities Act, construed not to absolve employer of considering a reasonable accommodation even if employee failed formally to request it); *Gordan v. Cummings*, 756 A.2d 942 (Me.2000) (relying on federal law decisions that limited employer liability in harassment cases as showing a need for the liability of individual defendants). *See also Zanni v. Medaphis Physician Servs. Corp.*, 240 Mich.App. 472, 612 N.W.2d 845 (2000) (permitting 31–year-old claimant to proceed with claim of "reverse" age discrimination, a theory generally rejected under the counterpart federal Age Discrimination in Employment Act and which is limited to claimants at least 40 years old). *But see Snead v. Metropolitan Property & Cas. Ins. Co.*, 237 F.3d 1080 (9th Cir.), *cert. denied* 534 U.S. 888, 122 S.Ct. 201, 151 L.Ed.2d 142 (2001) (applying *McDonnell-Douglas* burden-shifting scheme to Oregon disability discrimination statute); *Reilly v. Alcan Aluminum Corp.*, 272 Ga. 279, 528 S.E.2d 238 (2000) (declining to imply private damages action under state law for age discrimination or to create for age discrimination a public policy wrongful discharge exception to the doctrine of employment at will); *Carrisales v. Department of Corr.*, 21 Cal.4th 1132, 90 Cal.Rptr.2d 804, 988 P.2d 1083 (1999) (plaintiff's co-workers not personally liable under California Fair Employment and Housing Act, consistent with federal law); *Reno v. Baird*, 18 Cal.4th 640, 76 Cal. Rptr.2d 499, 957 P.2d 1333 (1998) (same re supervisors).

or employment discrimination claim, she must predict whether, on each likely determinative issue not yet authoritatively construed by the Supreme Court, a state or federal judge will offer the more favorable interpretation. For instance, if the plaintiff expects to face an immunity defense, he might opt to file in state court if that court routinely answers the "clearly established right" question by reference to state rather than lower federal court decisions, provided of course that the state's law is more likely to yield a positive answer to that question. If, however, a plaintiff expects to use claim or issue preclusion offensively, he may more often prefer federal court, where offensive preclusion has received somewhat greater acceptance. Similarly, the employment discrimination plaintiff may find a more favorable construction of federal law in a state court exercising concurrent subject matter jurisdiction over that claim.[6] For the defendant, of course, these considerations weigh in the decision whether to remove once the plaintiff opts for a state forum.[7]

State and federal court procedural and administrative differences also figure in the calculus. For example, agreements to arbitrate state law employment discrimination claims may be more closely scrutinized for unconscionability.[8] Less congested state court calendars may attract the plaintiff with the prospect of an earlier trial date. And if interim relief is important, plaintiff may choose a state system, which typically will support a larger number of judges who may decide such requests more quickly than their federal court counterparts. A party who prefers less judicial pretrial intervention may opt for state court to avoid the ever increasing involvement of federal district judges mandated by Rule 16 of the FRCP.[9] A state court may use a more liberal limitations period, or more liberal accrual approach (at least for a claim under state law), than the stringent federal definition adopted by the Supreme Court[10] and in federal law cases may apply a state law tolling rule more liberally than would a federal district court.[11] Also, a plaintiff might have better odds in state than in federal court of surviving a motion for summary judgment if the state court does not follow the burden-shifting scheme of federal employment discrimination law or the Supreme Court's *Celotex Corp. v. Catrett* and *Anderson v. Liberty Lobby* decisions that ease the defendant's

6. *But see Kohler v. Inter–Tel Technologies*, 244 F.3d 1167 (9th Cir.2001) (Under California state law, employers may defend against vicarious liability for hostile work environment sexual harassment claims in manner similar to that found in *Faragher* and *Burlington*); *Alberte v. Anew Health Care Servs., Inc.*, 223 Wis.2d 1, 588 N.W.2d 298 (1998) (following the "vast majority" of federal courts that had rejected individual liability under the federal Americans With Disabilities Act).

7. *See* § 5.50, *infra*.

8. *Armendariz v. Foundation Health Psychcare Services, Inc.*, 24 Cal.4th 83, 99 Cal.Rptr.2d 745, 6 P.3d 669 (2000).

9. See, e.g., Richey, *Rule 16 Revised, and Related Rules: Analysis of Recent Developments for the Benefit of Bench and Bar*, 157 F.R.D. 69 (1994).

10. *See Vielma v. Eureka Company*, 218 F.3d 458 (5th Cir.2000) (receipt of EEOC notice of right to sue does not trigger period for filing under state law); *Cisneros v. ABC Rail Corp.*, 217 F.3d 1299, 1305 (10th Cir.2000) (no need to comply with Title VII charge filing prerequisite in action to enforce conciliation agreement that is based on state law); *Romano v. Rockwell Int'l Inc.*, 14 Cal.4th 479, 59 Cal.Rptr.2d 20, 926 P.2d 1114 (1996) (applying plaintiff-friendly accrual definition).

11. *See* § 5.72, *infra*.

burden in making the motion and increase the plaintiff's burden in resisting it.[12]

State courts also frequently offer more liberal relation back where plaintiff has named a "Doe" defendant.[13] State court policy may allow discovery to proceed in situations where federal courts would stay discovery—for example, while an immunity question is being resolved.[14] State rules of evidence may be more, or less, favorable than the federal rules.[15] And state courts do not uniformly allow a defendant to limit his

12. *See Snead v. Metropolitan Property & Casualty Ins. Co.*, 237 F.3d 1080 (9th Cir.2001). The federal summary judgment decisions are discussed in § 5.100, *infra*.

13. *See* § 5.80, *infra*.

14. *Cf. Troupin v. Metropolitan Life Ins. Co.*, 169 F.R.D. 546 (S.D.N.Y.1996) (declaring in Title VII case, as a matter of federal common law, a "self-critical analysis" privilege that shields from discovery the evaluative, narrative, and analytical, but not the factual material of an employer's internal reports on diversity planning and results of employee survey). It is unclear if such decisions will be viewed to reflect substantive federal policy that is obligatory through Supremacy Clause preemption on state courts hearing federal employment discrimination and civil rights claims. See Section N, *infra*, on the question of federal preemption of state court procedural rules and customs.

15. Claims under the Reconstruction Acts and modern employment discrimination statutes are "federal question" claims within the meaning of 28 U.S.C.A. §§ 1331 & 1343; as such, federal rather than state common law governs questions of evidentiary privileges when those claims are brought in federal court. *See* Fed.R.Evid. 501. Most federal courts have rejected the physician-patient privilege, although many states recognize it. *See Patterson v. Caterpillar, Inc.*, 70 F.3d 503 (7th Cir.1995). On the other hand the Supreme Court has recognized a psychotherapist-patient privilege, one that is also recognized in some form by all fifty states. *Jaffee v. Redmond*, 518 U.S. 1, 116 S.Ct. 1923, 135 L.Ed.2d 337 (1996). In finding protection of confidential psychotherapist-patient communications sufficiently important to outweigh the ordinary need for probative evidence, the Court indicated it was obeying the Rule 501 command that federal courts "continue the evolutionary development of testimonial privileges." Further, it upheld the privilege broadly beyond psychiatrists and psychologists to include communications made to all licensed social workers. It recognized only the narrowest of possible exceptions, for example, in circumstances where a therapist's disclosure would be essential to avert serious harm to the patient or others.

The requirement of Federal Rule of Civil Procedure 35 that an order directing a physical or mental examination of a party may be made only upon "good cause shown" is more restrictive than the counterpart rules of some states. *See O'Quinn v. New York Univ. Med. Ctr.*, 163 F.R.D. 226 (S.D.N.Y.1995) (refusing to order plaintiff to undergo a medical examination despite what the court termed her "boilerplate" allegation of "mental anguish, emotional distress, and humiliation"). *But cf. Lahr v. Fulbright & Jaworski, LLP*, 164 F.R.D. 204 (N.D.Tex.1996) (ordering plaintiff to submit to mental examination with respect to Title VII prayer for compensatory damages for emotional distress and related state law tort claim).

The Supreme Court has facilitated the admissibility of expert scientific testimony under Federal Rule of Evidence 702, holding that the trial judge may evaluate the validity of the reasoning and methodology underlying such testimony and admit it even if it did not enjoy widespread "general acceptance" in the relevant scientific community. *Daubert v. Merrell Dow Pharmaceuticals, Inc.*, 509 U.S. 579, 113 S.Ct. 2786, 125 L.Ed.2d 469 (1993) (district court acts as gatekeeper and must determine that scientific evidence is relevant and reliable to be admissible). *See also Elsayed Mukhtar v. California State University*, 299 F.3d 1053 (9th Cir.2002) (district court's failure to exclude expert's testimony "decoding" white behavior and opining that race was a factor in tenure denial was prejudicial error because court abandoned gatekeeper function in assessing reliability of testimony); *Jenson v. Eveleth Taconite Co.*, 130 F.3d 1287 (8th Cir.1997), *cert. denied sub nom Oglebay Norton Co. v. Jenson*, 524 U.S. 953, 118 S.Ct. 2370, 141 L.Ed.2d 738 (1998) (psychological testimony relating defendant employer's actions to emotional distress damages of plaintiff admissible under *Daubert*). While the *Daubert* decision addressed only scientific testimony, the Court subse-

exposure to large fee awards by using offers of judgment as authorized by FRCP Rule 68.

Federal doctrinal limitations, mostly jurisdictional or quasi-jurisdictional, may also encourage filing in state court. State courts may, for example, impose looser standing requirements. Unless the parties are completely diverse and over $75,000 is at stake, a state law claim similar to its federal employment discrimination or civil rights counterpart but construed more liberally on a procedural point may survive only in a state court.[16] Further, state courts may provide the only avenue for

quently applied the *Daubert* holding to technical and other specialized knowledge in *Kumho Tire Co., Ltd. v. Carmichael*, 526 U.S. 137, 119 S.Ct. 1167, 143 L.Ed.2d 238 (1999), holding that the *Daubert* reliability factors such as testing, peer review, error rates, and "acceptability" in the relevant scientific community, can be utilized by a district court in assessing the reliability of an engineering expert's testimony "to the extent relevant." *See also Sheehan v. Daily Racing Form*, 104 F.3d 940 (7th Cir.1997), *cert. denied*, 521 U.S. 1104, 117 S.Ct. 2480, 138 L.Ed.2d 989 (1997) (statistician's analysis of and affidavit about employer list showing ages of employees slated for retention did not meet *Daubert* standards for admissibility due to failure to account for relevant variables and other defects reflecting lesser degree of care than would be used in scientific work).

But neither F.R.E. 702 nor *Daubert* allows the admission of expert testimony that is not helpful to the jury or draws inferences or reaches conclusions that the jury is competent to reach without the expert's testimony. *See, e.g., Nichols v. American Nat'l Ins. Co.*, 154 F.3d 875, 884 (8th Cir. 1998) (plain error to admit testimony that is a thinly veiled comment on a witness' credibility). And lay witnesses may not be permitted under F.R.E. 701(b) to opine about an employer's discriminatory motivation unless they have personal knowledge of facts giving rise to the adverse employment action plaintiff challenges. *Hester v. BIC Corp.*, 225 F.3d 178 (2d Cir.2000).

A district court's decision on admissibility of any evidence, including expert testimony, is reviewed for an abuse of discretion. *See Griffin v. City of Opa–Locka*, 261 F.3d 1295, 1301–02 (11th Cir.2001), *cert. denied* 535 U.S. 1033, 122 S.Ct. 1789, 152 L.Ed.2d 648 (2002) (no abuse of discretion to admit expert testimony on post-assault behavior of rape or sexual harassment victims, where expert did not comment on the particular plaintiff's own credibility, veracity, or version of events); *Swan v. Interstate Brands Corp.*, 333 F.3d 863 (8th Cir.2003) (exclusion of evidence impeaching employer witness in age discrimination action not clear and prejudicial abuse of discretion because evidence was not necessarily proper impeachment and may have been unduly prejudicial to employer); *Jones v. TEK Industries, Inc.*, 319 F.3d 355 (8th Cir.2003) (district court did not abuse discretion in admitting evidence of Title VII plaintiffs' felony convictions because evidence enabled jury to evaluate credibility of testimony of plaintiffs, state prisoners); *Anderson v. WBMG–42*, 253 F.3d 561 (11th Cir.2001) (exclusion of evidence of discipline received by compensation employer of different race not abuse of discretion because not substantially prejudicial to plaintiff); *Munoz v. Orr*, 200 F.3d 291, 301–302 (5th Cir.2000), *cert. denied*, 531 U.S. 812, 121 S.Ct. 45, 148 L.Ed.2d 15 (2000) (no abuse of discretion to exclude testimony of expert who failed to consider significant variables other than national origin and gender); *General Elec. Co. v. Joiner*, 522 U.S. 136, 118 S.Ct. 512, 139 L.Ed.2d 508 (1997) (reversing Eleventh Circuit which applied a more stringent standard of review; "while the Federal Rules of Evidence allow district courts to admit a somewhat broader range of scientific testimony ... [after *Daubert*] than would have been admissible under *Frye*, they leave in place the 'gatekeeper' role of the trial judge in screening such evidence"). *See also S.M. v. J.K.*, 262 F.3d 914 (9th Cir.2001) (no abuse of discretion to exclude evidence of plaintiff's sexual history where employer failed to file motion to introduce that evidence under seal, as required by F.R.E. 412(c)).

16. *See, e.g, Romano v. Rockwell Int'l, Inc.*, 14 Cal.4th 479, 59 Cal.Rptr.2d 20, 926 P.2d 1114 (1996) (regarding employment discrimination claim under California law, rejecting strict federal interpretation of "trigger" date for statute of limitations, under which charge-filing period begins to run when employee learns he will be discharged, holding instead that the clock does not start running until the employee is actually discharged).

damages relief against a state in view of the Supreme Court's rather restrictive interpretations of the Eleventh Amendment—although the state as such may no longer be sued under § 1983 in either state or federal court.[17] A given state may authorize attorney's fee awards to be enhanced for contingency, at least on state law claims, contrary to the apparent view of the Supreme Court respecting claims under the Reconstruction Acts or Title VII.[18] Federal decisionmaking may be pretermitted altogether or severely delayed by, respectively, the *Younger* and *Pullman* abstention doctrines.[19] And a plaintiff may choose state court because his action includes a colorable but tenuous pendent state law claim that a federal court might construe more narrowly because of its duty to decide in accordance with its prediction of the resolution that would be reached by the state's highest court.

State courts may not decline to entertain a Reconstruction Act claim in the absence of a valid excuse, i.e., one that refuses jurisdiction because of a neutral state rule of judicial administration. When a state court has entertained actions of a nature similar to the Reconstruction Act claim before it, the court may not discriminate against the federal claim. Where the defendants in the action would be subject to liability in the same action in a federal court, the state court may not grant them immunity.[20]

In one instance the Court has gone even further to hold that a state court may not bar a § 1983 action through application of the forum's notice-of-claim statute, even though that statute would have precluded litigation against a government entity on a wide variety of state claims as well. The Court concluded that compliance with the state statute would place an undue burden on a civil rights plaintiff by forcing her to comply with a requirement she would not face in federal court. In a reverse-*Erie* twist, the Court ruled the notice-of-claim statute superseded by virtue of the Supremacy Clause because it might produce different outcomes depending on whether the litigation were pursued in state or federal court.[21] Subsequent state appellate decisions have plumbed the limits of *Felder*. On one hand, may a state court, without discrimination against federal law claims, apply its own restrictions on obtaining orders allowing substituted service of process when those standards are more stringent than the requirements of due process and the Federal Rules of Civil Procedure?[22] On the other, may a state court refuse, consistent with its general practice, to afford a public official an immediate interlocutory appeal from the denial of that defendant's pretrial motion based on qualified immunity, even though the federal practice in such circum-

17. See discussion of *Will v. Michigan Dep't of State Police* in Chapter 2.

18. *Rendine v. Pantzer*, 141 N.J. 292, 661 A.2d 1202 (1995). *See* § 4.10, *supra*, for the Supreme Court's dim view of contingency enhancement under the Civil Rights attorney's Fee Act, 42 U.S.C.A. § 1988.

19. These doctrines are discussed in Sections C, D and E above.

20. *Howlett v. Rose*, 496 U.S. 356, 110 S.Ct. 2430, 110 L.Ed.2d 332 (1990).

21. *Felder v. Casey*, 487 U.S. 131, 108 S.Ct. 2302, 101 L.Ed.2d 123 (1988).

22. *See Britt v. Smith*, 446 Mich. 880, 522 N.W.2d 633 (1994), *cert. denied*, 513 U.S. 1151, 115 S.Ct. 1103, 130 L.Ed.2d 1070 (1995).

stances would be to treat the ruling as a "collateral order" subject to immediate appellate review?[23] The Supreme Court has held that it may, distinguishing *Felder* on the ground that a state's rule banning interlocutory appeals from denials of pretrial qualified immunity motions is a neutral rule regarding court administration, not targeted against civil rights defendants, and that it is less outcome determinative than the state notice-of-claim statute at issue in *Felder*.[24] The Court also asserted that the *Mitchell v. Forsyth* doctrine allowing federal court defendants such interlocutory appeals[25] represented only an interpretation of the general "final decision" section of the federal judicial code,[26] so that states are free to interpret as they please their own statutes governing the finality of lower court decisions. The residue of *Felder* and *Fankell* viewed together is that plaintiffs who pick state court get all of its advantages free of the disadvantages of filing a notice of claim, while defendants who find themselves in state court involuntarily are deprived of the tactically significant, policy-driven procedural advantage of an interlocutory appeal from an order denying them qualified immunity, an advantage they would have in federal court. Despite the dubious soundness of the Court's purported distinctions,[27] in the end the *Fankell*

23. *Turner v. Giles*, 264 Ga. 812, 450 S.E.2d 421 (1994), *cert. denied*, 514 U.S. 1108, 115 S.Ct. 1959, 131 L.Ed.2d 851 (1995) (denying collateral order review). *Cf. Nelson v. County of Allegheny*, 60 F.3d 1010 (3d Cir.1995), *cert. denied*, 516 U.S. 1173, 116 S.Ct. 1266, 134 L.Ed.2d 213 (1996) (observing that relevant state court practice was to permit immediate interlocutory review of order denying class certification, contrary to the federal practice then dictated by *Coopers & Lybrand v. Livesay*, 437 U.S. 463, 98 S.Ct. 2454, 57 L.Ed.2d 351 (1978)). The holding in *Coopers & Lybrand* was abrogated in 1998 by an amendment to Federal Rule of Civil Procedure 23(f), which permits a district court to certify for immediate appeal an order granting or denying class certification. The appellate court has discretion whether to hear the appeal. See the discussion in § 5.110 *infra*.

24. *Johnson v. Fankell*, 520 U.S. 911, 117 S.Ct. 1800, 138 L.Ed.2d 108 (1997).

25. The doctrine is discussed in detail in §§ 2.22 and 2.23.

26. 28 U.S.C.A. § 1291.

27. It was far from clear in *Felder* that, as Justice Brennan's opinion for the Court asserted, Wisconsin's notice of claim requirement was targeted against civil rights plaintiffs; it presented procedural roadblocks not only to them but also to the far greater number of ordinary tort plaintiffs suing local government in state court. Civil rights defendants seem similarly untargeted by the Idaho interpretation of its final decision rule at issue in *Johnson v. Fankell*, a rule that usually denies interlocutory appeals to all defendants in Idaho's courts. Nor was it evident, as Justice Brennan's opinion asserted in *Felder*, that Wisconsin's requirement was significantly outcome determinative to the detriment of plaintiffs. The claim statute served as a procedural obstacle only in cases where plaintiff's counsel had *elected* to assert a § 1983 claim in state rather than federal court, and where counsel may therefore have been aware of that requirement and negotiated its prerequisites to suit. For example, the Court had earlier held that a state's failure to provide for tolling of a § 1983 limitations period set by state law did not undermine the general § 1983 policies of compensation and deterrence sufficiently to enable a federal court to fashion one. *Board of Regents v. Tomanio*, 446 U.S. 478, 100 S.Ct. 1790, 64 L.Ed.2d 440 (1980), discussed in § 5.73, *infra*. By contrast, the application of the Idaho rule to civil rights defendants in Idaho state courts may significantly impair their defense as a practical matter, for it deprives them of the multiple tactical advantages of taking one or even multiple pretrial appeals. The Court's position that the *Mitchell* doctrine merely interprets a federal procedural statute is simply baffling. In a series of decisions beginning in the mid–1980's the Court frankly admitted that it developed the doctrine for a number of policy reasons specific to § 1983. See §§ 2.22 and 2.23, *supra*. It is difficult to see why those specific policies would fail to trigger federal preemption while the gener-

decision does little damage to the substantive, defendant-friendly policies underlying the *Mitchell* interlocutory appeal. While plaintiffs will now have an incentive to file in state court in states that deny defendants interlocutory appeals of this kind, individual defendants desirous of capitalizing on the ever-increasing number of tactical advantages surrounding assertion of the qualified immunity defense in federal court may, and presumably will, simply remove the action. Section 5.50, turns to that subject. Although the Court later agreed to consider further the extent to which state courts may apply their own law in actions under § 1983, after oral argument the Court dismissed, finding the writ of certiorari had been improvidently granted.[28]

Finally, there is the substantial risk that selection of a state forum will result in an adjudication triggering claim preclusion (res judicata) or issue preclusion (collateral estoppel) that would wholly or partially pretermit the plaintiff's subsequent resort to federal court. These possibilities will be discussed in Section U, below, beginning with § 5.116.

§ 5.46 Constitutional Tort Claims Under State Law

At least 21 states and Puerto Rico have recognized a claim for violations of state constitutional law–17 through an implied cause of action approved by the highest court of the state, and 4 others by statute.[1] Each of these states recognizes a claim against state government itself, filling the remedial gap created when the Supreme Court in *Will v. Michigan Dep't of State Police* held that no state or unit of state government is a "person" within the meaning of § 1983.[2]

In this way a cause of action squarely grounded on an alleged violation of a state's constitution can afford a remedy not available under federal law. Moreover, so long as the action does not meet the requirements for complete diversity (or, if so, one of the defendants is a citizen of the forum state), and provided no substantial federal law claim is alleged, such a claim should prove nonremovable as well. This ensures the plaintiff a state forum as a distinct and quite possibly advantageous alternative to the federal court to which a defendant may always remove a claim under § 1983.

There are several potentially dispositive procedural and remedial differences that might affect a plaintiff's choice to proceed under § 1983 (in which case the action would most likely end up in federal court through removal, even if the plaintiff initially filed in state court) or only under a state law constitutional tort theory in state court. Most dramati-

al remedial goals relied on to trigger preemption in *Felder* would.

28. *City of Tarrant, Ala. v. Jefferson*, 682 So.2d 29 (Ala.1996), *cert. dismissed*, 522 U.S. 75, 118 S.Ct. 481, 139 L.Ed.2d 433 (1997).

§ 5.46

1. The authors are indebted to Gail Donoghue and Jonathan Edelstein's *Life After Brown: The Future of State Constitutional Tort Actions in New York*, 42 N.Y.U.L.Rev. 447 (1998), for the information relied on in this subsection.

2. *Will* is discussed in detail in Chapter 2.

cally, two populous states, Illinois and New York, appear to permit the plaintiff to establish the government's liability for a violation of state constitutional law on the basis of simple vicarious liability or respondeat superior.[3] In other words plaintiffs in those states are free of the stringent *Monell* § 1983 doctrine[4] which requires proof that the government defendant at its highest levels encouraged, promoted, or ratified and thus ultimately "caused" the individual agent's unconstitutional act or omission as a matter of official government "policy." Most of the states to decide the question, by contrast, have adopted proof requirements similar to *Monell*'s.[5] Second, summary judgment practice may not be as defendant-favorable as under the federal courts' practice in cases under § 1983.[6] But third, the attorney's fees payable by defendants that are uniformly available to prevailing parties in actions under § 1983 may not be authorized under state law.

Not all of the states recognizing a state constitutional law claim against state government provide a similar remedy for constitutional torts committed by individual state agents. The remedial necessity that assertedly justifies a state law claim against the state itself[7] is absent in that situation, since § 1983 is available against those defendants.[8] States that do recognize such claims against individual state officers are not required to mimic the extraordinarily generous absolute or qualified immunities the Supreme Court has crafted for defendant government officers in actions under § 1983.[9] Most state courts that have considered the issue do afford individual government officers performing discretionary executive or administrative functions the same broad version of

3. *Brown v. New York*, 89 N.Y.2d 172, 652 N.Y.S.2d 223, 674 N.E.2d 1129 (1996); *Newell v. City of Elgin*, 34 Ill.App.3d 719, 340 N.E.2d 344, 347–48 (1976).

4. *Monell v. Department of Soc. Servs.*, 436 U.S. 658, 98 S.Ct. 2018, 56 L.Ed.2d 611 (1978). *Monell* and its progeny are discussed in detail in Chapter 2.

5. *See* cases cited at Donoghue and Edelstein, 42 N.Y.U.L.Rev. at 523 n.383.

6. For an illustration of the Supreme Court's own encouragement of the motion, *see Crawford–El v. Britton*, 523 U.S. 574, 118 S.Ct. 1584, 140 L.Ed.2d 759 (1998).

7. Courts implying a state law cause of action against the state have commonly reasoned by analogy to *Bivens v. Six Unknown Named Agents of Fed. Bureau of Narcotics*, 403 U.S. 388, 389, 91 S.Ct. 1999, 2001, 29 L.Ed.2d 619 (1971). There the Supreme Court implied a civil damages remedy available against an individual federal agent for a Fourth Amendment violation, in large part because § 1983 did not reach the case (for want of action "under color of" state law) and the Court considered a damages remedy essential to enforce the constitutional right at issue. *Bivens* has subsequently been extended to permit implied claims against federal officers for violations of the Fifth (including federal due process, with its equal protection "component"), Sixth and Eighth Amendments. *See* Donoghue and Edelstein, 42 N.Y.U.L.Rev. at 485 n.180 (citing cases). But the Court has subsequently declined to imply a similar claim for relief for constitutional violations against the U.S. government itself. *Federal Deposit Ins. Corp. v. Meyer*, 510 U.S. 471, 114 S.Ct. 996, 127 L.Ed.2d 308 (1994). And the Court has sharply constricted the reach of *Bivens* by holding that remedy impliedly precluded when Congress by statute has provided alternative relief for the violation in question, even when the procedures or remedies provided fall well short of those available under *Bivens*. Donoghue and Edelstein, 42 N.Y.U.L.Rev. at 487–488. *See also* § 2.22, *supra*.

8. *See, e.g., Corum v. University of North Carolina*, 330 N.C. 761, 413 S.E.2d 276 (1992); Donoghue & Edelstein, 42 N.Y.U.L.Rev. at 464–465 and 528–529.

9. *See* Chapter 2 for a full discussion of absolute and qualified immunity in § 1983 actions.

"objectively reasonable" qualified immunity that the Supreme Court accords them in defense of § 1983 claims. But other forms of immunity more faithful to the common law are a possibility, including those that require the defendant officer to establish her subjective good faith.[10]

If immunity from liability for a state constitutional tort is available, the procedures for asserting it may be less favorable to the defendant than they are in federal court under § 1983. There the individual defendant sued for damages would routinely move to dismiss, move for summary judgment or make both motions on the basis of qualified immunity; and if either or both motions were denied, she would be entitled to take one or more interlocutory appeals to seek review of the denial. By contrast, if the state court system would ordinarily not allow an interlocutory appeal from an order of the same general kind, the state court would not have to provide one for the individual officer sued for a state constitutional tort.[11] In addition, federal courts commonly facilitate the defendant's assertion of immunity by postponing merits discovery pending resolution of preliminary legal questions related to the defense;[12] some state courts will not, even if they do recognize some version of immunity.

§§ 5.47–5.49 [Reserved]

J. REMOVAL

§ 5.50 In General

Because state courts enjoy concurrent jurisdiction over both Reconstruction Act claims and claims under modern employment discrimination statutes, it is important to consider whether the defendant may defeat plaintiff's initial forum choice by removing such an action from state to federal court. Almost any claim arising under the Reconstruction Acts, Title VII, ADEA, ADA and EPA is, at least when pleaded alone, removable under 28 U.S.C.A. § 1441(a). That statute provides for the removal of "any civil action . . . of which the district courts of the United States have original jurisdiction" to the federal district court that embraces the venue of the pending action in state court.[1] Since original jurisdiction in virtually all actions in which a civil rights or employment discrimination claim is asserted could have been founded on § 1331,[2] the federal courts must also entertain these federal law claims, and, under § 1367, may also hear state law supplemental claims as well.[3] The first

10. Donoghue and Edelstein, N.Y.U.L.Rev. at 524–527.

11. This conclusion follows a fortiori from the Supreme Court's holding in *Johnson v. Fankell*, 520 U.S. 911, 117 S.Ct. 1800, 138 L.Ed.2d 108 (1997) (state court need not provide interlocutory appeal even when claim is under § 1983).

12. *See Crawford–El v. Britton*, 523 U.S. 574, 118 S.Ct. 1584, 140 L.Ed.2d 759 (1998).

§ 5.50

1. Except as otherwise provided by Congress. *See* 28 U.S.C.A. § 1441(a).

2. *See* § 5.6, *supra*.

3. A case falls with § 1331 original jurisdiction when, under the "well-pleaded

sentence of § 1441(b) confirms that because such actions contain at least one claim based on alleged violations of a federal constitutional or statutory right, they are "removable without regard to the citizenship or residency of the parties."[4]

As amended in 1991, § 1441(c) provides expansive authorization for the defendant to remove the "entire case," even when the federal civil rights or employment discrimination claim "is joined with one or more otherwise non-removable claims or causes of action."[5] This is true even if the case contains claims for monetary damages against a state or state officer in his official capacity (claims which are forbidden to federal courts by the Eleventh Amendment)[6] or claims calling for a deferential review of state administrative proceedings.[7]

In *Wisconsin Dep't of Corr. v. Schacht*,[8] the Court rejected plaintiff's contention that the presence of a claim against a state for monetary damages barred removal to federal court.[9] Schacht, a state employee, sued in state court the state of Wisconsin and his supervisors in both their official and individual capacities. Following removal, the district court dismissed the claims against the state and the official capacity claims on the basis of the Eleventh Amendment, and granted summary judgment on the personal capacity claims. On appeal, the Seventh Circuit sua sponte determined that removal was improper because the case contained claims forbidden to the federal courts by the Eleventh Amendment. The Supreme Court reversed, holding that even though a state's assertion of its Eleventh Amendment immunity defense in the district court would bar that court from hearing the claims against Wisconsin and the supervisors in their official capacities, neither the presence of these claims nor the proper assertion of the immunity defense destroys the original jurisdiction the district court has over the

complaint" rule, the plaintiff's own cause of action is based on federal law, *see Louisville & Nashville R.R. Co. v. Mottley*, 211 U.S. 149, 152, 29 S.Ct. 42, 43, 53 L.Ed. 126 (1908). Thus, a case may not be removed on the basis of a federal defense, at least unless Congress has completely preempted the field of law, as it has with ERISA. *See Rivet v. Regions Bank of La.*, 522 U.S. 470, 476–77, 118 S.Ct. 921, 925–26, 139 L.Ed.2d 912 (1998) (holding that although artful pleading doctrine may allow removal where federal law completely preempts a plaintiff's state-law claim, the affirmative defense of claim preclusion will not support removal jurisdiction) (citing *Metropolitan Life Ins. Co. v. Taylor*, 481 U.S. 58, 107 S.Ct. 1542, 95 L.Ed.2d 55 (1987) (ERISA) and *Avco Corp. v. Aero Lodge No. 735, Int'l Ass'n. of Machinists and Aerospace Workers*, 390 U.S. 557, 88 S.Ct. 1235, 20 L.Ed.2d 126 (1968) (Labor Management Relations Act)).

4. Because the claim retains its federal character after removal from state court, the characterization of the limitations period remains a question of federal law. Thus the same statute of limitations applies whether the § 1983 claim is heard in state or federal court. *Kuhnle Brothers, Inc. v. County of Geauga, Ohio*, 103 F.3d 516 (6th Cir.1997).

5. Subsection 1441(c) goes on to provide that, upon removal, "the district court may determine all issues therein, or, in its discretion, may remand all matters in which State law predominates."

6. *See Wisconsin Dep't of Corr. v. Schacht*, 524 U.S. 381, 118 S.Ct. 2047, 141 L.Ed.2d 364 (1998).

7. *See City of Chicago v. International Coll. of Surgeons*, 522 U.S. 156, 118 S.Ct. 523, 139 L.Ed.2d 525 (1997).

8. 524 U.S. 381, 118 S.Ct. 2047, 141 L.Ed.2d 364 (1998).

9. *See also Detroit Edison Co. v. Michigan Dep't of Envtl. Quality*, 29 F.Supp.2d 786 (E.D.Mich.1998)

personal capacity claims. The Court in *Schacht* expressly states that Eleventh Amendment immunity is a waivable affirmative defense that a court "can ignore" if the state does not assert it.[10] And Justice Kennedy, concurring, opined that the act of removal by a state or sub-state entity eligible to claim the defense constituted such a waiver. Indeed, a subsequent Supreme Court decision has unanimously adopted Justice Kennedy's view. But the holding is limited to state law claims that the state would have been required to defend in its own courts because it had waived its sovereign immunity.[11] So, if the state has not waived its immunity respecting a federal law claim, merely removing the action is unlikely to waive its Eleventh Amendment objection. On the other hand, only a few months before *Schacht*, the Court held that the affirmative defense of claim preclusion will not support removal of a case alleging only state law claims. That decision applied in a straightforward way the established *Mottley* principle that the plaintiff's own claim must arise under federal law.[12]

In *City of Chicago v. International College of Surgeons*,[13] the Court held that removal jurisdiction could be exercised over supplemental state law claims even when those claims called for a deferential review of state administrative findings. In *International College*, the plaintiff moved for a remand of its suit challenging on constitutional and state law grounds the Chicago Landmark Commission's denial of demolition permits after the Commission had removed based on federal question subject matter jurisdiction under § 1331. Plaintiff argued that because the suit called inter alia for a deferential, on-the-record judicial review of state administrative findings, a claim that normally lies in state circuit court, the action as a whole could not fall within the ambit of § 1441(a)—that is, it was not a "civil action ... of which the district courts of the United States have original jurisdiction." The Court clarified first, that when

10. 118 S.Ct. at 2052. But *need* not ignore. *Higgins v. State of Mississippi*, 217 F.3d 951, 953–54 (7th Cir.2000). *See also Branson Sch. Dist. RE–82 v. Romer*, 161 F.3d 619 (10th Cir.1998), *cert. denied*, 526 U.S. 1068, 119 S.Ct. 1461, 143 L.Ed.2d 546 (1999) (stating that *Schacht* holds that Eleventh Amendment immunity is "in the nature of an affirmative defense that may be asserted or waived at a state's discretion"); *Detroit Edison Co. v. Michigan Dep't of Envtl. Quality*, 29 F.Supp.2d 786, 790–91 (E.D.Mich.1998) (same).

The *Schacht* Court did not specifically address whether removal constitutes waiver. At least one circuit has so held. *See Sutton v. Utah State Sch. for Deaf and Blind*, 173 F.3d 1226 (10th Cir.1999) (holding that removal by a state constitutes an implicit waiver of Eleventh Amendment immunity). The opinion in *Detroit Edison Co.* takes the analysis one step further. If the state waives its Eleventh Amendment immunity defense through removal, § 1441(c) does not come into play and the federal court has no discretion under § 1441(c) to remand "matters in which State law predominates."

11. *Lapides v. Board of Regents of Univ. System of Georgia*, 535 U.S. 613, 122 S.Ct. 1640, 152 L.Ed.2d 806 (2002). *See Bank of Lake Tahoe v. Bank of America*, 318 F.3d 914 (9th Cir.2003) (state waived Eleventh Amendment immunity from state law claims by joining in co-defendant's effort to remove action to federal court).

12. *See Rivet v. Regions Bank of La.*, 522 U.S. 470, 476–77, 118 S.Ct. 921, 925–26, 139 L.Ed.2d 912 (1998), discussed *supra*.

13. 522 U.S. 156, 118 S.Ct. 523, 139 L.Ed.2d 525 (1997). *See also Lacks v. Ferguson Reorganized Sch. Dist. R–2*, 147 F.3d 718, 721 (8th Cir.1998), *cert. denied*, 526 U.S. 1012, 119 S.Ct. 1158, 143 L.Ed.2d 223 (1999) (relying on *Int'l College* to uphold removal of case involving claim challenging school board's administrative finding).

there is at least one federal claim (a claim arising under federal law under § 1331), all other transactionally related claims within the case fall within the federal court's supplemental jurisdiction as defined by § 1367.[14] Second, the Court rejected any suggestion that an exception to § 1367 exists for claims requiring a review of administrative findings.[15] Noting that district courts routinely conduct deferential review pursuant to their original jurisdiction over federal questions involving federal administrative actions, the Court stated that "[n]othing in § 1367(a) suggests district courts are without supplemental jurisdiction over claims seeking precisely the same brand of review of local [or state] administrative determinations."[16] The issue that must be decided by a district court, then, is whether the claim challenging the state administrative finding is properly within the district court's supplemental jurisdiction. The Court acknowledged, however, that district courts, after exercising subject matter jurisdiction, may be "obligated not to decide state law claims (or to stay their adjudication) where one of the abstention doctrines . . . applies."[17]

To grasp the rationale of these cases, recall that § 1441(a) sets out the threshold precondition to removal: that the action brought in state court be one "of which the district courts of the United States [would] have original jurisdiction."[18] The scope of a federal district court's *original* jurisdiction includes not only questions based on federal law under § 1331, however, but also related state law claims under § 1367(a) and (c), as amended in 1990.[19] Section 1367(a) extends federal courts' supplemental jurisdiction to state law "claims that are so related to" the federal question claim or claims on which original jurisdiction is founded that they "form part of the same case or controversy under Article III." Further, the second sentence of § 1367(a) extends that supplemental jurisdiction to such transactionally related state law claims even when they are asserted against different *parties*, i.e., parties against whom the plaintiff asserts no claim under federal law. As a result, common state tort law claims like intentional infliction of emotional distress and negligent retention [of a supervisory or managerial employee] may be filed as "pendent," in the pre–1990 terminology, or "supplemental," in the argot of the current § 1367(a), to the federal question claim on which federal jurisdiction is founded, provided only they are transactionally related to the degree that Article III requires under the Court's opinion in *United Mine Workers v. Gibbs*.[20] Finally, § 1367(c) serves as a discretionary check on the jurisdiction available under subsection (a). It authorizes the district courts to decline jurisdiction

14. *Id.* at 164–65, 118 S.Ct. at 529–30.

15. *Id.* at 166–67, 118 S.Ct. at 530.

16. *Id.* at 166, 118 S.Ct. at 530.

17. *Id.* at 174, 118 S.Ct. at 534.

18. A claim arising under a federal statute does not lose its removable character merely because the statute gives the plaintiff a choice of concurrent state court jurisdiction, even when it does so through language saying an action "may be maintained" in state court. *Breuer v. Jim's Concrete of Brevard, Inc.*, 538 U.S. 691, 123 S.Ct. 1882, 155 L.Ed.2d 923 (2003) (claim under Fair Labor Standards Act).

19. See § 5.40, *supra*.

20. *Gibbs* is discussed in § 5.40, *supra*.

over related state law claims where there are novel or complex state law issues; where state law predominates; where all claims founded on federal question jurisdiction have been dismissed, for example for failure to state a claim or on summary judgment; or under "exceptional circumstances" that present "compelling reasons" to decline to hear the state law claim.

Thus the federal district court in *International College* could adjudicate the state law claims challenging the administrative findings of the Landmark Commission under § 1367. And the mere presence of claims that are forbidden to the district court by a waivable defense such as Eleventh Amendment immunity (*Schacht*) or claim preclusion (*Rivet*) will not defeat the initial removal of the entire case because the court will then dismiss the claims that it is without power to hear.

Viewed in this light, what are the "otherwise non-removable claims" that 28 U.S.C.A. § 1441(c) says may be removed as part of "the entire case"? Essentially they are state law claims that are either insufficiently related, within the meaning of Article III or § 1367(a), to a jurisdictionally foundational federal question claim, or are sufficiently related but subject to discretionary dismissal under § 1367(c). The facial contrast between § 1441(c) and § 1367(a) might suggest that the scope of federal removal jurisdiction in these situations is broader than the scope of federal original jurisdiction—in other words, that the civil rights or employment discrimination defendant sued in state court has more recourse to federal court for ultimate trial and disposition of an entire action containing loosely related or unrelated state law claims than does the plaintiff who might wish to commence such an action in federal court. The contrast disappears, however, if the part of § 1441(c) that purports to authorize federal courts to hear removed state law claims that are "not otherwise removable" (because they are not part of the same Article III "case") is unconstitutional.[21] The only remaining respect in which federal question removal jurisdiction under § 1441 appears to exceed federal question original jurisdiction under § 1331 as supplemented by § 1367 is that § 1441(c) does not cabin the district judge's discretion to decline removal jurisdiction to the four circumstances spelled out in § 1367(c).

But what if the sole federal question claim on which original, and hence removal, jurisdiction is grounded fails not on the merits but because of a "quasi-jurisdictional" bar like sovereign immunity? Can it still serve as the neck on which related state law claims may pend? A decision holds that it cannot. Where the "stem" federal question claims against state officers sued in their official capacity were held barred by the *Hans v. Louisiana*[22] extension of Eleventh Amendment immunity, a

21. To this extent, § 1441(c) would appear to be authorizing federal subject matter jurisdiction that breaks even the flexible bounds of Article III as declared by the Court in *Gibbs*. *See* 136 Cong.Rec. S17581 (daily ed. October 27, 1990) (analysis by Sen. Grassley) (suggesting that the removal court must remand an insufficiently related state law claim).

22. 134 U.S. 1, 10 S.Ct. 504, 33 L.Ed. 842 (1890). The Eleventh Amendment and

panel of the Seventh Circuit held that related state law claims could not be heard by a federal district court after removal for lack of the "original jurisdiction" precondition to removal jurisdiction under § 1441(a).[23] The Supreme Court had earlier held that where the federal question claim on which removal hangs is voluntarily dismissed by the plaintiff, the removal court has the alternative of remanding rather than outright dismissing the state law claim, even though the removal statute did not provide that authority in express terms.[24] The statute has since been amended to provide expressly that if "at any time before final judgment" the court concludes subject matter jurisdiction is lacking, the case "shall" be remanded.[25] Thus while it was formerly uncertain if the federal court had any alternative to dismissal when the principal jurisdictional basis for removal disappeared, it now appears that remand is the only option in such circumstances.

In the foregoing discussion we have been assuming, as is often true with civil rights and employment discrimination claims between parties who have dealt with one another first-hand within one state, that not all requirements of the federal diversity statute, 28 U.S.C.A. § 1332, are satisfied. If, however, all plaintiffs are of diverse citizenship from all defendants, and if more than $75,000.00 is at stake, a federal court must exercise removal jurisdiction under § 1441(a) over *all* claims in the action, including those based on state law, whether or not they are interrelated.[26] Removal in "pure" diversity actions—those in which there is *no* claim founded on a federal question—is also possible,[27] but is limited by the second sentence of § 1441(b), which renders removal unavailable if any of the properly joined and served defendants is a citizen of the forum state.

Congress also created a special removal statute, 28 U.S.C.A. § 1443,[28] available for situations where a state proceeding, usually a criminal prosecution, is initiated in order to harass or intimidate a defendant for exercising his civil rights. Section 1443 removals, although rarely permitted, have a singular procedural advantage. An order remanding a civil rights action specially removed pursuant to § 1443 is immediately reviewable; an order remanding an action removed under § 1441 on the ground of a lack of federal court subject matter jurisdiction is not.[29]

the *Hans* decision are discussed in § 5.35, *supra*.

23. *Frances J. v. Wright*, 19 F.3d 337, 340–341 (7th Cir.1994), *cert. denied*, 513 U.S. 876, 115 S.Ct. 204, 130 L.Ed.2d 134 (1994).

24. *Carnegie–Mellon Univ. v. Cohill*, 484 U.S. 343, 108 S.Ct. 614, 98 L.Ed.2d 720 (1988).

25. 28 U.S.C.A. § 1447(c).

26. *See, e.g., Cemer v. Marathon Oil Co.*, 583 F.2d 830 (6th Cir.1978) (affirming that district court lacked discretion to dismiss state law claims where requirements of diversity are met).

27. *See Scheeler v. Crane Co.*, 21 F.3d 791 (8th Cir.1994) (civil rights employment claim under Iowa law).

28. Another special removal statute allows federal agencies and officers to remove any civil action commenced against them in a state court. *See* 28 U.S.C.A. § 1442.

29. *See* 28 U.S.C.A. § 1447(d). *See Quackenbush v. Allstate Ins. Co.*, 517 U.S. 706, 116 S.Ct. 1712, 135 L.Ed.2d 1 (1996) (only remands based on grounds specified

Any special removal advantage flowing from Section 1443 may be more apparent than real. Section 1443 has been construed almost out of existence. Subsection (1) provides for the removal before trial of any state action pending against any person "who is denied or cannot enforce" in state court a right under "any law providing for the equal civil rights of citizens." The Supreme Court has ruled that the denied right authorizing removal under § 1443 must arise from federal laws securing racial equality; alleged violations of other constitutional or statutory civil rights, including those protecting free speech and due process, will not suffice.[30] The asserted denial of rights must also take place in the state's courts.[31]

Even more restrictively, the denial of the racial equality right must usually be dictated by the facial terms of a state statute, for example a law explicitly barring African–Americans from serving on juries.[32] It is insufficient to allege that the state courts will not provide a fair trial because, for example, they have historically practiced discrimination or the subject prosecution is racially motivated.[33] The Court has insisted that the denial be "manifest in a formal expression of state law," for two reasons: first, so that the predicted denial by the state court of federal civil rights regarding racial equality will "appear with relative clarity prior to trial"; second, so that federal judges may avoid "the unseemly process of prejudging their brethren of the state courts."[34] A limited

in § 1447(c) are immune from review by virtue of § 1447(d); the grounds listed by 1447(c), in turn, are defects in removal procedure and an absence of basic subject matter jurisdiction; therefore a remand grounded in an *abstention* doctrine is not subject to the review prohibition of 1447(d) and is immediately reviewable under the collateral order exception to 28 U.S.C.A. Sec. 1291, the default provision that ordinarily allows appeals only from "final" federal district court decisions). *See also Hernandez v. Seminole County, Fla.*, 334 F.3d 1233 (11th Cir.2003) (remand based on district court finding of defect in removal procedure, after concluding that defendant who withheld consent from removal was not nominal or fraudulently joined party, was on a § 1447(c) ground and accordingly immune from review by virtue of § 1447(d)); *Cook v. Wikler*, 320 F.3d 431 (3d Cir. 20003); *In re Excel Corp.*, 106 F.3d 1197 (5th Cir.), *cert. denied sub nom. Rendon v. Excel Corp.*, 522 U.S. 859, 118 S.Ct. 159, 139 L.Ed.2d 104 (1997) (relying on *Quackenbush* to permit review by mandamus of remand order predicated on a lack of subject matter jurisdiction under 28 U.S.C.A. § 1445(c), as opposed to one of the grounds enumerated in § 1447(c)).

30. *State of Georgia v. Rachel*, 384 U.S. 780, 86 S.Ct. 1783, 16 L.Ed.2d 925 (1966); *City of Greenwood v. Peacock*, 384 U.S. 808, 86 S.Ct. 1800, 16 L.Ed.2d 944 (1966). *See also Johnson v. Mississippi*, 421 U.S. 213, 95 S.Ct. 1591, 44 L.Ed.2d 121 (1975); *Colorado v. Lopez*, 919 F.2d 131 (10th Cir.1990); *New York v. Galamison*, 342 F.2d 255 (2d Cir.1965), *cert. denied*, 380 U.S. 977, 85 S.Ct. 1342, 14 L.Ed.2d 272 (1965).

31. *State of Georgia v. Rachel*, 384 U.S. 780, 86 S.Ct. 1783, 16 L.Ed.2d 925 (1966) (upholding removal of criminal-trespass prosecutions as violating a specific right of racial equality provided by Civil Rights Act of 1964).

32. *See Strauder v. West Virginia*, 100 U.S. (10 Otto) 303, 25 L.Ed. 664 (1900).

33. *State of Georgia v. Rachel*, 384 U.S. 780, 86 S.Ct. 1783, 16 L.Ed.2d 925 (1966); *City of Greenwood v. Peacock*, 384 U.S. 808, 86 S.Ct. 1800, 16 L.Ed.2d 944 (1966); *Doe v. Berry*, 967 F.2d 1255 (8th Cir.1992), *cert. denied*, 507 U.S. 911, 113 S.Ct. 1258, 122 L.Ed.2d 656 (1993).

34. *State of Georgia v. Rachel*, 384 U.S. 780, 86 S.Ct. 1783, 16 L.Ed.2d 925 (1966). These restrictions on the narrow scope of removal under § 1443 seem to have been disregarded in *Borough of West Mifflin v. Lancaster*, 45 F.3d 780, 784 (3d Cir.1995), which, notwithstanding § 1447(d), approved appellate jurisdiction to review a remand order simply because the action was under § 1983 and therefore removal

exception to this requirement comes into play where a federal civil rights statute forbids even the *institution* of efforts to punish federally protected activity; in that event the mere commencement of the state court action denies the protected right, even absent any formal expression of state positive law.[35]

Section 1442, subsection (2) alternatively authorizes the removal of state judicial proceedings "for any act under color of authority derived from any law providing for equal rights, or for refusing to do any act on the ground that it would be inconsistent with such law." The Court has reined in the potentially broad reach of these words, too. It has construed removal under this section to be available only to federal civil or military officers or persons "authorized to act with or for them in affirmatively executing duties under any federal law providing for equal civil rights."[36] The section therefore cannot be invoked by private persons faced with state court prosecution as a result of their participation in civil rights advocacy activities.[37]

Section 1446(b) provides that defendants must file a "notice of removal ... within thirty days after the receipt by the defendant, through service or otherwise, of a copy of the initial pleading." There had been some dispute whether the clock began to run when the defendant received a courtesy copy of the complaint without prior formal service of summons. The Supreme Court has held that the thirty-day time period does not begin to run unless a formal service of summons either precedes or accompanies the defendant's receipt of a copy of the complaint or until defendant formally waives traditional service.[38]

§§ 5.51–5.54 [Reserved]

K. STANDING

§ 5.55 In General

Article III of the U.S. Constitution confines the federal judiciary to hearing actual "cases or controversies." The contemporary, judicially elaborated jurisprudence of standing, however, has both constitutional and "prudential," that is, judicially self-imposed, components. All these elements of standing are treated by the Court as jurisdictional, and as such a federal court will usually decide a defendant's challenge to standing at the outset of a case, often on the basis of the plaintiff's pleadings.[1] Further, upon challenge by the defendant, the burden is on

must have been under § 1443, rather than the general removal statute, § 1441.

35. *State of Georgia v. Rachel*, 384 U.S. 780, 86 S.Ct. 1783, 16 L.Ed.2d 925 (1966).

36. *City of Greenwood v. Peacock*, 384 U.S. 808, 86 S.Ct. 1800, 16 L.Ed.2d 944 (1966).

37. *Id.*

38. *Murphy Bros., Inc. v. Michetti Pipe Stringing, Inc.*, 526 U.S. 344, 119 S.Ct. 1322, 143 L.Ed.2d 448 (1999).

§ 5.55

1. Despite the characterization of standing as "jurisdictional" for purposes of the original subject matter jurisdiction of the federal district courts, a federal circuit court may lack pendent appellate jurisdiction to conduct interlocutory review of a

the plaintiff to prove the requisite jurisdictional facts. Standing is thus a potentially crippling roadblock to a federal court plaintiff who is unable to demonstrate the substantive requirements of standing doctrine without benefit of discovery.[2]

The constitutional dimension of standing doctrine requires that the plaintiff allege personal "injury in fact" that is "fairly traceable" to the allegedly unlawful acts of the defendant and "likely to be redressed" by the requested relief.[3] The injury in fact requirement ordinarily requires the plaintiff to allege and show personal harm that is "(a) concrete and particularized, and (b) actual or imminent, not conjectural or hypothetical."[4] An asserted right to have the government act in accordance with

standing issue presented together with a nonfinal decision that is eligible for interlocutory review under the "collateral order" exception to the usual rule, under 28 U.S.C.A. § 1291, that limits the jurisdiction of the courts of appeals to "final decisions" of the federal district courts. See § 2.23, *supra*, on the "collateral order" exception that permits interlocutory review of many orders denying a § 1983 defendant's motion to dismiss or summary judgment motion based on the defense of qualified immunity. The immediate reviewability of an order denying Eleventh Amendment immunity, for example, is another instance of the "collateral order" exception. But under *Swint v. Chambers County Comm'n*, 514 U.S. 35, 51, 115 S.Ct. 1203, 131 L.Ed.2d 60 (1995), other, nonfinal and hence ordinarily nonappealable orders may be addressed on interlocutory review of the denial of an Eleventh Amendment motion only if they raise issues "inextricably intertwined" with the appealable (e.g., Eleventh Amendment) decision, so that "review of the former ... [is] necessary to ensure meaningful review of the latter." Applying that standard, an appellate court that rejected state officials' Eleventh Amendment defense also declined to hear their objection to plaintiff's standing, because "we may resolve the Eleventh Amendment immunity issue without reaching the merits of standing." *Summit Med. Assocs., P.C. v. Pryor*, 180 F.3d 1326, 1335 (11th Cir.1999), *cert. denied*, 529 U.S. 1012, 120 S.Ct. 1287, 146 L.Ed.2d 233 (2000). *See also Moniz v. City of Ft. Lauderdale*, 145 F.3d 1278, 1281 (11th Cir.1998) (because qualified immunity issue could be resolved without reaching the merits of appellants' challenge to plaintiff's standing, the jurisdictional standing issue not within pendent appellate jurisdiction).

2. *Allen v. Wright*, 468 U.S. 737, 104 S.Ct. 3315, 82 L.Ed.2d 556 (1984).

3. *Id.*

4. *Lujan v. Defenders of Wildlife*, 504 U.S. 555, 559, 112 S.Ct. 2130, 2136, 119 L.Ed.2d 351 (1992) (citations, footnote, and internal quotations omitted). *See also Rizzo v. Goode*, 423 U.S. 362, 96 S.Ct. 598, 46 L.Ed.2d 561 (1976); *City of L.A. v. Lyons*, 461 U.S. 95, 103 S.Ct. 1660, 75 L.Ed.2d 675 (1983). An injury is not "particularized" if it is diffuse, that is widely shared by other members of the public. *See Crist v. Commission on Presidential Debates*, 262 F.3d 193 (2d Cir.2001) (per curiam). The injury must also be actual or imminent. Thus a lawyer who objected that his ability to practice law might be impeded by a religious sign over the entrance to a county courthouse (because he would not represent clients whose cases would be heard there) lacked standing where his practice was based elsewhere, he had never seen the courthouse in question and had no plans to open an office in that county, and could identify no case which had required or would require his presence there. *Doe v. County of Montgomery*, 41 F.3d 1156 (7th Cir.1994). *See also Morgan v. McCutter*, 365 F.3d 882 (10th Cir. 2004) (discharged state employee lacked standing to establish eligibility for reappointment absent evidence that he planned to continue employment with defendant). But the Supreme Court has held that on a motion to dismiss, general factual allegations of injury may suffice. *National Org. for Women, Inc. v. Scheidler*, 510 U.S. 249, 255, 114 S.Ct. 798, 803, 127 L.Ed.2d 99 (1994) (citing *Lujan*). And it distinguished *Lujan* in *Friends of the Earth v. Laidlaw Environmental Services*, 528 U.S. 167, 120 S.Ct. 693, 145 L.Ed.2d 610 (2000). In *Lujan* plaintiffs voiced only a general interest in species preservation but had no plans to visit the site. In *Laidlaw*, the Court treated plaintiffs' conditional statement that, but for defendant's pollution, they would use the site, as "actual or imminent" injury. *See Cleveland Branch, N.A.A.C.P. v. City of Parma, Ohio*, 263 F.3d 513 (6th Cir.2001) (organization had stand-

law is not sufficient. It has sometimes been held that even the stigmatizing injury of racial discrimination is insufficient unless plaintiffs have personally been denied equal treatment.[5] Nor will the "psychological consequence presumably produced by observation of conduct with which one disagrees" supply the requisite injury, if it is unaccompanied by more tangible or concrete harm.[6] But subjection of the plaintiff to unwelcome religious exercises may constitute adequate injury in fact even where the plaintiff is not thereby forced to assume any special burdens to avoid them.[7] It suffices that there has been an indirectly coerced, unwelcome exposure to a religious message that could have been avoided only by sacrificing the ordinary privileges of citizenship.[8]

Second, even where a serious, personal, economic or non-economic injury is properly alleged, the injury must be "fairly traceable" to the challenged government conduct—a constitutional requirement of causation.[9] A circuit court upheld a property owner's standing to challenge police officers' allegedly unreasonable execution of a search warrant, in the course of which they broke or mutilated portions of the house and the owner's personal property. Even though the owner lacked a reasonable expectation of privacy regarding the house, the injury could be linked to a distinct Fourth Amendment violation arising from the defendants' significant level of interference with the owner's possessory interest in the property.[10]

Finally, even if a plaintiff properly alleges injury to herself or her class that is traceable to the defendant's conduct, she still lacks standing if the requested relief is unlikely to redress that injury.[11] This is generally not a barrier to plaintiffs seeking retrospective, monetary relief, as they can usually show that money will redress their claimed injury.[12] But the "redressability" requirement means that § 1983 plain-

ing because one of its members met all requirements, including imminent injury, as evidenced by his repeated attempts to obtain employment). *But cf. Yeager v. General Motors Corp.,* 265 F.3d 389 (6th Cir. 2001) (white male's challenge to employer's racial and gender preference in ranking applicants for apprenticeship program alleged no imminent injury because employer could abolish program before plaintiff was ranked, or plaintiff might rank below other white males).

5. *Allen,* 468 U.S. 737, 104 S.Ct. 3315, 82 L.Ed.2d 556.

6. *Valley Forge Christian Coll. v. Americans United for Separation of Church and State, Inc.,* 454 U.S. 464, 485, 102 S.Ct. 752, 765, 70 L.Ed.2d 700 (1982).

7. *Id.* at 486–487 n.22.

8. *See, e.g., Lee v. Weisman,* 505 U.S. 577, 596–598, 112 S.Ct. 2649, 2660–2661, 120 L.Ed.2d 467, 486–487 (1992) (standing to challenge school prayer at graduation ceremony of public school where attendance was not prerequisite to receipt of diploma); *School Dist. of Abington Township, Pa. v. Schempp,* 374 U.S. 203, 224 n. 9, 83 S.Ct. 1560, 1572 n. 9, 10 L.Ed.2d 844 (1963) (standing to challenge classroom Bible reading although student could be absent or not participate). Thus citizens of a county who alleged that they were required to visit its courthouse to fulfill legal obligations or fully participate as citizens had standing to challenge a sign with a religious message that was displayed over the main and most prominent courthouse entrance. *Doe v. County of Montgomery,* 41 F.3d 1156 (7th Cir.1994).

9. *See Simon v. Eastern Ky. Welfare Rights Org.,* 426 U.S. 26, 38, 96 S.Ct. 1917, 1924, 48 L.Ed.2d 450 (1976).

10. *Bonds v. Cox,* 20 F.3d 697 (6th Cir.1994).

11. *Allen,* 468 U.S. at 752; *Goode,* 423 U.S. 362, 96 S.Ct. 598, 46 L.Ed.2d 561.

12. *See, e.g., PeTa, People for the Ethical Treatment of Animals v. Rasmussen,* 298 F.3d 1198 (10th Cir.2002) (even though

tiffs alleging excessive use of force by police or other conduct they seek to prohibit prospectively are often unable to obtain *injunctive* relief. For example, if, as the evidence may often show, excessive force is used by a "small minority of officers" and plaintiffs cannot show a "real and immediate" threat that they themselves will be repeat victims of the precise practice they seek to have enjoined, the Court views the requested relief as unlikely to redress the particular injury of which they complain.[13] Indeed the plaintiff in *City of L.A. v. Lyons*[14] was held to lack standing to seek an injunction against the Los Angeles Police Department's procedures concerning chokeholds even though, per *Monell* and its progeny, he would have to show in support of his companion damages claim that the force allegedly used against him was pursuant to official city policy. To have standing with respect to the injunction he sought, Lyons would have had to allege that the city authorized officers to apply chokeholds to suspects who offered no resistance or other provocation and "demonstrate" that he himself would likely again be stopped and choked by the police under those circumstances.[15] The upshot is that the court will test the plaintiff's standing with respect to each claim alleged, and the *Lyons* equitable requirements for standing, if not those under

protesters at junior high school would not again be threatened under statute prohibiting disruption of higher education institutions, they had standing to seek monetary damages); *Payton v. County of Kane*, 308 F.3d 673 (7th Cir.2002) (arrestees had standing to challenge county jail practice of setting bond fee for release above set bail amount, in part because their injury could be redressed by the monetary relief they sought).

13. *Goode*, 423 U.S. 362, 96 S.Ct. 598, 46 L.Ed.2d 561; *City of L.A. v. Lyons*, 461 U.S. 95, 103 S.Ct. 1660, 75 L.Ed.2d 675 (1983).

14. 461 U.S. 95, 103 S.Ct. 1660, 75 L.Ed.2d 675 (1983).

15. 461 U.S. at 106 n.7, 103 S.Ct. at 1667 n.7. The Court was unclear if its decision rested on Lyons' inability to satisfy Article III standing requirements or separate requirements justifying equitable relief that it had outlined in *O'Shea v. Littleton*, 414 U.S. 488, 499, 94 S.Ct. 669, 38 L.Ed.2d 674 (1974). As explained in *Lyons, O'Shea* had demanded as a precondition for equitable relief that the threat of a recurring violation be real and immediate and entail substantial and irreparable injury. 414 U.S. at 502. *See also Rizzo v. Goode*, 423 U.S. 362, 372, 96 S.Ct. 598, 46 L.Ed.2d 561 (1976) (claim of future injury too "attenuated" to warrant injunctive relief). Although one could view the police stop of Lyons as a chance encounter, the Court suggested that it was prompted by his misconduct. 461 U.S. at 105. And the Court has subsequently indicated that Lyons could not show standing because he could avoid engaging in illegal conduct prospectively, and would therefore likely avoid being stopped and then subjected to the chokehold he challenged, so that he could no show the required threat of further immediate injury. *Spencer v. Kemna*, 523 U.S. 1, 15, 118 S.Ct. 978, 140 L.Ed.2d 43 (1998). Thus *Lyons* was distinguished in a case where entirely innocent plaintiffs were stopped by the U.S. Border Patrol (as to which the federalism concerns expressed in *Lyons* would also not apply), and where further stops themselves would constitute the alleged injury, with no need to speculate about future chokeholds. The circuit panel was therefore willing to assume a sufficient likelihood of future injury to satisfy the Article III requirements of *Lyons*. It nevertheless held that even if federalism did not counsel application of the *Lyons/O'Shea/Rizzo* equitable requirements for injunctive relief, separation of powers doctrine did. And noting that plaintiffs encountered the Border Patrol regularly but had each been stopped only once in 10 years, it concluded that plaintiffs failed to meet the "sufficient likelihood of injury" equitable requirement because it was unduly speculative that they would likely be stopped by the Border Patrol again. *Hodgers–Durgin v. De La Vina*, 199 F.3d 1037, 1039 (9th Cir.1999). *See also Muhammad v. City of N.Y. Dep't of Corr.*, 126 F.3d 119 (2d Cir.1997). *Cf., Goff v. Harper*, 60 F.3d 518 (8th Cir.1995) (inability to show likelihood of recurrence of same violation fails "irreparable injury" requirement for injunction).

Article III itself, are so stringent as to require a plaintiff to show he is virtually certain to be a victim of the illegal practice soon or even immediately following the time he prays for an injunction. There is authority applying this and other standing requirements like injury in fact in a more relaxed fashion to claims based on the First Amendment, particularly where the plaintiff mounts an overbreadth challenge to statutes regulating speech.[16]

Lyons, then, makes it virtually impossible for the victim of police abuse to secure injunctive relief against a local government entity for practices of its police or sheriff's department. Evidently the Court places considerable faith in civil damage actions and, in criminal cases, the exclusionary rule to deter police misconduct. This faith, if not completely ill founded, is at least exaggerated. The ever-growing number of exceptions to the exclusionary rule that the Court has created in the last decade have been widely discussed elsewhere and will not be recounted here. But it is pertinent to observe that a great deal of police misconduct cannot be corrected through civil damage actions, either. For example, circuit courts generally do not permit § 1983 damage actions to be founded on violations of quasi-constitutional rules like the one announced in *Miranda*.[17] Even if the *Lyons* standing prerequisite to injunctive relief is met, a § 1983 plaintiff must also satisfy traditional requirements for equitable relief.[18]

Under the Court's *Heck v. Humphrey* decision, moreover, § 1983 damage actions brought by convicted criminal defendants that are based on unlawful searches and seizures may lie, at least in some circuits, only in the relatively rare event that the putative plaintiff has first succeeded in overturning his conviction on direct appeal or habeas.[19] And while police brutality claims are probably not subject to *Heck*,[20] many victims of that conduct are not prosecuted and therefore have no opportunity (or need) to invoke the exclusionary rule.

16. *See Ward v. Utah*, 321 F.3d 1263 (10th Cir.2003) (crediting plaintiff's statement that he intended again to engage in expression that might be elevated to a felony by arguable applicable hate-crimes statute); *Canatella v. State of California*, 304 F.3d 843 (9th Cir.2002) (finding likelihood that attorney would again be subject to bar discipline under state bar statutes and rule of professional conduct he challenged on First and Fourteenth Amendment grounds).

17. *See Jones v. Cannon*, 174 F.3d 1271 (11th Cir.1999) and other circuit decisions cited therein.

18. *See Switzer v. Coan*, 261 F.3d 985 (10th Cir.2001) (plaintiff's adequate remedy at law precluded equitable relief in *Bivens* action).

19. *See, e.g., Schilling v. White*, 58 F.3d 1081 (6th Cir.1995) (holding that § 1983 action alleging an unconstitutional search or seizure is premature, and must be dismissed without prejudice, if brought while the plaintiff still faces criminal punishment). *But see Kelley v. Myler*, 149 F.3d 641 (7th Cir.1998); *Gonzalez v. Entress*, 133 F.3d 551, 553–54 (7th Cir.1998); *Washington v. Summerville*, 127 F.3d 552 (7th Cir. 1997), *cert. denied*, 523 U.S. 1073, 118 S.Ct. 1515, 140 L.Ed.2d 668 (1998); *Perez v. Sifel*, 57 F.3d 503, 505 (7th Cir.1995) (per curiam) (Fourth Amendment claims accrue at time of alleged violation and are not subject to *Heck* bar).

20. *See, e.g, Lowery v. Stovall*, 92 F.3d 219 (4th Cir.1996), *cert. denied*, 519 U.S. 1113, 117 S.Ct. 954, 136 L.Ed.2d 841 (1997) (judicial estoppel, rather than *Heck* doctrine, precludes § 1983 excessive force claim after plaintiff's conviction upon guilty plea).

There are important additional pitfalls, described in detail in Chapter 2. For example, if, despite the powerful qualified immunity defense and the possible barrier of *Heck*, a plaintiff prevails on a damage claim for an unlawful search and seizure against an individual police officer, the damages are seldom great enough to have significant deterrent effect. If, despite qualified immunity, the plaintiff prevails on a claim against an officer for police brutality, the damages may be large but the defendant will often be unable to satisfy a significant judgment. Compensation in such a case would depend on the happenstance of whether the defendant is indemnified by his employing entity or otherwise insured.[21] And damage claims against the local government entity predicated on *any* sort of police misconduct are likely to founder on the Court's *Monell* decision. Plaintiffs can hurdle the *Monell* "policy" element only by showing a well-established pattern or custom of the kind of unconstitutional misconduct he alleges; or that the particular defendant's misconduct was affirmatively approved by the government entity official or board with final policymaking authority to make such determinations; or that an unconstitutional failure to aid or protect the plaintiff, or to screen the record of an applicant for law enforcement, was the result of "deliberate indifference" fairly chargeable to the government entity because of similar prior incidents that would have made the resulting constitutional violation "obvious."

In *Warth v. Seldin*,[22] the injury in fact requirement was held unsatisfied when a construction firm association sought to intervene to challenge a zoning ordinance on equal protection grounds because of its alleged effect of excluding people of low and moderate income from living in the community. Critically absent, wrote the Court, was an allegation that the ordinance "delayed or thwarted any project currently proposed by the association's members."

The Court has distinguished *Warth* in permitting a challenge by another contractors' association to a city's 10% set-aside program challenged as a form of preferential treatment for minority-owned businesses that violated equal protection under the criteria laid down by *City of Richmond v. J.A. Croson Co.*[23] In *Northeastern Florida Chapter of the Associated General Contractors of America v. City of Jacksonville*,[24] the court of appeals had found the association lacked standing because it had not shown that, absent the set-aside program, any of its members would have bid successfully for one of the covered contracts. The Supreme Court reversed, summarizing its cases as holding that when "government erects a barrier that makes it more difficult for members of one

21. Although courts and commentators alike have asserted that "a verdict against the municipal employee will almost always result in satisfaction of the judgment by the municipality because of the indemnification provisions typically found in bargaining agreements between municipalities and their employee unions," *Wilson v. Mendon*, 294 F.3d 1 (1st Cir.2002). *See also Jeffries*, *infra* this chapter; that assertion has not been empirically verified.

22. 422 U.S. 490, 516, 95 S.Ct. 2197, 2214, 45 L.Ed.2d 343 (1975).

23. 488 U.S. 469, 109 S.Ct. 706, 102 L.Ed.2d 854 (1989).

24. 508 U.S. 656, 113 S.Ct. 2297, 124 L.Ed.2d 586 (1993).

group to obtain a benefit than it is for members of another group, a member of the former group seeking to challenge the barrier need not allege that he would have obtained the benefit but for the barrier." It is enough if the plaintiff asserts that the barrier has denied him the right to be considered or compete for the benefit in question.[25] The Court observed that in *Warth*, by contrast, the claim was simply that the government would grant no variances or permits under the challenged ordinance; "there was no claim that the construction association's members could not apply for variances and building permits on the same basis as other firms."[26] The Court has applied this eased approach to equal protection standing to other "reverse discrimination" challenges, for example, white voters' Equal Protection challenges to race-conscious electoral redistricting and to affirmative action programs.[27]

Often the definition of a federal statutory right furnishes the requisite constitutional injury. In *Havens Realty Corp. v. Coleman*,[28] the Supreme Court upheld the standing of persons not themselves denied housing to seek relief under the Fair Housing Act.[29] That statute gives "any person" an enforceable legal right to truthful information about available housing—apart from the right to acquire or rent the housing itself[30]—and provides that this right may be enforced by civil action.[31]

25. *Id.* at 2302. The Court reaffirmed in *Texas v. Lesage*, 528 U.S. 18, 120 S.Ct. 467, 145 L.Ed.2d 347 (1999), that a plaintiff challenging an ongoing, expressly discriminatory policy—today, that would prototypically, and perhaps only, be a white or male plaintiff alleging reverse discrimination—has standing to seek declaratory and injunctive relief against the policy even if the defendant proves the benefit at issue would not have been received by the plaintiff even in a race-neutral competition. *But see Yeager v. General Motors Corp.,* 265 F.3d 389 (6th Cir.2001) (using possibility that plaintiff might be outranked by other white males, thus giving employer a "same-decision" argument, as a reason for rejecting standing). But the Court sharply distinguished actual, substantial damages relief, which is wholly barred if the defendant carries that "same-decision" showing. *Lesage*, which involved a challenge to a race-based educational admission policy, is discussed in detail in § 2.26, *supra. See also Thigpen v. Bibb County, Ga.*, 223 F.3d 1231 (11th Cir.2000) (promotion denial in county employment); *Price v. City of Charlotte, N.C.*, 93 F.3d 1241 (4th Cir.1996), *cert. denied*, 520 U.S. 1116, 117 S.Ct. 1246, 137 L.Ed.2d 328 (1997) (promotion denial in city employment; plaintiff denied promotion but accorded standing, prevailed on liability, and held eligible for all monetary remedies despite city's showing that even absent its reliance on race it would not have promoted plaintiff).

26. *Id.* at 2303.

27. *See, e.g., United States v. Hays*, 515 U.S. 737, 744–45, 115 S.Ct. 2431, 2436, 132 L.Ed.2d 635 (1995) (white voters have standing because they "may" be less well represented in a district drawn to enhance interests of African–Americans) and *Gratz v. Bollinger*, 123 S.Ct. at 2422–2423 (2003); *Grutter v. Bollinger*, 539 U.S. 306, 123 S.Ct. 2325, 156 L.Ed.2d 304 (2003). There the Court reaffirmed its minimalist view of standing in cases challenging express racial preferences, in the context of university admissions policies. It specifically cited with approval *Northeastern Fla. Chap., Associated Gen. Contractors of American v. Jacksonville* for the proposition that a party challenging a set-aside (or even a program giving lesser preference) "need only demonstrate that it is able and ready" to accept the government benefit in question, not that it would have received that benefit in a race-free competition. *See generally* §§ 2.26 and 7.45.

28. 455 U.S. 363, 102 S.Ct. 1114, 71 L.Ed.2d 214 (1982).

29. 42 U.S.C.A. § 3604(d).

30. The Act makes it unlawful to "represent to any person because of race ... that any dwelling is not available for inspection, sale, or rental when such dwelling is in fact so available." Section 804(d), 42 U.S.C.A. § 3604(d).

31. § 812, 42 U.S.C.A. § 3612(a).

The Court deemed the denial of that information sufficient injury in fact to satisfy Article III.

The Court has also devised three principal "prudential" limitations on standing. Both individuals, *Schlesinger v. Reservists Comm. to Stop the War*,[32] and organizations, *Simon v. Eastern Ky. Welfare Rights Org.*[33] lack standing if they assert only generalized grievances.[34] Thus an organizational plaintiff must allege concrete injury to its activities, not merely to its abstract social interests.[35] Second, plaintiffs must show an interest within the "zone of interests protected by the law invoked."[36] Third, plaintiffs must raise their own claims; in general they may not raise the claims of third parties.[37]

Although it is generally accepted that these "prudential" limitations on standing flow from Article III, a comprehensive analysis by a panel of the District of Columbia Circuit points out that they operate in fact as a constitutionally driven canon of statutory construction—a "set of presumptions" used to determine "whether the statutes in question confer

32. 418 U.S. 208, 217, 94 S.Ct. 2925, 2930, 41 L.Ed.2d 706 (1974).

33. 426 U.S. 26, 40, 96 S.Ct. 1917, 1925, 48 L.Ed.2d 450 (1976).

34. *See generally Warth v. Seldin*, 422 U.S. at 499, 95 S.Ct. at 2205.

35. *Havens Realty Corp. v. Coleman*, 455 U.S. 363, 379, 102 S.Ct. 1114, 1124, 71 L.Ed.2d 214 (1982).

36. *Allen*, 468 U.S. at 751, 104 S.Ct., at 3324; *Valley Forge*, 454 U.S. at 474–475, 102 S.Ct. at 759–760.

37. *Singleton v. Wulff*, 428 U.S. 106, 114, 96 S.Ct. 2868, 2874, 49 L.Ed.2d 826 (1976); *Warth*, 422 U.S. at 499, 95 S.Ct. at 2205; *Sierra Club v. Morton*, 405 U.S. 727, 735, 92 S.Ct. 1361, 1366, 31 L.Ed.2d 636 (1972). The Supreme Court has written that application of this prudential limitation on asserting the interests of third parties is context-dependent. In *Elk Grove Unified School District v. Newdow*, ___ U.S. ___, 124 S.Ct. 2301, ___ L.Ed.2d ___ (2004), for example, the Court denied standing to a parent, an atheist, who asserted that requiring his daughter to participate in a school's teacher-led pledge of allegiance that included the words "under God" violated the First Amendment's religion clauses. Although subject matter jurisdiction in *Elk Grove* rested on a substantial federal constitutional question, the majority wrote that its prudential standing rules should take into account the doctrine that excepts most domestic relations matters from federal diversity jurisdiction. Accordingly, the majority considered it critical that plaintiff was subject to a state court domestic relations order depriving him of the right to sue as his daughter's "next friend" and that the daughter's mother asserted that the child, as a Christian, would be harmed if the federal action proceeded. These considerations led to a narrow holding rejecting the standing of "a plaintiff whose standing to sue is founded on family law rights that are in dispute when prosecution of the lawsuit may have an adverse effect on the person who is the source of the plaintiff's claimed standing." The majority distinguished *Palmore v. Sidoti*, 466 US. 429, 432–434, 104 S.Ct. 1879, 80 L.Ed.2d 421 (1984) as a "rare instance . . . in which it is necessary to answer a substantial federal question that transcends or exists apart from the family law issue. . . ." As observed by Chief Justice Rehnquist, concurring in the judgment, it is difficult to see why the First Amendment issue in *Elk Grove* did not transcend or exist apart from the family law issue when the Court in *Palmore* upheld jurisdiction even though the federal issue there—constitutional concern about a state court ruling denying a mother custody based on the possible racial prejudice resulting from her interracial marriage—had "everything to do with the domestic relationship. . . ." *See Clay v. Fort Wayne Cmty. Sch.*, 76 F.3d 873 (7th Cir.1996) (only African–American applicants, not parents of African–American students, had standing to complain of race discrimination in a school board's search for a superintendent). But an inmate raised his own rights, not those of third parties, in seeking enforcement of a settlement agreement to which he was not party but for whose benefit the agreement was entered. *Floyd v. Ortiz*, 300 F.3d 1223 (10th Cir.2002).

a cause of action upon the plaintiff."[38] Put another way, "Congress legislates against the background of our prudential standing doctrine, which applies unless it is expressly negated."[39] Thus, prudential limits apply unless Congress defines within the statute at issue who may press a claim for a violation of the statute.[40] That is, where federal statutory rights are at issue, Congress has considerable authority to shape the prudential considerations governing standing. It may authorize standing up to the limits of Article III, permitting, for example, an individual who is not an intended beneficiary of a statute but who suffers injury in fact to sue for that statute's violation, or permitting someone to seek redress based on a violation of the statutory rights of others.[41]

Consider, for example, an organizational plaintiff that complains that its members have been deprived of the benefits of living in an integrated community by local ordinances that exclude people of low or moderate income. Such an allegation meets the Article III requirement of an injury in fact.[42] But whether that challenge is permissible under the "prudential" standing limits depends on whether it is asserted under a *statute* that permits a litigant to raise the putative rights of third parties. Section 1981 apparently does not.[43] It affords a cause of action only to those immediately injured by a denial of the right to contract, not to "persons whose injuries derive only from the violation of others' rights."[44] The Fair Housing Act clearly does. It confers a claim "upon

38. *Fair Employment Council of Greater Washington, Inc. v. BMC Mktg. Corp.*, 28 F.3d 1268 (D.C.Cir.1994) (holding testers lack standing under 42 U.S.C.A.Sec. 1981).

39. *Bennett v. Spear*, 520 U.S. 154, 163, 117 S.Ct. 1154, 1162, 137 L.Ed.2d 281 (1997) (holding that the Endangered Species Act's citizen—suit provision negates the zone-of-interests test (or, perhaps more accurately, expands the zone of interests) because the statute contains a broad definition of standing: "any person may commence a civil suit").

40. *See* the discussion of *Childress v. City of Richmond, Va.*, 134 F.3d 1205 (4th Cir.1998), *cert. denied*, 524 U.S. 927, 118 S.Ct. 2322, 141 L.Ed.2d 696 (1998), *infra* this section.

41. *See MX Group, Inc. v. City of Covington*, 293 F.3d 326, 335 (6th Cir.2002) (drug treatment provider seeking to open methadone clinic for which city had denied zoning permit had standing to sue city on its own behalf, without joining individual potential clients as plaintiffs, in action alleging violation of Rehabilitation Act and ADA); *Kyles v. J.K. Guardian Sec. Servs., Inc.*, 222 F.3d 289, 294 (7th Cir.2000).

42. *See Trafficante v. Metropolitan Life Ins. Co.*, 409 U.S. 205, 93 S.Ct. 364, 34 L.Ed.2d 415 (1972).

43. *Kyles v. J.K. Guardian Sec. Servs., Inc.*, 222 F.3d 289, 301–04 (7th Cir.2000); *Fair Employment Council of Greater Washington*, 28 F.3d 1268; *Mackey v. Nationwide Ins. Cos.*, 724 F.2d 419 (4th Cir.1984). *See Warth v. Seldin*, 422 U.S. at 512–514, 95 S.Ct. at 2212–2213. *But cf. Watts v. Boyd Properties, Inc.*, 758 F.2d 1482, 1485 (11th Cir.1985); *Meyers v. Pennypack Woods Home Ownership Ass'n*, 559 F.2d 894, 898 (3d Cir.1977), *overruled on other grounds by Goodman v. Lukens Steel Co.*, 777 F.2d 113 (3d Cir.1985), *aff'd*, 482 U.S. 656, 107 S.Ct. 2617, 96 L.Ed.2d 572 (1987) (testers have standing to challenge discriminatory housing practices under § 1982, which has similar phrasing and purpose as § 1981).

44. *Fair Employment Council of Greater Washington*, 28 F.3d 1268 (relying principally on *Warth*). The question whether a plaintiff is a "direct" victim of racial discrimination with standing to sue under § 1981 is particularly vexing when a corporation sues together with one of its principals. This is vividly illustrated by comparing the majority and partially dissenting opinions in *The Guides, Ltd. v. Yarmouth Group Property Management, Inc.*, 295 F.3d 1065 (10th Cir.2002). The majority concluded that because the corporation was the party denied the right to lease property, allegedly because of race, it was the "direct" victim and had standing. But it de-

everyone who meets the Article III requirements—that is, anyone 'genuinely injured by conduct that violates *someone's* ... rights'."[45]

Where does Title VII lie on this statutory continuum? Probably somewhere in between the Fair Housing Act and § 1981. The Equal Employment Opportunity Commission has at times used "testers" to ferret out evidence of unlawful discrimination in hiring and job referrals. The chief argument against standing in such cases is that the tester—the person, usually well qualified, who on behalf of EEOC or a private

nied standing to the co-plaintiff sole shareholder and president of the corporation in reliance on the circuit's "general rule" that a stockholder may not sue for harm to her corporation, holding in applicable the exception to this rule for cases where the stockholder can show unique injury to herself and not suffered by other stockholders. The dissent agreed that the corporate plaintiff had standing, but only as an "indirect" victim of unlawful race-based conduct aimed directly at the president and sole shareholder. It chided the majority's reason for according the corporation standing by quoting *Arlington Heights v. Metropolitan Housing Development Corporation,* 429 U.S. 252, 97 S.Ct. 555, 50 L.Ed.2d 450 (1977), a Fourteenth Amendment case not involving § 1981, to the effect that "a corporation ... has no racial identity and cannot be the direct target of the ... alleged discrimination." Instead, the dissent agreed that the corporation should be accorded standing as the indirect victim of discriminatory conduct aimed at the president and sole shareholder. It relied on post-*Arlington Heights* circuit decisions according corporations standing when they suffer injuries like lost profits resulting from unlawful discrimination directed at a human member of a protected class. 295 F.3d at 1080 (citing *Gersman v. Group Health Association, Inc.*, 931 F.2d 1565 (D.C.Cir.1991)), *vacated on other grounds*, 502 U.S. 1068, 112 S.Ct. 960, 117 L.Ed.2d 127 (1992) and *Hudson Valley Freedom Theater, Inc. v. Heimbach*, 671 F.2d 702, 708 (2d Cir.1982). The dissent also would have recognized the standing of the shareholder plaintiff as the "direct" victim of the discriminatory conduct, regardless of whether she was acting in her individual capacity in seeking the lease in question or was acting as a corporate agent.

45. *Id.* at 1278 (quoting *Gladstone, Realtors v. Village of Bellwood*, 441 U.S. 91, 103 n. 9, 99 S.Ct. 1601, 1609 n. 9, 60 L.Ed.2d 66 (1979)). *See also MX Group, Inc. v. City of Covington*, 293 F.3d 326, 335 (6th Cir.2002) (drug treatment provider seeking to open methadone clinic for which city had denied zoning permit had standing to sue city on its own behalf, without joining individual potential clients as plaintiffs, in action alleging violation of Rehabilitation Act and ADA); *Louisiana ACORN Fair Hous. v. LeBlanc,* 211 F.3d 298, 305 (5th Cir.2000) (holding that "an organization could have standing if it had proven a drain on its resources resulting from counteracting the effects of the defendant's actions"); *Ragin v. Harry Macklowe Real Estate Co.,* 6 F.3d 898 (2d Cir.1993) (fair housing organization had standing to sue real estate company for placing newspaper advertisements depicting white people only because the fair housing organization was forced to devote significant resources to identify and counteract the defendants' advertising practices and did so to the detriment of their efforts to obtain equal access to housing through counseling and other services); *Hooker v. Weathers,* 990 F.2d 913 (6th Cir.1993) (fair housing organization established standing by devoting resources to investigating and confirming defendant's discriminatory practices); *Village of Bellwood v. Dwivedi,* 895 F.2d 1521 (7th Cir.1990) (holding that fair housing organization had standing to sue real estate brokerage for violations of Fair Housing Act. "[T]he only injury which need be shown to confer standing on a fair-housing agency is deflection of the agency's time and money from counseling to legal efforts directed against discrimination."); *Arkansas ACORN Fair Hous., Inc. v. Greystone Dev., Ltd. Co.,* 160 F.3d 433 (8th Cir.1998) (acknowledging that "the deflection of an organization's monetary and human resources from counseling or educational programs to legal efforts aimed at combating discrimination, such as monitoring and investigation, is itself sufficient to constitute an actual injury [where] traceable to some act of the defendant" (citations omitted) but finding that plaintiff did not show specific facts establishing distinct and palpable injuries fairly traceable to defendant's advertisements); and *Central Ala. Fair Hous. Ctr., Inc. v. Lowder Realty Co., Inc.,* 236 F.3d 629 (11th Cir.2000) (fair housing organization has standing to recover in its own right for the diversion of its resources to combat the defendant's discrimination).

organization promoting equality of opportunity in employment presents himself to the employer or employment agency—has suffered no concrete injury for lack of any bona fide interest in an advertised position. The key question is whether the Title VII right sought to be enforced in a given case describes an aggrieved person in terms sufficiently broad to embrace the particular plaintiff. How the answer may varying depending upon the identify of the plaintiff and the relief sought is nicely illustrated by the District of Columbia Circuit's panel opinion mentioned above.

The plaintiff group in *Fair Employment Council of Greater Washington* included two African–American employment testers—"equipped with fake credentials intended to be comparable" to those of the two white testers with whom they were paired—and the Fair Employment Council. The defendant employment agency had allegedly denied the African–American testers employment referrals that it gave to the white testers. An alleged "pattern" of racial discrimination against other applicants for referral assertedly made it more difficult for the plaintiff Council to carry out its goal of promoting equal opportunity in the community.

The court first rejected both the testers' and the Council's claims under § 1981. The testers, the court found, could not state a claim under that statute, which gives a cause of action only to persons deprived of what would otherwise be a legal right to make or enforce a contract. The testers could not have enforced a contract offering them employment because they had to make material misrepresentations of fact about their intentions to secure employment in order to induce the defendant employment agency to make referrals. What they really lost was only "the opportunity to enter into a *void* contract—i.e., a contract that *neither* party can enforce." That, the court wrote, "is not an injury cognizable under Sec. 1981, for a void contract is a legal nullity."[46] As observed above,[47] the Council's § 1981 claim failed on prudential standing grounds. Only direct victims of an unlawful denial of the right to make or enforce a contract have standing to assert claims under that statute.[48]

The court was more equivocal about the standing of the individual testers to assert claims under Title VII. While expressly declining to decide whether testers lack standing because they have no bona fide interest in an employment position,[49] the court wrote that in general the Title VII scheme is more analogous to the Fair Housing Act provisions found to support standing in *Havens* than to the stricter requirements of § 1981. Nevertheless, the testers' claims were barred. Their claim for

46. *Fair Employment Council of Greater Washington*, 28 F.3d 1268. *But cf. Watts v. Boyd Properties*, 758 F.2d 1482 (11th Cir.1985) and *Meyers v. Pennypack Woods Home Ownership Ass'n*, 559 F.2d 894 (3d Cir.1977), *overruled on other grounds by Goodman v. Lukens Steel Co.*, 777 F.2d 113 (3d Cir.1985), *aff'd*, 482 U.S. 656, 107 S.Ct. 2617, 96 L.Ed.2d 572 (1987) (according fair-housing testers standing to sue under §§ 1982 and 1981, respectively, although not squarely addressing question whether the testers had suffered legal injury within the meaning of those statutes).

47. *See* text *supra*.

48. *Fair Employment Council*, 28 F.3d at 1280.

49. *Id.* at 1280 n.1.

damages failed because only equitable relief was available under Title VII for violations that occurred before the effective date of the Civil Rights Act of 1991. In turn, their prayer for injunctive or declaratory relief ran afoul of the *Lyons* limitations. To be eligible for prospective relief, they would have had to make "sufficient allegations that they are threatened with ... future illegality." That they could do only by showing a likelihood that the defendant agency would infringe their Title VII rights again, not simply that they would continue to suffer the ill effects of its alleged past violations. And like Lyons, or indeed virtually any imaginable civil rights plaintiff, how could they make such a case on the pleadings, even before discovery? It would be sheer "speculation" for them to allege that a future violation of their rights was probable, because that would depend—as it always will—upon matters within the defendant's control and knowledge.[50]

The Council fared somewhat better. Constitutional injury in fact was satisfied by its allegations that the defendant's conduct impaired the Council's ability to assist minorities in finding jobs, thereby undermining the effectiveness of its outreach efforts. Further, Title VII's plaintiff definition, like the Fair Housing Act's, provided prudential standing "to the extent that the effects of ... [the defendant's] discrimination have perceptibly impaired ... [the plaintiff's] programs." The court reached this conclusion in reliance on the language of Title VII that authorizes suit by any "person claiming to be aggrieved" by an unlawful employment practice.[51] Under such a statute, a person injured by conduct that violates its own or another's rights—that is, a person who suffers Article III injury in fact—also survives the prudential restrictions on standing. If the distinctions drawn by this decision ultimately prevail, EEOC's testers may ultimately be found to have standing to sue with respect to discriminatory job referrals, but not discriminatory refusals to hire.[52] Yet a considerably greater number of circuits have upheld Title VII standing by focusing on the significant differences in text and purpose between § 1981 and Title VII. The former protects only the right without regard to race to enter into and enforce a contractual relationship; the latter, prohibiting a wide range of discriminatory employment practices, accords

50. *Id.* at 1272. *See also Goff v. Harper*, 60 F.3d 518 (8th Cir.1995) (because recurrence of alleged violation was speculative, irreparable injury requirement for injunctive relief lacking).

51. 42 U.S.C.A. § 2000e–2(b).

52. *See Sledge v. J.P. Stevens & Co.*, 585 F.2d 625, 641 (4th Cir.1978), *cert. denied*, 440 U.S. 981, 99 S.Ct. 1789, 60 L.Ed.2d 241 (1979) (tester plaintiffs not harmed by refusal to hire for lack of serious interest in job, and hence lack standing); *Parr v. Woodmen of the World Life Ins. Soc'y*, 657 F.Supp. 1022 (M.D.Ga.1987) (plaintiff held ineligible to prosecute suit when court found he was not genuinely seeking employment but instead simply manufacturing the basis for a Title VII violation; the statutory provision in question, 42 U.S.C.A. § 2000e–2(a)(1), created a right to nondiscriminatory hiring, a violation the court found the plaintiff could not have suffered) and *Hailes v. United Air Lines*, 464 F.2d 1006 (5th Cir.1972) (in dictum denying possibility of suit against an employer that published an advertisement containing an unlawful discriminatory preference if the plaintiff had been a mere reader of the advertisement rather than, as was the case, a reader who actually applied for employment; the particular Title VII provision at issue, 42 U.S.C.A. § 2000e–3(b), did not specifically define the person aggrieved).

a substantive right to "any person claiming to be aggrieved" to be free from practices that attempt "to limit, segregate or classify" applicants and which "in any way ... would deprive or tend to deprive any individual" of employment opportunities. Thus while a tester's lack of interest in actually working for the defendant will limit the nature and extent of his injuries and consequently appropriate relief, it does not preclude relief for humiliation, embarrassment and like injuries that typically stem from discrimination.[53] Standing for testers under § 1981 also suffers by comparison with cases that have upheld standing for § 1983 plaintiffs who challenged race-based denials of public accommodations that they sought solely in order to initiate litigation.[54] The public accommodations tester actually uses, or attempts, to use those accommodations; the § 1981 tester, by contrast, is not attempting to form a contract or therefore to exercise the limited[55] right protected by that statute.

A related question concerns the standing of those who argue that a defendant having no direct employment relationship with the plaintiff interfered with the plaintiff's employment relationship with a third party. The circuits that have directly confronted the question have recognized standing in this situation.[56] These courts reason that while the Title VII defendant must be a defined "employer," the plaintiff need not be an "employee" but instead is referred to in the statute as a "person aggrieved." (For the same reason the statute applies to defendant labor unions and employment agencies, which also have no direct employment relationship with a plaintiff.) The plaintiff attempting to invoke "*Sibley* standing" must show that a defined Title VII "employer"

53. *Kyles v. J.K. Guardian Sec. Servs., Inc.*, 222 F.3d 289, 300 (7th Cir.2000). *See Anjelino v. New York Times Co.*, 200 F.3d 73, 91 & n. 25 (3d Cir.1999); *EEOC v. Mississippi Coll.*, 626 F.2d 477, 482–83 & n. 7 (5th Cir.1980), *cert. denied*, 453 U.S. 912, 101 S.Ct. 3143, 69 L.Ed.2d 994 (1981); *EEOC v. Bailey Co.*, 563 F.2d 439, 452–454 (6th Cir.1977), *cert. denied*, 435 U.S. 915, 98 S.Ct. 1468, 55 L.Ed.2d 506 (1978); *Waters v. Heublein, Inc.*, 547 F.2d 466, 469–470 (9th Cir.1976), *cert. denied*, 433 U.S. 915, 97 S.Ct. 2988, 53 L.Ed.2d 1100 (1977); *Gray v. Greyhound Lines, East*, 545 F.2d 169, 176 (D.C.Cir.1976). *See Trafficante v. Metropolitan Life Ins. Co.*, 409 U.S. 205, 209, 93 S.Ct. 364, 366–67, 34 L.Ed.2d 415 (1972).

54. *See Pierson v. Ray*, 386 U.S. 547, 558, 87 S.Ct. 1213, 1219–20, 18 L.Ed.2d 288 (1967) and *Evers v. Dwyer*, 358 U.S. 202, 79 S.Ct. 178, 3 L.Ed.2d 222 (1958) (both upholding standing to test right to use unsegregated public accommodations).

55. *Kyles v. J.K. Guardian Sec. Servs., Inc.*, 222 F.3d 289, 304 (7th Cir.2000).

56. *See, e.g., Bender v. Suburban Hosp., Inc.*, 159 F.3d 186, 188 (4th Cir. 1998); *Christopher v. Stouder Mem'l Hosp.*, 936 F.2d 870, 874–75 (6th Cir.1991), *cert. denied*, 502 U.S. 1013, 112 S.Ct. 658, 116 L.Ed.2d 749 (1991); *Zaklama v. Mt. Sinai Med. Ctr.*, 842 F.2d 291, 294–95 (11th Cir. 1988); *Gomez v. Alexian Bros. Hosp. of San Jose*, 698 F.2d 1019, 1021–22 (9th Cir. 1983); *Spirt v. Teachers Ins. & Annuity Ass'n*, 691 F.2d 1054, 1062–63 (2d Cir. 1982), *vacated on other grounds*, 463 U.S. 1223, 103 S.Ct. 3565, 77 L.Ed.2d 1406 (1983); *Sibley Mem'l Hosp. v. Wilson*, 488 F.2d 1338 (D.C.Cir.1973). *See also Graves v. Lowery*, 117 F.3d 723, 728 (3d Cir.1997) (discussing standing per *Sibley*). *But cf. Fields v. Hallsville Ind. Sch. Dist.*, 906 F.2d 1017, 1018–1019 (5th Cir.1990), *cert. denied*, 498 U.S. 1026, 111 S.Ct. 676, 112 L.Ed.2d 668 (1991) and *Diggs v. Harris Hosp.—Methodist, Inc.*, 847 F.2d 270, 271–272 (5th Cir.), *cert. denied*, 488 U.S. 956, 109 S.Ct. 394, 102 L.Ed.2d 383 (1988) (finding no direct employment relationship, but not directly passing on standing per *Sibley*).

used a position of power and control over a third party to wrongfully interfere with that party's employment relationship with the plaintiff.[57]

Unions have had no difficulty gaining standing to protest discrimination against their members,[58] and standing under Title VII has been liberally granted to employees who can show some personal harm resulting from their association with co-employees.[59] But where the Title VII plaintiff has himself suffered no personal injury, standing is typically denied. In *Childress v. City of Richmond, Va.*,[60] the Fourth Circuit, in an equally divided en banc decision, affirmed a district court's denial of standing to white male officers seeking to recover under Title VII for an alleged hostile work environment or retaliation created by the city's discriminatory and hostile treatment of women and blacks. In concurrence, Judge Luttig explained that the difference between the court's Title VII standing analysis in *Childress* and that employed by the Supreme Court in the Title VIII case *Trafficante*, is found in the different language employed in the statutes. Title VIII's term "aggrieved person" is broadly but expressly defined in the statute as "any person who claims to have been injured by a discriminatory housing practice."[61] Title VII, on the other hand, uses the term "aggrieved person" but

57. *See Sibley*, 488 F.2d at 1342. While courts that recognize *Sibley* standing are clear that the plaintiff need not have a direct employment relationship with the defendant, they do tend to require that the plaintiff have such a direct relationship with the third party. That relationship may be shown, however, through a test that considers the economic realities of employment but also relies on the degree of the third party's control over the plaintiff's conduct. *See, e.g., Alexander v. Rush N. Shore Med. Ctr.*, 101 F.3d 487, 492–493 (7th Cir. 1996), *cert. denied*, 522 U.S. 811, 118 S.Ct. 54, 139 L.Ed.2d 19 (1997); *Cobb v. Sun Papers, Inc.*, 673 F.2d 337, 341 (11th Cir.), *cert. denied*, 459 U.S. 874, 103 S.Ct. 163, 74 L.Ed.2d 135 (1982); *Spirides v. Reinhardt*, 613 F.2d 826, 831–832 (D.C.Cir.1979).

58. *See, e.g., International Woodworkers of Am. v. Chesapeake Bay Plywood Corp.*, 659 F.2d 1259 (4th Cir.1981); *International Woodworkers of Am., Local 5–475 v. Georgia–Pacific Corp.*, 568 F.2d 64 (8th Cir.1977); *Air Line Stewards & Stewardesses Ass'n, Local 550 v. American Airlines, Inc.*, 490 F.2d 636 (7th Cir.1973), *cert. denied*, 416 U.S. 993, 94 S.Ct. 2406, 40 L.Ed.2d 773 (1974).

59. *See, e.g., Maynard v. City of San Jose*, 37 F.3d 1396 (9th Cir.1994) (upholding plaintiff's standing to sue for retaliation against him based on his association with members of racial minorities); *Parr v. Woodmen of the World Life Ins. Co.*, 791 F.2d 888 (11th Cir.1986) (standing for plaintiff to complain of discrimination based on an interracial marriage); *Stewart v. Hannon*, 675 F.2d 846, 848–850 (7th Cir.1982) (whites have standing to complain that blacks excluded as school principals); *EEOC v. Mississippi Coll.*, 626 F.2d 477, 481–3 (5th Cir.1980) (same re failure to recruit or hire black faculty); *Waters v. Heublein, Inc.*, 547 F.2d 466, 469–70 (9th Cir.1976) (same re lower pay for black employees); *Rosenblatt v. Bivona & Cohen, PC*, 946 F.Supp. 298 (S.D.N.Y.1996) (white attorney fired allegedly because employer objected to his marriage to a black woman); *Chandler v. Fast Lane, Inc.*, 868 F.Supp. 1138 (E.D.Ark. 1994) (white plaintiff permitted to challenge discriminatory hiring and promotion practices directed only against African–American employees). *But see Leibovitz v. N.Y.C. Transit Authority,* 252 F.3d 179 (2d Cir.2001) (plaintiff suffered no injury herself based on alleged sexual harassment of co-workers that she neither witnessed nor knew about while it lasted); *Childress v. City of Richmond, Va.*, 134 F.3d 1205 (4th Cir.1998) (en banc), *cert. denied*, 524 U.S. 927, 118 S.Ct. 2322, 141 L.Ed.2d 696 (1998) (denying standing under Title VII to white male police officers claiming that sexually and racially derogatory remarks aimed at women and blacks harmed them by chilling teamwork).

60. 134 F.3d 1205 (4th Cir.1998) (en banc), *cert. denied*, 524 U.S. 927, 118 S.Ct. 2322, 141 L.Ed.2d 696 (1998).

61. § 810 (a) of the Fair Housing Act, codified at 42 U.S.C.A. § 3602(i)(1).

contains no definition. By defining the term in Title VIII, the Fourth Circuit reasoned, Congress "statutorily eliminated" all prudential standing requirements in Title VIII cases.[62] Conversely, by failing to define the term in Title VII, Congress impliedly incorporated the "term of art" definition of "aggrieved person" and all of the prudential limitations on standing. The white male plaintiffs had not themselves been the direct victims of discrimination but were instead asserting the rights of third party victims, and prudential standing limits denied standing.

Contrast this with the Seventh Circuit's 1982 decision in *Stewart v. Hannon*,[63] holding that a white employee could be aggrieved by the lack of black employees in the workplace if that produced "the loss of important benefits from interracial associations," described by the court as a personal loss. The Seventh Circuit cited *Stewart* with approval in *Bermudez v. TRC Holdings, Inc.*,[64] where, however, it expressed doubts about allowing nonminority plaintiffs to recover for an allegedly hostile environment based on an employer's negative treatment of minorities.

Standing in a Title VII retaliation case is limited to those persons who engaged in participation or opposition activities.[65] In *Karcher v. Emerson Electric Co.*, for example, a plaintiff was permitted to maintain a retaliation claim for emotional distress damages she suffered when her husband co-worker was dismissed after she filed a charge of discrimination against the employer. The court recognized plaintiff's claim despite the absence of a tangible employment detriment to her, because she suffered an injury ultimately traceable to her own protected participation.[66] In the converse situation, however, standing was denied to a spouse who alleged that he was retaliated against because of protected activity engaged in only by his wife.[67] And the claim of a police officer that he was retaliated against for opposing discrimination by other officers against citizens was not cognizable because he could not have reasonably believed that he was opposing an unlawful employment (as opposed to law enforcement) practice.[68]

Municipal taxpayers may possess standing to litigate "a good-faith pocketbook action."[69] To establish municipal taxpayer standing,[70] a plain-

62. *Childress*, 134 F.3d at 1209–10.

63. 675 F.2d 846, 850 (7th Cir.1982).

64. 138 F.3d 1176, 1180 (7th Cir.1998).

65. See the discussion of retaliation under Title VII generally in § 4.40, *supra*.

66. 94 F.3d 502 (8th Cir.1996), *cert. denied*, 520 U.S. 1210, 117 S.Ct. 1692, 137 L.Ed.2d 820 (1997).

67. *Holt v. JTM Indus., Inc.*, 89 F.3d 1224 (5th Cir.1996), *cert. denied*, 520 U.S. 1229, 117 S.Ct. 1821, 137 L.Ed.2d 1029 (1997).

68. *Wimmer v. Suffolk County Police Dep't*, 176 F.3d 125 (2d Cir.1999), *cert. denied*, 528 U.S. 964, 120 S.Ct. 398, 145 L.Ed.2d 310 (1999).

69. *Doremus v. Board of Education of Hawthorne*, 342 U.S. 429, 434, 72 S.Ct. 394, 96 L.Ed. 475 (1952).

70. The standing requirements for federal taxpayers are more stringent than those for municipal taxpayers. *See Massachusetts v. Mellon*, 262 U.S. 447, 486–87, 43 S.Ct. 597, 67 L.Ed. 1078 (1923); *Flast v. Cohen*, 392 U.S. 83, 102–03, 88 S.Ct. 1942, 20 L.Ed.2d 947 (1968); *Beaumont Indep. Sch. Dist.*, 173 F.3d at 282; *Board of Educ. of Mt. Sinai Sch. Dist. v. New York State Teachers Retirement Sys.*, 60 F.3d 106, 110 (2d Cir.1995); *Hawley v. City of Cleveland*, 773 F.2d 736, 741–42 (6th Cir.1985).

tiff must show only that he pays taxes to the relevant entity, and tax revenues are expended on the disputed practice.[71] The plaintiffs in *Doremus* were state and municipal taxpayers who challenged a state law mandating Bible reading in public schools. The Supreme Court found that the plaintiffs failed to establish a direct monetary injury that would confer standing to raise such a challenge, as they did not allege that the Bible reading was "supported by any separate tax or paid for from any particular appropriation or that it adds any sum whatever to the cost of conducting the school."[72] Likewise, the plaintiffs failed to provide any "information . . . as to what kind of taxes" they paid or to aver "that the Bible reading increase[d] any tax they [did] pay or that as taxpayers they are, will, or possibly can be out of pocket because of" the activity.[73] In short, the plaintiffs failed to establish more than a potential de minimis drain on tax revenues due to the challenged reading.[74] As a result, the plaintiffs lacked standing to sue. The Seventh Circuit reached the same conclusion in *Freedom From Religion Foundation, Inc. v. Zielke*,[75] in which plaintiffs sought to enjoin the display of a monument of the Ten Commandments in a park owned and maintained by the defendant city. While the city had spent money in 1899 to acquire the property for the park, the city had not spent any funds on maintaining the donated monument. The Seventh Circuit noted that "[a] plaintiff's status as a municipal taxpayer is irrelevant for standing purposes if no tax money is spent on the allegedly unconstitutional activity" and concluded that plaintiffs lacked standing to sue.[76]

§ 5.56 Standing After Bankruptcy Filed

A state appellate decision raises an interesting standing issue regarding the relationship between a plaintiff's previously filed bankruptcy case and a subsequent civil rights or employment discrimination case. In *United Technologies Corp. v. Gaines*,[1] the plaintiff's Chapter 7 bankrupt-

71. *Doe v. Beaumont Indep. Sch. Dist.*, 173 F.3d 274, 282 (5th Cir.1999); *United States v. New York*, 972 F.2d 464, 470 (2d Cir.1992) ("[M]unicipal taxpayers have standing to challenge allegedly unlawful municipal expenditures.") (collecting cases).

72. 342 U.S. at 433, 72 S.Ct. at 396, 96 L.Ed. 475.

73. *Id.*

74. *See id.* at 431–32, 72 S.Ct. at 396, 96 L.Ed. 475; *see also Doe v. Madison Sch. Dist. No. 321*, 177 F.3d 789, 794 (9th Cir. 1999) (en banc) (noting that "the school's expenditures for teachers' salaries, equipment, building maintenance, and the like were insufficient to confer taxpayer standing [in *Doremus*] despite their indirect support of the Bible reading").

75. 845 F.2d 1463, 1466 (7th Cir.1988).

76. *Id.* at 1470; *see also ACLU–NJ v. Township of Wall*, 246 F.3d 258 (3d Cir. 2001); *Clay v. Fort Wayne Community Schools*, 76 F.3d 873, 879 (7th Cir.1996) ("Municipal taxpayer status does not confer standing absent some allegation by the plaintiffs of an illegal use of tax revenues."); *Gonzales v. North Tp. of Lake County, Ind.*, 4 F.3d 1412, 1416 (7th Cir. 1993) ("Without evidence of expenditure of tax revenues [on a donated, maintenance-free crucifix in a public park], the plaintiffs cannot claim standing" as taxpayers.); *American Civil Liberties Union of Illinois v. City of St. Charles*, 794 F.2d 265, 267–68 (7th Cir.1986) (Plaintiffs' taxpayer status was irrelevant where there was no allegation "that any part of the expense of the [disputed display of a lighted] cross [was] paid for out of tax revenues.").

§ 5.56

1. 225 Ga.App. 191, 483 S.E.2d 357 (1997). *But cf. Dennis v. Dillard Dep't Stores, Inc.*, 207 F.3d 523, 525–526 (8th Cir.2000) (defendant granted leave to

cy case was closed before [or shortly after] she filed a tort action based on conduct that preceded her bankruptcy petition. Once the bankruptcy case was closed, the tort defendant moved to dismiss under the applicable state real party in interest provision, arguing that the bankruptcy trustee owned the claim under federal bankruptcy law. The plaintiff responded by successfully petitioning in bankruptcy court to reopen her bankruptcy case and name a new trustee. The new trustee and the plaintiff agreed, and the bankruptcy court ordered, that any legal action on the tort claim would be prosecuted in the name of the debtor—although the proceeds of any favorable judgment would accrue to the trustee, as the representative of the debtor's estate.

Despite this agreement and order, the tort defendant contended in state court that the new trustee, not the alleged tort victim, owned the claim. It was undisputed that upon the initial filing of the bankruptcy petition, federal law[2] had effected an instant transfer to the trustee, notwithstanding any contrary provision of state law, of all the debtor's legal and equitable interests, including pending or inchoate claims for relief. The tort defendant argued that after this transfer occurred by operation of law, the agreement between the new trustee and the debtor, blessed by the bankruptcy court, amounted to a partial assignment of the claim that violated a state statute prohibiting the assignment of a personal cause of action.[3] Accordingly, defendant moved to substitute the new trustee for the tort plaintiff-debtor as real party in interest.[4] After the trial court denied the motion, the state appellate court reversed. It agreed with defendant that although the federal statute effecting transfer of the debtor's claim to the trustee preempted contrary state law provisions respecting ownership of the claim, it did not alter the ordinarily prevailing state law rules prohibiting the trustee from assigning that claim thereafter.

The result in *Gaines* binds a plaintiff asserting a state law tort claim to state law limitations on assignability, despite contrary arrangements made during bankruptcy proceedings. It is of course quite possible that this holding does not affect claims under the federal employment discrimination or civil rights statutes. For one thing, the federal law provision automatically transferring ownership of the claim from the alleged victim to the trustee upon the filing of a petition in bankruptcy

amend answer in Equal Pay Act case to assert affirmative "factor other than sex" defense); *Pulliam v. Tallapoosa County Jail*, 185 F.3d 1182, 1189–96 (11th Cir. 1999) (defendant who failed to plead "mixed motives" defense in answer preserved it by raising defense in pretrial order). *See also Harris v. St. Louis Univ.*, 114 B.R. 647, 649 (E.D.Mo.1990) (debtor lacked standing to sue former employer under Title VII and ADEA); *In re Davis*, 158 B.R. 1000 (Bkrtcy.N.D.Ind.1993) (filing of complaint where debtors lacked standing and failed to substitute trustee as real party in interest warranted Rule 11 sanctions).

2. 11 U.S.C.A. § 541.

3. *See* O.C.G.A. § 44–12–24.

4. *See* O.C.G.A. § 9–11–17(a), providing that no action shall be dismissed because not prosecuted in the name of the real party in interest until a reasonable time after objection has been allowed for, among other things, substitution of the real party in interest. This provision echoes the language of F.R.C.P. 17(a), which would be relevant in similar situations arising in the course of employment discrimination or civil rights actions filed in federal court.

might not apply because of conflicting policies particular to the federal employment discrimination or civil rights statutes.[5] Second, even assuming the bankruptcy code provision automatically transferring ownership of the claim to the trustee does apply, and the trustee then assigns the claim to the plaintiff to the extent necessary for her to prosecute in her own name, those same federal policies might preempt state anti-assignment laws and uphold the assignment.[6] Third, even if the trustee acquires the claim under the bankruptcy laws and assigns its prosecution to the plaintiff, and if federal civil rights policies do not pre-empt state anti-assignment provisions, many states do not prohibit the assignment of personal claims.

Assuming, however, that the *Gaines* reasoning may permissibly be extended to federal employment discrimination or civil rights claims, the practical consequences to the debtor plaintiff in a state prohibiting assignments of personal claims may be grievous. First, the defendant would presumably be free to argue to the jury that any damages were suffered by, and any recovery will accrue to, the trustee, and, in turn, the victim's creditors—an argument not calculated to arouse jury sympathy for the plaintiff when it assesses liability or damages. Second, the alleged victim's share, if any, of whatever recovery is achieved despite this obstacle would potentially be substantially less than the victim could obtain in an action prosecuted in her own name, because that recovery would have to be distributed to the victim's creditors in accordance with the disposition of the bankruptcy proceeding. The authors are advised that the action in *Gaines* was in fact dismissed shortly after the appellate decision requiring the action to be prosecuted in the name of the new trustee.

If the bankrupt employment discrimination or civil rights plaintiff is found to have acted intentionally in failing to list the claim on the bankruptcy schedule of assets, the equitable doctrine of judicial estoppel may operate to preclude the plaintiff from asserting the discrimination or civil rights claim at all. As a debtor seeking shelter under the bankruptcy laws is under a continuing duty to disclose all assets, or potential assets, to the bankruptcy court,[7] several courts have concluded that intent can be inferred from the record. The Fifth Circuit stated that "the debtor's failure to satisfy its statutory disclosure duty is 'inadvertent' only when, in general, the debtor either lacks knowledge of the undisclosed claims or has no motive for their concealment."[8] In that

5. *But see Harris* and *Cain v. Hyatt*, 101 B.R. 440, 442 (E.D.Pa.1989) (both applying the ordinary automatic transfer provision so as to divest employment discrimination plaintiffs of standing). To same effect *see Walker v. Anderson Electrical Connectors*, 742 F.Supp. 591, 595 (N.D.Ala.1990), *aff'd*, 944 F.2d 841 (11th Cir.1991), *cert. denied*, 506 U.S. 1078, 113 S.Ct. 1043, 122 L.Ed.2d 352 (1993) (dictum).

6. *See, e.g.*, Section M, this Chapter, on 42 U.S.C.A. § 1988, which provides in pertinent part that state common law shall furnish the rule of decision in civil rights cases on remedial and procedural issues not specifically governed by the Title 42 statutes, but only "so far as the same is not inconsistent with the Constitution and laws of the United States."

7. 11 U.S.C.A. §§ 521(1); 541(a)(7).

8. *In re Coastal Plains, Inc.*, 179 F.3d 197, 210 (5th Cir.1999).

case, the court held that judicial estoppel barred the plaintiffs from asserting claims previously undisclosed to the bankruptcy court because the plaintiffs both knew about the undisclosed claims and had the motive to conceal them from the bankruptcy court.[9]

To reduce these potential risks, plaintiff's counsel should ask the client early in the representation if the client has filed for bankruptcy. If so, but she has not listed the employment discrimination or civil rights claim, counsel should seek leave of the bankruptcy court to amend the asset schedule (or, if the bankruptcy case has already closed, petition to reopen the case and amend that schedule) to list the claim.[10] Provided the claim is listed, the plaintiff may regain standing by persuading the trustee to "abandon" it,[11] either affirmatively or, once the bankruptcy case is closed, by operation of law.[12] In this way, even if the trustee declines to abandon the claim affirmatively, the plaintiff may prosecute a listed federal statutory claim in her own name as real party in interest once the bankruptcy case closes,[13] thereby avoiding the multiple tactical disadvantages inherent in prosecuting the case in the name of the trustee.

An employment discrimination defendant should inquire at the outset of investigation or discovery whether the plaintiff has filed a bankruptcy petition. If she has, but has not listed the claim in question

9. *Id.* at 212; *see also, Payless Wholesale Distrib., Inc. v. Alberto Culver, Inc.*, 989 F.2d 570 (1st Cir.1993) (holding that judicial estoppel barred a former debtor from asserting racketeering, antitrust and fraud claims because the debtor intentionally failed to disclose the claims in a prior bankruptcy proceeding, even though it knew about the claims and had the motive to conceal them).

10. But several courts have refused to allow the reopening of the estate. "The success of our bankruptcy laws requires a debtor's full and honest disclosure. Allowing [the debtor] to back-up, re-open the bankruptcy case, and amend his bankruptcy filings, only after his omission has been challenged by an adversary, suggests that a debtor should consider disclosing potential assets only if he is caught concealing them. This so-called remedy would only diminish the necessary incentive to provide the bankruptcy court with a truthful disclosure of the debtors' assets." *Burnes v. Pemco Aeroplex, Inc.*, 291 F.3d 1282, 1288 (11th Cir. 2002). *See also Traylor v. Gene Evans Ford, LLC,* 185 F.Supp.2d 1338, 1340 (N.D.Ga. 2002) (denying a debtor's request to back up and disclose a previously undisclosed claim to the bankruptcy court in the face of an adversary's challenge); *Scoggins v. Arrow Trucking Co.,* 92 F.Supp.2d 1372, 1376 (S.D.Ga.2000) (same); *Chandler v. Samford University,* 35 F.Supp.2d 861, 863–865 (N.D.Ala.1999) (applying the doctrine of judicial estoppel to bar a plaintiff from asserting a previously undisclosed tort claim, even though she eventually informed her attorney and the bankruptcy court of the claim).

11. "Abandonment" is a procedure allowed for and strictly controlled by the Bankruptcy Code, 11 U.S.C.A. § 554; its detailing workings are beyond the scope of this book. *See Harris*, 114 B.R. at 649 on plaintiff's regaining standing after trustee abandons claim.

12. For abandonment to happen automatically under 11 U.S.C.A. § 554 upon the closing of a bankruptcy case, the asset must have been properly scheduled, either originally or through an amended asset schedule. There is authority finding it an abuse of discretion for the bankruptcy court to deny that leave to amend. *Bittel v. Yamato Int'l Corp.*, 70 F.3d 1271 (6th Cir.1995) (unpublished opinion).

13. And plaintiff's counsel can safely refrain from filing the federal statutory claim until the bankruptcy case is closed. The limitations periods pertaining to the federal claims will be tolled from the time the bankruptcy petition is filed, so that the plaintiff need not file until 60 days after the bankruptcy case is closed. 11 U.S.C.A. § 108.

(or has listed the claim but the bankruptcy case has not closed), the defendant should move to dismiss any pending action on real party in interest grounds. The plaintiff may respond, of course, by amending the asset list to include the claim, or, if the case has closed, by petitioning to reopen the bankruptcy case and amending the list. But unless and until the trustee, either affirmatively or by operation of law, abandons the claim, the defendant may reap the significant tactical advantages attendant upon forcing the plaintiff to prosecute in the name of the trustee. In a jurisdiction with anti-assignment legislation and where there is no authoritative precedent exempting federal civil rights or employment discrimination claims from the automatic bankruptcy transfer, employment counsel on either side would be well advised to consult a bankruptcy expert to help negotiate these potentially perilous shoals.

§§ 5.57–5.64 [Reserved]

L. MOOTNESS

§ 5.65 In General

Because standing is a threshold jurisdictional or quasi-jurisdictional doctrine that bars the doors of the federal courthouse, the burden of its relatively restrictive application to constitutionally based claims for injunctive relief has been felt by plaintiffs. But the same Article III imperatives that underlie the standing doctrines are said to continue throughout the course of federal litigation under the rubric of the companion doctrine of "mootness," which may be thought of as standing redux. Mootness stops an action in its tracks either "when the issues presented are no longer 'live' or the parties lack a legally cognizable interest in the outcome."[1]

A variety of changed circumstances may render abstract a case that was initially sufficiently concrete for the plaintiff to have standing. Typical examples include the repeal or alteration of legislation challenged as constitutionally infirm, release of a prisoner on parole, or satisfaction of the plaintiff's claim by settlement or judgment. Indeed the requirement that issues be raised in a sharp adversary context between parties with concrete stakes persists at each federal appellate level as well. Thus a defendant desiring Supreme Court review of a court of appeals ruling might contend that a controversy remains live, while the plaintiff-appellee seeking to stave off reversal might contend that it is moot.

The Court of late has applied its mootness rules leniently, even as it construes standing stringently. *Lyons*[2] is a striking example. After the Court had granted certiorari to review the lower courts' preliminary injunction against Los Angeles' chokehold policies, the city imposed a

§ 5.65

1. *Powell v. McCormack*, 395 U.S. 486, 489, 89 S.Ct. 1944, 1947, 23 L.Ed.2d 491 (1969).

2. *See supra* § 5.55.

six-month moratorium on the use of one type of chokehold except where deadly force was authorized. The plaintiff resisted review on the grounds of mootness. The Court agreed with the city that the case was not moot because the moratorium was not permanent and therefore had not irrevocably erased the effects of the challenged practice. It nevertheless, for the reasons discussed above, concluded that the federal courts lacked standing ab initio to entertain plaintiff's claim for injunctive relief. The Court has also insisted that an action is moot only if the issue it presents is identical to one decided by a consent decree in related litigation against the same defendant; the new litigation is not moot if it would decide the rights of differently situated persons or impose fresh obligations on the common defendant.[3]

Indeed the Court in related contexts has declared that there is constitutional power to determine the legality of a practice even after the defendant's voluntary cessation of the activity in question.[4] For example, a defendant asserting mootness based on its voluntary compliance in the midst of litigation with a law or regulation or the constitutional standard at issue in the case "bears the formidable burden of showing that it is absolutely clear the allegedly wrongful behavior could not reasonably be expected to recur."[5] The issue has also arisen where a plaintiff seeks solely declaratory or injunctive relief against the operation of an unconstitutional statute that has expired or been repealed before the federal court rules. In that event a declaration of invalidity or prohibitory injunction concerning the old statute would not avail the plaintiff, ordinarily rendering the controversy moot.[6] But the Court has permitted such challenges where a legislature reenacted the challenged provisions in a form sufficiently altered that there was no reason to conclude that it was simply repeating the challenged conduct.[7]

The Court has similarly ruled that where there is a risk that the legislature will repeat its allegedly unconstitutional conduct by reenacting provisions identical or similar to those under challenge—as where

3. *Suter v. Artist M.*, 503 U.S. 347, 354 n. 6, 112 S.Ct. 1360, 1365 n. 6, 118 L.Ed.2d 1 (1992).

4. *Friends of the Earth v. Laidlaw*, 528 U.S. at 189–194, 120 S.Ct. at 708–711.

5. *Id.* at 190, 120 S.Ct. at 709. *See also Buckhannon Bd. and Care Home, Inc. v. West Va. Dep't of Health and Human Resources*, 532 U.S. 598, 121 S.Ct. 1835, 1842–1843, 149 L.Ed.2d 855 (2001): " 'It is well settled that a defendant's voluntary cessation of a challenged practice does not deprive a federal court of its power to determine the legality of the practice' unless it is 'absolutely clear that the allegedly wrongful behavior could not reasonably be expected to recur.' "Thus, for example, a prisoner's claim for injunctive relief in an action alleging he was exposed to unreasonably high levels of secondhand smoke was not mooted by his transfer to a different housing block or prison's implementation of a restrictive smoking policy where plaintiff asserted the new policy was not being enforced and he could have experienced the same high levels of smoke in the new cell block. *Davis v. New York*, 316 F.3d 93 (2d Cir.2002).

6. *See, e.g., Burke v. Barnes*, 479 U.S. 361, 107 S.Ct. 734, 93 L.Ed.2d 732 (1987) (expiration); *Board of Flour Inspectors v. Glover*, 160 U.S. 170, 16 S.Ct. 321, 40 L.Ed. 382 (1895) (repeal).

7. *Diffenderfer v. Central Baptist Church of Miami, Fla., Inc.*, 404 U.S. 412, 413–14, 92 S.Ct. 574, 575–76, 30 L.Ed.2d 567 (1972) and *Fusari v. Steinberg*, 419 U.S. 379, 380, 95 S.Ct. 533, 535, 42 L.Ed.2d 521 (1975).

the legislature announces the intention to do so,[8] or already has during the course of the litigation[9]—a federal court has discretion to determine the challenged practice's legality despite the defendant's voluntary, if perhaps only temporary, cessation. Mootness in this situation accordingly turns on the court's assessment of the degree to which reenacted legislation cures the originally alleged defect.[10] Review in this situation failed, however, where municipal legislation establishing a challenged "set-aside" affirmative action program for public contracts expired pending appeal by its own terms, rather than through voluntary action of the city.[11] The Second Circuit expressed confidence that in view of the Supreme Court's intervening decision in *City of Richmond v. J.A. Croson Co.*,[12] the plan struck down by the district court would not be reenacted in substantially similar form without an updated factual predicate reflecting the continuing effects of past discriminatory practices.

A traditional "capable of repetition, yet evading review" exception to mootness has been extended to and relaxed in the class action setting, significantly facilitating the civil rights group-based injunction. In its original, restrictive form, the exception kept within federal purview an otherwise mooted controversy that centered on an issue likely to recur between the same parties.[13] That is, the exception applied only when there was a "reasonable expectation that the same complaining party would be subjected to the same action again" after the mooting event.[14] An example is the Court's willingness to hear the claim of a formerly pregnant plaintiff in *Roe v. Wade*;[15] her issue was capable of repetition vis-a-vis the same state authorities but calculated to continue to evade review because more than nine months would likely elapse after the commencement of any civil action and the time her case could be heard and decided by the Supreme Court.[16] This form of the exception, still applicable in individual actions, requires the plaintiff to show that the

8. *City of Mesquite v. Aladdin's Castle, Inc.*, 455 U.S. 283, 289, 102 S.Ct. 1070, 1075, 71 L.Ed.2d 152 (1982).

9. *Northeastern Fla. Chapter of the Associated Gen. Contractors of Am. v. City of Jacksonville*, 508 U.S. at 660–61, 113 S.Ct. at 2300.

10. *Compare Northeastern Florida Chapter*, 508 U.S. at 660–61 & n.3, 113 S.Ct. at 2300 & n.3 (reenacted legislation that reduces only the degree of race-based preferential treatment without changing the mechanism for carrying it out is not "sufficiently altered") *with id.* at 674, 113 S.Ct. at 2307 (O'Connor, J., dissenting) ("I cannot say that these changes are 'insignificant' ... to petitioner's equal protection claim.").

11. *Associated Gen. Contractors of Conn., Inc. v. New Haven, Conn.*, 41 F.3d 62 (2d Cir.1994).

12. 488 U.S. 469, 109 S.Ct. 706, 102 L.Ed.2d 854 (1989).

13. *See, e.g., Southern Pac. Terminal Co. v. Interstate Commerce Comm'n*, 219 U.S. 498, 31 S.Ct. 279, 55 L.Ed. 310 (1911).

14. *Weinstein v. Bradford*, 423 U.S. 147, 149, 96 S.Ct. 347, 349, 46 L.Ed.2d 350 (1975) (per curiam). *See Russman v. Board of Educ. of Enlarged Sch. Dist. of City of Watervliet*, 260 F.3d 114 (2d Cir.2001) (case moot because reward did not indicate that parents of special education student would seek additional, available special education schooling).

15. 410 U.S. 113, 93 S.Ct. 705, 35 L.Ed.2d 147 (1973).

16. If a challenged practice is determinable via a claim for damages, however, it does not evade review even when the plaintiff lacks standing to secure an injunction. *Lyons*, 461 U.S. at 109, 103 S.Ct. at 1669.

challenged action is too short in duration to be fully litigated before its expiration or cessation and that there is a reasonable likelihood the same party will again be subjected to the same challenged action.[17]

When the Court transplanted the exception to the class action context, it no longer insisted that the otherwise mooted issue be represented by the same claimant. The named plaintiff in *Sosna v. Iowa*,[18] after obtaining class certification, also satisfied the residency requirement prerequisite to suit for an Iowa divorce before the class' challenge to that review—evading requirement could be heard on the merits. Although the issue was still live for others in her class, it seemed unlikely that she would face it again personally. The Court nevertheless held that the interest of the unnamed class members in the as yet undetermined issue could substitute for the vanished interest of the named plaintiff.

The Court soon wrenched the exception from its moorings by extending *Sosna* to embrace issues that would *not* evade review! In *Franks v. Bowman Transp. Co.*,[19] the Court permitted the sole named plaintiff in a previously certified Title VII subclass to pursue retroactive seniority relief on behalf of unnamed class members even though by then he lacked a personal interest in that relief and the unnamed plaintiffs would likely have other opportunities to obtain review of that issue. The Court thus appeared to accept that in a class action under Federal Rule of Civil Procedure 23, the concrete presentation sought to be assured by the "injury in fact" element of standing/mootness doctrine is met not by the named plaintiff but by the allegations on behalf of the class—they have a life of their own that survives his exit from the lawsuit.[20]

The question remained whether the federal courts' willingness to entertain the claims of unnamed class members after the mooting of the named plaintiff's claim was dependent on whether, as in *Sosna* and *Franks*, the mooting event occurred only after the class had been certified. The opinion in *Sosna* had so suggested.[21] The Court has since answered that question in the negative, permitting putative class members to obtain judicial review of rulings denying class certification issued after the mooting of the sole named plaintiff's claim. And it has permitted these appeals regardless of whether the named plaintiff's claim was mooted by his own favorable judgment on the merits—in which case it could be said that he still retains at least an economic interest in the statutory attorney's fees available to a prevailing party—or simply by expiration, as when a prisoner challenging parole release guidelines is

17. *See, e.g., First Nat'l Bank of Boston v. Bellotti,* 435 U.S. 765, 774, 98 S.Ct. 1407, 55 L.Ed.2d 707 (1978); *Porter v. Jones*, 319 F.3d 483, 489–490 (9th Cir.2003) (noting frequent application of the exception to election-related disputes).

18. 419 U.S. 393, 95 S.Ct. 553, 42 L.Ed.2d 532 (1975).

19. 424 U.S. 747, 96 S.Ct. 1251, 47 L.Ed.2d 444 (1976).

20. *Id.* at 754, 96 S.Ct. at 1259.

21. 419 U.S. at 399, 95 S.Ct. at 557.

released pending appeal.[22] If, upon such appeal, the denial of class certification is reversed, then *Sosna* authorizes adjudication of the merits.[23]

When a case becomes moot on appeal, the ordinary appellate court response is vacatur of the judgment below. The principal reason is that the judgment loser should not suffer the adverse res judicata or collateral estoppel effects of that judgment when, for reasons beyond its control, it is denied appellate review.[24] But where the parties render a case moot by settling their controversy on appeal, the equitable considerations favoring vacatur of the judgment under review evaporate and vacatur is not justified.[25]

Whereas mootness assumes that a plaintiff with a sufficiently concrete personal stake initially presented a live controversy suitable for judicial resolution, the separate doctrine of ripeness, another judge-made gloss on the requirements of an Article III "case or controversy," denies federal court cognizance of a case when the dispute hangs on future contingencies that may or may not occur. A classic instance would be a claim dependent on the occurrence of events that have not yet taken place.[26] In a sense, it could be maintained that every failure to exhaust administrative remedies is an instance of ripeness. Thus ripeness is one way that a court, presented with a claim under Section 1983, may rationalize dismissing an action brought before the plaintiff has exhausted available administrative remedies, notwithstanding the general rule[27] that a plaintiff need not exhaust administrative remedies before filing an action under Section 1983.[28]

§§ 5.66–5.69 [Reserved]

M. GAP–FILLING FROM STATE LAW UNDER SECTION 1988: SURVIVORSHIP AND LIMITATIONS

§ 5.70 42 U.S.C.A. § 1988

42 U.S.C.A. § 1988[1] provides, in terms that at first blush appear internally contradictory, that when federal law is "deficient in the

22. *See*, respectively, *Deposit Guaranty Nat'l Bank v. Roper*, 445 U.S. 326, 100 S.Ct. 1166, 63 L.Ed.2d 427 (1980) and *United States Parole Comm'n v. Geraghty*, 445 U.S. 388, 100 S.Ct. 1202, 63 L.Ed.2d 479 (1980).

23. *Geraghty*, 445 U.S. at 404, 100 S.Ct. at 1212.

24. *See United States v. Munsingwear, Inc.*, 340 U.S. 36, 71 S.Ct. 104, 95 L.Ed. 36 (1950) (referring to mooting that occurred "through happenstance"); *Associated Gen. Contractors of Conn., Inc. v. New Haven, Conn.*, 41 F.3d 62 (1994).

25. *U.S. Bancorp Mortgage Co. v. Bonner Mall Partnership*, 513 U.S. 18, 115 S.Ct. 386, 130 L.Ed.2d 233 (1994).

26. *See, e.g., Porter v. Jones*, 319 F.3d 483, 490–491 (9th Cir.2003) (defendant asserted plaintiffs' claim not ripe because based on their intended exercise of free speech during future election, but court found allegations concerned plaintiffs' activities during past election and hence presented "a fully developed factual scenario.").

27. *See Patsy v. Board of Regents*, 457 U.S. 496, 516, 102 S.Ct. 2557, 2568, 73 L.Ed.2d 172 (1982).

28. *See Bowers v. City of Flint*, 325 F.3d 758 (6th Cir.2003).

§ 5.70

1. 42 U.S.C.A. § 1988. Section 1988 reads in part:

provisions necessary to furnish suitable remedies" in a civil rights action, the law of the forum state shall apply unless that law is itself inconsistent with [the nonexistent?] federal law.

Section 1988 applies to actions under 42 U.S.C.A. §§ 1981, 1982, 1983 and 1985(3). "Its application involves three steps. First, the court must determine that federal law is deficient—that is, a positive provision of federal law does not address the question at issue. Second, the Court must identify the applicable state law. Third, the Court must apply that state law, but only to the extent it is "not inconsistent with the Constitution and laws of the United States." Of course, since the statute tells us to look to state law only when there is no positive federal statute on point, the federal law with which the state law may not be inconsistent must refer not to a statute but to the somewhat vaguer judge-made federal policies that surround the federal claim. That is, on the consistency question, a court must look not at "particular federal statutes and constitutional provisions"—if there were any, we wouldn't be repairing to state law in the first place—but at the policies that underlie these statutes and provisions.[2] A state statute or decision, however, cannot be considered "inconsistent" with federal law merely because it causes the plaintiff to lose the litigation.[3]

On some issues the Court has long taken it as self-evident that federal policy dictates judge-made solutions to problems not addressed in terms by the Reconstruction Acts themselves. Two salient examples are the question of immunities for both individual and government entity defendants and the measure of damages available to a prevailing civil rights plaintiff. In these areas the Court has sometimes borrowed state common law in forging a national approach but has sometimes frankly departed from the state tradition in the name of ancient civil rights policies or federal administrative or efficiency policies invented on the

> The jurisdiction in civil and criminal matters conferred on the district courts by the provisions of this Title, and of Title "CIVIL RIGHTS," and of Title "CRIMES," for the protection of all persons in the United States in their civil rights, and for their vindication, shall be exercised and enforced in conformity with the laws of the United States, so far as such laws are suitable to carry the same into effect; but in all cases where they are not adapted to the object, or are deficient in the provisions necessary to furnish suitable remedies and punish offenses against law, the common law, as modified and changed by the constitution and statutes of the State wherein the court having jurisdiction of such civil or criminal cause is held, so far as the same is not inconsistent with the Constitution and laws of the United States, shall be extended to and govern the said courts in the trial and disposition of the cause, and, if it is of a criminal nature, in the infliction of punishment on the party found guilty.

42 U.S.C.A. § 1988. A final sentence of the Section, added by the Civil Rights Attorney's Fees Awards Act of 1976, is omitted here. That Act is discussed in Chapter 4 on attorney's fees.

2. *Robertson v. Wegmann*, 436 U.S. 584, 590, 98 S.Ct. 1991, 1995, 56 L.Ed.2d 554 (1978).

3. *Id.* at 593, 98 S.Ct. at 1996.

spot.[4] Only rarely has the Court formally acknowledged that § 1988 constrains the applicable rule of decision. The discussion that follows illustrates the extreme difficulty the Court has had in applying the vague "inconsistency" test of § 1988 in a principled fashion.

§ 5.71 Survivorship

Federal law is deficient in providing for rights of survivorship in actions under the Reconstruction Civil Rights Acts. Therefore, pursuant to the terms of § 1988, it is necessary to borrow the applicable state survivorship law so long as it is consistent with the underlying federal cause of action. In *Robertson v. Wegmann*,[1] the Supreme Court held that Louisiana's survivorship law was not inconsistent with the federal policy underlying 42 U.S.C.A. § 1983, even though applying it caused the § 1983 action to abate in that case.[2] The Court stated that the "policies underlying § 1983 include compensation of persons injured by deprivation of federal rights and prevention of abuses of power by those acting under color of state law."[3] The Court concluded that because the state survivorship law was broad enough to encompass most situations of survivorship, and hence would permit compensation in most cases where a civil rights victim died before judgment, the mere failure of this particular case to meet the state's requirements for survival of the claim was insufficient to deem the state law inconsistent with federal law.[4]

Alabama has a survival statute that allows for punitive but not compensatory damages.[5] The Alabama Supreme Court held that the statute is not inconsistent with the Constitution and laws of the United States, citing *Robertson*, and that the statute applies in § 1983 suits, a holding that effectively immunizes municipalities from § 1983 wrongful death damages.[6] The Supreme Court granted certiorari and held oral argument,[7] but later dismissed the writ, finding that the Alabama Supreme Court order remanding the case was not a final order as required by 28 U.S.C.A. § 1257(a) for appellate review of state supreme court decisions.[8] Some courts have found a similar statutory scheme

4. *See* Chapter 2, on § 1983.

§ 5.71

1. 436 U.S. 584, 98 S.Ct. 1991, 56 L.Ed.2d 554 (1978).

2. *Id.* at 594–95, 98 S.Ct. at 1997–98. *See also Pluet v. Frasier*, 355 F.3d 381 (5th Cir. 2004) (Texas survival statute denies standing to guardian of person who was not deceased arrestee's biological son); *Pietrowski v. Town of Dibble*, 134 F.3d 1006, 1008–09 (10th Cir.1998) (holding § 1983 malicious prosecution claim abates after death of defendant, giving deference to state statute).

3. *Robertson*, 436 U.S. at 591, 98 S.Ct. at 1996.

4. *Id.* at 591–92, 98 S.Ct. at 1996.

5. § 6–5–410, Ala. Code 1975.

6. *City of Tarrant, Ala. v. Jefferson*, 682 So.2d 29 (Ala.1996), *cert. dismissed*, 522 U.S. 75, 118 S.Ct. 481, 139 L.Ed.2d 433 (1997). By contrast, adoption of the Georgia wrongful death statute in § 1983 actions via § 1988 had the effect of according standing to a mother whose son was murdered by his wife. *Carringer v. Rodgers*, 331 F.3d 844 (11th Cir.2003).

7. *Jefferson v. City of Tarrant, Ala.*, 520 U.S. 1154, 117 S.Ct. 1333, 137 L.Ed.2d 493 (1997).

8. *Jefferson v. City of Tarrant, Ala.*, 522 U.S. 75, 118 S.Ct. 481, 139 L.Ed.2d 433 (1997).

repugnant to the § 1983 remedial goal of compensation,[9] but others have even sustained statutes that call for total abatement of particular claims upon plaintiff's death.[10]

§ 5.72 Period of Limitations

Another area in which federal law is deficient, except as to most claims under section 1981,[1] is the period of limitations governing actions

9. *See Williams v. City of Oakland*, 915 F.Supp. 1074 (N.D.Cal.1996) (striking as inconsistent with § 1983 policies favoring victim compensation a California survivorship statute that precluded recovery for pain and suffering, since statute would substantially reduce the type and amount of damages recoverable in all § 1983 actions where the victim dies before entry of judgment); *County of L.A. v. Schonert*, 58 Cal.Rptr.2d 358 (Cal.Dist.Ct.App.1996) (refusing to apply in state court a state law that prevents successor plaintiff from recovering emotional distress damages after original plaintiff has died, on ground that law is too "inhospitable" to purposes of § 1983). *But see Los Angeles County v. Superior Court of L.A. County*, 21 Cal.4th 292, 87 Cal.Rptr.2d 441, 981 P.2d 68 (1999) (upholding against § 1983 preemption argument to California law authorizing survival action for pecuniary losses and punitive damages but precluding recovery for pain and suffering as providing adequate compensation and deterrence, at least where plaintiff died while action pending).

10. *Pietrowski v. Town of Dibble* 134 F.3d 1006, 1009 (10th Cir.1998) (no inconsistency between section 1983's policies and Oklahoma statute providing for abatement of malicious prosecution claims upon the plaintiff's death); *Evans v. Twin Falls County*, 118 Idaho 210, 796 P.2d 87 (1990), *cert. denied*, 498 U.S. 1086, 111 S.Ct. 960, 112 L.Ed.2d 1048 (1991) (no inconsistency between Idaho law of total abatement of personal causes of action and section 1983); *Parkerson v. Carrouth*, 782 F.2d 1449, 1455 (8th Cir.1986) (when widow sued not for her own injuries "derivatively suffered when defendants allegedly violated her husband's civil rights" but merely as executor of estate, overriding Arkansas law to mandate survival of action would not further section 1983's policy of compensating the person injured by a civil rights violation).

§ 5.72

1. In 1990 Congress passed 28 U.S.C.A. § 1658, which reads: "Except as otherwise provided by law, a civil action arising under an Act of Congress enacted after the date of the enactment of this section may not be commenced later than 4 years after the cause of action accrues." 28 U.S.C.A. § 1658 (Supp.1993). The language of § 1658, however, unambiguously applies only to acts of Congress *enacted after* December 1, 1990, the date of enactment of § 1658. Pub.L.No. 101–650, Title III, § 313(a), 104 Stat. 5114 (enacted Dec. 1, 1990). The Reconstruction Civil Rights Acts were originally enacted approximately a century and a quarter before December 1, 1990. But Section 1981, unlike the other Reconstruction Civil Rights Acts, was substantively amended by the Civil Rights Act of 1991, a post-December 1, 1990 act of Congress. As discussed in § 1.2, *supra*, the 1991 Act amended § 1981 by overruling the Supreme Court's decision in *Patterson v. McLean Credit Union,* 491 U.S. 164, 109 S.Ct. 2363, 105 L.Ed.2d 132 (1989), and thus restoring the application of § 1981 to terms and conditions of employment–like on-the-job harassment, failure to promote, demotion, and discharge—arising after initial contract formation. The question that then divided five circuit courts of appeals was whether a § 1981 claim asserting racial discrimination respecting a post-hire term of employment—that is, a claim made possible only by the Civil Rights Act of 1991's overruling of *Patterson*—was eligible for § 1658's 4–year statute of limitations even though the underlying statute that the 1991 Act amended, Section 1981, pre-dated December 1, 1990 by 124 years. In *Jones v. R.R. Donnelley & Sons Company*, ___ U.S. ___, 124 S.Ct. 1836, ___ L.Ed.2d ___ (2004), the Court held that it is. The Court concluded that a cause of action "aris[es] under an Act of Congress enacted after" December 1, 1990—and is therefore governed by § 1658's 4–year limitations period—if the particular plaintiff's claims were made possible by a post–1990 enactment. Because the *Jones* petitioners' hostile work environment, wrongful termination, and failure-to-transfer claims alleged § 1981 violations that, under *Patterson*, would not have stated a claim before December 1, 1990, but were actionable by virtue of the Civil Rights Act of 1991 amendments, they "ar[ose] under" the 1991 amendments to § 1981 and accordingly fit within the terms of § 1658.

under the Reconstruction Civil Rights Acts. Accordingly, pursuant to § 1988, state statutes of limitations will apply unless deemed inconsistent with federal law.[2] A state's period will be deemed repugnant to federal policy if there is an indication that it unfairly discriminates against the federal cause of action, as where a special statute geared specifically to actions under § 1983 is shorter than the state's limitations period applicable to personal injury actions in general.[3] But Section 1988 gives no general guidance as to which period of limitations a state should apply. In *Wilson v. Garcia*,[4] the Supreme Court concluded that for the purposes of "uniformity, certainty, and the minimization of unnecessary litigation," all claims under § 1983 should be characterized in the same manner[5]; and it chose the state period of limitations for tortious personal injury to govern.[6] In fact, all the Reconstruction Acts use the applicable state law period of limitations of the forum state for claims alleging tortious personal injury, as announced in *Wilson*.[7]

What period applies, though, when the forum state's law contains numerous limitation periods for different types of personal injury? In *Owens v. Okure*,[8] the Court acknowledged that the states have a broad range of limitations periods for intentional and unintentional injury to the person. But it also observed that each state has a general or residual statute for personal injury actions and held that period presumptively

Because the vast majority of claims under Section 1981, indeed virtually all such claims other than alleged racially discriminatory refusals to hire, depend on the 1991 amendments to § 1981 that overruled *Patterson*, almost all Section 1981 claims will now be eligible for § 1658's generous 4-year limitations period, regardless of shorter limitations periods of the forum state. By contrast, claims under the other Reconstruction Acts, principally claims under Sections 1982, 1983, and 1985, will remain subject to the forum state's general or residual limitations period governing claims of personal injury, because the rights created by those statutes have not been substantively amended after § 1658's cutoff of December 1, 1990.

In any event, the only deadline from accrual of the claim that need be followed is a statute of limitations. The Eleventh Circuit has refused to import a state statute of repose, reasoning that it was an unnecessary, distinct state statute. *Moore v. Liberty Nat'l Life Ins. Co.*, 267 F.3d 1209, 1216 (11th Cir. 2001) (noting that the court found no federal case in which a state statute of repose was borrowed to fill the gaps in a federal civil rights statute).

2. *See Wilson v. Garcia*, 471 U.S. 261, 266, 105 S.Ct. 1938, 1942, 85 L.Ed.2d 254 (1985).

3. *Arnold v. Duchesne County, Utah*, 26 F.3d 982 (10th Cir.1994), *cert. denied*, 513 U.S. 1076, 115 S.Ct. 721, 130 L.Ed.2d 626 (1995).

4. 471 U.S. 261, 105 S.Ct. 1938, 85 L.Ed.2d 254 (1985).

5. *Id.* at 275, 105 S.Ct. at 1946.

6. *Id.* at 280, 105 S.Ct. at 1949. *See also Shamaeizadeh v. Cunigan*, 182 F.3d 391, 394 (6th Cir.1999), *cert. denied*, 528 U.S. 1021, 120 S.Ct. 531, 145 L.Ed.2d 412 (1999) (applying Kentucky one-year personal injury limitations period); *Silva v. Crain*, 169 F.3d 608 (9th Cir.1999) (rejecting the use of California's special state notice-of-claim statute in favor of the state's general residual statute of limitations for personal injury actions, a one-year period).

7. *See Goodman v. Lukens Steel Co.*, 482 U.S. 656, 662, 107 S.Ct. 2617, 2621, 96 L.Ed.2d 572 (1987) (§ 1981 claims); *Village of Bellwood v. Dwivedi*, 895 F.2d 1521, 1528 (7th Cir.1990) (§ 1982 claims); *Bougher v. University of Pittsburgh*, 882 F.2d 74, 79 (3d Cir.1989) (§ 1985 claims).

8. 488 U.S. 235, 109 S.Ct. 573, 102 L.Ed.2d 594 (1989). *See also Huels v. Exxon Coal USA, Inc.*, 121 F.3d 1047 (7th Cir. 1997) (applying the Title VII doctrine of *Lorance v. AT & T Technologies*, 490 U.S. 900, 109 S.Ct. 2261, 104 L.Ed.2d 961 (1989) to ADA claim, even though *Lorance* was in relevant part overruled by the Civil Rights Act of 1991).

binding.[9] However, the Court also stated that each chosen residual period must be consistent with the policies underlying the federal cause of action. For example, if a court deems a residual period too short, it could hold that period inconsistent with the remedial goals of § 1983. Given the influence of the plaintiff's personal injury bar on state legislatures' selection of a general personal injury statute of limitations, however, it seems doubtful that a state's period will be deemed so short as to run afoul of the remedial objective of § 1983.

§ 5.73 Accrual of Period and Suspension or "Tolling" Circumstances

Federal and state courts must also ascertain the accrual or "trigger" date that starts the running of the applicable statute of limitations—that is, the applicable state limitations period—in Reconstruction Act cases,[1] or the federal deadlines for filing administrative charges and court complaints in cases under federal employment discrimination statutes. In Reconstruction Act cases, even though courts typically borrow (as a matter of federal law) the catalogue of *tolling* circumstances (circumstances that suspend the running of the limitations statute once it accrues) from the law of the state that provides the limitations period, they generally determine the claim's accrual date for themselves.[2] That

9. *Id.* at 236, 109 S.Ct. at 574. *See, e.g., Lovett v. Ray*, 327 F.3d 1181, 1182–1183 (11th Cir.2003) (applying Georgia 2-year general personal injury limitations period); *Sain v. Bend*, 309 F.3d 1134, 1139 (9th Cir.2002) (applying Oregon's personal injury limitations period, and citing authority rejecting use of Oregon Tort Claims Act); *Pearl v. City of Long Beach*, 296 F.3d 76,79 (2d Cir.2002) (citing *Okure*, applying three-year general or residual New York personal injury limitations period); *Ashafa v. City of Chicago*, 146 F.3d 459 (7th Cir.1998) (two-year general personal injury limitations period applied rather than five-year catch-all period); *Blake v. Dickason*, 997 F.2d 749 (10th Cir.1993) (applying Colorado's two-year residual personal injury statute of limitations, rather than a six-year statute of limitations for sexual assault against a minor, to a § 1983 claim concerning an alleged sexual assault by a teacher against a student).

§ 5.73

1. *See* § 5.72, *supra*.

2. *See, e.g., Lovett v. Ray*, 327 F.3d 1181 (11th Cir.2003) (holding federal law governs, stating the federal accrual rule of the circuit is that statute "does not begin to run until the facts which would support a cause of action are apparent or should be apparent to a person with a reasonably prudent regard for his rights" and relying on circuit authority that rejects use of continuing violation doctrine where plaintiff complains of continuing consequences of a one-time violation); *Shields v. Ft. James Corporation*, 305 F.3d 1280 (11th Cir.2002) (in effect deeming accrual a federal matter, by borrowing for § 1981 actions the Supreme Court-devised rules for the accrual of Title VII sexual or racial harassment claims); *RK Ventures v. City of Seattle*, 307 F.3d 1045 (9th Cir.2002) (determining as a matter of federal law that nightclub owners' § 1983 claims arising from city's enforcement of nuisance laws accrued when the city gave notice to plaintiffs of its decision to institute formal hearing under nuisance abatement ordinance, rather than the commencement of that hearing or subsequent prosecution, which was merely the inevitable consequence of the decision to initiate the proceeding); *Pearl v. City of Long Beach*, 296 F.3d 76, 80 (2d Cir.2002) (accrual determined by federal law and the rule of the circuit is that accrual occurs "when the plaintiff knows or has reason to know of the injury which is the basis of his action"); *Heard v. Sheahan*, 253 F.3d 316, 317–318 (7th Cir.2001); *Snodderly v. R.U.F.F. Drug Enforcement Task Force*, 239 F.3d 892 (7th Cir.2001) (false arrest claim akin to malicious prosecution accrues only when criminal prosecution dismissed); *Hughes v. Vanderbilt Univ.*, 215 F.3d 543, 548 (6th Cir.2000) (applying federal law

works well for the plaintiff, as the general federal approach provides that an action accrues when the plaintiff "knows or has reason to know of the injury which is the basis of the action."[3] In federal employment discrimination cases, the Supreme Court's fairly stringent nationally applicable accrual rule[4] generally prevails.

But there is considerable overlap and resulting confusion in the decisions between accrual and particular kinds of state "tolling" rules, i.e., rules that suspend the running of the limitations period after a claim accrues for a variety of circumstances including the plaintiff's infancy, insanity or other mental disability, or imprisonment. The taxonomy difference may be critical. While "accrual" of the claim may be defined by federal law, the Supreme Court held in *Johnson v. Railway Express*

standard that claim accrues when plaintiff knows or has reason to know of the injury of which she complains) (case under § 1983); *Harvey v. Waldron*, 210 F.3d 1008, 1013 (9th Cir.2000); *Shamaeizadeh v. Cunigan,* 182 F.3d 391, 398–99 (6th Cir.1999) (claim subject to *Heck* bar accrued when criminal charges against plaintiff were dismissed); *Gonzalez v. Entress*, 133 F.3d 551 (7th Cir.1998) (because Fourth Amendment claims not subject to *Heck* doctrine, they accrue at time of alleged unlawful arrest, search or seizure); *Ormiston v. Nelson*, 117 F.3d 69 (2d Cir.1997) (claim challenging unconstitutional medical or psychiatric confinement accrues on whatever date plaintiff has reason to know, or knows, of the constitutional injury, not invariably on the date of initial confinement or upon release therefrom); *Merriweather v. City of Memphis*, 107 F.3d 396 (6th Cir.1997) (in § 1983 excessive force claim based on shooting by police, Federal court decides that state's one-year statute begins to run on day of shooting); *Antonelli v. Foster*, 104 F.3d 899 (7th Cir.1997), *cert. denied*, 522 U.S. 834, 118 S.Ct. 104, 139 L.Ed.2d 58 (1997) (plaintiff detained pursuant to parole violator warrant had to successfully challenge that detention in habeas or parole revocation proceedings as precondition to accrual of § 1983 claim); *Smith v. Holtz*, 87 F.3d 108 (3d Cir.1996), *cert. denied*, 519 U.S. 1041, 117 S.Ct. 611, 136 L.Ed.2d 536 (1996) (§ 1983 claim accrued only when state supreme court dismissed murder charges, not earlier when conviction reversed and new trial ordered); *Schilling v. White*, 58 F.3d 1081 (6th Cir.1995) (because *Heck* doctrine does apply to Fourth Amendment claims, those claims do not accrue unless and until a conviction is reversed on state criminal appeal or invalidated on habeas); *Woods v. Candela*, 47 F.3d 545 (2d Cir.1995), *cert. denied*, 516 U.S. 808, 116 S.Ct. 54, 133 L.Ed.2d 18 (1995) (same); *Jackson v. Johnson*, 950 F.2d 263, 265 (5th Cir.1992). *Cf. Gutowsky v. County of Placer*, 108 F.3d 256 (9th Cir.1997), *cert. denied*, 522 U.S. 914, 118 S.Ct. 298, 139 L.Ed.2d 229 (1997) (a material fact question about a local government defendant's custom or policy triggers the continuing violations doctrine for a § 1983 claim, which has the effect of delaying the date the claim accrues). *But see Carreras–Rosa v. Alves–Cruz*, 127 F.3d 172 (1st Cir.1997) (borrowing Puerto Rico's accrual law).

3. *Jackson v. Johnson*, 950 F.2d 263, 265 (5th Cir.1992) (internal quotations omitted). See also the decisions cited in preceding footnote.

4. *Delaware State Coll. v. Ricks*, 449 U.S. 250, 101 S.Ct. 498, 66 L.Ed.2d 431 (1980) (Title VII claim accrues when plaintiff learns of impending termination, not subsequent date of preliminary or final grievance procedures or even later date of actual termination). For claims alleging intentional discrimination caused by changes in seniority systems, Congress provided its own rule in 1991. Section 706(e)(2) of the Civil Rights Act of 1991 partially overruled the Supreme Court's decision in *Lorance v. AT & T Technologies, Inc.*, 490 U.S. 900, 109 S.Ct. 2261, 104 L.Ed.2d 961 (1989), to provide that the applicable administrative charge-filing period begins to run either when a discriminatory seniority system change is adopted (that is, when the plaintiff might be presumed to know about it) *or* the later date when the plaintiff is actually affected by the change. *Cf. Romano v. Rockwell Int'l, Inc.*, 14 Cal.4th 479, 59 Cal. Rptr.2d 20, 926 P.2d 1114 (1996) (refusing to apply *Ricks* Title VII interpretation of "trigger" date to termination claim under California employment discrimination law, holding that the charge-filing clock does not start running until the employee is actually discharged).

Agency, Inc.,[5] that forum state law determines the circumstances that suspend or "toll" the running of the borrowed state statute of limitations on a claim under § 1981, so long as those tolling rules are not inconsistent with the policy of the underlying federal cause of action.[6]

> Any period of limitation ... is understood fully only in the context of the various circumstances that suspend it from running against a particular cause of action ... In borrowing a state period of limitation for application to a federal cause of action, a federal court is relying on the State's wisdom in setting a limit, and exceptions thereto.[7]

In *Johnson* the Court refused to create a federal tolling rule and held as a matter of federal law that the timely filing of a Title VII action did not suspend the running of the applicable state period of limitation on a claim under § 1981.[8] Similarly, in *Board of Regents v. Tomanio*,[9] the Court refused to create a federal tolling rule that would suspend the running of a § 1983 limitations period pending completion of an independent action in state court.[10] In *Tomanio* the plaintiff sought relief in federal court after suffering an adverse state court judgment on an independent cause of action. The defendants moved to dismiss on the ground that the § 1983 action was time barred under the applicable state period of limitations. The district court fashioned a rule tolling the limitations period during the pendency of the independent state court action, although state tolling provisions would not have tolled the period. The Supreme Court reversed, holding that the state's failure to provide for tolling did not unduly undermine the federal policies of deterrence and compensation underlying § 1983.

It is nevertheless important to keep in mind the caution in *Johnson* that federal judges may substitute their own tolling approach for that of a state when the state approach "would be inconsistent with the federal

5. 421 U.S. 454, 95 S.Ct. 1716, 44 L.Ed.2d 295 (1975).

6. 421 U.S. at 463, 95 S.Ct. at 1721.

7. 421 U.S. at 462–63, 95 S.Ct. at 1721–22. *See also Lucchesi v. Bar–O Boys Ranch*, 353 F.3d 691 (9th Cir. 2003) (tolling of § 1983 action pending state tort action arising from same events permitted by reference to California law); *Ellis v. City of San Diego*, 176 F.3d 1183 (9th Cir.1999) and *Martinez v. Gomez*, 137 F.3d 1124 (9th Cir.1998) (applying California law, inmate could claim benefit of state tolling statute of limitations for persons in execution under sentence of criminal court for term less than for life); *Cervantes v. City of San Diego*, 5 F.3d 1273 (9th Cir.1993) (equitable tolling under California law during period § 1983 plaintiff pursued administrative remedies, even though federal law does not require such exhaustion before § 1983 action may be brought); *Sierra–Serpa v. Martinez*, 995 F.2d 325 (1st Cir.1993) (holding that Puerto Rico's legislature implicitly repealed statute excluding time of imprisonment from period of limitations); *Harding v. Galceran*, 889 F.2d 906 (9th Cir.1989), *cert. denied*, 498 U.S. 1082, 111 S.Ct. 951, 112 L.Ed.2d 1040 (1991) (state criminal proceedings tolled federal action); *Winters v. Lynch*, 805 F.2d 1037 (6th Cir.1986) (incarceration of plaintiff tolled federal action); *Graffals Gonzalez v. Garcia Santiago*, 550 F.2d 687 (1st Cir.1977) (state administrative proceedings did not toll federal action).

8. *Johnson*, 421 U.S. at 463, 95 S.Ct. at 1722.

9. 446 U.S. 478, 100 S.Ct. 1790, 64 L.Ed.2d 440 (1980).

10. *Id.* at 491, 100 S.Ct. at 1799.

policy underlying the cause of action" in question.[11] In such cases of undue inconsistency, federal courts have applied either their own notions of equitable tolling[12] or federal-state hybrids.[13] But in the absence of such inconsistency, federal courts will not ignore state equitable tolling doctrines.[14] Thus, when equitable tolling would not apply to save a cause of action under state law, the federal court is bound to dismiss the federal case under the state's statute of limitations.[15] Federal courts have also sometimes been unwilling to fashion their own version of a "continuing violation" theory that would have the effect of extending the limitations period where the statute has run on the defendant's primary conduct targeted by the action but some of the defendant's subsequent conduct took place or its consequences were felt within the limitations period.[16]

Some questions have been raised about the position the plaintiff's attorney is left in after the decision in *Johnson* mandated that plaintiff file Reconstruction Act claims within the forum's own period of limitations. If the attorney chooses to seek relief under Title VII on the one hand and, on the other, § 1981 or § 1983, it is possible that a Title VII administrative proceeding focused on investigation and conciliation, and an adversarial judicial proceeding on the civil rights claim, may proceed concurrently. Indeed Title VII requires the plaintiff to complete administrative agency processing before filing a judicial action under that statute. The adversarial nature of the civil rights judicial proceeding could undermine the Title VII conciliation process; and absent a uniform federal tolling rule, the plaintiff will be obliged by the applicable state limitations statute to file the federal civil rights action before the related Title VII claim is administratively concluded. In addition, a final judg-

11. 421 U.S. at 465, 95 S.Ct. at 1722.

12. *See, e.g., Brown v. Morgan*, 209 F.3d 595, 596 (6th Cir.2000); *Harris v. Hegmann*, 198 F.3d 153, 157–159 (5th Cir.1999) (per curiam); *Cooper v. Nielson*, 194 F.3d 1316 (9th Cir.1999) (all holding that the state law limitations statute applicable to prisoners' federal civil rights action is tolled for the period of time that they are required by the Prison Litigation Reform Act, 42 U.S.C.A. § 1997e (1999) to exhaust whatever administrative remedies may be available); *Farmers & Merchants Nat'l Bank v. Bryan*, 902 F.2d 1520, 1522 (10th Cir.1990); *Gurley v. Documation Inc.*, 674 F.2d 253, 259 (4th Cir.1982).

13. *See, e.g., Smith v. City of Chicago Heights*, 951 F.2d 834, 840 (7th Cir.1992). *But cf. Nelson v. County of Allegheny*, 60 F.3d 1010 (3d Cir.1995), *cert. denied sub nom. Beddingfield v. County of Allegheny*, 516 U.S. 1173, 116 S.Ct. 1266, 134 L.Ed.2d 213 (1996) (tolling in § 1983 action ends when class certification denied, because that order is not immediately appealable in federal, unlike state court, and tolling until certification question ultimately resolved would therefore extend tolling period excessively). The holding in *Nelson* precedes the 1998 amendment to Federal Rule of Civil Procedure 23(f) which now allows, at the discretion of the appellate court, interlocutory review of district court orders granting or denying class certification. See discussion in § 5.110, *infra*.

14. *See Harris v. Hegmann*, 198 F.3d 153, 157–159 (5th Cir.1999) (applying Louisiana law to save claim).

15. *See Paige v. Police Dep't of City of Schenectady*, 264 F.3d 197 (2d Cir.2001) (per curiam); *Estate of Blue v. County of L.A.*, 120 F.3d 982 (9th Cir.1997), *cert. denied*, 522 U.S. 1111, 118 S.Ct. 1042, 140 L.Ed.2d 107 (1998).

16. *See, e.g., Russo v. Casey*, 15 F.3d 1089 (9th Cir.1993), *cert. denied*, 513 U.S. 813, 115 S.Ct. 65, 130 L.Ed.2d 22 (1994). In the wake of a recent Supreme Court reformulation of continuing violation theory under Title VII, at least one circuit has borrowed the Court's own new rules of accrual of sexual and racial harassment claims for action under Section 1981. *Shields v. Ft. James Corporation*, 305 F.3d 1280 (11th Cir.2002).

ment in the § 1981 or § 1983 judicial proceeding, if rendered prior to the conclusion of the Title VII administrative proceeding, may claim preclude a Title VII judicial action.[17]

In *Herrmann v. Cencom Cable Associates*,[18] Judge Posner suggests four methods by which the plaintiff may sidestep these pitfalls. First, the plaintiff may ask the state or federal agency to accelerate the Title VII administrative process so that it will be completed before a final Reconstruction Act judgment is entered. Second, in the hope of reaching an informal settlement in the Title VII administrative process, the employer may agree not to plead the Reconstruction Act statute of limitations. Third, the parties could agree to split the claims, so that the plaintiff avoids claim preclusion stemming from a prior judgment in the Reconstruction Act lawsuit.[19] Fourth, absent such an agreement, the employee could file suit on the Reconstruction claims, ask the court to suspend proceedings during the pendency of the Title VII administrative process, and then, if necessary, amend the complaint to include the Title VII claim after the administrative process concludes.[20]

How then to distinguish accrual, an issue clearly governed by federal law, from "tolling" (which, to make matters more confusing still, may be termed "equitable estoppel" in some states or federal circuits),[21] an issue governed by state law? The problem is most acute where the plaintiff argues that the defendant is responsible for fraudulent concealment of the facts underlying the claim until after the limitations period has expired; on that question the circumstances and considerations governing accrual are similar, and perhaps identical, to those encompassed by rules states often classify as rules of "tolling."[22] One guideline is that if the issue concerns plaintiff's awareness, actual or imputed, of actual injury, it may be considered a matter of accrual; whereas if the issue is concerned with plaintiff's awareness of the facts that would support a claim, and whether they have been fraudulently concealed, it may be considered a matter of equitable tolling.[23] Finally, even if a court concludes that the issue before it is one of "tolling," it is unclear from the Supreme Court's *Tomanio* opinion if federal courts should borrow only those rules that have been incorporated into state statutes or, as well, state common law rules that relieve a plaintiff from the limitations bar.[24]

17. *See* §§ 5.118–120, *infra.*

18. 999 F.2d 223, 225 (7th Cir.1993).

19. *See* Restatement Second of Judgments § 26(a).

20. *See Owens v. Kaiser Foundation Health Plan, Inc.*, 244 F.3d 708 (9th Cir. 2001) (Title VII claims were barred by res judicata though plaintiffs had not yet received their "right to sue" letters at the time of their first action); *Churchill v. Star Enter.*, 183 F.3d 184 (3d Cir.1999) (plaintiff could have presented ADA claim in prior action under Family Medical Leave Act despite necessity of pursuing administrative remedies before filing ADA claim).

21. *See Pearl v. City of Long Beach*, 296 F.3d 76, 81–86 (2d Cir.2002).

22. *Id.* at 80.

23. *Compare Forbes v. Eagleson*, 228 F.3d 471, 486 (3d Cir.2000) *with Oshiver v. Levin, Fishbein, Sedran & Berman* 38 F.3d 1380, 1387 (3d Cir.1994).

24. *See generally* the illuminating discussion of this subject in Judge Newman's opinion for the court in *Pearl v. City of Long Beach*, 296 F.3d 76, 81–86 (2d Cir. 2002) (ultimately not resolving circuit split as to whether fraudulent concealment should be governed by federal or state law,

§ 5.74 The Limitations "Cut-off" Event

State law, then, provides the applicable limitations period and the circumstances that suspend or "toll" the running of the statute on Reconstruction Act claims. Federal law, however, determines not just the accrual date but probably also whether the action has been commenced in federal court within the appropriate period. The Supreme Court wrote in *West v. Conrail*[1] that "[W]hen the underlying cause of action is based on federal law and the absence of an express statute of limitations makes it necessary to borrow a limitations period from another statute, the action is not barred if it has been 'commenced' in compliance with [Federal Rule of Civil Procedure] 3 within the borrowed period."[2] Rule 3 in turn provides that "[a] civil action is commenced by filing a complaint with the court."[3]

In *West* itself, the underlying claim arose from one federal statute and the statute of limitations was borrowed from another. Accordingly, its holding doesn't precisely answer whether, in a Reconstruction Act suit where the Supreme Court has commanded the borrowing of a *state* limitations period, timely commencement within the limitations period is governed by federal law—that is, FRCP 3's liberal "filing" approach—or a potentially more restrictive state law requiring completed service before the last date of the period. Regardless, a circuit court consensus has developed applying the *West* FRCP 3 "timely commencement by simple filing" rule, rather than any more restrictive approach that a given state may follow in its own courts, to actions under the Reconstruction Acts.[4] They reason that a rule prescribing which litigation event, filing or service, "beats the clock" on the running of a limitations period is not the kind of question "closely related" to tolling that the Supreme Court in *Wilson v. Garcia* said was governed by state law. Accordingly, civil rights plaintiffs unable to complete service of process before the last day of the limitations period may nevertheless timely commence a federal court action simply by filing a complaint with the clerk.[5]

reasoning that plaintiff's particular claim would meet the requirements of neither).

§ 5.74

1. 481 U.S. 35, 107 S.Ct. 1538, 95 L.Ed.2d 32 (1987). Thus, for example, circuits have applied the Supreme Court's liberal "mailbox rule" to measure the timely filing of a state prisoner's pro se complaint under § 1983. *Sulik v. Taney County*, 316 F.3d 813 (8th Cir.2003); *Cooper v. Brookshire*, 70 F.3d 377 (5th Cir.1995).

2. *West*, 481 U.S. at 39, 107 S.Ct. at 1541.

3. Fed.R.Civ.Pro. 3.

4. *Sain v. Bend*, 309 F.3d 1134, 1137–1138 (9th Cir.2002); *McIntosh v. Antonino*, 71 F.3d 29 (1st Cir.1995); *Moore v. State of Indiana*, 999 F.2d 1125 (7th Cir.1993); *Lewis v. Richmond City Police Dep't.*, 947 F.2d 733 (4th Cir.1991); *Martin v. Demma*, 831 F.2d 69 (5th Cir.1987).

5. Merely filing the complaint, however, does not fulfill all the plaintiff's obligations regarding timeliness. Rule 4(m) of the Federal Rules of Civil Procedure contains a distinct requirement for diligent prosecution of any federal civil action, including those that were timely commenced for limitations purposes:

> If a service of the summons and complaint is not made upon a defendant within 120 days after the filing of the complaint and the party on whose behalf such service was required cannot show good cause why such service was not made within that period, the action shall be dismissed as to that defendant with-

When federal court jurisdiction is based on diversity—or more precisely, where a particular claim is based on state law—state law determines the events necessary to commence the action within the applicable period of limitation.[6] But pendent state law claims annexed to Title VII or Reconstruction Act claims rest not on diversity jurisdiction but on a federal court's "supplemental" jurisdiction authorized by 28 U.S.C.A. § 1367. Hence although no reported cases on the point have been discovered, federal courts appear to assume that the lenient, plaintiff-friendly FRCP 3 "filing" rule that governs timely commencement of federal question claims also governs timely commencement of any pendent state law claims, even though the limitations period and "tolling" rules on both claims are supplied by state law.

The end result is a patchwork of rules about limitations that pay lip service to both national civil rights policy and state prerogatives but effectively serve neither. National uniformity is defeated because the states may apply general personal injury limitations periods of varying lengths to Reconstruction Act claims, as well as their own rules on tolling. Thus where the defendant is amenable to personal jurisdiction in more than one state, the plaintiff may forum shop for a longer period of limitations. This federalism-driven deference to state choice is only slightly offset by federal court decisions holding that federal law governs the determination of when a § 1983 claim accrues.[7] Yet viewed in another way the deference to state choice is little more than nominal, for the federal courts control the characterization of the Reconstruction Act claim as one involving personal injury; and what state is free as a practical matter to adjust its general personal injury limitations period based on considerations pertaining to the smaller number of claims in its courts that are based on violations of federal civil rights? Further, the liberal federal rules of civil procedure on timely commencement (FRCP 3) and relation back (FRCP 15) have the potential of defeating the state policy, embedded in its chosen limitations period, of ensuring that the defendant receives notice of the action within a specified time after the claim accrues.

The Supreme Court's decision in *Heck v. Humphrey*[8] will force some rethinking about how state limitations periods should be applied to prisoners' civil rights claims that, if successful, would invalidate their underlying convictions. Before *Heck*, for example, it was common for federal courts to conclude that a § 1983 damages claim based on an unconstitutional search, seizure or confession accrued when the alleged unconstitutional conduct occurred,[9] not at some later time when the

out prejudice upon the court's own initiative with notice to such party or upon motion.

6. *See Walker v. Armco Steel Corp.*, 446 U.S. 740, 752–53, 100 S.Ct. 1978, 1986–86, 64 L.Ed.2d 659 (1980).

7. *See, e.g., Morse v. University of Vt.*, 973 F.2d 122, 125 (2d Cir.1992).

8. 512 U.S. 477, 114 S.Ct. 2364, 129 L.Ed.2d 383 (1994).

9. *See, e.g., Day v. Morgenthau*, 909 F.2d 75, 79 (2d Cir.1990) (opinion on petition for reh'g).

conviction was overturned by a state court on appeal.[10] The federal court could then stay the § 1983 action pending the conclusion of the state criminal proceedings, on the rationale that those proceedings might have outcome—determinative effect on the civil rights claim by way of issue preclusion.[11] While this approach compelled the putative civil rights plaintiff to file an action that might not be able to proceed until after state criminal proceedings were final on appeal, it protected defendants by giving them early notice of the claims they would eventually face.

Heck, however, holds that no § 1983 claim which, if successful, would necessarily undermine the state conviction of a prisoner or former[12] prisoner, even comes into being until and unless that conviction is overturned on direct appeal or state or federal habeas. Presumably, therefore, the kind of § 1983 claim subject to *Heck* accrues for limitations purposes only when the underlying charges were dismissed or conviction is reversed or set aside; if so, an earlier filing would be both premature and unnecessary.[13] But far from assisting the plaintiff, *Heck* preserves the maximum opportunity for adverse fact findings to be preclusive against him in his federal civil rights damages action, by ensuring that state courts, or perhaps a federal habeas court, will have earlier decided the questions crucial to § 1983 liability.[14] And of course the several barriers to habeas relief that the Supreme Court has raised[15]

10. *Woods v. Candela*, 13 F.3d 574 (2d Cir.), *vacated for further consideration in light of Heck*, 513 U.S. 801, 115 S.Ct. 44, 130 L.Ed.2d 5 (1994).

11. *See, e.g., Mack v. Varelas*, 835 F.2d 995 (2d Cir.1987). Issue preclusion in this situation could be invoked against the civil rights plaintiff based on facts necessarily found in a successful criminal prosecution, under the doctrine of *Allen v. McCurry*, discussed later in this chapter.

12. Whether a former prisoner seeking damages under § 1983 is barred by *Heck* is not altogether clear. See text § 5.7, *supra.*

13. See discussion of which types of claims accrue only after a conviction is set aside in § 5.7, *supra. See Wiley v. City of Chicago*, 361 F.3d 994 (7th Cir. 2004) and *Covington v. City of N.Y.*, 171 F.3d 117 (2d Cir.1999), *cert. denied*, 528 U.S. 946, 120 S.Ct. 363, 145 L.Ed.2d 284 (1999) (plaintiff's false arrest claims would not accrue, for limitations purposes, until after the criminal charge or criminal prosecution was dismissed); *Smith v. Holtz*, 87 F.3d 108 (3d Cir.1996), *cert. denied*, 519 U.S. 1041, 117 S.Ct. 611, 136 L.Ed.2d 536 (1996) (§ 1983 claim accrued only when state supreme court dismissed murder charges, not earlier when conviction reversed and new trial ordered); *Woods v. Candela*, 47 F.3d 545 (2d Cir.1995), *cert. denied*, 516 U.S. 808, 116 S.Ct. 54, 133 L.Ed.2d 18 (1995); *Triplett v. Azordegan*, 478 F.Supp. 872 (N.D.Iowa 1977) (coerced confession claim did not "ripen" until state court ordered plaintiff released from prison, seventeen years after his conviction). *Cf. Gonzalez v. Entress*, 133 F.3d 551 (7th Cir.1998) (arrestee's § 1983 excessive force and illegal arrest claims accrued when events in question occurred, rather than when arrestee was eventually cleared of charges arising from arrest).

14. *See, e.g., King v. Goldsmith*, 897 F.2d 885 (7th Cir.1990) (state post-conviction court's determination that police officers did not offer false testimony at plaintiff's criminal trial precludes him from relitigating that issue in action under § 1983). *See Post v. Gilmore*, 111 F.3d 556 (7th Cir.1997) (per curiam) (inmate's § 1983 action should be stayed pending decision on habeas petition seeking restoration of his good-time credits subtracted because of prison discipline).

15. *See, e.g., Duncan v. Henry*, 513 U.S. 364, 115 S.Ct. 887, 130 L.Ed.2d 865 (1995) and cases cited therein. More recently, the Supreme Court held in *O'Sullivan v. Boerckel*, 526 U.S. 838, 119 S.Ct. 1728, 144 L.Ed.2d 1 (1999), that to avoid procedural default a habeas petitioner must have pursued each level of normal, nonexceptional appellate review provided by the state system, up to its highest court, even when that review is purely discretionary and in practice discouraged, unless the state formally and expressly stipulates that such review is unavailable.

significantly reduced the possibility that the criminal conviction will ever be overturned after direct appeal, thus forever barring the kinds of § 1983 claims that fall within *Heck*.

Federal and state courts have concurrent jurisdiction over claims under the Reconstruction Civil Rights Acts.[16] This raises the question whether federal civil rights claims brought in state court must comply with the timely commencement requirements of the forum state. There are three principal patterns of state commencement rules. About a third of the states follow the Rule 3 model for federal law claims by treating the filing of a complaint, without more, as commencing an action for purposes of limitations. These states require only that service be accomplished within a specified or reasonable time after filing. Roughly another third of the states require that the plaintiff not only file the complaint but also issue or deliver the summons to a designated officer before the limitations period runs; service may still be accomplished afterwards. The remaining states follow the strict approach, which demands that the defendant be served with process (or receive some substitute form of notice) before the limitations period expires.[17]

The question of what timely commencement rule governs in state court is sharpened by a Supreme Court decision, *Felder v. Casey*,[18] that federal civil rights plaintiffs in state court need not comply with state law "notice-of-claim" prerequisites to suits against municipalities and other local government entities, even though compliance would probably not derail any significant number of the federal claims. There is a residual irony of *Felder*. The Court, under the *Robertson* interpretation of § 1988,[19] respects insurmountable, quasi-*substantive* state obstacles to recovery (e.g., Louisiana's limited approach to survival of claims), in civil rights actions brought in *federal* court. At the same time, under *Felder*, it disrespects easily satisfied, nondiscriminatory state *procedural* prerequisites when civil rights actions are brought in *state* court. The former decision to some degree undermines the federal-court-access policy of § 1983, while the latter undermines the state comity/federalism shibboleth to which the Court elsewhere so frequently defers.

Despite *Felder*, it appears that the states should be free to apply their own definitions of timely commencement for limitations purposes to federal civil rights claims in their own courts. After all, the state's definition of what event "beats the clock" is as integral a component of the overall limitations calculation as the "tolling" circumstances that *Johnson* and *Tomanio* held governed by state law. And FRCP 3, like the FRCP 15(c) "relation-back" provision that can stretch a state's limitations period against misnamed defendants, is part of a body of rules

16. *See* § 5.1, *supra*.

17. Annotation, *Tolling of Statute of Limitations Where Process is Not Served Before Expiration of Limitation Period*, 27 A.L.R.2d 236 (1953 & Supps. 1970, 1978, 1981 & 1987); 54 C.J.S. *Limitations of Actions* §§ 265–68 (1948 & Supp.1987).

18. 487 U.S. 131, 108 S.Ct. 2302, 101 L.Ed.2d 123 (1988).

19. See text § 5.71, *supra*.

designed to "govern the procedure in the United States district courts,"[20] not in state courts. Even if, under *Felder*, a plaintiff need not comply with a state law *precondition* to suit, she should be bound by ordinary provisions of state court procedure—indeed that procedure is really the only thing that she chooses when she opts for a state rather than a federal forum.

Curiously, the only discovered reported decision touching on this issue goes the other way. In *Pimental v. Safeway Stores, Inc.*,[21] plaintiff brought suit in state court under the National Labor Relations Act. The court held that *West v. Conrail*, and therefore the simple filing requirement of FRCP 3,[22] defined the commencement of the action even in state court. The NLRA, however, unlike the Reconstruction Acts, has its own (federal) statute of limitations, which the court may have been loathe to impede by applying the stricter timely commencement rule used in the forum state's courts. The decision does not commend itself for use when the plaintiff chooses a state forum to pursue a civil rights or employment discrimination claim, where the applicable statute of limitations is supplied by state law.

Let us assume, however, that after applying a federally defined accrual date, state tolling principles, and the Federal Rule 3 complaint-filing timely commencement standard to a forum state period of limitations (determined through the federal characterization of the claim as one for tortious personal injury) a court deems a particular plaintiff's § 1983 claim timely commenced. Might this action filed within the limitations period nevertheless be barred by the doctrine of laches? A federal circuit, applying federal common law principles, has held there is no such independent defense to a claim under § 1983.[23]

§§ 5.75–5.79 [Reserved]

N. PLEADING

§ 5.80 In General

Rule 8(a)(2) of the Federal Rules of Civil Procedure requires "a short and plain statement of the claim."[1] It was in a civil rights case that

20. Fed.R.Civ.Pro. 1.

21. 196 Cal.App.3d 92, 241 Cal.Rptr. 568 (1987).

22. See text § 5.74, *supra*.

23. *Ivani Contracting Corp. v. New York*, 103 F.3d 257 (2d Cir.), *cert. denied*, 520 U.S. 1211, 117 S.Ct. 1695, 137 L.Ed.2d 821 (1997).

§ 5.80

1. *See, e.g., EEOC v. J.H. Routh Packing Co.*, 246 F.3d 850 (6th Cir.2001) (holding that ADA plaintiffs need not plead the major life activity, but must list the impairment in the complaint; collecting cases on both sides of the issue); *Gregory v. Daly*, 243 F.3d 687, 696–97 (2d Cir.2001) (asserting in complaint that supervisor made specific references to women as easy victims of sexual assault, added generally demeaning remarks about women, and wove vulgar and sexually explicit language into his tirades was sufficient to state a claim of discrimination because of sex); *Bennett v. Schmidt*, 153 F.3d 516, 518 (7th Cir.1998) (" 'I was turned down for a job because of my race' is all a complaint has to say"). A unanimous Supreme Court cited *Bennett* with approval in *Swierkiewicz v. Sorema, N.A.*, 534 U.S. 506, 122 S.Ct. 992, 996 n. 2, 152 L.Ed.2d 1 (2002), holding that a Title VII plaintiff need not allege a *McDonnell-*

the Supreme Court, in the late 1950's, announced its famous relaxed standard for compliance with Rule 8(a)(2): that a complaint should not be dismissed for failure to state a claim unless it "appears beyond doubt" that a plaintiff can prove no facts in support of her claim which would entitle her to relief.[2] The Court affirmed this standard in *Haines v. Kerner*,[3] adding that a prisoner's *pro se* complaint alleging denial of due process in steps leading up to his solitary confinement would be held to "less stringent requirements than formal pleadings drafted by lawyers."[4]

Subsequently, however, the Court's commitment to the permissive *Conley* brand of notice pleading was called into question. Most notably, and, considering the history of Rule 8(a)(2), somewhat ironically, the development has been most evident in civil rights actions. The phenomenon is illustrated by the Court's standing test articulated in *Allen v. Wright*.[5] The plaintiffs sought to enjoin the IRS from continuing to grant tax exemptions to racially discriminatory private schools across the nation. The Court acknowledged that the injury alleged—impairment of plaintiff's children's access to a desegregated education—was legally cognizable. But it wrote that injury could be fairly traceable to the IRS practice, and thus warrant standing, only if, *in their complaint*, the plaintiffs could offer evidentiary support about a number of interrelated factual propositions relating to the number of such private schools in each of their communities; the likely policy response of each such school if its tax exemption were withdrawn; and whether parents whose chil-

Douglas prima facie case in the complaint; "The prima facie case under McDonnell Douglas ... is an evidentiary standard, not a pleading requirement." *Id.* at 510, 122 S.Ct. at 997. As such, it "relates to the employee's burden of presenting evidence that raises an inference of discrimination," not to the pleading standard plaintiffs must satisfy to survive a motion to dismiss. *Id. See also Phillip v. University of Rochester*, 316 F.3d 291, 293–294 (2d Cir.2003) (relying on *Swierkiewicz* and applying its standard in § 1981 action, writing, "these liberal pleading rules apply with particular stringency to complaints of civil rights violations.")

But cf. Gregory v. Daly, 243 F.3d 687 (2d Cir.2001) (a simple declaration that defendant's conduct violated the ultimate legal standard at issue (e.g., it was "because of sex" or "severe or pervasive") does not suffice. But it is enough to assert facts from which, construing the complaint liberally and in the plaintiff's favor, one could infer such a violation). Failure to include in the complaint each type of claim, for example, where a plaintiff seeks to show both disparate treatment and disparate impact, however, will shut the door on the proffer of evidence to support the forgotten claim. *See, e.g., Coleman v. Quaker Oats Co.*, 232 F.3d 1271 (9th Cir.2000), *cert. denied*, 533 U.S. 950, 121 S.Ct. 2592, 150 L.Ed.2d 751 (2001) (affirming trial court's exclusion at summary judgment stage of evidence supporting disparate impact claim where plaintiffs did not plead it and failed to make it known they were proceeding under this claim during discovery phase); *Josey v. John R. Hollingsworth Corp.*, 996 F.2d 632, 641–42 (3d Cir.1993) (plaintiff barred from proceeding on disparate impact theory reasoning that adding a new theory of liability at the summary judgment stage would prejudice the defendant who faces different burdens and defenses under this second theory of liability).

2. *Conley v. Gibson*, 355 U.S. 41, 78 S.Ct. 99, 2 L.Ed.2d 80 (1957).

3. 404 U.S. 519, 92 S.Ct. 594, 30 L.Ed.2d 652 (1972).

4. There are a multitude of cases applying a more liberal reading of pro se complaints. *See, e.g., Spencer v. Doe*, 139 F.3d 107, 111–12 (2d Cir.1998) (under a liberal reading, finding that pro se plaintiff's complaint stated a claim against correctional officers in their individual capacities).

5. 468 U.S. 737, 104 S.Ct. 3315, 82 L.Ed.2d 556 (1984). *See supra* § 5.55.

dren attended such schools would, as a result of the schools' various responses, transfer their children to public schools in sufficient numbers to have a significant impact on the public schools' racial composition. To say the least, this kind of pleading is a far cry from *Conley*.

At the same time the federal courts of appeals considerably tightened pleading requirements not just on the jurisdictional requirement of standing but on the basic elements of claims under § 1983. Among the reasons offered for the trend were (a) to buttress Rule 11's deterrence of frivolous complaints; (b) to prevent public officials from being subjected to vexatious actions (on an analogy between vexatious suits and fraud claims which, by the express terms of Federal Rule of Civil Procedure 9(b), must be pleaded with specificity); (c) to slow the increase in the workload of federal courts, and particularly the § 1983 actions that constituted the largest single category on the federal docket; (d) to prevent the civil rights action from being misused as a device for litigating a state court claim in federal court; and (e) better to fulfill Rule 8's goal of providing the defendant fair notice.

To dam the flood of § 1983 actions after *Monell*, some courts devised "heightened pleading" requirements. The United States Court of Appeals for the Fifth Circuit began by imposing such a requirement on § 1983 suits against governmental actors in their individual capacities.[6] The Fifth Circuit's heightened pleading requirement forced the plaintiff to "alleg[e] with particularity all material facts on which he contends he will establish his right to recovery, which will include detailed facts supporting the contention that the plea of [qualified] immunity cannot be sustained."[7] In a later case, *Palmer v. City of San Antonio*,[8] the Fifth Circuit expanded the heightened pleading standard to cases involving municipal liability under § 1983.[9]

It remained to be seen if the Supreme Court would endorse the lower courts' rearguard action against *Conley* and in effect carve out a comprehensive exception to federal notice pleading for actions brought to enforce civil rights. An occasion for this decision was provided by a Fifth Circuit decision dismissing on the pleadings a *Monell/City of Canton* claim against a municipality alleging that the municipality had failed adequately to train and supervise its police officers. The Fifth Circuit had affirmed a district court ruling that the complaint failed to allege with sufficient factual detail and particularity "the requisite allegation that the municipality engaged in a policy or custom for which it can be held responsible" in conformance with the circuit's heightened pleading requirements.[10] The Supreme Court granted certiorari to resolve a conflict among the circuits as to the propriety of applying such requirements "to § 1983 actions alleging municipal liability."

6. *Elliott v. Perez*, 751 F.2d 1472, 1482 (5th Cir.1985).

7. *Id.*

8. 810 F.2d 514, 516–17 (5th Cir.1987).

9. *Id.*

10. *Leatherman v. Tarrant County Narcotics Intelligence and Coordination Unit*, 954 F.2d 1054 (5th Cir.1992).

Charlene Leatherman filed suit against the Tarrant County Narcotics Intelligence and Coordination Unit (TCNICU), Tim Curry (the director of TCNICU), the cities of Lake Worth, Texas and Grapevine, Texas, and Don Carpenter (the sheriff of Tarrant County).[11] There were two searches of homes by the TCNICU. The first involved plaintiff Leatherman, who, while driving in Fort Worth, Texas, was stopped and surrounded by police officers.[12] The police informed Ms. Leatherman that her home was in the process of being searched and that the police killed her two dogs.[13] Although nothing relevant to the investigation was found in the Leatherman home, the officers remained on the Leatherman's front lawn for over an hour "apparently celebrating their unbridled power."[14]

The second incident involved plaintiff Andert.[15] Andert's home was searched by the TCNICU after receiving reports that police officers detected odors "associated with the manufacture of amphetamines" coming from Andert's home.[16] Andert and his family were mourning the death of Andert's wife when the members of the TCNICU entered the Andert home without knocking or identifying themselves.[17] Andert was beaten and injured by the TCNICU, without provocation on Andert's part.[18] After a one and one-half hour search, the police, as with the Leatherman situation, found nothing associated with drug activity.[19]

The Plaintiffs (Leatherman and Andert) then sued the TCNICU, Tim Curry, the cities of Lake Worth, Texas and Grapevine, Texas, and Don Carpenter.[20] The Plaintiffs' amended complaint centered on a theory that the municipalities had failed to "formulate and implement an adequate policy to train its officers . . . on the proper manner to execute search warrants and respond when confronted by family dogs."[21] The Fifth Circuit deemed the allegations to be of the general, "boilerplate" variety.[22] Defendants TCNICU, Curry, and Carpenter moved to dismiss the complaint under Rule 12(b)(6) of the Federal Rules of Civil Procedure and alternatively for the court to enter summary judgment under Rule 56.[23]

The district court granted Defendants' motion, dismissing all Plaintiffs' claims even against defendants who failed to join in the motion.[24] The district court determined that Plaintiffs' complaint failed to meet the Fifth Circuit's heightened pleading standard, and even if it might have, the Defendants would be entitled to summary judgment as a

11. *Leatherman v. Tarrant County Narcotics Intelligence and Coordination Unit*, 755 F.Supp. 726, 727–28 (N.D.Tex. 1991).

12. *Leatherman*, 954 F.2d at 1055–56.

13. *Id.*

14. *Id.* at 1056.

15. *Id.*

16. *Id.*

17. *Id.*

18. *Id.*

19. *Id.*

20. *Id.*

21. *Id.*

22. *Id.*

23. *Id.*

24. *Id.* at 1057.

matter of law.[25] On appeal, the Fifth Circuit noted that the Plaintiffs' complaint did state the facts surrounding the two searches in detail but added that the complaint did not state "any facts with respect to the adequacy (or inadequacy) of the police training."[26] Therefore, the heightened pleading standard was not satisfied and the motion to dismiss was affirmed.[27]

In *Leatherman v. Tarrant County Narcotics Intelligence and Coordination Unit*,[28] a unanimous Court, per Chief Justice Rehnquist, reversed, repudiating special strict requirements for pleading the prima facie elements of civil rights claims against government entities. Moreover, although Justice Rehnquist's opinion specifically disclaimed any decision on the matter, the logic of the Court's opinion strongly suggested that the Court would reject the application of heightened pleading standards to claims against individual government officials as well.

The Court first addressed the county's assertion that *Monell*'s refusal to permit government entity liability via simple respondeat superior and its insistence instead on a showing of custom or policy[29] implied an immunity from suit that would be undermined by standard Rule 8 notice pleading. The Court replied that this argument falsely equated a mere heightened liability standard with a complete immunity from suit and overlooked the fundamental distinction between § 1983 actions against individual governmental official defendants, who enjoy a range of absolute or qualified immunity, and those against municipalities, which, the Court reaffirmed, enjoyed none. The Fourth Circuit expanded the application of *Leatherman* to a claim alleging a "failure to train" or other sort of government entity inaction, excusing the plaintiff from alleging multiple instances of prior, similar violations in order to state a claim for relief.[30] So applied, *Leatherman* facilitates § 1983 damage actions against entities in precisely the respect that *City of L.A. v. Lyons*[31] impedes injunctive relief against them: by obviating the necessity for pre-filing discovery of "pattern" facts difficult to obtain by private investigation.

Although the Court added that it therefore had "no occasion to consider whether our qualified immunity jurisprudence would require ... heightened pleading in cases involving individual government officials," the balance of its opinion suggests a negative answer to that suggestion. For the Court found it "impossible to square" the Fifth Circuit's heightened pleading standard "with the liberal system of 'no-

25. *Id.*

26. *Id.* at 1058.

27. *Id.* at 1055.

28. 507 U.S. 163, 113 S.Ct. 1160, 122 L.Ed.2d 517 (1993).

29. *See* Chapter 2 on § 1983.

30. *Jordan v. Jackson*, 15 F.3d 333 (4th Cir.1994). *Cf. Jackson v. Marion County*, 66 F.3d 151 (7th Cir.1995) (pro se prisoner's § 1983 complaint adequately stated claim against county for conspiring to "cover up the facts" of arrests allegedly made with excessive force despite absence of factual detail).

31. *See* discussion of *City of Los Angeles v. Lyons*, 461 U.S. 95, 103 S.Ct. 1660, 75 L.Ed.2d 675 (1983), in § 5.55, *supra*.

tice pleading' set up by the Federal Rules."[32] In the succeeding sentence it described the *Conley* construction of Federal Rule 8(a)(2) as affirming "that the Rule meant what it said"—the "Federal Rules ... do not require a claimant to set out in detail the facts."[33] Of course the Rules no more call for fact pleading with respect to civil rights claims against individual government officials than for claims against government entities.

The Court buttressed its conclusion by observing that in Rule 9(b) Congress imposed a pleading particularity burden in only two instances, fraud and mistake. It omitted "any reference to complaints alleging municipal liability under § 1983. Expressio unius est exclusio alterius." Since Rule 9(b) is equally as silent about claims against individual government officials, it should follow that the Court would not subject those claims, either, to a regime of fact pleading.[34] The thoroughgoing protection those defendants already enjoy in the form of absolute and qualified immunity and related procedural accommodations[35] should reassure the Court that notice pleading alone will not cause them to be unfairly dragged through trial or saddled with liability. By extension, the Court's reasoning should also shield Title VII and other employment discrimination claims from heightened pleading requirements, because Federal Rule 9(b) does not except them either from *Conley* or the general "friendly eye" of Rule 8(f).[36]

As observed above, however, Chief Justice Rehnquist, however, undermined the simplicity of the Court's conclusion based on Federal Rules 8 and 9 with the following statement: "We thus have no occasion to consider whether our qualified immunity jurisprudence would require a heightened pleading in cases involving individual government officials."[37] Relying on this caveat in *Leatherman*, some courts of appeals

32. 507 U.S. at 168, 113 S.Ct. at 1163.

33. *Id.* (quoting *Conley*, 355 U.S. at 47, 78 S.Ct. at 103).

34. *See Hall v. Dworkin*, 829 F.Supp. 1403, 1409 n. 5 (N.D.N.Y.1993). *See also Batiste v. Colonial Sugars, Inc.*, 1993 WL 149067 (E.D.La.1993) ("There is no logical reason to limit Leatherman's holding to claims of municipal liability, as the same Federal Rules of Civil Procedure govern all claims arising under § 1983. Imposing a heightened pleading standard for claims against individual public officials or private parties would conflict with the Federal Rules every bit as much as it would for claims against municipalities."); *Callaghan v. Congemi*, 1993 WL 114523, *5 (E.D.La. 1993) (*Callaghan* is much more blunt about the subject. "*Leatherman* ... appears to sound the death knell for *Elliott*'s requirement of heightened pleading in suits involving individual government officials."); *Timmons v. Cisneros*, 1993 WL 276863 (E.D.Pa. 1993) (also extending *Leatherman* to suits against individual "official[s] employed by a municipality."); *Hafley v. Lohman*, 90 F.3d 264 (8th Cir.1996), *cert. denied*, 519 U.S. 1149, 117 S.Ct. 1081, 137 L.Ed.2d 216 (1997) (circuit court lacks jurisdiction over interlocutory appeal after district court denied motion to dismiss on ground that plaintiff need not meet heightened pleading requirement to facilitate determination of fact-based qualified immunity defense).

35. *See* Chapter 2 on § 1983.

36. *Garus v. Rose Acre Farms, Inc.*, 839 F.Supp. 563 (N.D.Ind.1993).

37. *Leatherman*, 507 U.S. at 166–67, 113 S.Ct. at 1162. This unwillingness to extend the new rule beyond the parameters of municipal liability may trace not only to the Court's customary aversion to dictum but also to the views of Justice Kennedy. In *Siegert v. Gilley*, 500 U.S. 226, 111 S.Ct. 1789, 114 L.Ed.2d 277 (1991), his concurring opinion would have required the plaintiff to anticipate and overcome the individual government officer's affirmative defense

have refused to give plaintiffs the benefit of its notice pleading principle on their § 1983 claims against individual defendants. Acknowledging that "the Supreme Court's rationale would appear to apply in any case outside the fraud or mistake context," the Ninth Circuit nevertheless joined the District of Columbia Court of Appeals in retaining the heightened pleading standard for individual defendant cases.[38] Both courts cited the Supreme Court's limitation of its decision to entity actions and its refusal to address heightened pleading requirements as applied to cases where government officials are sued in their individual capacities and are therefore entitled to raise the defense of qualified immunity. The Fifth Circuit, too, has adhered to its heightened pleading rule as applied to individual defendants asserting qualified immunity.[39]

But the Supreme Court's subsequent decision in *Crawford–El v. Britton*[40] seems to extend the relaxed pleading permitted by *Leatherman* to cases against individual government defendants as well. The Court writes that plaintiffs need not in the usual case meet higher pleading standards in their initial pleading, or higher proof requirements at summary judgment or trial, respecting their prima facie cases, either because the particular constitutional tort requires proof of defendant's state of mind or because the individual defendant asserts the defense of qualified immunity.[41] The majority's opinion reiterates that qualified immunity is an affirmative defense that must be pleaded by the defendant in an Answer;[42] and it is settled that the plaintiff's Complaint need not anticipate or "plead around" an affirmative defense the defendant

of qualified immunity in accordance with a heightened pleading standard. *Id.* at 235, 111 S.Ct. at 1795. (Kennedy, J. concurring). Heightened pleading thus reinforces the qualified immunity defense the Court has devised in order to prevent discovery which would disrupt the work of the individual governmental official.

38. *Branch v. Tunnell*, 14 F.3d 449 (9th Cir.1994), *cert. denied*, 512 U.S. 1219, 114 S.Ct. 2704, 129 L.Ed.2d 832 (1994), *overruled, Galbraith v. County of Santa Clara*, 307 F.3d 1119 (even where improper motive was element of § 1983 claim, arrestee not required to plead with particularity coroner's alleged falsifications leading to prosecution of arrestee for murder); *Kimberlin v. Quinlan*, 6 F.3d 789 (D.C.Cir. 1993), *vacated*, 515 U.S. 321, 115 S.Ct. 2552, 132 L.Ed.2d 252 (1995), for consideration in light of *Johnson v. Jones*, 515 U.S. 304, 115 S.Ct. 2151, 132 L.Ed.2d 238 (1995) (*Bivens* claim). *See also Mendocino Envtl. Ctr. v. Mendocino County*, 14 F.3d 457 (9th Cir.1994) (heightened standard met).

39. *Cincl v. Connick*, 15 F.3d 1338 (5th Cir.1994), *cert. denied*, 513 U.S. 868, 115 S.Ct. 189, 130 L.Ed.2d 122 (1994). District courts, too, joined the chorus, relying for the most part on the Supreme Court's express refusal in *Leatherman* to decide whether to extend the standard notice pleading rule to cases against individual defendants. *See Harris v. Hayter*, 970 F.Supp. 500 (W.D.Va.1997); *Brown v. Stewart*, 910 F.Supp. 1064 (W.D.Pa.1996); *Verney v. Pennsylvania Turnpike Comm'n*, 881 F.Supp. 145 (M.D.Pa.1995); *McDonald v. City of Freeport*, 834 F.Supp. 921, 929 n. 2 (S.D.Tex.1993); *Orange v. County of Suffolk*, 830 F.Supp. 701 (E.D.N.Y.1993); *Idoux v. Lamar Univ. Sys.*, 828 F.Supp. 1252, 1256 n. 2 (E.D.Tex.1993). *But see Wood v. Cohen*, 1997 WL 59324 (E.D.Pa.1997); *Trusik v. Montgomery County*, 1997 WL 12135 (E.D.Pa.1997); *Johnson v. Dranov*, 1996 WL 547401 (E.D.Pa.1996); *Cap v. Hartman*, 1996 WL 266701 (E.D.Pa.1996) (all holding that *Leatherman* applies to individual defendant cases).

40. 523 U.S. 574, 118 S.Ct. 1584, 140 L.Ed.2d 759 (1998).

41. *Id.* at 600–01. *See Kimberlin v. Quinlan*, 199 F.3d 496, 502 (D.C.Cir.1999), *cert. denied*, 531 U.S. 871, 121 S.Ct. 172, 148 L.Ed.2d 118 (2000) (referring in dictum to the *Crawford–El* "Court's rejection of the so-called 'heightened pleading' standard in civil rights actions against government officials").

42. *Id.* at 586–87, 118 S.Ct. at 1591.

has not yet asserted. The majority approvingly summarizes prior decisions, including *Leatherman*, as refusing "to change the Federal Rules governing pleading by requiring the plaintiff to anticipate the immunity defense ... or requiring pleadings of heightened specificity in cases alleging municipal liability."[43]

The majority does suggest, however, that after the defense is raised, or even if it is not, district judges may require a more particularized pleading of particular claims, especially those requiring proof of improper motive, by ordering a Reply under F.R.C.P. 7(a) or granting a defendant's motion for a more definite statement under Rule 12(e).[44] Even before *Crawford–El*, the Fifth Circuit, sitting en banc, recognized that the Reply, rather than the Complaint, is the pleading in which the plaintiff should respond to the affirmative defense of qualified immunity which, unless defendant makes a motion before serving a responsive pleading, is not even asserted until defendant serves its Answer.[45] That court, in other words, abandoned its former insistence that the plaintiff "fully anticipate the defense in his complaint at the risk of dismissal under Fed.R.Civ.P. 12."[46] And in the wake of *Crawford–El*, the Fifth Circuit has recognized that even in the Reply the plaintiff need not plead "direct," only circumstantial evidence of discriminatory motive, and need not meet a "clear and convincing" standard of pleading.[47] The burden of pleading the affirmative defense of qualified immunity rests with the defendant.[48] And if the trial court does not invoke the *Crawford–El* option of ordering plaintiff to serve a Reply, the plaintiff need not and indeed may not[49] respond to the allegations in the Answer that assert qualified immunity. In any event, the plaintiff does not in such cases face a heightened burden of *proof* on the elements of her own

43. *Id.* at 595, 118 S.Ct. at 1595.

44. *Id.* at 597–98, 118 S.Ct. at 1596. *See Goad v. Mitchell*, 297 F.3d 497 (6th Cir.2002); *Brown v. Cochran*, 171 F.3d 1329, 1332–33 (11th Cir.1999); *Judge v. City of Lowell*, 160 F.3d 67, 74–75 (1st Cir.1998); *Kain v. Nesbitt*, 156 F.3d 669, 673 (6th Cir.1998) (interpreting *Crawford–El* as authorizing district judges to require heightened pleading by plaintiff in a Reply following a defendant's Answer in order for plaintiff to survive qualified immunity defense, at least respecting claims requiring proof of improper motive). *But cf. Kyle K. v. Chapman*, 208 F.3d 940, 943–44 (11th Cir. 2000) (rejecting heightened pleading argument, without citation to *Crawford–El*, simply by noting that initial Complaint met modest "short and plain statement of the claim" requirement of F.R.C.P. 8(a)).

45. *Schultea v. Wood*, 47 F.3d 1427 (5th Cir.1995) (en banc).

46. See *Todd v. Hawk*, 72 F.3d 443, 445 (5th Cir.1995) (per curiam) (reaffirming that the two-step *Schultea* process requires "plaintiff to file a short and plain statement ... pursuant to Rule 8(a)(2) followed by a more particularized reply pursuant to Rule 7," assuming that defendant in the interim has asserted the qualified immunity defense in the answer).

47. *Shipp v. McMahon*, 199 F.3d 256, 261 (5th Cir.2000) (reasoning that the Supreme Court, in *Crawford–El*, did not require clear and convincing plaintiff's evidence refuting qualified immunity even at summary judgment stage, so it follows that no such standard should apply in deciding a F.R.C.P. Rule 12(b)(6) motion to dismiss).

48. *Crawford–El*, 523 U.S. at 586–87, 118 S.Ct. at 1591; *Gomez v. Toledo*, 446 U.S. 635, 100 S.Ct. 1920, 64 L.Ed.2d 572 (1980).

49. Federal Rule 7(a) permits the plaintiff to reply, absent such a court order, only to the allegations of any *counterclaim* (not defense) the defendant might have asserted in its answer.

claim—the ordinary preponderance-of-the-evidence standard suffices[50] for all those elements.[51]

It seems likely after a recent Supreme Court decision relaxing pleading under Title VII that judges will not require heightened pleading in Reconstruction Act Cases, either, except in the rarest of circumstances. In *Swierkiewicz v. Sorema, N.A.*,[52] the Court held that a Title VII plaintiff need not allege the elements of a prima facie case in the complaint. The rationale of the opinion, coupled with the reliance in *Leatherman* on the transsubstantive nature of the Federal Rules of Civil Procedure, suggest that notice pleading is now the watchword for virtually all civil rights actions, including § 1983 actions against individual defendants who might assert qualified immunity as well as those against entities who will be liable only if the plaintiff at trial proves "policy."[53]

While civil rights complaints ordinarily need not plead a large number of facts to establish their claims, or rebut defenses like qualified immunity in anticipation of their being raised by a defendant in an Answer, the plaintiff does bear responsibility for the allegations he does make. Thus complaints will still be dismissed for legal insufficiency when

50. *See Tatro v. Kervin*, 41 F.3d 9 (1st Cir.1994) (jury instructions could not insist that § 1983 plaintiff had to prove that an arrest was "clearly" lacking probable cause or "clearly" effected with excessive force, for that would constitute a disguised, belated assertion of the qualified immunity defense that should have been determined at the outset of the action by the court as a matter of law). *Cf. Stephenson v. Doe*, 332 F.3d 68 (2d Cir.2003) (where jury in § 1983 action had no evidence, instructions, or argument about legal ambiguity or about defendant police officer's knowledge of excessive force law under the circumstances, special verdict according officer qualified immunity was legally inconsistent with special verdict in favor of plaintiff on excessive force and was set aside).

51. For example, plaintiff need only show by a preponderance that a defendant's unconstitutional conduct was a substantial cause of her injury, and the burden of proof then shifts to defendant to prove that all or part of plaintiff's harm was caused by other tortfeasors, whether or not they are named defendants. *See Northington v. Marin*, 102 F.3d 1564, 1567–69 (10th Cir.1996) (once plaintiff proves that a defendant's conduct, concurrently with the acts of other tortfeasors whether named as defendants or not, was a substantial cause of the harm plaintiff suffered, that defendant is liable for all the harm except to the extent that *he*, the defendant, proves the harm resulted from other concurrent causes) (citing cases).

52. 534 U.S. 506, 122 S.Ct. 992, 152 L.Ed.2d 1 (2002).

53. *See Educadores Puertorriquenos en Accion v. Hernandez* 367 F.3d 61 (1st Cir. 2004); *Alston v. Parker*, 363 F.3d 229 (3d Cir. 2004) (acknowledging that recent Supreme Court decisions abrogate those circuits' prior insistence on heightened pleading in § 1983 cases); *Phillip v. University of Rochester*, 316 F.3d 291, 293–294 (2d Cir. 2003) (relying on *Swierkiewicz* and applying its standard in § 1981 action, writing, "these liberal pleading rules apply with particular stringency to complaints of civil rights violations."); *Phelps v. Kapnolas*, 308 F.3d 180, 186–87 & n. 6 (2d Cir.2002) (per curiam); *Gabraith v. County of Santa Clara*, 307 F.3d 1119, 1121, 1123–26 (9th Cir. 2002); *Goad v. Mitchell*, 297 F.3d 497, 502–03 (6th Cir.2002); *Higgs v. Carver*, 286 F.3d 437, 439 (7th Cir.2002); *Currier v. Doran*, 242 F.3d 905, 911–17 (10th Cir.2001). *See generally Broam v. Bogan*, 320 F.3d 1023 (9th Cir.2003) (applying liberal *Conley v. Gibson* standard in allowing leave to amend). *Cf. Strong v. David*, 297 F.3d 646 (7th Cir.2002) (applying notice pleading to adequacy of prison grievance prisoner was required to file by the Prison Litigation Reform Act, and stating that as with judicial notice pleading, the grievance did not need to lay out the facts, articulate legal theories, or demand particular relief). *But see Davis v. Goord*, 320 F.3d 346 (2d Cir. 2003) (pro se prisoner complaint failed to state a claim for violation of free speech rights absent allegations of facts establishing an ongoing practice by officials of interfering with his mail or facts relating to resulting harm).

the plaintiff "pleads himself out of court." This will happen, for example, where plaintiff, after denominating defendants as "John Does" on the premise that their identities were unknown to him, later included one of those officials as a named defendant in the complaint[54]; where allegations negate an element of the claim[55]; or where plaintiff attaches an exhibit that negates an element of the claim.[56]

Moreover, on a few issues, plaintiffs should continue to have to plead with particularity. Damages under § 1983 are available against state officials only when they are sued in their individual or personal, rather than official, capacities.[57] Although a majority of the circuits give latitude to the plaintiff who fails to plead expressly the capacity in which he sues a state official, some do not.[58] It appears that a § 1983 "and laws" claim must plead particularly the sub-section of the statute on which plaintiff's claim relies.[59] And conspiracies between state and private actors sufficient to show state action by private actors are subject to heightened pleading requirements.[60]

Plaintiffs may, as in other cases in federal court, plead in the alternative, as authorized by Federal Rule of Civil Procedure 8(e)(2), and in doing so they are not making binding admissions. Thus an employment discrimination plaintiff may allege both that she is not guilty of misconduct attributed to her by the employer, and that she suffered harsher discipline for that misconduct because of her race, without conceding the truth of the employer's accusations.[61] By the same token, defendants may use Rule 8(e)(2) to set forth alternative defenses.[62]

The standard of pleading sufficiency applicable to cases that proceed in forma pauperis is governed by 28 U.S.C.A. § 1915(d), which calls for dismissal of complaints that are "factually frivolous." The Supreme Court has clarified that the quoted standard is met when the trial court deems the facts alleged to be "irrational" or "wholly incredible," even if they are not so far-fetched as to conflict with facts that are judicially noticeable. The Court also warned the federal circuits not to review

54. *Alejo v. Heller*, 328 F.3d 930 (7th Cir.2003).

55. *O'Connor v. Northshore Intern. Ins. Services*, 61 Fed. Appx. 722 (1st Cir. 2003) (per curiam) (in Title VII religious discrimination case, complaint came close to admitting that no representative of the employer with decisionmaking authority knew of her religious affiliation).

56. *Thompson v. Illinois Dept. of Professional Regulation*, 300 F.3d 750 (7th Cir. 2002) (civil rights plaintiff with burden of showing his position did not involve policymaking attached to complaint job description indicating policymaking function).

57. *See supra* § 2.35.

58. *Biggs v. Meadows*, 66 F.3d 56 (4th Cir.1995) (applying majority view and citing cases). *But cf. Colvin v. McDougall*, 62 F.3d 1316 (11th Cir.1995) (vacating damages award against county sheriff because caption in the complaint failed to specify that he was sued in his individual rather than official capacity).

59. *Blessing v. Freestone,* 520 U.S. 329, 117 S.Ct. 1353, 137 L.Ed.2d 569 (1997).

60. *Tahfs v. Proctor*, 316 F.3d 584 (6th Cir.2003); *Scott. v. Hern,* 216 F.3d 897, 907 (10th Cir.2000).

61. *Henry v. Daytop Village, Inc.*, 42 F.3d 89 (2d Cir.1994).

62. *See, e.g., Smith v. Cashland, Inc.*, 193 F.3d 1158, 1160–1161 (10th Cir.1999) (employer did not have to elect between the defenses that plaintiff resigned, or alternatively, was terminated for legitimate business reasons).

§ 1915(d) dismissals de novo, reminding them that the decision is confided to the discretion of the district courts and may be overturned only for an abuse of that discretion.[63]

The ease with which plaintiffs can withstand most motions to dismiss under FRCP 12(b)(6) contrasts sharply with the pro-defendant tilt embedded in current federal standards for ruling on motions for summary judgment.[64] Consequently, if no matters outside the pleadings have been offered and considered in support of a pretrial motion to dismiss, the plaintiff has an incentive to characterize the issue targeted by the motion as a jury triable element of her claim, rather than, for example, a fact-dependent question of subject matter jurisdiction for the court.[65]

Several circuit courts have expressed dismay both with so-called "shotgun" complaints and the manner in which district courts respond. The Seventh Circuit reversed a district court for dismissing a suit because of a "repetitious, rambling, and disorganized" but otherwise "intelligible" complaint; at the same time, the circuit encouraged the trial court to robustly employ Rule 12(e) by requiring a more definite statement from plaintiffs.[66] "Prolixity is a bane of the legal profession but a poor ground for rejecting potentially meritorious claims. Fat in a complaint can be ignored, confusion or ambiguity dealt with by means other than dismissal. It takes a lot worse than using 12 pages to set out a claim that could have been stated in 6 pages to justify a dismissal under Rule 8(a)."[67]

The Eleventh Circuit criticized both the litigants and the district court for mishandling a fifty-page, 173–paragraph complaint that began with thirty-seven paragraphs of general allegations that were incorporated by reference into each count of the complaint.[68] These general allegations "operated as camouflage, obscuring the material allegations of [plaintiff's] claims." The defendant "legitimized" this shoddy pleading by answering paragraph by paragraph instead of moving under Rule 12(e) for a more definite statement, or under Rule 12(f) to strike from each count the immaterial incorporated general allegations. The district court failed to demand repleader on its own initiative, and allowed the

63. *Denton v. Hernandez*, 504 U.S. 25, 112 S.Ct. 1728, 118 L.Ed.2d 340 (1992).

64. *See* § 5.100 *infra*.

65. *See Garcia v. Copenhaver, Bell & Assocs.*, 104 F.3d 1256 (11th Cir.1997) (plaintiff must show that defendant is an "employer" as an element of her prima facie case under ADEA, so the issue goes to the merits and should be decided by a jury at trial unless defendant is awarded summary judgment). *But see Scarfo v. Ginsberg*, 175 F.3d 957 (11th Cir.1999), *cert. denied*, 529 U.S. 1003, 120 S.Ct. 1267, 146 L.Ed.2d 217 (2000) (whether the defendants, corporations and their owner, constituted a "single employer" subject to Title VII was a question that, although not technically jurisdictional, determines whether Title VII applies and therefore must be decided by the court, which must answer it affirmatively before a jury may determine the related element of plaintiff's claim, i.e., whether 15 or more "employees" worked for such a "single employer").

66. *Bennett v. Schmidt*, 153 F.3d 516 (7th Cir.1998).

67. *Id.* at 518.

68. *See Johnson Enters. of Jacksonville, Inc. v. FPL Group, Inc.*, 162 F.3d 1290 (11th Cir.1998).

case to proceed to trial on a multitude of tort claims when the plaintiff's case was actually based on a simple breach of contract claim. This resulted in a $5.5 million plaintiff's verdict, a verdict ultimately set aside by the appellate court in favor of a $1 nominal damages award. Had the district court sorted through the complaint and answer, the appellate court stated, the district court would have concluded that the sum due plaintiff on the viable breach of contract claim was offset by sums owing on defendant's breach of contract counterclaim and avoided sending this suit to trial altogether. "If the trial judge does not quickly demand repleader, all is lost-extended and largely aimless discovery will commence, and the trial court will soon be drowned in an uncharted sea of depositions, interrogatories, and affidavits ... the case therefore proceeds to trial without proper delineation of issues.... The result is a massive waste of judicial and private resources."[69]

In a case applying Rule 12(b) to a Title VII action, the District of Columbia Circuit has held that an employer's affirmative statute of limitation defense under Title VII—that is, the ninety day time period afforded plaintiffs for filing suit after receiving a right to sue notice—may be raised in a pre-answer motion, even though that defense is not on Rule 12(b)'s narrow list[70] of defenses that may be raised in such a motion. The court reasoned that since a plaintiff's complaint necessarily includes certain facts about an alleged offense, the plaintiff does not suffer from lack of notice when a defendant bases a pre-answer motion on the facts as alleged in the complaint. Thus, where the plaintiff's complaint stated that she received her right to sue notice 92 days before filing suit, the court allowed the defendant to raise its 90-day defense by way of a pre-answer motion.[71]

Federal Rule of Civil Procedure 15(a) liberally authorizes discretionary amendments to complaints and answers, even after a brief window (generally before an opposing pleading is served) during which either party may amend its pleading without leave, as a matter of course. Thereafter, the district judge may grant leave to amend and in fact should deny leave, at least once, only where it would result in undue delay, bad faith, or dilatory motive on the part of the moving party, or after repeated failure to cure deficiencies in prior amendments, or where amendment would work undue prejudice to the opposing party, or would be "futile"—i.e., where on the facts and the law no plausible amendment could state a claim on which relief can be granted even under the lenient standard of Rule 8(a)(2).[72] Delay alone is insufficient reason to deny the

69. *Id.* at 1333.

70. Rule 12(b) states that a pre-answer motion may assert the following: (1) lack of jurisdiction over the subject matter, (2) lack of jurisdiction over the person, (3) improper venue, (4) insufficiency of process, (5) insufficiency of service of process, (6) failure to state a claim upon which relief can be granted, (7) failure to join a party under Rule 19.

71. *Smith–Haynie v. District of Columbia*, 155 F.3d 575, 578 (D.C.Cir.1998).

72. *Foman v. Davis*, 371 U.S. 178, 182, 83 S.Ct. 227, 230, 9 L.Ed.2d 222 (1962). *See also Henderson v. Bolanda*, 253 F.3d 928 (7th Cir.2001) (Rule 15(a) relation-back available only where first complaint was timely filed); *Curley v. Perry*, 246 F.3d 1278 (10th Cir.2001) (dismissal of a pro se complaint for failure to state a claim is proper

leave unless the opponent can also show prejudice.[73]

But what of the pleading that does not get formally amended, either as a matter of course or by leave under Rule 15(a), before trial? Are plaintiffs consequently flatly foreclosed from offering evidence in support of unpleaded claims, and defendants from offering evidence in support of unpleaded defenses? Federal Rule 15(b) provides a measure of flexibility here, particularly where an opponent is asleep at the wheel during trial and fails to object to such evidence unrelated to any pleading. Its first sentence treats that situation, providing:

> "When issues not raised by the pleadings are tried by express or implied consent of the parties, they shall be treated in all respects as if they had been raised in the pleadings."

Case law has established the sensible limitation, however, that no such consent will be implied against a party who offers evidence relevant to a claim that was properly pleaded, just because that evidence also tends to establish an unpleaded claim.[74]

The third and fourth sentences of Rule 15(b) authorize an alternative route to amendment of pleadings at trial for situations where the opponent of unpleaded evidence does timely object, and so his consent consent cannot be implied. They provide that if evidence is objected to at the trial on the ground that is not within the issues raised by the pleadings,

> "the court may allow the pleadings to be amended and shall do so freely when the presentation of the merits of the action will be subserved thereby and the objecting party fails to satisfy the court that the admission of such evidence would prejudice the party in maintaining the party's action or defense upon the merits. The court may grant a continuance to enable the objecting party to meet such evidence."

Thus the third sentence calls for the judge to strike the same kind of balance, common to the resolution of discovery disputes, between the proponent's need for the amendment and the resulting prejudice to the opponent. The proponent must persuade that the evidence is needed for a fair presentation of the merits, and the opponent bears the burden of persuasion respecting prejudice. The opponent typically carries his bur-

only where it is obvious that the plaintiff cannot prevail on the facts he has alleged and it would be futile to give him an opportunity to amend); *Owens v. Kaiser Foundation Health Plan, Inc.*, 244 F.3d 708 (9th Cir.2001) (affirming trial court's decision to allow defendant to amend answer to assert res judicata).

73. *Dennis v. Dillard Dep't Stores, Inc.*, 207 F.3d 523, 525 (8th Cir.2000) (defendant granted leave to amend answer in Equal Pay Act case to assert affirmative "factor other than sex" defense); *Pulliam v. Tallapoosa County Jail*, 185 F.3d 1182 (11th Cir.1999) (defendant who failed to plead "mixed motives" defense in answer preserved it by raising defense in pretrial order).

74. *See Pinkley, Inc. v. City of Frederick, Md.*, 191 F.3d 394, 400–401 (4th Cir. 1999), *cert. denied*, 528 U.S. 1155, 120 S.Ct. 1161, 145 L.Ed.2d 1072 (2000) (plaintiff's evidence which supported an unpleaded state law conversion claim also tended to establish plaintiff's pleaded claim under § 1983, so complaint would not be deemed amended by consent to include conversion claim).

den by showing that the discovery process failed to afford adequate notice that the unpleaded evidence would be presented.

The fourth sentence, by authorizing continuances to the objecting party where the amendment is granted, would seem to bias the inquiry in favor of the proponent. It seems to suggest that some types of prejudice may be cured by an additional opportunity for the opponent to conduct limited discovery on the facts raised by the issues allowed by amendment. In practice, however, it may be difficult to persuade a busy trial judge to admit evidence clearly outside the pleaded issues. One way trial and appellate courts have excluded that evidence, even without striking the Rule 15(b), sentence 3 balance in favor of the opponent, is to read these provisions as effectively eclipsed by the implication of Rule 16(e) that the pretrial order "shall control the subsequent course of the action." The expansive interpretations of that provision, discussed in § 5.98 below, in practice treat the opportunity to amend under Rule 15(b) as having been waived on the eve of trial. That interpretation of the interplay between the two sections is dubious, as it leaves no independent role for Rule 15(b), at least where the issues have not been tried by consent under the first sentence of that Rule.

Where Rule 15(b) amendments to the pleadings at trial are allowed by consent or by judicial determination that the proponent's need outweighs any uncurable prejudice to the opponent, the type of amendments allowed would appear unlimited by the Rule's language. The text of the Rule 15(b) would seem to embrace new claims for relief, new liability theories to support existing claims, and even new relief for claims and theories previously pleaded. But here Rule 15(b) intersects with the second sentence of Rule 54(c), which provides, in pertinent part:

> Except as to a party against whom judgment is entered by default, every final judgment shall grant the relief to which the party in whose favor it is rendered is entitled, even if the party has not demanded such relief in the party's pleadings.

Thus by its terms this provision seems to assume that even where the pleadings are *never* amended, either before trial or, per Rule 15(b), during trial, a party may receive whatever relief is warranted by the *evidence* actually presented at trial. But at least one circuit, reading Rules 15(b) and 54(c) together, concludes that the latter implicitly precludes a Rule 15(b) trial amendment designed to admit evidence of a type of relief not specified in the pleadings.[75] Yet an encumbrance on the scope of Rule 54(c) recognized by that circuit and at least two others makes it important that Rule 15(b) be construed to include amendments that seek only to expand relief. The encumbrance is that Rule 54(c) authorizes relief only on theories "squarely presented and litigated by the parties at some stage or other of the proceedings."[76] The theory on which Rule 54(c) relief is sought will not of course have been "squarely

75. *Pinkley*, 191 F.3d at 400.

76. *Evans Prods. Co. v. West Am. Ins. Co.*, 736 F.2d 920, 923–24 (3d Cir. 1984),quoted with approval in *Rodriguez v. Doral Mortgage Corp.*, 57 F.3d 1168, 1173 (1st Cir.1995) and *Pinkley*, 191 F.3d at 400.

presented and litigated" unless raised by the original pleadings or an express amendment under Rule 15(b).

One respect in which federal pleading disserves the policies of the Reconstruction Civil Rights Acts is its failure to permit "relation back" of "John Doe" complaints when the plaintiff is able to learn the identity of an intended defendant only after expiration of an applicable statute of limitations. As amended in 1991, FRCP 15(c)(3) permits relation back of an amendment that "changes the party or the naming of the party" respecting the same claim originally pleaded, but only if "within the period provided by Rule 4(m) for service of the summons and complaint," the intended defendant "(B) knew or should have known that, but for a mistake concerning the identity of the proper party, the action would have been brought against" him or her. In turn, the FRCP 4(m) deadline for completing service is 120 days after the filing of the original complaint–which in many cases will be long before the expiration of an applicable period of limitations. So even in cases where 15(c)(3) relation back is held available, it permits relation back only if the intended defendant learns within 120 days of the filing of the original complaint that, but for a mistake concerning her identity, she would have been named. And the latest that could be, where the complaint is filed on the last day of the limitations period, is 120 days thereafter.

Yet even this minimal degree of relation back under FRCP 15(c)(3)[77] has been held unavailable to plaintiffs who, as is not uncommon in excessive force cases, have no idea of the identity of a defendant when they commence an action and who therefore name one or more "John Does." The circuits are now in accord that an amendment of a John Doe complaint does not "change the party or the naming of the party," since no actual person was named originally, and does not correct a "mistake concerning the identity of the proper party." They therefore conclude that John Doe pleadings are ineligible for Rule 15(c)(3) relation back.[78]

§§ 5.81–5.84 [Reserved]

77. FRCP 15(c)(1) allows relation back much later than the somewhat stingy 120–day national minimum set by Rule 15(c)(3) if the law of the state that provides the statute of limitations, i.e., usually the forum state, happens to allow it. Rule 15(c)(3) authorizes relation back when "permitted by the law that provides the statute of limitations applicable to the action."

78. *See, e.g., Garrett v. Fleming*, 362 F.3d 692 (10th Cir. 2004) and *King v. One Unknown Federal Correctional Officer,* 201 F.3d 910, 914 (7th Cir.2000) (plaintiff's lack of knowledge of defendant's identity not a "mistake" curable through rule); *Wayne v. Jarvis*, 197 F.3d 1098, 1102–04 (11th Cir. 1999), *cert. denied*, 529 U.S. 1115, 120 S.Ct. 1974, 146 L.Ed.2d 804 (2000) ("John Doe" pleadings cannot be used to circumvent limitations statutes because replacement with named party effectively constitutes change in party sued, not "mistake" that can relate back under FRCP 15(c)(3)(B)); *Jacobsen v. Osborne*, 133 F.3d 315, 321–22 (5th Cir. 1998) (plaintiff made no "mistake" or "misidentification" within meaning of rule); *Cox v. Treadway*, 75 F.3d 230, 240 (6th Cir. 1996), *cert. denied*, 519 U.S. 821, 117 S.Ct. 78, 136 L.Ed.2d 37 (1996) (same); *Barrow v. Wethersfield Police Dep't*, 74 F.3d 1366 (2d Cir.1996), *modifying* 66 F.3d 466, 469–70 (2d Cir.1995) (plaintiff's amendment substituting named officers for "John Doe" defendants not permitted to relate back when plaintiff was unable or unwilling to comply with court's directive, issued within the limitations period, to name individual officer defendants; in effect, decision narrowly reads 1991 amendment to FRCP 15(c), extending relation-back period where original

O. FEDERAL RULE OF CIVIL PROCEDURE 11, AS AMENDED—RELATIONSHIP TO PLEADING

§ 5.85 In General

The amended Federal Rule of Civil Procedure 11 requires that a signature of a party or an attorney on a litigation document certify that the signer has: 1) read the document; and that the claims therein, upon knowledge, information and belief formed after a reasonable inquiry, are, 2) well grounded in fact and 3) warranted by existing law or a good-faith argument for the extension, modification, or reversal of existing law; and 4) that they are not being filed for improper purposes, such as harassment. If the court finds a violation of Rule 11, it shall, sua sponte or upon motion of the opposing party, impose sanctions, including monetary sanctions. Attorney's fees can also be awarded by motion.[1]

The disproportionate use of Rule 11 sanctions against plaintiffs, and civil rights plaintiffs in particular, is well documented.[2] Scholars differ on their interpretation of the disproportionate numbers. Some argue that more civil rights cases are frivolous as a proportion of the whole than are ordinary cases. Others argue that litigants and their attorneys in private law suits are less likely to "punish" each other by seeking Rule 11 sanctions, and that courts are more likely to "punish" unsuccessful civil rights plaintiffs in order to stem what they perceive to be a flood of civil rights litigation.

The Supreme Court denied certiorari to two important appeals from the Fourth Circuit in which sanctions were awarded against prominent civil rights attorneys.[3] In *Blue* in particular, the court upheld sanctions

pleading reflects a "mistake" concerning a defendant's identity as not applicable where unnamed defendant's identity is unknown); *Worthington v. Wilson*, 8 F.3d 1253, 1257 (7th Cir.1993) (lack of knowledge as to identity of defendant cannot be cured by relation back under 15(c)). *See also Singletary v. Pennsylvania Dep't of Corrections*, 266 F.3d 186, 201 (3d Cir.2001) (retreating from circuit authority preceding the 1991 amendment to Rule 15(c) that had upheld relation-back where original defendant was denominated "unknown," and terming it now "an open question" whether a plaintiff's ignorance of a target defendant's identity is a "mistake" curable under the Rule).

§ 5.85

1. *See Nuwesra v. Merrill Lynch, Fenner & Smith, Inc.*, 174 F.3d 87 (2d Cir. 1999) (Rule 11(c)(2) permits an award of attorney's fees only by motion); *Thornton v. General Motors Corp.*, 136 F.3d 450, 455 (5th Cir.1998) (per curiam) ("[W]here sanctions are imposed under Rule 11(c)(1)(B) by a district court on its own initiative, . . . the award of attorney's fees . . . [does not] constitute a valid sanction."); *Johnson v. Waddell & Reed, Inc.*, 74 F.3d 147, 152 n. 3 (7th Cir.1996) (per curiam) ("[W]here sanctions are imposed under Rule 11(c)(1)(B) by the district judge on his own initiative, Rule 11(c)(2) provides that payment of sanctions may be directed only to the court as a penalty."); Fed.R.Civ.P. 11 advisory committee's note to 1993 amendments ("The revision [to subsection (c)] provides that a monetary sanction imposed after a court-initiated show cause order be limited to a penalty payable to the court.").

2. *See, e.g., Rule 11 in Transition: The Report of the Third Circuit Task Force on Federal Rule of Civil Procedure 11, S. B. Burbank, Reporter; FJC Directions: Special Issue on Rule 11*, E. Wiggins, T. Willging, D. Stienstra; *Rule 11: A Critical Analysis*, G. M. Vairo.

3. *Blue v. United States Dep't of Army*, 914 F.2d 525 (4th Cir.1990), *cert. denied sub nom. Chambers v. United States Dep't of Army*, 499 U.S. 959, 111 S.Ct. 1580, 113 L.Ed.2d 645 (1991); *In re Kunstler*, 914

against Julius Chambers, despite the plaintiff's ability to establish a prima facie case, despite the fact that many plaintiffs in the large litigation had prevailed, and despite acknowledging that much of the landmark civil rights litigation of the century, such as *Brown v. Board of Educ.*, would never have been brought in the climate of sanctions existing today, given the controlling law of *Plessy v. Ferguson*.

The potential before *Leatherman* and *Crawford–El* of heightened pleading standards, coupled with the threat of sanctions under the former Rule 11 as amended in 1983 and thereafter interpreted, appeared to place civil rights attorneys and their clients at particular risk. In reaction there was considerable comment within the legal community that the ready use of sanctions against civil rights plaintiffs undermined the intent of Congress to encourage vindication of civil rights by providing for the shifting of attorneys fees to prevailing civil rights plaintiffs in § 1988.[4] The amendments to Rule 11, effective December 1, 1993, may halt this trend in its tracks.

The amendments, in brief, have reduced the number of Rule 11 motions made and pressed; reduce the percentage that will be granted; decrease the incidence of monetary sanctions even when the motion is found meritorious; often require that a monetary sanction, even if still appropriate, be paid to the court as a penalty rather than as reimbursement to the moving party; and ordinarily force a law firm to share liability for monetary sanctions with the individual lawyer responsible for violating one of the Rule 11 certifications. The changes relax the nature of the certifications made by a signer; create a "safe harbor" that gives the person who proffered the challenged paper a three-week window in which to withdraw or modify it without penalty; and provide extensive new limitations on the availability, nature, amount, and recipients of sanctions.

§ 5.86 The Certifications; The Papers They Initially Attach to; Subsequent Written and Oral Violations

The former Rule 11 drew no express distinction between plaintiffs and defendants. It provided that when either they or their counsel signed a pleading, motion or other paper, they made three certifications: (1) It is "well-grounded in fact"; (2) it is "warranted by existing law or a good faith argument for the extension, modification, or reversal of existing law"; and (3) it "is not interposed for any improper purpose, such as to harass or to cause unnecessary delay or needless increase in the cost of litigation." A violation of any of these certifications triggered sanctions, usually payable to the adversary.

A violation of the new rule similarly must trace back to a certification made in one of the same documents: "a pleading, a written motion,

F.2d 505 (4th Cir.1990), *cert. denied sub nom. Kunstler v. Britt*, 499 U.S. 969, 111 S.Ct. 1607, 113 L.Ed.2d 669 (1991).

4. *See* Chapter 4 *supra*.

or other paper." Rule 11(b). Indeed, subdivision (d) clarifies that the certifications and sanctions of Rule 11 do not apply to discovery disclosures, requests or materials, which are separately governed by the provisions of Rules 26–37. But there the similarity ends. On the one hand, the new certifications are, on balance, less stringent than those under the former rule as it was revised in 1983 and has been interpreted thereafter. On the other hand, each certification, although it initially arises only when a paper is signed, may be violated by re-"presenting" it in a later written or oral form. The litigant or lawyer continues to make a certification, and therefore risks violating the Rule, not only by "signing, filing, submitting" a paper, but also by "later advocating" it, either in writing or apparently through an oral presentation at a hearing or trial. New Rule 11(b).

The new certifications are set forth in Rule 11(b)(1)–(4). As the text confirms, Rule 11 may continue to be used to challenge particular contentions of law or allegations of fact, and need not challenge an entire paper. But the accompanying note warns that "Rule 11 motions should not be made or threatened for minor, inconsequential violations of the standards prescribed by subdivision (b)." And the new rule facilitates counterstrikes by parties who are unjustly targeted without the necessity of their filing a cross-motion. It permits the court to award to the prevailing party, including the party "opposing the motion," the reasonable expenses and attorney's fees incurred in resisting it. Rule 11(c)(1)(A).

a. The "Improper Purpose" Certification

The first and worst offense—the one most likely to result in monetary sanctions and a direction that they be paid to the moving party—is to violate the "improper purpose" certification. The substance of that certification, in proposed Rule 11(b)(1), is unchanged.

b. The Law Certification

New Rule 11(b)(2) is a somewhat relaxed certification concerning law. Henceforth the signer (or subsequent oral or written presenter) of the contention, if unable to certify that a contention is warranted by existing law, need no longer vouch for a "good faith" argument, only a "nonfrivolous" one, for extending, modifying, or reversing existing law. In addition, the signer may now vouch only that he is seeking to establish "new law." On its face the existing "good faith" certification may seem easier to satisfy. It requires only a subjective empty-head, pure-heart "state of mind," whereas the new "nonfrivolous" standard is, as the accompanying note confirms, objective.[1] But the new rule also specifically authorizes the signer to attempt to forge new law; and the related advisory committee note indicates that the certifier may bolster its position that a legal contention is nonfrivolous by pointing to "some

§ 5.86

1. *See Bethesda Lutheran Homes and Services, Inc. v. Born*, 238 F.3d 853 (7th Cir.2001) (where any reasonable attorney would know that suit was barred by res judicata, judicial estoppel, the Eleventh Amendment and qualified immunity, filing of frivolous suit and appeal warranted imposition of sanctions).

support for its theories even in minority opinions, in law review articles, or through consultation with other attorneys."[2]

c. *The Fact Certifications*

It is difficult to determine from the text or the advisory committee's note if the new Rule 11(b)(3) fact certification is stricter or more lenient than the current certification. Formerly a signer certified that the paper "is well grounded in fact." Now a signer/presenter must certify that the "allegations and other factual contentions" (not just the paper as a whole) have "evidentiary support."

Is "evidentiary support" a stricter standard than "well grounded in fact"? Possibly, because the explanatory note links "evidentiary support" with motions for summary judgment, where the party opposing the motion is ordinarily expected to produce potentially *admissible* evidence. Yet the note goes on to say, "That summary judgement is rendered against a party does not necessarily mean ... that it [initially] had no evidentiary support for its position. On the other hand, if the party has evidence with respect to a contention that would suffice to defeat a motion for summary judgment ... it would have sufficient 'evidentiary support' for purposes of Rule 11."

Another feature of the new fact certification appears specifically designed to help the plaintiff. The previous certification effectively required a plaintiff to certify about facts, upon pain of dismissal for failure to state a claim, even where further investigation or discovery was necessary to back up the factual contentions. The new provision allows a signer/presenter who cannot candidly certify that a factual contention has "evidentiary support" to identify specifically those allegations that "are likely to have evidentiary support after a reasonable opportunity for further investigation or discovery."[3] The note explains that the signer/presenter need not formally amend pleadings if further investigation and discovery fails to generate evidentiary support, but simply requires it to refrain thereafter from advocating claims or defenses that depend on those facts.

This alternative fact certification gives the plaintiff an option already enjoyed by defendants under Federal Rule 8(b) for pleading purposes: to deny allegations by stating that their initial investigation leaves them without sufficient information or knowledge to form a belief about the truth of an allegation. The final certification of new Rule 11, subparagraph (b)(4), confirms that the defendant has the same option for Rule 11 purposes as well: A signer/presenter who is unable to deny outright that a factual contention is "warranted on the evidence" may alternatively assert that specifically identified denials of those facts "are reasonably based on a lack of information or belief." But since defendants probably have already had this protection under the umbrella of

2. Further, contra the thrust of at least one Eleventh Circuit panel opinion, the signer/certifier need not specifically identify contentions that seek a change of law. But "a contention that is so identified should be viewed with greater tolerance under the rule." Advisory Committee Note to Subdivision (b).

3. Proposed Rule 11(b)(3).

Rule 8(b), the combined net effect of proposed Rule 11(b)(3) and (b)(4) is to assist plaintiffs by placing them under the same fact pleading regime as defendants. Under the new certification, a defendant's Rule 11 motion is less likely to succeed if it attacks fact allegations that the plaintiff has specifically identified as only "likely to have evidentiary support" after further investigation and discovery.

§ 5.87 The Target Party's "Safe Harbor"

Under the new procedure, even Rule 11 motions that appear promising despite the relaxed new certifications must be abandoned if the target party takes advantage of the new three-week "safe harbor." Proposed Rule 11(c)(1)(A) prohibits the moving party from filing the motion papers unless, within 21 days after they are served, the target party fails to withdraw or correct the challenged paper, claim, defense, contention, allegation, or denial. Apparently, then, the target party who invokes the safe harbor option and corrects or withdraws the offending paper or contention can avoid all Rule 11 sanctions no matter how egregious the initial violation of a Rule 11 certification.

The notes do, however, remind us that the federal courts have inherent power to punish for contempt or impose sanctions for improper litigation conduct and that Rule 11 does not supplant other rules or statutes providing for such sanctions or awards of attorney's fees to prevailing parties. See note to subdivision (d). Further, once the safe harbor is closed, nothing in the proposal attempts to alter the power of the court to impose sanctions, otherwise appropriate under Rule 11, even after a Rule 41(a) voluntary dismissal.[1]

§ 5.88 Permissive, Not Mandatory Sanctions

The most fundamental change in the sanctions area is that their imposition is no longer mandatory. The previous requirement of subdivision (b) that the court "shall impose" an appropriate sanction has yielded to subdivision (c)'s simple authorization: the court "may, subject to the conditions stated below, impose an appropriate sanction upon the attorneys, law firms, or parties that have violated subdivision (b) or are responsible for the law violation." This controversial change was added by the Judicial Conference's Standing Committee, and approved by the Judicial Conference, notwithstanding the approach of the Advisory Committee, which would have retained mandatory sanctions.

§ 5.89 Limitations on Nature, Purpose, and Magnitude of Sanctions: The Bias Against Monetary Sanctions

New subparagraph (c)(2) contains a general authorization for three types of sanctions: "Directives of a nonmonetary nature, an order to pay

§ 5.87

1. *See Cooter & Gell v. Hartmarx Corp.*, 496 U.S. 384, 110 S.Ct. 2447, 110 L.Ed.2d 359 (1990), or after a dismissal for lack of federal subject matter jurisdiction. *See Willy v. Coastal Corp.*, 504 U.S. 935, 112 S.Ct. 2001, 118 L.Ed.2d 596 (1992).

a penalty into court, or, if imposed on motion and warranted for effective deterrence, an order directing payment to the movant of some or all of the reasonable attorney's fees and other expenses incurred as a direct result of the violation."

In deciding between monetary or nonmonetary penalties the court must now take into account the overriding principle that the sanction, if any, imposed for a violation "shall be limited to what is sufficient to deter repetition of such conduct or comparable conduct by others similarly situated."[1] This approach subordinates the goal of compensating a party forced to incur costs as a result of an adversary's sanctionable conduct to the objective of preventing recurrences. The related note stresses a variety of additional factors that a court should consider in deciding whether to assess a nonmonetary or monetary penalty. These include the recklessness or willfulness of the violation, whether the violation infects only a small part of a paper or its entirety, whether the violator had engaged in similar conduct in the instant or other litigation, and "whether the responsible person is trained in the law."

The rule lists two specific circumstances in which no monetary sanction is available. First, no monetary sanction may be awarded against a represented party (as opposed to the party's lawyer) for violating the *law* certification of subdivision (b)(2). Second, when a court initiates Rule 11 procedures [which, under new (c)(1)(B) it must do by order to show cause], it may not impose monetary sanctions unless its show-cause order is issued before the plaintiff takes a voluntary dismissal or the parties settle the claims in question.[2] The advisory committee note details a variety of available nonmonetary sanctions, including striking the offending paper, admonishing or reprimanding the violator, or requiring the violator to participate in educational programs.[3]

§ 5.89

1. Rule 11(c)(2). The new rule adopts the approach taken in the minority of circuits that treated sanctions as exceptional, *see, e.g., Operating Engineers Pension Trust v. A–C Co.*, 859 F.2d 1336, 1344–45 (9th Cir.1988); *Doering v. Union County Bd. of Chosen Freeholders*, 857 F.2d 191, 194 (3d Cir.1988), or that insisted on the least severe sanction adequate to deter. *Ehrenhaus v. Reynolds*, 965 F.2d 916, 921 (10th Cir. 1992); *Orlett v. Cincinnati Microwave, Inc.*, 954 F.2d 414 (6th Cir.1992); *Miltier v. Downes*, 935 F.2d 660 (4th Cir.1991); *In re Kunstler*, 914 F.2d 505, 523 (4th Cir.1990), *cert. denied Kunstler v. Britt*, 499 U.S. 969, 111 S.Ct. 1607, 113 L.Ed.2d 669 (1991); *Traina v. United States*, 911 F.2d 1155, 1158 (5th Cir.1990); *White v. General Motors Corp.*, 908 F.2d 675, 684 (10th Cir. 1990), *cert. denied*, 498 U.S. 1069, 111 S.Ct. 788, 112 L.Ed.2d 850 (1991).

2. Rule 11(c)(2)(A) and (B). Additionally, courts may not impose any Rule 11 sanctions if they fail to comply with the procedural notice requirements of the Rule. *Bass v. E.I. Dupont de Nemours & Co.*, 324 F.3d 761 (4th Cir.2003) (although frivolousness of employee's conspiracy claims against employer warranted Rule 11 sanctions, they were vacated where court failed to comply with Rule's notice requirements and imposed sanctions months after resolution of claims on the merits). *Cf. Mickle v. Morin*, 297 F.3d 114, 123–126 (2d Cir.2002) (requiring notice and opportunity to be heard before court imposes sanctions on counsel pursuant to its inherent power to supervise and control its own proceedings).

3. The courts have imposed a wide variety of nonmonetary sanctions. The great majority of these impact the pending litigation: "dismissing a plaintiff's complaint with prejudice, entering a default judgment against a defendant, requiring the payment of the costs of filing and litigating the motion ... declaring that certain facts are established ... precluding the admission of evidence to support or attack certain propo-

§ 5.90 Does the Rule Erect a Further Presumption That Monetary Sanctions Be Paid as a Penalty to the Court Rather Than as Reimbursement to the Moving Party?

The note accompanying Rule 11(c)(2) asserts that the new rule creates a presumption that a monetary sanction

> "should ordinarily be paid into court as a penalty. However, under unusual circumstances, particularly for (b)(1) violations [papers or contentions presented for an 'improper purpose'] deterrence may be ineffective unless the sanction ... directs that some or all of this payment be made to those injured by the violation."

It is difficult to see where the note drafters find such a strong presumption in the text of the proposed new rule. The only specific textual limitations on directing payment of a monetary penalty to the movant are that the sanction be imposed as the result of a motion, rather than a court's show-cause procedure, and (like any sanction, monetary or not) be "warranted for effective deterrence."

The note drafters also expound on the limitation expressed by the text that monetary sanctions ordered paid to the moving party be limited to the "reasonable attorney's fees and other expenses incurred as a direct result of the violation." The note states that any monetary award payable to the movant "should not provide compensation for services that could have been avoided by an earlier disclosure of evidence or an earlier challenge to the groundless claims or defenses. Moreover partial reimbursement of fees may constitute a sufficient deterrent with respect to violations by persons having modest financial resources."

§ 5.91 Does the Rule Specially Restrict Monetary Recoveries by Movants in Civil Rights and Other Cases Brought Under Statutes That Provide for Fee-Shifting to Prevailing Parties?

Although the text of the Rule is silent on the point, the note drafters also assert that even when monetary sanctions are in order and appropriately paid to the movant, those expenses, including attorney's fees, may not be shifted "in a manner that would be inconsistent with the standards that govern the statutory award of fees." As an example of those "standards," the note drafters cite *Christiansburg Garment Co. v.*

sitions, barring the introduction of particular evidence." Imwinkelried and Blumoff, *Pretrial Discovery: Strategy & Tactics* § 1307, p. 8 (Callaghan 1986) (citations omitted). Nonlitigation sanctions have become more common. *See, e.g., Orlett v. Cincinnati Microwave, Inc.*, 954 F.2d 414 (6th Cir.1992) (directing consideration on remand of reprimand, censure, referral of offender to bar disciplinary committee); *Jennings v. Joshua Indep. Sch. Dist.*, 948 F.2d 194 (5th Cir.1991), *cert. denied*, 504 U.S. 956, 112 S.Ct. 2303, 119 L.Ed.2d 226 (1992) (similar sanctions); *In re Kunstler*, 914 F.2d 505 (4th Cir.1990), *cert. denied*, 499 U.S. 969, 111 S.Ct. 1607, 113 L.Ed.2d 669 (1991) (suspension and disbarment of attorney violator); *Figueroa–Ruiz v. Alegria*, 905 F.2d 545, 549 (1st Cir.1990) (reprimand); *Frantz v. United States Powerlifting Fed'n*, 836 F.2d 1063 (7th Cir.1987) (publicly censuring counsel).

EEOC.[1] That decision is now widely applied to civil rights, employment discrimination and other cases brought under statutes that provide for attorney's fees to prevailing parties—the biggest single category of cases in the federal docket. It precludes awarding attorney's fees to prevailing *defendants* unless the plaintiff's claim is manifestly without foundation or brought in subjective bad faith.

The note drafters are apparently suggesting that the *Christiansburg* standard should be applied to preclude civil rights defendants who prevail on Rule 11 motions from recovering their expenses except perhaps where the plaintiff has violated the (b)(1) "improper purpose" certification or where the violation of a (b)(2) law or (b)(3) fact certification is objectively and manifestly egregious. The note drafters' theory may make some sense in principle. That is, how can Rule 11 require a civil rights plaintiff whose claim has a colorable foundation to pay the defendant for the expenses incurred in resisting a *particular* baseless allegation or contention when, under *Christiansburg Garment*, such a plaintiff could not be ordered to pay *any* of the defendant's attorney's fees incurred in resisting an *entire claim*? But monetary sanctions could compensate the civil rights defendant itself, as opposed to its attorney, and in any event the text of new Rule 11 contains no such per se ban on defendants' collecting Rule 11 expenses from plaintiffs in this mammoth category of statutory fee-shifting cases.

§ 5.92 Presumption of Law Firm's Joint Liability With Signer/Presenter

Tucked away in the last sentence of subparagraph (c)(1)(A) is a new provision that changes the result decreed by *Pavelic & LeFlore v. Marvel Entertainment Group*,[1] which held that current Rule 11 does not authorize sanctions against a firm that employs the individual attorney who signs a groundless paper. The proposal provides: "Absent exceptional circumstances, a law firm shall be held jointly responsible for violations committed by its partners, associates, and employees." The rationale here is that under the proposed new safe harbor provision, the firm as an entity will ordinarily receive notice of the individual signer/presenter's alleged certification violation; will have 21 days in which to investigate and, if appropriate, withdraw or correct the offending allegation, contention, or paper; and thus, under established principles of agency, may properly be held responsible for persisting.

§ 5.93 Allocation of Responsibility Between Lawyer/Law Firm and Client

The Rule continues to permit sanctions to be imposed, where

§ 5.91

1. 434 U.S. 412, 98 S.Ct. 694, 54 L.Ed.2d 648 (1978).

§ 5.92

1. 493 U.S. 120, 110 S.Ct. 456, 107 L.Ed.2d 438 (1989).

appropriate, on represented as well as nonrepresented parties.[1] As noted above, however, it shields represented parties from *monetary* sanctions for the violation of the (b)(2) certification about *law*.[2] But *non*monetary sanctions may be imposed on a represented party even for violations of the subparagraph (b)(2) certification. Thus a client may still have to pay at least a litigation price, in the form of a stricken claim or defense, for any kind of Rule 11 violation by the lawyer. Further, monetary sanctions may be imposed on the client for violations of the (b)(1), (b)(3), or (b)(4) certifications.

§ 5.94 [Reserved]

P. DISCOVERY, EVIDENCE, PRE–TRIAL ORDERS, WAIVER OF OBJECTIONS, AND RELATED ISSUES

§ 5.95 Discovery in General

While *Leatherman* and *Crawford–El* thus appear to continue to countenance bare-bones notice pleading in civil rights cases, there is always the tactical question whether more detailed pleading is desirable. Pleading requirements are always related to the degree of discovery a court system permits or requires, as the December 1, 1993 amendments to the Federal Rules of Civil Procedure confirm. It is beyond the scope of this work to review in detail the Federal Rules of Civil Procedure that relate to discovery and the use of discovered materials at trial.[1] Two points, however, warrant brief mention.

First, several amendments to the discovery rules are likely to have particular impact on civil rights litigants. Rule 26 now mandates three phases of required disclosures—information to be revealed by each side to the other "without awaiting a discovery request."[2] Not only do these disclosures amplify formal discovery, but formal discovery may not proceed until the parties have met and conferred to discuss, among other things, the first round of required disclosures.[3] Within fourteen days after that meeting, each side is required to provide all other parties the names, addresses and telephone numbers of "each individual likely to have discoverable information that the disclosing party may use to support its claims or defenses, unless solely for impeachment,[4] identify-

§ 5.93

1. *See Business Guides, Inc. v. Chromatic Communications Enter.*, 498 U.S. 533, 111 S.Ct. 922, 112 L.Ed.2d 1140 (1991).

2. Rule 11 (c)(2)(A).

§ 5.95

1. A few differences from state procedure are mentioned in § 5.45 *supra*.

2. FRCP 26(a)(1).

3. FRCP 26(d) and 26(f).

4. This limitation that excepts from the mandatory disclosures evidence that could be used solely for impeachment is of course limited to the mandatory disclosures. Evidence that could be impeaching must be tendered upon receipt of a properly propounded discovery request that encompasses the evidence. *See Varga v. Rockwell Int'l Corp.*, 242 F.3d 693, 697 (6th Cir.), *cert. denied*, 534 U.S. 821, 122 S.Ct. 53, 151 L.Ed.2d 23 (2001) (defendant's argument that it had no obligation to produce impeaching documents because it viewed them

ing the subjects of the information"[5] and documents relevant to those facts.[6]

By providing for affirmative disclosure of core information without a discovery request from the adversary, an early discovery conference with opposing counsel, and a jointly prepared discovery plan and Rule 16 scheduling order, the new Rules are likely on balance to ease and speed the plaintiff's basic discovery. Correlatively, the new rules also severely limit the presumptively permissible number of interrogatories[7] and depositions.[8] Those limits should favor the defendant, because in most employment discrimination and many civil rights actions the defendant has knowledge of many more of the critical facts than the plaintiff.

Second, the fundamental admonition that information sought through discovery "need not be admissible at the trial if . . . [it] appears reasonably calculated to lead to the discovery of admissible evidence,"[9] has often been applied with particular vigor to civil rights actions. Document discovery under Rule 34 has also been permitted expansively, with corporate defendants often being required to produce or even create or reconstruct computer data bases to summarize data kept in the course of its business. And where a corporation's home office or corporate headquarters is involved in devising or approving the implementation of a policy that leads to the plaintiff's termination, discovery may extend to all the branches or units of the corporation that operate under the aegis of the central policymaking office, not just to the local unit at which plaintiff's termination was carried out.[10] Defendants are accorded similar liberality with respect to discovery relevant to potential defenses or limitations on liability.[11] But discovery of events in a plaintiff's life that are far remote in time may be prohibited.[12]

Discovery liberality under the Rules reaches overseas. In *Flavel v.*

as usable solely for impeachment purposes was "so devoid of merit as to be specious"; however, plaintiff's counsel did not object to the use of the evidence at trial and could not challenge the admission of the evidence on appeal).

5. FRCP 26(a)(1)(A).

6. FRCP 26(a)(1)(B).

7. The number of interrogatories is limited by Rule 33(a) to "twenty-five in number including all discreet subparts."

8. Rule 30 (a)(2)(A) provides that a "party must obtain leave of court . . . [if] a proposed deposition would result in more than ten depositions being taken under this rule or Rule 31 by the plaintiffs, or by the defendants, or by third-party defendants."

9. Rule 26(b)(1), as amended eff. December 1, 1993.

10. *See Kitchen v. Dial Page, Inc.*, 1995 WL 224547 (E.D.Tenn.1995) (case under Title VII and Tennessee law).

11. *See Vichare v. AMBAC, Inc.*, 106 F.3d 457 (2d Cir.1996) (permitting cross-examination in Title VII action based on discovery of employee misconduct relevant to the after-acquired evidence remedy limitation approved by *McKennon v. Nashville Banner Pub. Co.*, 513 U.S. 352, 115 S.Ct. 879, 130 L.Ed.2d 852 (1995)). *But see Rivera v. Nibco, Inc.*, 364 F.3d 1057 (9th Cir. 2004) (denying employer discovery of plaintiff-employees' immigration status as imposing undue burden on plaintiff and as chilling willingness of others to bring employment-based civil rights claims).

12. *See Jenson v. Eveleth Taconite Co.*, 130 F.3d 1287, 1292–93 (8th Cir.1997) (barring evidence of domestic abuse, earlier illnesses, and personal relationships that defendant sought in order to show alternate causes of plaintiff's emotional injury).

Svedala Indus. Inc.,[13] an ADEA plaintiff sought documents in the possession of the foreign parent of the defendant U.S. subsidiary. Although the defendant U.S. subsidiary's labor relations and personnel policies were not dictated by the parent, the interlocking management structure was such that the subsidiary could obtain the documents from the foreign parent on demand. The defendant argued that because the foreign parent was neither a named party nor an "alter ego" of the defendant U.S. subsidiary within the meaning of ADEA § 4(h), the parent was not subject to liability under ADEA and therefore also immune from discovery. The court accepted the former conclusion but rejected the latter. Relying on federal decisions construing the Federal Rules, the court observed that even if the relationship between the U.S. subsidiary and the foreign parent fell short of what the ADEA stipulated for subjecting the parent to substantive liability, it sufficed to require the subsidiary to respond to a demand for documents held abroad by the parent.

Finally, it should be remembered that the consequences of repeated, willful failure to comply with discovery orders can be fatal. Especially where a pattern of noncompliance prejudices the adversary and less drastic sanctions have proved ineffective, a district judge is fully authorized, after warning, to impose such draconian sanctions as dismissal of an action or striking of a defense.[14] An action has been dismissed even where the refusal to permit discovery was based on the employee's invocation of the Fifth Amendment privilege against self-incrimination.[15]

Courts have struggled to devise meaningful yet fair sanctions for "spoliation"—the failure to preserve evidence in pending or reasonably forseeable litigation, or the destruction of that evidence. The duty to preserve such evidence—chiefly documents or electronic files—arises when litigation is clearly contemplated. This may be well before a court complaint or administrative charge, such as an employment discrimination charge before the Equal Employment Opportunity Commission, is filed.[16] The duty extends to documents in a party's possession that it knows, or reasonably should know, is relevant to the action or contemplated action, reasonably calculated to lead to the discovery of admissible evidence, reasonably likely to be requested during discovery, or that is the subject of a pending discovery request.[17] And it extends to informa-

13. 1993 WL 580831 (E.D.Wis.1993).

14. *See, e.g.*, Fed.R.Civ.P. 37(b)(2)(C), (B). *See also Dotson v. Bravo*, 321 F.3d 663 (7th Cir.2003) (dismissal of prejudice of § 1983 action justified as sanction for discovery violations where plaintiff filed suit under false name and served unverified interrogatory answers containing lies about his true identity, birth date, and arrest record). *But cf. Rice v. City of Chicago*, 333 F.3d 780 (7th Cir.2003) (abuse of discretion to dismiss plaintiff's claims with prejudice as sanction for lawyer's failure to meet three discovery deadlines in excessive force case where defendant city's attorneys were equally disrespectful of court's orders but suffered no sanction).

15. *Serafino v. Hasbro, Inc.*, 82 F.3d 515 (1st Cir.1996). The court suggested that to avoid dismissal in such a situation, the civil plaintiff/potential criminal defendant should move for a stay of his action pending expiration of the criminal period of limitations.

16. *See, e.g., Silvestri v. General Motors Corp.*, 271 F.3d 583, 591 (4th Cir. 2001).

17. *Turner v. Hudson Transit Lines, Inc.*, 142 F.R.D. 68, 72 (S.D.N.Y. 1991)

tion relevant to the claims or defenses of any party or relevant to the subject matter of the action. In employment-based litigation, it extends to documents in the possession or under the control of employees likely to have relevant information.[18]

Sanctions for spoliation may include cost-shifting orders, including orders to pay the costs of additional depositions that a party may need when requested documents cannot be produced due to negligent or intentional spoliation. An alternative sanction is an "adverse inference instruction," whereby the jury is instructed that it may infer from the destruction of evidence that should have been preserved that the evidence would have been favorable to the requesting party and harmful to the spoliator. Some courts[19] deem this sanction extreme. A common formulation of the prerequisites for this sanction requires the party seeking the adverse instruction to show (1) that the party having control of the evidence had an obligation to preserve it when it was destroyed; (2) that the records were destroyed with a culpable state of mind; and (3) that the evidence destroyed was relevant to, in the sense that it would have supported, the claim or defense of the party seeking the sanction.[20] Yet element two virtually vanishes if "culpable state of mind" includes ordinary negligence, as it does in some jurisdictions.[21] By contrast, element (3) can be burdensome if relevance in this context means not just sufficiently probative to satisfy Federal Rule of Evidence 401 but that the party seeking the instruction must adduce evidence enabling a reasonable factfinder to infer that the destroyed or unavailable evidence would have been unfavorable to the spoliator or helpful to the sanction-seeker.[22]

Because claims under the Reconstruction Acts and Title VII arise under federal law, federal judges may apply federal standards in ruling on discovery sanctions, notwithstanding the *Erie* principle requiring deference to state law on "substantive" questions arising in connection with the trial of state law claims.[23] Federal courts accordingly enjoy considerable latitude in deciding whether to impose sanctions, their severity, and the circumstances warranting forgiveness of discovery violations.[24]

18. *Zubulake v. UBS Warburg LLC*, 220 F.R.D. 212, 218 (S.D.N.Y. 2003).

19. *Id.* at 219–220; *but see Mosel Vitelic Corp. v. Micron Technology, Inc.*, 162 F.Supp.2d 307, 315 (D.Del. 2000) (labelling the instruction "one of the least severe sanctions which the court can impose").

20. *See Byrnie v. Town of Cromwell*, 243 F.3d 93, 107–12 (2d Cir. 2001).

21. *See Residential Funding Corp. v. DeGeorge Fin. Corp.*, 306 F.3d 99, 108 (2d Cir. 2002).

22. *Id.*

23. *Park v. City of Chicago*, 297 F.3d 606 (7th Cir.2002).

24. *See, e.g., Perez v. Miami–Dade County*, 297 F.3d 1255 (11th Cir.2002) (holding district court abused discretion by denying defendant county's motion to withdraw admissions in § 1983 action that conclusively established county's liability, reasoning that plaintiff would not have suffered prejudice from withdrawal because he knew at outset of case he would have to prove elements subsequently deemed admitted). *Cf. Martinez v. Stanford*, 323 F.3d 1178 (9th Cir.2003) (granting summary judgment against inmate as sanction for failure to file timely opposition to defendants' motion for summary judgment was excessive punishment for violation of a local rule).

Normally, discovery orders are not "final" so as to authorize immediate appellate jurisdiction within the meaning of the "final decision" rule of 28 U.S.C.A. § 1291. Accordingly, they typically cannot be reviewed until after final judgment, by which time their significance may have been mooted by the subsequent course of litigation. There are exceptions, however, for discovery rulings deemed immediately appealable under the "collateral order" doctrine of *Cohen v. Beneficial Industrial Loan Corp.*[25] because the order conclusively determines a disputed question separable from the merits and would be effectively unreviewable in practical terms if review had to wait until entry of a final judgment. An example is a district court order that permits discovery despite invocations of the attorney-client privilege and the attorney work product doctrine.[26] Also, because sanctions raise issues collateral to the merits of an appeal, a district court retains jurisdiction to rule on them even after the filing of a notice of appeal deprives it of jurisdiction over the substance of a civil rights action.[27]

§ 5.96 Evidence in General

Although a full treatment of the Federal Rules of Evidence is beyond the scope of this book, a number of recurrent issues arise in employment discrimination and civil rights cases that merit attention.[1]

Testimony from coworkers that they were subject to similar discrimination is frequently offered; it is sometimes excluded under Rules 401 and 403 based on an absolute or relative lack of probative value and potential unfair prejudice.[2] If the other employees had different supervisors, their testimony is usually irrelevant.[3] Likewise, coworker testimony

25. 337 U.S. 541, 69 S.Ct. 1221, 93 L.Ed. 1528 (1949).

26. *In re Ford Motor Co.*, 110 F.3d 954 (3d Cir.1997). *See EEOC v. Lutheran Soc. Servs.*, 186 F.3d 959 (D.C.Cir.1999) (quashing EEOC subpoena for a report prepared by employer's attorney in anticipation of litigation over alleged Title VII violations). *See* F.R.C.P. 26(b)(3).

27. *Mahone v. Ray*, 326 F.3d 1176 (11th Cir.2003).

§ 5.96

1. Much of the ensuing discussion is based on Charles C. Warner, *Motions in Limine in Employment Discrimination Litigation*, 29 U.Mem.L.Rev. 823 (1999).

2. *See, e.g., Griffin v. City of Opa–Locka*, 261 F.3d 1295, 1308–1310 (11th Cir. 2001) (testimony by co-workers that alleged sexual harasser harassed them admissible against defendant city as evidence of § 1983 policy or custom); *Cummings v. Standard Register*, 265 F.3d 56 (1st Cir.2001) (no abuse of discretion to admit evidence that two employees other than plaintiff encountered age discrimination elsewhere in defendant corporation where probative value deemed to outweigh prejudicial effect); *Tennison v. Circus Circus Enterprises, Inc.*, 244 F.3d 684 (9th Cir.2001) (probative value of coworkers' testimony of sexual harassment was outweighed by danger of undue prejudice, and risk of "mini trial" provided basis to exclude coworker testimony of sexual harassment).

3. *See Wyvill v. United Cos. Life Ins. Co.*, 212 F.3d 296 (5th Cir.2000) (error to admit anecdotal evidence about alleged age-based discrimination against other employees where those employees had different supervisors, or worked in different parts of the company, or where those alleged age-based job actions are removed in time from the actions at issue in the case at bar); *Curtis v. Oklahoma City Pub. Sch. Bd. of Educ.*, 147 F.3d 1200, 1217–18 (10th Cir. 1998) (noting that the plaintiff and the potential witnesses had worked in different departments and had different supervisors); *Swanson v. General Services Administration*, 110 F.3d 1180, 1190 (5th Cir.1997) (affirming the exclusion of testimony from witnesses who did not work in plaintiff's

may have no probative value if the witness has no evidence regarding the particular decision or if the evidence is remote in time from the adverse job action at issue.[4] Such testimony may create the danger of unfair prejudice in the form of jury confusion. Thus, the jury might otherwise "assume a connection that was never proven between the terminations of the ... witnesses and that of [the plaintiff]."[5] Courts also have excluded such testimony under Rule 404(b) as improper character evidence of prior bad acts.[6]

Evidence in the form of lay opinion testimony offered from coworkers regarding whether discrimination occurred may be challenged under Rule 701. Thus, in *Visser v. Packer Engineering Associates*, coworker testimony that the plaintiff was terminated due to his age was excluded because their testimony was not based on personal knowledge and involved "amateur psychoanalysis."[7] Likewise, testimony that a supervisor had a "hostile and belligerent relationship with black employees" was excluded in *Hogan v. American Telephone & Telegraph Co.* on the basis that the testimony, although relevant, was prejudicial.[8]

Evidence of discriminatory statements or conduct by nondecisionmakers has been offered as both direct and circumstantial evidence of disparate treatment. Relying primarily on Rule 801(d)(2)(D), numerous courts have concluded that only conduct attributable to decisionmakers

office where their anecdotal accounts of discrimination were based on speculation) (race); *Schrand v. Federal Pac. Elec. Co.*, 851 F.2d 152, 156 (6th Cir.1988) (finding that testimony from former employees who worked in different offices from plaintiff and under different supervisors was irrelevant to plaintiff's age discrimination claim); *Goff v. Continental Oil Co.*, 678 F.2d 593, 596–97 (5th Cir.1982) (upholding the exclusion of testimony from former employees who did not work with plaintiff and who had no personal knowledge of the events surrounding plaintiff's discharge) (race).

4. *See, e.g., Williams v. Nashville Network*, 132 F.3d 1123, 1129–31 (6th Cir. 1997) (affirming exclusion of evidence that a co-worker applied for a different position with different qualifications and hiring requirements six years before plaintiff); *Haskell v. Kaman Corp.*, 743 F.2d 113, 122 (2d Cir.1984) (holding that testimony of a former employee regarding his and others' terminations should have been excluded since it was not probative of a pattern or practice nor was it related to the challenged decision); *Goff v. Continental Oil Co.*, 678 F.2d 593, 596–97 (5th Cir.1982) (affirming exclusion where "(a)ll the witnesses could have testified to was their own individualized dealings"), *overruled on other grounds*, *Carter v. South Cent. Bell*, 912 F.2d 832 (5th Cir.1990).

5. *Schrand*, 851 F.2d at 156.

6. *See Coletti v. Cudd Pressure Control*, 165 F.3d 767, 776 (10th Cir.1999).

7. 924 F.2d 655, 659 (7th Cir.1991).

8. 812 F.2d 409, 410–11 (8th Cir.1987). *See also Hester v. BIC Corp.*, 225 F.3d 178 (2d Cir.2000) (coworkers' testimony that supervisor's treatment of employee was race-based was not admissible lay testimony); *Curtis v. Oklahoma City Pub. Sch. Bd. of Educ.*, 147 F.3d 1200, 1219 (10th Cir. 1998) (affirming the exclusion of testimony by the plaintiff's former supervisor to counter charges of incompetence and neglect because the supervisor had no personal knowledge of the facts or issues in the case; therefore, his testimony was irrelevant); *Trotter v. Todd*, 719 F.2d 346, 349 (10th Cir.1983) (excluding co-employees' opinion testimony under Rule 701 since the jury "could draw their own conclusions of law as to the ultimate issue"). *But see Gossett v. Oklahoma ex rel. Bd. of Regents for Langston University*, 245 F.3d 1172 (10th Cir. 2001) (affidavit of former faculty member, which offered her opinion that plaintiff's involuntary withdrawal from the nursing program was the result of school-wide gender discrimination, was admissible under Rule of Evidence on lay opinion testimony).

is probative of disparate treatment.[9] The Sixth Circuit held that the admission of testimony of managers who said the plaintiff was discharged because of his age was reversible error because they had no role in the decision; therefore, "there was no basis for finding that the statements of these declarants concerned 'a matter within the scope of [their] agency.' "[10] Likewise, courts also have excluded evidence that other managers acted differently from the decisionmaking supervisor as being nonprobative or irrelevant.[11]

Evidence inadmissible in the liability phase of a trial may be probative on the issue of punitive damages. The Seventh Circuit held that while evidence regarding the terms of a collective bargaining agreement and the terms of an arbitration agreement were not admissible in support of an employer's explanation as to why it took no corrective action against a sexual harasser, the same evidence was probative as to the employer's liability for punitive damages.[12]

A district court's decision on admissibility of any evidence, including expert testimony,[13] is reviewed for an abuse of discretion.[14]

§ 5.97 [Reserved]

9. *See Armbruster v. Unisys Corp.*, 32 F.3d 768, 779 (3d Cir.1994); *Breneman v. Kennecott Corp.*, 799 F.2d 470, 473 (9th Cir.1986); *Hill v. Spiegel, Inc.*, 708 F.2d 233, 237 (6th Cir.1983). *See also Mason v. Southern Illinois University at Carbondale*, 233 F.3d 1036 (7th Cir.2000) (evidence that coworkers used racial epithets was inadmissible in suit alleging only supervisory racial harassment).

10. *Hill*, 708 F.2d at 237 (quoting Fed. R. Evid. 801(d)(2)(D)); *see also Williams v. Pharmacia*, 137 F.3d 944, 950–51 (7th Cir. 1998) (reaching the same conclusion regarding the testimony of five women in a sex discrimination case). *But see Ercegovich v. Goodyear Tire & Rubber Co.*, 154 F.3d 344, 356 (6th Cir.1998) (holding that comments by nondecisionmakers, while not supporting an inference of age discrimination standing alone, are not "categorically excludable" when offered as evidence of a long-standing "managerial policy").

11. *See Phelps v. Yale Sec., Inc.*, 986 F.2d 1020, 1025 (6th Cir.1993) (finding irrelevant the rehiring of younger employees by other managers after the plaintiff was laid off in a reduction in force); *Jones v. Gerwens*, 874 F.2d 1534, 1541–42 (11th Cir. 1989) (finding irrelevant evidence that other supervisors applied rules more leniently, since plaintiff must demonstrate his supervisor knew of violations and overlooked them).

12. *EEOC v. Indiana Bell Tel. Co.*, 256 F.3d 516, 528 (7th Cir.2001).

13. For a discussion of recent decisions regarding the considerations influencing the admission of expert testimony, see § 5.45, *supra*.

14. *See Griffin v. City of Opa–Locka*, 261 F.3d 1295, 1301–02 (11th Cir.2001), *cert. denied* 535 U.S. 1033, 122 S.Ct. 1789, 152 L.Ed.2d 648 (2002) (no abuse of discretion to admit expert testimony on post-assault behavior of rape or sexual harassment victims, where expert did not comment on the particular plaintiff's own credibility, veracity, or version of events); *Swan v. Interstate Brands Corp.*, 333 F.3d 863 (8th Cir.2003) (exclusion of evidence impeaching employer witness in age discrimination action not clear and prejudicial abuse of discretion because evidence was not necessarily proper impeachment and may have been unduly prejudicial to employer); *Jones v. TEK Industries, Inc.*, 319 F.3d 355 (8th Cir.2003) (district court did not abuse discretion in admitting evidence of Title VII plaintiffs' felony convictions because evidence enabled jury to evaluate credibility of testimony of plaintiffs, state prisoners); *Anderson v. WBMG–42*, 253 F.3d 561 (11th Cir.2001) (exclusion of evidence of discipline received by compensation employer of different race not abuse of discretion because not substantially prejudicial to plaintiff); *Munoz v. Orr*, 200 F.3d 291, 301–302 (5th Cir.2000), *cert. denied*, 531 U.S. 812, 121 S.Ct. 45, 148 L.Ed.2d 15 (2000) (no abuse of discretion to exclude testimony of expert who failed to consider

§ 5.98 Pre-Trial Orders and Other Potential Waivers of Objections Before Jury Retires

Federal Rule of Civil Procedure 16(e) provides that after every pre-trial conference,[1] a pre-trial order must be entered that shall "control the subsequent course of the action unless modified by a subsequent order" and may be "modified only to prevent manifest injustice." This rule operates to bind parties to factual stipulations,[2] the party's statement of issues, the lists of witnesses[3] and exhibits, and the evidence and theories of liability as reflected in the pre-trial order.[4] As an example of the sometimes harsh results of Rule 16(e), consider the Eleventh Circuit's holding that a plaintiff had abandoned his § 1981(a) claim for race discrimination in the making and enforcing of contractual rights because the pre-trial order failed to mention § 1981(a).[5] The pre-trial order did mention § 1981a, which amended Title VII and imposed a damages cap; despite the potential confusion between § 1981(a) and § 1981a, the circuit concluded that the drafter of the pre-trial order was (or should have been) aware of the difference. The end result was that the plaintiff was subject to the damages cap under Title VII, which is not applicable to § 1981(a) claims. But the Eleventh Circuit can be equally harsh with defendants—the court found that a municipal defendant had failed to preserve a seemingly meritorious *Monell* defense by failing to include

significant variables other than national origin and gender); *General Elec. Co. v. Joiner*, 522 U.S. 136, 118 S.Ct. 512, 139 L.Ed.2d 508 (1997) (reversing Eleventh Circuit which applied a more stringent standard of review; "while the Federal Rules of Evidence allow district courts to admit a somewhat broader range of scientific testimony ... [after *Daubert*] than would have been admissible under *Frye*, they leave in place the 'gatekeeper' role of the trial judge in screening such evidence"). *See also S.M. v. J.K.*, 262 F.3d 914 (9th Cir.2001) (no abuse of discretion to exclude evidence of plaintiff's sexual history where employer failed to file motion to introduce that evidence under seal, as required by F.R.E. 412(c)).

§ 5.98

1. Rule 16(f) allows a district court to dismiss an action for failure of a party to attend a pre-trial conference. The court has this power in order to "achieve the orderly and expeditious disposition of cases." *Link v. Wabash Railroad Co.*, 370 U.S. 626, 630–31, 82 S.Ct. 1386, 8 L.Ed.2d 734 (1962). However, the court shall not dismiss a case "without due warning to the plaintiff's counsel." *Ball v. City of Chicago*, 2 F.3d 752, 755 (7th Cir.1993). Due warning does not require the judge to "notify the plaintiff himself, as distinct from his lawyer, before dismissing." *Id.* at 756. Dismissal should be used "only in extreme situations, when there is a clear record of delay or contumacious conduct, or when other less drastic sanctions have proven unavailable." *Kruger v. Apfel*, 214 F.3d 784, 787 (7th Cir.2000) (internal quotations and citations omitted). In *Spain v. Board of Educ. of Meridian Community Unit School Dist. No. 101*, 214 F.3d 925 (7th Cir.2000), the Seventh Circuit upheld the dismissal of an action under Rule 16(f). Plaintiff's counsel failed to provide initial disclosures, failed to answer interrogatories, failed to pay a previously ordered $285 sanction for failing to make initial disclosures, displayed a lack of preparedness at an earlier pre-trial conference and finally failed to attend a second pre-trial conference.

2. *See, e.g., Islamic Republic of Iran v. Boeing Co.*, 771 F.2d 1279, 1291 (9th Cir. 1985), *cert. dismissed*, 479 U.S. 957, 107 S.Ct. 450, 93 L.Ed.2d 397 (1986).

3. *See R.M.R. ex rel. P.A.L. v. Muscogee County Sch. Dist.*, 165 F.3d 812, 818 (11th Cir.1999).

4. *See Pinkley, Inc. v. City of Frederick, Md.*, 191 F.3d 394, 400–401 (4th Cir.1999) (list of plaintiff's claims in pretrial order included only federal law claims under § 1983, not state law conversion claim, which was therefore waived); *Glismann v. AT & T Technologies, Inc.*, 827 F.2d 262, 267 (8th Cir.1987).

5. *Olmsted v. Taco Bell Corp.*, 141 F.3d 1457 (11th Cir.1998).

that defense in the pre-trial order as prescribed by F.R.C.P. 16(e).[6] On the other hand, defendants have sometimes been permitted to salvage defenses they should probably have earlier pleaded if they include them in the pretrial order.[7] Also, even where a Title VII defendant sought to amend the pretrial order to assert a good faith defense it had omitted from the order, and its motion was deemed untimely, it was granted because that defense had been declared only two months previously in a Supreme Court decision and any prejudice to the plaintiff could be cured by a continuance of the trial.[8]

Federal Rule of Civil Procedure 49(a) has been held to provide that failure to challenge the omission of an issue from the verdict form that rule describes before the jury retires waives the right to trial by jury on that issue.[9] A companion Federal Rule, 51, requires that objections to jury instructions must be made "before the jury retires to consider its verdict" or else will not be considered on appeal. Nevertheless, because the purpose of the rule is simply to require objections to be made at a time that leaves the trial judge an opportunity to correct an instruction, it is commonly accepted that objections made subsequently, for example when jurors are given additional instructions or the original instructions are reread, should be considered by the trial court and if not sustained may be raised on appeal.[10] But a party may receive only minimal "plain error" rather than more searching review if he fails to request an instruction at any time during trial.[11] And defendants who fail to seek Rule 50 judgment as a matter of law at the close of all the evidence may attack a verdict only for plain error or manifest miscarriage of justice, instead of the rational-jury test governing such motions as elaborated by the Supreme Court in *Reeves v. Sanderson Plumbing* discussed in § 5.100 immediately following.[12]

§ 5.99 [Reserved]

6. *Morro v. City of Birmingham*, 117 F.3d 508 (11th Cir.1997), *cert. denied*, 523 U.S. 1020, 118 S.Ct. 1299, 140 L.Ed.2d 465 (1998). *See also Hodges v. United States*, 597 F.2d 1014 (5th Cir.1979) (district court did not act arbitrarily in refusing to modify the pretrial order to conform to proof of taxpayers' liability; "any injury resulting from our [decision] . . . is a direct result of the IRS's own failure to properly present its case"); *Santiago v. Lykes Bros. S.S. Co.*, 986 F.2d 423 (11th Cir.1993) (decision of the trial court to modify or enforce a pretrial order will not be disturbed absent a showing of abuse of discretion); *Walker v. Anderson Elec. Connectors*, 944 F.2d 841, 844 (11th Cir.1991), *cert. denied*, 506 U.S. 1078, 113 S.Ct. 1043, 122 L.Ed.2d 352 (1993) (nominal damages sought under Title VII waived because not included in pretrial order); *Braswell v. ConAgra, Inc.*, 936 F.2d 1169, 1176 (11th Cir.1991); *Lexington Ins. Co. v. Cooke's Seafood*, 835 F.2d 1364, 1368 (11th Cir.1988).

7. *See Pulliam v. Tallapoosa County Jail*, 185 F.3d 1182, 1189 (11th Cir.1999) (defendant who failed to plead "mixed motives" defense in answer preserved it by raising defense in pretrial order).

8. *Davey v. Lockheed Martin Corp.*, 301 F.3d 1204 (10th Cir.2002).

9. *Bradway v. Gonzales*, 26 F.3d 313, 317 (2d Cir.1994).

10. *See Barrett v. Orange County Human Rights Comm'n*, 194 F.3d 341, 349 (2d Cir.1999) (quoting 91 Charles Alan Wright & Arthur R. Miller, *Federal Practice and Procedure* § 2553, at 415–17 (2d ed. 1995)).

11. *Griffin v. City of Opa–Locka*, 261 F.3d 1295, 1301 (11th Cir.2001).

12. *McKenzie v. Lee*, 259 F.3d 372 (5th Cir.2001) (per curiam) (plain error); *Fredrick v. District of Columbia*, 254 F.3d 156

Q. SUMMARY JUDGMENT (F.R.C.P. 56), SETTLEMENT, AND JUDGMENT AS A MATTER OF LAW UNDER F.R.C.P. 50(a) ("DIRECTED VERDICT") AND 50(b) ("J.N.O.V.")

§ 5.100 In General

Federal Rule of Civil Procedure 56 allows for summary judgment when, after opportunity for discovery, it appears that there is no genuine issue concerning the existence of a fact "material" under the substantive law, and that the moving party is therefore entitled to judgment as a matter of law.[1] For most of the Rule's history, the party that most commonly moves for summary judgment—a defendant attacking an element of the plaintiff's case—had the burden of adducing evidence that

(D.C.Cir.2001) (manifest miscarriage of justice). *Cf. Eaddy v. Yancey*, 317 F.3d 914 (8th Cir.2003) (plaintiff who failed to make either motion for judgment as a matter of law pursuant to FRCP 50 or motion for new trial pursuant to FRCP 59 could not obtain appellate review of adverse jury verdict, and denial of her motion for summary judgment could not be reviewed after trial on the merits).

§ 5.100

1. The local rules of the various district courts often require a Rule 56 statement of those facts that the movant asserts are undisputed, and a responsive statement from the opposing side in effect admitting or denying each of those asserted facts. *See, e.g.*, Local Rule 56 of the Middle District of Georgia ("LOCAL RULE 56: SUMMARY JUDGMENTS—STATEMENT OF FACTS REQUIRED. Upon filing any motion for summary judgment pursuant to Rule 56 of the Federal Rules of Civil Procedure, a separate, short, and concise statement of the material facts as to which the moving party contends there is no genuine issue to be tried, including specific reference to those parts of the pleadings, depositions, answers to interrogatories, admissions, and affidavits which support such contentions shall be filed with the motion and supporting memorandum. The papers opposing a motion for summary judgment shall include a separate, short and concise statement of the material facts as to which it is contended that there exists a genuine issue of material fact to be tried, including specific reference to those parts of the pleadings, depositions, answers to interrogatories, admissions on file and affidavits which support such contentions. All material facts set forth in the statement served by the moving party will be deemed to be admitted unless controverted by the statement required to be served by the opposing party."). Counsel opposing the motion must be careful to deny all those asserted facts that are central to the issues of the particular case. For example, in *Denney v. City of Albany*, 247 F.3d 1172 (11th Cir.2001), a reverse discrimination case arising out of the Middle District of Georgia, plaintiff's counsel failed to deny defendant's asserted fact that the decisionmaker did not consider race. Although the Eleventh Circuit stated that it did not affirm the district court's grant of summary judgment to defendant on that basis, it noted that it could have affirmed on that basis alone. *Id.* at 1184 (citing *Jones v. Gerwens*, 874 F.2d 1534, 1537 n. 3 (11th Cir.1989)) (treating fact as conceded, in accordance with local district court rule, where party opposing summary judgment failed to controvert the fact as described in the movant's statement of undisputed material facts); *American Nat'l Bank v. FDIC*, 710 F.2d 1528, 1536 (11th Cir.1983) (applying doctrine of judicial estoppel, which applies "to the calculated assertion of divergent sworn positions"). *See also Johnson v. Cambridge Industries Incorporated and Meridian Automotive Systems, Inc.*, 325 F.3d 892 (7th Cir.2003) (court of appeals would not reverse summary judgment granted to defendant on basis of evidence in the record that plaintiff failed to cite to district court as reason for denying motion, writing: "We have repeatedly assured the district courts that they are not required to scour every inch of the record for evidence that is potentially relevant to the summary judgment motion before them.")

virtually negated the fact plaintiff would have the burden of proving at trial. In *Celotex Corp. v. Catrett*,[2] however, the Court reallocated the burdens respecting the existence of a genuine issue: it placed it on the party resisting the motion if, as is usually the case, that party would bear the ultimate trial burden of persuasion on the targeted issue. Thus a defendant in a personal injury action may, by mere argument that the plaintiff has failed during discovery to turn up evidence tending to support any of the indispensable elements of her case (negligence or causation, for example), cast on the plaintiff the obligation to present such evidence in opposition to the motion.[3]

In *Anderson v. Liberty Lobby*,[4] the Court ruled that the evidence produced at the summary judgment stage must be sufficient to sustain

2. 477 U.S. 317, 106 S.Ct. 2548, 91 L.Ed.2d 265 (1986).

3. The same familiar tort questions presented in *Celotex*-was plaintiff exposed to defendant's product, and if so was that product the cause of plaintiff's injuries-will sometimes determine the outcome of summary judgment motions in civil rights cases, too. Compare the strikingly different results on these issues in two circuit opinions decided the same day. *Compare Henderson v. Sheahan*, 196 F.3d 839 (7th Cir.1999), *cert. denied*, 530 U.S. 1244, 120 S.Ct. 2691, 147 L.Ed.2d 962 (2000) (upholding summary judgment on claim that jail officials violated due process by exposing plaintiff to second-hand smoke, for want of sufficient evidence that the exposure would subject plaintiff to an increased risk of serious future medical harm) *with Warren v. Keane*, 196 F.3d 330 (2d Cir.1999) (material fact issue precludes summary judgment on same claim).

4. 477 U.S. 242, 106 S.Ct. 2505, 91 L.Ed.2d 202 (1986). Applying *Liberty Lobby* to summary judgment motions based on the individual defendant official's qualified immunity defense in § 1983 cases has proven especially vexing. *Liberty Lobby* of course requires the trial judge deciding a summary judgment motion to ascertain which party will bear at trial the burden of persuasion, and by what quantum, on the element of the case targeted by the motion. This is problematic with qualified immunity, however, because the Supreme Court has not decided which party bears what persuasion burden on each element of the defense. One might expect the defendant to bear the burden of persuasion on all those elements, since qualified immunity is an affirmative defense, *Gomez v. Toledo*, 446 U.S. 635, 100 S.Ct. 1920, 64 L.Ed.2d 572 (1980), that the defendant should plead in its Answer. And *Liberty Lobby* observes that summary judgment for the defendant will generally be unavailable respecting an affirmative defense, since the defendant would bear the unusually difficult burden of showing that any reasonable jury would be obliged to believe the facts underlying the defense by a preponderance of the evidence. 477 U.S. at 252–255, 106 S.Ct. at 2511–14. Yet the Supreme Court has held that it is the plaintiff's burden to prove the pure law element of the defense, by citing an authoritative case or cases demonstrating that the federal law violation alleged was "clearly established" at the time defendant acted. *Davis v. Scherer*, 468 U.S. 183, 197, 104 S.Ct. 3012, 3020–21, 82 L.Ed.2d 139 (1984). And the circuit decisions are sharply divided as to whether, once plaintiff makes that showing, defendant bears the burden of persuasion of proving that a reasonable person in his position would not have realized that his act or omission violated that clearly established law. *Compare Nelson v. McMullen*, 207 F.3d 1202, 1206 (10th Cir.2000); *DiRuzza v. County of Tehama*, 206 F.3d 1304, 1313 (9th Cir.), *cert. denied*, 531 U.S. 1035, 121 S.Ct. 624, 148 L.Ed.2d 533 (2000); *Black v. Coughlin*, 76 F.3d 72, 75 (2d Cir.1996); *Guffey v. Wyatt*, 18 F.3d 869, 871 (10th Cir.1994); *Elder v. Holloway*, 975 F.2d 1388, 1392 (9th Cir.1991), *rev'd on other grounds*, 510 U.S. 510, 114 S.Ct. 1019, 127 L.Ed.2d 344 (1994); *Benigni v. City of Hemet*, 879 F.2d 473, 479–80 (9th Cir.1988) (defendant bears burden) *with Gardenhire v. Schubert*, 205 F.3d 303, 311 (6th Cir. 2000); *Spiegel v. Cortese*, 196 F.3d 717, 723 (7th Cir.), *cert. denied*, 530 U.S. 1243, 120 S.Ct. 2688, 147 L.Ed.2d 961 (2000); *Hoard v. Sizemore*, 198 F.3d 205, 211 (6th Cir. 1999); *Crawford–El v. Britton*, 93 F.3d 813, 821–23 (D.C.Cir.1996) (en banc), *vacated and remanded on other grounds*, 523 U.S. 574, 118 S.Ct. 1584, 140 L.Ed.2d 759 (1998); *Shaw v. Stroud*, 13 F.3d 791, 801 (4th Cir.1994), *cert. denied*, 513 U.S. 813, 115 S.Ct. 67, 130 L.Ed.2d 24 (1994); *Ellis v. Wynalda*, 999 F.2d 243, 246 (7th Cir.1993);

the verdict at trial *by whatever standard will be required to support the burden of proof at trial*. Thus the public official plaintiff suing the press for libel must provide sufficient evidence to convince a reasonable fact finder of *New York Times* malice by a "clear and convincing" evidentiary standard. Mere production of some evidence of such malice will not sustain the denial of defendant's motion for summary judgment. Of course in civil rights and employment discrimination cases, the plaintiff's burden on prima facie elements is the ordinary "preponderance of the evidence" standard.[5] Therefore once the defendant properly makes the motion per *Celotex*, or by offering independent evidence of its own that suggests plaintiff cannot create a genuine issue about a material fact, the plaintiff can resist summary judgment only by producing admissible evidence—relevant,[6] reliable evidence that is either not hearsay or for which the Federal Rules of Evidence provide an exception.[7]

Pfannstiel v. City of Marion, 918 F.2d 1178, 1183–84 (5th Cir.1990), *abrogated on other grounds by Martin v. Thomas*, 973 F.2d 449 (5th Cir.1992) (plaintiff bears burden). An excellent discussion of both the burden of persuasion question and its implications for summary judgment may be found in Chen, "*The Burdens of Qualified Immunity: Summary Judgment and the Role of Facts in Constitutional Tort Law*," 47 Am.U.L.Rev. 1 (1997).

5. *See* § 5.80, *supra*.

6. For example, the Sixth Circuit reversed a trial court's decision, based on relevancy, to exclude a particularly offensive racially derogatory document circulated around the workplace with the supervisor's knowledge. *Robinson v. Runyon*, 149 F.3d 507, 513–15 (6th Cir.1998). The appellate court noted that even where a Title VII plaintiff proceeds not with direct evidence but rather via the inferential *McDonnell Douglas/Burdine* mode of proof, courts "must be mindful not to cripple a plaintiff's ability to prove discrimination indirectly and circumstantially by evidentiary rulings that keep out probative evidence because of crabbed notions of relevance" (internal quotation omitted). The court affirmed, however, the district court's exclusion of a hangman's noose which was displayed in the workplace for a short time period because the incident occurred over a year before the plaintiff's alleged harassment.

Because judges ruling on summary judgment motions can ordinarily consider only potentially admissible evidence, they must take into account the evidentiary rules that will govern relevance and the probative value/prejudicial effect balance at trial. In employment discrimination and civil rights cases, testimony about discrimination directed against other members of plaintiff's group commonly raises disputes about these issues. *See Heyne v. Caruso*, 69 F.3d 1475, 1479 (9th Cir.1995) (testimony of prior discriminatory acts against members of plaintiff's protected group by the particular employer agent alleged to have discriminated against plaintiff particularly probative of that agent's state of mind); *Palmer v. Board of Regents*, 208 F.3d 969, 972 (11th Cir. 2000) (affirming trial court's ruling that evidence of discriminatory acts by other decisionmakers in other departments was too remote to be relevant to motive of the decisionmaker at bar and accordingly was properly excludable as having greater prejudicial effect than probative value); *Roy v. Austin Co.*, 194 F.3d 840, 843 (7th Cir.1999) (approving trial court's use of general proposition "that showing disparate treatment by a different supervisor does not normally further a plaintiff's ability to make out a discrimination claim under Title VII."). *Beachy v. Boise Cascade Corp.*, 191 F.3d 1010, 1014 (9th Cir.1999), *cert. denied*, 529 U.S. 1021, 120 S.Ct. 1425, 146 L.Ed.2d 316 (2000) (to be relevant, the discrimination must evince hostility towards "a well-defined and protected group such as persons of a particular race" gender, national origin, religion, age or disability, and because of that group's status; employer agent's irritation with or hostility to such persons based solely on their work habits is not probative of unlawful discriminatory animus).

7. *See McMillian v. Johnson*, 88 F.3d 1573, 1583–85 (11th Cir.1996), *aff'd on other grounds*, 520 U.S. 781, 117 S.Ct. 1734, 138 L.Ed.2d 1 (1997), which construed the ambiguous passage on the subject in *Celotex*, 477 U.S. at 324, to mean that although evidence need not be reduced to a form that would be admissible at trial, it must be of the kind that would be admissible in substance. For example, where a letter produced in opposition to summary judgment would be inadmissible hearsay if offered at trial, the plaintiff could nevertheless rely on its contents to raise a genuine issue of fact where there was reason to believe that the writer could testify to its contents at trial. *Offshore Aviation v. Transcon Lines, Inc.*, 831 F.2d 1013, at 1015–1016 (11th Cir. 1987). By contrast, the panel in *McMillian* would not permit otherwise inadmissible hearsay statements to raise a genuine issue of fact where they would still be inadmissible when offered at trial. While those statements would be admissible at trial for impeachment purposes, the panel ruled that potential impeachment evidence could not be considered as substantive evidence to raise a genuine issue about the fact targeted by the motion.

In contrast, the Fifth Circuit has read Rule 56(e) to preclude the use of unsworn or handwritten statements. For example, in *Watts v. Kroger Co.*, 170 F.3d 505, 508–09 (5th Cir.1999), a Title VII sexual harassment case, the court held that several handwritten statements by plaintiff's co-workers that were signed but not sworn, notarized, or in the form of affidavits, were not competent summary judgment evidence for the purposes of Rule 56(e). The court rejected plaintiff's arguments that the touchstone for consideration is the ultimate admissibility of the evidence at trial. Similarly, in *Duplantis v. Shell Offshore, Inc.*, 948 F.2d 187, 191–92 (5th Cir.1991) the court relied on Rule 56(f): If the party opposing summary judgment has evidence which has not yet been reduced to admissible form but is germane to the existence of a genuine issue of material fact, then it is proper for the party opposing summary judgment to move for a continuance "to permit affidavits to be obtained or depositions to be taken or discovery to be had." The court acknowledged that *Celotex* gave "some indication" that the nonmoving party's Rule 56(e) evidence might not have to be in strictly admissible form. But it interpreted *Celotex* as merely dispensing with the necessity of full depositions, allowing other documents listed in Rule 56(c), such as "answers to interrogatories, and admissions on file, together with affidavits," to suffice as material that may resist the motion. The court stated that if unsworn statements or unauthenticated documents were allowed at summary judgment, courts would "get bogged down in a needless examination of the hypothetical ways the nonmoving party's evidence might be reduced to admissible form by the time of trial." Because unsworn statements and unauthenticated documents are not the kind of evidence described in Rules 56(c) and 56(e), and it was not the district court's duty to examine whether and how it might be reduced to acceptable form by the time of trial, the district court should disregard such evidence at summary judgment.

At the summary judgment stage, trial courts are forced to make a not-so-easy forecast of what would be admissible at trial, and their forecasts are sometimes invalidated by appellate courts. *Wright–Simmons v. City of Oklahoma City*, 155 F.3d 1264, 1268–69 (10th Cir.1998) is a case in point. When deciding a summary judgment motion, the district court did not consider a report, prepared by the defendant's personnel department in connection with its internal investigation of an employee's complaints about racial harassment, which concluded that the complaining employee's supervisor engaged in racial harassment. But the appellate court concluded that the failure to consider such a report constituted reversible error, relying on F.R.E. 801(d)(2)(B) (evidence is not hearsay if it "is offered against a party and is ... a statement of which the party has manifested an adoption or belief in its truth") and on evidence that the employer acted on the report when it sought the supervisor's resignation.

In *Stewart v. Henderson*, 207 F.3d 374, 377–378 (7th Cir.2000), the question was whether the trial court should have admitted evaluative statements made by others about the plaintiff that were contained in the affidavit of a supervisor-decisionmaker that he relied upon in recommending the adverse action plaintiff challenged. Referencing the Title VII substantive principle, that the employer's legitimate nondiscriminatory reason need only be sincerely held rather than correct, accurate, or wise, the court held that the affidavit was properly considered by the trial court in granting summary judgment. It was not hearsay, in short, because it was offered not for the truth of the matter asserted but instead to demonstrate that the supervisor-decisionmaker changed his opinion based on that of the evaluators. And "regardless of whether the committee members were correct" in their perception that plaintiff's application evinced an "adversarial quality that would be detrimental in the position," "their statement is relevant to show ... [the supervisor-decisionmaker's] state of mind when he made his [negative] recommendation." Similarly, in another case where evidence offered in opposition to summary judgment was germane to the state of mind of defendant's decisionmakers, it was not offered to prove the truth of the matter asserted, was therefore not hearsay as defined by F.R.Evidence 801(c), and could ac-

This potentially admissible evidence may be in the form of affidavits, documents, deposition testimony, interrogatory answers, admissions or otherwise, but it must be sufficient taken as a whole for a reasonable jury to find plaintiff's way on that fact by a preponderance of the evidence. Still, plaintiff's own affidavit can suffice to resist a motion for summary judgment.[8]

In Title VII and ADEA cases, the defendant may rebut the element of discriminatory intent by showing neutral, non-discriminatory reasons for the employee's discharge. The plaintiff must then produce evidence that the defendant's explanation is pretextual. The Supreme Court denied certiorari in *Hardin v. Pitney–Bowes*,[9] where the Sixth Circuit had granted summary judgment on that issue. Justice Rehnquist dissented vigorously from the denial of certiorari, maintaining that summary judgment is never appropriate on issues of intent. Circuit courts have continued to uphold summary judgment on the ultimate intent question that lies at the heart of the individual disparate treatment case, consistent with the *Celotex* and *Anderson* standards. They have applied those decisions to require that the plaintiff, to survive summary judgment, must do more than offer some evidence that an employer's assertion of non-discriminatory intent was false, or even a pretext for unlawful discrimination; rather, the plaintiff must present evidence *sufficient* to enable a *reasonable* jury to find such pretext by a preponderance of the evidence, the plaintiff's ultimate burden at a trial.[10]

An example illustrates the risk faced by a plaintiff resisting summary judgment after the Supreme Court's restatement in *St. Mary's Honor Ctr. v. Hicks*,[11] of the trial burden on "pretext." The Seventh Circuit, applying *St. Mary's*, has held that an ADEA plaintiff, to counter employer evidence of a legitimate nondiscriminatory reason in opposing a summary judgment motion, need only "produce evidence from which a rational factfinder could infer that the company lied"; it was not essen-

cordingly be considered. *Wright v. Southland Corp.*, 187 F.3d 1287, 1304 n. 21 (11th Cir.1999). Other times, of course, district courts correctly predict admissibility on difficult questions of evidence law. *See, e.g., Zaben v. Air Products & Chemicals, Inc.*, 129 F.3d 1453, 1455–57 (11th Cir.1997) (affirming trial court's exclusion of hearsay statements after an arduous double hearsay analysis under F.R.E. 801, 802 and 805).

Sometimes evidence law prohibiting hearsay confronts the principle of *Johnson v. Jones* that a § 1983 individual defendant official may not appeal a district court's summary judgment order denying him the defense of qualified immunity on the sole ground that the pretrial record reveals a genuine issue of fact requiring trial. One circuit has held that in this situation, *Johnson* precludes interlocutory appellate jurisdiction even when, in the view of the circuit court of appeals, the decision denying summary judgment depended on "the rankest type of inadmissible hearsay." *Ellis v. Washington County*, 198 F.3d 225, 229 (6th Cir.1999), *cert. denied*, 529 U.S. 1087, 120 S.Ct. 1720, 146 L.Ed.2d 642 (2000).

8. *Danzer v. Norden Sys., Inc.*, 151 F.3d 50, 57 (2d Cir.1998) (recognizing that disregarding a plaintiff's own affidavit would substantially alter the Rule 56(c) convention that all inferences must be drawn in favor of nonmovant).

9. 451 U.S. 1008, 101 S.Ct. 2345, 68 L.Ed.2d 861 (1981) (denying certiorari).

10. *See, e.g., Healy v. New York Life Ins.*, 860 F.2d 1209 (3d Cir.1988), *cert. denied*, 490 U.S. 1098, 109 S.Ct. 2449, 104 L.Ed.2d 1004 (1989), where the Third Circuit reversed its prior adherence to Justice Rehnquist's position, and *Alphin v. Sears Roebuck*, 940 F.2d 1497 (11th Cir.1991).

11. 509 U.S. 502, 113 S.Ct. 2742, 125 L.Ed.2d 407 (1993).

tial, in other words, for the plaintiff to offer other, affirmative evidence of pretext, for example, that similarly situated employees were treated differently.[12] But because, under *St. Mary's*, such a showing would merely permit, not require, the factfinder at trial to find intentional discrimination because of age by a preponderance of the evidence, plaintiff takes a risk in limiting his summary judgment showing to evidence that attacks the employer's asserted legitimate reason.

In the case at hand, for example, the court viewed the plaintiff's evidence that the employer had lied about its stated reason as insufficient to avoid summary judgment, apparently because it believed that a jury acting reasonably could not find such a lie by a preponderance of the evidence submitted on the motion.[13] The lesson for plaintiff's counsel seems to be that although *St. Mary's*, and therefore summary judgment practice, may *require* only one kind of evidence of pretext (e.g., evidence that the employer lied), plaintiff acts at her peril even on summary judgment if she withholds other available evidence of pretext. This is because, now that *Anderson* has equated the summary judgment standard with that required for directed verdict, her evidence in response to a defendant's summary judgment motion must meet the same preponderance—standard *weighing* she will encounter at trial, notwithstanding the Supreme Court majority's rhetorical protestations to the contrary.

In § 1983 cases, the confusion these standards sow is apparent in two cases in the Eleventh Circuit. Plaintiffs must show evidence of a municipal policy or practice that allows or encourages constitutional violations by its employees to render the municipality liable under § 1983.[14] In two cases decided one month apart, the Eleventh Circuit granted and denied the defendant municipalities' motions for summary judgment, although plaintiffs had produced similar evidence in each case.[15]

Summary judgment is also the individual § 1983 defendant's preferred vehicle for raising the defense of qualified immunity. An individual government official will qualify for immunity either if the federal law he allegedly violated was not then clearly established or if he can show that a reasonable official in his position would not have understood in the particular circumstances that his challenged conduct violated that clearly established law.[16] Even though qualified immunity is an affirmative defense on which the defendant bears the burden of pleading,[17] production and persuasion, the "clearly established" prong is a question of law well suited for summary disposition.[18]

12. *Anderson v. Baxter Healthcare Corp.*, 13 F.3d 1120 (7th Cir.1994).

13. *Id.*

14. *See* §§ 2.30–2.32, *supra*.

15. *Samples v. Atlanta*, 846 F.2d 1328 (11th Cir.1988); *Brown v. Clewiston*, 848 F.2d 1534 (11th Cir.1988).

16. *See* § 2.22, *supra*.

17. *Gomez v. Toledo*, 446 U.S. 635, 100 S.Ct. 1920, 64 L.Ed.2d 572 (1980); *Moore v. Morgan*, 922 F.2d 1553 (11th Cir.1991).

18. *See* § 2.23, *supra*.

Even when, as is so frequently the case in employment discrimination and civil rights litigation, the issue on the motion concerns a defendant's intent or other state of mind, summary judgment is, contrary to an older school of thought, now clearly available.[19] The Supreme Court apparently recognizes the propriety of summary judgment grants even on the issue of malice.[20] Summary judgment would therefore also seem available to dispose of claims based on 42 U.S.C.A. § 1985(3) for lack of evidence of the required invidiously discriminatory class-based animus.[21] Further, partial summary judgment could sometimes be granted on punitive damages, in cases where they are alleged to be dependent on a wrongful state of mind.[22]

The tilt toward the defendant in the summary judgment decisional calculus ushered in by *Celotex* and, especially, *Anderson*, has altered settlement dynamics both before and after the motion is decided. A defendant who is able and chooses to make the bare-bones initial supporting showing permitted by *Celotex* can make the motion rather inexpensively. Yet once the defendant makes the motion, *Anderson*'s insistence on *enough* evidence to enable a reasonable jury to find for the plaintiff *by a preponderance* places great pressure on the plaintiff to respond by offering all or virtually all evidence that he has unearthed during the course of discovery that is likely to raise a genuine issue about the fact targeted by the motion. This process is quite expensive, but once complete represents a significant advance investment on the plaintiff's preparation for trial.

After the motion is made, then, plaintiffs are perhaps more likely than they were before *Celotex* and *Anderson* to settle to avoid the greater costs of resisting and the greater risk of losing the motion. On the other hand, if the motion is made and denied, plaintiff's price to settle is probably higher than in pre-*Anderson* days, for three reasons. First, the judge, by denying the motion, has pre-certified it as one a reasonable jury might find plaintiff's way by the required trial quantum of evidence. Second, there is less risk than previously that the plaintiff will suffer judgment as a matter of law, now that the Supreme Court equates the summary judgment standard with the standards for directed verdict and judgment notwithstanding the verdict. Third, the plaintiff's demand must now account for front-loaded, full-scale pretrial preparation costs that he has probably already incurred in order to resist the motion. Of

19. *See Crawford–El v. Britton*, 523 U.S. 574, 600–601, 118 S.Ct. 1584, 140 L.Ed.2d 759 (1998) (observing also that even if plaintiff can prove the wrongful state of mind, defendant may prevail on the qualified immunity defense by showing that the law was not clearly established when defendant acted). *See also Borgo v. Goldin*, 204 F.3d 251 (D.C.Cir.2000) (triable fact questions remained as to whether supervisor acted with reverse discriminatory motive); *Kimberlin v. Quinlan*, 199 F.3d 496, 502 (D.C.Cir.1999), *cert. denied*, 531 U.S. 871, 121 S.Ct. 172, 148 L.Ed.2d 118 (2000) (summary judgment possible on question of defendant's motive to interfere with plaintiff's First Amendment rights) (citing *Crawford–El*).

20. *See Anderson v. Liberty Lobby*, 477 U.S. at 254, 106 S.Ct. at 2513.

21. *See* § 1.5, *supra*.

22. *See* § 2.25, *supra*, on the *Smith v. Wade* standard under which juries may award punitive damages in Reconstruction Act cases.

course even if the motion is granted, the defendant may still have some reason to negotiate, given the possibility of a meritorious plaintiff's appeal.[23]

Despite the Supreme Court's observation in *Anderson* formally equating the directed verdict and summary judgment standards, it is not inevitable in practice that the same evidence sufficient to resist summary judgment will also suffice to authorize or uphold a verdict. In general, the F.R.C.P. 50(a) and (b) motions for judgment as a matter of law (corresponding, in former terminology, to the motions for directed verdict and j.n.o.v.) should only be granted when the court determines that there is insufficient evidence from which a jury reasonably could find (directed verdict) or could have found (j.n.o.v.) an issue favorably to the party that bears the burden on an issue by the applicable quantum of evidence—normally, a preponderance. A common test used by the lower federal courts in a wide variety of cases to assess such sufficiency is whether there is "substantial evidence" on the issue in question, defined as "evidence of such quality and weight that reasonable and fair-minded men [sic] in the exercise of impartial judgment might reach different conclusions."[24] But to some uncertain degree this formulation implicitly assumes that directed verdict or j.n.o.v. will sometimes be warranted despite the admission of evidence supporting the proponent's position when that evidence is "overwhelmed by contrary proof."[25] The Fifth Circuit applied these tests to the burden the Supreme Court placed on the ADEA plaintiff[26] of proving that age had a "determinative influence" on the challenged employment decision. In dictum, the Fifth Circuit concluded that evidence tending to show that the employer's proffered neutral explanation is false—sufficient under *St. Mary's* to resist summary judgment under Rule 56 because it would permit a fact-finder to determine that the false explanation was a pretext for age discrimination—may nevertheless in some cases fail to support a verdict if that evidence is not "substantial" in the sense used to decide Rule 50 motions for judgment as a matter of law.[27] Another circuit's formulation, somewhat more respectful of the jury's fact-finding role, limits the rule 50 inquiry as follows: " 'whether the evidence presented, combined with all reasonable inferences therefrom, is sufficient to support the verdict [by the requisite preponderance of the evidence] when viewed in the light most favorable to the party against whom the motion is directed . . . In other words, we are limited to assessing whether no rational jury could

23. *See Sheng v. Starkey Laboratories, Inc.*, 117 F.3d 1081 (8th Cir.1997) (affirming validity and enforceability of agreement settling Title VII action even though parties executed it after a district court order, of which they were unaware, granted defendant's motion for summary judgment). Presumably defense counsel can guard against such a possibility by providing in a draft or oral settlement agreement that a condition of the accord's finality is that any pending summary judgment motion not be granted in the interim.

24. *Boeing Co. v. Shipman*, 411 F.2d 365 (5th Cir.1969).

25. *Neely v. Delta Brick and Tile Co.*, 817 F.2d 1224 (5th Cir.1987).

26. *Hazen Paper Co. v. Biggins*, 507 U.S. 604, 113 S.Ct. 1701, 123 L.Ed.2d 338 (1993).

27. *Rhodes v. Guiberson Oil Tools*, 82 F.3d 615 (5th Cir.1996) (en banc).

have found for the plaintiff.' In doing so, 'this court may not step in and substitute its view of the contested evidence for the jury's.' "[28]

In perhaps its most significant plaintiff-friendly employment discrimination opinion in decades, the Supreme Court has now resolved the post-*St. Mary's* debate, and the general standard governing FRCP 50 motions, consistent with the jury—respectful approach taken by the majority of the circuit courts. As the discussion that follows explains, however, the decision will probably have even more significant impact in the resolution of the vastly greater number of motions for summary judgment in employment discrimination and civil rights case and civil litigation generally.[29]

In *Reeves v. Sanderson Plumbing Prods., Inc.*,[30] a case under the Age Discrimination in Employment Act ("ADEA"), the Court, taking note of the differing *St. Mary's* passages, wrote that the jury may find the ultimate fact of discrimination on a prohibited ground simply from (1) *evidence* establishing a prima facie case, coupled with (2) "sufficient" *evidence* that the employer's asserted legitimate nondiscriminatory explanation is false. The Court considered this approach consistent with general evidence law: "the factfinder is entitled to consider a party's dishonesty about a material fact as 'affirmative evidence of guilt' "; and once the employer's asserted reason is rejected, unlawful discrimination "may well be the most likely alternative explanation."[31] Of course, as *St. Mary's* had held, the jury may properly find liability in such a case only if properly charged that it must, from these two kinds of evidence, make dual *findings*: (1) that the reason or reasons offered by the employer for taking the adverse action against plaintiff were not its real reasons, *and* (2) that the employer's real reason was in fact the unlawful ground. But the Court disapproved the circuit cases that had required plaintiffs to adduce evidence not only that the employer's asserted legitimate reason was false but also sufficient, independent *evidence* that the employer's actual reason was an *unlawful* one.[32]

That of course still left the Court to explain what it meant by the required "sufficient" or "enough" evidence that an employer's proffered legitimate reason is false. On this point the Court was refreshingly precise. Resolving a long-standing uncertainty as to the general standard for directed verdict (now the Federal Rule of Civil Procedure 50 motion

28. *Mathur v. Board of Trustees*, 207 F.3d 938, 941 (7th Cir.2000) (internal citations omitted).

29. *See, e.g., Mickle v. Morin*, 297 F.3d 114, 120–123 (2d Cir.2002) (explicitly applying *Reeves* standard to Rule 50(a) motion in action under § 1983 and accordingly finding error in district court's failure to credit plaintiff's testimony in ruling on motion).

30. 530 U.S. 133, 120 S.Ct. 2097, 147 L.Ed.2d 105 (2000).

31. 530 U.S. at 146, 120 S.Ct. at 2108–09.

32. But, as several circuits have held, the jury should not be charged with the elements of plaintiff's prima facie case under Title VII when plaintiff seeks to meet it through the inferential evidence formula of *McDonnell Douglas v. Green*. Rather, the instructions should focus the jury on the ultimate question whether the residue of all the evidence persuades them by a preponderance that the defendant intentionally discriminated against the plaintiff on a ground prohibited by Title VII. *See Sanghvi v. City of Claremont*, 328 F.3d 532 (9th Cir.2003) (citing cases).

for "judgment as a matter of law") in the federal courts, the Court wrote that a trial or appellate court should consider the entire record, not merely evidence favoring the non-moving party—i.e., in the *St. Mary's* context, the plaintiff.[33] But it stressed that the deciding court must draw all reasonable inferences in favor of the nonmovant, refraining from making credibility determinations itself or weighing the evidence. And it clarified that in order to avoid intruding on that jury function, the court "must disregard all evidence favorable to the moving party [the defendant, in the *St. Mary's* setting] that the jury is not required to believe.... That is, the court should give credence to [all] the evidence favoring the nonmovant [plaintiff] as well as [only] that 'evidence supporting the moving party that is uncontradicted and unimpeached, at least to the extent that that evidence comes from disinterested witnesses.' "[34]Accordingly, as long as plaintiff's counsel substantially impeaches or contradicts defendant-favorable evidence, a court should not consider that evidence in determining whether to uphold a plaintiff's verdict.

In elaborating these Rule 50 standards, the Court relied heavily on *Anderson v. Liberty Lobby*,[35] its most recent principal guidance on deciding motions for summary judgment. Indeed the Court repeated the *Liberty Lobby* observation that the inquiry under the summary judgment and directed verdict (judgment as a matter of law) motions is "the same." So it now appears settled in cases under ADEA (and, as discussed below, under Title VII) that it is possible for a disparate treatment plaintiff to survive summary judgment and proceed to trial, or to survive a motion for judgment as a matter of law during trial or after a favorable verdict, provided only it has offered evidence establishing the minimal, *McDonnell Douglas* prima facie case and "sufficient" evidence of the falsity of the employer's asserted legitimate nondiscriminatory reason. The plaintiff need not also have presented evidence of an employer decisionmaker's ageist, racist or sexist remarks, or evidence that a similarly situated comparator who was younger or of a different race, sex, religion, or national origin received more favorable treatment. (Although such additional evidence had been presented in *Reeves*, the opinion made clear that only *McDonnell Douglas* prima facie evidence, plus "sufficient" evidence that the employer's stated reason is false, is necessary to permit a jury to reach the ultimate conclusion that the employer relied on an unlawful factor.) And in considering when evidence of falsity suffices, the trial court should take into account only evidence favoring the plaintiff and unimpeached, uncontradicted testimony favoring the defendant.

Summary judgment (and, even more directly, judgment as a matter of law) should accordingly now be granted only in the presumably rare case that a court, considering such evidence alone, determines that a jury could not rationally find (or could not have rationally found) by a

33. *Id.* at 147–48, 120 S.Ct. at 2109–10.

34. *Id.* at 148, 120 S.Ct. at 2110.

35. 477 U.S. 242, 106 S.Ct. 2505, 91 L.Ed.2d 202 (1986).

preponderance of that evidence the ultimate fact of unlawful race, sex, religious, national origin, or age discrimination, despite its acceptance of the prima facie case and the falsity of the employer's stated legitimate, nondiscriminatory reason. The Court observed that this could happen where, for example, the record "conclusively revealed" affirmative evidence that the employer's challenged decision was taken for a different nondiscriminatory reason—as where the employer gave the false, nondiscriminatory explanation to conceal a lawful but embarrassing reason, or a reason unlawful under some law other than Title VII or ADEA. Or, the Court added, judgment as a matter of law may be warranted where the employer presents "abundant and uncontroverted independent evidence" that it did not act on an unlawful ground *and* the plaintiff "created only a weak issue of fact as to whether the employer's reason was untrue." As Justice Ginsburg observed in her concurring opinion, conclusive demonstrations by unimpeached and uncontradicted evidence that discrimination could not have been the employer's actual motivation will be "atypical." Accordingly, in her words, a plaintiff will have to produce evidence beyond the two minimally required categories—the *McDonnell Douglas* prima facie showing and evidence that the employer's stated nondiscriminatory reason is false—only in "uncommon" circumstances. Consequently, "the ultimate question of liability ordinarily should not be taken from the jury once the plaintiff has introduced" the two minimally required categories of evidence.

It seems apparent from the *Reeves* opinion that the Supreme Court intends these rules to apply to cases under Title VII, not just to cases under ADEA. Citing and adopting the approach taken by the courts of appeals, the Court assumed arguendo that the Title VII, *McDonnell Douglas* evidentiary framework for cases based on "circumstantial," as opposed to "direct" evidence, as that framework was elaborated in *St. Mary's*, was "fully applicable" to the ADEA case at hand. This conclusion follows logically as well. The Court repeated its statement from *Hazen Paper Co. v. Biggins*[36] that in ADEA actions, the plaintiff must show that his age played not just a role but had a "determinative influence" on the outcome of the employer's decisionmaking process. In Title VII cases, by contrast, the statute as amended in 1991 provides that a plaintiff need only prove that race, sex, religion or national origin was a "motivating" factor in the employer's decision. It is therefore to be expected that Title VII plaintiffs should be able to survive Rule 56 summary judgment motions and Rule 50 motions for judgment as a matter of law at least as readily as ADEA plaintiffs will be able to under the standards announced in *Reeves*. More broadly, the general Rule 50 (and by extension rule 56) standards announced in *Reeves* will likely be held applicable to the other employment discrimination and civil rights claims considered throughout this book, and indeed to civil litigation generally. The Court has usually hewed to a "transsubstantive" approach to the Federal Rules of Civil Procedure, construing and applying them uniformly without regard to the nature of a particular claim except

36. 507 U.S. 604, 610, 113 S.Ct. 1701, 1706, 123 L.Ed.2d 338 (1993).

where the Rules themselves specifically provide otherwise.[37] Furthermore, its discussion in *Reeves* relied and elaborated on authority arising from ordinary civil litigation.[38] The application of summary judgment to employment discrimination "pretext" cases is discussed more fully in § 5.10.

§ 5.101 Interlocutory Appeals of Orders Denying Summary Judgment on the Defense of Qualified Immunity

The *Mitchell v. Forsyth*[1] collateral order exception to the 28 U.S.C.A. § 1291 final decision requirement permits the individual government defendant in § 1983 actions an immediate, interlocutory appeal from orders denying a motion for summary judgment (or motion to dismiss for failure to state a claim) based on the qualified immunity defense. Indeed it has been held that even a trial court's *refusal* to rule before trial on the qualified immunity defense is immediately appealable under the *Mitchell* principle, because once the trial proceeds the defendant will have permanently lost the immunity from the burdens of suit that interlocutory appeal is designed to protect.[2] A fuller discussion of the procedural complications surrounding these interlocutory appeals may be found in Chapter 2, § 2.23. Here we will note only that there is no exception to the "law of the case" doctrine applicable to a civil rights defendant's interlocutory appeal of an order denying qualified immunity; thus a defendant who loses in the trial court on the "clearly established law" prong of the defense, but appeals only a ruling rejecting his argument that the complaint was deficiently alleged in other respects, will, assuming the initial appeal is unsuccessful, be bound in both the trial court on remand and on any successive appeal by the ruling on the unappealed issue.[3] The result might be different if the defendant, in the trial court, withholds a fact-based summary judgment motion on qualified immunity, raising and losing only a rule 12(b)(6) motion challenging whether the complaint adequately pleads a violation of clearly estab-

37. *See, e.g., Crawford–El v. Britton*, 523 U.S. 574, 118 S.Ct. 1584, 140 L.Ed.2d 759 (1998) (§ 1983 plaintiff generally need not meet heightened pleading requirements to plead an element of intent required by particular claim or to overcome the individual defendant officer's anticipated defense of qualified immunity, subject to trial court's authority in individual cases to order a Reply); *Leatherman v. Tarrant County Narcotics Intelligence and Coordination Unit*, 507 U.S. 163, 113 S.Ct. 1160, 122 L.Ed.2d 517 (1993) (the legal sufficiency of allegations about the "failure to train" variant on "custom" in a § 1983 action against a government entity should also be measured against the usual, liberal "notice pleading" standard of F.R.C.P. 8).

38. For example, the Court cited *Boeing Co. v. Shipman*, 411 F.2d 365 (5th Cir.1969), cited *supra* this section, as part of its discussion requiring federal trial courts, in deciding Rule 50 motions, to consider only evidence favoring the resisting party (usually the plaintiff) plus the uncontradicted and unimpeached evidence favoring the movant (usually the defendant).

§ 5.101

1. 472 U.S. 511, 105 S.Ct. 2806, 86 L.Ed.2d 411 (1985).

2. *Parton v. Ashcroft*, 16 F.3d 226 (8th Cir.1994).

3. *Kimberlin v. Quinlan*, 199 F.3d 496, 501–02 (D.C.Cir.1999).

lished law, and appealing on the latter issue only. On remand after an unsuccessful appeal, defendant may well then be able to move for summary judgment on the factual ground that no reasonable person in his position would have realized he was violating clearly established law. He has "split" his defense, it is true, but the Supreme Court appears to contemplate just such successive motions and interlocutory appeals n these legal and factual aspects of qualified immunity.[4] And he has not failed to appeal a ruling on an issue presented to and ruled upon by the trial court, thereby avoiding the defense of "law of the case."

For somewhat similar reasons, the Court, relying by analogy on the *Mitchell v. Forsyth* decision, has held that the denial of a defendant's motion to dismiss based on the quasi-jurisdictional Eleventh Amendment objection is also immediately appealable.[5] In that setting it is the supposed harm to the sovereignty of the states resulting from the extended exercise of federal jurisdiction that is deemed to warrant an immediate ruling.

§ 5.102 Settlement

The Supreme Court's approach to summary judgment heavily influences settlement dynamics, as discussed in § 5.100 above. When a settlement agreement is intended by the parties to dispose of all issues between them, the failure of a party to raise an issue during settlement negotiation can constitute waiver of the issue.[1] Parties who desire the option of invoking a federal court's subject matter jurisdiction to enforce an agreement settling a federal court employment discrimination or civil rights action should take pains to have the agreement embodied in a court order or judgment or prevail on the court to reserve jurisdiction pending implementation of the agreement.[2] Courts ordinarily employ normal state law contract principles in deciding whether to enforce agreements settling litigation under federal employment discrimination laws.[3] The same principle should apply to agreements settling litigation under the Reconstruction Civil Rights Acts.[4]

4. *Behrens v. Pelletier*, 516 U.S. 299, 116 S.Ct. 834, 133 L.Ed.2d 773 (1996), discussed in detail in §§ 2.22 and 2.23, *supra*.

5. *Puerto Rico Aqueduct and Sewer Auth. v. Metcalf & Eddy*, 506 U.S. 139, 113 S.Ct. 684, 121 L.Ed.2d 605 (1993).

§ 5.102

1. *See, e.g, Wray v. Clarke*, 151 F.3d 807 (8th Cir.1998) (failing to raise issue of attorney's fees constitutes waiver).

2. *See Kokkonen v. Guardian Life Ins. Co.*, 511 U.S. 375, 114 S.Ct. 1673, 128 L.Ed.2d 391 (1994) (rejecting the proposition that a federal court that failed to retain jurisdiction over a primary controversy has "ancillary" jurisdiction to hear a separate action to enforce a settlement agreement reached in the underlying action).

3. *See Hayes v. National Serv. Indus.*, 196 F.3d 1252 (11th Cir.1999) (applying Georgia law on scope of attorney's authority to enter into agreement on client's behalf). *Cf. Doi v. Halekulani Corp.*, 276 F.3d 1131 (9th Cir.2002) (state law limiting the circumstances under which an attorney can settle a claim on behalf of client was irrelevant where plaintiff herself orally agreed to terms of settlement agreement in open court).

4. *See* §§ 5.70 through 5.74, *supra*, on the state law "gap-filling" role commanded by 42 U.S.C.A. § 1988.

§ 5.103 Appeal

Courts reviewing trial errors[1] in employment discrimination cases have applied the version of the "harmless error" standard predominant in civil cases. Under that standard, the court need only conclude "with fair assurance" that the judgment was not "substantially swayed" by the error below.[2] In different circumstances, appellate courts will attempt to satisfy themselves of that in different ways. Erroneously admitted evidence may have represented a very small part of otherwise "one-sided" evidence supporting a verdict.[3] The court may deem the inadmissible matter of "minor importance."[4] Or the appellate court may consider that the district court sufficiently instructed the jury that they were not misled by erroneously admitted evidence.[5]

One Supreme Court decision in 2000, *Weisgram v. Marley Co.*,[6] expands the potential for circuit courts of appeals to enter judgment as a matter of law pursuant to Federal Rule of Civil Procedure 50 in favor of a verdict loser when the appellate court determines that the verdict is unsustainable because evidence supporting it was erroneously admitted.The Court held that a federal appellate court may itself enter judgment as a matter of law, without remanding for a new trial, either where it views the evidence presented at trial as originally insufficient to support a verdict, as in *Neely v. Martin K. Eby Construction Co.*,[7] or, as in *Weisgram*, where the jury's verdict becomes insufficient only after the appellate court rules that evidence supporting the verdict was improperly admitted.

But the Court's decision in *Reeves v. Sanderson Plumbing Prods., Inc.*[8] later in the same year significantly tightens the standard for the

§ 5.103

1. For an overview of limitations on the subject matter jurisdiction of the federal circuit courts of appeals, *see* § 5.8, above.

2. *See Taylor v. Virginia Union Univ.*, 193 F.3d 219 (4th Cir.1999) (en banc), *cert. denied*, 528 U.S. 1189, 120 S.Ct. 1243, 146 L.Ed.2d 101 (2000) (citing cases). *See also Monroe v. City of Phoenix, Ariz.*, 248 F.3d 851 (9th Cir.2001) (failure to give plaintiff requested instruction on the limited permissible use of deadly force under Fourth Amendment was harmless error in action by arrestee who was shot by police officer; jury, after being instructed on use of deadly force under state law, must have found that officer believed deadly physical force was immediately necessary to protect himself against arrestee's use or imminent use of unlawful deadly physical force when it found in officer's favor on arrestee's state-law tort claims, and therefore jury must have concluded that officer had probable cause to believe that arrestee posed threat of serious physical harm to officer or others, supporting verdict for officer on excessive force claim.) Cf. *Stafne v. Unicare Homes*, 266 F.3d 771 (8th Cir.2001) (an error not to give jury instruction about reasonable accommodation when even with accommodation, plaintiff's ADA claim would fail because she would not have been able to perform essential functions of job). *But see Rose v. N.Y.C. Bd. of Educ.*, 257 F.3d 156, 162–63 (2d Cir.2001) (even though jury found age not determinative, it was harmful, not harmless error to deny plaintiff the *Price–Waterhouse* burden-shifting instruction she requested).

3. *See Alexander v. Fulton County*, 207 F.3d 1303, 1329–1330 (11th Cir.2000).

4. *Lubbock Feed Lots, Inc. v. Iowa Beef Processors, Inc.*, 630 F.2d 250, 271 (5th Cir.1980).

5. *Alexander*, 207 F.3d at 1329.

6. 528 U.S. 440, 120 S.Ct. 1011, 145 L.Ed.2d 958 (2000).

7. 386 U.S. 317, 87 S.Ct. 1072, 18 L.Ed.2d 75 (1967).

8. 530 U.S. 133, 120 S.Ct. 2097, 147 L.Ed.2d 105 (2000).

grant of a Rule 50 motion by either a federal trial or appellate court. *Reeves*, discussed in detail in § 5.100, above, severely limits an appellate court's freedom to affirm a trial court's grant of a Rule 50 motion or to order judgment as a matter of law itself so long as the jury could reasonably have reached its verdict by reference solely to all the evidence favoring the verdict winner and only the unimpeached and uncontradicted evidence favoring the verdict loser.

§ 5.104 [Reserved]

R. SECTION 1983 ACTIONS AGAINST INDIVIDUAL AND ENTITY DEFENDANTS—BIFURCATION OF CLAIMS FOR TRIAL

§ 5.105 In General

Section 1983 actions are often brought against individual and government entity defendants together. The police conduct depicted in the videotaped arrest of Rodney King by Los Angeles law enforcement officers is characteristic of the factual situation that would prompt a plaintiff to file against both individual defendants and their government entity employer or principal. A review[1] of the elements of proof and defense in § 1983 claims against individual and entity defendants furnishes the necessary backdrop for understanding why entity defendants in these dual defendant actions frequently move for bifurcation.

Beginning in 1978 with *Monell v. Department of Soc. Servs.*[2] and continuing more recently with *City of Canton v. Harris*[3], the Supreme Court has sustained § 1983 claims against municipal and county governments, departing in that respect from *Monroe v. Pape.*[4] *Monell* overruled *Monroe* to the extent that it prevented suits against local government entities, but the price for allowing suits was the requirement that the constitutional injury suffered resulted from an implementation of government "policy."[5] Under *Monell* and its progeny, policy could be shown as a policy statement,[6] an ordinance or regulation,[7] or a discrete decision officially adopted by a final policy making official.[8] All these are affirmative act situations. *City of Canton v. Harris*[9] provided a significant, if limited, alternative method of demonstrating "policy" where the conduct complained of more closely resembled omissions than actions. Under *City*

§ 5.105

1. These prerequisite elements of proof and available defenses to claims under § 1983 are surveyed in detail in Chapter 2.

2. 436 U.S. 658, 98 S.Ct. 2018, 56 L.Ed.2d 611 (1978).

3. 489 U.S. 378, 109 S.Ct. 1197, 103 L.Ed.2d 412 (1989).

4. 365 U.S. 167, 81 S.Ct. 473, 5 L.Ed.2d 492 (1961).

5. *Monell*, 436 U.S. at 663, 690, 98 S.Ct. at 2022, 2035.

6. *Id.* at 690, 98 S.Ct. at 2035.

7. *Pembaur v. City of Cincinnati*, 475 U.S. 469, 480–82, 106 S.Ct. 1292, 1298–99, 89 L.Ed.2d 452 (1986).

8. *City of St. Louis v. Praprotnik*, 485 U.S. 112, 124–25, 108 S.Ct. 915, 924–25, 99 L.Ed.2d 107 (1988) (plurality opinion); *Jett v. Dallas Indep. Sch. Dist.*, 491 U.S. 701, 737, 109 S.Ct. 2702, 2724, 105 L.Ed.2d 598 (1989) (majority opinion).

9. 489 U.S. 378, 109 S.Ct. 1197, 103 L.Ed.2d 412 (1989).

of Canton, a municipality can be held liable for a failure to act if the circumstances evidence the municipality's "deliberate indifference" to the probable resulting harm.[10]

"Deliberate indifference," in turn, can be established by evidence that the unconstitutional harm likely to result from the failure to act was "so obvious" from prior similar experience of the defendant government that its policymakers could be said to have been "deliberately indifferent" to the need to act.[11] Proving that a failure to act or other omission was the cause of the particular plaintiff's harm may be more difficult than proving that the harm was caused by the affirmative act of a final policymaker. But the issue that is usually dispositive in the "act" setting—who is a final policymaker—is one of law, for the court, determinable before trial.[12] The "omissions" case *begins* with a question of law: did the entity's inaction violate a specific constitutional guarantee.[13] But the *City of Canton* "so obvious" issue, as well as whether a failure to act was the cause of plaintiff's harm, appear to be questions of fact for the jury.[14] Thus despite the substantive differences between the standards, it may be more difficult to sell the "affirmative act" variant of policy to a judge than to sell the "failure to act" variant to a jury. The plaintiff relying on an "omission" can exploit the possibility that a jury could be "fooled" into deciding that an individual agent's isolated, negligent "failure to act" actually reflects the more than negligent deliberate entity indifference the Court demanded in *Canton*.[15]

The references in *Canton* to the jury as factfinder on the question of pattern or custom of indifference seem advertent. In their brief on the merits, Harris's counsel had addressed the point:

> The application of *Monell* frequently requires, as it did here, that the finder of fact resolve conflicting evidence and draw inferences regarding policies, custom and causation. But nothing in *Monell* suggests that the factual issues made critical by that decision are to be resolved by judges rather than juries. There is "no reason, so long as the jury system is the law of the land, and the jury is made the tribunal to decide disputed questions of fact, why it should not decide such questions as these as well as all others." Jones v. East

10. *Id.* at 388–89, 109 S.Ct. at 1205.

11. *Id.* at 390, 109 S.Ct. at 1205. *Monell* foreshadows *Canton* by referring to actionable custom, which must be so "permanent and well settled," *id.* at 690, to amount to a "de facto official policy." 1 Sheldon H. Nahmod, *Civil Rights And Civil Liberties Litigation: The Law of Section 1983* § 6.07 (1991).

12. *Jett*, 491 U.S. at 737, 109 S.Ct. at 2724 ("[T]he identification of those officials whose decisions represent the official policy of the local governmental unit is itself a legal question to be resolved by the trial judge before the case is submitted to the jury."). *See also Pembaur*, 475 U.S. at 483, 106 S.Ct. at 1300; *Praprotnik*, 485 U.S. at 124, 108 S.Ct. at 924.

13. *City of Canton*, 489 U.S. at 387, 109 S.Ct. at 1204.

14. *Id.* at 391, 109 S.Ct. at 1206.

15. Justice O'Connor, dissenting, seems to be concerned that if such claims go to the jury, it "would only invite jury nullification of Monell." *Id.* at 399, 109 S.Ct. at 1210.

Tennessee, V. & G.R. Co., 128 U.S. 443, 446, 9 S.Ct. 118, 118, 32 L.Ed. 478 (1888).[16]

Justice Scalia (who dissented in *City of Canton*) apparently raised the issue of allowing a jury to determine causation during oral argument.[17] Justice O'Connor, dissenting, asserted that allowing a failure to act claim to go to the jury "would only invite jury nullification of *Monell*."[18] Justice White for the majority almost brushes off the dissent's concern:

> Predicting how a hypothetically well-trained officer would have acted under the circumstances may not be an easy task for the factfinder, particularly since matters of judgment may be involved, and since officers who are well trained are not free from error and perhaps might react very much like the untrained officer in similar circumstances. But judge and jury, doing their respective jobs, will be adequate to the task.[19]

The opinions of lower courts since *City of Canton* have accordingly concluded[20] or assumed[21] that the key "failure to act" issues are indeed for the jury.

A caveat is in order here. The assumed advantage of jury trial when the complaint is cast as a "failure to act" claim under *City of Canton* may be undermined by the more lenient standards the Court has approved for granting summary judgment motions, discussed above.[22] *Celotex Corp. v. Catrett*[23] relieves the defendant whose motion for summary judgment is directed against an element of plaintiff's claim from supporting its motion with evidentiary materials.[24] *Anderson v. Liberty Lobby*[25] picks up where *Celotex* leaves off, holding that the ultimate summary judgment inquiry is "whether reasonable jurors could find by a preponderance of the evidence [or whatever other burden of persuasion plaintiff would bear at trial] that the plaintiff is entitled to a verdict."[26] *Celotex*, in other words, significantly eases the moving defendant's initial summary judgment burden. *Anderson* then makes it more difficult for the nonmoving party to resist summary judgment unless she offers a sufficient quantum of evidentiary material to persuade the court that a reasonable juror could find plaintiff's way on the controverted issues—in

16. Resp't's Br. at 19, No. 86–1088.

17. *See* Tr. of Oral Argument, *City of Canton v. Harris*, No. 86–1088, 50.

18. 489 U.S. at 399, 109 S.Ct. at 1210.

19. *Id.* at 391.

20. *Reynolds v. Borough of Avalon*, 799 F.Supp. 442, 447 (D.N.J.1992).

21. *Rellergert v. Cape Girardeau County, Mo.*, 924 F.2d 794, 797–98 (8th Cir. 1991); *Mateyko v. Felix*, 924 F.2d 824, 826 (9th Cir.1990), *cert. denied*, 502 U.S. 814, 112 S.Ct. 65, 116 L.Ed.2d 40 (1991); *Davis v. Mason County*, 927 F.2d 1473, 1485 (9th Cir.1991), *cert. denied*, 502 U.S. 899, 112 S.Ct. 275, 116 L.Ed.2d 227 (1991); *Buffington v. Baltimore County*, 913 F.2d 113, 123 (4th Cir.1990), *cert. denied*, 499 U.S. 906, 111 S.Ct. 1106, 113 L.Ed.2d 216 (1991). *Cf. Farmer v. Brennan*, 511 U.S. 825, 114 S.Ct. 1970, 128 L.Ed.2d 811 (1994) ("juries should be instructed" on the Eighth Amendment's "subjective" indifference test, which the Court contrasted with the "objective" indifference required for entity liability under § 1983).

22. *See* § 5.100, *supra*.

23. 477 U.S. 317, 106 S.Ct. 2548, 91 L.Ed.2d 265 (1986).

24. *Id.* at 323–24, 106 S.Ct. at 2553.

25. 477 U.S. 242, 106 S.Ct. 2505, 91 L.Ed.2d 202 (1986).

26. *Id.* at 252, 106 S.Ct. at 2512.

the omissions setting, deliberate indifference and causation—by the required preponderance of the evidence.[27] Persuasive defendant's evidence may convince a judge that reasonable jurors would not be able to find deliberate indifference or causation by a preponderance of the evidence. The plaintiff would then never get to the jury that *Canton* makes available in theory.

One last point concerning entity liability needs to be reconsidered. The Court held in *Owen v. City of Independence*[28] that municipalities do not enjoy an immunity defense from § 1983 damages liability akin to that with which the Court has endowed their individual agents. Still, as the foregoing review reflects, proving prima facie that a local government entity is responsible for its agent's deprivation of federal constitutional or statutory rights is far from an easy task. Where the entity is sought to be held liable on the basis of its agent's unconstitutional conduct,[29] the plaintiff must do more than prove that the agent's action or decision violated federal law. In addition, establishing the entity's liability requires proof that the agent's conduct was pursuant to an entity policy or a manifestation of a long-standing entity custom that caused the plaintiff's harm. The entity must have conferred on the agent final policymaking authority to make the challenged decision or take the challenged action; ratified that decision after the fact; or acted with "deliberate indifference" in failing to train an agent or screen an applicant in a way that would have avoided the injury-producing conduct.[30]

§ 5.106 Why Bifurcation?

Proving the case against the entity has been further complicated by *City of Los Angeles v. Heller*,[1] which approved the use of bifurcated trials where a local government and its individual agents are sued together.[2] Entity defendants in such actions have often invoked the strategy of seeking bifurcated trial, urging the court to try the individual claims first. Under Federal Rule of Civil Procedure 42, bifurcation or separate trial of claims is committed to the discretion of the trial judge. Bifurcation is appropriate to minimize prejudice to the parties; avoid jury

27. *Id.* at 256, 106 S.Ct. at 2514.

28. 445 U.S. 622, 638, 100 S.Ct. 1398, 1409, 63 L.Ed.2d 673 (1980).

29. The claim configuration discussed in this section does not exhaust the universe of claims that might be brought against a government entity in an action where it is joined as a defendant with its agent. So long as the plaintiff satisfies Federal Rule of Civil Procedure 20's requirements for joining defendants—the claims against each arise out of the same transaction or occurrence and involve at least one common question of law or fact—the claims against the two defendants may be predicated on distinct federal law violations.

30. See Chapter 2 for a detailed discussion of the several ways a plaintiff may prove entity "policy."

§ 5.106

1. 475 U.S. 796, 106 S.Ct. 1571, 89 L.Ed.2d 806 (1986).

2. As noted *infra* § 5.107, the Court does not mention why bifurcation was accomplished, just that it was. Federal Rule 42 allows for bifurcation of claims when bifurcating would serve to "further[ ] convenience ... avoid prejudice ... [and] be conductive to expedition and economy." Fed.R.Civ.P. 42(b). Its application to bifurcation under *Heller* is discussed in § 5.108 that follows.

confusion; and promote judicial efficiency and economy. In a typical excessive force case, for example, evidence of other incidents involving the use of excessive force by the entity's agents will often be presented to establish the required policy, custom, or failure to train. That evidence is often inflammatory and may prejudice the jury as to the culpability of the particular officer involved in the particular incident.[3] More generally, trying the claim against the individual officer first may promote judicial efficiency by obviating the need to consider the claim against the entity.[4]

The prima facie liability of the individual defendant for a federal constitutional or statutory violation is in these cases a necessary prerequisite to the prima facie liability of the entity.[5] The Supreme Court accordingly held in *Heller* that if the entity and one or more of its agents are sued together[6] on a claim that predicates entity liability entirely on proof of the liability of a single[7] agent/co-defendant, and if that individual defendant is absolved on the ground that the plaintiff failed to establish the violation of a federal right, there is no basis for the liability of the entity. If, however, there is a finding that an individual defendant violated the plaintiff's federal right, the case against the entity defendant should proceed. This is true even where the plaintiff recovers only nominal damages against the individual (and thus is limited to nominal damages against the entity), because any subsequent verdict against the entity would hold the entity responsible for its own actions and may encourage the entity "to reform the patterns and practices that led to constitutional violations, as well as alert the municipality and its citizenry to the issue."[8]

§ 5.107 The *Heller* Decision

Heller was a motorist, stopped by two Los Angeles police officers.[1] The officers suspected that Heller was intoxicated and subjected him to

3. *See, e.g., Amato v. City of Saratoga Springs, N.Y.*, 170 F.3d 311, 316 (2d Cir. 1999) (upholding trial court's bifurcation on judicial economy and evidentiary grounds).

4. *See Id.*

5. It is not *sufficient* for entity liability, however, which also requires that the conduct violating federal law be fairly attributable to the entity as a matter of its official policy or custom. *See* §§ 2.30–2.32, *supra.*

6. A plaintiff need not "in principle" (although for tactical reasons ordinarily will) name an individual officer as defendant together with the government entity, even when she seeks to hold the government entity liable solely by virtue of that officer's conduct. *Wilson v. Mendon*, 294 F.3d 1 (1st Cir.2002) (but finding on the facts of the case that plaintiff could not pursue § 1983 claim against municipality based on police officer's alleged use of excessive force where officer was not named as defendant, as the failure to name the officer unfairly precluded municipality from introducing evidence that arrestee had obtained acquittal on criminal charge resulting from arrest through officer's perjured testimony).

7. But where the combined conduct of several employees, acting pursuant to a government policy or custom, violates plaintiff's rights, the local government body may be liable even where the acts or omissions of individual employee-defendants do not violate those rights. *Barrett v. Orange County Human Rights Comm'n*, 194 F.3d 341, 350 (2d Cir.1999); *Anderson v. City of Atlanta*, 778 F.2d 678, 686 (11th Cir.1985); *Garcia v. Salt Lake County*, 768 F.2d 303, 310 (10th Cir.1985).

8. *Amato v. City of Saratoga Springs, N.Y.*, 170 F.3d 311, 318 (2d Cir.1999).

§ 5.107

1. *Heller v. Bushey*, 759 F.2d 1371, 1372–73 (9th Cir.1985), *rev'd per curiam sub nom. City of L.A. v. Heller*, 475 U.S. 796, 106 S.Ct. 1571, 89 L.Ed.2d 806 (1986).

various field sobriety tests. Apparently, the policemen were not satisfied with the results, so they arrested Heller to take him to the station house for a breath analysis test.[2] Heller was not pleased with the arrest and began to struggle with the officers.[3] One of the officers attempted administering a "chokehold" on Heller, who, as a result, fell through a plate glass window.[4]

Heller sued the City of Los Angeles, the Los Angeles Police Commission, and individual police officers under § 1983.[5] He alleged that the officers arrested him without probable cause and subjected him to excessive force.[6] Heller also alleged that the city and the police department adopted a policy "condoning excessive force in making arrests" and that he was injured as a direct result of the policemen's application of the policy.[7]

At trial, the suit was bifurcated into two phases: the first against the individual officers and the second against the municipality.[8] The record did not reflect the rationale for the decision, but does state that the Plaintiff's counsel opposed bifurcation.[9]

The trial proceeded against one of the police officers[10] and the case went to the jury.[11] The jury was instructed that Heller could establish a constitutional claim if he "were arrested without reasonable cause, or if he were arrested with 'unreasonable force' that exceeded the force necessary under the circumstances to effect arrest."[12] However, the jury received no instruction on qualified immunity or any other affirmative defenses.[13] The jury found for the Defendant officer and against Heller.[14] The District Court dismissed the remaining action against the municipality and the remaining defendants, determining that since the individual officer was exonerated by the jury, there was no basis for entity liability.[15] The Ninth Circuit reversed with respect to the government defendants, apparently agreeing with Heller's counsel that a " 'jury could have believed that Bushey [the police officer] . . . was entitled in

2. *Id.*

3. *Id.*

4. *Id.*

5. *City of Los Angeles v. Heller*, 475 U.S. at 797, 106 S.Ct. at 1572.

6. *Id.*

7. *Id.* at 801, 106 S.Ct. at 1574 (Stevens, J. dissenting).

8. *Id.*

9. *Id.* at 801 n.3, 106 S.Ct. at 1574 n.3 (Stevens, J., dissenting) (The minutes of a chambers conference indicate that the only mention in the record made of bifurcation was as follows: . . . [B]ifurcation of case. Plaintiff's counsel opposes bifurcation. Defendant does not oppose bifurcation.). Apparently, the judge's entry of a sua sponte bifurcation order surprised Heller's counsel, who when interviewed by one commentator stated that it "was the first time I had ever encountered such a motion." Douglas L. Colbert, *Bifurcation of Civil Rights Defendants: Undermining Monell in Police Brutality Cases*, 44 Hastings L.J. 499, 538 n.220 (1993).

10. The other police officer was granted summary judgment by the District Court. 475 U.S. at 797, 106 S.Ct. at 1572.

11. *Id.* at 797, 106 S.Ct. at 1572.

12. *Id.*

13. *Id.* at 797–98, 106 S.Ct. at 1572.

14. *Id.*

15. *Id.* at 798, 106 S.Ct. at 1572.

substance to a defense of good faith. Such a belief would not negate the existence of a constitutional injury.' "[16]

The United States Supreme Court reversed per curiam. Since the jury was not charged on any affirmative defense, the Ninth Circuit could not assume that the jury "consider[ed] and base[d] their decisions on legal questions with respect to which they [were] ... not charged."[17] The Court considered the finding against Heller to be conclusive with respect to the city and the Police Commission.[18] The Court's theory is summed up this way: "[I]f the [individual defendant, Bushey] inflicted no constitutional injury on respondent, it is inconceivable that [the government entities] could be liable to respondent."[19]

Justice Stevens in dissent, joined by Justice Marshall, sounded a warning that the majority's reading of the case is "unprecedented, ill-considered, and far-reaching" and if it is correct will provide defendants "with a tactical weapon of great value."[20] If correct, the majority will "persuad[e] trial judges to bifurcate trials in which both the principal and its agents are named as defendants, and [by] requir[ing] the jury to bring in its verdict on the individual claim first, they [municipal defendants] may obtain the benefit of whatever intangible factors have prompted juries to bring in a multitude of inconsistent verdicts in past years; defendants will no longer have to abide the mechanisms that courts have used to mitigate and resolve apparent inconsistencies.[21] Perhaps that is an appropriate response to the current widespread concern about the potential liabilities of our municipalities, but I doubt it."[22]

The *Heller* majority took pains to observe that the City and its police Commission were "sued only because they were thought responsible for Bushey's actions."[23] That is, the entities' alleged liability was wholly derivative of the individual officers, so exoneration of the latter for want of a constitutional violation naturally exonerated the entities as well. Put otherwise, no independent predicate violations actionable under § 1983 were asserted against the entities.[24] In similar circumstances, federal appellate courts since *Heller* have followed its reasoning by dismissing "failure to train" omission claims asserted against entities pursuant to *City of Canton v. Harris*[25] whenever a common predicate claim against their individual officers or agents has failed.[26] It is clear, though, that if a federal constitutional or statutory claim asserted against the entity is

16. *Id.* at 798, 106 S.Ct. at 1572 (quoting 759 F.2d at 1373–74).

17. *Id.* at 798, 106 S.Ct. at 1572.

18. *Id.* at 799, 106 S.Ct. at 1583.

19. *Id.*

20. *Id.* at 807, 106 S.Ct. at 1577.

21. *Id.* (footnote omitted).

22. *Id.*

23. *Id.* at 799, 106 S.Ct. at 1573.

24. *Fagan v. City of Vineland*, 22 F.3d 1283, 1292 (3d Cir.1994), *amended*, 22 F.3d 1296 (3d Cir.1994) (discussing *Heller*). *Fagan* is discussed and criticized in another respect in the text immediately following.

25. 489 U.S. 378, 109 S.Ct. 1197, 103 L.Ed.2d 412 (1989).

26. *See Temkin v. Frederick County Comm'rs*, 945 F.2d 716, 724 (4th Cir.1991), *cert. denied*, 502 U.S. 1095, 112 S.Ct. 1172, 117 L.Ed.2d 417 (1992); *Roach v. City of Fredericktown, Mo.*, 882 F.2d 294, 297–98 (8th Cir.1989).

clearly distinct from another asserted against its agents, the demise of the latter should not doom the former. This would be the case, for example, where a jury decides that a police "officer's on-the-scene decision to use canine force was reasonable under the circumstances," but the plaintiff asserts liability of the municipality for equipping the officer with a dog trained to bite and seize all concealed suspects, including those attempting to surrender, without training its dogs to perform more selectively.[27]

But a panel opinion of the Third Circuit, *Fagan v. City of Vineland*,[28] held it permissible to predicate the entity's liability *solely* on its failure to train an officer to respond to events from which the officer defendant was absolved of liability. The court viewed this failure-to-train claim as distinct from the underlying Eighth Amendment substantive due process claim against the entity's officers for an allegedly reckless high-speed police pursuit. In that setting, the court wrote, "an underlying constitutional tort can still exist even if [because the police behavior did not 'shock the conscience'] no individual police officer violated the Constitution."[29] The court purported to distinguish *Heller* by observing first that the excessive force claim there was under the Fourth Amendment, unlike the Eighth Amendment substantive due process claim at hand, and that the Supreme Court had recently highlighted the difference between those claims.[30] Second, the court stressed that in *Heller*, the City of Los Angeles was sought to be held liable "only because they were thought legally responsible" for the individual officer's conduct.[31] It was somehow different, according to the panel opinion, that the City of Vineland was sought to be held responsible for a failure to train under the strict guidelines for showing entity "policy" approved in *City of Canton*. The court concluded that if it could be shown that the individual officer's lack of constitutionally adequate training caused the plaintiff's injury, and if that lack of training was the result of the city's deliberate indifference, "the City is directly liable under section 1983 for causing a violation of the plaintiff's Fourteenth Amendment rights."[32]

With respect, it is submitted that the Third Circuit panel's purported distinctions will not withstand scrutiny and that the court's holding ignores controlling Supreme Court precedent. In the case relied on by the panel, the Supreme Court insisted that certain claims akin to malicious prosecution are actionable only under the Fourth Amendment and not under the Eighth Amendment's substantive due process clause;[33] it in no way suggested that a failed Eighth Amendment claim against an entity's agent somehow leaves standing an independent claim against

27. *Chew v. Gates*, 27 F.3d 1432, 1445–1446 (9th Cir.1994), *cert. denied*, 513 U.S. 1148, 115 S.Ct. 1097, 130 L.Ed.2d 1065 (1995).

28. 22 F.3d 1283 (3d Cir.1994), *amended*, 22 F.3d 1296 (3d Cir.1994).

29. *Id.* at 1292.

30. *Id.*, citing *Albright v. Oliver*, 510 U.S. 266, 114 S.Ct. 807, 127 L.Ed.2d 114 (1994).

31. *Id.*, quoting *Heller*, 475 U.S. at 1073.

32. *Id.*

33. *Albright v. Oliver*, 510 U.S. 266, 114 S.Ct. 807, 127 L.Ed.2d 114 (1994).

the entity directly under the Fourteenth Amendment or § 1983. Moreover, it was as true in *Fagan* as it was in *Heller* that the plaintiff sought to fasten liability on the city because, and only because, of the conduct of its officer. The real difference between the cases is simply that in *Heller* the police acted, in *Fagan* they failed to act. That distinction is the basis of the different proof requirements the Supreme Court has mandated for showing entity accountability under § 1983: a formal policy pronouncement or the act of a final policymaker, in an action case; "deliberate indifference" as defined by *City of Canton* in an omissions case. But, as the Supreme Court has twice underlined,[34] showing entity accountability in one of these ways is no substitute for proving that the entity's agent committed an independent federal law violation.[35] Yet the *Fagan* opinion identifies no constitutional provision applicable through the Fourteenth Amendment that the City might have violated; surely it did not have in mind the Eighth Amendment, which it had already found was not abridged. A Seventh Circuit decision applying *Heller* to dismiss a claim against a city after a jury exonerated its police officer on a claim of excessive force also rejects the logic of *Fagan*.[36]

Where the combined conduct of several employees, acting pursuant to a government policy or custom, violates plaintiff's rights, the situation is quite different. Then the local government body may be liable for a violation resulting from entity "policy" or "custom" even where the acts or omissions of individual employee-defendants do not violate those rights.[37]

§ 5.108 Post–*Heller* Developments on Bifurcation

As we have seen, prima facie evidence of "policy" is necessary before an entity bears responsibility under § 1983, a requirement absent in cases against individuals. On the other hand, only the individual defendant may invoke the qualified and absolute immunity defenses. Simultaneous trial of common claims against all these defendants therefore poses more than the usual risk of jury confusion. Trial courts have accordingly frequently granted entity defendants' motions to bifurcate, proceeding to the claim against the individual defendant first.[1]

34. *Farmer v. Brennan*, 511 U.S. 825, 114 S.Ct. 1970, 128 L.Ed.2d 811(1994); *Collins v. City of Harker Heights*, 503 U.S. 115, 118, 112 S.Ct. 1061, 1065, 117 L.Ed.2d 261 (1992).

35. The same error can be seen even by examining *City of Canton* on its own terms. Justice White's opinion insisted that liability depends on proof that the plaintiff's injury was caused, not just by the entity's agents, but by the entity's own unconstitutional failure to train those agents to safeguard an emotionally disturbed detainee-a question of constitutional law the Court in *Canton* explicitly reserved. See discussion of *Canton* in Chapter 2.

36. *Thompson v. Boggs*, 33 F.3d 847, 859 n. 11 (7th Cir.1994), *cert. denied*, 514 U.S. 1063, 115 S.Ct. 1692, 131 L.Ed.2d 556 (1995).

37. *Barrett v. Orange County Human Rights Comm'n*, 194 F.3d 341, 350 (2d Cir. 1999); *Anderson v. City of Atlanta*, 778 F.2d 678, 686 (11th Cir.1985); *Garcia v. Salt Lake County*, 768 F.2d 303, 310 (10th Cir. 1985).

§ 5.108

1. *See, e.g., Ismail v. Cohen*, 706 F.Supp. 243 (S.D.N.Y.1989), *aff'd*, 899 F.2d 183 (2d Cir.1990); *Marryshow v. Town of Bladensburg*, 139 F.R.D. 318 (D.Md.1991).

Under *Heller*, the claim against the entity disappears if the claim against the individual defendant on which entity liability is predicated fails prima facie for lack of a currently cognizable federal claim. But failure of the claim against the individual should not always foreclose the claim against the entity when the individual defendant prevails on the affirmative defense of qualified immunity.[2] For the sustaining of that defense does not necessarily mean there is no current constitutional violation; often it merely recognizes that the defendant violated a constitutional right not clearly established at the time she acted, or that she could not reasonably have appreciated that her conduct would violate clearly established law.[3] Similarly, a legislator's, prosecutor's or judge's assertion of an absolute immunity defense potentially relieves them of liability regardless of the legal sufficiency of the predicate federal law claim (a cognizable constitutional or statutory violation) and accordingly should not necessarily bar a derivative claim against the entity for the same conduct.[4]

But the Court's decision in *Siegert v. Gilley*[5] and its progeny may make trial judges in these combined individual-entity actions even more receptive to entity defendants' motions to stay discovery against them and, if necessary, bifurcate the trial. *Siegert* in effect requires that henceforth more qualified immunity motions will be granted on the ground that the complaint fails to state a currently sufficient claim—the predicate for *Heller* extinction of the claim against the entity. *Siegert* and its progeny direct trial judges, in ruling on an individual defendant's motion to dismiss based on qualified immunity, to decide whether the plaintiff has stated any currently cognizable claim of a federal law violation *before* deciding, if the answer is affirmative, whether that claim was also "clearly established" at the time of the challenged conduct.[6]

2. In the alternative, a finding of no entity liability does not preclude a finding of individual liability. *See, e.g., Springdale Educ. Ass'n v. Springdale Sch. Dist.*, 133 F.3d 649, 653 (8th Cir.1998) (reversing a trial court's holding that because the individual defendant was not the final policymaker for the entity, he was not subject to individual § 1983 liability).

3. *Wachtler v. County of Herkimer*, 35 F.3d 77 (2d Cir.1994) (county potentially liable for an unconstitutional policy of strip searching without reasonable suspicion that arrestee had concealed weapon or contraband, even after defendant individual officers accorded qualified immunity); *Chew v. Gates*, 27 F.3d 1432, 1439 (9th Cir.1994), *cert. denied*, 513 U.S. 1148, 115 S.Ct. 1097, 130 L.Ed.2d 1065 (1995); *Garner v. Memphis Police Dep't*, 8 F.3d 358, 364–65 (6th Cir.1993), *cert. denied*, 510 U.S. 1177, 114 S.Ct. 1219, 127 L.Ed.2d 565 (1994); *Medina v. City and County of Denver*, 960 F.2d 1493, 1499–1500 (10th Cir.1992); *Barber v. City of Salem, Ohio*, 953 F.2d 232, 237–38 (6th Cir.1992).

4. Cf. *Spallone v. United States*, 493 U.S. 265, 110 S.Ct. 625, 107 L.Ed.2d 644 (1990) (claim against individual legislators who asserted absolute immunity proceeded after City found liable). *But cf. Brown v. Crawford County*, 960 F.2d 1002, 1012 n. 17 (11th Cir.1992) (ordering dismissal of claims against the county after its legislators received absolute immunity).

5. 500 U.S. 226, 111 S.Ct. 1789, 114 L.Ed.2d 277 (1991). *Siegert* is discussed in detail in §§ 2.22 and 2.23, *supra*.

6. *See also County of Sacramento v. Lewis*, 523 U.S. 833, 840–42 n. 5, 118 S.Ct. 1708, 1713–14 n. 5, 140 L.Ed.2d 1043 (1998); *Conn v. Gabbert*, 526 U.S. 286, 289, 119 S.Ct. 1292, 1295, 143 L.Ed.2d 399 (1999); *Wilson v. Layne*, 526 U.S. 603, 609, 119 S.Ct. 1692, 1697, 143 L.Ed.2d 818 (1999) (suggesting, and finally mandating, the *Siegert* sequencing—namely a court must first determine whether plaintiff has alleged the deprivation of an actual constitutional right).

Trial judges obedient to the issue sequencing prescribed by *Siegert* and progeny will thus more often determine qualified immunity motions—which are typically made at the outset of the action—by ruling that the federal law claim against the individual defendant is legally insufficient as of the day of decision. Such a ruling, in turn, would abort the action against the entity, under *Heller*. And the prospect of a greater number of qualified immunity defenses succeeding on that ground, either on motion or at trial, thereby obviating the need for discovery or trial against the entity, should enhance trial judges' willingness to defer discovery against the entity and, if trial is necessary, grant bifurcation.

Countervailing this argument is the possibility that trial judges will be chastened by the Court's reminder in *Leatherman v. Tarrant County Narcotics Intelligence and Coordination Unit*, and in *Crawford–El v. Britton*, both discussed earlier in this chapter, that motions to dismiss for failure to state a claim made by entity and individual defendants, respectively, should rarely be granted. Then, even though *Siegert* and progeny require trial judges to turn first to the question of the complaint's legal sufficiency in deciding the "clearly established law" prong of a qualified immunity defense, relatively few such motions will be granted on the ground that they currently fail to state a cognizable claim. We will now consider the combined impact on *Heller*-driven bifurcation of *Leatherman*'s relaxation of pleading requirements, *Siegert*'s direction to decide legal sufficiency questions early, and *Liberty Lobby*'s facilitation of summary judgments.

Heller does not explain why bifurcation is desirable. It may be that the use of bifurcation can lead to an earlier and less costly disposition of § 1983 claims brought against a municipality and individual defendants, thus advancing the convenience and economy goals of Rule 42(b).[7] Another reason advanced is that it may serve to prevent a "prolonged examination of government policy and custom before trial."[8] Where the individual defendant is exonerated on a finding that she committed no constitutional violation, discovery bifurcation gives the municipal defendant, through a procedural decision, a form of immunity from suit—an immunity it lacks in substance.[9] On the other hand, if the individual defendant is found liable or exonerated for reasons other than the absence of a constitutional violation, e.g., qualified immunity, bifurcation may result in a greater total expenditure of litigant and judicial resources.

Especially problematic is that *Heller* fails to provide guidance to lower courts about how and when a case should be bifurcated under Rule 42. In fact, the only mention of bifurcation was to note that it was done by the district court.[10] So it has been left to the lower courts to determine what circumstances meet the requirements of Rule 42.

7. *Ricciuti v. New York City Transit Auth.*, 796 F.Supp. 84, 85 (S.D.N.Y.1992).

8. *Id.* at 86.

9. *Owen v. City of Independence*, 445 U.S. 622, 100 S.Ct. 1398, 63 L.Ed.2d 673 (1980).

10. *Id.* at 797, 801.

In *Ismail v. Cohen*,[11] the United States District Court for the Southern District of New York addressed the propriety of bifurcation in a § 1983 claim. Under Rule 42, a court may order bifurcation in order to: "1) avoid prejudice; 2) provide for convenience; or 3) expedite the proceedings and be economical."[12] To order a separate trial, only one of the three conditions needs to be met.[13]

Avoiding prejudice to the parties is usually concerned with the effect of trying several issues before a jury.[14] For example, prejudice could occur when the jury is confronted with evidence admissible for one purpose only, and having the jury exposed to that evidence may prejudice or confuse the jury on related issues.[15] Specifically in the § 1983 context, evidence on the *Monell* claim against the municipality may "contaminate" the minds of the members of the jury in determining the individual defendant's liability.[16]

The promotion of judicial efficiency and economy is served when the separate trial "disposes of one charge or establishes a necessary element of a second charge."[17] As *Heller* instructs us, if the individual defendant is absolved of liability on the ground that no constitutional violation by the individual defendant is established, then no claim can lie against the municipal defendant.[18] Bifurcation manages to dispose of the charge against the municipal defendant, *if* no constitutional injury by the individual defendant can be established. But if the constitutional injury *can* be established, then there must be a full-scale separate trial against the municipal defendant, even if the individual defendant was absolved of liability by way of qualified immunity.

Whether bifurcation is convenient also turns on whether the proof relevant to the bifurcated issues overlaps.[19] The *Monell* claim against the municipality includes evidence essential to establish the individual defendant's liability but also requires the production of evidence that would be unnecessary to the resolution of the individual claim.[20] Resolving the *Monell* claim may require, for example, evidence of similar instances preceding the incident at issue[21] or evidence about the status of

11. 706 F.Supp. 243 (S.D.N.Y.1989), *aff'd*, 899 F.2d 183 (2d Cir.1990).

12. *Id.* at 251 (citation omitted).

13. *Id.*

14. *Id.*

15. *Id.*

16. *Id.* ("For example, evidence concerning a de facto policy encouraging discrimination of the City, or that the City failed to train adequately its officers, could prejudice the jury in its determination of the culpability of defendant Cohen based on the specific incident involving plaintiff. Likewise, if the jury determines that Officer Cohen is culpable this might unfairly influence its determination of whether the City had a de facto policy leading to discriminatory treatment.")

17. *Id.*

18. *Heller*, 475 U.S. at 799.

19. *Id.* (citation omitted).

20. *Id.* (citation omitted).

21. *Id. See City of Canton v. Harris*, 489 U.S. 378, 109 S.Ct. 1197, 103 L.Ed.2d 412 (1989). See *Griffin v. City of Opa–Locka*, 261 F.3d 1295, 1301 (11th Cir.2001), *cert. denied* 535 U.S. 1033, 122 S.Ct. 1789, 152 L.Ed.2d 648 (2002) (refusal to bifurcate not abuse of discretion even though plaintiff included evidence of individual defendant's prior bad acts in order to show a custom or policy that would establish liability of co-defendant city, where individual defendant failed to object to the prior bad acts evidence at trial or ask for a limiting instruction).

an official as a "final policymaker."[22] Admission of this additional evidence could lead to jury confusion or, more likely, prejudice.

Most judges grant or deny bifurcation with little, if any comment.[23] It is clear, however, that even though it is not difficult to satisfy the requirements of Rule 42(b), bifurcation is not automatic. But in some districts it is becoming commonplace. In the Central District of California, judges apparently bifurcate approximately ninety-five percent of all § 1983 trials.[24] In both the Southern and Eastern Districts of New York, judges are apparently granting bifurcation motions almost as "a matter of routine practice and over the objection of plaintiff's counsel"[25]—notwithstanding the case-specific inquiry demanded by Rule 42(b). In the District of Massachusetts, one attorney estimated that "of the twelve sitting district court judges, only one or possibly two have refused to grant bifurcation motions."[26] In contrast, federal judges[27] in Philadelphia rarely grant bifurcation motions.[28] The situation in the Eastern District of Michigan is similar.[29]

Where the motion is granted, there appear to be two primary models,[30] trial and discovery bifurcation.[31] Trial bifurcation, used in the federal courts in Los Angeles and Boston,[32] does not preclude discovery against the entity pending the settlement or trial disposition of the claim

22. *See City of St. Louis v. Praprotnik*, 485 U.S. 112, 108 S.Ct. 915, 99 L.Ed.2d 107 (1988).

23. For example, in *Vaughn v. Salinas*, 1990 WL 11055 (D.Kan.1990), an unpublished, one page opinion, the United States District Court for the District of Kansas merely stated the text of Rule 42(b) and then, without any analysis, that "the court finds that considerations of convenience, expedition and economy favor a single trial in this matter ... [t]he court also finds that any potential prejudice to defendants can be avoided through the use of limiting instructions." *Id.* at *1. Likewise, the Southern District of New York, in another unreported, one page opinion, did grant bifurcation. *Deagle v. City of N.Y.*, 1991 WL 267765 (S.D.N.Y.1991). *Deagle* just quoted the text of Rule 42(b) and without real analysis decide that "the interests of judicial economy will be served by separate trials." *Id.* at *1. *See Alexander v. Fulton County*, 207 F.3d 1303, 1323, 1324–25 (11th Cir.2000) (reviewing trial court's determination under Rule 42(b) as to whether "the efficiency of a consolidated trial is outweighed by its potential prejudice to the litigants" by abuse of discretion standard, and in effect holding that the common questions of fact or law required for claim joinder under F.R.C.P. 20 also suffices to permit district court to deny separate trials under Rule 42(b)).

24. Colbert, 44 Hastings L.J. at 554 (information obtained by telephone interviews with attorneys in the Los Angeles area.).

25. *Id.* at 556.

26. *Id.* at 558. (Again, this information, in the absence of reported cases, comes from attorneys in the locality.).

27. Of course, while litigants may have a right to have their § 1983 claim heard by an Article III United States District Judge, they may, upon special designated by the district court, expressly consent to trial before a United State Magistrate Judge as contemplated by a provision of the Federal Magistrate Act of 1979, 28 U.S.C.A. § 636(c); alternatively, their litigation conduct—e.g., making a general appearance before the magistrate judge despite having been told of their right to be tried by a district judge—may give that consent. *Roell v. Withrow*, 538 U.S. 580, 123 S.Ct. 1696, 155 L.Ed.2d 775 (2003).

28. *Id.* at 559. (David Rudovsky, the Philadelphia attorney interviewed by Professor Colbert, did note that defendants rarely move for bifurcation.).

29. *Id.* at 560. (based on telephone interviews).

30. *Marryshow v. Town of Bladensburg*, 139 F.R.D. 318, 319 (D.Md.1991).

31. Colbert, 44 Hastings L.J. at 553–54.

32. *Id.*

against the individual defendant. This approach denies the government defendant one of the signal benefits of bifurcation, the chance to delay and perhaps avoid altogether time-consuming and expensive discovery.[33]

Discovery bifurcation, used in federal courts in New York,[34] halts discovery on plaintiff's claim against the entity until after the case against the individual defendant is decided or settled.[35] The only discovery allowed is that which relates to the individual defendant's liability.[36] But in some circumstances, the individual defendant should be permitted to conduct discovery that as a practical matter also implicates the potential liability of the entity. This arises from one of the potential conflicts, in the kind of case under consideration, between the interests of the individual defendant and those of the entity.

The individual defendant may not wish to contest that his conduct constitutes a constitutional violation, relying instead on the remaining escape valves of qualified immunity: the conduct did not violate a right clearly established at the time, or, even if it did, a reasonable person in defendant's position would not have realized that his conduct would violate that right. Then the discovery the individual defendant would desire if the defense is denied would not conflict with the interests of the entity; the entity will eventually be permitted to conduct discovery designed to defeat a showing of constitutional violation. By contrast, suppose, as in a false arrest, wrongful imprisonment or excessive force case, the plaintiff must demonstrate that the defendant officer or agent acted with a culpable state of mind in order to establish the predicate constitutional violation, and the plaintiff has a companion failure to train claim against the entity employer. The individual defendant (once a qualified immunity defense fails) may try to negate a prima facie violation by showing that she was merely following orders as part of a pattern of supervisory indifference to the conduct in question. Here the nature of the discovery desired by the individual defendant obviously conflicts with the interests of the entity, because the entity's liability turns, under *City of Canton*, on whether such a pattern or custom exists. In that situation fairness to the individual defendant counsels permitting discovery about past similar incidents; yet if that discovery is permitted, the entity will lose the ordinary advantages of discovery bifurcation.

On occasion, *Heller* has been misapplied to situations where the individual defendant is found nonliable strictly on the basis of the qualified immunity defense. In *Heller* itself, Officer Bushey was absolved of individual liability by the general verdict of a jury.[37] The jury had heard evidence both on the constitutional violation as well as on defenses like qualified immunity, but the judge instructed it only about the

33. *Ricciuti*, 796 F.Supp. at 86. (But note that this is a court which participates in the discovery bifurcation model.)

34. Colbert, 44 Hastings L.J. at 556–57.

35. *Marryshow*, 139 F.R.D. at 318.

36. *Fisher v. City of N.Y.*, 1992 WL 77606, *3 (S.D.N.Y.1992).

37. *Heller*, 475 U.S. at 798, 106 S.Ct. at 1572.

predicate violation.[38] Although conceivably the jury may have rested its verdict on the defense of qualified immunity, the Court reasonably assumed that the finding of no liability meant that the jury had found no constitutional injury inflicted by the defendant.[39]

Some district courts have apparently overread *Heller* to mean that if "the individual officers are not held liable [for any reason], the City cannot be held liable under a *Monell* claim."[40] But *Heller* cannot stand for this broad proposition. If the Court had so intended, its subsequent holdings in *City of St. Louis v. Praprotnik*[41] and *City of Canton v. Harris*[42] would be inexplicable.[43] Both *Praprotnik* and *Harris* exonerated the individual defendants yet proceeded to consider the terms of entity liability.[44] If *Heller*, decided years earlier, meant that exoneration of individual defendants on any ground mandated exoneration of the municipal defendant, the Court could not have decided the way it did in either of these cases.[45] As the United States Court of Appeals for the Eighth Circuit noted in *Doe v. Sullivan County, Tenn.*,[46] a dismissal of a claim against an officer who asserts qualified immunity may mean no more than that "an officer in the defendant's position could reasonably have believed that the conduct in question did not violate law that was clearly established at the time.... To read *Heller* as implying that a municipality is immune from liability regardless of whether the plaintiff suffered a constitutional deprivation simply because an officer was entitled to qualified immunity would, we are convinced, represent a misconstruction of its holding and rationale."[47]

The road map drawn by *Siegert v. Gilley*,[48] for sequencing judicial decision on the distinct elements of the qualified immunity defense, should absolve a greater number of individual and in turn government entities before discovery. *Siegert* reaffirms that the trial judge, when ruling on the individual defendant's motion to dismiss or for summary judgment based on the defense of qualified immunity, must determine at the outset whether the plaintiff alleged the violation of a clearly established constitutional right.[49] The Court added, however, that "[a] neces-

38. *Id.* at 798–99, 106 S.Ct. at 1572.

39. *Id.*

40. *Myatt v. City of Chicago*, 816 F.Supp. 1259, 1264 (N.D.Ill.1992).

41. 485 U.S. 112, 108 S.Ct. 915, 99 L.Ed.2d 107 (1988).

42. 489 U.S. 378, 109 S.Ct. 1197, 103 L.Ed.2d 412 (1989).

43. Barbara Kritchevsky, *Making Sense of State of Mind: Determining Responsibility in Section 1983 Municipal Liability Litigation*, 60 Geo.Wash.L.Rev. 417, 440 (1992).

44. Colbert, 44 Hastings L.J. at 544; *Praprotnik*, 485 U.S. at 128, 108 S.Ct. at 926; *Harris*, 489 U.S. at 388 n.8, 109 S.Ct. at 1205 n.8 (The cited note only assumes that the right to receive medical care was denied by the city's employees. However, the case touched only on the City of Canton's liability, never the individual defendant's).

45. Colbert, 44 Hastings L.J. at 544.

46. 956 F.2d 545 (6th Cir.1992), *cert. denied*, 506 U.S. 864, 113 S.Ct. 187, 121 L.Ed.2d 131 (1992).

47. *Id.* at 554. *See also Marryshow*, 139 F.R.D. at 320 n.7 and text accompanying; *Ricciuti*, 796 F.Supp. at 86.

48. 500 U.S. 226, 111 S.Ct. 1789, 114 L.Ed.2d 277 (1991).

49. *Id.* at 231, 111 S.Ct. at 1793. *See also County of Sacramento*, 523 U.S. at 840–42 n.5; *Conn*, 119 S.Ct. at 1295; *Wilson*, 119 S.Ct. at 1697.

sary concomitant to the determination of whether the constitutional right asserted by a plaintiff is 'clearly established' at the time the defendant acted is the determination of whether the plaintiff has asserted a violation of a constitutional right at all."[50] The Court accordingly directed the district courts to decide these defenses initially on the pleadings to "weed out" poorly founded actions and save individual defendants from the "expensive and time consuming preparation to defend a suit on its merits."[51]

Most courts of appeals have accepted *Siegert* and its progeny as the new blueprint for evaluating § 1983 actions against government officials. Specifically, the determination whether the plaintiffs "asserted a violation of a constitutional right at all" must be made before the court evaluates the "clearly established" law prong or the "reasonable official" fact prong of qualified immunity.[52] If the court determines that no constitutional violation is stated at all, then the individual defendant will be absolved of all § 1983 liability (not just damages liability) on the ground that the complaint fails to state a claim for relief. Under *Heller*, the claim against the municipal defendant should accordingly be dismissed.[53] Circuits that initially flouted the suggestion in *Siegert* have been reminded by observations in two 1999 Supreme Court decisions that the sequencing is mandatory.[54]

The potential of *Siegert* for early absolution of individual and hence entity defendants on grounds of legal insufficiency may be somewhat offset by the Court's reaffirmation in *Leatherman v. Tarrant*[55] that all Federal Rule of Civil Procedure 8 requires, at least against government entities, is " 'a short and plain statement of the claim' that will give the defendant fair notice of what the plaintiff's claim is and the grounds upon which it rests."[56] While *Leatherman*'s narrow holding is limited to municipal liability, its notice pleading rationale suggests that it is also applicable to the liability of individual defendants, and the Supreme Court has subsequently so indicated.[57] The Eighth Circuit anticipated this result when it ruled that a district court's dismissal of a plaintiff's suit against an individual defendant for failure to state a claim "may not

50. *Id.*

51. *Id.*

52. *Watterson v. Page*, 987 F.2d 1, 7 (1st Cir.1993). *See also Hale v. Townley*, 45 F.3d 914 (5th Cir.1995); *Triad Assoc., Inc. v. Robinson*, 10 F.3d 492, 496 (7th Cir. 1993); *Buchholtz v. Dugan*, 9 F.3d 106 (6th Cir.1993); *Figueroa v. United States*, 7 F.3d 1405, 1409 (9th Cir.1993), *cert. denied*, 511 U.S. 1030, 114 S.Ct. 1537, 128 L.Ed.2d 190 (1994); *Post v. City of Fort Lauderdale*, 7 F.3d 1552, 1556 (11th Cir.1993), *modified*, 14 F.3d 583 (1994); *Calhoun v. New York State Div. of Parole Officers*, 999 F.2d 647, 652 (2d Cir.1993); *American Civil Liberties Union of Md., Inc. v. Wicomico County, Md.*, 999 F.2d 780, 784 (4th Cir.1993); *Hinton v. City of Elwood, Kan.*, 997 F.2d 774, 780 (10th Cir.1993); *Cole v. Bone*, 993 F.2d 1328, 1332 (8th Cir.1993).

53. *Heller*, 475 U.S. at 799, 106 S.Ct. at 1573.

54. *Wilson v. Layne*, 526 U.S. 603, 119 S.Ct. 1692, 143 L.Ed.2d 818 (1999); *Conn v. Gabbert*, 526 U.S. 286, 119 S.Ct. 1292, 1295, 143 L.Ed.2d 399 (1999).

55. 507 U.S. 163, 113 S.Ct. 1160, 122 L.Ed.2d 517 (1993). *Leatherman* is discussed in detail earlier in this Chapter.

56. 113 S.Ct. at 1163 (quoting *Conley v. Gibson*, 355 U.S. 41, 47, 78 S.Ct. 99, 103, 2 L.Ed.2d 80 (1957)) (footnotes omitted).

57. *Crawford–El v. Britton*, 523 U.S. 574, 118 S.Ct. 1584, 140 L.Ed.2d 759 (1998).

be sustainable in view of the holding in *Leatherman*" so long as the complaint meets the requirements of Rule 8.[58]

§ 5.109 [Reserved]

S. CLASS ACTIONS

§ 5.110 In General

Claims of systemic disparate treatment or of neutral practices having a disproportionate adverse impact will often be advanced through class actions. In theory, maintenance of actions in class form should expedite the presentation of evidence on behalf of large numbers of claimants. In fact, after receiving class actions quite hospitably in the early years of the Act, federal courts have erected substantial barriers to class certification through interpretations of Federal Rule 23.

The most formidable obstacle was declared by a Supreme Court decision construing the "commonality" and "typicality" requirements of Rule 23(a)(2) and Rule 23(a)(3). *General Telephone Co. of the Southwest v. Falcon*,[1] precludes named plaintiffs complaining of discrimination in one term and condition of employment (for example, promotion) from representing persons complaining about the same kind of discrimination with respect to other terms and conditions of employment (for example, hiring). The Court stressed that the requisite commonality and typicality must extend to defendant employer practices, not merely the general type of discrimination—race, gender, religion, or national origin—alleged.

Employment discrimination and civil rights cases are classic examples[2] of the kind of class action permitted by Rule 23(b)(2): where "the party opposing the class has acted or refused to act on grounds generally applicable to the class, thereby making appropriate final injunctive relief or corresponding declaratory relief with respect to the class as a whole." So where class treatment is denied in these cases it is usually because the claims fail to meet one or more of the compound requirements of Rule 23(a):

(1) "a class so numerous that joinder of all members is impracticable"[3];

58. *Kohl v. Casson*, 5 F.3d 1141, 1148 (8th Cir.1993). *See also Hall v. Lopez*, 823 F.Supp. 857, 865–66 (D.Colo.1993) (under *Leatherman*, even if a plaintiff's claim of § 1983 liability is based on nothing more than a "bare allegation," it is sufficient to survive a summary judgment motion. Nevertheless, the Eighth Circuit in *Kohl* sustained the dismissal on the grounds that the defendant officers acted as reasonable officers would have under the circumstances, thus meeting the final prong of qualified immunity. And the municipality was absolved of liability because "there was no causal relationship between ... [plaintiff's] arrest and any inadequacy in the training provided by the" municipality).

§ 5.110

1. 457 U.S. 147, 102 S.Ct. 2364, 72 L.Ed.2d 740 (1982).

2. *See Amchem Products, Inc. v. Windsor*, 521 U.S. 591, 117 S.Ct. 2231, 138 L.Ed.2d 689 (1997) (case under Rule 23(b)(3)).

3. Where the plaintiff class is not sufficiently numerous—e.g., if 20 or fewer plaintiffs compose the putative class—they may

(2) "questions of law or fact common to the class";

(3) "the claims ... of the representative parties are typical of the claims ... of the class";

(4) "the representative parties will fairly and adequately protect the interests of the class."

As for Rule 23(a)(4), the Court in *Falcon* did note that named plaintiffs complaining of one term or condition of employment could represent class members complaining of another where the employer used a common testing procedure or where different kinds of employees could be shown to have suffered discrimination "in the same general fashion," *e.g.*, through "entirely subjective decision making processes" or at the hands of the same employer personnel.[4] Nevertheless, many lower courts have taken a grudging approach to class action certification since *Falcon*. In any event, in applying the Falcon tests, district courts find it extremely challenging to obey the Supreme Court's separate admonition[5] that they avoid considering the merits of the underlying claim when deciding class certification.

Plaintiffs' counsel have tried to comply with the Court's strictures by assembling class-representative complements composed of applicants, employees and former employees complaining of varied terms and conditions of employment, with each named plaintiff offering to represent a discrete subclass. Defendants routinely reply with objections and motions asserting the existence of conflicts among the proposed subclasses and challenging plaintiffs' adequacy to represent them. When these motions succeed and class certification is denied, they may doom the class action as a practical matter, since orders denying certification are appealable only at the discretion of the appellate court after certification by the district court.[6] Even when defendants' objections are not sustained, they usually necessitate extensive discovery and briefing about the propriety of certification that can rob the class action of its intended expedition and efficiency.

join their claims under the far more permissive standard of Federal Rule of Civil Procedure 20. That rule permits joinder provided only that the claimants assert rights to relief arising out of the same transaction or occurrence and at least one question of law or fact common to all persons proposing joinder. *See Alexander v. Fulton County*, 207 F.3d 1303, 1324 (11th Cir.2000) (common allegations of systemic pattern or practice of race-based discrimination arising from same series of transactions, coupled with discriminatory character of defendant's conduct, suffices, even though plaintiffs suffered different effects—promotion denials, transfers, assignments, or discipline—resulting therefrom); *Grayson v. K Mart Corp.*, 79 F.3d 1086, 1097 (11th Cir.), *cert. denied sub nom Helton v. Kmart Corp.*, 519 U.S. 982, 117 S.Ct. 435, 136 L.Ed.2d 332 (1996) (a unified policy, plan or scheme of discrimination satisfies Rule 20 commonality requirement); *Mosley v. General Motors Corp.*, 497 F.2d 1330, 1332, 1334 (8th Cir.1974) (the discriminatory character of defendant's conduct, apparently even without the kind of common policy or scheme often required for Rule 23 class action certification under *Falcon*, can satisfy the commonality requirement of Rule 20).

4. *Falcon*, 457 U.S. at 159 n.15, 102 S.Ct. at 2371 n.15. *See also Bazemore v. Friday*, 478 U.S. 385, 106 S.Ct. 3000, 92 L.Ed.2d 315 (1986).

5. *Eisen v. Carlisle & Jacquelin*, 417 U.S. 156, 177, 94 S.Ct. 2140, 2152, 40 L.Ed.2d 732 (1974).

6. *See* 1998 amendment to Rule 23 adding § 23(f). *See* text, *infra*.

Now that the Civil Rights Act of 1991 permits compensatory and punitive damages in claims under Title VII and the Americans with Disabilities Act, employer representatives have suggested that class treatment would be inappropriate in such cases because issues concerning individualized relief would predominate over issues of liability common to the class.[7] Formally, however, there is no such "predomination" requirement for class certification under Rule 23(b)(2), only under Rule 23(b)(3), which has sometimes successfully been invoked to support class action treatment for mass torts.[8] Although the Supreme Court recently underscored that high individual stakes and significant disparities among class members' demands for relief in mass tort cases may undermine the predomination necessary for (b)(3) certification, the same opinion specifically distinguished the requirements of (b)(2).[9] And while the Court also discussed the requirement of Rule 23(a)(4), elaborated in *Falcon*, that the named class representatives fairly and adequately protect class interests, the Court's (a)(4) concern in the mass tort setting focused on the divergence of remedial goals between currently asbestos injury claimants who desired immediate compensation and those who had been exposed but were not yet suffering provable injury and who therefore sought delayed compensation through the creation of a massive fund.[10] By contrast, while civil rights and employment discrimination class members would seek damages in varying amounts for compensatory or punitive damages or both, these individual relief questions have typically been handled by bifurcating the systemic treatment class action

7. *See, e.g., Allison v. Citgo Petroleum Corp.*, 151 F.3d 402 (5th Cir.1998) (plaintiffs' Title VII and § 1981 disparate impact claims for money damages and constitutional right of both parties to jury trial, as now provided under Civil Rights Act of 1991, rendered case unsuitable for class certification). District courts have reached varying conclusions on the effect of the 1991 Amendments on class action suits. *See, e.g., EEOC v. McDonnell Douglas Corp.*, 960 F.Supp. 203 (E.D.Mo.1996); *Morgan v. United Parcel Serv. of Am., Inc.*, 169 F.R.D. 349 (E.D.Mo.1996); *Griffin v. Home Depot, Inc.*, 168 F.R.D. 187 (E.D.La.1996); *Zapata v. IBP, Inc.*, 167 F.R.D. 147 (D.Kan.1996); *Bremiller v. Cleveland Psychiatric Inst.*, 898 F.Supp. 572 (N.D.Ohio 1995); *Arnold v. United Artists Theatre Circuit, Inc.*, 158 F.R.D. 439 (N.D.Cal.1994) *See also* Daily Labor Report (December 10, 1996), at pp. A–4 and A–5.

In 1997, the Supreme Court decertified a 23(b)(3) "settlement only" class because the court found numerous conflicts of interest among group members, as well as differing issues and claims. That decision, *Amchem Products v. Windsor*, dealt with a mass tort (asbestos) but it may have effects on employment class actions as well. Employment classes after 1991 may have many of the same qualities. For example, individual claims for back pay or front pay may undercut the class' cohesiveness. High stakes could induce individual plaintiffs to seek to control the litigation. Representing both current and former employees could make adequacy of representation questionable.

8. *See Amchem Products, Inc. v. Windsor*, 521 U.S. 591, 117 S.Ct. 2231, 138 L.Ed.2d 689 (1997). Where plaintiffs' claims require case-specific fact inquiries surrounding each alleged discriminatory practice, they have failed Rule 23(b)(3)'s predomination requirement, which is more demanding than the commonality requirement of Rule 23(a). *Allison*, 151 F.3d at 420; *Jackson v. Motel 6 Multipurpose, Inc.*, 130 F.3d 999, 1006 (11th Cir.1997).

9. *Id.* at 4644, 4641. *See Allen v. International Truck and Engine Co.*, 358 F.3d 469 (7th Cir. 2004) (remanding for certification of employment discrimination class for equitable issues).

10. *Id.* at 4644.

into a second, remedial stage following an initial determination on liability.[11]

Class actions certified under 23(b)(3) must provide putative class members the option of excluding themselves from the suit.[12] Normally, 23(b)(1) or 23(b)(2) classes are mandatory, which means that the absent class members cannot opt out of the class. Most federal appellate courts have allowed district courts to provide opt out rights to some or all of the absent class members included in a mandatory class in limited circumstances. They have acted under the authority of Rule 23(d),[13] which permits a court, inter alia, to enter orders "determining the course of proceeding." For example, the District of Columbia Court of Appeals allows opt outs from mandatory classes in two situations: (1) if the court finds that the assumption of cohesiveness underlying the certification of a mandatory class is inapplicable to the individual class members claims for money damages, then it may fashion a hybrid class where class members have a limited right to opt-out to individually pursue their money damage claims; and (2) if the court finds that particular plaintiffs' claims are unique or sufficiently distinct from the claims of the class as a whole, then it can permit opt outs on a selective basis.[14] In any case, once reasonable opt out procedures are put into place and approved by the court, and putative class members are notified of the procedures, any deviation from the procedures justifies the court denying that opt out election.[15]

11. *See Tardiff v. Knox County*, 365 F.3d 1 (1st Cir. 2004) (issues about county policies concerning suspicionless strip searches predominated and were certifiable despite individually variable damages claims).

12. *See* F.R.C.P. 23(c)(2).

13. Rule 23(d) allows "the court [to] make appropriate orders: (1) determining the course of proceedings or prescribing measures to prevent undue repetition or complication in the presentation of evidence or argument; (2) requiring, for the protection of the members of the class or otherwise for the fair conduct of the action, that notice be given in such manner as the court may direct to some or all of the members of any step in the action, or of the proposed extent of the judgment, or of the opportunity of members to signify whether they consider the representation fair and adequate, to intervene and present claims or defenses, or otherwise to come into the action; (3) imposing conditions on the representative parties or on intervenors; (4) requiring that the pleadings be amended to eliminate therefrom allegations as to representation of absent persons, and that the action proceed accordingly; (5) dealing with similar procedural matters." This authority is limited, however. The Eleventh Circuit vacated two class communication orders as an abuse of the district court's discretion because the nationwide advertisements and mass mailings, issued before class certification, and made pursuant to the communications orders, were causing "serious and irreparable harm to the [defendant's] reputation and to its relationship with its employees." Communication with putative class may be made before certification, but districts "must strive to avoid authorizing injurious class communications that might later prove unnecessary." *Jackson v. Motel 6 Multipurpose, Inc.*, 130 F.3d 999 (11th Cir. 1997).

14. *See Thomas v. Albright*, 139 F.3d 227, 234–35 (D.C.Cir.1998), *cert. denied*, 525 U.S. 1016, 119 S.Ct. 539, 142 L.Ed.2d 448 (1998) (reversing the district court's decision allowing opt outs where neither prong of the test was met).

15. *See, e.g., Grilli v. Metropolitan Life Ins. Co.*, 78 F.3d 1533, 1538 (11th Cir. 1996), *cert. denied sub nom.* Coulter v. Metropolitan Life Ins. Co., Inc., 519 U.S. 1040, 117 S.Ct. 608, 136 L.Ed.2d 533 (1996) (denying late opt out elections where purported electors did not satisfy excusable neglect standard); *In re Painewebber Ltd. Partnerships Litig.*, 147 F.3d 132, 135 (2d Cir.1998) (same).

The Supreme Court had held that orders denying class action certification are not appealable before final judgment on the merits, even as it recognized that this decision would often induce a plaintiff to abandon his claim.[16] However, the Congress modified Federal Rule of Civil Procedure 23 in 1998 by adding section 23(f). It provides specific authority for a permissive interlocutory appeal of an order granting or denying class certification, subject to the discretion of the court of appeals. Appeals must be made within 10 days of entry of the class certification order, and provides for no stay of the action unless otherwise ordered. The rule took effect on December 1, 1998, and governs proceedings in civil cases commenced after December 1, and in pending proceedings "insofar as just and practicable."[17]

§§ 5.111–5.115 [Reserved]

T. CLAIM AND ISSUE PRECLUSION IN ACTIONS UNDER TITLE VII AND THE RECONSTRUCTION CIVIL RIGHTS ACTS

§ 5.116 Overview

An increasingly important procedural issue is the extent, if any, to which court actions will be barred by prior agency or court determinations.[1] EEOC reasonable cause determinations cannot prevent timely filed Title VII actions from being heard on the merits. Nor will the decisions of state or local administrative deferral agencies have preclusive effect on subsequent Title VII actions: it would make no sense to preclude a federal court when EEOC is merely required to give those decisions "substantial weight."[2] Resolving a conflict in the circuits, and reaching a result consonant with *University of Tennessee v. Elliott*,[3] the Supreme Court has held that the unreviewed administrative determinations of state or local agencies do not preclude private plaintiff actions under ADEA, either.[4] An ADEA lawsuit brought by EEOC, in contrast, will generally preclude private relief.

16. *Coopers & Lybrand v. Livesay*, 437 U.S. 463, 98 S.Ct. 2454, 57 L.Ed.2d 351 (1978).

17. *See* Amendments to Federal Rules of Civil Procedure, 118 S.Ct. 399 (April 24, 1998). Some state courts also permit interlocutory review of orders denying class certification. *See* § 5.45, *supra*.

§ 5.116

1. It is clear that no preclusion doctrines, statutory or common law, operate in the absence of an underlying judgment or administrative finding. *See Carver v. Nall*, 172 F.3d 513, 515 (7th Cir.1999) (settlement of union grievance proceedings before the Illinois State Labor Relations Board (ISLRB) did not have res judicata effect precluding deputy sheriffs' § 1983 suit). Thus, a settlement agreement that has not been integrated into a consent decree is not a judgment and cannot trigger preclusion.

2. *University of Tennessee v. Elliott*, 478 U.S. 788, 106 S.Ct. 3220, 92 L.Ed.2d 635 (1986). *But see Mitchell v. Albuquerque Bd. of Educ.*, 2 F.3d 1160 (10th Cir.1993), *cert. denied*, 510 U.S. 1045, 114 S.Ct. 693, 126 L.Ed.2d 660 (1994).

3. 478 U.S. 788, 106 S.Ct. 3220, 92 L.Ed.2d 635 (1986). *Elliott* is discussed in § 5.121, *infra*.

4. *Astoria Fed. Sav. & Loan Ass'n v. Solimino*, 501 U.S. 104, 111 S.Ct. 2166, 115 L.Ed.2d 96 (1991).

When, on the other hand, a state administrative determination is reviewed by a state court, a judgment of non-liability may bar a Title VII action in federal court by force of the Full Faith and Credit Act,[5] at least where the judicial review was sought by the employee.[6] *Kremer*, declining to create a Title VII exception to the preclusion required by the terms of § 1738, holds that a federal court presented with a Title VII claim must give the same deference to the state appellate judgment as would a court of the rendering state under the state's principles of preclusion.[7] Consistent with *Kremer*, a state court judgment reviewing a state administrative determination will be accorded the same preclusive effect in a federal court ADEA action that it would receive in the courts of the state.[8] Preclusion under the applicable *state's* law is, however, an important precondition to *Kremer* preclusion; where the state law does not bar subsequent federal employment discrimination suits, *Kremer* will not bar federal court relitigation.[9] Nevertheless, *Kremer* stands as a warning to prospective Title VII plaintiffs that they may lose their Title VII claim by seeking state judicial review of an adverse agency determination.

Kremer has been extended by some lower courts to reach the situation where the *employer* seeks state court review of the administrative agency decision.[10] This approach is questionable. Employment discrimination claimants in most states—those designated by EEOC as "deferral" jurisdictions—are required by Title VII itself to institute state administrative agency proceedings as a prerequisite to the effective filing of a charge with EEOC and therefore ultimately as a condition of prosecuting a Title VII claim in state or federal court. If preclusion of the Title VII claim follows from an employer—instituted review of a state administrative proceeding that Title VII requires the potential plaintiff to commence, the employer in those states may avoid a judicial defense of Title VII claims by its own unilateral action whenever the agency

5. 28 U.S.C.A. § 1738.

6. *See Kremer v. Chemical Constr. Corp.*, 456 U.S. 461, 102 S.Ct. 1883, 72 L.Ed.2d 262 (1982). Usually, as in *Kremer* itself, relitigation is barred by issue rather than claim preclusion. This is because most state courts reviewing underlying agency decisions have appellate jurisdiction to review only claims brought under their own state anti-discrimination laws, not claims asserted under Title VII. In *Maniccia v. Brown*, 171 F.3d 1364 (11th Cir.1999), plaintiff, a deputy sheriff, was terminated for various offenses. During her state administrative process, she admitted she committed the violations, but contended her punishment—termination—was harsher because of her gender, but the state administrative proceeding, and the state judicial forum on appeal, excluded all evidence she tried to introduce to support her claim of sex discrimination. The federal court found that she was issue precluded on whether she committed these violations, and the Eleventh Circuit affirmed on the precedent set by *Kremer*.

7. 456 U.S. at 485, 102 S.Ct. at 1899.

8. *See, e.g., Hogue v. Royse City, Texas*, 939 F.2d 1249 (5th Cir.1991).

9. *See Brye v. Brakebush*, 32 F.3d 1179 (7th Cir.1994); *McNasby v. Crown Cork & Seal Co.*, 888 F.2d 270 (3d Cir.1989), *cert. denied*, 494 U.S. 1066, 110 S.Ct. 1783, 108 L.Ed.2d 784 (1990).

10. *See, e.g., Zanders v. National R.R. Passenger Corp.*, 898 F.2d 1127 (6th Cir. 1990); *Trujillo v. County of Santa Clara*, 775 F.2d 1359 (9th Cir.1985); *Hickman v. Electronic Keyboarding, Inc.*, 741 F.2d 230 (8th Cir.1984); *Unger v. Consolidated Foods Corp.*, 693 F.2d 703, 710 n. 11 (7th Cir. 1982); and *Gonsalves v. Alpine Country Club*, 727 F.2d 27 (1st Cir.1984). In *Zanders* the court even precluded the Title VII claim where the *employer* instituted state court proceedings not based on employment discrimination. 898 F.2d at 1130.

finds for the claimant. The Supreme Court has repudiated a similar result under Title VII or ADEA in two decisions after *Kremer*.[11]

Against this background, *University of Tennessee v. Elliott*[12] creates an awkward dichotomy; it rejects preclusion based on judicially unreviewed state agency proceedings of the kind that underlie Title VII actions, but allows such preclusion in actions under the Reconstruction statutes. The plaintiff in *Elliott* presented both types of federal claims to the federal court, but found himself precluded only on the civil rights claim.

Federal courts have also barred Title VII claims by according preclusive effect to prior federal judgments in actions arising out of the same employment setting. In *Woods v. Dunlop Tire Corp.*,[13] for example, a Title VII claim was barred by res judicata because plaintiff had failed to raise that claim in a previous action that challenged her termination under the Labor Management Relations Act ("LMRA"). The Court invoked the broad, contemporary approach to claim preclusion, observing that it is "the identity of facts surrounding the occurrence which constitutes the cause of action" that triggers res judicata, even if the legal theories advanced in the two actions are distinct. That the short statute of limitations on the labor claim ran before EEOC had finished administrative processing of plaintiff's claim did not persuade the court to relieve plaintiff of the ordinary consequences of federal common law preclusion. The court noted that plaintiff could have demanded a notice of right to sue from EEOC 180 days after filing her EEOC charge, or if necessary sought a stay of the LMRA action pending completion of EEOC proceedings, and then amended the LMRA complaint to include a claim under Title VII.

In the class action employment discrimination setting, however, the Supreme Court has somewhat eased the subsequent sting of an adverse federal court judgment. Federal common law accords preclusive effect to judgments rejecting pattern–type discrimination claims in subsequent actions asserting the same theory. But adverse class action or group—based judgments (e.g., rejecting claims of disparate treatment against protected group members or claims alleging the disproportionate adverse impact of a neutral practice) do not bar the claims of individual class members alleging disparate treatment à la *McDonnell Douglas/Burdine*.[14] Moreover, when a court denies class action certification, individual class members' claims may still be timely, because the filing of a class

11. See § 5.121, *infra*.

12. 478 U.S. 788, 106 S.Ct. 3220, 92 L.Ed.2d 635 (1986).

13. 972 F.2d 36 (2d Cir.1992), *cert. denied*, 506 U.S. 1053, 113 S.Ct. 977, 122 L.Ed.2d 131 (1993). *See also Owens v. Kaiser Foundation Health Plan, Inc.*, 244 F.3d 708 (9th Cir.2001) (Title VII claims were barred by res judicata though plaintiffs had not yet received their "right to sue" letters at the time of their first action); *Churchill v. Star Enter.*, 183 F.3d 184 (3d Cir.1999) (precluding ADA claim based on judgment in prior Family Medical Leave Act action alleging illegal termination based on disability, because plaintiff could have joined ADA claim with FMLA claim in prior action despite necessity of pursuing administrative remedies under ADA).

14. *See Cooper v. Federal Reserve Bank of Richmond*, 467 U.S. 867, 104 S.Ct. 2794, 81 L.Ed.2d 718 (1984).

action has been held to toll the 90–day period for filing suit until the denial of certification.[15]

§ 5.117 The Full Faith and Credit Act[1] and State Court Proceedings; Section 1738

When an aspect of a Reconstruction Act claim, previously decided by a state court judgment, reappears in another action in a court of the same state, that state's preclusion law applies. Where the second action is in the court of another state, however, the Full Faith and Credit Clause of Article IV of the Constitution governs. Article IV, § 1 of the United States Constitution provides that "Full Faith and Credit shall be given in each State to the . . . judicial Proceedings of every other State."[2] This has long been understood to require the second state's courts to give as much effect to the first state court's judgment as would the courts of the first state under its own principles of preclusion.

If the preclusion possibility is presented by the effect of a federal court judgment in another federal court, the governing rules are furnished by a federal common law of preclusion as exemplified by the Supreme Court's decisions in *Blonder–Tongue Laboratories v. University of Ill. Found.*[3] and *Parklane Hosiery Co. v. Shore.*[4] Finally, the Supremacy Clause of the Constitution, Article VI, dictates the preclusive effect of a federal court decision, in accordance with that federal common law, in a subsequent action in state court.

But are federal courts precluded by prior *state* court judgments determining a claim of federal civil rights? Federal courts are not constrained by the requirements of the Full Faith and Credit Clause. However, shortly after the ratification of the Constitution, Congress established legislation "specifically to insure that federal courts, not included within the constitutional provision, would be bound by state judgments."[5] On May 26, 1790, Congress passed the first version of the Full Faith and Credit statute.[6] Subsequently re-enacted by Congress,[7] the Full Faith and Credit statute has existed in substantially the same form ever since.

Currently, this statute is located at 28 U.S.C.A. § 1738.[8] Section 1738 is divided into three parts. First, § 1738 provides for the authentication of the acts of the legislature "of any State, Territory, or Posses-

15. *Crown, Cork & Seal Co. v. Parker*, 462 U.S. 345, 103 S.Ct. 2392, 76 L.Ed.2d 628 (1983).

§ 5.117

1. 28 U.S.C.A. § 1738 (1988).

2. U.S. Const. Art. IV, § 1.

3. 402 U.S. 313, 91 S.Ct. 1434, 28 L.Ed.2d 788 (1971).

4. 439 U.S. 322, 99 S.Ct. 645, 58 L.Ed.2d 552 (1979).

5. *Kremer v. Chemical Constr. Corp.*, 456 U.S. 461, 482 n. 24, 102 S.Ct. 1883, 1898 n. 24, 72 L.Ed.2d 262 (1982); *see also Davis v. Davis*, 305 U.S. 32, 40, 59 S.Ct. 3, 6, 83 L.Ed. 26 (1938).

6. Act of May 26, 1790, ch. 11, 1 Stat. 122.

7. Act of Mar. 27, 1804, ch. 56, 2 Stat. 298–99.

8. 28 U.S.C.A. § 1738 (1988).

sion of the United States."[9] Second, § 1738 provides the means by which the "records and judicial proceedings of any [ ] State, Territory, or Possession . . . shall be proved and admitted in other courts within the United States."[10] Third, § 1738 provides that:

> [s]uch Acts, records and judicial proceedings or copies thereof, so authenticated, shall have the same full faith and credit in every court within the United States and its Territories and Possessions as they have by law or usage in the courts of such State, Territory or Possession from which they are taken.[11]

As understood by the Supreme Court, § 1738 requires "all federal courts to give preclusive effect to state-court judgments whenever the courts of the State from which the judgments emerged would do so."[12] Federal courts must therefore accord a state court decision the same preclusive effect as to claims ("res judicata," in the familiar earlier terminology) and issues ("collateral estoppel") that state courts would give. Of course a strong motive behind the passage of the Civil Rights Act of 1871[13] and the Civil Rights Act of 1964[14] was the "grave congressional concern that the state courts had been deficient in protecting federal rights."[15] Neither statute, however, specifically mentions § 1738, and the United States Supreme Court has held that federal court actions under the Reconstruction civil rights acts and Title VII do not escape state court preclusion through an implied exception to § 1738.[16] We will turn to this issue shortly.

§ 5.118 Claim and Issue Preclusion

42 U.S.C.A. § 1738[1] requires the federal courts to give state court judgments the same[2] preclusive effect that other courts in that state would. A federal court applying that statute may therefore have to consult the preclusion law of any of the fifty states. As a representative introduction to the modern law of claim and issue preclusion prevailing among the states, this Chapter will refer to the widely followed Second Restatement of Judgments, which is also the model for the contemporary federal common law of preclusion. It is settled that when a federal court

9. 28 U.S.C.A. § 1738.

10. *Id.*

11. *Id.*

12. *Allen v. McCurry*, 449 U.S. 90, 96, 101 S.Ct. 411, 415, 66 L.Ed.2d 308 (1980).

13. 42 U.S.C.A. § 1983.

14. 42 U.S.C.A. § 2000e *et seq.*

15. *McCurry*, 449 U.S. at 98, 101 S.Ct. at 417. *See also Kremer v. Chemical Constr. Corp.*, 456 U.S. 461, 467, 472, 102 S.Ct. 1883, 1890, 72 L.Ed.2d 262 (1982) (stating that although Congress intended the states to play a role in Title VII enforcement, the federal courts would be "entrusted with ultimate enforcement responsibility.").

16. *See Allen v. McCurry,* 449 U.S. 90, 101 S.Ct. 411, 66 L.Ed.2d 308 (1980); *Kremer v. Chemical Construction Corporation,* 456 U.S. 461, 102 S.Ct. 1883, 72 L.Ed.2d 262 (1982); *Migra v. Warren City Sch. Dist.*, 465 U.S. 75, 104 S.Ct. 892, 79 L.Ed.2d 56 (1984); and *University of Tennessee v. Elliott*, 478 U.S. 788, 106 S.Ct. 3220, 92 L.Ed.2d 635.

§ 5.118

1. *See supra* § 5.117.

2. One objection to the *Rooker–Feldman* doctrine, *supra* § 5.27, is that in effect it uses jurisdictional principles to accord *more* preclusion to state court judgments than is called for by the applicable state law.

decides a *federal question* claim—including claims under any of the federal civil rights or employment discrimination statutes—the preclusive effect of the judgment in a later filed action is governed by federal, judge-made law.[3]

a. Claim Preclusion

Claim preclusion, or res judicata, refers to the preclusive effect of prior adjudications on entire causes of action asserted in subsequent litigation. A "valid final adjudication of a claim precludes a second action on that claim or any part of it."[4] The essential elements a defendant must plead and prove to preclude a claim, therefore, are : (1) a final judgment "on the merits" in the prior action; (2) identity of claims in the two actions; and (3) identity or privity between the parties in those actions.[5] In addition, for the first judgment to be "valid," it must have been rendered by a court of competent jurisdiction.[6]

Identity not only of claims but of parties in the two actions is required; in the subsequent litigation, the same plaintiff or someone in privity with him must be suing the same defendant or her privy.[7] Under the Second Restatement, claim preclusion is divided into the Rule of Merger and the Rule of Bar, depending on whether the plaintiff (merger)

3. *See Stoll v. Gottlieb*, 305 U.S. 165, 59 S.Ct. 134, 83 L.Ed. 104 (1938). But if an issue decided by a federal court under *state* law reappears identically in a federal civil rights or employment discrimination case in federal court, the federally prescribed rule of preclusion is that which would be used by courts of the state in which the federal court sits, except for situations in which the federal court determines that the state preclusion law is inconsistent with federal policy. *Semtek International, Inc. v. Lockheed Martin Corp.*, 531 U.S. 497, 121 S.Ct. 1021, 149 L.Ed.2d 32 (2001).

4. *Baker by Thomas v. General Motors Corp.*, 522 U.S. 222, 233 n. 5, 118 S.Ct. 657, 664 n. 5, 139 L.Ed.2d 580 (1998).

5. *Frank v. United Airlines, Inc.*, 216 F.3d 845, 850 (9th Cir.2000), *cert. denied* 532 U.S. 914, 121 S.Ct. 1247, 149 L.Ed.2d 154 (2001).

6. *Jang v. United Technologies Corp.*, 206 F.3d 1147, 1149 (11th Cir.2000).

7. *See, e.g., Andrews v. Daw*, 201 F.3d 521, 525–526 (4th Cir.2000) (government official sued under § 1983 in original action in his official capacity not in privity with himself when subsequently sued, also under § 1983, in his individual capacity, so plaintiff not precluded); *De Llano v. Berglund*, 183 F.3d 780 (8th Cir.1999) (§ 1983 action against university employees involved in plaintiff's termination not precluded by plaintiff's adverse judgment in Title VII action against university for lack of privity between defendants); *Tice v. American Airlines, Inc.*, 162 F.3d 966 (7th Cir.1998), *cert. denied*, 527 U.S. 1036, 119 S.Ct. 2395, 144 L.Ed.2d 795 (1999) (pilots not precluded from asserting ADEA claim despite prior suit challenging same employment policy because their interests were neither adequately represented nor "virtually represented" in prior litigation); *Delew v. Wagner*, 143 F.3d 1219 (9th Cir.1998), *cert. denied*, 525 U.S. 1015, 119 S.Ct. 538, 142 L.Ed.2d 448 (1998) (§ 1983 suit arising from alleged police misconduct in the investigation of motor vehicle was not barred by prior wrongful death suit; § 1983 defendants differed from wrongful death defendant); *Headley v. Bacon*, 828 F.2d 1272, 1279–80 (8th Cir.1987) (litigation against city officials sued in their personal capacity under § 1983 not precluded by prior litigation against them in their official capacities under Title VII). See Restatement (Second) of Judgments § 36 cmt.e (determination in action against public official sued in official capacity binding on government but not on official personally). *But see McGuinness v. Regents of Univ. of N.M.*, 183 F.3d 1172 (10th Cir.1999), *cert. denied*, 528 U.S. 932, 120 S.Ct. 332, 145 L.Ed.2d 259 (1999) (defendant university regents successfully invoked claim preclusion in ADA action based on prior judgment in favor of university's medical school, with which regents were in privity) (depublished).

or defendant (bar) succeeded in the initial litigation.[8] The general Rule of Merger is that

> [w]hen a valid and final[9] judgment is rendered in favor of the plaintiff:
>
> (1) The plaintiff cannot thereafter maintain an action on the original claim or any part thereof, although he may be able to maintain an action upon the judgment.[10]

This prohibition against a plaintiff's "splitting" her "cause of action" is sweeping. In particular, so long as the first forum had subject matter jurisdiction to entertain the unasserted claims and provide the same remedies,[11] merger precludes the plaintiff from bringing a subsequent action based on the same real-life transaction or event, either to obtain greater or different relief from that sought originally or to assert a distinct legal theory,[12] or to bring forth new or different evidence or arguments.[13]

8. Restatement (Second) of Judgments [hereinafter, "Restatement"] § 17.

9. For the purposes of both claim and issue preclusion, a judgment is final from "the date of its rendition, without regard to the date of commencement of the action in which it is rendered or the action in which it is to be given effect." *Id.* § 14. The definition includes trial court judgments on appeal, until and unless reversed.

10. Restatement (Second) of Judgments § 18.

11. *Id.* § 26(1)(c) (exception to § 24 definition of "claim") (discussed *infra* this section and § 5.119). Where a state habeas court lacked authority to award damages, a § 1983 claim that arose out of the same transaction and would therefore ordinarily have been claim precluded was held not barred by res judicata. The court observed, however, that fact findings reached by the habeas tribunal might have collateral estoppel effect in the judicial action under § 1983. *Burgos v. Hopkins*, 14 F.3d 787 (2d Cir.1994).

12. Thus, a federal § 1983 action challenging the constitutionality of land use regulations was precluded by a prior state court action where plaintiff could have asserted their constitutional arguments. *See Wilkinson v. Pitkin County Bd. of County Comm'rs*, 142 F.3d 1319 (10th Cir.1998) (per curiam).

13. Restatement (Second) of Judgments §§ 18, 24. *See, e.g., Wilkes v. Wyoming Dep't of Employment Div. of Labor Standards*, 314 F.3d 501 (10th Cir.2002) (claim preclusion barred Title VII action in view of prior action alleging equal pay violation that arose out of same employment relationship; although plaintiff had not received EEOC right to sue letter when first action commenced, she could have requested one and amended her equal pay action to add the Title VII claim or sought stay of equal pay action pending completion of EEOC administrative process); *Havercombe v. Department of Educ. of Com. of P.R.*, 250 F.3d 1 (1st Cir.2001) (after successful ADEA and Title VII suit, plaintiff was precluded from asserting new suit alleging substantially the same facts); *Jang v. United Technologies Corp.*, 206 F.3d 1147, 1149 (11th Cir.2000) (after suffering dismissal of Americans With Disabilities Act claim for want of an EEOC notice of right to sue, plaintiff precluded from asserting same claim in new action after obtaining right to sue letter). Preclusion applies where both the prior and current claims were based on federal law, *see Rivers v. Barberton Bd. of Educ.*, 143 F.3d 1029 (6th Cir.1998) (barring Title VII claim) and where plaintiff splits what for claim preclusion purposes is a "single" cause of action by bringing state law claims in one suit and then, after obtaining an administrative notice of right to sue, bringing a federal claim for relief. *See Heyliger v. State Univ. & Cmty. College Sys.*, 126 F.3d 849, 855–56 (6th Cir.1997), *cert. denied*, 522 U.S. 1117, 118 S.Ct. 1054, 140 L.Ed.2d 117 (1998) (observing that plaintiff could and should have requested right to sue letter and, upon receipt, amended state court complaint to add federal law claim); *Brzostowski v. Laidlaw Waste Sys., Inc.*, 49 F.3d 337, 339 (7th Cir.1995) (plaintiff precluded for bringing state law claim first, federal law claim later); *Woods v. Dunlop Tire Corp.*, 972 F.2d 36, 41 (2d Cir.1992) (explaining how plaintiffs may

The general Rule of Bar, in contrast, is triggered by "a valid and final personal judgment rendered in favor of the defendant"—it too prevents "another action by the plaintiff on the same claim."[14] Bar precludes in fewer situations than does merger, because it is subject to an exception for judgments rendered on certain procedural grounds. The first-action outcomes that do not bar include dismissals based on lack of jurisdiction, venue, nonjoinder, misjoinder, failure to satisfy a precondition to suit, prematurity, initial voluntary dismissals, and any grounds of termination that, according to the forum state's or federal court's procedural law or rules, do not bar another action on the same claim.[15] The exception is often said to apply to judgments "not on the merits." This terminology is misleadingly overinclusive, because in contemporary practice repetitive voluntary dismissals as well as involuntary dismissals for failure to state a claim, for untimeliness, or for failure to prosecute or obey court rules or orders all trigger bar even though they plainly do not determine the factual substance of the plaintiff's claim.

A threshold prerequisite for claim preclusion, therefore, is that the claim sought to be precluded in a subsequent action be the same as that asserted in a prior action. In sharp contrast to earlier, more technical and limited definitions, Restatement § 24 provides that the claim capable of extinction (by merger or bar) includes "all rights of the plaintiff to remedies against the defendant with respect to all or any part of the

preserve both state and federal law claims by filing the former, seeking a stay pending conclusion of Title VII administrative process and receipt of notice of right to sue, and then amending complaint to add Title VII claims). In *Herrmann v. Cencom Cable Assoc.*, 999 F.2d 223, 226 (7th Cir.1993), discussed below, Judge Posner elaborated on the ways that plaintiffs required to obtain an administrative clearance before filing a federal employment discrimination claim could avoid preclusion even if the clearance is unavailable when the limitations period expires on companion federal or state law claims arising out of the same transaction and occurrence. *See* § 5.73, *infra*.

14. *Id.* § 19 (emphasis added).

15. *See Id.* § 20 (1) and (2). For a representative list of first-action dismissal grounds that do not usually bar another action on the same claim, see FRCP 41(a)(1) and 41(b). The grounds specifically listed there include only initial voluntary dismissals and involuntary dismissals based on the dilatory defenses of jurisdiction, venue or failure to join a necessary or indispensable party. But the Federal Rule goes on to provide that an order dismissing on any other ground operates as an "adjudication upon the merits"—that is, the order bars unless it "otherwise specifies." The Restatement, by including dismissals for prematurity or failure to satisfy a precondition to suit among the grounds that do not bar relitigation of the claim even where the dismissal order is silent on that point, thus bars on fewer grounds than Federal Rule 41 would suggest. A federal court using the Restatement as its guide for fashioning a federal common law of preclusion would accordingly not bar on those two grounds despite the contrary implication of the Federal Rules. Compare Restatement §§ 20(2) with 20(1)(c). The same result follows if F.R.C.P. 41(b) itself is read to except from bar dismissals based on prematurity. *See Lundquist v. Rice Memorial Hospital,* 238 F.3d 975 (8th Cir.2001) (denial of motion to amend that led to dismissal of first action not on merits and so does not preclude subsequent action under Americans With Disabilities Act on same claim); *Curtis v. Citibank, N.A.,* 226 F.3d 133 (2d Cir.2000) (same under Title VII); *Criales v. American Airlines, Inc.*, 105 F.3d 93 (2d Cir.1997), *cert. denied*, 522 U.S. 906, 118 S.Ct. 264, 139 L.Ed.2d 190 (1997) (relying on *Costello v. United States*, 365 U.S. 265, 81 S.Ct. 534, 5 L.Ed.2d 551 (1961) as support for construing F.R.C.P. 41(b) to deny bar effect to dismissals for failure to comply with a prerequisite to a determination on the merits, and accordingly holding Title VII action based on timely EEOC charge not barred by dismissal of separate Title VII action based on untimely charge).

transaction, or series of connected transactions, out of which the action arose."[16] So long as the two actions stem from the same core of real-life events, claim preclusion is possible: the same claim is presented even if the plaintiff proceeds on different legal theories,[17] offers different supporting evidence, or seeks different or additional relief.[18] On the other hand, a prisoner's § 1983 damages claim predicated on unconstitutional conditions of confinement is spatially and temporally distinct from his habeas claim challenging an underlying criminal conviction. Accordingly, the § 1983 claim will not be claim precluded by a previous habeas determination—for res judicata purposes, these are different claims.[19]

Migra requires the federal court to follow whatever preclusion rules are followed in the forum state's own courts. In this connection it should be borne in mind that some states follow older, more restrictive definitions of claim identity that antedate the 2d Restatement of Judgments. Thus where state claim preclusion law deemed claims distinct because based on significantly different elements, a federal court could not preclude a § 1983 claim alleging a deprivation of substantive due process based on the resolution of a state court negligence action, even though it involved the same parties and had been decided on the merits.[20] Where, by contrast, the applicable state preclusion law followed the Second Restatement's broader definition—claims are the same for claim preclusion purposes if they simply arise out of the same real-life transaction and occurrence, that is, spatially and temporally—federal court civil rights and employment discrimination claims were precluded based on a state court judgment reviewing a police board's denial of disability pension benefits.[21]

The definition of claim identity prevents the relitigation not only of causes of action actually raised and adjudicated but of any causes that could have been raised with respect to the same real-life transaction. Thus in the lexicon of modern preclusion, claims based on state law and federal law arising from the same police arrest or employment discharge are considered part of the same transaction; if either is not raised in the original action it may be precluded in subsequent litigation, provided, as would usually be the case, the first forum had subject matter jurisdiction

16. Restatement (Second) of Judgments § 24.

17. *See N.A.A.C.P., Minneapolis Branch v. Metropolitan Council*, 125 F.3d 1171 (8th Cir.1997), *vacated on other grounds*, 522 U.S. 1145, 118 S.Ct. 1162, 140 L.Ed.2d 173 (1998) (action brought under state constitution by class of schoolchildren alleging that council's housing policies deprived them of adequate education was barred by previous action by class of minority persons living in low-income housing alleging that council's policies violated Fair Housing Act; "[t]he same cause of action framed in terms of a new legal theory is still the same cause of action"); *Brzostowski v. Laidlaw Waste Sys., Inc.*, 49 F.3d 337 (7th Cir.1995) (ADEA claim arising from discharge precluded by judgment in action asserting discharge violated employment contract).

18. *See* comments to Restatement § 24.

19. *See Rhodes v. Hannigan*, 12 F.3d 989 (10th Cir.1993).

20. *Stemler v. Florence*, 350 F.3d 578 (6th Cir. 2003)(Kentucky law).

21. *Garcia v. Village of Mount Prospect*, 360 F.3d 630 (7th Cir. 2004)(Illinois law).

to entertain both claims.[22] Only if the second proceeding is significantly predicated on spatially or temporally distinct real-life events will it normally be considered a separate claim free of the preclusion defense.[23]

These principles are easier to state than to apply. Take, for example, *Herrmann v. Cencom Cable Assoc., Inc.*[24] There the Seventh Circuit Court of Appeals defined "transaction" under the Restatement as follows: "[the] two claims are one for purposes of res judicata if they are based on the same, or nearly the same, factual allegations."[25] The plaintiff, after being discharged by the defendant, filed a charge of discrimination with the EEOC. A few months later the plaintiff also filed suit in federal court against the defendant under the continuation of benefits provision of ERISA ("COBRA"). On defendant's motion, the district court granted summary judgment in the defendant's favor. After obtaining a right-to-sue letter from the EEOC, plaintiff then instituted a Title VII action against the defendant. The district court held the action precluded (by merger) because the claim under ERISA and the Title VII claim should have been brought in one lawsuit.

22. *See* § 26(1)(c), Restatement (Second) of Judgments. Before claim precluding § 1983 claims, federal judges routinely take pains to observe that the plaintiff would have been free under state law to assert the precluded claim in the prior state proceeding. *See, e.g., Hutcherson v. Lauderdale County, TN,* 326 F.3d 747 (6th Cir.2003); *Wilhelm v. County of Milwaukee,* 325 F.3d 843 (7th Cir.2003). They apparently recite this because the inability to assert a claim in a prior proceeding because of a subject matter or perhaps personal jurisdiction barrier constitutes an exception to claim preclusion under the state preclusion law that federal courts must respect under § 1738, as construed in *McCurry* and, most pertinently, *Migra. Cf. Staats v. County of Sawyer,* 220 F.3d 511 (7th Cir.2000) (where no one state or federal original administrative agency or court had jurisdiction over plaintiff's state law and Americans With Disabilities Act claims, subsequent ADA claim in federal court not precluded, despite possibility that Wisconsin courts on review of state agency decision might have entertained ADA claim as well). *But see Froebel v. Meyer,* 217 F.3d 928 (7th Cir.2000), *cert. denied* 531 U.S. 1075, 121 S.Ct. 769, 148 L.Ed.2d 669 (2001) (state administrative tribunal had jurisdiction to hear both state and federal environmental claims, so state court's judgment reviewing agency's decision precludes later separate federal action on withheld federal claim.) *Humphrey v. Tharaldson Enters.*, 95 F.3d 624 (7th Cir. 1996) (civil rights claims barred even though state agency where plaintiff first sought relief lacked jurisdiction over those claims); *Davis v. City of Chicago*, 53 F.3d 801, 803 (7th Cir.1995) (precluding federal law claim that § 1983 plaintiff failed to assert when he invoked state court review of local administrative agency determination, even though it was not clear that state court would exercise jurisdiction over the § 1983 claim); *Misischia v. Pirie*, 60 F.3d 626 (9th Cir.1995) (res judicata invoked because § 1983 plaintiff did not seek judicial review in state court of administrative agency decision).

23. *See, e.g., Frank v. United Airlines, Inc.*, 216 F.3d 845, 850–852 (9th Cir.2000) (flight attendants' claims challenging weight policy under Title VII not claim precluded because based on alleged violations arising after date of post-judgment settlement and because it challenged a different, post-judgment policy); *Pleming v. Universal–Rundle Corp.*, 142 F.3d 1354 (11th Cir.1998) (summary judgment against employee on prior discrimination claim, involving one hiring decision, did not have res judicata effect so as to bar current claims based on two other hiring decisions occurring after filing of prior claim); *Perkins v. Board of Trustees*, 116 F.3d 235 (7th Cir. 1997) (no preclusion of Title VII claim alleging employer refused to permit plaintiff to sit for civil service examination based on prior adverse judgment on plaintiff's Title VII claim that employer had refused to permit him to sit for another such examination two years before).

24. 999 F.2d 223, 226 (7th Cir.1993).

25. *Id.* at 227.

The plaintiff appealed and the Seventh Circuit reversed. The court of appeals, Judge Posner writing, held that although the proceedings stemmed from a common fact—the discharge of the employee—the Title VII claim concerned primarily events before, and the COBRA claim primarily events after, the discharge. The factual overlap was therefore insufficient to constitute one claim for purposes of res judicata.[26] On the other hand, the court hypothesized a situation in which an employee has an employment contract that protects her from being fired without cause. After the employee is fired, the employee brings suit alleging that the termination was in violation of both the contract and Title VII. In this situation, the "two claims would be the same for purposes of res judicata because, although they would not have identical elements, the central factual issue," whether the employee was fired for cause, would be "at the center of litigation of both claims."[27]

A subsequent appellate decision presents slightly variant facts that may fall between the categories sketched in *Hermann*. A federal employee filed suit alleging that his nonselection for promotion violated Title VII. The employee then filed a class action asserting that the employer had a policy of retaliating against employees who had filed discrimination complaints by denying their subsequent personnel grievances. The Eleventh Circuit upheld a district court decision that the class action was barred by res judicata because it involved the same parties and arose from the same nucleus of operative facts as the discrimination claim.[28] Here the events at issue in the two actions both concern conduct during the term of the plaintiff's employment, in contrast to the situation in *Hermann*. But the alleged retaliation occurred subsequent to the alleged discrimination, and the two claims concern somewhat different employer conduct. Is the retaliation claim barred because it would not have arisen "but for" the underlying claim of discrimination, a measure of claim identity expressly rejected by *Hermann*? A somewhat better rationale for the result is that plaintiff would probably have been allowed to amend his federal court complaint alleging unlawful discrimination to add a claim of unlawful retaliation without being required to initiate separate administrative proceedings on the latter claim.

Because administrative exhaustion in Title VII actions is not a jurisdictional element, but rather a condition precedent, a dismissal of one suit for failure to obtain an EEOC right-to-sue notice, for example, would bar a second suit arising from the same operative facts because the first suit would be decided "on the merits."[29]

Where any of the elements of claim preclusion is not met, or an exception to claim preclusion applies, the advocate for a party who

26. *Id.* at 226.

27. *Id.*

28. *Stephens v. Department of Health and Human Servs.*, 9 F.3d 121 (11th Cir. 1993), *cert. denied*, 512 U.S. 1236, 114 S.Ct. 2740, 129 L.Ed.2d 860 (1994).

29. *See Rivers v. Barberton Bd. of Educ.*, 143 F.3d 1029 (6th Cir.1998). *But see Criales v. American Airlines, Inc.*, 105 F.3d 93 (2d Cir.1997), *cert. denied*, 522 U.S. 906, 118 S.Ct. 264, 139 L.Ed.2d 190 (1997) (dismissal of Title VII action because EEOC charge untimely does not bar separate action based on timely charge).

prevailed in prior litigation of one or more issues embedded in that claim should consider asserting the separate defense of issue preclusion.[30]

b. Issue Preclusion

Issue preclusion prevents the relitigation not of entire claims but only of particular, actually litigated, issues that were identifiably and necessarily determined by a prior judgment. The general rule of issue preclusion is that "[w]hen an issue of fact or law is actually litigated and determined by a valid and final judgment,[31] and the determination is essential to[32] the judgment, the determination is conclusive in a subsequent action ... whether on the same or a different claim."[33] Therefore, in contrast to claim preclusion, an issue must have been actually litigated to enjoy preclusive effect in subsequent litigation.

The issue must have been the same,[34] although sometimes courts will reach that conclusion by inference.[35] Of course to find issue identity,

30. *See Staats v. County of Sawyer,* 220 F.3d 511, 517 (7th Cir.2000).

31. *See Kent v. Katz,* 312 F.3d 568 (2d Cir.2002) (arrestee not estopped from pursuing § 1983 probable cause claim by judge's mere inscription on criminal information finding probable cause for arrest, because the issue of probable cause to arrest was never litigated and judge's finding did not constitute the kind of final judgment necessary to trigger collateral estoppel).

32. *See, e.g., Sullivan v. Gagnier,* 225 F.3d 161 (2d Cir.2000) (resisting arrest conviction does not necessarily preclude excessive force claim by former criminal defendant, because review of pleadings, evidence and jury instructions in criminal trial may reveal that facts necessary to support excessive force claim were not litigated in or not essential to the resisting arrest conviction). *Gammage v. West Jasper Sch. Bd. of Educ.,* 179 F.3d 952 (5th Cir.1999) (precluding ADA claim based on state court finding that plaintiff had not notified employer of disabling condition, a finding essential to judgment approving her nonrenewal). *But cf. Zamarripa v. City of Mesa,* 125 F.3d 792 (9th Cir.1997) (Arizona trial court's pretrial finding that defendant's confession was voluntary was neither judgment nor essential to eventual acquittal, and, thus, could not have collateral estoppel effect in subsequent civil rights action alleging that his confession to crime had been coerced).

33. See § 27 Restatement (Second) of Judgments. It may be wondered why issue rather than claim preclusion would be invoked if the issue common to the two actions were re-presented in a claim that meets the Restatement § 24's broad concept of claim identity and hence is subject to claim preclusion. The reason is that some prerequisite of claim preclusion other than claim identity might be lacking. For example, the original judgment may not be "final" or, in the "bar" situation, a judgment may fall within a § 20 exception for procedurally-grounded judgments deemed "not on the merits."

34. *See Hinchman v. Moore,* 312 F.3d 198 (6th Cir.2002) (prior finding at preliminary hearing in criminal prosecution that evidence was sufficient to establish probable cause for arrest could not estop arrestee in § 1983 action that challenged the integrity of that evidence by asserting defendant police officers who caused her to be arrested had lied to establish probable cause); *Phelps v. Hamilton,* 122 F.3d 1309 (10th Cir.1997) (prior state trial court ruling finding some prosecutions of protestors were brought in bad faith did not have collateral estoppel effect regarding whether subsequent prosecutions were brought in bad faith). *Cf. Zukowski v. St. Lukes Home Care Program,* 326 F.3d 278 (1st Cir.2003) (prior state court judgment finding employee's dismissal unjust had no preclusive effect because it did not decide issue material to employee's subsequent Title VII action, that is whether employer's stated reason for discharge was a pretext of national origin discrimination).

35. *Compare Bechtold v. City of Rosemount,* 104 F.3d 1062 (8th Cir.1997) (a finding in prior state court action that plaintiff's termination was proper implies that it was nondiscriminatory so as to defeat subsequent action under Age Discrimination in Employment Act) *with McClendon v. Indiana Sugars, Inc.,* 108 F.3d 789 (7th Cir.1997) (Title VII plaintiff's attempted use of offensive issue preclusion fails in part because issue decided in his favor in state unemployment compensation proceed-

the court applying issue preclusion must be able to ascertain from the first order or judgment that the same issue[36] was actually determined and how it was determined. That is clearly more difficult, for example, in the case of a general verdict for plaintiff in a case presenting more than one claim, or a general verdict for defendant on any claim, than where the plaintiff prevails on a single claim. Moreover, the second court must be able to ascertain that the common issue was determined favorably to the party invoking preclusion.[37] And any error in refusing to apply the doctrine will be held harmless if the issue has little relevance to a material issue in the discrimination or civil rights action in which preclusion is asserted.[38]

The Second Restatement of Judgments contains a number of exceptions to the general rule of issue preclusion.[39] Most of these are necessary to temper the judicial development that permits issue preclusion, unlike claim preclusion, to be invoked "nonmutually," that is, by (but not against—Due Process forbids that) a nonparty to the prior proceeding.[40] The most important Restatement escape from § 1738 issue preclusion in actions under Title VII and the Reconstruction civil rights acts permits relitigation if

> [t]here is a clear and convincing need for a new determination of [an] issue . . . because the party sought to be precluded, as a result of the conduct of his adversary or other special circumstances, did not have an adequate opportunity or incentive to obtain a full and fair adjudication in the initial action.[41]

Thus, subject only to the restraints imposed by the Second Restatement's flexible exceptions, a defendant not party to a prior action may assert issue preclusion "defensively" against a plaintiff who was a party

ings did not necessarily show that employer's proffered reason for discharging him was a pretext for unlawful discrimination).

36. But not all courts are equally exacting in insisting on issue identity. *See Estes v. Joerling*, 318 F.3d 794 (8th Cir. 2003) (per curiam) (prior federal judgment, declaring insurance claim not covered because insured's own criminal acts caused fire and she misrepresented destruction in fire of certain personal property, precludes insured as civil rights plaintiff from showing that county and police officers framed her in violation of her constitutional rights).

37. *See, e.g. Sullivan v. Gagnier, supra*; *Johnson v. Watkins*, 101 F.3d 792 (2d Cir.1996) (§ 1983 false arrest and malicious imprisonment claim not precluded because arrestee had been *acquitted* of the charge for which he had been arrested) (applying New York law).

38. *Biggins v. Hazen Paper Co.*, 111 F.3d 205 (1st Cir.1997), *cert. denied*, 522 U.S. 952, 118 S.Ct. 373, 139 L.Ed.2d 290 (1997).

39. *See* Restatement (Second) of Judgments §§ 28, 29.

40. *See Bills v. Aseltine*, 52 F.3d 596, 604 (6th Cir.1995), *cert. denied*, 516 U.S. 865, 116 S.Ct. 179, 133 L.Ed.2d 118 (1995) (permitting § 1983 defendants to assert collateral estoppel nonmutually based on jury's finding, through ascertainable answers to special interrogatories, against plaintiff and in favor of co-defendant).

41. Restatement § 28; *see Kremer v. Chemical Constr. Corp.*, 456 U.S. 461, 480, 102 S.Ct. 1883, 1896, 72 L.Ed.2d 262 (1982). In addition, "[a] party precluded from relitigating an issue with an opposing party . . . is also precluded from doing so with another person unless the fact that he lacked full and fair opportunity to litigate the issue in the first action or other circumstances justify affording him an opportunity to relitigate the issue." Restatement § 29.

to that action[42] or in privity with such a party.[43] Further, a plaintiff not party to the prior proceedings may assert issue preclusion "offensively"[44] —although again, because of Due Process, only against a defendant who was a party, personally or through a privy, to the earlier litigation.

§ 5.119 State Court to Federal Court Preclusion; The Civil Rights Act of 1871

In *Allen v. McCurry*,[1] the United States Supreme Court held that actions under the Civil Rights Act of 1871 are not exempt from the mandate of § 1738, at least in regard to issue preclusion.[2] Civil rights plaintiffs have no special right to relitigate an issue in a federal forum as long as the state court was "acting within its proper jurisdiction [and] has given the parties a full and fair opportunity to litigate" the issue.[3]

42. *See Blonder–Tongue Laboratories v. University of Ill. Found.*, 402 U.S. 313, 91 S.Ct. 1434, 28 L.Ed.2d 788 (1971). In an unusual defensive preclusion context, the police officers convicted in federal court of violating Rodney King's civil rights after their state court acquittal on felony assault charges were unable to avail themselves of one of the standard exceptions to issue preclusion. The officers sued the City of Los Angeles to recover their costs in defending a subsequent civil suit King brought against them. The City was relieved of the obligation to pay for that defense because the court found that their convictions on federal criminal charges showed they had acted with actual malice in effecting King's arrest; and malice forfeited their entitlement to a City-paid defense. They were estopped from denying that they had acted with actual malice even though that finding, which the court deemed implicit in the federal criminal conviction, had been at least implicitly rejected by the prior state court verdict of acquittal. *Allen v. City of L.A.*, 92 F.3d 842 (9th Cir.1996). *But see Quinn v. Monroe County*, 330 F.3d 1320 (11th Cir.2003) (declining to expand the exceptions, in the context of defensive collateral estoppel from one civil action to another, to the Florida law requirement of mutuality of parties, and concluding that individual defendant administrator not named as respondent in prior administrative proceedings or as party in prior state court proceeding was not a prior party in any capacity and therefore could not invoke collateral estoppel).

43. *See Tyus v. Schoemehl*, 93 F.3d 449 (8th Cir.1996), *cert. denied sub nom. Miller v. Schoemehl*, 520 U.S. 1166, 117 S.Ct. 1427, 137 L.Ed.2d 536 (1997) (alderman challenging vote dilution allegedly violative of Voting Rights Act held issue precluded based on decision in prior action brought by voters challenging same district boundaries); *Shaw v. Hahn*, 56 F.3d 1128 (9th Cir.1995), *cert. denied*, 516 U.S. 964, 116 S.Ct. 418, 133 L.Ed.2d 336 (1995) (§ 1983 plaintiff attacking her peremptory, allegedly race-based exclusion from a civil jury in prior action held to have been in privity with plaintiffs in that action who unsuccessfully challenged her exclusion under *Batson v. Kentucky*, 476 U.S. 79, 106 S.Ct. 1712, 90 L.Ed.2d 69 (1986), on theory that she shared identity of interest with them as a matter of law; plaintiff accordingly bound by determination against prior plaintiffs on that issue). *But see Cunningham v. Gates*, 312 F.3d 1148 (9th Cir.2002) (decedent's family members asserting § 1983 excessive force claim not estopped by criminal conviction of decedent's robbery accomplice, with whom they were not in privity); *Gentile v. Bauder*, 718 So.2d 781 (Fla.1998) (plaintiff's effort offensively to estop defendant police officer in § 1983 action fails because officer not in privity with State of Florida, which had prosecuted plaintiff). *Unimex, Inc. v. United States Dep't of Hous. & Urban Dev.*, 594 F.2d 1060, 1061 n. 3 (5th Cir.1979) (per curiam) (suit against official sued in official capacity cannot have collateral estoppel effect in subsequent suit against him in his personal capacity).

44. *See Parklane Hosiery Co. v. Shore*, 439 U.S. 322, 99 S.Ct. 645, 58 L.Ed.2d 552 (1979).

§ 5.119

1. 449 U.S. 90, 101 S.Ct. 411, 66 L.Ed.2d 308 (1980).

2. *Id.* at 103, 101 S.Ct. at 419.

3. *Id.* at 103, 101 S.Ct. at 419.

The decision in *McCurry* stemmed from a state court adjudication of a Fourth Amendment search and seizure issue in the context of a suppression hearing and the subsequent attempt to relitigate the issue under § 1983 in federal court. In 1977, St. Louis, Missouri undercover police officers arrested McCurry and charged him with possession of heroin and assault with intent to kill. The undercover officers had gone to McCurry's home to attempt to purchase heroin from him. A gun battle ensued between McCurry and the undercover officers, and McCurry surrendered in front of his home. The officers then entered the home to conduct a "sweep" for other persons and also seized several items. At a pretrial suppression hearing McCurry contested the admission of the items, relying on the Fourth Amendment's prohibition of a search and seizure without a valid warrant. The judge excluded some of the seized items, but admitted the rest as falling within the "plain view" exception. Subsequently, McCurry was convicted on both the possession and assault counts.[4]

McCurry then filed a § 1983 action in federal court against the officers, the city of St. Louis and the police department, alleging a violation of his Fourth Amendment rights. The general requirements of issue preclusion appeared to be in place: the second action presented the same issue; that issue had been actually litigated, leading to a determination that was necessary to the criminal conviction; and preclusion was being asserted against a party who had enjoyed a full and fair opportunity in the prior proceeding to object to the constitutionality of the police conduct.

The district court granted the defendants' motion for summary judgment, holding that issue preclusion prevented McCurry from relitigating the Fourth Amendment issue in the federal courts. McCurry appealed. The court of appeals reversed and remanded.[5] It held that because *Stone v. Powell*[6] barred McCurry from seeking habeas corpus relief in federal court, issue preclusion should not prevent McCurry from litigating his constitutional claim in a federal forum under § 1983.[7] The court of appeals was careful to note that it was not creating a general

4. *Id.* at 92, 101 S.Ct. at 413.

5. *Id.* at 93, 101 S.Ct. at 414.

6. 428 U.S. 465, 96 S.Ct. 3037, 49 L.Ed.2d 1067 (1976). In *Stone* the Supreme Court held that when a state prisoner has been provided a full and fair opportunity to litigate a Fourth Amendment claim, federal habeas review is not available to attack collaterally the conviction as resting on evidence obtained through an unconstitutional search and seizure. *Id.* at 474. The Court has refused numerous times to extend the holding in *Stone* to other areas of federal habeas review. *See, e.g., Withrow v. Williams*, 507 U.S. 680, 113 S.Ct. 1745, 123 L.Ed.2d 407 (1993) (refusing to extend *Stone* to claims that conviction was based on statements obtained in violation of *Miranda*); *Kimmelman v. Morrison*, 477 U.S. 365, 106 S.Ct. 2574, 91 L.Ed.2d 305 (1986) (refusing to extend *Stone* to Sixth Amendment claim of ineffective assistance of counsel); *Rose v. Mitchell*, 443 U.S. 545, 99 S.Ct. 2993, 61 L.Ed.2d 739 (1979) (refusing to extend *Stone* to equal protection claim of racial discrimination in the selection of a grand jury foreman); *Jackson v. Virginia*, 443 U.S. 307, 99 S.Ct. 2781, 61 L.Ed.2d 560 (1979) (refusing to extend *Stone* to prevent federal habeas review of Fourteenth Amendment due process claim of insufficient evidence to support a state conviction).

7. *Allen*, 449 U.S. at 93, 101 S.Ct. at 414.

exemption for § 1983 actions from the preclusive effect under 28 U.S.C.A. § 1738 of issues previously litigated in a state court.[8] However, "invoking 'the special role of the federal courts in protecting civil rights,' the court concluded that the section 1983 suit was McCurry's only route to a federal forum for his ... [fourth amendment] claim and directed the trial court to allow him to proceed to trial unencumbered by [issue preclusion]."[9]

The Supreme Court granted certiorari and reversed.[10] The Court examined the text and legislative history of §§ 1738 and 1983 and found no intent on the part of Congress to deny preclusive effect to issues of fact or law decided by a state court, so long as that court has jurisdiction to entertain the civil rights claim and gives the parties a full and fair opportunity to litigate.[11] In the absence of any express or implied repeal of § 1738, the federal court must give the conviction as much preclusive effect as under the law of Missouri,[12] but no more.[13] The Court assured

8. *Id.*

9. *Id.*

10. *Id.* at 91, 105, 101 S.Ct. at 413, 420.

11. *Id.* at 103, 101 S.Ct. at 419. The majority opinion focuses on the ability of the state-court to provide "fair procedures" for the determination of the constitutional claims. *Id.* at 98, 103, 101 S.Ct. at 417, 419. The dissent rejects the idea that Congress "was [ ] concerned solely with procedural regularity." *Id.* at 108, 101 S.Ct. at 422. The dissent argues that "[t]he availability of a federal forum was not meant to turn on whether, in an individual case, the state procedures were adequate." *Id.* at 108–09, 101 S.Ct. at 422–23. Rather, Congress was concerned with the question as to whether "substantive justice" was obtainable in the state forum. *Id.* at 108, 101 S.Ct. at 422. On the several possible Congressional purposes underlying enactment of the Civil Rights Act of 1871, see the discussion of *Monroe v. Pape* in Chapter 2 on § 1983. *See Haberer v. Woodbury County*, 188 F.3d 957 (8th Cir. 1999) (§ 1983 plaintiff suffers issue preclusion on common issue of constructive discharge based on state court's affirming of state agency ruling against him on that issue, despite absence of discovery in state agency proceedings).

12. *Allen*, 449 U.S. at 105, 101 S.Ct. at 420.

13. *See Haring v. Prosise*, 462 U.S. 306, 103 S.Ct. 2368, 76 L.Ed.2d 595 (1983), in which the Court held that § 1738 does not preclude a § 1983 action contesting the legality of a search and seizure when the prior criminal conviction was by guilty plea. The Court reasoned that because state law would not preclude, for want of actual litigation of the issue in the criminal proceeding, there could be no preclusion under § 1738. *Id.* at 317, 103 S.Ct. at 2375. *Cf. Johnson v. Watkins*, 101 F.3d 792 (2d Cir.1996) (§ 1983 false arrest and malicious imprisonment claim not precluded because arrestee had been acquitted of the charge for which he had been arrested) (applying New York law). *But cf. Lowery v. Stovall*, 92 F.3d 219 (4th Cir.1996), *cert. denied*, 519 U.S. 1113, 117 S.Ct. 954, 136 L.Ed.2d 841 (1997) (admission made in guilty plea hearing precludes subsequent § 1983 action under doctrine of "judicial estoppel"). In addition, the Court in *Haring* rejected the petitioners' proposal that the Court fashion a federal common-law rule of preclusion to bar the § 1983 claim. 462 U.S. at 323, 103 S.Ct. at 2378. The Court stated that "[a]doption of petitioners' rule of preclusion would threaten important interests in preserving federal courts as an available forum for the vindication of constitutional rights." *Id.* at 322, 103 S.Ct. at 2377. *See also* Marjorie A. Silver, *In Lieu of Preclusion: Reconciling Administrative Decisionmaking and Federal Civil Rights Claims*, 65 Indiana L.J. 367, 381 n.77 (1990).

However, just three years later in *University of Tennessee v. Elliott*, 478 U.S. 788, 106 S.Ct. 3220, 92 L.Ed.2d 635 (1986), the Supreme Court did create a federal common-law rule of preclusion for state agency factfinding in actions under 1983. *See infra* § 5.121. *Elliott* concerned factfinding in state administrative proceedings; by its own terms, therefore, § 1738 was not applicable. Even though § 1738 did not apply, the Court made it clear that nothing in the text or legislative history of the Reconstruction Civil Rights Act suggested that Congress intended to prevent the further develop-

itself that issue preclusion would not be unfair because the collateral estoppel rules of the states, to which the Court held § 1738 demanded deference,[14] themselves contain a built-in exception that denies preclusion whenever the party opposing it has not received a full and fair opportunity to litigate the issue in question. That principle, incidentally, explains why police officers are not collaterally estopped by a finding in a prior criminal prosecution of the Section 1983 plaintiff that the search of his house was illegal: the police officers, nonparties to the state's prosecution, will ordinarily not have been in privity with the state because they neither control such prosecutions nor are their own interests represented by the state.[15]

The burden is on the party asserting preclusion to show that the issue as to which estoppel is claimed was actually adjudicated in a prior proceeding. Accordingly, if there is doubt whether the prior judgment was broad enough to embrace a finding on the issue subsequently presented, estoppel will be denied. It follows that where the prior judgment is based on a general verdict, estoppel will be granted only if rational jurors must have determined the common issue a discernible way.[16]

These principles were applied in an appellate decision involving an action by a criminal suspect against the police officer who released against him a police dog named Volker, as well as the officer's superiors and the city of Los Angeles. A jury had awarded Chew, the plaintiff (not the dog), $13,000 against Officer Bunch, and a threshold question was whether that verdict represented only compensation for the kicks that Officer Bunch administered to Chew, or also, even in part, for Volker's bites. In the latter event Chew, as well as the remaining defendants,

ment of preclusion law. The Court fashioned a federal common-law rule of issue preclusion for state agency factfinding in actions under the Reconstruction Civil Rights Acts. 478 U.S. at 798, 106 S.Ct. at 3226.

The *Elliott* approval of administrative preclusion of § 1983 claims appears to ignore or discount the value enunciated in *Haring* of maintaining an available federal forum for the vindication of federal constitutional rights. A distinction, however, may lie in the involuntary nature of the state proceedings in *Haring*—a criminal prosecution-and the voluntary nature of the state proceedings in *Elliott*—in which the plaintiff submitted his discrimination claims to a state administrative agency although not required to do so by § 1983. This is one of the distinctions the Court has recognized, both before and after *Elliott*, between statutory employment discrimination claims-which a plaintiff is first required to submit to the appropriate state administrative agency-and Reconstruction Act claims, which have no such prerequisite. See *Elliott* (holding that unreviewed administrative proceedings do not preclude Title VII claims) and *Astoria Fed. Sav. & Loan Ass'n v. Solimino*, 501 U.S. 104, 112–14, 111 S.Ct. 2166, 2172–73, 115 L.Ed.2d 96 (1991) (same holding re ADEA claims).

14. Federal courts weighing whether to give preclusive effect to a state court judgment must apply that state's law of collateral estoppel. *Wood v. Kesler*, 323 F.3d 872, 879–880 (11th Cir.2003); *cf. Travers v. Jones*, 323 F.3d 1294 (11th Cir.2003) (applying state law of collateral estoppel in case where issue had been litigated in local administrative hearing).

15. *See McCoy v. Hernandez*, 203 F.3d 371 (5th Cir.2000) (finding that officers not in privity because they did not participate in questioning witnesses in the criminal trial, or influence trial strategy, or have a right to appeal).

16. *Chew v. Gates*, 27 F.3d 1432, 1438 (9th Cir.1994), *cert. denied*, 513 U.S. 1148, 115 S.Ct. 1097, 130 L.Ed.2d 1065 (1995).

would be collaterally estopped from relitigating the issue of dog bite damages. Then, because the $13,000 judgment had been paid in full, the "one-satisfaction" rule would preclude Chew from pursuing additional damages for dog-bite injuries from the remaining defendants. Because the court could not ascertain from a general plaintiff's verdict that the prior damages were awarded solely with respect to Volker's bites, and because the burden on that issue was on the remaining defendants who asserted collateral estoppel, the court presumed that the verdict compensated Chew for Bunch's kicks alone. On such facts the plaintiff's name, Chew, now seemed peculiarly appropriate: he got a second bite at the remaining defendants. Even more remarkable—and this is a bit much to chew—the court went on to hold that Chew could seek to hold those defendants liable for the very same bites with respect to which it presumed the first jury had absolved Officer Bunch.[17]

Four years later the Supreme Court in *Migra v. Warren City Sch. Dist.*[18] expanded *McCurry* by permitting preclusion under § 1738 of entire civil rights claims. On April 17, 1979, the Warren City School District Board of Education offered Dr. Ethel Migra a renewal of employment for the 1979–80 school year. Dr. Migra accepted this renewal by letter to the Board. Subsequently, the Board voted to withdraw Dr. Migra's renewal and terminated her employment. Dr. Migra brought suit in state court against the Board and its members for breach of contract and wrongful interference by the Board members with her contract of employment. The court ruled in her favor on the issue of the contract breach and thereafter she moved for voluntary dismissal of the wrongful interference claim.

Dr. Migra then filed an action in federal court under 42 U.S.C.A. §§ 1983 and 1985 against the Board, its individual members and the superintendent of schools. The defendants moved for summary judgment on the basis that the prior state-court judgment precluded the litigation of these claims. The ordinary prerequisites of claim preclusion appeared satisfied: the federal law claims, although on different legal theories, arose from the same employment termination that gave rise to the state cause of action, and as such they met Restatement § 24's expansive definition of claim identity; the same parties were aligned in the federal action in the same positions they occupied in the prior state proceedings; the prior judgment was final; and the state court could have exercised concurrent jurisdiction over the federal civil rights claims had Dr. Migra presented them. The district court granted the defendant's motion. The Court of Appeals for the Sixth Circuit affirmed and the Supreme Court granted certiorari.

In equitable terms, the argument for claim preclusion, as in *Migra*, may seem stronger than for the issue preclusion supported in *McCurry*

17. *Id.* at 1438–1439. How the supervisory defendants and the city might be liable for those bites, even when Officer Bunch was not, is related as part of a discussion on the distinct liability of supervisors that is contained in § 2.36, *supra* and of entities, in § 5.106, *supra*.

18. 465 U.S. 75, 104 S.Ct. 892, 79 L.Ed.2d 56 (1984).

because the plaintiff who is claim precluded chose the state forum willingly when she might first have proceeded to federal court.[19] In federalism terms, however, there is a stronger argument for issue preclusion: federal judicial relitigation of issues adjudicated by the state court may affront the state judiciary, while permitting federal court adjudication of a federal claim not previously asserted in state court can cause no offense and may even promote comity by encouraging state law claims to be heard in state court.[20]

The Court glossed over these competing concerns, writing woodenly that the policies underpinning § 1983 do not "justify a distinction between the issue preclusive and claim preclusive effects of state-court judgments."[21] "Having rejected in [*McCurry*] the view that state-court judgments have no issue preclusive effect in § 1983 suits," the Court also rejected "the view that § 1983 prevents the judgment in [Migra's] state-court proceeding from creating a claim preclusion bar."[22] Under the standard approach to claim preclusion, this holding should mean not only that the claim of a state court plaintiff is "merged" into her judgment when she wins in state court,[23] but that when she loses there on the "merits" of her claim[24] any subsequent federal civil rights action will be "barred" when it concerns the same transactionally defined claim. Putting *McCurry* and *Migra* together, then, § 1738 has been held to mandate that in actions under the Reconstruction civil rights acts a state judgment be given the same issue and claim preclusive effect in federal court as it would have in its own courts.

Migra compounds the consequences of Supreme Court decisions that in effect compel a Reconstruction Act plaintiff to resort first to state court. We have already seen that potential § 1983 plaintiffs initially sued or shunted into a state court proceeding—either because they were

19. See Blackmun, J., dissenting in *McCurry*, 449 U.S. at 105, 101 S.Ct. at 420.

20. Shapiro, *The Application of State Claim Preclusion Rules in a Federal Civil Rights Action*, 10 Ohio N.U.L.Rev. 223 (1983). Despite this argument, the local federal appellate court continues to respect Ohio's claim preclusion principles, holding § 1983 claims foreclosed to the full extent of all relief that could have been obtained in earlier filed, transactionally related actions in the Ohio courts. *Thomson v. Harmony*, 65 F.3d 1314 (6th Cir.1995) *cert. denied*, 517 U.S. 1105, 116 S.Ct. 1321, 134 L.Ed.2d 473 (1996) (where prior action filed in Ohio Court of Claims, which could award legal but not equitable relief, § 1983 claim precluded with respect to damages, with only equitable claims for prospective relief preserved).

21. *Migra*, 465 U.S. at 83, 104 S.Ct. at 897.

22. *Id.* at 84, 104 S.Ct. at 897.

23. *See, e.g., Hutcherson v. Lauderdale County, TN*, 326 F.3d 747 (6th Cir.2003) (landowner and corporation that had prevailed in state court action where they did not but could have sought money damages were claim precluded by § 1738, applying Tennessee law, from bring § 1983 damages action for constitutional violations arising from same facts); *Wilhelm v. County of Milwaukee*, 325 F.3d 843 (7th Cir.2003) (county employee's § 1983 claims barred by prior action in Wisconsin state court, also arising from the interruption of his employment by county, in which he had sought interest on back pay and could have joined his § 1983 claims). *But cf. id.*, plaintiff's § 1983 claims not precluded by another of his prior Wisconsin state court actions in which he sought certiorari review of county's decision terminating him, because under Wisconsin preclusion law he was not required to assert his civil rights claims in that proceeding.

24. See discussion of the dimensions of merger and bar in § 5.118, *supra*.

criminally prosecuted, as in *Allen v. McCurry*, or because of *Younger* nonintervention or *Pullman* abstention—may later find their day in federal court clouded by issue preclusion under the Full Faith and Credit Statute according to the rules of the state court that rendered the prior judgment. A similar fate awaits civil rights plaintiffs who have initiated or defended quasi-judicial administrative proceedings; they will be bound by agency factual determinations according to the federal common law of issue preclusion the Supreme Court announced in *University of Tennessee v. Elliott*.[25]

Another possibility for issue preclusion is provided by the Court's decisions holding legally insufficient any § 1983 claims by a convicted criminal that, if successful, would lead to his immediate or speedier release[26] or, more broadly, would simply impugn the validity of his criminal conviction.[27] In *Heck v. Humphrey*[28] the Court elaborated that, in order to respect the integrity of state judicial proceedings, such § 1983 claims, even if they are only for damages, are not cognizable unless and until the state conviction is overturned on direct appeal or invalidated by the habeas corpus decision of a state or federal court. Will the decision overturning the conviction have issue preclusive effect in the plaintiff's favor when she is free of the *Heck* bar and can sue under § 1983, by analogy to the issue preclusion that, pursuant to the Court's decision in *Allen v. McCurry*,[29] works against her after a conviction?

Heck's criminal conviction was affirmed by the state appellate court on direct appeal while his appeal to the Seventh Circuit of the district court's dismissal of his § 1983 action was pending. (In addition, *Heck*'s two federal habeas petitions had failed.) The Supreme Court disclaimed that it was taking a position on the application to this situation of "res judicata"—in context, a broad use of the term intended to include collateral estoppel or issue preclusion.[30] Nevertheless, citing *Migra v. Warren City Sch. Dist. Bd. of Educ.*[31] (which went beyond *McCurry* to subject § 1983 actions to claim as well as issue preclusion), it wrote in *Heck* that the "res judicata effect of state-court decisions in § 1983 actions is a matter of state law." In this way the Court alludes to its conclusion in both *Migra* and *McCurry* that the only possible impedi-

25. 478 U.S. 788, 106 S.Ct. 3220, 92 L.Ed.2d 635 (1986). *See Travers v. Jones*, 323 F.3d 1294 (11th Cir.2003) (firefighter precluded from relitigating in § 1983 action certain factual issues relevant to whether his chief had disciplined him in retaliation for his union activity in violation of his First Amendment rights, based on findings at administrative hearing in which plaintiff had full and fair opportunity to litigate those issues). One circuit describes as follows the circumstances under which it will consider issue preclusion based on a prior administrative proceeding: "when a state agency acts in a judicial capacity and resolves issues of fact properly before it which the parties have had an adequate opportunity to litigate, we give the agency's fact-finding the same preclusive effect to which it would be entitled in the state courts." *Quinn v. Monroe County*, 330 F.3d 1320 (11th Cir.2003).

26. *Preiser v. Rodriguez*, 411 U.S. 475, 93 S.Ct. 1827, 36 L.Ed.2d 439 (1973).

27. *Heck v. Humphrey*, 512 U.S. 477, 114 S.Ct. 2364, 129 L.Ed.2d 383 (1994).

28. *Id.*

29. 449 U.S. 90, 101 S.Ct. 411, 66 L.Ed.2d 308 (1980).

30. *See Heck*, 114 S.Ct. at 2368 n.2.

31. 465 U.S. 75, 104 S.Ct. 892, 79 L.Ed.2d 56 (1984).

ment to preclusion stemming from a prior criminal conviction and affirmance might be any state law limitations on the preclusive use of that judgment. This reading of *Heck* is fortified by the Court's reminder that because of its "concerns for finality and consistency," it "has generally declined to expand opportunities for collateral attack."[32]

Thus fact determinations made by a state appellate or habeas court (or, for that matter, a federal habeas court)[33] when it overturns a criminal conviction and hence gives life to the kind of § 1983 claim covered by *Heck*, presumptively cannot be relitigated in the action under § 1983. In theory, this could help rather than hinder the § 1983 plaintiff if the prior fact findings were favorable to him, as would often be true on our hypothesis that the judgment of conviction has been reversed. But in practice this kind of offensive issue preclusion will seldom work. Both issue and claim preclusion, it will be recalled, may be used only against a party to the prior proceeding or someone in privity with that party. The § 1983 plaintiff would therefore usually be able to issue preclude only the state or local government subdivision against which the criminal appeal or habeas proceeding was brought. If that was the state, there will be no preclusion because the Court has held that § 1983 claims do not lie against a state sued in its own name.[34] In any event, the § 1983 plaintiff whose conviction has been overturned will usually be suing a police officer or prosecutor rather than state, or for that matter local government. In short, there will usually be no § 1983 defendant, who was also party to the prior criminal proceeding, against whom or which the plaintiff may use issue preclusion.

32. *Heck*, 114 S.Ct. at 2371.

33. A federal court entertaining a § 1983 claim would not be compelled to respect federal habeas factfinding by virtue of the Full Faith and Credit Statute, 28 U.S.C.A. § 1738, which directs federal courts to respect state court judgments, but rather by virtue of a judge-made federal common law of preclusion. One can imagine thorny conflicts between efficiency and sovereignty if a federal habeas court resolves an issue contrary to the finding of the state criminal or appellate court and then the same issue is presented in litigation under § 1983. If, in the § 1983 action, the state court's resolution of the issue is binding under *Allen v. McCurry*, what was the purpose of federal habeas? If, on the other hand, it is not, we compound the affront to state judicial factfinding first created by the federal habeas court's contrary finding. *See* Comment, *The Collateral–Estoppel Effect to be Given State–Court Judgments in Federal § 1983 Damage Suits*, 128 U.Pa.L.Rev. 1471 (1980).

Perhaps the issue is solved by the standard preclusion law of the Restatement (2d) of Judgments that is used by many state civil courts and must then, under the terms of § 1738, be applied by a federal court hearing a § 1983 claim. Issue preclusion would usually be invoked in the civil rights action by a person who was not a party to the prior criminal proceeding. (The state will have initiated many criminal proceedings, and under the Court's decision in *Will v. Michigan Dep't of State Police*, 491 U.S. 58, 109 S.Ct. 2304, 105 L.Ed.2d 45 (1989), the state is not a "person" suable in its own name under § 1983.) When a nonparty invokes issue preclusion, § 29 of the Restatement declares it a circumstance justifying relitigation if the prior determination (e.g., federal habeas) is itself inconsistent with another determination of the same issue (e.g., the state criminal court's factfinding). Thus a federal court, in permitting relitigation rather than deferring to either the state *or* federal habeas court's determination of the fact, would be obedient to state preclusion law made applicable under § 1738.

34. *See Will v. Michigan Dep't of State Police*, 491 U.S. 58, 109 S.Ct. 2304, 105 L.Ed.2d 45 (1989), discussed in detail in Chapter 2.

Migra ups the ante past these forms of issue preclusion. It deprives the putative plaintiff of any day in court on a § 1983 claim if she earlier sued on the same transaction. It should also have the same preclusive effect on § 1983 plaintiffs who as state (or federal) court civil defendants in previous litigation failed to assert compulsory counterclaims.[35] So when decisions of the Court direct a plaintiff to present "first" to the state court a claim growing out of the same transaction that gives rise to a claim under § 1983, "first" may as a practical matter become "final."

An example is furnished by *Pennhurst II, supra* § 5.35, which construed the Eleventh Amendment to forbid federal courts from entertaining *state* law claims asserted against a state. Suppose the plaintiff, as in *Pennhurst* itself, also wishes to assert federal civil rights claims stemming from the same events. *Migra* would presumably prevent her from filing an action in federal (or state) court on those claims after the state law claim goes to judgment in state court, where *Pennhurst* requires the state claim to be brought. To preserve a federal forum for the federal civil rights claims, the plaintiff must file there first, either foregoing the state law claim or asserting it in a separate action in state court.[36]

§ 5.120 Title VII

In *Kremer v. Chemical Construction Corp.*,[1] the Supreme Court held that Title VII, like § 1983, contains no express or implied exemption from the mandate of § 1738,[2] so that in Title VII actions federal courts are required to accord state court judgments full preclusive effect.

In 1975 Rubin Kremer lost his engineering job with Chemical Construction Corporation after being laid off. After several attempts to be rehired, Kremer filed a discrimination charge with the Equal Employment Opportunity Commission (EEOC) under Title VII. Pursuant to Title VII, the EEOC referred the charge to a state administrative agency for proceedings under the parallel state antidiscrimination laws. The state agency made a finding of no discrimination and this finding was upheld on administrative appeal. Kremer then sought review of the

35. § 22(2) of the Restatement (Second) of Judgments, which is the model for preclusion law in many states, places the defendant who fails to assert a "compulsory" counterclaim-one arising from the same transaction that underlies the plaintiff's claim-in the same position as the plaintiff who fails to assert an additional, related claim against the defendant. That is, after judgment in that action, the defendant will be precluded from asserting that claim in a new action.

36. It may be wondered why the plaintiff who follows this script, and files first in federal court but only on the federal law claim, would not encounter the claim preclusion problem in *state* court. Why, that is, should she not be precluded from bringing her state law claim there when, by hypothesis, it arises from the same transaction that gave rise to the federal civil rights claims previously asserted in federal court? The reason is that, because of *Pennhurst*'s view of the Eleventh Amendment, she *could* not have asserted the state law claim in a prior, federal court action, and § 26(1)(c) of the Second Restatement excepts from the ban of res judicata claims that the first forum could not have entertained for lack of jurisdiction.

§ 5.120

1. 456 U.S. 461, 102 S.Ct. 1883, 72 L.Ed.2d 262 (1982).

2. *Id.* at 476, 102 S.Ct. at 1895.

administrative decision to the state's intermediate appellate court, which affirmed.[3] Thereafter, a District Director of the EEOC made the determination that "there was no reasonable cause to believe that the charge of discrimination was true and issued a right-to-sue notice."[4] Kremer nevertheless instituted a Title VII action in federal district court. The defendants moved to have the claim dismissed on the ground that the state-court decision precluded relitigation in federal court, and the district court ultimately dismissed Kremer's complaint. The court of appeals affirmed and the Supreme Court granted certiorari.

As in *McCurry* and *Migra*, the Court in *Kremer* framed the issue as "whether Congress intended Title VII to supersede the principles of comity and repose embodied in section 1738."[5] The Court noted that although Title VII requires the EEOC to give "substantial weight" to state proceedings, including presumably state judicial proceedings, that direction is simply a floor on the level of deference required, not a ceiling as suggested by the dissent.[6] Accordingly, the Court held that in actions under Title VII, as under the nineteenth century civil rights acts, § 1738 requires federal courts to give as much[7] preclusive effect to court

3. *Id.* at 463–64, 102 S.Ct. at 1888.

4. *Id.* at 465, 102 S.Ct. at 1889.

5. *Id.* at 462, 102 S.Ct. at 1887.

6. *Id.* at 470 n.8, 488, 102 S.Ct. at 1892 n.8, 1901. The *Kremer* majority distinguished federal court review of state court proceedings, the issue there, from federal court review of state administrative agency proceedings. (The *Kremer* dissent, by contrast, viewed the state appellate court's affirmance of the agency's finding as merely a continuation of the state agency proceedings. *Id.* at 490, 102 S.Ct. at 1902 (Blackmun, J., dissenting)). The majority thus laid the foundation for one of the holdings in *University of Tennessee v. Elliott*, 478 U.S. 788, 106 S.Ct. 3220, 92 L.Ed.2d 635 (1986), discussed below, asserting in dictum that "it is clear that [judicially] *unreviewed administrative* determinations by state *agencies* ... [*under Title VII*] should not preclude [federal court] review [of federal claims under statutes that mandate prior resort to state administrative agencies] even if such a decision were to be afforded preclusive effect in a State's own courts." *Kremer*, 456 U.S. at 470 n.7, 102 S.Ct. at 1891 n.7 (emphasis added). The Court would later expand that holding from *Elliott* to permit federal court actions under the Age Discrimination in Employment Act notwithstanding a contrary state administrative determination. *Astoria Fed. Sav. & Loan Ass'n v. Solimino*, 501 U.S. 104, 111 S.Ct. 2166, 115 L.Ed.2d 96 (1991).

Justice Stevens, also dissenting, redefined the issue as whether the state judicial review of the agency proceedings involves a substantive review of the claims presented at the agency level-in which case the judgment would be entitled to preclusive effect-or a more deferential "arbitrary and capricious" standard-in which case the judgment would have no preclusive effect. *Kremer*, 456 U.S. at 507, 102 S.Ct. at 1910 (Stevens, J., dissenting). Although the majority stated that "[t]here is no requirement that judicial review must proceed de novo if it is to be preclusive," it did seem to require that the state court's holding must at least "constitute a finding 'one way or the other' on the merits of petitioner's claim." *Id.* at 480 n.21, 102 S.Ct. at 1896 n.21.

In a footnote, the Court cited several cases indicating that the state-court review in *Kremer* was a review on the merits. *Id.* In *Bray v. New York Life Ins.*, 851 F.2d 60 (2d Cir.1988), the United States Court of Appeals for the Second Circuit held that a state court dismissal on statute of limitation grounds of an appeal from an administrative determination of no probable cause served to preclude a relitigation of those issues in federal court under Title VII and § 1981. *Id.* at 61. Citing *Kremer*, the court concluded that "[b]ecause New York treats a dismissal on statute of limitation grounds as a final judgment on the merits for res judicata purposes," the state court judgment served to preclude relitigation in federal court. *Id.* at 64.

7. *Kremer*, 456 U.S. at 476. If state law would not accord a prior state court judgment preclusive effect in other courts of that state, neither would § 1738 give the judgment preclusive effect in a subsequent

judgments as would other courts of that state.[8]

The Court observed that prior decisions, including *McCurry*, which insisted that the person to be precluded had received a "full and fair opportunity to litigate," did not define the extent of that requirement.[9] The Court in *Kremer* did, holding that "where we are bound by the statutory directive of section 1738, state proceedings need do no more than satisfy the minimum procedural requirements of the Fourteenth Amendment's Due Process Clause in order to qualify for the full faith and credit guaranteed by federal law."[10]

The *Kremer* majority opinion apparently limits its holding by emphasizing that "[n]o provision of Title VII requires claimants to pursue in state court an unfavorable state administrative action."[11] That is, an important undercurrent to the Court's opinion appears to be the idea that the petitioner/employee in *Kremer* was precluded only because he went beyond Title VII's mandated administrative agency exhaustion by pursuing the state law employment discrimination claim to the state appellate court. Nevertheless, some lower courts have downplayed the "voluntary" nature of the state-court review and have purported to give preclusive effect to state-court judgments even when it was the defen-

Title VII action in federal court. *See Pavon v. Swift Transp. Co.*, 192 F.3d 902 (9th Cir.1999) (under Oregon law, Title VII claim dependent upon proof of discriminatory intent not part of same "claim" as prior unpaid wage state court action that required only evidence of failure to pay off wage due, so no preclusion even though both claims arose from common events); *Dici v. Pennsylvania*, 91 F.3d 542 (3d Cir. 1996) (state court affirmance of workers compensation ruling on fact issues not issue preclusive in subsequent Title VII action because workers compensation and Title VII legal issues differed and a Pennsylvania state court would not give preclusive effect even to fact issues under those circumstances); *McNasby v. Crown Cork and Seal Co.*, 888 F.2d 270, 271 (3d Cir.1989), *cert. denied*, 494 U.S. 1066, 110 S.Ct. 1783, 108 L.Ed.2d 784 (1990) (denying preclusive effect in a Title VII action to a state court judgment because the judgment would not be entitled to preclusive effect in other courts of that state). *See* discussion of *Haring v. Prosise, supra* § 5.119.

8. *See Heyliger v. State Univ. and Cmty. Coll. Sys. of Tenn.*, 126 F.3d 849 (6th Cir.1997) (federal court Title VII action precluded by adverse state court judgment arising from same termination decision), *cert. denied*, 522 U.S. 1117, 118 S.Ct. 1054, 140 L.Ed.2d 117 (1998); *Bechtold v. City of Rosemount*, 104 F.3d 1062 (8th Cir.1997) (plaintiff's ADEA claim collaterally estopped by finding in his prior state court action that his termination was proper, implying it was also nondiscriminatory).

9. *Kremer*, 456 U.S. at 480–82, 102 S.Ct. at 1896–98.

10. *Id.* at 482, 102 S.Ct. at 1898. In *Clark v. Clark*, 984 F.2d 272 (8th Cir.1993), *cert. denied*, 510 U.S. 828, 114 S.Ct. 93, 126 L.Ed.2d 60 (1993), the United States Court of Appeals for the Eighth Circuit held that the due process requirement of *Kremer* does not require a state court specifically to address each contention raised by a litigant in order for that decision to have preclusive effect. *Id.* at 273. In *Clark* the plaintiff raised several constitutional contentions in her state-court action claiming title to real property. The state court ruled against the defendant, but failed to address any of the plaintiff's constitutional arguments in its opinion. Plaintiff then brought suit under § 1983 in district court seeking an injunction. The district court dismissed the suit and the plaintiff appealed. *Id.* The court of appeals affirmed, holding that due process does not require "any particular technique of opinion-writing [and that] [c]ourts frequently reject by implication arguments urged by parties." *Id.* Although the decision in *Kremer* dealt with actions under Title VII, the Supreme Court's discussion of what constitutes a "full and fair opportunity to litigate" merely expands on the same terminology earlier used in *McCurry*, an action under § 1983. *See supra* § 5.119.

11. *Kremer*, 456 U.S. at 469, 102 S.Ct. at 1891.

dant employer, not the employee, who appealed the administrative finding.[12]

In one such decision, the employee, as required by Title VII, filed a state law claim with the appropriate state administrative body, which found liability. The employer appealed to state court, which reversed. The state agency appealed that ruling and an appeals court reversed and reinstated the agency's determination of liability. At the same time, the employee filed an action in federal court alleging violations of Title VII, § 1983 and § 1981, seeking remedies beyond those available through the state agency. The Ninth Circuit approved a district court decision dismissing the action as precluded by the state court decisions.[13] The court acknowledged that the *Kremer* plaintiff's resort to state court was voluntary, but it also noted the Supreme Court's statement that "the finality of state court judgments should not 'depend on which side prevailed in a given case[ ].' "[14] The Ninth Circuit also found that the Supreme Court's 1985 decision in *Marrese v. American Acad. of Orthopaedic Surgeons* (holding that the preclusive effect of a state-court judgment is determined solely by reference to applicable state law principles)[15] dictated that regardless of whether the federal plaintiff's trip to state court was voluntary, § 1738 mandated that the state-court judgment be given the same preclusive effect it would enjoy in courts of the state.[16]

These lower court decisions seem to miss the Supreme Court's point. That *Kremer* was not concerned with which side prevailed in state court does not diminish the significance of its emphasis that the employee in *Kremer* chose the state judicial forum voluntarily, not by compulsion of federal law. There is something manifestly unfair, and hence seemingly contrary to Due Process[17] as well as the law of preclusion, about permitting the employer to deprive the employee of a federal judicial forum on a federal claim simply by seeking judicial review of a state administrative proceeding that federal law required the employee to initiate. The Supreme Court's apparent recognition of this unfairness, and the supremacy of federal law in such situations, is implicit in two post-*Kremer* decisions that declined to preclude plaintiffs' Title VII or ADEA claims as the result of administrative proceedings that federal law obliged them to exhaust.[18]

12. *See Zanders v. National R.R. Passenger Corp.*, 898 F.2d 1127 (6th Cir.1990); *Trujillo v. County of Santa Clara*, 775 F.2d 1359 (9th Cir.1985); *Hickman v. Electronic Keyboarding, Inc.*, 741 F.2d 230 (8th Cir. 1984); and *Gonsalves v. Alpine Country Club*, 727 F.2d 27 (1st Cir.1984).

13. *Trujillo*, 775 F.2d at 1359–63, 1369.

14. *Id.* at 1364 (quoting *Kremer*, 456 U.S. at 470, 102 S.Ct. at 1891 (footnote omitted)).

15. 470 U.S. 373, 105 S.Ct. 1327, 84 L.Ed.2d 274 (1985).

16. *Trujillo*, 775 F.2d at 1363.

17. *See Logan v. Zimmerman Brush Co.*, 455 U.S. 422, 102 S.Ct. 1148, 71 L.Ed.2d 265 (1982) (once state creates a claim and hence a contingent property right of the plaintiff, it may not adopt procedures that effectively ensure that the claim will fail).

18. *See University of Tennessee v. Elliott*, 478 U.S. 788, 106 S.Ct. 3220, 92 L.Ed.2d 635 (1986) (Title VII plaintiffs); *Astoria Fed. Sav. & Loan Ass'n v. Solimino*, 501 U.S. 104, 111 S.Ct. 2166, 115 L.Ed.2d

§ 5.121 Federal Common Law Preclusion: State Agency to Federal Court

As noted above,[1] the Court squarely held in *Patsy v. Board of Regents*[2] what it had stated many times in the preceding nineteen years: that a potential plaintiff (other than prisoners)[3] need not pursue administrative agency exhaustion as a precondition to bringing suit under § 1983.[4] In so holding the Court relied principally on the intention of the 1871 Congress that federal courts would play a paramount role in protecting federal rights and its suspicion of the ability or willingness of the "state authorities" to protect those rights or punish those who violated them. In effect it found these policies surrounding the enactment of § 1983 sufficiently weighty as to warrant an exception to the modern rule requiring exhaustion of administrative remedies before the institution of civil litigation.[5]

96 (1991) (ADEA plaintiffs). *Elliott is discussed in the text immediately following.*-

§ 5.121

1. *See* § 5.7, *supra*.

2. 457 U.S. 496, 102 S.Ct. 2557, 73 L.Ed.2d 172 (1982). The precedents the Court cited traced from *McNeese v. Board of Educ.*, 373 U.S. 668, 83 S.Ct. 1433, 10 L.Ed.2d 622 (1963).

3. The Prison Litigation Reform Act of 1996 ("PLRA"), which revised remedies for prison condition lawsuits, does require administrative exhaustion for prisoners. See 42 U.S.C.A. § 1997e ("No action shall be brought with respect to prison conditions under section 1983 of this title, or any other Federal law, by a prisoner confined in any jail, prison, or other correctional facility until such administrative remedies as are available are exhausted.") The PLRA imposes requirements to exhaust all possible administrative remedies before bringing actions "with respect to prison conditions." Thus a prisoner plaintiff must allege exhaustion of all administrative remedies and submit proof, such as document showing final disposition of grievance. The Supreme Court held in *Porter v. Nussle*, 534 U.S. 516, 122 S.Ct. 983, 152 L.Ed.2d 12 (2002), that the PLRA exhaustion requirement applies to all inmate suits about prison life, whether they involve general circumstances or particular episodes, and whether they allege excessive force or some other wrong. The term "prison conditions" thus applies to suit for excessive force by correction officers and exhaustion is required. The Supreme Court has also held that PLRA demands full administrative exhaustion even where an inmate (state or federal) seeks only monetary relief not available administratively, so long as the administrative process could provide any other sort of relief. *Booth v. Churner*, 532 U.S. 731, 121 S.Ct. 1819, 149 L.Ed.2d 958 (2001).

4. The Court took note of a statutory exception to this proposition, the requirement of the Civil Rights of Institutionalized Persons Act that adult inmates "in any jail, prison, or other correctional facility" must exhaust for ninety days any available administrative procedure that the U.S. Attorney General has certified as meeting minimum standards for the "plain, speedy, and effective" resolution of grievances. 42 U.S.C.A. § 1997(e). The Supreme Court had held the requirement inapplicable to a federal prisoner's claim for damages, *McCarthy v. Madigan*, 503 U.S. 140, 149, 112 S.Ct. 1081, 1088, 117 L.Ed.2d 291 (1992), but the subsequently enacted PLRA has held applicable to federal prisoners' *Bivens* claims. See § 2.48, *supra*. *Harris v. Hegmann*, 198 F.3d 153, 157 (5th Cir.1999) (§ 1997e, as amended by the Prison Litigation Reform Act, requires state prisoners to exhaust available administrative remedies before filing suit under Section 1983); *Knight v. Kenai Peninsula Borough Sch. Dist.*, 131 F.3d 807 (9th Cir.1997), *cert. denied sub nom Anchorage Educ. Ass'n v. Patterson*, 524 U.S. 904, 118 S.Ct. 2060, 141 L.Ed.2d 138 (1998) (only prisoner plaintiffs are required to exhaust administrative remedies under § 1983; nonunion school teachers were not required to exhaust union remedies to which they never agreed). Dismissal for failure to exhaust a certified grievance procedure as required by PLRA may be with prejudice, *see Pedraza v. Ryan*, 18 F.3d 288 (5th Cir.1990) or if the prisoner tried in good faith to exhaust, may not. *See Rocky v. Vittorie*, 813 F.2d 734 (5th Cir.1987).

5. *Patsy*, 457 U.S. at 518, 102 S.Ct. at 2568 (White, J., concurring) (citing *Myers v.*

Interestingly, the Court could have easily reached the opposite conclusion by adopting one of the rationales it had used two years earlier in *Allen v. McCurry* to support application of collateral estoppel via 28 U.S.C.A. § 1738. There the Court expressed its assurance that § 1983 litigants would not be unfairly estopped by fact findings made in prior state criminal prosecutions because one of the standard exceptions to collateral estoppel invalidates its use where the prior litigation of the issue common to the actions was not "full and fair." Similarly, exhaustion of administrative remedies has not been required where the plaintiff challenged the lawfulness of the administrative system, its practical efficacy, or the adequacy of the administrative remedy.[6] Putting *McCurry* and *Patsy* together, it might be said that § 1983's goals are not important enough to except it from ordinary rules of federal issue preclusion but are important enough to permit the plaintiff to escape the ordinary requirement of administrative exhaustion. It is unclear why the Court thinks unimpeded access to federal court is essential in the latter setting but not the former.

In *University of Tennessee v. Elliott*,[7] the Supreme Court reached divergent conclusions about the preclusive effect of unreviewed state agency factfinding on federal court actions under, respectively, Title VII and the Reconstruction civil rights acts. The Court held that state agency factfinding not judicially reviewed has no preclusive effect on Title VII claims.[8] By contrast, the Court did fashion a federal common-law rule of issue preclusion for state agency factfinding in actions under the Reconstruction civil rights statutes.[9]

In 1981 the University of Tennessee informed Elliott that he was being discharged for poor work performance. He requested an administrative hearing to determine the validity of the discharge but also filed a federal action under Title VII and § 1983alleging that the discharge was racially motivated. The administrative law judge found no racial motivation behind the discharge,[10] and Elliott did not appeal this result to state court. The university moved the federal court for summary judgment on the basis that the state administrative agency factfinding precluded any further action on the Title VII or § 1983 claims.[11]

The Supreme Court, reinstating a summary judgment granted by the trial judge, first noted that § 1738 was inapplicable. Section 1738 does not cover state administrative factfinding; by its own terms it

Bethlehem Shipbuilding Corp., 303 U.S. 41, 58 S.Ct. 459, 82 L.Ed. 638 (1938)).

6. *See Patsy v. Florida Int'l Univ.*, 634 F.2d 900 (5th Cir.1981) (en banc), *reversed*, 457 U.S. 496, 102 S.Ct. 2557, 73 L.Ed.2d 172 (1982).

7. 478 U.S. 788, 106 S.Ct. 3220, 92 L.Ed.2d 635 (1986).

8. *Id.* at 796, 106 S.Ct. at 3225. This holding was extended to federal court litigation under the Age Discrimination in Employment Act in *Astoria Fed. Sav. & Loan Ass'n v. Solimino*, 501 U.S. 104, 111 S.Ct. 2166, 115 L.Ed.2d 96 (1991).

9. *Elliott*, 478 U.S. at 798, 106 S.Ct. at 3226.

10. However, the administrative law judge did feel that the discharge was too harsh a response to the petitioner's poor work performance and ordered that the petitioner merely be transferred to another position with the university. *Id.* at 791, 106 S.Ct. at 3222.

11. *Id.* at 792–94, 106 S.Ct. at 3222.

requires prior state "judicial proceedings" like those in *McCurry, Migra*, and *Kremer*.[12] Yet federal courts have frequently devised federal common-law rules of preclusion.[13] The Court accordingly defined the issues as whether it should fashion a common law rule of preclusion "first with respect to respondent's Title VII claim, and next with respect to his claims under the ... Reconstruction civil rights statutes."[14]

In regard to the Title VII claim, the Court referred to the directive in 42 U.S.C.A. § 2000e–5(b) that EEOC must accord state administrative factfinding "substantial weight."[15] The Court stated that "it would make little sense for Congress to write such a provision if state agency findings were entitled to preclusive effect in Title VII actions in federal court."[16] In addition, the Court cited *Chandler v. Roudebush* as supporting the view that state administrative findings are not entitled to preclusive effect in Title VII actions.[17] *Chandler* held "that a federal employee whose discrimination claim was rejected by her employing agency after an administrative hearing was entitled to a trial de novo in federal court on her Title VII claim."[18] The Court felt that it would be inconsistent with the decision in *Chandler* to deny Elliott a trial de novo on his Title VII claim. It therefore held that in actions under Title VII, unreviewed state administrative factfinding has no preclusive effect either under § 1738 or federal common law.[19]

12. *See supra* §§ 5.117, 5.119–120.

13. *Elliott*, 478 U.S. at 794, 106 S.Ct. at 3224.

14. *Id.* at 794, 106 S.Ct. at 3224.

15. *Id.* at 795, 106 S.Ct. at 3224. *See, e.g., Heyne v. Caruso*, 69 F.3d 1475 (9th Cir.1995) (overruling trial court's exclusion from evidence of a state antidiscrimination agency's finding of probable cause). *But see Beachy v. Boise Cascade Corp.*, 191 F.3d 1010, 1014 (9th Cir.1999), *cert. denied*, 529 U.S. 1021, 120 S.Ct. 1425, 146 L.Ed.2d 316 (2000) (state agency's determination of insufficient facts to continue investigating inadmissible in jury trial; in effect such a determination amounts to final ruling of no probable cause, and as such entails a much greater risk of unfair prejudice than a more tentative agency determination finding probable cause to believe violation occurred). Similarly, EEOC's own probable cause determination is usually admissible in a subsequent judicial action under Title VII, because its probative value outweighs its potential prejudicial effect, a determination within the discretion of the trial judge. *See* text *infra*. *But see Walker v. NationsBank*, 53 F.3d 1548 (11th Cir.1995) (noting that EEOC determinations are routinely admissible in bench trials, but only when the determinations are detailed and of high quality in jury trials).

The IDEA requires federal courts to give state administrative proceedings "due weight." *See Board of Educ. of Hendrick Hudson Central Sch. Dist., Westchester County v. Rowley*, 458 U.S. 176, 206, 102 S.Ct. 3034, 3051, 73 L.Ed.2d 690 (1982) ("the fact that § 1415(e) [of the IDEA] requires that the reviewing court 'receive the records of the [state] administrative proceedings' carries with it the implied requirement that due weight shall be given to these proceedings"). This does not mean however that a district court may adopt the state findings wholesale; the 525 U.S. 813, 119 S.Ct. 47, 142 L.Ed.2d 36 judge must conduct an independent examination of the evidence. *See Doe v. Metropolitan Nashville Pub. Sch.*, 133 F.3d 384 (6th Cir.1998), *cert. denied*, 525 U.S. 813, 119 S.Ct. 47, 142 L.Ed.2d 36 (1998).

16. *Elliott*, 478 U.S. at 795, 106 S.Ct. at 3225 (citing *Kremer v. Chemical Constr. Corp.*, 456 U.S. 461, 470, 102 S.Ct. 1883, 1891, 72 L.Ed.2d 262 (1982)).

17. *Id.* at 795, 106 S.Ct. at 3225 (citing 425 U.S. 840, 96 S.Ct. 1949, 48 L.Ed.2d 416 (1976)).

18. *Id.* at 795, 106 S.Ct. at 3225.

19. *Id.* at 796, 106 S.Ct. at 3225. *See also Bishop v. City of Birmingham Police Dep't.*, 361 F.3d 607 (11th Cir. 2004) (per curiam) and *Crapp v. City of Miami Beach*, 242 F.3d 1017, 1021 (11th Cir.2001) (court and city personnel board's respective findings of fact not entitled to any preclusive

The decision in *Elliott* concerned an attempt by an employer to use a favorable administrative finding to preclude a subsequent federal suit against that employer under Title VII. Several lower courts have refused to limit the *Elliott* Title VII holding, which concerned a defendant employer's attempt to invoke collateral estoppel, by giving preclusive effect when the Title VII *plaintiff* invokes the doctrine offensively.[20] The United States Court of Appeals for the Third Circuit, for example, has held that the *Elliott* condemnation of Title VII administrative preclusion by defendants also serves to prevent the offensive use of issue preclusion "in a Title VII action by an employee who has previously filed a successful [administrative] claim."[21] These courts have relied on *Elliott*'s broad language, which denied preclusive effect to unreviewed state administrative determinations unfavorable to defendants, without indicating specifically that the Court also recognized the normal Title VII policy of affording claimants unimpeded access to a judicial forum;[22] or they have noted that the employer bore a heavier burden of persuasion on the common issue in the earlier proceeding, so that estoppel would be unfair.[23] But at least one court has found otherwise, in part by finding

effect); *Rao v. County of Fairfax, Va.*, 108 F.3d 42, 45 (4th Cir.1997); *Roth v. Koppers Indus., Inc.*, 993 F.2d 1058, 1060–63 (3d Cir.1993); *McInnes v. California*, 943 F.2d 1088, 1093–94 (9th Cir.1991); *DeCintio v. Westchester County Med. Ctr.*, 821 F.2d 111, 114–15 (2d Cir.1987); *Duggan v. Board of Educ.*, 818 F.2d 1291, 1293–95 (7th Cir. 1987); *Abramson v. Council Bluffs Community School Dist.*, 808 F.2d 1307, 1308–09 (8th Cir.1987).

The *Elliott* holding has recently been applied notwithstanding an employer's argument that the particular agency that rendered the finding on the common issue was "an actual court" because it enjoyed quasi-adjudicatory powers. The Fourth Circuit held that the existence of such powers did not transform the agency into a court for preclusion purposes, noting that either party could have petitioned a court for enforcement of the agency's decisions. *Rao v. County of Fairfax, Va.*, 108 F.3d 42 (4th Cir.1997).

20. *See, e.g., Herron v. Tennessee Bd. of Regents*, 42 F.3d 1388 (6th Cir.1994), *cert. denied*, 515 U.S. 1102, 115 S.Ct. 2246, 132 L.Ed.2d 255 (1995); *Roth v. Koppers Indus., Inc.*, 993 F.2d 1058, 1062–63 (3d Cir.1993); *United States v. Board of Educ. of Piscataway*, 798 F.Supp. 1093, 1100 (D.N.J.1992); *Gallo v. John Powell Chevrolet, Inc.*, 765 F.Supp. 198, 207–08 (M.D.Pa. 1991); *Johnson v. Halls Merch., Inc.*, 1989 WL 23201, at *2 (W.D.Mo.1989); *Caras v. Family First Credit Union*, 688 F.Supp. 586, 589 (D.Utah 1988).

21. *Roth v. Koppers Indus., Inc.*, 993 F.2d 1058 (3d Cir.1993).

22. *See Roth*, 993 F.2d at 1062.

23. *See Herron v. Tennessee Board of Regents*, 42 F.3d 1388 (6th Cir.1994). Of course an employer in an administrative proceeding under state law may often bear the burden of demonstrating some sort of "cause" or "just cause" for termination or other adverse employment action. If plaintiff proceeds to court under Title VII, and produces only inferential, *McDonnell Douglas*-type evidence of race, gender, religious or national origin discrimination, then she, rather than the employer, would bear the burden of persuasion on the ultimate issue of unlawful discrimination; and the employer would bear only a production burden to raise the defense of a legitimate nondiscriminatory reason. In such a case it may therefore be unfair to permit the plaintiff, based on the prior administrative proceedings, to invoke issue preclusion against the employer on the issue of "cause" or other issues impliedly decided as a result. *McClendon v. Indiana Sugars, Inc.*, 108 F.3d 789 (7th Cir.1997) (offensive issue preclusion in Title VII action fails in part because plaintiff had lesser burden of proof in prior administrative proceedings). If, on the other hand, the plaintiff offers "direct" evidence of unlawful discrimination, the *defendant*, per Title VII § 703(m), must persuade that it would have taken the same employment action for a reason or reasons (e.g., "just cause") independent of the unlawful one. In such a case, at least, it is not shifting any burden of persuasion to preclude the employer from relitigating the issue of cause, on which it must carry the persuasion burden in both proceedings.

Elliott distinguishable because the plaintiff is more favorably situated in terms of Title VII policies.[24] Moreover, given the Court's other holding in *Elliott*, that Reconstruction Act plaintiffs, unlike Title VII plaintiffs, are vulnerable to defensive issue preclusion based on prior, optional administrative proceedings, § 1983 plaintiffs should be able to use preclusion offensively (subject to the exceptions in Restatement § 28) when they have prevailed in those proceedings.[25] Finally, it should be noted that a state (or federal) administrative agency's decision may, like that of an arbitrator,[26] be admissible in the employment discrimination lawsuit even if it is denied preclusive effect.[27]

24. *Driscoll v. Greene County Sch. Dist. and Phil Brock*, No. 94–71 (M.D.Ga. 1995) (precluding defendants from relitigating state administrative agency's quasijudicial, unreviewed findings concerning facts related to Title VII defenses, and adhering to that decision on reconsideration). One of the authors was co-counsel for plaintiff in *Driscoll*.

25. See text *infra*.

26. *Alexander v. Gardner–Denver Co.*, 415 U.S. 36, 94 S.Ct. 1011, 39 L.Ed.2d 147 (1974), discussed in § 6.6 above.

27. The clear majority of circuits hold that the admissibility of EEOC determinations in jury trials depends on Fed.R.Ev. 403 probative value/prejudice balancing and is within the discretion of the trial judge. That is to say, even when an EEOC letter of determination finding reasonable cause to believe that an employer unlawfully discriminated is not challenged as untrustworthy pursuant to Fed.R.Ev. 803(8)(C), and is thus presumptively probative and admissible hearsay, it may still be excluded under Fed.R.Ev. 403 if its probative value is substantially outweighed by that Rule's countervailing factors—needless presentation of cumulative evidence, danger of misleading the jury, risk of unfair prejudice or confusion, undue delay or waste of time. *Coleman v. Home Depot*, 306 F.3d 1333 (3d Cir.2002) (district court's exclusion of report because of high risk of unfair prejudice and confusion affirmed on the different grounds of undue delay and waste of time, especially in view of conclusions about systemic discrimination in EEOC letter evaluation claim of single charging party); *Amantea Cabrera v. Potter*, 279 F.3d 746 (9th Cir.2002) (no per se rule of admissibility); *Lathem v. Department of Children and Youth Servs.*, 172 F.3d 786 (11th Cir.1999) (no cause determination was properly excluded as too prejudicial); *Paolitto v. John Brown E. & C., Inc.*, 151 F.3d 60 (2d Cir.1998) (no per se rule of admissibility); *EEOC v. Ford Motor Co.*, 98 F.3d 1341 (6th Cir.1996) (no error in refusal to admit EEOC determinations in either bench or jury trials); *Hall v. Western Prod. Co.*, 988 F.2d 1050, 1057–58 (10th Cir. 1993); *Barfield v. Orange County*, 911 F.2d 644, 650–51 (11th Cir.1990), *cert. denied, Barfield v. Lamar*, 500 U.S. 954, 111 S.Ct. 2263, 114 L.Ed.2d 715 (1991); *Johnson v. Yellow Freight Sys., Inc.*, 734 F.2d 1304, 1309 (8th Cir.1984), *cert. denied*, 469 U.S. 1041, 105 S.Ct. 525, 83 L.Ed.2d 413 (1984); *McCluney v. Jos. Schlitz Brewing Co.*, 728 F.2d 924, 929–30 (7th Cir.1984); *United States v. MacDonald*, 688 F.2d 224, 229–30 (4th Cir.1982); *Walton v. Eaton Corp.*, 563 F.2d 66, 75 & n. 12 (3d Cir.1977) (en banc); *Cox v. Babcock & Wilcox Co.*, 471 F.2d 13, 15 (4th Cir.1972) (admissibility within discretion of district court). *But see EEOC v. Manville Sales Corp.*, 27 F.3d 1089, 1095 (5th Cir.1994), *cert. denied*, 513 U.S. 1190, 115 S.Ct. 1252, 131 L.Ed.2d 133 (1995); *Plummer v. Western Int'l. Hotels Co.*, 656 F.2d 502, 505 (9th Cir.1981) (appearing to adopt a per se rule that a plaintiff may introduce an EEOC probable cause determination in a Title VII lawsuit); *Gilchrist v. Jim Slemons Imports, Inc.*, 803 F.2d 1488, 1500 (9th Cir.1986) (same). *But see Beachy v. Boise Cascade Corp.*, 191 F.3d 1010, 1014 (9th Cir.1999), *cert. denied*, 529 U.S. 1021, 120 S.Ct. 1425, 146 L.Ed.2d 316 (2000) (state agency's determination of insufficient facts to continue investigating inadmissible in jury trial; in effect such a determination amounts to final ruling of no probable cause, and as such entails a much greater risk of unfair prejudice than a more tentative agency determination finding probable cause to believe violation occurred).

In bench trials, EEOC determinations are routinely admissible. *See Bell v. Birmingham Linen Serv.*, 715 F.2d 1552, 1554, n. 4 (11th Cir.1983), *cert. denied*, 467 U.S. 1204, 104 S.Ct. 2385, 81 L.Ed.2d 344 (184); *Garcia v. Gloor*, 618 F.2d 264, 272 (5th Cir.1980), *cert. denied*, 449 U.S. 1113, 101 S.Ct. 923, 66 L.Ed.2d 842 (1981); *Peters v. Jefferson Chemical Co.*, 516 F.2d 447, 450 (5th Cir.1975); *Smith v. Universal Servs., Inc.*, 454 F.2d 154, 157 (5th Cir.1972). In

The Court in *Elliott* next addressed the preclusive effect of state administrative findings on actions under the Reconstruction civil rights acts. Although the Court acknowledged that the decisions in *McCurry* and *Migra* were not controlling, it found them supportive of the view that Congress, in passing the Reconstruction acts, did not intend "to create an exception to general rules of preclusion."[28] Thus, although § 1738 was not applicable, the Court found nothing in the legislative history of the Reconstruction acts to suggest that Congress intended to foreclose the further development of federal common-law rules of preclusion.

The Court then recited a number of policy reasons for giving preclusive effect in Reconstruction Act cases to "the factfinding of administrative bodies acting in a judicial capacity": to further repose as well as facilitate "the parties' interest in avoiding the cost and vexation of repetitive litigation[,] the public's interest in conserving judicial resources ... and the value of federalism."[29] It held accordingly that in actions under the Reconstruction civil rights acts, "[w]hen an administrative agency is acting in a judicial capacity and resolves disputed issues of fact properly before it which the parties have had an adequate opportunity to litigate," the federal courts must give the findings of the state agency the same preclusive effect, if any, that the findings would have in that State's courts.[30] Most but not all federal appellate courts that have considered the question have limited the scope of *Elliott*'s administrative preclusion of Reconstruction Act claims to an agency's findings of fact; they have denied preclusion to an agency's conclusions of law.[31]

Walker v. NationsBank, 53 F.3d 1548 (11th Cir.1995), the court observed that EEOC administrative determination letters have been held routinely admissible in bench, but not in jury trials; those determinations, the court wrote, vary significantly in their degree of detail and quality, and have the potential to create unfair prejudice in the minds of jurors. In jury trials the Circuit's approach is a case-by-case evaluation of the reliability of the particular EEOC determination letter which is then factored in to the F.R.E. 403 balance of probative value versus prejudicial effect. *See Lee v. Executive Airlines, Inc.*, 31 F.Supp.2d 1355 (S.D.Fla.1998).

28. *Elliott*, 478 U.S. at 797, 106 S.Ct. at 3225. In fact, the Court states that the result in *McCurry* could probably have been reached even in the absence of § 1738. *Id.*

29. *Id.* at 797–98, 106 S.Ct. at 3225–26. *See, e.g., JSK v. Hendry County Sch. Bd.*, 941 F.2d 1563, 1568 (11th Cir.1991).

30. *Elliott*, 478 U.S. at 797–98, 106 S.Ct. at 3226–26 (quoting *Utah Constr. & Mining Co.*, 384 U.S. at 421–22, 86 S.Ct. at 1559–60). State courts apply similar issue preclusion principles with respect to determinations made in prior administrative proceedings. *See, e.g., Nummer v. Treasury Dep't*, 448 Mich. 534, 533 N.W.2d 250 (1995), *cert. denied*, 516 U.S. 964, 116 S.Ct. 418, 133 L.Ed.2d 335 (1995). At least one lower court has found the *Elliott* procedural prerequisites for preclusion unsatisfied. In *Yates v. Philip Morris, Inc.*, 690 F.Supp. 180, 184 (S.D.N.Y.1988), the court concluded that: (1) the state administrative proceedings did not afford the plaintiff an adequate opportunity to litigate the claim; and (2) in any event the state's own courts would refuse to give preclusive effect to the findings of the state administrative proceedings. *Id.* at 184. *See also Wehrli v. Orange County*, 175 F.3d 692 (9th Cir.1999), *cert. denied, 528 U.S. 1004, 120 S.Ct. 498, 145 L.Ed.2d 384 (1999) (no preclusive effect where no judicial review of state administrative decision was available under state law).*

31. *Edmundson v. Borough of Kennett Square*, 4 F.3d 186, 189 (3d Cir.1993); *Gjellum v. City of Birmingham*, 829 F.2d 1056, 1064–65 n. 21 (11th Cir.1987); *Peery v. Brakke*, 826 F.2d 740, 746 (8th Cir.1987).

Justices Stevens, Brennan and Blackmun dissented from the holding that administrative fact findings were entitled to preclusive effect in actions under the Reconstruction civil rights acts.[32] The dissenters were skeptical about the Court's assertion that giving preclusive effect to the findings would serve the policies of federalism and conservation of judicial resources. Justice Stevens noted that although *Elliott* may prevent federal court relitigation of issues under the Reconstruction civil rights acts, it permits the trial of a companion Title VII claim.[33] He predicted that this "schizophrenic approach" would generate inconsistent findings as between the state administrative agency and the federal court, with consequent damage to federal-state comity.[34]

In a sense it was the *Patsy* decision that made it possible for the Court in *Elliott* to apply judicially crafted preclusion to actions under § 1983. Had *Patsy* required exhaustion of administrative remedies, a vast number of putative plaintiffs would find their § 1983 claims halted in their tracks by virtue of *Elliott*-type preclusion. The contrary conclusion reached in *Patsy* means that the sting of *Elliott* is principally felt only by those claimants who for tactical reasons voluntarily pursue a quasi-judicial state administrative remedy despite the risks of preclusion. Only the § 1983 plaintiff unlucky enough to be embroiled in government-initiated administrative proceedings—like McCurry, a § 1983 plaintiff unlucky enough to have been criminally prosecuted—will suffer preclusion à la *Elliott*, involuntarily. The potential plaintiff, in other

Contra, Miller v. County of Santa Cruz, 39 F.3d 1030, 1032–33 (9th Cir.1994), *cert. denied*, 515 U.S. 1160, 115 S.Ct. 2613, 132 L.Ed.2d 856 (1995); *Eilrich v. Remas*, 839 F.2d 630, 634 n. 2 (9th Cir.1988), *cert. denied*, 488 U.S. 819, 109 S.Ct. 60, 102 L.Ed.2d 38 (1988). *Cf. Raju v. Rhodes*, 7 F.3d 1210 (5th Cir.1993), *cert. denied*, 511 U.S. 1032, 114 S.Ct. 1543, 128 L.Ed.2d 194 (1994) (according collateral estoppel effect to decision by grievance committee affirmed by state court). In according both collateral estoppel and res judicata effect to the decision of a county civil service commission in an action under § 1983, the Ninth Circuit stressed that the plaintiff had failed to pursue available state judicial review of the agency's decision. *Miller v. County of Santa Cruz*, 39 F.3d 1030 (9th Cir.1994). It has not been authoritatively decided if the availability of state judicial review is a precondition to preclusion based on prior state administrative proceedings. In *Elliott* the Supreme Court mentioned that the civil rights plaintiff had not pursued such an appeal but did not indicate whether the availability of appellate review would be essential to preclusion in another case.

32. *Elliott*, 478 U.S. at 799–802, 106 S.Ct. at 3226–28.

33. *Id.* at 800, 106 S.Ct. at 3227 (Stevens, J., concurring in part, dissenting in part).

34. *Id.* at 800 n.1, 106 S.Ct. at 3227 n.1 (quoting C. Wright, A. Miller, & E. Cooper, *Federal Practice and Procedure* 4471, p.169 (Supp. 1985)). As Justice Stevens predicted, subsequent to Elliott several cases arose in which plaintiffs brought actions in federal court under both Title VII and one or more of the Reconstruction Civil Rights Acts; the Reconstruction Act claims were precluded by prior administrative fact findings, while the Title VII claim proceeded to a trial de novo. *See Buckhalter v. Pepsi–Cola Gen. Bottlers, Inc.*, 820 F.2d 892 (7th Cir.1987) (1981 claim dismissed) and *DeCintio v. Westchester County Med. Ctr.*, 821 F.2d 111 (2d Cir.1987), *cert. denied*, 484 U.S. 965, 108 S.Ct. 455, 98 L.Ed.2d 395 (1987) (1983 and 1981 claims dismissed).

A distinct problem is presented by prior *judicial* litigation of a Reconstruction Act claim, which would ordinarily have claim preclusive effect on a Title VII claim. *See* § 5.130, *infra*. Plaintiffs do have ways, however, of avoiding that kind of preclusion. *See Herrmann v. Cencom Cable Assocs., Inc.*, 999 F.2d 223 (7th Cir.1993) (discussed in text § 5.73, *supra*).

words, may preclude himself out of a § 1983 remedy by initiating internal disciplinary proceedings first.[35]

Elliott permitted a defensive use of issue preclusion in a Reconstruction Act lawsuit—that is, the federal court defendant used state administrative findings of fact to prevent relitigation in federal court of an issue decided favorably to it by the agency. However, what happens if the state agency findings are adverse to the defendant? May the plaintiff use them offensively to prevent relitigation of the issue in a subsequent Reconstruction Act action? Apparently, there is no federal bar to the offensive use of administrative collateral estoppel in a Reconstruction Act action and the ultimate answer depends instead on the forum state's law. In *Frazier v. King*,[36] the federal court plaintiff attempted to use a state administrative finding offensively to prevent relitigation of the issue in federal court. A state agency had found that the plaintiff's employment had been terminated in violation of her right "to speak out."[37] Plaintiff then brought suit in federal court under § 1983 claiming that the defendant's actions violated her rights under the First and Fourteenth Amendments. The plaintiff contended that the state findings were entitled to preclusive effect on the First Amendment issue. The district court agreed and the defendants appealed.[38] The court of appeals reversed, ruling that the administrative agency findings did not prevent relitigation of the First Amendment issue. But it reached that conclusion, it said, only because the applicable *state* law did not happen to provide for the offensive use of collateral estoppel.[39] There would have been no reason for the court to reach that issue unless it assumed that preclusion was permitted under *federal* (common) law as adumbrated by *Elliott*. A circuit court stated, albeit in dicta, that if the EEOC prevailed against a defendant for injunctive relief, the federal court's finding of discrimination would have preclusive collateral estoppel effect if an individual employee-plaintiff pursued monetary damages in an arbitration proceeding.[40] And a federal district court has granted the plaintiff's motion in a civil rights and employment discrimination action to preclude the defendants from relitigating an administrative body's findings that rejected defendants' allegations that the plaintiff had performance deficiencies and accordingly recommended renewal of her contract.[41]

35. *Hunter v. City of Warner Robins*, 842 F.Supp. 1460 (M.D.Ga.1994) (precluding plaintiff based on prior administrative proceedings deemed quasi-judicial because of the presence of counsel, the opportunity to present evidence and cross-examine witnesses, and the tribunal's recitation of findings of fact and conclusions of law).

36. 873 F.2d 820 (5th Cir.1989), *cert. denied*, 493 U.S. 977, 110 S.Ct. 502, 107 L.Ed.2d 504 (1989).

37. *Id.* at 822.

38. *Id.*

39. *Id.* at 825. *See also, Ward v. Harte*, 794 F.Supp. 109 (S.D.N.Y.1992); *Gore v. R.H. Macy & Co.*, 1989 WL 65561 (S.D.N.Y. 1989); *Farley v. North Bergen Township Bd. of Educ.*, 705 F.Supp. 223 (D.N.J.1989).

40. *EEOC v. Kidder, Peabody & Co.*, 156 F.3d 298, 303 (2d Cir.1998).

41. *Driscoll v. Greene County Sch. Dist. and Phil Brock*, No. 94–71 (M.D.Ga. 1995). One of the authors was co-counsel for plaintiff in the *Driscoll* litigation. The motion papers respecting preclusion and the court's order are included among the forms in Lewis and Norman, *Litigating Civil Rights and Employment Discrimination Cases* (2d ed. West 1999).

A threshold issue in *Frazier* was whether the state agency finding had *claim* preclusive effect—that is, precluded the plaintiff from asserting in court claims not advanced before the state agency regardless of the outcome of those proceedings. The court of appeals first stated that the decision in *Elliott* did not answer whether state or federal preclusion law governed this question.[42] The court did suggest that federal preclusion law applies[43] but reserved judgment on the question because neither federal nor state law, under the facts in *Frazier*, would have precluded the federal claim. The Second Restatement creates an exception to § 24(1)'s broad definition of "claim" if "[t]he plaintiff was unable . . . to seek a certain remedy or form of relief in the first action because of the limitations on the subject matter jurisdiction of the courts."[44] In *Frazier*, the remedies available under § 1983 were not available through the agency proceedings. Thus because of a standard exception to preclusion under federal or state law, the plaintiff's federal claim could not be merged in the agency decision. Yet the court's discussion does appear to assume that in other circumstances a Reconstruction Act claim could be halted by merger based solely on prior administrative proceedings.[45] And given the Supreme Court's view in *Migra* and *McCurry* that issue and claim preclusion stand on the same footing in terms of their capacity to foreclose or limit the litigation of civil rights actions, in principle offensive preclusion based on prior administrative proceedings should also avail the plaintiff seeking to preclude a civil rights defendant on only one or more issues, rather than an entire claim.

Finally, even where there is some technical barrier to both claim and issue preclusion, the administrative claimant runs the risk of having her subsequent judicial action barred by the doctrine of "judicial estoppel" if, but only if, her employment discrimination or civil rights claim is predicated on an assertion—e.g., her ability to perform a job—that is undermined by a position taken in the administrative proceeding—e.g., that she was unable to work.[46]

§§ 5.122–5.124 [Reserved]

42. *Frazier*, 873 F.2d at 823.

43. *Id.* (citing *Gjellum v. City of Birmingham*, 829 F.2d 1056 (11th Cir.1987)).

44. Restatement (Second) of Judgments § 26(1)(c). Thus where a state habeas court lacked authority to award damages, a § 1983 claim that arose out of the same transaction and would therefore ordinarily have been claim precluded was held not barred by res judicata. The court observed, however, that fact findings reached by the habeas tribunal might have collateral estoppel effect in the judicial action under § 1983. *Burgos v. Hopkins*, 14 F.3d 787 (2d Cir.1994). Further, at least where it is arguable that the prior tribunal might exercise jurisdiction over the federal claim, the plaintiff must attempt to assert it there or face subsequent preclusion. *Davis v. City of Chicago*, 53 F.3d 801, 801–803 (7th Cir. 1995). *See also Waid v. Merrill Area Pub. Sch.*, 91 F.3d 857 (7th Cir.1996) and 130 F.3d 1268 (7th Cir.1997) (appeal after remand) (Title IX employment discrimination claim not precluded by prior state administrative proceeding where state administrative agency clearly had jurisdiction under state law only over employment discrimination claim, not Title IX claim, and state law claims could be pursued only in that agency; agency's finding that district discriminated against teacher in violation of state law did not, under doctrine of issue preclusion, prevent teacher from demonstrating that district's disciplinary and financial concerns over hiring teacher were pretextual). *But see* § 5.118, *supra*.

45. *See also Healy v. Town of Pembroke Park*, 831 F.2d 989 (11th Cir.1987).

46. *Compare Carrasca v. Pomeroy*, 313 F.3d 828 (3d Cir.2002) (Hispanic state park visitor alleging that park officials arrested

U. ARBITRATION

§ 5.125 In General

Two years prior to *Elliott*, in *McDonald v. City of West Branch*,[1] a § 1983 action, the Court had held that § 1738 does *not* provide for preclusion in Reconstruction Act actions based on prior arbitration awards. The Court noted "that Congress intended the statute ... at issue ... to be judicially enforceable and that arbitration could not provide an adequate substitute for judicial proceedings in adjudicating claims under [§ 1983]."[2] The vitality of *McDonald* is drawn in question by decisions holding that a wide variety of federal statutory rights may be authoritatively and finally determined by arbitration awards resulting from an individual's pre-dispute agreement to arbitrate.[3] In any event,

her but not non-Hispanic visitors for swimming after hours not judicially estopped by plea of guilty for swimming after hours, as plea did not undermine any aspect of her civil rights claim) *with Rissetto v. Plumbers and Steamfitters Local 343*, 94 F.3d 597 (9th Cir.1996) (estopping age discrimination plaintiff from asserting that she was performing her job adequately when she had filed a workers compensation claim based on inability to work). *See McNemar v. The Disney Store, Inc.*, 91 F.3d 610 (3d Cir. 1996), *cert. denied*, 519 U.S. 1115, 117 S.Ct. 958, 136 L.Ed.2d 845 (1997) (Americans With Disabilities Act claim barred by judicial estoppel based on plaintiff's representation to Social Security Administration and state agencies that he was totally disabled). The Supreme Court has since held that the possibility of judicial estoppel under the ADA must be assessed in each case by reference to the particular allegedly inconsistent prior representation, with the burden of persuasion on the defendant. *Cleveland v. Policy Mgmt. Sys. Corp.*, 526 U.S. 795, 119 S.Ct. 1597, 143 L.Ed.2d 966 (1999). *Compare Lane v. BFI Waste Systems of No. America*, 257 F.3d 766 (8th Cir.2001) (ADA plaintiff precluded by statement in applying for social security that he could not perform any substantial work); *Ahrens v. Perot Sys.*, 205 F.3d 831, 833–836 (5th Cir.), *cert. denied*, 531 U.S. 819, 121 S.Ct. 59, 148 L.Ed.2d 26 (2000) (position in ADA action that plaintiff was discharged by employer because discrimination inconsistent with position taken by plaintiff in, and relied on by federal court in remanding her prior action in which she alleged that her employer terminated her as the result of tortious interference by others with her employment contract) *with Parker v. Columbia Pictures Indus.*, 204 F.3d 326 (2d Cir.2000) (plaintiff's statement in seeking Social Security benefits that he was completely incapacitated merely an explanation for his termination rather than a description of his physical disabilities and thus not sufficiently inconsistent for estoppel with his statement in ADA action that he could work with reasonable accommodation). *Cf. Lowery v. Stovall*, 92 F.3d 219 (4th Cir.1996), *cert. denied*, 519 U.S. 1113, 117 S.Ct. 954, 136 L.Ed.2d 841 (1997) (invoking judicial estoppel based on admission made in guilty plea hearing to preclude subsequent § 1983).

§ 5.125

1. 466 U.S. 284, 104 S.Ct. 1799, 80 L.Ed.2d 302 (1984).

2. *Id.* at 289, 104 S.Ct. at 1802. The Court had expressed similar suspicion of the arbitration process a decade earlier in *Alexander v. Gardner–Denver Co.*, 415 U.S. 36, 94 S.Ct. 1011, 39 L.Ed.2d 147 (1974), a Title VII action. There the Court refused to give preclusive effect to arbitration awards entered pursuant to a collectively bargained agreement to arbitrate, but did allow lower courts to admit the awards as evidence and give them such weight as they deemed appropriate under the circumstances. *See also Barrentine v. Arkansas–Best Freight Sys.*, 450 U.S. 728, 101 S.Ct. 1437, 67 L.Ed.2d 641 (1981) (arbitration agreement does not preclude judicial action under the Fair Labor Standards Act).

3. *See, e.g., Mitsubishi Motors Corp. v. Soler Chrysler–Plymouth, Inc.*, 473 U.S. 614, 105 S.Ct. 3346, 87 L.Ed.2d 444 (1985) (action under the Sherman Act); *Shearson/American Express, Inc. v. McMahon*, 482 U.S. 220, 107 S.Ct. 2332, 96 L.Ed.2d 185 (1987) (action under the Securities Ex-

preclusion of a subsequent Reconstruction Act or contemporary federal employment discrimination claim is somewhat more likely where a state court has confirmed the arbitral award, at least if the judicial review proceedings are on the merits rather than merely procedural.[4]

A plaintiff who loses her Title VII claim in court may still have a chance of arbitrating those claims under a collective bargaining agreement. In *Weaver v. Florida Power & Light Co.*,[5] the district court had entered an injunction staying arbitration because the plaintiff had lost her gender and disability discrimination claim in federal court. The Eleventh Circuit vacated the injunction because the defendant had an adequate remedy at law—the employer could assert res judicata in the arbitration proceeding.

§§ 5.126–5.129 [Reserved]

V. INTER–ACTION AND INTRA–ACTION PRECLUSION

§ 5.130 In General

Ordinarily, a plaintiff will be required to assert all available Title VII and Reconstruction Act claims arising from the same real-life events in the same judicial action. State courts have subject matter jurisdiction concurrent with federal courts to entertain both Title VII and Reconstruction Act claims. Accordingly, the jurisdiction exception to claim preclusion[1] is inapplicable and a final, prior state court judgment on one of these federal statutory claims should preclude asserting any other such claim in a federal court, pursuant to the *Migra* interpretation of § 1738.[2] Similarly, a prior final *federal* court judgment on one of those

change Act of 1934 and the Racketeer Influenced and Corrupt Organization Act); *Rodriguez de Quijas v. Shearson/American Express, Inc.*, 490 U.S. 477, 109 S.Ct. 1917, 104 L.Ed.2d 526 (1989) (action under Securities Act of 1933 and the Securities and Exchange Act of 1934); *Gilmer v. Interstate/Johnson Lane Corp.*, 500 U.S. 20, 111 S.Ct. 1647, 114 L.Ed.2d 26 (1991) (action under Age Discrimination in Employment Act). In *Gilmer* the Court expressly repudiated the "mistrust of the arbitral process" reflected in its earlier decisions, even when arbitration is used to resolve claims arising from statutory rights.

4. *Compare Jaworowski v. New York City Transit Auth.*, 182 F.3d 900 (2d Cir.), *cert. denied*, 528 U.S. 1046, 120 S.Ct. 580, 145 L.Ed.2d 482 (1999) (§ 1983 constitutional challenges to arbitration award determining disciplinary charges against plaintiff precluded because award confirmed by state court); *Caldeira v. County of Kauai*, 866 F.2d 1175 (9th Cir.1989), *cert. denied*, 493 U.S. 817, 110 S.Ct. 69, 107 L.Ed.2d 36 (1989) *and Rider v. Pennsylvania*, 850 F.2d 982 (3d Cir.1988), *cert. denied*, 488 U.S. 993, 109 S.Ct. 556, 102 L.Ed.2d 582 (1988) (precluding, respectively, § 1983 and Title VII claims after state judicial review in which plaintiff had an opportunity to or did challenge the merits of the award) *with Kirk v. Board of Educ. of Bremen Cmty. High Sch.*, 811 F.2d 347 (7th Cir.1987); *Bottini v. Sadore Mgmt. Corp.*, 764 F.2d 116 (2d Cir.1985) *and Aleem v. General Felt Indus., Inc.*, 661 F.2d 135 (9th Cir.1981) (denying preclusion of federal civil rights claims, principally by reasoning that state judicial review of awards was not or under state law could not have been on the merits).

5. 172 F.3d 771 (11th Cir.1999).

§ 5.130

1. See § 5.121, *supra*, concerning Restatement § 26(1)(c).

2. See § 5.119, *supra*. For this reason it also would appear that claim as well as issue preclusion should be applied in Title

claims would usually preclude the subsequent prosecution of any other such claim in another federal action, per the federal common law of preclusion.

Nevertheless, there will be situations in which a subsequent action would not be claim precluded. For example, there may be no final judgment in the first action before the second action is commenced; the parties may have agreed that the plaintiff may split her claims; the second action may be adjudged to be based on a different "claim"; or, most obviously, the second action is brought by a different plaintiff against the same employer or civil rights defendant, thereby destroying identity of parties. In such cases the second action may proceed, although common issues will then be subject to *issue* preclusion.

Of course, as is always true when for some reason claim preclusion fails, the court in the second action must take care to invoke issue preclusion only to the degree that its distinct requirements and exceptions demand. A decision involving successive Title VII actions by different employees against the same employer makes the point. Two female employees commenced separate actions alleging discriminatory rejection for promotion to the same supervisory position in favor of a less qualified male. Coworker 1, whose action first proceeded to judgment, prevailed on bench determinations that (1) the employer's stated reason for preferring the male was a pretext for gender discrimination and (2) she, rather than the male or coworker 2, was best qualified for the lone supervisory position. In the second action, coworker 2, after establishing a prima face case which the employer rebutted by asserting the same ostensibly legitimate nondiscriminatory reason, asked the court to estop the defendant from denying that its rejection of her was pretextual. The employer objected, and asked the court to estop the plaintiff from denying that coworker 1 was best qualified and that only she, not coworker two, was eligible for a remedy.

The court of appeals ruled that the plaintiff could (offensively) estop the employer from denying pretext, but that the employer could not (defensively) estop the plaintiff from relitigating who among the three candidates for the position was best qualified.[3] On issue (1), pretext, the standard for prerequisites of collateral estoppel were in place: the party against whom estoppel was asserted, the employer, was a party to action 1; the pretext issue was identical; that issue was litigated and determined; and the determination of the pretext issue was essential to the judgment in favor of coworker 1. Further, no exception to issue preclusion pertained, because the employer had received a full and fair opportunity with ample incentive to defend the first action in a tribunal that afforded no lesser procedural advantages than the second.

VII actions under the court's decision in *Kremer*. Since state trial courts have concurrent jurisdiction to entertain Title VII claims as a matter of federal law, it is not unfair to preclude such a claim that could have been asserted in a prior state court proceeding.

3. *Meredith v. Beech Aircraft Corp.*, 18 F.3d 890 (10th Cir.1994).

By contrast, the court rejected the use of defensive issue preclusion by the employer on the issue of which of the candidates was best qualified. It is a fundamental requirement not only of issue (as well as claim) preclusion but also due process that only parties to the action in which the prior judgment was rendered, or their narrowly defined privies, can be precluded, because only they have had an opportunity to litigate. Coworker 2 was not a party to the action that first came to judgment. Nor was she represented in it, actually or virtually, by coworker 1, whose interests were indeed adverse in the sense that only one of the plaintiffs could be deemed entitled to the promotion.

Suppose a plaintiff first brings an equitable suit under Title VII, triable only to a court, then a legal, jury-triable action under § 1981 or § 1983, and that, for one of the reasons given above, claim preclusion does not bar or merge the claims.[4] If an adverse bench determination of an issue common to the two lawsuits could preclude relitigation of that issue in the subsequent action at law, a party could lose the right to jury determination of that issue when the legal claim is tried. In *Parklane Hosiery Co. v. Shore*,[5] a securities law case, the Supreme Court held that the ordinary rules of issue preclusion applied despite the consequent loss of the jury trial right. Presumably the same result obtains when the two actions presenting the common issue involve civil rights or employment discrimination claims.[6]

But sometimes legal and equitable claims are presented in the same action. By hypothesis there is no prior judgment, so *Parklane*-type preclusion does not apply. In this setting the Court does preserve the right to jury trial at the risk of inconsistent determinations of the common issue. In *Lytle v. Household Mfg., Inc.*,[7] the Court held that an adverse ruling on the common issue as part of a district judge's dismissal (ultimately reversed on appeal) of a Title VII claim could not preclude the jury from deciding the same issue differently in deliberating on the § 1981 claim. This holding was in accord with decisions that had condemned prior bench determinations of issues common to legal and equitable claims because the judicial ruling would, as law of the case,[8]

4. A claim under 42 U.S.C.A. § 1985 would *not* be allowed, for reasons wholly distinct from claim preclusion, if it arises from facts that would also support liability under Title VII. See Chapter 1 discussing *Great Am. Fed. Sav. & Loan Ass'n v. Novotny*, 442 U.S. 366, 99 S.Ct. 2345, 60 L.Ed.2d 957 (1979).

5. 439 U.S. 322, 99 S.Ct. 645, 58 L.Ed.2d 552 (1979).

6. In *Allen v. McCurry* and *Migra*, for example, civil rights claims were denied any special exemption from the ordinary workings of § 1738. *See supra* § 5.119.

7. 494 U.S. 545, 110 S.Ct. 1331, 108 L.Ed.2d 504 (1990).

8. The "law of the case" doctrine is a softer form of claim or issue preclusion within one civil action (and therefore not dependent on a prior final judgment) that rests on the premise that an issue once decided and not overturned by a subsequent appeal should, if presented a second time in the same case and court, be decided consistently with the first ruling. For the most part, the parties, having not challenged the ruling when able to do so on an initial appeal, are deemed to have waived the right to challenge that decision subsequently,

bar relitigation of the common issue and in turn effectively deprive a party of a Seventh Amendment or statutory right to jury trial.[9] And where a jury decides, for example, the amount of a back pay award, the judge in a subsequent bench trial is bound by the jury's determination.[10]

The problem of mixed legal and equitable claims should arise less often in the employment context because of the Civil Rights Act of 1991, which amended Title VII. The Act provides that Title VII claims of intentional discrimination, like claims under § 1981 or § 1983, are triable to a jury. The problem should persist, and *Lytle* and *Parklane* remain pertinent, primarily when the Title VII plaintiff challenges only a neutral practice (alleging its disproportionate adverse impact), a claim triable solely to the court even under the Civil Rights Act of 1991. That plaintiff would be well advised, if desirous of preserving jury trial on a related Reconstruction Act claim, to present both claims in the same action, so that *Lytle* would protect the right to jury trial. Alternatively, if separate actions are permissible despite the restrictions of claim preclusion, and are tactically desirable or necessary to fulfill procedural prerequisites or avoid limitations problems,[11] the plaintiff may still avoid the effect of *Parklane* by pressing for a judgment on the jury-triable Reconstruction Act claim before another court adversely determines the equitable Title VII claim.

§§ 5.131–5.134 [Reserved]

subject only to an intervening change in the law or a showing that the previous decision was clearly erroneous and manifestly unjust. *See Kimberlin v. Quinlan*, 199 F.3d 496, 500 (D.C.Cir.1999), *cert. denied*, 531 U.S. 871, 121 S.Ct. 172, 148 L.Ed.2d 118 (2000). While the question is not free from doubt, it has been held that the doctrine applies not just when an issue has been decided by an appellate court ruling at a previous stage of the case but also on remand to a district court where its previous ruling was not challenged, reviewed or decided on an initial appeal. *Id.* at 500. *Compare Crocker v. Piedmont Aviation, Inc.*, 49 F.3d 735 (D.C.Cir.1995), *cert. denied*, 516 U.S. 865, 116 S.Ct. 180, 133 L.Ed.2d 118 (1995) ("law of the case" not applicable where party failed to appeal appealable issue on first appeal or present it on remand to district court but raised it for first time on second appeal, so only possible bar to appellate court's consideration of issue on second appeal would be a species of equitable waiver).

In a bizarre First Circuit case, *Alberty-Velez v. Corporacion De Puerto Rico Para La Difusion Publica*, 242 F.3d 418 (1st Cir. 2001), the district court judge ignored the law of the case doctrine, and well after the plaintiff had ended her case in chief and on the fifth and last day of a jury trial under Title VII, granted a Rule 50 motion for judgment as a matter of law by the defendant on the issue of whether the plaintiff was an independent contractor, a question it had decided in the negative in a summary judgment motion months earlier. Plaintiff's motion for a new trial was denied; on appeal, the appellate court held that the district court, which had incorporated its earlier finding that the plaintiff was an employee and therefore covered by Title VII into the pretrial order, erred in allowing testimony on the issue of the plaintiff's employment status and ordered a new trial based on the prejudice that arose from unfair surprise.

9. *See Beacon Theatres, Inc. v. Westover*, 359 U.S. 500, 79 S.Ct. 948, 3 L.Ed.2d 988 (1959); *Curtis v. Loether*, 415 U.S. 189, 94 S.Ct. 1005, 39 L.Ed.2d 260 (1974).

10. *See, e.g., Troy v. Bay State Computer Group, Inc.*, 141 F.3d 378 (1st Cir.1998) (state law claim was triable to a jury, but Title VII claimant was limited to a bench trial for claim that accrued prior to the 1991 amendment).

11. See §§ 5.72–5.74, *supra*.

W. FORECLOSURE OF RECONSTRUCTION ACT CLAIMS BY RELEASE—DISMISSAL AGREEMENTS

§ 5.135 In General

In *Town of Newton v. Rumery,*[1] the Supreme Court held that an agreement by a criminal defendant to release a potential § 1983 claim in exchange for the dismissal of pending criminal charges will be enforced if (1) the agreement is voluntarily entered into by the defendant; (2) the prosecutor has an "independent, legitimate reason" to make the agreement, a reason "directly related to [ ] prosecutorial responsibilities"; and (3) enforcement of the agreement would not "adversely affect the relevant public interests."[2]

In 1983 Bernard Rumery was arrested by the Chief of Police of Newton, New Hampshire and charged with tampering with a witness in a pending sexual assault case. After being contacted by Rumery's attorney, the Deputy County Attorney agreed to dismiss the charges against Rumery if he would release any future claims against the town or its officials. Rumery's attorney drafted an agreement, which Rumery signed after discussing the matter with his attorney and waiting three days. Ten months later Rumery nevertheless brought a § 1983 action in district court against the town and its officials for violations of his constitutional rights. Upon defendants' motion and in reliance on the release-dismissal agreement, the district court dismissed. On appeal, the Court of Appeals for the First Circuit reversed and the Supreme Court granted certiorari.[3]

The Court rejected a per se rule invalidating all release-dismissal agreements as violative of public policy. The Court noted that the criminal justice system constantly requires a defendant to make difficult choices.[4] " 'Although a defendant may have a right, even of constitutional dimensions, to follow whichever course he chooses, the Constitution does not by that token always forbid requiring him to choose.' "[5] The Court rejected the per se rule because a defendant's desire to enter into a release-dismissal agreement may reflect a carefully considered decision that the "certain benefits of escaping criminal prosecution exceed the speculative benefits of prevailing in a civil action."[6]

The Court found that Rumery's "voluntary" decision to enter into the release-dismissal agreement reflected this rational balancing of interests.[7] Furthermore, the Court held that "in this case" the prosecution

§ 5.135

1. 480 U.S. 386, 107 S.Ct. 1187, 94 L.Ed.2d 405 (1987).

2. *Id.* at 398, 107 S.Ct. at 1195.

3. *Id.* at 389–91, 107 S.Ct. at 1190–91.

4. *Id.* at 393, 107 S.Ct. at 1192.

5. *Id.* at 393, 107 S.Ct. at 1192 (quoting *Crampton v. Ohio*, 408 U.S. 941, 92 S.Ct. 2873, 33 L.Ed.2d 765 (1972)). Although the Court recognized the possibility of coercion and involuntariness in entering into these agreements, it stated that these policy concerns were not enough to outweigh a voluntary release of the right to sue. *Id.* at 394, 107 S.Ct. at 1192.

6. *Id.* at 393, 107 S.Ct. at 1192.

7. *Id.* In particular, the Court noted that Rumery was a "sophisticated businessman," was not in jail at the time the agreement was entered into, "was represented by an experienced criminal lawyer," and had considered the agreement for three days before signing it. *Id.*

had "an independent, legitimate reason to make this agreement directly related to his prosecutorial responsibilities."[8] The only reason identified was the prosecutor's concern that the victim in the sexual assault case would be forced to testify in another criminal case, and perhaps a civil case as well. The Court concluded "that enforcement of this agreement would not adversely affect the relevant public interests."[9] Those interests were not specified, however; it appears that a valid prosecutorial reason for seeking the agreement also suffices to show that the agreement does not violate public policy. No affirmative showing of the public interests furthered by the agreement was required.

In a part of the opinion joined by only three other justices, Justice Powell acknowledged two potentially negative consequences of release-dismissal agreements: prosecutors may be tempted (1) to bring frivolous criminal charges—for example, to create a bidding chip to forestall a civil rights action against local government; or (2) to dismiss "meritorious charges ... to protect the interests of other officials." On the other hand, the plurality recognized that § 1983 actions further "the vindication of constitutional rights and the exposure of official misconduct."[10] Nevertheless, the plurality asserted that release-dismissal agreements relieve government of the cost of defending civil lawsuits and facilitate the wise allocation of resources.[11] These "legitimate prosecutorial and public interests" led five justices[12] to reject a per se ban on release-dismissal agreements.[13]

In *Woods v. Rhodes*,[14] the United States Court of Appeals for the Eighth Circuit applied *Rumery* in upholding a release-dismissal agreement. The agreement dismissed pending charges of driving while intoxicated in exchange for the release of any claims defendant might bring against the city or its officers. In 1987 plaintiff was arrested by the Sioux City, Iowa police department and charged with various offenses. In the course of her arrest, plaintiff received several bruises. After learning that the prosecution's key witness might be unavailable for trial, the County Attorney offered to dismiss the charges if plaintiff would release all civil claims she might have against the city. After considering the release-dismissal offer for approximately two months, plaintiff signed the agreement.

8. *Id.* at 398, 107 S.Ct. at 1195.

9. *Id.* at 398, 107 S.Ct. at 1195.

10. *Id.* at 395, 107 S.Ct. at 1193.

11. *Id.* at 395, 107 S.Ct. at 1193.

12. Justice O'Connor, who provided the fifth vote for Parts I, II, III–A, IV, and V of the Court's opinion, declined to join in Part III–B of Justice Powell's opinion. Part III–B primarily addressed the various public interests weighing in favor of and against release-dismissal agreements. *Id.* at 394, 107 S.Ct. at 1192. Justice O'Connor agreed that a per se ban on release-dismissal agreements was unnecessary. However, because it is the burden of the party seeking to uphold the agreement to prove its validity, she believed that courts should not presume that the agreement is in the public interest. Justice O'Connor feared that Part III–B of the opinion implied such a presumption. *Id.* at 401, 107 S.Ct. at 1196 (O'Connor, J., concurring in part and concurring in judgment).

13. *Id.* at 397, 107 S.Ct. at 1194. Although only a plurality of the Court joined Part III–B of Justice Powell's opinion, lower federal courts have adopted its examination of the relevant public interests as a part of the *Rumery* test for the validity of release-dismissal agreements. *See Woods v. Rhodes*, 994 F.2d 494 (8th Cir.1993).

14. 994 F.2d 494 (8th Cir.1993).

First, the court listed factors that led it to find that the civil rights plaintiff had voluntarily signed the release-dismissal agreement: "the sophistication of the signer[,] cost/benefit considerations by the signer[,] the circumstances of the signing, i.e., whether the signer is in custody at the time of the signing[,] whether the signer was represented by counsel[,] the time with which the signer considered the document[,] whether the signer's attorney drafted the document[,] whether the signer expressed any unwillingness, and whether the release is clear on its face."[15] The court noted that although the plaintiff's attorney did not draft the document, plaintiff was represented by competent counsel, was well aware of the benefits and consequences of signing the document, had two months to consider the document, was not in custody at the time the release was executed, and the release was clear on its face.[16]

Next, the court found legitimate prosecutorial reasons for the release-dismissal agreement and that it did not contravene public policy. The court noted that the list of acceptable reasons included concern for the cost and burden of litigation, "docket control and the efficient resolution of criminal charges, ... and the avoidance of questionably valid civil rights litigation."[17] The court held that the prosecution's concern for the cost of prosecuting the respondent was a legitimate reason for seeking the release.[18] Additionally, the court held that the prosecution had a legitimate concern for the cost of a possibly unsuccessful prosecution and that this concern "did not contravene public policy."[19]

In finding the release-dismissal agreement in *Town of Newton* valid, the Supreme Court had stated that the "agreement was voluntary, ... there is no evidence of prosecutorial misconduct, and that enforcement of this agreement would not adversely affect the relevant public interests."[20] Although the Eighth Circuit's opinion in *Woods* has a cursory discussion of prosecutorial misconduct and the relevant public interests, the only part of the opinion with any real bite is the voluntariness prong. If there is a legitimate prosecutorial motive for the release-dismissal agreement—and it would appear from the generalized interests found acceptable there always will be—then it seems that the similarly generalized public interests will almost never be found adversely affected. In the end it is really only the "voluntariness" factors that control the validity of release-dismissal agreements. And they must be scrutinized with

15. *Id.* at 499 (citations omitted).

16. *Id.* at 497.

17. *Id.* at 500.

18. *Id.* at 501. The cost of prosecuting the respondent had increased significantly since her arrest. The prosecution believed that because the key witness against the respondent had moved a considerable distance from Sioux City, the cost of transporting him to the trial was not worth the benefit of a successful prosecution. Additionally, the court noted that the charges filed against the respondent were filed by the police, not by the prosecutor's office, and that there was no evidence that the police were in any way retaliating against the respondent when she was charged. *Id.* at 500. These factors, however, are present in many criminal prosecutions. Given the pervasiveness of these concerns, it is hard to envision a release-dismissal agreement that would not be held supported by a legitimate prosecutorial reason.

19. *Id.* at 502.

20. 480 U.S. at 398, 107 S.Ct. at 1195.

particularity; voluntariness, unlike the question whether the agreement is in the public interest, may not be presumed.[21]

The Third Circuit has held that when the release-dismissal agreement is oral, the prosecution bears the risk of error resulting from lack of a written document and accordingly bears the burden of proving voluntariness by clear and convincing evidence.[22] This higher proof standard has been rejected by the Sixth Circuit, however, in favor of the ordinary preponderance of the evidence standard, at least where the oral agreement was "read" into the record in the context of the plea agreement.[23]

In *Hill v. City of Cleveland*,[24] the Sixth Circuit, in upholding an agreement, focused principally on its voluntary nature and the lack of prosecutorial overreaching. Although the Court recited that the agreement was not contrary to the public interest, its support for that proposition was simply that there was uncertainty about the facts underlying the § 1983 action—an observation that could as readily be made about any other.

Several circuits also approve the validity of releases of § 1983 claims in exchange not for outright dismissal of criminal charges, but for lesser punishment upon a plea of guilty,[25] and even for a mutual release of civil liability granted by the government.[26]

§§ 5.136–5.139 [Reserved]

X. THE PRECLUSIVE EFFECT OF EMPLOYMENT DISCRIMINATION CONSENT JUDGMENTS ON NONPARTIES

§ 5.140 In General

A 5–4 Supreme Court majority held in *Martin v. Wilks*[1] that nonminority employees who object to a consent judgment adverse to their interests are not required to intervene in a Title VII action but instead may collaterally attack the judgment in independent actions. Since the Court had several times recognized that employers are principally motivated to adopt "voluntary" affirmative action programs, or settle pending lawsuits by consent agreements, in order to avoid the costs of extended litigation, the *Wilks* decision appeared to remove much of the

21. *Coughlen v. Coots*, 5 F.3d 970 (6th Cir.1993).

22. *Livingstone v. North Belle Vernon Borough, Pa.*, 91 F.3d 515 (3d Cir.1996), *cert. denied*, 520 U.S. 1142, 117 S.Ct. 1311, 137 L.Ed.2d 474 (1997).

23. *Burke v. Johnson*, 167 F.3d 276 (6th Cir.1999).

24. 12 F.3d 575 (6th Cir.1993).

25. *See Burke v. Johnson,* 167 F.3d 276 (6th Cir.1999); *Ashley v. City of Huntsville, Ala.*, 85 F.3d 645 (11th Cir.1996), *cert. denied*, 519 U.S. 1110, 117 S.Ct. 947, 136 L.Ed.2d 835 (1997) (civil rights plaintiff got lesser sentence and fine as consideration for release).

26. *Dye v. Wargo*, 253 F.3d 296, 300–02 (7th Cir.2001).

§ 5.140

1. 490 U.S. 755, 109 S.Ct. 2180, 104 L.Ed.2d 835 (1989).

incentive for these arrangements. But the Civil Rights Act of 1991,[2] discussed below, substantially overrules *Wilks*, striking a balance between the minority plaintiffs' interest in comprehensive, efficient litigation involving all parties and the interest of nonminority persons potentially affected by a group-based decree.

The Act responds to the Court's decision in *Wilks* by foreclosing many collateral challenges, typically by whites or males, to employment practices adopted under the authority of litigated or consent judgments. These attacks customarily assert that the underlying judgments unlawfully provide group-based, reverse-discriminatory relief to minority or female applicants or employees, including those not shown to have suffered discrimination at the hands of the defendant employer. The Court in *Wilks* permitted such attacks even when the attackers knew about the underlying litigation but did not try to intervene. It relied on the familiar due process principle that a judgment cannot bind a litigant who was not a party or privy and therefore lacked an opportunity to be heard.[3] Yet the 1991 Act purports to bar the white or male challengers from later challenging decrees entered under the federal[4] antidiscrimination laws if they had a reasonable opportunity, after adequate notice, to raise their objections during the primary proceedings and failed to intervene, or if they were adequately represented in those proceedings by a similarly situated litigant.[5]

2. Pub.L.No. 102–166, 105 Stat. 1071.

3. *See, e.g., Parklane Hosiery v. Shore*, 439 U.S. 322, 327 n. 7, 99 S.Ct. 645, 649 n. 7, 58 L.Ed.2d 552 (1979); *Hansberry v. Lee*, 311 U.S. 32, 40–41, 61 S.Ct. 115, 117–118, 85 L.Ed. 22 (1940).

4. The Act does not explicitly provide protection to consent judgments or orders entered under *state* discrimination laws. Andrea Catania and Charles A. Sullivan argue, however, that although § 703(n)(1)(B) does not mention subsequent challenges to decrees based on state law, "the drafters probably did not intend to allow state-based claims against court ordered restructuring in the workplace[ ]." Andrea Catania & Charles A. Sullivan, *Judging Judgments: The 1991 Civil Rights Act and The Lingering Ghost of Martin v. Wilks*, 57 Brooklyn L.Rev. 995, 1035 (1992). "Such a view ... would tend to eviscerate the whole purpose of the [Act]." *Id.*

Another effect of § 703(n)(1)(A) is that state court consent judgments or orders under *federal* discrimination laws are given preclusive effect if the requirements of § 703(n)(1)(B) are met. *Id.* at 1033. This effectively alters and expands for the covered consent decrees the sphere of influence of 28 U.S.C.A. § 1738: so long as the requirements of the Act have been met, federal courts must give preclusive effect to state-court judgments even if courts of a state would deny preclusive effect to the consent decree, which they probably would if the challengers were not party to the prior proceedings. *See supra* § 5.118 (discussing party identity requirement of claim preclusion).

5. Pub.L.No. 102–166, § 703(n)(1)(A)–(B), 105 Stat. 1071. Section 703(n)(1)(A)–(B) reads:

> (A) Notwithstanding any other provision of law, and except as provided in paragraph (2), an employment practice that implements and is within the scope of a litigated or consent judgment or order that resolves a claim of employment discrimination under the Constitution or Federal civil rights laws may not be challenged under the circumstances described in subparagraph (B).
>
> (B) A practice described in subparagraph (A) may not be challenged in a claim under the Constitution or Federal civil rights laws—
>
> > (i) by a person who, prior to the entry of the judgment or order described in subparagraph (A), had—
> >
> > (I) actual notice of the proposed judgment or order sufficient to apprise such person that such judgment or order might adversely affect the interests and legal rights of such per-

On the other hand, the Act also makes it more difficult for the parties to the primary lawsuit—the minority or female plaintiffs and the defendant employer—to achieve assurance that a judgment in their litigation will effectively end the controversy among all relevant parties. They will have to give actual notice to identifiable incumbent employees who might be adversely affected by a proposed judgment that, for example, commands group-based goals or quotas for a training program or promotion or adjustments to seniority. And when such notice is given, the Act leaves intact another of the Court's 1988 Term decisions[6] that generally[7] relieves intervening challengers from liability for the attorney's fees incurred by the primary parties in defending the group protection features of the proposed underlying judgment.

The difficulties faced by the primary parties are even greater with respect to contemplated relief—goals or quotas concerning hiring or, in the case of a union defendant, membership—that will affect nonminority employees who are not readily identifiable and accordingly cannot be given actual notice. In those situations the primary parties, if they seek a durable, comprehensive judgment, will have to join as additional parties persons or groups who will be deemed adequate representatives of the absentees likely to be affected by the judgment.

On balance, then, the Act makes it riskier for a putative challenger to wait to attack such a judgment until after it is entered and he is denied hire or promotion pursuant to its terms. Further, it encourages his intervention in the underlying action by continuing to shield him from liability for the plaintiff's attorney's fees in most cases. In these respects the Act affords indirect support for group protection remedies in the context of completed or, in the case of a consent judgment, partial litigation. But in cases that involve proposed group-based hiring or membership remedies, the primary parties may still be reluctant to enter into consent judgments for fear that they cannot locate and join as parties adequate representatives of all potentially affected nonminority persons; these persons would then remain free to attack the judgment collaterally. To that extent, the Act moderately discourages the group-based remedy.

> son and that an opportunity was available to present objections to such judgment or order by a future date certain; and
>
> (II) a reasonable opportunity to present objections to such judgment or order; or
>
> (ii) by a person whose interests were adequately represented by another person who had previously challenged the judgment or order on the same legal grounds and with a similar factual situation, unless there has been an intervening change in law or fact.

Id.

Paragraph (2) explains that paragraph (1) shall not alter the standards for intervention under FRCP 24, apply [directly] to the rights of the parties to the underlying action in which the judgment was entered, or prevent challenges to judgments procured by collusion or fraud.

6. *Independent Fed'n of Flight Attendants v. Zipes*, 491 U.S. 754, 109 S.Ct. 2732, 105 L.Ed.2d 639 (1989).

7. The Court had saddled such a challenger with liability only when its position was "frivolous, unreasonable, or without foundation." 491 U.S. at 768 (Blackmun, J., concurring) (quoting *Christiansburg Garment Co. v. EEOC*, 434 U.S. 412, 98 S.Ct. 694, 54 L.Ed.2d 648 (1978)).

Appendix

RESEARCHING CIVIL RIGHTS LAW

Analysis

Section 1. Introduction

Civil Rights Law and Practice provides a strong base for analyzing even the most complex problem involving issues related to civil rights law. Whether your research requires examination of case law, statutes, expert commentary, or other materials, West books and Westlaw are excellent sources of information.

To keep you informed of current developments, Westlaw provides frequently updated databases. With Westlaw, you have unparalleled legal research resources at your fingertips.

Additional Resources

If you have not previously used Westlaw or if you have questions not covered in this appendix, call the West Reference Attorneys at 1–800–REF–ATTY (1–800–733–2889). The West Reference Attorneys are trained, licensed attorneys, available 24 hours a day to assist you with your Westlaw search questions. To subscribe to Westlaw, call 1–800–344–5008 or visit westlaw.com at **www.westlaw.com**.

Section 2. Westlaw Databases

Each database on Westlaw is assigned an abbreviation called an *identifier*, which you can use to access the database. You can find identifiers for Westlaw databases in the online Westlaw Directory and in the printed *Westlaw Database Directory*. When you need to know more detailed information about a database, use Scope. Scope contains coverage information, lists of related databases, and valuable search tips.

The following chart lists selected Westlaw databases that contain information pertaining to civil rights law. For a complete list of civil rights law databases, see the online Westlaw Directory or the printed *Westlaw Database Directory*. Because new information is continually being added to Westlaw, you should also check the tabbed Westlaw page and the online Westlaw Directory for new database information.

Selected Civil Rights Law Databases on Westlaw

Database	Identifier	Coverage
Federal and State Materials Combined		
Americans with Disabilities Cases	AWD–CS	Begins with 1945
Americans with Disabilities Statutes	AWD–ST	Varies by jurisdiction
Andrews Disability Litigation Reporter Court Documents	ANDISLR–DOC	Begins with 2000
Andrews Employment Litigation Reporter Court Documents	ANEMPLR–DOC	Begins with 2000
Andrews Sexual Harassment Litigation Reporter Court Documents	ANSEXHLR–DOC	Begins with 2000
National Disability Law Reporter	NDLRPTR	Begins with 1990

Database	Identifier	Coverage
Federal Case Law		
Federal Case Law	ALLFEDS	
Federal Civil Rights–Cases	FCIV–CS	Begins with 1789
Federal Civil Rights–Supreme Court Cases	FCIV–SCT	Begins with 1790
Federal Civil Rights–Courts of Appeals Cases	FCIV–CTA	Begins with 1891
Federal Civil Rights–District Courts Cases	FCIV–DCT	Begins with 1789
State Case Law		
Multistate Civil Rights Cases	MCIV–CS	Varies by state
Individual State Civil Rights Cases	XXCIV–CS (where XX is a state's two-letter postal abbreviation	Varies by state
Federal Statutes and Regulations		
Federal Civil Rights–U.S. Code Annotated	FCIV–USCA	Current data
Federal Civil Rights–Code of Federal Regulations	FCIV–CFR	Current data
Federal Civil Rights–Federal Register	FCIV–FR	Begins with July 1980
Americans with Disabilities Code of Federal Regulations	AWD–CFR	Current data
Americans with Disabilities Federal Register	AWD–FR	Begins with July 1980
Arnold & Porter Legislative History: Americans with Disabilities Act of 1990	ADA–LH	Full history
Federal Administrative Materials		
Americans with Disabilities Act Technical Assistance Manuals	ADA–TAM	Informational booklets: 1991 Manuals: 1992
Fair Housing Administrative Decisions	FAIRHOUS	Begins with 1989
Federal Labor and Employment–Equal Employment Opportunity Commission (EEOC) Multibase	FLB–EEOC–ALL	Varies by source
Federal Labor and Employment–Equal Employment Opportunity Commission Decisions	FLB–EEOC	Begins with June 1969

Database	Identifier	Coverage
Federal Labor and Employment–Equal Employment Opportunity Commission (EEOC)–Enforcement Guidances and Related Documents	FLB–EEOCGUID	Begins with 1990
Federal Labor and Employment–Equal Employment Opportunity Commission (EEOC)–Compliance Manual	FLB–EEOCCM	Current data
Federal Labor and Employment–U.S. Equal Employment Opportunity Management Directives	FLB–EEOCMD	Begins with 1983
Office of Federal Contract Compliance Programs Decisions	OFCCP	Begins with 1968
State Administrative Materials		
California Fair Employment and Housing Commission Decisions	CA–FEHC	Begins with 1978
Chicago Commission on Human Relations Decisions	CHICIV–ADMIN	Begins with 1992
City of New York Commission on Human Rights	NYCCIV–ADMIN	Begins with 1970
Illinois Human Rights Commission Decisions	ILCIV–ADMIN	Begins with 1991
Massachusetts Commission Against Discrimination Decisions	MACIV–ADMIN	Begins with 1999
Ohio Civil Rights Commission Decisions	OHCIV–ADMIN	Begins with 1980
Legal Texts and Periodicals		
Civil Rights–Law Reviews, Texts, and Bar Journals	CIV–TP	Varies by publication
ADA and People with Mental Illness: A Resource Manual for Employers	ABA–DISMAN	1994 edition

Database	Identifier	Coverage
African-American Law and Policy Report	AALPR	Full coverage begins with 1994 (vol. 1)
American Bar Association Disability Law Texts, Combined	ABA-DIS	Varies by source
Americans with Disabilities Act Handbook	JW-ADA	Current data
Americans with Disabilities Practice and Compliance Manual	AMDISPCM	Current data
Americans with Disabilities Texts and Periodicals	AWD-TP	Varies by source
Berkeley La Raza Law Journal	BERKLARLJ	Selected coverage begins with 1992 (vol. 5); full coverage begins with 1994 (vol. 7)
Berkeley Women's Law Journal	BERKWLJ	Selected coverage begins with 1990 (vol. 5); full coverage begins with 1994 (vol. 9)
California Civil Practice–Civil Rights Litigation	CCP-CIVRGT	Current data
Columbia Human Rights Law Review	CLMHRLR	Selected coverage begins with 1984 (vol. 15); full coverage begins with 1993 (vol. 25)
Columbia Journal of Gender and Law	CLMJGL	Selected coverage begins with 1991 (vol. 1); full coverage begins with 1993 (vol. 3, no. 2)
Disability Law Compliance Manual	DLCM	Current edition
George Mason University Civil Rights Law Journal	GMUCRLJ	Selected coverage begins with 1990 (vol. 1); full coverage begins with 1993 (vol. 4)
Government Discrimination: Equal Protection Law and Litigation	GOVDISCRIM	Current data
Harvard Civil Rights–Civil	HVCRCLLR	Full coverage begins with 1981
Liberties Law Review		(vol. 16)
Harvard Latino Law Review	HVLATLR	Begins with 2002 (vol. 5)

Database	Identifier	Coverage
Into the Jury Box: A Disability Accommodation Guide for State Courts	ABA–DISJURY	1994 edition
Journal of Gender, Race, and Justice	JGRJ	Full coverage begins with 1997 (vol. 1)
Law and Inequality	LAWINEQ	Selected coverage begins with 1985 (vol. 3); full coverage begins with 1993 (vol. 11, no. 2)
Law and Sexuality: A Review of Lesbian and Gay Legal Issues	LSEX	Full coverage begins with 1993 (vol. 3)
Litigating Age Discrimination Cases	LITADCS	Current data
Manual on Employment Discrimination and Civil Rights Actions in the Federal Courts	MEDCRA	Current edition
Mental and Physical Disability Law Reporter	MPHYDLR	Selected coverage begins with 1987 (vol. 11)
National Black Law Journal	NBLJ	Selected coverage begins with 1993 (vol. 12, no. 3); full coverage begins with 1994 (vol. 13, no. 3)
New England Journal on Criminal and Civil Confinement	NENGJCCC	Selected coverage begins with 1989 (vol. 15)
Police Misconduct and Civil Rights: Federal Jury Practice and Instructions	PMCIV–FJPI	Second edition
Public Accommodations Under the Americans with Disabilities Act	ADA–PUBACC	2004 edition
Scholar: St. Mary's Law Review on Minority Issues	SCHOLAR	Full coverage begins with 1999 (vol. 1)
Statistics of Discrimination	STATDIS	Current data
Temple Political and Civil Rights Law Review	TMPPCRLR	Selected coverage begins with 1992 (vol. 1); full coverage begins with 1993 (vol. 2, no. 2)
Texas Journal on Civil Liberties and Civil Rights	TXJCLCR	Full coverage begins with 1996 (vol. 2)

Database	Identifier	Coverage
Washington and Lee Race and Ethnic Ancestry Law Journal	WLLREALJ	Full coverage begins with 1995 (vol. 1)
Yale Human Rights and Development Law Journal	YHRDLJ	Full coverage begins with 1998 (vol. 1)
News and Information		
Access Currents	ACCURR	Begins with January 1997
ADA Update	ADAUP	Begins with January 1997
Andrews Disability Litigation Reporter	ANDISLR	Begins with November 2003
Andrews Employment Litigation Reporter	ANEMPLR	Begins with November 1996
Andrews Sexual Harassment Litigation Reporter	ANSEXHLR	Begins with November 1996
Disability Law Report	OAKDLR	Begins with October 2001
Discrimination Law Update	DISCRIMLU	Begins with January 1997
Employment Discrimination Law Update	OAKEDLU	Begins with October 2001
Human Rights Brief	HUMRTB	Begins with 2000
Special Education Law Update	OAKSELU	Begins with October 2001
Directories		
West Legal Directory®–Civil Rights	WLD–CIV	Current data
West Legal Directory–Constitutional Law	WLD–CON	Current data

Section 3. Retrieving a Document with a Citation: Find and Hypertext Links

3.1 Find

Find is a Westlaw service that allows you to retrieve a document by entering its citation. Find allows you to retrieve documents from any page in westlaw.com without accessing or changing databases. Find is available for many documents, including case law (state and federal), the *United States Code Annotated*®, state statutes, administrative materials, and texts and periodicals.

To use Find, simply type the citation in the *Find this document by citation* text box at the tabbed Westlaw page and click **GO**. The following list provides some examples:

To find this document:	Access Find and type:
Jett v. Dallas Indep. School Dist. 109 S. Ct. 2702 (1989)	**109 sct 2702**
Mittl v. New York State Div. of Human Rights 794 N.E.2d 660 (N.Y. 2003)	**794 ne2d 660**
42 U.S.C.A. § 2000a	**42 usca 2000a**
28 C.F.R. § 36.104	**28 cfr 36.104**
Cal. Civ. Code § 52	**ca civ s 52**
Ariz. Rev. Stat. Ann. § 41–1491.21	**az st s 41–1491.21**

For a complete list of publications that can be retrieved with Find and their abbreviations, click **Find** on the toolbar and then click **Publications List**.

3.2 Hypertext Links

Use hypertext links to move from one location to another on Westlaw. For example, use hypertext links to go directly from the statute, case, or law review article you are viewing to a cited statute, case, or article; from a headnote to the corresponding text in the opinion; or from an entry in a statutes index database to the full text of the statute.

Section 4. Searching with Natural Language

Overview: With Natural Language, you can retrieve documents by simply describing your issue in plain English. If you are a relatively new Westlaw user, Natural Language searching can make it easier for you to retrieve cases that are on point. If you are an experienced Westlaw user, Natural Language gives you a valuable alternative search method to the Terms and Connectors search method described in Section 5.

When you enter a Natural Language description, Westlaw automatically identifies legal phrases, removes common words, and generates variations of terms in your description. Westlaw then searches for the concepts in your description. Concepts may include significant terms, phrases, legal citations, or topic and key numbers. Westlaw retrieves the documents that most closely match the concepts in your description, beginning with the document most likely to match.

4.1 Natural Language Search

Access a database, such as the Federal Civil Rights–Cases database (FCIV–CS). Click **Natural Language** and type the following description in the text box:

reasonable accommodation for employees under the americans with disabilities act

4.2 Browsing Search Results

Best Mode: To display the best portion (the portion that most closely matches your description) of each document in a Natural Language search result, click the **Best** arrows at the bottom of the right frame.

Term Mode: Click the **Term** arrows at the bottom of the right frame to display portions of the document that contain your search terms.

Previous/Next Document: Click the left or right **Doc** arrow at the bottom of the right frame to view the previous or the next document in the search result.

Section 5. Searching with Terms and Connectors

Overview: With Terms and Connectors searching, you enter a query consisting of key terms from your issue and connectors specifying the relationship between these terms.

Terms and Connectors searching is useful when you want to retrieve a document for which you know specific details, such as the title or the fact situation. Terms and Connectors searching is also useful when you want to retrieve all documents containing specific terms.

5.1 Terms

Plurals and Possessives: Plurals are automatically retrieved when you enter the singular form of a term. This is true for both regular and irregular plurals (e.g., **child** retrieves *children*). If you enter the plural form of a term, you will not retrieve the singular form.

If you enter the nonpossessive form of a term, Westlaw automatically retrieves the possessive form as well. However, if you enter the possessive form, only the possessive form is retrieved.

Compound Words and Abbreviations: When a compound word is one of your search terms, use a hyphen to retrieve all forms of the word. For example, the term **non-discrimination** retrieves *non-discrimination*, *nondiscrimination*, and *non discrimination*.

When using an abbreviation as a search term, place a period after each of the letters to retrieve any of its forms. For example, the term **a.c.l.u.** retrieves *ACLU*, *A.C.L.U.*, *A C L U*, and *A. C. L. U.* Note: The abbreviation does not retrieve the phrase *american civil liberties union*, so remember to add additional alternative terms such as **"american civil liberties union"** to your query.

The Root Expander and the Universal Character: When you use the Terms and Connectors search method, placing the root expander (!) at the end of a root term generates all other terms with that root. For example, adding the ! to the root *violat* in the query

"civil right" /s violat!

instructs Westlaw to retrieve such terms as *violate*, *violated*, *violating*, and *violation*.

The universal character (*) stands for one character and can be inserted in the middle or at the end of a term. For example, the term

withdr*w

will retrieve *withdraw* and *withdrew*. Adding two asterisks to the root *jur*

jur**

instructs Westlaw to retrieve all forms of the root with up to two additional characters. Terms such as *juror* or *jury* are retrieved by this query. However, terms with more than two letters following the root, such as *jurisdiction,* are not retrieved. Plurals are always retrieved, even if the plural form of the term has more than two letters following the root.

Phrase Searching: To search for an exact phrase, place it within quotation marks. For example, to search for references to *deliberate indifference*, type **"deliberate indifference"**. When you are using the Terms and Connectors search method, you should use phrase searching only if you are certain that the terms in the phrase will not appear in any other order.

5.2 Alternative Terms

After selecting the terms for your query, consider which alternative terms are necessary. For example, if you are searching for the term *constitutional*, you might also want to search for the term *unconstitutional.* You should consider both synonyms and antonyms as alternative terms. You can also use the Westlaw thesaurus to add alternative terms to your query.

5.3 Connectors

After selecting terms and alternative terms for your query, use connectors to specify the relationship that must exist between search terms in your retrieved documents. The connectors are described below:

Type:	**To retrieve documents with:**	**Example:**
& (and)	both terms	**age & discriminat!**
a space (or)	either term or both terms	**sex! gender**
/p	search terms in the same paragraph	**religion neutral!**
/s	search terms in the same sentence	**bifurcat! claim**
+**s**	the first search term preceding the second within the same sentence	**burden +s proof prov!**
/n	search terms within *n* terms of each other (where *n* is a number from 1 to 255)	**rac! /5 discriminat!**
+**n**	the first search term preceding the second by *n* terms (where *n* is a number from 1 to 255)	**qualified +3 immunity**

" "	search terms appearing in the same order as in the quotation marks	**"state action"**
Type:	**To exclude documents with:**	**Example:**
% (but not)	search terms following the % symbol	**"due process" % criminal**

5.4 Field Restrictions

Overview: Documents in each Westlaw database consist of several segments, or *fields*. One field may contain the citation, another the title, another the synopsis, and so forth. Not all databases contain the same fields. Also depending on the database, fields with the same name may contain different types of information.

To view a list of fields and their contents for a specific database, see Scope for that database. Note that in some databases not every field is available for every document.

To retrieve only those documents containing your search terms in a specific field, restrict your search to that field. To restrict your search to a specific field, type the field name or abbreviation followed by your search terms enclosed in parentheses. For example, to retrieve a U.S. Supreme Court case titled *Younger v. Harris*, access the Federal Civil Rights–Supreme Court Cases database (FCIV–SCT) and search for your terms in the title field (ti):

ti(younger & harris)

The fields discussed below are available in Westlaw case law databases you might use for researching issues related to civil rights.

Digest and Synopsis Fields: The digest (di) and synopsis (sy) fields summarize the main points of a case. The synopsis field contains a brief description of a case. The digest field contains the topic and headnote fields and includes the complete hierarchy of concepts used by West's editors to classify the headnotes to specific West digest topic and key numbers. Restricting your search to the synopsis and digest fields limits your result to cases in which your terms are related to a major issue in the case.

Consider restricting your search to one or both of these fields if

- you are searching for common terms or terms with more than one meaning, and you need to narrow your search; or
- you cannot narrow your search by using a smaller database.

For example, to retrieve federal courts of appeals cases that discuss age as a bona fide occupational qualification, access the Federal Civil Rights–Courts of Appeals Cases database (FCIV–CTA) and type the following query:

sy,di(age /p "bona fide occupational qualification" b.f.o.q.)

Headnote Field: The headnote field (he) is part of the digest field but does not contain the topic names or numbers, hierarchical classification information, or key numbers. The headnote field contains a one-sentence summary for each point of law in a case and any supporting citations given by the author of the opinion. A headnote field restriction is useful when you are searching for specific statutory sections or rule numbers. For example, to retrieve headnotes from federal courts of appeals cases that cite 42 U.S.C.A. § 2000a, access the FCIV–CTA database and type the following query:

he(42 +s 2000a)

Topic Field: The topic field (to) is also part of the digest field. It contains the hierarchical classification information, including the West digest topic names and numbers and the key numbers. You should restrict search terms to the topic field in a case law database if

- a digest field search retrieves too many documents; or
- you want to retrieve cases with digest paragraphs classified under more than one topic.

For example, the topic Civil Rights has the topic number 78. To retrieve federal district court cases that discuss religious discrimination in the context of civil rights, access the Federal Civil Rights–District Courts Cases database (FCIV–DCT) and type a query like the following:

to(78) /p religio /5 discriminat!**

To retrieve cases classified under more than one topic and key number, search for your terms in the topic field. For example, to retrieve recent federal cases discussing race discrimination, which may be classified to such topics as Civil Rights (78), Constitutional Law (92), Elections (144), and Federal Courts (170B), access the Federal Case Law database (ALLFEDS) and type a query like the following:

to(rac! /5 discriminat!) & da(aft 2002)

For a complete list of West digest topics and their corresponding topic numbers, access the Custom Digest by choosing **Key Numbers and Digest** from the *More* drop-down list on the toolbar.

> *Note*: Slip opinions and cases from topical services do not contain the West digest, headnote, and topic fields.

Prelim and Caption Fields: When searching in a database containing statutes, rules, or regulations, restrict your search to the prelim (pr) and caption (ca) fields to retrieve documents in which your terms are important enough to appear in a section name or heading. For example, to retrieve federal statutes regarding voting rights, access the Federal Civil Rights–U.S. Code Annotated database (FCIV–USCA) and type the following:

pr,ca(vot! /s right)

5.5 Date Restrictions

You can use Westlaw to retrieve documents *decided* or *issued* before, after, or on a specified date, as well as within a range of dates. The following sample queries contain date restrictions:

da(2003) & hostile /s environment

da(aft 1998) & "disparate treatment"

da(6/14/1995) & injunct! /s relief

You can also search for documents *added to a database* on or after a specified date, as well as within a range of dates, which is useful for updating your research. The following sample queries contain added-date restrictions:

ad(aft 1999) & qualified /5 immunity

ad(aft 11/9/2001 & bef 6/23/2002) & same-sex /s harass!

Section 6. Searching with Topic and Key Numbers

To retrieve cases that address a specific point of law, use topic and key numbers as your search terms. If you have an on-point case, run a search using the topic and key number from the relevant headnote in an appropriate database to find other cases containing headnotes classified to that topic and key number. For example, to search for federal cases containing headnotes classified under topic 78 (Civil Rights) and key number 1036 (Threats, Intimidation, and Harassment), access the FCIV–CS database and enter the following query:

78k1036

For a complete list of West digest topics and their corresponding topic numbers, access the Custom Digest by choosing **Key Numbers and Digest** from the *More* drop-down list on the toolbar.

> *Note*: Slip opinions and cases from topical services do not contain West topic and key numbers.

6.1 Custom Digest

The Custom Digest contains the complete topic and key number outline used by West attorney-editors to classify headnotes. You can use the Custom Digest to obtain a single document containing all case law headnotes from a specific jurisdiction that are classified under a particular topic and key number.

Access the Custom Digest by choosing **Key Numbers and Digest** from the *More* drop-down list on the toolbar. Select up to 10 topics and key numbers from the easy-to-browse outline and click **Search selected**. Then follow the displayed instructions.

For example, to research issues involving civil rights, scroll down the Custom Digest page until topic 78, *Civil Rights*, is displayed. Click the plus symbols (+) to display key number information. Select the check box next to each key number you want to include in your search, then click **Search selected**. Select the jurisdiction from which you want to retrieve headnotes and, if desired, type additional search terms and select a date restriction. Click **Search**.

6.2 KeySearch

KeySearch is a research tool that helps you find cases and secondary sources in a specific area of the law. KeySearch guides you through the selection of terms from a classification system based on the West Key Number System® and then uses the key numbers and their underlying concepts to automatically formulate a query for you.

To access KeySearch, click **KeySearch** on the toolbar. Then browse the list of topics and subtopics and select a topic or subtopic to search by clicking the hypertext links. For example, to search for cases that discuss public accommodations in the context of civil rights, click **Civil Rights** at the first KeySearch page. Then click **Public Accommodations** at the next page. Select the source from which you want to retrieve documents and, if desired, type additional search terms. Click **Search**.

Section 7. Verifying Your Research with Citation Research Services

Overview: A citation research service, such as KeyCite, is a tool that helps you ensure that your cases, statutes, regulations, and administrative decisions are good law; helps you retrieve cases, legislation, articles, or other documents that cite them; and helps you verify the spelling and format of your citations.

7.1 KeyCite for Cases

KeyCite for cases covers case law on Westlaw, including unpublished opinions. KeyCite for cases provides the following:

- direct appellate history of a case, including related references, which are opinions involving the same parties and facts but resolving different issues
- negative indirect history of a case, which consists of cases outside the direct appellate line that may have a negative impact on its precedential value
- the title, parallel citations, court of decision, docket number, and filing date of a case
- citations to cases, administrative decisions, secondary sources, and briefs on Westlaw that have cited a case
- complete integration with the West Key Number System so you can track legal issues discussed in a case

7.2 KeyCite for Statutes and Regulations

KeyCite for statutes and regulations covers the *United States Code Annotated* (USCA®), the *Code of Federal Regulations* (CFR), statutes from all 50 states, and regulations from selected states. KeyCite for statutes and regulations provides

- links to session laws or rules amending or repealing a statute or regulation
- statutory credits and historical notes
- citations to pending legislation affecting a federal statute or a statute from selected states
- citations to cases, administrative decisions, secondary sources, and briefs that have cited a statute or regulation

7.3 KeyCite for Administrative Materials

KeyCite for administrative materials includes the following:

- National Labor Relations Board decisions beginning with 1935
- Board of Contract Appeals decisions (varies by agency)
- Board of Immigration Appeals decisions beginning with 1940
- Comptroller General decisions beginning with 1921
- Environmental Protection Agency decisions beginning with 1974
- Federal Communications Commission decisions beginning with 1960
- Federal Energy Regulatory Commission (Federal Power Commission) decisions beginning with 1931
- Internal Revenue Service revenue rulings beginning with 1954
- Internal Revenue Service revenue procedures beginning with 1954
- Internal Revenue Service private letter rulings beginning with 1954
- Internal Revenue Service technical advice memoranda beginning with 1954
- Public Utilities Reports beginning with 1974
- U.S. Merit Systems Protection Board decisions beginning with 1979
- U.S. Patent and Trademark Office decisions beginning with 1984
- U.S. Tax Court (Board of Tax Appeals) decisions beginning with 1924
- U.S. patents beginning with 1976

7.4 KeyCite Alert

KeyCite Alert monitors the status of your cases, statutes, regulations, and administrative decisions and automatically sends you updates at the frequency you specify when their KeyCite information changes.

Section 8. Researching with Westlaw: Examples

8.1 Retrieving Law Review Articles

Recent law review articles are often a good place to begin researching a legal issue because law review articles serve as an excellent introduction to a new topic or review for an old one, providing terminology to help you formulate a query; as a finding tool for pertinent primary authority, such as cases, statutes, and rules; and in some instances, as persuasive secondary authority.

Suppose you need to gain background information on immunity of public officials from liability for civil rights violations.

Solution

- To retrieve recent law review articles relevant to your issue, access the Civil Rights–Law Reviews, Texts, and Bar Journals database (CIV–TP). Using the Natural Language search method, enter a description like the following:

immunity of public officials for civil rights violations

- If you have a citation to an article in a specific publication, use Find to retrieve it. For more information on Find, see Section 3.1 of this appendix. For example, to retrieve the article found at 75 Cornell L. Rev. 462, access Find and type

75 cornell l rev 462

- If you know the title of an article but not the journal in which it was published, access the CIV–TP database and search for key terms in the title field. For example, to retrieve the article "Qualified Immunity for Civil Rights Violations: Refining the Standard," type the following Terms and Connectors query:

ti(qualified & refining & standard)

8.2 Retrieving Case Law

Suppose you need to retrieve federal cases dealing with the burden of proof in an action brought under the Americans with Disabilities Act (ADA).

Solution

- Access the FCIV–CS database. Type a Terms and Connectors query such as the following:

burden /5 proof prov! /p "americans with disabilities" a.d.a.

- When you know the citation for a specific case, use Find to retrieve it. For more information on Find, see Section 3.1 of this appendix. For example, to retrieve *Raytheon Co. v. Hernandez*, 124 S. Ct. 513 (2003), access Find and type

124 sct 513

- If you find a topic and key number that is on point, run a search using that topic and key number to retrieve additional cases discussing that point of law. For example, to retrieve U.S. Supreme Court cases containing headnotes classified under topic 78 (Civil Rights) and key number 1540 (Discrimination by Reason of Handicap, Disability, or Illness), access the FCIV–SCT database and type the following query:

78k1540

- To retrieve cases written by a particular judge, add a judge field (ju) restriction to your query. For example, to retrieve federal courts of appeals cases written by Judge Benavides that contain headnotes classified under topic 78 (Civil Rights), access the FCIV–CTA database and type the following query:

ju(benavides) & to(78)

- You can also use KeySearch and the Custom Digest to retrieve cases and headnotes that discuss the issue you are researching.

8.3 Retrieving Statutes and Regulations

Suppose you need to retrieve federal statutes and regulations addressing discrimination in employment

Solution

- Access the FCIV–USCA database. Search for your terms in the prelim and caption fields using the Terms and Connectors search method:

pr,ca(discriminat! & employment)

- When you know the citation for a specific statute or regulation, use Find to retrieve it. For example, to retrieve 42 U.S.C.A. § 1981a, access Find and type

42 usca 1981a

- To look at surrounding sections, use the Table of Contents service. Click **Table of Contents** on the Links tab in the left frame. To display a section listed in the Table of Contents, click its hypertext link. You can also use Documents in Sequence to retrieve the section following 42 U.S.C.A. § 1981a even if the subsequent section was not retrieved with your search or Find request. Choose **Documents in Sequence** from the Tools menu at the bottom of the right frame.

8.4 Using KeyCite

Suppose one of the cases you retrieve in your case law research is *Monell v. Dep't of Social Services of City of New York*, 98 S. Ct. 2018 (1978).

Solution

- Use KeyCite to retrieve direct and negative indirect history for *Monell*. Access KeyCite and type **98 sct 2018**.
- Use KeyCite to display citing references for *Monell*. Click **Citing References** on the Links tab in the left frame.

8.5 Following Recent Developments

If you are researching issues related to employment discrimination, it is important to keep up with recent developments. How can you do this efficiently?

Solution

One of the easiest ways to follow recent developments in employment discrimination law is to access the Westlaw Topical Highlights–Labor and Employment database (WTH–LB). The WTH–LB database contains summaries of recent legal developments, including court decisions, legislation, and materials released by administrative agencies in the area of labor and employment law. When you access the WTH–LB database, you automatically retrieve a list of documents added to the database in the last two weeks.

You can also use the WestClip® clipping service to stay informed of recent developments of interest to you. WestClip will run your Terms and Connectors queries on a regular basis and deliver the results to you automatically. You can run WestClip queries in legal and news and information databases.

Table of Cases

A

B

C

Campanelli v. Bockrath, 100 F.3d 1476 (9th Cir.1996)—**§ 2.41, n. 12.**
Campbell v. City of San Antonio, 43 F.3d 973 (5th Cir.1995)—**§ 2.32, n. 4.**
Campbell v. Peters, 256 F.3d 695 (7th Cir. 2001)—**§ 2.22, n. 60.**
Campos–Orrego v. Rivera, 175 F.3d 89 (1st Cir.1999)—**§ 2.25, n. 8, 14; § 2.26, n. 4, 5, 24.**
Canary v. Osborn, 211 F.3d 324 (6th Cir. 2000)—**§ 2.2, n. 35, 36.**
Canatella v. State of California, 304 F.3d 843 (9th Cir.2002)—**§ 5.55, n. 16.**
Cannon v. City of West Palm Beach, 250 F.3d 1299 (11th Cir.2001)—**§ 2.41, n. 12.**
Cannon v. University of Chicago, 441 U.S. 677, 99 S.Ct. 1946, 60 L.Ed.2d 560 (1979)—**§ 3.9; § 3.9, n. 13; § 3.19, n. 1.**
Canton, Ohio, City of v. Harris, 489 U.S. 378, 109 S.Ct. 1197, 103 L.Ed.2d 412 (1989)—**§ 2.1, n. 7; § 2.31; § 2.31, n. 80; § 2.32; § 2.32, n. 1, 70; § 2.34, n. 4; § 2.41, n. 41; § 2.42, n. 4, 41, 49; § 2.61, n. 2; § 2.62, n. 23; § 5.105; § 5.105, n. 3, 9; § 5.107; § 5.107, n. 25; § 5.108; § 5.108, n. 21, 42.**
Canty v. Old Rochester Regional School Dist., 66 F.Supp.2d 114 (D.Mass.1999)—**§ 3.20; § 3.20, n. 32.**
Canup v. Chipman–Union, Inc., 123 F.3d 1440 (11th Cir.1997)—**§ 4.5, n. 57.**
Canutillo Independent School Dist. v. Leija, 101 F.3d 393 (5th Cir.1996)—**§ 3.20, n. 2.**
Cap v. Hartman, 1996 WL 266701 (E.D.Pa. 1996)—**§ 5.80, n. 39.**
Caras v. Family First Credit Union, 688 F.Supp. 586 (D.Utah 1988)—**§ 5.121, n. 20.**
Carey v. Nevada Gaming Control Bd., 279 F.3d 873 (9th Cir.2002)—**§ 2.22, n. 112.**
Carey v. Piphus, 435 U.S. 247, 98 S.Ct. 1042, 55 L.Ed.2d 252 (1978)—**§ 1.2, n. 53; § 2.3, n. 4, 7; § 2.24, n. 1; § 2.25, n. 3, 8, 23; § 2.26; § 2.26, n. 3, 4, 6, 9; § 2.61, n. 16; § 3.9, n. 17; § 4.5, n. 20.**
Carlos v. Santos, 123 F.3d 61 (2nd Cir. 1997)—**§ 2.2, n. 26, 35.**
Carlson v. Green, 446 U.S. 14, 100 S.Ct. 1468, 64 L.Ed.2d 15 (1980)—**§ 2.47, n. 3.**
Carnegie–Mellon University v. Cohill, 484 U.S. 343, 108 S.Ct. 614, 98 L.Ed.2d 720 (1988)—**§ 5.40, n. 3; § 5.50, n. 24.**
Carney v. American University, 151 F.3d 1090, 331 U.S.App.D.C. 416 (D.C.Cir. 1998)—**§ 1.2, n. 60.**
Carpenter's Produce v. Arnold, 189 F.3d 686 (8th Cir.1999)—**§ 2.48, n. 16.**
Carr v. City of Florence, Ala., 916 F.2d 1521 (11th Cir.1990)—**§ 5.35; § 5.35, n. 12.**
Carr v. O'Leary, 167 F.3d 1124 (7th Cir. 1999)—**§ 5.7, n. 16.**
Carrasca v. Pomeroy, 313 F.3d 828 (3rd Cir.2002)—**§ 5.121, n. 46.**
Carreras–Rosa v. Alves–Cruz, 127 F.3d 172 (1st Cir.1997)—**§ 5.73, n. 2.**
Carringer v. Rodgers, 331 F.3d 844 (11th Cir.2003)—**§ 5.71, n. 6.**
Carrion v. Yeshiva University, 535 F.2d 722 (2nd Cir.1976)—**§ 2.32, n. 86.**
Carrisales v. Department of Corrections, 90 Cal.Rptr.2d 804, 988 P.2d 1083 (Cal. 1999)—**§ 5.45, n. 5.**
Carroll v. General Acc. Ins. Co. of America, 891 F.2d 1174 (5th Cir.1990)—**§ 1.8, n. 1.**
Carroll v. Yates, 362 F.3d 984 (7th Cir. 2004)—**§ 5.7, n. 71.**
Carter v. City of Philadelphia, 181 F.3d 339 (3rd Cir.1999)—**§ 2.31, n. 68, 77; § 5.35, n. 16.**
Carter v. District of Columbia, 795 F.2d 116, 254 U.S.App.D.C. 71 (D.C.Cir. 1986)—**§ 2.32, n. 61.**
Carter v. Morris, 164 F.3d 215 (4th Cir. 1999)—**§ 2.31, n. 19; § 2.32, n. 4, 61.**
Carter v. Sedgwick County, Kan., 36 F.3d 952 (10th Cir.1994)—**§ 4.5, n. 100.**
Carter v. South Cent. Bell, 912 F.2d 832 (5th Cir.1990)—**§ 5.96, n. 4.**
Carteret Sav. Bank, F.A. v. Shushan, 919 F.2d 225 (3rd Cir.1990)—**§ 5.8, n. 2.**
Cartwright v. Stamper, 7 F.3d 106 (7th Cir.1993)—**§ 4.5, n. 24, 32.**
Carver v. Foerster, 102 F.3d 96 (3rd Cir. 1996)—**§ 2.2, n. 36.**
Carver v. Nall, 172 F.3d 513 (7th Cir. 1999)—**§ 5.116, n. 1.**
Case v. Kitsap County Sheriff's Dept., 249 F.3d 921 (9th Cir.2001)—**§ 2.21, n. 3; § 2.22, n. 17, 40.**
Cash v. Granville County Bd. of Educ., 242 F.3d 219 (4th Cir.2001)—**§ 5.35, n. 17.**
Cason v. Seckinger, 231 F.3d 777 (11th Cir.2000)—**§ 5.7, n. 56.**
Cassidy v. Indiana Dept. of Corrections, 199 F.3d 374 (7th Cir.2000)—**§ 5.7, n. 65.**
Castaneda by Castaneda v. Pickard, 781 F.2d 456 (5th Cir.1986)—**§ 3.9, n. 9.**
Castano v. Nebraska Dept. of Corrections, 201 F.3d 1023 (8th Cir.2000)—**§ 5.7, n. 71.**
Castillo v. Cameron County, Tex., 238 F.3d 339 (5th Cir.2001)—**§ 5.7, n. 56.**
Cathey v. Guenther, 47 F.3d 162 (5th Cir. 1995)—**§ 2.41, n. 35.**
Catone v. Spielmann, 149 F.3d 156 (2nd Cir.1998)—**§ 2.23, n. 13.**
Causey, United States v., 185 F.3d 407 (5th Cir.1999)—**§ 2.15, n. 6.**
Cavalieri v. Shepard, 321 F.3d 616 (7th Cir.2003)—**§ 2.22, n. 112.**
Ceaser v. Pataki, 2002 WL 472271 (S.D.N.Y.2002)—**§ 3.9, n. 16.**
Celotex Corp. v. Catrett, 477 U.S. 317, 106 S.Ct. 2548, 91 L.Ed.2d 265 (1986)—

Commonwealth of (see name of commonwealth)
Comstock v. McCrary, 273 F.3d 693 (6th Cir.2001)—**§ 2.42, n. 43.**
Congress of Racial Equality v. Clemmons, 323 F.2d 54 (5th Cir.1963)—**§ 1.5, n. 1.**
Conley v. Gibson, 355 U.S. 41, 78 S.Ct. 99, 2 L.Ed.2d 80 (1957)—**§ 5.80, n. 2; § 5.108, n. 56.**
Conn v. Gabbert, 526 U.S. 286, 119 S.Ct. 1292, 143 L.Ed.2d 399 (1999)—**§ 2.22; § 2.22, n. 44, 96, 100; § 2.41, n. 50, 51; § 5.108, n. 6, 54.**
Connecticut v. Doehr, 501 U.S. 1, 111 S.Ct. 2105, 115 L.Ed.2d 1 (1991)—**§ 2.12; § 2.12, n. 38; § 2.41, n. 27.**
Connick v. Myers, 461 U.S. 138, 103 S.Ct. 1684, 75 L.Ed.2d 708 (1983)—**§ 2.22, n. 113.**
Connolly v. National School Bus Service, Inc., 177 F.3d 593 (7th Cir.1999)—**§ 4.5, n. 32.**
Consolidated Rail Corp. v. Darrone, 465 U.S. 624, 104 S.Ct. 1248, 79 L.Ed.2d 568 (1984)—**§ 3.10, n. 5.**
Construction Industry Retirement Fund of Rockford, Ill. v. Kasper Trucking, Inc., 10 F.3d 465 (7th Cir.1993)—**§ 4.5, n. 75.**
Cook v. Tadros, 312 F.3d 386 (8th Cir. 2002)—**§ 2.10, n. 1.**
Cook v. Wikler, 320 F.3d 431 (3rd Cir. 2003)—**§ 5.50, n. 29.**
Cooper v. Brookshire, 70 F.3d 377 (5th Cir. 1995)—**§ 5.74, n. 1.**
Cooper v. Casey, 97 F.3d 914 (7th Cir. 1996)—**§ 5.7, n. 53.**
Cooper v. Dupnik, 963 F.2d 1220 (9th Cir. 1992)—**§ 2.21, n. 2.**
Cooper v. Federal Reserve Bank of Richmond, 467 U.S. 867, 104 S.Ct. 2794, 81 L.Ed.2d 718 (1984)—**§ 5.116, n. 14.**
Cooper v. Nielson, 194 F.3d 1316 (9th Cir. 1999)—**§ 5.73, n. 12.**
Cooper v. Parrish, 203 F.3d 937 (6th Cir. 2000)—**§ 2.24, n. 48, 65.**
Cooper Distributing Co., Inc. v. Amana Refrigeration, Inc., 63 F.3d 262 (3rd Cir. 1995)—**§ 2.26, n. 4.**
Coopers & Lybrand v. Livesay, 437 U.S. 463, 98 S.Ct. 2454, 57 L.Ed.2d 351 (1978)—**§ 5.45, n. 23; § 5.110, n. 16.**
Cooter & Gell v. Hartmarx Corp., 496 U.S. 384, 110 S.Ct. 2447, 110 L.Ed.2d 359 (1990)—**§ 5.87, n. 1.**
Copper Liquor, Inc. v. Adolph Coors Co., 701 F.2d 542 (5th Cir.1983)—**§ 4.5, n. 126.**
Cornelius v. Town of Highland Lake, Ala., 880 F.2d 348 (11th Cir.1989)—**§ 2.32, n. 80.**
Cornell v. Woods, 69 F.3d 1383 (8th Cir. 1995)—**§ 2.25, n. 29.**
Cornfield by Lewis v. Consolidated High School Dist. No. 230, 991 F.2d 1316 (7th Cir.1993)—**§ 2.31, n. 61.**
Cornforth v. University of Oklahoma Bd. of Regents, 263 F.3d 1129 (10th Cir. 2001)—**§ 5.35, n. 57.**
Correa v. Nampa School Dist. No. 131, 645 F.2d 814 (9th Cir.1981)—**§ 2.26, n. 29.**
Correctional Services Corp. v. Malesko, 534 U.S. 61, 122 S.Ct. 515, 151 L.Ed.2d 456 (2001)—**§ 2.12, n. 16; § 2.47, n. 5.**
Cort v. Ash, 422 U.S. 66, 95 S.Ct. 2080, 45 L.Ed.2d 26 (1975)—**§ 2.55, n. 57.**
Corum v. University of North Carolina Through Bd. of Governors, 330 N.C. 761, 413 S.E.2d 276 (N.C.1992)—**§ 5.46, n. 8.**
Cosgrove v. Sears, Roebuck & Co., 191 F.3d 98 (2nd Cir.1999)—**§ 4.1, n. 2.**
Costello v. United States, 365 U.S. 265, 81 S.Ct. 534, 5 L.Ed.2d 551 (1961)—**§ 5.118, n. 15.**
Cotterell v. New York City Transit Police Dept., 1995 WL 604700 (E.D.N.Y. 1995)—**§ 1.12, n. 10.**
Cottone v. Jenne, 326 F.3d 1352 (11th Cir. 2003)—**§ 2.22, n. 112; § 2.36, n. 9.**
Cottrell v. Caldwell, 85 F.3d 1480 (11th Cir.1996)—**§ 2.22, n. 109, 110; § 2.23, n. 31.**
Coughlen v. Coots, 5 F.3d 970 (6th Cir. 1993)—**§ 5.135, n. 21.**
County of (see name of county)
Courtney v. Canyon Television & Appliance Rental, Inc., 899 F.2d 845 (9th Cir. 1990)—**§ 1.8, n. 1.**
Cousin v. Small, 325 F.3d 627 (5th Cir. 2003)—**§ 2.2, n. 18.**
Coutin v. Young & Rubicam Puerto Rico, Inc., 124 F.3d 331 (1st Cir.1997)—**§ 4.5, n. 84.**
Covington v. City of New York, 171 F.3d 117 (2nd Cir.1999)—**§ 5.7, n. 35, 37; § 5.74, n. 13.**
Cox v. Babcock & Wilcox Co., 471 F.2d 13 (4th Cir.1972)—**§ 5.121, n. 27.**
Cox v. Treadway, 75 F.3d 230 (6th Cir. 1996)—**§ 5.80, n. 78.**
Cozzo v. Tangipahoa Parish Council–President Government, 279 F.3d 273 (5th Cir. 2002)—**§ 2.2, n. 6; § 2.22, n. 40; § 2.31, n. 55, 72; § 2.32, n. 60; § 2.36, n. 22; § 5.35, n. 17.**
Cozzo v. Tangipahoa Parish Council–President Government, 262 F.3d 501 (5th Cir. 2001)—**§ 2.32, n. 59; § 2.41, n. 24; § 5.35, n. 16.**
Crabill v. Trans Union, L.L.C., 259 F.3d 662 (7th Cir.2001)—**§ 4.5, n. 48.**
Craig v. Eberly, 164 F.3d 490 (10th Cir. 1998)—**§ 5.7, n. 53.**
Craig v. Gregg County, Tex., 988 F.2d 18 (5th Cir.1993)—**§ 4.5, n. 43.**
Craig v. Secretary, Dept. of Health and Human Services, 864 F.2d 324 (4th Cir. 1989)—**§ 4.10, n. 7.**
Cramblit v. Fikse, 33 F.3d 633 (6th Cir. 1994)—**§ 4.5, n. 40.**

Crampton v. Ohio, 408 U.S. 941, 92 S.Ct. 2873, 33 L.Ed.2d 765 (1972)—**§ 5.135, n. 5.**

Crapp v. City of Miami Beach, 242 F.3d 1017 (11th Cir.2001)—**§ 5.121, n. 19.**

Crawford v. Davis, 109 F.3d 1281 (8th Cir. 1997)—**§ 2.55, n. 53; § 3.19, n. 12, 13; § 3.21, n. 4; § 5.35, n. 45.**

Crawford–El v. Britton, 523 U.S. 574, 118 S.Ct. 1584, 140 L.Ed.2d 759 (1998)—**§ 2.22; § 2.22, n. 15, 48, 50, 89, 118, 122, 123; § 2.26; § 2.26, n. 50, 51; § 5.46, n. 6, 12; § 5.80; § 5.80, n. 40; § 5.100, n. 19, 37; § 5.108, n. 57.**

Crawford–El v. Britton, 93 F.3d 813, 320 U.S.App.D.C. 150 (D.C.Cir.1996)—**§ 2.22, n. 136; § 5.100, n. 4.**

Crawford Fitting Co. v. J. T. Gibbons, Inc., 482 U.S. 437, 107 S.Ct. 2494, 96 L.Ed.2d 385 (1987)—**§ 4.5, n. 122.**

Creative Goldsmiths of Washington, D.C., Inc., In re, 119 F.3d 1140 (4th Cir. 1997)—**§ 5.35, n. 47.**

Crenshaw v. Baynerd, 180 F.3d 866 (7th Cir.1999)—**§ 2.2, n. 9.**

Criales v. American Airlines, Inc., 105 F.3d 93 (2nd Cir.1997)—**§ 5.118, n. 15, 29.**

Crissman v. Dover Downs Entertainment Inc., 289 F.3d 231 (3rd Cir.2002)—**§ 2.12, n. 47.**

Crissman v. Dover Downs Entertainment, Inc., 2001 WL 617503 (3rd Cir.2001)—**§ 2.12, n. 72.**

Crist v. Commission on Presidential Debates, 262 F.3d 193 (2nd Cir.2001)—**§ 5.55, n. 4.**

Criswell v. Wayne County, Kentucky, 165 F.3d 26 (6th Cir.1998)—**§ 2.32, n. 52.**

Crocker v. Piedmont Aviation, Inc., 49 F.3d 735, 311 U.S.App.D.C. 1 (D.C.Cir. 1995)—**§ 2.23, n. 19; § 5.130, n. 8.**

Crockett v. Cumberland College, 316 F.3d 571 (6th Cir.2003)—**§ 2.23, n. 25, 47.**

Croker v. Boeing Co. (Vertol Division), 662 F.2d 975 (3rd Cir.1981)—**§ 4.1, n. 2.**

Crosby v. Paulk, 187 F.3d 1339 (11th Cir. 1999)—**§ 2.22, n. 103.**

Cross v. General Motors Corp., 721 F.2d 1152 (8th Cir.1983)—**§ 1.6, n. 5.**

Crossman v. Marcoccio, 806 F.2d 329 (1st Cir.1986)—**§ 4.20, n. 15, 16.**

Crowley v. Prince George's County, Md., 890 F.2d 683 (4th Cir.1989)—**§ 2.31, n. 66.**

Crown, Cork & Seal Co., Inc. v. Parker, 462 U.S. 345, 103 S.Ct. 2392, 76 L.Ed.2d 628 (1983)—**§ 5.116, n. 15.**

Cruz v. City of Laramie, Wyo., 239 F.3d 1183 (10th Cir.2001)—**§ 2.22, n. 43.**

Cruz v. Kauai County, 279 F.3d 1064 (9th Cir.2002)—**§ 2.22, n. 111.**

Crymes v. DeKalb County, Ga., 923 F.2d 1482 (11th Cir.1991)—**§ 2.2, n. 48.**

Cuesta v. School Bd. of Miami–Dade County, Fla., 285 F.3d 962 (11th Cir.2002)—**§ 2.32, n. 61.**

Cullen v. New York State Civil Service Commission, 435 F.Supp. 546 (E.D.N.Y. 1977)—**§ 2.4, n. 20.**

Cullinan v. Abramson, 128 F.3d 301 (6th Cir.1997)—**§ 2.24, n. 53, 65.**

Cummings v. Koehnen, 568 N.W.2d 418 (Minn.1997)—**§ 5.45, n. 3.**

Cummings v. Standard Register Co., 265 F.3d 56 (1st Cir.2001)—**§ 5.96, n. 2.**

Cummins v. Campbell, 44 F.3d 847 (10th Cir.1994)—**§ 2.22, n. 111.**

Cunningham v. Gates, 312 F.3d 1148 (9th Cir.2002)—**§ 5.118, n. 43.**

Cunningham v. Gates, 229 F.3d 1271 (9th Cir.2000)—**§ 2.22, n. 111.**

Cureton v. National Collegiate Athletic Ass'n, 198 F.3d 107 (3rd Cir.1999)—**§ 3.6, n. 4; § 3.16; § 3.16, n. 13.**

Curley v. Perry, 246 F.3d 1278 (10th Cir. 2001)—**§ 5.80, n. 72.**

Currie v. Group Ins. Com'n, 290 F.3d 1 (1st Cir.2002)—**§ 5.28, n. 1.**

Currier v. Doran, 242 F.3d 905 (10th Cir. 2001)—**§ 2.22, n. 111; § 5.80, n. 53.**

Curtis v. Citibank, N.A., 226 F.3d 133 (2nd Cir.2000)—**§ 5.118, n. 15.**

Curtis v. Loether, 415 U.S. 189, 94 S.Ct. 1005, 39 L.Ed.2d 260 (1974)—**§ 5.130, n. 9.**

Curtis v. Oklahoma City Public Schools Bd. of Educ., 147 F.3d 1200 (10th Cir. 1998)—**§ 5.96, n. 3, 8.**

Cushing v. City of Chicago, 3 F.3d 1156 (7th Cir.1993)—**§ 2.41, n. 35.**

Cutting v. Muzzey, 724 F.2d 259 (1st Cir. 1984)—**§ 2.2, n. 26, 36, 41.**

D

Dababnah v. Keller–Burnside, 208 F.3d 467 (4th Cir.2000)—**§ 2.2, n. 15.**

Dacey v. Dorsey, 568 F.2d 275 (2nd Cir. 1978)—**§ 1.5, n. 3.**

D'Aguanno v. Gallagher, 50 F.3d 877 (11th Cir.1995)—**§ 2.22, n. 3; § 2.41, n. 48.**

Dahlem by Dahlem v. Board of Educ. of Denver Public Schools, 901 F.2d 1508 (10th Cir.1990)—**§ 4.5, n. 41.**

Dalehite v. United States, 346 U.S. 15, 73 S.Ct. 956, 97 L.Ed. 1427 (1953)—**§ 2.49, n. 2.**

D'Amato v. Wisconsin Gas Co., 760 F.2d 1474 (7th Cir.1985)—**§ 1.6, n. 17, 36.**

Danco, Inc. v. Wal–Mart Stores, Inc., 178 F.3d 8 (1st Cir.1999)—**§ 1.2, n. 2.**

Danese v. Asman, 875 F.2d 1239 (6th Cir. 1989)—**§ 2.36, n. 15; § 2.41, n. 37; § 2.42, n. 4.**

Daniel v. Loveridge, 32 F.3d 1472 (10th Cir.1994)—**§ 4.5, n. 87.**

E

F

Feliciano v. City of Cleveland, 988 F.2d 649 (6th Cir.1993)—§ **2.31, n. 61.**
Felix de Santana v. Velez, 956 F.2d 16 (1st Cir.1992)—§ **2.24, n. 55.**
Felton v. Polles, 315 F.3d 470 (5th Cir. 2002)—§ **1.2, n. 11, 46, 60, 69, 84, 88; § 1.8, n. 3; § 1.11, n. 10; § 1.12, n. 10.**
Ferens v. John Deere Co., 494 U.S. 516, 110 S.Ct. 1274, 108 L.Ed.2d 443 (1990)—§ **5.9, n. 4.**
Fernandez, Matter of Estate of, 123 F.3d 241 (5th Cir.1997)—§ **5.35, n. 47.**
Ferrill v. Parker Group, Inc., 168 F.3d 468 (11th Cir.1999)—§ **1.2, n. 49, 70.**
Fiedler v. Marumsco Christian School, 631 F.2d 1144 (4th Cir.1980)—§ **1.2, n. 33.**
Fields v. Durham, 909 F.2d 94 (4th Cir. 1990)—§ **2.41, n. 36.**
Fields v. Hallsville Independent School Dist., 906 F.2d 1017 (5th Cir.1990)—§ **5.55, n. 56.**
Figueroa v. Rivera, 147 F.3d 77 (1st Cir. 1998)—§ **5.7, n. 8, 16, 17.**
Figueroa v. United States, 7 F.3d 1405 (9th Cir.1993)—§ **5.108, n. 52.**
Figueroa–Ruiz v. Alegria, 905 F.2d 545 (1st Cir.1990)—§ **5.89, n. 3.**
Fincher v. State of Fla. Dept. of Labor and Employment Sec. Unemployment Appeals Com'n, 798 F.2d 1371 (11th Cir. 1986)—§ **1.2, n. 33; § 1.21, n. 2; § 5.35, n. 64.**
Finley v. United States, 490 U.S. 545, 109 S.Ct. 2003, 104 L.Ed.2d 593 (1989)—§ **5.40, n. 4.**
Finnegan v. Fountain, 915 F.2d 817 (2nd Cir.1990)—§ **2.22, n. 50.**
Finsel v. Cruppenink, 326 F.3d 903 (7th Cir.2003)—§ **2.22, n. 112.**
First English Evangelical Lutheran Church of Glendale v. Los Angeles County, Cal., 482 U.S. 304, 107 S.Ct. 2378, 96 L.Ed.2d 250 (1987)—§ **2.62, n. 8.**
First Nat. Bank of Boston v. Bellotti, 435 U.S. 765, 98 S.Ct. 1407, 55 L.Ed.2d 707 (1978)—§ **5.65, n. 17.**
Fish v. St. Cloud State University, 295 F.3d 849 (8th Cir.2002)—§ **4.5, n. 55.**
Fishburn v. Brown, 125 F.3d 979 (6th Cir. 1997)—§ **2.48, n. 4.**
Fisher v. City of New York, 1992 WL 77606 (S.D.N.Y.1992)—§ **5.108, n. 36.**
Fisher v. Flynn, 598 F.2d 663 (1st Cir. 1979)—§ **2.26, n. 28, 29.**
Fisher v. Stolaruk Corp., 110 F.R.D. 74 (E.D.Mich.1986)—§ **4.20, n. 18.**
Fite v. First Tennessee Production Credit Ass'n, 861 F.2d 884 (6th Cir.1988)—§ **4.10, n. 7.**
Fitzpatrick v. Bitzer, 427 U.S. 445, 96 S.Ct. 2666, 49 L.Ed.2d 614 (1976)—§ **5.35, n. 24, 41, 42.**
Flagg Bros., Inc. v. Brooks, 436 U.S. 149, 98 S.Ct. 1729, 56 L.Ed.2d 185 (1978)—§ **2.12, n. 12, 25.**
Flagner v. Wilkinson, 241 F.3d 475 (6th Cir.2001)—§ **2.22, n. 111.**
Flast v. Cohen, 392 U.S. 83, 88 S.Ct. 1942, 20 L.Ed.2d 947 (1968)—§ **5.55, n. 70.**
Flavel v. Svedala Industries, Inc., 1993 WL 580831 (E.D.Wis.1993)—§ **5.95; § 5.95, n. 13.**
Fletcher v. O'Donnell, 867 F.2d 791 (3rd Cir.1989)—§ **2.31, n. 19.**
Flores v. Cameron County, Tex., 92 F.3d 258 (5th Cir.1996)—§ **2.31, n. 51, 57.**
Flores v. Morgan Hill Unified School Dist., 324 F.3d 1130 (9th Cir.2003)—§ **2.22, n. 81, 103.**
Florida Dept. of Health and Rehabilitative Services v. Florida Nursing Home Ass'n, 450 U.S. 147, 101 S.Ct. 1032, 67 L.Ed.2d 132 (1981)—§ **5.35, n. 4.**
Florida Prepaid Postsecondary Educ. Expense Bd. v. College Sav. Bank, 527 U.S. 627, 119 S.Ct. 2199, 144 L.Ed.2d 575 (1999)—§ **5.35; § 5.35, n. 46.**
Flowers v. Jefferson Hosp. Ass'n, 49 F.3d 391 (8th Cir.1995)—§ **4.15, n. 9.**
Floyd v. Ortiz, 300 F.3d 1223 (10th Cir. 2002)—§ **5.55, n. 37.**
Floyd v. Waiters, 171 F.3d 1264 (11th Cir. 1999)—§ **3.20, n. 2, 7.**
FOCUS v. Allegheny County Court of Common Pleas, 75 F.3d 834 (3rd Cir.1996)—§ **5.11, n. 8.**
Foley v. University of Houston System, 355 F.3d 333 (5th Cir.2003)—§ **1.2, n. 65, 74, 87.**
Foley v. University of Houston System, 324 F.3d 310 (5th Cir.2003)—§ **1.2, n. 60; § 2.22, n. 112.**
Foman v. Davis, 371 U.S. 178, 83 S.Ct. 227, 9 L.Ed.2d 222 (1962)—§ **5.80, n. 72.**
Forbes v. Eagleson, 228 F.3d 471 (3rd Cir. 2000)—§ **5.73, n. 23.**
Ford v. City of Rockford, 1992 WL 309603 (N.D.Ill.1992)—§ **1.12; § 1.12, n. 5.**
Ford, Estate of v. Ramirez–Palmer, 301 F.3d 1043 (9th Cir.2002)—§ **2.22, n. 115.**
Fordice, United States v., 505 U.S. 717, 112 S.Ct. 2727, 120 L.Ed.2d 575 (1992)—§ **3.9, n. 8.**
Ford Motor Co. v. Department of Treasury of State of Indiana, 323 U.S. 459, 65 S.Ct. 347, 89 L.Ed. 389 (1945)—§ **2.42, n. 32.**
Ford Motor Co., In re, 110 F.3d 954 (3rd Cir.1997)—§ **5.95, n. 26.**
Forrester v. White, 484 U.S. 219, 108 S.Ct. 538, 98 L.Ed.2d 555 (1988)—§ **1.4, n. 5; § 2.2, n. 8.**
Foster v. City of Lake Jackson, 28 F.3d 425 (5th Cir.1994)—§ **2.22, n. 111.**
Fottler v. United States, 73 F.3d 1064 (10th Cir.1996)—§ **5.7, n. 10.**
Foy v. Holston, 94 F.3d 1528 (11th Cir. 1996)—§ **2.22, n. 132; § 2.26, n. 25.**

G

H

Hopp v. City of Pittsburgh, 194 F.3d 434 (3rd Cir.1999)—**§ 1.12, n. 11.**
Hopwood v. State, 1994 WL 242362 (W.D.Tex.1994)—**§ 4.15, n. 18.**
Hopwood v. State of Texas, 236 F.3d 256 (5th Cir.2000)—**§ 4.10, n. 3; § 4.15, n. 18.**
Hopwood v. State of Texas, 78 F.3d 932 (5th Cir.1996)—**§ 2.26, n. 2, 42.**
Hopwood v. State of Texas, 861 F.Supp. 551 (W.D.Tex.1994)—**§ 3.9, n. 17.**
Horne v. Coughlin, 178 F.3d 603 (2nd Cir. 1999)—**§ 2.22, n. 97.**
Horne v. Coughlin, 191 F.3d 244 (2nd Cir. 1999)—**§ 2.22, n. 103.**
Horner v. Kentucky High School Athletic Ass'n, 43 F.3d 265 (6th Cir.1994)—**§ 3.22, n. 51, 52.**
Horseshoe Entertainment, In re, 305 F.3d 354 (5th Cir.2002)—**§ 5.9, n. 9.**
Hosty v. Carter, 325 F.3d 945 (7th Cir. 2003)—**§ 2.22, n. 112.**
Howard v. Adkison, 887 F.2d 134 (8th Cir. 1989)—**§ 2.36, n. 24, 26.**
Howard v. Military Dept., State of Cal., Air Nat. Guard of California, 5 F.3d 537 (9th Cir.1993)—**§ 4.10, n. 14.**
Howell v. Evans, 922 F.2d 712 (11th Cir. 1991)—**§ 2.23, n. 2.**
Howell v. Tanner, 650 F.2d 610 (5th Cir. 1981)—**§ 5.9, n. 8.**
Howerton v. Gabica, 708 F.2d 380 (9th Cir. 1983)—**§ 2.24, n. 55.**
Howlett By and Through Howlett v. Rose, 496 U.S. 356, 110 S.Ct. 2430, 110 L.Ed.2d 332 (1990)—**§ 5.1, n. 20; § 5.45, n. 1, 20.**
Huang v. Johnson, 251 F.3d 65 (2nd Cir. 2001)—**§ 5.7, n. 26.**
Hubbard v. Beatty & Hyde, Inc., 343 Mass. 258, 178 N.E.2d 485 (Mass.1961)—**§ 2.24, n. 44.**
Hubbard v. Haley, 262 F.3d 1194 (11th Cir.2001)—**§ 5.7, n. 59.**
Hudgins v. City of Ashburn, Ga., 890 F.2d 396 (11th Cir.1989)—**§ 2.23, n. 2.**
Hudson v. Hall, 231 F.3d 1289 (11th Cir. 2000)—**§ 2.22, n. 111.**
Hudson v. New York City, 271 F.3d 62 (2nd Cir.2001)—**§ 2.21, n. 6.**
Hudson v. Palmer, 468 U.S. 517, 104 S.Ct. 3194, 82 L.Ed.2d 393 (1984)—**§ 2.41; § 2.41, n. 15.**
Hudson Valley Freedom Theater, Inc. v. Heimbach, 671 F.2d 702 (2nd Cir. 1982)—**§ 1.2, n. 32; § 5.55, n. 44.**
Huels v. Exxon Coal USA, Inc., 121 F.3d 1047 (7th Cir.1997)—**§ 5.72, n. 8.**
Huey v. Stine, 230 F.3d 226 (6th Cir. 2000)—**§ 5.7, n. 16.**
Huffman v. Pursue, Ltd., 420 U.S. 592, 95 S.Ct. 1200, 43 L.Ed.2d 482 (1975)—**§ 5.10; § 5.10, n. 12.**
Hufford v. McEnaney, 249 F.3d 1142 (9th Cir.2001)—**§ 2.22, n. 113.**
Hughes v. Lott, 350 F.3d 1157 (11th Cir. 2003)—**§ 5.7, n. 35.**
Hughes v. Ortho Pharmaceutical Corp., 177 F.3d 701 (8th Cir.1999)—**§ 1.2, n. 12.**
Hughes v. Vanderbilt University, 215 F.3d 543 (6th Cir.2000)—**§ 5.73, n. 2.**
Hukill v. Auto Care, Inc., 192 F.3d 437 (4th Cir.1999)—**§ 5.6, n. 5.**
Hull v. Cuyahoga Valley Joint Vocational School Dist. Bd. of Educ., 926 F.2d 505 (6th Cir.1991)—**§ 1.6, n. 5.**
Humphrey v. Staszak, 148 F.3d 719 (7th Cir.1998)—**§ 2.22, n. 111.**
Humphrey v. Tharaldson Enterprises, Inc., 95 F.3d 624 (7th Cir.1996)—**§ 5.118, n. 22.**
Hundertmark v. State of Florida Dept. of Transp., 205 F.3d 1272 (11th Cir. 2000)—**§ 5.35, n. 45.**
Hunger v. Leininger, 15 F.3d 664 (7th Cir. 1994)—**§ 4.5, n. 79.**
Hunt v. Uphoff, 199 F.3d 1220 (10th Cir. 1999)—**§ 5.7, n. 62.**
Hunter v. Bryant, 502 U.S. 224, 112 S.Ct. 534, 116 L.Ed.2d 589 (1991)—**§ 2.23; § 2.23, n. 10.**
Hunter v. City of Warner Robins, Ga., 842 F.Supp. 1460 (M.D.Ga.1994)—**§ 5.121, n. 35.**
Hunter v. District of Columbia, 943 F.2d 69, 291 U.S.App.D.C. 355 (D.C.Cir. 1991)—**§ 2.22, n. 98.**
Hutcherson v. Lauderdale County, Tennessee, 326 F.3d 747 (6th Cir.2003)—**§ 5.118, n. 22; § 5.119, n. 23.**
Hutchinson v. Proxmire, 443 U.S. 111, 99 S.Ct. 2675, 61 L.Ed.2d 411 (1979)—**§ 2.2, n. 34.**
Hutto v. Finney, 437 U.S. 678, 98 S.Ct. 2565, 57 L.Ed.2d 522 (1978)—**§ 2.35, n. 11; § 4.5, n. 111; § 5.35, n. 22, 59.**
Hutton v. Strickland, 919 F.2d 1531 (11th Cir.1990)—**§ 5.35, n. 13.**
Hyde v. Small, 123 F.3d 583 (7th Cir. 1997)—**§ 4.5, n. 30.**
Hyland v. Wonder, 117 F.3d 405 (9th Cir. 1997)—**§ 2.22, n. 113; § 2.31, n. 61.**
Hysten v. Burlington Northern and Santa Fe Ry. Co., 296 F.3d 1177 (10th Cir. 2002)—**§ 1.2, n. 74.**

I

Iacobucci v. Boulter, 193 F.3d 14 (1st Cir. 1999)—**§ 2.25, n. 29.**
Ibrahim v. District of Columbia, 208 F.3d 1032, 341 U.S.App.D.C. 63 (D.C.Cir. 2000)—**§ 5.7, n. 61.**
Idaho v. Coeur d'Alene Tribe of Idaho, 521 U.S. 261, 117 S.Ct. 2028, 138 L.Ed.2d 438 (1997)—**§ 5.35, n. 8, 58.**
Idoux v. Lamar University System, 828 F.Supp. 1252 (E.D.Tex.1993)—**§ 5.80, n. 39.**

J

K

L

L.W. v. Grubbs, 974 F.2d 119 (9th Cir. 1992)—**§ 2.31, n. 24; § 2.32; § 2.32, n. 77.**
Lyes v. City of Riviera Beach, Fla., 166 F.3d 1332 (11th Cir.1999)—**§ 1.6, n. 18.**
Lyte v. Sara Lee Corp., 950 F.2d 101 (2nd Cir.1991)—**§ 4.5, n. 17; § 4.20; § 4.20, n. 4.**
Lytle v. Household Mfg., Inc., 494 U.S. 545, 110 S.Ct. 1331, 108 L.Ed.2d 504 (1990)—**§ 5.130; § 5.130, n. 7.**

M

Maag v. Wessler, 993 F.2d 718 (9th Cir. 1993)—**§ 4.15, n. 4.**
Mabra v. United Food & Commercial Workers Local Union No. 1996, 176 F.3d 1357 (11th Cir.1999)—**§ 1.2, n. 23, 53.**
Mabrey v. Farthing, 280 F.3d 400 (4th Cir. 2002)—**§ 2.23, n. 32.**
Mabry v. State Bd. of Community Colleges and Occupational Educ., 813 F.2d 311 (10th Cir.1987)—**§ 3.19, n. 5.**
MacDonald, United States v., 688 F.2d 224 (4th Cir.1982)—**§ 5.121, n. 27.**
Mack v. Varelas, 835 F.2d 995 (2nd Cir. 1987)—**§ 5.74, n. 11.**
Mackensworth v. S.S. American Merchant, 28 F.3d 246 (2nd Cir.1994)—**§ 5.8, n. 1.**
Mackey v. Dickson, 47 F.3d 744 (5th Cir. 1995)—**§ 5.7, n. 35.**
Mackey v. Nationwide Ins. Companies, 724 F.2d 419 (4th Cir.1984)—**§ 5.55, n. 43.**
Macuba v. Deboer, 193 F.3d 1316 (11th Cir.1999)—**§ 2.2, n. 35, 36.**
Madison v. IBP, Inc., 330 F.3d 1051 (8th Cir.2003)—**§ 1.2, n. 46.**
Magnetic Engineering & Mfg. Co. v. Dings Mfg. Co., 178 F.2d 866 (2nd Cir.1950)—**§ 5.8, n. 2; § 5.9, n. 14.**
Mahone v. Ray, 326 F.3d 1176 (11th Cir. 2003)—**§ 5.95, n. 27.**
Maine v. Thiboutot, 448 U.S. 1, 100 S.Ct. 2502, 65 L.Ed.2d 555 (1980)—**§ 2.3; § 2.3, n. 32; § 2.31, n. 6; § 2.55; § 2.55, n. 1, 58; § 2.60, n. 5; § 5.6, n. 1.**
Maitland v. University of Minnesota, 260 F.3d 959 (8th Cir.2001)—**§ 2.2, n. 36.**
Maitland v. University of Minnesota, 155 F.3d 1013 (8th Cir.1998)—**§ 2.22, n. 111.**
Maldonado–Denis v. Castillo–Rodriguez, 23 F.3d 576 (1st Cir.1994)—**§ 2.36, n. 18, 22, 26.**
Malinowski v. DeLuca, 177 F.3d 623 (7th Cir.1999)—**§ 2.12, n. 16, 17; § 2.24, n. 62, 65.**
Mallett v. Wisconsin Div. of Vocational Rehabilitation, 130 F.3d 1245 (7th Cir. 1997)—**§ 2.55, n. 18, 31, 47, 57.**
Malley v. Briggs, 475 U.S. 335, 106 S.Ct. 1092, 89 L.Ed.2d 271 (1986)—**§ 2.22, n. 28, 39.**
Mallory v. Eyrich, 922 F.2d 1273 (6th Cir. 1991)—**§ 4.20, n. 19.**
Malloy v. Monahan, 73 F.3d 1012 (10th Cir.1996)—**§ 2.25, n. 3.**
Manarite By and Through Manarite v. City of Springfield, 957 F.2d 953 (1st Cir. 1992)—**§ 2.36, n. 22.**
Mandel v. Doe, 888 F.2d 783 (11th Cir. 1989)—**§ 2.31, n. 56, 60.**
Manders v. Lee, 338 F.3d 1304 (11th Cir. 2003)—**§ 2.31, n. 72; § 5.35, n. 14, 17.**
Maniccia v. Brown, 171 F.3d 1364 (11th Cir.1999)—**§ 5.116, n. 6.**
Manis v. Corrections Corp. of America, 859 F.Supp. 302 (M.D.Tenn.1994)—**§ 2.12, n. 16.**
Manley v. City of Chicago, 236 F.3d 392 (7th Cir.2001)—**§ 5.27, n. 4.**
Manley v. Engram, 755 F.2d 1463 (11th Cir.1985)—**§ 5.9, n. 1.**
Mann v. Conlin, 22 F.3d 100 (6th Cir. 1994)—**§ 5.10, n. 23.**
Manning v. Jones, 696 F.Supp. 1231 (S.D.Ind.1988)—**§ 2.15, n. 26.**
Manning v. Metropolitan Life Ins. Co., Inc., 127 F.3d 686 (8th Cir.1997)—**§ 1.2, n. 80.**
Manor Healthcare Corp. v. Lomelo, 929 F.2d 633 (11th Cir.1991)—**§ 2.31, n. 53.**
Marbley v. Bane, 57 F.3d 224 (2nd Cir. 1995)—**§ 4.5, n. 43.**
Marek v. Chesny, 473 U.S. 1, 105 S.Ct. 3012, 87 L.Ed.2d 1 (1985)—**§ 4.20; § 4.20, n. 3.**
Mark v. Borough of Hatboro, 51 F.3d 1137 (3rd Cir.1995)—**§ 2.12, n. 10.**
Markham v. White, 172 F.3d 486 (7th Cir. 1999)—**§ 2.22, n. 60.**
Marks v. Carmody, 234 F.3d 1006 (7th Cir. 2000)—**§ 2.22, n. 40.**
Marquart v. Lodge 837, Intern. Ass'n of Machinists and Aerospace Workers, 26 F.3d 842 (8th Cir.1994)—**§ 4.15, n. 7.**
Marquez v. Gutierrez, 322 F.3d 689 (9th Cir.2003)—**§ 2.22, n. 45, 115.**
Marrero v. City of Hialeah, 625 F.2d 499 (5th Cir.1980)—**§ 2.25, n. 2.**
Marrese v. American Academy of Orthopaedic Surgeons, 470 U.S. 373, 105 S.Ct. 1327, 84 L.Ed.2d 274 (1985)—**§ 5.27, n. 11; § 5.120, n. 15.**
Marryshow v. Town of Bladensburg, 139 F.R.D. 318 (D.Md.1991)—**§ 5.108, n. 1, 30.**
Marsh v. Butler County, Ala., 268 F.3d 1014 (11th Cir.2001)—**§ 2.22, n. 70, 75, 113.**
Marsh v. Butler County, Ala., 225 F.3d 1243 (11th Cir.2000)—**§ 2.35, n. 8; § 2.36, n. 27.**
Marsh v. Fulton County, 77 U.S. 676, 19 L.Ed. 1040 (1870)—**§ 2.42, n. 27.**
Marsh v. State of Alabama, 326 U.S. 501, 66 S.Ct. 276, 90 L.Ed. 265 (1946)—**§ 2.12, n. 9, 10.**

McDonnell Douglas Corp. v. Green, 411 U.S. 792, 93 S.Ct. 1817, 36 L.Ed.2d 668 (1973)—**§ 1.2; § 1.2, n. 20.**

McElligott v. Foley, 182 F.3d 1248 (11th Cir.1999)—**§ 2.42, n. 43.**

McGeorge v. Continental Airlines, Inc., 871 F.2d 952 (10th Cir.1989)—**§ 5.8, n. 1.**

McGuinness v. Regents of University of New Mexico, 183 F.3d 1172 (10th Cir. 1999)—**§ 5.118, n. 7.**

McInnes v. State of Cal., 943 F.2d 1088 (9th Cir.1991)—**§ 5.121, n. 19.**

McIntosh v. Antonino, 71 F.3d 29 (1st Cir. 1995)—**§ 5.74, n. 4.**

McIntosh v. Turner, 861 F.2d 524 (8th Cir. 1988)—**§ 2.48, n. 10.**

McKeesport Hosp. v. Accreditation Council for Graduate Medical Educ., 24 F.3d 519 (3rd Cir.1994)—**§ 2.12, n. 4, 6, 49.**

McKennon v. Nashville Banner Pub. Co., 513 U.S. 352, 115 S.Ct. 879, 130 L.Ed.2d 852 (1995)—**§ 2.26, n. 39; § 5.95, n. 11.**

McKenzie v. Cooper, Levins & Pastko, Inc., 990 F.2d 1183 (11th Cir.1993)—**§ 4.5, n. 108.**

McKenzie v. Lee, 259 F.3d 372 (5th Cir. 2001)—**§ 5.98, n. 12.**

McKesson Corp. v. Division of Alcoholic Beverages and Tobacco, Dept. of Business Regulation of Florida, 496 U.S. 18, 110 S.Ct. 2238, 110 L.Ed.2d 17 (1990)—**§ 2.42, n. 27.**

McKnight v. General Motors Corp., 908 F.2d 104 (7th Cir.1990)—**§ 1.8, n. 1.**

McKnight v. Rees, 88 F.3d 417 (6th Cir. 1996)—**§ 2.12, n. 16.**

McLaughlin v. Board of Trustees of State Colleges of Colorado, 215 F.3d 1168 (10th Cir.2000)—**§ 5.35, n. 33, 62.**

McLaughlin v. Watson, 271 F.3d 566 (3rd Cir.2001)—**§ 2.22, n. 111.**

McMillian v. Johnson, 88 F.3d 1573 (11th Cir.1996)—**§ 2.31, n. 71; § 5.100, n. 7.**

McMillian v. Johnson, 88 F.3d 1554 (11th Cir.1996)—**§ 2.2, n. 22; § 2.22, n. 45, 58, 60, 130; § 2.23, n. 31.**

McMillian v. Monroe County, Ala., 520 U.S. 781, 117 S.Ct. 1734, 138 L.Ed.2d 1 (1997)—**§ 2.31, n. 68; § 2.35; § 2.35, n. 12.**

McNair v. Coffey, 279 F.3d 463 (7th Cir. 2002)—**§ 2.22, n. 44, 46.**

McNasby v. Crown Cork and Seal Co., Inc., 888 F.2d 270 (3rd Cir.1989)—**§ 5.116, n. 9; § 5.120, n. 7.**

McNeese v. Board of Ed. for Community Unit School Dist. 187, Cahokia, Ill., 373 U.S. 668, 83 S.Ct. 1433, 10 L.Ed.2d 622 (1963)—**§ 5.16, n. 6; § 5.121, n. 2.**

McNemar v. Disney Store, Inc., 91 F.3d 610 (3rd Cir.1996)—**§ 5.121, n. 46.**

McRorie v. Shimoda, 795 F.2d 780 (9th Cir.1986)—**§ 2.36, n. 5.**

McSurely v. McClellan, 697 F.2d 309, 225 U.S.App.D.C. 67 (D.C.Cir.1982)—**§ 2.23, n. 2.**

Meade v. Grubbs, 841 F.2d 1512 (10th Cir. 1988)—**§ 2.36, n. 3.**

Medberry v. Butler, 185 F.3d 1189 (11th Cir.1999)—**§ 5.7, n. 62.**

Medical Institute of Minnesota v. National Ass'n of Trade and Technical Schools, 817 F.2d 1310 (8th Cir.1987)—**§ 2.12, n. 49.**

Medina v. City and County of Denver, 960 F.2d 1493 (10th Cir.1992)—**§ 2.22, n. 53; § 5.108, n. 3.**

Meloy v. Bachmeier, 302 F.3d 845 (8th Cir. 2002)—**§ 2.36, n. 7.**

Memphis Community School Dist. v. Stachura, 477 U.S. 299, 106 S.Ct. 2537, 91 L.Ed.2d 249 (1986)—**§ 2.25, n. 1, 3, 10; § 2.34, n. 1; § 2.61, n. 16.**

Mendocino Environmental Center v. Mendocino County, 14 F.3d 457 (9th Cir. 1994)—**§ 5.80, n. 38.**

Mendoza v. Block, 27 F.3d 1357 (9th Cir. 1994)—**§ 2.22; § 2.22, n. 31.**

Mennone v. Gordon, 889 F.Supp. 53 (D.Conn.1995)—**§ 2.55, n. 49; § 3.19, n. 11.**

Mentavlos v. Anderson, 249 F.3d 301 (4th Cir.2001)—**§ 2.12, n. 15.**

Mercer v. Duke University, 190 F.3d 643 (4th Cir.1999)—**§ 3.22; § 3.22, n. 38.**

Meredith v. Beech Aircraft Corp., 18 F.3d 890 (10th Cir.1994)—**§ 5.130, n. 3.**

Meredith v. Oregon, 321 F.3d 807 (9th Cir. 2003)—**§ 5.10, n. 8.**

Meriwether v. Coughlin, 879 F.2d 1037 (2nd Cir.1989)—**§ 2.36, n. 26.**

Merrell Dow Pharmaceuticals Inc. v. Thompson, 478 U.S. 804, 106 S.Ct. 3229, 92 L.Ed.2d 650 (1986)—**§ 5.6, n. 8.**

Merrill Lynch Business Financial Services, Inc. v. Nudell, 363 F.3d 1072 (10th Cir. 2004)—**§ 5.27, n. 3.**

Merritt v. Mackey, 932 F.2d 1317 (9th Cir. 1991)—**§ 2.26, n. 15.**

Merriweather v. City of Memphis, 107 F.3d 396 (6th Cir.1997)—**§ 5.73, n. 2.**

Mertik v. Blalock, 983 F.2d 1353 (6th Cir. 1993)—**§ 2.41, n. 12, 36.**

Mesquite, City of v. Aladdin's Castle, Inc., 455 U.S. 283, 102 S.Ct. 1070, 71 L.Ed.2d 152 (1982)—**§ 5.65, n. 8.**

Metheny v. Hammonds, 216 F.3d 1307 (11th Cir.2000)—**§ 5.7, n. 27.**

Metropolitan Government of Nashville v. Doe By and Through Doe, 525 U.S. 813, 119 S.Ct. 47, 142 L.Ed.2d 36 (1998)—**§ 5.121, n. 15.**

Metropolitan Life Ins. Co. v. Taylor, 481 U.S. 58, 107 S.Ct. 1542, 95 L.Ed.2d 55 (1987)—**§ 5.50, n. 3.**

Meyers v. City of Cincinnati, 14 F.3d 1115 (6th Cir.1994)—**§ 2.31, n. 61.**

N

National R.R. Passenger Corp. v. Morgan, 536 U.S. 101, 122 S.Ct. 2061, 153 L.Ed.2d 106 (2002)—**§ 1.2; § 1.2, n. 45.**

National Wrestling Coaches Ass'n v. Dept. of Educ., 366 F.3d 930 (D.C.Cir.2004)—**§ 3.22, n. 52.**

Native Village of Venetie IRA Council v. State of Alaska, 155 F.3d 1150 (9th Cir. 1998)—**§ 2.55, n. 30, 51.**

Navarro v. Block, 250 F.3d 729 (9th Cir. 2001)—**§ 2.22, n. 129.**

Navarro v. Block, 72 F.3d 712 (9th Cir. 1995)—**§ 2.31, n. 19; § 2.32, n. 61, 62.**

Naylor v. State of Louisiana, Dept. of Corrections, 123 F.3d 855 (5th Cir.1997)—**§ 2.23, n. 13.**

Neal v. Board of Trustees of California State Universities, 198 F.3d 763 (9th Cir.1999)—**§ 3.22, n. 42, 51.**

Neal v. Goord, 267 F.3d 116 (2nd Cir. 2001)—**§ 5.7, n. 71.**

Neal v. Howell, 689 F.2d 473 (4th Cir. 1982)—**§ 2.26, n. 31, 33.**

Neal v. Shimoda, 131 F.3d 818 (9th Cir. 1997)—**§ 5.7, n. 27.**

Neely v. Delta Brick and Tile Co., Inc., 817 F.2d 1224 (5th Cir.1987)—**§ 5.100, n. 25.**

Neely v. Feinstein, 50 F.3d 1502 (9th Cir. 1995)—**§ 2.36, n. 31.**

Neely v. Martin K. Eby Const. Co., 386 U.S. 317, 87 S.Ct. 1072, 18 L.Ed.2d 75 (1967)—**§ 5.103; § 5.103, n. 7.**

Neighbour v. Covert, 68 F.3d 1508 (2nd Cir.1995)—**§ 2.21, n. 2.**

Nekolny v. Painter, 653 F.2d 1164 (7th Cir.1981)—**§ 2.26, n. 29.**

Nelson v. County of Allegheny, 60 F.3d 1010 (3rd Cir.1995)—**§ 5.45, n. 23; § 5.73, n. 13.**

Nelson v. Heiss, 271 F.3d 891 (9th Cir. 2001)—**§ 2.22, n. 114.**

Nelson v. Jashurek, 109 F.3d 142 (3rd Cir. 1997)—**§ 5.7, n. 43.**

Nelson v. Kline, 242 F.3d 33 (1st Cir. 2001)—**§ 2.22, n. 44.**

Nelson v. McMullen, 207 F.3d 1202 (10th Cir.2000)—**§ 2.22, n. 135; § 5.100, n. 4.**

Nelson v. Murphy, 44 F.3d 497 (7th Cir. 1995)—**§ 5.11, n. 7.**

Nelson v. Temple University, 920 F.Supp. 633 (E.D.Pa.1996)—**§ 3.19, n. 11.**

Nephew v. City of Aurora, By and Through Its Mayor and City Council, 830 F.2d 1547 (10th Cir.1987)—**§ 4.5, n. 22.**

Nevada v. Hall, 440 U.S. 410, 99 S.Ct. 1182, 59 L.Ed.2d 416 (1979)—**§ 5.35, n. 5, 68.**

Nevada Dept. of Human Resources v. Hibbs, 538 U.S. 721, 123 S.Ct. 1972, 155 L.Ed.2d 953 (2003)—**§ 5.35, n. 42.**

Nevel v. Village of Schaumburg, 297 F.3d 673 (7th Cir.2002)—**§ 2.32, n. 84.**

Newell v. City of Elgin, 34 Ill.App.3d 719, 340 N.E.2d 344 (Ill.App. 2 Dist.1976)—**§ 5.46, n. 3.**

Newell v. Sauser, 64 F.3d 1416 (9th Cir. 1995)—**§ 2.22, n. 113.**

New Hampshire, State of v. Adams, 159 F.3d 680 (1st Cir.1998)—**§ 4.5, n. 43.**

Newman v. Soballe, 871 F.2d 969 (11th Cir.1989)—**§ 2.49, n. 2.**

New Orleans Public Service, Inc. v. Council of City of New Orleans, 491 U.S. 350, 109 S.Ct. 2506, 105 L.Ed.2d 298 (1989)—**§ 5.10, n. 29; § 5.30; § 5.30, n. 5, 8.**

Newport, City of v. Fact Concerts, Inc., 453 U.S. 247, 101 S.Ct. 2748, 69 L.Ed.2d 616 (1981)—**§ 1.2, n. 51; § 2.3, n. 16; § 2.33, n. 3; § 2.34; § 2.34, n. 2; § 2.61, n. 15, 20; § 2.62, n. 22.**

Newton, Town of v. Rumery, 480 U.S. 386, 107 S.Ct. 1187, 94 L.Ed.2d 405 (1987)—**§ 5.135; § 5.135, n. 1.**

New York v. Galamison, 342 F.2d 255 (2nd Cir.1965)—**§ 5.50, n. 30.**

New York v. United States, 505 U.S. 144, 112 S.Ct. 2408, 120 L.Ed.2d 120 (1992)—**§ 2.32, n. 83.**

New York, City of, United States v., 972 F.2d 464 (2nd Cir.1992)—**§ 5.55, n. 71.**

New York Gaslight Club, Inc. v. Carey, 447 U.S. 54, 100 S.Ct. 2024, 64 L.Ed.2d 723 (1980)—**§ 4.5; § 4.5, n. 58, 64.**

New York State Federation of Taxi Drivers, Inc. v. Westchester County Taxi and Limousine Com'n, 272 F.3d 154 (2nd Cir.2001)—**§ 4.5, n. 45.**

New York Urban League, Inc. v. State of N.Y., 71 F.3d 1031 (2nd Cir.1995)—**§ 3.9, n. 9.**

Ngiraingas v. Sanchez, 495 U.S. 182, 110 S.Ct. 1737, 109 L.Ed.2d 163 (1990)—**§ 2.60, n. 6.**

Nicholas v. Tucker, 114 F.3d 17 (2nd Cir. 1997)—**§ 5.7, n. 59.**

Nichols v. American Nat. Ins. Co., 154 F.3d 875 (8th Cir.1998)—**§ 5.45, n. 15.**

Nihiser v. Ohio E.P.A., 269 F.3d 626 (6th Cir.2001)—**§ 5.35, n. 45.**

Nishiyama v. Dickson County, Tenn., 814 F.2d 277 (6th Cir.1987)—**§ 2.62, n. 9.**

Nivens v. Gilchrist, 319 F.3d 151 (4th Cir. 2003)—**§ 5.10, n. 7.**

Nixon v. Condon, 286 U.S. 73, 52 S.Ct. 484, 76 L.Ed. 984 (1932)—**§ 2.12, n. 8.**

Nixon v. Fitzgerald, 457 U.S. 731, 102 S.Ct. 2690, 73 L.Ed.2d 349 (1982)—**§ 2.2, n. 3; § 2.48, n. 3.**

Nixon v. Herndon, 273 U.S. 536, 47 S.Ct. 446, 71 L.Ed. 759 (1927)—**§ 2.25, n. 11.**

Nobby Lobby, Inc. v. City of Dallas, 970 F.2d 82 (5th Cir.1992)—**§ 5.10, n. 11.**

Nonnette v. Small, 316 F.3d 872 (9th Cir. 2002)—**§ 5.7, n. 16.**

Norman v. Housing Authority of City of Montgomery, 836 F.2d 1292 (11th Cir. 1988)—**§ 4.10, n. 8.**

Norris v. Sysco Corp., 191 F.3d 1043 (9th Cir.1999)—**§ 4.5, n. 57.**

O

P

S

T

U

V

W

Y

Z

*

Index

References are to Sections

†

0–314–15011–0